THE ENCYCLOPEDIA OF STRIKES IN AMERICAN HISTORY

THE ENCYCLOPEDIA OF STRIKES IN AMERICAN HISTORY

AARON BRENNER
BENJAMIN DAY
IMMANUEL NESS
EDITORS

M.E.Sharpe
Armonk, New York
London, England

Library of Congress Cataloging-in-Publication Data

The encyclopedia of strikes in American history / Aaron Brenner, Benjamin Day, Immanuel Ness [editors].
p. cm.
Includes bibliographical references and index.
ISBN 978-0-7656-1330-1 (cloth : alk. paper)
1. Strikes and lockouts—United States—Encyclopedias. I. Brenner, Aaron. II. Day, Benjamin, 1979–
III. Ness, Immanuel.

HD5324.E39 2008
331.892′97303—dc22 2007036072

Printed in the United States of America

The paper used in this publication meets the minimum requirements of
American National Standard for Information Sciences
Permanence of Paper for Printed Library Materials,
ANSI Z 39.48-1984.

MV (c) 10 9 8 7 6 5 4 3 2 1

Publisher: Myron E. Sharpe
Vice President and Editorial Director: Patricia A. Kolb
Executive Editor: Lynn Taylor
Production Director: Carmen Chetti
Production Editor: Angela Piliouras
Editorial Assistants: Kathryn Corasaniti and Nicole Cirino
Typesetter: Nancy Connick
Cover Design: Jesse Sanchez

CONTENTS

EDITORS AND CONTRIBUTORS

Editors

Aaron Brenner is a researcher, editor, and consultant in the areas of labor and finance, and he is currently employed as a senior research analyst with the Service Employees International Union. He has written on labor, labor history, finance, and economics for such publications as *New Labor Forum, Labor's Heritage, Business History Review,* and *Labor Notes.* He is a contributor to *A Troublemaker's Handbook* 2 and editor of such publications as *Human Rights Watch World Report 2003; Immigrants, Unions, and the New U.S. Labor Market;* and *Local Area Network Magazine.* He has taught history, social relations, finance, and research at Columbia University, Cornell University, Marymount Manhattan College, and Michigan State University. He earned a Ph.D. from Columbia University.

Benjamin Day is the Executive Director of Mass-Care: The Massachusetts Campaign for Single Payer Health Care, and the Statewide Coordinator for Massachusetts Physicians for a National Health Program. He received his Master's in social and political thought at the University of Sussex in the United Kingdom under a Fulbright Scholarship, and is a doctoral student in Labor Law, Labor History, and Collective Bargaining at the New York State School of Industrial and Labor Relations at Cornell University.

Immanuel Ness is a professor of political science at Brooklyn College, City University of New York, and teaches at the Brooklyn College Graduate Center for Worker Education. He has written a number of books on labor, including *Trade Unions and the Betrayal of the Unemployed: Labor Conflict in the 1990s* and *Organizing for Justice in Our Communities: Central Labor Councils and the Revival of American Unionism.* He is also editor of *World Protest and Revolution 1500–Present.* His articles have appeared in *New Political Science, Labor Studies Journal, National Civic Review, The Nation,* and *Z Magazine.* He is a former union organizer.

Contributors

Jon Amsden
The WritersCoach.com

Edward Beechert
University of Hawaii

Jon Bekken
Albright College

Mary H. Blewett
University of Massachusetts Lowell

Jeremy Brecher
Journalist and Author

Stephen Brier
CUNY Graduate Center

Cecelia Bucki
Fairfield University

Robert Bruno
Institute for Labor and Industrial Relations, University of Illinois

Theresa Ann Case
University of Houston-Downtown

Deirdre Clemente
Carnegie-Mellon University

Dorothy Sue Cobble
Rutgers, The State University of New Jersey

Andrew Dawson
University of Greenwich

Victor G. Devinatz
Illinois State University

Myrna Cherkoss Donahoe
California State University, Dominguez Hills

Greg Downey
University of Wisconsin-Madison

Steve Early
Communications Workers of America, Retired

Gerald Friedman
University of Massachusetts Amherst

Jackie S. Gabriel
Colorado State University

David J. Goldberg
Cleveland State University

Ian Collin Greer
Leeds University Centre for Employment Relations Innovation and Change

Lisa Hayes
University at Buffalo—The State University of New York

John Hinshaw
Lebanon Valley College

Michael Hirsch
Labor Journalist

Mandi Isaacs Jackson
UNITE-HERE

Daniel Jacoby
University of Washington, Bothell

Howard Karger
University of Queensland

Dan La Botz
Independent Scholar

Paul Le Blanc
La Roche College (Pittsburgh)

Michael Z. Letwin
Association of Legal Aid Attorneys, Former President

Nathan Lillie
University of Groningen

John P. Lloyd
California State Polytechnic University, Pomona

Timothy P. Lynch
College of Mount St. Joseph

Christopher R. Martin
University of Northern Iowa

William Mello
Indiana University

Jack Metzgar
Roosevelt University

Rachel Meyer
University of Michigan

Todd Michney
Tulane University

Vernon Mogensen
Kingsborough Community College—The City University of New York

Scott Molloy
University of Rhode Island

Roxanne Newton
Mitchell Community College

Paul J. Nyden
Charleston Gazette

Daniel J. Opler
College of Mount Saint Vincent

Christopher Phelps
The Ohio State University at Mansfield

Kim Phillips-Fein
Gallatin School of New York University

Nicola Pizzolato
Queen Mary, University of London

James S. Pula
Purdue University

Damone Richardson
United Association for Labor Education

Gerald Ronning
Albright College

Michael Schiavone
Flinders University

Anthony J. Silva
National Coalition of Independent Scholars

Joseph Slater
University of Toledo College of Law

Robert Smith
Sinclair Community College

Stan Sorscher
Labor Representative at SPEEA

David J. Walsh
Miami University

Calvin Winslow
Institute of International Studies, University of California, Berkeley & The Mendocino Institute

James Wolfinger
DePaul University

John L. Woods
University of Indianapolis

Gary Zabel
University of Massachusetts Boston

LIST OF ABBREVIATIONS

9to5	National Association of Working Women
AAA	Agricultural Adjustment Administration
AAUP	American Association of University Professors
ACA	American Communications Association
ACSU	Atlantic Coast Seamen's Union
ACWA	Amalgamated Clothing Workers of America
ACTU	Association of Catholic Trade Unionists
ACTWA	Amalgamated Clothing and Textile Workers of America
ADT	American District Telegraph
AEA	Actors' Equity Association
AFA	Association of Flight Attendants
AFGE	American Federation of Government Employees
AFL	American Federation of Labor
AFM	American Federation of Musicians
AFSCME	American Federation of State, County, and Municipal Employees
AFSCME DC 37	District Council 37 of the American Federation of State, County, and Municipal Employees
AFT	American Federation of Teachers
AFTRA	American Federation of Television and Radio Artists
AFW	Association of Federation Workers
AGVA	American Guild of Variety Artists
AISI	American Iron and Steel Institute
AIU	American Industrial Union
ALAA	Association of Legal Aid Attorneys
ALPA	Air Line Pilots Association
ALRA	Agricultural Labor Relations Act (California)
AMBWNA	Amalgamated Meat Cutters and Butchers Workmen of North America ("The Amalgamated")
AMPAS	Academy of Motion Picture Arts and Science
ANA	American Nurses Association
APA	Allied Pilots Association
APFA	Association of Professional Flight Attendants
ARTA	American Radio Telegraphists' Association
ARU	American Railway Union
ATA	African American Teachers' Association
ATWA	Amalgamated Textile Workers of America
AWF	Alternative Work Force
AWIL	Agricultural Workers Industrial League
AWO	Agricultural Workers' Organization
AWU	Auto Workers Union
AWUE	Association of Western Union Employees
BCLU	Boston Central Labor Union
BCOA	Bituminous Coal Operators Association
BLA	Black Lung Association
BLE	Brotherhood of Locomotive Engineers
BLF	Brotherhood of Locomotive Firemen
BLS	Bureau of Labor Statistics
BSAU	Bookkeepers, Stenographers and Accountants' Union
BUSOC	Boston University Staff Organizing Committee
CAB	Civil Aeronautics Board
CASE	Cornell Association of Student Employees
CAWIU	Cannery and Agricultural Workers Industrial Union
CC	Central Casting
CF & I	Colorado Fuel & Iron (now Rocky Mountain Steel)
CFT	Chicago Federation of Teachers
CGEU	Coalition of Graduate Employee Unions
CGT	Confederation generale du travail
CIO	Congress of Industrial Organizations
CIR	Commission on Industrial Relations
CIW	Coalition of Immokalee Workers
CLA	Communist League of America
CLUW	Coalition of Labor Union Women
CND	Council of National Defense

COLA	Cost of Living Allowance
COME	Citizens on the Move for Equality
CPUSA	Communist Party USA
CRA	Catholic Radical Alliance
CSU	Canadian Seamen's Union
CSU	Coastal Seamen's Union
CSU	Conference of Studio Unions
CTJ	Commercial Telegraphers' Journal
CTU	Commercial Telegraphers' Union of America
CUE	Coalition of University Employees
CWA	Communications Workers of America
DGA	Directors Guild of America
DPOWU	Distributive Processing and Office Workers Union
DRUM	Dodge Revolutionary Union Movement
EFC	Emergency Fleet Corporation
EHRB	Emergency Home Relief Bureau
ERP	Employee Representation Plan
FAA	Federal Aviation Administration
FAIR	Fairness and Accuracy in Reporting
FEIA	Flight Engineers International Association
FEPC	Fair Employment Practices Committee
FHUE	Federation of Hospital and University Employees
FLCFWU	Farm Laborers and Cotton Field Workers Union
FLOC	Farm Labor Organizing Committee
FMCS	Federal Mediation and Conciliation Service
FMPC	Federated Motion Picture Crafts
FTA	Food, Tobacco, Agricultural, and Allied Workers (formerly UCAPAWA)
GEOC	Graduate Employees Organizing Committee
GESO	Graduate Employees and Students Organization
GET-UP	Graduate Employees Together
GSEU	Graduate Student Employees United (Columbia)
GSOC	Graduate Students Organizing Committee
HDC	Highway Drivers Council of California
HERE	Hotel Employees and Restaurant Employees International Union
HNA	Hawaiian Nurses Association
HSPA	Hawaiian Sugar Planters Association
HUAC	House Un-American Activities Committee
IABSIW	International Association of Bridge and Structural Iron Workers
IAFF	International Association of Fire Fighters
IAM	International Association of Machinists
IAM-AW	International Association of Machinists and Aerospace Workers
IATSE	International Alliance of Theatrical Stage Employees (also called IA: the Alliance)
IAWOC	Insurance and Allied Workers Organizing Committee
IBEW	International Brotherhood of Electrical Workers
IBP	Iowa Beef Packers
IBT	International Brotherhood of Teamsters
ICC	Interstate Commerce Commission
ICF	International Federation of Chemical and General Workers Unions and International Federation of Chemical, Energy and General Workers
ICSOM	International Conference of Symphony and Opera Musicians
IFFA	Independent Federation of Flight Attendants
IFPTE	International Federation of Professional and Technical Employees
ILA	International Longshoremen's Association
ILD	International Labor Defense
ILGWU	International Ladies' Garment Workers' Union
ILWU	International Longshore and Warehouse Union
IMF	International Monetary Fund
IMU	International Moulders' Union
IPPAU	International Printing Pressman and Assistants Union
IRIC	Redwood Industrial Relations Committee
IRT	Interborough Rapid Transit Company
ISU	International Seamen's Union
ITC	Iron Trades Councils
ITF	International Transport Workers' Federation
IUFA	International Union of Flight Attendants
IUMSWA	Industrial Union of Marine and Shipbuilding Workers of America
IWU	Insurance Workers Union
IWW	Industrial Workers of the World (a.k.a. Wobblies)
JMSC	Joint Maritime Strike Committee
KofL	Knights of Labor
KWA	Kohler Workers Association
LCA	Lakes Carriers Association
LFLRA	Lowell Female Labor Reform Association
LUPA	Longshoremen's Union Protective Association
MAP	Mutual Assistance Pact

MASE	Mutual Alliance of Studio Employees
MEBA	Marine Engineers Beneficial Association
MESA	Mechanics Educational Society
MFD	Miners for Democracy
MFLU	Mississippi Freedom Labor Union
MFU	Maryland Freedom Union
MGA	Musicians Guild of America
MLB	Major League Baseball
MLBPA	Major League Baseball Players' Association
M&M	Merchants and Manufacturers Association (Los Angeles)
MMA	Metal Manufacturers Association
MMP	Masters, Mates, and Pilots
MMWIU	Metal Mine Workers' Industrial Union
MNA	Massachusetts Nurses Association
MNPA	Musicians National Protective Association
MPPA	Motion Picture Producers Association
MPPDA	Motion Picture Producers and Distributors of America
MRF	Member Relief Fund
MTA	Motor Truck Association of California
MTWU	Marine Transport Workers Union
MWIU	Marine Workers Industrial Union
NAACP	National Association for the Advancement of Colored People
NAB	National Association of Broadcasters
NABET	National Association of Broadcast Employees and Technicians
NAM	National Association of Manufacturers
NASW	National Association of Social Workers
NBA	National Basketball Association
NBPA	National Basketball Players' Association
NCC	National Coordinating Committee
NCDDC	North Central District Drivers Council
NCF	National Civic Federation
NEA	National Erectors Association
NFA	National Founders Association
NFFE	National Association of Federal Employees
NFL	National Football League
NFLPA	National Football League Players' Association
NFLU	National Farm Labor Union
NFWA	National Farm Workers Association
NHL	National Hockey League
NHLPA	National Hockey League Players' Association
NIOSH	National Institute of Occupational Safety and Health
NIRA	National Industrial Recovery Act (1933)
NJEA	New Jersey Education Association
NLM	National League of Musicians
NLRA	National Labor Relations Act (also called the Wagner Act)
NLRB	National Labor Relations Board
NLU	National Labor Union
NMB	National Mediation Board
NMTA	National Metal Trades Association
NMU	National Maritime Union
NMU	National Miners Union
NOW	National Organization of Women
NRA	National Recovery Administration
NTU	Newark Teachers' Union
NTWIU	Needle Trades Workers Industrial Union
NTWU	National Textile Workers Union
NWLB	National War Labor Board
NYSA	New York Shipping Association
NYSNA	New York State Nurses Association
OEIU	Office Employees International Union
OEMs	Original Equipment Manufacturers
OPEIU	Office and Professional Employees International Union
OPU	Operative Pottery Union
ORC	Order of Railway Conductors
ORIT	Inter-American Regional Organization of Laborers
OSHA	Occupational Health and Safety Administration
PACE	Paper, Allied-Industrial, Chemical and Energy Workers International Union
PATCO	Professional Air Traffic Controllers Organization
PEBs	Presidential Emergency Boards
PERC	Public Employment Relations Commission
PFL	Pacific Freight Lines
PHWIU	Packing House Workers Industrial Union
PMA	Pacific Maritime Association
PRTEU	Philadelphia Rapid Transit Employees Union
PWOC	Packinghouse Workers Organizing Committee
RCIPA	Retail Clerks International Protection Association
RED	Railway Employees' Department
RLB	Railroad Labor Board
RMA	Record Musicians' Association
ROPA	Regional Orchestra Players' Association
RUM	Revolutionary Union Movement
RWDSU	Retail Wholesale and Department Store Union (formerly United Retail Employees of America)
SAG	Screen Actors Guild
SBA	Studio Basic Agreement

SCLC	Southern Christian Leadership Conference
SCMWA	State, County, and Municipal Workers of America
SCU	Alabama Share Croppers Union
SEIU	Service Employees International Union
SFFT	San Francisco Federation of Teachers
SFTU	Southern Tenant Farmers Union
SIPCO	Swift Independent
SIU	Seafarers' International Union
SIUNA	Seafarers' International Union of North America (formerly SIU)
SLAB	Shipbuilding Labor Adjustment Board
SLC	Stockyards Labor Council
SLU	Shipyard Laborers' Union
SLWIU	Shoe Leader Workers Industrial Union
SMWIU	Steel and Metal Workers Industrial Union
SNCC	Student Nonviolent Coordinating Committee
SPD	German Social Democratic Party
SPEEA	Society of Professional Engineering Employees in Aerospace
SSWU	Social Service Workers Union
STLA	Socialist Trade and Labor Alliance
SUB	Supplemental Unemployment Benefits
SUP	Sailors' Union of the Pacific
SWDC	Social Worker's Discussion Club of New York
SWG	Screen Writers Guild
SWOC	Steel Workers' Organizing Committee
TAA	Teaching Assistant Association
TDU	Teamsters for a Democratic Union
TNG	The Newspaper Guild
TPL	Telegraphers Protective League
TU	Trainmen's Union
TUEL	Trade Union Educational League
TURF	Teamsters United Rank and File
TUUL	Trade Union Unity League
TWOC	Textile Workers' Organizing Committee
TWU	Transport Workers' Union
TWUA	Textile Workers Union of America
UAW	United Automobile, Aerospace and Agricultural Implement Workers of America
UBC	United Brotherhood of Carpenters
UCAPAWA	United Cannery, Agricultural, Packing and Allied Workers of America (renamed FTA: Food, Tobacco, Agricultural, and Allied Workers)
UE	United Electrical, Radio and Machine Workers of America
UFA	Union of Flight Attendants
UFCW	United Food and Commercial Workers (formerly AMBLONA)
UFT	United Federation of Teachers
UFW	United Farm Workers (formerly NFWA)
UFWOC	United Farm Workers Organizing Committee (merger of NFWA and AWOC, later called UFW: United Farm Workers)
UIS	Union of International Seafarers
UMW or UMWA	United Mine Workers of America
UNITE	Union of Needletrades, Industrial and Textile Employees
UOPWA	United Office and Professional Workers of America
UPWA	United Packinghouse Workers of America (formerly PHWIU)
URW	United Rubber Workers
USS	United States Steel Corporation (now USX)
USTG	United Studio Technicians Guild
USWA	United Steel Workers of America
UTLA	United Teachers of Los Angeles
UTW	United Textile Workers of America
VEBA	Voluntary Employee Benefits Association
VISTA	Volunteers in Service to America
WCI	Women Consolidated Industries
WFM	Western Federation of Miners
WGA	Writers Guild of America (formerly SWG)
WMC	War Manpower Commission
W-P	Willing-Pittsburgh
WP	Workingmen's Party
WSB	Wage Stabilization Board
WTUL	Women's Trade Union League

TIMELINE

1636 First organized work stoppage in colonial America on Richmond Island, Maine; fishermen struck to protest withholding of wages.

1659 Strike by New York City master bakers protesting low prices.

1663 Maryland indentured servants strike to demand meat in their food rations; judge sides with master, but suspends sentence of 30 lashes.

1677 New York City cartmen are first workers to face criminal prosecution for striking.

1768 Journeymen printers in New York City strike for "three shillings and six pence per day with diet."

1786 Journeymen printers in Philadelphia strike for a dollar a day and set up a strike fund to support their effort; they disband the fund after their strike succeeds.

1791 Journeymen carpenters initiate first building trades strike in Philadelphia.

1792 Philadelphia journeymen cordwainers (shoemakers) form first permanent local union and launch strike against a wage reduction.

1805 New York City cordwainers establish first permanent strike fund.

1806 In *Commonwealth v. Pullis,* the United States Supreme Court rules that an 1805 strike for higher wages by Philadelphia journeymen cordwainers is a criminal conspiracy, setting a precedent that lasts into the twentieth century.

1824 Strike by female cotton mill operatives in Pawtucket, Rhode Island, is first strike by factory workers in the United States.

1825 United Tailoresses Society of New York goes on strike.

1828 Textile mill workers and machinists in Paterson, New Jersey, strike against the changing of their dinner hour and demand a ten-hour day; they win the first demand but not the second.

1829 The Workingmen's Party of New York forms.

1834 More than 800 female mill workers in Lowell, Massachusetts, strike to protest a wage reduction; mill owners defeat the strike by hiring scabs and refusing to bargain.

1834 President Andrew Jackson sends federal troops to Williamsport, Maryland, to quell a labor conflict among workers on the Chesapeake and Ohio Canal.

1835 Navy yard workers in Washington, D.C., are the first federal government workers to strike.

1836 More than 1,500 female mill workers in Lowell, Massachusetts, form a Factory Girls' Association and strike to protest an increase in the cost of room and board in company-owned boarding houses; in response, several mill owners rescind the increase.

1836 A strike by New York City journeymen tailors sparks strikes of stevedores, laborers, carpenters, and others; violent conflicts rock the city's workshops; 30,000 workers rally at City Hall for formation of workingmen's party; it is the largest protest gathering in American history to that point.

1842 Anthracite miners in Schuylkill County, Pennsylvania, walk out for higher wages and payment in cash instead of in "store orders" for goods at local stores; this first coal miners' strike dissipates after several weeks when state militia and local sheriffs protect scabs.

1842 Pittsburgh puddlers (iron workers) and boilermakers engage in the first sit-down strike when they seize a mill.

1850 New York City journeymen tailors strike for higher wages and a closed shop; several violent clashes take place; at rallies, sympathetic workers renew the call for a workingmen's party; the strike ends with the formation of the Cooperative Union Tailoring Establishment.

1861 Civil War begins; during the conflict, Southern slaves leave plantations for Union lines and free themselves in the largest strike in American history.

1863 Emancipation Proclamation ends legal slavery.

1866 National Labor Union is the first national union federation formed, composed primarily of construction unions; led by William H. Sylvis, it favors arbitration over strikes, advocates the eight-hour day, and supports the exclusion of Chinese workers from the United States; it lasts until 1872.

1868 Congress establishes eight-hour day for laborers, women, and mechanics who work for the federal government.

1869 The Knights of Labor is formed as a fraternal society advocating the establishment of cooperative ownership of mines and factories; it officially opposes strikes, but it grows and evolves over the years to become a diverse labor union that engages in strikes, pushes for the eight-hour day, recruits women and African-American workers, and advocates Chinese exclusion; it declines after the 1886 Haymarket affair and a failed strike against the Missouri Pacific railroad the same year.

1869 Colored National Labor Union is founded; Isaac Myers, a free-born African American ship caulker is its first leader; it demands equal representation in the workforce and admits workers regardless of race or gender; Frederick Douglass becomes its president in 1872.

1872 Lynn, Massachusetts, shoemakers in the Knights of St. Crispin, the country's largest trade union at the time, strike to renew an agreement that had set wages for the city's shoemakers; the strike fails and their union collapses as employers refuse to employ union members in a period of high unemployment.

1876 Workingmen's Party forms; it is the first Marxist party in the United States.

1877 In the Great Strike, railroad workers across the country protest wage cuts; supporters in dozens of communities join the demonstrations, many of which include the destruction of railroad property; more than 80,000 railroad workers and half a million other workers participate; the Workingmen's Party leads protests in several cities, including a general strike in St. Louis; the U.S. government sends thousands of federal troops to occupy the city; state and local authorities mobilize police and militia to crush the strike in Martinsburg, West Virginia, Baltimore, Pittsburgh, Toledo, Terre Haute, Indiana, Chicago, and other cities.

1878 Socialist Labor Party forms; it incorporates the Workingmen's Party.

1881 Federation of Organized Trades and Labor Unions of the United States of America and Canada is formed, precursor to the American Federation of Labor.

1883 Cowboys in the Panhandle of Texas strike for higher wages, better food, and the right to graze their small herds on public range land; ranchers crush the strike by hiring scabs and having Texas Rangers guard their cattle.

1885 Workers on railroads controlled by robber baron Jay Gould strike against wage reductions and win; two months later a second strike protests the dismissal of Knights of Labor members; again the strikers win; the victories lead nearly 600,000 workers to join the Knights over the next year.

1886 The Federation of Organized Trades and Labor Unions is reorganized as the American Federation of Labor (AFL); it includes primarily craft unions; Samuel Gompers is its president; it is the most important and powerful labor federation in the country.

1886 In early May, approximately 350,000 workers nationwide strike to demand the eight-hour day; police shoot into a crowd of striking McCormick Harvesting Machine workers outside Chicago; the next day a bomb is thrown into a crowd of 3,000 people protesting the police brutality in Chicago's Haymarket Square; eight anarchists are arrested, tried, and found guilty although no evidence links any of them to the bomb or a conspiracy; they are sentenced to death, one commits suicide, and four are executed.

1886 Local assemblies of the Knights of Labor strike Jay Gould's southwest railroad lines to enforce wage agreements made after the 1885 strikes; with the aid of state and federal judges, the companies crush the strike; the Knights of Labor begins a rapid decline.

1887 Longshoremen, led by the Knights of Labor, shut down the waterfronts of New York and New Jersey; when police and Pinkerton agents begin guarding scab ships, the strike collapses, along with the Knights of Labor on the docks.

1890 Carpenters strike for the eight-hour day and win in 137 cities, involving more than 46,000 workers.

1890 The Sherman Antitrust Act prohibits cartels in restraint of trade; the act is used in 1894 against the American Railway Union during the Pullman strike.

1892 A lockout of the Amalgamated Association of Iron, Steel, and Tin Workers by Carnegie Steel in Homestead, Pennsylvania, includes a violent conflict in which workers defeat 300 Pinkerton guards trying to reopen the plant; seven guards and nine strikers die; National Guard troops then occupy the town and reopen the plant; the defeat is a mighty blow to the cause of unionism in the steel industry.

1892 Unionized miners in Coeur d'Alene, Idaho, strike to protest a wage reduction; they seize several mines; widespread support for the miners, including from the local sheriff, leads mine owners to import strikebreakers and convinces the governor to mobilize the National Guard; the military force, including mass arrests, breaks the strike, but not the unions, who soon form the Western Federation of Miners.

1892 Multi-racial workers in the New Orleans Teamsters, Scalesmen, and Packers unions strike together to demand a ten-hour day, overtime pay, and a closed shop; the strike spreads into a general strike for the closed shop throughout the city, with more than 20,000 workers participating; the governor declares martial law and the strike ends; the workers win their wage and hour demands, but not union recognition; the strike illustrates the possibilities for multi-racial unionism in the South.

1894 Miners in Cripple Creek, Colorado, win a strike for the eight-hour day when Governor Davis H. Waite mobilizes the state's resources to protect the strikers from local sheriffs and private guards employed by the mine owners; the strike demonstrates the centrality of government action in many labor disputes.

1894 Members of the American Railway Union working at the Pullman Palace Sleeping Car Company outside Chicago strike to protest a cut in wages and rents in the company town; the ARU, led by Eugene V. Debs, shuts down much of the nation's rails by refusing to handle Pullman cars; skilled unions in the AFL, including the railroad brotherhoods, refuse to support the strike, which is crushed by injunctions, arrests, and thousands of federal troops; Debs spends six months in jail.

1895 In *In re Debs*, the United States Supreme Court upholds the use of injunctions against strikes affecting interstate commerce.

1898 The Erdman Act establishes mediation and arbitration for settling disputes between railroad companies and their workers; it outlaws yellow dog contracts that prohibit railroad employees from joining unions; the Supreme Court declares the section on yellow dog contracts unconstitutional in 1908.

1899 A strike by Buffalo grain shovelers against Great Lakes shipping companies, elevator owners, and railroads paralyzes the nation's largest grain port; the strike wins an end to the contract labor system and the implementation of a closed shop; it establishes the International Longshoremen's Association in the Great Lakes.

1900 Five thousand Chicago machinists strike; settlement includes a board of arbitration having equal representatives of the union and the employers to decide wages, grievances, and apprenticeship rules.

1901 Two thousand San Francisco restaurant workers strike for a six-day week and pay raises; their strike fails, but they win their demands by organizing individual restaurants the next year.

1901 Socialist Party of America forms.

1902 Chicago Teamsters strike against the "big six" oligopoly of meatpacking companies; popular anger at the oligopoly leads to several days of rioting over meat prices and to stop the movement of nonunion meat; the strikers do not win formal union recognition but do win arbitration, a wage increase, and overtime pay.

1903 Twelve hundred agricultural workers in the Japanese-Mexican Labor Association in Oxnard, California, more than 90 percent of the workforce, strike against the contracting system; they overcome racial division, win an end to the contracting system, and nearly double their wages.

1904 The New York City Interborough Rapid Transit strike, one of the first large "wildcat strikes," fails when union leaders condemn the walkout by rank-and-file workers as a breach of the union's contract with the employer.

1904 Approximately 40,000 skilled and unskilled packinghouse workers in nine cities strike for a floor on the wages of the unskilled; despite workers' unity across lines of skill, race, gender, and ethnicity, the strike fails when the packers restart the plants with foremen and various groups of scabs, including a large group of African-American strikebreakers; the strike illustrates the difficulties of sustaining solidarity across divisions among workers.

1905 The Industrial Workers of the World (IWW) (Wobblies) forms to promote revolutionary unionism; it opposes the AFL's conservative focus on skilled workers with the motto "An injury to one is an injury to all"; early organizers include William "Big Bill" Haywood, Daniel DeLeon, Eugene V. Debs, and Mother Jones.

1908 In Missoula, Montana, IWW organizers flood the city, hold open-air meetings, distribute literature, advocate revolutionary unionism, get arrested, clog the jails and courts, and win support from workers and liberal leaders; it is the first of more than thirty "free-speech fights" that help build the IWW.

1909 In the "Uprising of the 20,000," Jewish and Italian women shirtwaist makers in New York City strike for the union shop; they win support from middle-class women, who legitimize the strike in the public's eye; despite intense solidarity from the city's workers, the strike fails after three months.

1909 A strike at the Pressed Steel Car Company in McKees Rocks, Pennsylvania, involves both skilled American-born and unskilled foreign-born workers, demonstrating that unskilled workers are capable of union organizing; IWW organizers enter after the strike begins; the strike fails due to ethnic divisions among the workers and the force of strikebreakers and the government.

1910 Metal trades unions in Los Angeles strike against the open shop; *Los Angles Times* publisher Harrison Gray Otis is an outspoken critic of the strike; a bomb destroys the *Times'* building; employers crush the strike with injunctions and strikebreakers; the City of Angels remains an open-shop bastion into the 1930s.

1910 A labor dispute at the Philadelphia Rapid Transit Company sparks a citywide general strike.

1911 Fire at Triangle Shirtwaist factory in New York City kills 146 workers trapped by locked doors and blocked fire escapes.

1912 In what comes to be called the "Bread and Roses Strike," IWW organizers lead a walkout of approximately 10,000 immigrant textile workers in Lawrence, Massachusetts, protesting a pay cut and demanding "bread and roses, too"; the strike inspires national attention when the IWW arranges to send strikers' children to live with supporters in other cities for the duration of the strike, which wins a pay raise; within a year the employers use various tactics, including dismissals and private detectives, to rout the IWW from the city's mills.

1913 IWW organizers lead a strike by Paterson, New Jersey, silk workers; to support the strike, radical intellectuals and cultural figures organize the "Paterson Strike Pageant," which plays to overflow crowds at Madison Square Garden in New York City and wins the strike nationwide attention; despite massive solidarity, the strike is defeated by physical attacks on pickets, the arrests of IWW leaders, injunctions, scabs, and ethnic and skill divisions among the strikers.

1914 During a strike by coal miners against the Colorado Fuel and Iron Company, owned by John D. Rockefeller, state militia attack a tent camp in Ludlow, Colorado, with machine guns, setting fire to the camp and killing five miners, two women, and eleven children; the Ludlow Massacre horrifies the nation, but little is done to restrain attacks on striking workers.

1914 In spite of strong organization by the United Textile Workers, a long strike by several thousand textile workers at the Fulton Bag and Cotton Mills Company in Atlanta fails when the employers evict workers from company housing, employ scabs, and launch a public relations campaign that eventually discredits the union.

1915 During a strike by stillcleaners at Standard Oil in Bayonne, New Jersey, armed strikebreakers protected by police fire into a crowd of strikers and sympathizers, killing four; despite public outcry, the company and city continue the physical attacks and launch a public campaign to alienate American workers from their Polish, Hungarian, and Italian comrades; the strike fails.

1916 Some 5,000 miners, three-quarters of them of Mexican heritage, strike in Arizona for wage equality, wage increases, and payment in cash; Anglo miners support the strike, which wins elimination of racial distinctions in the mines and union recognition.

1916 Mesabi Range miners in Minnesota strike over economic grievances and against the contract-labor system; the 8,000 strikers call off the strike after the arrest of veteran IWW leaders, attacks by AFL leaders, and four months of company intransigence.

1917 The United States enters World War I.

1917 Vigilantes armed and employed by the Phelps-Dodge copper company in Bisbee, Arizona, round up 1,200 striking miners led by the IWW; they herd the strikers into cattle cars and ship them to a stockade in the desert near Hermanas, New Mexico; no one is punished for atrocity.

1917 When a strike by lumber workers loses steam in the Pacific Northwest, IWW organizers suggest members go back to work but act as if they do not know what they are doing; this "strike on the job" hurts production and encourages government intervention that results in better wages and working conditions.

1918 National War Labor Board forms.

1919 In support of a strike by 35,000 Seattle shipyard workers demanding higher wages and shorter hours, radicals at the head of the city's Central Labor Council call a citywide general strike and run the city for five days, mobilizing to maintain food, water, heat, and electricity for residents; the strike is crushed when, amid nationwide and local anti-radical hysteria, the mayor calls in federal troops; the strike is the first major event in a massive postwar strike wave that lasts into 1920.

1919 Massachusetts governor Calvin Coolidge breaks a strike by Boston police with militia and scabs.

1919 Eight thousand women telephone operators defy male union leaders and paralyze New England communications for six days with a strike that wins seniority rights.

1919 A strike by 250,000 workers, mostly unskilled immigrants, paralyzes the nation's steel industry; employers hire scabs and mobilize anti-immigrant vigilantes to attack picketers; despite the attacks the immigrant workers remain on strike; eventually leaders of the American-born skilled workers' union order its workers back and the strike fails; it is another major defeat for the labor movement in basic industry.

1920–1922 A series of strikes by miners in West Virginia turns into virtual war as the employers and their government allies use force to crush the walkouts; the miners fight back with considerable success in a series of skirmishes; to end the conflict, the governor declares the strike an insurrection, and President Warren Harding orders regular army troops into the state.

1922 Four hundred thousand railroad shopmen strike against wage cuts, contracting out and the abolishment of overtime pay; the nationwide strike fails; nearly half the strikers lose seniority rights; company unionism expands in the locomotive shops.

1929 A Communist-led strike by approximately 30,000 textile workers in Gastonia, North Carolina, is the first in a series of Southern textile strikes over the next five years; the strike demands the elimination of piecework, a minimum wage, a forty-hour week, equal pay for equal work, and union recognition; the strike all but collapses after anti-Communist propaganda divides the strikers; it ends for good after a series of attacks on the remaining strikers and the arrest of strike leaders.

1931 Radical immigrant cigar workers strike for three days in Tampa, Florida, after employers ban readers who read to the workers as they make the cigars; the employers then lock out the cigar makers and eventually hire only three-quarters of the original strikers.

1932 Led by Communist organizers, 400 Mexican, Filipino, Japanese, and Anglo tree pruners walk out to protest a wage cut; the employers defeat the two-month strike with a combination of scabs, arrests, and racist rhetoric.

1932 A strike against Century Airlines is the first by the Air Line Pilots Association.

1933 Section 7(a) of the National Industrial Recovery Act gives workers the right to organize and bargain collectively through representatives of their own choosing and free from coercion by their employer; the Supreme Court declares the act unconstitutional in 1935.

1933 Auto workers at Briggs Manufacturing Company strike to protest a wage cut and unsafe conditions; their actions inspire strikes at other parts companies and idle 100,000 workers at auto assembly plants; the strikers win a minimum wage and establish momentum for the cause of auto worker unionism.

1934 Rubbers workers "sit down" in a strike against General Tire and Rubber in Akron, Ohio; the plant occupation is one of the first in the United States during the period, and it is also the first in a series of major strikes during the year that revive the labor movement.

1934 During a strike led by the American Workers Party at Electric Auto-Lite in Toledo, Ohio, organizers undermine strikebreaking by mobilizing mass pickets of unemployed workers and strikers; despite injunctions, arrests, and violent clashes, the continued mass mobilizations eventually win a wage increase and union recognition.

1934 A Teamsters strike in Minneapolis led by the Communist League of America, a small Trotskyist organization, becomes a general strike that paralyzes the city; the strikers set up a food service operation, a communication network, and mobilize roving pickets to make sure only necessary deliveries continue; in several battles with police, the union's overwhelming popular support carries the day, though police kill several strikers; political intervention from the governor eventually leads to a compromise solution, which establishes Teamster Local 574 as one of the most powerful local unions in the country.

1934 During a Communist-led strike by San Francisco longshoremen, police kill two strikers; the violence inspires the city's Central Labor Council to authorize a general strike, which lasts several days and encourages intervention from the federal government; the longshoremen win a wage increase, union-run hiring halls, and reduced hours.

1935 Responding to a rise in strikes, Congress passes the National Labor Relations Act (also called the Wagner Act); it establishes the rights of workers to organize unions and bargain collectively; it creates the National Labor Relations Board and establishes the legal infrastructure for the recognition of unions and the procedures of collective bargaining; it is the labor movement's most important legislative victory in U.S. history.

1935 The Committee for Industrial Organization (CIO), led by United Mine Workers president John L. Lewis, brings together several AFL unions with the aim of building unions that represent all workers in an industry, as opposed to those in particular crafts; it soon splits with the AFL and becomes the Congress of Industrial Organizations in 1937.

1936 The Byrnes Act makes it a felony to transport persons in interstate commerce with the intent to employ them to obstruct the rights of peaceful picketing.

1936 Rubber workers strike five different rubber companies over the course of several months, including a massive sit-down at industry leader Goodyear Tire and Rubber in Akron, Ohio; though the United Rubber Workers opposes the sit-down tactic, the new CIO union nonetheless capitalizes on the success of the strikes to become the major union in the industry.

1936–1937 Auto workers in Flint, Michigan, occupy several General Motors plants for forty-four days; when the governor refuses to remove the workers from the plants, the "sit-downs" win union recognition from the world's largest corporation; it is the most important victory for the industrial labor movement, which grows by leaps and bounds over the next years; it inspires workers around the country to adopt the sit-down tactic in their own unionization fights.

1937 Between 1,000 and 2,000 workers at the Hershey Chocolate factory in Hershey, Pennsylvania, sit down and win union recognition.

1937 Workers, mostly women, stage a sit-down at Woolworth's stores in several major cities, including Detroit and New York City; they win union recognition and wage increases.

1937 The newly formed Steelworkers Organizing Committee of the CIO leads a strike against "Little Steel," the four major steel companies that are not industry giant U.S. Steel; in Chicago on Memorial Day, police attack strikers and their supporters, shooting many of them in the back and leaving ten dead; violence occurs in other cities, including Massilon and Cleveland, Ohio; company resistance defeats the strike, but not the union, which wins recognition at all four companies by 1942.

1938 The Fair Labor Standards Act establishes a forty-hour work week and a minimum wage and bans child labor.

1939 In *NLRB v. Fansteel Metallurgical Corporation* (1939), the United States Supreme Court rules sit-down strikes illegal.

1940 The Alien Registration Act makes it a criminal offense for anyone to advocate overthrowing the government of the United States and requires noncitizen adult residents to register with the government; the act is used against foreign-born union organizers.

1941 Communists in the United Auto Workers lead a strike for union recognition at North American Aviation in Inglewood, California; top UAW officials oppose the strike, as does the Roosevelt administration, which uses the army to occupy the plant and crush the walkout; the strike signals CIO officials' growing unwillingness to risk militancy for fear of alienating the government.

1941–1943 On several dozen occasions, white workers in Detroit, Michigan, strike against the employment or promotion of African-American workers; the strikes are often the result of management manipulation, but they rarely succeed.

1941–1945 During World War II, AFL and CIO officials agree to a "no-strike pledge" committing their members to refrain from any work stoppages and to settle all labor-management disputes through the National War Labor Board.

1943 The War Labor Disputes Act (Smith-Connally Act) gives the federal government the ability to seize industries threatened by strikes.

1944 Philadelphia bus drivers strike against the employment of African-American drivers and lose.

1945–1946 A postwar wave of strikes washes across the United States; 4.5 million workers participate, resulting in 116 million man-hours lost; the strikes are mostly for higher wages and better benefits as workers try to make up for wartime inflation.

1945–1946 The United Auto Workers strikes General Motors for 113 days; in negotiations, UAW vice-president Walter P. Reuther demands that the company open its books to show why it cannot provide a wage increase without raising the price of its automobiles; the company refuses what it sees as union encroachment on management rights; rather than push for greater say in company operations, the union settles for a wage increase, accepting the company-imposed limits on its ability to affect management decisions.

1946 In support of striking department store employees, 100,000 workers in Oakland, California, engage in a three-day general strike.

1947 The Labor-Management Relations Act (Taft-Hartley Act) prohibits jurisdictional strikes, wildcat strikes, solidarity or political strikes, secondary boycotts, "common situs" picketing, closed shops, and monetary donations by unions to federal political campaigns; it requires union officers to sign non-Communist affidavits with the government and allows states to pass "right-to-work laws" outlawing union shops; it empowers the federal government to block strikes that imperil "national health or safety."

1947 In a nationwide strike against American Telephone & Telegraph, 350,000 telephone workers, two-thirds of whom are women, seek wage increases, a union shop, and other demands; the strike is one of the largest of women in U.S. history; it lasts a month and achieves only some of its demands.

1950 President Truman orders the U.S. Army to seize all national railroads to prevent a general strike.

1950 General Motors and the United Auto Workers sign the "Treaty of Detroit," in which the union gives up the right to strike during the contract and the right to bargain over some workplace issues; in exchange the UAW wins guaranteed wage increases over the life of the contract, extensive health, unemployment, and pension benefits, expanded vacation time, and cost-of-living adjustments to wages; the contract becomes a model for employer-provided social welfare programs, which leave U.S. unions less motivated to fight for the public provision of health care, pensions, and other social benefits.

1952 President Truman orders the U.S. Army to seize nation's steel mills to avert a strike; the U.S. Supreme Court rules the act illegal.

1953 African-American sugar cane workers in Louisiana strike for union recognition; the planters defeat the strike by evicting workers from their homes and winning injunctions against picketing.

1954 The United Auto Workers launches a strike against the Kohler Company, a plumbing manufacturer in Wisconsin; led by the virulently anti-union Herbert Kohler, the company resists the union's mass pickets; the strike moves to the courts and drags on for more than a decade, when the courts finally order strikers rehired and the two sides negotiate a settlement and a new contract; the strike illustrates the ability of employers to use the National Labor Relations Board and courts to delay unionization and the growing sophistication of their anti-union activity.

1955 The AFL and the CIO merge.

1959 The Labor-Management Reporting and Disclosure Act (Landrum-Griffin Act) bars members of the Communist Party and convicted felons from holding union office, requires unions to submit annual financial reports to the Department of Labor, establishes that union officers must act as fiduciaries in handling the assets and conducting the affairs of the union, and limits the power of unions to put subordinate bodies in trusteeship; the act mandates that businesses report to the Secretary of Labor any agreement with labor relations consultants hired to persuade employees in regard to their rights to bargain collectively; this provision is routinely ignored.

1959 Approximately 500,000 steelworkers shut down the steel industry for 116 days; the ostensible issues are wages and benefits, but the workers stay out to preserve work rules that protect their jobs; they succeed and win wage and benefit gains.

1960 A strike by the International Union of Electrical Workers (IUE) at General Electric for better wages and protection of the existing cost-of-living allowance is an utter failure; the defeat results largely from divisions among the workforce sewn a decade earlier when the CIO expeled the Communist-led United Electrical Workers (UE), which represented 80 percent of the GE workforce, and chartered the anti-Communist IUE, led by James R. Carey; in 1960 the IUE represents only 70,000 of GE's 251,000, with another 35,000 workers sprinkled between the UE, the International Association of Machinists, and several smaller unions; these unions, along with the nonunion majority of workers, refuses to follow Carey's ill-prepared strike call; the fiasco leads to Carey's eventual ouster from the IUE.

1965 A group of Filipino grape pickers in the Agricultural Workers Organizing Committee launch a strike for union recognition in the central valley of California; the mostly Mexican National Farm Workers Association joins the strike and the two unions soon merge to create the United Farm Workers' Organizing Committee, led by César Chávez; despite early recognition from two major companies, the strike continues against other growers; since agricultural workers are exempt from the National Labor Relations Act as modified by the Taft-Hartley Act, the UFWOC can and does call for a boycott of grapes; the campaign lasts for five years but eventually wins union recognition and a contract that improves wages and benefits for farm workers.

1966 To win their demands for a major wage increase, improved pensions, longer vacations, and other benefits, New York City transit workers violate state law and shut down the city for twelve days; despite the jailing of their leaders, they win a 15 percent wage increase, wage equality with other city workers, and a supplemental pension.

1967–1976 A wave of official and wildcat strikes washes across the U.S. economy; public sector workers, especially teachers and city workers, are prominent.

1968 A series of New York City teachers strikes against local control in the Ocean Hill–Brownsville district pits the union against civil rights activists and alienates many African-American workers from the union movement.

1968 After two co-workers are killed in industrial accidents, African-American sanitation workers in Memphis walk out to demand equality on the job and union recognition; the mayor declares the strike illegal, but it continues nonetheless; using nonviolent civil disobedience, rallies, marches, and other forms of protests, the strikers win support from the city's African-American community and from civil rights leaders across the South, including Dr. Martin Luther King, Jr.; after violence breaks out during a march of 5,000 strike supporters, the governor mobilizes the National Guard; Dr. King vows to return to lead a nonviolent march in support of the strike and when he does he is assassinated, leading the federal government to step in and settle the strike; the result is union recognition, a wage increase, a merit-promotion plan, a no-discrimination clause, and the establishment of a powerful public sector union in Memphis.

1969 African-American women hospital workers strike for 100 days, demanding union recognition and an end to discrimination; using tactics similar to those employed by Memphis sanitation workers and inspiring support from civil rights groups and unions around the country, they win most of their demands, but not union recognition.

1970 A wildcat strike by New York City postal workers spreads nationwide; the strike by 200,000 post office workers is the largest ever against the federal government and wins substantial wage increases for the woefully underpaid postal workers.

1970 Though union officials are still negotiating, tens of thousands of rank-and-file Teamsters in thirty-seven cities walk off the job when the National Master Freight Agreement expires; most go back to work the next day when a settlement is reached, but wildcats demanding local improvements continue in Ohio, Missouri, California, and elsewhere; in Ohio, strikers clash with National Guard troops; though they last for weeks, only in Chicago do the wildcat strikes win improvements.

1970 Despite having hammered out the basic outlines of an agreement, officials of the United Auto Workers lead a fifty-eight-day strike against General Motors; rather than pressuring the company, the strike is designed to get rank-and-file auto workers to approve the agreement; the strike succeeds in "blowing off steam," and the workers ratify a wage and benefit increase.

1972 Auto workers in Lordstown, Ohio, strike against the unbearable speed of the assembly line at one of General Motors' most advanced plants; the strike wins national attention of media fascinated with the "blue collar blues," the discontent and alienation caused by mind-numbing work.

1972–1973 Philadelphia teachers defy injunctions and strike to win significant wage and benefit improvements; the strike is just one example of dozens of teachers' strikes during the period.

1977 Women bank workers in Willmar, Minnesota, strike to protest workplace gender discrimination in hiring and promotion.

1977–1978 The United Mine Workers engages in its longest national walkout, a 110-day strike centered on the right to strike over grievances and health care improvements; the strike culminates nearly a decade of wildcat strikes during which rank-and-file miners took grievances into their own hands; the strike continues despite court injunctions and the intervention of President Jimmy Carter; the settlement ending the strike includes a significant wage increase, but not the right to strike over grievances; the industry's troubled health care fund is disbanded and replaced with weaker company-based private plans; the union is left considerably divided.

1981 President Ronald Reagan fires striking air traffic controllers and decertifies their union, the Professional Air Traffic Controllers Association; the president's union-busting activity signals a sea change for the American labor movement and the number of strikes begins a precipitous decline.

1981 The Major League Baseball Players Association strikes to protect free agency and wins.

1982 The National Football League Players Association strikes for an increased percentage of gross revenue, but wins only a one-time payment.

1983–1986 A coalition of unions at Phelps-Dodge in Arizona strikes to preserve a cost-of-living allowance; the company refuses and begins a campaign to break the unions; almost a thousand National Guard troops protect strikebreakers, while police arrest and beat strikers; despite the company's power, the strikers maintain their efforts and raise considerable support from unions around the country; but depression in the copper industry means scabs are available and the company eventually succeeds in decertifying the unions.

1984–1985 Yale University clerical workers strike to win a first contract and comparable worth for women workers; the university hires union-busting lawyers, but worker solidarity carries the day; new salary structures allow women workers to advance from dead-end jobs and take time off to have children without losing seniority.

1985 In Austin, Minnesota, Local P-9 of the United Food and Commercial Workers resists the concessionary bargaining of the national union during its negotiations with Hormel; instead it launches a corporate campaign and then a strike, which succeeds in shutting the plant for several weeks; the company hires hundreds of replacement workers and National Guard troops protect them as they reopen the plant; in response, Local P-9 sends roving pickets to other Hormel plants, but workers who honor the pickets are fired; the strike polarizes Austin and much of the labor movement; after six months, the UFCW takes over Local P-9 and negotiates a new concessionary contract.

1986 Flight attendants at TWA, newly taken over by corporate raider Carl Icahn, strike against pay cuts and work rule changes; pilots and machinists, who offered concessions to get Icahn to buy the airline, refuse to support the strike; the company hires and trains replacements and the strike collapses.

1989 Workers at NYNEX, the telephone company in the Northeast, strike for four months against company demands for higher employee health care contributions and flexible compensation schemes; strike preparation builds the necessary solidarity, while coordinated negotiations by the Communications Workers of America and the International Brotherhood of Electrical Workers create a united front of the unions; company public relations gaffs, particularly the application for rate increases, alienate public officials and turn popular sentiment toward the strikers; the strike succeeds in protecting workers' existing level of wages and benefits.

1989–1990 The Pittston Coal Company withdraws from the Bituminous Coal Operators Association and provokes a strike by demanding concessions, including weaker work rules, irregular schedules, Sunday shifts, and drastic limitations on health and pension benefits for retired and disabled workers; to protect themselves, miners in the United Mine Workers organize mass pickets, demonstrations, and civil disobedience; dozens are arrested and the union is hit with massive fines; nonetheless, the miners keep up the strike and manage to inflict enough damage to bring the company to the table; the final compromise protects health and pension benefits, but allows subcontracting and Sunday shifts.

1993–1995 Labor disputes in Decatur, Illinois, at construction equipment maker Caterpillar, tire maker Bridgestone-Firestone, and sugar refiner A.E. Staley turn the city into a war zone for several years; the disputes arise from the companies' demands for concessions, particularly in the form of new work rules and cuts in health care benefits; in marches, demonstrations, and civil disobedience, workers at each plant draw on each other for solidarity; the companies use strikebreakers, the courts, and intransigence at the bargaining table to defeat the strikes.

1994–1995 The National Hockey League loses an entire season when it locks out its players.

1997 A strike by the International Brotherhood of Teamsters at United Parcel Service goes against the tide of concessions and failure; in preparation for a possible walkout, the union involves its members in negotiations and strike planning; it develops the popular slogan "Part-time America doesn't work" and makes its central demand the conversion of part-time work into full-time jobs; the intense solidarity of the workforce along with widespread public support quickly convince the company to agree to the union's main demand.

2003–2004 A badly prepared four-month strike by 70,000 Southern California grocery workers against several major supermarket chains ends with the United Food and Commercial Workers accepting lump-sum payments in place of wage increases for current workers and a two-tier system under which new hires earn less in wages and benefits.

2005 New York City transit workers strike for two-and-a-half days when contract negotiations over wages and pensions break down; the strike is illegal under New York state law, so strikers lose two days' pay for each day on strike, the union must pay fines, and its president receives a ten-day jail sentence, of which he serves four; in the end, the union agrees to employee pension contributions in exchange for not having to pay employee health care contributions.

2008 Engineers at Boeing strike successfully for nearly two months to prevent outsourcing and increase job security, wages, and benefits.

2008 After managers at Republic Windows and Doors in Chicago inform them that they will shut the plant, the mostly African-American and Latino workers occupy the factory; their action galvanizes support around the country; their union, the United Electrical Workers Local 1110, publicizes their plight and attacks Bank of America for failing to provide credit to keep the plant open; after six days, the workers win severance pay and two months of health care coverage.

TOPIC FINDER

Civil Rights Unionism

Communism/Communist Party

Constitutional Issues

Contemporary Strikes

Decline of Strikes

Globalization

Latino-Americans

Human Rights

Immigrants

Labor Movement, Organizational History of

News Coverage/Press and Strikes

Organizing

Public Sector

Religion and Strikes

Social Activism

Socialists

Strikebreakers

Women

INTRODUCTION TO THE ENCYCLOPEDIA OF STRIKES IN AMERICAN HISTORY

Aaron Brenner

Strikes have been ubiquitous in American labor-management relations from the colonial era to the present. No one knows for sure how many strikes there have been since the first Europeans colonized North America, but a conservative estimate would put the number well above 300,000. That is an average of more than two per day for every day since the founding of the Jamestown Settlement in Virginia in 1607. Strike statistics are notoriously spotty and unreliable, but since they usually underestimate the incidence of strikes they still indicate the extent of strike activity over the decades. The twenty-five years from 1881 to 1905 saw an average of 1,492 strikes, or more than four per day, with an average of 381,000 workers walking out each year. From 1914 to 1980, on average, 1.7 million workers engaged in 3,448 strikes each year. Clearly strikes have been a prevalent phenomenon in American history.

Strikes have also been fierce, even violent, affairs that have enveloped entire communities in conflict and change. Struggles over workplace issues have spilled into the public arena, as both sides have battled for the support of the police, politicians, and the rest of the community. At times, physical clashes have taken place, and while no definitive count of injuries and fatalities exists, in few other industrialized countries have workers shed (or drawn) more blood in the course of their struggles than in the United States. Even where strikes have not been violent, they have shaped not only the terms and conditions of work, but also the wider economy and society. As a result of strikes, the balance of power between employers and workers has shifted back and forth, setting limits on what each side could accomplish and changing the way participants understood themselves and their world. Victorious strikers have usually demanded better wages and working conditions, but many have also insisted upon greater political power, higher social status, or expanded influence in their communities. By contrast, defeated strikers have rarely been in a position to make such demands, but their employers have gained greater control over their workplaces and their communities as well as enhanced social standing. In these ways, strikes have been key events in the creation of class division and class consciousness, and the prevalence and ferocity of strikes represent compelling evidence of the long-term, widespread class conflict that has run through American history.

Strike Diversity

The level of strike activity has not been consistent through the years. Rather, it has ebbed and flowed over the decades. This variability illustrates an essential characteristic of strikes: they tend to come in waves—periods of heightened strike activity. The twentieth century alone witnessed several significant strike waves—1919, 1934–39, 1946, and 1967–73—involving millions of workers each time. The second half of the nineteenth century also saw massive strike waves in 1877, 1886, and 1892–94. Smaller strike waves occurred in the late 1830s and the late 1860s. In some periods, strike waves were interspersed with periods of relatively high levels of labor conflict, such as the early 1900s and early 1950s, but at other times strike activity declined precipitously, as in the period since the early 1980s. Still, it has been a rare day when not one person has been on strike anywhere in the United States.

Just as the level of labor conflict has not been

consistent over time, it has varied across space. In the early years of the republic, strikes took place mostly in urban centers, such as Philadelphia and New York City. By the 1830s and 1840s, workers were going on strike in the mill towns of the Northeast, including Fall River, Massachusetts, and Woonsocket, Rhode Island. At the dawn of the twentieth century mining counties in Appalachia, such as Kanawha, West Virginia, became strike centers, as did company manufacturing towns like Pullman south of Chicago or Homestead near Pittsburgh. Once companies spanned larger geographic areas, so could strikes. The first of these were the railroad companies that emerged in the middle of the nineteenth century, and they faced strikes that crossed half a dozen or more states. Still, few companies have developed a national footprint, and those that have managed a level of ubiquity like McDonald's, Sears, or Starbucks have never faced a national strike. Truly national strikes have been extremely rare. The 1970 strike by post office workers and the 1997 strike against United Parcel Service are two exceptions that prove the rule that for the most part strikes have been local affairs.

Work stoppages have taken a wide variety of forms, including stay-aways, walkouts, pickets, protests, sit-downs, pitched battles, boycotts, and general strikes. Some lasted years, while others just minutes. Some involved hundreds of thousands of workers, while some just a handful. Some were peaceful, while some were violent. Some were routine—almost scripted—affairs, while some were raucous free-for-alls that swept entire communities into the fray. Some involved workplace grievances, while some were about wages and benefits. Some were legal, while some were illegal. Some aimed to exclude workers of color or women, while some united men and women from multiple racial and ethnic backgrounds. Some have challenged enormous multinational corporations, while some have faced owners of small businesses. The diversity of work stoppages has been remarkable.

Strikes have taken such a broad array of forms because there have been such a wide variety of workers toiling for an incredibly diverse set of employers located in myriad places governed by assorted laws and customs fashioned by varied histories. Strikes have been shaped first and foremost by the workers involved, and in the United States workers have differed in innumerable ways, including age, race, skill, religion, gender, social status, and experience. These workers have labored in a diversified economy that has included thousands of differing and changing occupations; it is not surprising that the strikes of cartoonists would differ from the strikes of plumbers or aerospace engineers or newsboys or nurses. Even within the same occupations and industries there have been significant geographic differences, so miners' strikes in Colorado have been different from miners' strikes in West Virginia.

As industries changed over time, so did their strikes. It took dozens of workers to load a ship docked in New York City harbor in 1907, and the dock strike that year involved thousands of immigrant dockworkers in mass protests, parades, and even sailing pickets that patrolled the harbor to prevent the movement of scab cargo. Despite the huge number of strikers, they had no established union organization that could bring them together in the face of an even larger force of strikebreakers supported by the mayor, the police, and the employers. Demoralized, the strikers returned to work defeated. Nearly a century later, containerization had automated dock work and shrunk the workforce, but it had also increased the skills required to load ships. Moreover, ports had become key choke points in the transportation chain that supported the national economy. As a result, the International Longshore Workers Union could stand toe-to-toe with the employers in the Pacific Maritime Association during the 2002 West Coast port lockout. Even the president of the United States could not break the workers' resolve, and they won significant job protections and benefit gains. They accomplished what their predecessors could not, because so much in their industry had changed.

Strikes have had decidedly mixed results and meanings. Some, like the 1881 strike of Atlanta's black washerwomen, achieved little in material terms, but revealed much about race, class, and gender relations in America. Others, such as the 1969 wildcat strike of miners, led directly to the passage of landmark health and safety legislation. Still others, like the 1981 strike of professional air traffic controllers, represented epochal shifts not just in labor relations but also in national political culture and party power. Strikes like these have exposed the most pressing public issues of the day, whether it was segregation in the hate strikes by white autoworkers in 1943; the eight-hour day in the 1886 strike at the Chicago McCormick works that inaugurated May Day; or the poverty of government workers in the 1970 postal walkout. Strikes have secured enormous gains not only for workers but for all citizens, yet they have also led to the destruction of workers' organizations, the loss of workers' jobs, and even the loss of workers' lives. Strikes have expanded the power of workers and enlarged the labor movement, but they have also been weapons of exclusion wielded by racist and sexist workers and their unions trying to maintain privileges associated with white skin and male gender. Strikes have constituted the single most important method workers have employed to expand their rights and improve their conditions, both on and off the job. Strikes have shaped not only the labor and lives of workers, but also the fate of corporations, the development of the economy, the character of political culture, and the extent and nature of local and national government—usually, but not always, for the better.

Whatever their size and scope, strikes have had profound impacts on America's economy and society. At the most basic level, strikes have changed the lives of workers and their employers. While some strikes have been unremarkable, many have plunged workers into a caldron of collective activity that has forced them to confront a number of life-defining questions. For most workers considering a strike, "Which side are you on?" has been a simple question in the abstract, but far more complicated when they have to put food on the table. Should they risk their livelihoods for union rights? Should they cross the picket line and face the wrath of their coworkers? Should they trust their union brothers and sisters, their union leaders, and their community allies in the heat of battle with employers, police, and politicians? How should they handle the violence that could occur? What should they do if the strike fails and they lose their jobs? How should they cope with the public ridicule that strikers often face? What should they do if their families are divided by the strike? Should they live by their ideals, when doing so could lead to job loss, ostracism, or possibly violence?

In addition to raising such personal questions, strikes have repeatedly thrust a number of enduring questions to the forefront of public consciousness. Do workers have collective interests? If so, what are those interests and are they opposed to the interests of employers? What role, if any, should unions play? What are the rights of workers in a society based on private property? What are the limits to the power of capital? What role should the state play in regulating the workplace? Is there another way to organize the economy other than capitalism?

As all these questions make clear, strikes are complex events. Even where a walkout appears to be a simple conflict over wages and benefits, more is involved, because strikes, by their very nature, challenge the usual relations of power at the workplace. Simply by going on strike, workers make it clear that they no longer accept the employer's unrestricted right to run his or her business. Instead, strikers insist that their needs are at least as important as those of their employer. This can lead to radical ideas, such as the notion that the returns to ownership should be commensurate with those to labor or that workers' control of the workplace should match that of management. Usually, the break with routine is only temporary; once the strike is over control reverts to ownership or its representatives in management. Yet even in these situations, strikes can shift the balance of power in the workplace and change the ideas of workers. Moreover, by going on strike workers acknowledge, implicitly or explicitly, their collective destiny and forge a level of solidarity. This experience of collective action not only illustrates the meaning and power of unity. It is one of the ways workers come to understand themselves as members of the working class. That identity can have profound social, economic, cultural, and political ramifications for individuals and for the rest of the community. In this way, strikes, even when they are routine, can have profound, life-changing impacts.

Strikes Today

The number of strikes in the United States has declined dramatically each year since the 1970s.

In 2006, according to the Bureau of Labor Statistics (BLS), there were just twenty strikes in the United States involving 1,000 or more workers, what the BLS calls major work stoppages. Seventy thousand workers went on strike for a total of 2.7 million workdays. The total number of strikes of all sizes was approximately 247, according to the Federal Mediation and Conciliation Service. By comparison, there were 424 major work stoppages in 1974, twenty-one times the number in 2006. These major strikes involved 1.8 million workers, who missed 31.8 million days of work. The total number of strikes of all sizes in 1974 was 6,074, involving 3.5 percent of the workforce, who missed 48 million work days.

To see just how low recent strike figures are, look at strike statistics from 1947 to 1979, when each year saw an average of 303 major strikes involving 1.5 million workers missing 24.5 million days. In the recent period, from 1980 to 2006, the average number of major strikes each year was just fifty, involving an average of 325,000 workers missing 7.3 million workdays.

Despite the decline, strikes remain significant in America. During 2006, 12,600 workers at Goodyear Tire and Rubber struck for eighty-six days, missing a total of 718,000 days of work. Their strike, which took place at plants in ten different states, preserved health benefits for workers and retirees and convinced the company to invest more heavily in its existing American plants to preserve jobs. In another strike, 9,500 Detroit teachers defied the law and walked out for three weeks to stop the Detroit School Board's attempt to cut their wages by 15 percent.

A strike of janitors at the University of Miami in February 2006 involved only 400 workers, but it epitomized what it takes for workers to win these days. The janitors, most of whom were from Latin America and the Caribbean, walked out demanding that their employer, Massachusetts-based contractor Unicco, allow them to form a union through a card-check/neutrality agreement that would skip the employer-dominated National Labor Relations Act election process. The workers mobilized support from various constituencies in the university and off-campus communities. Along with students and local clergy, they held demonstrations that stopped traffic, organized sit-ins at university offices, and launched a hunger strike that galvanized support locally and nationally. They reached out to University of Miami alumni, Unicco workers at other universities, and Unicco investors. The strike lasted two months, but the workers' solidarity, their constant activity, and the community support they received led to victory. By the end of June the workers had a union. They also had a renewed level of commitment to each other and a set of union leaders with the knowledge, experience, and confidence to sustain that commitment. Strikes like these, and several hundred more in 2006, demonstrate that, despite their infrequency, strikes continue to shape U.S. labor relations.

Organization of the Encyclopedia

The Encyclopedia of Strikes in American History attempts to illuminate the complex history of strikes in the United States by exposing it to analysis from many viewpoints. Despite its title, *The Encyclopedia of Strikes* is not encyclopedic. A comprehensive explanation of the hundreds of thousands of strikes in U.S. history would be impossible. Rather, *The Encyclopedia of Strikes* seeks to give readers the tools to analyze not only the strikes included in its pages but also the strikes that have been excluded for reasons of space.

To provide analytical tools for understanding strikes, *The Encyclopedia of Strikes* has two types of essays: those focused on an industry and those focused on a theme. Industry essays provide an analytical framework for understanding the chronological progression of strikes within an economic sector (e.g., agriculture) or industry (e.g., auto assembly), or among a group of workers (e.g., miners). Each essay introduces a group of workers and their employers and places them in their economic, political, and community contexts. With this background established, each essay describes the industry's strikes, including the main issues involved and outcomes achieved, and assesses the impact of the strikes on the industry over time.

Thematic essays answer questions that can only be answered by looking at a variety of strikes across industries, groups of workers, and time.

They address questions such as why the number of strikes has declined since the 1970s, or why there was a strike wave in 1946. They offer various analytical viewpoints and cover a wide array of themes.

Each essay concludes with references to additional essays in the encyclopedia, where appropriate, and includes a brief bibliography of essential sources. Additional sources, organized by section, are included in the Bibliography.

The essays are organized into five parts, each with a brief introduction. The first part, "Strikes: Theory and Practice," includes a set of thematic essays dealing with theoretical and practical issues raised by strikes in the United States. It gives readers an overview of how various theorists have understood strikes, how corporations have tried to thwart strikes, and the lessons unions can draw from strikes.

The second part is entitled "Strikes and Working Class Culture," and its thematic essays examine various aspects of striker identity, such as race, gender, ethnicity, religion, and politics. Taken together, essays in this part introduce the incredible diversity of strikes and strikers and delve into the ways strikes have shaped and been shaped by working-class identity.

The third part, "Strike Waves," looks at four of the most important strike waves in U.S. history, as well as strikes since World War II. It provides a sense of how strikes have changed and stayed the same over time.

The fourth and fifth parts are devoted to industry essays. The fourth, "Public Sector Strikes," demonstrates that the militancy of publicly employed workers goes back at least a century and continues today. The fifth, "Strikes in the Private Sector," has three sections: "Manufacturing, Mining, and Agricultural Strikes," "Infrastructure Industry Strikes," and "Service Industry Strikes." It conveys the ubiquity and diversity of strikes in American history.

Like the strikes they write about, the contributors to *The Encyclopedia of Strikes in American History* are a diverse group. Included are historians of various fields; numerous sociologists, anthropologists, and philosophers; and a variety of current and past activists from unions and other social movement organizations. Each has been allowed to advance his or her own perspective; the editors have not sought to impose any unifying theoretical or political approach to the topics covered. Our hope is that with these perspectives *The Encyclopedia of Strikes in American History* reflects the multifaceted nature of the workers and activities it covers.

TYPES OF STRIKES

Aaron Brenner

Strikes are usually categorized by their purpose or by the tactics they use, or sometimes both. For example, the strike of autoworkers in Flint, Michigan, in late 1936 and early 1937 was a sit-down strike because the workers occupied the factory. It was also a recognition strike because the workers demanded that the company recognize their union and engage in collective bargaining. Sometimes, legislation or court/agency decisions define categories of strikes for legal and regulatory purposes. It is common for strikes to fall into multiple categories.

Here are the most prevalent types of strikes:

Economic Strike. A strike to improve the terms of employment, such as better wages, benefits, and working conditions. Most strikes in American history have been economic strikes. Under U.S. law, employers may permanently replace workers engaged in an economic strike.

Unfair Labor Practice Strike. A strike protesting an unfair labor practice (ULP) by the employer. The National Labor Relations Act (NLRA; 1935) and subsequent amendments to it, along with decisions by the National Labor Relations Board (NLRB) and federal courts, define what constitutes an unfair labor practice. In broad terms, ULPs include interference with an employee's right to organize and bargain collectively, employer domination of a labor union, discrimination in hiring and employment to encourage or discourage union membership, discharge of employees who have filed charges under the NLRA, and refusal to bargain with a legally recognized union. Employers may not legally permanently replace workers engaged in a ULP strike, and there are times when an economic strike can be converted to a ULP strike, as when the employer illegally refuses to bargain. Not all workers are covered by the NLRA. Those in the airline and railroad industries are covered by the Railway Labor Act (RLA; 1926), which treats strikes differently. Some, such as agricultural workers, are not covered by either the NLRA or the RLA, which sometimes gives them more options when it comes to strikes and boycotts.

Grievance Strike. A strike to address a particular grievance. Workers usually have grievances over workplace issues that may or may not be a subject of collective bargaining, such as the work process or the nature of discipline. Contracts between employers and workers have generally included procedures to settle grievances without strikes. Workers have essentially traded workplace peace for greater economic benefits. Nonetheless, workers have gone on strike over workplace grievances, whether or not their union contracts prohibit such action. For many years, the International Brotherhood of Teamsters negotiated contracts that actually allowed them to strike over an unresolved grievance. More often, workers have gone on grievance strikes despite the existence of a contract prohibition. This type of strike also goes by the name of wildcat strike (see paragraph below on "wildcat strikes").

Recognition Strike. A strike to persuade an employer or group of employers to recognize and engage in collective bargaining with a union. Recognition strikes were more common in the United States before the NLRA established procedures for unions to win recognition through an election. Before the NLRA, many unions found that the only way to convince a company to bargain over wages and working conditions was to strike. After the NLRA, recognition strikes declined. However, they have not disappeared altogether. Some unions have used them as an alternative to the NLRB election process, which has become increasingly more difficult for unions. Such strikes often seek a card check/neutrality agreement in which the employer agrees to remain neutral while the union has a short period of time, say ninety days, to sign up a supermajority, say 60 percent, of the workers.

Wildcat Strike. A strike unauthorized by union officials, usually during the term of a union contract. Wildcats tend to be short-lived walkouts by workers protesting a specific problem at work, such as unsafe conditions or abusive supervision. They have been powerful tools for workers to win immediate change, but because they are generally illegal—they violate no-strike clauses in union contracts—they can also lead to dismissal. Measuring the number of wildcats has been difficult because short strikes have not always been reported to government authorities who collect strike statistics. The largest wildcat strike ever involved 200,000 postal workers in 1970 and lasted a week. Wildcat strikes tend to increase during strike waves.

Sympathy Strike. A strike by one set of workers in support of another set of workers at a different employer. Sympathy strikes are also known as secondary strikes. These strikes can be very powerful because they create widespread solidarity to magnify the power of any single group of workers. One of the most famous sympathy strikes was the Pullman Strike in 1894, in which railroad workers struck in support of wildcat strikers who were protesting a wage cut at the Pullman Palace Car Company. U.S. law has treated sympathy strikes differently over the years, but it has generally been hostile, precisely because sympathy strikes can be so powerful. Before the National Labor Relations Act, judges sometimes invoked the Sherman Antitrust Act (1895) to prohibit sympathy strikes. The Taft-Hartley Act (1947) amended the NLRA to explicitly prohibit sympathy strikes. The Railway Labor Act does not prohibit sympathy strikes. Some unions, such as the Teamsters, have had contract clauses that allow them to respect picket lines—for example, unionized delivery workers have legally refused deliveries to grocery stores on strike.

Secondary Boycott. Technically not a strike; a boycott of one business in support of workers striking another business. The Taft-Hartley Act of 1947 made secondary boycotts illegal. Because they work in agriculture, the United Farm Workers are not subject to this law, which is why they could launch boycotts of grapes and lettuce in the 1960s and 1970s.

Hot Cargo Strike. Similar to a secondary strike, a refusal by one set of workers to handle, process, or transport goods because they deem the work to be unfair due to a labor conflict at the source of the goods. Some unions were able to negotiate hot cargo clauses in their contracts that allowed such refusals. For example, construction unions had contract clauses under which employers could subcontract only to firms paying union wages. Because they constituted a restraint on an employer's ability to do business, hot cargo clauses and strikes were of dubious legality after the Taft-Hartley Act and definitively prohibited by the Labor-Management Reporting and Disclosure Act (Landrum-Griffin Act).

Jurisdictional Strike. A strike to assert a set of workers' rights to particular jobs. These took place mostly in the construction industry, where different unions fought over who would do different jobs on construction sites. Eventually, the unions set up an adjustment system to settle their disputes. Jurisdictional strikes also occurred in the 1930s and 1940s in the local delivery, grocery, and warehouse industries, when the United Retail, Wholesale, and Department Store Employees, an affiliate of the Congress of Industrial Organizations, challenged the International Brotherhood of Teamsters, an affiliate of the American Federation of Labor, for the right to represent the industries' workers. The Taft-Hartley Act empowered the National Labor Relations Board to settle jurisdictional strikes.

Employer Lockout. A strike by the employer, who shuts down his or her business as part of a strategy to defeat a union. Lockouts are generally legal for any reason other than as a means to keep employees from exercising their rights under the National Labor Relations Act. It is illegal to lock out employees to avoid collective bargaining, stop an organizing drive, or break a union, but it is difficult for workers to prove intent. Lockouts are a powerful tool for employers in collective bargaining.

Political Strike. A strike designed to win a specific political outcome, such as the passage of legislation or a change in regulation. These strikes are quite rare in the United States. In 1969, West Virginia coal miners launched a twenty-three-day wildcat strike that succeeded in prompting the legislature to pass a Black Lung law to compensate miners for pneumoconiosis.

General Strike. A strike by workers at multiple employers in a particular location, usually occurring during a strike wave. The threshold for the number of businesses that must be on strike to constitute a general strike is hard to pinpoint. In the United States, general strikes have been infrequent but spectacular. They occurred at least in St. Louis (1877), Seattle (1919), San Francisco (1934), Minneapolis (1934), Toledo (1934), and Oakland (1946). General strikes are usually short, but can involve the temporary reorganization of society because the essential services that strikers provide are not available.

Blow-Off-Steam Strike. A strike led by union officials with the implicit or explicit approval of the employer in an effort to subdue rank-and-file protest. Such a strike is not designed to win more concessions from the employer. Instead, it is designed to convince workers that union officials have done everything possible to win a better contract. It is based on an assumption that militant workers are more likely to vote for a contract that appears to have been won through their collective action than simply negotiated by union officials. Since employers and union leaders rarely acknowledge their motivations in public, it is difficult to know when a strike is designed to blow off steam. Such strikes take place most often during strike waves, as employers and union leaders try to reduce the militancy of rank-and-file workers. A famous example was the 1970 strike at General Motors. Before the strike, union officials and GM management negotiated the basic outline of a contract, but they did not make it public. Since rank-and-file workers were extremely angry about wages and working conditions, union officials worried that they would reject the contract in the belief that they could get more by going on strike. With the approval of GM management and without any intention of extracting additional concessions, union officials called a strike, allowing rank and filers to vent their anger at the company through pickets and protests. After two months on strike, union officials presented the already-negotiated contract to union members as if it were the result of the strike, making it appear as if it was the best possible contract and making union members more likely to vote for it, which they did.

Sit-Down Strike. A strike in which workers occupy their place of work. The Industrial Workers of the World used the tactic on occasion early in the twentieth century. A wave of sit-down strikes occurred in 1937, inspired in part by factory occupations in Europe at the time. By the end of the 1930s, the National Labor Relations Board and the courts had declared sit-downs illegal.

PART I
STRIKES: THEORY AND PRACTICE

Introduction by Aaron Brenner

Strikes are multifaceted events involving complex interactions between workers, unions, employers, governments, and other members of the community. By walking off the job, workers try to restrict the revenue going to their employer, thereby pressuring the employer into improving the terms and conditions of their work. In this sense, a strike is an economic act. However, walking off the job has other implications. In doing so, workers implicitly or explicitly challenge their employer's unfettered control over his or her property. In this sense, a strike is a political act, a contest for power over how production will take place. But a strike can be even more. For some workers, participation in a strike can be transformative, because it involves them in a collective project that changes the way they understand society and their position in it. In this sense, strikes can be mechanisms for the creation of class consciousness, a moment when workers come to see themselves not only as individuals but as members of a working class in opposition to the employer class and its government allies. Or, strikes can do the opposite, convincing workers and others of the futility of collective action.

This section tries to comprehend the multiple meanings of strikes by looking at them in theory and practice. The essays have no single theme, but they deal with issues common to many strikes in American history. Why do workers go on strike? What can they accomplish? How have employers resisted? How have outside observers, including the media, understood strikes? What explains the rising and falling prevalence of strikes? What lessons can be learned from strikes?

Two of the essays, by Gerald Friedman and Christopher Phelps, review how various observers have understood strikes. Given that conflict is inherent in every work stoppage, it is not surprising that there is considerable disagreement about the causes, nature, and value of strikes. Are they manifestations of individual workers' pursuit of economic goals, the inevitable result of unavoidable class conflict, the outcome of failed interest group negotiation, the consequence of unscrupulous manipulation by union leaders, or something else altogether? In assessing the purposes and outcome of strikes, observers have differed along political lines. Those on the conservative end of the spectrum have argued that strikes are coercive, trample employers' property rights, disrupt the economy, and reward lawlessness. More liberal observers prefer to avoid strikes but recognize that they are legitimate expressions of workers' collective economic interests, as long as they are contained within manageable legal and economic boundaries. By contrast, radicals see in strikes the potential to educate workers about their exploitation, challenge the foundations of capitalist labor relations, and, in the extreme case, create the nascent arrangements of a socialized economy. Hopefully, by reviewing what others have had to say about strikes, readers can develop their own methods for analyzing strikes.

From a more practical perspective, essays by Robert Smith and Kim Phillips-Fein trace the methods bosses have used to prevent and defeat strikes. The repertoire has been extensive and includes the employment of scabs (replacement workers), racist or sexist propaganda to divide the strikers, creation of anti-strike committees composed of workers and community members, appeals to the legal system for injunctions against strikers and their unions, requests of the executive branch to arrest strikers, physical attacks on pickets, eviction of strikers and their families from company housing or property, formation of employer groups to spread the cost of lost production, declaration of bankruptcy to reopen without a union contract, and simply waiting out the workers. Since the formation of the United States, employer anti-strike rhetoric has consistently naturalized market relations and characterized the employment relationship as the result of impersonal economic force rather than the result of conscious choice by real people with power over others. Because this market ideology is so prevalent and carries a grain of truth, employers have had not only resources but rhetoric on their side in many strikes.

The essays by Jeremy Brecher and Steve Early focus on the recent history of strikes. Brecher wants to know why the number of work stoppages has declined so precipitously. Early attempts to draw lessons from recent strike victories and defeats. Both are sympathetic to the labor movement and draw similar conclusions about the challenges facing workers and their unions. They both recognize that globalization of manufacturing makes it easier for employers to shift production away from striking workers. Similarly, restructuring—downsizing, outsourcing, automation, work reorganization—reduces the power workers have over their jobs, while the increased flexibility of corporations gives them additional resources to fight strikes. The government, particularly the courts and the National Labor Relations Board, has grown much less sympathetic to workers, unions, and strikes, and in fact has mobilized its resources on numerous occasions to defeat work stoppages. Compounding the problem, many unions have been unwilling to mount the broad challenges necessary to restore workers' collective power. That is why both Brecher and Early look first to the things unions can do to make their strikes more successful. These include comprehensive campaigns that target every aspect of a corporation in an effort to find its vulnerabilities. Workers can also exploit some of the changes brought about by restructuring; the use of just-in-time production, for example, makes corporations vulnerable to well-timed and well-placed strikes, if unions are willing to engage in them. Early notes that certain tactics make strikes more likely to win, including widespread community involvement, the advocacy of issues that resonate with the broader public, and the creation of a meaningful strike fund. Thus, despite somber assessments of the labor movement's recent history, Brecher and Early remain convinced that strikes can work.

Taken together, the essays in this section familiarize readers with general concepts related to strikes and provide them with background for reading the rest of *The Encyclopedia of Strikes in American History.*

STRIKES IN AMERICAN HISTORY

Aaron Brenner

The term *strike,* in its connotation as work stoppage, derives from a nautical term: to strike sail, which means to lower or fold a ship's sail. According to historians Peter Linebaugh and Marcus Rediker, as a form of protest, merchant mariners in the eighteenth century would strike sail to prevent a ship from delivering its cargo. Their work stoppages became known as strikes, and the term soon applied to work stoppages on land. Of course, work stoppages are considerably older than the word *strike.* No doubt, as long as some people have worked for other people, there have been work stoppages. The first recorded, and apparently successful, work stoppage took place in Egypt in the twelfth century BCE, when builders of the royal necropolis of Ramses III laid down their tools to demand their food rations, which they then received. But it should be no surprise that the first modern work stoppages were carried out by merchant mariners, since in many ways they represented the first modern working class: laborers without access to the means of subsistence working for people who brought together capital and labor in profit-seeking endeavors. Their work stoppages, like so many that followed, reflected the conflicts inherent in capitalist production between employers' pursuit of profit in a competitive market on the one hand, and workers' desire to control their labor and the fruits thereof on the other. It is to be expected, then, that these first modern workers also generated a new term—strike—for their work stoppages.

Work stoppages in America predate the strikes of merchant mariners. In colonial America, indentured servants often ran away or shirked their duties, but the first organized work stoppage appears to have occurred in 1636, on Richmond Island off the coast of Maine. Fishermen there struck to protest the withholding of their wages, but it is not known if they won. Five years later, carpenters on the same island refused to work when they did not receive meat in their food rations. They had a labor shortage on their side, and won their demand. In 1663, indentured servants in Maryland were not as lucky. They quit work when they, too, were denied meat by their masters. Dragged to court, the servants argued that they were too weak to work without meat, but the judge decided against them. Fortunately, he suspended the sentence of thirty lashes after hearing the servants' pleas for forgiveness. These early work stoppages involving indentured servants exhibited few of the features of later American strikes.

More characteristic of later work stoppages were strikes in late eighteenth-century Philadelphia. In 1786, journeymen printers there went on strike for wages of a dollar a day. Having earlier established a strike fund, they were able to hold out long enough to win their demand. Five years later, the Journeymen Carpenters of the City and Liberties of Philadelphia struck to demand a ten-hour day and overtime pay. During this and other strikes at the time, the union sent "tramping committees" to striking workplaces to prevent "scabs," or replacement workers, from taking their jobs. Master carpenters who employed the journeymen competed fiercely for the business of the city merchants and landowners who financed building projects. Because the financiers refused to pay the masters more, the masters, in turn, refused to meet the journeymen's demands. After losing the strike, the journeymen formed a cooperative society and advertised themselves at rates 25 percent below the master carpenters. The next year, journeymen shoemakers formed The Federal Society of Journeymen Cordwainers and struck against a reduction in the prices they received for the shoes they made. They lost the strike, and their organization fell apart, but reformed the next year and lasted long enough to participate in an 1805 strike during which they were arrested, tried, convicted, and declared by the United States Supreme Court in *Commonwealth v. Pullis* (1806) to be criminal conspirators for engaging in collective action to set the price of their labor. Their case set a legal precedent branding strikers as criminal conspirators that lasted into the twentieth century.

Despite the *Commonwealth* decision, over the next two centuries more than 130 million workers engaged in at least 275,000 strikes in the United States. Many of these later strikers used the same tactics and experienced the same consequences as their Philadelphia forebears. Like the strikes of late eighteenth- and early nineteenth-century printers, carpenters, and cordwainers, later work stoppages involved union organization, wage and hour demands, worker and community solidarity, strike funds, tough bargaining, the use of scabs, the squeeze of economic competition, and government intervention on the side of employers. In response to economic change, political development, and workers' own changing experiences, later strikers expanded the repertoire of strike activities and goals. They invented whole new categories of work stoppage—the general strike, the political strike, the hate strike—and they involved important new groups of workers—the unskilled, women, immigrants, African Americans. The result was a rich and diverse history of striking in the United States that defies easy generalization but nonetheless shaped the American economy, polity, society, and culture in myriad ways.

Nasty, Brutish, and Long

Strikes in American history have been nasty, brutish, and long. Given the stakes, labor conflict in the United States has usually been heated, with no love lost between the two sides and often fierce rhetoric. In the 1840s, striking New England textile workers drew on prevalent notions of liberty when they denounced their work as "wage slavery" and called their supervisors "slave drivers," an increasingly powerful insult as free-labor ideology developed in the antebellum North. During the Great Strike of 1877, Peter H. Clark, an African-American leader of the Workingmen's Party in Cincinnati, called railroad owners "princes," while his Workingmen's Party comrade in Chicago, Albert Parsons, denounced them as "tyrants." Eight years later, a worker complained before Congress that he and a coworker suffered "under insolent, unscrupulous bosses, rapacious foremen, greedy and unsympathetic managers, wealthy and avaricious contractors, brutal and egotistical capitalists." Because they most directly confronted strikers, scabs—justly or unjustly—usually received more than their fair share of contempt. Most famously, a poem, "The Scab," generally attributed to Jack London, summed up strikers' attitude toward their replacements:

> After God had finished the rattlesnake, the toad and the vampire, he had some awful stuff left with which he made a SCAB.
>
> A SCAB is a two-legged animal with a corkscrew soul, a waterlogged brain, and a combination backbone made of jelly and glue. Where others have hearts he carries a tumor of rotten principles. . . .
>
> A strike breaker is a traitor to his god, his country, his family and the working class.

Employer rhetoric has rarely been as colorful, but it has been just as derogatory. The prosecution in the 1806 journeymen cordwainers' case labeled the strikers criminal conspirators. Later, employers regularly called strikers "anarchists," "Communists," and "hooligans." More recently, employers and their government allies have adopted a new lexicon to describe strikers. New York City Mayor Michael Bloomberg said striking transit workers in 2005 had "thuggishly turned their backs on New York" and "hijacked" the city, managing to combine a racist slur ("thugs") against the largely African-American and Latino workers with an obvious allusion to the September 11, 2001 attacks on the city ("hijackers"). Likewise, in 2004, United States Secretary of Education Rodney Paige called the National Education Association a "terrorist organization." Two years earlier, Homeland Secretary Tom Ridge warned International Longshore and Warehouse Union leader James Spinosa that a strike by dockworkers would threaten national security. Though often little more than a tactic in the public relations contest between the two sides, heated rhetoric can also reflect deeply held antagonisms between employers and workers, fueling lingering conflict and preventing reconciliation.

The hostility of strikers and employers has led to relatively long strikes in the United States, compared to, for example, Europe, as P.K. Edwards has shown. According to Bureau of Labor Statistics (BLS) data, over the last seventy-five years of the twentieth century, strikes averaged slightly more than three weeks in duration, with the duration getting longer toward the end of the period. The only years when strikes averaged less than two weeks long were during World War II, when union officials adopted a no-strike pledge and the federal government moved quickly to suppress strikes in war industries. Outside wartime, the superior economic and political power of corporations meant that responsibility for lengthy strikes generally lay with employers' hostility to labor organizations. While there are many reasons for this, one is simply that workers preferred shorter strikes, since they were more likely to win. Edwards presents data "which shows a very marked tendency for the proportion of successes to decline, and of failures to rise, as the length of stoppages increases." Where workers could, they imposed their will as quickly as possible, knowing that their organizational strength would likely ebb over time as their resources dwindled. By contrast, employers could wait out strikers; they could entice or force workers back to work with the carrot of pay or the stick of law and violence; or they could hire scabs and restart production. The exceptions to this pattern occurred when the particularities of production favored workers, as when farm workers timed their strikes to coincide with the harvest, threatening employers with the loss of their perishable crops, or when hotel workers struck during high tourism season, threatening to drive away the most profitable customers.

The brutish part of American strike history is the violence endemic on both sides. But again, due to the unequal distribution of power, employers bear greater liability for the deaths, injury, and destruction. The examples are legend: more than 100 killed, most by police, the National Guard, and U.S. army troops, during the Great Strike of 1877; three Pinkerton security guards and seven workers dead in a shootout at the Carnegie steel works in Homestead, Pennsylvania in 1892; forty-eight men, women, and children killed, most by National Guard troops, during the United Mine Workers strike at Ludlow, Colorado, in 1914; ten demonstrators shot in the back and sixty wounded by Chicago police at Republic Steel in 1937; the forced deportation of 1,185 Industrial Workers of the World strikers and their sympathizers in Bisbee, Arizona in 1917; or four unionists killed by a sheriff's posse in Bogalusa, Louisiana, in 1919. No one has counted the number of strike-related fatalities, but it is in the many hundreds, while the number of injuries is in the tens of thousands. At times, strikers fought back, as at Homestead, though rarely with any success. "Bloody Mingo" was just one of three counties where the United Mine Workers battled Baldwin-Felts detectives trying to break their union during the West Virginia "Mine Wars" of 1920–21. The Mine Wars included dynamited mines, hijacked trains, machine-gunned tent colonies, murdered strikers and detectives, shootouts, numerous beatings, indicted sheriffs, hundreds of arrests, and the intervention of 2,500 federal troops supported by an air squadron, probably the only time air power has been used against U.S. civilians. Less dramatically but equally deadly, Teamsters and scabs fought throughout the summer of 1905 during a strike in Chicago, leaving 416 people injured and 21 dead.

Strike-related injuries and deaths diminished as the twentieth century progressed, but violence remained significant. In 1967 and 1970, wildcat strikes by truckers involved shooting between strikers, union officials, scabs, police, and National Guard. During the 1977–78 miners' strike, someone (most likely miners) destroyed a massive coal auger (drill) at a strip mine in Georgia, and state police in riot gear teargassed a demonstration of 400 striking miners in Kentucky. Police gassed, beat, and arrested strikers and their supporters during strikes at Hormel in Austin, Minnesota, in the mid-1980s; at Pittston Coal in West Virginia in 1989–90; and at Caterpillar, Bridgestone/Firestone, and A.E. Staley, three strike/lockouts that turned Decatur, Illinois, into what workers dubbed the "War Zone" in the early 1990s.

Interestingly, there was no definitive relationship between violence and victory. While violence instigated by employers usually crushed strikes, it sometimes failed. Miners and Teamsters sometimes won because of *their* violence, but they also won because the other side could not or would not mobilize enough force. The same was true for others. In the famous 1937 "Battle of the Running Bulls," Flint sit-down strikers occupying a General Motors plant fended off attacks by police, but won their strike in part because Michigan Governor Frank Murphy was unwilling to mobilize enough law enforcement to dislodge them. In this sense, the level and success of strike violence often reflected the balance of other forms of power rather than a simple accounting of physical force.

Of course, most strikes in American history were not violent. Compared to the number of strikes and strikers, the incidence of strike-related deaths and injuries was minuscule. Nonetheless, strikes were fierce, coercive affairs, as both strikers and employers used more than rhetoric to advance their cause.

Carpenters, Miners, and Tailors

Virtually every American industry experienced strikes. Familiar are strikes by workers in mining, auto, steel, construction, trucking, printing, meatpacking, retail, grocery, professional athletics, and teaching. Still, the diversity of strikers is astounding. African-American washerwomen in Atlanta walked out in 1881. Cartoonists at Walt Disney Studios laid down their pens several times in the 1930s and 1940s. Tugboat workers shut down New York City harbor in 1946 and 1959. Thoroughbred jockeys picketed Aqueduct racetrack in the fall of 1988 to demand higher wages—and won. Librarians went on strike in several cities in the decades after the Wagner Act. Surgeons in Wheeling, West Virginia, walked off their jobs in 2003 to protest rising medical malpractice insurance costs. This brief list suggests that all kinds of workers have seen the strike as a method to advance their interests, both on and off the job. It is a testament to the fact that the collective ability of workers to withhold their labor is a powerful source of strength against employers and other authorities.

Despite the diversity of strikers, some workers have been much more strike-prone than others. By far the largest number of strikes has taken place in the building construction industry, and this has been true since the American Revolution. Aggregate statistics do not exist before the 1880s, but according to data compiled by Edwards, between 1880 and 1905 construction workers accounted for 26 percent of the strikes, 14 percent of all strikers, and 39 percent of the firms struck. From 1927 to 1940, they accounted for 12 percent of walkouts and 6 percent of strikers, and in the years 1950 to 1972 carpenters and their comrades accounted for between 19 percent and 20 percent of all strikes and between 15 percent and 18 percent of all strikers. Two characteristics of the industry help to explain the frequency and consistency of construction strikes. First, construction has always employed a large number of workers; in 1900, for example, construction constituted about 12 percent of employment outside agriculture, and in 2005 it was about 5 percent of a much larger economy. Second, most construction firms are small; even in the early twenty-first century after tremendous consolidation, all residential and most commercial building construction is performed by regionally based companies. All else being equal, having a large number of workers at a larger number of small firms is likely to produce more strikes.

Of course, not all else is equal. Huge numbers of retail workers have labored at many small firms, but they have not engaged in anywhere near the same number of strikes as construction workers. The type and skill of the work, its seasonality, its project nature, the weakness of construction firms, and the workers' knowledge, history, and traditions have also contributed to the number of strikes in construction. Skilled construction workers have not been as easily replaced as unskilled retail workers, which means their strikes have been harder to break. Knowledge of their power has given carpenters, bricklayers, electricians, plumbers, ironworkers, and other construction workers greater confidence to walk out. They have had greater motivation to strike, too, because usually their jobs have lasted only until completion of the current construction project. By acting quickly, as opposed to engaging in long negotiations, they have employed maximum leverage over their building firm employers.

These employers have been locally or regionally based, with fewer resources to hire scabs, and they have often faced financial penalties for construction delays, which have given them incentive to settle strikes quickly. For construction workers, the skill, danger, and cooperation involved on the job have provided common bonds, and they have built enduring unions that have reinforced workplace cultures of solidarity and the willingness to strike. Further buttressing construction workers' solidarity has been, until very recently, the disgraceful exclusion of African-American, Latino-American, and women workers from construction jobs and construction unions. While not its main source, strikes have played a role in this race and gender exclusion. Employers have often used workers of color as scabs, reinforcing the racist view that workers of color could not be organized into the construction unions. By increasing the strength of racial exclusion and by bringing workers together in common struggle, strikes have magnified the workplace solidarity of white male construction workers, which, in turn, has emboldened them to go on more strikes.

No other group of workers has been as consistently militant over as long a period as construction workers, but one group has come close: miners. And in some senses, miners have been even more militant. Based on data from Edwards, from 1881 to 1905, miners were only 4.5 percent of nonagricultural employees, but they accounted for 10 percent of the strikes and 31 percent of the workers on strike. Miners engaged in the biggest and longest strikes of the period, involving three times as many workers as the average and lasting 50 percent longer. Construction strikes, by contrast, were nearly 50 percent shorter than average. From 1927 to 1940, miners were less than 3 percent of the workforce, yet they accounted for a disproportionate number of strikes (4 percent), strikers (21 percent), and days lost to strikes (31 percent). Again, they had the biggest and longest strikes, averaging 2,160 workers and over twenty-seven days per strike, compared to 427 workers and eighteen days per strike for the rest of the economy. More than 20 percent of miners went on strike each year during the period, and in 1938–41 some 63 percent of miners participated in work stoppages. By comparison, the average level of strike participation for all industries was less than 5 percent, as it was for construction. Mining strikes declined after the 1940s, but miners remained far more strike prone than all other workers. Representing 1.3 percent of all workers, miners accounted for 8 percent of strikes, 7 percent of workers on strike, and 7 percent of days lost to strikes in the period between 1950 and 1972. In the late 1960s and 1970s, miners were again extremely militant. In addition to dozens of official strikes, they engaged in a wave of wildcat strikes to protest not just conditions in the mines but the failure of their union leaders to protect their interests. One set of wildcats succeeded in directly prompting the West Virginia Legislature to pass a Black Lung bill to compensate miners for pneumoconiosis.

Even more than construction workers, miners developed enduring cultures of workplace solidarity. To build the trust in each other necessary to survive a very dangerous job, they developed and enforced detailed work practices that everyone had to follow if they were all to leave the mine safely at the end of each shift. Old miners taught the work rules to new miners, and the practices bound workers together on the job across the generations. One of these rules was that when one worker went on strike, usually signaled by pouring out the water each miner carried, everyone went on strike. Given the deplorable record of the mine owners, walkouts like this over safety were common.

Off the job, miners shared similar experiences that also reinforced solidarity. They often lived in company towns, where their employer was also their landlord, the local storeowner, the mayor, and the police. Class lines in such communities were stark. On one side were the miners and their families. On the other side were the mine owners and their hired hands who ran the town. In such circumstances, workplace conflict was community conflict, and vice versa, and collective action was a means of survival. Strikes became community affairs, with spouses and children helping to organize pickets, relief, and other necessities. Upon this base of solidarity, the United Mine Workers built a powerful organization that overcame divisions among the workers of skill, ethnicity, and often race. By harnessing miners' solidarity into a powerful force that could stand up to the brutality of the mine owners and win strikes, union organizers magnified miners' collective consciousness, further amplifying their solidarity, so they could walk out again if necessary.

In the period between 1880 and 1940, one additional group of workers nearly matched miners and carpenters in their militancy—tailors and their fellow garment workers. With 3.5 percent of workers in the period 1880 to 1905, clothing workers accounted for 7 percent of the strikes, 10 percent of the strikers, and 13 percent of the firms struck, according to data compiled by Edwards. Statistics do not exist for the period between 1905 and 1927, but garment workers were extremely militant. In a series of massive strikes focused mostly in the garment centers of New York and Chicago, they established two major unions, the Amalgamated Clothing Workers and the International Ladies Garment Workers Union. From 1927 to 1940, garment workers were but 3 percent of the workforce, yet they accounted for a higher portion of strikes (13 percent) than any other group, including construction workers. They were 12 percent of all strikers and accounted for 8 percent of all days lost to strikes. The years 1930 to 1937 were particularly militant, with more than 25 percent of garment workers going on strike.

Like miners' strikes, garment worker strikes were community affairs, in large part because garment work was done by the men, women, and children of the ghettos where garment contractors concentrated. Unlike mining, garment work was done by women and girls as well as men and boys. Garment workers did their cutting and sewing in their apartments or in tenement sweatshops near their homes. In this way, they lived like miners, concentrated together, with similar experiences at home and work. When they went on strike, they struck together. Unlike miners, garment workers sometimes won the support of middle- and upper-class urban social reformers, many of whom believed that the deplorable work and home lives of garment workers demonstrated the need to regulate employers and reform city government. Their power and money deflected some of the most repressive tactics of garment contractors, government officials, and police. Yet the reform impulse of native-born socialites often clashed with the radically egalitarian socialist vision brought from Europe and nurtured by immigrant garment workers and their descendents. This vision, which infused the International Ladies Garment Workers Union, nurtured class consciousness in garment workers and inspired their militancy. Though garment unions had an inexcusable blind spot when it came to African-Americans, they attempted to unite everyone in the industry regardless of skill or ethnicity, giving their strikes added force. The unions also provided myriad social benefits, including subsidized housing, education, and cultural events. The collective experience that came from these benefits further reinforced garment workers' solidarity, encouraging them to strike more often.

It is no coincidence that the three most consistently militant groups of workers toiled in relatively labor-intensive industries for relatively small employers subject to fierce competition and weak regulation. Since labor costs composed a high portion of total costs, construction, mining, and garment firms competed by driving down wages and benefits. Barriers to entry were low, meaning new businesses could form, hire cheaper labor, and undercut existing firms. To survive, existing firms had little choice but to cut workers' pay. Even when they did, they often still went bankrupt. Construction, garment, and, to a lesser extent, mining firms went out of business far more than those in oligopolistic industries such as railroad, steel, and chemicals. As a result, carpenters, miners, and tailors had to fight more consistently to win and keep union recognition and to set and maintain wage and benefit standards. Yet because they faced weaker employers, they were more often successful, thereby encouraging more strikes.

Recent changes in all three industries have altered the conditions that made them so strike-prone. Key have been consolidation, automation, and employers' decisions to move away from areas with strong unions. These trends manifested first in the garment industry, when manufacturers fled to nonunion areas of the southern United States in the 1950s and 1960s and then to low-wage countries in Latin America and Asia starting in the 1970s. Capital flight was not as dramatic in mining and construction, but the geographic center of gravity of each industry shifted toward nonunion regions: from Appalachia to the Rockies in mining; and from the Northeast and Midwest to the South and Southwest in construction. More important for these two industries were consolidation and automation. In mining, ten companies produced more than 60 percent of the country's coal output by the turn of the twenty-first century. They did so with automated techniques that had more than doubled the industry's output of fifty years earlier while shrinking the workforce by two-thirds. In construction, consolidation has been regional and automation has taken the form of ready-made materials that reduce the number and skill of the workers needed to construct a building. All these changes have reduced the leverage workers have over their employers, but their impact has been magnified by the failure of the unions in each industry to organize under the new conditions. Without organizations to maintain solidarity, workers' willingness to strike has ebbed. Once-militant carpenters, miners, and tailors are now some of the least strike-prone workers in America.

Mass-Production Workers

In comparison to carpenters, miners, and tailors, workers in the iron, steel, machine, glass, and tobacco industries faced a very different set of conditions. As these industries developed in the second half of the nineteenth century, they became increasingly more capital intensive. Machines replaced skilled workers, and management directed more aspects of workers' productive activity. Companies merged into regional and national corporations. Then, in a process dubbed vertical integration, they bought their suppliers and distributors so they could control both the inputs for their products and the sales and marketing of those products. As each industry consolidated, a few massive corporations came to dominate production, distribution, and sales. Such enormous concentrations of capital created significant barriers to entry, meaning it was very difficult for new companies to compete. Oligopolies formed and persisted, often for decades. Corporations became so huge, hiring so many workers and making so much money that they dominated the economic and political life of cities, regions, and even the nation. To win strikes against these behemoths required massive effort. Workers tried often, but mostly lost.

Many late nineteenth-century work stoppages in developing mass production industries sought to resist the process of de-skilling, which given its often piecemeal nature took years to implement. Iron molders and puddlers, glassblowers, butchers, coopers, coal miners, machinists, boilermakers, typographers, and other skilled workers exercised considerable control over the production process. Individually and through their unions, they established work rules, terms of apprenticeship, standard wages for their trade, and other aspects of work activity. They even hired and fired their helpers. As Industrial Workers of the World (IWW) leader "Big" Bill Haywood put it, "The manager's brains are under the workman's cap." As they grew, employers were determined to gain control over more aspects of work. In order to do so, they applied "scientific management," which not only applied technology to production but attacked the collectivist ethic upon which craft control depended. They consciously and collectively launched an "open shop drive." Employers thus sought not only to reduce their dependence on workers' skill, but also to undermine workers' reliance on each other. The conflict over workplace control sparked thousands of work stoppages over many decades.

The de-skilling process changed the nature of production and the workers who populated the expanding factories. The introduction of machinery led to the hiring of thousands, and eventually millions, of semiskilled and unskilled operatives. For them, the challenges of work centered not as much around control as the terms and conditions of labor. Operatives, many of them immigrants, worked long hours for little pay at dangerous jobs in steel mills, glass factories, chemical works, meatpacking plants, and other mass production sites. They were fired often and faced horrendous living conditions. Their destitution contrasted sharply with the monumental fortunes they created for their employers in the Gilded Age and later. The boom and bust cycles of industrial capitalism exacerbated wealth disparities, since workers received disproportionately less in the booms and suffered disproportionately more in the busts. The indignities of work and the vast inequalities of wealth fueled workers' resentment and willingness to strike. In the period 1880 to 1905, strikers in the tin, steel, and machinery industries faced massive corporations determined to resist and armed with vast resources, including private armies, spies, and friendly government. Because of these obstacles, they lost more strikes than they won. During the same period, tobacco and glass workers, who faced automation a bit later, did only slightly better, winning just 51 percent of their strikes. The success rate for semiskilled and unskilled workers in these industries was considerably lower.

It took the profound social, economic, and political dislocations of the Great Depression, the New Deal, and World War II to create the context for the successful, long-term unionization of semiskilled and unskilled workers in basic industry. It also took the longest and most audacious wave of mass strikes in the country's history. This wave, which rose and fell several times over the decade between 1933 and 1943, involved millions of workers in a diverse set of industries fighting for union recognition, living wages, decent working conditions, and industrial democracy. Their activity, in combination with the political accomplishments of the New Deal, tripled the number of union members and increased the proportion of workers represented by unions from 7 percent in 1933 to 23 percent of nonagricultural employees in 1941. Though numerical membership growth was greater in old-line American Federation of Labor (AFL) unions, the rise of the Congress of Industrial Organizations (CIO), which sought to unionize basic industry, provided the wave's driving force. Yet even before the CIO's formation in 1935, workers were on the march. The year 1934 saw a successful mass strike of auto parts workers in Toledo; general strikes in Minneapolis and San Francisco sparked by teamsters and dock workers, respectively; and a strike of 400,000 textile workers along the Eastern seaboard. This activity suggested to union leaders that industrial workers might be unionized, and spurred the formation of the CIO, which led the next upsurge in 1937. The meteoric rise of sit-down strikes in February and March of that year signaled a new level of militancy. Following the United Auto Workers' astonishing victory over General Motors in Flint, Michigan, workers initiated dozens of sit-downs, not just in heavy industry but also at five-and-dimes and department stores, which resulted in one stunning victory after another. As Rachel Meyer describes in this volume, sit-downs quickly disappeared, but the strike impulse continued off and on through World War II.

Throughout the decade, one strike's success spurred another. Rank-and-file participation was high. Ordinary workers engaged in an extraordinarily wide range of strike activities. They occupied their workplaces, held mass demonstrations, organized unemployed workers to prevent scabbing, collected strike funds, ran strike kitchens, coordinated community support, arranged health care, talked to reporters, wrote their own strike newspapers, fought police and vigilantes, and lobbied politicians. Spirits were often high; as historian Dana Frank recounts, striking female Woolworth workers continually sang songs, danced, and played games while they occupied their Detroit store. But their effort was serious; they held out for a week and won a 25 percent wage increase, time and a half for overtime, union shop, and half their pay for the time they were on strike.

Radical strike leadership was prevalent in the 1930s; union officers, organizers, and stewards were often some type of New Dealer, Socialist, or Communist. Despite their competing political visions, radicals provided essential organizational leadership, experience, and dedication. A group of Trotskyists, including James P. Cannon, Ray Dunne, and Carl Skoglund, played crucial leadership roles in the 1934 Minneapolis Teamsters strike. They initiated the Voluntary Organizing Committee, suggested the formation of a Women's Auxiliary, edited the *Daily Strike Bulletin of General Drivers Local 574,* and organized roving pickets to prevent scab trucks, all of which were major contributions to the strike's victory. In the Toledo Auto-Lite strike of the same year, the socialist American Workers Party cadre, led by A.J. Muste, organized unemployed workers to participate in mass pickets, which proved decisive. Recognizing their labor leadership qualities, Congress of Industrial Organizations (CIO) leader John L. Lewis consciously hired Communists and Socialists to work on the CIO's organizing campaigns, though he maneuvered to make sure they did not win control of the unions. When criticized for hiring radicals, he replied, "Who gets the bird, the hunter or the dog?" Nonetheless, Socialists and Communists won leadership positions in many of the new unions, including the International Longshore and

Warehouse Union; the United Electrical Workers; the Food, Tobacco, Agricultural and Allied Workers; the United Packinghouse Workers; and the United Auto Workers. Even where they were not top union leaders, they were organizers, stewards, and rank-and-file activists.

The strikes of the 1930s transformed the American labor movement and democratized American society. The experience of being on strike, battling employers, challenging the government, and building community solidarity radicalized millions of workers and their families. In conflict, they learned who controlled American economic and political life and discovered the potential of their own collective action to alter the balance of power in the American workplace. They built unions that could contest the largest corporations in the world and in the process altered the nature of economic life in the United States. Workers won a voice in setting the rewards and conditions of their employment and established new rights and benefits, including paid vacations, overtime pay, protection from arbitrary discipline and dismissal, pensions, and health care. And they went beyond the workplace. Using the political power of their unions and guided by an expanded social consciousness, they elected new political leaders, locally and nationally, who adopted sweeping social legislation that protected many Americans from the vicissitudes of economic life, including Social Security, unemployment insurance, and fair labor standards. The exclusion of millions of Americans, particularly agricultural workers and many African Americans, from the new unions and the New Deal's most important provisions demonstrated the limits of the unions' vision and power, as well as the resistance of employers and their conservative political allies. Nonetheless, the strike wave of the 1930s and 1940s profoundly changed American economic and political life for the better. It also provided perhaps the most far-reaching example of how strikes, because they involve conflict, can change the consciousness of individual workers.

Strike Waves

The strike wave of the 1930s and early 1940s was unique in America in its size, scope, and radicalism, but it nonetheless illustrated many of the characteristics typical of other strike waves in American history. The United States experienced four major strike waves in the 140 years after the Civil War: 1877, 1919, 1933–43, and 1946. Numerous smaller strikes waves also occurred, for example, in 1886, 1892–94, 1901, 1912–13, 1952–53, and 1967–73. The "demonstration effect" is one reason strikes came in waves. Work stoppages in part reflected workers' confidence in their collective activity, and the example of some striking workers often inspired others, even in different industries or far-flung parts of the country. Solidarity played a role, too, as strikers recognized that their walkouts could both draw strength from and reinforce those already in progress. This is why strike waves often included citywide general strikes, such as those in St. Louis in 1877, Seattle in 1919, Minneapolis in 1934, or Oakland in 1946. The activity of one group of workers—railroad workers in St. Louis, shipyard workers in Seattle, teamsters in Minneapolis, and department store workers in Oakland—sparked a chain reaction of strikes that led workers to shut down their cities. The wave of sit-down strikes in 1937 was similar. Success first in the 1936 Goodyear Tire and Rubber strike in Akron and then, most famously, at General Motors in Flint in 1937, touched off a wave of sit-downs across the country that swept up Woolworth's workers, hotel workers, and restaurant workers in New York City, Detroit, and elsewhere. Most were successful.

Equally if not more important in stimulating strike waves was the larger economic, political, and social context. Strike waves were invariably associated with forms of crisis and conflict that went beyond the workplace. In 1877, as John P. Lloyd chronicles in his essay in this volume, workers protested not just wage cuts and brutal working conditions, but also the community destruction and economic disparities created by the growth of the railroads. In 1919 and 1946, workers sought to recapture the economic losses inflicted by wartime inflation and build upon their wartime organizational successes, and they were also inspired by the wartime rhetoric of freedom and democracy, which they believed should be applied at home if it were to have any real meaning. In 1919, workers were encouraged, too, by the revolutionary movements in Europe, especially the 1917 Russian Revolution.

Democracy, freedom, and respect, in addition to decent wages, also motivated the strike wave of the 1930s, which drew inspiration from the social and political atmosphere of the New Deal and encouragement from the activity of radicals, Socialists, and Communists. Thus, strike waves became expressions of larger societal conflicts over economic and political power, not just struggles over wages and working conditions. And, because they offered alternative scenarios for the distribution of that power, strike waves threatened the rule of corporate executive and their government allies.

For this reason, strike waves faced extreme repression. Federal troops and local police shot and beat strikers during the strike wave of 1877; the conflict was so violent that it inspired the construction of armories in cities across the country to make sure authorities always had the necessary firepower to defeat mass strikes. Similarly, in 1919 the Justice Department's Bureau of Investigation, National Guard troops, local police, and vigilantes attacked strikers and their organizations, especially the IWW, as part of a nationwide Red Scare that resulted in thousands of arrests and deportations. Violence was common in the 1930s, too—so much so it has been memorialized in pithy phrases: the Memorial Day Massacre in Chicago (1937), the Battle of the Running Bulls in Flint (1937), the Battle of the Overpass in Dearborn (1937), Bloody Friday in Minneapolis (1934), and Bloody Thursday in San Francisco (1934). The difference in the 1930s was that workers and their unions generally prevailed, in large part due to the favorable political climate for which their political mobilization deserved some credit. The 1946 strike wave saw little violence, due in no small part to the legislative, legal, and political victories that had established the legitimacy of unions and strikes in the 1930s and early 1940s.

Because they were one way workers responded to political and economic conflict, strike waves could have profound impacts on the country. The workplace militancy of the 1930s prompted the establishment of an extensive regime of labor regulation through the National Labor Relations Act and the formation of the National Labor Relations Board. This legislation drew on the precedent nearly two decades earlier of the War Labor Board, which was created in response to an earlier strike wave during World War I. These legislative and administrative actions aimed to prevent strike waves by creating dispute resolution mechanisms to channel labor conflict. They did not succeed in stopping strikes waves, but they did profoundly alter American labor relations law and practice. No similar expansion of government involvement in labor relations occurred during the Great Strike in 1877, but the aforementioned construction of a system of armories to quell worker militancy increased the repressive apparatus of American government. Legislation passed in response to widespread workplace and radical protest during strike waves, such as the Espionage Act (1917), Sedition Act (1918), and the Smith Act (1940) similarly expanded the ability of government to crush dissent.

At a different level, strike waves often bolstered the union movement, establishing or expanding workers' organizations and their power on the job. The most dramatic example of this was the creation of the CIO unions during the militancy of the 1930s, but smaller strike waves contributed to the growth of the Knights of Labor in the 1870s and 1880s, garment workers' unions at the turn of the twentieth century, and public sector workers' unions in the 1960s and 1970s. These successes expanded the political power and social weight of workers beyond the workplace and inspired the spread of democratic and radical ideas. However, strike waves could also have disastrous consequences for workers' organizations. Defeats during the 1886 strike wave broke many local chapters of the Knights of Labor and the vicious government response to the 1919 strike wave crippled the IWW. The ripple effect of these defeats reinforced the conservative policies pushed by employers and their government allies, further dampening union support among workers.

Some strike waves had contradictory impacts on the power of workers and their organizations. Workers won most of their strikes during the massive 1946 strike wave, leading to better wages and benefits and stronger unions. Yet the sheer size and success of the work stoppages motivated employers and anti-union politicians to lead a political backlash against unions, successfully winning passage of the anti-union Taft-Hartley Act (1947), which severely restricted workers' right to strike by banning secondary boycotts and sympathy strikes. Thus, whatever their outcome, strike waves shaped American politics and society in important ways.

Winning and Losing

Strikes and the labor movement have a reciprocal history. The success and failure of strikes reflected the strengths and weaknesses of the labor movement, which fluctuated over time. Likewise, the power of workers rose and fell with their ability to win strikes. And strikers did win, at times more than they lost. There are no statistics on strike success for the entire history of American strikes, but according to Edwards, workers won 47 percent and lost 38 percent of strikes between 1881 and 1905; the rest were compromised. During the period from 1927 to 1941, the percentage of strikes won increased from 34 percent from 1927 to 1929 to 53 percent from 1938 to 1941. Clearly, the rate of success varied over time. Similarly, the formula for victory changed often and involved many different elements.

Unions helped to win strikes, but not as much as one might think. Edwards found that workers won 49.5 percent of strikes ordered by unions between 1881 and 1905, but they won only 33.8 percent of those not ordered by unions. Yet in certain years, such as 1886, 1889, and 1894, strikes without a union's initial involvement were more successful than those led by unions. Most of the time, union organization probably helped workers win, but it was no guarantee of success. Then again, there were never any guarantees of success for strikers.

The size of strikes probably played a role in their success, though there is no definitive evidence. Smaller strikes involving fewer workers seem to have been won more often than large strikes. For example, between 1887 and 1894, boot and shoe worker strikes involved half as many workers as textile strikes, yet boot and shoe workers won 42 percent of their strikes compared to 31 percent for textile workers. This does not mean large strikes were never won—they were just not won as often as smaller strikes. Most likely, smaller strikes succeeded more often because they faced smaller employers who had fewer resources, or because unions found it easier to organize smaller groups of workers. Perhaps, too, smaller strikes were more likely to involve skilled workers, who were fewer in number but exerted greater economic power.

Along the same lines, skilled workers who struck were generally more successful than unskilled workers, simply because they had more power over their employers. For example, within the boot and shoe industry, Edwards found that between 1887 and 1894 skilled shoemakers won 65 percent of their strikes compared to less-skilled lasters (shoe mold makers), who won just 31 percent of their walkouts. In the textile industry, mule spinners who operated the complex machines that created thread won 61 percent of their strikes in the period, compared to 33 percent for less-skilled weavers. Interestingly, a far higher proportion of mule spinners' strikes, 77 percent, were over working conditions, whereas 70 percent of weavers' strikes were over wages and hours. Thus, it may be the issues involved and not the skill that determined mule spinners' success. This was the case at times in the mid-twentieth-century strikes of auto and steel workers, who found it easier to win wage and benefit improvements than control over the pace and content of work.

Strike success had many other causes, including low unemployment, sympathetic government authorities, improving economic conditions, favorable media coverage, public support for the strikers, strategic timing of the walkout, workers' organization and determination, competent union leadership, and community mobilization. The 1997 strike by the International Brotherhood of Teamsters at United Parcel Service exhibited many of these elements. The union mobilized workers months before the strike, preparing them for picket duty, educating them to talk to the media, and convincing them of the importance of solidarity. The union picked an issue—the need to change part-time workers to full time—and a slogan—"Part-time America doesn't work"—that resonated throughout much of the nation's workforce. As a result, other unions lined up to support the Teamsters publicly. Once the strike began, picketers were orderly and articulate. Public opinion polls indicated that sizable majorities supported the workers. It helped that the company was enjoying rapid growth and profitability and that President Bill Clinton would not use the powers granted under the Taft-Hartley Act to intervene. The result was a resounding victory and an agreement by the company to turn 10,000 part-time jobs to full-time ones.

The success of the 1997 Teamster strike defied the recent trend. Far more common recently have been disasters like the 2003–4 strike of Southern California grocery workers. After four-and-a-half months on the picket line, the workers returned to work and accepted a contract that was mostly worse than the contract offered before the strike. They agreed to a two-tier wage structure, which undermines union solidarity, and a cap on the employers' contributions to their health care benefit plan. The strike's failure reflected the industry's economic conditions, the determination of the employers, and the unimaginative and confused leadership of the United Food and Commercial Workers (UFCW) union. Facing intense competition from other grocery chains, non-chain stores, and big-box stores like Wal-Mart, the employers signed a mutual-aid agreement to share losses in the case one or more faced a strike. This undermined the possibility of isolating each chain by striking one at a time.

In response, the UFCW showed no imagination, offered no leadership, and did nothing to prepare the workers for the strike. As a result, enough of them crossed picket lines to keep most of the stores running. The union organized little community support, despite the popularity of the workers, as demonstrated in numerous opinion polls, and the willingness of other organizations and unions to help. Shoppers' refusals to cross the picket lines led to losses totaling more than $1.5 billion for the three chains involved. Union officials also refused to link up strikes by UFCW locals in other cities against the same chains, further dividing and weakening the workers against united employers. A management lawyer not involved in the dispute called the strike "tepid and apathetic." The defeat also reflected the increasingly precarious situation of organized labor, including its shrinking political clout, the hostile legal and political environment, economic changes that have undermined unions' traditional strengths, and the union movement's public obscurity.

Beyond Victory and Defeat

It is tempting to see in the UPS and grocery strikes only success and defeat, respectively, but the impact of strikes is extremely complex. Victorious strikes do not come without costs, just as strike defeats inevitably contain small victories. UPS workers lost two weeks of wages, which essentially eliminated the negotiated wage increase for the year. The company's lost income due to the strike lowered the workers' profit-sharing bonuses. In addition, the union accepted a five-year contract instead of the usual three-year contract, meaning workers would go longer without the ability to fight for better wages and benefits. Undoubtedly, these were trade-offs Teamsters were willing to make, but they were costs nonetheless.

For grocery workers, the gains salvaged in defeat were less material. There was the pride and solidarity they built on the picket line, in demonstrations, at civil disobedience actions, and at other events during four and a half months on strike, the longest strike in UFCW history. After Teamster officials refused to honor UFCW pickets at warehouses, rank-and-file Teamsters at one warehouse organized a walkout in support of the grocery strikers, which gave a huge boost to local UFCW strikers. More concretely, the final settlement required grocery workers to pay less in health care premiums than the employers' original proposal; all minor victories, but victories nonetheless.

If war is the continuation of politics by other means, strikes are the continuation of labor relations by other means. They are the most extreme form of the contest between workers and employers for workplace control. They represent the breakdown of workplace conflict resolution mechanisms, whether those be negotiation, collectively bargained grievance procedures, or official agencies like the Federal Mediation and Conciliation Service. During a strike, the two sides escalate their disagreements and transform their conflict into, at its most fundamental level, an economic contest between the workers' ability to survive without wages and the employer's ability to survive without revenue. Employers work to get production restarted as quickly as possible on their own terms, while strikers withhold their labor to impose their terms on employers. As in the UPS and grocery strikes, this basic struggle usually gets much more complicated and moves far beyond just employers and strikers to include scabs, other unions, community and religious groups, businesspeople, and government officials. Historian Josiah Bartlett Lambert notes:

> Strikes, however, are more than instruments in the collective bargaining process; they are also expressive activities through which groups of workers voice their grievances and proclaim their allegiances. They are a form of protest, an expression of defiance, and one of the most powerful ways for wage earners to say they will not accept arbitrary treatment at work. . . . [S]trikes enable workers to express both dissent and dignity against powerlessness, meaninglessness, and self-estrangement generated by mass-production work. Strikes also give wage earners a voice in the firm and thus serve to extend democracy and justice into economic institutions.

By walking off the job, strikers make clear their position that production cannot continue under the employer's terms. Indeed, they go further. They challenge the employer's absolute right to determine the terms and conditions of their labor. Whether or not they realize it, they call into question the nature of capitalist production, where a powerful minority owns the businesses and the vast majority survives only by selling their labor power. Few strikers make the leap to question capitalism, but most explicitly or implicitly demand, as Lambert says, democracy and justice at work.

See also: Corporate Strike Strategy, 66; Strike Lessons from the Last Twenty-Five Years: What It Takes to Walk Out and Win, 81.

Bibliography

Bernstein, Irving. *Turbulent Years: A History of the American Worker, 1933–1941*. Boston: Houghton Mifflin, 1969.

Brecher, Jeremy. *Strike!* Boston: South End Press, 1972.

Brody, David. *Workers in Industrial America: Essays on the Twentieth Century Struggle*. New York: Oxford University Press, 1993.

Edwards, P.K. *Strikes in the United States 1881–1974*. New York: St. Martin's Press, 1981.

Lambert, Josiah Bartlett. *"If the Workers Took a Notion": The Right to Strike and American Political Development*. Ithaca, NY: Cornell University Press, 2005.

Linebaugh, Peter, and Marcus Rediker. *The Many-Headed Hydra: Sailors, Slaves, Commoners, and the Hidden History of the Revolutionary Atlantic*. Boston: Beacon Press: 2000.

Zinn, Howard, Dana Frank, and Robin D.G. Kelley. *Three Strikes: Miners, Musicians, Salesgirls and the Fighting Spirit of Labor's Last Century*. Boston: Beacon Press, 2002.

THEORIES OF STRIKES

Gerald Friedman

The Strike

In the late nineteenth century, the strike became the dominant form of social protest in industrial societies. Involving more workers in meaningful struggle than any other form of social action, strikes have been both an index of working-class attitudes and one of the most important forms of working-class self-creation. A strike is a collective protest that asserts a noncapitalist political economy. Rather than quitting as individuals, strikers assert a collective ownership over their work, including the right to return to their jobs and to prevent the hiring of replacements. By challenging the capitalist's control over access to productive property, this claim to ownership in work makes all strikes fundamental challenges to capitalism. It makes the very act of striking a political statement—a collective demand for fundamental social change.

Formative events in the creation of a working class, strikes have also been central in the evolution of civil and political liberties. Fought over pay and working conditions, strikes are economic struggles that erupt when the bargaining process between buyers and sellers of labor power has failed. Strikes spread an alternative vision of the economy to workers and to the outsiders mobilized to support the strike. Mobilization fosters a new sense of class unity by challenging established power in the name of the collective workers. Participation in strikes leads workers to form new social institutions, labor unions to sustain their collective protest, and radical political parties to punish state officials for their complicity with the capitalist. Strike action requires space for rallies and picket lines; conflict over access to public space, including streets and sidewalks and workplaces, can lead to broader campaigns for free speech and the right to assemble against the right to private property.

Strikes have a dual nature. They are both part of a bargaining process between workers and their employers and challenges to capitalist relationships and to the state authority that sustains them. This duality has led to two approaches to the study of strikes. One approach views strikes as narrow economic conflicts, bargaining disputes following a breakdown of negotiations between workers and their employers. Scholars in this approach focus on the economic gains workers and employers seek from strikes. By contrast, those who view strikes as political disputes focus on popular consciousness, ideology, and the use of strikes to mobilize workers and to transform the political and economic environment. Without discounting the importance of production technology and the specifics of the labor contract involving wages and working conditions, these scholars emphasize the forms and ideology of labor organizations, relations among workers, and the workers' consciousness of themselves as a distinct group, or a class with common and collective interests.

With these differences, it is ironic that both approaches to strikes, the bargaining and the political models, have roots in the work of Karl Marx. And it is doubly ironic that Marx would probably condemn much of the work done in either tradition for neglecting the dynamic side of social action. One of the first social scientists to appreciate the importance of strikes, Marx associated strikes with the rise of capitalism and the separation of workers from control over the means of production. Capitalism, Marx argued, gives workers economic reasons to strike. It also fosters political attitudes and social consciousness that lead to the mobilization of workers for collective action. However, more important for Marx than a simple dichotomy between economic and political views of strikes was the strike's ability to transform both economics and politics by developing the consciousness and the institutions to revolutionize society.

These three approaches to understanding strike determination also carry over to the study of strike outcomes. Those who work from a simple economic perspective where strikes are determined by external material structures disregard strike outcomes as secondary epiphenomena. Determined by external structures, strike outcomes have no independent significance because, by assumption, social conflict has no impact on these material and technological structures. Little more attention has been given to strike outcomes from the political perspective. There, too, it is assumed that strike outcomes are determined by structures outside of the strike, such as political institutions, union organization, or the development of popular consciousness. Therefore, strike outcomes themselves are assumed to have no independent impact on society. Strike outcomes are seen to have an independent impact only in the Marxist dialectical approach because there it is held that the organization and mobilization of workers and of their opponents, including employers and state officials, reflect social experience, including the impact of participation in strikes. In this dialectical approach, participation in strikes and the outcome of strikes shape future social developments.

Capitalism and the Strike

The strike is unique to capitalism because the capitalist labor exchange, where workers sell their labor time to capitalists for wages, is necessarily incomplete. In other markets, the conditions of exchange are fully specified. Both consumers and store owners, for example, know the price, size, and characteristics of a can of soup for sale on the store shelves, and consumers who refuse the offered price leave with no claim on the soup. By contrast, labor is a "variable" element of production because the exact conditions of employment, including notably the amount of labor to be performed in any time period, are not fully specified. Instead, capitalists hire workers for a period of time in hopes of driving them to produce enough to cover their wage and allow for a profit. The incomplete nature of capitalist-labor contracts makes the labor process a contested terrain where conflicts extend to all areas that influence workers' productivity, including the authority of supervisors, management's right to hire and to fire workers, and workers' speech at work.

Capitalists use their control over access to the means of production to enforce their version of the labor contract by threatening to discharge individuals who work too slowly or lack labor discipline. Control over access to the means of production and the weight of a powerful and wealthy capitalist against an individual worker give employers leverage against workers. Strikers challenge the capitalist labor contract in two ways: by rejecting the capitalist's control over access to productive property and by rejecting the individualist premise of the labor exchange. There are always disputes between individual buyers and sellers where one side walks away from the exchange. However, strikes are fundamentally different because strikers insist on their right to bargain collectively with their employer, balancing their numbers against the employer's wealth and power, and because strikers insist on their right to control access to the means of production, what capitalists consider their private property. So all strikes are incipient rebellions against the capitalist system itself, because capitalism rests on the authority of the capitalist over the workers, authority that comes from the capitalist's control over access to productive property and the leverage the capitalist has over individual workers. No dispute over the price of soup can raise such fundamental issues.

Of course, strikes are not the only form of social protest. On the contrary, the strike changed the nature of social protest, elevating the concerns of some groups at the expense of others. As the strike developed in the nineteenth century, it supplanted forms of popular protest where workers acted as members of communities rather than as wage workers with grievances specific to that social status. Since medieval times, for example, French workers had joined their neighbors in *charivaris* to defend a traditional moral economy linking all members of the community in webs of reciprocal obligations and responsibilities without regard for the ownership of capital or wage labor. As historian Charles Tilly described them, these highly routinized—even scripted—protests were sparked by perceived violations of rights rooted in community membership. Angry that an old widower had married a young woman, for example, or that a marriage was held without the customary wedding ball for the community, workers would gather with others in the middle of the night outside the home of the miscreant master or merchant. The *charivariseurs* would then serenade the house, accompanying themselves on makeshift and improvised musical instruments while singing mocking, even obscene, songs describing and condemning the miscreants' misdeeds. For small offenses, a gift of money or drinks would suffice to end the protest. More serious offenses might require larger gifts, and might even require the departure from the community of the tainted individual or couple.

Charivaris resembled other forms of community-based protest in defense of established moral claims, including bread riots and urban insurrections. By treating workers as members of communities, these struggles linked workers with their nonwage-earning neighbors. Conducted outside of the production process and without institutional support, *charivaris* united workers with homemakers, students, and others in defense of established claims. By contrast, the strike is particular to proletarians fighting to advance new interests; and it came to involve a range of new institutions, notably trade unions and working-class political parties. Focused on the development of the working class, many scholars and activists have discounted nonstrike protests. But emphasizing grievances associated with capitalist labor relations discounts the concerns of women and others whose oppression comes from outside the production process. The older protest repertoire still retains some special strength, including the support of traditional moral and clerical authorities. This has helped the older repertoire to survive, and even flourish, in civil rights demonstrations, feminist and environmental actions, "living-wage" and anti-sweatshop campaigns, and anti-war protests.

The Rise of the Strike

The first strikes came with the emergence of a wage-earning proletariat and the clear subjugation of labor to capital. Before capitalism, guilds united artisans and their employees, setting minimum prices and quality and regulating wages, employment, and output. Controlled by independent craftsmen—the masters, who then employed journeymen and trained apprentices—these guilds regulated industry to protect the comfort and status of the masters and the future position of the apprentices and journeymen. In the eighteenth century, European and North American merchants undermined the guilds by employing partly trained workers in factory settings without regard for guild regulations. By the mid-nineteenth century, few Americans could anticipate moving up to become master artisans. There may have been a surge in *charivari* and other popular protests in response to the collapse of the guild system. But eventually some wage earners abandoned the defense of past positions to seek a collective regulation of their employment as wage workers.

Trained craftsmen conducted the first strikes in industries like shoemaking and carpentry, when proletarian relations began to supplant the traditional guild order. Representing the interests of wage-earning journeymen, these strikes and craft unions sought a collective labor monopoly to balance their employers' control over the machinery of production. Historians such as Alan Dawley believe that, notwithstanding their narrow and exclusive orientation, these early actions and organizations represented a radical and democratic challenge to the emerging capitalist order. Even the narrowest craft organization or strike advances the fundamental idea of the labor movement, which is that employees should have a voice in the management of industry comparable to citizens' rights to a voice in the management of public affairs.

There were very few strikes in these early years, and most were conducted by well-paid workers in a few skilled urban crafts. The mass of the factory proletariat of the new industrial revolution joined the strike movement only at the end of the nineteenth century. Strike activity exploded with the May Day campaigns for an eight-hour workday in 1886 in the United States and in 1890 in Europe. The inaugural May Day campaign in the United States inspired an explosion of strike activity; the number of strikers in 1886 was more than triple the number in the previous year. This "strike wave" spread the strike from urban craftsmen to railroad workers, miners, and factory workers; strikes entered the consciousness of the community.

The importance of the May Day campaigns illustrates a general principle of strikes. Strike patterns are irregular and discontinuous; long periods of little activity are punctuated by sudden bursts of action, often inspired by observing the actions of others. These are strike waves, which occur when large numbers of workers previously outside of the labor movement join in and discover the power of collective action. Strike waves inspire new groups to demand changes in conditions previously seen to be beyond their ability to change. In these "moments of madness," to use a phrase from Aristide Zolberg, a new repertoire of collective action is created by workers whose consciousness has been transformed in the crucible of collective struggle.

Strike waves are unusual. Depending on the definition used (50 percent or 100 percent more than the average number of strikes for the preceding five years), there were only between four and fourteen strike waves in the United States from 1880 to 2000; and there were strike waves in other countries in fewer than 10 percent of those years. But these waves have been crucial for the development of the strike as an instrument of collective protest. Strike waves raise the base level of strike activity by involving new workers in collective action. Observing others on strike encourages workers to join in and to strike by showing that it is possible to challenge capitalist authority and that these challenges will be supported by their fellow workers and may even succeed. Sociologist Michael Biggs has shown that once workers have struck once, the experience of participating in a strike can be transformative and lead them to make a lifelong commitment to working-class collective action. Joining across firms in an industrial and regional strike wave, workers forge a new repertoire of collective action, new ways to advance their collective interests. In the French department of the Nord, for example, the May Day strike wave of 1890 initiated a century of strike action and support for industrial unions and socialist politics. To take another example, the sit-down strikes of the mid-1930s left behind an entrenched militant movement among metal workers in Michigan in the United States and in the Paris suburbs in France. One indication of the impact of strike waves is the acceleration of union membership growth. As this author has demonstrated elsewhere, in six countries studied, union growth rates were ten times as great in strike wave years as in other years.

The association of union growth and strike militancy with strike waves can also undermine the development of the labor movement by frightening employers, state officials, and the broader public. Fearful of exploding labor militancy, employers unite and rally state officials and their middle-class constituents against reform and to the defense of order and capitalist property. Some of the most famous strike waves were disasters for organized labor because they provoked such extreme reactions. The American strike wave of 1886, for example, was followed by the country's first "red scare," a wave of repression that destroyed the Knights of Labor; a similar backlash of repression rolled back labor's gains after the strike waves in 1919 and 1946. More recently, the British strike wave of 1979 led to the election of the conservative Margaret Thatcher as prime minister and a general assault on organized labor.

Explaining Strikes I: Marx

Karl Marx, the founder of modern socialism, was the first to appreciate the importance of the strike as a new social act specific to capitalism and as a means of transforming social consciousness. In *The Communist Manifesto*, Marx and Friedrich Engels develop these two themes. Strikes, they argue, are responses to structural changes in the economy; by striking, workers develop the class consciousness to revolutionize society. Marx's own writings recognize the role of both material structure and human consciousness; he appreciates workers both as historical subjects and as independent agents. Rejecting both pure idealism and the determinism of simple materialism, Marx argues that workers could create their revolutionary movement and new social forms through historical and social action.

Marx argues that capitalist development causes strikes, but he also appreciates the role of political concerns and past social action in shaping strikes. The search for higher profits drives capitalists to lower wages and to make the worker "an appendage of the machine," whose work is "repulsive" to the worker. In response to these structural circumstances, "the workers begin to form combinations (Trade Unions) against the bourgeoisie; they club together in order to keep up the rate of wages; they found permanent associations in order to make provision beforehand for these occasional revolts."

Because Marx associated capitalist development with strikes, Marxism has been associated with materialism and the idea that structural circumstances determine social development. But Marx also saw a political side to class development. Moreover, he saw a reciprocal connection between social action and the economic and social structures of society. His theory is better called *dialectical materialism* because of this interaction of ideas and consciousness with material structures. He relates worker militancy to structural economic circumstances in order to make the larger point that structural circumstances provide context for social action that forges social consciousness. It is a "distinctive feature" of "[o]ur epoch, the epoch of the bourgeoisie," Marx and Engels conclude in *The Communist Manifesto*, that "it has simplified the class antagonisms: Society as a whole is more and more splitting up into two great hostile camps . . . Bourgeoisie and Proletariat." Technological changes are important because by lowering wages they give workers an interest in social struggle; but they are more important because they remove barriers that have divided workers according to training and craft. "Masses of laborers, crowded into the factory, are organized like soldiers. . . . Differences of age and sex have no longer any distinctive social validity for the working class. All are instruments of labor."

But Marxism is neither simple materialism nor idealism where consciousness and ideas alone cause social change. Instead, under this theory material circumstances affect social action, but it is social action and its outcomes that build consciousness, shaping future actions. In particular, strikes shape social consciousness by sharpening the divide between capital and labor. Occasionally, the workers will win their strikes, "but only for a time" because state intervention and competitive pressures soon drive wages back down to bare subsistence. Experience thus teaches workers that they must go beyond these local struggles. "The real fruit of their battles," Marx and Engels say, "lies, not in the immediate result, but in the ever-expanding union of the workers." It is this play of structures, consciousness, and social action that gives Marxism its dynamism. Because social developments depend on social outcomes that are specific to each nation and history, dialectical Marxism is neither a universal nor a predictive social science. Instead, Marxism can only identify areas of social conflict. Moreover, because class conflict shapes consciousness, dialectical Marxism is not dismissive of any sides of the class struggle. Employers and state officials have roles just as vital those of workers.

Explaining Strikes II: The Simple Materialism of the Second International

Much of the subtle dialectic between structure and consciousness in Marx's writings disappeared in the work of his immediate followers in the Second Socialist International. Scholar-activists like Karl Kautsky used a theory of working-class development that was closer to the simple materialism of the early nineteenth-century German materialist philosopher Ludwig Feuerbach than to the ideas of Marx, Feuerbach's critic. Kautsky predicted that workers would bring on a socialist revolution because capitalism would revolutionize production in ways that would lead workers to strike and to seek revolutionary social change. But capitalists have no role apart from their relentless search for profits; even the workers have no independent role in causing strikes or revolution because material structures alone guarantee that they will become socialists.

Paradoxically, Kautsky's materialism left no room even for activists like himself in creating the inevitable social revolution. Still, rising strike militancy and the support given by Marxists to strikes fed conservatives' fears that the growing strike movement presaged a general revolution.

Rather than associate strike action with material circumstances or with any legitimate grievances held by workers, many blamed strikes on the work of militants and revolutionary activists. Conservatives like the French scholar Gabriel Tarde and the American E.L. Godkin blamed outside agitators for promoting strikes by confusing the workers and making impossible promises. Even the French reformer Emile Zola associated the miners' strike he described in *Germinal* with a shadowy Socialist International and its agents. As recorded by historian Richard Wayne Sanders, Joseph Lasies, a French conservative politician, explained rising strike activity in the early twentieth century by telling the French Chamber of Deputies that "I am convinced that some outside agitators (*meneurs interlopes*) must have infiltrated the ranks of the French workers, who are by nature good, generous, and incapable of any meanness or villainy, and stirred them up." Neatly tying radical politicians to the rising strike action, Lasies charged that "outside agitators" learned their inflammatory ideas from socialist politicians like Jean Jaurès. Addressing Jaurès, Lasies said: "There is no reason to be surprised when violence occurs. You do not preach your doctrines in vain to the masses. When you preach such doctrines, it is because you really hope that they will be put into practice."

Explaining Strikes III: Reformers, Liberals, and Economists

The involvement of revolutionary socialists in strikes was a problem for moderates and reformers who defended unions and strikes in the hope that they would defuse revolutionary demands by raising wages and improve working conditions. Reformers such as the American statesman Carroll Wright or the French economist Charles Rist agreed with Marx and Kautsky that strikes were caused by material conditions such as low wages and poor working conditions. But the reformers hoped that workers would overcome these problems through collective action and state regulation, without a revolutionary transformation. Rejecting the Marxist view that strikes were inevitable because of the fundamental conflict between labor and capital, reformers believed that there was a natural harmony of interest between workers and their employers. Both employers and workers benefited from labor peace and business prosperity. Strikes, therefore, must be accidents, due to mistakes and miscommunication. The first U.S. Commissioner of Labor, Carroll Wright, said: "[L]abor troubles are as often the result of a lack of information as to the true state of a trade as of any other thing."

Wright and his fellow reformers feared that involvement in strikes could lead workers to embrace socialism. Instead, reformers would divert workers from strikes to peaceful collective bargaining that would undermine radicalism by raising wages and improving working conditions. Stable labor unions and constructive collective bargaining were their preferred vehicles for social reform; they expected that these would obviate the need for revolutionary politics and strikes by facilitating communication and cooperation between management and labor, raising wages, and even teaching workers that their interests were joined to their employers. "The age of lock-outs and strikes is fast passing away," Wright intoned, "and the rule of reason is rapidly asserting itself; and, when it shall hold sway, capital and labor will learn that their interests are reciprocal and not antagonistic." This was, of course, the opposite of the lesson that Marx hoped workers would learn from strikes.

Conservatives pressed for police action against unions and strikers by associating rising strike activity with revolutionary politics. This advocacy made it urgent for reformers to develop a nonrevolutionary explanation of strikes that would associate strikes with innocuous demands for higher wages and better working conditions. French economist Charles Rist, for example, argued that even in the period of the greatest revolutionary syndicalist agitation during the early twentieth century, French strike activity increased no faster than did strikes elsewhere. Using pioneering econometric analysis, he argued that strike rates in France and in other countries had no political intent because they all were linked to the same economic conditions, price changes, and unemployment rates. Far from radical politics causing strikes, Rist argued that strikes had the conservative intent of simply improving the economic condition of workers within capitalism.

Although not all of Rist's empirical findings

bear rigorous scrutiny, his work has been embraced by other liberals seeking to defend workers' collective action against state or employer repression by distancing strikes from revolutionary politics. The reformers provided an agenda for moderate trade unionists: strikes and unions were to raise wages and improve working conditions without regard for any broader political goals, and many reform-minded scholars have argued that this narrow approach reflects the true concerns of workers. According to U.S. labor economist Selig Perlman, once the employment relationship is improved and wages raised, workers will be "content to leave the employer in the unchallenged position of his property and business." On their own, workers will never develop a socialist consciousness; instead, they will adopt a job consciousness, using collective action to protect their jobs and to raise their wages. Organic labor militancy, the worker's own ideology, begins and ends with conditions at work. Rather than politics and grand designs, unions should advance the workers' real material interests through collective bargaining backed by carefully planned strikes. By raising wages and improving working conditions, unions could obviate the need for revolutionary action; indeed, they could prevent such action by diverting the workers' collective energies away from radical politics and toward constructive collective bargaining.

Following Rist, other reformers argued for a narrow economic approach to strikes that linked labor militancy with the business cycle. In 1904, the reformist American labor leader Samuel Gompers pronounced what he called the "law of growth in organized labor," associating union membership and strike activity with the business cycle. Following Gompers and Rist, labor economist John R. Commons associated labor militancy with economic prosperity, arguing that price inflation caused strikes by lowering real wages. This approach led to a "time-series school" of economists, including George Bain and Farouk Elsheikh, who explain strikes and other labor unrest as a product of business cycle conditions.

It was a short step from this liberal defense of unions and working-class collective action to the economists who separate strikes entirely from any other working-class collective politics and then discount strikes as mistakes due to bad communication or errors in perception. In 1932, the English economist John R. Hicks published his *Theory of Wages*, where he argued that all strikes were "the result of faulty negotiation" and "ignorance by one side or the other of the other's dispositions." Rational actors, Hicks argued, would avoid the expense and unpleasantness of strikes by moving immediately to their final settlement by making whatever concessions they would finally make at the beginning rather than waiting to make the same concessions at the end of an expensive strike. Changes in relative bargaining power, whether due to changes in technology or in market conditions, should be reflected in the terms of the wage contract rather than in strikes. Strikes are simply mistakes or accidents due to a failure to communicate properly.

Later bargaining theorists developed Hicks's argument by specifying reasons for mistakes and communication breakdowns. Assuming that union and business leaders are well informed and seek to maximize their side's economic returns, Orley Ashenfelter and George Johnson expect that on their own they could easily agree on contract terms. There are strikes, these economists argue, because union leaders need to prove to their membership that they have done everything possible to win concessions. Strikes, therefore, will be most common where workers' expectations diverge from the real economic conditions understood by the management of the enterprise and the union. Other economists, such as Michel Cousineau and Robert Lacroix, and John Kennan and Robert Wilson, agree that strikes are accidents due to misperceptions and miscommunication. They will be most common, therefore, in industries where rapid changes in technology or the product market make it difficult to perceive economic conditions correctly or for one party to communicate its views to the other side.

Focusing on the material interest workers and managers share in avoiding wasteful strikes, reformers sought to establish institutions to promote better and clearer communication between workers and management. Wright, for example, favored the establishment of state mediation boards to serve as honest brokers between management and labor. Later theorists predicted a "withering away" of the strike after countries established trade unions and systems for peaceful collective bargaining. American industrial relations economists, including Arthur Ross and Paul Hartman, Richard Lester, and Clark Kerr, associated declining strike activity in the 1950s with the institutionalization of labor unions and the regularization of labor relations. Such theories fell out of favor with the revival of labor unrest in the late 1960s.

Support for the narrow economic approach to strikes has remained strong despite a lack of empirical evidence. Looking across occupations and industries, strike activity depends less on conditions in the industry than on the degree of organization, formal and otherwise, among the workers. Despite low wages and poor working conditions, for example, there are few strikes among agricultural or domestic day laborers. Instead, there are many strikes among relatively well-paid and highly unionized craft workers and among some professionals, such as teachers. Nor does the instrumentalist approach find much empirical support in time-series analysis of annual strike activity. Indeed, business cycle conditions such as inflation, rates of unemployment, or economic growth cannot explain dramatic surges and drops in strike activity. Almost none of the variation in strike activity in the United States and Germany from 1880 to 2000, for example, is explained by business cycle conditions. Strikes are associated with economic prosperity in the United Kingdom and France, but even there, business cycle conditions explain less than 10 percent of the variation in strike activity. And in no country do economic conditions explain the timing of strike waves.

Explaining Strikes IV: Lenin, Consciousness, and Resource Mobilization

It is easy to understand why so many Marxists have emphasized economic structures rather than ideas and consciousness; social analysis is much simpler when it can be expressed in terms of economic interests alone. Marx's writings left a confusing legacy for socialist activists who found his dialectical approach too sophisticated for political sloganeering. Already by 1900, however, it was clear even to committed Marxists that despite the interests workers may have in it, a socialist revolution was not coming soon. A growing socialist dissident movement then sought to restore consciousness to Marxian analysis.

Disappointed with the loss of revolutionary vigor among most European unions and socialists, Lenin argues in his classic pamphlet "What Is to Be Done?" that capitalism would not spontaneously lead to revolutionary working-class consciousness. Instead, he agrees with reformers that economic conditions alone will only lead workers to develop "reformist" or "trade union consciousness" where they try to improve their wages and working conditions without regard for broader concerns. Strikes and other trade-union struggles are only over wages; at best, they will improve conditions for a few workers, perhaps creating a "labor aristocracy" of privileged workers whose trade unions raise their wages even while separating them from the rest of the working class. Agreeing with reactionaries like Lasies, Lenin argues that socialist and revolutionary working-class consciousness does not develop spontaneously among workers but must be brought to them by revolutionary intellectuals. Without this leadership, Lenin argues, workers would only attain the "false consciousness" of trade unionism and class harmony.

Lenin meant to restore politics to the study of strikes by showing how political activists could lead workers to militant strike action. In doing so, he reopened the door to a dialectical or a historical interpretation of strikes because his focus on leadership and consciousness also implied that events can shape class consciousness. Recalling the experience of the 1905 Russian Revolution, Lenin writes that "in every strike there lurks the hydra of revolution," because "struggle educates the exploited class . . . discloses to it the magnitude of its own power, widens its horizon, enhances its abilities, clarifies its mind, forges its will." Economic struggle, Lenin continues, "is capable of rousing the most backward strata of the exploited masses, gives them a real education and transforms them—during a revolutionary period—into an army of political fighters within the space of a few months."

Turning attention back to the formation of class consciousness through the work of labor leaders and revolutionary militants, Lenin also examines the outcomes of social conflicts and the actions of labor's antagonists. For Lenin, labor is no longer the sole master of its destiny because the development of revolutionary class consciousness depends on the outcomes of conflicts influenced by employers, state officials, and others.

It was over fifty years before Lenin's theories significantly broadened the theoretical discussion of strikes. Lenin made a revolution and created a Communist movement around the idea that a vanguard of intellectual activists could lead workers to socialism. In practice, Communists understood how collective action could shape consciousness and Lenin's followers encouraged strikes. But few used his insight to broaden their view of class dynamics to include employers, state officials, and others whose behavior influenced the outcome of conflicts and consciousness. Official Communist ideology remained stalled in the simple materialism of the Second International.

Even before the revival of strike activity and class conflict in the late 1960s, disappointment with Soviet Communism and simple materialism had led scholars and activists associated with the "New Left" of the 1950s and 1960s to go beyond these ideas to explore the way politics and social action shape popular consciousness. In his magisterial *The Making of the English Working Class*, Edward P. Thompson illustrated how class consciousness arose out of the full social environment, including popular culture and political action as well as material circumstances. Returning to Marx's original dialectic, Thompson saw class not as a thing but as "an *historical* phenomenon," not a "structure, nor even as a category, but as something which in fact happens . . . in human relationships." Class identity sprang from material interests, and also from involvement in political reform, democratic activism, and community life. The working class created itself, Thompson argued, through "conscious working-class endeavor," through mutual aid, community self-policing, and friendly societies. Strikes and other militant actions contributed directly to the creation of the working class.

The Making of the English Working Class inaugurated a new approach to understanding strikes, where class consciousness is studied as a work of self-creation through collective action. The economist Mancur Olson first articulated the theoretical underpinnings of this broader approach. In *The Logic of Collective Action*, Olson showed that rational, self-interested individuals would rarely contribute to collective projects that produce *public* goods, enjoyed by all regardless of their contribution. Instead, they will try to "free ride," leaving the production of public goods to others while concentrating their own energies on producing private goods for themselves. Obviously there are limits to Olson's analysis, but he highlights the cultural or social mechanisms, the "social capital," that sustain community life by leading individuals to contribute to collective action rather than pursuing their own narrow selfish interests.

Following Olson and Thompson, scholars of strikes have explained variations in strike activity as a result of the ability of different groups to overcome the collective action problem and to mobilize the resources of individuals for achieving collective ends. Thus, they have highlighted the dialectical relationship between strike activity and the institutions and social attitudes that foster strikes and which can also be products of strike involvement. They have associated strike activity not only with the availability of resources, such as the wealth and social influence of members of the group, but with the nature of community life, including the presence of institutions and social values encouraging collective action.

The role of the dialectic between social action and attitudes and institutions is shown in one of the first major works in the political interpretation of strikes, written before Thompson and Olson: Clark Kerr and Abraham Siegel's 1954 article, "The Interindustry Propensity to Strike." Kerr and Siegel associate strike activity with socially isolated groups of workers, such as miners, fishermen, and lumberjacks, because they argue that these groups are able to form communities that can sustain collective action. Physically and socially removed from the rest of society, these workers form homogeneous communities, an "isolated mass" of workers nursing grievances and "capable of cohesion" for collective action.

For several decades, the Kerr-Siegel hypothesis was the standard interpretation of interindustry differences in strike propensity. It lost favor in the 1970s and 1980s when a variety of studies showed that strike activity was more common in urban areas and among workers integrated into their broader community. Also, the Kerr-Siegel approach neglected the other ways that communities are able to build a capacity for collective action, including dialectically through participation in social action and in social institutions. Nonetheless, a valid kernel remains to Kerr and Siegel's argument: strikes require the mobilization of resources for collective action, which is more easily done when workers belong to communities. Working with an array of graduate students, Charles Tilly has shown how the strike developed as a new element in working people's repertoire of action among urban craft workers who had the material resources and community connections to sustain collective action and to attract outside support. Historical studies showed that the first strikes were conducted by relatively privileged and well-paid craft workers; the low-wage workers who had the greatest objective need for collective action rarely struck because they had fewer available resources and had more difficulty in mobilizing them for collective projects. The idea and the means for collective action had to be brought to them by others, through unions and political organizations and often during strike waves.

Through the establishment of new social institutions guiding collective action, the resource mobilization approach associates strikes with broader historical developments, including the genesis of unions and radical political organizations. Most early strikes, including a majority of American strikes as late as 1881 and French strikes into the 1890s, were conducted without unions. Unions were often formed in the course of a strike when experience taught workers the advantage of prior organization or after strikers when workers were caught up in the spirit of the strike and had observed the support others were giving the collective project. But once established, unions developed an institutional life of their own, developing and extending a new repertoire of working-class action, including strikes, union organization, and political action, to other craft workers and even beyond to the mass of the new industrial working class. Formal union organization helped to sustain strikes by accumulating resources, and they spread strikes by supporting formal leadership and providing connections that facilitated resource mobilization. Through the agency of these new institutions, the strike ceased to be a rare, spontaneous outburst among relatively privileged craft workers and spread to other craft workers and to the whole working class.

Winning and Losing Strikes

By viewing consciousness as a product of social action and organizations, the dialectical approach connects the analysis of strike rates with studies of strike outcomes, because strike activity depends on social consciousness and institutions created through strikes and other forms of social conflict. Until recently, strike outcomes have been less studied than have strike rates. There was an early debate over the form of worker organization best designed to conduct effective strikes. In 1909, for example, a German union leader, Josef Steiner, argued in *Voix du Peuple* that German unions were better at winning strikes than their French counterparts because they focused on narrow economic goals rather than radical politics. He was seconded by Samuel Gompers, longtime head of the American Federation of Labor (AFL), who also made invidious comparisons between the AFL's politically moderate craft unions and the politically active industrial and regional unions in the Knights of Labor in the United States in the 1880s and 1890s. French unionists answered these arguments.

Reviewing official statistics on strike outcomes, the revolutionary-syndicalist head of the French *Confédération générale du travail* (CGT), Victor Griffuelhes, declared that they "show that despite defeats . . . the French working class knows how to struggle. They prove also that the concern for immediate gains is not obscured by the affirmation renewed daily for the revolutionary ideal." "In the absence of strong reserves," he concluded, "French unions supplement with enthusiasm, energy, the sentiment of sacrifice and a superior sense of struggle." His comrade Ėmile Pouget agreed that French unions were able to conduct effective strikes through "*élan revolutionnarie.*" Rather than pitting the "*sous* of the worker against the capitalist's millions," they won through "the vigor deployed in battle, the spread of the revolutionary ideal among the French workers, and not to the power of their union reserves." American radicals agreed. Concluding that French syndicalism was the result of "natural selection" and the best organization for conducting effective strikes, syndicalists William Foster and Earl Ford argued in *Syndicalism* that high dues and benefit funds weaken unions by supporting union bureaucrats and alienating workers from unions. "They prostitute the unions from their true functions as aggressive organizations to the false ones of defensive organizations."

By defending a narrow focus on wages and working conditions, Steiner and Gompers advocated the union strategy promoted by political reformers. Perhaps this is why many historians have accepted their arguments without careful analysis. To be sure, the aggregate comparisons made by activists like Steiner, Griffuelhes, and Pouget are not very useful. Few workers strike without a reasonable expectation of success, and unions do not survive if they cannot win strikes. Therefore, workers in most countries will win a high proportion of their strikes and the unions that survive in any country will be reasonably well suited to win strikes under the prevailing circumstances. Different union strategies, therefore, will be reflected more in different types of strikes and varying characteristics of unions than in the aggregate success rates of strikes.

For these reasons, meaningful analysis of strike outcomes depended on the investigation of strikes below the aggregate level using microdata sets with characteristics of individual strikes. This analysis was first done for French strikes by Edward Shorter and Charles Tilly in the 1970s and, building on Shorter and Tilly's work, by this author in a comparative study of France and the United States. An analysis of data on the characteristics of individual strikes in these two countries before World War I found that in both countries union involvement increased the probability of strikers gaining at least some of their demands. Different paths led to strike success in the two countries. French unions won strikes by increasing the number of strikers and by involving government officials as mediators. American unions won strikes by limiting the number of strikers to avoid state intervention and by providing financial aid to help strikers to hold out longer.

These different strike strategies were closely related to different forms of union organization in the two countries. The French formed industrial and regional unions and set dues levels low enough to attract even the poorest-paid workers. American unions, by contrast, formed exclusive craft unions and used high dues to accumulate benefit funds to sustain longer strikes. In both countries, unions that followed strategies different from the national norm were relatively unsuccessful. Narrow craft organizations conducted less successful strikes in France, and inclusive unions, like the Knights of Labor, promoted larger but less successful strikes in the United States.

Previous studies of strike outcomes have suffered from implicit structuralist and worker-centric assumptions. The same structural circumstances, such as the size of industrial establishments, can have different effects on strike outcomes and unionization rates in different political contexts. Before World War I, larger establishments are associated with strike success and stronger unions in France but with less successful strikes and weaker unions in the United States. The difference was due to different state politics. In France, the early Third Republic, before 1914, was beset by challenges from the monarchist right and the Republic's leadership depended on the support of the working class, including political radicals. Sympathetic state officials were ready to favor labor in disputes with employers associated with reactionaries and monarchists opposed to the Republic itself.

In the United States, however, after the end of slavery and Reconstruction, there were no such divisions in the political and economic elite, and few state officials were ready to sympathize with strikers. Studying strike rates and outcomes solely from the perspective of workers and acting as if labor was the only party to the class conflict able to determine social outcomes solely according to their conditions and consciousness misses crucial differences in the social and political context around strikes. Strikes involve at least three parties: labor, management, and the government, and variations in strike rates and strike outcomes therefore reflect changes in the behavior or attitudes of any of these three and in their interactions.

The extent and forms of labor militancy and union organization reflect differences in state politics or employer policy as well as differences among workers. Inclusive unions and broad strike strategies flourish when labor has political leverage because of division in the economic and political elite; the reverse is also true: inclusive strategies are relatively ineffectual where state officials are unsympathetic with labor from fear of political radicalism. And union movements can go from one to another form when, as in the United States after the Haymarket Affair of 1886, a backlash against labor militancy united political and economic leaders against labor. Thus the study of strike outcomes returns the discussion of strikes to politics and to the history behind any political regime.

Future of the Strike?

For the last quarter of the twentieth century, there has been a sharp decline in strike activity throughout the advanced capitalist world. Since 1980, the share of workers striking has fallen by nearly 80 percent in the United States. Union membership and support for working-class political organizations has also fallen sharply since the 1970s. These declines have raised questions about the future of the strike and whether the working-class repertoire that emerged from the nineteenth century has now reached the end of the line. Are unions, as some critics say, a relic of an old, industrial age of conformist, unskilled workers? Do the more educated workers of today resent the conformity imposed by collective bargaining and prefer to look out more effectively for their own interests through individual bargaining?

A dialectical perspective suggests that we should hesitate before reaching such conclusions. Rather than viewing the decline in strike activity as a reflection of changes in the working class, it should be seen as a consequence of broader changes in the political economy of advanced capitalist states effecting workers, employers, state officials, and the interactions among them. One lesson from the study of strikes over the past century is that we should be careful not to lapse into any simple conclusions. Scholars have broadened our analysis of past strikes to see them as political, emerging from the full body of working-class life and history. Our analysis of recent strike behavior should be as broad and nuanced.

See also: Socialist Theories of Strikes, 28.

Bibliography

Cronin, James E. "Theories of Strikes: Why Can't They Explain the British Experience?" *Journal of Social History* 12 (1978): 194–221.

Dawley, Alan. *Class and Community: The Industrial Revolution in Lynn.* Cambridge, MA: Harvard University Press, 1976.

Friedman, Gerald. "Revolutionary Syndicalism and French Labor: The Rebels Behind the Cause." *French Historical Studies* 20 (Spring 1997): 155–81.

______. "The State and the Making of the Working Class, France and the United States 1880–1914." *Theory and Society* (May 1988): 403–30.

———. "Strike Success and Union Ideology, the United States and France, 1880–1914." *Journal of Economic History* 48 (March 1988): 1–25.

Haimson, Leopold, and Charles Tilly, eds. *Strikes, Wars, and Revolutions in an International Perspective: Strike Waves in the Late Nineteenth and Early Twentieth Centuries*. Cambridge, UK: Cambridge University Press, 1989.

Katznelson, Ira, and Aristide Zolberg. *Working-Class Formation: Nineteenth-Century Patterns in Western Europe and the United States*. Princeton, NJ: Princeton University Press, 1986.

Kerr, Clark, and Abraham Siegel. "The Interindustry Propensity to Strike—An International Comparison." In *Industrial Conflict*, ed. Arthur Kornhauser, Robert Dubin, and Arthur M. Ross. New York: McGraw-Hill, 1954.

Lenin, Vladimir. "The Lessons of the Revolution." In *Collected Works, vol. 16: September 1909–December 1910*. Moscow: Foreign Languages Publishing House, 1963.

Olson, Mancur. *The Logic of Collective Action: Public Goods and the Theory of Groups*. Cambridge, MA: Harvard University Press, 1965.

Scott, Joan. *The Glassworkers of Carmaux: French Craftsmen and Political Action in a Nineteenth-Century City*. Cambridge, MA: Harvard University Press, 1974.

Shorter, Edward, and Charles Tilly. *Strikes in France, 1830–1968*. Cambridge, UK: Cambridge University Press, 1978.

SOCIALIST THEORIES OF STRIKES

Christopher Phelps

The socialist worldview, which advocates emancipation from capitalism and common ownership of the means of production, originated in the late eighteenth and early nineteenth centuries as a legatee of revolutionary Enlightenment liberalism and an answer to the social misery produced by factory production. Initially, socialists opposed strikes, seeing them as damaging to social harmony. Over the course of the nineteenth century, however, they came to identify with labor and embraced the strike as an indispensable tactic. With the legitimacy of strikes established, new differences arose over such issues as optimal strike strategies, the role of political parties in strike organization, and the analysis of particular strike forms. At every step, American socialist strike theory was influenced by both European ideas and American experience.

Artisan Radicalism and Utopian Socialism

Between the American Revolution and the Civil War, radicals saw strikes as illustrative of the barbarism, irrationality, and antagonism inherent in private production. They considered strikes coercive, violent, selfish, and fruitless and advised consensual change instead. This is partly explained by the republican discourse of early American labor radicalism. Skilled craftsmen, invoking the tradition of 1776 and a language of virtue, equality, manliness, and independence, looked upon capitalists as aristocratic and foppish. They sought liberty and opportunity, not abolition of private property. Theirs was the vanishing ideal that every apprentice ought to be able to become a master, the owner of his own shop. This labor republicanism favored producers, whether manufacturers, apprentices, or wage earners, against decadent and parasitic merchants and bankers. It lingered on in a host of late nineteenth-century social rebels—single-taxers, monetary reformers, critics of monopoly, populist farmers—whose agrarianism was the predominant radical mode in a country shaped by frontier and agriculture.

Although the word *socialism* entered the English language around 1837, the reforms advocated earlier by the British industrialist Robert Owen (1771–1858) are typically classified as socialist. When Owen traveled to the United States in 1825, he spoke before Congress, met with President James Madison and President-elect John Quincy Adams, visited with Thomas Jefferson, and organized an ambitious but short-lived colony at New Harmony, Indiana. Owen and his American followers, including Frances Wright (1795–1852), condemned squalor, poverty, and inequality as the result of improper social practices. A benevolent philanthropist, Owen saw strikes as counterproductive and advised workers to set aside class enmity. "Be assured that whatever tends to irritation and violence," he lectured a British audience in his "Address to the Working Classes" (1819), "proceeds from the most gross ignorance of human nature and evinces an utter inexperience in those practical measures by which alone society can be relieved from the evils which it has so long suffered."

When desires for social reform revived again after the fervent evangelical Protestant awakening of the 1830s, the French socialist Charles Fourier (1772–1837) eclipsed Owen as leading inspiration. Fourier's "associationism" called for *phalanxes,* communities of 1,620 members who would share responsibilities and rewards. Fourier disavowed strikes, along with all class struggle. His American followers emphasized Christian reconciliation. Pierre-Joseph Proudhon (1809–1865), Fourier's most prominent French disciple, espoused a doctrine of "mutualism" through producer cooperatives and rejected strikes as forcible and futile, merely presaging price increases. In the first half of the 1840s, Fourier's and Proudhon's ideas were popularized in the United States by Albert Brisbane (1809–1890), author of *The Social Destiny of Man* (1840), and Horace Greeley (1811–1872), a former printer's apprentice and editor of the *New York Tribune.* Given its land mass, America was a favored site for utopian experiments. Dozens of small-scale communities, including New England's Brook Farm, were established on Fourierist principles, but most foundered because of internal disputes or economic failure. Not only did Owenites and Fourierists consider strikes anathema, but other antebellum social reformers—abolitionists, temperance activists, feminists—tended to be indifferent to labor, further mitigating against the emergence of a socialist theory in favor of strikes.

When labor did down its tools, contradictory impulses tugged at socialists, as may be seen in the communism of Wilhelm Weitling (1808–1871). A journeyman tailor and founder of German socialism, Weitling moved to New York after the failed revolution of 1848, part of an emigration making Germans second only to Irish among American antebellum immigrants. Weitling published *Die Republik der Arbeiter (The Workers' Republic),* a newspaper that reported on strikes, albeit with skepticism. To Weitling, strikes in pursuit of wages fostered egoistic, avaricious desires. He advocated that all workers join a mutual aid society to supply old-age pensions while educating for a general revolutionary transformation. But when the New York tailors' strike of 1850 broke out, Weitling led the sizeable cohort of Germans, penning their declaration, "The Rights of Labor *versus* the Rights of Thieves." He remained in their leadership even after the strikers, in pitched battle with police, shattered shop windows and tore up unfinished garments in a Broadway riot. The discrepancy between Weitling's practice and theory showed the difficulty of hewing to socialist doctrines that proposed to emancipate labor while renouncing class antagonism.

Marx and Engels

A more consistent theory of the strike was espoused by Karl Marx (1818–1883) and Friedrich Engels (1820–1895). German revolutionaries who relocated to England, Marx and Engels thought perfectionist communities and small-scale cooperatives powerless to halt the remorseless advance of capitalist manufacturing. They grounded socialism in the activity of the working class, including fledgling trade unions, labor parties, and strikes. Although they lived in London, the pair strongly influenced socialism in the United States. They corresponded with Joseph Weydemeyer (1818–1866), Friedrich A. Sorge (1828–1906), and other German Americans. After the 1848 "spring of peoples" in Europe, when reaction set in, the only newspapers steadily open to Marx's writings were American—especially Greeley's widely circulated *Tribune,* whose foreign editor Charles A. Dana, a onetime Fourierist, asked Marx to write a column.

The starting point for Marx and Engels was analysis of the capitalist mode of production. Capitalism was in their definition a system in which workers sell their labor power in return for a wage, while capitalists buy that labor power and sell the goods and services it produces on the market for private profit. The source of profit was the "surplus value" produced by workers above and beyond their wages. Wage strikes resulted when workers seeking to extract maximum price for their labor power clashed with employers wishing to reduce the price of labor power so as to maximize their rate of profit. Strikes manifested an irrepressible conflict between *proletariat* (the wage-earning working class) and *bourgeoisie* (the possessing class, owners of capital, including machinery, factories, and raw materials). Far from being unethical, fruitless, or wasteful, strikes and other forms of class struggle presaged a coming progressive transition to socialism, which would abolish class divisions. Strikes were both assertions of workers' immediate interests and experiences that prepared workers to govern society themselves.

Although Engels was junior partner to Marx in many respects, he blazed the way for this analysis of strikes in *The Condition of the Working Class in England* (1845), whose first English-language publication was in the United States in 1887. Engels viewed strikes as a collective effort to diminish wage competition, a more sophisticated sign of worker discontentment than crime or smashing of machines. Strikes, he observed, were disadvantageous to capital, causing productive investment to rest idle. The threat of strikes therefore helped to check capital's basic impulse to reduce wages. Engels conceded that strikes usually ended badly for trade unions and did not always raise wages. Nevertheless, he judged strikes morally and politically significant:

> It will be asked, "Why, then, do the workers strike in such cases, when the uselessness of such measures is so evident?" Simply because they must protest against every reduction, even if dictated by necessity; because they feel bound to proclaim that they, as human beings, shall not be made to bow to circumstances, but social conditions ought to yield to them as human beings; because silence on their part would be a recognition of these social conditions, an admission of the right of the bourgeoisie to exploit the workers in good times and let them starve in bad ones.

The Condition of the Working Class in England focused especially on the 1842 strikes of factory operatives in Manchester, then the most advanced industrial center in the world. The Manchester strikes, Engels wrote, were provoked by the bourgeoisie, which hoped to mobilize workers against the Corn Laws benefiting the landholding aristocracy. Once industrial workers struck, however, they passed beyond opposition to the Corn Laws to call for fair wages, the ten-hour day, and constitutional reforms known as the "People's Charter." The bourgeoisie then turned ferociously against the strikers, who were defeated because they were "unprepared, unorganized, and without leadership." Nevertheless, the conflict proved that workers have the capacity for collective action and that political action is a necessary accompaniment to workplace struggles.

Marx, elaborating upon Engels's insights, viewed strikes as insufficient, for they left capitalist labor relations intact. He dissented, however, from Ferdinand Lassalle's "Iron Law of Wages," which argued that wages in the long run reach equilibrium at subsistence level, making strikes futile. The general tendency of capitalism, Marx acknowledged, was to push labor's value down to its "minimum limit," the barest required to reproduce workers' existence. Marx emphasized, however, the partial effectiveness of strikes in improving living standards. Despite pontifications about the market's "invisible hand" and natural laws of supply and demand, he wrote in the *New York Tribune* in 1854, "Under certain circumstances, there is for the workman no other means of ascertaining whether he is or not paid to the actual market value of his labor, but to strike or threaten to do so."

Since the state intervened persistently on behalf of employers, Marx anticipated that workers would carry their activity "over to the political field." He also held that socialists were obliged to assist strikers. When the International Workingmen's Association (or "First International") was founded in 1864, with Marx a leader, it aided strikes in England, Switzerland, Belgium, and France. Marx was proud of this record but rejected allegations that revolutionaries caused strikes. In an address to the First International in 1869, he referred to "the guerrilla fights between capital and labor—we mean the strikes which during the last year have perturbed the continent of Europe, and were said to have sprung neither from the misery of the laborer nor the despotism of the capitalist, but from the secret intrigues of our Association." Strikes, Marx rejoined, arose from real grievances. Marx and Engels enjoined the labor movement to pass beyond the slogan "A fair's day's wage for a fair day's work!" to the motto "Abolition of the wages system!"

The chief initial followers of Marx and Engels in the United States were German émigrés, but in a few instances Marx's theories had wider influence. "During a big strike which broke out in New York," writes Paul Lafargue, Marx's son-in-law, "extracts from *Capital* were published in the form of leaflets to inspire the workers to endurance and show them how justified their claims were." (Lafargue himself made a modest contribution to the socialist theory of the strike with his apt characterization of lockouts as "employers' strikes.") During an 1853 New York strike wave, 800 German Americans formed the American Workers' League, with Weydemeyer a principal. One League resolution envisioned industry-wide general strikes for union recognition, stating that "if a trade in the United States is organized, and it can achieve its rights from the employers only by a general work stoppage, such a stoppage, if it one day takes place throughout the United States, should have our complete solidarity."

Such declarations were, however, exceptional. Even labor leaders discountenanced strikes at this time, thinking them provoked by employers desirous of labor's ruination. One exception was the Pennsylvania-born iron molder's union leader William H. Sylvis (1828–1869), a member of the First International who founded the National Labor Union (NLU) (1866–1872). During the Civil War, Sylvis, in a quotation cited by his biographer Charlotte Todes, defended the unprecedented U.S. strike movement of 1864 and repudiated the proposition that labor and capital have mutual interests:

> If workingmen and capitalists are equal co-partners, composing one vast firm by which the industry of the world is carried on and controlled, why do they not share equally in the profits? Why does capital take to itself the whole loaf, while labor is left to gather up the crumbs? Why does capital roll in luxury and wealth, while labor is left to eke out a miserable existence in poverty and want? Are these the evidences of an identity of interests, of mutual relations, of equal partnership? No sir. On the contrary they are evidences of an antagonism. This antagonism is the general origin of all "strikes." . . . There is not only a never-ending conflict between the two classes, but capital is in all cases the aggressor.

The NLU, however, set aside strikes after Sylvis's death, launching a party of greenback currency reform. Strikes seemed a cautionary tale because of their dubious legal standing, the opprobrium of respectable society, the prevalence of subsistence wages and unemployment, and the precariousness of labor organizations. However, since workers had few options as compelling as the collective withholding of labor, in the long run American socialists had to come to terms with the tactic.

Gilded-Age Ambivalence

Reservations about strikes persisted long after the Civil War. Middle-class socialists were repelled by the violence of the Paris Commune in 1871 and disturbed by the destructiveness of late nineteenth-century American strikes. They could not help being influenced by the denunciations that poured from press, podium, and pulpit against "class legislation," such as the eight-hour day, as an unnatural intrusion into the market economy—although use of militia and legal injunctions to break strikes was not deemed contrary to natural law.

Socialist opinion was split regarding the first nationwide strike in the history of the United States, the 1877 walkout sparked by railroad workers in West Virginia. *The American Socialist* newspaper, published by the communitarian society of John Humphrey Noyes (1811–1886) at Oneida, New York, remonstrated that laborers "have a right to quit work and seek better pay elsewhere, but have no right to make war or destroy property, or prevent others from taking their places at the reduced wages." But socialists in the Workingmen's Party of the United States, influenced by Marx, led the strike when it reached St. Louis, where the socialist Thomas Curtis jubilantly proclaimed it "not a strike but a social revolution."

The two leading American radicals of the Gilded Age disapproved of strikes. In *Progress and Poverty* (1879), Henry George (1839–1897), advocate of a single tax on land, labeled the strike "a destructive contest" which "must, like the organization for war, be tyrannical" and "lessens wealth." The most widely read socialist text in the United States of the late nineteenth century, more popular than Marx by far, was *Looking Backward* (1888), a fictive variation upon Rip Van Winkle by Edward Bellamy (1850–1898). *Looking Backward* features a cultivated Bostonian who awakens magically one century in the future, when a new order has relegated "labor troubles" to the distant past. "Disturbances of industry" were so frequent in the 1870s and 1880s, Bellamy's futuristic narrator reflects, that "it had come to be the exceptional thing to see any class of laborers pursue their avocation steadily for more than a few months at a time." Strikers advanced "demands which it was impossible to see the way to granting unless the world were to become a great deal richer than it then was." In *Looking Backward,* strikes are irrational disturbances that will disappear once peaceful economic evolution consolidates capital into a single firm owned by the nation.

The Gilded Age was punctuated by strikes, however, making it increasingly difficult for socialists to sustain a policy of conciliation. Nowhere was this more evident than in the 1885–86 strikes by members of the Knights of Labor, a fraternal labor federation. Terence V. Powderly (1849–1924), Grand Master Workman of the Knights, was a social reformer who sought a cooperative republic but shrank from conflict. "I will never advocate a strike unless it be a strike at the ballot box," he wrote in *Thirty Years of Labor* (1889). Under Powderly, whose thought descended from early artisan radicalism, the Knights sought to abolish "wage slavery," eliminate "parasites," and restore harmony between capital and labor. Employers who sold union-made goods or employed union workers were admitted into the order, as were women, immigrants, the unskilled, and African Americans. Despite Powderly's program of education, cooperatives, land reform, and arbitration, strikes were what accounted for the union's explosive growth. Hundreds of thousands flooded the membership rolls in the belief that the union was a dynamo of labor militancy—and proceeded to make it exactly that. The "Great Upheaval" of 1885–86 was a strike on the Southwest railway lines, owned by Wall Street millionaire Jay Gould, stretching from Kansas City to Fort Worth. The strike ended in bitter defeat for the Knights at the hands of state militias and Gould's intransigence, in large part because the Knights leaders' reticence hamstrung the union's ability to shape the outcome.

Powderly's desire to reorganize society without strikes was frustrated again when a popular movement arose for a shorter workday, culminating in a call for a general strike on May 1, 1886. "Lay down your tools," ran one circular, "cease your labor, close the factories, mills and mines," and demand "eight hours of work, eight hours for rest, eight hours for what we will." Once again, rank-and-file Knights responded with enthusiasm. Powderly abstained, leaving the eight-hour-day movement in the hands of others, notably anarchists: revolutionary socialists inclined to favor individual acts of violence against representatives of the state or business. The Haymarket affair in Chicago, in which a bomb was thrown in the midst of police at a rally following the May strike, brought down opprobrium. To the public, the labor movement seemed a frightening mix of foreigners, radicalism, and violence.

Caution was the lesson some social visionaries took from the massive class battles of 1877 and 1885–86, but by the end of the nineteenth century, such explosions had the cumulative effect of promoting among socialists a view of the strike as inevitable in a society rife with deep inequalities. The Civil War had resolved slavery, that most urgent issue of property and labor, but the Gilded Age posed the question of whether the economic surplus was justly distributed between labor and capital. As the eclipse of proprietary capitalism by large-scale corporate capitalism came to seem irrevocable, artisan radicalism looked archaic. Strikes increasingly seemed the indispensable instrument of a modern labor movement.

Gompers and De Leon

Such developments favored Marxism becoming the argot of the left, but a complicating factor was the stabilization of skilled trade unions and attendant labor conservatism. The representative figure of this trend was Samuel Gompers (1850–1924), an English immigrant cigarmaker who advocated a practical-minded "pure and simple" trade unionism. Gompers, while schooled in Marxism, had concluded after 1886 that radicalism was a public relations disaster. Gompers presided over the American Federation of Labor (AFL), the mainstream labor association created in 1886, for all but one year of its existence until his death in 1924. Gompers thought unions were weakened when walkouts were uncoordinated and unplanned but had no qualms about strikes per se. Enabling strikes, he thought, was one of the primary functions of a union and its treasury. Gompers fashioned business unionism, in which unions support private enterprise so that, in theory, capital could grant shorter working hours and pay higher wages, in turn enabling workers to pay high union dues, build up union strike funds, and thereby attain "more, more, more now."

Radicals, for their part, held that to sever immediate goals from ultimate aims was self-defeating. The first concerted challenge in American Marxist theory to Gompers came from Daniel De Leon (1852–1914). Caribbean-born and European-educated, De Leon taught at Columbia University before leading the Socialist Labor Party (SLP), the most significant American socialist organization of the 1880s and 1890s, originating out of the remnants of the First International in the United States. In *What Means This Strike?* (1898), based on a lecture to striking textile workers in New Bedford, Massachusetts, De Leon criticized "pure and simple" unionism and the AFL desire to restore the balance between the capitalist class and the working class as chimerical, given the irrepressible hostility between capital and labor.

Strikes, De Leon suggested, were all too easily broken because of the large pool of unemployed, the application of machinery to diminish need for skilled labor, and transportation improvements that made the unemployed easily available to employers nationwide. Given these conditions, the only effective method of winning a strike was industrial unionism. Craft unions like those in the AFL were based upon job function (such as butcher) on the supposition that skilled labor had the greatest leverage because it was not easily replaceable. Industrial unions, by contrast, sought to represent all workers, regardless of task, in a particular plant or economic sector (such as meatpacking). De Leon viewed craft unionism as divisive and business unionism as collaborationism and treason. He held that industrial unionism would benefit even relatively privileged workers, whose interests were not served well by anachronistic attempts to preserve craft categories. All workers would benefit from plant-wide, company-wide, and, preferably, industry-wide organization.

Few workers joined De Leon's dwindling sectarian unions in the Socialist Trade and Labor Alliance (STLA). However, De Leon's writings, with their vigorous defenses of the right to strike and industrial unionism, helped forge an emergent consensus among socialists. As corporate organization, product standardization, and scientific management became intrinsic to production, deskilling rendered craft organization obsolete. Karl Kautsky (1854–1938), a German Marxist influential among American socialists, wrote in *The Class Struggle* (1910) that skilled workers held "important strategic advantage" because "it was difficult to find substitutes for them in case of a strike." However, he wrote, "as mechanical production advances, one craft after another is tumbled into the abyss of common labor," a fact that teaches "even the most effectively organized divisions that in the long run their position is dependent upon the strength of the working-class as a whole."

American Socialism in the Debs Era

American socialism blossomed in the first two decades of the twentieth century. The Socialist Party of America, created in 1901, enjoyed extensive electoral success. Its members had significant influence in the labor movement and published hundreds of local papers. A mass party linked up with the substantial Second International, whose largest party was the German Social Democratic Party (SPD), the American Socialist Party included Christian Socialists and revolutionary Marxists, New York garment trades workers, and hardscrabble Oklahoma farmers. The Socialists had no uniform labor outlook, but in general they upheld the validity of the strike, favored both industrial unionism and socialist activity within AFL unions, and supported solutions at the ballot box.

The personification of this synthesis was Eugene V. Debs (1855–1926), who received 6 percent of the vote for president in 1912 and more than one million votes in 1920. In the way Debs told his own story, he became a socialist because of a strike. In 1893–94, he was head of the American Railway Union (ARU), an industrial organization of engineers, firemen, conductors, brakemen, switchmen, and trackmen. In 1894, the ARU won a brief strike against Great Northern, then walked out in sympathy with workers on strike against the Pullman Company, a Chicago passenger car manufacturer. When President Grover Cleveland, a Democrat, sent in federal troops, the Pullman strike was broken, the union demolished, and Debs jailed six months for defying an injunction. Writing in 1902 in *New York Comrade,* Debs called this "my first practical lesson in socialism, though wholly unaware that it was called by that name," for "in the gleam of every bayonet and the flash of every rifle *the class struggle was revealed.*" While behind bars, he read many socialist books and pamphlets, resulting in his heightened understanding of socialism. To Debs, the Pullman strike proved "pure and simple" unionism misguided, for disputes at the point of production invariably involve police, the military, the judiciary, legislation—the whole apparatus of the capitalist state. The working class, Debs concluded, had to act politically to establish democratic public ownership of property.

By the twentieth century, socialist opinion favored strikes. "He who opposes strikes," wrote William English Walling in *Labor-Union Socialism and Socialist Labor-Unionism* (1912), "opposes labor unions." Strikes, held socialists, were about more than wages or conditions. A.M. Simons wrote in *Class Struggles in America* (1903) that "strikes, boycotts, lockouts, and injunctions" are "the birth pangs of a new society in which for the first time in the world, the workers shall rule, and all shall be workers, and thereby rulership and slavery shall pass from off the earth." Socialists threw themselves fervently into assisting strikes, as when Socialist women picketed and held mass meetings for the "Uprising of 20,000," the landmark 1909–10 strike of young, mostly Jewish women in more than 500 shops in New York's garment district.

Occasional anxiety was still expressed about strike violence. H.G. Wells, the English Fabian, writing in *New Worlds for Old* (1908), faulted revolutionaries for imagining that "when strikers take to rifles and explosives, as they do in Pennsylvania and Colorado," it meant "something more than the promise of the class war." But as Homestead, Cripple Creek, and Ludlow came to have the same meaning for socialists that Antietam or Gettysburg had for other Americans, they were inclined to think of labor's crusade as a civil war that might very well justify force. Mother Jones, the Irish-American socialist mineworker organizer, whose speeches have been collected by Philip Foner in *Mother Jones Speaks,* spoke at a meeting of 13,000 steelworkers in Monessen, Pennsylvania, in 1919:

> One chap said to them: "You know we are going to have a strike. Now you must be peaceful, we must have peace." Imagine what a statement to make to men who were going on strike! I wonder if Washington was peaceful when he was cleaning hell out of King George's men. I wonder if Lincoln was peaceful. I wonder if President Wilson was. And then this gentleman gets up and says we must be peaceful! When he sat down I said: "I want to take issue with you"—an old fossilized thing that hadn't worked for twenty years, but he drew his salary—"I want to tell you we're not going to have peace, we're going to have hell! Strikes are not peace. We are striking for bread, for justice, for what belongs to us."

Most socialists, however, portrayed the destructiveness of strikes as the fault of capitalism, not strikers. Novelist Jack London, in "Strike Methods: American and Australian" (1905), anthologized by Philip Foner in *Jack London: American Rebel,* suggested that violence in American labor relations resulted from classifying unions and strikes as conspiracies in restraint of trade:

> For with us a strike is practically civil war—a revolt against all the powers of government. Deny a union picket the right to attempt to exercise moral suasion on a blackleg, and he will all the more readily hit the blackleg with a brick. Violence begets violence. Suppression causes explosion. Force is met with force, and when capital bombards labor with rifle-bullets, court injunctions, and suits for damages, Labor fights back with every weapon it can lay hands on.

London predicted that the "irrational anarchy of strikes and lockouts" would end only when "the system of production for profit will have been replaced by the system of production for service."

"Wobblies" and Socialists

The establishment in 1905 of the Industrial Workers of the World (IWW), a revolutionary industrial union commonly known as the Wobblies, gave rise to discussion of the "general strike." The phrase was not new. It was already used to describe walkouts that paralyzed whole localities or nations—even industries, although application to economic sectors was a declining usage. Advocacy of the general strike as a revolutionary goal had antecedents in the First International, where Mikhail Bakunin, the Russian anarchist, championed it. As Engels parodied in the pamphlet "The Bakuninists at Work" (1873), Bakunin imagined that "one fine morning all the workers in every industry in a country, or perhaps in every country, will cease work, and thereby compel the ruling classes either to submit in about four weeks, or launch an attack on the workers so that the latter will have the right to defend themselves, and may use the opportunity to overthrow the old society." This, Engels objected, was a fantasy. In another sense, however, the general strike was simply a tactic. Socialists had employed the political mass strike to try to obtain universal suffrage in Europe, and some, including Helen Keller in an article "Strike Against War" (1916), advocated a general strike to prevent war. This occurred despite August Bebel's sage prediction in a speech at the Mannheim Congress of 1906 that anti-war feeling would be drowned out by nationalistic fervor upon outbreak of war.

To the Wobblies, however, the general strike was more than a tactic. It was the climactic insurrectionary goal. They drew upon French syndicalism, whose major theorist Georges Sorel (1847–1922) argued that the general strike could be effective as eschatology even if it never materialized by sustaining workers' spirits. The Wobblies also emulated the French "pearled strike" or passive resistance while staying on the job. Such radical visions could lead to extraordinary feats of imagination, as when in 1905 at the IWW's founding convention, Lucy Parsons (1853–1942), herself a widow of a Haymarket martyr, forecast the sit-down strike:

> The trouble with all the strikes in the past has been this: the workingmen like the teamsters in our cities, these hardworking teamsters, strike and go out and starve. Their children starve. Their wives get discouraged. . . . My conception of the strike of the future is not to strike and go out and starve, but to strike and remain in and take possession of the necessary property of production. If any one is to starve—I do not say it is necessary—let it be the capitalist class. They have starved us long enough, while they have had wealth and luxury and all that is necessary.

The Wobblies advocated "striking on the job," or slowdowns, which they called "sabotage," a French term derived from a wooden shoe lodged in the machine. Although in IWW usage "sabotage" did not necessarily denote property destruction or violence, the word's ambiguity and shock value left the IWW vulnerable to prosecution and slander. None of this diminished their romantic appeal. "We want bread and roses too," read a banner carried in the 1912 textile strike of young female immigrant mill workers in Lawrence, Massachusetts. Such poetry threw the AFL's pinched unionism into highly unfavorable relief, as did the solidarity of New York Socialists who opened their homes to the children of Lawrence strikers.

In *Syndicalism* (1912), Earl C. Ford and William Z. Foster looked to a strike in which "the whole working class will disorganize all the industries and force the whole capitalist class to give up its ownership of them." Ford and Foster denied the need for extensive preliminary organization, since "great strikes break out spontaneously" and "spontaneously produce the organization so essential to their success." In actuality, general strikes tended to arise out of unions and limited strikes, as in Seattle and Winnipeg in 1919, and required coordination to sustain. Ford and Foster also held that vast strike funds "cause centralization and weaken the action of the unions by placing large funds in the hands of powerful national committees, who keep these funds intact by preventing strikes," but they did not explain how a large strike could be sustained without funds to support strikers and their dependants.

Revolutionary industrial unionism and socialism were not incompatible. De Leon drafted the IWW's preamble that "the working class and the employing class have nothing in common," and Debs bridged the Socialist Party and IWW. In 1912, however, the Socialist Party's right wing took measures to disassociate the party from sabotage, fearing it a liability at the polls. Socialist leader John Spargo, author of *Syndicalism, Industrial Unionism and Socialism* (1913), called it an individualistic practice destructive of working-class solidarity. Meanwhile, the IWW increasingly sneered at political action in any form, preferring, in Ralph Chaplin's words in *Wobbly: The Rough-and-Tumble Story of an American Radical* (1948), "the strike, rather than the ballot, as a weapon of class war." The Wobbly suspicion of politics flowed in good part from a highly specific contingency: the exclusion of many workers from the polls. In "The General Strike" (1911), Wobbly leader Big Bill Haywood (1869–1928) emphasized that a majority of the American working class—women, African Americans, boys, girls, and many immigrant men—could not cast ballots, making the strike their only reliable method of power. The anarchist dogma that on-the-job action is the only road to proletarian emancipation persisted, however, long after the extension of the franchise to most groups mentioned by Haywood.

Revolutionary socialist Austin Lewis's *The Militant Proletariat* (1911) bore marks of the Wobbly criticism of parliamentarism and endorsed the general strike, but even Lewis noted that "the general strike advocate who sees in it the great, sole, and infallible remedy is like all peddlers of panaceas—somewhat in danger of becoming a quack." Recommendations to forego politics seemed to socialists to miss the lesson Debs learned at Pullman, namely that the nature of the modern state required political action. Victor Berger, the first Socialist elected to Congress, stated in *Berger's Broadsides* (1912) that "every lost strike—and every strike won—teaches the trades union man that his economic struggle alone is entirely inadequate."

In this period, socialists began, haltingly, to confront matters of race and gender in strikes, including employers' use of African-American strikebreakers. Writing in the *International Socialist Review* in 1912, Hubert Harrison, a West Indian immigrant who belonged to both the IWW and Socialist Party, held the labor movement's own racism responsible for African-American strikebreaking: "These are the same men who denounce Negro strike-breakers. They want them out of the unions and also want them to fight for the unions. Presumably they would have them eating air-balls in the meantime." In *The Great Steel Strike and Its Lessons* (1920), William Z. Foster, who led the 1917 meatpacking and 1919 steel-organizing drives for the AFL, concluded that unions "must open their ranks to negroes, make earnest effort to organize them, and then give them a square deal when they do join" so as to overcome the "large and influential black leadership" which looks upon "strike-breaking as a legitimate and effective means of negro advancement." Growing socialist support for interracial solidarity in labor unions contrasted with socialist skepticism about cross-class gender solidarity. In the 1909–10 shirtwaist strike, an innovative initial alliance between immigrant strikers and wealthy woman suffragists disintegrated when privileged feminists issued a public criticism of socialists and their involvement in the strike. Socialist organizer Theresa Malkiel, as reported by historian Meredith Tax in *The Rising of the Women* (1980), decried bourgeois reformers who come "down from the height of their pedestals to preach identity of interests to the little daughters of the people."

Reverberations of the Russian Revolution

Toward the end of the First World War, revolution shook Russia. The Bolshevik Party ("Bolshevik" meant "majority") assumed power in Petrograd in October 1917, announcing its intention to transfer "All Power to the Soviets"—councils of workers, peasants, and soldiers. The heady news of the establishment of a proletarian republic was greeted with exhilaration by all parts of an American left which, in contrast to the Second International's capitulation to nationalism and war in Europe, had opposed the war and suffered relentless blows from government and vigilantes. American radicals were spellbound by the Bolsheviks' internationalist opposition to imperialism, stated intention of workers' control, and sharp criticisms of social-democratic reformism. The 1919 American strike wave owed much to the inspiration of workers' rule in Russia, and revolutionary socialists gained ground rapidly in the Socialist Party. Once again, socialist theory of the strike was refashioned.

No theoretician was more important in this radicalization than Louis Fraina (1892–1953), an Italian-born immigrant and former De Leon protégé who edited *The Class Struggle* and *Revolutionary Age*. According to Fraina, a new stage of "imperialistic State Capitalism" had resulted in sharpened competition, war, crisis, and revolution. Organized capitalism required "the machine proletariat, the proletariat of average labor," with a propensity for aggressive mass action. In 1919, Fraina took note of the wave of mass strikes in "larger, basic industry" by "unorganized, unskilled" workers. Writing in

The Class Struggle, he urged socialists to approach this upsurge in a fresh way:

> But if, as in the past, the Socialist Party uses these great strikes to prove to the workers the futility of strikes, and the power of the vote—then a great opportunity will be wasted. That is the petty bourgeois policy, which tries to compress the elemental action of the proletariat within the stultifying limits of parliamentary action, as such. The Socialist Party, revolutionary Socialism, should use these strikes and mass industrial revolts to develop in the proletariat the consciousness of revolutionary mass action, to develop the conception and practice of political strikes, to make it realize that its action should centre in the large plants, that when it wants to act, its action should develop out of the mill, mine and factory. . . . To broaden the strike into a demonstration, to develop, out of these, revolutionary mass action against Capitalism and the state—that is the policy of revolutionary Socialism.

Revolutionary socialists, held Fraina, should greet mass strikes as "the proletariat itself in action" and "marshal and direct the proletariat for the conquest of power."

The influence of European revolutionary Marxism could not have been more evident. Fraina owed something to Rosa Luxemburg (1870–1919), the Polish-Jewish revolutionary, whose writings against nationalism and war and in favor of the Russian October Revolution he translated and published in *The Class Struggle.* Her pamphlet *The Mass Strike* (1906) on the attempted 1905 revolution in Russia that gave birth to the "soviet" (workers' council) called the uprising a "political mass strike" for freedom against absolutism. But Luxemburg's strike pamphlet was not widely known in the United States at this time, as its only English translation was published by an obscure group in Detroit. Far more axiomatic to the culture of the left in 1919 and after—and to Fraina in particular—were the writings of V.I. Lenin, the Bolshevik leader, whose prestige was immense following the Soviet revolution.

In *What Is to Be Done?* (1902), Lenin argued against "economism," reducing "the working-class movement and the class struggle to narrow trade-unionism and to a 'realistic' struggle for petty, gradual reforms." Revolutionary socialists, said Lenin, should push "not only for better terms for the sale of labor-power, but for the abolition of the social system that compels the propertyless to sell themselves to the rich." Lenin articulated the need for a party to combine working-class militants with radical intellectuals like Marx and Engels from bourgeois backgrounds, who would develop revolutionary theory. According to Lenin, "the working class, exclusively by its own effort, is able to develop only trade union consciousness, i.e., the conviction that it is necessary to combine in unions, fight the employers, and strive to compel the government to pass necessary labor legislation, etc."

The Bolshevik model offered a powerful alternative to business unionism, syndicalism, and reformist socialism alike. Acquiescence to spontaneity, Lenin argued, would merely strengthen the hold of the bourgeoisie, able to disseminate its ideology through the press, churches, and schools. Revolutionaries did not belong "at the tail-end of the movement," but must form its forward guard, acting "in such a way that *all* the other contingents recognize and are obliged to admit that we are marching in the vanguard." Lenin's position was that revolutionaries should not merely assist strikes but shape them, pointing the way to the seizure of state power. This view rapidly superseded the Debsian view of trade unions and party as having distinct, complementary functions—one economic and the other political. In 1919, Fraina took hope from Seattle, Butte, and Winnipeg, where he saw "the strike broadening its character, becoming not only a general strike but a strike in which the workers consciously try to usurp the functions of government."

The Communist Party

When the Socialist Party's energized left-wing majority was expelled by the party's center-right, which feared loss of control, it sought affiliation with the Third International, or Comintern, established by the Soviets in 1919. This American Communist movement would be the dominant strand of American radicalism until 1956. Its initial premise, derived from Lenin, was that the revolutionary party organized into shop nuclei should embed itself in industry. The 1920s, however, proved far from revolutionary as the IWW collapsed, the AFL declined, and the number of strikes dwindled.

The most substantial contribution to socialist theories of the strike in the 1920s came from William Z. Foster, by then head of the Communist-led Trade Union Educational League (TUEL). Foster called on revolutionaries to work inside unions to encourage amalgamation along industrial lines, militancy, and interracial organizing. The TUEL supported industrial unionism but rejected "dual unions" such as the IWW as a "secession" that isolated militants. Foster called upon a "militant minority" in the AFL to challenge corruption and business unionism by propounding fighting approaches, including use of the strike weapon. Other socialists drew similar conclusions. In *Left Wing Unionism* (1926), David Saposs of Brookwood Labor College held that the Wobblies had won many strikes but put too little priority on stable organization and too much on syndicalist propaganda.

Accumulated American experiences formed the basis for Foster's pamphlet *Strike Strategy* (1926). Foster observed that even defensive strikes, such as to prevent a wage cut, must take the offensive to win. He emphasized the element of surprise, maintaining morale, mobilizing allies, involving the rank-and-file in activities beyond meetings, and encouraging group cooperation in strike leadership. Foster warned against "too advanced" demands, dragging out strikes beyond workers' psychological or material capacities, and placing too much value in "public opinion," although he recommended "dramatizations" to capture workers' imaginations.

When capitalism entered into worldwide crisis after 1929, Communists contributed to labor's revival by leading the San Francisco waterfront strike of 1934 and achieving positions of leadership in mainstream unions. In the final analysis, however, Communist strike theory was hostage to the party's changing line. In this sense, the Communist supplanting of the Socialists as the main organization of American radicalism in the 1930s and 1940s was disastrous. As a bureaucratic dictatorship was consolidated in the Soviet Union under Joseph Stalin, Lenin's successor, the receptiveness to European theory that was long a mainstay of American radicalism transmogrified into obedience. Foster had to eat his words in 1929 as the TUEL's progressive union strategy was replaced by sectarian "Red" unions, a policy in turn replaced by the Popular Front in 1935, when Communists opened their arms to progressives they had been denouncing as "social fascists." With every such twist of line—and there were many—the Communist view of strikes shifted. By 1942, Foster was calling on labor to "insure the continuance of production by the avoidance of strikes," a policy originating in the Soviet Union's needs in the Second World War. The Communist labor left's record of subordination to Stalin's foreign policy was its Achilles' heel in the McCarthy era and a moral catastrophe for a movement launched out of social idealism.

Anti-Stalinist Marxism

A varied left existed independent of the Communist Party during the Great Depression of the 1930s, contributing to a renaissance of American Marxism. Broadly speaking, this left's understanding of strikes shared Lenin's valuation of socialist organization, militancy, mass mobilization, and leadership. A 1937 article in the independent *Marxist Quarterly* on the 1877 railroad strikes, for example, found lack of "solid organizational foundations" to be the reason the strikes "succumbed to force and loss of momentum," but denied that they were "spontaneous," saying they arose out of informal, ongoing organization. The most creative leap in historical imagination during the Depression-era labor upsurge occurred in 1935 when W.E.B. Du Bois, then an independent Marxist, in *Black Reconstruction in America,* recast the Civil War slave exodus as "a general strike" to "stop the economy of the plantation system." Additional insights arose from practical experimentation. In 1934, the American Workers Party, led by A.J. Muste, organized an Unemployed League that mobilized out-of-work pickets outside the Toledo Auto-Lite factory gates, turning the unemployed from strikebreakers into strike supporters. Many socialists on the non-Stalinist left began to reconsider Comintern models of leadership as manipulative and arrogant. In 1938,

Jay Lovestone, whose small group had a presence in the needle trades, criticized, in "Marxists and the Unions" in *Workers Age,* the "commissarship" attitude that "we have the plan, the patent, the monopoly, just what the labor movement needs to be a 'real' labor movement."

As socialists made fitful starts to reconcile leadership and democracy, they combated mortal threats to the right to strike, especially in the rise of Nazism. Leon Trotsky (1879–1940), a Bolshevik associate of Lenin's who had become the premier international Marxist critic of Stalinism and whose American followers led the 1934 Minneapolis Teamsters strike, delivered a penetrating assessment of the rise of German fascism in which he emphasized the right to strike as one of the basic democratic freedoms the Nazis sought to extinguish. Although Chicago's Little Steel Memorial Day massacre in 1937 showed that strikes could still be violently repressed in the United States, momentum ran in the opposite direction, as by 1935 the New Deal sought to restore purchasing power through Social Security, union recognition, and the right to strike. The Wagner Act fostered an upsurge already under way of second-generation workers homogenized by mass culture, who poured into the Congress of Industrial Organizations (CIO), a breakaway from the AFL, in 1935–37. The CIO's cadre were semiskilled machine operators, tool-and-die makers, and machinists, not precisely the "average labor" Louis Fraina had pictured, although his prediction of shopfloor insurgency was vindicated.

The sit-down strikes of 1936 and 1937, in which workers remained inside factories to prevent production from resuming, reflected both mass awakening and the conscious leadership of working-class militants, often radicals. "Many revolutionaries, so-called, talk about 'spontaneous combustion of the workers,'" observed Genora Johnson Dollinger, a socialist militant and spark plug of the Flint, Michigan, sit-down that created the United Auto Workers (UAW), in *Not Automatic: Women and the Left in the Forging of the Auto Workers Union* (2000). "I can't see that at all, because it took time for the organizers in the various plants of this whole General Motors empire to talk to the workers and to bring them to classes—to make some contact, create a bond." Known in Europe as "occupation strikes" or "factory seizures," sit-downs had never before been employed so widely in America. In *Labor's New Millions* (1938), Mary Heaton Vorse, a journalist with socialist and feminist leanings, listed the advantages of remaining in the plant instead of walking out: employers hesitated to authorize attacks for fear of injuring their property, strikers were shielded from the elements, and extensive internal education could take place. But for Marxists, sit-downs held a far greater significance. "Mass sit-down strikes shake the principle of bourgeois property," wrote Trotsky in "The Transitional Program" (1938). Revolutions in miniature, they went "beyond the limits of 'normal' capitalist procedure," posing "in a practical manner the question of who is boss of the factory: the capitalist or the workers?"

Mid-century: Bureaucracy, Wildcats, and a New Left

The sit-downs compelled union recognition. By 1945, almost a third of Americans were organized. This did not augur revolution, but it did teach the power of the strike. The period from 1936 to 1946 was among the most militant in American labor history, even though the Supreme Court, as if with ear cocked toward Trotsky, ruled in 1939 that companies could fire sit-down strikers, putting an effective halt to that tactic. When the Second World War arrived, a no-strike, no-lockout pledge was agreed upon by union leaders, management, and the White House, with Communists concurring. Virtually the only support for wartime strikes came from small Trotskyist organizations.

"Wildcats"—irregular strikes lacking union authorization—exploded during the war. The socialist C.L.R. James (1901–1989) saw wildcats as proof of the elemental revolutionary impulses of the self-emancipating working class. In this he drew upon Marx's largely unknown philosophical and economic manuscripts of 1844, which underscored alienation in work as a source of discontent. In *State Capitalism and World Revolution* (1950) and *Facing Reality* (1958), James and his colleagues depicted union leadership as "an instrument of capitalist production" that traded away the "struggle in production" for "the struggle over consumption, higher wages, pensions, education, etc." The resultant speed-up and mindlessness led inevitably to "revolt, wildcat strikes, a desperate attempt of the working class to gain for itself conditions of labor that are denied to it by the employers and the labor bureaucracy." Variations on this theme were espoused by Raya Dunayevskaya in *Marxism and Freedom* (1958) and Martin Glaberman in *Punching Out* (1952) and *Wartime Strikes* (1980). Critics noted, however, that wildcats often had informal, organic leadership from shop stewards and radicals, and reflected not sentiment against unions so much as a desire that contracts be respected. Nor were wildcats invariably heroic. George Lipsitz's *Rainbow at Midnight* (1994) documents "hate strikes," white supremacist wildcats during the Second World War sparked by transfers of African-American workers into all-white departments.

The ebb of labor militancy presented a larger problem. Socialists in the 1940s and 1950s confronted the possibility that unions, rather than representing a new world within the shell of the old, were wholly integrated into the capitalist system. With union density at its peak, the CIO united with the AFL in 1955, creating a behemoth. Industrial unionism was joined to business unionism, with craft organization remaining in large areas such as the building trades. Academic discourse, governed by pluralist theories of industrial relations, saw labor as a mere pressure group and strikes as the consequence of feckless bargaining that could be minimized through proper management techniques.

In this atmosphere of unprecedented affluence, when some conjectured that capitalism was creating a classless society, radicals began to rethink labor. In his "Letter to the New Left" (1960), C. Wright Mills spoke of a "labor metaphysic" held by those who cling to images of the working class "as *the* historic agency, or even as the most important agency, in the face of the really impressive historical evidence that now stands against this expectation." Herbert Marcuse's *One-Dimensional Man* (1964) concluded that the proletariat was no longer the bearer of "historical transformation," since workers were complacent, with an "overriding interest in the preservation and improvement of the institutional status quo." Similar impressions were given by Paul A. Baran and Paul M. Sweezy's *Monopoly Capital* (1966) and James Boggs's *The American Revolution* (1963). Even Harry Braverman's *Labor and Monopoly Capital* (1974) portrayed worker cynicism but did not mention strikes. As the New Deal alliance of labor, liberals, and the left unraveled over race and the Vietnam War, radicals at times saw strikes as embedded in consumer acquisition, rituals within the system.

Beneath that tendency, however, ran countervailing currents, particularly from Europe. *New Left Review* editor Perry Anderson refused to relinquish the classical Marxist understanding of trade unions as "dialectically both an opposition to capitalism and a component of it." The British historian E.P. Thompson's *The Making of the English Working Class* (1964), with its thesis that class consciousness is "made," not "given," provided an alternative model to mechanical Marxism and inspired new labor studies. Most critical of all were the massive strikes in France in May 1968 that nearly brought down the state as workers linked arms with revolutionary students in defiance of Communist trade union leaders. As reporter Daniel Singer put it in *Prelude to Revolution: France in May 1968* (1970), the May strike movement was so "internationalist and egalitarian, spontaneous and libertarian," that it "suddenly recalled what socialism once stood for and showed what it could mean again in our times." A youth rebellion from Czechoslovakia to Mexico and an upturn in African-American militancy seemed to place socialist revolution on the historical agenda once again. After 1968, labor was no longer a metaphysic, Marxism no longer a nineteenth-century relic.

Rosa Luxemburg's *The Mass Strike* (1906) was read widely among American socialists only after the May 1968 events. Whereas she had once been grouped with Lenin as a revolutionary critic of empire, war, and reformism, her reputation was now recast to emphasize her libertarianism. Contesting the staid German trade union officials of the Second International, Luxemburg held that mass strikes are not made, propagated, or planned. They emerge spontaneously, not out of the "rigid, mechanical-bureaucratic conception" of all workers taking direction from "the central committee of a party" by being organized into trade unions. Indeed, wrote Luxemburg, it may well be the least organized (miners, textile workers), not the best organized (printers), who prove most revolutionary. Originally directed primarily at reformist social democracy, Luxemburg's pamphlet took on new meaning when read against sclerotic Soviet Marxism-Leninism after May 1968—although some readers overlooked Luxemburg's differences with syndicalist theories of a general strike and her commitment to the revolutionary socialist party.

By the beginning of the 1970s, American radicals were looking anew at the working class. Students aided the grape boycott in the Chicano-led United Farm Workers strikes, and a wave of wildcats erupted in 1968–72, some sparked by Detroit's League of Revolutionary Black Workers. New left socialists were receptive to strikes that harmonized demands of new social movements of women, people of color, and gays and lesbians. Union WAGE, for example, founded in the 1970s by feminist socialists, pressed labor to negotiate contracts granting paid maternity leave and equal pay for equal work. Stanley Aronowitz, in *False Promises: The Shaping of American Working Class Consciousness* (1973), deprecated "revolutionary cheerleading of every strike for higher wages" while pointing to a confluence of youth culture, African-American militancy, and worker discontent in the 1972 strike at General Motors in Lordstown, Ohio.

While some new leftists reverted to Stalinism in Maoist guise or developed new permutations of Trotskyism, the tendency was toward spontaneity. Theories of workers' control underwent a revival. Longshoreman Stan Weir, historians Staughton Lynd and George Rawick, and other contributors to *Radical America* emphasized "working-class self-activity." Jeremy Brecher's *Strike!* (1972) held that mass strikes in American history entailed "workers' challenge to authority, direction of their own activity, and spreading solidarity."

Demise of the Strike?

Those who looked carefully could see the warning signs. In 1967, in "The Role of the American Working Class," Staughton Lynd foresaw "a concerted attack by American capitalism on the right to strike." In 1969, the Belgian Trotskyist Ernest Mandel, in "Where Is America Going?" predicted "a far more ruthless attack on the real wage levels of American workers." Few others perceived the corporate offensive so early, but it was under way already and would accelerate in the 1970s. Socialists were less prescient in anticipating the fight to come. Lynd believed industrial workers "may once more become militant when their very right to collective existence—the right to strike—is threatened." Mandel expanded on Lenin's *What Is to Be Done?* by observing that "trade-union consciousness" is "neither reactionary nor revolutionary," for it may create "a major revolutionary potential once the system is no longer capable of satisfying basic trade-union demands."

No grand working-class upsurge materialized, however. The hopes of 1968 ran aground on the shoals of 1973 as economic stagnation and political cynicism ushered in a shift culminating in the election of Republican President Ronald Reagan in 1980. The ranks of socialists committed to labor thinned, particularly as many intellectuals rushed to join what historian Ellen Meiksins Wood called, in the title to a 1986 book, social theory's "retreat from class." Meanwhile, the AFL-CIO responded so ploddingly to the siege on its citadel that Thomas Geoghegan used the words *mastodon*, *dumb*, *stupid*, and *arthritic* to describe organized labor on the first page of his clever 1991 defense of it, *Which Side Are You On? Trying to Be for Labor When It's Flat on Its Back.*

Socialists interpreted the thirty-year decline in strike frequency and magnitude as intimately related to the decline of labor unions. They blamed several factors, one of which being the unequal playing field of law and state. Reagan-era normalization of "replacement" workers made strikes into losing propositions, so much so that historian Peter Rachleff talked of "the eradication of a meaningful right to strike." A second factor was a declining rate of profit, prompting capital to drive down labor costs to preserve "competitiveness." Production was shifted to the non-union American South or abroad. Hundreds of thousands of union jobs were wiped out in steel, auto, and other sectors. Especially after the collapse of Soviet-bloc Communism in 1989–91, the market became global. Socialists urged cross-border solidarity to meet the challenge.

What most distinguished socialist theory from mainstream commentary on the decline of strikes was the extent of its attention to labor's own flawed internal structures, practices, and vision. Kim Moody, Mike Parker, Jane Slaughter, and others associated with the Detroit-based *Labor Notes* observed that autocratic union structures made leaders remote and unaccountable to the rank and file, and that this was a primary factor in disastrous concessionary bargaining that eroded wages, pensions, and health care benefits. The labor bureaucracy, described as a "distinct social layer" by historian Robert Brenner in *Against the Current*, was willing to accept retreat and failure rather than rock the boat by striking. As Michael Goldfield observed in *The Decline of Organized Labor in the United States* (1987), business unionism's tendency to see the union "primarily as a solvent financial organization" led to a desire to avoid strikes even when clearly in the interests of members so that the union will "not deplete its resources unnecessarily." Socialists chafed at contract clauses that forbade strikes for the contract's duration. Goldfield noted that unions have "bargained away, in many cases, the right to strike during the life of their contracts." Socialists had come full circle: two centuries later, they now faulted unions for *insufficient* commitment to the strike.

Left-wing socialists sought a labor movement revitalized from below by the rank-and-file. They hoped to "put the *movement* back in the labor movement," as *Labor Notes* expressed it. Strikes could succeed when they mobilized members, had national union support, and engaged broad sympathies, as in the 1997 Teamsters strike that put United Parcel Service on the defensive by dramatizing dead-end, part-time, reduced-benefit positions. Even militant democratic social unionism in heroic rank-and-file struggles could falter, though. Despite support from labor activists around the country, Local P-9's strike against wage cuts at the profitable Hormel plant in Austin, Minnesota, in 1985–86 was betrayed by United Food and Commercial Workers leaders at the national level. To win such strikes, some socialists stressed the imperative of preventing revived production by blocking scabs from entering plants. Shrugging off worries about illegality, they observed that the great strikes of 1934—Toledo, San Francisco, Minneapolis—all involved confrontations with the National Guard. Others advised "inside campaigns" or "work to rule," taking pains to follow every recommended company quality procedure, filing safety complaints, and otherwise slowing production without giving the company just cause to fire workers.

At the outset of a new century, some theorists began to return to themes of political action, pointing to the limitations of the strike. Historian Nelson Lichtenstein, in *State of the Union: A Century of American Labor* (2002), questioned collective bargaining itself, arguing that a private welfare program for the membership was no substitute for broad gains for the whole class, such as universal health care. He suggested that labor adopt a civil rights discourse comparable to that successfully employed by African Americans, women, and other groups, and think beyond "extremely detailed, firm-centered collective bargaining contracts" toward social-democratic reforms. Massive demonstrations of millions of Latino, Asian, Muslim, and Irish immigrants on behalf of immigration law liberalization on May 1, 2006, resulted in what author Mike Davis told the British *Socialist Worker* was a "near general strike in the Latino neighborhoods of California," and spoke to the enduring potential for working-class mobilization premised on social solidarity. Davis observed that American radicalism's fortunes often correlated to upturns in immigrant workers' struggles, but it remained to be seen whether the American working class would at last awaken to challenge the freefall in union density, stagnant real wages, and the nonunion status of Wal-Mart, the nation's largest employer. Nothing short of such an awakening could resuscitate the strike.

See also: Theories of Strikes, 16; The Decline of Strikes, 72; Strikes Led by the Trade Union Unity League, 1929–1934, 166; The Strike Wave of 1877, 177; World War I Era Strikes, 191; Strikes in the Nineteenth-Century Cotton Textile Industry in the Northeast United States, 314; Labor Upheaval on the Nation's Railroads, 1877–1922, 483.

Bibliography

Anderson, Perry. "The Limits and Possibilities of Trade Union Action." In *The Incompatibles: Trade Union Militancy and Class Consciousness*, ed. Robin Blackburn and Alexander Cockburn. Harmondsworth, Middlesex, England: Penguin, 1967.

Cooper, Jake. *Lessons of the P-9 Strike.* San Francisco: Socialist Action, 1988.

Davis, Mike. *Prisoners of the American Dream: Politics and Economy in the History of the US Working Class.* New York: Verso, 1986.

Fraina, Louis. "Laborism and Socialism." *The Class Struggle* II, no. 4 (September–October 1918): 410–31.

———. "The Mass Strike in Action." *The Revolutionary Age* 1, no. 32 (May 24, 1919): 4.

Herreshoff, David. *American Disciples of Marx.* Detroit: Wayne State University Press, 1967.

Lynd, Staughton. "The Role of the American Working Class." *Monthly Review* 19, no. 7 (December 1967): 52–57.

Marx, Karl. *The First International and After,* ed. David Fernbach. New York: Vintage, 1974.

Moody, Kim. *An Injury to All: The Decline of American Unionism.* London: Verso, 1988.

Oberman, Karl. *Joseph Weydemeyer: Pioneer of American Socialism.* New York: International, 1947.

Rachleff, Peter. "Workers' Rights & Wrongs." *Against the Current* 125 (November/December 2006): 27–31.

Trotsky, Leon. *The Transitional Program for Socialist Revolution.* New York: Pathfinder, 1973.

THE NEWS MEDIA AND STRIKES

Christopher R. Martin

There is a tendency in each generation of media critics to believe that news coverage never has been as horrible as in the present. That tendency holds true when considering mainstream national news media coverage of strikes. Yet in a review of news coverage of strikes in U.S. history, one would be hard pressed to discover any Golden Era in which the national news media presented honest and accurate accounts of strikes.

The problem with the news media's coverage of strikes—and their coverage of organized labor in general—is that the news media are both social institutions designated to practice the First Amendment freedoms of speech and press and corporate entities designed to generate profits for their media magnates and stockholders. Particularly in strike stories, the news media's built-in conflict between the practice of journalism and the business of media is most evident. Thus, the news media have rarely served as independent storytellers of strikes, but instead have told stories that are aligned with the generally anti-labor interests of corporate America—which includes their publishers and parent media corporations.

But, news organizations that serve their own corporate interests risk undermining their greatest asset—people's trust. In their work *The Elements of Journalism*, press critics Bill Kovach and Tom Rosenstiel argue that the first loyalty of journalism is to citizens, not media owners. That loyalty, they note, "is the basis of why we as citizens believe a news organization. It is the source of its credibility." Because of the significant stakes for corporations, labor, and citizens, news organizations' coverage of strikes has long invited debate about the news media's credibility and their institutional loyalties.

News About Strikes: 1870s to 1934

Observers of the U.S. labor movement have been critical of how news media cover strikes and other labor activities for more than a century. In his 1920 book *The Brass Check,* Progressive Era muckraking journalist Upton Sinclair identified several decades of dishonest newspaper stories designed to discredit unionists and paint them as anarchists and terrorists. Sinclair reserved particular ire for the Associated Press (AP), a news cooperative of leading mainstream news organizations, which was (and still is) a dominant force in the American press, especially in distributing—via its news wire service—what might be the only version of strike stories to the rest of the nation:

> Great strikes are determined by public opinion, and public opinion is always against strikers who are violent. Therefore, in great strikes, all the efforts of the employers are devoted to making it appear that the strikers are violent. The greatest single agency in America for making it appear that strikers are violent is the Associated Press. . . . There are some violent strikers, needless to say, and Capitalist Journalism follows this simple and elemental rule—if strikers are violent, they get on the wires, while if strikers are not violent, they stay off the wires; by which simple device it is brought about that nine-tenths of the telegraphic news you read about strikes is news of violence, and so in your brain-channels is irrevocably graven the idea-association: Strikes—violence! Violence—strikes!

In a letter to the AP in 1912, labor leader Eugene Debs also argued that the wire service acted against

FRANK LESLIE'S
ILLUSTRATED WEEKLY
HOMESTEAD TROUBLES.
NEW YORK, JULY 14, 1892.

The lockout/strike at the Carnegie steel works in Homestead, Pennsylvania, as depicted in *Frank Leslie's Illustrated Weekly*, July 14, 1892. After locked-out workers occupied the mill to prevent scabs from taking their jobs, a gun battle took place when hired Pinkerton agents attacked the plant. The workers repelled the attack and captured some of the agents. The newspaper chose to display the scene after the battle, when the workers and their sympathizers taunted and beat some of the Pinkerton men. (Drawn by Miss Ge.A. Davis, from a sketch by C. Upham. *Courtesy:* Library of Congress.)

the interest of working people: "If there is in this country a strictly capitalist class institution it is the Associated Press."

Anti-labor sentiment in the press can be traced back at least as far as the 1870s, when English-language dailies in Chicago were "uniformly hostile to strikes, picketing, class-based politics, and labor methods generally, although they were sympathetic to educational and cooperative ventures," according to journalism historian Jon Bekken. Yet, some instances of news coverage were careful not to resort to simple characterizations of strikers. For example, in coverage of the Great Strike of July 1877, *Frank Leslie's Illustrated Newspaper,* a popular newsmagazine of the time, drew distinctions between railroad strikers and the relatively few "idle roughs" and "malcontents" who were violent, and went so far as to state "the element of disorganization and plunder, or incendiarism and murder, must not be confounded with the railroad strikers." Moreover, *Frank Leslie's,* as well as *Harper's Weekly,* carried illustrations of a Sixth Regiment of the Maryland National Guard firing on strikers in Baltimore, clearly indicating the bloodshed and imbalance of power. *Frank Leslie's* argued "it should need no political economist to demonstrate to corporations the necessity of fostering labor instead of grinding it into the dust."

Nevertheless, nuanced accounts were rare, and accurate reports on labor and strikes even more difficult to find; most press reports from this era marked unionists as violent radicals, regardless of any factual evidence. In the 1880s, says Bekken, Chicago's English-language daily newspapers "cheered the execution" of the alleged Haymarket conspirators, four working-class radicals who were questionably convicted of bombing a Haymarket Square rally in 1886. Labor historian Melvyn Dubofsky calls the newspaper and magazine coverage of the Haymarket bombing and trial the first national Red Scare campaign, linking all trade unionism to anarchy and murder.

By the turn of the century, according to Bekken, the commercial dailies of the heavily industrialized Chicago area "generally claimed to champion the interests of workers, but believed that the interests of labor and capital were fundamentally the same—and that both were subordinate to the 'public interest.' They strongly backed arbitration of labor disputes, opposed sympathy strikes, and called for forcible suppression of strike-related disorder."

On the West Coast, one of the Associated Press's great allies in capitalist journalism was the *Los Angeles Times,* purchased by Harrison Gray Otis in 1882. Otis (like his son-in-law and successor, Harry Chandler) was notoriously anti-labor and schemed to stop unionizing campaigns not only at his newspaper but also at businesses throughout the Los Angeles area, as historian John Nerone relates. A strike by *Los Angeles Times* workers in September 1910 elicited this denunciation in the newspaper's editorial page under the title "The Wolves Are Howling." It reveals the newspaper's sentiments toward strikes:

> [The strikers] are mostly of the anarchic scum of Europe. They are envious, idle, brawling, disorderly men who hang about the deadfalls and, between drinks, damn as a scab every non-union industrious worker. They hate law, hate order, and hate the men and the conditions which compel them to work occasionally. Their instincts are criminal, and they are ever ready for arson, riot, robbery, and murder. . . . They combine in labor unions whose honest purpose they pervert . . . to prohibit the skillful and the industrious mechanic from accomplishing any more work in a day than the unskillful and lazy man.

News About Strikes, Post-Wagner Act: 1935 to Present

Portraying striking unionists as violent—despite the fact that violence was often ignited by corporate-sponsored thugs, or corporate-aligned local police, state troopers, and federal troops—is still a common news frame, but it ceased to be the single dominant frame after passage of the National Labor Relations Act (also called the Wagner Act, after its chief sponsor, U.S. Senator Robert F. Wagner of New York) in 1935. The Wagner Act established the legal infrastructure for labor unions to exist and collectively bargain with industry. According to historian Robert Zieger, passage of the act and its favorable review by the U.S. Supreme Court in 1937 ended a period of violent confrontation in which "literally hundreds of workers had been killed and thousands injured in a long history of disputes stretching back into the nineteenth century." The act "shifted the focus of labor conflict away from violent confrontation toward the hearing rooms and courts." A report by the Machinists Union Media Monitoring Project, authored by Jerry Rollings, found that of all labor-related issues, strikes receive the most press attention. With the Wagner Act, however, news frames about strikes changed. The law legitimized unions, but the press recast their activities—particularly their now-legal strikes—in ways that still worked to marginalize workers.

HARPER'S WEEKLY.
A JOURNAL OF CIVILIZATION
Vol. XXI.—No. 1076.] NEW YORK, SATURDAY, AUGUST 11, 1877.

The caption from *Harper's Weekly*, August 11, 1877, reads "The Great Strike—the Sixth Maryland Regiment Fighting Its Way Through Baltimore." Maryland governor John Lee Carroll mobilized the troops, who dislodged protesting workers and their sympathizers from Camden Station by force, arrested hundreds, killed ten protesters, and wounded scores more. (From a photograph by D. Bendann. *Courtesy:* Library of Congress.)

Even as unions were gaining strength, when it came to labor there was still a "considerable body of news which the commercial press suppresses or buries, or distorts," journalism critic George Seldes wrote in 1938. He charged that "the commercial press only pretends that the interests of labor are its first interest also." A 1945 content analysis of American radio news stories on labor in *Journalism Quarterly* by academic Leila Sussman verified Seldes's concerns and found that unions were usually portrayed as the "wrong" party in workplace disputes. The radio stories typically quoted prominent government officials, political leaders, business executives, and even union members to construct management's "side" of the story. Only labor leaders were used to provide quotes supporting the labor position, suggesting that the union had few advocates beyond its own leadership.

Other studies of mainstream news media coverage of strikes and unions have come to similar conclusions. Several studies, including those by Yorgo Pasadeos, Hayg Oshagan and Christopher Martin, and Paul Walton and Howard Davis have noted that in coverage of strikes and other labor-management disputes, quotes and interviews are most typically from management representatives, occasionally from union representatives, and least likely from regular workers. Citing workers might seem to be redundant when union representatives are already quoted. But, when workers undertake strikes that are not endorsed by union leadership (wildcat strikes) or when workers disagree with their union leadership and form opposition groups within the union (such as the New Directions caucus in the UAW, or Teamsters for a Democratic Union group in the Teamsters), quoting rank-and-file workers is essential to an accurate story.

The extensive Machinists Union Media Monitoring Project of television entertainment and news broadcasts in 1980 and 1981 found that "television typically casts unions as violent, degrading, and obstructive." Media coverage of labor-management conflict in Great Britain is often similar. Three major studies titled *Bad News* by the Glasgow University Media Group in the 1970s and 1980s on British television's coverage of industrial news demonstrated the consistently poor coverage of labor issues. The Media Group found that events reflecting negatively on management, such as industrial accidents, were "systematically underreported," whereas labor's reasons for striking were reported irregularly or not at all. The British studies also show that the credibility of labor's position is always in question in the description of industrial conflict:

> [I]ndustrial reporting relies on the assumption that industrial disputes are about "trouble"—trouble for us as customers, commuters and members of the public, trouble for the managers of industry, trouble for the nation; but never trouble for the workers involved. In the detailed examination of the vocabulary used we have demonstrated that in disputes the traditional *offers* of management are inevitably countered by the *demands* of workers—to the point where the nouns and verbs describing management actions are generally positive while the matching vocabulary for workers' actions is negative.

Studies suggest that the visual language of news reports is also damaging to labor's image. Television news interviews typically portray management representatives speaking directly to the camera in the calm, rational environment of business offices. Conversely, workers are depicted in the often chaotic, noisy environment of a street picket line, and are rarely interviewed face-to-face. In *Inventing Reality: The Politics of Mass Media*, published in 1986, Michael Parenti summarized studies of labor coverage in the news and cataloged seven generalizations about the way the news media portray labor:

1. The larger struggle between capital and labor is ignored, making it possible to present labor struggles as senseless conflicts that could be solved if only the union would be willing to negotiate in good faith.
2. Company "offers" are emphasized, while company takebacks, employee grievances, and issues such as job security, health insurance, and safety are underplayed or ignored.
3. While big labor wages are reported, management compensation usually isn't. When workers are asked to make concessions, no coverage is typically given to management salaries, bonuses, and other perquisites.
4. The problems a strike brings to the economy and public convenience are emphasized to the detriment of in-depth coverage on the cause(s) of the strike.

5. Reports fail to consider the impact on the workers if the workers were to give up the strike and accept management's terms.
6. The class dimensions of a strike are absent, as instances of union solidarity and broader public support are rarely covered.
7. Governmental agencies are cast as neutral entities upholding the public interest. Nevertheless, the president, the courts, and police often act to protect corporate property, force workers back into production, and bodyguard strikebreakers.

In his *Through Jaundiced Eyes: How the Media View Organized Labor*, William Puette has further detailed mass media stereotypes of labor unions, including "unions protect and encourage unproductive, usually fat, lazy and insubordinate workers," and "unions institutionalize conflict . . . they remain to dredge up conflict where there would otherwise be perfect harmony." Such stereotypes create popular images of labor inefficiencies and aggressiveness, despite the fact that less than 2 percent of all contract talks actually result in strikes, and Richard B. Freeman and James L. Medoff have illustrated in *What Do Unions Do?* that unionized establishments are often more productive than non-union establishments.

One of the most important characteristics of mainstream news coverage of labor is that the media often do not cover labor at all. Jonathan Tasini's 1990 study of more than 1,000 network news broadcasts (approximately 22,000 minutes) found that only slightly more than 1 percent of the airtime (265 minutes) was devoted to covering American unions, confirming Seldes's observation decades earlier that the commercial press "suppresses or buries" labor news. A strike by Eastern Airlines employees accounted for 72 percent of all union airtime, leaving just a few minutes for all other union issues.

National broadcast and cable news networks have no regular labor beats. In the print media, the labor beat has almost disappeared, as editors have cut labor reporting in recent decades, while beefing up business news. The decline in the labor beat is connected to the news media's general shift since the 1980s away from working-class news readers to a more affluent readership. This is a shift that moves journalism away from its loyalty to all citizens in order to appeal to a select group of consumers and increase already often-substantial news organization profits.

By 2006, only ten of the top twenty-five newspapers in the United States had full-time labor or workplace reporters. Of those ten, there were clear qualitative differences in approaches to the beat, as some reporters wrote more about work issues and others about lifestyle issues, according to this author's analysis. Emblematic of the problem was the loss of the *Los Angeles Times'* only labor beat reporter in 2005. Nancy Cleeland, who led a team that won the 2004 Pulitzer Prize in National Reporting for a series on Wal-Mart's effects on American towns, workers, suppliers, and developing countries, said she left the labor beat and moved to an education staff writer position "out of frustration." The *Times'* labor beat was under the Business Desk, and Cleeland told writer Michael Massing that her editors "really didn't want to have labor stories." The move left the leading newspaper in the nation's second-largest media market with no labor beat reporter, and marked a century-long transition at the *Los Angeles Times* from vehemently anti-labor journalism to journalism of complete indifference to labor and working-class issues.

Some studies argue that the news media is biased against business, although none have concluded that the news media is biased in favor of labor. A Freedom Forum survey of business executives, reporters, and editors suggested that business executives believe the news media is dangerous, mean-spirited, and arrogant. Yet, Warren Phillips, former Dow Jones chairman and a former executive editor of the *Wall Street Journal*, notes that business executives have particular expectations of the press: "The majority of business leaders are really looking for cheerleaders, just like the majority of government people are mostly looking for people to support their policies in government."

More common are complaints from the political right that the news media represent the views of the liberal elite. In their book *The Media Elite*, Robert S. Lichter, Stanley Rothman, and Linda S. Lichter, argue that an elitist liberal East Coast media strongly influences the general tone of America's national news coverage. In 1979–80, they surveyed 238 journalists at the *New York Times*, *Washington Post*, *Wall Street Journal*, *Time*, *Newsweek*,

U.S. News and World Report, and ABC, CBS, NBC, and PBS news divisions, along with 216 business leaders (though from only six different major corporations). They found that the elite group of journalists was generally in favor of liberal social positions, which were out of step with surveyed business leaders' opinions. Thus, these authors conclude, the media is biased against business. But their conclusion of an anti-business bias is problematic, in part because they also found that the media elite are broadly supportive of pro-business policies. Large majorities of the elite news workers responded that they believe "people with more ability should earn more," "private enterprise is fair to workers," and "less regulation of business is good for the U.S." Thus, the elite media worker's liberalism apparently does not extend to the concerns of labor.

The news watchdog organization FAIR (Fairness and Accuracy in Reporting) came to a similar conclusion in 1998 when they found that on a wide variety of economic issues—including the expansion of NAFTA, taxing the wealthy, concern over corporate concentration of power, and government-guaranteed medical care—the press was to the right of the public's views. Media critic Eric Alterman's extensive study of bias in the news also found a clear slant against labor coverage, "even in alleged bastions of left-liberalism like NPR, which prefers to offer its listeners regular 'NPR business updates' frequently during the day along with the daily program *Marketplace,* augmented by the weekly *Sound Money.*" National Public Radio's news programming is part of what Alterman argues is the "media's total embrace of corporate values in virtually all matters of political economy."

News for the Consumer, Not the Citizen

In the early twentieth century, labor-management conflict "was likely to be caught, framed, and illuminated by the stark contest between organized capital and organizing labor," Dan Schiller notes. In the late twentieth century, labor-management conflict was more likely to be characterized as a consumer issue, with no class implications. By framing coverage of labor and strikes around the narrow interests of the consumer (concerns about the price and availability of goods and services) and not the broader interests of the citizens (which can involve issues of class equality and economic democracy), news coverage of strikes and labor conflict appears to take a neutral ground, not favoring management or labor. Maintaining a neutral appearance helps the news media maintain an appearance of fairness and objectivity. However, consumer-oriented coverage is not neutral or objective; it ultimately leads to a pro-capital bias.

This author's book-length study of how the news media framed labor and strike stories in the 1990s illustrates this shift in coverage. The narrative frame of a news report is the particular structure of the story—its typical setting, characters, courses of action, and discourse. Five central frames consistently emerged in the news media coverage of major labor stories in the 1990s:

1. *The consumer is king.* Because the consumer and his or her consumption are fundamental to the U.S. economy and culture, treating the individual consumer as a hallowed entity is the unstated assumption of all news.
2. *The process of production is none of our business.* The role of the consumer is to decide whether or not to buy a product or service and not to inquire about the production process. The news treads lightly on the topic of production because it would often undermine the myths and imagery of their sponsors' advertising and public relations.
3. *The economy is driven by great business leaders and entrepreneurs.* Instead of workers, who are largely invisible, the news chooses to represent the economy with heroic profiles of the CEO and entrepreneur, staples of business journalism in the 1990s.
4. *The workplace is a meritocracy.* This frame suggests that "you get what you deserve" in the workplace based on the myth that good people rise to the top and are compensated likewise.
5. *Collective economic action is bad.* The notion here is that collective action such as strikes, protests, or boycotts by workers, communities, and even consumers will upset

> the well-functioning American consumer economy and the decisions of great business leaders and entrepreneurs.

Of course, there are exceptions to such consumer-oriented news coverage, and they have been motivated by public opinion in favor of striking or protesting workers, which has forced the news media to reformulate their news frames. For example, during the fifteen-day United Parcel Service (UPS) strike in 1997, the Teamsters (with new, progressive leadership) won public support with their popular slogan "Part-Time America Won't Work" and with effective rank-and-file coordination that allowed ordinary strikers to speak for themselves. A reservoir of public goodwill for UPS workers had been generated by their daily contact with many Americans, by UPS's own advertisements celebrating its hardworking employees, and by the company's record-high profits. A *USA Today*/CNN/Gallup Poll showed that 55 percent of Americans supported the strikers, while only 27 percent supported UPS. This level of public support precipitated news frames that seriously considered workers' concerns.

Similarly, the 50,000 labor, environmentalist, and human rights protesters who filled the streets during the 1999 World Trade Organization (WTO) meeting in Seattle caused a shift away from the consumer-oriented news frames that characterized early coverage of the WTO meeting. A *Business Week* poll conducted just a few days after the end of the WTO meeting in Seattle verified that the majority of Americans supported the Seattle protesters. Fifty-two percent of respondents said they were sympathetic toward the protesters at the summit, compared to 39 percent who said they were not sympathetic. The mainstream corporate news media stumbled in its efforts to get beyond typical news frames emphasizing the problems caused by the protesters, but finally addressed concerns of citizens and developed stories that discussed the problems of international trade policies.

Beyond the Mainstream: The Labor News Media

As noted earlier, Upton Sinclair, the well-known muckraking reporter of the early twentieth century, was outraged by press coverage of labor in his time. Sinclair charged, "Whenever it comes to a 'show-down' between labor and capital, the press is openly or secretly for capital—and this no matter how 'liberal' the press may pretend to be." Given the shortcomings of labor coverage in the mainstream press, it is no surprise that labor activists resolved to take the matter into their own hands by publishing labor-oriented newspapers.

Bekken reports that at the beginning of the twentieth century, "the U.S. labor movement published hundreds of newspapers in dozens of languages, ranging from local and regional dailies issued by working-class political organizations and mutual aid societies to national union weeklies and monthlies." These alternative publications served an important organizing function, and many invited readers to submit articles for publication. Some of these partisan presses with pro-union messages were as popular as any commercial newspaper. In *The New Labor Press: Journalism for a Changing Union Movement*, Sam Pizzigati and Fred J. Solowey note that "just after the turn of the century, the largest-circulation weekly newspaper in the United States was the *Appeal to Reason,* an unofficial Socialist Party paper that circulated over 760,000 copies at its peak in 1913. During the Great Depression, the newspaper of the Communist Party USA, the *Daily Worker,* saw its paid circulation climb to 100,000." The high circulation of these weeklies (significant even by today's standards) was difficult to sustain, especially with the government-led antiradical campaign during and after World War I. The U.S. government banned certain publications from the mails, while other working-class newspapers suffered libel suits, destruction of presses, or deportation of editors. In *Violence Against the Press: Policing the Public Sphere in U.S. History*, John Nerone notes that those "years saw the destruction of a large chunk of the radical network that had been built over the past two decades. By the end of the war, 1,500 of the more than 5,000 Socialist Party locals—about one-quarter of the organizational base—had been eliminated. Most of the lost locals were in small communities. The attrition rate for Socialist newspapers was similar; losses there were likewise concentrated in small towns."

There has long been the idea for a national,

general-interest labor newspaper. Media critic George Seldes imagined in 1938 a labor newspaper with popular appeal. "To get millions of readers the labor press will have to supply the comic strips, the stories dealing with sex, money and crime, which have made many tabloids successful, the baseball scores, all the stuff the general public wants and now gets in the non-labor or anti-labor press." But no such national labor press emerged, and labor and worker-oriented newspapers developed only at the local level. By the end of the twentieth century, local working-class newspapers such as *Racine* [Wisconsin] *Labor* had mostly faded away. Union publications have not come close to Seldes's dream. They typically have limited readership, and have most often served as undemocratic mouthpieces for union leaders. There are persistent calls for reform in labor news media. The International Labor Communications Association has called for opening up labor publications to dissent, and the International Association of Machinists has proposed a labor cable channel. There is still no national general-interest labor newspaper, but in the era of the Internet, a Web-based labor newspaper with lower costs and international reach is more feasible.

Outside of unions, closer to the mainstream but still on the margins, reside independent labor monthlies like *Labor Notes,* Web sites like workdayminnesota.org, public affairs magazines of the left (including *The Nation, The Progressive, In These Times,* and *Z Magazine*), radio news programs like Democracy Now and syndicated radio service Workers Independent News, and satellite/cable channels like Free Speech TV and Link TV. These news organizations—not beholden to the corporate imperatives of the mainstream corporate news media—consistently provide the most truthful and accurate coverage of the labor movement and strikes.

See also: Corporate Strike Strategy, 66; Newsboy Strikes, 609.

Bibliography

Alterman, Eric. *What Liberal Media?* New York: Basic Books, 2003.

Bekken, Jon. "The Working Class Press at the Turn of the Century." In *Ruthless Criticism: New Perspectives in U.S. Communication History,* ed. William S. Solomon and Robert W. McChesney. Minneapolis: University of Minnesota Press, 1993.

Croteau, David. "Challenging the 'Liberal Media' Claim." *Extra!* July/August 1998, 4–9.

Haggerty, Mike, and Wallace Rasmussen. *The Headline vs. The Bottom Line: Mutual Distrust Between Business and the News Media.* Nashville, TN: The Freedom Forum First Amendment Center, 1994.

Martin, Christopher R. *Framed! Labor and the Corporate Media.* Ithaca, NY: Cornell University Press, 2004.

Schiller, Dan. *Objectivity and the News: The Public and the Rise of Commercial Journalism.* Philadelphia: University of Pennsylvania Press, 1981.

Seldes, George. *Lords of the Press.* New York: Julian Messner, 1938.

Sinclair, Upton. *The Brass Check: A Study of American Journalism.* Pasadena, CA: The Author, 1920.

Tasini, Jonathan. "Lost in the Margins: Labor and the Media," *Extra!* 3, no. 7 (1990): 2–11.

Walton, Paul, and Howard Davis. "Bad News for Trade Unionists." In *Trade Unions and the Media,* ed. Peter Beharrell and Greg Philo. London: Macmillan, 1977.

THE BUSINESS COMMUNITY'S MERCENARIES: STRIKEBREAKERS AND UNION BUSTERS

Robert Smith

For more than a century and a half, a uniquely American institution—the professional strikebreaking agency—has proved an effective tool in the business community's efforts to discipline its workforce. The early years of the labor movement witnessed open warfare between unionists, whose activities many regarded as un-American, and their employers' first mercenary forces—private armies of armed guards. As the public's attitude toward organized labor slowly changed from open hostility to acceptance, anti-union entrepreneurs demonstrated the spirit of American inventiveness by adapting their tactics to the new realities. More subtle than armies of armed guards was the use of professional scabs and undercover operatives, the former protected by long-cherished American economic axioms and the latter by stealth. With the institutionalization of labor relations after World War II, the business community relied less on sleuths, saboteurs, or blackjacks and more on labor relations consultants. Sporting expensive suits and carrying briefcases, these professionals proved even shrewder in helping their clients avoid or eliminate unionization. In recent years, they have played a key role in the deterioration of organized labor's strength. Once again, the anti-union tactics are marginalizing labor unions, much as they did during the age of industrial violence a century ago.

Private Police Entrepreneurs

In the years after the Civil War, as an increasingly large and unruly proletariat threatened the established order, private policing emerged as the first form of commercial union busting. Well aware of labor's precarious position, employers felt little need for subtlety. Moreover, they recognized, as did the members of the United States Industrial Commission in 1902, that city police came largely from the working class, making them "unwilling to enforce order effectively." Allan Pinkerton, founder of the most well-known detective agency in the United States, was the first to foresee the profits to be earned by supplying armed guards to businessmen frightened by union organizing. By the last decades of the nineteenth century, Pinkerton men were such a common sight that "Pinkertons" became the eponym applied to all armed guards.

Although the professional and efficient service they promised must have seemed a godsend, the violence associated with armed strikebreakers often generated hostility against their clients. The death of a young boy at the hands of Pinkerton men during a Jersey City coal handlers strike in 1886, as well as the actions of Pinkerton guards during the New York Central Railroad strike in 1890, stoked public antipathy toward the agency. While the official organ of the Knights of Labor spoke for wage earners when it argued that these guards were "from the lowest class of society—a class notoriously unprincipled, worthless and venal," editors of *The Nation* argued that businesses' reliance on mercenary forces was evidence that the "nation had sunk into a form of medieval barbarism similar to the feudalism of the twelfth century."

After the New York Central strike, John Quinn, a New York congressman, presented a petition to Congress asking that they outlaw the private guard industry, but little came of his efforts. A thorough investigation into the armed guard industry awaited one of the bloodiest labor disputes of the late nineteenth century: the Homestead strike in 1892. Only after William Jennings Bryan eloquently told Congress that "governments are organized to protect life and property. These functions should not be transferred to private individuals and hired detectives until we are ready to acknowledge government a failure" did the national legislature consider a proposal from Tom Watson, the populist congressman from Georgia, to outlaw hired guards.

When workers walked out of the Carnegie steel works at Homestead, Pennsylvania, plant manager Henry Clay Frick (according to his testimony in a congressional investigation) recalled that during a strike three years earlier, police "were driven off, their hats and coats taken from them . . . driven back to Pittsburgh." So he contracted for 300 Pinkerton men. As they landed their boat at the Homestead works in the early morning hours of July 6, 1892, hundreds of angry strikers greeted them at the plant's entrance along the Monongahela River. After a twelve-hour siege in which the strikers set the river ablaze with oil and fired a Civil War cannon acquired from the town green, Frick's mercenaries surrendered. Marched through town, "the character of the injuries inflicted upon the Pinkertons . . . were too indecent and brutal to describe," a congressional committee later reported.

With public interest and debate over this incident at a fever pitch, both houses of Congress established subcommittees to investigate the battle of the Monongahela. In spite of the anti-Pinkerton rhetoric that dominated the proceedings, an overriding concern for private property influenced much of Congress's thinking. Nonetheless, the investigations awakened the American people to the tactics of privately paid armed guards, and prompted state lawmakers in twenty-six states to prohibit the importation of armed men from neighboring states.

Although Robert Pinkerton, who followed his father as head of the family-named agency, was initially undaunted by these legislative efforts, within months of the Homestead strike, a spokesman for his agency, quoted by historian James Horan in his book *The Pinkertons: The Detective Dynasty That Made History*, declared that the "work of supplying watchmen [during labor disputes] is extremely dangerous and undesirable and for that reason we prefer not to furnish watchmen in such cases." For the image-conscious Pinkerton National Detective Agency, the realization that many Americans questioned the presence of private armies for hire in a modern republic provided the impetus it needed to end its armed guard service.

Where Pinkerton retreated, others attacked. Private policing agencies flourished throughout

The 1892 lockout/strike at the Carnegie steel works in Homestead, Pennsylvania, was one of those rare instances when professional strikebreakers lost. As these images from *Harper's Weekly*, July 16, 1892 illustrate, the workers set fire to the Pinkerton agents' barge and then imprisoned them briefly in the Eintracht Saenger Halle (Harmony Singers Hall). In the end, however, the state militia proved to be the ultimate strikebreakers, and the strike was defeated. (*Courtesy:* Library of Congress.)

the country, as they found ways to circumvent state legislation. By 1893, Chicago alone could boast more than twenty such agencies, including the U.S. Detective Agency. Organized more than a decade earlier, its clients included the Frog & Crossing Company, Carnegie Steel, the Wabash Railroad, and the Baltimore and Ohio Railroad. Its well-armed men played a major role in a lumber strike in Bay City, Michigan in 1885. Twenty of them provided protection during a streetcar strike in Cleveland in 1892. Other strikebreaking firms included the Illinois Detective Agency, the Standard Detective Agency, Alexander's Detective Agency, the American Detective Service, and the Veteran's Police Patrol and Detective Agency. The principal of this last firm, John L. Manning, furnished over 100 guards to the Western Indiana Railroad and thirty more to the Wabash Railroad when their switchmen walked off the job in 1886.

After the Homestead debacle, although much of the business community came to rely less and less on private police, in isolated mining communities, private mercenaries remained a viable union-busting alternative well into the twentieth century. Found in nearly every mining community in the southern part of West Virginia, by 1910 guards in the employ of the Baldwin-Felts Agency provided the mine owners with feudal-like control over their workers. Guarding the payroll, collecting rents, and determining access to company towns, they barred gamblers, prostitutes, and union organizers. Before 1909, United Mine Workers of America (UMWA) organizers could move freely about the state, but after that time the UMWA discouraged them from even setting foot in southern West Virginia.

Although one of the firm's founders, Thomas Felts, claimed that his men had eliminated "all semblance of unionism" in that part of the state, the introduction of his guards often proved more of a liability than an asset. For example, shortly after he boasted of their prowess, guards' brutality prompted the miners in Kanawha County to rise up in what came to be known as the Paint Creek-Cabin Creek strike of 1912–13. During the early phase of this dispute, in addition to escorting strikebreakers, Baldwin-Felts men constructed concrete forts throughout the area and equipped them with machine guns. On Cabin Creek, they placed one such weapon on a building owned by Carbon Fuel Company. From portholes this gun could sweep the valley in all directions.

Poet, writer, artist, and Industrial Workers of the World organizer Ralph Chaplin captured the miners' antipathy to the Baldwin-Felts mercenaries in his poem "Mine Guard," published in a Socialist newspaper:

> You Cur? How can you stand so calm and still
> And careless while your brothers strive and bleed?
> What hellish, cruel, crime-polluted creed
> Has taught you thus to do your master's will,
> Whose guilty gold has dammed your soul until
> You lick his boots and fawn to do this deed—
> To pander to his lust of boundless greed,
> And guard him while his cohorts crush and kill?
> Your brutish crimes are like a rotten flood—
> The beating, raping, murdering you've done—
> You psychopathic coward with a gun:
> The worms would scorn your carcass in the mud;
> A bitch would blush to hail you as a son—
> You loathsome outcast, red with fresh-spilled blood.

Through inquiries sponsored by the state of West Virginia and the United States Senate, the public learned about the brutality of the mine owners' mercenaries, including one incident in early February 1913, during which the local sheriff, a coal operator, and fourteen guards machine-gunned a strikers' tent colony at Holly Grove from a tent train known as the "Bull Moose Special." Before the year was over, state lawmakers enacted the Wertz bill, making it unlawful for any "deputy to act as, or perform any duties in the capacity of guards . . . for any private individual or, firm or corporation." The men of the Baldwin-Felts Agency continued to rule southern West Virginia, however, for few took the Wertz bill seriously, since legislators failed to include a penalty clause.

When the UMWA decided to challenge the mine owners in southern West Virginia less than seven years later, the men of the Baldwin-Felts

Agency became involved in a bloody shoot-out in Matewan that led to the West Virginia Mine Wars of 1920–21. Violence erupted in the spring of 1920, when one of the largest coal producers in the region, the Red Jackett Coal Company, turned to Baldwin-Felts to remove miners residing in their Stone Mountain coal camp. Tom Felts assigned the Red Jackett job to his two brothers, Albert and Lee, and a posse of ten guards who arrived in Matewan, the nearest railroad town. Although they carried out their orders without incident, news of their action spread quickly. When they attempted to board the train back to Bluefield, the town mayor, Cabell Testerman, and the chief of police, Sid Hatfield, blocked their path. The Baldwin-Felts men particularly disliked Hatfield, who enforced the law in a way that favored the miners. Frustrated by his intransigency, Tom Felts had gone so far as to offer him $300 a month for his loyalty. When Hatfield informed Felts that he held a warrant for his arrest, Felts responded by saying he had a warrant of his own, and that the sheriff would have to return to Bluefield with the detectives. They exchanged more heated words, then suddenly gunfire. From hiding places on either side of the street came a murderous fusillade. In the first volley, five guards fell. The miners killed two more as they tried to escape. In all, only five managed to save themselves. Hatfield later told the *Philadelphia Public Ledger*, "it was a question of life or death for me" and "it was all over in two minutes." In addition to the Baldwin-Felts men, including Albert and Lee Felts, Testerman and two miners died in the shootout.

After the U.S. Coal Commission and the Senate Committee on Education and Labor concluded their inquiries into the Matewan dispute, coal operators relied less and less on agencies like Baldwin-Felts. Rather than risk further negative publicity, the mine operators employed more official means to discipline their workers, including a state police system that grew increasingly more professional after its inception in 1919. Owners also forced their workers to sign "yellow dog" contracts legally prohibiting them from joining a union. The death knell of the Baldwin-Felts Agency finally came in 1935, when the West Virginia legislature made the deputization of private guards illegal.

King of the Strikebreakers

Long before West Virginia lawmakers moved to restrict deputization, private police agencies were on the wane. In addition to anti-Pinkerton laws regulating the shipment of armed guards across state lines, public police began to usurp the agencies' function. Moreover, most businessmen were coming to realize that the introduction of Pinkerton-like forces, even in isolated rural environments, resulted in bloodshed and public outrage. Well aware of their clients' need to find new ways to discipline their workers, anti-union entrepreneurs showed their ability to adapt to the changing economic and political environment.

Around the turn of the century, the muckraker F.B. McQuiston alerted the public to a new trend in labor discipline when he wrote in *The Independent* that "within the past decade the strikebreaker has become indispensable to the successful mill operator." He was referring not to African-American or immigrant workers who had been tricked into selling their class loyalty for the opportunity to work, but to professional strikebreakers whose function was to convince striking workers that their coworkers had returned to work. While many Americans regarded the armies of guards who surrounded strike-bound plants as a remnant of a feudal past during which princes hired mercenaries to impose their will on others, much of the public looked upon strikebreakers differently. Many would have agreed with the one-time president of Harvard University, Charles W. Eliot, who referred to such men as "the heroes of American industry." To Eliot and others, strikebreakers defended the American worker, who possessed the right to work for whomever he liked. Moreover, although the introduction of strikebreakers enraged striking workers and their allies, the public often proved indifferent to their arrival, for few dared challenge a businessman's right to hire whomever he desired. Indeed, while state legislatures outlawed the ruse of private police, they upheld the right of businessmen to employ strikebreakers. For example, according to writer Edward Levinson, one could be arrested for addressing "any offensive, derisive or annoying words" to strikebreakers in New Hampshire and in Michigan state law prohibited strikers from interfering with strikebreakers by means of "threats, intimidation, or otherwise." Not until Congress enacted the Byrnes Act in 1936 did the federal government try to control the strikebreaking industry.

Glorified for their efforts, the captains of these strikebreaking armies, such as James A. Farley and Pearl L. Bergoff, developed national reputations. For a fee they supplied hundreds, and on occasion even thousands, of workers to restart their clients' plants, or at least make it appear that workers were returning to their posts. While some strikebreakers possessed the skills needed, just as commonly their ranks included drifters, vagabonds, or people who were too old or enfeebled to tend machinery. It mattered little, however, because the effect was the same: discouraged strikers.

In 1904, muckraker B.T. Fredricks wrote of James Farley in *Leslie's Magazine:* "In no single case where he has responded and taken hold of capital's end of a fight with labor, has labor won the fight. That is his business. He is the boss strikebreaker." Farley opened his agency in New York City in 1902. In addition to regular detective work, he took on industrial cases, specializing in streetcar strikes, which blossomed as the industry grew rapidly through boom and bust cycles in virtually every major city in the country. Although many communities were at odds with their traction companies due to their poor service, popular support for streetcar employees was not enough to overcome state lawmakers who usually protected Farley's strikebreakers.

To traction companies, Farley was a good ally and earned the title "King of the Strikebreakers" in the *New York Tribune.* According to labor historian Philip Foner, editors for the *St. Louis Globe-Democrat* wrote that "the Amalgamated Association of Street and Electric Railway Employees would have been a mighty power but for Farley, the man who is the cause of most of its failure in strike episodes." By that time he had crushed twenty strikes, including streetcar walkouts in Philadelphia, Scranton, Cleveland, Providence, Richmond, and New York City.

In 1904, when the Amalgamated Association of Street and Electric Railway Employees began preparations for a strike against the Interborough Rapid Transit Company (IRT) in New York City, Farley mobilized an army of sixty men. The *New York Times* believed they were "a strange crew, who blow together with all the four winds of heaven the moment there is trouble," but noted that they were all experienced railroad men, each selected with "a special view to physical courage and staying qualities." Because they were highly skilled, each veteran received $20 to $25 per day. This pay compared quite favorably to the $2 per day earned by ordinary motormen and conductors. To supplement his gathering army, Farley set up a recruiting station in the city. Thousands of men thronged to his offices "until far into the night. Each carried a card bearing these instructions: 'Call at No. Ten Dey Street, nine o'clock Monday morning, one flight up. Bring this with you. Yours truly, James Farley.'" While he preferred to hire experienced streetcar crews, he told the *New York Times* that "courage and a strong skeleton is what I look for in selecting men." In the end, Farley's army went unused. At the last minute before the strike, August Belmont (head of the IRT) met with the union, which agreed to his offer of $3 per day.

When negotiations with the carmen's union broke down less than six months later, Farley once again put together an army of 5,000 men, "each knowing what he had to do and with a fair knowledge of how to do it," according to the *New York Times.* Included in Farley's army was Leroy Scott, a writer for *World's Work,* who later wrote that amongst his new colleagues he found "a sprinkling of the upper grade of hoboes; a large number of cheap 'sports'—devil-may-care young fellows, whose ideal life seemed to be a week of work, a week of the Bowery" and a number workmen "with the strained look of a man long out of a job." Rather than lofty ideologies about the right of private property, it was money that motivated these men, he reported. While far short of the scale Farley paid battle-tested veterans, his strikebreaking station platform men, ticket choppers, and agents made $2.50 per day; second-class conductors and guards received $3 per day. Farley paid motormen and engineers $3.50 per day. He charged his clients $5 per day for each worker.

An hour after the strikers left their cars, Farley's men assumed the controls. From a back room in an office building he commanded his troops, working the phones and giving orders to a string of messenger boys. When Scott asked if August

Belmont ran the line, Farley responded by saying, "Who the ___ is Belmont, Farley's running this road." Although the trains ran poorly, within four days the walkout came to an end. According to William Brown Meloney, a reporter for *Public Opinion,* if it "had not been for [Farley] the strike would still be in full swing, or the corporation would have capitulated." The local union folded and better than 60 percent of the strikers lost their jobs. The *New York Times* reported that the IRT paid Farley $300,000 for breaking the strike. It was money well spent, as the IRT remained union-free for years, according to Foner.

After a string of successes, Farley became a national figure. Editors referred to him as "the best known strikebreaker in the United States" (*Richmond Times-Dispatch)* and "the best hated man in this country" (*New York Herald*). He became richer than "he had ever dreamed of being," according to Fredricks. The San Francisco streetcar strike of 1907 brought Farley his greatest rewards. Rumors circulated that he earned $1 million for his efforts to break the strike. Doing more than $10 million worth of business by 1914, he paid assistant Frank Curry handsomely. Much of this income he earned from retainer work for employers, including the IRT, which awarded him $1,000 per day for his services in the months leading up to another strike less than six months after the 1904 victory. To a fascinated public, his life became legendary. Rumors circulated, for instance, that he paid a $100 bonus to any conductor who rode the first trolley out of the car barn with him. His hometown newspaper, the Plattsburgh *Daily Press,* contributed to his growing stature, reporting that he was "absolutely without fear" and his methods even "compel the admiration of his enemies." Editors for *Public Opinion* joined in the adulation, telling their readers that he carried two bullets in his body, though the *New York Herald* mentioned only one.

As the first decade of the twentieth century came to a close, so too did Farley's days of fame. Suffering from tuberculosis, he rejected the job of breaking the 1910 Philadelphia streetcar strike. Too weak to work, he claimed to have turned down the job because "the strikers were in the right," according to journalist Edward Levinson. In September 1913, the *New York Times* reported that he spent his last days surrounded by ten guards, watching the races at the Empire City Track in Yonkers. "My horses are all I have to live for now," he reportedly claimed as he lay dying.

Strikebreaking Efficiency Expert

Amongst the dozens of strikebreaking entrepreneurs who stood ready to inherit Farley's mantle as "King of the Strikebreakers" were John "Black Jack" Jerome, who helped break the Denver Tramway strike in 1920, R.J. Coach of the Coach Detective Agency in Cleveland, and Archie Mahon and James Waddell of the Waddell and Mahon Agency. However, one contender, Pearl Louis Bergoff, stood above the rest. According to W.P. Mangold writing in *The New Republic* in 1934, by the end of his career, Bergoff could claim that while others "may break a buttonhole miners' strike . . . when it is steel or utilities or railroads they come to me. I'm dean—been at it thirty years and made millions breaking strikes in this country." Although he was prone to exaggeration and self-promotion, this proved no idle boast. Sending his army against workers in more than 300 strikes, Bergoff became the most important strikebreaker of the twentieth century.

After nearly ten years of plying his trade for others, in 1905 Bergoff formed his own company, the Vigilant Detective Agency of New York. Two years later he joined with his three brothers and changed the name of the firm to Bergoff Brothers Strike Service and Labor Adjusters. They entered the growing field of labor relations convinced, according to an October 25, 1934, *New York Post* article, that "there was more money in industrial work." When frightened businessmen enlisted Bergoff's services, they turned to a specialist in labor control who claimed to have "never steered them wrong," according to Mangold. Rather than a loosely organized army of ruffians, the Bergoff agency joined in written contracts with clients, employed a sales staff, and developed a command structure. Bergoff expected "to take care of everything from toothpicks in the commissary to general managership" of a strike, according to Levinson's book. Events proved him correct. From the end of the depression of 1907 until the early 1920s, the Bergoff brothers enjoyed one banner year after another. Many of the contracts they won proved bloody, including an order to end a two-month walkout at the Pressed Steel Car Company of McKees Rocks, Pennsylvania in the summer of 1909.

Shortly after the Pressed Steel Car walkout began, plant manager James Rider contracted with the Bergoff brothers, who agreed to "produce promptly . . . a total of 500 able bodied workmen," as well as guards to "assist in any capacity about our shops and act as guards day and night," according to Levinson's book. Rider promised to pay a rate of $5 per day per worker. Bergoff's managers, who were generally permanent employees and organized into a military-like chain of command, assembled recruits, made out the payroll, and strategically positioned the men. The lieutenants, or as they were known in strikebreaker parlance, "the nobles," acted as guards and front-line leaders, shielding the rank and file from angry strikers. Bergoff estimated that his agency supplied one guard for every fifteen to twenty strikebreakers. Speaking about his armed and deputized guards, he told Mangold that "we have a tentative understanding with local sheriffs, as has any large agency like ours that knows its business." Setting up a recruiting headquarters in a basement office on West 33rd Street in Manhattan, his brother Leo filled his quota of guards with men from the Bowery within hours. Such a rough and tumble stream of men pushed in and out of this office that the owner believed the renters had opened "a gambling establishment," said the *New York Times* in August 1909.

On the bottom rung of Bergoff's army were the foot soldiers, commonly known as "finks." While some accepted these jobs because they were too incompetent or old to find other employment, many were shiftless men who "don't really want to work . . . what they want is excitement and easy money," the *New York Post* wrote in 1934. Many others were shipped "direct to McKees Rocks from immigrant vessels without realizing that they were to assume the part of strikebreakers and without understanding . . . what perils they would encounter," wrote the *New York Times* in late August 1909. Fred Reiger, a German immigrant, who told a governmental inquiry that he and five other men answered an advertisement for "machinists" in a Manhattan newspaper, was among those recruited in New York City. Shipped to the strike zone in boxcars after two days without any food, Reiger and his fellow machinists found themselves in the yards of the Pressed Steel Car Company. Strikers greeted the men with rocks, bottles, and other debris. Inside the compound, a second skirmish broke out when the terrified strikebreakers demanded the guards escort them out of the stockade. Later that same day, the major battle of the strike took place when a company-owned vessel, the "Steel Queen," crossed the Ohio River and attempted to land 350 strikebreakers at the yards. Met by an equal number of strikers, the "Steel Queen" made for the opposite shore after the two sides exchanged more than 100 shots. Although strikers won the "Battle of the Ohio," throughout the next month 1,200 men in Bergoff's employ poured into the yards.

At the end of August, the tide turned against the Pressed Steel Car Company. Angry at the conditions in the plant, the citizens of Pittsburgh and McKees Rocks were additionally horrified when strikers and strikebreakers clashed. City officials counted six dead, six dying, and nearly fifty injured. Local papers that were at first generally sympathetic to the company now called for an end to the strike. During the troubles at McKees Rocks, a total of twenty-two people died, including two of Bergoff's men. He later told a reporter, quoted by writer Albert Kahn, "We paid four or five thousand dollars for each of our men killed. The income was so large that this expense made no difference."

The debacle at McKees Rocks did little to hurt Bergoff's business. The next year proved one of his best, as the Erie Railroad and the Chicago, Burlington and Quincy Railroad called on his services. Later that winter, when 5,000 conductors and motormen called a strike against the Philadelphia Rapid Transit Company, he secured "one of the biggest jobs I handled," he told the *New York Post* later. When he needed additional men, he spread the word to places where unemployed men gathered, charity employment agencies, and flophouses. Shortly after the Philadelphia strike, he handled a comparatively small job for the Delaware and Hudson Railroad, and years later he boasted to the *New York Post* that not only had he earned $35,000 for his efforts, the head of the railroad wrote him a personal letter thanking him for his "efficient service in breaking the strike." The next year brought work at the Baldwin Locomotive Works and a trip to New York to break a strike of the city's street sweepers. A strike along the piers in Boston, a hotel walkout in New York, and a dispute on the Lehigh Valley Railroad occupied Bergoff's attention for the next two years. During this time, Bergoff assumed the title "Red Demon," which he claimed to the *Post* came from "my red hair and reputation in strikes." Although "I look gentle . . . when I'm directing 1,000 men in the midst of a mob of strikers, I'm a different man." In 1913, executives called upon the "Red Demon" to break a strike of telegraph operators on the Missouri, Kansas, and Texas Railroad. Other clients that year included the Erie Railroad and the Philadelphia and Reading Railroad.

In the years before World War I, professional strikebreakers prospered in an environment in which the middle class lauded their tactics as justifiable excesses in defense of the rights of free enterprise. As the well-worn concepts of a laissez-faire economy gave way to a growing wave of social reform, the role of strikebreakers in labor relations came under scrutiny. Established two decades after the Homestead inquiries, the Commission on Industrial Relations (CIR) provided a sweeping denunciation of strikebreakers. The majority of commissioners deemed the activities of anti-union mercenaries a contributing element in the "Denial of Justice," one of the four factors they listed as leading to industrial violence. Moreover, they challenged those economic beliefs that protected strikebreakers, pointing out that the long-held axiom guaranteeing a man's right to work "seems to be based on the conception that the strikebreaker is normally a working man who seeks work and desires to take the place of a striker." Almost without exception, the commission argued, "the strikebreaker is a not a genuine workingman but is a professional who merely fills the place of a worker and is unable or unwilling to do steady work, or, if he is a bona fide workingman, that he is ignorant of conditions or compelled to work under duress." They also questioned a businessman's "right to do business," arguing that the prerogatives of business may be restricted ". . . whenever it is dangerous or in any way deleterious to the public." Although a number of the commissioners called for legislation regulating private detective agencies (strikebreaking agencies) in order to "insure the character of their employees and limit their activities to the 'bona fide' business of detecting crime," the commission lacked the unanimity required to stimulate congressional action. World War I further distracted the public interest.

As the CIR called witness after witness, Bergoff never slowed his operation. In 1915, as the commission released its final report, he joined forces with James Waddell of the Waddell and Mahon Agency. By creating a national strikebreaking firm with offices in Philadelphia, Boston, Baltimore, and Chicago, the officers of Bergoff Brothers and Waddell could boast of breaking dozens of strikes, including a bloody copper miners' walkout at the Calumet and Hecla mines in Michigan during the winter of 1913–14. After defeating striking transit worker in Wilkes Barre, Pennsylvania, Bergoff Brothers and Waddell earned $204,000 for breaking a strike of trolley crews on the New York Interborough Rapid Transit system.

The increasing strike activity of the immediate postwar years brought Bergoff Brothers and Waddell more work. In 1920, the agency helped end the Erie Railroad switchmen's walkout by supplying railroad officials with thousands of strikebreakers. Bergoff boasted that he grossed $2 million on the job. Later, he brought 3,000 strikebreakers to New York City four days after the Brooklyn Rapid Transit (BRT) strike began. BRT officials paid Bergoff Brothers and Waddell $712,000, prompting the mayor to launch "a special and exhaustive inquiry," according to the *New York Times*.

While the postwar decade began well for Bergoff Brothers and Waddell, opportunities quickly vanished with the relative prosperity and decline of strikes during the Coolidge years. More importantly, with labor union membership falling from 5 million to less than 3.5 million, businessmen basked in the public's growing reverence for the material accomplishments of the age. The postwar period also brought even more sophisticated forms of worker control, including welfare schemes. According to historian Irving Bernstein in his book *Lean Years: A History of the American Worker, 1919–1929*, during the 1920s the strike "had fallen into almost total disuse." Finding little work, Bergoff told Levinson later that "business got so goddamn lousy I closed the office in 1925 and went to Florida."

The Great Depression reversed the fortunes of many, including Bergoff Brothers and Waddell. They were well aware that the business community's growing fear of labor conflict represented a golden opportunity. "I can see so much strike ahead I don't know which way to turn," Bergoff told Levinson. Employers felt increasingly besieged by their workers as a number of the nation's lawmakers came to sympathize with organized labor and the public's reverence for businessmen waned.

In the summer of 1936, Bergoff Brothers and Waddell found themselves playing an important role in an ingenious anti-union campaign drafted by the head of the Remington Rand Corporation, James H. Rand Jr. The campaign was later known as the "Mohawk Valley Formula," after its place of origin in upstate New York. Less than two weeks after workers at seven Remington Rand plants walked away from their posts, Rand began his program of deception. He posted a "for sale" sign outside his plant in Middletown, Connecticut, and company officials began advertising for millwrights to assist in "dismantling machinery and skidding machinery for shipment," according to National Labor Relations Board (NLRB) records. Rand never planned to hire those who applied, however, for Bergoff had agreed to supply fifty-nine "millwrights." Although each carried a millwright card, they knew little about tearing down a plant. Bergoff later testified to this fact when he told the NLRB, "A man, a fink, as you call him in the newspapers, he is anything; he may be a carpenter today, a plumber tomorrow, a bricklayer the next day; this particular day they were millwrights." When Rand announced that he had decided not to relocate his facility, and with only a few positions to fill, strikers quickly returned to their posts. He paid the Bergoff Service Bureau (the new name of his reopened agency) and seven other detective agencies $145,000 for the two months of the strike.

Shortly after Rand's workers returned to their posts, the United States District Court for the District of Connecticut indicted Bergoff and Rand for transporting strikebreakers across state lines. After years of discussion but no action, Congress had finally acted. On June 24, 1936, the day before Bergoff shipped his men to Rand's plant in Middletown, President Roosevelt had signed the Byrnes Act into law, making it a felony to transport persons in interstate commerce with the intent to employ them to obstruct the rights of peaceful picketing. Although a federal judge acquitted Bergoff and Rand, the "Red Demon" retired in 1936, nearly three decades after opening his first detective agency.

Anti-Union Espionage

The year Bergoff retired, a son of Robert Pinkerton announced that the eponymous firm would no longer "furnish its employes [*sic*] to any client for the exclusive purpose of providing workmen to take the place of a client's striking employees, nor to physically protect employes [*sic*] . . . while a labor strike in progress." Moreover, restricted not only by the Byrnes Act but by public condemnation of strikebreaking, many employers rejected such blatant tactics. Once again, however, they did not stand alone. Rather than turn their backs on a lucrative market, the Pinkerton Agency and many similar firms "preferred to place emphasis on its undercover work, which being secret, created less antagonism."

While spying on workers was nothing new, espionage came to play a larger role in the business community's offensive against labor during the Depression. By the late 1930s, more than 200 anti-union agencies offered undercover operatives to their clients.

Under the direction of Allan Pinkerton, the Pinkerton National Detective Agency first began offering "spotters" to expose dishonest and lazy railroad conductors in 1855. In 1873, Robert Pinkerton ended this service, concluding that, in the eyes of the business community, individual acts of dishonesty paled in comparison to the growing threat of collective conspiratorial violence. But his agency's anti-labor espionage did not end—in fact, it grew. In 1874, Pinkerton operative James McParlan infiltrated the secret society of Irish-American coal miners known as the Molly Maguires, gathering enough "information" to hang ten of them. After helping to break a number of strikes, including the Chicago, Burlington, and Quincy Railroad strike in 1888, Pinkerton undercover operatives proved themselves so formidable that the Brotherhood of Locomotive Engineers held all meetings behind closed doors during their convention that fall. Delegates also organized a special committee to search out hiding places spies might use. Their efforts failed, as two Pinkerton operatives attended the convention and recorded the minutes of the meeting.

As strikes came to dominate industrial relations during the next two decades, the Pinkertons skillfully played upon the business community's fears by asking "would [it] not be well for employers . . . to keep a close watch for designing men among their own employees?" The appeal worked. The Pinkerton agency added fifteen new offices between 1890 and 1910. Social reform activity in the Progressive Era, which turned public opinion against strikebreaking, encouraged employers to turn to espionage services. E.H. Murphy, head of an espionage service, wrote to a potential client that "we have a reputation of being several jumps ahead of the old way of settling capital labor difficulties. . . . Our service aims to keep clients informed through the medium of intelligence reports." As early as 1904, AFL leader Samuel Gompers concluded that liberal public opinion prompted employers to become more clandestine in their anti-union activities. A few years later, delegates to the Massachusetts state AFL convention resolved that private detective agencies had not only "assumed formidable proportions" but threatened to "Russianize" American society. Reflecting the changing approach, Captain B. Kelcher of the CBK Detective Bureau in New York informed one prospective client that his firm did "not handle strike work but rather "prevent[ed] strikes."

By the twentieth century, besieged industrialists could find, in the telephone directories of any large city, a host of labor spy services listed under such euphemisms as "industrial engineers," "private detectives," or "labor conciliators." Others advertised their services in business journals. "We are prepared," one agency informed potential customers in the May 1905 issue of *American Industries,* "to place secret operatives who are skilled mechanics in any shop, mill or factory, to discover whether any [labor] organizing is being done." By the end of the steel strike of 1919, spying on workers had become such an accepted business practice that steel company executives freely handed to Interchurch World Movement investigators 600 spy reports compiled by the Sherman Service Company and the Corporations Auxiliary Company.

By the middle of the Depression decade, espionage came "to be a common, almost universal, practice in American industry," as a virtual "blue book of American industry," including thirty-two mining companies, twenty-eight firms associated with the automotive industry, and an equal number of food-processing concerns relied upon labor spies. Testifying before a Senate hearing on anti-union practices, one member of the NLRB estimated that American industrialists spent over $80 million a year spying on their workers. General Motors, for example, paid $994,000 for undercover work during a two-year period surrounding the Congress of Industrial Organization's drive to unionize the auto industry. In addition to the Pinkerton Agency, GM employed thirteen spy agencies. Its dependence upon espionage services reached its final addictive stages when it employed Pinkerton agents to spy on operatives of other agencies in their plants. In addition to GM, the Pinkerton Agency provided spy service for 300 other firms during the 1930s. In 1935, it operated out of twenty-seven offices and grossed more than $2 million. Between 1933 and 1935, Pinkerton clients hired over 1,200 undercover operatives.

Pinkerton had sixty-four spies within the railroad brotherhoods. Seventeen operatives held union cards in the United Textile Workers of America, and the ranks of the International Brotherhood of Electrical Workers included twenty Pinkerton men. In all, Pinkerton operatives wormed their way into ninety-three unions. Other agencies were also well established behind union lines. By 1935, the Cleveland office of the Corporations Auxiliary Company controlled thirty spies, twenty-three of whom were union members. These men submitted reports on activities within their clients' plants and union halls and on picket lines. In their most important function—ascertaining the names of union sympathizers—some of these men, such as Pinkerton operative Fred Weber, who obtained a job as a night janitor in a union office in Cincinnati, proved ingenious. Alone for hours, he recorded the names of union members and meeting minutes. Sadly, while operatives directly in the employ of these agencies generated most reports, some were written by workers who had been duped, or in the spy's parlance "hooked," into this sordid activity. Roped in gradually, they first reported on innocuous offenses, such as malingering, then later the thoughts and opinions of their coworkers. During the first half of 1936, the Pinkerton Agency paid $240,000 to such workers.

With the help of this fifth column, anti-union employers quietly ended their labor problems by discharging those who were less than loyal. In early 1935, for example, the Fruehauf Trailer Company in Detroit fired nine workers and threatened to dismiss three others for involvement in union activity after the treasurer of one local, a Pinkerton operative, turned union rosters and dues ledgers over to management. Commenting on the case, J. Warren Madden, chairman of the NLRB, said, "The mystery and deadly certainty with which this scheme operated was so baffling to the men that they each suspected the others, were afraid to meet or to talk and the union was completely broken." Nearly one-third of Pinkerton operatives held high union positions, including one national vice president, fourteen local presidents, eight local vice presidents, and numerous secretaries. They also controlled forty-three operatives within company unions, among them one president, three recording secretaries, and one chairman. From these lofty positions these operatives crafted factions and disagreements or, in the case of a veteran Pinkerton operative in the International Association of Machinists, incited a premature strike. Earlier, he boasted to his supervisors, "This is an easy one to handle as there are only about two men in it that are really interested in the organization work and they are easily discouraged."

In addition to supplying undercover operatives and agent provocateurs, many anti-union contractors conducted whispering campaigns for their clients as far back as World War I. By the Depression decade, the NLRB stated in its first annual report that propaganda disseminated by espionage agencies was "the most common form of interference with self-organization engaged in by employers." As revealed in the La Follette Hearings on Violations of Free Speech and the Rights of Labor, among the dozens of letters of solicitation Republic Steel Corporation received before the Little Steel Strike in 1937 at least three detective agencies offered such services. An executive of one agency, W. Howard Downey and Associates, wrote, "We have a whole kit of expressions . . . that have proved themselves in the handling of industrial disturbances time and again. After hearing a few remarks that we have up our sleeves you should see how apprehensive a striker becomes." The NLRB believed the "pressure exerted on workers" by these operatives was "overwhelming."

White-Collar Union Busting

Shifting political winds, particularly the rise of the New Deal Democrats in the 1930s, brought new scrutiny to Pinkerton and other union-busting agencies. In March 1936, Senator Robert M. La Follette Jr. initiated an investigation into violations of workers' civil liberties. After distributing over 800 questionnaires to the most notorious anti-union agencies, the Senate members of what came to be know as the La Follette Committee held hearings at which victimized workers and union officials testified. The committee then demanded the testimony of corporate chieftains who used strikebreaking agencies and officials from the five largest union-busting firms: Railway Audit and Inspection Company, Pinkerton National Detective Agency, Corporations Auxiliary Company, National Corporation Service, and William J. Burns International Detective Agency. The committee impounded the records of the mercenary agencies and subpoenaed many of their clients' records. When investigators suspected that files had been discarded, they dug through trash bins and found scraps of bills, receipts, and secret reports, which they painstakingly pieced back together. What they found shocked the nation. "In various business quarters record keeping has gone out of fashion and systems of bookkeeping seem to have given way to systemized book-cooking," the committee's investigators wrote upon discovering that many of the agencies deliberately destroyed incriminating evidence. In one case, while being served a subpoena at the front door, Pinkerton employees spirited company records out the back.

Starting in March 1939, after nearly three years of hearings, La Follette introduced legislation prohibiting industrial espionage, strikebreaking, the purchase and use of armaments, and the use of private armed guards beyond the premises of their employers. The Oppressive Labor Practices bill won approval in the Senate but not the House.

Eventually the bill died, lost in the growing debate over national defense. Nonetheless, the revelations of the La Follette committee sparked strong public outrage against the anti-union industry. In April 1937, according to historian James Horan, the Pinkerton board of directors unanimously agreed that "this agency in the future not furnish information to anyone concerning lawful attempts of labor unions or employees to organize and bargain collectively." "That is the phase of our business that we are not particularly proud of and we're delighted we are out of it. However, there was nothing illegal about it at the time," Allan Pinkerton, the grandson of the Pinkerton Agency's founder, told the *New York Times*. The decline of spying, however, did not eliminate the union-busting industry.

In the latter half of the 1940s, a new breed of anti-union practitioner arose to meet the changing needs of businesses trying to avoid unionization. Labor relations consulting firms, including Equitable Research Associates of New York, the Vincent J. Squillante Company, and the Marshall Miller Company began offering a more sophisticated anti-union service. The largest of these was Labor Relations Associates, formed under the auspices of Sears & Roebuck in late 1939, and led by the retail giant's head of employee relations, Nathan W. Shefferman. During the late 1940s, the company expanded its operations beyond its parent company and their suppliers. With branch offices in New York and Detroit and a staff of thirty-five, Shefferman was the most successful union buster in the country by the mid-1950s. According to a Senate Committee on Improper Activities in the Labor Management Field, for nearly 400 clients, including many national firms such as Whirlpool, Shefferman's operatives set up anti-union employee groups called "Vote No Committees," designed tricks to uncover pro-union workers, and helped arrange "sweetheart" contracts with friendly unions.

In the spring of 1957, Democratic Senator John L. McClellan looked into the activities of Labor Relations Associates as part of his larger investigation into corruption in the Teamsters and other national unions. Alarmed by the discovery that "the National Labor Relations Board is impotent to deal with Shefferman's type of activity," Congress included in the Labor-Management Reporting and Disclosure Act of 1959 (the Landrum-Griffin Act) a clause mandating that businesses report to the Secretary of Labor any agreement with a labor relations consultant "where an objective thereof, directly or indirectly, is to persuade employees" in regards to their rights to bargain collectively. Although he defended his labor relations career by releasing his side of the story, *Man in the Middle*, in 1961, Shefferman closed his office and retired the following year.

Despite ending Shefferman's career, the Landrum-Griffin Act had little impact on his successors. In 1962, the Department of Labor weakened the law by requiring consultants to report their activities only after communicating directly with their clients' workers. This ruling provided the loophole anti-union firms like John Sheridan and Associates needed. In the late 1970s, Sheridan said that his firm, like many other labor relations consultants, did not file reports with the government because his agents did not speak directly to their clients' workers. Armed with degrees in industrial psychology, industrial relations management, and labor law, the new breed of union-busting consultants developed more sophisticated techniques. According to a 1985 Bureau of National Affairs report: "The role of labor relations consultants is not to block union representation but rather to help employers to . . . provide a safe and financially secure workplace for their employees." The new anti-union agencies proved skilled at sidestepping the provisions of both the National Labor Relations and Landrum-Griffin acts.

As the public came to look less critically upon the business community's anti-union efforts, "the number of consultants and the scope and sophistication of their activities . . . increased substantially," according to testimony by Assistant Secretary of Labor William Hopgood before the House Subcommittee on Labor Management Relations in 1980. This assessment was corroborated by consultants like the founder of Modern Management Methods, Inc., Herbert G. Melnick, who testified before the same committee that he knew of a "dozen firms of substance" involved in labor consulting and that his industry had undergone a "tenfold growth in ten years." Melnick's company reportedly assisted employers in 696 union organizing drivers from 1977 to 1979, with a win rate of 93 percent. West Cost Industrial Relations Associates served 1,500 clients in one year, while John Sheridan boasted that his firm intervened in hundreds of union elections at large companies.

The business community learned about the anti-union consultants at numerous seminars they began offering on union avoidance strategies during the 1970s. For a fee of $250 to $550, executives who attended these clinics picked up tips from specialists in industrial psychology, labor law experts, and one-time union officials on the intricacies of employee relations programs that "make union unnecessary," according to an April 1977 *Wall Street Journal* article. "Any company that gets a union deserves it, and you deserve the one you get," Charles Hughes told executives who attended a seminar offered by Executive Enterprises, Inc., in Atlanta in 1977.

Although they claimed to tailor their strategy to each client's needs, most modern union busters employed a standardized three-pronged attack. Cognizant of the Landrum-Griffin Act's guidelines requiring consultants to report their activity only when engaged directly in persuading employees in regards to their right to bargain collectively, most consulting teams used supervisory personnel as "the critical link in the communication network," according to testimony before the House Subcommittee on Labor Management Relations. In one of its pamphlets, West Coast Industrial Relations Associates advised its clients that "in any campaign where the issue is 'union or not?' the one thing every supervisor should not be is 'non-committal.'" Upon such advice employers waged unremitting psychological warfare, bombarding workers, in some cases hour by hour, with posters, leaflets, personal letters and speeches. For example, during a 1980 countercampaign during a union organizing drive at Mercy Hospital in Watertown, Massachusetts, operatives for Modern Management Methods, Inc., mailed letters to workers informing them of their right to work "without threats of strikes" or being forced to pay "union dues or fines."

While remaining within National Labor Relations Act (NLRA) guidelines, these and other tricks created an environment far from what the NLRA described as ideal: one in which workers have the time to make a free and rational decision regarding unionization. Drafted in the 1930s and amended in the 1940s when anti-union tactics were far less subtle, the NLRA offered numerous opportunities for those skilled in labor law to circumvent its intent. One labor relations consultant, Martin J. Levitt, referred to the NLRA as a "union buster's best friend." One common tactic called for management's negotiators to contest every nuance of an NLRB election. As one consultant told Congress, "Even though a 'consent' election may be 'quicker' it has the same results as a shot in the head . . . always go to a hearing. It always works in your favor."

Back to the Future of Strikebreaking

By the 1980s, public and government support for unions had disintegrated, allowing the return of agencies that supplied replacement workers and security firms that provided armed guards. Their methods differed little from the union-busting tactics of a century earlier. The importance of the political milieu is highlighted by the fact that the growth in the use of permanent replacement workers relied for legal support on a 1938 Supreme Court ruling that allowed companies to hire permanent replacements for strikers who walked out for "economic reasons," rather than unfair labor practices reasons. Few paid attention to the ruling until the 1980s, when using permanent replacements no longer stimulated massive public outrage. William Gould, chairman of the NLRB at the time, conceded to the *New York Times* in April 1994 that while the activities of strikebreaking agencies were hardly "equitable or sensible" they remained legal.

Today, temporary employment agencies, like Worldwide Labor Support of Pascagoula, Mississippi, provide strikebreakers. During a walkout by union workers at Caterpillar in the mid-1990s, this company supplied 200 welders who helped break the strike. Manufacturing Technical Search of Westchester, Illinois, and Strom Engineering Corporation, a temporary employment agency in Minnetonka, Minnesota, supplied replacement workers trained in other trades. Other firms include BE&K, which maintains a data bank of names of thousands of workers willing to cross picket lines, and Denver's U.S. Nursing Corporation, which in September 1994 brought more than

100 nurses to Port Jervis, New York, to break a strike at that city's Mercy Community Hospital.

To protect replacement workers, strike-bound employers hire today's equivalent of Pinkerton guards: security specialists. At the outset of the Detroit newspaper strike in 1995, newspaper executives contracted with Alternative Work Force (AWF) for 600 replacement workers and hired Huffmaster Security, which supplied nearly 500 armed guards. In four months, the Detroit newspapers paid Huffmaster and AWF $2.3 million for their services. Huffmaster was eventually replaced by the most notorious security specialist, Vance International's Asset Protection Team. Since 1984, this subsidiary has worked more than 600 strikes, with revenues reaching $89 million. Charles Vance promised his clients that "our tactical security teams ensure a safe operating environment for non-striking employees, replacement workers, corporate executives. . . . [Their] strong presence has neutralized many turbulent situations." In reality, security specialists are employed not so much to guard private property as to intimidate and provoke strikers into acts of violence. While violence often proved counterproductive for their predecessors, when employed in conjunction with cameras and camcorders to "document acts of violence or strike related incidents," Vance's heavy-handed tactics enable its clients to secure "restraining orders, injunctions, arbitration or criminal or civil actions," according to one of the company's pamphlets. In eleven months of work during the United Mine Workers of America's dispute at Pittston in 1989, Vance cameramen shot miles of videotape and more than 50,000 still photographs. "Coupled with incident reports and testimony," this evidence resulted in $64 million in fines levied against the UMWA in state courts and $1 million in federal court fines. "Although most of the fines were later forgiven, they helped to return the labor officials to the bargaining table," Vance boasted.

Vance is not the only security agency specializing in strike breaking. Executives of Special Response Corporation, based in Baltimore, Maryland, claim to have participated in 1,000 labor disputes since the start of the 1990s. Their advertisement features a uniformed agent holding a riot shield standing beneath a headline that reads: "A Private Army When You Need It Most." It promises the security clients need to continue operations during a strike.

Agencies like Vance, Huffmaster, and U.S. Nursing Corporation are heirs to a long line of commercial union-busting agencies whose efforts have enabled American businesses to avoid bargaining collectively with their workers for more than a century. The longevity and utility of the anti-union industry has rested on the ability of firms to devise new tactics to meet their clients' changing needs. The strategies they developed have grown in sophistication and subtlety, reflecting the public's evolving sympathy to organized labor. Incredibly, union busting today is little different from union busting a century ago.

See also: Corporate Strike Strategy, 66; Strike Lessons from the Last Twenty-Five Years, 81; The Strike Wave of 1877, 177; Steel Strikes Before 1935, 351; Labor Upheaval on the Nation's Railroads, 1877–1922, 483.

Bibliography

Bernstein, Irving. *The Lean Years: A History of the American Worker, 1919–1929.* Boston: Houghton, Mifflin, 1960.

Foner, Philip. *History of the Labor Movement in the United States: The Policies and Practices of the American Federation of Labor, 1900–1909.* New York: International Publishers, 1964.

Fredricks, B.T. "James Farley, Strikebreaker." *Leslie's Magazine* 59 (March 1939).

Hadsell, Richard M., and Coffee, William E. "From Law and Order to Class Warfare: Baldwin-Felts Detectives in the Southern West Virginia Coal Fields." *West Virginia History* (Spring 1979).

Kahn, Albert. *High Treason: The Plot Against the People.* New York: Lear Publishers, 1950.

Levinson, Edward. *I Break Strikes.* New York: Robert M. McBride & Co., 1935.

———. "The Right to Break Strikes." *Current History* 45 (February 1937).

Levitt, Martin J., with Terry Conrow. *Confessions of a Union Buster.* New York: Crown Publishers, 1983.

Morn, Frank. *The Eye That Never Sleeps: A History of the Pinkerton National Detective Agency.* Bloomington: Indiana University Press, 1982.

Savage, Lon. *Thunder in the Mountains: The West Virginia Mine Wars, 1920–1921.* Pittsburgh, PA: University of Pittsburgh Press, 1990.

Scott, Leroy. "'Strikebreaking' as a New Occupation." *World's Work* 10 (May 1905).

CORPORATE STRIKE STRATEGY

Kim Phillips-Fein

The history of employer strategies to undermine and break strikes is as long as the history of labor itself. Strikes, regardless of the particular issues at stake, often represent deep challenges to the power of management in the workplace and, in some sense, in society at large. By disrupting normal economic operations, they demonstrate the usually invisible power that workers wield over production. Thus on some level, strikes call into question the privileged role of the manager and the owner in society. Strikes create a community of protest and a sense of common purpose among workers who are normally docile. In organizing to fight strikes, employers are seeking to regain their control over the company, not only in order to resume production in the short term, but with an eye to the long-term relationships of workers and management. This is why employers often prolong labor conflict in a way that may appear irrational and against their economic interest in resuming production—they are attempting to beat the strike, defeat the union, and adjust the balance of power. At the same time, corporate strike strategy is always influenced by the overall political climate, the community perception of the union, and the nature of the industry itself. Even as management seeks to intimidate and coerce workers into stopping a strike, they must also find ways to justify their actions in ways that make sense to the rest of the community. Strikebreaking, like striking itself, is a fundamentally political act.

Over the course of American history, corporate anti-strike strategies have changed in a variety of ways, with a general trend away from the open use of force to break unions to an emphasis on propaganda and intimidation. An increased public interest in monitoring and restricting the free rein of employers in strike situations has led to a decline of the large strikebreaking companies that played such a central role in strike strategies in the period before the New Deal, although in recent years permanent replacements have once again become an important part of anti-strike strategy. Yet some elements of corporate strike strategy have remained constant: the essential project of demonstrating management control over the company is still the underlying principle of anti-strike strategy today, just as it has been for hundreds of years. Corporate strike strategy seeks to reassert the power and dominance of the company and the weakness and impotence of the workers, even in their collective institutions. Anti-strike rhetoric still seeks to portray the strikers as violators of a natural economic order that would be running smoothly were it not for this abrupt interruption, and the organization against the strike continues to attempt to show that the employer, not the strikers, stands for community interests and the good of the whole society.

Enforcing the Natural Order

The vision of strikes as aberrations in an organic industrial order dates back to the earliest days of industrialization in the United States. The ante bellum period in American history was a time of transition from craft production, artisanship, and small-property ownership to wage labor. Frequently the emerging class of workers consisted of frustrated journeymen, the same people who could previously have counted on rising to become masters of their own shops. Strikes dramatized their changing relationship to their work and their product and their increasing sense of themselves as an economic class separate from the class of master craftsmen.

Even in these early years, masters took concerted steps to penalize strikers and mark strikes as criminal conspiracies, violations of the natural order of society. Most labor struggles in the antebellum period were waged on the state or local level, and hence most responses were similarly local. The federal government rarely intervened in labor disputes in the antebellum period—in 1834, Andrew Jackson sent federal troops into Maryland to quell riots among Irish immigrants laboring on the canals, as historian Melvyn Dubofsky describes, but this was an unusual episode. Local masters would form their own associations to set terms and conditions within the industry, creating blacklists of workers who might be trouble. Frequently employers would seek to use the courts to break strikes and threaten to punish strikers. One of the earliest of such efforts was the New York City 1809 trial of the leaders of the Journeymen Cordwainers' Society, who organized a strike against shoemaker employers who hired nonunion workers. Historian Sean Wilentz tells their story. The shoemakers sued two dozen union leaders, charging them with conspiracy to interfere with trade and prevent the nonunion workmen from practicing their vocations. While the trial was inconclusive—the union leaders were found guilty, but they were punished only with light fines, and the mayor who adjudicated the case ratified that workers had the basic right to gather and push for improved conditions—this was the type of concerted action that master employers took in the effort to suppress strikes and unionism among their employees in craft centers like New York City.

The uncertain legal status of unions and the absence of a clear sense of workers' rights during organizing drives and strikes continued to make possible all kinds of draconian responses to strikes during the Gilded Age. Corporate response to strikes shifted in the era of rapid industrialization that followed the Civil War. During this period, both companies and unions began to be organized on a national level. Taking advantage of the mass markets made possible by railroads, themselves some of the first national firms, corporations began for the first time to span the entire country. In an effort to cope with the new challenges of concentrated industry, workers started to form national labor organizations. Both strikes, and the responses to them, started to become more premeditated. Strikes in the 1880s and 1890s were increasingly concerted actions that were initiated and planned by unions to win particular objectives (a union shop, a formal contract, better pay), rather than defensive actions (like preventing a wage cut) undertaken by workers with little organization or planning. Just as workers became better organized and more able to stage offensive battles, the tools available to corporations to fight and break strikes also became more elaborate, with the development of a national industry of strikebreaking companies and detective firms devoted to anti-union activities.

The private strikebreaking industry played an integral role in corporate anti-strike strategies during the 1880s and 1890s. While the federal government used military troops to help quell certain well-publicized labor struggles—most dramatically the railroad strike of 1877 and the Pullman strike of 1894—private strikebreakers played a central part in many other disputes. Strikebreaking companies like the Pinkerton Detective Agency appealed to corporate management because they provided a way for the company to use the most aggressive anti-strike tactics possible without themselves being held accountable, and also because they possessed resources on a national scale (such as hiring centers across the country in communities distant from the one where the strike was taking place) that individual corporations did not have.

Perhaps the most famous instance of strikebreaking by a private agency came in 1892 at the Homestead, Pennsylvania steel factory of Andrew Carnegie. After breaking off contract negotiations with the Amalgamated Association of Iron and Steel Workers, the company locked out several thousand workers and then hired strikebreakers to resume operations in a clear attempt to break the union. The workers then seized the mill and attempted to prevent the strikebreakers from entering the town, leading to open battles between the Pinkertons and the workers, until National Guardsmen came out to retake the mill. The breaking of the strike led to the crushing of the union and the death of unionism in the steel industry for nearly forty years. Strikebreakers had been used not only to regain control of the company in a particular instance, but to demonstrate the awesome power of the corporation, and the toll it would exact on anyone who tried to resist the direction in which it wanted to take American industry. In the words of historian James Holt, quoted by Paul Krause in *The Battle for Homestead, 1880–1892: Politics, Culture and Steel*, the Homestead strike demonstrated that "a great corporation could refuse to negotiate with a strong trade union, use the most oppressive strike-breaking tactics available, and ignore the flood of adverse publicity which resulted."

In the early years of the twentieth century, public sentiment began to turn against the use of strikebreakers, and more broadly against the use of physical violence to end strikes. One of the central turning points was the United Mine Workers strike of 1913–14 against the Colorado Fuel & Iron Corporation, owned by John D. Rockefeller. Howard Zinn, among others, has written of the strike. The company hired the Baldwin-Felts Detective Agency to import strikebreakers. During the strike, the National Guard of Colorado attacked one of the strikers' camps at Ludlow, setting tents on fire and burning strikers' families alive. The events at Ludlow took place only a few years after the Triangle Shirtwaist Fire, at a time when more middle-class reformers were becoming anxious about the conditions of life for the American working class. After the Ludlow Massacre, the *New York Times* editorialized, "Worse than the order that sent the Light Brigade into the jaws of death, worse in its effect than the Black Hole of Calcutta, was the order that trained the machine guns of the state militia of Colorado upon the strikers' camp at Ludlow, burned its tents, and suffocated to death the scores of women and children who had taken refuge in the rifle pits and trenches." A congressional committee convened to investigate the strike. Rockefeller was sufficiently unnerved by the public attention his mines were receiving and by the pickets that followed him from his New York City offices to the church where he worshipped to his estate in Tarrytown that he hired a public relations expert to reinvent his image and distance him from the violence at Ludlow.

The labor uprisings that followed the end of World War I—including the massive steel strike—were crushed with the use of state force. In western Pennsylvania, for example, one of the centers of the steel strike, policemen sought to prevent virtually every public meeting or gathering. People were arrested and held indefinitely, or arrested and then released only with large fines. Thousands of immigrants were arrested for deportation. Employers sought to spread division among workers in whatever ways they could, including spreading racial propaganda and seeking to intensify ethnic divisions between workers, according to historian Jeremy Brecher. Following the quelling of the strikes, employers sought a new degree of coordination in their attempts to weaken unions, as in the Open Shop Campaign organized by the National Association of Manufacturers. Many also began to institute a range of benefits thought to make the need for unions or for strikes less intense, although in some companies (for example, Ford or General Motors) management made new efforts to intensify levels of spying on their workers. The combination of reliance on the state for assistance to end strikes, the networks of private strikebreaking firms, the organized coordination between employers, and the careful use of "welfare capitalism" to increase worker loyalty proved highly effective in lowering the number of strikes during the 1920s.

Iron Fist in the Velvet Glove

In the 1930s virtually all of these conditions changed. Instead of being seen as violations of a natural and organic industrial order, political leaders like Senator Robert Wagner of New York began to envision unions as a solution to the Depression and an extension of American principles of self-governance into the workplace. The articulation of the legal right to organize unions in the National Labor Relations Act (NLRA) made certain strike-breaking techniques, such as espionage, threats and intimidation, and the use of violence, illegal. A 1936 law (the Byrd Act) prohibited the importation of strikebreakers across state lines. As demonstrated in highly publicized confrontations such as the sit-down strikes at General Motors in 1937, the state could no longer be counted upon as a strikebreaker. Even in the most radical strikes, in which workers literally prevented owners from accessing their property, the government refused to intervene to end the conflict and break the strike. Congressional investigations of strikebreaking companies, combined with the recognition of legal rights to organize and strike, forced many of the venerable old strikebreakers and detective companies out of business. Even outbursts of violence such as the Little Steel massacre of 1937 seemed remnants of an older order, a way of fighting strikes that no longer seemed in accord with the new acknowledgment of unionism as an expansion of democracy.

Almost immediately, corporations began to experiment with ways to break strikes. Most famous was the "Mohawk Valley Formula." The formula was developed by the Remington Rand Company of upstate New York in 1936. As analyst John Steuben recounts in his description of the formula, after breaking a strike, the company president announced, "Two million businessmen have been looking for a formula like this and business has hoped for, dreamed of and prayed for such an example as you have set." According to political scientist Richard Walter Gable, the National Association of Manufacturers enthusiastically publicized the formula, describing it in detail in its Labor Relations Bulletin and pronouncing it "a real contribution to civic dignity." The formula was a self-conscious effort to reformulate strikebreaking for a post-NLRA era. It replaced violence as the central tool in the strikebreaking arsenal with propaganda aimed at discrediting the union, appeals to workers to return to work, and creating a Citizens Committee composed of community elites to vociferously insist on the importance of returning to work. The Mohawk Valley Formula acknowledged the essentially political nature of strikes and provided strategies that employers could use to mold public opinion, transform community awareness, and undermine the confidence of workers in their union and their ability to act collectively. There was some mention of violence in the formula; employers were urged to create a large police force to intimidate strikers, using deputies from other neighborhoods with few personal loyalties to the workers who would be trained to respond harshly to unlawful assemblies, inciting to riot, and disorderly conduct. "Unhampered by any thought that the strikers may also possess some rights, they will be ready and anxious to use their newly acquired authority to the limit," the formula read. But even here the real role of violence was as a threat, demonstrating the power of the company and the impotence of the strikers, rather than as a tool to break the strike.

Another important innovation of the Mohawk Valley Formula—and connected to its eschewing of open physical force—was its emphasis on enticing strikers to return to work, rather than using strikebreakers. The main way to do this was through the creation of an employees' committee, loyal to the boss, which would issue propaganda and attempt to organize workers to return to their jobs. Employers were instructed to "heighten the demoralizing effect of the above measures—all designed to convince the strikers that their cause is hopeless—by a 'back-to-work' movement, operated by a puppet organization of so-called 'loyal employees' secretly organized by the employer." By focusing on getting workers to cross their own picket line, the formula attacked the very principles of solidarity, thus undermining the ideological and political foundation of the union itself. Instead of simply using violence to crush the strike and restarting production with strikebreakers, the formula represented a new awareness of strikebreaking as an opportunity for the company to assert its power over its employees and reaffirm its political position by turning the workers against the union.

"Boulwarism" and Beyond

Despite the Taft-Hartley Act of 1947, which permitted the federal government to intervene in strikes that were thought to provoke national emergencies, the 1950s were a decade of strikes. Workers engaged in an average of 352 major strikes (involving 1,000 or more workers) a year, a record for the century (there were also wildcat work stoppages at companies like Chrysler and in the steel industry, where according to trade association records there were 788 unauthorized strikes in the period 1956–58, and thousands of strikes at smaller companies). Labor historians Nelson Lichtenstein, David Brody, and Steve Jeffreys have each written about this period. However, in contrast to earlier periods, these strikes rarely meant the death of the unions undertaking them. The strength and power of the postwar industrial unions, bolstered by the labor laws of the New Deal, had successfully limited the types of actions that employers felt able to take in strike situations. For most people, striking no longer appeared a dangerous and potentially illegal threat to the economic order; rather, it was generally recognized as a civil and political right, a legitimate tool that workers could use to press for their interests in economic disputes. Given this new sense of striking as an appropriate act, many employers confronted with strikes became more reluctant to hire permanent replacements in order to break the strike. While in rare instances employers in the 1950s and 1960s did act to replace strikers—such as the Lone Star Steel and Kohler Company strikes—more frequently employers declined to do so, even though it remained technically legal.

More common during these years were anti-strike strategies that resembled the Mohawk Valley Formula, with heavy use of propaganda, subtle economic threats, and encouragement of workers to cross the picket line and return to work. General Electric (GE), under the leadership of Vice President for Employee and Community Relations Lemuel Ricketts Boulware, adopted elaborate strategies in its showdown with the International Union of Electrical Workers (the anti-Communist union founded in 1949 as a rival to the United Electrical Workers). Boulware was hired at GE in 1945, shortly before the major strike wave that swept the nation in the wake of World War II. Most of GE's production workers struck during that upsurge, marching in mass pickets that kept not only strikebreakers but even management out of the company's plants. Boulware and other top executives at GE vowed never to let something like the 1946 strike happen again. To prevent it, Boulware developed tough negotiating strategies designed to undermine the union, making it appear that collective action could obtain nothing. He balanced his bargaining strategies with a daily propaganda barrage at the workers, constantly sending the message that the company, not the union, was the source of any benefit in their lives.

The company's strategies successfully averted major strikes until 1960. When the union, troubled by pay and benefits falling farther behind auto and steel as well as by GE's relocation of plants from the North and Midwest to the South, finally called a strike in 1960, the company was ready to employ full-scale anti-strike strategies. First and foremost, for months leading up to the strike, GE insisted that it would not close its plants and that it would take a long strike rather than accept a settlement forced upon it by the union. Management sent letters to the homes of employees, telling them that the company would protect their right to work, that it would not permit strikers to close the factories, and that "if you do not cross a peaceful picket line, you have joined the strike." Before the strike began, employees received letters attacking the union leadership and urging them to report to work. Once the strike started, in addition to sending letters, managers began to pay home visits to workers, and to call them, asking them to return. At the same time, the company contacted shareholders, put ads in both national and local newspapers, and tried to rally support among local businessmen, clergy, and other community authorities. GE even encouraged secretaries and women employees to call local radio shows posing as disgruntled workers or as the wives of strikers eager for the strike to end. In the end, the strike fell apart after two weeks, demonstrating the continued willingness and ability of certain anti-union employers to develop anti-strike strategies, relying heavily on community mobilization, economic intimidation, and propaganda instead of violence or strikebreakers, even at the height of the postwar liberal order.

Reinstalling the Natural Order

As postwar liberalism came under increasing attack from a resurgent conservative movement in the 1970s, anti-unionism and opposition to strikes became more vehement and widespread. Anti-union arguments had new resonance in the era of economic strife of the 1970s, when American industry faced greater international competition and manufacturers were fleeing south in search of lower wages. At the same time, unions were losing their power—they represented a smaller proportion of the labor force, even as newly militant unions were organizing in the public sector and in some parts of the service sector (for example, hospitals). The combination of militancy in particular sectors and overall weakness may have made the labor movement newly vulnerable to conservative attacks. On the one hand, at least in certain sectors, labor seemed on the march; on the other, it was weak enough to beat. Underlying this new confidence among businesspeople was an important ideological and political shift. For the growing conservative movement, in which business activists played a central role as both organizers and participants, striking was an essentially violent act. By seeking to undermine the free market, it was in its nature coercive. As free-market intellectual Ludvig von Mises put it, "The labor unions are practically free to prevent by force anybody from defying their orders concerning wage rates." Collective bargaining, in his view, was "not a market transaction"; it was "bargaining at the point of a gun." Friedrich von Hayek described the picket line as an "instrument of intimidation" that represented "organized pressure upon individuals which in a free society no private agency should be permitted to exercise." Strikes, and by extension labor unions, did not advance the public interest—they were fundamentally at odds with it.

During the 1980s, many employers once again began to use permanent replacements to break strikes. When President Ronald Reagan fired 13,000 striking air traffic controllers, barred them from federal employment for life, and hired all-new replacements, the message to business was clear: hiring replacements was a civic good. Permanent replacements were used in nearly one-fifth of strikes between 1985 and 1989 by companies including Greyhound, International Paper, Caterpillar, Pittston Coal, Eastern Airlines, Phelps-Dodge, and Continental Airlines. As the use of permanent replacements became more widespread, so did the presence of armed security guards, who not only guarded the plants and protected the strikebreakers but harassed strikers. For example, during the UAW strike at Caterpillar in 1991, Vance guards stood on company rooftops, videotaping strikers as though their marching was illegal. As Stephen Norwood has described, the company was able to break the strike by advertising for permanent replacements; when it received tens of thousands of phone calls from workers desperate for the jobs in the Caterpillar factories, the strike was over. The suggestion of military force, the willingness of the company to do whatever was necessary to break the union, and the absence of solidarity and sympathy from lower-wage or unemployed workers in the region ultimately doomed the strike. Today, despite the existence of a legal right to strike, employers are often willing to use permanent replacements, armed guards, and a steady stream of propaganda intended to demoralize the union and emphasize the company's power in order to break the strike. The underlying ideological support for this comes from the free-market faith, according to which unions pervert a natural market order—a language reminiscent of that used against labor 200 years ago, in the early days of the republic.

See also: The Business Community's Mercenaries: Strikebreakers and Union Busters, 52; The 1945–1946 Strike Wave, 216; Strikes in the United States Since World War II, 226; Steel Strikes Before 1935, 351.

Bibliography

Brecher, Jeremy. *Strike!* San Francisco: Straight Arrow Books, 1972.

Brody, David. *Workers in Industrial America: Essays on the Twentieth-Century Struggle.* New York: Oxford University Press, 1993.

Dubofsky, Melvyn. *The State and Labor in Modern America.* Chapel Hill: University of North Carolina Press, 1994.

Gable, Richard Walter. "A Political Analysis of an Employers' Association, The National Association of Manufacturers." Ph.D. Dissertation, University of Chicago, 1950.

Hayek, Friedrich. *The Constitution of Liberty.* Chicago: University of Chicago Press, 1960.

Jeffreys, Steve. *Management and Managed: Fifty Years of Struggle at Chrysler.* New York: Cambridge University Press, 1986.

Lichtenstein, Nelson. *State of the Union: A Century of American Labor.* Princeton, NJ: Princeton University Press, 2002.

Norwood, Stephen. *Strikebreaking and Intimidation: Mercenaries and Masculinity in Twentieth-Century America.* Chapel Hill: University of North Carolina Press, 2002.

Phillips-Fein, Kim. "Top-Down Revolution: Businessmen, Intellectuals and Politicians against the New Deal, 1945–1964." Ph.D. diss., Columbia University, 2005.

Steuben, John. *Strike Strategy.* New York: Gaer Associates, 1950.

von Mises, Ludvig. *Human Action: A Treatise on Economics.* New Haven, CT: Yale University Press, 1949.

Wilentz, Sean. *Chants Democratic: New York City & the Rise of the American Working Class, 1788–1850.* New York: Oxford University Press, 1984.

Zinn, Howard, Dana Frank, and Robin D.G. Kelley. *Three Strikes: Miners, Musicians, Salesgirls and the Fighting Spirit of Labor's Last Century.* Boston: Beacon Press, 2001.

THE DECLINE OF STRIKES

Jeremy Brecher

In the capitalist economic system, labor power is treated as a commodity that can be bought and sold in the market. Therefore, strikes can be viewed as a normal feature of capitalist markets. Workers, like any other vendors, can withdraw their commodity from the market if they are dissatisfied with the price offered for it. This is a way that strikes are commonly viewed, for example, by economists.

However, workers are in fact more than just the purveyors of labor power. Even at work they remain people with thoughts, feelings, social relationships, and a claim to the rights of human beings and of members of society. Yet at work they must accept an employer's authority—an authority normally backed by law—in order to make a living. A strike viewed in this aspect represents not just a withdrawal of a commodity from the market, but also a withdrawal of consent from authority, an act of noncooperation—even of resistance to authority.

Further, the employer is not the only authority that strikes can challenge. General strikes, mass strikes, and political strikes have been used repeatedly around the world to challenge social structures and governmental policies and power.

Strikes in U.S. History

Strikes were rare in the United States before the nineteenth century, though a few did occur. During the American Revolution, for example, iron workers in the frontier of northwestern Connecticut did not like their working conditions, so they stopped work. The revolutionary legislature of the Connecticut colony sent a committee to negotiate with them and settle their grievances. But this was a rather atypical occurrence.

Over the early decades of the nineteenth century, the era of the Industrial Revolution, a growing proportion of the workforce became what we think of today as "workers"—people who work for someone else for a wage. With that change came the development of strikes as a normal part of life in the United States.

Initially, strikes were treated legally as criminal conspiracies. Nonetheless, they continued to occur. As more and more Americans became propertyless wage laborers, their power as individuals diminished but their power as a group became greater. The strike provided a way to exercise some power over their conditions of life and work.

For most of the nineteenth century and well into the twentieth, most strikes occurred in the context of craft unionism. Workers who could monopolize the skills and knowledge required to do the job in a particular craft could organize a union and withdraw their labor power, often at a critical juncture. They could thereby exercise economic power and thus force higher wages or changes in their working conditions. Such craft union economic strikes became part of the core strategy of the American Federation of Labor (AFL), long the dominant U.S. trade union center, under its longtime leader Samuel Gompers.

A related aspect of craft union strategy was exclusionism. The unions that formed the AFL, with some exceptions, excluded African-American workers; many also excluded Asian workers. Women also found themselves excluded from many unions. Such exclusion was part of the unions' strategy to control the labor supply for a particular craft.

Craft unions often faced pressures from within to go beyond the "pure and simple unionism" advocated by Gompers. In many instances, AFL unions formed coalitions, joined sympathy strikes, and engaged in other, more inclusive forms of action. But the dominant theme of craft unionism reflected what their critics in the radical Industrial Workers of the World (known as the "Wobblies") used to say: the American Federation of Labor should be called the "American Separation of Labor." The Wobblies published a pamphlet around 1911 called "Why Strikes Are Lost." It told the story of the "union scab," recounting strikes in which workers who were members of craft unions continued to work while other unionized workers at the same job site were on strike. One by one the strikes would fail, because of the separate, rather than joint, efforts of the two groups.

More inclusive groups within the American labor movement included the Knights of Labor, the American Railway Union, and the Industrial Workers of the World. They tried to bring together a more diverse set of workers, although the Knights of Labor and the American Railway Union were not without exclusionism of their own.

Ever since the Civil War, the United States has repeatedly experienced periods of worker upheaval: strike waves, general strikes that paralyzed entire cities, and other expressions of widespread worker protest. In such periods, worker actions tended to extend beyond one group of workers, a process often described as "spreading by contagion." These periods of upheaval fit in many ways what the German revolutionary socialist leader Rosa Luxemburg characterized as "periods of mass strike." These periods tended not only to have a very wide range of different kinds of labor struggles but to be related to economic, political, military, and social crises, rather than just to what was going on in the workplace.

Perhaps the first major mass strike in the United States, known at the time as "The Great Upheaval," occurred in 1877. What started as a local wildcat railroad strike in the midst of a deep depression spread into a nationwide railroad strike and then into strikes and mass marches in dozens of cities, including street battles with the police, state guards, and ultimately the U.S. Army. It included a general strike in St. Louis, perhaps the first in U.S. history.

In 1886, labor conflict again came to a peak over the issue of working hours, in what was essentially a general strike in Chicago and a number of other cities. It is often remembered in relation to what is generally referred to as the "Haymarket riot"—which was actually more of a police riot than anything else. Hundreds of thousands of workers were on strike across trades and industries in dozens of cities at the beginning of May 1886, all striking around the demand for shorter hours, usually an eight-hour day.

In 1894, the Pullman strike again shut down the railroads of the country. The strike began in sympathy and support for a group of people who were not even railroad workers but who were working in the shops of the Pullman Company, making Pullman cars and not making enough money to be able to afford to eat. After strikes and mass actions throughout the country, the movement was suppressed by federal injunctions and large-scale military and police force.

Throughout this period there was in practice no right to strike. Though the prosecution of strikers for conspiracy became rare, it was a normal practice during strikes for employers to go before a judge to get an injunction against the strike, and then have workers and union leaders declared in contempt of court for violating the injunction. From the nineteenth century to the 1930s, the government frequently acted systematically as a strikebreaker.

Until World War I, most employers opposed unions and worker organizations, and fought to maintain unilateral control of the workplace. They generally found support from government. During World War I, the tremendous demand for labor caused the government to adopt a two-pronged policy. One prong was to suppress the more radical parts of the labor movement quite violently: labor leader and Socialist Party presidential candidate Eugene Victor Debs spent World War I in prison and the IWW was decimated by violent lynchings and beatings, while law enforcement officials either turned a blind eye or participated in the process. The other prong was the opening of government-sanctioned collective bargaining, with the right to organize and bargain for the more conservative, mainstream unions protected by the government and accepted by most large employers.

After World War I, employers, with government acquiescence, tried to roll back these changes by eliminating whatever institutionalization of worker power had developed. It is in that context that the great strike wave of 1919 occurred, which had as one of its first expressions the Seattle General Strike of 1919—an event that should also be seen as part of the global crisis and revolt of the post–World War I era.

The postwar effort to roll back the beachhead that workers had made in major parts of American industry was quite successful. During the 1920s, the so-called open shop, the exclusion of unions from workplaces, was close to universal. Strikes were few and largely regarded as relics of the past.

In the mid-1930s, a wave of sit-down strikes—mass occupations in auto and rubber factories and many other workplaces—shook the country. They played a central role in establishing a different form of unionism, known as industrial unionism, which was pioneered by the Congress of Industrial Organizations (CIO) and later imitated by the AFL. This was a much more inclusive form of labor organization, but one with its roots still very much in the AFL tradition in the sense of viewing labor organization as a relation between a group of workers and their employer.

There was also a fundamental shift in the legal status of strikes and of labor organizations. The National Labor Relations Act (NLRA) established the right of workers to organize and to take concerted action. It thereby seemed to guarantee workers' right to strike, which was not the norm during most of American history.

In the wake of the NLRA's passage, however, courts interpreted the act as guaranteeing not the rights of workers but the rights of unions. Once workers were represented by a union, the right to strike became a right of the union as an organization. Therefore, if the union had a contract with the employer that provided for no strikes during the course of the agreement, strikes again became illegal. According to labor analyst Fred Joiner, by 1947 no-strike clauses were included in 90 percent of contracts. Eventually the courts declared that even if there was not a no-strike clause in the contract, a no-strike agreement was implied simply by the existence of a contract.

Further limitation on the right to strike came with the Taft-Hartley Act after World War II, which outlawed so-called secondary strikes and boycotts. A strike could only be protected under American labor law if it was a strike against the immediate employer regarding issues with the employer. Extraneous issues, such as what was happening to other workers someplace else, were not legally acceptable subjects for a strike. Solidarity became, in effect, illegal.

In sum, only an extremely narrow range of strikes were legally protected. Generally, they had to be called by a union, there had to be no contract in place, and they could only be about wages, hours, and working conditions of the immediate employer.

The quarter century that followed World War II has often been called the "golden age of capitalism." From 1947 to 1973, the global economy had an unprecedented average annual growth rate of 5 percent a year. There were very few deep recessions. In the United States, there was unprecedented stability in economic growth and in the business cycle.

This coincides with what is often called the "era of institutionalized collective bargaining," the beginning of which could be marked with the strike wave of 1946. As happened after World War I, employers wanted to roll back the gains that the labor movement had made during the war. This time, however, the battle was fought to a standstill. Major employers thereupon decided that they were going to accept the existence of unions in their plants. According to historian Howell John Harris, Henry Ford II said in 1946, "We of the Ford Motor Company have no desire to 'break the unions' or to turn back the clock." Instead, Ford said, "We must look to an improved and increasingly responsible [union] leadership for help in solving the human equation in mass production." That acceptance continued for another quarter century.

The most recent period of mass strike, though rarely recognized as such, was the Vietnam era. In addition to the more widely recognized forms of protest by students, African Americans, and soldiers, there were large-scale wildcat strikes by miners, postal workers, teamsters, and many other groups that were very similar to the patterns of previous mass strikes. It also marked the end of the era in which most large employers bargained collectively with most of their workers.

The Decline of Strikes

In the years from 1950 to 1975, the "era of institutionalized collective bargaining," the Department of Labor statistics on "large strikes" (1,000 or more workers for one or more shifts) typically show between 200 and 450 large strikes per year. Since then, the decline has been dramatic. The number of large strikes declined almost every year from 1980 to 1999. In 1999, the number of major strikes hit a fifty-year low. There were only seventeen strikes involving 1,000 or more workers in the United States, which is one-twelfth of the number two decades before. After a slight rebound to thirty-nine in 2000, the number of major strikes resumed its decline, hitting a new low of fourteen in 2003. Since then, there has been little rebound.

Why have strikes declined so dramatically in the United States?

First, there is the economic context: a long period of economic stagnation worldwide. The quarter century that began in 1973 saw average annual global growth fall from 5 percent to 2.5 percent. According to economics reporter Louis Uchitelle, in the United States, the years from 1973 to 1997 represent by some measures the longest period of weak economic growth since the Civil War.

The decline of strikes is sometimes attributed to the alleged fact that workers simply have no need to strike any more, but this is not an effective explanation. The period of declining strikes saw a 15 percent reduction in workers' real wages and a 30 percent reduction in real incomes for young families, according to labor economists Lawrence Mishel, Jared Bernstein, and John Schmitt. The United States has also seen the rise of the twelve-hour day and the seven-day workweek; the loss of health, pension, and social safety net protections; downsizing; outsourcing; and the erosion of job security. These reverse the prime historical accomplishment of strikes and the labor movement: modifying the idea that labor is just something traded in a market to the idea that workers are human beings with human rights, labor rights, the kinds of democratic rights that are provided in the U. S. Constitution, rights to health and social security, and so on. Over the past twenty years, the United States has seen a return to the idea that labor is just a commodity.

Another explanation that some have offered is that the decline of strikes is just a result of high unemployment. True, much of the era of strike decline was marked by high unemployment. But strikes have not rebounded much during the booming employment of the late 1990s and 2000s. This contrasts with the long-run historical pattern in which strikes tend to go up very sharply when wages decline and employment surges. With or without unions, workers have normally turned to strikes at a very high rate in that situation, and that has not occurred in the past couple years. Why?

Strikes in the past twenty-five years were nasty, brutish, and long. A string of catastrophic strike defeats runs from the Professional Air Traffic Controllers Organization (PATCO) in 1981 to the three-year strike/lockout of Staley workers in Decatur, Illinois, in 1992–95. One case, occurring in a stronghold of unionism, demonstrates some of the sources of failure.

The Caterpillar Corporation is the world's largest manufacturer of earth-moving equipment. It has plants all over the world, from Scotland to Mexico to Indonesia. It has been a center of class struggle all around the world. Caterpillar workers conducted a 103-day factory occupation in Scotland in 1987 and a six-day occupation in Canada in 1991.

In the United States, the company and the United Auto Workers (UAW) union had a cooperation program in the 1980s that was oriented toward creating more efficient production so that American plants would be more competitive. While that was happening, the company also pursued its own restructuring program, which reduced the workforce by 30 percent and built new, nonunion plants. In 1991, the Caterpillar Company demanded a whole range of concessions, including a two-tier pay scale, changes in health insurance, and a familiar litany of similar takebacks. Caterpillar Chairman Donald V. Fites said he needed greater flexibility to set wages, benefits, and working conditions to protect Caterpillar's preeminent position in competition with companies in Japan and Europe.

Workers at the Caterpillar plant in Decatur struck in November 1991 and the bargaining chair of the largest local told *Labor Notes* in May 1992, "As long as we hold the line, and don't take our experience in there, we're going to be all right." In other words, the withdrawal of labor power by this group of workers in itself would be sufficient to win the strike and protect them from the company's attacks.

After five months, Caterpillar threatened to bring in replacement workers. Caterpillar workers were afraid of permanently losing their jobs, and the UAW leadership ordered the workers back to work. The *New York Times* commented, "The abrupt end of a five-month strike against Caterpillar showed that management can bring even a union so mighty and rich as the United Automobile Workers to its knees."

Two and a half years later, the UAW ordered its members back on strike. The company attempted to continue production with strikebreakers, and to a considerable extent it was successful. After seventeen months on strike, the UAW negotiated a new agreement with Caterpillar, which the workers voted down by nearly 80 percent. Then the UAW "recessed" the strike and ordered union members back to work anyway.

Conditions upon their return were horrendous: according to *UAW Solidarity*, the National Labor Relations Board (NLRB) filed over 250 separate complaints for unfair labor practices against Caterpillar and found that the company's "pattern of unlawful conduct convinces us that, without proper restraint, Caterpillar is likely to persist in its attempts to interfere with employees' statutory rights." That prediction proved correct. Caterpillar workers referred to their workplace as "Stalag Caterpillar."

Why did strikes so often become disasters? Five reasons are visible in the story of Caterpillar; they reflect deeper structural trends, and no doubt many more could be added.

First, corporations have gone global. They can threaten to move their work or their facilities. They are able to whipsaw globally: to play workers in their different plants against each other, forcing the workers to compete with each other for work. They also function in global markets in which they compete on labor costs—a practice the labor movement hoped to eliminate. The result is what has been called a "race to the bottom," as corporations scour the globe looking for the cheapest labor.

The labor movement, meanwhile, is very divided globally. There was little response among American workers, for example, to the Scottish and Canadian Caterpillar occupations. Most UAW members in the United States probably did not know about them. In the United States, the union attempted to make plants more efficient in order to compete with the foreign Caterpillar plants. Rather late in the Caterpillar struggle, the UAW tried to bring together a Caterpillar World Council, which had one meeting. Little came of it, and it is not hard to see why there was not much interest among Caterpillar workers in other parts of the world in supporting workers at U.S. plants, given U.S. workers' previous disinterest in supporting Caterpillar workers elsewhere. In short, workers face a "global separation of labor" as a sequel to the "American Separation of Labor" of the period of national capitalism.

Second, corporations have restructured in pursuit of what Chairman Fites referred to as "the need for flexibility." This is referred to as downsizing, outsourcing, lean production, and the like. Restructuring generally means a change from vertically integrated and horizontally integrated corporations to today's trendy "core/ring" structure, as labor economist Bennett Harrison has chronicled. This means eliminating everything except the core functions and then contracting with a group of satellite suppliers for everything from janitorial services to computer management. The result might be called, in contrast to the integrated corporation, the "dis-integrated" corporation. This makes any one group of workers even more powerless vis-à-vis their employer.

Just within the United States, there are dozens of unions that negotiate with most major corporations. There are no bargaining councils in most of these companies. There is little connection and coordination among those dozens of unions within each corporation; this is still an American separation of labor.

Third is the end of class compromise. Caterpillar's shift from cooperation to combat was explicit. It is representative of a shift by American corporations from cooperation with unions to elimination of any independent power in the workplace.

Emblematic of the anti-union shift is the widespread use of permanent replacement workers, which was virtually unknown in the United States from the institutionalization of labor law in the 1940s to Ronald Reagan's firing of the PATCO workers in 1981. It is hard to imagine a more powerful symbol of the recommodification of labor than the idea that a company can take an entire labor force, decide it does not like its attitude, and just get rid of it to hire a completely new workforce. That is "labor as a commodity" back with a vengeance.

Employers' primary goal in such cases appears to be unilateral management control; that is, the elimination of labor as an independent force. To achieve this goal, it is not necessary to eliminate unions. The companies have often accepted the continued existence of unions, as long as they do not function as an independent force. This is a different strategy than was followed by the open-shop movement in the 1920s, but the results are uncomfortably similar.

Fourth is the changing role of the state. One important aspect of this is the atrophy of the collective bargaining institutions that were created under the NLRA. Today, 12 percent of workers are represented by unions. This is the lowest proportion of workers unionized since 1936. Union density is right back where it was before the passage of the NLRA. There is also a breakdown of NLRB protections for workers. One study found that 10,000 workers are fired annually for attempting to organize unions. The Congress recently refused to reappoint an NLRB head primarily because he had shown an interest in defending workers' statutory rights. The gassing and beating of striking Caterpillar and Staley workers in Decatur in the early 1990s, and in many other strikes of the past two decades, also indicate that the government's hostility to strikes is quite in keeping with the long-term historical pattern going back to the nineteenth century.

Finally, there is the question of union acquiescence in these conditions. At Caterpillar, as in many companies, the union actively pursued a cooperation program it hoped would preserve U.S. jobs, even at the expense of Caterpillar workers elsewhere. Such support for workplace, company, and national "competitiveness" has been a hallmark of organized labor's approach throughout this period. So has the limitation of struggles summarized by those memorable words, "As long as we hold the line and don't take our experience in there, we're going to be all right."

Were there alternatives? At the time of the Caterpillar strike, there were three major strikes in the Decatur area: Caterpillar, A.E. Staley, and Bridgestone/Firestone. Locals from all three did actually form an alliance in the city. There were several other companies that were on the verge of strikes. There was serious thought given by some workers to the idea that this situation was moving toward a local general strike. Staley striker Dan Lane, who conducted a sixty-five-day hunger strike, was very conscious that he was trying to move the situation toward a general strike in the city of Decatur. That idea provides one vision of what it would mean to move toward broader solidarity, something more like the Seattle general strike, for example. However, the unions involved rejected this approach, preferring instead to settle these strikes separately, as quickly as possible, and on almost any terms the companies would accept.

New Tactics in Social Conflict

There are some developing approaches that begin to counter these serious problems. Organized labor is beginning to respond to globalization, for example. Although the Caterpillar World Council and solidarity support never got off the ground, there have been a number of strikes where international solidarity has played a crucial role. In the Bridgestone/Firestone lockout, pressure on the company from workers all over the world, including Japan, Brazil, and Europe, was a major factor in persuading Bridgestone/Firestone to reverse itself and rehire the workers it had permanently replaced. The 1997 United Parcel Service (UPS) strike was one of the shining moments of labor success of the past few years. In that situation, international pressure, especially by European workers—some in unions, some trying to organize in UPS—played a major role in UPS's decision to back down and come to a settlement. There have been numerous examples of grassroots international labor activity, including campaigns for labor rights, the anti-sweatshop movements, and support for the strike at the Han Young maquiladora (foreign-owned export factory) in northern Mexico. However, labor is still very far from redefining itself as a global movement with the breadth and depth of solidarity needed to have any chance of dealing with global corporations.

There are also some interesting responses to corporate restructuring. The corporate campaigns that accompany many strikes now are, among other things, a way of taking on a company as a whole and trying to find all of the places it is vulnerable to pressure, rather than just focusing on the strike of one group of workers trying to take on the company in isolation.

There are also ways that the reorganization of corporations strengthens workers. For example, there have been a series of local strikes at General Motors plants that have taken advantage of the introduction of just-in-time production. Under just-in-time production, factories receive the parts they need just as they are about to be used, so if a strike paralyzes a parts plant all the other plants in the assembly chain must shut down. In this way, the whole North American operation of General Motors, with hundreds of thousands of workers, was stopped on several occasions by a couple thousand workers in Flint, Michigan, and Dayton, Ohio.

In Flint, overwork was the problem because the company was not hiring new workers. But the workers' objectives went beyond reducing overwork for those currently employed. The workers made an alliance with the broader community, notably black ministers. The alliance fought against the hiring of temporary workers, insisting instead on the hiring of permanent workers because the city of Flint needed jobs.

The rise of organizing by labor markets is another interesting response. In Los Angeles, Service Employees International Union (SEIU) led a big victory of home health care workers, and part of its strategy was not to think about organizing employer by employer, but rather to organize an entire workforce that represents a labor market. They did this by winning legislation to create a single employer—a county agency—to "employ" the homecare workers whose traditional employers had been individual patients. Then they won organizing rights with the county agency. Organizing by market is also happening through the creation of workers' centers, which are also not based on organizing by employer. These most often organize by ethnic group. In Boston, a contingent worker center serves as a base for people who are part-time and temporary workers and contract workers in a wide range of occupations. The living wage campaigns and similar efforts that put a floor under social conditions represent another way of trying to address the problem of corporate restructuring by moving beyond one group of workers organizing or striking just to deal with the immediate employer.

The end of employer indulgence of worker organization and the onset of corporate class war is something that the labor movement has only begun to address. Despite all the changes in the AFL-CIO, President John Sweeney repeatedly says that there is a natural community of interest between American business and American workers. The question of whether that has any meaning in the era of global capitalism is one that the labor movement is going to have to face. The era of class compromise is over. Global capital is essentially uninterested in dealing with organized workers.

Labor also needs to recognize the reality of unequal power. Labor law essentially maintains that collective bargaining establishes equality between workers and corporations. Most unions similarly maintained that they were as strong as the companies, but in reality they are not. Labor needs to recognize this and think in terms of the tactics and strategies that are appropriate for a weak force trying to deal with a stronger force.

One example is "the inside game." This uses the power of workers' withdrawal of labor and noncooperation—but not by going on strike, leaving the workplace, and marching around in front of it. Instead, it uses what the Wobblies used to call "striking on the job" or "the withdrawal of efficiency." Now it is sometimes called "making the workplace run backward."

In response to the changing role of the state, the labor movement is now trying publicly to define the right to organize as a basic human right. It is linking international labor rights and the right of workers to organize in the United States, which is something that has long been outside the paradigm of the U.S. labor movement. A logical corollary would be to expand the same concept to assert the right to strike as a basic human right: to assert that, if workers cannot strike, they are living under a form of slavery. Such an approach is necessary because there is no way that workers are going to get any significant power or be able to be an independent force within the limits imposed by current labor law.

One of the most significant developments in labor struggles in the past twenty years is the widespread use of nonviolent civil disobedience. The labor movement has always been primarily a nonviolent movement, but when it has been attacked by state power, its response has been varied. In general, there has been a consistent policy not to respond violently in such situations, but to instead respond by some kind of nonviolent mass mobilization. The use of Gandhian techniques and the tactics of Martin Luther King Jr. and the civil rights movement have become a regular staple of labor struggles over the past twenty years. That provides a way of asserting the unacceptability of government repression without the danger of alienating the public and making it feel it is dealing with a violent force that the state could legitimately suppress.

Finally, the labor movement's acquiescence in corporations' plans for the "recommodification of labor" has begun to change. This is not just a matter of greater militancy, but more of the goals of strikes. When the Teamsters and UPS workers put the focus of the UPS strike on the problem of part-time work and defined it as a social problem not just for UPS workers but for all American workers, they hit a huge responsive chord. It was one reason the strike was successful.

Mass Strike Worldwide

Worldwide, general strikes and political strikes have been burgeoning. According to labor journalist Kim Moody in 1997, "In the last couple of years, there have been at least two dozen political general strikes in Europe, Latin America, Asia, and North America. There have been more political mass strikes in the last two or three years than at any time in the twentieth century." Since 1996 there have been general strikes in Argentina, Belgium, Brazil, Canada, Columbia, Denmark, Ecuador, France, Greece, Haiti, Italy, Puerto Rico, South Korea, and Spain, among others.

The characteristics of these strikes are very different from the typical U.S. strike. Most of these strikes were not about problems with particular employers. Rather, they contested government austerity programs, privatization, denial of labor and human rights, and the slashing of basic services. In most cases they were responses to the pressures of globalization. Generally these strikes had the support of the vast majority of the population. And, while they often had roots in earlier events and activities, they did not occur primarily in places that had long traditions of general strikes of this kind.

France is interesting because it is one of the few industrial countries that has a labor union density as low as that of the United States at around 12 percent. It also has a very divided labor movement. When the government announced that it was going to cut France's equivalent of social security, workers, both union and nonunion, began forming local assemblies that cut across union lines. They began organizing a strike, which became a nationwide general strike with huge mass demonstrations and marches.

One of the main demands that emerged from the worker assemblies was that the unions start cooperating. They were forced to cooperate with each other in challenging what everyone saw as a threat: the destruction of the social security system (cut in the name, of course, of international competitiveness). Within a few weeks the government was forced to withdraw its plan. Since then the struggle has continued in a myriad of forms. It also had something to do with why there is no longer a conservative government in France.

Strikes have also played a crucial role in the people power movements that have brought down undemocratic regimes from Poland to the Philippines to Indonesia to Korea. And they have been central to the resistance to IMF "structural adjustment" plans imposed in the wake of global financial crisis in the late 1990s.

It would be premature to describe all this as a "global mass strike." But global capitalism may be creating the conditions for such a phenomenon.

Conclusion: The Future of Strikes

One lesson of history is that new conditions will create new challenges. The kinds of strikes that marked the United States in the heyday of collective bargaining from the 1940s through the 1970s seem unlikely to occur again in significant numbers. It is hard to see what will ever restore the power of one group of workers to make gains simply by withdrawing their labor power from their employer.

Strikes may serve again as a vehicle for working people to express their power, but if so they will be strikes of a very different character.

During the world wars of the past century, it was often said that workers were being pitted against workers militarily in global warfare. Today workers are being pitted against workers economically in a global race to the bottom. For those who accept this situation, the strike probably has little to offer. For those who choose to challenge it, strikes are likely to be an essential means of action for a long time to come.

See also: The Business Community's Mercenaries: Strikebreakers and Union Busters, 52; Corporate Strike Strategy, 66; Strike Lessons From the Last Twenty-Five Years: What it Takes to Walk Out and Win, 81; Strike Waves (Part III Introduction), 175; Strikes in the United States Since World War II, 226.

Bibliography

Brecher, Jeremy. *Strike!* Boston: South End Press, 1997.

Brecher, Jeremy, and Tim Costello. "Labor and the Challenge of the 'Dis-Integrated Corporation.'" *New Labor Forum* Spring (1998).

Buhle, Paul. *Taking Care of Business.* New York: Monthly Review Press, 1999.

Harris, Howell John. *The Right to Manage: Industrial Relations Policies of American Business in the 1940s.* Madison: University of Wisconsin Press, 1982.

Harrison, Bennett. *Lean and Mean: The Changing Landscape of Corporate Power in the Age of Flexibility.* New York: Basic Books, 1994.

Luxemburg, Rosa. "The Mass Strike, the Political Party and the Trade Unions." In *Rosa Luxemburg Speaks,* ed. Mary-Alice Waters. New York: Pathfinder, 1970.

Mishel, Lawrence, Jared Bernstein, and John Schmitt. *The State of Working America, 1996–97.* Armonk, NY: M.E. Sharpe, 1997.

Montgomery, David. *The Fall of the House of Labor.* Cambridge, UK: Cambridge University Press, 1987.

Moody, Kim. *Workers in a Lean World: Unions in the International Economy.* London: Verso, 1997.

Trautmann, William. "Why Strikes Are Lost." Reprinted in *Rebel Voices: An I.W.W. Anthology,* ed. Joyce L. Kornbluth. Ann Arbor: University of Michigan Press, 1964.

Uchitelle, Louis. "That Was Then and This Is the 90's." *The New York Times,* June 18, 1997.

STRIKE LESSONS FROM THE LAST TWENTY-FIVE YEARS: WHAT IT TAKES TO WALK OUT AND WIN

Steve Early

In the fall of 2002, streets and office buildings in downtown Boston were the scene of inspiring immigrant worker activism during an unprecedented strike by local janitors. The walkout was backed by other union members, community activists, students and professors, public officials, religious leaders, and even a few socially minded businessmen. The janitors had long been invisible, mistreated by management and, until recently, ignored by their own Service Employees International Union local. Simply by making their strike such a popular social cause, they achieved what many regarded as a major victory.

On the same day that the janitors' dispute was settled, a much larger strike—at Overnite Transportation—ended quite differently. Faced with mounting legal setbacks and dwindling picket line support, the Teamsters were forced to call off their nationwide walkout against America's leading nonunion trucker. The 4,000 Overnite workers involved were not able to win a first contract. And, since their three-year strike was suspended, all have lost their bargaining rights in a series of "decertification" elections.

The intersecting trajectory of these two struggles—one hopeful and high-profile, the other tragic and now almost forgotten—raises important questions about the state of the strike at the start of a new century. But one answer seems clear: maintaining "strike capacity" is no less important to the future of unions than shifting more resources into organizing or political action, two popular union strategies. Unfortunately, developing new ways to walk out and win has not been a major component of the debate among unions and their supporters about how to regain bargaining clout. For example, it was completely absent from the year-long debate that preceded the 2005 split in the AFL-CIO that led to the formation of the Change to Win union federation.

Labor's strike effectiveness and organizational strength have long been connected. Throughout history, work stoppages have been used for economic and political purposes to alter the balance of power between labor and capital within single workplaces, entire industries, or nationwide. Strikes have won shorter hours and safer conditions through legislation or contract negotiation. They have fostered new forms of worker organization—like industrial unions—that were badly needed because of corporate restructuring and the reorganization of production. Strikes have acted as incubators for class consciousness, rank-and-file leadership development, and political activism. In other countries, strikers have challenged—and changed—governments that were dictatorial and oppressive (often against union leadership no longer accountable to the membership).

In some nations—like Korea, South Africa, France, and Spain—where strike action helped democratize society, general strikes are still being used for mass mobilization and political protest. In the last decade, millions of Europeans have participated in nationwide work stoppages over public sector budget cuts, labor law revisions, or pension plan changes sought by conservative governments. In Brazil, voters have even chosen a one-time strike leader, Luis Inacio ("Lula") da Silva, to serve as president of their country.

Meanwhile in America, "major" work stoppages have become a statistical blip on the radar screen of industrial relations. Every year, more than 20,000 union contracts are negotiated. Yet, since 1992, each year there is an average of fewer than forty walkouts by 1,000 or more workers. In 2004, there were just seventeen, with only 316,000 union members participating (100,000 of them in a single four-day telephone strike). In contrast, at the peak of labor's post–World War II strike wave in 1952, there were 470 major strikes affecting nearly 3 million workers nationwide.

Today, hardly anyone strikes for union recognition (although New York University teaching assistants did conduct a lengthy work stoppage in 2005–6 to regain recognition after it was withdrawn in the wake of an NLRB ruling that stripped private sector graduate student employees of NLRA protection). Most workers win bargaining rights via representation elections or card checks. Then, they negotiate first contracts which, like almost all American labor agreements, contain binding arbitration and no-strike clauses. This means they are legally barred from walking out during the life of the contract to protest unresolved grievances. As recently as the 1970s, such strictures were routinely ignored by tens of thousands of coal miners and other union members—despite fines, injunctions, damage suits, and contempt citations. Now, "wildcat" strikes—of any size—are extremely rare. When 18,000 General Electric workers staged an authorized strike in 2003 against impending medical plan changes—while their national agreement was still in effect—this option was available only because the GE contract is one of the few left with an "open-ended" grievance procedure.

Thanks to court decisions sanctioning the use of "permanent replacements," even contract strikes are a high-stakes venture in the private sector. If management chooses to play hard ball and hire a substitute workforce, it can in effect "fire" strikers, thereby also nullifying their "right to strike" at contract expiration. This countermeasure was deployed with devastating effect during the nationwide walkout by Northwest Airlines mechanics and cleaners in 2005. In the public sector, the legal and financial risks of striking lie in severe statutory restrictions on work stoppages themselves. Except in a handful of states, public employee unions that walk out are automatically subject to injunctions and/or fines. In New York, members of the Transport Workers Union—who stopped NYC subway operations for three days in December 2005—incurred the unusually heavy penalties of the Taylor Act, which apply to both labor organizations and their individual members.

Labor's current timidity about using the strike weapon can be traced back to the Professional Air Traffic Controllers Organization (PATCO) disaster in 1981. Twelve thousand striking employees of the Federal Aviation Administration (FAA) were fired and replaced by President Ronald Reagan. The government's success in breaking the strike sent an unmistakable message to workers and employers everywhere. The 1980s soon became a dark decade of lost strikes and lockouts, in which many other anti-concession battles—at Phelps-Dodge, Greyhound, Hormel, Eastern Airlines, and International Paper—ended badly. The response to these strikes on the part of the national AFL-CIO and many of its central labor councils (CLCs) was feeble indeed; too many CLCs had become hollow shells, more preoccupied with protocol and political endorsements than mobilizing members around strikes or boycotts.

Fortunately, the resulting vacuum was filled by a variety of unofficial groups that organized mass picket lines and rallies, conducted plant-gate collections and solidarity tours, and "adopted" strikers' families. In the late 1980s, with backing from a few national unions, some of these rank-and-file groups coalesced into the Jobs with Justice (JWJ) network. JWJ soon developed a strained relationship with the Lane Kirkland and Tom Donahue administrations of the AFL-CIO. By 1995, due in part to discontent with the AFL-CIO's paltry strike support efforts, JWJ was part of the climate for change enabling a reform slate to win control over the labor federation. But even John Sweeney's "New Voice" victory did not occur in time to alter the balance of power on picket lines in places like Decatur, Illinois, where factories operated by Caterpillar, Bridgestone/Firestone, and A.E. Staley all became part of single strike-bound "war zone" in the mid-1990s.

Not the least of labor's strike failings in the pre- and post-1995 periods was its seeming inability to learn from either defeats or victories. Without summing up and sharing the lessons of these battles, how could anyone expect them to become the basis for future success rather than a reoccurring pattern of failure? Nevertheless, most unions still shy away from any systematic strike postmortems. Particularly during the 1980s—when the landscape of labor was littered with the wreckage of lost walkouts—the dominant tendency was to bury the dead and move on, quickly, to the next fiasco. Even when these fights cost millions of dollars and the workers involved made enormous sacrifices over many months or years (including losing their jobs), few union representatives ever filed the labor equivalent of an "after-action report"—the kind of data routinely collected by the Pentagon to guide future military training and campaign planning.

Labor's own lack of bureaucratic interest in what went right or wrong on the industrial battlefield reinforces the idea that strikes are now futile, even suicidal. Meanwhile, the steady decline in work stoppages has reduced the pool of union activists with any strike background. Few unions compensate for this experience gap by publishing and distributing up-to-date strike manuals, offering in-depth training on strike strategy and tactics, or using their own (or other unions') organizational case studies. Anyone interested in the subject must turn to literature from academics, journalists, and activists, such as *Labor Notes* from the Detroit-based Labor Education & Research Project (LERP). LERP also holds biannual educational conferences featuring panels and workshops on strike activity. In 1991 and again in 2005, LERP published *A Troublemaker's Handbook,* which contains much useful information about the planning and execution of successful contract campaigns and strikes. A more recent book by attorney Robert Schwartz, entitled *Strikes, Picketing and Inside Campaigns: A Legal Guide for Unions*, is equally essential reading for would-be strikers.

Despite the hostile bargaining climate of the last twenty-five years and labor's haphazard approach to processing its own history, the vital lessons to be learned and applied in future strikes point in much the same direction. Among the necessary (if not always sufficient) conditions for strike effectiveness are the following: careful preparation and financing; membership mobilization and involvement; creative tactics and tactical flexibility; a message that resonates with the broader public; and a comprehensive campaign plan, which enlists all possible labor and community allies, at home and abroad.

Make Your Strike a Community/ Labor Cause Célèbre

Even during the 1980s, there were contract campaigns that bucked the tide of concession bargaining. In 1989, simultaneous strikes by miners in Appalachia and telephone workers in the northeastern United States both became successful examples of worker militancy and social movement unionism rather than disheartening displays of labor disarray.

The United Mine Workers of America (UMWA) succeeded in making their twelve-month walkout against Pittston into a national labor cause even though it involved only several thousand strikers in geographically isolated coal field communities. The union mobilized other UMWA members for sympathy strikes at non-Pittston mines, linked arms with recent presidential candidate Jesse Jackson, orchestrated waves of mass arrests, staged one of the few plant occupations since the 1930s, and created an encampment in southwest Virginia (Camp Solidarity) that became a magnet for strike supporters of all types from throughout the country. As labor historian James Green describes:

> Throughout the summer of 1989, the UMWA employed a corporate campaign, roving pickets, mass demonstrations, direct action, and civil disobedience. Whenever the company got a court injunction against certain activity, the miners responded by developing new tactics or reviving tactics of the past. Sometimes the strike resembled the non-violent civil rights movement of 40 years earlier. Other times, it was a pitched battle in what [then] UMWA Vice President Cecil Roberts dubbed "class warfare in southwest Virginia."

UMWA organizers "promoted and supported a local culture of solidarity and consciously transformed the strike into a people's resistance movement against corporate greed."

In August of 1989—after a New York City rally addressed by Pittston strike leader (and then UMWA President) Rich Trumka—60,000 members of CWA and IBEW joined the miners in fighting medical benefit givebacks. Like Pittston, their employer—NYNEX—was trying to shift the burden of medical cost inflation onto its unionized workforce, and for the first time require employee premium contributions for health coverage. The forty telephone worker locals involved had spent more than eighteen months getting ready for this showdown in New York and New England. They built up an active network of 4,000 stewards and "mobilization coordinators" to distribute literature, organize displays of workplace solidarity, and counter management propaganda about the need for wage and benefit concessions.

When negotiations deadlocked, months of membership education and on-the-job activity had already laid the groundwork for a high-impact strike. Strikers participated in mobile picketing that was militant and creative. They followed scab trucks more aggressively and systematically than ever before while also targeting top company executives and board members at their homes, businesses, universities, social clubs, and many corporate-sponsored events. There were mass arrests (about 400 in all), rallies of up to 15,000 people, 250 strike-related suspensions or firings (which took many months to contest in arbitration proceedings after the return to work), and numerous incidents of sabotage (which became the subject of full-page company newspaper ads offering $100,000 rewards.)

The strikers distributed tens of thousands of stickers calling for "Health Care For All, Not Health Cuts At NYNEX." They formed alliances with the Rainbow Coalition, National Organization for Women, Citizen Action, the Physicians for a National Health Program, and other health care reform groups. In Boston, weekly mass meetings featured speakers from these groups and fellow strikers from Pittston and Eastern Airlines, plus innumerable public officials and labor and community supporters. Strike-related rallies and publicity all emphasized the common bond between union and nonunion, insured and uninsured, workers and their mutual need for national health insurance (particularly after the strikers' own medical benefits were cut off).

In New York, NYNEX made the bad mistake of applying to the state's Public Service Commission (PSC) for a $360 million rate hike right in the middle of the four-month strike. CWA strikers gathered 100,000 signatures from consumers opposing the increase and got 130 state legislators—over 60 percent of the total—to lend their name to full-page anti-rate-hike ads in the *New York Times* and other papers. The union also formed a coalition with religious, student, senior citizen, and community organizations to intervene in the regulatory process. Press conferences were held with Jesse Jackson and consumer advocate Ralph Nader, and strikers distributed tens of thousands of pamphlets urging residential customers to "hang up" on NYNEX's attempt to double their monthly bills.

In the fourth month of the strike, facing a major defeat at the PSC and the risk of longer-term disruption of its carefully cultivated relationships with politicians and regulators, NYNEX finally realized it was time to settle. The company threw in the towel on its efforts to introduce weekly payroll deductions for medical coverage; seventeen years later, telephone workers at Verizon (NYNEX's New York/New England successor firm) are still among the 5 percent of all workers with employer coverage who make no premium contributions. "You don't know how grateful the Mine Workers are," Trumka told a group of NYNEX strikers at the AFL-CIO convention in November 1989—just after their settlement and on the eve of one at Pittston. "Our struggle would have been that much more difficult if you had not won your outstanding victory."

Frame Strike Issues Broadly So They Resonate With the Public

In 1997, the contract strike made its biggest comeback in the post-PATCO era with the now-famous walkout by nearly 200,000 United Parcel Service (UPS) workers. How the International Brotherhood of Teamsters (IBT) framed their dispute with UPS was a critical factor in gaining broader public sympathy, along with a tremendous outpouring of rank-and-file union support for UPS drivers and package handlers. The IBT's main objective was to create more full-time jobs by thwarting management's strategy of converting the UPS workforce into a largely part-time one. As in the NYNEX strike, union activists tried to invest the contract fight with larger social meaning—in this case, by declaring in research reports, press releases, and innumerable interviews that "Part-Time America Doesn't Work!" The UPS strike not only beat back the company's concession demands and won the creation of more full-time jobs—it also became a rallying point for everyone concerned about the societal impact of part-timing, with its accompanying erosion of job-based benefits.

Unlike his predecessors, then-Teamster President Ron Carey refused to treat the second-largest contract talks in the country—only General Motors' bargaining was bigger at the time—as a special interest game played out of sight from the membership, their families, and the public. Carey-era IBT staffers Matt Witt and Rand Wilson recall that just "a few hours after picket lines went up, Reuters quoted UPS driver Randy Walls from Atlanta saying, 'We're striking for every worker in America!'" Walls was just one of thousands of rank-and-filers who stayed "on message." Many months of intensive education, discussion, and internal communication within the union's newly created "member-to-member networks" built a broad consensus about UPS bargaining goals and how best to articulate them. UPS is notorious for its authoritarian systems of workforce control and internal propagandizing; nevertheless, the company was caught off guard by the public pummeling it took. "If I had known that it was going to go from negotiating for UPS to negotiating for part-time America, we would have approached it differently," UPS executive John Alden confessed later to *Business Week*.

According to Witt and Wilson, "Polls showed that the public supported the strikers by more than 2 to 1. . . . While some argue that unions must shun the 'militant' image of their past in order to maintain support from members and the public, the UPS experience shows the broad appeal of a labor movement that is a fighter for workers' interests."

Some unions have tried to borrow from the Teamsters' playbook at UPS in more recent contract struggles against health care cost shifting. Between 2001 and 2003, there were plenty of opportunities to do this: health care–related strikes or lockouts broke out among state employees in Minnesota, teachers in New Jersey, janitors in Massachusetts, candymakers in Pennsylvania, food processors in Wisconsin, uranium-plant workers in Kentucky, truck builders in Tennessee, and aerospace workers in Texas. In 2003, major contracts were also up in the telecom, auto, and grocery industries. In each case, management sought to shift the burden of medical cost inflation to active and retired workers.

The question facing unions was how to broaden their defense of negotiated medical benefits when 40 million Americans have no coverage at all, most retirees lack employer-paid health benefits, and workers without unions pay much more for their medical insurance than union members do. If organized labor resists benefit cuts in a way that projects the broader demand for "Health Care for All," it can help create pressure for a political solution that replaces job-based coverage with a system of national health insurance. By positioning themselves as the champion of all workers—not just those with a membership card—unions also stand to gain far greater public sympathy and support.

Labor's record in this regard has been mixed, even as the difficulty of fending off benefit concessions has increased due to the emerging simultaneous management attack on health insurance and pensions. One of the best local examples of coordinated contract-related agitation for health care reform was the June 5, 2003, "Health Care Action Day" sponsored by Massachusetts Jobs with Justice. This cross-union effort at rank-and-file education and workplace activity was endorsed by more than fifty community groups and labor organizations, including nurses, state employees, and utility workers. The sponsors distributed more than 65,000 stickers demanding "Health Care for All." Then, they did the mobilization necessary to get many of their members to wear their stickers on the job on June 5. To increase public visibility and press coverage that day, JWJ also organized informational picketing and noontime rallies around the state, which called for a health care system that "covers everyone, is publicly financed, and saves money . . . by reducing bureaucratic waste." Among the most active participants were General Electric workers (whose national contract was due to expire in several weeks and who had already struck for two days in January over medical coverage) and members of CWA and IBEW at Verizon, whose regional negotiations had just gotten under way.

The UFCW's 2003–4 grocery workers walkout

in Southern California was far less successful in making the connection between management demands for benefit cuts and the need for universal medical coverage. The strike involved 60,000 workers at three major supermarket chains. Many of the strikers were twenty-hour-a-week part-timers whose plight could easily have dramatized the need for real health care reform. Instead, as David Bacon observes, UFCW "picket lines had an air of desperation after the first few weeks." The protracted walkout failed to develop anything near its full potential for community and political support or favorable media coverage; instead of striking a strong and popular political theme, it became a monument to union dysfunction and disorganization. (Since this debacle, the UFCW has become more active in funding state-level health care reform initiatives.)

If Circumstances Require, Stay on the Job—Or Strike Selectively

Union members with a long history of strike activity are sometimes reluctant to deviate from past practice when a contract expires. Yet responding flexibly and creatively to management strike preparations makes more sense than a knee-jerk response that may lead to disaster. Even in the UMW, where the tradition of "no contract, no work" was deeply ingrained, miners at Pittston worked without a contract for fifteen months before their nine-month strike began in 1989. As Dan LaBotz notes in *A Troublemaker's Handbook* 2, "Some strikes are lost when a union simply hits the bricks, without taking the measure of the opponent and what it will take to win." That is why smarter unions are now experimenting with limited-duration walkouts, combined with inside campaigns, to reduce the risk and cost of protracted shutdowns. Working to rule, working without a contract, and "striking while on the job" before walking off the job are good ways of "testing the waters" and "looking before you leap" while gradually ratcheting up the pressure against employers.

Between 1968 and 2003, blue-collar workers at Yale—later joined by white-collar university staffers organized in the mid-1980s—went on strike eight times. In March of 2003, Hotel Employees and Restaurant Employees International Union (HERE) Locals 34 and 35 had been working without a contract for thirteen months. So, joined by graduate student teachers and Yale-New Haven hospital workers, they organized a high-impact five-day strike to press their joint demands. The walkout was accompanied by daily rallies and picketing, culminating in a march by 10,000 strikers and community supporters—the largest demonstration in New Haven in more than thirty years.

As in the past, the union's strike schedule was tactically flexible, tied into the academic calendar, and, at least initially, limited in duration. "As negotiations continued through the summer, the unions built for an open-ended strike," write Steve Hinds and Rob Baril in *A Troublemaker's Handbook* 2. "That strike began in August, when Yale students returned for the Fall semester. The Rev. Jesse Jackson played another active role in this strike, spending an entire week at strike-related events, including a 24-hour sit-in with Yale retirees demanding pension improvements." Faced with civil disobedience, community pressure, and mounting bad publicity, Yale sued for peace in the form of a long-term contract that doubled pension benefits by 2009.

During the same summer and fall, thousands of telephone workers—who had struck five times in the previous two decades—were engaged in regional bargaining with Verizon. In the words of New York Verizon tech Pam Galpern in *A Troublemaker's Handbook* 2, it is a firm with "deep pockets, a highly automated work process, and virulently anti-union top management." According to Galpern:

> Verizon was itching for a strike. . . . Management thought it could outlast the unions, impose its concession demands, raise health co-pays, and eliminate strong job security language that was limiting its ability to move jobs to lower cost states or overseas.

A walkout in August 2003 would have temporarily nullified the effect of an arbitrator's ruling in late July that directed the company to rehire 3,400 workers laid off the previous year in violation of the contract. Confronted with widespread evidence of effective contingency planning by management, IBEW and CWA shifted gears, throwing their corporate adversary off balance. For more than a month, 75,000 union members took the unprecedented step of working without a contract while welcoming back the thousands of laid-off workers who were beneficiaries of the arbitration victory. Verizon incurred enormous strike-preparation costs without getting the opportunity to replace its existing workforce, as planned, with an army of 30,000 managers and contract workers it had lined up around the country.

Instead, there was a high level of on-the-job activity and public agitation against the company from Maine to Virginia. Noted Galpern, "The combined pressure of working to rule, informational pickets, community-supported demonstrations, the arbitrator's ruling upholding the job security language, and the expense of the company's unused contingency plan led Verizon to abandon two of its most important concession demands: that workers pay health care premiums and accept the loss of lay-off protection."

Less than a year later, an even larger group of telephone workers—nearly 95,000 at SBC Communications—faced similar threats to existing medical coverage for active and retired members. Prior to expiration, there had been considerable membership education and mobilization activity in a twelve-state area. However, some CWAers at SBC had not been on strike in twenty years, and their bargaining unit included right-to-work bastions in the South and Southwest. After working under an extension for more than a month, it was time to up the ante. But if the union called an open-ended strike, there was a high risk of immediate picket-line crossing by nonmembers in open-shop states. So instead, CWA organized a four-day warning strike in May 2004 that spanned a weekend when work schedules would be lighter and there could be greater family and community participation in strike rallies, marches, and picnics. Encouraged by strong union member support and workplace organization, almost all 15,000 nonmembers stayed off the job as well—much to SBC's surprise. By the night of the scheduled return to work, a tentative agreement was reached that thwarted health care premium sharing and made job security gains.

Use Employer Lockouts to Union Advantage

Sometimes an effective "inside campaign" will lead an employer to lock out the union members to avoid paying workers for "striking while working" after their contract has expired. Whatever the claimed reason for a lockout, such action puts the onus of responsibility for the dispute on management. This can make it easier to generate public sympathy for the workers involved and definitely puts them in a stronger legal position than strikers under state and federal law.

As attorney Robert Schwartz points out in his book *Strikes, Picketing, and Inside Campaigns*, employers who lock out their employees "may have to pay for unemployment benefits, cannot hire permanent replacements, and may incur an NLRB back-pay order" if the board finds evidence of bad-faith bargaining, unilateral changes, or other unfair labor practices affecting negotiations. In thirty-four states, locked-out workers can qualify for jobless pay, while strikers are eligible for unemployment insurance benefits in just one state (New York). Most important of all, as Schwartz notes, "hiring permanent replacements makes a lockout unlawful." In a strike, if the board finds no bargaining-related unfair labor practices (ULPs) and management properly implements its permanent replacement strategy, workers who walk out may have to wait a lot longer to reclaim their jobs after the dispute ends, because an employer is under no legal obligation to displace their replacements.

Relying on these relative advantages alone is not a winning strategy, however. Seventeen hundred West Virginia mill workers, locked out by Ravenswood Aluminum Company, applied many of the lessons of the Pittston strike in a wide-ranging corporate campaign orchestrated by the United Steel Workers of America (USWA). As Kate Bronfenbrenner and Tom Juravich report, the USWA used international union connections to create problems for key financial institutions and investors tied to the employer. In particular, the union targeted fugitive financier Marc Rich, with the help of European labor allies. Despite massive hiring of replacement workers and other union-busting measures (which produced remarkably little scabbing), Ravenswood was finally forced to end its lockout and settle with the USWA.

> It took the union twenty-two months and an estimated $20 million to beat the company. . . . Rarely had a union plotted such a complex strategy aimed at a company's pressure points away from the picket line. And best of all, Ravenswood's shareholders revolted, leading to the downfall of the company's hard-line president.

A more recent lockout—which shut down all West Coast ports in September 2002—also ended in an important defensive victory because of similar union dexterity in handling a complex bargaining showdown. When their agreement with the Pacific Maritime Association (PMA) expired on July 1, 10,000 members of the International Longshore and Warehouse Union (ILWU) initially worked under day-to-day contract extensions for two months. Meanwhile, its corporate and political enemies raised the specter of dire threats to "homeland security" if the ILWU chose to strike.

There was little progress in negotiations, so the union refused to extend any further. Amid mounting tension, the negotiating committee called for strict membership adherence to all waterfront safety standards. According to journalist and photographer David Bacon, management in turn "accused the union of 'working to rule' and using safety complaints to slow work down." The ensuing retaliatory lockout triggered "doomsday predictions about the economic damage of a 'strike'" with the mainstream media "often forgetting or ignoring the fact that the PMA had locked out the workers." As ILWU organizing director Peter Olney noted:

> Under increasing pressure from the PMA and its biggest customers, President Bush acted on October 8 and went to Federal District Court in San Francisco to enjoin the lock-out and open up the ports. The 80-day cooling-off period prescribed by the Taft-Hartley legislation, never before used against an employer lock-out, provided that both parties had to work at a "normal and reasonable rate" during the 80 days and continue to negotiate and seek an agreement.

The PMA's original strategy was to get this "injunctive relief" and "then press for severe economic and criminal sanctions against the ILWU" based on evidence of a renewed "employee slowdown." Fortunately, the employers association "overplayed its hand." Just prior to Bush's filing for a Taft-Hartley order, federal mediator Peter Hurtgen—with backing from the White House—proposed a thirty-day extension of the old contract instead. The union agreed but the PMA did not.

According to Olney, "When it came time for the Justice Department to decide whether to go after the ILWU for criminal contempt citations, the Department demurred and signaled to the PMA that they would have to negotiate a contract with the ILWU without the increased leverage of court-imposed penalties." The subsequent settlement, which was ratified overwhelmingly in January 2003, increased pensions substantially and averted health care cost shifting, while restoring some outsourced work in return for gradual elimination of about 400 clerk jobs due to the introduction of new technology.

Never Strike Alone

Successful strikes require multiple forms of solidarity—preferably from other workers at the same company, nonstriking members of the same union, and unionized workers generally. There is no sadder sight in labor than a small group of workers—not to mention a large one—ending up on picket lines powerless, impoverished, and alone. In Barbara Koppel's 2002 documentary on the Overnite strike, "American Standoff," we meet many such victims of what *Newsday* labor reporter Ken Crowe called a "banzai strike." As Crowe reported, "1,500 unprepared, unsupported workers" were called off the job in 1999 at forty Overnite trucking facilities around the country. The drivers and dock workers who participated in Teamster President James Hoffa's much-hyped "unfair labor practice" strike had little success, even at the outset of their three-year attempted shutdown. The company's nonunion workforce was four times larger than the minority of Overnite workers who had voted for union representation earlier in the 1990s, when Ron Carey was

IBT president and the union had a well-funded, patiently developed, and nationally coordinated Overnite campaign.

However, by 1999 the union's Overnite worker support apparatus was no longer in place. Teamster freight locals failed to sustain effective mobile picketing of Overnite trucks and some quickly became "no-shows" at other strike events. "From the very beginning," complained one dismayed AFL-CIO field mobilization staffer, "it was a quasi-strike—a virtual walk-out, with no strategy behind it other than taking the workers out. . . ."

"When we went out, we was [*sic*] guaranteed we would have 100,000 Teamsters to back us," says one embittered striker who appears in Koppel's film. "And what have we had? We've had a little money, yeah, but we haven't had shit from the damn Teamsters!"

High-profile strikes and/or lockouts in the 1980s at Hormel and International Paper were among the many that foundered for similar reasons. In much stronger, long-established bargaining units only one part—or a small part—of an employer's total workforce was engaged in the struggle. Workers in other plants had no union or were represented by different unions; union contracts had no common expiration date; and locals pursued their own bargaining agenda due to management pressure or through a lack of national union coordination. The result was contract concessions elsewhere that undercut strike resistance to the same give-back demands, regardless of how determined the strikers themselves proved to be.

In the airline industry, lack of coordinated bargaining, fragmentation in the pattern of union representation, and acrimony between unions have produced some of the worst-case examples of this "divide and conquer" scenario. Strike preparation in such an environment should include a careful assessment of management's ability to weather a walkout and a realistic estimate of the union's likely strike impact, including the reaction of necessary allies. Instead, amidst dreadful choices and angry members, magical thinking sometimes prevails when strike decisions are made.

As labor historian Peter Rachleff observed about the 2004–5 strike by the Aircraft Mechanics Fraternal Association at Northwest Airlines:

> AMFA members, particularly the mechanics, were confident that NWA could not operate effectively without them. Not only were their skills, licenses, and certificates of value, but they felt that their informal knowledge of their airline's plans, rules, and practices made them irreplaceable.

While feisty, democratic, and militant, AMFA was still "a small union" with "no strike fund." It was "not affiliated with the AFL-CIO" and "had little connection with other unions since its emergence on NWA property six years ago." Nevertheless, Rachleff writes:

> With the other NWA unions . . . facing demands for major concessions, AMFA hoped for significant support, perhaps even sympathy strikes (Taft-Hartley's prohibition of which doesn't apply in industries regulated by the Railway Labor Act). AMFA also hoped for help from non-NWA, non-airline unions, who they expected would recognize what stakes they had in this struggle.

When AMFA struck, however, pilots, flight attendants, and IAM-represented baggage handlers at NWA all continued to work while trying to negotiate their own separate concessionary deals under the gun of the company's Chapter 11 bankruptcy proceedings. The 4,400 striking mechanics and cleaners were quickly replaced and reduced to futile airport terminal picketing. As Rachleff, a leading Twin-Cities AMFA supporter, painfully concludes, Northwest management effectively implemented "a well-conceived, well-funded union-busting strategy [that] has caught the attention of corporate managers not only in the airlines industry but throughout the economy."

Rather than recognizing everyone's stake in a major fight against wage cuts and contracting out, many labor officials either denounced AMFA (because it had defeated the IAM, IBT, or Transport Workers in National Mediation Board elections) or simply ignored its pleas for help. Some national unions did discourage their members and staffers from flying on the airline. More significantly, the UAW donated $800,000 to AMFA from its own substantial strike fund. But, most revealingly, neither the AFL-CIO nor its new rival, the Change to Win federation, played any helpful official role (with the AFL actually sending out directives discouraging central labor council assistance to AMFA).

The lesson of AMFA should not be lost on a new generation of would-be strikers expecting to rely on the generosity or strike support capacity of national labor federations. Before (rather than after) walking out, workers must line up solid commitments of grassroots labor and community support by approaching local solidarity coalitions, such as those affiliated with Jobs with Justice.

Take Strike Financing Seriously

Regardless of what form worker militancy takes, it is essential to provide adequate financial support for workers and their families. Even if members of a union are not all out on strike together and most are still working, they can help each other out by setting aside a fixed portion of their dues money for strike assistance. One bottom-line requirement in every union should be a national fund that pays out guaranteed weekly benefits of at least $200 to $300 for strikers, for workers fired for alleged "picket line misconduct," or for the disciplinary casualties of concerted in-plant activity.

In 1989, the 20,000 CWA members who struck NYNEX for four months did not have that kind of safety net. They depleted the entire $28 million balance of CWA's then-underfunded Defense Fund, which doled out the money through local strike committees based on determinations of individual need. To make it through the final weeks of the walkout, CWA had to arrange a special $15 million low-interest loan from the Japanese telephone workers federation, Zendentsu. In the wake of this experience, convention delegates voted to raise CWA's standard dues from 1.15 percent to 1.3 percent of base pay, with the additional revenue earmarked for a new Member Relief Fund (MRF) that would pay out fixed weekly benefits (which increase to $300 in the fifth week of any strike). Local unions were also strongly encouraged to build up their own supplemental strike funds, which the larger ones have done.

Seventeen years later, CWA's MRF is now the second largest in the labor movement (after the UAW's $900 million fund). It has a balance of more than $375 million and is able to pay out large sums even in relatively short strikes. CWA's 75,000-member walkout at Verizon in 2000 lasted less than three weeks but involved a $20 million MRF expenditure. In addition, the union maintains its original Defense Fund, which provides separate contract campaign funding for workers who are prohibited by law from striking and which also pays for strikers' medical expenses and/or COBRA premiums.

Skeptics of this "strike benefit" approach cite the experience of the United Auto Workers during the second of its two Caterpillar strikes in the early 1990s. As *Chicago Tribune* reporter Stephen Franklin reported in his 2001 book, *Three Strikes*, the UAW boosted its payouts to $300 a week for Caterpillar strikers and also paid about $600 per member each month for health benefits. By December 1995, however, between 1,000 and 5,000 UAW members had deserted the fight and the union was forced to sue for peace under terms overwhelmingly rejected by the remaining strikers.

The alternative strike-financing philosophy is best expressed by the always independent—and tough-minded—United Electrical Workers (UE). In its excellent and very detailed guide to "Preparing for and Conducting a Strike," the 25,000-member UE parts company with the few national unions "that pay strikers a set amount per week, regardless of need." UE believes that "the purpose of such financial assistance is not to pay people for being on strike but to make sure that no one is forced back to work because they cannot afford the basic necessities of life. . . . The goal is make sure that all strikers are able to survive for as long as it takes to win an acceptable settlement."

To drive this point home, the UE guide includes the text of a fiery 1968 speech by national officer Jim Matles explaining the basis for the union's "policy on strike assistance":

> Somehow, the idea has gotten around among working people that there is a painless way of striking. A striker doesn't have to picket anymore—he just comes down to the Union to get a weekly check since he is not getting it from his boss. If the Union doesn't give him a check, it's like the company not paying on pay day. . . . We are not going to create any such illusions among our people. We have to try to handle strikes in the way the labor movement has handled them

> for generations. Our people have got to know, in the first place, that a strike means sacrifice.

Matles went on to provide a still-relevant warning about top-down control of fixed-benefit funds. He noted that, "time and again, the rank-and-file turned down the terms of a strike settlement negotiated by the International, but the membership was forced back to work when the International cut off payment of weekly strike benefits." One recent example of this practice occurred during the disastrous 141-day southern California supermarket strike in 2003–4; faced with dwindling funds and, in the view of some observers, the need to soften up strikers for a settlement, UFCW leaders cut their weekly strike pay to $150 or less.

From Matles's perspective in the late 1960s, the fact that "the real meaning of working people striking has been prostituted and corrupted" was "one of the most fundamental problems facing the American trade union movement." Some forty years later, a far bigger problem is the lack of labor movement–wide mechanisms for sustaining strikers and their families. Less than a month before that UFCW's grocery walkout ended in February 2004, the AFL-CIO announced a belated "national campaign" to aid the 60,000 strikers. Yet, having no national relief fund of its own, the labor federation was unable to supplement dwindling UFCW benefits, except through ad hoc fund raising.

During the deliberations a year later about how the AFL-CIO should be changed, CWA lobbied for a system of "national strike insurance for all federation unions." Under CWA's plan, all strikers would be guaranteed to receive "at least $200 per week" and these benefits would "be funded from AFL-CIO per capita dues with rebates for unions that can fund their own benefits at this level." Unfortunately, this proposal received little serious consideration. Thus, in twenty-first century America, labor as a whole continues to handle strikes "the way the labor movement has handled them for generations"—which is to say, not as well as the UE. And the challenge of shifting resources to expand individual union strike capacity has gone largely unmet. Those who will pay the price for this in the future are, of course, rank-and-file members—who deserve better from unions.

See also: The Decline of Strikes, 72; Strikes in the United States Since World War II, 226; Three Strikes Against the New York City Transit System, 277; Strikes in the U.S. Airline Industry, 1919–2004, 577; Teamster Strikes and Organizing, 1934–1964, 601; Striking the Ivory Tower: Student Employee Strikes at Private Universities, 685.

Bibliography

Bacon, David. "A Union on the Line." *The Nation,* October 28, 2002.

Bronfenbrenner, Kate, and Tom Juravich. *Ravenswood: The Steelworkers Victory and the Revival of American Labor.* Ithaca, NY: Cornell University Press, 1999.

Devinatz, Victor G. "A Heroic Defeat: The Caterpillar Labor Dispute and the UAW, 1991–1998." *Labor Studies Journal* 30, no. 2 (Summer 2005): 1–18.

Early, Steve. "The NYNEX Strike: A Case Study in Labor-Management Conflict Over Health Care Cost Shifting." *Proceedings of NYU Annual National Conference on Labor.* New York: Little, Brown & Co., 1991.

Fantasia, Rick, and Kim Voss. *Hard Work: Remaking the American Labor Movement.* Berkeley: University of California Press, 2004.

Franklin, Stephen. *Three Strikes: Labor's Heartland Losses and What They Mean for Working Americans.* New York: Guilford Press, 2001.

Green, James. *Taking History to Heart: The Power of the Past in Building Social Movements.* Amherst, MA: University of Massachusetts Press, 2000.

Kochan, Tom, Andrew von Nordenflycht, Robert McKersie, and Jody Hoffer Gittel. "Airborne Distress: How Can Labor Recover in the Airline Industry?" *New Labor Forum* 14, no. 2 (Summer 2005): 39–51.

Olney, Peter. "On the Waterfront: An Analysis of the ILWU Lockout." *New Labor Forum* (Summer 2003): 33–40.

Witt, Matt, and Rand Wilson. "Part-Time America Won't Work: The Teamsters' Fight for Good Jobs at UPS." In *Not Your Father's Union Movement: Inside the AFL-CIO,* ed. Jo-Ann Mort. New York: Verso Press, 1999.

PART II

STRIKES AND WORKING-CLASS CULTURE

Introduction by Benjamin Day

Labor historians of the past two generations have greatly expanded our understanding of the role that working-class culture plays in shaping the politics of work at every level, from the shop floor to national policy. On the heels of a long debate over the formation of class consciousness within modern capitalism, the 1960s and 1970s brought us a generation of labor historians who moved beyond the history of workers' institutions to focus on the lived experiences of workers and to emphasize the role that sociocultural groupings play in shaping those experiences and the labor movement. This literature has brought the history of strikes into closer proximity to the disciplines of anthropology and sociology, and created a space for labor history to be informed by feminist research, African-American and post-emancipation studies, queer theory, religious studies, immigration histories, and many other fields of study.

The rich sociocultural backdrop against which every strike plays out directly informs its outcome as well as its importance for other workers. Beyond the impact that working-class cultures have on individual strikes, the cultural institutions that shape the labor movement as a whole mold the norms of who may and who may not strike and when, and they often set the boundaries of solidarity. Strikes are significant not only for their economic goals or their attempts to win dignity, respect, and self-control over working lives, but also for their ability to challenge and transform these cultural institutions. By striking, workers often challenge a broader set of norms and social institutions, for better or for worse, from civil rights strikes through hate strikes.

The lived experience of striking, as glimpsed through strikers' cultural backgrounds and cultural innovations, also offers a unique window into labor history and the transformation of work. A growing amount of literature in the United States has explored the importance of workplace control as a locus of class conflict, as opposed to "bread and butter" demands such as wages and benefits. This literature has led labor historians to reevaluate the cause and purpose of strikes and has generated a renewed emphasis on the relationships between workplace and working-class cultures, particularly as these relationships shape who controls work and how. Employers have long attempted to create shop-floor institutions of control that echo broader social institutions, relegating women, people of color, or immigrants to an underclass of workers. Unions have often participated in these processes. Strikes have constituted an important form of resistance to workplace subjugation, and they have often been part of broader movements in opposition to social subjugation.

Culture connects labor markets to other social institutions—from the church to the political party. Through these ties, a strike becomes more than a struggle between workers and their employers, but a struggle that mobilizes and challenges society and indelibly etches workplace relations with the mark of social relations.

DRESSED FOR DEFIANCE: THE CLOTHING OF FEMALE STRIKERS, 1910–1935

Deirdre Clemente

Long before latter-day feminists worried about the glass ceiling, their great grandmothers, from the garment shops of the Lower East Side to the cotton mills of North Carolina, strode picket lines for better working conditions, higher wages, and freedom from sexual harassment. From 1881 to 1905 workers in the clothing, hat, millinery, hosiery, and knit goods industries went on 2,500 strikes that involved more than 850,000 workers. From 1914 to 1926, the number of strikes rose to 3,563 and the number of strikers reached over a million. While modern-day scholars have neglected to examine the clothing of these "girl strikers" (a term the press applied to all women on the picket line, regardless of age), the contemporary press paid close attention to their ensembles, interpreting their outfits down to the last bit of lace. In 1913, the *New York Times* reported of strikers, "They were well-dressed and did not show the life of drudgery to which the strike leaders say they are exposed." Even when women strikers were on trial for their actions on the picket line, the press paid more attention to their togs than their testimony. When Sophie Melvin faced murder charges in 1929 for an accidental death of a plant guard in Gastonia, North Carolina, the papers focused on her dress; it was "powder blue" and "set off perfectly the natural beauty for which she was praised by so many of the people outside the courtroom."

The attention paid to the appearance of the female strikers speaks to the importance of women's clothing in the development of their social, cultural, and political identities. Malcolm Bernard, a scholar of material culture, has contended that clothing is "used not only to constitute and communicate a position in [the] social order, but also to challenge and contest positions of relative power within it." Historian Nan Enstad has written that fashion carries "a diverse range of cultural meanings that have political valences in the context of a strike" and that "it should not be surprising that public discussion of the mass strike recurrently focused on women's styles."

This essay focuses on two periods of women's strike activity in the garment and textile industries. The first is the period from 1909 to 1913, during which garment and textile workers engaged in dozens of strikes, including the Shirtwaist Strike of 1909 and the "Bread and Roses" strike in Lawrence, Massachusetts, in 1912. The second period, which is the late 1920s and early 1930s, involved the next generation of American working women and included the deadly conflicts in Gaston County, North Carolina, in 1929 and the General Textile Strike of 1934. These strikes exposed how women on the picket line used clothing to redefine their place on the American socioeconomic landscape.

This evolution, of course, was inevitably affected by the sweeping changes that took place between 1909 and 1929—suffrage, World War I, the "flapper" era, the rise of media culture, especially the film industry. Nevertheless, with clothing worn on the picket line at the center of the analysis, much can be learned about how these strikers defined themselves as both Americans and women. To differing degrees, both generations used tricolored pins and flags to remind onlookers that they, too, were Americans. The strikers' clothing also illustrated the changing notions of femininity; the first wave of strikers dressed in elaborate hats and fur muffs to associate themselves with prevailing ideals of ladylike behavior, while strikers in the late 1920s and early

1930s often wore men's work clothing. Strikers also used their clothing as a show of solidarity; white, a color with no gradations, was the shade of choice. These fashion choices illuminate the changing notions of what it meant to be a modern American working woman.

Clothing as a Reflection of National Identity

Garment and textile workers were but one group of American women to protest labor conditions during the first half of the twentieth century. Domestic workers, waitresses, and department store clerks also took to the picket line in an effort to improve their circumstances. However, garment and textile workers offer unique case studies for two distinct reasons. First, such workers, by the very nature of their occupation, were kept abreast of fashion trends and many of these women coveted *au courant* clothing. Turn-of-the-century sweatshop workers operated machinery in calfskin heels and saved for silk underwear. In the 1930s, *Labor News,* whose primary audience was factory workers, carried multiple articles in each issue on the latest styles, including reports from Paris. As producers of clothing, these working women experienced the ebb and flow of the American fashion system; their very livelihoods were tied to it.

Second, and more significantly, the garment and textile industries were plagued by labor unrest during the first half of the century, markedly so in the years around 1910 and then again in the early 1930s—years that saw great social and cultural change in the United States. The Shirtwaist Strike of 1909 and the textile strikes two decades later are informative because they involved women strikers who had previously not been organized. Young and systematically neglected by male-dominated unions, both sets of strikers arose in protests that were spontaneous in nature and heavily documented in the popular and labor press.

Women textile and garment workers in the early twentieth century were either immigrants themselves or the children of immigrants; on strike, they cautiously waved American flags and marched in sync to protest songs. Their daughters in the early 1930s, however, felt entitled to their rights as Americans and draped their bodies in flags as they threw rocks at national guardsmen. This shift in self-perception was the outgrowth of social and cultural changes, including a pronounced sense of national pride during and after World War I and the growth of female-friendly labor unions.

In the waning months of 1909, nearly 30,000 shirtwaist makers went on strike, and 80 percent of them were women. Estimates from the era placed half of the women working in the dress and waist industry as under the age of twenty; most were single immigrants. Historian Kathie Friedman-Kasaba noted that the majority of the shirtwaist strikers were Jewish women (nearly 21,000 by her account) and at least 2,000 were Italian women. Only seven percent of the strikers were native born. Their employment was largely seasonal and they were laid off according to the tides of production. Busy seasons were three months in the spring and another three in the early fall. In between these bursts of activity, it was common for 30 percent of the workforce to be dismissed, and few women were able to sustain yearlong employment.

To a large degree, these newcomers to America viewed the garment shops as an intermediary phase between childhood and marriage. Sociologist Roger Waldinger wrote that during this era "female participation in the labor force reflected the income dynamics and life-cycle patterns of the immigrant family." The transience of the labor supply, coupled with the seasonality of production, had historically kept the shirtwaist workers from organizing—fewer than 10,000 of New York City's 350,000 female workers were unionized at the turn of the century. Perhaps more poignant than practical obstacles, social dicta severely hampered immigrant women's involvement with organized labor.

The social constraints of an immigrant family were aptly documented in *The Diary of a Shirtwaist Striker,* a propagandistic journal written by Theresa Serber Malkiel, a female participant in the labor movement, and published in 1912. The young woman had confrontations with both her boyfriend and her immigrant father due to her involvement with the strike. Her father argued, "I don't think it's a woman place to be hangin' around street corners, fighting with rowdies. [The] Union . . . was never meant for the women."

Labor newspapers of the era also illustrated the difficulty of organizing female workers. *The Labor Leader* wrote in 1910, "When you first invite girls to a union meeting most of them will poke their pompadours up a little on the side, arrange their belts before the mirror and give you a superior smile. They are altogether too ladylike to attend trade union meetings." Divisions based on ethnic background contributed to the lack of organization of female garment and textile workers because the first generation of strikers still considered themselves to be Italian, Russian, or Polish rather than American. Indeed, the workplace served as a means of helping these women reconstruct their ethnic identities. As labor historian Sarah Eisenstein wrote, "Going to work was sometimes an important influence, along with school, in the 'Americanization' of immigrant women, particularly the younger among them."

One symbol of cross-ethnic alliance was the American flag. Photographs of the shirtwaist strikers showed women wearing tricolored pins on their coat lapels and hats. It was also common to see the shirtwaist strikers and those participating in strikes around the same time waving American flags or carrying one as a banner while they walked. As one newspaper reporter noted, "Most of the marchers carried small American flags to show their patriotism."

As the children of the earlier strikers became Americanized, spoke English, and participated in the development of consumer culture, a stronger sense of national identity emerged among them, and the clothing of the hopeful "girl strikers" reflected this change. Two decades and a war later, the sense of patriotism illustrated on the picket line in 1909 again resurfaced, but in a much more overt manner. When mill owners in New Bedford, Massachusetts, announced a 10 percent wage cut in early April 1928, they violated a promise to give workers a thirty-day notice of pay changes. The result was one of the longest and most violent strikes in the history of the textile industry. More than 20,000 strikers actively picketed for six months in the face of New England summer weather and police brutality. Half of New Bedford's mill workers were women; they became militant and dedicated strikers.

Mass protests saw many of these women take to the streets dressed in red, white, and blue. They were known as "liberty girls," and some, such as Mary Costa, dressed as Lady Liberty herself. Following the actions of the liberty girls via newspapers and accounts by union organizers, other female strikers in other areas of the country picked up on the style and used it on their own picket lines.

In March 1929, the Bemberg plant and Glanzstoff rayon mill in Elizabethton, Tennessee, saw one of the first in a series of textile strikes that would plague the South well into the mid-1930s. Women held 30 percent of the jobs at Bemberg and 44 percent at the larger Glanzstoff mill. The clash between strikers and the National Guard resulted in 1,250 arrests, including many women. On the first day of the strike, "hundreds of girls had driven down main street in buses and taxis shouting and laughing at people who watched them from windows and doorsteps." Many of the women wore American flags as shawls and were dressed in red, white, and blue. As flag-clad picketers marched down the town's Bemberg Highway, their patriotic apparel "forced guardsmen to present arms each time they passed."

Historian Jacquelyn Dowd Hall wrote about the most flamboyant of the Elizabethton girl strikers, Trixie Perry and her friend Texas Bill, named for her affinity for cowboy-inspired attire. A single mother, Perry worked as a reeler at the Glanzstoff mill and was brought to trial for taunting the National Guard. In a dress made from tricolored fabric and a cap sewn from a small American flag, Trixie Perry took the stand. A prosecuting attorney began his questioning not with the events of the day in question but with the striker's queer ensemble.

> "You have a United States flag as a cap on your head?"
>
> "Yes."
>
> "Wear it all the time?"
>
> "Whenever I take a notion."
>
> "You are dressed in a United States flag, and the colors?"
>
> "I guess so. I was born under it, guess I have a right to."

The words of Trixie Perry illustrate the fundamental shift in how women workers came to identify themselves. The influence of immigrant parents and the divisions over ethnic identities that had marked *The Diary of a Shirtwaist Striker* held less sway over a second generation of women who considered themselves Americans. Unions that had for twenty years been struggling to retain women were by the mid-1930s a powerful and vocal force on the American labor scene.

During the 1920s, however, the trade union activities of women were on the decline. In her 1929 article "Trade Union Activities of Women," economist Theresa Wolfson analyzed the decrease of female union members in the 1920s. According to the 1920 census, there were 368,508 women working in the clothing industry and 471,466 working in textiles. Wolfson's figures suggested that between 1920 and 1927, the number of female union members in the clothing industry dropped from 172,700 to 101,409. In the textile industry, they dropped from 40,500 to 20,700. She attributed these decreases to unstable leadership and a depressed market.

Yet the late 1920s saw the return of workers to unions, as membership drives fueled by labor unrest revived interest. Organizing and keeping Southern members proved to be a difficult task, however. In his 1931 *Journal of Political Economy* article "Aspects of Southern Textile Unionism," economist G.T. Schwenning discussed the difficulty in keeping cotton-mill workers interested in the union as "few are cognizant of the history and objectives of the labor-union, or its possibilities in advancing their collective cause."

While the sustained membership and staying power of these unions was limited, the image of the American working woman proved enduring. As political and cultural currents stressed the importance of being "American," girl strikers from the second generation felt they were entitled to the same standard of living as the rest of the country. The government's call for patriotism shown via war work had cast a new kind of American working woman nearly a decade before. As historian Maureen Weiner Greenwald wrote, "Economic, social, and political conditions unique to the war gave women confidence in their power to improve their economic status." The picketing cotton-mill worker may not have been one of the women working in the artillery industry during the war, but in many respects she was her legacy.

Clothing as a Reflection of Changing Notions of Gender

As these working women claimed their rights as Americans, their behavior and attire reflected changing notions of femininity. While working women at the turn of the century saved to buy a new hat or to treat a friend to a movie, the second generation of girl strikers was surrounded by a popular culture brimming with store-bought clothing and long-lasting lipstick. Newspapers from both eras described the girl strikers as "well dressed." Interestingly, while women in both the 1910s and the 1930s attempted to look their best on the picket lines, their motivation stemmed from generally different aims. Early shirtwaist strikers used their clothing to associate themselves with traditions of ladyhood; the second generation used clothing to attract attention to themselves as liberated, sexual beings and to flaunt their financial independence. This shift in gender identity specific to the picket line was illustrative of broader social change. As historian Kate De Castelbajac noted, in post–World War I America there existed "an emphasis on beauty that was sexually, rather than socially codified."

In the case of the first generation of strikers, the evolution of the ready-made clothing industry, advancements in textile production, and more media outlets for disseminating current trends ensured working-class women access to and knowledge of the clothing deemed fashionable by the upper classes. While their actions flew in the face of tradition, their clothing, to a large degree, was in keeping with society's vision of feminine attire.

Photographs from the strikes showed women marching in styles that could also be seen at any gathering of middle-class women; their garments were, at first glance, very similar. Girl strikers used form-altering undergarments to achieve the cinched waist that dominated fashion in the first decade of the twentieth century, and few went without the era's omnipresent oversized picture hat. Fur accessories, jewelry, and lace collars were symbolic of the women's adherence to society's standards of female attire. Enstad noted that when the shirtwaist strikers walked off the job in late 1909, they "did so as ladies; they could not do otherwise. The practices of ladyhood had shaped who they were and had centrally formed their public identities."

While the clothing of the shirtwaist strikers reinforced their "ladyhood," it also represented the working-class woman's creative take on fashionable styles—an interpretation that spoke clearly to the goals and aspirations of the immigrant women. As sociologist Diana Crane asserted in her book *Fashion and Its Social Agendas*, "For these [working] women, dressing in fashionable clothes was a way of showing their knowledge of American culture, of rejecting their traditional ethnic culture, and of expressing their own identities." The clothing indicated not only who the girl strikers were but who they hoped to become.

Much to the chagrin of middle-class union organizers, working women tended to overdo their attempts to be in vogue, and in doing so created a style uniquely their own. Barbara Schreier wrote in a study of Jewish garment workers in New York, "They sampled, mixed, and reassembled the decorative with the practical to create a range of hybrid styles . . . [A]sserting their cultural agency, working-class young women actively created their own standards of dress." With cheap trimmings, working women adorned hats with multiple feathers, faux flowers, and oversized bows for an ultra-fussy style in an already fussy era of fashion.

When a number of middle- and upper-class women who were mostly suffragettes joined the lines to assist the strikers, the laborers' colorful ensembles became a particular issue of contention. While the Edwardian palette leaned toward the conservative, the bright hues of the women's wardrobes enraged suffragettes and labor leaders who thought the colors were garish and distracting to the cause. One suffragette, Rose Pastor, wrote, "Now, you cannot deny, girls, that some of you wear a combination of dress that equals Joseph's coat of many colors."

Anzia Yezierska's novel of immigrant life on the Lower East Side, *Bread Givers,* offered one explanation for their efforts: "Give a look only on these roses for my hat (cried Mashas) . . . Like a lady from Fifth Avenue I look, and for only ten cents, from a pushcart on Hester Street." These exaggerated styles, complete with oversized bows and silk stockings, were an attempt to remind the public—and themselves—that, despite their status as working class, they were first and foremost ladies.

The appearance of these women—some clad in fur, others sporting watches and lockets—was a problem to middle-class strike leaders who played to society's pity and sought to portray the workers as frail and downtrodden. Reports in the press continually noted the elaborateness of the strikers' clothing. In *Collier's,* Sarah Comstock wrote of the shirtwaist strikers in 1909, "I had come to observe the Crisis of a Social Condition, but apparently this was a Festive Occasion. Lingerie waists were elaborate, puffs towered; there were picture turbans and di'mont pendants." Labor leaders reacted by reiterating time and again that while the girls' clothing was fashionable, it was poorly made and unable to withstand the rigors of their relentless toil. A 1913 study of Italian women in the garment industry reaffirmed this notion. The author documented the clothing purchases for several different working women, and most had to buy three or more pairs of shoes a year due to their poor quality.

Interestingly, the girl strikers could blend in with middle-class women when they so aspired—or were instructed. On several occasions, "college girls" from Vassar and Bryn Mawr came to picket alongside the strikers. The *New York Times* reported on December 19, 1909, "The public does not know and can not discriminate the college girls" who also "wore the garment of contention." The involvement of these college-educated young women saved many girl strikers from going to jail, as police were afraid to arrest the "wrong" protesters.

Southern women's clothing on the picket line in the late 1920s and early 1930s revealed new notions of femininity, but their ensembles attracted just as much inquiry from the popular press. Gaston County, North Carolina had 100 cotton mills, more than any other county in the nation. It was home to cities such as Belmont and Gastonia, which were locations of persistent labor unrest. Cora Harris, a reporter for the *Charlotte Observer*, covered the strikes in Gaston County in 1929. She wrote that strikers were "dressed in their gay Easter frocks and a few with spring coats. I was particularly attracted by the popularity of silk stockings." Again, the press was expecting the strikers to appear downtrodden and ill-clad.

The young women on the picket lines were active consumers of fashion, as illustrated by the tale of Flossie Cole, a striker from the Bemberg plant. While Flossie's mother "could look at a picture in a catalog and cut a pattern and make a dress just like it," upon receiving her first paycheck she went to the store and bought "a blue dress and black shoes—patent leather, honey, and real high heels—and a blue hat."

While many Southern women strikers embraced feminine accoutrements, such as hosiery and high heels, others did not. One culturally charged article of clothing seen time and again on the picket line were overalls, a favorite of young women. The masculine styles of the era might have made overalls more acceptable. For middle- and upper-class women, the oversized cardigan sweaters and two-piece suits of Gabrielle "Coco" Chanel reflected the subtle appropriation of men's clothing that characterized the times. Such clothing tended to androgynize the body, as did flat, two-dimensional silhouettes and child-like cropped haircuts. Nonetheless, the outright adoption of men's working wear in a public forum was nearly revolutionary.

Female workers had first worked in "special 'feminine' trousered uniforms" in the munitions factories during the war. Women and magazine writers alike feared the social repercussions of females wearing overalls—even in a patriotic capacity. *World's Work* had promised in June 1917 that women's contribution to the war "will not consist in putting on trousers or an unbecoming uniform and trying to do something that a man can do better." The publication was soon proven wrong; newspaper accounts of war workers told of women who "wear overalls, do a man's work and receive a man's wages." After the war, when men returned to the factories, women—even those who remained in heavy labor—commonly went back to wearing more feminine work clothing.

When overalls were seen on the picket line in the late 1920s, community reaction was most often outrage. The local newspaper correspondent for the *Gastonia Daily Gazette* wrote in disbelief, "I have seen young girls, I mean strikers, going up and down the street with old overalls on and men's caps, with the bills turned behind, cursing us, calling the cops all kind of dirty things." The correspondent for the *Labor Defender,* the paper of the Communist-controlled International Labor Defense, mentioned the overalls with much less disdain in May 1929. He noted, "How happy they are, the young folks, to be taking part in the strike. They are thrilled; the young girls laugh; some have on overalls; they flirt."

Perhaps more pertinent than the fact that women were wearing overalls on the picket lines were the accessories they selected. *The Charlotte News* noted on April 6, 1929, "To the younger girls in the mill village, the strike is a thrilling affair. Many of them wear knickers or overalls, not at all disconcerted by the contrast of these utilitarian garments with long collars or other feminine adornments." Here, just as with the shirtwaist strikers' creative take on middle-class clothing twenty years before, the girl strikers of the late 1920s exhibited their own hybridized style. The juxtaposition of "feminine adornments" with masculine working garments seemed to embody the girl strikers' fundamental struggle for a cultural identity. Hair barrettes, necklaces, and blouses were worn with the overalls and were readily apparent in photographs of the era.

Unlike the exaggerated feminine accoutrements of the previous generation, the clothing worn by the "modern" girl striker was not meant to reinforce established notions of femininity. On the contrary, these "girls" were asserting themselves as a new wave of American working women. As opposed to the frail, downtrodden shirtwaist strikers who were the charity cases of socially conscious Fifth Avenue ladies, the girl strikers emerging in late 1920s were not looking for pity. The newspaper *Hosiery Worker* reported in 1932, "Be it cotton, be it silk, the American working girl wears what Fashion dictates with a dash and a verve. She manages to look like a debutante, much to the amazement and chagrine [*sic*] of the cotton kings' daughters." The girl strikers sported clothing that represented a redefinition of what women wore and how they wore it.

White Clothing as a Symbol of Solidarity

The clothing worn by women on the picket line between 1909 and 1934 speaks to the development of an American identity and changing notions of femininity. The difference between the prim shirtwaist striker and the cursing cotton-mill girl was profound, but commonalities existed. During both eras, female garment and textile strikers commonly wore white to speak to the strikers' uniformity in action.

White accessories such as ribbons, armbands, and hats appeared at strikes both in the United States and abroad in an effort to distinguish between those who were with the cause and those who were not. Armbands often carried slogans or words of encouragement. In Lawrence, Massachusetts, in 1912, strikers wore white armbands that read, "Don't be a scab!" Dressing entirely in white was a technique commonly used by women, particularly during parades or rallies. When a general garment workers strike was declared in Cleveland in 1909, women from a diverse range of industrial backgrounds took to the streets in protest. The younger ones were "garbed in white" and "wore bright ribbons and gay flowers." White was again the color of choice when the mill girls marched in a Labor Day parade just days before the General Textile Strike of 1934. Many were clad in above-the-knee skirts and short-sleeved white shirts. Some had on white sailor hats. Many wore signs on their backs that read, "Textile Workers Get Ready."

Why strikers continually selected the color white is unclear. Suffragettes used a similar technique in their campaign for the vote. Perhaps the strikers were attempting to associate themselves with innocence or purity. More likely, strikers wore white because it was a common color and one that most would have in their wardrobes.

Curiously, while women strikers used white to show unity, their leaders often wore a single color to distinguish themselves on the picket line. Union leader Ann Burlak, known as "the Red Flame," was a key player in New England during the General Textile Strike of 1934. She was a vibrant orator and always dressed entirely in red from hat to suit to matching shoes. Another lesser-known figure was sixteen-year-old Rita Brouliette, known to police and guardsmen as "the girl in green." She was spotted in a green sweater at a strike-turned-riot in Saylesville, Rhode Island, in 1934 before reappearing at demonstrations in Worchester, Massachusetts, where she wore a green dress. Burlak's color of choice connoted her political sympathies; Brouliette's reasoning is as mysterious as the girl herself. Both would have been easy to spot in a crowd.

Conclusion

The study of the clothing of these two groups of girl strikers sheds light on the evolution of women in the workforce during the first third of the twentieth century. The first generation of strikers held American flags as they picketed; the second generation dressed in American flags. The first protestors used clothing to flaunt their femininity; their daughters dressed in ways that redefined what it meant to be feminine.

While their wardrobes were as different as their mind-sets, both groups of girl strikers developed a "hybrid" style of dress to wear on the picket line. For the shirtwaist strikers, it was overstylized frills and furbelows. For the mill worker, it was menswear mixed with makeup. Each generation creatively juxtaposed socially acceptable trends with more radical attire. In doing so, these "girl strikers" demonstrated that they both simultaneously adhered to and rejected society's image of womanhood.

In each era, the public presentation of this dichotomy was met with contempt and confusion from the popular press. While both sets of strikers established their own customized styles, their ensembles were remarkably different, reflecting fundamental shifts in American culture. On the most basic level, women's fashion did change radically beginning in 1912, with the introduction of new styles that allowed for more freedom of movement and called for less constraining undergarments. The fashion industry and the manufacturing world underwent dramatic change as well, due in part to the turnover in clothing trends, the birth of modern media, and the shift in textile production from the North to the South. Yet the clothing these women chose to wear in the public sphere in the context of a strike offers much insight into social and cultural change. The evolution of the girl striker is but one example of how the study of clothing can add texture and tangibility to American history. By examining what she wore on her body, one can see how the face of the girl striker changed in the first half of the last century—mirroring the mindset of the American woman.

See also: Better Than a Hundred Speeches: The Strike Song, 103; North Carolina Women on Strike, 154; Twentieth-Century Textile Workers, 330; Garment Worker Strikes, 342.

Bibliography

Barnard, Malcolm. *Fashion as Communication.* London: Routledge, 1996.

De Castelbajac, Kate. *The Face of the Century: 100 Years of Makeup & Style.* New York: Thames & Hudson, 1995.

Eisenstein, Sarah. *Give Us Bread But Give Us Roses: Working Women's Consciousness in the United States, 1890 to the First World War.* London: Routledge & Kegan Paul, 1983.

Enstad, Nan. "Fashioning Political Identities: Cultural Studies and the Historical Construction of Political Subjects." *American Quarterly* 50, no. 4 (December 1998): 745–82.

Enstad, Nan. *Ladies of Labor, Girls of Adventure: Working Women, Popular Culture, and Labor Politics at the Turn of the Twentieth Century.* New York: Columbia University Press, 1999.

Friedman-Kasaba, Kathie. *Memories of Migration: Gender, Ethnicity, and Work in the Lives of Jewish and Italian Women in New York, 1870–1924.* Albany: State University of New York Press, 1996.

Greenwald, Maurine Weiner. *Women, War, and Work: The Impact of World War I on Women Workers in the United States.* Westport, CT: Greenwood Press, 1980.

Hall, Jacquelyn Dowd. "Disorderly Women: Gender and Labor Militancy in the Appalachian South." *Journal of American History* 73 (September 1986): 354–82.

Schreier, Barbara. *Becoming American Women: Clothing and the Jewish Immigrant Experience, 1880–1920.* Chicago: Chicago Historical Society, 1994.

Waldinger, Roger. "International Ladies Garment Workers Union: Women, Industry Structure and Collective Action." In *Women, Work & Protest,* ed. Ruth Milkman. Boston: Routledge & Kegan Paul, 1985.

Wolfson, Theresa. "Trade Union Activities of Women." *Annals of the American Academy of Political and Social Science* 143 (May 1929): 120–31.

Yezierska, Anzia. *Bread Givers.* New York: Persea Press, 1990 (1925).

"BETTER THAN A HUNDRED SPEECHES": THE STRIKE SONG

Timothy P. Lynch

As Ella May Wiggins's coffin was lowered into the ground, Katie Barrett sang Ella May's best-loved song, "Mill Mother's Lament."

> We leave our homes in the morning,
> We kiss our children good bye
> While we slave for the bosses
> Our children scream and cry.
>
> And when we draw our money
> Our grocery bills to pay,
> Not a cent to pay for clothing,
> Not a cent to lay away.
>
> And on that very evening,
> Our little son will say:
> "I need some shoes, Mother,
> And so does sister May."
>
> How it grieves a heart of a mother,
> You everyone must know,
> But we can't buy for our children
> Our wages are too low.
> It is for our little children,
> That seem to us so dear,
> But for us nor them, dear workers,
> The bosses do not care.
>
> But understand, all workers,
> Our union they do fear;
> Let's stand together, workers,
> And have a union here.

Wiggins's five children stood by the gravesite, hearing the words their mother had composed. Perhaps only the eldest, Myrtle, understood why her mother had died. Her coworkers, however, believed she had been singled out, shot to death as she rode in a truck with other strikers to a union meeting. As one striker, quoted in *Strikes Songs of the Depression Decade,* explained, "The bosses hated Ella May because she made up songs, and was always at the speakings. They aimed to git Ella May. They was after her." There had, in fact, been an earlier attempt to poison her water supply.

Whether or not the shooting of Ella May was a deliberate act may never be proven. But what is certain is that Ella May's music, which emerged from a textile strike in Gastonia, North Carolina, in 1929, tells a compelling and revealing story. In "Mill Mother's Lament," mill work not only creates family disruption by separating mothers from their children, but this sacrifice fails to bring in enough money to raise a family. In an industry dominated by female labor, it is not surprising that strike songs, such as Ella May's composition, address the particular concerns of women as they struggled with the dual roles of breadwinner and caregiver for their families. Ella May's song, which was so popular with her fellow workers, promotes unionization in the name of motherhood, inextricably connecting class with gender. And by modeling her song on "Little Mary Phagan," Ella May drew upon the memories of many workers who were familiar with the 1913 murder of Mary Phagan at an Atlanta pencil factory allegedly by her boss, Leo Frank. This connection, between the victimization of Mary Phagan and that of mill children by company bosses, would have conjured powerful images and emotions in the minds and hearts of the workers who heard Ella May's song. Presented in this manner, striking and union organizing become an extension of the role of mother: protecting, nurturing, and caring for her children.

Moreover, the fact that "Little Mary Phagan" had been released on Columbia Records in 1925, selling approximately 300,000 copies, suggests the influence of the emerging mass consumer culture on song-making during the strike.

As "Mill Mother's Lament" illustrates, strike songs could send a message of collective action and worker solidarity in terms reflective of workers' gender and class identity. In addition, the shared experience of singing strike songs provided the very means by which that message was communicated. As workers' most common form of performative expression, singing brought strikers together both physically and emotionally. The communal experience of singing provided striking workers with an opportunity to vent their frustrations and assert their strength, instilling in them a sense of their own power. Although strike songs were most often the creation of one individual, sometimes two, they communicated shared feelings, thoughts, and values. In this way, strike songs helped build community and class consciousness among workers.

The spontaneity with which many strike songs were written rendered them roughhewn. But the fact that they were composed as events unfolded makes them particularly valuable documents of the labor unrest that engendered them. Strike songs capture the sorrows and desires, complaints and worries, concerns and anxieties of strike participants. As statements from the strikers themselves, then, strike songs provide insight into the lives of workers, giving voice to those who might otherwise be deemed inarticulate.

For their part, union organizers knew well the practical uses of song-making and singing during a strike. Strike songs stated the union's demands and provided potent propaganda for the cause. Singing boosted the morale of those on picket lines and in union halls. Singing was also used to raise strike funds, providing needed financial support for striking workers. Singing was sometimes used to open and conclude union meetings, as if to serve as an invocation and benediction to the proceedings. Singing was even employed as a diversionary tactic during one strike, distracting company police as strikers took possession of a critical factory. Union organizers understood what journalist Margaret Larkin, quoted in *Strike Songs of the Depression,* had recognized in 1929 as she listened to Ella May's "song ballets." Strike songs were "better than a hundred speeches."

Labor, Freedom, and God

Singing within the labor movement was long believed to be uncommon in the nineteenth century, before the rise of the Industrial Workers of the World with their *Little Red Song Book.* However, the publication of Philip Foner's *Labor Songs of the Nineteenth Century* exploded this misconception. Foner gathered more than 550 songs from the pages of the American labor press. Moreover, virtually every issue that faced American labor during the nineteenth century was addressed in song. As Foner writes: "The songs and ballads in labor papers dealt with the organizations and struggles of working people, their hatred for the oppressor, their affirmation of the dignity and worth of labor, their determination to endure hardships together and to fight together for a better life. There is scarcely a single important issue of labor struggle in nineteenth-century America which is not represented in . . . song." Of course, not all labor songs emanated from strikes—but many did, representing various industries and a range of labor issues.

It is difficult to know how many of these songs were actually sung, since publication in the labor press does not necessarily mean that the composition was ever performed. Undoubtedly some were, and others were not. There is much evidence that singing did occur at meetings, strikes, and demonstrations. Clearly workers were advancing their cause in song long before the Wobblies' concerted efforts.

In 1836, young women mill workers in Lowell, Massachusetts, went on strike to protest a series of wage cuts. They formed the Factory Girls Association and as 1,500 of them paraded in a strike demonstration, according to Foner they sang:

> Oh! Isn't it a pity that such a pretty girl as I
> Should be sent to the factory to pine away
> and die?
> Oh! I cannot be a slave;
> I will not be a slave,
> For I'm so fond of liberty
> That I cannot be a slave.

Still in the afterglow of the American Revolution and at a time of increasing sectional tensions, the references to liberty and slavery drew on rhetoric common to the period. The Lowell girls' association of their situation with slavery invoked a comparison often made in antebellum America between the slave-based economy of the South and the wage-labor system of the North.

The Lowell strike collapsed after a month, with many of the girls returning home after being evicted from their boarding houses. But others followed the example of their "pretty sisters at Lowell." The same year, strikers at a mill in Steubenville, Ohio, sang of the dignity of labor when they demanded "Reward for toil by us is craved." They, too, according to Foner, invoked liberty and denounced wage slavery:

> Reward for toil by us is craved,
> And Fortune has a scheme contrived:
> Then why should Weavers be enslaved
> And basely of their rights deprived?
> Weavers, be firm, and never flee,
> We have been bound but will be free!

A large strike occurred just months before shots were fired at Fort Sumter when wage reductions among shoemakers set off a walkout that began in Lynn and Natick, Massachusetts, and spread to a number of other New England towns. Unions emerged in over twenty-five towns, as some 20,000 workers went out on strike. Commenting on the strike, the Republican candidate for the presidency, Abraham Lincoln, connected the struggle of the shoemakers with the anti-slavery cause that would soon bring civil war. According to Foner, he said, "I am glad to see that a system of labor prevails in New England under which laborers can strike when they want to, where they are not obliged to labor whether you pay them or not. I like the system which lets a man quit when he wants to, and wish it might prevail elsewhere. One of the reasons why I am opposed to slavery is just here." The shoemakers' strike lasted a month and secured a wage increase for the workers, spreading the influence of unions in many towns previously unorganized. "The Shoemakers' Song," sung to the tune of "Yankee Doodle," gave the composition a patriotic mantle. Quoted by Foner, the first verse and refrain went as follows:

> Ye jours and snobs throughout the land,
> 'Tis time to be astir;
> The Natick boys are all on hand,
> And we must not demur.
>
> *Refrain:*
> Up and let us have a strike;
> Fair prices we'll demand.
> Firmly let us all unite,
> Unite throughout the land.

Following the Civil War, with the decline of artisan production, the rise of mass industries, and the commodification of labor, strike songs increasingly touched on the widening divide between workers and employers. The strike wave of 1877, which included a national railroad strike, general strikes in St. Louis and Chicago, and the government's use of force to suppress workers' protest in multiple states, inspired several such songs. "The Strike" clearly articulates the class antagonisms that energized the struggle. Indeed, as quoted by Foner, the song celebrates "grand palace cars blazing," as part of this "labor uprising" designed "to crush down the robbers of men."

> Aye, listen, ye millionaires, listen!
> Tread light o'er your carpeted floors,
> And see the red flames as they glisten,
> And hear the wild shout of the boors,
> Or slaves, as you've long tried to make them,
> Hark! hark! That dread sound's drawing nigher.
> Have you ventured at last to awake them
> To spirits of vengeance and fire?
> See! See! Your grand palace cars blazing!
> They light up the mountains, and glen,
> And see maddening labor uprising,
> To crush down the robbers of men!

Likewise, in "The General Strike," also inspired by the events in 1877 and quoted by Foner, "the labors sensation" battles "men in high station."

> The labors sensation spread fast over this nation,
> While men in high station do just as they like;
> They'll find out their mistake when it will be too late,

When they see the results of a general strike.
The butchers, the whalers, the tinkers, the tailors,
Mechanics and sailors will surely agree,
To strike and stand still, let the rich run the mill,
While I sing of the sights that I fancy we'll see.

Both of these songs speak of the class divisions created by industrial capitalism. Labor's struggle is against "millionaires" and "the rich." This theme is echoed in hundreds of other songs and song-poems of the nineteenth century. As battle cries during strikes and demonstrations, and as literary submissions to the labor press, songs and song-poems defined the interests of the working class as distinct from capitalist employers. In so doing, historian Clark Halker argues labor songs expressed "the ceaseless defense of labor's cause and caustic criticism of the rising order."

Although the Great Strike of 1877 spread quickly, the use of federal troops to bust the strike and the workers' lack of organization brought the strike to a quick end. The Noble and Holy Order of the Knights of Labor attempted to provide workers with such organization. Established by a group of Philadelphia tailors in 1869, the Knights attempted to organize all workers—skilled and unskilled, men and women, black and white, native born and immigrant. Victories against two of the nation's largest railroad companies in the early 1880s drew workers to the ranks of the Knights, and at their height in the 1880s, the Knights boasted approximately 800,000 members in a wide variety of occupations.

The Knights were at the vortex of labor struggles in the 1880s. Their hope was to create a cooperative society in which laborers worked for themselves and not for the profit-oriented capitalists. They supported educational efforts toward this end, sponsoring lectures and establishing reading rooms. They also believed poems and songs could have educational benefit.

Terence Powderly, the Knights grand master, preferred to avoid strikes, believing them a distraction from the goal of a cooperative society. Nonetheless, strikes did occur, including one among coal miners in the anthracite region of Pennsylvania in 1887–88. Scabs and Pinkerton guards were brought in, and strikers were evicted from company houses and denied credit at the company store. In an industry with a long history of singing, the miners told the story of their failed strike, as quoted by Foner, in "The Knights of Labor Strike."

We're brave and gallant miner boys
That work in underground,
For courage and good nature
None like us can be found.
We work both late and early,
And get but little pay
To support our wives and children,
In free Americ-a.

Here's to the Knights of Labor,
That brave and gallant band,
That Corbon and old Swigard
Is trying to disband.
But stick and hang brave union men,
We'll make them rue the day
They thought to break the K. of L.
In free Americ-a.

If Satan took the blacklegs,
I'm sure 'twould be no sin,
What peace and happiness 'twould be
For us workingmen.
Eight hours we'd have for labor,
Eight hours we'd have for play,
Eight hours we'd have for sleeping,
In free Americ-a.

The reference in the third verse to the eight-hour movement suggests how widespread that demand had become by the late 1880s. In fact, the effort to "disband" the Knights mentioned in the second verse was a direct response to agitation for the eight-hour day. The growth of the eight-hour movement and the demonstrations that took place in Chicago and other cities and towns across the nation inspired a number of songs advancing the cause. The most popular was "Eight Hours," written by I.G. Blanchard. It originally appeared as a poem in 1866 in the *Workingman's Advocate.* In the early 1870s, the Reverend Jesse H. Jones, who was associated with an eight-hour league in Boston, set the poem to music. By the time the May 1, 1886, demonstrations took place, it had become the rallying cry of the movement. Foner quotes it as follows:

> We mean to make things over, we're tired of toil and naught,
> While bare enough to live upon, and never an hour for thought;
> We want to feel the sunshine, and we want to smell the flowers,
> We're sure that God has willed it, and we mean to have eight hours.
> We're summoning our forces from shipyard, shop and mill;
> Eight hours for work, eight hours for rest, eight hours for what we will!
> Eight hours for work, eight hours for rest, eight hours for what we will!

The certainty that "God has willed it," expressed in this verse, echoes a common theme in labor songs and song-poems of the nineteenth century. The songs workers wrote and sang often verbalized the fervent conviction that God was on their side. Labor's fight was not only a class struggle against the forces of industrial capitalism; it was a crusade for the human dignity that should be afforded all God's children. Another verse of "Eight Hours" articulated this conviction of the righteousness of the workers' cause—that the workers possessed "the true religion for which Christ had died," as Halker puts it.

> The voice of God within us is calling us to stand
> Erect, as is becoming to the work of his right hand,
> Should he, to whom the Maker his glorious image gave,
> The meanest of his creatures crouch, a bread and butter slave!
> Let the shout ring down the valleys and echo from ev'ry hill.
> Eight hours for work, eight hours for rest, eight hours for what we will!
> Eight hours for work, eight hours for rest, eight hours for what we will!

In the wake of the eight-hour-day demonstrations, the Knights faced severe repression from employers and the state and saw their membership fall to 100,000 by 1890. The meteoric rise and fall of the Knights inspired the American Federation of Labor (AFL), established in 1886 under the leadership of Samuel Gompers, to abandon notions of a different society and seek accommodation with employers. The AFL organized along craft lines, using workers' skills as leverage in negotiations to secure wage concessions and improve working conditions. Despite their preference for negotiation, AFL affiliates were willing to use strikes to advance their cause.

Songs to Organize By

One of the most celebrated and disappointing AFL strikes took place in 1892, when Henry Clay Frick attempted to break the Amalgamated Association of Iron and Steel workers at Andrew Carnegie's steel mill in Homestead, Pennsylvania. On July 6, workers fought Pinkerton guards in a twelve-hour battle that killed nine strikers and seven guards and wounded many more. Despite winning the battle and inspiring sympathy strikes at other mills, the Amalgamated eventually lost the strike and any significant presence in the steel for the next four decades. The dramatic events of July 6 and the subsequent effort of the union to hold out inspired a number of songs. One of them, "Father Was Killed by the Pinkerton Men," written by William W. Delaney, tells the story of the strike, triggered by a "reduction of their pay" and broken when Frick "closed the works till starved they would obey." In the song, quoted by Foner, the haughty power of Carnegie, the "millionaire employer with philanthropic show," is contrasted with the "grieving" and "affliction" of the children orphaned by the Pinkertons.

> 'Twas in a Pennsylvania town not very long ago
> Men struck against reduction of their pay
> Their millionaire employer with philanthropic show
> Had closed the works till starved they would obey
> They fought for home and right to live where they had toiled so long

But ere the sun had set some were laid low
There're hearts now sadly grieving by that sad
 and bitter wrong
God help them for it was a cruel blow.

Refrain:
God help them tonight in their hour of affliction
Praying for him whom they'll ne'er see again
Hear the orphans tell their sad story
"Father was killed by the Pinkerton men."

In the second verse, the alignment of government forces with the mill's management provides "protection for the rich man." But for the workers, it is "the freedom of the grave."

Ye prating politicians, who boast protection
 creed,
Go to Homestead and stop the orphans' cry,
Protection for the rich man ye pander to his
 greed,
His workmen they are cattle and may die.
The freedom of the city in Scotland far away
'Tis presented to the millionaire suave,
But here in free America with protection in
 full sway
His workmen get the freedom of the grave.

The collapse of the Homestead strike dramatically underscored the changing nature of labor in an industrial age. Technological change reduced the power of craft unionism by increasing the proportion of unskilled workers in the mines, mills, and factories. Employers required fewer skilled hands and more willing ones, who were easily replaced by strikebreakers. As a result, the balance of power shifted further from craft workers toward employers. Moreover, the support management enjoyed from government, as pliant civil authorities provided police and militia "protection," further undermined efforts toward labor solidarity. Clearly, the new realities necessitated a different approach to labor organization. For many, the Industrial Workers of the World (IWW) offered just such an approach.

Popularly known as the "Wobblies," the IWW sought, in the words of founding member and leader William "Big Bill" Haywood, "the emancipation of the working class from the slave bondage of capitalism." Like the Knights of Labor, the IWW sought to organize all workers irrespective of skill, gender, race, ethnicity, or place of birth. This "one big union" would then provide labor the strength necessary to overthrow capitalism, abolish the wage system, and run industry in a decentralized, democratic manner. In its endeavor to promote economic justice and an egalitarian society, the IWW developed an extensive literature of poems, stories, skits, cartoons, and, especially, songs. With their *Little Red Songbook,* the Wobblies hoped "to fan the flames of discontent," as inscribed on its cover. Widely distributed among IWW members, the *Little Red Songbook* went through thirty-five separate editions, featuring almost 200 different songs. Within its pages were traditional labor songs, original compositions, and parodies of church hymns and contemporary tunes. For the Wobblies, songwriting and singing played a central role in radicalizing the working class. Richard Brazier, who helped compile the first *Little Red Songbook* in 1909, described the lofty hopes the IWW had for singing within the labor movement.

> Songs are easily remembered but dull prose is soon forgotten . . . and our aims and principles can be recorded in songs as well as in leaflets and pamphlets—in some cases even better. For songs for workers will be more apt to reach the workers than any dry-as-dust polemic. . . .
>
> We shall run the gamut of emotions in our songs. . . . We will have songs of anger and protest, songs which shall call to judgment our oppressors and the Profit System they have devised. Songs of battles won (but never any songs of despair), songs that hold up flaunted wealth and thread-bare morality to scorn, songs that lampoon our masters and the parasitic vermin, such as the employment-sharks and their kind, who bedevil the workers. These songs will deal with every aspect of the workers' lives. They will bring hope to them, and courage to wage the good fight. They will be songs sowing the seeds of discontent and rebellion. We want our songs to stir the workers into action, to awaken them from an apathy and complacency that has made them accept their servitude as though it had been divinely ordained. We are sure that the power

> of song will exalt the spirit of Rebellion, and we want that new and better songbook.

The Wobblies' noble vision met considerable resistance as they battled against factionalism, government harassment, and economic depression. But the IWW gained national attention when it led a massive textile strike in 1912 in Lawrence, Massachusetts. Approximately 25,000 textile workers, half of whom were young, immigrant women, participated in the ten-week strike. To deal with the ethnic diversity of the workers, the IWW translated speeches and strike literature into the various languages the strikers spoke. The union also organized picket lines and street demonstrations during which a good deal of singing took place. Song seemed to bridge the ethnic divisions that could potentially undermine the strike. Journalist Ray Stannard Baker, covering the strike for *The American Magazine,* wrote: "It is the first strike I ever saw that sang. I shall not soon forget the curious lift, the strange sudden fire of mingled nationalities at the strike meetings when they broke into the universal language of song. And not only at the meetings did they sing, but in the soup houses and in the streets." Baker's comments document well the central role singing played for the IWW. In song the message of solidarity could be expressed in a "universal language" capable of drawing all workers into "one big union." During the strike, strikers grafted new lyrics to popular tunes. The Irving Berlin song "Everybody's Doing It" became "Few of Them Are Scabbing It." "The Good Old Picket Line," a parody of "In the Good Old Summertime," made direct reference to the ethnic diversity of the strikers who "are from every place, from nearly every clime."

> In the good old picket line, in the good old picket line,
> The workers are from every place, from nearly every clime,
> The Greeks and Poles are out so strong, and the Germans all the time,
> But we want to see more Irish in the good old picket line.

After clashes with the police, government investigations, and widespread sympathy action by socialist supporters, including temporary foster care for hundreds of Lawrence children, the workers won a stunning victory. Wages increased in the Lawrence mills, as well as other mills in New England.

Solidarity Forever

The success of the IWW at organizing such a large number of unskilled, foreign-born workers challenged the craft-based, native-born approach of the AFL. The strike was denounced by Samuel Gompers, AFL president, and John Golden, the president of the AFL United Textile Workers (UTW). In a parody of "A Little Talk with Jesus," the IWW's "John Golden and the Lawrence Strike" suggested collusion between AFL leadership and the president of the American Woolen Company, William Wood.

> John Golden had with Mr. Wood a private interview,
> He told him how to bust up the "I double double U."
> He came out in a while and wore the Golden smile.
> He said: "I've got all labor leaders skinned a mile."
>
> *Refrain:*
> A little talk—
> A little talk with Golden
> Makes it right, all right;
> He'll settle any strike,
> If there's coin enough in sight;
> Just take him up to dine
> And everything is fine—
> A little talk with Golden
> Makes it right, all right.

This lyrical attack on the UTW chieftain was written by the greatest of the many Wobbly bards, Joe Hill. Born Joel Emmanuel Haaglund in Sweden, he came to the United States in 1901 at the age of nineteen. By 1910 he was an IWW member, active in the port of San Pedro, California. He then migrated to Utah. There he would be accused of the fatal shooting of a grocer on January 14, 1914. His guilt is still disputed. But before his execution for the crime in November 1915, his case involved President Wilson, the Swedish ambassador to the United States, and Samuel Gompers, among thousands of others, securing him martyr status within the labor movement. His songs, which became very popular among Wobblies, chastised strikebreakers ("Casey Jones—The Union Scab"), promoted solidarity ("There Is Power in a Union"), described the plight of the homeless ("The Tramp"), ridiculed the Salvation Army's evangelizing ("The Preacher and the Slave"), and offered commentary on a host of other issues of interest to workers. Joe Hill himself became memorialized in a song by Alfred Hayes and Earl Robinson, which became a standard among protest singers. The verses of "Joe Hill" speak of his eternal spirit that came to represent striking workers everywhere as they struggle for justice.

> I dreamed I saw Joe Hill last night
> Alive as you and me
> Said I, "But Joe, you're ten years dead,"
> "I never died," says he, "I never died," says he.
>
> "In Salt Lake Joe, by God," says I
> Him standing by my bed,
> "They framed you on a murder charge"
> Says Joe, "But I ain't dead," says Joe, "But I ain't dead."
>
> "The copper bosses shot you, Joe
> They killed you, Joe," says I.
> "Takes more than guns to kill a man"
> Says Joe, "I didn't die," says Joe, "I didn't die."
>
> And standing there as big as life
> And smiling with his eyes
> Says Joe, "What they forget to kill
> Went on to organize, went on to organize."
>
> "Joe Hill ain't dead," he says to me
> "Joe Hill ain't never died
> Where workingmen are out on strike
> Joe Hill is at their side, Joe Hill is at their side."
>
> "From San Diego up to Maine
> In every mine and mill
> Where workers strike and organize,"
> Says he, "You'll find Joe Hill," says he, "You'll find Joe Hill."

Although Joe Hill was the most renowned of the union's many songwriters, the single greatest Wobbly song was Ralph Chaplin's "Solidarity Forever." Set to the tune of "John Brown's Body"/"Battle Hymn of the Republic," "Solidarity Forever" has become the anthem of the labor movement. Long after the Wobblies vanished from the scene, Chaplin's lyrics can still be heard on picket lines and in union halls. Its stirring lyrics and patriotic melody combine with a powerful force.

> When the Union's inspiration through the workers' blood shall run,
> There can be no power greater anywhere beneath the sun.
> Yet what force on earth is weaker than the feeble strength of one?
> But the Union makes us strong.
>
> *Refrain:*
> Solidarity Forever!
> Solidarity Forever!
> Solidarity Forever!
> For the Union makes us strong.
>
> They have taken untold millions that they never toiled to earn,
> But without our brain and muscle not a single wheel can turn.
> We can break their haughty power; gain our freedom when we learn
> That the Union makes us strong.
>
> In our hands is placed a power greater than their hoarded gold;
> Greater than the might of armies, magnified a thousand-fold.
> We can bring to birth a new world from the ashes of the old
> For the Union makes us strong.

Chaplin's classic had more staying power than the union that gave it birth. For many reasons, including most importantly government repression, the Wobblies had all but disappeared by the

1920s. Nevertheless, their passionate and irreverent songs lived on.

Appalachian Roots

The IWW was not the only workers' organization to draw on American folk and religious music. Strikers in Gastonia, North Carolina, in the late 1920s, also found inspiration in traditional songs. After being evicted from company housing, they took refuge in a tent camp provided by the Communist-affiliated National Textile Workers Union (NTWU). Most union meetings there ended with much singing. Strike leader Fred Beal later described a typical evening:

> No evening passed without getting a new strike song from our Ella May, the minstrel of our strike. She would stand somewhere in the corner, chewing tobacco or snuff and fumbling over notes of a new poem scribbled on the back of a union leaflet. Suddenly some one would call for her to sing and other voices would take up the suggestion. Then in a deep resonant voice she would give us a simple ballad. . . . The crowd would join in with an old refrain and Ella May would add verse after verse to her song. From these the singers would drift into spirituals or hymns and many a "praise-the-Lord" would resound through the quiet night.

By employing familiar folk melodies and religious hymns, these strike songs expressed workers' thoughts and feelings in a manner everyone could understand. "On Top of Old Smokey" became "On Top of Old Loray," describing the deplorable conditions in the Loray mill, the focus of the strike. Composed by an eleven-year-old millhand, the song begins:

> Up in old Loray
> Six stories high,
> That's where they found us,
> Ready to die.

This use of traditional song forms closely tied to the workers' religious beliefs and mountain culture helped legitimize the promotion of a union. The ideals of unity and solidarity were advanced as compatible with the workers' own attitudes and values. Grafting new ideas to traditional cultural forms, as journalist Margaret Larkin, quoted in *Strike Songs of the Depression*, observed, gave these songs "a strange persuasiveness. . . . Their curious mingling of old and new is the true reflection of the lives of the workers."

A similar mingling of Appalachian musical traditions and radical politics occurred during the strikes in the coalfields of eastern Kentucky in the early 1930s, in what became known as "Bloody Harlan County." Aunt Molly Jackson was the most important balladeer to emerge from Bloody Harlan. As a nurse and midwife, she testified before a visiting committee of literary luminaries, including Theodore Dreiser, John Dos Passos, and Sherwood Anderson, regarding the malnutrition and diseases affecting miners' families. Following her testimony, she sang "Kentucky Miner's Wife Ragged Hungry Blues."

> I'm sad and weary, I got those hungry ragged blues;
> I'm sad and weary, I got those hungry ragged blues;
> Not a penny in my pocket to buy one thing I need to use.
>
> I woke up this morning with the worst blues I ever had in my life;
> I woke up this morning with the worst blues I ever had in my life;
> Not a bite to cook for breakfast, poor coal miner's wife.

So touched were the committee members by this bitter musical lament that they included it in the published product of their inquiry, *Harlan Miners Speak*. They also asked Aunt Molly and her half-brother Jim Garland to travel to New York City to help raise relief funds for the miners. There they appeared before an estimated 21,000 people in New York's Bronx Coliseum. In all, Aunt Molly toured thirty-eight states soliciting funds for Kentucky miners.

As the Communist-affiliated National Miners Union tried to organize in eastern Kentucky, it faced intense and violent opposition from mine owners, the local press, and county officials. Sam

Reece was one of the miners who had joined the NMU. Knowing that he was being targeted by coal operators and their hired thugs, he was laying low. Feeling that she "just had to do something to help," Sam's wife Florence composed "Which Side Are You On?" The song was written on the back of a calendar since "we didn't have any stationery cause we didn't get nothing, we was doing good to live." Fusing a militant battle cry with a traditional melody, "Lay the Lily Low," this song would become the anthem of the Harlan County miners, and was adopted and adapted by other workers in other industries. Unlike so many of Aunt Molly's compositions, which described the class division between the coal operators and the miners, Reece's famous song addressed the split between the miners themselves. "I was asking the miners," she later recalled, "all of them, which side they were on. They had to be on one side or other; they had to be for themselves or against themselves." As Reece saw it, one was either for the union or against it; neutrality was not an option. One was either "a union man / Or a thug for J.H. Blair," the county sheriff and ally of the mine owners.

Come all you poor workers
Good news to you I'll tell
How the good old union
Has come in here to dwell.

Refrain:
Which side are you on?
Which side are you on?

We're starting our good battle
We know we're sure to win
Because we've got the gun-thugs
A-lookin' very thin.

If you go to Harlan County
There is no neutral there
You'll either be a union man
Or a thug for J.H. Blair.

Reece did not ignore class divisions. Her song, like many of Aunt Molly's, describes the miners' struggle to form a union as an effort to provide for their families. It characterizes the class distinctions in terms of the coal operators' children who "live in luxury" and the miners' children who are "almost wild." To "be a union man" was to defend one's family against those who would "take away our bread."

They say they have to guard us
To educate their child
Their children live in luxury
Our children almost wild.

With pistols and with rifles
They take away our bread
And if you miners hinted it
They'll sock you on the head.

Gentlemen, can you stand it?
Oh, tell me how you can?
Will you be a gun thug
Or will you be a man?

In one of the conflicts of Bloody Harlan, a Young Communist League and NMU organizer named Harry Hirsh, alias Harry Simms, was shot as he set out to meet writer Frank Waldo and a visiting committee in Pineville. Jim Garland, who had befriended Simms, wrote "The Ballad of Harry Simms," eulogizing him in mountain ballad style:

Comrades, listen to my story,
Comrades, listen to my song.
I'll tell you of a hero
That now is dead and gone.
I'll tell you of a young boy
Whose age was just nineteen.
He was the bravest union man
That ever I have seen.

Harry Simms was a pal of mine,
We labored side by side,
Expecting to be shot on sight
Or taken for a ride
By the dirty operator gun thugs
That roam from town to town
To shoot and kill our Comrades
Wherever they may be found.

Sit-Down Songs

Hard times forced Aunt Molly, Jim Garland, and their sister Sarah Ogan Gunning, who also sang, to move to New York City. There they became involved in the urban folk movement of the late 1930s and 1940s, associating with the likes of Woody Guthrie, Earl Robinson, Will Geer, Pete Seeger, Huddie Ledbetter, Burl Ives, Cisco Houston, and others. Through his association with a professor at New York University, Jim Garland lectured on Kentucky folklore and for a short time had his own radio program on the university's station. All three members of the Garland clan were also recorded for the Library of Congress. Years had passed since the NMU pulled out of Harlan County defeated, but the experience of that struggle had left its mark on the Garland family and their music. That influence would also affect a number of other musicians whose music would become an integral part of the labor movement, as well as that of other progressive causes, up to the present day.

When a new strike tactic—the sit-down—emerged in the mid-1930s, it inspired several new songs. The first was written by Maurice Sugar, an attorney for the United Auto Workers (UAW), whose sit-down strike in Flint, Michigan, in 1936–37 has been described by Sidney Fine as "the most significant labor conflict in the twentieth century." Written while the strike was in progress, "Sit Down" was an immediate hit among the sit-down strikers in Flint. Sugar later recalled, "They went for 'Sit Down' in a big way." The song promoted the power of collective action in fighting against low wages, poor working conditions, and the intimidation and bad faith of bosses. With driving force, "Sit Down" implored workers to join together for their common benefit.

When they tie the can to a union man,
Sit down! Sit Down!
When they give him the sack, they'll take him back.
Sit Down! Sit Down!

Refrain:
Sit down, just take a seat,
Sit down, and rest your feet,
Sit down, you've got 'em beat.
Sit down! Sit down!

When they smile and say, "No raise in pay,"
Sit down! Sit down!
When you want the boss to come across,
Sit down! Sit down!

When the speed-up comes, just twiddle your thumbs.
Sit down! Sit down!
When you want them to know they'd better go slow,
Sit down! Sit down!

When the boss won't talk, don't take a walk.
Sit down! Sit down!
When the boss sees that, he'll want a little chat.
Sit down! Sit Down!

Another song, "The Fisher Strike," told the story of the Flint sit-down, explaining how workers responded to news spread that GM was loading dies on freight cars outside Fisher Body No. 1 bound for plants in Grand Rapids and Pontiac, Michigan, so as to circumvent a strike in the Fisher plant. Sung to the tune of "The Martins and the Coys," the song begins:

Gather round me and I'll tell you all a story,
Of the Fisher Body Factory Number One.
When the dies they started moving,
The Union Men they had a meeting,
To decide right then and there what must be done.

Refrain:
These 4000 Union Boys,
Oh, they sure made lots of noise,
They decided then and there to shut down tight.
In the office they got snooty,
So we started picket duty,
Now the Fisher Body shop is on a strike.

Now this strike it started one bright Wednesday evening,
When they loaded up a box car full of dies.
When the union boys they stopped them,
And the Railroad Workers backed them,
The officials in the office were surprised.

Published within a week of the event in the local UAW newspaper, the *Flint Auto Worker,* "The

Fisher Strike" popularized and perpetuated a version of the strike's origin as "Union Men" heroically responding to a company action openly and deliberately hostile to the workers—the threat of production relocation. In so doing, the song enhanced the image of the union in the eyes of GM workers, both union and nonunion, while depicting the corporation as conniving and sinister. This was no small matter. For both GM and the union, public image during the strike was critical. GM tried to present itself as the good employer that had become the captive victim of a radical minority. By forcing a halt in production, this radical minority was depriving the mass of workers access to their jobs. On the other hand, for the strike to be successful, the union had to increase its ranks by winning the minds and hearts of the workers. The fact that the union could successfully seize a key plant and bring production to a standstill provided impressive testimony to the union's power. Consequently, songs such as "The Fisher Strike," which applauded the union's ability to exert its influence over GM, served to promote the union among the workers.

Another event during the Flint sit-down also inspired a song. Thirteen days into the sit-down, the company attempted to evict the strikers from the Fisher Body plant. However, when police (whom the workers called "bulls") attempted to disperse the crowd outside the plant with tear gas, the wind carried the fumes back toward them. When they then rushed the plant to oust the strikers, the sit-downers sprayed high-pressure water hoses on them while also heaving two-pound car-door hinges. The drenched policemen beat a hasty retreat, literally freezing as the temperature hovered around sixteen degrees. A second assault by police was met with a barrage of bottles, rocks, and hinges, forcing the police to retreat again. This time though, as the police left, they fired into the crowd, wounding fourteen strikers and sympathizers. Several policemen also sustained injuries, including Sheriff Thomas Wolcott, who had his car overturned by strikers with him still in it. "The Battle of the Running Bulls" was an important victory for the strikers, and two strikers composed new lyrics for "There'll Be a Hot Time in the Old Town Tonight" to memorialize the triumph. The song both heralded the courage of "The boys . . . sticking fast" and reveled in the humiliation of plant manager Evan Parker and the police who "never ran so fast."

Cheer, boys, cheer,
For we are full of fun;
Cheer, boys, cheer,
Old Parker's on the run;
We had a fight last nite
And I tell you, boys, we won,
We had a hot time in the old town last nite.

Tear gas bombs
Were flying thick and fast;
The lousy police,
They knew they couldn't last.
Because in all their lives they never ran so fast,
As in that hot time in this old town last nite.

The police are sick
Their bodies they are sore
I'll bet they'll never
Fight us any more;
Because they learned last nite
That we had quite a corps.
We had a hot time in the old town last nite.

Now this scrap is o'er;
The boys are sticking fast
We'll hold our grounds
And fight here to the last
And when this strike is o'er
We'll have our contract fast,
We'll have a hot time in the old town that-nite!

Days later, the union again seized the initiative when it feigned a sit-down strike at Chevrolet No. 9. When police came to the plant, a larger body of workers seized a critical engine plant, Chevrolet No. 4. As Henry Kraus, the managing editor of the union newspaper during the strike, later recalled in *The Many and the Few:* "The boys had been told as they were passing police headquarters to sing out as though in triumph and they did so well . . . that they might easily have impressed observers that they were returning from victorious battle." This ruse proved successful and gave momentum to the union's cause. Eleven days later, GM effectively accepted the UAW as the workers' collective bargaining agent.

Many of those who participated in the union's ploy to capture Chevrolet No. 4 were women. Organized into a Women's Auxiliary and a Women's Emergency Brigade, women performed an array of tasks from cooking meals to picketing in support of the sit-downers inside the plants. They, too, wrote and sang strike songs. Unlike the songs male strikers wrote that stressed male camaraderie and solidarity—"the boys . . . sticking fast"—the songs composed by women depicted their efforts in support of the strike as an extension of their familial roles as wives and mothers. The connection between the family responsibilities women bore and their participation in the strike pervades the "Women's Auxiliary Song." Put to the tune of "Let's All Sing Like the Birdies Sing," the song's emphasis on the familial concerns of women echoes a theme present in the songs of Ella May Wiggins, Aunt Molly Jackson, and Florence Reece:

> Auxiliary women are in the fight
> In the fight to stay
> They will battle with all their might
> Onward every day
> For their homes and their kiddies too
> For their union men
> You can bet your last dime
> They'll be there every time
> Fighting to the end.

Music and singing played a major role at Flint, largely because of the nature of a sit-down strike. The very fact that workers were together occupying a number of plants for over six weeks made boredom and idleness commonplace. Writing and singing songs were effective ways of maintaining morale and passing the time. The importance of singing was not lost on union leaders. Less than four months after the strike, Merlin Bishop, educational director for the UAW, noted that music and singing "were extremely worthwhile during the sit-down strikes." He recognized singing as a valuable means of rousing workers during a strike and vital "for the enrichment of a real working class culture." Indeed, in the wake of the Flint sit-down strike, much was done to promote singing within the labor movement. Bands and orchestras formed, glee clubs assembled, and songbooks were printed. Singing and songwriting had become an integral part of labor organizing.

United Front Folk

Many of the industries that unionized during the 1930s were also industries key to the war effort of the 1940s. During organizing drives in these decades, the music of the Almanac Singers could often be heard. This group of leftist musicians included Lee Hays, Millard Lampell, Josh White, Will Geer, Huddie Ledbetter, Sis Cunningham, Woody Guthrie, and Pete Seeger, among others. At the vortex of the urban folk revival in New York City, the Almanac Singers used their musical talent to promote various left-wing causes, including support of organized labor and, after Germany invaded the Soviet Union in June 1941, American involvement in World War II. Their pro-labor and anti-fascist politics conjoined to inspire scores of songs advancing both the war effort and the labor movement, including "The Union Train," "The Union Maid," "Belt Line Girl," and "Deliver the Goods." "Talking Union," first performed in Madison Square Garden in May of 1941 during a Transportation Workers' Union strike, became their signature song when playing at labor rallies and union meetings. Performed in the talking blues style, the song combines caustic humor and biting sarcasm to send its message of unionization, as illustrated in the first two verses:

> Now, if you want higher wages let me tell you what to do
> You got to talk to the workers in the shop with you.
> You got to build you a union, got to make it strong
> But if you all stick together, boys, it won't be long.
> You get shorter hours, better working conditions
> Vacations with pay. Take your kids to the sea shore.
>
> It ain't quite that simple, so I better explain
> Just why you got to ride on the union train.

'Cause if you wait for the boss to raise your pay
We'll all be waiting 'til Judgement Day.
We'll all be buried, gone to heaven
St. Peter'll be the straw boss then.

The last verse offers a reminder of labor's successes, providing a litany of employers that have been unionized, and cautioning against the tactics of union busting.

But out at Ford, here's what they found
And out at Vultee, here's what they found
And out at Allis-Chalmers, here's what they found
And down at Bethlehem, here's what they found
That if you don't let red-baiting break you up
And if you don't let stoolpigeons break you up
And if you don't let vigilantes break you up
And if you don't let race hatred break you up
You'll win. What I mean, take it easy, but take it!

The war disrupted the short career of the Almanac Singers, with various members entering the service or taking war production jobs. Their popularity did, however, influence other socially conscious musicians to promote the war and labor's cause. Among them were The Priority Ramblers, associated with the United Federal Workers Union, and The Union Boys, which included many former members of the Almanac Singers. Songwriting and musical performance had reached a level of professionalism within the labor movement previously unseen. Increasingly, unions commissioned musicians to perform at union rallies and strikes. Songs were written, records were pressed and distributed, and concerts were scheduled, providing many leftist musicians with employment in the service of labor organizing.

This relationship continued after the war, leading to the formation of People's Songs. Organized by Pete Seeger, Lee Hays, and a number of other musicians, People's Songs hoped to promote a truly democratic society, as Seeger later said, through "every kind of musical expression which can be of use to people's organizations: folk, jazz, popular, or serious cantatas for union choruses." People's Songs musicians played for striking workers, supported progressive candidates for office, and advanced civil rights for African Americans. Hoping to build upon the gains labor made during the war years, People's Songs embraced the progressive agenda of the CIO following the war. In 1946, Alan Reitman, the director of public relations for the CIO's Political Action Committee, echoed Seeger's optimism and praised People's Songs' contribution to labor organizing, stating: "The talented song writers and musicians who have banded together in this organization insure the production of outstanding songs. Union groups should lose no time in presenting these songs to their membership and working with People's Songs to prepare special songs for specific issues and occasions."

But this relationship began to fray by the end of the 1940s. The passage of the Taft-Hartley Act in 1947 restricted union activity and required that unions certify their members were not associated with the Communist Party. Amidst these Cold War fears, unions purged their memberships of radicals. Most notably, in 1949 the CIO expelled nine unions representing 900,000 workers. Similarly, organized labor distanced itself from those with left-wing ties, which included the artists in People's Songs. The Cold War had a chilling effect on the labor movement. Its radical vision of promoting economic democracy had been replaced by business unionism. Increasingly, unions focused on the "bread and butter" issues of higher wages and better benefits. The militancy of the thirties and forties seemed long past when the AFL and the CIO merged in 1955. The union's new chief, George Meany, captured well the limited goals of the AFL-CIO when he said, "We do not seek to recast American society in any particular doctrinaire or ideological image. We seek an ever rising standard of living."

To be sure, strikes continued to be used for leverage when renegotiating contracts. But more often than not, labor issues were fought behind closed doors between labor chieftains and management, or by influencing labor's political ally, the Democratic Party. Less emphasis was put on recruiting new members and more on protecting existing union turf. Union membership was dropping; labor's muscle weakening. This decline was accompanied by a marked absence of singing within the labor movement. Merlin Bishop, the UAW educational director who had hailed the benefit of singing during the Flint sit-down strike, later lamented the drop in singing in the labor movement. In 1963, he commented, "One thing I think is lacking today is the use of songs. . . . People really sang. There was a real life and spirit. We have lost that in the CIO. I think there is a great need for it. Maybe if we had more of it, we would be growing instead of slipping backwards as we are at the present time." Two years after Bishop's commentary, Pete Seeger made a similar observation. He queried, "Whatever happened to singing in the union?" Like Bishop, Seeger remembered a time in American labor history when workers lifted their voices in song as they walked picket lines and held union rallies. He pondered the powerful benefits that singing once had for strikers as they demanded higher wages, improved working conditions, and recognition for their union. Both Bishop and Seeger bemoaned the disappearance of such a formidable tool for union organizing. They remembered the dramatic labor struggles of the thirties and forties, and the important role singing had played.

In his 2001 autobiography, *Labor's Troubadour,* folksinger and labor organizer Joe Glazer maintains such claims are overblown and exaggerated. He acknowledges that "labor songs have always come in cycles," and that "the relative prosperity labor enjoyed during the 1950s and 1960s . . . did not develop many militant labor songs." But "the best [labor songs] have emerged from struggle," he argues. Consequently, labor's present situation provides "many opportunities for labor songs about union busters, jobs, scabs, solidarity, plant safety, automation, and cheap imports." Indeed, in two chapters he introduces the reader to "some of the new voices of labor" who have been advanced through the Labor Heritage Foundation, a nonprofit organization he helped establish to promote music, art, and culture within the labor movement. But the very fact that such an initiative was necessary suggests something of the hard times the union movement has experienced in recent years—and the desperate need for revival. The singing has all but stopped. Whether or not there will be strike songs in the future depends largely on the health of the labor movement. If present trends continue, rousing choruses of "Solidarity Forever" may only be known to the past.

See also: North Carolina Women on Strike, 154; Automobile Workers' Strike, 389.

Bibliography

Bird, Stewart, Dan Georgakas, and Deborah Shaffer. *Solidarity Forever: An Oral History of the IWW*. Chicago: Lake View Press, 1985.

Brazier, Richard. "The Story of the I.W.W.'s 'Little Red Songbook.'" *Labor History* 9 (Winter 1968): 91–105.

Chaplin, Ralph. *Wobbly: The Rough and Tumble Story of an American Radical.* Chicago: University of Chicago Press, 1948.

Cohen, Ronald D., and Dave Samuelson, comps. and eds., *Songs for Political Action: Folkmusic, Topical Songs, and the American Left, 1926–53.* Hamburg, Germany: Bear Family Records, 1996.

Foner, Philip S. *American Labor Songs of the Nineteenth Century*. Urbana: University of Illinois Press, 1975.

Glazer, Joe. *Labor's Troubadour*. Urbana: University of Illinois Press, 2001.

Halker, Clark D. *For Democracy, Workers, and God: Labor Song-Poems and Labor Protest, 1865–95*. Urbana: University of Illinois Press, 1991.

I.W.W. Songs: Songs of the Workers: To Fan the Flames of Discontent, 1st–35th eds. Chicago: I.W.W., 1909–76.

Joyce Kornbluh, ed. *Rebel Voices: An I.W.W. Anthology*. Ann Arbor: University of Michigan Press, 1964.

Lynch, Timothy P. *Strike Songs of the Depression*. Jackson: University Press of Mississippi, 2001.

CIVIL RIGHTS STRIKES

Todd Michney

Since 1988, when a seminal article by Robert Korstad and Nelson Lichtenstein located the origins of the Black Freedom Struggle in World War II–era labor activism, a diverse and wide-ranging literature on what Korstad would later term "civil rights unionism" has burgeoned. Historians have documented numerous instances where African Americans, other racial minorities, and women mounted collective challenges to segregated workplaces, discriminatory pay scales and job classifications, and poverty-level wages paid to service industry workers deemed ineligible for the protections of the emergent New Deal state. In discussing what she describes as the "powerful social movement sparked [in the 1930s] by the alchemy of laborites, civil rights activists, progressive New Dealers, and black and white radicals, some of whom were associated with the Communist Party," Jacquelyn Dowd Hall has contended that this fortuitous convergence "was not just a precursor of the modern civil rights movement. It was its decisive first phase." Yet despite the oneness of the labor and equal rights struggles in the minds of many minority and female union members—as they themselves recount in Michael Honey's collection, *Black Workers Remember*—it would seem that comparatively few full-blown strikes were motivated first and foremost by civil rights issues. The clearest examples of this are the strikes waged by hospital workers in New York City in 1962 and in Charleston in 1969, as well as the 1968 sanitation workers' strike in Memphis, during which Martin Luther King Jr. was assassinated. In addition, it should be recalled that in the mid-1960s, at least two civil rights organizations actually organized union locals whose minority members struck in response to discriminatory and degrading treatment by their employers. Finally, numerous smaller-scale work stoppages and wildcat strikes, particularly during World War II, are noteworthy for having turned the spotlight directly on the issue of discrimination against racial minorities and women.

The First Phase

Even prior to World War II, there were examples of minority workers using strikes to protest discriminatory treatment. In a particularly large action recounted by Zaragosa Vargas, 10,000 Latina pecan shellers went out on strike in San Antonio in 1938, demanding pay equal to that of their white coworkers. It was the largest strike the city had ever seen, and it served to unify and politicize the city's Mexican-American community. But with the mass entry of African Americans, other minorities, and women into industrial jobs during the war, the incidence, scope, and potential for such conflicts increased dramatically. In Detroit, as August Meier and Elliott Rudwick recount in *Black Detroit and the Rise of the UAW*, African-American war workers would repeatedly walk out in protest against discrimination and the "hate strikes" staged by their white coworkers. Amid conversion to war production at Ford's plants in the summer of 1941, black autoworkers walked off the job three different times because transfers into the new defense industries were not being administered on the basis of seniority as stated in the contract, but rather on a whites-preferred basis. In early 1943, black workers at one of the city's Chrysler plants conducted work stoppages when they were passed over for promotions and again when black female janitors were assigned unreasonably heavy labor. That April, continued inequities in transfer policies and the persistence of race-based job lines provoked

3,000 African-American autoworkers at the massive River Rouge plant to mount a three-day wildcat. And as white autoworkers' hate strikes in response to black promotions built to a summertime climax, African-American foundry workers at Packard retaliated with walkouts to protest the union's lack of resolve in confronting the intransigent white strikers. A final walkout in November 1943 finally achieved significant transfer gains for the city's African-American war workers.

The June 1943 strike at the R.J. Reynolds Co. that forms the centerpiece of Korstad's work on tobacco workers began as a work stoppage by black female tobacco stemmers. Key demands to emerge from the plant's African-American unionists included the equalization of pay scales, improved conditions, and more respectful treatment. Also in 1943, as Michael Honey recounts, African-American workers at a cellulose plant in Memphis responded with a wildcat to a federal settlement that froze them in Jim Crow job classifications. At that point, their own CIO union, the United Cannery, Agricultural, Packing and Allied Workers of America, brought them back under threat of fines because it had signed the wartime no-strike pledge. With the same issue still unresolved the following year, however, these same workers would again walk off the job in protest. In January 1944, African-American workers at a Memphis rubber-mixing plant struck when their employer attempted to switch their newly acquired jobs back to white-only positions. In June and again the following March, black workers at the same plant walked out over incidents of mistreatment by company guards; the latter action sparked a response in kind by white workers that shut the plant down for three days.

White women, as well as black women and men, engaged in these types of tactics. Dorothy Sue Cobble asserts that "during the war, labor [union] women resorted to sit-downs and other direct action to adjust pay rates," in addition to seeking legal redress. Female electrical workers were particularly active in demanding wage equity during this period, using strategies that included filing grievances, picketing, striking, and litigating. Some carried this tradition into the postwar years. For example, in 1953 and 1954 several locals of the International Union of Electrical Workers struck in pursuit of equal pay for women. But, as Martha Biondi details in *To Stand and Fight*, the racial divide was sometimes formidable for female workers as well as male. In New York City in 1946, black women in Local 121 of the United Gas, Coke, and Chemical Workers Union struck and picketed a cosmetics-manufacturing company over blatant race-based wage discrepancies and segregated working conditions. Their white co-unionists declined to join in the protest, which lasted for several weeks. According to Bruce Fehn, the United Packinghouse Workers of America (UPWA) more successfully confronted both employer discrimination and racism in its own ranks. In 1951, after gathering proof of discriminatory hiring practices at Swift & Co., activists in Chicago's black-led UPWA Local 28 organized rallies, work stoppages, and slowdowns until government intervention resulted in black women being hired on the production line—with back pay. At the Rath Co. in Waterloo, Iowa, in 1953, white female workers' threat to walk off the job in response to the hiring of black women in the sliced bacon department prompted African-American workers in other departments to counterstrike, after which the company instituted nondiscrimination policies. In another incident from the 1950s at one Chicago packinghouse, black and white women in the racially integrated pork trimming unit went from department to department, encouraging others to join a wildcat that quickly succeeded in getting African-American women placed in the formerly all-white sliced bacon department.

The 1960s

The late 1960s saw a resurgence of shop-floor strike actions by Detroit's black autoworkers around the issues of fairness and persistent racism, which has been chronicled by Heather Thompson, among others. Perhaps ironically, the origins of the militant Revolutionary Union Movement (RUM) apparently date to a May 1968 wildcat over line speedups staged by white female autoworkers that were subsequently joined by African-American women from their department. Over the next several years, RUMs sprang up in nearly every Detroit auto plant, and their members conducted numerous wildcat strikes in response to intolerable working conditions and racist treatment at the hands of white foremen on the shop floor.

Anywhere from hundreds to thousands of black autoworkers participated in these demonstrations; in the largest such action, a July 1968 walkout at Dodge Main, some 4,000 participated.

Minority and female workers resorted to direct action in the face of discrimination because of the glacial pace of change in the direction of equal opportunity, not to mention white male workers' often spirited defense of their own job prerogatives. To be sure, some union locals—especially left-led ones like United Auto Workers (UAW) Local 248 at the Allis-Chalmers Corp. in Milwaukee—proved strongly supportive of African-American civil rights during World War II. As the existing scholarship has established, however, even Communist-led unions were not always willing to push for equal rights for black workers if it threatened to alienate the white rank and file. Alan Draper has concluded that militant interracial unionism historically stood a good chance of success only in those settings where African Americans either made up a majority of the workforce or where blacks controlled a key step in the production process, as in the case of meatpacking. Bodies like the CIO's Committee to Abolish Racial Discrimination (formed in 1942), the United Steelworkers of America's Committee on Civil Rights (1950), and the UAW's Trade Union Leadership Conference (1957) were relegated mainly to conducting surveys, trying to reeducate the white membership, winning black representation on executive boards, or networking with organizations like the NAACP around legislative issues.

In the end, disgruntled minority and female workers proved most likely to confront discrimination not through existing union grievance channels or direct action, but by litigating and filing complaints with government agencies like the Fair Employment Practices Commission, War Labor Board, War Manpower Commission, National Labor Relations Board, or later, the Equal Employment Opportunity Commission. Despite various limitations of these agencies, federal intervention—especially in the South—often proved "indispensable," to quote Korstad. After the passage of the Civil Rights Act in 1964, African-American workers effectively used litigation to gain access to jobs, most notably in the Southern textile and paper industries.

At least two civil rights organizations actually organized union locals whose minority members struck to demand fair treatment, respect, and a living wage. In 1965, the Student Nonviolent Coordinating Committee organized the Mississippi Freedom Labor Union (MFLU), intended as "a union for all kinds of workers who are underpaid—field hands, tractor drivers, maids, and others." Black laborers in the MFLU subsequently went on strike to demand the federal minimum hourly wage. In Baltimore in 1966, according to Michael Flug, the Congress of Racial Equality formed the Maryland Freedom Union (MFU), which was modeled on the MFLU. It took up the cause of winning the federal minimum for the city's laundry, nursing home, and hospital workers, as well as those in retail establishments serving West Baltimore's black community. One local nursing home was struck, with picket signs targeting its owner, Asa Wessels, that read: "WESSELS PLANTATION. THE BLACK PEOPLE SLAVE IN BALTIMORE SO WESSELS CAN LIVE LIKE A KING IN FLORIDA. SUPPORT FREEDOM LOCAL #1." Workers at another nursing home joined the cause, forming "Freedom Local #2" and their own picket line. While these actions did not succeed in getting wages raised to the federal minimum, they did prompt modest increases. Over the course of 1966, the MFU also assisted striking laundry workers and picketed on behalf of black department store employees.

Local 1199 New York City

Hospital workers—nurses' aides, orderlies, and support staff—proved particularly inclined to interpret their struggle in terms of civil rights. They came from overwhelmingly minority backgrounds (mostly African American and Latina) and were disproportionately female; often experienced condescension on the job from white administrators, doctors, and nurses; and, at private institutions beyond the scope of the federal minimum wage, were compensated at extremely low rates that frequently kept them mired in poverty. "For this portion of the 'new working class,'" Leon Fink and Brian Greenberg have written, "the organizing process increasingly involved not only economic and job-related issues but a larger civil rights identity, a sense of community empowerment, and moral-political appeals directed to a larger audience." "By the late sixties," they continue, "the rank-and-file mobilization of hospital workers developed using what [Local] 1199 leaders dubbed a 'union power, soul power' model."

Local 1199 of the Drugstore Workers Union, which rose to the occasion of organizing hospital workers first in New York City and subsequently in Charleston and elsewhere, hailed directly from the left-labor coalitions of the 1930s, its leadership (embodied in the person of President Leon Davis) having ridden out the purges of the McCarthy years. The union had African-American members since its early days, including intimate connections with the North Harlem Pharmaceutical Association. Local 1199 would form its own Fair Employment Committee in 1949, begin celebrating Black History Month in 1950, and later solicit donations from its members during the 1956 Montgomery Bus Boycott. In its first strike against six New York hospitals in 1959, union recognition had been the main demand, although 1199 had also skillfully couched the conflict in terms of a "fight for emancipation," and in building support for their cause tapped a coterie of civil rights leaders and their constituents. Individuals, groups, and community institutions including Adam Clayton Powell, Bayard Rustin, Eleanor Roosevelt, the local National Association for the Advancement of Colored People (NAACP), Urban League, ACLU, Federation of Hispanic-American Societies, Democratic ward clubs, black churches, and schoolteachers all came forward in support of the strike. In the end, 1199 acceded to a settlement that fell short of recognition, but that did establish a "Permanent Administrative Committee" (PAC) as a means of allowing hospital, community, and union representatives to negotiate in a setting akin to collective bargaining.

Local 1199's explicit civil rights orientation crystallized around a two-month-long strike in 1962 against Beth-El Hospital, located in Brooklyn's Brownsville neighborhood. The union emerged from the strike with "Freedom Now!" as its anthem. It subsequently sponsored "Freedom Days" and in "Operation First-Class Citizenship" lobbied the New York state legislature for legalized collective bargaining rights. Interestingly, the strike both showcased the interracialism that had characterized the civil rights movement to that point and foreshadowed its turn toward Black Power later in the decade. Historian Wendell Pritchett has written that the conflict "revealed the promise of a northern movement that crossed racial and ethnic lines, as members of New York's liberal community vigorously backed the Jewish-led union and their predominantly black and Puerto Rican rank and file." But with at least a third of Beth-El's low-wage employees drawn from the surrounding area, the strike additionally evidenced growing assertiveness and unity between local African-American and Latino residents. According to Pritchett, it effectively "awakened the whole Brownsville community to the possibility of organization and helped bring about the political maturation of this rapidly changing neighborhood."

As in its previous battles to organize New York hospitals that had led to the formation of the PAC, Local 1199 was motivated by issues of recognition and of poverty-level wages; the starting rate paid to female employees stood at 90 cents per hour, while that paid to male employees was hardly better at $1.03, as compared to the federal minimum wage of $1.30. Frustrated by the emerging pattern of hospitals joining the PAC voluntarily to take advantage of its no-strike protection, in the fall of 1961 Local 1199 withdrew its pledge not to strike new joiners. With momentum gathering behind a community-backed organizing drive ongoing since 1960 at Beth-El, the hospital's decision to join the PAC in January 1962 was therefore rejected by the union. Then, when several months of agitation and negotiations with the hospital administration failed to result in the implementation of collective bargaining, Local 1199 declared a strike in late May, as Pritchett has described.

Even in preliminary picketing before the strike was declared, Local 1199 had couched its struggle in terms of "equal rights" and "fair pay." Frequent instances of picket-line police brutality once the strike began, including unduly harsh punishment meted out to African-American and Latino pickets, served to make race a central issue. Brownsville residents sustained the strike with picketing assistance and by providing food and supplies where possible. Sympathetic college students participated by sitting-in at the Beth-El lobby in early June, while CORE, the NAACP, the Jewish Labor Committee, the United Federation of Teachers, the city's CIO Council, and the local black press swung their support behind the strikers. A "Committee for Justice to Hospital Workers" was established with A. Philip Randolph among its members, while additional labor and civil rights leaders (including Malcolm X) lent their support. Although the hospital proved intransigent, Governor Nelson Rockefeller eventually intervened (citing the dangers of "explosive" potential and "racial considerations and tensions"), which forced a settlement whereby Local 1199 would return to work in exchange for a promise of legislation to permit genuine collective bargaining. The hospital workers subsequently got raises, bringing their pay level up to the federal minimum wage, and 1199 grew as a result of the strike's outcome, but it would take yet another strike against suburban Lawrence Hospital to get a law passed extending collective bargaining rights to all New York state hospital workers.

Local 1199B Charleston

By the late 1960s, 1199's success in organizing the New York metropolitan area's hospitals had inspired it to carry the struggle elsewhere. In 1968, hospital workers from Charleston, South Carolina, approached the union, resulting in the chartering of Local 1199B that October to represent approximately 500 nurses' aides, orderlies, and food and maintenance workers at two Charleston hospitals. All of these workers were African American and the vast majority of them were women. They would go on strike the following March in what Fink and Greenberg describe as "one of the South's most disruptive and bitter labor confrontations since the 1930s." They had an existing history of on-the-job activism dating to a dispute the previous year in which five black nurses' assistants at Medical College Hospital had been fired for protesting against disrespectful treatment; with the backing of the local African-American community and an investigation by the Department of Health, Education, and Welfare, these women subsequently won reinstatement under the provisions of the 1964 Civil Rights Act. Following this incident, the hospital workers clandestinely started building an organization, getting vital advice from Isaiah Bennett, the president of a tobacco workers' local in town, as well as use of his union's meeting facilities. Their cause also began to be publicized by Bill Saunders, a local Black Power activist and community organizer, in his bulletin called the *Lowcountry Newsletter.* After hospital administrators repeatedly ignored the workers' requests for a meeting to address their grievances, they approached Local 1199 for representation on Bennett's advice.

Local 1199 increased the pressure on the administration at Medical College Hospital to meet, picketing in December 1968 and lobbying state legislators and local government officials. When Medical's president, Dr. William McCord, finally agreed to a scheduled meeting, 1199B's representatives who showed up were surprised to find a contingent of anti-union loyalists awaiting them. This in turn led about 100 union supporters to crash the meeting and stage an impromptu sit-down in McCord's office, which was broken up by police. When twelve union activists were subsequently fired for their involvement in this incident, 1199B declared a strike on March 20, 1969, and Medical's hospital workers walked out, followed by workers at Charleston County Hospital one week later. 1199B's demands were straightforward: recognition with dues check-off (automatic payroll deduction), and reinstatement of the twelve fired activists. McCord's condescending early comment to the press that "I am not about to turn a $25 million complex over to a bunch of people who don't have a grammar school education" indicated that the administration had no intention of capitulating. The hospital sought and got an injunction to crack down severely on picketing; over the following weeks hundreds (more than 350 over one four-day period) were arrested as the city police, State Law Enforcement Division, and ultimately the National Guard were called in to quell the numerous demonstrations in conjunction with the strike.

"While already an important element of the union's message," Fink and Greenberg wrote, "the civil rights theme assumed an unprecedented centrality in the Charleston strike." Seeking to transform the conflict into a national-level civil rights issue, Local 1199 invited the Southern Christian Leadership Conference (SCLC) on board. SCLC leaders such as Ralph Abernathy and Andrew Young provided much-needed visibility, while the organization coordinated near-daily marches and picketing actions and built a wide-ranging community network to provide strikers with financial assistance, food, and services. As honorary chair of the union's 1968 national organizing campaign, recently widowed Coretta Scott King showed up to lead one major march while the UAW's Walter

Reuther arrived for another. Individual strikers attended church services in their hospital uniforms to promote their cause, and black churches from across the state donated generously. SCLC organized local high school students in a protest that kept as much as 30 percent of the student body out of school and coordinated boycotts of Charleston stores. "Support Our Soul Power with Your Green Power!!!" read one widely posted flyer; on May 24, the SCLC got more confrontational, staging "shop-ins" that clogged aisles on King Street, the city's main tourist and business artery. Bill Saunders, the local Black Power activist, organized an armed militia that guarded union meetings and appeared at some demonstrations. Occasional instances of window breaking, gunshots, and firebombings were reported during the conflict. Meanwhile, individual New York hospital workers and other labor unions helped raise a $185,000 strike fund that offset strikers' rent and food expenses; local Catholic priests spoke out on their behalf; the International Longshoremen's Association considered shutting down the port in sympathy; and several congressmen offered to mediate. In Fink and Greenberg's words, the Charleston strike became a "liberal cause célèbre."

Despite the negative publicity and pressure from local business owners for a settlement, the two hospitals stood firm. Operations were scaled back, with volunteers and some strikebreakers filling in to keep the hospitals running, while the administration pursued legislation to have the SCLC's school boycott outlawed. With resources flagging, toward the end of May Local 1199 began to look for an exit strategy, but a breakthrough came when the union discovered that Medical College Hospital's federal funding had been under threat since the previous September due to a litany of civil rights violations. Behind-the-scenes pressure from the Department of Health, Education, and Welfare succeeded in bringing the hospitals to the table, but a compromise settlement fell through at the last minute when management refused to rehire the twelve fired union activists, claiming that white nurses would quit if the activists were reinstated. As the strike again escalated, a federal mediator from the Department of Labor came in to negotiate a settlement. The resulting agreement, announced on June 27, did not include union recognition, but 1199's leadership was able to claim victory since the settlement did provide pay raises, a grievance procedure, and dues check-off through an employee credit union. Unfortunately for the workers, the hospitals ultimately circumvented the latter two conditions, and without continued support from the national office, 1199B lost ground.

Memphis Sanitation Strike

The 1968 strike by Memphis sanitation workers offers another clear-cut example of a strike where civil rights concerns predominated. As in the case of hospital work, garbage disposal was an industry where minority workers toiled for low wages with little or no chance to rise into the supervisory ranks reserved for white workers. In addition, sanitation work was uniquely dirty, degrading, and potentially dangerous. The Memphis city government's desire to keep costs low led it to resist investing in labor-saving equipment, leaving black sanitation workers to hand-carry leaking garbage containers long distances and deal with old, unreliable compactors. Mayor Henry Loeb ran the city on a paternalistic basis, condescendingly referring to African-American municipal employees as "my Negroes," in what the strikers would characterize as a "plantation mentality." Their choice of "I AM A MAN" as a slogan not only demanded that their basic human dignity be recognized, but also underscored their feelings of emasculation and powerlessness to work under such conditions. In Michael Honey's words, the Memphis sanitation workers' strike "quickly developed into a stark confrontation pitting supporters of the old racial-economic order against practically the entire Memphis African-American community and major portions of the city's organized labor movement," and their struggle took on national-level significance in the ongoing freedom struggle.

Memphis sanitation workers had shown an interest in organizing as early as 1960, in tandem with the growing civil rights consciousness among black students organizing sit-ins at the time. A brief walkout that year in response to the city's refusal to negotiate had failed as support from local Teamsters evaporated. In 1963, sanitation workers again attempted organizing with help from the Retail Clerks Local 1529, an effort that was forced underground after their leading activist was fired. The following year, the sanitation workers successfully formed an association that affiliated with AFSCME

When African-American Memphis sanitation workers went on strike for union recognition in February 1968, they chose the phrase "I AM A MAN" as their rallying cry. By asserting the workers' humanity and dignity, the slogan made clear that their strike was not simply about wages and working conditions, but part of the larger African-American struggle for justice. Dr. Martin Luther King Jr. came to Memphis several times to build support for the strike. The strikers' determination, the scrutiny of the nation, intervention by an undersecretary of labor, and the outrage after Dr. King's assassination in Memphis finally brought victory in April, when the city signed a contract with AFSCME Local 1733 that addressed all the workers' demands. (*Courtesy:* Special Collections, University of Memphis Libraries.)

to become Local 1733, which the city adamantly refused to recognize. In 1966, Local 1733 actually voted to strike and some members even walked off the job, but an injunction won by the city and threats of firings quickly brought the workers back. Then in February 1968, a convergence of events served to stiffen the sanitation workers' resolve.

First, a rainstorm caused black workers to be sent home while white truck drivers and supervisors remained on the job to collect a full day's pay, a typical occurrence representing a long-standing grievance among black sanitation workers. Two days later, another rainstorm caused a malfunctioning trash compactor to crush two African-American workers who had temporarily taken shelter inside of it, and these men's families were deemed ineligible for either workmen's compensation or a life insurance settlement. With their anger boiling over, Local 1733 members at a February 12 union meeting voted unanimously to strike, and an ambitious list of demands—subsequently pared down by the national AFSCME office—was drawn up, including recognition with dues check-off, higher wages, overtime, back pay for rainy days when black workers had been sent home, and safety upgrades.

The city administration was particularly adamant on the matter of recognition, fearing this could set a "bad precedent" for other municipal workers. Mayor Loeb, in typical paternalistic style, announced his intention to "protect" sanitation workers from the rapacious designs of organized labor. In the meantime, he got an injunction against picketing, deployed police to intimidate the strikers, and began hiring scab replacements. On February 22, Local 1733 held a mass meeting and crashed City Council deliberations to demand that a resolution on the strike be formulated. When the Council's promise to do so proved empty, sanitation workers staged an ad hoc march to a local black church serving as strike headquarters. The march ended violently when police sprayed mace on the demonstrators. This turn of events galvanized black Memphians of all backgrounds behind the strike. The NAACP and local black press had advocated on behalf of the sanitation workers from the outset; now numerous black ministers and other community leaders came forward to form Citizens on the Move for Equality (COME), which sponsored daily marches and nightly mass meetings, as well as a boycott of downtown businesses. Working-class black women organized themselves into the Concerned Citizens for the Sanitation Workers and Their Families. COME prevailed upon nationally prominent civil rights leaders to lend their support, with the result that Roy Wilkins, Bayard Rustin, and Martin Luther King Jr. arrived to address crowds numbering in the thousands. White and black trade unionists in the Memphis Trades and Labor Council donated financially and expressed solidarity with the strikers, with 500 of them marching on March 4. The AFL-CIO's national office also lent financial aid, paying $100,000 over the course of the two-month-long strike.

Reverend King in particular clearly understood the linkages between race and class that characterized this kind of low-wage work, as well as the direction in which the civil rights movement had been evolving after the passage of the

1964 Civil Rights Act. "Now our struggle is for genuine equality, which means economic equality," King made clear in one speech. "What does it profit a man to be able to eat at an integrated lunch counter if he doesn't earn enough money to buy a hamburger and a cup of coffee?" he went on to ask. On March 28, a demonstration that King was at the head of turned violent when police clashed with young participants, some belonging to groups advocating armed resistance like the "Invaders." Angry youths broke windows and looted as the police beat dozens of demonstrators, shot one black man, called in the National Guard, and imposed a curfew. King, banned from leading any more demonstrations, returned to Memphis on April 3 and delivered his famous "Mountaintop" speech; the following day he was assassinated. The spontaneous outbreak of rioting in Memphis and around the country that followed the murder, the unrelenting media spotlight, and the intervention of the undersecretary of labor finally succeeded in bringing the Memphis city administration to the table. On April 16 a contract was announced that addressed all the strikers' demands: a wage increase, effective recognition, dues check-off, and merit-based promotion. It was approved unanimously by the union membership. As a result of this victory, AFSCME Local 1733 grew to be the city's single largest union local and inspired sanitation workers elsewhere in the South to organize.

During the middle decades of the twentieth century, minority and female workers stood up on numerous occasions for equal rights, more often in ad hoc protest actions and sometimes in full-blown strikes that escalated to become major battlegrounds in the national freedom struggle. Clearly, in the minds of many such workers, labor rights and civil rights were one and the same. As for how to assess the phenomenon of civil rights strikes, there would appear to be no clear formula for success—although it is worth noting that in most of these struggles strikers sought to improve their chances by cultivating support in the local community and by appealing to regional and national civil rights and labor leaders and organizations. In some industries, as in meatpacking and auto manufacturing, even wildcat strikes in pursuit of fair treatment could bring significant gains; in other cases, as in the Charleston Hospital Strike of 1969, victory proved elusive despite a strong community orientation and advocacy from nationally prominent figures. As with many episodes in labor history, the significance lies not in whether the workers were ultimately victorious, but in the fact that they engaged in these battles at all.

See also: World War II Hate Strikes, 126; Strikes in the United States Since World War II, 226.

Bibliography

Cobble, Dorothy Sue. *The Other Women's Movement: Workplace Justice and Social Rights in Modern America.* Princeton, NJ: Princeton University Press, 2004.

Draper, Alan. *Conflict of Interests: Organized Labor and the Civil Rights Movement in the South, 1954–1968.* Ithaca, NY: ILR Press, 1994.

Fehn, Bruce. "African American Women and the Struggle for Equality in the Meatpacking Industry, 1940–1960." *Journal of Women's History* 10 (Spring 1998): 45–69.

Fink, Leon, and Brian Greenberg. *Upheaval in the Quiet Zone: A History of Hospital Workers' Union Local 1199.* Urbana: University of Illinois Press, 1989.

Flug, Michael. "Organized Labor and the Civil Rights Movement of the 1960s: The Case of the Maryland Freedom Union." *Labor History* 31 (Summer 1990): 322–46.

Hall, Jacquelyn Dowd. "The Long Civil Rights Movement and the Political Uses of the Past." *Journal of American History* 91 (March 2005): 1245.

Honey, Michael K. "Martin Luther King, Jr., the Crisis of the Black Working Class, and the Memphis Sanitation Strike." In *Southern Labor in Transition, 1946–1995*, ed. Robert H. Zieger. Knoxville: University of Tennessee Press, 1997.

———. *Southern Labor and Black Civil Rights: Organizing Memphis Workers.* Urbana and Chicago: University of Illinois Press, 1993.

Korstad, Robert. *Civil Rights Unionism: Tobacco Workers and the Struggle for Democracy in the Mid-Twentieth Century.* Chapel Hill: University of North Carolina Press, 2003.

Korstad, Robert, and Nelson Lichtenstein. "Opportunities Found and Lost: Labor, Radicals, and the Early Civil Rights Movement." *Journal of American History* 75 (December 1988): 786–811.

Pritchett, Wendell E. "A Northern Civil Rights Movement: Community Race Relations and the Beth El Hospital Strike of 1962." *Labor's Heritage* 10 (Fall 1999/Winter 2000): 4–23.

Vargas, Zaragosa. *Labor Rights Are Civil Rights: Mexican American Workers in Twentieth-Century America.* Princeton, NJ: Princeton University Press, 2005.

WORLD WAR II HATE STRIKES

James Wolfinger

In the American popular imagination, World War II was a moment of national unity when the United States came together to fight the obvious evil of fascism. Among others, the historian Stephen Ambrose and the journalist Tom Brokaw have told well this popular American story. And to be sure, there is some truth to it. After Pearl Harbor, American men and women overwhelmingly supported the war overseas. Thousands rushed to join the military, and millions made sacrifices to support the war effort. But the tale of national unity and sacrifice is only part of the story. Equally telling are the conflicts that buffeted American society during the war. Obvious examples include the internment of Japanese Americans, the African-American Double V campaign for victory over fascism abroad and Jim Crow racism at home, and the demands of women and black workers for equal pay and fair treatment in the workplace. These conflicts demonstrated that while there may have been unanimity on the question of fascism abroad, there were still deep divisions in many realms of American life.

These divisions often emerged most noticeably on the shop floor. Officially, organized labor adopted a "no-strike pledge" shortly after Pearl Harbor in December 1941, effectively promising not to strike with the United States at war. In reality, workers, who had gained some power during the organizing campaigns of the 1930s, knew that with the nation at war and in need of their labor they had a great opportunity to improve their workplace lives. The strike, they understood, was their most potent weapon, and in every year of the war American workers ignored their leadership's pledge and launched thousands of so-called wildcat strikes (strikes without the consent of their leaders), usually over matters of wages, working conditions, and union recognition.

Wildcat strikes often proved effective in improving shop-floor conditions, but at times white workers used them not against management but against a different "threat": African Americans and, less frequently, women, who they saw as dangerous competitors for "their" jobs. These "hate strikes" against African Americans and women shook every region of the country, from Detroit to Mobile, Philadelphia to Portland, and dozens of places in between. They also hit a multitude of industries, including armaments, shipbuilding, autos, and transportation. The problem grew so bad that government official Robert Weaver worried that an "epidemic" of work stoppages threatened vital war production.

Weaver's concern was warranted, although it is difficult to determine exactly how many hate strikes took place. The federal government's Bureau of Labor Statistics tracked strikes, but only recorded job actions that affected at least six employees and lasted for a full day or shift. Many racially motivated walkouts were too brief to show up in the statistics. Still, in 1943 and again in 1944, the Bureau's *Monthly Labor Review* reported some fifty strikes over racial issues. Government statistics did not adequately capture the arc of hate strike activity. There were few of these strikes in 1941 and 1942, they peaked in 1943 and 1944, and then largely faded away by 1945. Despite their limited history, hate strikes at their height had a significant impact on the war effort by, for example, sapping the nation of 2.5 million hours of war production in just a three-month period from March to May 1943.

Although they had a relatively brief history,

these strikes offer an important window to examine not only racial cleavages in the working class, but also other related issues. One of those issues was gender relations. Women were generally expected to take care of the home and children while men went off to work. The labor shortages of World War II brought hundreds of thousands of women into the country's workplaces, where men often regarded them as at best a drag on their wages (since women generally earned less than men for the same work) and at worst a threat to their jobs. Moreover, white women in the workforce came into contact with black men, which raised the taboo of interracial sex.

Internal union politics also played a major role in the hate strikes. In the 1930s, unions in the newly created Congress of Industrial Organizations (CIO) organized workers throughout an industry, regardless of their occupation. This meant enrolling all workers in the union, including African Americans. Many white workers disliked having black people in their union, but CIO leaders argued that strong unions required workers to set aside racial divisions and present a united front to management. In general, CIO unions, especially those in the North, offered at least tepid support of black workers' demands for equality. The older, craft-based American Federation of Labor (AFL) organized workers according to their particular jobs, which meant skilled workers ran the unions. African Americans were largely barred from the AFL and segregated in most unions that they could join. These unions, stronger in industries that required more skilled labor, offered little support to black workers and seldom tried to settle hate strikes to the satisfaction of African Americans. The two labor bodies had basic differences in their approach to black workers, and as they competed to organize American industry during World War II, their divergent attitudes helped spark hate strikes.

Management played a key role in the hate strikes as well. Managers saw the racial divisions in organized labor and worked to exacerbate them. Companies had long used racial antagonisms in the working class to divide the workforce, undermine workers' solidarity, and keep wages down, but the growth of the CIO made matters more urgent for corporate America. CIO unions often made stronger demands than the AFL, and companies believed the best way to stymie the new unions was to play on the working class's racial antipathies by encouraging white workers to feel threatened by African Americans. Management not only inflamed already tense situations, it often created openly racist workplaces that made workers believe a hate strike could succeed. Hate strikes on the whole were short and poorly planned; without management support, or at least benign neglect, white workers would have had trouble getting them started.

The government also played a crucial part in the course these strikes followed. Despite a long history of ignoring the rights of African-American workers, the federal government in 1941 committed itself to nondiscrimination with the promulgation of Executive Order 8802, which established the Fair Employment Practices Committee (FEPC). President Franklin Roosevelt created the FEPC under pressure from black labor leader A. Philip Randolph, who wanted the government to halt discrimination in war industries, government employment, and the military. The FEPC had little power (it only had authority to investigate war industries), but for many African Americans it represented a long-awaited government commitment to their rights. That commitment only held strong, however, when it coincided with the nation's war production needs. In most cases the government ignored its obligation to African Americans, especially in the South, if doing so meant white workers would settle their grievances and return to their jobs more quickly. The willingness or unwillingness of federal authorities to enforce antidiscrimination policies ultimately played a critical role in the outcome of many hate strikes.

Finally, it is no coincidence that hate strikes took place during World War II. The war caused massive changes in American society: cities grew explosively; housing became outrageously expensive when it was available at all; and black people and women, emboldened by the fight against fascism abroad, demanded their equal rights as citizens at home. The war was a watershed that changed where and how people lived and gave them new ideas about what it meant to be American citizens. Just as importantly, the war ended the Great Depression, giving workers a sense of security for the first time in a decade. But they remembered the bad times and worried they would return. Any threat to the jobs of white males, particularly from more assertive black and women workers, scared white men, especially when they thought about the 1930s. Thus, hate strikes grew out of a context of massive change, especially in gender, race, and labor relations. In this unsettling and sometimes threatening environment, some workers resorted to hate strikes to protect their jobs. The case studies that follow highlight how these multiple themes emerged in hate strikes in different cities and industries across the country.

Philadelphia

Of all the hate strikes during World War II, the costliest took place at the Philadelphia Transportation Company (PTC), when 8,000 white employees walked out in August 1944. The strike shut down the nation's third-largest war production center for six days and forced President Roosevelt to use armed troops to end it. At the time, the strike was widely regarded as a terrible blow to America's war effort, which it certainly was. But the strike also revealed the explosive mix of race, gender, and union-management relations that roiled many workplaces during World War II.

Philadelphia, like the rest of the nation's industrial centers, grew tremendously during the war. From a population of 250,000 in 1940, the number of black Philadelphians grew to 375,000 by 1950, an increase of 50 percent that mostly came during World War II. At the same time, the white population remained steady at about 1.7 million people, which meant African Americans went from 13 percent to over 18 percent of the population. New African-American migrants found that housing discrimination confined them to the oldest, most rundown buildings, many of which lacked basics such as running water. At the same time, their children attended segregated schools; adults described the police force as "brutal"; and, perhaps most disheartening, African Americans encountered pervasive employment discrimination in most of the city's businesses. According to one study, 90 percent of Pennsylvania's companies discriminated against African-American workers in their hiring practices.

The experiences of black Philadelphians during World War II mirrored those of African Americans across the country who found discrimination in employment and housing hypocritical. The war, African Americans argued in their Double V campaign, had to be about defeating fascism abroad and Jim Crow at home. In Philadelphia, they took the battle to such discriminatory companies as the Pennsylvania Railroad, AT&T, and, most prominently, the Philadelphia Transportation Company (PTC). The PTC had hired black workers for decades and had some 500 African-American workers in the early 1940s, but they were relegated to menial labor. Black employees were not allowed to drive transit vehicles or interact with the public. As the New York newspaper *PM* put it, "PTC has operated along Southern lines [for years and white workers have] simply accepted the fact that [driving] is a white man's job, and no Negro is going to get it." This attitude galled black Philadelphians because the PTC was a semi-public company that received taxes as well as fares from the black community. PTC discrimination was, according to the African-American newspaper the *Pittsburgh Courier,* "tantamount to discrimination by the City of Philadelphia."

Angered by the discrimination, black Philadelphians, with the support of the National Association for the Advancement of Colored People (NAACP), pressed PTC management for driving jobs. PTC president Ralph Senter refused to consider the idea, saying the company could not promote African Americans without the consent of the Philadelphia Rapid Transit Employees Union (PRTEU), a company union unaffiliated with the AFL or the CIO. PRTEU leaders worked closely with the company, keeping wages down as a *quid pro quo* for white workers' control of the best jobs. Rank-and-file white workers knew their wages were about 10 percent below the rates in Chicago, Detroit, and New York, but they accepted their lower pay in exchange for the racial prerogatives they received. This arrangement, observed the NAACP's *Crisis,* meant that "regardless of [qualifications] a Negro could never hope to fill certain jobs, such as conductors, motormen, [or] bus drivers." Both PTC management and its white workers believed they benefited from the arrangement, and neither felt obliged to open jobs to African Americans.

This cozy relationship changed for two reasons. First, on the heels of a new PRTEU-PTC contract that provided terrible provisions for pay and working conditions, the CIO's Transport Workers Union (TWU), a fairly racially egalitarian union, challenged the PRTEU in a representation election in the spring of 1944. In the campaign, the TWU downplayed its commitment to the CIO's racial egalitarianism, instead arguing that a vote for the TWU was a vote for a better-paying contract. The PRTEU and rival AFL unions, which also wanted to represent PTC workers, countered with racist attacks, sending out speakers to argue that "a vote for [the] CIO is a vote for Niggers on the job." This ugly rhetoric swayed some workers, but the TWU won the election with 55 percent of the vote. Despite downplaying black workers' rights, the TWU stood by its commitment to black workers' access to PTC jobs, which gave African Americans a powerful ally in their campaign for equal work at the transit company.

The second reason the relationship between the PTC and its workers changed was a decision by the Fair Employment Practices Committee that ordered the company to cease its discrimination. Confronted by black workers' demands, TWU bargaining agents, and FEPC orders, management backed down and agreed to employ black workers as drivers, starting August 1, 1944.

In the weeks leading up to the black drivers' start date, a number of white PTC employees (many of whom were former leaders of the deposed PRTEU) made it clear they would not accept African-American promotions. Some of these workers came from the Jim Crow South, especially Virginia and the Carolinas, and the thought of working as equals with African Americans infuriated them. However, many of the workers were longtime residents of Philadelphia: Irish and Italian Philadelphians made up 70 percent of the transit company's workforce and they had participated in the PTC's discriminatory employment system for decades. Longtime Philadelphians and new immigrants from the South were equally willing to discriminate against African Americans. These white workers circulated leaflets in the carbarns, telling their coworkers they had to form a "white supremacy movement" to protect the jobs of white PTC employees serving overseas. This was a false but powerful claim that tapped into many workers' fears about losing their jobs just a few years after the Depression.

A series of meetings on PTC property soon followed, with white workers vowing to walk off the job if the transit company went through with its plan to give driving jobs to African-American workers. Rather than stamp out this movement, PTC management allowed it to grow, believing it would anger white PTC workers and weaken the TWU. The CIO union had realized the company's worst fears during contract talks by demanding a 15 percent pay raise and a better pension. Management knew these demands would cost millions, but they also knew the Smith-Connally Act prohibited wartime strikes and gave the government power to abrogate any contract and toss out a union if it led a strike against a war production company. Management used its workers' racism to undermine the CIO union.

At 4:00 A.M. on August 1, 1944, a few dozen white drivers refused to work and asked the rest of the employees to join them. By noon, the transit system had come to a halt and the city was at a standstill. Philadelphia's key industries fell idle because their employees could not get to work. In all, manufacturers reported the first few days of the strike cost them 3 million hours of lost labor (25 percent of the city's production capacity). One military official warned that if the strike continued it would "delay the day of victory."

PTC management demonstrated its complicity in the hate strike from the start. Rather than trying to break the strike by having supervisors and willing workers drive, the PTC shut down the high-speed lines and closed its ticket windows. It left its carbarns open so strike leaders could meet to plot strategy and hold rallies to inflame the workforce. And it blamed the FEPC for fomenting the strike, which the company argued would only end if African Americans, the government, and the TWU backed down and accepted discrimination on the transit lines. Government officials replied that such an arrangement was out of the question, so the PTC happily stepped aside from further deliberations, hoping the strike would lead to the TWU's demise.

In strike meetings, the drivers made it clear that their greatest fears were the loss of their jobs and the denigration of their status as white Americans. "We don't want Negroes and we won't work with Negroes," Frank Carney, one of the strike leaders, told a cheering crowd "[because] this is a white man's job." For many of the workers, this was not just a matter of keeping blacks down, but of whites maintaining their status, too. "This is a case of the white race keeping *its place* [emphasis in original]," observed one man. Meanwhile another strike leader, James McMenamin, claimed that merely sharing a bench with black drivers between runs would contaminate white workers. "Their standard of living," he told a reporter, "is very far below the standard of operators." White workers would get "bedbugs" if they had to sit next to African Americans.

While the preservation of white workers' exclusive access to jobs and racial status was key to the strikers, it was not the only issue at stake. White drivers also believed black workers' promotions threatened their neighborhoods and the virtue of Philadelphia's white women. Black drivers supposedly endangered white neighborhoods, especially in North Philadelphia, because the PTC generally placed its drivers at depots near their homes and many of these stations were on the outer edge of the city's expanding black neighborhoods. So African Americans taking jobs at these depots would mean not only more black workers at the PTC, but also more African Americans with the income and desire to buy homes in the white neighborhoods near the carbarns. This development, in the words of one defender of the strikers, would leave white neighborhoods "demoralized by inroads of Negro residents." The FEPC and black drivers countered this argument, saying, "Non-white workers will not make an 'invasion' of white workers' preserves," but this assurance brought little calm to the PTC workforce.

For many white PTC workers, African Americans' entrance into their depots and communities was bad enough, but the fact that black men would then have more contact with white women made matters far worse. The transit company employed some 500 white women, many as drivers in place of their husbands who were serving overseas. Even before the strike began, these women complained about the "attention" they received on late night runs and reported that black passengers threatened to "get" them in the middle of the night. Strike leaders knew the kind of feelings such threats inspired and brought a woman to the carbarns to tell everyone how she had "been slashed by a Negro." Other strike leaders asked the crowds, "Do you know what colored people want—it's social equality with white women. Do you want your wife or mother to ride with them on empty trolleys?" The threats black men allegedly posed led female drivers to swear they would never work with African Americans.

Although the strikers were adamant in their refusal to work with black workers, the walkout's damage to war production just two months after D-Day meant President Roosevelt had to crush the strike. On August 3 he ordered the military to seize the PTC, and on August 5 General Philip Hayes led 5,000 troops into Philadelphia. They came prepared to drive buses and trains and enforce the black workers' promotions. At the same time, the Selective Service threatened to revoke the draft deferments of all striking workers. In this case, the power of the federal government came down squarely on the black workers' side and forced white PTC employees to bring their hate strike to an end one week after it began. Racial tensions lingered at the company, but military intervention coupled with the TWU winning a more lucrative contract stopped any revival of the nation's costliest hate strike.

Although the strike lasted only a week and ended in failure for the PTC's white workers, it highlighted a number of critical issues for understanding American labor history. First, it demonstrated the profound racial cleavages that divided the working class, not just in the South but across the nation. Second, it revealed how management manipulated white racism in an attempt to undermine industrial unionism and protect corporate profits. Finally, this hate strike showed the power the federal government had to enforce equal opportunity in the workplace. When white PTC workers in control of a vital industry in Philadelphia brought the city to a halt, federal force quickly ended the walkout and demonstrated that hate strikes could not succeed if national authorities thought the war effort was in danger, or if they simply acted to enforce their stated policy of nondiscrimination.

Mobile

Like Philadelphia and many other American cities, the port city of Mobile, Alabama, had a painful experience with massive population growth during World War II. The city, which had some 79,000 residents in 1940, grew to 125,000 in 1943, while the metropolitan area went from 174,000 to 260,000 people in the same period. Almost overnight, it seemed to observers, Mobile changed from a tired Gulf seaport to a bustling city "overrun by war workers." Tens of thousands of migrants came, mostly to work at area shipyards, the largest being the Alabama Dry Dock and Shipbuilding Company (ADDSCO). They left Mobile, in the novelist John Dos Passos's terms, as quoted by historian Bruce Nelson, looking "trampled and battered like a city that's been taken by storm."

This growth created a number of problems, including poor health care and a lack of schools, but nothing caused the city more trouble than its housing and job markets. A housing shortage caused rents to double at the start of the war and forced workers to live in homes that often had no sewage system or running water. Bad problems for white residents were far worse for black Mobilians, whose population grew from 29,000 to 45,000 in the 1940s. Private black housing consisted mostly of what journalists and government investigators called "ancient slums" while the National Housing Agency, which had built 14,000 units for white Mobilians, constructed only 934 units for black residents. In one case, twenty-seven people lived in a home with only one toilet and one water faucet.

As bad as housing conditions were for black Mobilians, the workplace was equally troublesome. The two major employers in the city were Alabama Drydock and the Gulf Shipbuilding Corporation. The former, ADDSCO, employed only about 1,000 people in the late 1930s, but boosted that number to 30,000 in 1943, including 7,000 black male and female workers. Black Mobilians widely regarded ADDSCO as the fairest employer around, even though the company limited African Americans to unskilled and semiskilled jobs. When pressed, management swore it would never "employ a negro in a skilled capacity." Gulf Shipbuilding was far worse. The company opened in 1940 and eventually employed some 10,000 workers. As late as 1942, only twenty of these workers were black. When asked why Gulf had so few black workers, a company vice president explained that "work stoppages might develop from the employment of Negroes even in unskilled jobs," which made it "much simpler not to hire them in the first place." Later in the war, when there were few white men left to hire, some 700 African Americans found work at Gulf, but they were confined to unskilled jobs. This racism on the part of company officials helped set a context that made hate strikes likely, if not inevitable, when African Americans finally gained skilled jobs.

In addition to the city's overcrowded conditions and the attitude of the shipyards' management, the employment of white women added to workplace tensions. Women first began working in the shipyards in 1942, when some 100 female welders joined ADDSCO. Within two years, the yard had increased its female labor force to 3,000. Many of these women worked in clerical positions rather than performing skilled labor, and their hiring, as Nelson pointed out, "could be rationalized as a temporary phenomenon that would not undermine the system of social relations in the Jim Crow South." Temporary or not, the employment of a large white female workforce opened the possibility of interracial sexual contact when black men got jobs in the yards and made ADDSCO an even more explosive environment.

An increasingly restive black population, led by local NAACP president John LeFlore, compounded matters. LeFlore made it clear World War II would change the city. "The Negro," he said on one occasion, "is the real American, he is patriotic, he wants Democracy but has none of it, and he does not feel like fighting for Democracy until Democracy becomes more of a reality to him." Black members of the International Longshoremen's Association stood behind LeFlore during this speech, nodding in agreement. With LeFlore leading the way, black Mobilians demanded equal treatment on the city's public transportation system, in the housing market, and—most importantly—at the shipyards.

To augment the NAACP's efforts, African Americans turned to the FEPC. They urged the committee to help them break down employment barriers at the shipyards, and in November 1942 the FEPC ordered ADDSCO and Gulf Shipyard to hire African Americans and promote them to skilled jobs. The shipyards' managers were reluctant to comply, however, arguing that their white workers would never stand for such a situation. Management was right to suggest white working-class racism could cause problems, but ADDSCO and Gulf never tried to soothe racial antagonisms. Instead, the companies fanned any potential conflict by implying that racial clashes were an ordinary outcome of black employment.

African Americans also looked to local unions for help. AFL unions, which controlled much of the skilled organized labor force in the yards, dismissed talk of black workers' promotions and relegated their few black members to auxiliaries, which limited African Americans' rights to shape union policy or train for skilled jobs. Most black workers understood the AFL's stance and, as one union official put it, "stay[ed] away in droves." The CIO, though far from perfect in its support of black workers' rights, was far better than the AFL. CIO leaders such as Phil Murray consistently told black audiences his unions "should admit to membership upon a basis of absolute equality every man and woman . . . regardless of race, creed, political or religious belief." Despite the CIO's growing national power, leaders of its Industrial Union of Marine and Shipbuilding Workers of America (IUMSWA) found only limited support in Mobile, and that mostly came from black workers. White workers evidently had little use for a union that preached racial equality. In 1943, IUMSWA counted only 800 members in a workforce of some 30,000 ADDSCO employees, and organizers worried that with the overwhelming majority of their support coming from the black community, they were in danger of becoming a "nigger union." If the company promoted African Americans, IUMSWA leaders knew they would have little power to keep white workers from reacting violently.

On May 25, 1943, all of these issues—the weak CIO, the presence of white women on the job, the racism of the white workers, and company-sponsored discrimination—came to a head in one of World War II's most violent hate strikes. ADDSCO needed as many as 2,500 more welders to keep up with demand and turned to black workers for help. Twelve men received promotions and worked as a segregated unit on the night of May 24 without a problem. But the next morning small groups of white workers began to gather in the yards, stoking their anger by passing rumors of black violence and sexual assault. As company guards passively looked on, 4,000 workers beat African-American employees with bricks, hammers, and pieces of steel. Luckily no one was killed, but FEPC officials estimated at least fifty people were injured, all of them black. The riot lasted most of the day, and subsequent turmoil slowed production for three more days.

Investigators searching for the causes of the riot pointed to two issues: white workers' fear of African-American competition in the workplace and the possibility of interracial sexual contact. Company officials and union leaders argued that much of the violence came from recent white migrants from rural areas, but their arguments reflected their bias against poor migrants more than the reality of the strike. Since the early 1940s, when war contracts first rolled into Mobile, city residents had called migrant workers "the lowest type of poor whites" who were "ferocious [and] unreliable . . . specimens . . . from the mountain areas." Certainly these young migrants joined the hate strike, but there was little difference between their behavior and that of other white workers at the shipyard. They all feared losing welding positions or any other jobs. This was a company that just a few years earlier had employed only 1,000 workers. Whites may have had the best jobs in 1943, but they knew the end of the war would cut thousands of positions and they wanted to control any available work. When they rioted, white workers did not attack just black welders (in fact there were none on the ADDSCO premises at the time), but instead turned on any African-American employees, including those in the repair yards where African Americans had always worked. Across ADDSCO, black workers reported that white workers ordered them to "get going [because] this is our shipyard."

The fear of lost jobs was tinder, but the spark came from the possibility of interracial sexual contact. Controversy over black-white sexual relations was common to America in the 1940s, but Mobile's location in the Deep South made any rumors extremely dangerous for black workers at the shipyards. Some of the most inflammatory rumors circulating on the morning of the strike included the story of "a Negro welder [who] had killed a white woman the night before" and, as the *Mobile Register* put it, the "indiscreet mingling of white and negro workers." Men were not the only ones angered by suggestions of interracial sex: white women, who may have found their femininity challenged by the dirty, physical labor of the shipyards, led many of the attacks. IUMSWA officials and other investigators argued white women started the riot when they attacked African Americans with bricks, iron bars, and broom handles.

In the aftermath of the riot, black and white workers found it difficult to resolve the situation. For African Americans, the hate strike demonstrated exactly where the bulk of white Mobile residents stood, and more than 1,000 black workers asked the War Manpower Commission (WMC) to transfer them to other employers. ADDSCO's labor shortage made their exodus impossible, so some African Americans returned on Wednesday night, but did so warily. The next morning thousands of whites quit working again. They wanted, in the words of one union official, to make the company promise "never to employ any negroes in any capacity." ADDSCO could promise no such thing, so the cycle of strikes, minus the violence, continued. Black workers went to work; some white workers struck for a time and then returned when it was apparent they could not win. Over the course of the week, this pattern of walkouts cut production by about 50 percent, leading the federal government to get more involved in settling matters.

On Friday, leaders from IUMSWA, the FEPC, and the WMC met with ADDSCO management. Some of the managers argued the only solution was to remove the black welders, but the FEPC refused to give up skilled jobs for African Americans. Finally an ADDSCO official proposed the creation of four segregated yards that would be staffed entirely by African Americans. Black workers could work in the other yards as laborers, but if they got promoted to skilled work, then they would have to transfer to one of the segregated yards. The FEPC did not like the idea of workplace segregation, but believed there was no other solution. Over the next several months, black workers decided they liked separate yards, where they earned nearly twice the wages of unskilled labor and took pride in building their own ships. IUMSWA embraced the yards too, since they soothed white workers and lowered the internal racial pressure on the union. The FEPC also grudgingly lauded the black shipyards as one of the few places in Mobile where "Negroes are advanced without any restriction."

The hate strike at least superficially achieved what white Mobilians wanted: It removed the "threat" to white workers' jobs and sharply reduced the chance of interracial sexual contact. Black leaders around the nation denounced the segregated arrangement as "a step backward," but their protests brought no change. The strike had convinced the government that in the Jim Crow South, as opposed to Philadelphia, it was best to retreat on racial democracy when war production was at stake. Black Mobilians accepted the arrangement, at least until the end of the war, when they learned the segregated yards offered no protection against layoffs and, in fact, made it easier to fire African Americans. V-J Day brought an end to government contracts and ADDSCO reduced its workforce from 30,000 to 3,000 employees. African Americans suffered most, as the company closed the segregated yards and put nearly all of its black employees out of work. The irony was that ADDSCO's hate strike seemed to work for white workers by cementing segregation in the shipyards, but in fact it did not save white workers' jobs: the end of government funding was the true threat, not the competition of black workers. No hate strike could save Mobile's white workers when the war drew to a close.

Detroit

Detroit was perhaps America's greatest war production city. Michigan received 10 percent of the government's contracts during the war, with 70 percent of that amount going to the Detroit area. Federal money brought people: the city's population grew by 286,000 in the early 1940s, mostly because of migration from the Midwest and upper South. These new arrivals (approximately 100,000 white people and 150,000 black people) sought work in the city's war industries, most prominently at Ford's River Rouge and Willow Run plants. The new white residents brought with them a racist worldview that helped fuel the hate strikes that flared during the war. Overall, Detroit's labor force more than doubled: from 396,000 workers at the end of the 1930s to 867,000 workers in 1943. Wages improved, too, as the work week lengthened and pay rose by 9 percent during the war. Everyone, it seemed on the surface, could find a job and get ahead in America's "Arsenal of Democracy."

Things were less promising away from the shop floor. Despite the growing population, government and private builders constructed little new housing. Detroit's vacancy rate was a scant 0.5 percent during the war, and in 1943 each housing ad received seven responses. Education, mass transit, and other municipal systems also failed to meet residents' needs. Everywhere, the city was crowded and uncomfortable, and the fact that so many white Southern migrants mixed with tens of thousands of black residents exacerbated the situation. Detroit was, in the words of *Life* magazine, "Dynamite."

Two events in the first three years of the war proved *Life* right. In 1941, the federal government and the Detroit Housing Commission announced plans to build the Sojourner Truth housing project for black residents. White residents in neighborhoods adjoining the proposed site opposed the project and the government initially backed down. But the outcry from the black community and city officials led federal authorities to reverse themselves, promising the homes to black war workers after all. When the first black families moved into the project in February 1942, a crowd of over 1,000 black supporters and white opponents filled the streets. In the ensuing melee forty people were injured and 220 arrested. African Americans ultimately got their homes, but some white Detroit residents made it clear they would defend their racial prerogatives—with violence if necessary.

The second event that demonstrated Detroit's tense atmosphere took place a year later in June 1943. One hot Sunday late that month, tens of thousands of city residents headed to Belle Isle, a park in the Detroit River. Black and white youth, uncomfortable in the heat and angered by rumors of interracial sexual violence, engaged in a number of altercations throughout the afternoon. Radio reports inflamed tempers, telling listeners, "A Negro had attempted to rape a white girl on a bus and had been caught and beaten up by some white men." The growing interracial conflict culminated in a riot that involved thousands of white and black people brawling with each other, smashing shop windows, and destroying property. The police eventually suppressed the violence, taking out their aggression on black residents by killing seventeen African Americans but not a single white resident. Overall, the riot claimed thirty-four lives (twenty-five black victims), injured 675 people, and led to 1,893 arrests. Even more, it, along with the Sojourner Truth riot, showed how race, sex, and the city's overcrowding had created a volatile atmosphere.

That atmosphere also crystallized in the hate strikes that swept the city. Plants owned by Packard, Chrysler-Dodge, Hudson Naval Ordnance, and Timken Roller Bearing all experienced hate strikes by the end of 1942. One of the largest of these strikes was at Packard, where black workers protested to their union, the United Auto Workers (UAW), a CIO affiliate, that management was unfairly favoring white workers in hiring and promotion decisions. UAW leadership held talks with Packard officials, who argued the promotions could lead to racial violence, but ultimately agreed to upgrade black workers. By suggesting violence might follow black promotions rather than promoting African Americans and saying it would brook no dissent, the company helped open the door for white workers to walk out. Officials knew a strike would not only keep the workforce divided against itself, but would undermine the power of the CIO. Sure enough, the day two black metal polishers started skilled jobs in September 1941, 250 white workers staged a walkout. Within forty minutes, the company agreed to stop the promotions until further negotiations took place. Just as in Philadelphia and Mobile, white workers' racism merged with a corporate agenda, leading white workers to believe their interests differed from African Americans and the CIO union that supported them.

After this initial conflict, Packard became a battleground for three years as white workers sought to control access to skilled work. In that time, management continued to exploit the racial divisions. As the scholar George Lipsitz argued,

"Management officials quietly encouraged the white hate-strikers . . . to undermine the UAW International officers," persistently telling workers to "defy their union and refuse to work with blacks." African Americans, despite the resistance, continued to fight for fair employment at Packard and finally got four black women assigned to skilled work in March 1943. The day they started, 3,000 white workers walked off the job in protest. Black workers countered with a walkout of their own until the union agreed to back their rights. But this agreement did not stop the hate strikes: each time African Americans started skilled jobs, white workers staged another hate strike, which then led to a counterstrike by black workers who demanded the company and union use fair employment practices or live without their labor. This vicious circle of walkouts lasted until the company finally agreed to warn all supervisors against racism and forced its workers to accept the promotions of African-American workers.

While events at Packard highlighted racial divisions in Detroit's workplaces, a strike at the Kelsey-Hayes Wheel Company demonstrated how hate strikes could grow from gender conflicts, too. Kelsey-Hayes, a manufacturer of auto wheels, got a contract in 1940 to build a defense plant in Plymouth, on the western edge of Detroit. Management began hiring workers in 1941 and almost immediately heard complaints from the UAW about women getting jobs. Men, the argument went, should have first rights to the jobs, with women getting any leftover work. Kelsey-Hayes officials bought this argument and agreed to hire women only for "light work," but cautioned that a shortage of men would lead to "all girls out there the same as the last war." That shortage came quickly and tensions grew when Kelsey-Hayes resumed hiring women. The local union president told an investigator that male employees believed "women [were] edging in on all the jobs." The men particularly worried the company would use women to undercut men's wages since men earned fifteen cents more an hour than women did. Rather than demanding equal wages for equal work, male workers sided with management in supporting wage differentials, which weakened working-class solidarity and tied men to discriminatory company policies.

In response to the threat women workers allegedly posed to "their" jobs, male employees walked out in October 1941. The strikers demanded the "removal of all girl employees from machine work," which was in their view "a man's job," and asked management to define a small number of low-skilled jobs as "female work." They also wanted management to stipulate that the workforce would be comprised of no more than 25 percent women, who could earn no more than 85 percent of what men made in the same jobs. The strikers found management quite pliant in negotiations and quickly achieved all their goals, so they returned to work only thirty-six hours after walking off the job. Both sides were happy: management had a divided workforce and the strikers kept their higher pay and control of the best jobs.

While the strike lasted only a day and a half, it revealed the way gender relations created fissures in the working class during World War II. Commentators across the country noted the divisions, with *BusinessWeek* calling the issue "one of the most dangerous and troublesome ones Washington will have to meet" and the U.S. Women's Bureau chastising the strikers for going against "the usual democratic policies of the C.I.O." and worrying that the UAW would now ignore women's issues in favor of protecting men. The bureau was right, as the UAW made good on its 1941 pledge to oppose "any attempt to train women to take the place of men on skilled jobs until such time as all the unemployed men have been put back to work." With companies and unions supporting men's claims on defense jobs in auto plants, the number of female autoworkers fell from 31,000 to 28,000 in 1941, even as more than half a million men obtained work in the industry. Women also found themselves on different seniority lists, which allowed employers to hire and upgrade laid-off male workers rather than promote women. When women complained about their treatment, the public generally remained unsympathetic to their cause. Faced with hostile employers and fellow employees willing to undercut the war effort to protect male privilege, women had few options.

The growth of war contracts and the conscription of millions of men changed the industry enough that women finally got fair opportunities at Kelsey-Hayes and other defense plants. Women's employment in auto plants grew from

69,000 in October 1942 (12 percent of the workforce) to 203,000 in November 1943 (26 percent of the workforce). Women also broke down many of the job assignment barriers, working in foundries, driving trucks, and so on. Despite these breakthroughs, wage differentials remained in place and companies still referred to jobs as either "male" or "female." Women continued to complain about the discrimination, arguing they could "see that they are doing exactly the same jobs that the men are [and that] they have not been getting a square deal." Gender conflict, female workers added, had undermined working-class solidarity and would continue to do so if men did not start basing pay on the job performed rather than on the gender of the person doing it.

This was a persuasive argument and one that male leaders in the UAW were inclined to heed by the end of the war as the female workforce reached its peak. In 1945, the UAW's executive board, feeling pressure from 200,000 female autoworkers, announced it would seek the elimination of gender-based job categories. This was a good faith effort, but by the end of the war it was too late: the auto industry had cemented its policy of treating men and women unequally. This had dire consequences for tens of thousands of female defense workers who were forced out of the auto industry when management reconverted to production for civilian use after the war. Women had greater power within the union in 1945 than they had in 1941, but the discriminatory settlement reached between male workers and management at Kelsey-Hayes and elsewhere made it easier for the companies to treat women workers as second-class citizens. Hundreds of thousands of women lost their good-paying jobs in auto and other defense plants across the country at least in part because of the pattern of shop-floor and contractual relations that World War II's hate strikes helped establish.

Conclusions

Hate strikes afflicted a variety of industries in many cities during World War II. In most cases they were driven by racial antagonisms in the workplace. Whatever problems white workers had with weak unions, low income, and little say on the shop floor, they had the color of their skin, and that brought material as well as psychological advantages. As W.E.B. DuBois pointed out, even the poorest white Americans understood the importance of race and used it to set themselves apart from their black counterparts. In American industry, white workers held the cleanest, best-paying jobs, while black workers were relegated to the dirtiest, most dangerous labor. Hate strikes quite often grew from white workers' attempts to keep control of the best jobs in the face of black workers' demands.

In staging these strikes, however, white workers were not simply giving vent to their most basic racist impulses. To be sure that was partly the case, but they were also making, at least at a subconscious level, a calculation that they were better off striking against their fellow employees than uniting across the color line. If the government waffled on its commitment to anti-discrimination in the workplace, if employers sided with the white men who walked out, and if many unions (particularly outside the CIO) tolerated segregation, then it is understandable that many white workers believed hate strikes could protect their marginally superior position in the workplace. Granted, these strikes failed to secure lasting benefits, but they nonetheless represented a strategy by white workers to control their work lives.

The wave of hate strikes, especially the fact that it ultimately lasted only a few years, tells us something about black workers as well as whites. While the rise of hate strikes early in the war showed how white workers had come to feel that they had greater control over the workplace and that they saw the strike as their most powerful tool, the decline of these strikes by 1945 tacitly demonstrated that by the end of the war white workers knew they could not dislodge African Americans from industrial jobs. More assertive black workers, often with help from the government and more racially egalitarian unions, won jobs and consolidated their place in the workforce—especially in the urban North. Hate strikes certainly roiled America's shop floors and revealed the limits of working-class solidarity, but their quick decline showed that African Americans, at least in the war years, made significant advances in their battle for workplace equality.

In the end, hate strikes, while often focused on racial issues, must be considered in a much broader context than just race relations on the shop floor. Employers played a major role in these strikes, helping pit white workers against black in the interest of stymieing the CIO and keeping the workforce split along racial and gender lines. The internal politics of the AFL and CIO also played a role, as each organization grappled with how to deal with racial issues while simultaneously trying to win the allegiance of the nation's working class. The growing numbers of women in the workforce played a part as the possibility of interracial sexual contact came up again and again in hate strikes across the country. At the same time, as events at Kelsey-Hayes showed, women could become the objects of hate strikes, as white men worried female employment would lower their pay and limit their claims on the best jobs. The government also played a part by selectively choosing to enforce its policy of nondiscrimination based on the perceived needs of war production, which for most federal officials overshadowed all other issues. Finally, the importance of the context of World War II cannot be overestimated. The war moved millions of people across the land, gave African Americans and women new ideas about their rights as American citizens, and helped challenge the racial order in the nation's neighborhoods and workplaces. In short, hate strikes were about race, but they were also about how white Americans, usually men, attempted to deal with a multitude of issues shaping the country in the midst of the world's greatest war.

See also: Civil Rights Strikes, 118; The 1945–1946 Strike Wave, 216.

Bibliography

Boris, Eileen. "'You Wouldn't Want One of 'Em Dancing with Your Wife': Racialized Bodies on the Job in World War II." *American Quarterly* 50 (March 1998): 77–108.

Gabin, Nancy. "The Hand That Rocks the Cradle Can Build Tractors, Too." *Michigan History Magazine* 76 (March/April 1992): 12–21.

Glaberman, Martin. *Wartime Strikes: The Struggle Against the No-Strike Pledge in the UAW During World War II.* Detroit, MI: Bewick, 1980.

Kryder, Daniel. *Divided Arsenal: Race and the American State During World War II.* New York: Cambridge University Press, 2000.

Lichtenstein, Nelson. *Labor's War at Home: The CIO in World War II.* New York: Cambridge University Press, 1982.

Nelson, Bruce. "Organized Labor and the Struggle for Black Equality in Mobile during World War II." *Journal of American History* 80 (December 1993): 952–88.

Reed, Merl. *Seedtime for the Modern Civil Rights Movement: The President's Committee on Fair Employment Practice, 1941–1946.* Baton Rouge: Louisiana State University Press, 1991.

Weaver, Robert. *Negro Labor: A National Problem.* New York: Harcourt Brace & Co., 1946.

Winkler, Allan. "The Philadelphia Transit Strike of 1944." *Journal of American History* 59 (June 1972): 73–89.

POLISH WORKERS AND STRIKES, 1900–1937

James S. Pula

Between 1880 and 1914, immigrants from Poland were the second-largest nationality group to arrive in America, surpassed in number only by those from Italy. By the beginning of the twentieth century, Poles had established vibrant ethnic communities throughout the industrial heartland of America, from the textile mills of New England to the coal mines of Pennsylvania and West Virginia and on to the steel mills and slaughterhouses of Chicago. Largely a movement of agricultural workers seeking better economic conditions than those in rural Eastern Europe, they migrated, as they said, "*za chlebem*"—for bread. They found employment in the expanding backbone of American industrial development—in textiles, mines, steel, and petroleum, and specialized industries such as meatpacking. By 1900, the communities they established, whether in large cities or small towns, had developed into relatively self-sustaining neighborhoods with their own social and cultural organizations, churches, schools, entrepreneurs, and civic and religious leaders. The first decade of the twentieth century marked a watershed in the development of these communities and their relationships with the dominant American culture, especially the emerging labor activism.

The Development of American "Polonia"

During the second half of the nineteenth century, in response to foreign powers that had partitioned Polish lands among themselves in the late eighteenth century, an indigenous self-help movement swept Poland. Political leaders of the time referred to it as "organic work." According to Aleksander Swietochowski, a leader in the movement quoted by historian Frank Renkiewicz, its purpose was "to extend work and learning in society to discover new resources, to utilize existing ones, and to concern ourselves with our own problems." As Poles migrated to America, this movement spread with them, with Polish immigrants banding together into various societies to attain through collective action the pooling of human and financial resources necessary to construct churches, establish schools, meet unexpected expenses such as funerals, and provide for other community needs. Successes they enjoyed in these arenas reinforced their belief in the benefits of collective action for mutual gain. This attitude was fully ingrained in Polish-American communities by the beginning of the twentieth century, forming a collective psyche receptive to the entreaties of the emerging labor movement.

Part of the "organic work" immigrants undertook in America was the establishment of local religious and secular organizations, with the inevitable attempts to organize these on the national level. Chief among these "umbrella" organizations were the Polish National Alliance (*Zwiazek Narodowy Polski*), a secular organization open to all who traced their origins to the inhabitants of the old Polish-Lithuanian Commonwealth regardless of religious or ethnic affiliation, and the Polish Roman Catholic Union (*Zjednoczenie Polskie Rzymsko-Katolickie*), which sought to organize Polonia for the purpose of maintaining immigrant allegiance to Roman Catholicism. The sometimes vicious antagonism between these two organizations led the former to support labor causes, while the latter, in keeping with its Catholic roots, feared the spread of socialism and potential for violence among the early labor activists. By 1905, the generally pro-labor PNA counted over 600 lodges in twenty-five states, a number that grew steadily to 1,670 lodges in thirty-two states in the early 1920s and 1,907 lodges in 1935. As its size grew, so did its assets. By 1900 the PNA commanded a net worth of $98,400, a figure that grew dramatically each decade thereafter: $1,100,000 in 1910, $5,700,000 in 1920, $20,300,000 in 1930, and, despite the Depression, $30,400,000 in 1940. What Renkiewicz labeled the "communal capitalism" of these early immigrant organizations resulted in not only an organizational apparatus well suited to support worker organization, but a source of institutional funding for future collective action and a training ground for labor organizers.

Along with the development of ethnic organizations, leadership expertise, and financial resources, another important phenomenon within the Polish-American community—"Polonia"—was the widespread growth of the Polish-language press, a development that provided support for worker organization by informing communities throughout the country about unionization activities outside their immediate purview. Tracing its origins to the émigré newspaper *Orzel Polski* (Polish Eagle), which was published briefly beginning in 1863, by 1900 a diverse Polish press provided local news and information from Poland for people unable to speak English; carried organizational news; imparted information about American customs, laws, and naturalization procedures; and generally assisted in the adjustment of immigrants to their new environment. In this sense, the Polish press was both an educational instrument and a change agent. When Henryk Nagiel surveyed the Polish press in 1893, he found over fifty periodicals with a plethora of perspectives. The Polish National Alliance, the largest secular fraternal organization, published *Zgoda* (Harmony) as its house organ, while the Polish Roman Catholic Union, the largest religious organization, published *Naród Polski* (The Polish Nation). The combined circulation of the two exceeded 100,000. In addition, smaller local newspapers reprinted much of the news and opinion from the larger tabloids for their own readers, thus spreading the influence of these publications to a national audience.

Since the Roman Catholic Church stood staunchly against the growing influence of socialism, it was not a strong advocate of labor unions and strikes, generally preferring to focus on maintaining religious allegiance and stressing adherence to law and order. The Polish National Alliance, because of its secular control and longstanding rivalry with the Polish Roman Catholic Union for hegemony over the Polish immigrant communities, tended to be much more sympathetic to worker issues and labor organization. Among the more influential publications, aside from the fraternal organs, was the leading liberal, anti-clerical publication *Ameryka-Echo* (American Echo) founded in Toledo by Antoni Paryski in 1889. Paryski, a radical labor agitator often referred to as the "Polish Hearst," also produced hundreds of thousands of copies of books, pamphlets, and other publications that his traveling agents sold throughout Polonia. Many of these focused on immigrant organization and topics consonant with the labor movement. Other publications that tended to be pro-labor included the weekly *Gwiazda Polarna* (The Northern Star); *Robotnik Polski* (The Polish Worker), the New York organ of the Polish Socialist Alliance in America (*Zwizek Socjalistów Polskich w Ameryce*); the socialist *Dziennik Ludowy* (The People's Daily), which later became *Głos Ludowy* (The People's Voice), published by the Polish Bureau of the Communist Party of the United States; and *Górnik* (The Miner), a moderate to conservative newspaper that was the house organ of the Polish Union of the United States of America. By 1918, *Dziennik Ludowy* enjoyed a circulation of 18,000, the eleventh-largest of some 300 English- and foreign-language socialist papers. Though perhaps not apparent from their circulation, *Dziennik Ludowy* and the other labor-oriented journals enjoyed widespread circulation among working-class communities. They were passed from person to person in taverns, union halls, and fraternal meetings, increasing their influence beyond the actual number of subscriptions.

Thus, by the beginning of the twentieth century, Polish immigrants in America possessed the leadership expertise, organizational structure, communications tools, and history of recent successes with "organic work" that propelled them to think of extending collective action to their workplaces. At the same time, some American labor organizers were beginning to take a more active interest in immigrant workers.

The Formative Period of Polish American Labor Organization, 1900–1909

While organized labor in nineteenth century America was dominated, sometimes exclusively, by skilled craft unions, by 1900 the widespread use of new technology and the continuing influx of hundreds of thousands of unskilled workers each year decreased the importance of skilled workers and led to a rising interest in the organization of the unskilled masses, two-thirds of whom were newly arrived immigrants by the middle of the first decade of the century. In fact, union membership exploded from some 447,000 in 1897 to 2 million in 1903. At the same time, however, prominent business owners and leaders of the American Federation of Labor (AFL) formed the National Civic Federation dedicated to keeping labor peaceful through conciliatory relationships between the AFL and industry. Part of this movement for a closer relationship between labor and business was the leadership of Samuel Gompers, president of the AFL, in the movement to lobby the federal government for the restriction of immigration.

Symptomatic of the conflicting forces that pulled the labor movement in diverging directions at the beginning of the twentieth century was the steel industry. By 1900, the steel industry was one of the primary sources of employment for Poles in Chicago and the surrounding communities in Illinois and Indiana. Yet labor organization mirrored the divisions that lobbied against unionism both nationally and within the Polish community. Nationally, while the Carnegie, Federal, and National Steel companies combined into United States Steel, unions found it difficult to effectively organize the workforce. Ethnic divisions, the large number of unskilled workers that were not served by existing unions, and the rival craft unions that did not generally cooperate with unskilled workers all combined to retard effective unionization. At the same time, rival factions within the Polish community also resulted in a lack of cohesive support for organized labor. In 1894, for example, when the anarchist leader J. Rybakowski led an attempt to form the Workers Alliance to organize steel workers in Chicago, the Catholic newspaper *Dziennik Chicagoski* (Chicago Daily News) commented, according to historian Jan Kowalik, that an "anarchic pestilence is creeping even into peaceful South Chicago." Anyone who accepted this "socialism," it asserted, was not a true Pole. Naturally, the active opposition of the Catholic Church impeded labor organization.

The results can be seen in the 1901 strike of the fledgling Amalgamated Association of Iron, Steel and Tin Workers against the United States Steel Corporation. An organization of skilled workers that eschewed the large majority of immigrant and unskilled laborers, the Amalgamated lacked the support of national leaders Samuel Gompers and John Mitchell, both of whom refused overtures by the Amalgamated's leaders, and of the two major organizations in Chicago's South Works, both of which rejected entreaties to walk out. As unskilled workers, Poles were not generally engaged in the work stoppage. After three months, the strike was so decisively defeated that the owners were gradually able, over the next seven years, to extinguish any significant labor organization in the steel industry by closing mill operations and then reopening them with nonunion workers.

In contrast to the disorganized state of labor in the steel industry, early in the new century miners in the Pennsylvania fields succeeded in overcoming many of the barriers to organization. Mining unions were among the first to make direct appeals to unskilled immigrant labor. A random sampling of Pennsylvania anthracite mines in 1903 revealed that Poles formed the largest immigrant group employed in the industry. Recognizing this potential, the Knights of Labor began publishing its *United Mine Workers Journal* in several languages, scheduling speeches in various languages at its functions, and hiring Polish organizers as early as the mid-1880s. The first distinctly Polish strike occurred in 1888, so that by 1900 the United Mine Workers (UMU) was well ahead of most other industries in organizing Polish labor. Although he remained at heart a conservative, Poles associated UMW President John Mitchell with their newfound welcome in the mining union, many of them placing his photograph on their walls next to the traditional religious symbols of their faith.

A series of violent confrontations in the Pennsylvania coal fields in the 1890s resulting in the deaths of several Polish workers galvanized the immigrant community against the mine owners, a position actively supported by the schismatic Polish National Catholic Church, whose headquarters was located in Scranton, and its newspaper *Straz* (The Guard). A further catalyst to the organization of Polish mine workers was the aggressive attitude of Irish labor leader John Fahy who insisted on hiring Polish organizers and reserving a vice presidency in each district for a Slavic leader. Under his guidance, Paul Pulaski began an effective UMW organizing effort in 1900, as did John Bednarski, John Feleski, and the Polish-speaking Cornell S. Pottier. Their concerted efforts led to significant increases in union membership in Districts 1 and 9, including the formation of new locals. Further, the new members were more inclined toward activism than their Anglo-Saxon coworkers. In Shenandoah, for example, the *Evening Herald* reported that "almost all the English speaking people, as distinguished from the Poles, Lithuanians and Austrians, expressed themselves as opposed to a strike." The *Public Ledger* commented that the heavily Polish Shamokin-Mt. Carmel area was unionized, while in Ashland "there are none of the undesirable class of foreigners that are making trouble in the other districts, the men here are all American, Irish, Germans, and Welsh, none of them members of the Mine Workers' organization." Clearly the Poles and other Slavs were the most active in the growing UMW movement.

When mine workers went on strike in 1900, Slavic workers joined en masse. Wishing to bring an end to the walkout during an election year, Mitchell negotiated a quick end to the walkout by gaining a 10 percent wage increase. When the 1900 accord expired in 1902, a new strike by some 150,000 anthracite miners began. The miners were seeking a reduction in work hours and union recognition. Poles were its most avid supporters, remaining loyal to the union in the face of provocations by the owners' Coal and Iron Police, the owners' hiring of 1,000 secret detectives, and the deployment of some 9,000 Pennsylvania state militia in support of the owners. With the economic impact of the 165-day strike mounting, President Theodore Roosevelt intervened to promote the negotiation of a settlement on the basis of a small increase in wages, a reduction in work hours, but no union recognition. Despite the limited gains and the continued conservative stance of Mitchell, the strike both demonstrated and solidified the continuing loyalty of the Poles to the mining union.

The relative success of the anthracite strikes, in contrast to the failure of the steel strike led by the Amalgamated, demonstrated that active appeals to Polish unskilled workers by organizers and publications using their own language could be successful in galvanizing support for strikes. It also demonstrated that the support of the ethnic press and local ethnic business owners for striking workers were powerful tools in supporting the longevity of labor walkouts.

A similar occurrence in the Chicago meatpacking industry demonstrated both the support of Poles for organized labor and the remaining division in their community. Although about one-third of the nation's meatpackers worked in Chicago in 1900, the city's meatpacking industry was largely unorganized. In 1901, Michael Donnelly moved the headquarters of the Amalgamated Meat Cutters and Butcher Workmen to Chicago, where he succeeded in forming seven new locals within the year. Although the Amalgamated originally opposed the enlistment of unskilled workers, Donnelly believed it should be open to all workers and argued effectively that skilled workers could not hope to win a major strike on their own. Donnelly also recognized, as Fahy had in the mining industry, the need to employ organizers who could speak to workers in their native languages. He found willing supporters among the Poles who not only joined, but elected a president of the Pork Butchers Local in 1904. Polish women also joined the meatpacking unions in large numbers, while the local secular Polish press contained frequent reports on union organization with appeals to all workers to support the union cause.

Faced with a growing union movement, the owners attempted to drive a wedge between the workers by favoring the skilled workers to keep them from forming a united front with the unskilled. When a national strike began in July 1904, about half of the 50,000 affected workers were located in Chicago. To overcome the strikers, the owners resorted to provocations and imported some 18,000 black workers to keep the slaughterhouses operating. Racial tensions arose as a result, with the strikers throwing bricks and other objects at strikebreakers and police, the latter responding by firing into the crowd. A full-scale riot broke out on August 3 in which several Poles were beaten by the police. Although labor leaders and clergy stressed the need to avoid violence, unity once again eluded the Polish community. The religiously oriented Polish newspapers generally blamed the retailers for increasing prices during the strike rather than the owners, and refrained from reporting on working conditions, the treatment of employees, decreasing pay, or any of the other worker complaints. The influential Catholic *Dziennik Chicagoski* did not print a single article favorable to the unions in either the Pennsylvania Coal Strike of 1902 or Chicago Packinghouse Strike of 1904, focusing instead on articles supporting efforts by the police to maintain order with frequent portrayals of the workers as troublemakers. At the same time, the secular Polish press spotlighted the plight of workers, emphasizing the universal nature of the workers' struggle. The differing approaches of the religious and secular Polish press were no doubt more a function of the ongoing struggle for ethnic hegemony between these two factions, colored by unrelenting Catholic antipathy for anything that smacked of socialism, than they were a direct result of the activities of the union or the workers themselves.

When Donnelly eventually called off this bitter strike in September, the workers, overwhelmed by a deep sense of betrayal, turned on him, beating him severely and chasing him out of the city. Although wages did gradually increase, a sense of union treachery pervaded Chicago's Polish working class after the end of the strike and led to very low morale. In fact, following the 1904 strike, large numbers of Poles abandoned the union, and future calls for organization met with only lukewarm support from a community that recalled with vivid memory what it regarded as the duplicity of union leaders.

Characteristics of Polish-American Strikes

The experience of Polish immigrants in Europe before their migration was largely one of communal life and organization, with the concept of "community" being a respected and closely held value. In rural Poland, the extended family was the most important social unit, followed by one's neighborhood and village. Work, social activities, and religious observances were all communal activities undertaken with family, friends, and neighbors. Further, in the late nineteenth century protest was also a communal activity. As Polish historian Adam Walaszek observed, peasant demonstrations were generally ritualistic, taking the form of a noisy crowd, preceded by a band, moving to the gateway of the manor to press whatever claims they might have upon the landlord. This tradition was easily adapted to the collective actions of organized labor in America.

Polish-American unions elected their officers as a communal affair. These officers usually included not only the typical positions found in most American organizations, but also a *cenzor* (censor), a uniquely Polish official whose responsibility it was to make sure that all the officers acted in accordance with the group's rules and that no actions were taken in violation of the organization constitution and by-laws. In this, the "censor" often combined the authority of a judge, parliamentarian, and occasionally sergeant-at-arms. Union meetings were open affairs with any member enjoying the right to speak. Major decisions were made by group vote, with the officers managing the union local's affairs in accordance with its constitution and the will of the group as expressed through votes.

Polish entrepreneurs were called upon to provide money, food, and the other requirements to support the strikers. Community residents who did not work in the industry being struck were expected to contribute to the support of the strikers. Where a Polish-language newspaper was available, it carried news of the strike, with even local strikes frequently enjoying coverage in periodicals with a more regional or national audience. Particularly important was the support of the local priest, since the parish was the heart of the Polish-American community. Yet throughout most of the period between 1900 and 1930 there was a rift between the Roman Catholic hierarchy and labor activists that sometimes led local clergy to be less than supportive. This rift was often reflected in the press—where secular newspapers tended

Polish strikers at New York Mills, near Utica, New York, in the early twentieth century. (*Courtesy:* Library of Congress.)

to be outspoken in their support of strikers, the Catholic-controlled press generally took a more conservative approach by supporting worker rights while at the same time avoiding endorsement of unions and advocating peaceful means for achieving worker goals. Despite these divisions, local parish priests often supported the workers in their struggle against owners, although with the caveat that protests remain peaceful.

Polish labor organizations typically employed rhetoric strongly laced with references to both their European experience and well-known aspects of American history. Owners were typically referred to as "czars" or "Kaisers" and their minions—whether company officials, hired guards or detectives, or local police—were invariably referred to as "Cossacks." Appeals might be made to Polish history, but more characteristically there were references to Kazimierz Pułaski and Tadeusz Kościuszko, Polish heroes of the American Revolution who embodied the dual symbolism of establishing Polish roots deep within the historical fabric of America and reminding the immigrants that they, too, were fighting for "freedom" and "democracy" in their new country. While Polish union halls were decorated with both Polish and American symbols, public parades generally showcased the American flag as a symbol to the general public that the workers considered themselves Americans and were striking for the same rights as other Americans.

Frequently, Polish unions reached out to other ethnic groups, to organized labor of every nationality, and to the general public for support. They sought donations to sustain the strikers, encouraged other unions to honor their picket lines and assist their efforts, and often encouraged workers of other nationalities to establish their own union locals. In Baltimore, for example, a Polish local held meetings with Czech officials to coordinate activities. In Buffalo and Rochester, the Poles organized joint meetings and social events with other groups. In Cleveland, Polish and Italian leaders held regular joint meetings at the Polish National

Hall to which all were invited. In New York Mills (New York), Polish union officials assisted Italians and Syro-Lebanese workers in establishing their own locals, while at the same time reaching out for support to the Anglo-Saxon dominated umbrella labor organization in nearby Utica. Such examples were legion.

The Rise of Polish-American Militancy, 1909–17

By 1905, only 6 percent of American workers belonged to the AFL, which remained predominantly interested only in enrolling skilled trade unionists. The movement toward industrial unionism received a boost in that same year when 200 delegates representing forty-three organizations enrolling some 60,000 workers met in Chicago to form the Industrial Workers of the World (IWW). Led by William D. "Big Bill" Haywood and Eugene V. Debs, the IWW welcomed unionists, anarchists, Socialists, and anyone else who supported workers' rights and the establishment of a single industrial union. The fledgling IWW moved into the vacuum created by the reluctance of the AFL to actively organize immigrant workers, preaching militant unionism to create "one big industrial union" and eventually forcing AFL member unions to reassess their position on unskilled workers.

While the formation of the IWW did much to stimulate the organization of unskilled workers in both new and existing unions, events in Europe also influenced the receptiveness of Polish immigrants to the union message in America. As quoted by historian Victor Greene, early labor historian John R. Commons captured the prevalent sentiments of turn-of-the-century America when he wrote: "The peasants of Catholic Europe, who constitute the bulk of our immigration of the past thirty years, have become almost a distinct race, drained of those superior qualities which are the foundation of democratic institutions." This view was reinforced by prominent progressive Americans such as Woodrow Wilson, who wrote: "There came multitudes of men of lowest class from the south of Italy and men of the meaner sort out of Hungary and Poland, men out of the ranks where there was neither skill nor energy nor any initiative of quick intelligence and they came in numbers which increased from year to year, as if the countries of the south of Europe were disburdening themselves of the more sordid and hapless elements of their population" (quoted by Stephen A. Garrett). Indeed, the prevailing stereotype of Polish unskilled workers was that their docility well suited them to work in the numbing repetitiveness of industrial America. As more recent historians have concluded, the truth was somewhat more complex. John J. Bukowczyk noted that the docility was most often observed and commented on during the 1880s and into the early 1890s, while Poles became more assertive in their support for labor organization and strikes after 1900.

Part of this transformation in the Polish worker stemmed from events in Europe. Early Polish emigration to America came largely from the German-occupied lands of the partitioned nation, areas that were more industrialized and in which Poles were allowed less freedom to express their cultural and political traditions. Beginning in the mid-1880s, however, the origins of Polish migration changed dramatically to the agrarian areas of the Austrian and Russian partitions. In the same years, there developed in these sections a strong peasant populist movement characterized by increasingly intense rhetoric directed at the landowning class. A traveler through this area in the 1890s, quoted by Victor Greene, noted that the peasants were "losing their old-time respectful manners, and, with the modern ideas of democracy . . . acquiring an offensive manner of independence." Concurrently, the spread of socialism that took root among agricultural workers in both the Austrian and Russian sections fanned the flames of peasant discontent. By 1906, some 700 agrarian strikes took place in Russian Poland alone, while spates of strikes swept Austrian Poland in 1898, 1900, and 1902. With the immigration of some 100,000 Poles per year between 1900 and 1914, nearly all of whom were from the areas affected by the rise of populism and socialism, the new attitudes of activism spread wherever the new immigrants settled. Evidence of this can be seen in the formation of the Polish Section of the Socialist Party of the United States of America in 1907 and the founding in Chicago, in the same year, of *Dziennik Ludowy* (The People's Daily), the aggressively pro-labor organ of Polish Socialist Party in America. Further evidence rests with the increasing number of articles on the exploitation of workers carried in the Polish National Alliance organ *Zgoda* (Harmony) and its successor *Dziennik Zwiazkowy* (Alliance Daily), as well as articles on the plight of female workers in the Polish Women's Alliance journal *Głos Polek* (Polish Womens' Voice).

As Bukowczyk explained:

> . . . while migrants from rural Poland had little acquaintance with radical ideologies or progressive politics in the 1880s, the opposite held true for post-1890 migrants. Leaving a rural society now gripped by popular agitation for peasant land reform, strikes by agricultural wage laborers, and a full-fledged rural socialist movement, they carried an assortment of democratic and egalitarian notions which hardly fitted contemporary—and latterday—stereotypes. Moreover, after the repression of the Revolution of 1905 by tsarist authorities in Russian Poland, Polish settlements in America also received an infusion of political radicals, trade unionists, and insurrectionaries who had fled literally for their lives. That many settled in New York City and environs is evident from the sudden rise of the Polish left there during the subsequent period.

The arrival of these new, more assertive immigrants coincided with the movement of the IWW and some of the older labor organizations, such as the United Mine Workers, toward the active organization of unskilled workers, providing fertile ground for the growth of unions and the spread of strikes through various industries. The result can be seen in an upsurge of strikes between 1909 and 1922, coupled with an increase in distinctly Polish participation in labor agitation. In 1910, for example, Polish workers in a Brooklyn, New York, sugar refinery went out on strike when the company insisted they work on Easter Sunday in disobedience of Polish religious traditions. In the same year, Polish steel workers in Gary, Indiana, knelt before a Roman Catholic crucifix to pledge not to act as scabs during planned strikes.

Historian David Brody found that by 1909 Poles had become organized and confident enough in the steel industry to become overtly militant in their support of labor organization. During 1909–10, Poles were actively involved in steel strikes in McKees Rocks, Bethlehem, and elsewhere. In the McKees Rocks strike, the Wobblies led some 8,000 workers of fourteen nationality groups in a bloody industrial action against the Pressed Steel Car Company that included pitched battles with the State Constabulary resulting in the deaths of a dozen strikers and a similar number of Constabulary officers, as well as the injuring of some fifty others.

By 1900, Poles predominated in the refinery industry in Bayonne, New Jersey. In July 1915, about 1,000 employees went out on strike in protest of poor working conditions and ill treatment, choosing as their spokesman local attorney Paul Supinski. Historian John J. Bukowczyk tells the story. The strike spread rapidly, but the Standard Oil Company retaliated by engaging Italian strikebreakers and calling in the Bayonne police as allies against the workers. The latter was possible because the city's mayor, Pierre Garven, was also employed as counsel for Standard Oil. On July 20 a riot broke out, following which organizers arrived from the rival AFL and the IWW. To meet this threat, the mayor advised the company to employ guards from a private detective agency. "Get me two hundred and fifty husky men who can swing clubs," an oil company executive commanded. "If they're not enough, get a thousand or two thousand. I want them to march up East Twenty-second Street through the guts of Polacks." Bukowczyk described the result: "For the next four days . . . [the] private army of so-called 'nobles' terrorized the strikers by sniping at pickets and launching armed sorties into the assembled crowds. No fewer than five strikers died and several more sustained gunshot wounds before the corporate reign of terror at the hands of . . . 'armed thugs' finally subsided. In the end, force—and persuasion—applied from another quarter finally restored order to the city of Bayonne. Hudson County Sheriff . . . broke up the striker's organization, beat up their young socialist leader Jeremiah Baly, dispersed . . . [the private company] forces, arrested IWW organizer [Frank] Tannenbaum and banned the sale of the radical newspaper the *New York Call*."

The 1915 strike ended with the workers winning a salary increase, but little else. In 1916, however, they again walked off the job, forcing Standard Oil to increase wages and adopt a policy of "welfare capitalism" including benefits such as "accident, sickness, and death provisions." Yet the most telling examples of the new labor militancy displayed by Polish workers in the years following 1909 can be seen in the textile industry. Although Poles were not the dominant worker group in the famous Lawrence textile strike of 1912 in Massachusetts, the walkout began on January 11 when weavers, nearly all Polish women, walked off the job in the Everett Mill in a reaction to a reduction in wages. As the walkout spread, two Poles were elected to the fifty-six-member strike committee, and Polish workers remained loyal union supporters throughout. Even Chicago's Catholic newspaper *Dziennik Chicagoski*, which usually opposed unions because of the perceived Socialist influence in these worker organizations, opined on January 12: "Workers are justified in demanding the right to create their own organizations . . . as long as the organizations remain loyal to the existing laws of the society and the governments." The role of Poles in this landmark textile strike was verified by the research of Donald B. Cole, who concluded in his book *Immigrant City: Lawrence, Massachusetts, 1845–1921* that Poles and other Slavic workers in Lawrence formed a cohesive group that supported organized labor.

But the Lawrence strike was not the only significant textile action in which Poles were involved during this period. A similar strike occurred in Little Falls, New York, when the owners of the Phoenix and Gilbert Knitting Mills reduced salary levels. From October 1912 to January 1913, more than 1,300 workers, most of whom were Polish, Slovak, and Italian, struck in a dispute characterized by physical and emotional bitterness that more than matched the inclement weather of a brutal winter. Robert E. Snyder has written a history of the strike, which took place against the background of the growing rivalry between the AFL and the IWW for control of unskilled workers, with "Big Bill" Haywood traveling to Little Falls to argue the IWW case against Charles A. Miles of the AFL. In the end, the IWW proved more influential, possibly because of the egregious actions of local officials that called forth a stronger response from the workers.

The Little Falls strikers were faced with a company that successfully manipulated the local law enforcement officials to their side. Labor activists, and even the Socialist mayor of Schenectady, were refused permission by the city police to address a meeting of workers, while the county sheriff commented to the local press that "Socialist speeches at this time would tend to 'rioting' among the strikers, a thing we intend to prevent if we have to call out every regiment of the national guard in the state." The city police chief explained further that "we have a strike on our hands and a foreign element to deal with. We have in the past kept them in subjugation and we mean to continue to hold them where they belong." To overcome this attitude, and the restrictions placed upon them, the workers turned for support to the IWW. They adopted a strategy of insisting upon the constitutional right of free speech, while provoking mass arrests to overcrowd the local penal system and draw attention to the violation of legal rights and due process by local law enforcement officials. Eventually this strategy proved effective, as Governor John A. Dix reminded Little Falls officials that "your attention is invited to the fact that the Constitution of the State of New York guarantees the right of free speech and the right of people peacefully to assemble and discuss public questions. The people of the State of New York wish to see that these rights are not unnecessarily curtailed, but are respected in spirit as well as in letter, within your jurisdiction."

On October 30, when pickets failed to move quickly enough in clearing a path for scabs to enter the mills, mounted police attacked the strikers with clubs, beating some into unconsciousness. When the strikers fled, police pursued them across the Mohawk River into the immigrant section of town, where the officers assaulted the strike headquarters in Slovak Hall. The police threw women bodily from the steps, broke down the doors, destroyed the musical instruments of the Slovak Society Band, smashed the framed IWW charter, confiscated several cases of beer and liquor, and arrested the entire strike committee and other supporters. Despite the denial of basic constitutional rights and the brutality of the police, the Poles and their Slovak and Italian brethren continued the strike to a successful conclusion, winning an agreement to reemploy all strikers without prejudice, an increase in salary, and other concessions.

Less violent examples were the two strikes waged by Polish workers against the New York Mills Corporation in 1912 and 1916. In the first example, Poles suffering under poor working conditions, maltreatment, and economic deprivation organized Local 753 of the United Textile Workers of America and, in 1912, when their overtures to company officials were rebuffed, they went on strike. Company officials retaliated by recruiting strikebreakers, swearing in foremen and other company officials as deputy sheriffs, and calling in the New York National Guard to protect their property. The deputized company officials provoked fights with strikers, ran horses through picket lines, and engaged in other provocative activities. The strikers, however, maintained a strict discipline and called upon fellow unionists for support. They also won over the National Guard with their peaceful discipline and the distribution of coffee and sandwiches to guardsmen on picket duty. Ironically, the guardsmen brought in to protect company property, effectively protected the strikers from the excesses of company thugs. In the end, through the intervention of New York State officials, a compromise settlement was reached wherein the workers received a pay increase and assurances of better treatment. No sooner had the ink on the agreement dried, however, than company officials began firing union organizers, cutting salaries, and otherwise violating the strike settlement.

In 1916, Local 753 began another strike, this time attempting to encourage Italian, Syro-Lebanese and other workers to join them. The company once again retaliated by hiring private detectives, deputizing company officials, hiring strikebreakers, and provoking violence. They also attempted to drive wedges between the various ethnic groups and eventually evicted workers from company housing despite epidemics of infantile paralysis and influenza. When these were not enough to defeat the strikers, company officials filed legal actions against union officials for lost profits and also began a smear campaign claiming that strike leaders were profiting from collections intended for the strikers.

The Polish union members reacted with considerable thought, sending representatives to other Polish communities to raise funds, forming alliances with English-speaking unionists in the local area, and raising funds by selling postcards of those evicted from their homes. As with most Polish strikes, it was a community affair, with the parish priest strongly supporting the strikers, entrepreneurs donating food and other supplies, and community members contributing whatever they could. In the end, after four grueling months, the Poles won a complete victory, gaining every concession they sought. In fact, John Golden, president of the national United Textile Workers of America, proclaimed it one of the most successful strikes ever waged.

Still another strike in this series of textile walkouts resulted from efforts by the AFL to organize Polish and Italian workers in Syracuse and Auburn, New York, in 1913, as Kenneth Fones-Wolf has shown. Once again, the union utilized the effective techniques of employing Polish- and Italian-speaking organizers, developing cooperative efforts with local religious and civic leaders, and renting immigrant facilities for meetings. Polish workers attended smokers in Garbinski's Hall in Auburn, with Joseph Minczewski speaking to them in their native language. Faced with the organization of Polish workers, the Columbian Rope Company in Auburn fired the presidents of the Polish and Italian locals in March 1913. Some 900 workers immediately struck, followed within a week by 550 Poles, Russians, and Italians at the International Harvester factory. In this instance, the strikes failed when other workers arrived to reopen the factories, with the result that the employers were able to enforce an open shop.

The conclusion to be drawn from these strikes, which represent only a few of the hundreds of labor actions in which Polish Americans played leading or supportive parts between 1909 and World War I, is that far from being the stereotypical passive pawns of corporate capitalism, Poles were quite interested in and supportive of organized labor as a means of obtaining equal treatment, a better life for themselves, and a better future for their children.

World War I

The outbreak of the First World War dramatically reduced the number of immigrants arriving on

America's shores. This combined with an increase in industrial production due to wartime orders for everything from food and clothing to munitions created a more favorable environment for unionization.

As a result, in April 1918 the AFL determined to renew efforts to organize the steel industry, which resulted in the formation of the National Committee for Organizing Iron and Steel Workers in Chicago. When the War Labor Board acted in July to prohibit anti-union policies at the Bethlehem Steel Works in Pennsylvania, the government effectively recognized the right of workers to organize. This along with the continuing wartime economy led labor leaders to believe the time was ripe for success in the steel industry. Efforts focused on the Chicago area, where unionists distributed a piece entitled "Forward to Bleed and Die!" This was translated into Polish with a title that, when translated back into English, was roughly the equivalent of "Forward to Wade Through Blood!" According to Dominic A. Pacyga, a historian of Polish workers in Chicago, the Polish leader refused to distribute the piece, explaining that "my people are all good Catholics. They won't stand for advice like that."

When the strike began in September 1919, about 98 percent of the workers in heavily Polish South Chicago voted in favor of the strike, yet divisions within the community remained. The South Chicago newspaper *Polonia* carried an article by Rev. Francis M. Wojtalewicz titled "We Do Not Want a Strike!" that argued against a walkout because winter was coming and the workers would have no means of survival. The same issue ran a story about the outbreak of violence in nearby Hammond, Indiana, urging "Americans and Poles [to] stand up as citizens to protest these things done to our countrymen!" Although the Catholic *Dziennik Chicagoski* generally supported the workers, an editorial cartoon published on September 28 "portrayed a steelworker with a demon marked 'radicals' sitting on his shoulder and whispering in his ear." The caption read: "The Son of Vulcan Listens to Seducers." Despite the dissension, Polish workers once again turned out in large numbers to support the strike. The records of Illinois Steel's South Works, for example, reveal that some 20.8 percent of its employees remained at work through the strike. Of these, half were native-born whites, 57 percent blacks, 7 percent Germans, and less than 1 percent Poles. The Polish workers remained steadfast supporters of the strike through weeks of bitter weather, disappointments, and the importation of some 30,000 to 40,000 black workers as strikebreakers. Finally, on January 8, 1920, the strike ended in failure. The only consolation for the Poles was the acknowledgement of the secretary-treasurer of the Chicago District Organizing Committee that the Slavic workers had better attendance at meetings and exhibited more supportive behavior than any other group.

The 1920s

The First World War marked in some respects a transformation for Polonia and Polish-American workers. Prior to the war, as many as half of the Poles who came to America could be classified as "birds of passage," people who came in search of opportunity but with the intention of returning to Poland. As such, few actively pursued citizenship, while many were willing to endure hardships they believed to be temporary expedients necessary until they could return to Poland with enough money to make a better life for themselves and their families. With the end of World War I, and the emergence of a free Poland after more than a century of subjugation, the vast majority of Poles in America made a conscious decision to remain in their adopted homeland. Once they overcame this psychological barrier, Polish immigrants began to exhibit a stronger interest in citizenship, learning English and participating in unions to obtain a better future in what they now knew to be their permanent home. Further, since the war had been widely proclaimed to be a fight between democracy and autocracy, Poles in the postwar years began more frequently to equate their struggle for political and economic equality with the ideals for which they freely gave their resources and sons to America in 1917 and 1918. According to John Bukowczyk, one newspaper account of a strike in 1919 read: "Casimir Mazurek, who fought on foreign soil to make the world free for Democracy, was shot to death by hirelings and thugs of the Lackawanna Steel Co. because he fearlessly stood for industrial Democracy on American soil." Such allusions were commonplace in the aftermath of the war.

Two other postwar factors also influenced the future of the union movement among Polish Americans. First, the advent of new immigration laws in 1921 and 1924 imposed strict restrictions on the number of immigrants the United States would accept each year, while also establishing nationality quotas that eventually reduced the number of Polish immigrants each year to a small fraction of what it had been in the prewar years. The dramatic limitation on immigration reduced the surplus of unskilled labor, thus providing workers with more leverage in negotiations with employers. Second, the growing radicalism in postwar Europe spread fears that immigrants from Eastern Europe would bring with them waves of anarchists, socialists and other violent elements. The resulting "Red Scare" brought suspicion on both Poles and organized labor.

One of the first major strikes to occur in this postwar atmosphere was the Great Steel Strike of 1919. In the previous year, John Fitzpatrick and William Z. Foster began organizing steel workers, paying particular attention to unskilled immigrant labor. Working in ethnic neighborhoods, union leaders allied themselves with officers of ethnic fraternal organizations and other community leaders such as Antoni Pilawski, a socialist and leader in the Polish National Alliance who emerged as the most important leader in the movement to organize steel workers in the Cleveland area. Pilawski organized thousands of Polish workers into Locals 114 and 140. But once again there were community divisions. Cleveland judge Joseph Sawicki spoke out against unions, which he blamed for creating tensions within the Polish community. Similarly, when the weekly newspaper *Ognisko Domowe* (The Home Hearth) from Detroit came out against unions and strikes, workers in Cleveland burned it in the streets and boycotted those who brought it into the city. In most cases, however, Poles remained committed to union organization, according to Bukowczyk. In Gary, Indiana, for example, a Polish worker wrote to organizer Fitzpatrick to inquire why unionization had not progressed any faster. "We do not know what you are up to," he wrote, "has the company bought you up or something, it's almost half a year since you started organizing a union and nothing has yet come out of it, and possibly nothing will." Fitzpatrick should either do something, the annoyed worker wrote, or stop taking people's money.

The strike that began in September 1919 encompassed almost 400,000 workers in ten states: an estimated 98 percent of all unskilled employees in the steel industry. Although announced through the offices of the National Committee and the AFL, the strike was characterized by leadership initiatives at the local and shop level, offices that were more often held by Polish or other elected ethnic officials. Once again, however, although Polish workers supported the strike in exceptional numbers, the strike received little support from other national unions. It was eventually called off by the AFL in January when funds to support the strikers were expended and President Woodrow Wilson sent in federal troops to assist strikebreakers in entering the factories. As a result, Polish workers once again felt betrayed by Anglo-Saxon workers and the AFL, increasing their suspicions and decreasing their willingness to participate in AFL activities in the future. Because of this, the steel industry was not organized until 1937.

Another early postwar walkout occurred among meatpackers in Chicago beginning in 1921. The wartime atmosphere of increased demand and decreased labor sources encouraged the Chicago Federation of Labor to begin organizing efforts among the city's slaughterhouse workers in 1916. With assistance of the Butcher Workmen, they formed the Stockyard Labor Council (SLC) in July 1917 as an umbrella group for several unions. In January 1918 the Polish local in the SLC numbered 12,000; by the end of the year, membership was up to 20,000. Much of the success was due to the efforts of Jan Kikulski, the acknowledged Polish leader and president of the Amalgamated Meat Cutters District No. 9 as well as organizer and secretary of the SLC, who was a strong advocate of industrial unionism and equality between black and white workers. No doubt due to the lingering sense of betrayal the Poles harbored from the failed strike of 1904, they repeatedly violated union rules by organizing locally and appointing their own leaders to negotiate with employers outside the formal activities of the parent union.

Considerable tension resulted from the organizing efforts. Initially there was acrimony between Polish workers and their Anglo-Saxon coworkers, who were less likely to support unionization. By August 1919 the Polish newspaper *Dziennik Zwiazkowy* reacted to anti-union articles in the English language press by attacking the newspapers as "tools of the meatpackers." But ethnic divisions paled in comparison to the struggle for control between the Amalgamated Meat Cutters and the Stockyard Labor Council for control of the workers. Although the Chicago Federation of Labor attempted to mediate the dispute, acrimonious charges were made against Kikulski, who became embroiled in the dispute. At the height of conflict, attackers accosted Kikulski on his way home and murdered him. *Dziennik Chicagoski* blamed the Irish labor leaders J.W. Johnstone and Martin Murphy, but no arrests were made. Kikulski's replacement Stanisław Rokosz was killed in the same manner less than a year later.

In February 1921 the meatpackers announced they would no longer be bound by the wartime agreements. Negotiations with the owners dragged on sporadically from April into the fall, when the owners announced their intention to reduce wages. In November the Amalgamated Meat Cutters voted to strike, claiming 100,000 members nationwide including 40,000 in Chicago. The meatpacking firms responded with a plan to reduce wages even further. In Chicago, the strike began on December 5, with the first violence following only two days later when strikers beat up workers attempting to enter the factories and police opened fire on the crowd, killing one and wounding several others. *Dziennik Zwiazkowy* labeled the affair "Bloody Wednesday," branding the police as agents of the "Swine Barons" and accusing them of charging into crowds of women and children. *Dziennik Ludowy* likewise accused the owners of planting agents provocateur in the crowd designed to incite the violence. Polish newspapers encouraged the workers to maintain solidarity and remain peaceful. On December 8, snipers were active in the largely Polish Back of the Yards neighborhood, with 150 people injured.

Chief among the strike leaders was Mary Janek, with women forming a significant portion of the strikers, and perhaps a majority of those on the picket lines. In response to continuing demonstrations by the strikers, the police rode horses into crowds, but Polish women threw red pepper in the horses' eyes—and in the eyes of police once they dismounted. Police resorted to motorcycles, but the Poles scattered tacks and broken glass in the streets to counter this tactic. Twenty-three Poles were injured in the melee, including nine women. "The whole trouble in this strike lies with the women," opined a Chicago police captain, quoted by Dominic A. Pacyga. "They are behind the men, pushing them on." But the violence served to coalesce support for the strikers among the Polish press. *Dziennik Chicagoski* informed its readers that "the fight between labor and capitalism has finally started. The strikers are battling for their rights, but the police are interfering." The socialist *Dziennik Ludowy* assured its readers that the strike was apolitical: "The strike in the stockyards does not have a political nor a revolutionary character. It is simply an economic problem. . . . There are no communists involved. When the provocations are stopped, when the police treat strikers as citizens and not like huns then there will be peace." The Catholic *Dziennik Zjednoczenia*, noted for its lack of support for unions and strikes, revealed some lingering reservation; it supported the strike while at the same time cautioning against violence and intimidation. "If someone desires to strike let him do so," the editors opined, "but if anyone desires to work he should not be compelled to strike by beating, threatening, or any other violence; for such action would be terrorism, a limitation of personal liberty, which is despotism not democracy."

On December 9 the owners obtained an injunction against the union, while they at the same time importing 8,000 strikebreakers. Although the strike continued on through the cold winter weather in December and January with frequent outbursts of violence, the skilled unions, comprised largely of Irish, German, and native-born workers, ignored calls for support, and assistance from unions outside Chicago was scant. This, too, increased the chasm between the skilled and unskilled, as well as between the Poles and those ethnic groups that did not support the strike.

The strike ended in defeat for the workers on February 1. Nearly the entire Polish community had supported the strike, everyone from workers and their families to priests, entrepreneurs, and journalists. With its failure, the community felt abandoned by the English-language press, skilled workers, national union leaders and the Irish, Germans, and native-born Americans who refused to support their efforts. The bitterness engendered by these feelings struck deeply, with no further serious organizing efforts undertaken in the stockyards for the next fifteen years.

The textile industry was yet another site of strikes in the immediate postwar years. While the United Textile Workers of America, affiliated with the AFL, remained somewhat conservative in its efforts in accordance with AFL beliefs, the Amalgamated Clothing Workers of America adopted an aggressive organizing campaign basing the formation of locals on specific job specialization or ethnic affiliation. Concerned especially with Polish workers because of their number in the industry, the Amalgamated included immigrants among its leadership and published a Polish-language version of their journal titled *Przemysłowa Demokracja* (Industrial Democracy). Their efforts were rewarded with a significant number of defections from the UTWA, particularly in the textile centers of Lawrence, Massachusetts, and Passaic and Patterson, New Jersey. Six of these were Polish locals, with the largest of them, Local 38, enrolling 4,000 workers in Chicago. When strikes broke out in these cities in 1919 and 1922, ethnic groups chose their own representatives to strike committees. Because the UTWA and ACWA both encouraged Polish participation in leadership and organizing positions and made other accommodations to ethnic sensitivities, Poles remained actively committed to textile unionism throughout this period.

At the same time, the influx of more radical ideas from the growing Socialist movement in Europe led other Polish workers to support one form or another of American Socialism. While the existing Alliance of Polish Socialists was in truth a nationalist organization linked to Marshal Józef Piłsudski's political party in Poland, there was in fact a small but active Polish socialist movement that enjoyed somewhat of a heyday in the early to mid-1920s. Although never numbering more than 5 to 12 percent of Polish workers, socialists nevertheless succeeded in motivating Polish workers to actively participate in the union movement and in strikes. Among the most effective socialist leaders was Stanley Nowak, who began editing the leftist newspaper *Głos Robotniczy* (Workers' Voice) in Detroit in 1924. He was later employed as an organizer for United Auto Workers. Another important socialist leader was Leo Krzycki from Milwaukee, a well-known Midwestern orator and politician.

The Depression

The staggering unemployment of the Depression created an unfriendly environment for organized labor. It also threatened the employment and home ownership of Polish-Americans, two of the most important factors in Polonia's stable ethnic communities. "The insecurity, anger and militance that resulted," historian Thaddeus Radzilowski observed, "marked henceforth the culture and psychology of second generation Polish Americans. Their major response was to join the battle for unions and even to lead it. Between 1936 and 1938, 500,000 to 600,000 Polish Americans joined the new CIO unions." According to Homer Martin, first president of the United Auto Workers, Poles were "the most militant and progressive workers" in America. "The CIO victory is one of the major Polish American contributions to American history," concluded Radzilowski. "At the time when the descendants of the founding fathers sought to limit civil and political rights and to prevent participation of workers in setting the terms and conditions of their employment, Polish Americans through their resistance helped to widen the meaning of justice and democracy."

The labor orientation of Polish Americans also solidified another aspect of American life that would last for the balance of the century and beyond. Prior to the end of the 1920s, the "Polish vote" might have been very real at the local level, but there was little evidence that it was solidified at the national level. Polish support for the Democratic Party began to crystallize in 1928 when Alfred E. Smith, a Catholic, proved very popular as the Democratic standard-bearer. This tendency was solidified by the perception of Franklin D. Roosevelt's policies as pro-union, and the New Deal legislation designed to promote economic recovery and ease the impact of the Depression on workers. By the mid-1930s, Poles had become, largely because of their active adherence to the cause of labor, a mainstay of the urban-ethnic/working class/black coalition that would prove to be the backbone of the post–World War II national Democratic Party.

Conclusions

Some scholars have theorized that Poles were well suited to the rugged demands of industrial America because of their cultural background. According to Victor Greene, John R. Commons concluded that the Slavic worker was both too passive and too radical for organized labor. Each extreme, he commented, weakened unions. In general, he felt that the dull immigrants were much too ignorant to be organized, forming instead a leaderless mob that was so malleable it could be bent to the wishes of exploitive capitalists. Conversely, he noted that some Slavs, "once moved by the spirit of unionism . . . are the most dangerous and determined of unionists," but these were particularly dangerous because they could not be controlled by American leaders. Thus, in Commons's view, immigrants who showed little enthusiasm for unions were unwitting pawns of big business while those who did support unionism were dangerous radicals. Either way, they were a threat to American society.

Only recently have more sophisticated researchers uncovered ties between Polish immigrant behavior and their Old World past. Ewa Morawska maintains that Polish peasant society contained both a "basic survival orientation" and "the image of and desire toward accomplishment as measured by the standards of the peasant-immigrant society—the 'positive wish.' In the ongoing interaction with the surrounding environment, the actions of peasants who left their villages and settled in American cities were motivated by both these elements." The survival orientation of the rural peasant village taught Poles to live from day to day and make the best of every situation, while the desire for accomplishment manifested itself in a positive work ethic and the desire for home ownership.

John Bukowczyk found Poles used similar cultural supports to endure and even thrive in the often-difficult world of industrial America. According to Bukowczyk, "Peasant fatalism, reinforced by the dolorous world-view of Polish Roman Catholicism, helped inure Polish immigrant workers to these harsh conditions. But it was the purpose that many Poles had in mind when they emigrated which actually encouraged them to endure industrial hardship. Many young Galician [Austrian Poland] and Russian Poles left behind families in Poland who struggled to hold on to undersized parcels of land. Less immigrant than migrant, these Poles considered their sojourn in American factories a temporary expedient. They fully intended to return to Poland and use their American wages to buy land or to bail out debt-ridden rural households."

The desire to succeed, whether to return to Poland or to better one's life in America, combined with a cultural socialization to hard work, no doubt provided Poles with a psychological makeup that was compatible with the industrial system. Indeed, it appears that the Poles behaved, as Renkiewicz concludes, in a "culture-specific" manner that was not the Protestant work ethic. One of the problems with this was that the American labor union had no obvious counterpart in the experience of immigrants from rural Poland; thus, the immigrant was left to piece together a coping mechanism from other past experiences that often had little in common with industrial America. However, later research by Polish historian Adam Wasaszek has shown that agricultural organization and strikes were actually quite commonplace in the Poland the turn-of-the-century immigrants left.

The organization of Polish workers was not easy not because they were unwilling, but because of the language and cultural differences and the early predilection of established unions to see unskilled immigrant workers as a problem or threat rather than an opportunity. Among the most important and effective strategies that unions employed in the decade before World War I were the employment of Polish-speaking organizers and translators, the printing of Polish-language materials, and the attempt to cooperate with local immigrant civic and religious leaders. Union officials soon came to realize the importance, both symbolic and financial, of renting immigrant-owned halls for labor meetings and advertising in the local Polish-language press. Once unions determined to organize the masses of unskilled

Polish workers and adopted strategies to appeal to their ethnic sensitivities, Polish workers became willing and active participants in the union movement. As James R. Barrett has concluded, "Where the American labor movement reached out to the immigrants, the Poles made splendid union men and women."

See also: The Business Community's Mercenaries: Strikebreakers and Union Busters, 52; The Catholic Church and Strikes, 162; Steel Strikes Before 1935, 351; Unionizing the "Jungle": A Century of Meatpacking Strikes, 375.

Bibliography

Brody, David. *The Steelworkers in America: The Non-Union Era*. Cambridge, MA: Harvard University Press, 1960.

Bukowczyk, John J. "Polish Rural Culture and Immigrant Working Class Formation, 1880–1914." *Polish American Studies* vol. XLI, no. 2 (Autumn 1984): 23–44.

———. "The Transformation of Working-Class Ethnicity: Corporate Control, Americanization, and the Polish Immigrant Middle Class in Bayonne, New Jersey 1915–1925." *Labor History* 25, no. 1 (1984).

Fones-Wolf, Kenneth. "Revivalism and Craft Unionism in the Progressive Era: The Syracuse and Auburn Labor Forward Movements of 1913." *New York History* (October 1982).

Garrett, Stephen A. "Eastern European Ethnic Groups and American Foreign Policy." *Political Science Quarterly* 93, no. 2 (1978): 319.

Greene, Victor R. "The Polish American Worker to 1930: The 'Hunky' Image in Transition." *The Polish Review* 21, no. 3 (1976).

Kowalik, Jan. *The Polish Press in America*. San Francisco: R & E Research, 1978.

Morawska, Ewa. "'For Bread with Butter': Life-Worlds of Peasant-Immigrants from East Central Europe, 1880–1914." *Journal of Social History* 17, no. 3 (1984): 387.

Pacyga, Dominic A. *Polish Immigrants and Industrial Chicago: Workers on the South Side, 1880–1922*. Columbus: Ohio State University Press, 1991.

Radzilowski, Thaddeus C. "Class, Ethnicity and Community: The Polish Americans of Detroit and the Organization of the CIO." Paper presented at annual meeting of the American Association for the Advancement of Slavic Studies, November 4, 1984.

Renkiewicz, Frank A. "Polish American Workers, 1880–1980." In *Pastor of the Poles: Polish American Essays Presented to Right Reverend Monsignor John Wodarski in Honor of the Fiftieth Anniversary of His Ordination*, ed. Stanislaus A. Blejwas and M.B. Biskupski. New Britain, CT: Polish Studies Program, Central Connecticut State University, 1982.

Snyder, Robert E. "Women, Wobblies, and Workers' Rights: The 1912 Textile Strike in Little Falls, New York." *New York History* (January 1979).

Walaszek, Adam. "Was the Polish Worker Asleep? Immigrant, Unions and Workers' Control in America, 1900–1922." *Polish American Studies*, vol. XLVI, no. 1 (Spring 1989): 74–96.

NORTH CAROLINA WOMEN ON STRIKE

Roxanne Newton

Participation in a strike is often a life-altering experience. It was for the North Carolina women strikers (whose names have been changed to protect their privacy) interviewed by this author. They participated in labor disputes from the General Textile Strike of 1934 to the Paper, Allied Chemical, and Energy (PACE) strike of 2001. When they went on strike, they faced many of the same challenges as their union brothers on the picket line: lost wages, disputes with nonunion coworkers, vindictive management, and condemnation by members of their communities. As with their brothers, their strike and union experiences often led to opportunities for greater education, community activism, and leadership. And they took advantage, despite working in a state that has consistently maintained the lowest rate of unionization in the nation.

But because they were women, they put their experiences to some different uses than their union brothers. The women interviewed developed confidence, knowledge, and skills, which they used to combat the sexism and racism prevalent at their workplaces. They developed strong political and union consciousness, emphasizing solidarity with their union sisters and brothers. Many of these women also embraced union feminism, promoting gender and racial equality, workplace democracy, and social justice in their communities. They assumed leadership roles in their unions and empowered other women in the ongoing struggles to realize access, parity, and agency in the American workplace.

Education

Education is one step toward achieving equity and access for women at the workplace. For several of the women interviewed, their education began when they joined the union and continued during strikes. Annie is one such woman. She participated in the 1934 General Textile Strike as a "scab," or replacement worker. At the time, Annie was a fifteen-year-old child whose father had abandoned the family. Annie was the oldest of three children whose mother was unable to work due to illness. Since she was underage, Annie was unable to work for pay, so the mill management "hired" her for no pay for two months until she turned the legal age of sixteen. After the strike was over, she was a trained worker, with a good job and a willingness to do "whatever it takes" to get the work done.

World War II led Annie in a different direction. She was recruited, along with other women working in the textile mill, to work at a munitions factory. As a "Rosie the Riveter," Annie worked at a union plant and eventually became shop steward. The women in her area called for a "wildcat," or unsanctioned, strike because they found out that the men were making more money per hour. Annie told the women that she would appeal to the union before they went out on strike. When the union was able to negotiate wage equity for the women in the company, Annie realized the power of a union.

After the war, she returned to her textile mill job, eager to learn more about unions. When enough workers at her factory had joined the Textile Workers Union of America in 1950, the union leadership called for an election. During the organizing drive, management targeted Annie because she had organizers staying at her home, where she also hosted union meetings. When she missed a day of work because of a sick child, Annie was illegally fired. She took her case to the

National Labor Relations Board, which ruled in her favor and for five other workers who were also illegally fired for union activity. Annie fought the company for six years, finally winning her case, and the company paid her all back wages and reinstated her with seniority at her old job. While she was unemployed during that six-year period, Annie could not find work elsewhere. She was, as she recalls, "blackballed," or blacklisted, because she was a "troublemaker." Since much of Annie's identity was constructed by her working life, her inability to work hurt her as much as any of the other difficulties that she had faced. She said, "All I wanted to do was work. But I didn't back off. I never would say that I would do what they wanted me to do [to be reinstated]." Annie experienced the poverty that caused her to cross the picket line and learned firsthand that unions give workers the power of solidarity and the power to change their conditions for the better.

Another woman who gained an education through her union experiences, Sally, a telecommunications worker, is a longtime member of the Communication Workers of America (CWA). The union and her strike experience provided her with an invaluable education. Sally had been employed at the telephone company for two years when the union membership voted to go on strike in 1971. Since her father was a manager at a nonunion cotton mill, Sally grew up with no knowledge of union membership or of solidarity with her fellow workers. Her lack of awareness became a painful and enduring lesson when she crossed the picket line in the 1971 strike. Sally recalled that at the time of the strike, "I didn't even know that you could sign up [with the union]."

In 1984, Sally was able to put her lesson into practice when the CWA again went on a nationwide strike. The dispute was, as Sally recalls, "the best three weeks I ever had in my life." She was able to rectify her earlier wrong and to march on the picket line with her union sisters and brothers. When other strikers recall the "good times" on the picket line, they often remember the solidarity and camaraderie among the workers, but Sally expresses a deeper satisfaction with being a part of the event that would lead to improved working conditions for all workers. Since she felt that her ignorance during the 1971 strike was detrimental to her fellow workers when she "betrayed" them by crossing the picket line, Sally could now show her support for the union and the common struggle. "I felt like a different person. I wouldn't have cared if we had stayed out [on strike] longer. And it didn't matter about the money because of that first time." In 1971, Sally had worked and had drawn "a pay, even if it's just four days," while her striking coworkers lost compensation for the same number of days. Sally describes her experience crossing the picket line:

> That was just such an eye-opener for me. And I'm so glad it happened because I feel like the union has been so important. I make good money. I got good benefits, and I just really feel like there's people that went out on strike for me, and I got these benefits, and by not going out, I was saying, "Well, I'll let somebody else do my dirty work, but I'll reap from it."

Ultimately, what Sally reaped was a strong devotion to the union and a desire to advocate for her fellow workers. She now attends carefully to her coworkers and their involvement in the union, and she makes sure that she invites all new employees to join, explaining the benefits of union membership.

Sally remains an ardent supporter of the union, crediting the union with opening jobs for women that previously were held only by men. Sally has worked in jobs that were considered to be the domain of men for more than half of her thirty-three-year tenure with the company. "If it hadn't been for the union, I don't think jobs would have been as available as they are for women." In addition, she states that the union is also responsible for the excellent benefits that she enjoys, including an impending retirement that will take care of her in later life. Since Sally is cynical about the company's motives with respect to workers, pay, and benefits, she hopes that the unions can continue to fight effectively for workers' rights. "My work experience as a woman with a union company has been great. I do hope unions stay strong because workers need somebody to stand up for them. You need a place to go and grieve things that you see are wrong. And you need support." Finally, she returns to her early experience during the strike of 1971: "When we had the strike, and I crossed the picket line, I learned that everybody needs to stand together to make things better for all."

Naomi, a member of the Paper, Allied Chemical and Electrical (PACE) union, also credits the union with winning her the opportunity to do a "man's job" at the paper company where she worked for several decades. The union set up the schools and training courses for the various skilled jobs and invited women to apply in order to gain access to the jobs traditionally reserved for men. Naomi states that the union "actually encouraged women to join maintenance." However, the stigma attached to being the first woman in a lucrative, male-dominated field was often difficult. She reported that the discrimination and sexism were apparent early in her career as an electrician. "It's odd being the only woman. Most of the men can only see us as women."

Naomi worked diligently for the union during the strikes. In 1971, she walked the picket line for herself and her husband for six weeks, since he had a part-time job that they needed to support their young family during the strike. However, Naomi and her husband both were supportive of the union and the strike, so they thought it was important that at least one of them would take both turns on the picket line. Naomi also praises the safety advances that unionization brought to the company. Because of PACE guidelines, workers were required to wear safety glasses, earplugs, and appropriate safety shoes and clothing. Prior to that, Naomi often went to work in shorts and sandals. In addition to safety, the union brought real bargaining power to the workers. In 2001, while the union fought the drastic pay and benefits cuts proposed by the foreign investor who had bought the plant, Naomi and her coworkers learned that their strike was a failure. Refusing to bargain in good faith, the owner closed the company, as he had threatened to do early in the negotiations. Naomi said the cuts he proposed were "criminal." Instead of the promised 10 percent pay cut, the company would take up to 60 percent of workers' pay. "I sat down and figured mine up, and I was going to lose forty-nine percent." As Naomi states, "There was no give and take. So it ended up a stalemate." Though the union brought job and pay equity to women and living wages for all workers when it formed in the 1960s, PACE had lost much of its bargaining power to the global economy by 2001.

Social Activism

While education remains an important aspect of their participation in unions and strikes, women workers also gained newfound interest in political and social activism in their workplaces, unions, and communities. Workers in North Carolina have alternately resisted and promoted social justice through labor unions over the course of their history. One notable example of a woman who made a difference was Theodosia Gaither Simpson, who worked at R.J. Reynolds Tobacco in Winston-Salem. In 1943, Gaither Simpson worked stemming tobacco leaves, a job that was primarily done by women. The war simultaneously drove demand for cigarettes and cut the supply of workers, leading Reynolds managers to insist on overtime. Despite the extra hours, workers' income fell, because the cost of living in Winston-Salem was nearly double the earnings of even the best and most highly paid workers. "Few stemmers made more than 10 cents above minimum wage, even those who had worked at Reynolds for many years," according to historian Robert Korstad. The increased demands on workers and the constant monitoring and disciplining of the women by the foremen led to even greater dissatisfaction.

Nearly desperate, the women in the stemmeries knew that conditions would have to change because they could not keep up the pace and could no longer endure the oppressive conditions in the factory. A union-organizing drive began under the auspices of the United Cannery, Agricultural, Packing, and Allied Workers of America–Congress of Industrial Organizations (UCAPAWA-CIO), through a local Tobacco Workers Organizing Committee. Workers were ready for a change. One woman, quoted by Korstad, noted:

> We was catching so much hell in Reynolds that we had to do something [. . .] . In the first place they gave you a great big workload, more than you could do [. . .] . Instead of cutting down on

> the boxes of work, if the foreman discovered a box not tightly packed, he would roll it back to the casing room to be repacked. If you'd tell them they put too much work on you, they'd fire you. And then they stood over you and cussed you out about doing it: "If you can't get this work out, get your clothes and get out" [. . .] . Everybody would almost cry every day the way they would work you and talk to you. Working conditions was so bad you needed God and a union.

Simpson was outraged at this mistreatment and secretly called a few women together in the bathroom to discuss a sit-down strike in protest. When the foreman heard of this, he warned the women that they would lose their jobs if they stopped work. Not to be deterred, 200 women held their strike that afternoon, earlier than the original plan to strike the next morning.

Eventually workers on other floors heard of the strike and joined it. Simpson was spokesperson for the workers, and she met the members of management in a battle of wills that pitted her knowledge and skills against those of company officials. Wrote Korstad:

> Never before had these women, en masse, spoken so honestly and fearlessly to the chief representative of a company that wielded tremendous control over their lives. Equally important, they challenged management's monopoly on expert knowledge, one of the prerogatives of power, and aligned themselves with the federal government, whose ability to intervene in labor-management disputes was at an all-time high.

Simpson and her coworkers successfully fought a powerful company whose injustices were intolerable. Ultimately, 10,000 workers participated in the strike at a firm whose workers were 56 percent women and 60 percent African American.

Another important union activist from North Carolina is Crystal Lee Jordan. Popularized in the film *Norma Rae,* Jordan's struggle for economic justice in textile mills in North Carolina illustrates how education and activism can result from involvement in union organizing. Born into a family employed in textile mills in Roanoke Rapids, Jordan suffered financial hardships and the degradation of being considered mill "trash." Both her parents worked in the mill, and in the eleventh grade, Jordan began working full-time in the mill on the second shift. Throughout her life in the small town, Jordan tried to escape mill work but always returned. In 1973, Jordan was working at JP Stevens folding towels when the Textile Workers Union of America launched a campaign to organize at least half of the seventy-five Stevens mills in North Carolina. The company had been very effective in opposing organizing efforts in 1963, resulting in "dozens of charges against JP [Stevens] by the union in federal courts in the South," according to Jordan's biographer Henry Leifermann. One of the charges—that workers were illegally fired for joining the union—led to a judgment requiring Stevens to pay tens of thousands of dollars in back pay to those workers and to post an embarrassing apology letter to all of those workers on each bulletin board in every Stevens plant. Though the company complied, they continued to use intimidation and racist tactics to deter the union.

Jordan became involved in the organizing effort and began to talk to other workers during breaks and at lunch. "I would talk union to my friends, and I started getting a lot of membership cards signed," she told Leifermann. In response to the union activity, the plant manager posted a threatening four-page letter on bulletin boards, which was especially intimidating to African-American workers because the letter suggested that black workers who joined were a militant group. Since 80 percent of the workers were white, the management hoped to discredit the union by pandering to the racism among the white workers. If the white workers thought that the union was a "black" enterprise, the organizing drive would be defeated. Because the union needed a copy of the letter, organizer Eli Zivkovich asked Crystal Lee Jordan to copy it. Copying the letter was considered hostile activity, and Jordan could only take down parts of it at a time during breaks and lunch. When she was observed copying the letter, her supervisor told her to stop. The plant manager later told her not to copy the letter, but she defiantly completed her task. Jordan was fired for her involvement in the organizing drive and then began working for the union organizing campaign full-time. Jordan brought black and white workers together in the campaign, defying the company's racist tactics. In 1974, the union was voted in by a narrow margin, and the victory was attributed to the efforts of Crystal Lee Jordan.

A former paper worker, Stella is a contemporary North Carolina woman unionist fighting for justice. She views life in her small mountain community from an analytical framework that includes questioning authority and resisting the status quo. Stella comments about the many injustices perpetrated against poor and working-class people. "My parents were growing up here, and this was a very poor county. They couldn't afford to buy a home. All they had was money for groceries. With four children to feed, there was nothing left." Stella indicated that their poverty was caused by unorganized workers looking out "for number one." Further, she notes, "My grandfather worked at [a lumber company] where they gave the workers just enough money to live on. This also was a result of not having a union." Stella also recounted her family's experiences with wealthy and powerful men and women who have what she calls the "Big Me-Little You" concept "that rich people have." One of the most dramatic examples of this idea occurred late in the nineteenth century. Stella reports that "George Vanderbilt stole 100 acres that my grandfather had bought for $30 in the Pisgah Forest. He's another one of those rich bastards who made money off the poor people." The series of unfair and oppressive actions taken against the working people of her community led Stella to become an active unionist and a fighter for justice.

Stella worked forty-nine years for the paper company that provided the livelihood of the majority of people in her community. Prior to its arrival in 1939, the community was dependent on pulpwood and tanneries, which added to the wealth of the very few individual owners while keeping the workers in poverty. "That's what happens when you got an economy where it's 'Big Me and Little You.' They're going to keep you that way. If they ever get you like that, they're going to keep you there. That's why it is so important to have unions." In the 1960s, a major corporation bought the plant and eliminated benefits and cut wages to boost their profits. When the cuts began affecting the workers, a union was formed to help preserve workers' rights and their benefits. As a result of the union, workers benefited from improved wages and medical and retirement benefits.

Stella became a fervent union supporter, learning more about how the union could fight injustice during two major strikes. She learned that workers' solidarity and working together could combat the oppression by the rich and the powerful. The first strike lasted eight weeks, and Stella gained important knowledge about the power of unions during that time. "It helped me an awful lot, the strike. It helped me to see that there were times in a person's life where it was more important to stand together than to be selfish. Everybody helped everybody." After the dispute was settled, Stella was convinced that unions were the workers' only power. She says, "I one hundred percent believe in the unions." In 2001, however, a multinational company bought and eventually closed the plant, concluding a long strike. She further notes that the current conditions for workers in the county, state, and nation are indicative of the unions' loss of power. "Of course, it's going back [to the pre-union conditions] now. [Many people] can't afford to buy houses now." Stella's activism is firmly situated in the tradition of economic justice carried on by many unions.

Another union activist, Millie, is a member of the United Steelworkers of America (USWA) and works in a tire manufacturing plant in North Carolina. She participated in a yearlong strike in 1999. As a result of her involvement in the USWA, Millie has developed a strong sense of social activism. From her beginnings at the male-dominated workplace, Millie learned how to challenge the status quo. Her first day of work was challenging. She says, "I was a tire builder. Those guys bet that I wouldn't make it. Those men didn't know they gave me the incentive to stay. I was one of the best tire builders they had." Her determination has served Millie well as a social activist. She now focuses her attention on helping other women achieve success. "I tell other women to . . . decide in their mind what they want to do, stick to it, and do it. You see another person do it, you can do it too." In addition, she said, some supervisors intimidate women workers, but that "once you let them know one time that you won't be pushed around, then you got it [made]." Through the USWA, Millie is able to negotiate the conditions of her work in a nontraditional field for women.

Millie has assumed several leadership roles in her local and on the central union council. As a member of the local executive board, she says, "I get to vote and help make some of the decisions for the union." Her feminism motivated her effort to become a leader. "I want to be in the decision making. During the election there were nine men and one female, which was me, and I got it." In her local there are 113 women out of 1,100 members. With a membership of only 10 percent women, Millie's election is a testimony to the members' respect for and admiration of her capabilities, irrespective of gender. For Millie, her leadership position enables her to gain firsthand knowledge of situations that affect workers. She says, "I like to know up front. I like to hear firsthand what's going on." Unions have provided the means for women to overcome the sexism in their trades, offering them influential roles. Currently Millie is working to develop greater involvement among women and to address their needs in the union. "We have a Silver Lights committee, we have a welfare committee, we have a Women of Steel [group]. You know, just that women can come together and voice their opinion on what's going on." She reports that "women'll get stuff done. We are trying to help [women] get active and trying to make the local better." Her own work in the union has enabled her to grow politically and to develop new leadership abilities. Millie's social activism is based on her realization that she has "important work to do for women and all workers."

Leadership

Ellen is another North Carolina unionist who gained educational, activist, and leadership experience from her involvement with the union. A thirty-one-year veteran of the telecommunications industry, she faced harassment and discrimination at several points in her career. Ellen has worked in a number of areas ranging from the female-dominated operator section to clerical work for a male supervisor, and finally to an outside job in repair. Eventually she moved into what is considered a man's job, underground cable splicing. As Ellen reports, "The women's jobs don't pay as much as the outside jobs, so we started going outside." She tells of dealing with sexism. "There was one guy in my group who told me to my face he didn't want to work with me." Ellen notes that all women had to prove their worthiness for the repair jobs. The sexism and discrimination that Ellen repeatedly faced in her early career only served to fuel her union feminism. However, Ellen's own work experiences were not the only ones that encouraged her fight for social justice.

When Ellen served as a United Way volunteer, going to various companies to talk with their workers, she gained personal insights into the ways that unions help empower female workers. At an Asheville shirt factory, Ellen noted that the workers—all women—were subjected to oppressive conditions. The factory manager would allow the United Way presentation only during the workers' lunchtime. After her presentation, all of the women donated to the charity, and many of them gave their "fair share," or one hour's pay per month. When Ellen looked at their donation cards, she asked the personnel officer who was assisting her if the donations had been calculated correctly. Ellen could not believe their low wages. "They make so little, and here they are giving that much." At that time the factory manager walked up and overheard Ellen. "And so [the manager] tapped me on the shoulder and said, 'I don't need no Norma Rae in here. I think you can leave now.'" Years later, Ellen continues to be outraged by the conditions in that factory. "I was so used to being treated fair at all times because I had worked for a union company."

Ellen became a union leader in her years with the Communication Workers of America. She attributes her success in part to her early involvement with the Western North Carolina Central Labor Council. "I was offered opportunities that men were used to getting, but women weren't. [The council president] gave me my first opportunity to become involved in politics because he made me the volunteer political coordinator for the labor council. That opened up a whole lot of doors." The president of that group, a man, had given her the opportunity, while other men tried to take it away. In the union as well as on the job, Ellen faced discrimination when she tried to represent her local as a member of the labor council. Whenever she went to meetings as a delegate for the council, Ellen was told how to vote while previous male delegates had not been so advised. "Usually women were told what position they were going to take on certain issues. And before I left town, I knew how I was supposed to vote because it had kind of been given to me."

When it came to endorsing a candidate for the United States Senate, Ellen voted against what she had been advised. As she says, "God gave me a mind, and I'm going to have to use it. And I appreciate all the information that you can give me to help me make up my mind. But if there's an alternative route that's better, I'm going to take it." Even though she had not "followed orders," she says that she eventually won the council members' respect because she "had actually researched it and not just done it on a whim." In the face of this overt discounting of her intellectual capacity, Ellen had the good fortune to meet P.R. Latta, the so-called "godfather of the union" in North Carolina, who empowered Ellen to think for herself and to find her own voice. This man helped Ellen to gain the confidence and the skills to become a high-level leader in the union.

Another empowered leader, Joan, was a local representative of the International Ladies' Garment Workers' Union (ILGWU) and was involved in a strike at her company in 1988. The company, which was making huge profits, planned to cut medical and retirement benefits, pensions, and workers' salaries while extending the workweek from thirty-five to forty hours. This was an outrage to Joan and the other workers. When the company refused to negotiate these demands over the bargaining table, union leadership suspected that the company was engaging in "union-busting." She explains: "In 1988, we [. . .] feared when we was in the plant that the company said that they had wanted to get rid of the union. And that they were no longer going to have a union contract because it was too expensive." In a unanimous vote, the workers agreed to go on strike. As Joan notes, "They cleared the plant. Even people that wasn't in the union came out of the plant with us." Joan reports that none of the company's overtures were serious offers. The company hired attorneys from a known anti-union law firm that included then–U.S. Senator Jesse Helms. "They were determined not to negotiate a contract with us, and they were determined that [the striking workers] were never going to go back to work in that plant." Nevertheless, the workers on the picket line were just as determined as the company and their legal team.

Since the owner would not agree to their demands, the strikers began to picket showrooms and corporate buyers in various states who were considering their company's products. "We let them know that we were on an unfair labor strike, and the company wasn't bargaining in good faith with us." The workers even went to stores where their garments were sold. "We went to those stores and we handed out flyers, and we told them our story." They then picketed the company's subcontractors. The "tough strike" was made even more difficult by its duration. The women who were walking the picket line grew weary of the constant stress but refused to yield. "They would never give up. We went on strike in July, spent Thanksgiving on the strike line, and come Christmas, then we walked in the snow." The union was supportive, and the women were persistent. "I would say that we were some determined women. We did not give up. I mean those women out there really had pride in what they were doing." Joan was right by their side through the worst of it, counseling and leading them in solidarity with the faith that they would win this fight for workers' justice.

Their efforts were rewarded at least in the short term when the company finally lost so much money that the owner began to negotiate in earnest. "We got everything back we had lost. That's the first strike [in North Carolina] that we ever had where we won the strike and won full, full benefits that we had prior to the strike." Though the company closed its doors four years after the strike, Joan still works for the union, continuing her fight against injustice. Her colleagues note that she is a positive force in her union, for workers and for members of her community. She organizes food drives and helps the homeless, among her many other efforts. "I believe that if there's any way that I can help anybody I'm always out there. I believe that if you have lived your life and not have made some difference in someone else's life, it's all been in vain." Clearly Joan's lessons of leadership enabled her to make a powerful difference in the fight for justice.

Kim is another member of the USWA whose education and activism have resulted in leadership roles. She works at a tire company where she went on strike in 1999. She explains that before she began working in a union plant, she was woefully ignorant about the economic and political climate in which she found herself. Union information and activities raised Kim's consciousness about the issues. "I know what's happening in politics, what's happening around the world. Even with different countries. [The union teaches] a lot of things. And the women are doing more, and I think that's because now [the union is] more inclusive." Kim hopes that all workers can gain the knowledge and skills that unions offer to women. "I just wish every company would have a union. I listen to some people talk about how their supervisors talk to them or have let them go and don't have an explanation and don't warn them or don't tell them." With the realization that unions empower workers, Kim hopes to widen the net to include her sisters and brothers in the plant and in other disputes. "Now, when we know somebody's having a strike, or somebody's trying to organize, we try to back them and help them."

Because of the extensive knowledge that Kim has gained through her work with the union—locally, nationally, and internationally—she understands the political implications of her work. "The union teaches you a lot." Her political activism, born of her own struggles as a single mother trying to raise her children, keeps her strong and laboring for the cause. This passion for family, solidarity, justice, and independence all combine to make Kim a powerful advocate for the union. Kim is developing her leadership skills in the union environment. Women are "doing better" in the USWA, Kim acknowledges, with increased participation. "This was the first year we've ever had a woman district rep. We had a woman to run, and she got it and now we have an international women's conference, so they're doing better." She goes on to report that women are gradually moving into leadership positions in the male-dominated union. "They're more active now than they used to be, and I can understand it. I think once a woman starts to work in a union, then she kinda gets passionate about it." Prior to her union experience, Kim notes that she "didn't pay any attention to politics." Her new political awareness—together with her union activity—results in a positive, feminist leadership.

Women who have been involved in labor disputes in North Carolina have gained a powerful new tool in union feminism; these women are resisting injustice, sex discrimination, sexual harassment, and economic oppression. For the union feminist, power is defined by equality, access, and involvement in constructing a more democratic workplace and a more inclusive, equitable society. Union feminism incorporates some of the multiple viewpoints and different voices of feminism, ultimately affording working-class women the means to achieve agency in their work and personal lives. For these women struggling in the anti-union South, their work is essential to achieving social justice for the working class.

See also: Dressed for Defiance: The Clothing of Female Strikers, 1910–1935, 95; Twentieth-Century Textile Strikes, 330; Garment Worker Strikes, 342; Steel on Strike: From 1936 to the Present, 360.

Bibliography

Balser, Diane. *Sisterhood and Solidarity: Feminism and Labor in Modern Times.* Boston: South End, 1987.

Braunstein, Jill, Lois Shaw, and Robin Dennis. "What Do Unions Do for Women?" In *Women: Images and Realities*, ed. Amy Kesselman, Lily D. McNair, and Nancy Schniedewind. Mountain View, CA: Mayfield, 1998.

Fonow, Mary Margaret. *Union Women: Forging Feminism in the United Steelworkers of America.* Minneapolis: University of Minnesota Press, 2003.

Korstad, Robert R. *Civil Rights Unionism: Tobacco Workers and the Struggle for Democracy in the Mid-Twentieth Century South.* Chapel Hill: University of North Carolina Press, 2003.

Leifermann, Henry P. *Crystal Lee: A Woman of Inheritance.* New York: Macmillan, 1975.

THE CATHOLIC CHURCH AND STRIKES

Dan La Botz

The Catholic Church's attitude toward strikes in the United States is complicated, sometimes inconsistent and contradictory, but always significant. The complexity and contradictory character of the church's role arise from tensions between Catholic social teaching, church practice and community, and individual decisions. The Catholic Church's social teachings have evolved throughout the nineteenth and twentieth centuries, permitting and then encouraging Catholic involvement in unions. Catholic Church practice in different periods and regions has its own history, however—a history that is not always completely consistent with the church's teachings. Finally, Catholic communities and individuals may act on their own interpretation of the teachings and understanding of the practices or independently of them. We can say, nevertheless, that since the late nineteenth century the Catholic Church has accepted the fact that Catholics will join labor unions, bargain collectively, and strike. Catholic labor leaders have led strikes; Catholic activists have organized them; and Catholic workers in every period have participated in them.

The Period of the Knights

With the immigration of millions of Catholics from Ireland, Germany, Italy, Poland, Mexico, and other Catholic countries in the nineteenth century, the United States grew to have a significant Catholic population. The majority of the Catholic immigrants became workers and many became swept up in the great labor movements of the period, joining the National Labor Union in the 1860s and later the Knights of Labor in the 1870s. As part of such organizations, Catholic workers struck with their unions, even though the church did not support unions or strikes in the 1860s and 1870s.

The Catholic Church hierarchy, without clear guidelines at the time, tended to be critical of labor unions for various reasons: because unions were often secret societies influenced by Free Masonry, because the unions sought a labor monopoly, or because some unions advocated socialism. The church opposed socialism and defended private property, the cooperation of capital and labor, and class harmony. The church before 1888 generally advised workers to keep clear of unions and to stay out of strikes, though some Catholic priests previously supported unions. The church tended to be more sympathetic to unions and strikes in some areas. In Philadelphia, the Diocesan newspaper, *The Catholic Standard,* supported anthracite miners and railroad workers' strikes, according to historian Ken Fones-Wolf.

As more and more Catholic workers joined the Knights of Labor, some in the American Catholic hierarchy believed that the church should relent and permit them to do so. Some church leaders came to believe that if they failed to permit Catholics to join the Knights, as Protestant Americans did, that the church would be perceived as foreign, leading to a Know Nothing backlash against Catholics. Moreover, some in the hierarchy worried that if forced to make a choice, Catholic workers might well choose the Knights over the church. American Catholic leaders were divided over the Knights, so they took the issue to Rome. Cardinal James Gibbons argued that Catholic unions were not possible or necessary in the United States; at the same time, while opposed to strikes, he recognized that they formed part of modern social life. Pope Leo XIII ruled in 1888 that Catholics were now permitted to join the Knights. Pope Leo XIII's decision was a turning point, permitting American Catholics to participate in unions and, as union members, in strikes. Still, many Catholic bishops and priests opposed both unions and strikes.

The AFL Period

Responding to the growth of labor unions and the spread of strikes throughout Europe and America, in 1891 Leo XIII issued the Papal Encyclical *Rerum Novarum* on labor and capital, a major revision of the church's position on unions. The Pope continued to condemn socialism and reject class conflict, but recognized the importance of the labor question and granted the legitimacy of labor unions, permitting and encouraging Catholics to join them. The Catholic Church, its priests, and Catholic union officials emphasized the right of a male breadwinner to a family wage, a wage that would permit him to support his family. Protestants during this period also supported this right.

In the United States, Catholic bishops and priests generally opposed strikes, though there were exceptions. For example, Bishop William Elder of Cincinnati supported the creation of a fund for the benefit of 150,000 striking anthracite miners in 1902, according to historian Roger Fortin. In any case, regardless of whatever their bishops and priests thought, Catholic workers continued to join unions and engage in strikes. If one considers the great industrial conflicts of the late nineteenth century, such as the Pullman and Homestead strikes, factory workers' strikes in the East, and the Rocky Mountain mining battles, in many cases a large minority—if not a majority—of the strikers must have been Catholic.

Catholics, and particularly Irish Catholics, played a large role in the American Federation of Labor (AFL), a majority of whose members were Catholic, says historian Marc Karson. Father Peter E. Dietz worked to draw the Catholic Church into a closer relationship with the AFL. In 1910 he spoke at the AFL convention in support of conservative unionism, and at that same meeting he organized the Militia of Christ for Social Service as a permanent Catholic association within the AFL. The Militia supported labor unionism and collective bargaining and worked to oppose the socialist group, which represented about one-third of AFL members at the time. While the Catholic Church often advocated arbitration, Catholic workers struck with their AFL craft locals.

The Industrial Workers of the World (IWW), established in 1905 on a revolutionary anti-capitalist basis, embraced many Catholic workers in its union and its strikes, whether in factories in the East or in mines or forests in the West. The Catholic Church, of course, would not support the IWW's strikes because of the union's revolutionary syndicalist ideology.

The CIO Period

The Great Depression of the 1930s led to the development of new currents within the Catholic Church, some of which embraced industrial unions and actively supported strikes. The Catholic Worker, an anarchist Catholic organization based in New York City and founded by Peter Maurin and Dorothy Day, had not generally supported unions and strikes. However, under the influence of the growing labor insurgency, in 1936 the Catholic Worker published a pamphlet, "Catholic Worker Stand on Strikes," which called for support for the Congress of Industrial Organizations (CIO) and its strikes. The *Catholic Worker* newspaper praised the CIO sit-down strikes in the auto plants as labor's way to nonviolently challenge capital. Later the Catholic Worker organization would return to its disinterest in unions and strikes.

The Chicago Catholic Worker organization had a greater commitment to unions and strikes than did its New York counterpart. Catholic Worker members participated in 1937 in the strike at Republic Steel, site of the famous Memorial Day massacre. Catholic Worker activists in Chicago were arrested for their participation in other labor and strike action.

In April 1937, Catholic priests Charles Owen Rice and Carl Hensler founded the Catholic Radical Alliance (CRA) in Pittsburgh to support the rising industrial union movement. The CRA worked actively in the Steel Workers Organizing Committee strikes in Pennsylvania. During the strike at Heinz by the Canning and Pickle Workers Union, the priests spoke to hundreds of strikers on the picket line in support of their strike. The CRA movement organized labor schools in which they argued against strikebreaking and criticized scabs from a Catholic point of view.

In New York in the winter of 1937, a group of mostly Irish Catholic workers created the Association of Catholic Trade Unionists (ACTU). By 1941, the organization had expanded to Boston, Pittsburgh, Detroit, Rochester, Corning (NY), San Pedro (CA), Toledo, Cleveland, San Francisco, Glassport (PA), Newark and Ponca (OK), South Bend, Chicago, Milwaukee, Saginaw (MI), and Bay City. The ACTU defended the right to strike and picket peacefully, and members were involved in many of the CIO unions and quite active in strikes in the organizing period.

While organizations like the Catholic Worker, the CRA, and the ACTU played a significant role, the impact was much greater when the church hierarchy itself supported strikes. In Chicago in 1936, Saul Alinksy, not himself a Catholic but rather a Russian Jew, created the Back-of-the-Yards Organization, which sought to win support from Catholic churches for the Packinghouse Workers union. With the backing of Auxiliary Bishop Bernard Shiel, Alinsky succeeded in getting parish priests and their congregations to back the union and its strikes. With the Catholic Church's support, the Packinghouse Workers union's strikes won recognition and contracts from the Chicago meatpackers.

With the beginning of the Cold War in the late 1940s, the Catholic Church and Catholic organizations like ACTU continued to support unions and sometimes strikes, but most of their emphasis was on fighting communism. The era of the 1930s when worker priests stood beside strikers on the picket line was definitely over.

The UFW Period

In 1962 César Chávez, a Mexican-American farm worker and devout Catholic, established the union that would become the United Farm Workers (UFW). Chávez, trained in organizing by Catholic priests and by Saul Alinsky, founded a union made up of mostly Catholic Mexican workers who prayed, fasted, made pilgrimages, and carried the banner of the Virgin of Guadalupe. In the 1960s and 1970s, the UFW engaged in the largest and most important strikes in agriculture since the 1930s. Dependent on the growers, Central Valley Catholic churches initially declined to support his organizing efforts, but over time many Catholic churches and priests became strong supporters of the union. Chávez helped revive the radical Catholic labor movement and its strike tradition, forcing the church to move in a more liberal direction.

In 1981, Pope John Paul II published his encyclical *Laborem Exercens* on human work, which reiterated the church's support for Catholic workers' participation in labor unions and made clear the church's support for the right to strike. The Pope revised the Catholic position on labor to argue that while capital and labor are both necessary to society, labor has primacy. John Paul II's encyclical represents the fullest and most complete discussion of workers' rights by a Pontiff. Regarding strikes, John Paul II wrote:

> *One method* used by unions in pursuing the just rights of their members is *the strike* or work stoppage, as a kind of ultimatum to the competent bodies, especially the employers. This method is recognized by Catholic social teaching as legitimate in the proper conditions and within just limits. In this connection workers should be assured the *right to strike,* without being subjected to personal penal sanctions for taking part in a strike. While admitting that it is a legitimate means, we must at the same time emphasize that a strike remains, in a sense, an extreme means. It *must not be abused;* it must not be abused especially for "political" purposes. Furthermore it must never be forgotten that, when essential community services are in question, they must in every case be ensured, if necessary by means of appropriate legislation. Abuse of the strike weapon can lead to the paralysis of the whole of socioeconomic life, and this is contrary to the requirements of the common good of society, which also corresponds to the properly understood nature of work itself.

Since 1965 and the shift to racial inclusion in U.S. immigration law, the United States has experienced an enormous expansion of immigrants, most of them from Latin America and overwhelmingly Catholic. As unions such as the Service Employees

International Union (SEIU), UNITE-HERE, the Carpenters, and the Laborers International Union (LIUNA) have undertaken to organize these workers, they have sometimes called upon local Catholic parishes and priests to support them. Thus there has developed a fairly consistent involvement of the Catholic Church at the local level in support of strikes by Catholic immigrant workers, and of other workers as well.

The Catholic Church and the Strike: A Critique

While the Catholic Church, with the development of modern society and the rise of labor unions, came to recognize the strike as a legitimate form of workers' struggle for a better life, in general the Catholic Church's impact on the labor movement and on strikes has been negative. Despite John Paul II's argument for the primacy of labor, Catholic practice often emphasizes the protection of private property. The church continues to seek the harmony of capital and labor, the balance between management and workers. The emphasis on harmony and balance works against attempts to strengthen unions vis-à-vis employers. When conflicts occur, the Catholic Church often seeks mediation or arbitration rather than mobilizing full support for unions and workers in order to defeat employers.

Because of its close ties to employers and its links to political parties and the state, the Catholic Church tends through its influence on unions and workers to undermine union independence and militancy. The church is a fundamentally conservative organization interested in maintaining order. Consider the experience of the Latino immigrant movement, which had been supported by the church until its leaders called for a May 1, 2006, general strike. The church refused to support the strike and urged Catholic immigrants to take some other action. The church, with its hierarchical organization and powerful institutions, also tends to undermine democracy insofar as it involves itself in union affairs. Feminists would also argue that the church's historic positions on women's subordination in church, society, and family and its emphasis on the male breadwinner's family wage both tend to diminish women. However, whatever the church teachings are, individual Catholic workers often have their own views of God, church, and society and their own conception of social justice. This reconstitution of worker activist networks, along with politically savvy strategic thinkers capable of linking workers' power across industries and national boundaries, represents the future of the labor movement.

See also: Polish Workers and Strikes, 1900–1937, 138; Unionizing the "Jungle": A Century of Meatpacking Strikes, 375; Agricultural Strikes, 415.

Bibliography

Abell, Aaron I. "The Reception of Leo XIII's Labor Encyclical in America, 1891–1919." *The Review of Politics* 7, no. 4 (October 1945).

Fones-Wolf, Kenneth. *Trade Union Gospel: Christianity and Labor in Industrial Philadelphia, 1865–1915.* Philadelphia: Temple University Press, 1989.

Fortin, Roger. *Faith and Action: A History of the Archdiocese of Cincinnati, 1821–1996.* Columbus: Ohio State University Press, 2002.

Griswold del Castillo, Richard, and Richard A. Castillo. *César Chávez: A Triumph of the Spirit.* Norman: University of Oklahoma Press, 1995.

John Paul II, "Laborem Exercens," at http://www.vatican.va/holy_father/john_paul_ii/encyclicals/documents/hf_jp-ii_enc_14091981_laborem-exercens_en.html, accessed March 12, 2007.

Karson, Marc. "The Catholic Church and the Political Development of American Trade Unionism (1900–1918)." *Industrial and Labor Relations Review* 4, no. 4 (July 1951).

Leo XIII, "Rerum Novarum," at http://www.vatican.va/holy_father/leo_xiii/encyclicals/documents/hf_1-xiii_enc_15051891_rerum-novarum_en.html, accessed March 17, 2007.

Piehl, Mel. *Breaking Bread: The Catholic Worker and the Origin of Catholic Radicalism in America.* Philadelphia: Temple University Press, 1982.

Seaton, Douglas P. *Catholics and Radicals: The Association of Catholic Trade Unionists and the American Labor Movement, from Depression to Cold War.* Lewisburg, PA: Bucknell University Press, 1981.

Sicius, Francis Joseph. "The Chicago Catholic Worker Movement: 1936 to the Present." Ph.D. diss., Loyola University of Chicago, 1979.

STRIKES LED BY THE TRADE UNION UNITY LEAGUE, 1929–1934

Victor G. Devinatz

Much of the Communist Party USA's (CPUSA) trade union activity during "Third Period Communism" (1928–34) focused on the creation of independent "revolutionary" or "red" industrial unions in opposition to the craft-oriented American Federation of Labor (AFL) unions. This represented a change from the prior strategy of "boring from within" the AFL, which had been CPUSA policy for most of the 1920s. To implement the new strategy, in 1929 the CPUSA remade its trade union arm—the Trade Union Educational League (TUEL), which was formed in 1921—into the Trade Union Unity League (TUUL). This was done with the explicit purpose of organizing Communist-led "dual unions" in industries where AFL unions already existed.

Largely based on several major TUUL strikes in highly visible industries, the standard interpretation in the historical literature, including that of historian Harvey Klehr and radical writer Bert Cochran, is that strikes led by the TUUL were dismal failures and led to few, if any, gains for the workers. In addition, scholars claim that the TUUL strikes failed because during these disputes the trade union federation advanced revolutionary rhetoric, including such slogans as "class against class" and "defend the Soviet Union." In essence, the argument is that the TUUL unions attempted to use these strikes to promote a frontal assault on capitalism at every conceivable opportunity, as opposed to focusing primarily on achieving economic and trade union demands for the strikers, including the fight against wage cuts and speedups, improvement of low wages, the implementation of forty-hour work weeks, and recognition of shop committees or unions. This essay will test the veracity of these standard historical interpretations by investigating the dynamics of TUUL-led strikes conducted in a wide variety of industries, including needle trades, textile, shoe, mining, agriculture, steel, auto, and maritime.

TUUL-led strikes were qualitatively different from AFL-led strikes in two dimensions. First, the demographics of the workers involved in TUUL-led strikes differed from those who participated in AFL-led strikes. Second, the TUUL attempted to promote a more democratic, activist, and participatory unionism among its rank-and-file membership during strikes, although there is no direct evidence that the federation was successful in this regard, as opposed to the AFL unions' more bureaucratic approach. TUUL-led strikes experienced differential success rates across two distinct time periods delineated by the passage of the National Industrial Recovery Act (NIRA). Prior to the NIRA's passage in June 1933, strikes were more likely to have emerged spontaneously, been taken over by TUUL cadre external to the employees, and to have been lost. After the NIRA's passage, TUUL-led strikes were more likely to have been organized by TUUL members employed at the work site and to have resulted in a union victory.

TUUL-Led Strikes in the Pre-NIRA Period

Harvey Klehr argues that the revolutionary trade union federation had dramatically different goals than the conservative, craft-union-oriented AFL. Strikes were not restricted to achieving workers' economic demands but were a methodology for obtaining revolutionary power. In 1930, the Red International of Labor Unions, an international grouping of Communists active in trade unions known by its Russian abbreviation "Profintern," called for its affiliated organizations to utilize "the development of the mass political strike" as a mechanism for attacking capitalism. The TUUL interpreted the Profintern's orders as meaning that it must inject their strikes with "more of a class and political character" and direct them against the capitalist state as well as employers as part of the working class's struggle to promote revolution. Because of these objectives, in TUUL-led strikes the union not only fought against employers but attacked the state and other reformist organizations, especially the AFL and independent unions.

Not long after the Profintern's pronouncement, the Executive Committee of the Communist International (ECCI), the guiding body of the international organization to which individual Communist parties were affiliated, modified its instructions to the TUUL concerning strikes. In October 1930, as Klehr describes, the ECCI requested that the TUUL focus its strikes on immediate economic demands, such as "wages, hours, speed-up, unemployment, increasing accidents and growing oppression in the factories," rather than emphasizing the "abstract politicizing of strikes," but the ECCI did encourage the raising of "political demands which correspond to the strike struggles."

According to Bert Cochran, the TUUL's formation on the eve of the Great Depression came during a period of declining class struggle. From 1930 to 1932, there were few strikes conducted, with most being "desperate rear-guard actions to fend off wage cuts." Furthermore, strike statistics from this period indicate that the average number of strikes per year was much lower than in the previous three decades. Because AFL unions were disinclined to lead workers in defensive struggles in primarily unorganized industries, the TUUL took over this role during this period.

Much of the TUUL unions' membership recruitment activities during the early 1930s were intricately connected with strikes it led. Although many of these strikes by unorganized workers involved fights against wage cuts and speed-up, some TUUL-led strikes during this period were offensive actions and were launched to obtain wage increases or to improve working conditions. Many of these strikes were spontaneous so that the TUUL did not have the opportunity to prepare adequately. Instead, the TUUL came to offer leadership once the strikes had commenced. Once a strike took place, the CPUSA would bring in its forces, ranging from top party and TUUL leaders to rank-and-file activists to its relief organizations such as the Workers International Relief and the International Labor Defense to take over the leadership of the strike. Although TUUL unions were able to mobilize thousands of strikers, the trade union federation did not have the manpower or the financial resources to see the strikes through to a successful conclusion, according to Klehr and historian Fraser Ottanelli.

The TUUL was confronted with carrying out two major activities during these walkouts: it provided leadership and organizational resources to these often spontaneous struggles and it sought to recruit members to the TUUL unions. Although many (but not all) of these TUUL-led strikes were lost, a number of these strikes resulted in concrete gains for the workers. These gains did not necessarily lead to either a long-term increase in membership or organizational stability for the TUUL unions.

Many, but not all, large TUUL-led strikes in this period unfolded in the following manner. Initially, the CPUSA exhibited a tremendous commitment and enthusiasm at the start of the walkout, followed by violence against the strikers, resulting in the defeat of the strike. From 1929 to 1932, according to Cochran, the National Textile Workers Union (NTWU) led a number of disastrous strikes in Gastonia (North Carolina), in Lawrence (Massachusetts) at the American Woolen Mills, and in the silk mills of Allentown, Pennsylvania. Other unsuccessful TUUL-led strikes, which also failed to result in the establishment of stable organizations, included cigar makers in Tampa, shoe workers in New York, and Mexican agricultural workers in the California Imperial Valley. As Klehr recounts, Jack Stachel, a leading TUUL official, stated, "We were so happy to have strikes we didn't want to end them."

One strike in the pre-NIRA period representative of the pattern was the farm workers' strike of January 1930 in Imperial Valley, California. On New Year's Day 1930, hundreds of Mexican and Filipino lettuce workers in Brawley, California, participated in a spontaneous work stoppage over wage cuts and unbearable working conditions. Within a week, 5,000 farm workers joined the original strikers, turning the Imperial Valley strike into an important struggle. Early on, the strike was threatened by the arrest of strikers and employer attacks on strike meetings organized by the Mexican Mutual Aid Society. However, according to historian Kate Bronfenbrenner, the strike was reinvigorated after the TUUL sent in three youthful organizers, Frank Waldron, Harry Harvey, and Tsuji Horiuchi, from its affiliated Agricultural Workers Industrial League (AWIL).

Upon arriving in Imperial Valley, the three organizers spent a number of days working underground to develop the strike's rank-and-file leadership. When they came out in the open, the organizers immediately created an AWIL chapter and incorporated Filipino workers into all strike activities. By encouraging rank-and-file activism and emphasizing trade union issues rather than promoting revolutionary ideology, the AWIL revived the failing strike. Nevertheless, after authorities arrested the three organizers, blocked strike relief, and threatened to arrest and deport Mexican strikers, the union leaders called off the strike on January 23 without obtaining any of the workers' demands.

However, not all TUUL-led strikes during this period resulted in a total defeat for the union. For example, the February 1930 strike of unorganized workers at American Woolen originated as a fight against speed-up involving only thirty-three workers in one department of one mill. Within two weeks, 10,000 to 12,000 workers were on strike, calling for union recognition, overtime pay at time and a half, the right to elect departmental committees, the removal of "efficiency men" who timed the workers and sped the work process, and a reduction in the number of machines that each worker had to operate from nine to three. According to a report by CP organizer Jack Stachel in the CPUSA records at the Library of Congress, the employer agreed to all of the strikers' demands, except time-and-a-half-pay for overtime, and 650 workers became members of the NTWU during the first week of the strike, but upon the strike's conclusion the employer immediately set out to destroy the union.

According to documents in its records at the Library of Congress, the TUUL unions led more strikes in 1931 than in 1930. For example, of 67,000 workers on strike during July 1931, the TUUL was leading a strike of 10,000 textile workers in Lawrence (Massachusetts) and a coal miners' strike of 40,000 in western Pennsylvania, eastern Ohio, and western Virginia. Other major TUUL-led strikes that year included a strike of 20,000 textile workers in Rhode Island, Connecticut, Massachusetts, and New Jersey; a cannery strike of 2,000 workers in San Jose, California; and a furriers' strike in New York City.

The National Miners Union's (NMU) strike of 40,000 miners against the Carnegie Coal Company (and other companies) over wage cuts in May 1931 was the largest miners' strike in 1931 and the largest walkout that had been led by the CPUSA up to that time. The CPUSA lacked the requisite resources to lead the strike, and it ended in defeat. The same analysis applies to the other disastrous miners' strike led by the NMU in 1931 in Harlan, Kentucky. Cochran concludes, "In the big strikes, the Communists piled up a perfect negative score," while Klehr's assessment of the CPUSA's leadership role in TUUL strikes is that the TUUL "organizers demonstrated an eerie talent for losing what strikes they did succeed in calling."

The CPUSA's examination of the failed miners' strike resulted in an analysis that applied to other defeated TUUL-led strikes. The party argued that NMU organizers failed to develop and train "necessary new cadres from below" to take over the strike's leadership; the organizers performed all of the strike leadership work without involving the workers' duly-elected leaders. The CPUSA also claimed that the strike could not be consolidated because of the failure to build "local and pit organizations" that had "daily contact with the central strike leadership." Another reason for the strike's failure, according to the CPUSA, was that the union did not sufficiently "develop a strong relief movement from the beginning of the strike." Finally, the party stated that the NMU failed to build a united front from below with the miners led by the Musteites, followers of the radical minister A.J. Muste, in southern West Virginia.

While the TUUL languished on a national scale, it fared considerably better in New York City.

From the middle of August 1931 to the middle of February 1932, the New York City district TUUL, the Trade Union Unity Council (TUUC), led approximately 11,000 workers in defensive strikes against wage cuts and in offensive strikes for wage increases. About 65 percent of these strikes ended in victory. The union won most of the defensive strikes, and in the "well organized" offensive strikes it won employer-provided wage increases and either shop committee or union recognition.

The last major strike in heavy industry led by a TUUL union before the passage of the NIRA in June 1933 was the Briggs Strike in Detroit, which began on January 23, 1933. Due to a wage cut, speed-up, and dangerous working conditions, 6,000 workers struck four Briggs plants and turned to the Auto Workers Union (AWU) for organizational help. According to Cochran and historian Roger Keeran, the union and the CPUSA provided strike leadership, organized soup kitchens, and attempted to raise funds for the strikers. However, public red-baiting resulted in the removal of Communists from the strike committee. This combined with a lack of funds caused the strike to founder by early March, and the strikers returned to work having achieved only a few minor concessions.

TUUL-Led Strikes in the Post-NIRA Period

With the passage of the NIRA and the inclusion of Clause 7(a), most private-sector workers won a federally protected right to organize, and union membership in all types of labor organizations dramatically increased. Since Clause 7(a) was ambiguous with respect to workers' legal rights to collective bargaining representation, many employers established company unions in an attempt to prevent workers from joining AFL, TUUL, or independent unions, according to Klehr. Nevertheless, by the end of October 1933, the TUUL had benefited from this legislation through a dramatic increase in membership. According to its records at the Library of Congress, the TUUL estimated its membership between 125,000 and 130,000, with 30,000 in the Needle Trades Workers Industrial Union (NTWIU), 10,000 in the Steel and Metal Workers Industrial Union (SMWIU), and 10,000 in the Shoe Leather Workers Industrial Union (SLWIU).

Even though the CPUSA believed that a major purpose of the NIRA was to undermine labor militancy, the legislation reinvigorated the strike movement in 1933, leading to triple the number of strikers when compared with 1932. By the end of August 1933, the party estimated that nearly 670,000 workers had taken part in strikes during the first eight months of 1933, with the TUUL itself leading walkouts in more than fifteen industries.

Of the 666 strikes that took place in the first eight months of 1933, AFL unions led 311 strikes, TUUL unions led 125 strikes, independent unions led 129 strikes, and 101 were spontaneous. The AFL-led strikes were concentrated in three industries—mining, needle trades, and textiles—while a majority of TUUL-led strikes occurred in four industries: mining, needle trades, auto, and shoe. Two months later, the CPUSA estimated that since the beginning of 1933, 1 million workers had at some point been on strike and that AFL unions had led 45 percent of these strikers, the TUUL unions had led 20 percent, independent unions had led 17.5 percent, and 17.5 percent were spontaneous.

Given that at the end of 1933 the AFL had approximately 2,318,000 members and the TUUL had 125,000 members, the AFL led one strike for every 7,453 members while the TUUL led one strike for every 1,000 members. Through October 1933, the AFL led approximately one-fifth of the number of members in its organization on strike while the TUUL led 1.6 times the number of members in its organization on strike.

One industry in which neither AFL nor independent unions led strikes during the second half of 1933 was agriculture. The only union that led strikes in this industry in the last six months of 1933 was the TUUL-affiliated Cannery and Agricultural Workers Industrial Union (CAWIU), previously named the Agricultural Workers Industrial Union (AWIU) and before that the AWIL. Since leading 5,000 Mexican and Filipino lettuce workers on strike in California's Imperial Valley in early January 1930, the AWIL and its successor organizations had retained a strong presence among California agricultural laborers. Despite earlier failures, the CAWIU achieved some success in conducting walkouts among California agricultural workers, as recounted by historians Cletus Daniels and Harvey

Levenstein. Of at least eighteen strikes held in this industry in California in 1932 and 1933, the CAWIU won thirteen among cotton pickers, pea pickers, strawberry pickers, lettuce workers, cherry pickers, pear pickers, and beet workers, the largest of which was the strike by 18,000 cotton pickers in the fall of 1933 in the San Joaquin Valley.

Although it is unclear the percentage of TUUL-led strikes that were won on the national level during this time period, the New York City–based TUUC unions prospered in the post-NIRA era, according to TUUL documents. By the end of October 1933, there were 45,000 members in the New York City district with the NTWIU and the SLWIU having 18,200 and 8,500 members, respectively. From the NIRA's enactment to the beginning of October 1933, 177,100 workers struck in New York City, with the AFL unions leading strikes of 112,700 workers and the TUUL unions conducting walkouts encompassing 64,400 workers. In virtually all of the TUUL-led strikes, workers struck to obtain wage increases, establish minimum-wage scales, reduce hours with an "equal division of work during the slow period in seasonal trades," and achieve union recognition.

The TUUC unions won most of the strikes they led during this period. More than half of the TUUC-led strikers (35,000) were found in the needle trades. Among this group of workers, successful strikes occurred among fur workers, bathrobe workers, custom tailors, and knit-good workers. The 2,500 knit-good strikers and the 2,000 bathrobe strikers obtained wage increases ranging from 20 to 35 percent, and the former won implementation of the thirty-five-hour workweek, while the latter won union recognition. Fur industry workers won substantial wage increases along with a thirty-five-hour workweek. However, in the dressmakers' strike and the white-good workers' strikes, the CPUSA admitted that the NTWIU failed to achieve "any organizational gains."

In the other New York City industry where a TUUL union had more than a nominal presence, the SLWIU led a number of walkouts that culminated in wage increases of 20 to 50 percent for the vast majority of strikers. Upon the conclusion of these strikes, the union increased its membership more than sevenfold, from 1,200 to 9,000 members. As in a number of other successful industrial actions, the CPUSA attributed its success to a united front from below with shoe workers who were members of independent unions. Among the 4,000 striking workers led by the SMWIU, 1,000 silver hollowware workers obtained "substantial gains" but not union recognition.

In several small shops in the light-metal industry, the SMWIU moved quickly to assume the leadership of several spontaneous strikes at companies such as Majestic (350 workers) and Durable (200 workers), which resulted in wage increases of $2 to $8 per week and increased union membership. In smaller strikes led by TUUC unions, such as the mirror workers (500) and pipe makers (900), the strikers wrested "considerable gains" from employers, according to CPUSA records.

Not all strikes led by the TUUC unions at this time were successful. Strikes of 2,000 tobacco workers and 2,000 cleaners and dyers ended in defeat, while, according to a TUUL report, a strike of 1,000 laundry workers won only "shop committees with some improvements in the conditions of the workers."

Virtually all TUUC-led strikes in the latter half of 1933 took place in light industries. No strikes occurred in heavy industries, such as steel, transport, railroad, or marine. The CPUSA admitted that the TUUC unions were having problems recruiting in these industries. In addition, many of these strikes occurred in relatively small shops, which was characteristic of the industries where TUUC unions had the most success.

A representative example of a TUUL-led strike from the post-NIRA period was the walkout by 1,100 workers led by the Food Workers Industrial Union (FWIU) against the Chase Commissary Corporation in New York City in October 1934. Prior to the strike, the FWIU organized the workers in each of the company's cafeterias, and when the strike began each store's shop chairman brought the workers out to the picket line. By forming a united front with other AFL unions in the company, specifically the Teamsters Union and AFL Locals 16 and 302, and by getting students involved in strike support work through the National Student League, the FWIU achieved victory after nine days. Major gains included company recognition of the FWIU and its shop committees, substantial wage increases for lower-paid workers, full pay for the strikers during the week that they were on strike, reinstatement of all strikers and those terminated two weeks prior to the strike, union-controlled hiring procedures, and the establishment of a grievance committee to be composed of two union and two management representatives, according to labor journalist J. Rubin.

Although the TUUL began to fold up shop due to orders from Moscow towards the end of 1934, it still led strikes in the first half of the year concentrated primarily in the auto, steel, and metal industries. However, the last successful strike conducted by a TUUL-affiliated union might very well have been the strike against the Chase Commissary Corporation in October 1934.

How TUUL-Led Strikes Differed From AFL-Led Strikes

While AFL-led strikes occurred among unionized workers, the TUUL-led strikes took place primarily among unorganized workers. In addition, the TUUL unions attempted to promote a more democratic, activist, and participatory unionism, or "bottom up unionism," among their rank-and-file members during strikes, as opposed to the bureaucratic, or "top down," approach of the AFL. Evidence of the TUUL's desire for an alternative unionism comes from the TUUL's continual self-criticism, which critiqued the lack of democracy and worker participation during the walkouts of its affiliated unions. There is no evidence that the TUUL ameliorated this problem. In addition, during the TUUL-led strikes, the unions continually attempted to address the concerns and develop the leadership capacity of workers traditionally ignored by the AFL unions—young, female, and/or African-American workers. Although the TUUL did not always achieve these lofty objectives, the radical trade union federation worked to turn its vision into a reality.

In analyzing the failure of certain TUUL-led strikes from 1930 to 1932, the organization felt that insufficient involvement on the part of the workers was a major drawback, according to a report in the CPUSA records. For example, in the 40,000 strong NMU-led strike in the late spring and summer of 1931, the TUUL argued that a major problem was "the failure to activise [sic] [the workers] for the building of local and pit organisations [*sic*]." In addition, noting the important role that young workers played in the mining industry, the radical trade union federation pointed out that the NMU failed to develop "special youth commissions attached to the strike leadership" to recruit young workers as strike leaders. Finally, although it was acknowledged that the African-American miners "showed themselves as brave fighters in the strike," the TUUL criticized the NMU for not sufficiently drawing this group of workers into the strike leadership, for failing to address the "specific discriminations" against the African-American workers, and for not conducting "a systematic campaign against all manifestations of chauvinism among the white workers."

This failure to address adequately the specific grievances of African-American workers and to confront "the chauvinism of white workers" during strikes was a recurring problem throughout the 1930 to 1932 period, noted the union leadership. For example, leaders criticized a strike led by the SMWIU in September 1932 at the Trumbell Mill of the Republic Steel Corporation in Warren, Ohio, on the grounds that the union did insufficient work in organizing among the African-American workers and failed to include their specific demands in the strike program. In addition, the TUUL criticized the SMWIU local leadership for capitulating to the chauvinist attitudes of the white, native-born American workers during the strike.

Even after the TUUL-affiliated unions led many more successful strikes in the post-NIRA period, the TUUL leadership remarked in a report that "there are still many serious shortcomings to be overcome" concerning the affiliated unions' strike leadership. While applauding that "the strike committees were organized on a democratic basis consisting of shop representatives elected by the workers in the shop," the TUUL criticized these committees for not being "placed in full leadership" of the strikes. In many of these strikes, the TUUL observed that the strike committees served more of an agitational role than one of actually "leading the strikes," while the direction of the strike "remain[ed] in the hands of the top leadership."

In the more successful walkouts in the latter half of 1933, the TUUL took notice of the continuing deficiencies of its organizing work among African-American, female, and young workers. Local leaders failed to incorporate these workers' special demands into strike programs and integrate them sufficiently into strike leadership. Finally, the TUUL unions did not do enough to combat the "white chauvinism among the workers" and allowed African-American workers to receive "lower prices than white workers" for performing the same work.

Conclusion: A Reevaluation of TUUL-Led Strikes

While the widely held view of TUUL strikes is that they were an abject and total failure, this essay suggests their results were more mixed. TUUL unions took over many spontaneous strikes, especially in the pre-NIRA period. While they lost many of them, they provided a voice and leadership to many groups of workers, including African Americans, women, immigrants, and the unskilled, who received little or no support from larger AFL and independent unions, as historian Edward Johanningsmeier notes. Although the TUUL never developed an industrial concentration in heavy industry and was fairly weak (or nonexistent) in many parts of the United States, it did develop a base of support in New York City, where it had considerable success in organizing and leading strikes in smaller shops in light industries, particularly in the needle trades and shoe industry. In a number of these strikes, the TUUL unions were victorious when they successfully implemented united front tactics from below with workers who were members of competing unions. In addition, in these industries, the TUUL unions had their largest and most stable memberships, resulting in viable labor organizations.

Although much of the TUUL literature directed toward public consumption was filled with political slogans, such as "Defend the Soviet Union," at the workplace and in their daily activities TUUL organizers downplayed such mottos during their strikes. In fact, one complaint of TUUL leaders was that "our organizers" and the "leading comrades" in the party were not willing to "bring forward the party or even to explain the revolutionary character" of the TUUL unions to rank-and-file members.

According to Ottanelli, the CPUSA did not politicize the TUUL's strikes by invoking revolutionary rhetoric during strike meetings. Rather, the TUUL's demands and activities focused on increasing inadequate wages, alleviating hazardous working conditions, and obtaining both a forty-hour workweek and union recognition. Instead of emphasizing the overthrow of capitalism, the TUUL practiced a far-sighted, multiethnic, integrationist industrial unionism that was meant to appeal to a wide variety of employees, such as African Americans, women, and young workers, in industries not traditionally represented by the AFL unions.

If the Communist International had not put an end to the TUUL in 1934, could it have become the foundation of a viable left-wing industrial trade-union federation in the post-Wagner Act period commencing in 1935, when organizing both strikes and industrial unions became considerably easier? Based on the TUUL's strength being centered in the light industries in and around New York City combined with its difficulties penetrating heavy industry, it is unlikely that the TUUL would have been able to achieve such a status. In addition, when industrial militancy intensified in 1934 and AFL unions led three of the four major strikes that year, the TUUL was in the process of being eclipsed by a reinvigorated AFL.

While, according to Cochran, TUUL unions had difficulty holding on to membership and achieving organizational stability after strikes, they did fight when the AFL and independent unions would not. Their strikes provided real gains for workers, even in strikes ostensibly lost, including better wages and working conditions and more seasoned shop-floor leaders. The experience of shop-floor leaders became particularly important when CPUSA trade union activists reentered the AFL in 1934 and 1935, at the start of the Popular Front period. They contributed key organizational and leadership skills to unions in the Committee of Industrial Organization (CIO) after 1935, helping to construct mass industrial unionism in the country's major industries. More than any balance sheet accounting of union victories and defeats, the training and experience that served as a crucial foundation for the rise of the CIO is perhaps the most important legacy of TUUL-led strikes.

See also: Types of Strikes, xxxvii; Theories of Strikes, 16; Garment Workers Strikes, 342; Agricultural Strikes, 415.

Bibliography

Bronfenbrenner, Kate. "Imperial Valley, California, Farmworkers' Strike of 1930." In *Labor Conflict in the United States*, ed. Ronald L. Fippelli. New York: Garland Publishing, 1990.

Cochran, Bert. *Labor and Communism: The Conflict that Shaped American Unions*. Princeton, NJ: Princeton University Press, 1977.

Daniels, Cletus E. *Bitter Harvest: A History of California Farmworkers, 1870–1941*. Ithaca, NY: Cornell University Press, 1981.

Johanningsmeier, Edward P. "The Trade Union Unity League: American Communists and the Transition to Industrial Unionism: 1928–1934." *Labor History* 42, no. 2 (2001): 159–77.

Keeran, Roger. *The Communist Party and the Auto Workers Unions*. Bloomington: Indiana University Press, 1980.

Kimeldorf, Howard. *Reds or Rackets? The Making of Radical and Conservative Unions on the Waterfront*. Berkeley: University of California Press, 1988.

Klehr, Harvey. *The Heyday of American Communism: The Depression Decade*. New York: Basic Books, 1984.

Levenstein, Harvey A. *Communism, Anticommunism, and the CIO*. Westport, CT: Greenwood Press, 1981.

Nelson, Bruce. *Workers on the Waterfront: Seamen, Longshoremen, and Unionism in the 1930s*. Urbana: University of Illinois Press, 1988.

Ottanelli, Fraser M. *The Communist Party of the United States: From the Depression to World War II*. New Brunswick, NJ: Rutgers University Press, 1991.

Recent History of the Labor Movement in the United States, 1918–1939. Moscow: Progress Publishers, 1977.

Rubin, J. "Victory for the New York Food Workers." *Labor Unity* (November 1934): 19–21.

Stepan-Norris, Judith and Zeitlin, Maurice. *Left Out: Reds and America's Industrial Unions*. Cambridge: Cambridge University Press, 2003.

Steuben, John. "The TUUL in New York." *Labor Unity* (January 1932): 23–24.

Steuben, John. "Factory Work–The Major Work." *Labor Unity* (March 1932): 28–29.

PART III
STRIKE WAVES

Introduction by Aaron Brenner

Since the Industrial Revolution in the middle of the nineteenth century, strike waves have periodically swept over the United States, with profound impact on the country's social, economic, and political life. Major strike waves occurred in 1877, 1919, 1937, and 1946. Smaller but still significant strike waves took place in 1886, 1890, 1892–94, 1901, 1912–13, 1916–17, 1933–34, 1941, 1952–53, and 1967–74. In each case, the number of strikes and the number of workers on strike jumped appreciably from the pre-strike-wave period. For example, both totals more than doubled in 1937 compared to 1936. In 1890, the number of strikes was more than ten times the number in 1889. Yet strike waves were not defined simply by statistics. Rather, the strikes that composed a strike wave often had something in common, something that drove so many workers to walk off their jobs.

In 1919 and 1946, for example, the experience of World War, both positive and negative, inspired workers in many different industries to strike as they sought to recover wages lost to wartime inflation and to achieve in the workplace the ideals of democracy for which they had fought on the battlefield. Violence, or the lack thereof, sometimes united strikes. In 1877, strikes convulsed the country, involved tens of thousands of workers and their families, and sparked the mobilization of the U.S. Army, but the 1946 strike wave was almost without violence of any kind despite the involvement of millions of workers. The Great Strike, as the 1877 strike wave has been called, was generally a defeat for workers. By contrast, the strikes in 1946 mostly succeeded. As these two examples illustrate, strike waves could share common characteristics but could also vary tremendously in their character.

It is no coincidence that strikes tended to cluster in waves. Striking was, and still is, risky, so anything that reduced the risk of failure and increased the chances of success encouraged workers to strike. Particularly encouraging was the example of an effective strike. Successful strikes inspired workers and boosted their confidence to engage in a strike of their own. Strike success begat strike success, and when the process happened quickly the number of strikes rose to become a wave that crashed over multiple industries.

But what accounted for the first success? Many things were possible. Sometimes a change in the political landscape, particularly the government's increased involvement in the economy, could inspire workers. In 1933, for example, many workers saw the passage of the National Industrial Recovery Act, with its famous section 7(a), as a signal that President Franklin D. Roosevelt endorsed unionization and would protect their interests in the case of a strike. The result was a huge increase in the number of strikes. In other cases, such as the 1946 strike wave, government's role was minimal; instead, workers were determined to increase their wages. In the early 1970s, wages were important, but frustration with shop-floor conditions was the main inspiration for the strike wave, which was characterized by a large number of wildcat strikes led by rank-and-file workers instead of union officials.

Interestingly, defeat could also inspire a strike wave. Especially in the nineteenth century, workers often responded to wage cuts by fighting back, sometimes on a massive scale. These paroxysms of protest were rooted in frustration but rested on solidarity. Workers struck in sympathy with each other, believing that they had strength in numbers.

Understanding the similarities and differences within and between strike waves is the purpose of this section. Four essays look at some of the major strike waves in U.S. history. A fifth essay looks at what has happened to strikes in the years since the last major strike wave. Each essay asks why so many workers decided to strike at the same time and what their actions accomplished. The approach, however, differs from essay to essay, much as the strike waves themselves differed. John Lloyd compares the progress and outcome of the Great Strike of 1877 in different geographic locations, finding what united and divided the participants. Cecelia Bucki looks at the long strike wave during World War I, when the expansion of government involvement in the economy altered the balance of class forces. By contrast, Rachel Meyer narrows her focus to the sit-down strikes that constituted a minority of strikes in the 1930s but were the most dramatic and successful form of worker militancy during the strike wave. Jack Metzgar stresses the political and economic context of the 1946 strike wave, as well as the choices that determined its outcome.

These essays reveal strike waves to be complex, even contradictory events shaped by the historically specific conditions and unique personalities of their times. They also show that strike waves had far-reaching consequences for the nation, whether it was the establishment of armories around the country to put down strikes inspired by the Great Strike of 1877, the "Red Scare" that doused the flames of workplace radicalism in 1919, or the creation of employer-based welfare programs that arose from the strikes of the 1930s. Strike waves may have been sporadic, but they were not inconsequential.

THE STRIKE WAVE OF 1877

John P. Lloyd

The strike wave of July 1877 began as a spontaneous reaction to a 10 percent wage cut on the Baltimore & Ohio (B&O) railroad, but quickly grew into a nationwide strike wave that shook the nation's political system to its very core. Virtually every major urban industrial area from coast to coast was touched by what historian Philip Foner aptly termed the "great labor uprising." While most of the significant strike activity was concentrated in the Northeast and Midwest, the West saw unrest, as did pockets in the South.

In many instances, railroad workers were quickly joined by the unemployed as well as other workers who shared their misery and privation. In St. Louis, the strike was so widespread that it became, in Foner's words, "the first truly general strike in history," and it effectively shut down several other cities, including Pittsburgh and Chicago. So unprecedented was the uprising that it gave rise to a fear among some authorities that revolution was at hand. In many cities, as historian David Stowell has noted, the strike became the spark for "generalized antirailroad violence" that brought whole segments of the working-class population into the streets. Working-class anger against the railroads stemmed not only from their exploitation of workers, he argues, but also from the fact that they encroached on city streets in working-class neighborhoods in ways that angered a broad section of the community.

The strikes were also notable for the scope and ferocity of the federal government's response. At a time when federal troops were mostly stationed in the South or in the West, President Rutherford B. Hayes made the fateful decision to use federal troops to break the strike by force. By the time the strike wave of 1877 was over, more than 100 Americans—almost all of them workers, their supporters, and bystanders—lay dead, and many more were wounded. The strikes of 1877 marked the beginning of a tumultuous era in labor relations in the United States.

Industrial Growth and Hard Times

The decade following the end of the Civil War witnessed dramatic growth in American industry and commerce, and the railroad industry stood at the center of this growth. Railroad mileage roughly doubled during the decade as the growing network of roads knitted together the country's markets, linking producers in the West with manufacturers in the East. But while the railroad owners and financiers often amassed magnificent fortunes, those who built and worked on them received very little for their hard, dangerous work.

A financial panic in 1872, sparked by the failure of the banking house of Jay Cooke and Company, sent the nation into a severe economic depression that exacerbated living and working conditions for the working class. Nearly 50,000 businesses went bankrupt and 5 million people were thrown out of work. Railroad building came to a halt. With approximately 20 percent of the workforce unemployed, millions of workers—lacking any social safety net—took to the roads in search of work and food, giving rise to what middle-class newspapers often referred to as the "tramp problem." Advertisements for handguns appeared in newspapers touting their value as protection against "tramps" and "vagrants." On average, wages for many workers, which were not high to begin with, fell by nearly half during the seven-year depression. The issue of wage cuts would be at the heart of the great uprising of labor in 1877.

Working people faced tremendous hardship during the depression, and rumblings of discontent could be seen around the country. In New York City in 1872, a young cigar maker, Samuel Gompers, who would later become head of the American Federation of Labor (AFL), witnessed police brutally beat workers in Tomkins Square during a demonstration protesting the lack of work, food, and clothing. In Pennsylvania, coal miners went on what became known as the "Long Strike" of 1875–76, protesting the harsh conditions under which they lived and worked. In the strike's wake, twenty miners alleged to have been members of a secret order called the "Molly Maguires" were hanged on the testimony of James McParlan. McParlan was a company spy hired by the president of the Reading Railroad, Franklin B. Gowen, who would also play a role in the strike wave a year later.

In spite of the bleak economic conditions and the constant threat of reprisals by employers and the state, workers nonetheless continued to organize. Workers in many skilled occupations often organized nascent unions along craft lines. Railroad workers, for example, formed "brotherhoods" by occupation. While quite conservative, the brotherhoods provided an independent forum for workers to air grievances and defend their interests. At the top of the labor hierarchy on the railroads were the engineers, but they were closely aligned with the firemen, for in reality the firemen assisted the engineers and many engineers had begun their careers as firemen. In 1876, the Brotherhood of Locomotive Engineers (BLE) successfully struck the Central Railroad of New Jersey to rescind a wage cut and the Grand Trunk Railway of Canada over the firing of several of its leaders. With these modest victories under its belt, the BLE grew to some 14,000 members and 192 locals by 1877. Though the majority of white male workers continued to vote for one of the two major political parties, new political movements in the 1870s such as the Greenback Party and the Workingmen's Party gained new adherents by appealing to workers.

The railroad owners, squeezed by falling revenues, organized in turn. Many followed the lead of Charles Francis Adams II, head of the Boston & Maine line, who had been waging a campaign to rid the railroads of organized labor using a "carrot and stick" approach. By 1869, he had overseen the creation of a State Board of Railroad Commissioners in Massachusetts, the "controlling mind" of the industry as he saw it, and had himself appointed one of the three commissioners. In 1876, he took on the BLE and won, cutting their wages on the Boston & Maine by 10 percent and ending the year with a surplus for his shareholders. When the BLE struck the Boston & Maine in February 1877, the company hired strikebreakers, used police to disperse strikers, and fired striking engineers. In March of 1877, he authored an influential series of articles on the brotherhood in *The Nation*, saying that the BLE had become "a public menace," and a threat to good order in society. He proposed that railroad interests push for passage of laws with stiff penalties for organized work stoppages on railroads and in turn a regularized system of promotions, pensions, and benefits for loyal (in other words, nonunion) workers. "The men would [not] . . . sacrifice, by joining in strikes, what represented the accumulation of years of service," he argued. Lest any of his readers mistake the purpose of his proposal, he was clear in his aim: "The Brotherhood of Locomotive Engineers," he wrote, "has got to be broken up."

Franklin Gowen, fresh from his victory over the Mollies, seems to have followed Adams's advice in dealing with the brotherhoods, for his actions were cut from the same cloth. In April 1877, when the engineers and firemen petitioned the Philadelphia & Reading management for a 20 percent raise, management responded by saying the petitioners could either quit the brotherhood or lose their jobs. The company would also thereafter provide loyal employees with a company-run substitute for the brotherhood's insurance, though any money the employee paid into the company plan would be forfeited in case of strike or dismissal.

BLE Grand Chief Peter Arthur was determined to meet Gowen head on, and after the Reading's superintendent refused the workers' request for arbitration, the union called a strike. Half the engineers walked out, but Gowen managed to hire enough strikebreakers to keep the trains running, which gradually wore down the engineers. Other railroad owners looked to Gowen for inspiration, writing to him asking for copies of the Reading insurance plan and sending lobbyists to state legislatures to push for legislation making it illegal for an engineer to abandon his train "at any place other than the scheduled or otherwise appointed destination." With seven states passing such laws, the BLE was in full retreat. Two weeks later, the Missouri Pacific cut engineers' pay by 12 percent with no resistance. By the end of May, other lines, including the Pennsylvania, the Lehigh Valley, the Lackawanna, the Michigan Southern, the Indianapolis & St Louis, the Vandalia (on which a young Eugene V. Debs worked as secretary for the Brotherhood of Locomotive Firemen [BLF] local in Terre Haute), the New York Central & Hudson, and the Northern Central all ordered 10 percent wage cuts, according to historian Robert B. Bruce.

The situation for trainmen was desperate. Not only were the trainmen "down to hard pan," as a result of previous wage cuts, but their work routine generated its own unique grievances. Railroad work in the 1870s was notoriously dangerous, and the law usually made employees themselves liable for any injuries suffered on the job. The workload of railroad workers led to grievances as well. Train crews were expected to "lay over" at the end of their run at their own expense. Moreover, train crews went unpaid during such downtime, which could last for days. As economic conditions worsened in the 1870s, management required crews to run "double headers," or trains with twice as many cars, effectively doubling the workload and increasing the likelihood of dangerous accidents. There was no institutionalized means for employees to air grievances over these issues, and those who complained about work conditions could be summarily fired. In the words of one trainman quoted by Foner, the crews were treated "like dogs" by authoritarian company supervisors.

During the economic depression of the 1870s, railroads cut rates for many of their largest clients. John D. Rockefeller's Standard Oil Company, for example, extracted deep cuts in rates and rebates from the roads, forcing them to find ways to cut costs. Other roads, having incurred heavy debt loads to finance their expansion during the boom times, teetered on the edge of bankruptcy as the credit squeeze dried up capital. In the year prior to the great strike wave alone, 7,225 miles of track went into receivership, according to Bruce.

Responding to the economic crisis, a number of executives of several large Eastern trunk lines met in Chicago to negotiate a pooling agreement to fix freight rates. Rates on westbound traffic were raised a whopping 50 percent, though the wage cuts would continue. The executives who concluded the agreement never admitted to explicitly colluding to cut wages, but the wage cuts were almost all identical (10 percent) and Baltimore & Ohio president John Garrett wrote to his banker that "the great principle upon which we all joined to act was to earn more and to spend less."

The Long, Hot Summer of 1877

On the surface it appeared that the railroad workers were thoroughly beaten when Tom Scott, president of the giant Pennsylvania Railroad system, dictated a 10 percent wage cut to take effect on June 1, 1877. This action was bound to have widespread consequences, if for no other reason than that it covered workers on more than 6,500 miles of road. On June 4, a grievance committee of engineers and firemen met with Scott and described the hardship the wage cut would cause. They asked him to reverse the wage cut, demanded a stable work schedule, and either extra pay or passes home during long layovers. Scott listened to his workmen and then explained that the rate war had caused immense losses and that the dividends of stockholders had been reduced by 40 percent. At such times, he asked them, was it too much to ask the workers to bear their share of the pain? The grievance committee left the office and accepted the cut. Later, the *Engineers' Journal* reported that the company had made enough to pay an 8 percent dividend and set aside $1.5 million in 1876, and that, thus far, the company's earnings were higher than the previous year.

A meeting of Pennsylvania workers narrowly defeated a strike vote for the time being, but their anger simmered just below the surface. Some felt the engineers only looked after themselves and that greater unity among railroad workers was needed. In Allegheny City, Pennsylvania, workers formed a new "Trainmen's Union" (TU), open to all railroad workers—unlike the brotherhoods, which were organized along craft lines. Trainmen elected Robert Ammon, a brakeman, head of the new union and within weeks the Allegheny City Local grew to more than 500 members.

Baltimore & Ohio

In June, B&O president John Garrett announced a 10 percent wage cut for all his workers to take effect on July 16. He cited the need to cut costs during the difficult economic climate and expressed confidence that his workers would "cheerfully recognize" the necessity of the action. Trainmen bitterly complained that at the reduced wages of ninety cents a day they would be forced to "steal or starve" at a time when it was reported that the B&O was making a profit and that the board of directors had recently voted to maintain a 10 percent dividend for stockholders. That afternoon, the fireman on Engine 32 walked off the job, leaving his train at Camden junction, and soon other firemen on the line did likewise. The next day, thirty-eight engineers on the B&O joined the firemen, as did members of the Baltimore Boxmakers' and Sawyers' Union and the tin can workers, whose wages had also been cut recently. Mayor Ferdinand Latrobe ordered police, at the request of the railroad, to arrest striking railroad workers for "inciting a riot." Initially, Baltimore remained relatively quiet and, despite pleas from B&O officials, Maryland Governor John Lee Carroll felt that no federal troops were needed.

On July 16, as workers seethed in Baltimore, B&O crews in Martinsburg, West Virginia, halted the trains in protest of the 10 percent wage reduction. When firemen locked engines in the B&O freight roundhouse and announced that no freight trains would be moved until the wage reduction was rescinded, Martinsburg mayor A.P. Schutt, who had close ties to B&O management, ordered police to arrest the strikers and prepare the way for strikebreakers to be brought in. Sympathy in the town was with the strikers, however, and the mayor's order was ignored. A large crowd of bystanders gathered around the freight yards to watch the excitement. The following day, a B&O official convinced West Virginia governor Henry Matthews to call out the local militia to suppress what he called a "riot," even though crews were still moving passenger trains and there was no evidence that a riot had occurred or that any property had been destroyed. On Matthews's order, one company of volunteer militia from Martinsburg (many who were themselves railroad workers) assembled at the freight depot. As a scab engineer attempted to run a freight train through the yards, twenty-eight-year-old William Vandergriff, a striker armed with a pistol, threw a switch that threatened to derail the train. When John Poisal, a militiaman, attempted to move the switch back to its original position, Vandergriff fired at him twice, one shot grazing him on the temple. Poisal and several other militiamen then shot Vandergriff, who died a week later of his wounds, leaving behind a pregnant wife. After the gunfire, no one could be found willing to move any trains, and the militia commander dismissed his men until further notice. By the evening of July 17, strikers in Martinsburg had succeeded in stopping freight traffic out of the town.

The following day (July 18) the strike spread rapidly along the line in West Virginia and the B&O was effectively shut down as no scabs could be found to run freight trains. The strike had by now become big news, and many Eastern papers sent reporters to cover the rapidly spreading strike. In the small towns throughout West Virginia, they noted the remarkable support the strike had from the surrounding communities, as family members, neighbors, and friends joined the strikers. Large numbers of women—many of them wives, mothers, and daughters of the trainmen—also joined in support of the strikers. One woman told a reporter that she would rather join the walkout and "starve outright" than to "die by slow starvation." Another report noted that black workers had also joined the strike in Keyser, West Virginia. The strong support for the strike in these communities suggested it had touched a nerve and that many members of these communities—black and white, men and women—felt aggrieved by the brutal economic conditions in general and the railroads in particular.

That afternoon, Governor Matthews cabled President Hayes that "unlawful combinations and domestic violence" existed all along the B&O line, and these made it "impossible with any force at my command to execute the laws of the state." He asked Hayes to send 200–300 federal troops to protect the state from "domestic violence" and to maintain "the supremacy of the law." Hayes gath-

The Great Strike of 1877 started along the Baltimore and Ohio Railroad, particularly in Martinsburg, West Virginia, where strikers blockaded the engines. It spread to other lines, including the Reading Railroad, and strikers burned down that line's Lebanon Valley Railroad Bridge, which crossed the Schuylkill River. (From *Harper's Weekly*, August 11, 1877. *Courtesy:* Library of Congress.)

ered with members of his cabinet to consider this request. Federal troops had been used against striking workers only one other time in U.S. history: when Andrew Jackson had sent troops to quell a strike by canal workers on the Chesapeake and Ohio in the 1820s (ironically, the Chesapeake and Ohio canal men would be among those striking in 1877). During the Civil War and Reconstruction, however, the federal government had significantly expanded its role in putting down insurrectionary activities in the states. The question was whether the strike rose to the level of "insurrection." B&O president John Garrett, having seen his railroad virtually shut down, argued that it was. He cabled Hayes that the situation in West Virginia was grave, that the state had done all it could "to suppress this insurrection," and that federal troops were necessary to restore "for public use . . . this great national highway." According to Bruce, Garrett's telegram emphasized the public nature of the road, even though the roads were privately owned and operated, and skillfully created a sense of national emergency. Hayes dispatched federal troops to Martinsburg to quell the "insurrection," though when they arrived the next morning (July 19) they found the town, in the words of a correspondent for the *New York Sun*, "quiet as a Sunday."

With troops occupying Martinsburg, the B&O planned to bring in scores of strikebreakers under armed escort from Baltimore on July 20. The sympathy of thousands of workers in Baltimore was with the strikers, and thousands took to the streets in protest. According to Bruce, one Baltimore strike leader told a reporter:

> The working people everywhere are with us. They know what it is to bring up a family on ninety cents a day, to live on beans and corn meal week in and week out, to run in debt at the stores until you cannot get trusted any longer, to see the wife breaking down under privation and distress, and the children growing sharp and fierce like wolves day after day because they don't get enough to eat.

The crowd gathered at Camden Station, where they prevented the trains from leaving. Thousands from the factories, mills, canals, and docks, as well as "roughs," gathered in the streets and harassed the militias as they attempted to retake the city streets around Camden Station. At several points, clashes between the crowds and the militias resulted. Pistol fire and brickbats thrown by the crowds were returned by rifle fire from the militias. The militias, aided by the Baltimore police, arrested hundreds and eventually managed to secure the depot, but not before at least ten protesters were killed and scores more badly wounded. The following day, with more than 2,000 troops occupying the city, including 500 federals, the protests ended. Over the next several days, B&O workers wrote up their grievances and proposed a restoration of pay, but were summarily rebuffed by B&O management and Maryland officials. As Baltimore quieted, however, the strikes spread westward along the rail lines.

Pennsylvania

While strikers shut down the B&O that Thursday, the Pennsylvania Railroad announced that all eastbound freights would be run as double headers. The double-header policy meant that some crews would be laid off and the remaining crews would have their work doubled. With anger running high over the recent wage cuts and the B&O strike roiling nearby, Pennsylvania management could not have picked a worse moment to announce its policy. Pennsylvania Railroad superintendent Robert Pitcairn, who issued the order, was not worried about worker anger, for as he told a reporter, "the men are always complaining about something." To make matters worse, Pittsburgh in July 1877 was a social tinderbox, with sympathy for the railroad strikers running high in the city's rolling mills, foundries, and factories. While the city had begun to recover from the depression, large numbers of unemployed "tramps" were encamped around the outskirts of the city, providing a volatile mix of poverty and anger.

As a morning double header prepared to leave the station, flagman Gus Harris decided not to go out. The rest of his crew joined him, and twenty-five other brakemen and conductors in the trainmen's room also refused to take the train. There is no evidence that this was a premeditated effort—the walkout appears to have been spontaneous. All were fired on the spot. When a dispatcher was able to round up a crew of yardmen, the striking crews blocked the train and the volunteer crew gave up. When told by a supervisor that the strikers had no legal right to interfere with other trains, flagman Andrew Hice replied, "It's a question of bread or blood, and we're going to resist."

The strike spread rapidly on the morning of July 19, and by noon other freight crews had joined the strikers. By mid-afternoon the railroad strikers were outnumbered by others from the surrounding neighborhoods who gathered at the yards in support of the strike. As in Baltimore and Martinsburg, many in the city of Pittsburgh sympathized with the strikers, including many small merchants who depended on the patronage of the workers and had no love for the Pennsylvania Railroad. As recounted by Foner, Phoenix Hall, reporter for the *National Labor Tribune*, wrote "There is no disguising the matter. . . . The people of this city sympathize with the strikers. They are incensed beyond measure with the cold, corrupt legislature which has fostered the colder and more corrupt organization known as the Pennsylvania Railroad."

The Trainmen's Union called a mass meeting for the following day, drew up a set of demands, and elected a committee to take the demands to Pitcairn. They asked management to rescind the wage cut, withdraw the double-header order, and rehire those strikers who had been fired. Pitcairn and the other officials dismissed even the very idea of negotiating with workers over pay or working conditions on the road. To have entered into negotiations, in management's view, would have meant acknowledging the workers' committee as a legitimate partner in the operation of the road. It would have meant surrendering the absolute power and authority of management over every decision. As Pitcairn later explained, "They [the workers] proposed taking the road out of our hands."

With freight traffic completely shut down, Pennsylvania Railroad officials appealed to the governor's office to send the militia. Pennsylvania governor John Hartranft was out of the state at the time—on a junket sponsored by Tom Scott and the Pennsylvania Railroad. The state's Adjutant General, James W. Latta, had been authorized to act in his absence, and he called out the Pittsburgh militia—even though to this point, as historian Robert Bruce noted, "total injuries so far consisted of an official's bruised eye, a brakeman's aching ribs, and a sheriff's hurt feelings."

The militia call presented railroad officials with a dilemma, however. As Bruce recounted, the Pittsburgh men were from the same neighborhoods as the strikers. Many had family members who were now on strike, and some even worked for the hated Pennsylvania Railroad themselves. Pittsburgh militiamen sympathized with their working-class brethren and some even fraternized with the strikers. When told that he might have to "clear the tracks" of strikers, one Pittsburgh militiaman replied, "They may call on me, and they may call pretty damn loud before they will clear the tracks." Militia commanders soon concluded that the Pittsburgh militia could not be trusted to confront the strikers. The commander of the Pittsburgh militia himself, Major General Alfred Pearson, struggled with the feelings of ambivalence: "Meeting an enemy on the field of battle, you go there to kill. . . . But here you had men with fathers and brothers and relatives mingled in the crowd of rioters. The sympathy of the people, the sympathy of the troops, my own sympathy, was with the strikers proper. We all felt that those men were not receiving enough wages." After the call-up, some regiments had seen only a tiny fraction of their men heed the call for duty. In the Fourteenth Regiment not a single man had yet shown up. Meanwhile the strikers and their supporters seemed to be gaining confidence. Word in town was that miners and other workers from the Monongahela Valley, Wilkes-Barre, and Mansfield were on their way to lend support to the strikers.

After being informed of the situation in Pittsburgh by Major General Alfred Pearson of the Pennsylvania National Guard, Adjutant General Latta, hoping to find a more obedient force, ordered the Philadelphia militia to be sent to Pittsburgh. On the afternoon of July 21, more than 600 Philadelphia troops arrived by train, bristling with guns, to take control of the depot and run the Pennsylvania Railroad's freight at the point of a bayonet if necessary. They were greeted with a chorus of boos, hisses, and catcalls, as stones, bricks, and other objects were thrown at the passing train. Company vice president Alexander Cassatt, who was among the officials who greeted the troops when they arrived, was urged to wait until Monday in order to let the crowd cool down but refused, replying, "We must have our property." Looking at his watch, he claimed that enough time had been lost already.

The soldiers unloaded two Gatling guns and proceeded to the freight crossing, which was then in the hands of a crowd of between 5,000 and 7,000. Hundreds more onlookers followed behind the troops and stood on surrounding hillsides. Bystanders, among them some members of the Pittsburgh militia, shouted at the Philadelphia troops to "take it easy." As the troops drew near, the order was passed to fix bayonets and clear the tracks. The troops moved into the crowd, pushing back the people with bayonets, but the crowd was too thick and could not be moved back quickly. Several men in the front were pierced with bayonet points as they tried to move back. Angry shouts from the crowd grew louder, and stones, bricks, and coal were hurled into the ranks of the soldiers. The crack of a gun was heard. No one is sure who fired first, but within seconds, the militia unleashed a volley of rifle fire that left approximately twenty dead and scores more wounded. Fifteen Philadelphia troops suffered injuries but none were killed. According to Foner, a grand jury investigation into the shooting concluded that the Philadelphia militia's action that afternoon amounted to "unauthorized, willful, and wanton killing . . . which the inquest can call by no other name than murder."

Word spread quickly throughout the city just as thousands of factory workers were getting off work. Incensed crowds of workers and citizens surrounded the Philadelphia militia and forced them to retreat to the huge roundhouse at the freight depot. As night fell, crowds looted and set fire to the hundreds of freight cars in the yard, bathing the city in an eerie reddish glow. Witnesses reported that women played a prominent role in the looting, carrying off goods and encouraging the men to keep up their resistance to the hated Pennsylvania Railroad and its armed minions in

During the Great Strike of 1877, strikers and other citizens expressed their deep hostility toward the railroad companies, whose inordinate economic and political power seemed to contradict the country's democratic traditions. One way they demonstrated their anger was by burning stations and roundhouses, such as this one in Pittsburgh. (*Source:* James D. McCabe, *The History of the Great Riots* [1877]).

the roundhouse. Several times during the night the roundhouse was threatened as crowds pushed burning freight cars towards it.

In the predawn hours of Sunday morning, a group of young men captured a cannon from the Pittsburgh militia and rolled it up the street that led to the roundhouse. As they prepared to fire the gun on the roundhouse, the Philadelphia militia opened fire, killing eleven and scattering the rest. The besiegers attempted several more times to fire the cannon, but were driven off each time by rifle fire from the roundhouse. As the sun came up over the clouds of smoke and ash, the fire forced the militia to flee the roundhouse. They marched up Penn Avenue, followed by an infuriated crowd. As they marched out of the city, they were forced to engage in a running gun battle with snipers all along the route, one soldier falling dead in the exchange. The militia did not stop until they reached Sharpsburg, by which time the crowd had left them, apparently satisfied that the Philadelphians had been driven from the city.

By Sunday the fire continued to spread throughout the yards. First the roundhouse burned, and then the fire spread to Union Depot. Few in Pittsburgh that day seemed to mourn the loss of Pennsylvania Railroad property. A machinist from the nearby Jones and Laughlin steel mill watching the Union Depot burn told his friend that he did not care if everything belonging to the hated Pennsylvania Railroad burned. "It's got to come down," he said. "It's a monopoly and we're tired of it." Meanwhile, looters made off with anything left to carry. Pittsburgh police arrested more than 130 suspected looters, who were labeled as "tramps" or from "the poorer class of people." Police were overwhelmed by the sheer size of the crowds surrounding the freight yards. On Monday morning federal troops arrived in the city to find little but rubble in the Pittsburgh yards. The Pittsburgh militia reassembled and marched through the streets. Officials put the weekend's toll at twenty-four dead, including five Philadelphia soldiers, though the toll was probably higher as an uncounted number were likely buried without notice.

As Pittsburgh reeled, the strike now became general. Across the Allegheny River from Pittsburgh, as the fires still burned, workers on the Pittsburgh, Fort Wayne & Chicago Railroad, a subsidiary of the Pennsylvania, voted to strike. Robert Ammon of the Trainmen's Union (TU) took control of the dispatcher's office as workers shut down all freight traffic out of Allegheny City. The TU strike committee stationed strikers in defensive positions on all the routes into the city in case troops should be sent. So completely would the workers control the road that when Pennsylvania Governor Hartranft arrived from his western tour on July 24, it was Ammon who assured him safe passage.

On Monday morning, July 23, other workers in Pittsburgh went on strike. More than a thousand striking workers from the McKeesport Tube Works marched through the city behind a brass band, calling other workers to join in demanding $1.50 a day for laborers and a raise of twenty-five cents a day for all. They marched to Andrew Carnegie's massive Edgar Thomson Steel Works and convinced the mill workers there to walk out. One by one, they marched to the mills and shut them down. One mill owner in Allegheny responded by offering a twelve-and-a-half cent raise to keep his workers from striking. On Monday evening the railroad strikers issued a statement placing blame for the destruction on the Pennsylvania Railroad, whose heavy-handed tactics had enraged the city. The strikers still wanted to negotiate and twice requested meetings with officials, but the company refused to meet with them, saying that it was up to the military to "settle" the matter.

Meanwhile the strike spread across Pennsylvania to industrial cities such as Altoona, Harrisburg, Erie, Johnstown, and Reading, terminus of the Philadelphia & Reading Railroad. P&R president Franklin Gowen had engendered real hostility among workers for his role several years earlier in prosecuting the Molly Maguires, and he was determined to prevent the strikers from getting the upper hand on his road. Gowen contacted the Reading militia, but the militia sympathized with the workers and told him that "they are workingmen and do not desire to kill other workingmen." On July 22, Gowen called on the Pennsylvania National Guard, which sent troops to Reading even though city authorities had not been consulted. While clearing the tracks of strikers and onlookers, National Guardsmen opened fire and killed an estimated ten people and wounded at least forty more. Within two days, Reading was back under the control of the company, as the combined forces of the First United States Artillery and the P&R "Coal and Iron Police," a private force hired by Gowen, kept the city under guard.

Dozens of other minor strikes took place in smaller cities and towns in Pennsylvania as well. Coal miners went on strike throughout the anthracite region of western Pennsylvania. In Allentown, striking miners marched behind a brass band, stoned police, and were dispersed by the militia. In Shamokin, unemployed miners marched through town demanding work or bread. They got bullets from an armed posse instead. Thousands of mill and mine workers struck in and around Scranton, but the strike lost steam when the railroad strikes were crushed.

By July 25, as strikes spread across the state of Pennsylvania, Governor Hartranft wired President Hayes that the situation in Pennsylvania had "assumed the character of a general insurrection" which the state was unable to suppress and requested federal troops. By July 27, Hartranft had used federal and state troops to break the strikes in Harrisburg and Altoona, and the next day, after refusing to meet with strikers in Pittsburgh, ordered troops to break the blockade and reopen the railroad. On Monday, both the Pennsylvania and the Philadelphia & Reading Railroads announced they would resume freight operations the following day. That week, the steel mills reopened, though workers at the Jones and Laughlin American Iron Works stayed out for another month before returning to work for the same wages. On October 19, Governor Hartranft wired Hayes that the state was secure and federal troops could be withdrawn.

Erie and New York Central

Like the other eastern trunk lines, the Erie Railroad based in upstate New York cut its workers' wages by 10 percent on July 1, 1877. Erie workers elected a committee to meet with Erie president Hugh Jewett, but Jewett apparently convinced them that the pinch of falling revenues had left no choice in the matter. After a lengthy debate, the men decided to accept the wage cut and ask for an increase when "better times" returned. Confident that he had the upper hand, Jewett decided to press the advantage over his workers and fired the members of the workers' committee. Still, Erie workers stayed on the job until word of the B&O and Pennsylvania strikes reached them. Emboldened by the growing labor uprising, they delivered a list of demands to Jewett that included a restoration of their old wages, the reinstatement of those fired for labor activity, lower rent for company housing, and a restoration of pass rights for the trainmen. They threatened to strike unless these demands were met by July 19. When Jewett rejected the demands out of hand, Erie workers struck the next morning, July 20. The strike began in Hornellsville and quickly spread along the Erie line to Port Jervis, Corning, Buffalo, and other points.

The Erie strike was notable for the strikers' discipline. Strikers pledged to abstain from alcohol for the duration of the strike, and strike committees told saloons not to serve strikers. Despite the absence of a single report of violence along the Erie, the *New York Times* described Erie strikers as drunken and dangerous. When Erie officials attempted to run a passenger train out of Hornellsville, women aiding the strikers quickly brought buckets of soap and soaped the tracks along the uphill grade leading out of town. When the train slid harmlessly back into town, the crowd along the tracks let out a cheer. Later that day, as another train attempted to leave, strikers boarded it, expelled everyone aboard, disabled the engine, and sent it back to the station. A third train was boarded and left stranded out of town, its boiler drained and its fire extinguished.

As was the case in a number of other cities, local militias sympathized with the strikers and "looked the other way" as trains were prevented from leaving the station. With this violation of state law forbidding interference with rail traffic, the *New York Times* called for military force. New York Governor Lucius Robinson thereupon declared martial law, saying, "It is no longer a question of wages, but the supremacy of the law." The Twenty-Third Regiment from Brooklyn was sent to Hornellsville and the order was issued that any striker entering the yards would be shot. The strike quickly ended after the company agreed to meet with strikers and a settlement was reached—most likely, historian Philip Foner believes, because the strikers were so effective in shutting the line down completely. While firemen and brakemen would have to accept the 10 percent wage cut, trackmen would have their wages restored and no worker would be fired for strike activity. It was the most amicable settlement of any railroad strike of 1877.

In Buffalo, trainmen of the New York Central, having also suffered a 10 percent wage cut, were convinced by their Erie brethren to strike against the Vanderbilt road. On July 22, strikers halted all traffic on the Central except mail and passenger trains. Management subsequently ordered all traffic stopped, and then pleaded with the federal government to intervene, claiming interference with the U.S. mail. The following day, factory workers in Buffalo joined the railroad workers and at least a thousand strikers blockaded the Erie roundhouse, overwhelming the local militia company. When strikers stopped a trainload of militia outside of town, a melee ensued, and at least half a dozen strikers were killed by soldiers before the strikers overpowered them.

The strike quickly spread to Albany, Rochester, and Syracuse. Governor Robinson mobilized the National Guard, which with the aid of local police established virtual martial law in those cities. A curfew was imposed and police and militia freely clubbed or shot at strikers who dared to gather in the streets. New York Central strikers had asked for company president William H. Vanderbilt to rescind the wage cut, but he gave a variety of evasive answers to their pleas—arguing, for example, that the company could not acquiesce to allowing workers to dictate company policy. "The owners of the railroads," he told reporters, "cannot afford to let the employees manage it." He also claimed that his workers did not want to strike and that they were being influenced by intemperate voices outside the company. When strikers approached prominent leaders in New York and asked them to deliver their petition requesting a restoration of wages, the businessmen assented, but the petition was never delivered. Finally, strike leaders were arrested and workers were told they would lose their jobs if they did not return to work by July 30. Faced with overwhelming military force and an ultimatum, most grudgingly went back to work.

Midwest

On July 22, as angry crowds expelled the Philadelphia militia from Pittsburgh, strikes spread throughout the Midwest, including Ohio, Illinois, and Indiana. In Columbus, Ohio, brakemen and firemen on the Pittsburgh, Cincinnati, St. Louis & Chicago Railroad voted to strike for a return to 1874 wages. The local BLE chapter soon joined in the strike. By the following day, strikers marched through city streets calling on workers in the rolling mills to join them. Many heeded the call until thousands were in the streets and the rolling mills were shut down. That day, railroad workers in Cleveland struck the Cleveland, Columbus, Cincinnati & Indianapolis Railroad, but management rescinded the 10 percent pay cut and the workers went back to their jobs. The Atlantic & Great Western, also in Cleveland, never issued the 10 percent cut, so they were spared the strike. In all, Cleveland was relatively quiet. The same could not be said of Cincinnati, however. In that city, trainmen on the Cincinnati, Hamilton, & Dayton announced a strike, but it was called off when management hurriedly rescinded the cut. Workers on the Ohio & Mississippi (O&M) also walked off the job in protest of the 10 percent cut, but the O&M officials refused to negotiate. A crowd estimated at nearly 3,000 gathered at the O&M depot, and later set fire to the nearby O&M trestle.

At the same time, Cincinnati's branch of the Workingmen's Party (WP) held a rally in support of the strikers in Pittsburgh and elsewhere. Peter H. Clark, leader of the city's WP and a prominent African-American labor leader in Cincinnati, spoke energetically for public ownership of the railroads and other means of production. According to Foner, Clark condemned railroad owners who lived like "princes" while "the man whose labors earn these vast sums" lived in virtual penury. "When they complain," he continued, "they are told they are at liberty to quit and take their services elsewhere. This is equivalent to telling them that they are at liberty to starve." On Tuesday crowds in Cincinnati continued to clash with police until heavy rainfall finally dispersed most of them by evening. The following day the strike was brought to an end when police arrested strike leaders and restored "law and order" with billy clubs.

In Toledo, what was initially a significant degree of support for workers and the strike by trainmen blossomed into a general strike throughout the city. At a rally in support of the strike on July 23, the city's police commissioner even encouraged the strikers, as did the commander of the local militia. Workers set up a "Committee of Safety" and drew up a list of demands calling for the establishment of a minimum wage level for various types of work. After an orderly march through the city's manufacturing district, some manufacturers agreed to pay the higher wages. The *Toledo Blade* reported that by the afternoon of July 24, the city was virtually shut down. The next day, the city government, under pressure from employers, changed course—arresting strike leaders, deputizing 400 police, and patrolling the streets with militia. The general strike in Toledo was over the following day.

In Indiana, the railroad brotherhoods had long prided themselves on their conservatism. The newsletter of the BLF local was often filled with articles that stressed the virtue of punctuality, sobriety, and hard work. As historian Nick Salvatore has shown, they adopted the language and the posture of class harmony and identity of interest between themselves and their employer, the Vandalia Railroad. When Vandalia president Riley McKeen followed the example of the Eastern trunk lines and cut the workers' pay by 10 percent (this after a cumulative 23 percent cut from 1873 to 1876), the firemen and brakemen met in Terre Haute to "respectfully request" a 15 percent raise. McKeen said he would wait to see what happened in the East before making a decision, and the men expressed "faith" in his "honor and integrity." While the brotherhoods briefly halted freight traffic, they turned down an offer of assistance from 300 miners nearby, thus ensuring that the strike would be limited in scope.

The deference and conservatism of the brotherhoods did not prevent McKeen from ultimately refusing the wage "request" and allowing federal troops to be used to break the strike. After the strike, McKeen suspended strike leaders and even testified against them during their trial for contempt of court. One of the members of the Terre Haute Local of the BLF was young Eugene V. Debs, and his experience in the Great Strike of 1877 left an impression. The fate of the brotherhoods exposed the weaknesses of the old craft-based unionism and also demonstrated that workers' deference made little difference unless it was backed by workers' power. Eventually, the experience also convinced Debs that, given the political power of capital, strikes had to be coupled with labor's political power in order to have a reasonable chance of success.

Chicago was a booming city in 1877. Railroads brought livestock and agricultural products to its doorstep and it was fast becoming a manufacturing and commercial center for the nation's economy. More than 11,000 Chicagoans were employed by the railroads in 1877. Chicago was also a deeply divided city, with a largely native-born middle and upper class and an immigrant working class. While extravagant new fortunes were being made at one end, poverty and want stalked the other. On the eve of the strike, the *Chicago Times* estimated that the city had more than 15,000 unemployed. When the railroad strikes broke out in the East, working-class Chicago sympathized. Chicago's Workingmen's Party held two mass meetings in support of the strikers on Saturday, July 21. A German-language meeting held outdoors at the corner of Halstead and 12th streets attracted "several thousand" and an English-language meeting at Stack's Hall was packed "almost to suffocation," according to the *Chicago Tribune*. The WP called for the nationalization of the railroads and for an eight-hour workday for all workers. The highlight of the mass meeting was a speech by a twenty-nine-year-old printer and WP member named Albert Parsons, who brought the crowd to its feet with his denunciations of the "monopolies and tyrants" who ran the city's businesses and its government. He rejected the *Chicago Tribune*'s claim that workers should accept employers' right to set wages, responding that if workers followed the advice of the *Tribune*, "We are bound hand and foot—slaves, and we should be perfectly . . . content with a bowl of rice and a rat a week apiece." It was labor, he argued, that had the right to say what it was worth.

The following night the WP sponsored a huge rally and torchlight parade on Market Street attended by an estimated 15,000. Within hours of the rally, workmen on the Michigan Central struck for higher wages. The next day, the Michigan Central workers marched to the Chicago freight yards of the B&O and the Illinois Central and called those workers out. As the crowd of strikers grew, it fanned out to the machine shops, iron works, and mills near the yards, where still more workers joined the strike. The lumberyards and huge packinghouses were next. By mid-afternoon on Tuesday, July 24, press dispatches from Chicago were calling the strike "general." As the strikers marched through the streets, they were joined by women and children in one massive parade of humanity.

In the face of this working-class demonstration, Chicago's authorities planned a counterattack. Parsons had gone to his printing job only to be told that he was fired. As he left, he was taken to police headquarters and grilled by the city's police commissioner, who told him that there were powerful men on the Board of Trade who wanted to see him hang. That night, as 5,000 gathered at a WP meeting, Chicago police broke into the hall and began wildly swinging their clubs. WP general secretary Philip Van Patten was taken to police headquarters and "given the Parsons treatment." The following day, police opened fire on a crowd at the Burlington & Quincy yards, killing three and wounding at least eight. That afternoon, police used clubs to break up a peaceful WP rally. On Thursday, crowds of strikers and others—including many women—clashed with police, leaving a number of workers dead. By the end of the week, the strike was crushed, as Chicago became a city occupied by federal troops. The death toll from the week's violence was at least eighteen killed: all workers.

St. Louis General Strike

In St. Louis, workers had been watching the strike unfold across the nation, and the leaders of the WP in St. Louis called a meeting to support the strikes at Traubel's Hall in East St. Louis, Illinois, on the evening of July 22. During the meeting, which was attended by an estimated 500 workers, a large contingent of men from the BLF local marched in and announced that they were on strike. A great cheer went up from the crowd and it was decided that the workers would march to the nearby East St. Louis relay depot, where they would be joined by still more workers as news of the strike spread. As the huge crowd approached the depot, flying the red banner and singing the *Marseillaise*, they were greeted with cheers by the striking railroad workers and a huge open-air meeting was held.

The Trainmen voted not simply for the companies to rescind the most recent 10 percent wage cut, but for a restoration of wages to pre-depression levels. They also elected a strike committee and resolved to stay out until the companies met their demands. The strikers then marched to the St. Louis freight yards behind a fife and drum corps. A Strike Executive Committee was formed by members of the WP and strikers to coordinate strike activities. The committee first issued "General Order No. 1" stipulating that all freight traffic was to be stopped. By the end of the first night, all freight traffic had been halted and other workers began to join the strike. So complete was the Strike Committee's control of the city by this point, that East St. Louis Mayor John Bowman proposed that the Strike Committee appoint strikers as special officers to guard railroad property. The committee agreed and also ordered all saloons closed.

The next day, managers of the Missouri Pacific Railroad offered to rescind the 10 percent wage cut, but the committee issued an order forbidding any piecemeal settlement of the strike, declaring that any settlement offers would have to go through the Executive Committee. That night, the WP sponsored a huge rally at Lucas Market attended by thousands, including many workers the *St Louis Globe-Democrat* identified as those of "the better class." Fiery speeches calling for an eight-hour day and public ownership of the railroads were heard, but the meeting was generally peaceful. The following day, scores more shops and businesses shut down as other workers heeded the strike call. In the meantime, James H. Wilson, a court-appointed receiver of the St Louis & Southeastern Railroad in St. Louis, had contacted officials in Washington and called for federal troops.

On Tuesday, six companies of federal troops from the 23rd U.S. Infantry arrived in the city and announced they were there to safeguard railroad property, not to run the trains. That night, the WP led a "Grand Procession" and rally of an estimated 10,000 strikers through the heart of St. Louis. At the rally, WP officials called for a general strike demanding passage of an enforceable eight-hour work law, and the crowd roared its approval. The following day, the WP printed handbills announcing the general strike and held another rally at Lucas Market. The strike continued to gain strength, as dockworkers and deckhands on Mississippi riverboats—many of them African American—began to strike as well. That day, a multiracial crowd of workers marched through the south side of St. Louis calling on workers to join the strike. Thousands heeded the call and attended a WP-sponsored rally that night.

The rally on July 25 was the high-water mark of the strike. An estimated crowd in excess of 10,000 jammed the area around Lucas Market and heard speeches calling for workers to unite behind the WP and emancipate working people as Lincoln had emancipated the slaves a decade before. Resolutions called on Congress to pass an eight-hour law, public ownership of the railroads, and a public jobs program for the unemployed. The Executive Committee by this time was virtually running the city. Flour mills were allowed to remain open so that the city would not go hungry. Employers were encouraged to feed strikers so as to avoid looting and riots. In the absence of management authority, railroad workers continued to run passenger trains and collect fares. But the strike began to break under the strain of internal weakness and external pressure.

City authorities had met with several businessmen and formed a "Committee of Public Safety" that charged Sheriff John Finn with the task of raising a 5,000-man posse. Prominent St Louis merchants raised over $20,000 to arm a citizens' militia as federal soldiers arrived from Kansas. As the armed noose closed around the city, the Executive Committee wavered in its commitment to worker solidarity. By Thursday, July 26, large crowds of workers, black and white, native born and immigrant, had walked off their jobs in support of the strike. Then, perhaps fearing a white backlash, or perhaps because of the racism of strike leaders themselves, black strikers began to be turned away from WP mass meetings. Albert Currlin, an Executive Committee member, later admitted that he turned away a group of 500 African-American workers from a strike meeting and ordered the white workers present to have "nothing to do with them."

While the WP leadership failed to unite workers as a class, they missed an opportunity to divide the employers. When the Executive Committee announced that no road would be allowed to settle individually, they ensured that the railroad owners would be united in opposition. Had they allowed the wavering employers such as the Missouri Pacific to settle and begin operations, they might have weakened the position of the hard-line roads. The WP was not primarily interested in individual workplace settlements, however. Their preponderant focus on a broader political agenda thus turned out to be a weakness. As historian Philip Foner has pointed out, many of the WP leaders were Lassallean in their orientation, more given to political action than trade union organizing. As a result WP leaders made little effort to integrate the city's existing trade union leadership into a cohesive unit. Finally, as historian David Burbank has argued, while the WP had issued a series of demands, it had no coherent plan for how to implement its objectives in the short run. Workers in St. Louis were nowhere near being ready to force Congress to act on a far-reaching political program that would require seizing railroad property and regulating labor and unemployment policy beyond anything contemplated in Washington to that point. Thus, when thousands of soldiers and police marched into the city, the strike collapsed almost immediately. Within two days, members of the Strike Committee had been arrested, as had many other WP members.

Conclusion

By July 21, 1877, the strike wave had spread from coast to coast. In California, anger at the railroad barons who ran the state's political machinery mutated into white working-class racism against Chinese immigrant workers and anti-Chinese riots spread throughout the state. WP-sponsored rallies in New York City, Boston, Philadelphia, Paterson and Newark, New Jersey, and Louisville, Kentucky, roused thousands more workers into the streets. Dockworkers in New Orleans briefly struck. All major U.S. railway lines were affected, and the nation's transportation and manufacturing system came to a virtual standstill. Even businesses whose workers did not strike were often forced to shut down because of the strike, such as Standard Oil, whose massive refineries sat idle during the strike. In New York City, the WP organized a mass rally in Tomkins Square, site of a police attack on workers in 1872. An estimated 20,000 people assembled peacefully and listened to speeches in support of the strikers and for a political party based on the "natural rights of labor." As the speeches ended and the peaceful crowd began to disperse, hundreds of New York City police chased and clubbed many as they tried to make their way home from the rally.

At the strike's height, the *New York World* estimated that more than 80,000 railroad workers and half a million other workers went on strike. In the cities affected by the strikes, countless other citizens joined the strikers. Reports told of thousands of women, "boys," and sometimes even merchants and small-business owners who came into the streets out of sympathy or just plain curiosity. And, in each instance, countless unemployed workers—"tramps" in the press accounts of the day—joined in solidarity with the strikers. Indeed, the presence of so many members of the community in the strikes has led historian David Stowell to argue that the Strike Wave of 1877 was as much an urban-historical phenomenon as a labor strike. In his analysis, long-simmering anger against the railroads—the most tangible symbol of the social dislocation produced by the industrial revolution—was at the root of the Great Uprising.

See also: Labor Upheaval on the Nation's Railroads, 1877–1922, 483.

Bibliography

Bruce, Robert B. *1877: Year of Violence*. Indianapolis: Bobbs-Merrill, 1959.

Burbank, David T. *The Reign of the Rabble: The St. Louis General Strike of 1877*. New York: A.M. Kelley, 1966.

Dacus, James A. *Annals of the Great Strikes in the United States*. New York: B. Franklin, 1969; orig. 1877.

Foner, Philip S. *The Great Labor Uprising of 1877*. New York: Monad Press, 1977.

Salvatore, Nick. *Eugene V. Debs: Citizen and Socialist*. Urbana: University of Illinois Press, 1982.

Stowell, David O. *Streets, Railroads, and the Great Strike of 1877*. Chicago: University of Chicago Press, 1999.

WORLD WAR I ERA STRIKES

Cecelia Bucki

The Great War provided the context for the expansion of the federal government into more areas of social and economic life than ever before. It also created the possibility for organization of workers in mass-production industries for the first time. The strikes generated by the Great War came in two waves: first, the workplace activity that accompanied the economic boom created by the start of hostilities in Europe in August 1914; and second, the labor disputes that arose after U.S. entry into the war in April 1917. The second wave brought the federal government systematically into the industrial-relations arena for the first time. But the first strike wave was most indicative of workers' goals and consciousness, and this activity determined the response of both the federal government and the American Federation of Labor (AFL).

The World War I era revealed very starkly the dissonance between the nineteenth-century craft union movement and the modern industrial system that was undermining it—a system to which the AFL was only slowly adapting. By 1914, the AFL had gained a place within federal government circles, but had not fully integrated itself into the political world of power. Industrialists had yet to solve basic problems in modern industrial relations. Indeed, with the exception of the National Civic Federation, employers were generally hostile to union representation. What emerged by 1918 was a four-way battle among the AFL, radical unionists inside and outside the AFL, employers, and the federal government to create a workable industrial-relations system. By the postwar year of 1919, the federal government revealed itself to be only temporarily committed to peaceful industrial relations; the business community was split between cooperative employers and fierce open-shop advocates; and the mainstream union movement was at the height of its membership but internally split along skill, ethnic, race, and gender lines and struggling between right and left. That situation gave rise to the massive postwar strike wave of 1919.

Any analysis of the strikes of the World War I era must work on three tracks: first, within workplace activities of workers themselves; second, within the halls of the AFL, where unskilled industrial workers still had no place; and third, within the new government apparatus of industrial relations and its complex relationship with union officialdom.

Strike Activities, 1915–17

The Progressive Era labor movement was a volatile mix of AFL business unionists, socialists, and syndicalists, who had support in some mainstream unions as well as in independent industrial unions, whether moderate like the independent Amalgamated Clothing Workers or revolutionary like the Industrial Workers of the World (IWW). Socialist Party union members were split between those who supported the craft-based approach of the AFL and those who heeded Eugene Debs's call for industrial unionism. The masses of unskilled immigrant workers who filled the workplaces of America could find no place in most AFL unions. Unions were relatively stagnant during the economic doldrums of 1914. Only the economic boom created by influx of orders from European belligerents after August 1914 made successful labor activity possible. However, this 1915 activity also revealed the weaknesses of traditional AFL craft unionism.

Table 1

Strikes, 1914–1919

Year	Number of Strikes and Lockouts	Number of Employees*	Principal Causes (%) ** Wages	Hours	Union Recognition
1914	1,080	n.a.	47.6	10.1	11.8
1915	1,405	504,275	44.3	17.8	6.6
1916	3,786	1,599,610	66.8	22.9	18.5
1917	4,359	1,213,000	63.3	18.1	15.8
1918	3,285	1,235,459	67.6	15.5	14.4
1919	3,374	4,112,507	66.0	29.5	23.7

* Not all events reported.
** Alone or with other demands.
Source: Adapted from Alexander Bing, *Wartime Strikes and Their Adjustment* (New York, 1921), 293.

The AFL affiliates had been struggling, rather unsuccessfully, with the new rationalization of production that some industrialists were attempting to introduce. Metal-trades employers were fascinated with the promises of industrial engineer Frederick Winslow Taylor and his scheme of scientific management, which claimed to bring efficiency to the workplace. Employers were experimenting with reorganizing the production process to eliminate highly skilled operations and break them down into machine operations that semiskilled workers could perform, and introducing incentive pay to ratchet up the amount of production. But many craft unionists argued that Taylorism was designed to undercut the control of the work process that craftsmen still enjoyed. They called this trend "dilution" of the craft. At this point, few employers had actually implemented all these Taylorist reforms. But now the demands of war production, which included a large volume of standardized products, allowed them to revamp their shop floors. The munitions industry and the machinists who worked in those factories were on the cutting edge of this new development.

AFL unions took advantage of the new war-boom economy to expand their power in areas where they already had a presence. Workers were able to leverage labor scarcity to their advantage. The International Association of Machinists (IAM), bruised from a decade of fierce open-shop drives by major employers and their associations, now chose to flex its muscle. The IAM's first move came in Bridgeport, Connecticut, a war-boom town where a massive expansion of munitions factories was in progress. The building trades unions in Bridgeport started by striking on war-industry construction sites in spring 1915. In late spring, following the building trades' successful strike demanding an eight-hour day and union recognition, the IAM announced a strike of all Bridgeport machinists for the same demands. The IAM had significant membership in the toolrooms and small metal manufacturers of the city, and this strike succeeded in forcing the large Remington Arms-Union Metallic Cartridge (UMC) Company to agree to its demands. The company did so in order to put into immediate production the massive rifle factory it had just built on the city's East Side, where it had a lucrative contract to produce rifles for the Russian czar's army. As Remington-UMC was the major munitions producer in the city and the driving engine for the wartime Bridgeport economy, its decision compelled almost every other metalworking shop in the city to accept the IAM's demands. This organized union activity using tried-and-true craft methods of striking and negotiating with all employers of machinists in the city at once was a major step forward in labor's goal of an eight-hour day—or forty-eight-hour workweek, since the work-week was a standard six days. It also established traditional IAM craft contracts in the city's major metalworking factories.

What was totally unexpected was the massive uprising of unorganized men and women in most workplaces in the city for the same demands—an eight-hour day, union recognition, wage increases, and the end of irksome rules and fines. Following the spontaneous walkout of 1,600 women machine operators at the Warner Corset Company in mid-August, unskilled foreign-born men and women in other corset and garment shops, textile plants, foundries, laundries, and other service industries walked out of their workplaces. They conducted strike meetings in Italian, Hungarian, and Polish, while sympathy strikes spread the movement to practically every workplace. Nearly 12,000 workers were on strike in August, largely without formal AFL involvement, but with locally elected shop committees. By the end of September, most strikes were settled and the eight-hour day won in most workplaces.

The AFL unions scrambled to send organizers to the city to enroll unskilled workers in various federal (directly affiliated) locals. These were designed to hold unionized workers until they could be parceled out to the appropriate craft union. The IAM, for example, had already reluctantly enlarged its membership categories to include both "specialists" who worked in only one area of the craft and "handymen," rather than only machinists who had finished a full apprenticeship; this was a recognition that the trade had changed irreparably. But other craft unions still lagged behind in their membership practices. IWW organizer Joseph Ettor came to town to enroll eager strikers into the IWW, where all-grades organization in mass industry was standard. But little formal recognition occurred in most workplaces as Bridgeport employers remained strongly opposed to the recognition of union shop committees. Only those employers who had already recognized traditional craftsmen's unions continued to do so, and these AFL locals reveled in their newfound clout.

This eight-hour movement in the summer of 1915 was two-tiered. While the eight-hour demand had first been raised in industry by the IAM, most of the 2,500 striking machinists were back at work when strikes swept the rest of the city. The separate walkouts of nearly 12,000 unskilled laborers and machine operatives carried the movement and the drive to unionize the city. Indeed, machinists were not eager to aid the women machine operatives at the UMC plant when the women complained that the eight-hour-day rule was being ignored. The contrast between the craft unionists' aloofness and the mass strike movement among the unskilled indicated the considerable distance separating these two groups of workers, one skilled and old-stock American, and the other unskilled and new-immigrant. These tensions would be present for much of the war years.

The IAM was so pleased with its campaign for the eight-hour day in Bridgeport in 1915 that it proclaimed a nationwide drive for the eight-hour day on May 1, 1916, as part of an expansion of its strength. The IAM called some 600 strikes on that day. The union hoped to consolidate its power at those metalworking plants where they had made inroads in 1912–13, such as in Los Angeles and Buffalo. They even returned to Westinghouse Electric in Pennsylvania's Turtle Creek Valley, where efforts had been thwarted before and where a more militant industrial union modeled on the IWW had emerged in 1914. The Allegheny Congenial Industrial Union, which soon changed its name to the American Industrial Union (AIU), attracted the majority of workers in Pennsylvania's Turtle Creek Valley metalworking shops, even though its emphasis was on an IWW-style struggle around demands, not contract negotiation. Its demands for a rotation system for handling layoffs and for an end to piecework and incentive-pay plans were prompted by the continued hard times at Westinghouse, which had not yet seen the effects of the war economy. Here, skilled and unskilled workers joined the job action, and even the clerical workers voted to join the strike. The early 1915 strike failed, but in late 1915 the company had to relent and agree to some demands. More importantly, when the spring 1916 eight-hour-day campaign of the IAM got under way, there was already a strike in progress over the firing of an AIU union leader. That strike escalated into a broad strike in the whole valley, jointly administered by the AIU and the IAM, and marches and picket lines were met with bloody resistance by company guards and coal-and-iron police. In spite of the involvement of the federal Mediation Commission, the 1916 Westinghouse strike failed. This strike exemplified, both in its shop-floor organizing and in its street actions, the sort of collective action undertaken in many workplaces and cities from the war years to the early 1920s.

In its aftermath, Turtle Creek Valley workers drafted a resolution to the Secretary of Labor William B. Wilson (quoted by David Montgomery in *The Fall of the House of Labor*), which appealed for a federal investigation of the "abuse of corporate power" and proclaimed that "injustice has dulled our patriotism, Mans [*sic*] equality before the law will make us patriots instead of paupers." Here was an indication of how things had changed in Woodrow Wilson's Washington, where the AFL had made an alliance with the Democratic Party in return for relief from debilitating court battles and for a place in the halls of political power. William B. Wilson had been a miner and an officer in the United Mine Workers. As a congressman from Pennsylvania, he had crafted the bill that created the Department of Labor in 1913. He was then nominated by President Wilson as the first Secretary of Labor. Under William B. Wilson's leadership, by 1914 the department began mediating industrial disputes, often encouraging recognition of AFL affiliates in those cases. Moreover, for the last decade, the AFL had a potentially rewarding relationship with the National Civic Federation (NCF), a prominent business organization, and the Department of Labor mediation service was inspired by the NCF's previous attempts to soften other employers' open-shop drives. The AFL had succeeded in getting the Clayton Antitrust Act passed in 1914, limiting court injunctions and antitrust lawsuits against labor activities. The AFL proclaimed the legislation to be labor's "Magna Carta," even though it was ultimately a rather limited bill in protecting workers' rights.

More importantly, the Wilson administration set up a U.S. Commission on Industrial Relations (CIR) to investigate the causes of industrial conflict. The CIR idea had been in process under the Taft administration since the 1910 bombing of the *Los Angeles Times* building during a labor dispute. When Woodrow Wilson took office, he reassessed Taft's appointees and restructured the commission to give it a more pro-labor cast. His key appointment was Kansas City labor lawyer Frank P. Walsh as chairman of the commission. Walsh's CIR spent two years taking testimony around the country, most dramatically in the wake of the bloody 1914 Ludlow (Colorado) massacre. At various points in Walsh's remarks at CIR hearings, he had appealed to the principle of Industrial Democracy, arguing that the way toward that goal was organization by workers themselves. The main report of the CIR, written in mid-1915 by Walsh's assistant Basil Manly, was endorsed by Walsh and the three labor representatives. It was rejected by the public and business representatives as too pro-labor and they wrote two minority reports. The Manly Report strongly endorsed federal government action on behalf of working Americans to overcome the "deplorable conditions" the investigations had uncovered. For these progressive reformers, this meant primarily removing obstacles to workers' organizing on their own behalf, guaranteeing equal pay for equal work of men and women, and expanding social services, education, and public works remedies for unemployment. As a counterpoint, the minority report, written by the public representative economist John R. Commons, urged government-sponsored mediation of disputes as the solution, without workers' active participation. Out of the Manly Report came the ideas for handling labor disputes in wartime.

During President Wilson's reelection campaign year of 1916, Congress passed a remarkable series of pro-labor bills. The Railroad Brotherhoods, not members of the AFL, had achieved the eight-hour day due to President Wilson's direct intervention. With these developments, the AFL reluctantly modified its voluntarist and anti-statist politics and acquiesced to modest state intervention into workplace issues. In addition to supporting Wilson for reelection, since October 1916 Gompers had been sitting on the Council of National Defense (CND), an agency coordinating a war-preparedness campaign and had already pressed the AFL executive board to support war if it should come. Thus the AFL was prepared when President Wilson asked Congress for a declaration of war on April 2, 1917. Gompers then moved quickly in the CND labor committee to pledge a "strike as a last resort" principle for the duration. In return, Gompers expected that the Wilson administration would listen to labor's demands. The AFL Executive Board, it should be noted, did not endorse a "no-strike pledge." Nonetheless, the federal machinery was slow, and it was only in September 1917 that the President's Mediation Commission was established to quell the rising surge of labor unrest.

War-time Strikes 1917–18

The year 1917 turned out to be the year with the most labor unrest. National union discipline waned as workers took advantage of the booming war economy to press for the eight-hour day, wage increases, and union representation. There were nearly 3,000 strikes reported in the first six months of 1917, with the largest (both in numbers of workers involved and in number of workdays lost) in metalworking, followed by shipbuilding, coal mining, copper mining, textiles, lumber, clothing, and railroads.

The increased cost of living meant that demands for wage increases were among the top causes of strike activity. Inflation also caused some important nonworkplace organizing, as cost-of-living protests, or "food riots" to use the common newspaper label, swept through a number of large cities, beginning with the Jewish neighborhoods of the Lower East Side of Manhattan and Brooklyn, New York. In mid-February 1917, housewives spontaneously protested the skyrocketing price of basic foodstuffs, in some cases 20 to 30 percent overnight, accusing suppliers of starving the domestic market in order to sell abroad. By the end of the month, the protests had spread to Philadelphia, Boston, and Chicago. In New York City, Socialists, including Congressman Meyer London, championed the women's cause in calling for government control of food prices. The protests dwindled in March, due mostly to success in lowering the price of commodities, and then were obviated by U.S. entrance into the war in April, which resulted in federal oversight of the food market. These actions were a strong indication of working-class community sentiment.

In northern industry, craft unions focused on changes on the shop floor instituted by management. The key to understanding the outcomes of governmental actions in different industries was the prewar nature of labor relations in each industry. Railroads and shipbuilding were two sites of coordinated labor action before the National War Labor Board (NWLB) was created in early 1918; indeed, events in these two industries helped shape NWLB practice. Railroads were an anomaly, since their industrial relations had been heavily monitored by the U.S. government since the 1890s. The unions had a systems-federation approach, which meant that craft union members formed joint committees in each company to deal with issues. The new Railroad Administration's Wage Commission ordered wage increases in 1917, and the Administration also agreed to unions' demands that the dilution of craft be limited and temporary and skilled workers protected. The railroads were nationalized in January 1918 to aid in the war effort, and there were no strikes on the railroads during the war due to this war corporatism. However, the accommodation reached between management and unions during the war set up postwar labor agitation leading to the great 1922 railroad shopmen's strike, just as the 1919 political fight over the Plumb Plan had its roots in the wartime arrangement. The Plumb Plan, named after Glenn E. Plumb, a Chicago lawyer who was counsel to the Four Railroad Brotherhoods during the war, was an important piece of proposed legislation that would keep the railroads nationalized and administered by a joint committee of railroad workers and shippers.

Shipbuilding represented another economic sector where the federal government was instrumental in shaping the industry and in regulating industrial relations. The Emergency Fleet Corporation (EFC) was established in April 1917 to oversee rapid shipbuilding. The EFC and the AFL's Metal Trades Department agreed to establish the Shipbuilding Labor Adjustment Board (SLAB). This was not effective, as summer 1917 saw numerous locally directed strikes in private shipyards and some Navy yards as well. National union leaders were instrumental in getting the men back to work, and in return, national union leaders achieved decision-making power. However, local unions often refused to abide by national decisions to forgo closed shops or second-class designations on some jobs or mass-production techniques on others, and wildcat strikes (without union leadership approval) were a constant disturbance. Organization of less-skilled workers began in 1916, with the IWW organizing laborers and helpers, and later with the Shipyard Laborers' Union (SLU), an AFL federal union created in early 1917. The SLU began organizing apprentices and semiskilled operatives in late 1917, especially in the San Francisco Bay area. The summer 1917 strikes in West Coast shipyards were handled by the Iron Trades Councils (ITC), which embraced unskilled as well as skilled workers in AFL affiliates. The ITC maintained local solidarity across craft lines even as national union leaders were trying to get individual locals back to work. More revealing, the ITC in San Francisco also asked for higher wage hikes for less-skilled employees than for craftsmen and demanded that the agreement cover all factories, not just shipyards.

These strikes revealed the adaptability of craft unions within the AFL on the local level, even as national leaders were trying to regularize industrial relations in keeping with their new cooperative relationship with the federal government. Locals of craft unions found it beneficial to include unskilled and semiskilled workers in their organizing and demands. Since the AFL had done little in general to organize mass-production workers in the metal trades, many of these activities were led by radical industrial unionists, like the anti-war socialist machinists at General Electric in Schenectady, IWW activists, or by the seemingly pro-war industrial-union IAM in Bridgeport. Here could be found the impulse called "workers' control," which went beyond craft solidarity to embrace broad worker solidarity and a larger, potentially syndicalist goal of self-management of industry. Radical industrial unionists won leadership positions in the evolving unions in both Bridgeport and Turtle Creek, where they pursued industrial-union goals. In Bridgeport, the IAM organizing committee fell under the influence of radical industrial-unionists in 1916, some purportedly with training in IWW tactics. With Russian-born Samuel Lavit as its elected business agent, Bridgeport IAM District 55 set out to organize the city. In addition to the traditional craft Lodge 30, which represented all machinists in the area and had led the 1915 machinist strikes, the new District 55 created three new lodges: one a Remington-UMC Lodge (breaking with craft practice by creating one plant-based lodge) and two ethnic lodges, Scandinavian and Polish, for machinists of those ethnicities. District 55 later established a Women's Lodge as well. All were indications that the Bridgeport IAM intended to embrace all workers in the city's munitions and machine shops, regardless of their craft status.

More importantly for all AFL unions, these activities revealed a new intention on the part of organized workers to engage in sympathy strikes for other workers, regardless of what contracts were already in place. This willingness flew in the face of accepted AFL practice and harkened back to the Gilded Age labor movement, as well as forward to future activities. All of these developments took place before the National War Labor Board was established.

The President's Mediation Commission was established in September 1917 in response to all the strikes that had taken place in the previous six months. It was established by presidential proclamation, not by agreement with the unions (as had been the case with previous war adjustment boards) and its jurisdiction included the entire economy. The ongoing disputes in copper mining, lumbering, street railways, and among telephone operators were addressed and in some cases successfully adjudicated. But the strikes in lumber, copper, and agriculture were led by the IWW, and were met with fierce violence and repression—first by employers and then by the federal government itself. The IWW, which never endorsed the war and acted with revolutionary flair, was highly successful in organizing such rural workers. Copper owners, in particular, were adamant about crushing the miners' strike and organized local vigilantes who carried out the infamous Bisbee Deportation.

In summer 1917, nearly 1,200 striking copper miners were rounded up in Bisbee, Arizona, and transported by train to the New Mexico desert; these were followed by other minor deportation incidents in fall 1917 around the Southwest. Six weeks later, a mob lynched IWW organizer Frank Little in the copper-mining town of Butte, Montana. Many states passed "criminal syndicalism" laws, and these efforts were joined by the federal government's passage of the Espionage Act in 1917

To break a strike of copper miners led by the Industrial Workers of the World in Bisbee, Arizona, in July 1917, vigilantes, organized by the companies and local sheriff and armed with rifles and a machine gun, herded nearly 1,200 striking miners into boxcars and shipped them to a desert town in New Mexico. Despite national protest, no one was ever punished for the Bisbee Deportation. (*Courtesy:* Arizona Historical Society/Tucson, AHS #43182.)

and the Sedition Act in 1918. The federal government carried out a concerted campaign against the IWW in September, indicting 166 officials and organizers under the Espionage Act. Most of these IWW-led strikes demanded no more than what other war-industry workers had been granted—the eight-hour day, wage increases, and the right to organize. Though these repressive actions were condemned by Frank Walsh, few in the AFL raised a cry on behalf of their IWW rivals. Particularly revealing of government goals was the decision by the War Department, after the Mediation Commission failed to get lumber operators to deal with the IWW, to set up an alternative "union," the Loyal Legion of Loggers and Lumbermen, to overcome the disruption in vital lumber delivery to shipyards. The IWW was subsequently hounded nationwide and nearly destroyed.

An intriguing industrial-union experiment in Chicago's packinghouses represented a version of what a progressive labor movement could do. The Chicago Stockyards Labor Council (SLC) was created in July 1917 by the Chicago Federal of Labor, whose president John Fitzpatrick was committed to organizing mass-production industrial workers, particularly those in meatpacking. The industry was ripe for organizing, since sporadic strikes in 1916 and early 1917 over wages combined with very high turnover rates as workers individually sought higher wages and better working conditions. The AFL's Amalgamated Meat Cutters and Butcher Workmen continued to have some presence in the plants, but they were not up to the task of organizing the entire workforce. That job fell to the SLC, which consisted of representatives from twelve AFL unions. William Z. Foster was its key organizer. Foster, with recent membership in the North American Syndicalist League and the International Trade Union Education League, had developed the theory and practice of industrial unionism for an American situation. He modeled the SLC after the railroad-systems federation. Allying the craft unions into one coherent organization proved more daunting than originally thought, and in some cases merely reinforced traditional craft and ethnic lines. One great stumbling block was most AFL unions' color bar against African-American members, whose numbers had increased in packinghouses as a result of the Great Migration of African Americans from the South.

To solve all these problems, the SLC created neighborhood-based locals. Packinghouse workers flooded into the SLC and pressure mounted for a strike in November 1917, when the packers refused to listen to the SLC's demands and then fired committee members. The unions appealed to the president's new Mediation Commission for a system of binding arbitration in exchange for a no-strike pledge. The packers finally agreed, and the Commission appointed Judge Samuel Alschuler of Illinois as the arbitrator. Many union demands were thus settled by government-sponsored negotiations. But shop committees elected by the rank and file took over day-to-day handling of grievances. Historian James R. Barrett notes that Poles and African Americans were particularly prominent on these committees, but in the 1918 organizing drive newer arrivals in the black community tended not to join the union. This highlights the special presence of immigrant and African-American workers in the workforce and in the briefly successful union drive.

The migration by some 450,000 African Americans from the deep South to industrial jobs in the North was one of the results of the halting of European migration due to the war. But African-American men were hired only in certain niches in industry where they already had a presence, notably in steel, auto (mostly Ford Motor Company), and meatpacking. Notably, they had often gained these niches as a result of earlier strike-breaking activities by employers. Often they were placed in the most hazardous and undesirable jobs, such as coke furnace tenders in steel. Black men found themselves in hostile circumstances when they were hired into more desirable jobs. For example, in June 1917, machinists at the Schenectady GE plant struck over the hiring of an African American to operate a drill press. Only when management explained that he was one of the college students that they were accustomed to hiring temporarily during the summer did the machinists return to work. African Americans also had strained relationships within their own communities, as longtime residents were wary of the newcomers whose presence threatened to upset the careful racial harmony built up in previous decades in these northern cities. Union leaders emerged from these settled African-American communities, at the same time as they included community leaders beholden to the meatpacking companies.

In the South, black communities tried to improve their conditions by engaging in organized activity in 1917. On the waterfront and in the shipyards of the Norfolk-Portsmouth-Newport News area of Virginia, African-American union members participated in the Norfolk Labor Day Parade. Later that month, 300 African-American women struck against the American Cigar Company and were joined by machinists' helpers. Unfortunately, they were replaced by white scabs. At that time, the National Brotherhood Workers of America, supported by A. Philip Randolph and Chandler Owen from the black journal *The Messenger,* became the organizing center for African-American workers in Virginia. Though the postwar economic downturn and the aggressive organizing of African-American longshoremen by AFL unions soon robbed the brotherhood of momentum, it was a significant example of African-American workers' organizing outside of the traditional union channels. Many AFL unions at that time had color bars to membership and were often hostile to African-American workers, unless the African-American workers organized on their own. It was no wonder that recent African-American arrivals in 1918 Chicago were unmoved by the appeals of the Stockyards Labor Council. The general racist hostility by white communities led to the East St. Louis race riot of July 2, 1917, which was a precursor of the 1919 race riots in many cities.

The presence of women workers in war work further complicated unionization attempts. White women (few African-American women were hired in northern industry) entered war jobs in order to earn more money, offset the rising cost of living, or replace lost wages if their husbands or fathers were in the military. Most women in war jobs were not new to the paid workforce but were switching to better-paid jobs outside of the traditional women's jobs. Indeed, the wages for women machine operators in munitions plants were so lucrative that teacher and nursing shortages were reported in war-boom towns as working women flocked to the metal trades. The growth in demand for women came about because of the disruption of European immigration as well as the increased production needs. Employers, with the help of reformers in the newly created Women's Branch of the Army Ordnance Department and the Women's Section of the U.S. Railroad Administration, intended to make a smooth transition to a mixed-sex labor force. But they also intended to use the war emergency to introduce women workers as part of their dilution of metal-working craft jobs. Managers argued that untrained women workers needed the specialized production machinery and carefully monitored production process that scientific management sought. Thus employers revamped the production process by dividing skilled metalworking procedures into semiskilled machine operations, which needed only machine operatives trained for a few weeks on that specific task. Thus women could be brought in at much lower wages than skilled machinists. Because of this, the women often faced the hostility of male craft unionists.

In 1917 and early 1918, women workers who were introduced into the workplace but not in competition with craftsmen were likely to be encouraged to form unions and often struck alongside men for increased wages or better working conditions. For example, Kansas City laundry workers struck in February 1918 when women laundresses joined with male laundry drivers to win a wage increase, and where the women also complained about unhealthy workplace conditions. This strike mushroomed into a general strike for one week in March when most Kansas City workers struck in sympathy with the laundry workers. After the National Guard was called out to control violence against scabs in the streetcars, the mayor negotiated a settlement between the laundry owners and workers that included a wage increase and the right to organize. Kansas City had the unusual experience of an active Women's Trade Union League (WTUL) chapter with a strong working relationship with the city Central Labor Union to organize women and men in various jobs. Kansas City WTUL leader Sarah Green persuaded the Amalgamated Association of Street and Electric Railway Employees local to welcome women conductors into their ranks, only to discover that the company was paying the women a substantially lower wage. The Amalgamated, rather than react with anger toward the women, petitioned the new National War Labor Board for equal pay.

Other examples of general strikes in 1917 and early 1918 reveal a broader sense of worker solidarity. The general strike in Springfield, Illinois, erupted in September 1917 after striking streetcar workers were blocked from holding a parade to publicize their cause; the labor council, and especially the miners, protested this denial of free assembly for a week before the sheriff's office relented. The spring 1918 general strikes in Waco, Texas, and in Billings, Montana, began as lockouts of streetcar workers and laundry workers, respectively, where other workers then struck in sympathy. All this activity presaged the bigger strikes that would erupt in 1919. These were service-sector workers. The most vital action was taking place in the metal trades, where workers were making the munitions, rifles, cannon, tanks, trucks, and submarines being used by the armed forces.

Immigrants provided a significant proportion of the workers in wartime American shops. Unskilled immigrant men often benefited from the reorganization of production in metalworking, as more semiskilled jobs became available. But they were pressed by a forceful "100 percent Americanism" patriotism, even as they were concerned with events in their European homelands. Immigrants tied to the Allied countries were more welcomed. Those hailing from the Central Powers nations found their lives more difficult. Employers with U.S. war contracts began demanding citizenship papers or "intent to file" papers from their employees, and the War Department set up perimeters around war plants within which "enemy aliens" could not reside. Employers were faced with both new workers and recalcitrant skilled workers who needed to be disciplined. So employers began plantwide personnel efforts. Various amenities, such as cafeterias and sponsorship of "victory gardens," were provided. Employers instituted exit interviews to curb turnover. They also included Americanization programs, such as English classes for immigrants, along with instruction in arithmetic and civics. Liberty Loan campaigns became festive events within plants complete with flags and parades and competition to see which department could produce the highest sales. Buying war bonds was expected and was one way for workers to save the wages earned by overtime work. Those immigrants who stayed after 1919 often cashed their bonds to buy houses, while others sought to return to the newly created nation-states of Eastern Europe. The politics of immigrant patriotism were complex, but all ethnics had to be mindful of potential accusations of disloyalty once the United States entered the war.

Most importantly, the reorganization of production had the unexpected result of heightening the power of skilled machinists and other metal craftsmen in the toolrooms of the large plants, who were responsible for creating the specialized jigs and fixtures for the new machines and who were required to maintain and repair those machines, since semiskilled operators could not. Here was a potential split within the workforce, as skilled toolroom machinists were tempted to go it alone.

Thus craft workers in AFL unions had two tendencies in 1917: one was to continue in the traditional craft way, organizing only their own, though easing membership requirements in some cases and cooperating with other craft unions in coordinated actions against employers; another was to organize in "all-grades" unions where everybody working in that factory regardless of skill could join, in spite of national union orders to the contrary. This latter tendency was usually led by radical craftsmen who saw that mass industrial unionism was the only way to guarantee workers' power given management's determination to subdivide or dilute skilled jobs; radical craftsmen often termed this effort within the AFL an "amalgamation" of the crafts. The industrial-union and amalgamation efforts of these radical craftsmen were a constant affront to AFL leaders and continued to be so through 1919.

The National War Labor Board

The continuing reality of strikes forced the federal government to create an agency to handle labor disputes in companies with government contracts. The Mediation Commission had little power, and various government agencies in shipbuilding and railroads were making divergent decisions. Thus a presidential executive order created the National War Labor Board (NWLB) in April 1918, one full year after the United States had entered the war.

The NWLB consisted of five labor representatives and five business representatives, along with "public" representatives Frank Walsh and former president William Howard Taft, who were chosen as joint chairmen. The labor representatives were Frank J. Hayes (president, United Mine Workers), William L. Hutcheson (president, United Brotherhood of Carpenters), Thomas A. Rickert (president, United Garment Workers), Thomas J. Savage (executive board, International Association of Machinists), and Victor Olander (executive board, International Seamen's Union). The business representatives were Loyall A. Osborne (vice president, Westinghouse Electric Manufacturing Company), William H. VanDervoort (president of an engineering firm, an automobile company, and an ordnance firm in East Moline, Illinois), Leonor F. Loree (president of Delaware & Hudson Railroad and numerous coal and iron companies), B.L. Worden (president of the Lackawanna Bridge Company and the Submarine Boat Corporation), and C. Edwin Michael (president of Virginia Bridge and Iron Company). NWLB principles derived from previous rulings of their predecessor committees as well as common practice in each industry. Thus their rulings had a different impact on each city or industry, depending on previous conditions or level of union organization in those industries.

The NWLB under Frank Walsh operated under the general principle of Industrial Democracy, which had as many meanings as there were participants in the negotiation. To labor, it meant the homefront equivalent of the "war for democracy" abroad, for workers' voice without employer retaliation. To radicals, it was a weak substitute for "workers' control" of production. To Taylorist reformers, it was a way to harmonize scientific management and trade unionism. To Progressive reformers, it meant a cooperative, organic relationship between employer and worker, to the benefit of both and of the nation.

The NWLB attempted to maintain stable industrial relations through its principle of "existing standards"—in other words, to rule in favor of unions when they already had a presence in that workplace but not to favor unions where their previous presence had been negligible. Radical industrial unionists used that principle to advantage through 1918 to press forward the mass organizing within these craft unions, arguing to both the AFL and the NWLB that these new workers had to be admitted and their grievances addressed under the guiding principle. To compromise between the labor movement's demand for government protection of the rights of workers to organize in return for wartime cooperation and nonunion employers' demand for the open shop, the NWLB settled on the model of the shop committee. This solved the competing demands by giving workers a voice but not union representation.

The shop committee structure derived from a number of directions: Gompers cited the British model of the Whitley councils; Taylorist reformers had already experimented with shop committees; John D. Rockefeller Jr. had established an employee representation plan at the Colorado Fuel and Iron Company after the 1914 Ludlow massacre. The latter had a different twist from the NWLB practice in that it was a joint council with employer veto rights. On the contrary, the NWLB shop committee, which had been elected in about 125 cases by the end of the war, was to be representative of workers only, though foremen were allowed to vote in their own departments. The NWLB implemented rules for elections under federal supervision and off the company premises in most cases. It insisted on industrial-style representation, not craft-based representation, to the chagrin of AFL craft unions everywhere. Most significantly, many of the NWLB shop committee elections resulted in the selection of union activists and strike leaders, who were often the industrial unionists among the craftsmen. These workers had already formed shop committees while engaging in actions during the previous years.

NWLB rulings smoothed the way for management reorganization of production, just as employers wanted, and gave wage increases to semiskilled machine operatives, who with piecework and incentive pay took home nearly as much as craftsmen. This tempted craft workers in another direction: to hang on to their craft privilege, which still remained strong in toolrooms and specialty machine shops. The best example of both the craftsmen's go-it-alone impulse and the NWLB's inclination was the 1918 machinists' strike in Bridgeport. Some Bridgeport machinists, who chafed under increased dilution of skill as well as the increased numbers of semiskilled women and immigrant workers in their ranks, rebelled against business agent Lavit's industrial union approach and struck on Good Friday 1918 for holiday pay and a wage increase. They were encouraged by the recent NWLB ruling in the Smith & Wesson case in Springfield, Massachusetts, in which the War Department seized the munitions plant and forced recalcitrant employers to give large wage increases and implement shop committees.

In the Bridgeport case, the NWLB instead decided to investigate all metalworking wages in the city, not just those of the IAM members on strike. Hearings during the spring and summer kept Lavit running between Bridgeport and Washington, DC, where he simultaneously argued the case of Bridgeport workers and argued with machinists at home to be patient and wait for the government ruling. He also shrewdly used the NWLB's penchant for factory-wide labor units to extend his goal of industrial unionism. His organizing committee had already demanded a wage scheme based on new job classifications for machine-shop workers. The seven classifications, which included semiskilled operators as well as skilled positions, went well beyond the two or three traditional IAM categories and reflected the changes that scientific management had wrought on the shop floor. When the NWLB ruling came in late August, it rejected the local's classification demands and surprisingly ordered large wage increases for most lower-skilled workers and only a five-cent raise for skilled workers, noting that lower-paid workers had lost out more than higher-paid workers in the wartime inflation. The skilled machinists, now insulted, rejected the ruling and struck again, in spite of national union orders. It was only when President Wilson threatened to end the strikers' military draft exemptions that the strike ended. In the stormy aftermath, the Bridgeport machinists under Lavit created an American Labor Party to run in the November 1918 elections. Its platform revealed a wide-ranging worldview, proclaiming the goal of "exercising their political rights as an instrument of industrial emancipation thus paving the way for an autonomous Industrial Republic (shop control in the factories, mines, mills, and other establishments)." This was a far more ambitious agenda than Walsh's Industrial Democracy or simple industrial unionism.

Debate: Workers Control or Industrial Democracy?

Historian David Montgomery was the first to analyze the wave of strikes during World War I as part of an evolving struggle for "workers' control," labeling that impulse among skilled machinists to consider their craft skills as controlling their workplaces in the context of a radical industrial-union goal. Historian Jeffrey Haydu found the same thing in his comparative study of workers' control struggles among the Bridgeport metalworkers and Coventry, England, shop stewards' movement during the war years. This was confirmed by this author's investigation of the Bridgeport strikes, though that investigation revealed a fissure between old-line craftsmen who clung to traditional IAM practice and those who espoused a radical industrial-unionism. Historian Joseph McCartin has most thoroughly critiqued this interpretation, emphasizing the more moderate Industrial Democracy idea as the defining ideology of the moment. McCartin revealed, in the patterns of 1917 and 1918 worker activity, the immense impact that the Mediation Commission and then the NWLB had on worker aspirations as well as on employer intransigence. Workers would not have been as successful as they were without the NWLB's championing of Industrial Democracy.

But to pose the question as one of workers' control versus Industrial Democracy presents a misleading choice, as both ideas were present in different strikes or even within the same strike. The fact that an atmosphere of coercive patriotism had built up by 1918 and that the most successful labor leaders would be using patriotic rhetoric acceptable to the government and the public is not surprising. What should be kept in mind are the various innovative campaigns for workplace representation that existed before the NWLB. These shop committees and strike actions from 1915 through 1917 ran the gamut from craft initiatives to mass union actions to sympathy strikes for service workers. The proper analysis depends on what strike and which evidence base are being investigated, but only the totality of those models of behavior can explain the mass strikes that took place in 1919, after the NWLB shut its doors.

What was remarkable in the postwar period was the degree to which employers used the NWLB model of industrial relations, now adapted to their own liking but with the same patriotic rhetoric. Thus the old open-shop drive became the "American Plan" with employee representation committees. The 1919 industry-wide strikes in opposition to this renewed open shop offensive included large numbers of less-skilled immigrant workers as well as craft workers, and included city-wide general strikes such as in Seattle. This was not a revolutionary moment in the United States. The wartime strikes presaged the industrial unionism of the 1930s CIO, just as the NWLB anticipated the New Deal industrial relations system. But the wartime strikes also briefly revealed a glimpse of some workers' aspirations beyond elementary industrial relations.

See also: The Strike Wave of 1877, 177; The 1945–1946 Strike Wave, 216; Steel Strikes Before 1935, 351; Unionizing the "Jungle": A Century of Meatpacking Strikes, 375; Rubber Workers' Strikes, 398; Labor Upheaval on the Nation's Railroads, 483; Trolley Wars, 519; Longshoremen's Strikes, 1900–1920, 547.

Bibliography

Barrett, James R. *Work and Community in the Jungle: Chicago's Packinghouse Workers, 1894–1922.* Urbana: University of Illinois Press, 1987.

Bing, Alexander. *Wartime Strikes and Their Adjustment.* New York: E.P. Dutton, 1921.

Brody, David. "World War I and Industrial Democracy: Or, Why We Have No Works Councils in America." In *Labor Embattled: History, Power, Rights.* Urbana: University of Illinois Press, 2005, 62–81.

Bucki, Cecelia F. "Dilution and Craft Tradition: Bridgeport, Connecticut, Munitions Workers in 1915–1919." *Social Science History* 4, no. 1 (February 1980): 105–24. Anthologized in *The New England Working Class and the New Labor History*, ed. Herbert G. Gutman and Donald M. Bell. Urbana: University of Illinois Press, 1987.

Connor, Valerie Jean. *The National War Labor Board: Stability, Social Justice, and the Voluntary State in World War I.* Chapel Hill: University of North Carolina Press, 1983.

Fasce, Ferdinando. *An American Family: The Great War and Corporate Culture in America.* Columbus: Ohio State University Press, 2002.

Frank, Dana. "Housewives, Socialists, and the Politics of Food: The 1917 New York Cost-of-Living Protests." *Feminist Studies* 11, no. 2 (Summer 1985): 255–85.

Greenwald, Maurine Weiner. *Women, War, and Work: The Impact of World War I on Women Workers in the United States.* Westport, CT: Greenwood Press, 1980.

Haydu, Jeffrey. *Between Craft and Class: Skilled Workers and Factory Politics in the United States and Britain, 1890–1922.* Berkeley: University of California Press, 1988.

———. *Making American Industry Safe for Democracy: Comparative Perspectives on the State and Employee Representation in the Era of World War I.* Urbana: University of Illinois Press, 1997.

Lichtenstein, Nelson, and Howell John Harris, eds. *Industrial Democracy in America: The Ambiguous Promise.* New York: Cambridge University Press, 1993.

McCartin, Joseph Anthony. *Labor's Great War: The Struggle for Industrial Democracy and the Origins of Modern American Labor Relations, 1912–1921.* Chapel Hill: University of North Carolina Press, 1997.

Montgomery, David. *The Fall of the House of Labor: The Workplace, the State, and American Labor Activism, 1865–1925.* New York: Cambridge University Press, 1987.

———. "The 'New Unionism' and the Transformation of Workers' Consciousness in America 1909–22." *Journal of Social History* 7 (Summer 1974): 509–29.

———. *Workers' Control in America: Studies in the History of Work, Technology, and Labor Struggles.* New York: Cambridge University Press, 1979.

THE RISE AND FALL OF THE SIT-DOWN STRIKE

Rachel Meyer

The sit-down strike is here to stay. Of that workers are resolved. The law may change slowly, but change it must.

—Joel Seidman, "Sit-Down," 1937

The defining feature of a sit-down strike is that strikers occupy the workplace instead of leaving to set up pickets outside. Compared to traditional strikes, sit-down strikes offer many advantages for workers, including a greater ability to deter strikebreakers and stop production. Employers are less able to maintain even low levels of production, as they often do with traditional strikes. They avoid ousting strikers aggressively for fear of damaging their own property. At the same time, strikers can defend their position from behind closed doors instead of on an exposed picket line.

Without strikebreakers and with strikers sharing close quarters around the clock, sit-downs forge solidarity among workers. Although morale can erode if a strike drags on for an extended period of time, sit-downers often develop a strong sense of camaraderie. Instead of manning picket line shifts in the cold and fighting back strikebreakers, sit-down strikers spend long periods together engaging in a variety of solidarity-building activities, such as preparing meals and cleaning, entertainment with singing and games, regular union meetings, and so on. According to historian Dana Frank, sit-down strikes are simply much more fun:

> . . . sit-down strikes raised the morale of the strikers. Squished in together, rather than isolated at home or in small conversations on the picket line, the strikers' spirits rose and an enormous group feeling developed—precisely the sense of solidarity that working-class struggle is all about.

A psychologist quoted by historian Sidney Fine noted about one sit-down strike that "'the atmosphere of cooperativeness' in the sit-down reoriented the thought of the sit-downers and created 'a veritable revolution of personality' so that the pronoun 'We' came to replace the pronoun 'I.'" Subjecting participants to close and enclosed quarters, the sit-down strike has particularly strong potential to create cohesion among the workers involved.

At the same time, sit-downs are easier to organize than traditional strikes—which rely on a large base of rank-and-file support to stop production and hold the picket line—because a relatively small number of workers can shut down a large factory, workplace, or even an entire company. Focusing on key departments or plants in the production process, sit-downers can affect production far from their own workplace. As journalist Louis Adamic described a 1936 rubber factory sit-down of 7,000: "Some realized for the first time how important they were in the process of rubber production. Twelve men had practically stopped the works! Almost any dozen or score of them could do it! In some departments six could do it!" Although not all sit-downs occur in this way, the ability of a small number of workers to cause major disruptions in production at a large factory—or many factories—is one of the sit-down strike's most distinctive features.

From a tactical point of view, the sit-down strike is extremely effective. Its ability to stop production, build solidarity, and bring victory to workers—even when relying on support from only a minority of the workforce—is almost unparalleled in the history of working-class collective action. And so it gained prominence during the upsurge of American labor struggle of the 1930s, as a wave of sit-down strikes hit a variety of U.S. workplaces in 1936–37.

The Rise and Fall of the Sit-Down Strike

It is unclear when and where the sit-down strike was first used. Historians most often cite examples from Europe and the United States, although it seems unlikely that the tactic was never tried elsewhere in the world. Early sit-downs were generally short-lived and not well documented, and use of the tactic did not become widespread until the mid-1930s. The earliest sit-downs in the United States were isolated events. Pittsburgh steelworkers occupied a mill in 1842 in what was perhaps the first American sit-down strike, according to historian Philip Foner. In 1884, brewery workers in Cincinnati "barricaded themselves behind beer barrels for sixty-five hours," according to Frank. And Foner cites New York City laundry workers who sat down in 1896 in support of a garment workers' strike. The Industrial Workers of the World were involved in an occupation—perhaps the most prominent early sit-down in the United States—at the General Electric plant in Schenectady, New York, in 1906. And workers in Minnesota sat down for three days at the Hormel Packing Corporation in 1933, according to comparative historian Michael Torigian.

Sit-down strikes became more widely used in the mid-1930s. Miners across Europe were sitting down at the time. Sit-down strikes then spread throughout France in the spring of 1936, when almost a fifth of all French workers were involved in sit-downs, as both Frank and Torigian note. American workers followed suit. In the words of Frank, they "began to perfect the 'quickie' sit-down, by which a short strike for modest demands could produce results in a matter of hours." Although the sit-down was used regularly by seamen around this time, it first gained prominence in the Akron, Ohio, rubber industry, which saw an occupation of General Tire in June 1934 and then a series of spontaneous sit-downs at the major rubber companies in late 1935. Journalist Louis Adamic, historian Daniel Nelson, and labor specialist Joel Seidman have each described these events. The Akron rubber industry sit-downs continued into 1936—with more than sixty occupations between March and December—serving as a precursor to the great wave that would wash into other industries, especially auto production.

While preceding years saw some increase in sit-down activity—especially the short "quickie" variety where workers were unlikely to remain in the workplace overnight—it was not until the end of 1936 and early 1937 that the sit-down strike developed into a prominent mode of collective action. The auto industry's first overnight occupation—sometimes called a "stay-in"—began on November 17, 1936, at Bendix Products in South Bend, Indiana, and resulted in the United Auto Workers (UAW) gaining exclusive bargaining rights after a weeklong strike, as described by Torigian. Two more successful UAW sit-downs soon followed, both in Detroit: an eight-day occupation of Midland Steel that began on November 27, and a two-week sit-down in December at Kelsey-Hayes, which supplied brakes to Ford Motor Company. The Midland Steel strike was particularly important in demonstrating the power of the sit-down. When 1,200 day-shift steelworkers sat down and halted the production of steel frames, within a few days they idled at least 53,000 autoworkers at other plants, according to Fine. Just six days after the Kelsey-Hayes strike was settled with the workers emerging from the factory victorious, workers in Flint, Michigan, sat down in what was to be a defining event in the history of sit-down strikes in the United States.

Having discovered the virtues of this new organizing tactic and emboldened by their success with sit-downs at Bendix, Midland Steel, and Kelsey-Hayes, UAW activists set their sights on a more formidable foe: the General Motors Corporation (GM), which was at the time one of the largest, most powerful companies in the world. Preceded by occupations of GM Fisher Body plants in Atlanta, Kansas City, and Cleveland, two of the company's main shops located in Flint were hit by sit-downs on December 30, 1936. Although the UAW had intended to use the tactic in Flint, sit-downs spontaneously erupted earlier than union leaders had planned. At 7:00 A.M. workers at the Fisher Body No. 2 plant sat down, followed at 10:00 P.M. that night by their comrades at the more im-

Sit-down strikers occupied the General Motors Fisher Body plant in Flint, Michigan, from December 30, 1936 to February 11, 1937. The strike, which spread to other GM factories, forced management to recognize the United Auto Workers as the exclusive representative of the workers. It also sparked a wave of sit-down strikes that rippled throughout the country over the course of 1937. (*Courtesy:* Library of Congress.)

portant Fisher Body No. 1 plant. In the immediate aftermath, a series of sit-downs and conventional strikes hit GM plants around the country, including an occupation at the strategically important Chevrolet plant No. 4 in Flint, where all Chevrolet motors were assembled. Although a relatively small minority of the workforce took part in the occupations, workers succeeded in stopping production at one of the largest, most powerful corporations in the world. According to a UAW source quoted by Seidman, "By early February almost all of the 200,000 General Motors employees were idle, and the weekly production of cars had declined to 1,500 from the mid-December peak of 53,000."

The Flint GM sit-down lasted over six weeks. Because it was logistically difficult to maintain a large group of strikers inside the shop, a core group stayed while other workers left to fight from beyond the plant gates. Some sit-downers found the experience difficult emotionally, particularly those who were away from spouses and children, and physically, as the company would periodically turn off heat and electricity. But "for many of the strikers the sit-down was a truly enjoyable experience, a glorious moment in their otherwise drab lives. Sitting down and participating in the life of the new plant community were more pleasurable than the tedium of work on the assembly line," according to Fine. Inside the plants, workers made themselves at home. They slept on car seats. They entertained themselves with games, sports, music, and reading. And they prepared for a possible attack, fashioning weapons from the materials at hand and barricading doors and windows. There was a strong sense of community and a high degree of organization, with committees for all purposes, including a strike committee, a sanitation committee, and a patrol committee that was in charge of security. Strikers came together on a daily basis for union meetings.

The support of allies outside the plant was also important, since the sit-downers had to rely on

This sit-down strike by about 100 women at a Woolworth's store in Detroit in February 1937 lasted seven days and won significant gains in wages, hours, and working conditions. The strike inspired a sit-down strike by workers at Woolworth's in New York City, as well as sit-down strikes of other service workers. (*Courtesy:* Walter P. Reuther Library, Wayne State University.)

others for food, picketing, publicity, and plant gate monitoring. While business interests in the Flint community mobilized against the strikers, fellow unionists from the surrounding area—especially from Detroit and Toledo—came to their side and even occupied other plants. Of particular importance were the Women's Auxiliary and its offshoot, The Women's Emergency Brigade, which was committed to protecting the strikers from outside attack. Genora Johnson Dollinger was a leader of the Women's Auxiliary.

Although the sit-downers had seized GM property, they did not destroy it. As was typical of the sit-down, strikers were extremely careful with machinery, equipment, and parts while occupying the factories. They were in possession of company property as a means to an end, but would not destroy the materials on which their livelihoods were based.

After sitting down for forty-four days, workers achieved a clear victory, gaining union representation and establishing collective bargaining at General Motors. By demonstrating the power of workers' solidarity against a corporate giant, the sit-down strike became an effective tool for building the union. After the union's victory against GM, UAW membership rose from about 88,000 in February 1937 to almost 400,000 by mid-October. More than any other single labor struggle in America, this strike was pivotal to the establishment of industrial unionism and the growth of the labor movement in the United States.

After gaining prominence in Flint, the sit-down quickly spread to other locations and industries. Indeed, the UAW victory against GM in February 1937 was followed by "a wave of sit-down strikes unparalleled in the annals of American labor," in the words of Wyndham Mortimer, an early UAW leader. In nearby Detroit, the effects of the Flint victory were particularly strong: "For a few days local people absorbed the news. Then all hell broke loose in Detroit. In the second week after the General Motors settlement, four or five thousand working people at twenty or thirty different workplaces throughout the city went on strike," according to Frank. As Fine noted, the importance of this sit-down wave to the labor movement both in and outside of Michigan is indicated by the diversity of industries where it took place:

> The sit-downs involved every conceivable type of worker—kitchen and laundry workers in the Israel-Zion Hospital in Brooklyn, pencil makers, janitors, dog catchers, newspaper pressman, sailors, tobacco workers, Woolworth girls, rug weavers, hotel and restaurant employees, pie bakers, watchmakers, garbage collectors, Western Union messengers, opticians, and lumbermen.

The impressive diversity of industries (from submarine builders to hosiery makers) and locations (from "building service workers in New York City" to "motion picture extras in California," said Seidman) betrays the prominence of the sit-down as a form of collective action. A reporter in Detroit quoted by Fine noted that "sitting down has replaced baseball as a national pastime, and sitter-downers clutter up the landscape in every direction."

Although the sit-down is most closely associated with the auto and rubber industries where the tactic was first widely used, it was crucial to the growing unionization of many other industries. Moreover, its use was not restricted to what was at the time the male-dominated world of the factory. Witnessing the nearby success of the UAW against GM, in February and March 1937 white-collar workers took on the retail giant Woolworth's, also one of the largest companies in the country at the time. Over 100 young women in Detroit sat down for seven days in a strike that resulted in a clear victory; the workers won a long list of demands regarding wages, hours, and working conditions. Their victory inspired other service sector workers—hotel, restaurant, and retail workers—in Detroit and elsewhere to follow suit and sit down, often winning substantial concessions from their employers. As Daniel Opler describes, in mid-March, New York City store clerks at two five-and-dime chains, Woolworth's and F&W Grand, secured groundbreaking contracts through a sit-down strike that was, "for the first time in the union's history, a clear-cut victory." White-collar women in the service sector used the same powerful tactic in struggles with employers and enjoyed similarly victorious results as their male counterparts in other industries. Just as the sit-down established unionism in the auto industry, its ramifications for retail unionism were perhaps equally important.

From 1936 to 1937, the sit-down strike's prominence grew by many measures, including the total number of sit-downs, percentage of strikes that were sit-downs, and number of workers involved. In March 1937, the sit-down wave peaked, with 170 occupations involving 167,210 workers. In light of the widespread use of the sit-down in early 1937, its dramatic decline shortly thereafter appears even more striking.

The decline was sudden and steep. After the sit-down's popularity peaked in March, April saw only fifty-eight sit-downs affecting 33,339 workers, and its incidence declined even further during the remainder of the year. December 1937 saw only four sit-downs affecting merely 357 workers. Within eight months, the number of sit-downs fell from the March peak of 170 to the December low of four—a profoundly swift decline. After dramatically decreasing through 1937, the tactic all but disappeared shortly thereafter.

The imminent downfall of the sit-down was not apparent to labor leaders at the time. As the sit-down strike gained popularity in 1937, the fate of the tactic remained unclear. One possibility was that the sit-down would become a legitimate form of protest, a permanent feature on the landscape of American labor struggle. Unionists and their supporters expected—or at least hoped—that it would eventually be declared legal, along with other protest tactics that had followed the same route. Their vision was of an expansion of civil rights, of a progressive acceptance of protest tactics that originated outside the mainstream power structure, where tactics of the oppressed that were at first demonized eventually gained legitimacy. But this vision was not realized. Instead of becoming legal, the sit-down strike was crushed and criminalized.

What explains the sudden rise and fall of this powerful mode of working-class collective action? If it was such a useful strategy for workers, how and why did it disappear? Why didn't the sit-down strike become a permanent feature of American labor relations? When the wave of occupations began, repression on the part of the authorities—the courts, government officials, the police—was minimal. As the tactic gained popularity, there was a conspicuous absence of violence and police intervention on behalf of employers. But as the state shifted its approach to the tactic with increased police intervention and legal challenges, use of the sit-down strike rapidly declined.

State Intervention and the Sit-Down Strike

Opportunity

The weeklong sit-down strike at Bendix in November 1936 was the longest American sit-down to date. It was a nonviolent struggle. The courts imposed no injunction against the strikers, and the police made no attempt to oust them by force—and the union prevailed. The successful sit-downs that immediately followed exhibited a similarly conspicuous absence of anti-union action on the part of public authorities. Fine notes that during the string of sit-downs that hit Detroit in December of that year:

> The UAW must have noted with keen interest that only in the Gordon Baking strike was a war-

National Guard troops boarding trucks and on duty during the January 1937 sit-down strike against General Motors in Flint, Michigan. (*Courtesy:* Walter P. Reuther Library, Wayne State University.)

> rant charging trespass issued against the strikers, and only here was an effort made by police, constables, and some company employees to eject the sit-downers. The UAW must also have been heartened by the opinion of the Wayne County prosecutor . . . that, although employers might seek redress in the civil courts, the police could not interfere with a peacefully conducted sit-down since no statue forbade such a strike and since the applicable common law did not authorize police intervention. The sit-downers, the prosecutor declared, were inside the plant by the invitation of their employers, "so there can be no trespass."

When the UAW decided to use the tactic against GM, it was aware of the fact that, with only one exception, during previous sit-downs neither the courts nor Michigan's public officials had made an effort to eject strikers from the shops. As the tactic gained popularity, its legality had not been determined. With courts for the moment on the side of the strikers and the legal status of sit-downs still ambiguous, employers found their ability to evict sit-downers significantly curtailed.

In addition to the ambiguity of the law, the political climate was crucial to explaining the lack of state intervention against the strikers. The great wave of sit-down strikes coincided with the electoral success of labor-sympathetic governments on both the state and national level. Franklin D. Roosevelt's victory in the presidential election of 1936 emboldened labor, as did Frank Murphy's election as governor of Michigan.

The importance of the political climate became especially clear during the pinnacle of sit-down success—the Flint strikes against GM. Torigian describes how the New Deal president assisted the strikers in a number of ways:

> Roosevelt refused to intervene against the strikers, acted behind the scenes to set up negotiations . . . leaned on the GM management . . . and at several stages in the conflict threatened the corporation with new federal statutes that would have imposed additional limitations on it and other businesses. At the same time, his labor secretary declined to characterize the strikes as illegal and did everything possible to coerce the reluctant GM management into negotiating.

Although Roosevelt's intervention was important, he was sometimes hesitant to get involved. It was Governor Murphy who had a more direct effect on the crucial Flint strikes and whose actions were central to UAW success. Perhaps Murphy's most important act was his refusal to use force against the Flint strikers. According to historian Henry Kraus, he publicly assured the strikers many times that he "would not permit force or violence to be used in ousting [them] from the plant." Averse to the use of state violence, Murphy's acts "consisted largely of a series of abstinences—refusal to obtain evacuation of the plants by force, refusal to help serve three hundred John Doe warrants against the sitdowners, refusal to publicly condemn the sitdown, and so on."

One of the most important of Governor Murphy's actions in the Flint GM strike was when he refused to enforce an injunction directing the sit-downers to evacuate the plants. When the National Guard was brought to Flint under Murphy's direction, he refused to use them to break the strike. According to Fine, the National Guard at one strategically important plant "in effect, protected the sit-downers from any outside attack—the strikers referred to the Guardsmen as 'pickets.'" Governor Murphy's "position with respect to the use of force in the strike and the necessity of settling the dispute by negotiation was the *single most important factor in bringing the strike to a conclusion that was not unfavorable to the union*" (emphasis added). If at any point Murphy had decided to evict the strikers by force, it is most likely that the outcome would have gone against the union.

Union leaders were not the only people to recognize the importance of this labor-friendly political context. Corporate leaders and their allies also took note. A Republican politician quoted by Torigian suggested that one word from Roosevelt is all it would have taken to break up the strike, but that "no such word was forthcoming from the White House." Anti-union politicians, corporate managers, and civic leaders criticized Murphy for failing to eject the strikers from the plants and for protecting them with the National Guard. According to one U.S. congressman quoted by Kraus, Murphy had "supported mob rule with troops." As the sit-down wave reached its peak, both sides recognized the crucial role of the state in shaping the sit-down's fate.

Repression

Although early sit-downers were rarely attacked, once labor set its sights on companies as powerful as GM there were bound to be ramifications. Not coincidentally, repression of the tactic began right as the sit-down wave peaked and the UAW succeeded in bringing GM to the bargaining table. Indeed, one of the first major outbreaks of violence against sit-down strikers occurred during the GM struggle, prior to Governor Murphy's intervention with the National Guard. In the famous Battle of the Running Bulls, Flint police (called "bulls" by many workers) attacked sit-downers in the Fisher Body No. 2 plant with tear gas and firearms. The strikers fought back by opening fire hoses and hurling auto parts at the police, who soon beat a hasty retreat. According to Kraus, prior to this incident "nothing of the sort had ever been attempted before" against sit-downers. The GM struggle also saw violence at Chevrolet plant No. 9, where clubs and tear gas were used against workers as they attempted to take possession of the shop. Although violence did not succeed in crippling workers' struggle against GM, it was a dress rehearsal for what was to come.

The sit-down's swift decline coincides with major changes in the extent of state repression, the legality of the tactic, and the nature of police intervention. In 1937, the conditions that made the sit-downs possible were changing rapidly as the political tide turned against the practice. Writing for the UAW in 1937, Joel Seidman documented the change:

> Attacks upon the sit-down strike have already begun, and many more may be expected. Governor Hoffman of New Jersey, for example, has warned that the entire resources of the state, if necessary, would be used to eject sit-downers. . . . Early in 1937, legislation to outlaw the sit-down strike was being considered in Alabama and Vermont. New York City police at first refused to intervene against sit-downers. In February, 1937, however, more stringent rules were put in force, under which strikers will be ejected and arrested if a formal complaint is made by the owner of the plant.

Likewise, according to Fine, when "the sit-down strike reached epidemic proportions in March, an increasing number of members of Congress began to direct their fire at the tactic." Police violence against sit-downs increased. Even Murphy appeared more willing to use force against strikers after the GM settlement. According to

Frank, "Throughout the nation, state and local governments moved swiftly to restore private property rights at the point of a gun, ending the sit-down wave."

While early Flint sit-downs saw almost no police intervention, those following the GM strike saw, in the words of Kraus, "an all-out attack launched by the city's resurgent anti-union forces." Instead of protecting strikers or leaving them alone, police treated them roughly. There was a similar crackdown against sit-downers in Detroit just after the GM victory. The attacks started on smaller shops, but the ultimate goal was to oust strikers from the large and strategically important Chrysler shops where workers were sitting down. According to Wyndham Mortimer, a UAW activist at the time, "In early April, the Detroit police began a 'get tough' campaign of ousting sit-down strikers from their plants. They went from one struck plant to another, in what was clearly a dress rehearsal of what they planned to do at Dodge and Plymouth." Although these Chrysler strikes were ultimately resolved without such measures, police violence and intervention had intensified so much during this time that the UAW held a mass demonstration in protest.

The battle intensified in the courts as well as in the factories. GM attacked the legality of the sit-down, looking for legal justification for the eviction of strikers. While early on the legal status of the sit-down was ambiguous, this changed over time. The tactic was officially criminalized in 1939 when the Supreme Court declared the practice illegal.

The sit-down strike was extremely effective, and this accounts for its popularity and for why it was the tactic of choice in struggles against even very powerful corporations. The capacity of the sit-down to stop production while deterring strikebreakers—even with only a minority of workers involved—was crucial to its effectiveness in extracting concessions from employers. But it was precisely the success of the tactic for unions and the crescendo of sit-down strike activity that precipitated the employer counterattack and state repression that let to its demise.

Institutionalization

The rise and fall of the sit-down strike occurred in the context of increasing institutionalization and bureaucratization of labor relations. The passage of the 1935 National Labor Relations Act (NLRA or Wagner Act) is often linked to the demise of the sit-down strike and a general reduction in worker militancy. As Torigian describes it, "After the Supreme Court accepted the constitutionality of the Wagner Act in March 1937, which protected unions from employer interference and enabled the National Labor Board to conduct certifying elections, U.S. sit-downs drastically dropped off, as unions pursued their goals through procedural means." But what exactly is the relationship between this increasing institutionalization of labor relations and the fate of the sit-down tactic? How does it relate to the increased repression and violence against strikers?

The absence or presence of state repression greatly affected use of the sit-down, and so its demise cannot be explained by legislation alone. Indeed, changes in the level of state repression mirror the tactic's rise and fall more closely than the general trend of institutionalization of labor relations. Though the Wagner Act did give unions other venues to pursue grievances, the sit-down strike still afforded great advantages for labor. Given these advantages, the mere existence of an alternative bureaucratic option cannot explain its demise. During the sit-down wave of 1936–37, workers actually had the option of going to the National Labor Relations Board (NLRB) for a federally monitored election, but the existence of that option did not discourage workplace occupations. The UAW went out of its way to avoid an NLRB election in the GM strike because, among other reasons, they feared that they did not have majority support.

Why was the sit-down—so advantageous and successful from the union perspective—abandoned for the institutional route? Generally speaking, institutionalized methods are less desirable from the perspective of union power unless there is a high cost associated with more militant methods—that is, unless tactics like the sit-down strike are explicitly repressed. It is only in the context of such repression that pursuing union recognition through the NLRB became more desirable. Institutionalization did not, in other words, single-handedly rechannel impulses of worker insurgency. Instead, worker insurgency was rechanneled because institutionalized options became available at the same time that the option of using the successful sit-down tactic was made more difficult due to robust state repression. Two distinct mechanisms were thus operating at once—repression of the more militant sit-down strike and institutionalization of other strategies, such as NLRB elections. As sociologist Sidney Tarrow describes for social movements more generally, this is a situation where "forms of disruption that invite repression are discarded as participants learn to avoid them," while at the same time "there are compensations for groups that choose the institutional path."

Sit-Down Strikes After the Great Wave

Beset by the twin pressures of repression and institutionalization, the sit-down strike was largely eliminated from the American labor movement's repertoire of collective action. No longer a major organizing strategy, sit-downs became isolated events. After being used during the wave to establish bargaining rights in a variety of industries and workplaces, the sit-down came to be used once again primarily as a short "quickie" strike to rapidly address grievances on the shop floor. Limited in scope and duration and no longer a tool of mass mobilization, such actions were rarely recorded in newspapers and history books. Documented cases of sit-downs are all but nonexistent since the great wave of 1936–37.

But the sit-down strike did not disappear completely. Relegated to the ranks of illegal and illegitimate protest, it was retooled as a weapon of the militant rank and file. With labor relations solidly institutionalized through the NLRB, sit-downs after the 1930s were less likely to be sanctioned by unions. They were often wildcat strikes, taking place outside of the normal routine of labor relations—without regard to contractual limits and timelines and pursued by the rank and file when union channels failed. Once used by the mainstream labor movement, the sit-down became a tool of those marginalized by union bureaucracy and alienated by the routinized nature of contemporary labor relations.

Such was the nature of the sit-down strike that occurred at Chrysler's Jefferson Assembly Plant in Detroit in 1973. According to James Geschwender, at 6:00 A.M. on July 24, two African-American spot welders, Issac Shorter and Larry Carter, scaled a ten-foot fence, locked themselves in the power cage, turned off the electricity, and stopped the assembly line. After circulating a petition to fire an abusive, racist supervisor and unable to address the problem through union channels—and in a climate of speed-ups, overtime, and poor working conditions—they decided to take matters into their own hands. Inspired by this bold act, recounts Heather Thompson, "more than 150 workers surrounded the structure where the duo had barricaded themselves and actually placed their hands on its cable to prevent a Chrysler maintenance crew from removing them from the power cage." Workers refused to let union officials resolve the conflict and instead insisted that management talk to strikers directly. After thirteen hours, management capitulated to their demands that the supervisor be fired and that there be no reprisals against strikers. The sit-down idled 5,000 workers and cost Chrysler "about 950 cars, or something over a million dollars," wrote Geschwender.

The power of the sit-down strike was once again betrayed by the tactic's success at Jefferson Assembly. Despite the fact that the illegality of the tactic had been entrenched for decades, a small minority of workers was able to stop production and cause significant economic disruption almost instantaneously, thus winning concessions from a powerful employer in a short period of time.

Since the practice was illegal, the police were prone to intervene, as they did when a second group of Detroit workers sat down a month after Shorter and Carter cut the power in their shop. In August 1973, seventy-five Detroit workers sat down for thirty hours at Chrysler Corporation's Mack Avenue stamping plant. The occupation followed a series of events that originated in a dispute about the welding department's substandard ventilation system. Workers were confronted by both police, who forcibly removed the strikers, and the court, which issued a restraining order to keep the workers from striking. As at the Jefferson Assembly Plant, this was a wildcat that occurred only after workers had attempted and failed to solve their problems through standard grievance procedures. In both cases, the sit-downs occurred because the institutionalized channels of labor-management relations—the grievance procedure, stewards, the contract—did not work. In both cases workers challenged the very structures that early sit-downers were fighting to achieve.

As displayed in both 1973 strikes, post-wave sit-downers had an additional foe: unions. According to Carter, "We couldn't even tell the difference between the union representatives and management, the way they were begging us to come out of that cage." One UAW leader called the Jefferson Assembly sit-downers "hijackers." As described by Geschwender in the Mack Avenue case, union representatives had come to accept the illegality of the tactic: "[Douglas] Fraser continued to sound more like a Chrysler executive than a UAW vice-president in stating that 'We don't place a premium on lawlessness.'" The union then mobilized to prevent picketing after police expelled workers from the plant:

> The difficulty in telling management from union people continued as 1,000 UAW members wearing arm bands stating Sergeant-at-Arms assembled at the plant gates in order to insure that work was resumed. The "loyal unionists" prevented any picketing and physically roughed-up several workers who attempted to maintain a picket line.

While union leaders that had once embraced the sit-down had come to reject it, workers most marginalized by the union—labor dissidents, African Americans, the most militant of the rank and file—had come to adopt it as their own.

Not all union officials have rejected the sit-down strike. In fact, the United Mine Workers embraced the tactic during the Pittston Coal strike in Virginia in September 1989. In the middle of a protracted traditional strike, ninety-eight miners and a clergyman entered the company's main coal-processing plant and occupied it for over three days. Called "Operation Flintstone" by some of the participants in honor of the historic Flint sit-downs, workers left the plant hours after a court-ordered deadline to vacate had passed. The workers prevailed in the strike months later—gaining job security and health benefit provisions and beating back the company's concessionary demands—but this was not due to the sit-down alone. The occupation was one small, though significant, tactic among a large repertoire of actions executed in support of a strike that lasted nine months. The Pittston strike is noteworthy for its reliance on both national and international worker solidarity and for the variety of tactics that were used throughout the campaign, including civil disobedience, sympathy strikes by other miners, community support, corporate campaigns, and the involvement of peace activists. The success of this strike depended on maintaining this broad and diverse campaign. While the three-day plant occupation helped to put pressure on the company, use of the sit-down tactic was hindered by its illegal status, and it was cut short by a court order. Despite the fact that the union supported the occupation, they could not rely on it to bring resolution to the conflict as labor leaders of the 1930s had.

While the plant occupations at Chrysler in 1973 were used to quickly resolve shop-floor grievances, state sanctions against the sit-down are such that during more protracted labor struggles other tactics come to the fore. Although the sit-down was most prominent in 1936–37, since then it has been used only rarely, as just one tactic—one marginalized tactic—among a variety of other kinds of working-class collective action.

Conclusion: The Contradictions of a Rank-and-File Tactic

Although it was once part of the mainstream labor movement, the sit-down has always shared some qualities with the wildcat strike, characterized as it is by spontaneity and relying on workers themselves to take the lead in protest. As Louis Adamic noted in 1936:

> The beauty of the sitdown or the stay-in is that there are no leaders or officials to distrust. There can be no sell-out. Such standard procedure as strike sanction is hopelessly obsolete when workers drop their tools, stop their machines, and sit down beside them. The initiative, conduct, and control of the sitdown come directly from the men involved.

These anti-bureaucratic tendencies are true not only of "quickie" strikes, but also of the large-scale mobilizations that took place during the great wave of sit-downs. During the upsurge of sit-downs in the rubber industry, for example, many if not a majority of them took place without the encouragement of organizers, as according to Adamic, "sudden, spontaneous affairs, springing out of immediate conditions in the department." Other major 1936–37 sit-downs were worker-led, even though unions were involved as they tried to establish exclusive representation and bargaining rights with employers. In the case of the Flint GM occupations, the UAW—which was heavily involved in planning the strikes—intended to wait for Governor Murphy to take office before initiating them, but the rank and file took the union by surprise. Workers sat down before they were "supposed to" and the union went along for the ride. This quality of rank and file worker control can be found throughout the history of the sit-down—from the earliest "quickies," through the great wave, to the Jefferson Assembly wildcat.

Because of its rank-and-file character, union officials had an ambivalent relationship with the sit-down even before it was criminalized. According to Adamic: "[Union leaders] at once like and fear it. Some fear it, perhaps, because it deprives the regular labor official of much of his authority; others because the sitdown is too spontaneous and seemingly haphazard. It threatens to play the devil with the collective bargaining idea." United Rubber Workers leaders, for example, actually opposed the tactic as it came into widespread use in Akron in the mid-1930s. During the great wave, union leaders tended to sanction the sit-down for use in establishing representation and collective bargaining, but once a contract was in place they preferred to go through the grievance procedure to settle conflicts. As labor-management relations became increasingly institutionalized, union leaders felt more secure acting within the bureaucratic constraints of collective bargaining.

While the sit-down remains a rank-and-file tactic, it has been criticized—most often by employers—as undemocratic. It is seen as elitist, since a minority of workers can carry out the action without the participation or approval of the majority. This feature is a great contradiction: while the ability to use only a minority of workers is a strength of the tactic, at the same time it exhibits the weakness inherent in any minority-driven movement. The sit-down strike demonstrates the power that workers have on the shop floor at the point of production, but it does not require the kind of mass mobilization featured in many traditional strikes.

Alternatively, the sit-down can be seen as quintessentially democratic, with the rank and file acting against corporate and union power alike. As a tactic that allows an activist minority to take the lead in bringing other workers into the fold, it is more appropriately seen not as anti-democratic but as an organizing tool. Indeed, with the sit-down strike, the minority often motivates the majority. One major consequence of the great sit-down wave, for example, was an overall increase in union membership. Rather than relying on mass mobilization, the sit-down inspired it.

Despite the contradictory implications of minority power, there is one way in which the sit-down has clear radical implications—its seizure of private property. Neither the relatively modest goals of "quickie" strikes nor the establishment of union representation and collective bargaining are revolutionary aims. In general, sit-down strikers were not fighting for socialism or any change in the ownership of the means of production; as Fine notes, during the great wave "the mass of the sit-down strikers were utterly without revolutionary intent." But although the unions and most strikers were ultimately fighting for collective bargaining rights and not a change in property relations, the revolutionary implications of the sit-down were apparent to radical rank and filers and leftist sympathizers. Writing for the UAW in 1937, Seidman notes that although the sit-down strike was not a revolutionary tactic, it "exhibits a healthy disregard of the property rights held supreme under our present system of law." The radical implications were also apparent to social scientists of the time, one of whom, Melvin Vincent, saw the sit-down strike as "teeming with proletarian threats to do away with private property altogether." Sit-down strike opponents and the companies themselves emphasized this point. As Kraus relates, GM framed the sit-down as being about "the priority and sanctity of property rights," which was not a difficult conclusion to make given that they were denied access to their own factories for a full six weeks.

It is doubtful that companies thought property relations would be altered in any fundamental way as a result of the sit-down wave. Surely they called attention to the property issue in part as standard anti-union red-baiting propaganda. Nonetheless, the connection was not hard to make, especially in light of the circumstance that some of the most powerful capitalist enterprises in the world lost effective control over their own factories for extended periods of time. Since the transformation of ownership is a main tenet of left-wing working-class politics, it is an unavoidable backdrop to any labor struggle where property becomes a central theme. Despite the fact that neither union leaders nor most workers were aiming to challenge capitalist property rights, the tactic was nonetheless discussed in those terms.

In the United States the sit-down strike has been a tactic of revolutionary means pursuing modest or reformist ends, a tactic that has seized private property without seeking a fundamental change in property relations. It has been a tactic more radical than its demands. Such has been the great paradox of the American sit-down strike. More than any other single tactic, the sit-down established collective bargaining and the institutionalization of labor relations in major American industries. But while sit-downers were fighting for the basic provisions of a union contract or to resolve shop-floor grievances, at the same time they were almost inadvertently challenging the very keystone of capitalism—private property. Although in the United States the sit-down strike has not been linked historically with radical ideology, goals, or demands, its radicalism resides in the way that it seizes property, exerts workers' power, forces the hand of capital, and affects social change. Despite the fact that it is no longer used as a tool of mass mobilization or union organization, it maintains a privileged position in the historical landscape of American labor struggle.

See also: Steel Strikes Before 1935, 351; Automobile Workers' Strikes, 389; Rubber Workers' Strikes, 398; Retail Workers, 620; Waitress Strikes, 633.

Bibliography

Adamic, Louis. "Sitdown." *The Nation* 143, no. 23 (December 5, 1936): 652–54.

———. "Sitdown: II." *The Nation* 143, no. 24 (December 12, 1936): 702–4.

Carter, Larry, and Issac Shorter. Interview. *The Black Voice* 3, no. 16 (September 1973): 5–6, 10.

Dollinger, Sol, and Genora Johnson Dollinger. *Not Automatic: Women and the Left in the Forging of the Auto Workers' Union.* New York: Monthly Review Press, 2000.

Fine, Sidney. *Sit-Down: The General Motors Strike of 1936–1937.* Ann Arbor: University of Michigan Press, 1969.

Foner, Philip S. *First Facts of American Labor.* New York: Holmes & Meier, 1984.

Frank, Dana. "Girl Strikers Occupy Chain Store, Win Big: The Detroit Woolworth's Strike of 1937." In *Three Strikes: Miners, Musicians, Salesgirls, and the Fighting Spirit of Labor's Last Century,* ed. Howard Zinn, Dana Frank, and Robin D.G. Kelley. Boston: Beacon Press, 2001.

Geschwender, James A. 1977. *Class, Race, and Worker Insurgency: The League of Revolutionary Black Workers.* Cambridge: Cambridge University Press.

Green, Jim. "Camp Solidarity: The United Mine Workers, the Pittston Strike, and the New 'People's Movement.'" In *Building Bridges: The Emerging Grassroots Coalition of Labor and Community,* ed. Jeremy Brecher and Tim Costello. New York: Monthly Review Press, 1990.

Kraus, Henry. *Heroes of Unwritten Story: The UAW, 1934–39.* Urbana: University of Illinois Press, 1993.

Nelson, Daniel. "Origins of the Sit-Down Era: Worker Militancy and Innovation in the Rubber Industry, 1934–38." *Labor History* 23, no. 2 (Spring 1982):198–225.

Opler, Daniel. "For All White-Collar Workers: The Possibilities of Radicalism in New York City's Department Store Unions, 1934–1953." Ph.D. diss., New York University, 2003.

Seidman, Joel. *Sit-Down.* League for Industrial Democracy, 1937.

Tarrow, Sidney. *Power in Movement: Social Movements and Contentions Politics,* 2nd ed. Cambridge: Cambridge University Press, 1998.

Thompson, Heather Ann. *Whose Detroit?: Politics, Labor, and Race in a Modern American City.* Ithaca, NY: Cornell University Press, 2001.

Torigian, Michael. "The Occupation of the Factories: Paris 1936, Flint 1937." *Comparative Studies in Society and History* 41, no. 2 (April 1999): 324–47.

Vincent, Melvin J. "The Sit-Down Strike." *Sociology and Social Research* 21 (July–August 1937): 524–33.

THE 1945–1946 STRIKE WAVE

Jack Metzgar

When World War II ended on August 14, 1945, so did the no-strike-for-the-duration pledge that had bedeviled workers and their unions since 1942. According to the Bureau of Labor Statistics, over the next eighteen months, some 7 million workers engaged in the largest, most sustained wave of strikes in American history. About 144 million days of work were lost in those eighteen months, more than in the entire decade of the 1980s or the 1990s and just slightly less than the total "days idled by work stoppages" in both those decades combined.

The number of strikes was not substantially higher than during the war, when they were not sanctioned by national unions, but their length and mass were of a completely different character. Most strikes during the war involved a small number of workers, a single plant or department, and lasted a short time, during which union leaders scurried (or made a show of scurrying) to get strikers back to work. The postwar strikes, by contrast, included massive feats of national organization. The Auto Workers, for example, shut down eighty General Motors plants in fifty cities, with 175,000 workers on strike for 113 days. The Steelworkers were out for only twenty-five days, but there were 750,000 of them from nearly all steel and steel-related companies in the United States. Some 400,000 United Mine Workers of America (UMWA) struck twice during 1946, shutting down the coal industry. Many fewer railroad workers actually struck in May 1946, but two of the rail brotherhoods, the Locomotive Engineers and the Trainmen, shut down the nation's transportation system for the two days they were out and precipitated a national crisis when President Truman threatened to draft the strikers.

The big national strikes were political events involving the federal government and some of the largest, most powerful corporations in the world. However, most strikes were local and involved every kind of worker and workplace imaginable. Of the nearly 5,000 strikes in 1946, only thirty-one involved more than 10,000 workers. Seamen and longshoremen on both coasts in different unions struck at different times. Other strikers included lumber workers in the Northwest; oil workers in the Southwest; retail clerks in Oakland; utility workers, transit workers, and truck drivers all over; teachers and other local government workers, and even the first airline pilots strike. Several of these local strikes, especially in workplaces that were not well organized nationally, led to general strikes like those in Rochester, Pittsburgh, and Oakland.

The strike wave was, in the words of radical labor reporter Art Preis, a "wage offensive," with the vast majority of strikes focused purely and simply on wage increases in a way that is actually quite rare in labor disputes. Most prewar strikes involved union recognition, but only 13 percent of 1945 strikes and 14 percent of 1946 strikes did. Likewise, jurisdictional strikes and other strikes caused by union rivalry were rare. Issues that would become important in the next decade—job security, workload, shop conditions, and policies—were involved in less than a fifth of the 1945–46 strikes. What a few years later would be dubbed "fringe benefits"—health insurance and pensions—were not an issue in any of the strikes, according to a detailed analysis by the Bureau of Labor Statistics.

The general result of the wage offensive was 18½ cents an hour. Given that a 1946 penny would be worth about a 11 cents today (2008), that is $2 an hour in today's money and about an 18 percent increase then and now. It was not enough, however, to achieve the general union goal or to overcome inflation in the next few years. The economics of the strike are explained in upcoming sections. Here it should be noted that bargaining was done in pennies per hour rather than in percentage terms, and this had the effect of giving larger percentage raises to lower-wage workers than to higher-wage ones. This was an explicit goal of the Congress of Industrial Organizations (CIO), but government mediators and American Federation of Labor (AFL) unions mostly followed this practice as well. Though nobody called it a "solidarity wage" at the time, that is what it was.

The strike wave was noteworthy for the relative absence of violence. The big national strikes were simply too large and widespread for employers to try to operate with scabs (or "replacement workers"). Smaller and more local employers sometimes tried to operate with a combination of supervisors and scabs, and this resulted in scores of picket-line skirmishes and some damage to supervisors' personal property. However, unlike previous decades, police and public officials were almost uniformly neutral, with a goal of controlling picket-line behavior rather than of helping employers break strikes. Employers, in response, usually did not endeavor to hire scabs and instead tried to outlast workers in long strikes during a time of increasing postwar unemployment.

Though strikes occurred everywhere, the vast majority of work time lost was in the Northeast and the Great Lakes industrial belt. In 1946, Pennsylvania alone accounted for 17 percent of "man days idled." Along with New York, Ohio, Michigan, and Illinois, these five states experienced more than half the total work time lost nationally. Massachusetts, Connecticut, New Jersey, West Virginia, Indiana, and Wisconsin accounted for another 25 percent. Outside this arc of "northern" states, only California had a significant percentage of the national work time lost (5 percent). These twelve states were the most populated and urbanized areas of the United States, which had a population about half of its current total (140 million in 1946). But though they included about half the population, these states accounted for more than 80 percent of strike activity.

These demographics are important to understanding how the widespread and often very deep local support strikers usually enjoyed coincided with a backlash that resulted in a Republican sweep of Congress in 1946, which then passed the anti-union Taft-Hartley Act in 1947. Though the backlash was nationwide, it was particularly strong in the more than thirty states where unions were weak. The Congress that was seated in 1947—long before the Supreme Court's "one-man, one-vote" rulings in the early 1960s—was heavily biased toward the representation of rural and small-town America not just in the Senate, but in the House of Representatives as well.

There is no comprehensive study of the 1945–46 strike wave as it was organized and experienced by workers and their unions. Most studies have focused on the policies and attempted policies of the Truman administration and the high-level negotiations that occurred with CIO and AFL leaders. Studies of individual unions and labor leaders cover the big national strikes—the CIO, the miners, and the railroad strikes—but the vast majority of strikes (as opposed to work time lost) were local and involved AFL-style unions, where the local union typically had much more power, financial resources, and autonomy than in the more centralized CIO unions, the UMWA, and the railroad brotherhoods. The American labor movement in 1946 was divided, often bitterly so, into these four parts. Not only were the CIO and the AFL rival federations, the rail unions were not affiliated with either, and John L. Lewis and the UMWA had been in and out of both federations over the previous decade and were always an independent force regardless of their current affiliation. The following account of the strike wave is organized by these four parts.

The Context: Reconversion Economics

During World War II, wages and prices were controlled by the federal government. In a full-employment war economy, inflation would have run riot without these controls. Indeed, the cost of living increased 11 percent in 1942, and government controls successfully reduced that to 1.7 percent in 1944 and 2.3 percent for all of 1945. The economic problem of converting to a peacetime economy was how to avoid both massive unemployment and runaway inflation. Unemployment was a threat due to the loss of production for war and the return of soldiers to the civilian labor force. As companies converted to producing consumer products for which demand had been bottled up during the war, they were eager to shed price controls. However, this would inevitably lead to the kind of inflation that would eventually depress the economy, particularly if pushed by wage increases for which workers were eager.

These macroeconomic dynamics were familiar to business, labor, and government, even though Keynesian macroeconomics was just emerging as an academic discipline and was not yet officially accepted by both political parties. Top leaders often confirmed the wisdom of "moderation" in wage and price increases and in basic power relations as they tried to prepare for the end of the war. The leaders of the AFL, CIO, and U.S. Chamber of Commerce, for example, signed a "Charter" in March 1945 that involved the Chamber accepting labor law and policy as it stood (versus repealing or amending the Wagner Act) and labor leaders pledging to continue a no-strike policy into the reconversion period. As historian Howell John Harris has commented, "The right or power of any one of [these] three men to sign on behalf of his organization, to say nothing of actually delivering the membership's practical assent, was very questionable"—and as it turned out, impossible. A larger and more representative gathering of business and labor leaders in November 1945, during the early stages of the strike wave, dealt mostly with principles of labor-management relations—that is, power relations—but provided no guidance on wages and prices. Meanwhile, union workers and local leaders focused on wages, and they developed a powerful public argument for a large increase of 30 cents per hour.

During the war, large companies—particularly those producing for the war, which was most of them—were assured of profits, but the so-called "Little Steel Formula" for allowing hourly wage increases was patently unfair to workers. As a result, hourly real wages had stagnated for most workers and declined for many. But with steady work and consistent overtime during the war (forty-eight hours a week was standard and fifty-two was not uncommon) and with overtime hours paid at time-and-a-half under the Fair Labor Standards Act of 1938, annual real incomes had risen substantially—by more than 30 percent since 1940. Since the average manufacturing wage was $1.02 an hour in 1945, a 30-cent hourly increase would be roughly 30 percent, which was the amount union researchers figured it would take to maintain workers' incomes while cutting back to forty hours a week. Furthermore, this magnitude of increased wages was necessary to replace war spending with adequate consumer demand; without it, the economy would slip back into a depression. By October 1945 this had become the unions' plan and program—first with CIO unions, then with others—despite ongoing attempts at moderation and labor statesmanship by CIO and AFL leaders. Unions argued that employers could afford this increase without raising prices, while companies maintained that they could not. The Auto Workers at General Motors, under the leadership of Walter Reuther, famously made a strike demand for a

This picket line was part of a strike by the United Auto Workers union against General Motors that lasted from November 21, 1945, to March 19, 1946. The strike was part of a widespread, postwar strike wave in which workers across the economy demanded higher wages to make up for the large price increases that took place during the war. Company leaders insisted they could not afford the wage increases, but refused to open their books to prove their professed poverty. (*Courtesy:* Walter P. Reuther Library, Wayne State University.)

30-cent increase without an increase in car prices and challenged GM to "open the books" to prove it could not afford the raise. This demand for increased wages without price increases was a common one. American unionists by 1945 thoroughly understood how a pay raise could be eaten away by an increase in the cost of living.

GM never opened its books and neither did any other company. In fact, management uniformly took special offense to the "open books" demand. Instead, President Truman appointed a series of fact-finding committees to study each industry and make recommendations. During the steel strike in January and February 1946, the fact finders came to the conclusion that 18½ cents was what the companies could afford to pay if steel prices were allowed to rise by $5.00 a ton. President Truman adopted this conclusion as official government policy, and Philip Murray, head of both the CIO and the United Steelworkers, accepted it as the basis for ending the steel strike. After that, 18½ cents was the official government standard, and though many unions resisted it as an unjustified limitation (including the Auto Workers at GM), most settled their 1946 contracts based on that standard (many without resorting to strikes).

As union researchers and many local leaders had argued, 18½ cents was not enough. Based on subsequent negotiations, the average manufacturing wage eventually increased to $1.33 an hour by 1948—the 30 percent increase sought in 1946—but by that time inflation had increased by 34 percent. What the wage increase gave, price increases took away.

The CIO Strikes

The CIO unions were not able to coordinate their bargaining and strike activity in the way that Phil Murray had hoped, but after acting independently (and sometimes antagonistically) the unions came together pretty impressively in the first three months of 1946. By January 21 more than 1.5 million CIO workers in four unions—the Auto Workers, Steelworkers, Electrical Workers, and Packinghouse Workers—were on strike at the same time. Though 18½ cents was not enough and though the government-brokered deal would unleash inflation, by March the CIO unions had set a national standard well above the 8 to 10 cents initially offered. They also demonstrated the feasibility of industry-wide bargaining that took wages out of competition, as well as the power and potential of disciplined collective action on a massive scale.

Murray had wanted to avoid postwar strikes and more than once had signaled his willingness to accept a smaller wage package if the government would continue to keep a lid on prices. It is doubtful that this approach had even a sliver of support among rank-and-file workers and local leaders, who faced layoffs and the loss of overtime work immediately after the war ended. From victory in Europe in May until October 1945, for example, average take-home pay had dropped almost 25 percent. The unauthorized "wildcat" strikes during the war increased after August 14, except now they sometimes received authorization after they began. The Auto Workers counted ninety such wildcats in the Detroit area alone in August and September, including one at Kelsey-Hayes where 4,500 strikers eventually idled some 50,000 Ford workers as well. Many of these were driven by local issues involving shop-floor power just as they had been during the war, but now the fear of returning to prewar living standards was the main driver. There was also a widespread desire among rank-and-file workers to demonstrate, to themselves and others, the ability they now thought they had to bring management to heel by shutting down production.

Postwar wildcats were often authorized by AFL unions, like the Teamsters and Machinists, after a strike had begun. AFL unions had and desired less centralized control, and in general they were happy to deal with one location and/or one employer at a time. Postwar wildcats were much more of a problem for CIO unions, whose industrial union concept required bargaining across entire industries, including every company and all its plants. This aspiration put CIO union leaders in the position of continuing to suppress wildcat strikes after the no-strike pledge no longer applied. They wanted national wages and national standards, and they expected help from their Democrat allies in the White House and Congress. They got less help than expected from the Truman administration, and what help they eventually did get required a complicated dance of substantive defiance and rhetorical statesmanship, always with an eye toward general public opinion, which sometimes ended up stoking their own members' restive militancy.

The CIO's strategy was to get some kind of government-pressured general agreement to raise wages and contain prices, and the Truman administration did call for a Labor-Management Conference in early November for a similar purpose. Though not without its accomplishments, that conference showed major corporations to be just as militantly resistant to large wage increases and any continued government interference with prices as rank-and-file workers were to returning to prewar living and working conditions. Wages were hardly even discussed at the conference, while by November the strike wave was well under way. As historian Robert H. Zeiger has chronicled, 200,000 coal miners had struck in September and were joined in October by 44,000 AFL lumber workers in the Northwest, 35,000 wildcatting AFL longshoremen in New York, and thousands of AFL truck drivers in the Midwest. Even CIO unions were out on authorized strikes by then–43,000 oil workers beginning in mid-September, glass workers in Pittsburgh, textile workers in New England, and a coalition of AFL and CIO machinists in the San Francisco Bay area. In addition, CIO auto, rubber, and steel workers were engaged in hundreds of usually short, local strikes—some authorized, some not.

After the November conference failed, the CIO's special relationship with the Democrats continued to be a yoke around Phil Murray's neck, though he skillfully made adjustments in just how tight the yoke was at any given time. On the other hand, according to historian Nelson Lichtenstein, Walter Reuther, who was then head of the Auto Workers' General Motors division (not yet president of the union), concluded it was past time to lead the ranks rather than follow or suppress them. In a move that broke not only with Murray but with UAW President R.J. Thomas and most other CIO union presidents, Reuther called the GM strike, which began November 21 and continued until March 19, 1946. Reuther invited 30,000 CIO Electrical Workers at GM to join the strike but their leadership refused, opening a wound that never did heal. Other CIO unions also held off, still trying to maneuver for a general government-brokered deal. America's giant corporations, however, made clear that they would not grant any significant wage increase without correlative price increases. It was also clear that they had no fear of strikes in 1945, during which a provision of the wartime excess profits tax allowed them tax deductions for any loss of income, such as those incurred in a strike.

Though high-level negotiations continued with both employers and politicians, as 1946 began it was evident to all those paying attention that large CIO strikes would be necessary to force the Truman administration to make a decision that the companies could then be bullied into accepting by a combination of political and direct economic pressure. With the UAW strike at GM and many others grinding on (plus hundreds more flashing into and out of existence locally and regionally), the United Electrical, Machine & Radio Workers Union (UE) was the first to go on January 15. The UE finally put GM's last 30,000 production workers on the street, and, more importantly, 200,000 additional UE workers shut down each and every General Electric and Westinghouse plant in the United States and Canada. The next day 125,000 CIO Packinghouse Workers, in coalition with 90,000 AFL Amalgamated Meat Cutters, shut down Armour, Swift, Wilson, Cudahy, and Morrell—the major meatpackers of the time. Five days later, on January 21, three-quarters of a million Steelworkers finally got their chance to participate, shutting down not only all of basic steel from Baltimore to Oakland, Buffalo to Birmingham and everything in between (including Pittsburgh, Cleveland, Gary, and Chicago), but also hundreds of fabricating plants that bent and shaped steel and other metals.

Despite continued sniping among CIO leaders and still more between the AFL and the CIO, late January and early February witnessed the single greatest display of worker solidarity in American history. Unlike all the wildcat strikes during and after the war—many of which pitted department against department, plant against plant, leadership against ranks, and sometimes white against black—the 1946 CIO strikes brought everybody together for the same purpose. This included everyone from the same company in all its locations, everybody (or almost everybody) in the same industry and, indeed, in several different industries at once.

Shutting down the operations of the likes of GE, GM, U.S. Steel, and Armour & Company, let alone entire industries, and doing so in a highly disciplined and orderly way must have been exhilarating for the strikers. From 1892 until 1946, for example, steelworkers had never conducted a successful strike, with everybody going out (and coming back) at the same time. Historian Ronald Schatz marveled at the UE's "success in shutting down every GE and Westinghouse plant . . . a feat which had never before been accomplished [or tried] in the history of the industry." Reuther biographer Nelson Lichtenstein comments: "The UAW had never before been able to shut down all of General Motors, so for even veterans of the 1930s the postwar stoppage was exhilarating and cathartic."

The 1946 settlement (18½ cents) was inferior not only as measured against the 30-cent-an-hour goal, but even against the 19½ cents that Truman's auto fact-finders had recommended in late 1945. Even so, the companies resisted it for three or four weeks, until the strikes started to bite economically and the government relented on price increases. Still, if the unions did not get all they wanted, for the first time ever they had a hand in determining the national result. Reuther and his Auto Workers held out for that extra penny until mid-March (and did not get it), but by then most big corporations had fallen in line, including RCA, Ford, Chrysler, and the Big Four rubber companies, without company-wide strikes.

In the end, the CIO had forced a nationally standardized wage increase. It was not large enough, but it was the first and only time such a thing has ever happened. The well-organized, highly disciplined strikes across entire industries, especially as so many of them came together in late January, were stirring affirmations of the old union slogan "in unity there is strength"—and, in this case, 18½ cents.

Coal and Rail Strikes

With the conclusion of the CIO strikes in March, the main act of the postwar strike wave was over. The rest of the wave would be about unions and employers who resisted the steel settlement. In the end, almost all ended up accepting it or something very similar. On the union side, the UMWA, a powerful union in an essential industry, was the primary exception. The miners pocketed the 18½ cents, and then fought for and won a new welfare and retirement fund based on a 5-cent royalty for each ton of coal mined. Other exceptions were the Locomotive Engineers and Railroad Trainmen who, unlike the other rail brotherhoods, refused to arbitrate their wage demands and instead engaged in a politically disastrous strike.

Both contemporary observers and historians have seen the strike wave in general as a primary cause of the Republican takeover of Congress in 1946 and the resulting Taft-Hartley Act in 1947. The voting public was inconvenienced, sometimes seriously so, by one strike after another, and it would defy common sense if many of them were not fed up with strikes, even if they were workers who had been on strike themselves. But the CIO strikes and, as we will see, many local strikes had strong popular support (as well as bitter opposition from the business class and the press), with many picket lines reportedly "festive" and "celebratory" as nonstrikers mingled with pickets. Most unions, especially those belonging to the CIO, routinely made the case that they were fighting not just for themselves, but for a general wage increase and an "American standard of living," and at different times and places this resonated deeply with a wide public. The mine and rail strikes were the very opposite of this. Whatever public approbation had been won through the CIO strikes in the first three months of 1946 was dissipated and worse by the big national strikes of April and May. Had these negotiations been settled without strikes, the politics of 1946 would have had a very different cast.

According to his biographers Melvyn Dubofsky and Warren Van Tine, UMWA President John L. Lewis was "one of the most hated men in America" in the 1940s. The nation's dependence on coal for home heating and industrial uses also made him one of the most powerful men in America, and he used that power to deny the nation coal while it was at war. He had defied government agencies, President Roosevelt, and the public with a series of strikes in 1943 that won miners "portal-to-portal pay" and Lewis the damnation of the Army's popular newspaper *Stars and Stripes*: "Speaking for the American soldier, John L. Lewis, damn your coal-black soul." To be fair, Lewis was mostly reacting to spontaneous wildcat strikes that swept through the coal fields in 1943, and he never technically violated the no-strike pledge, though the various winking and nodding he did with his members through the public press was transparent to all. The public often sympathized with the miners, so politicians (above all, Franklin Roosevelt) focused all their ire on Lewis, who seemed to relish the attention, even the public contempt, and worked hard to foster the notion that he was in control.

In 1946 Lewis was in firm control as he strutted upon the national stage with a series of flamboyant maneuvers that resulted in a six-week nationwide strike beginning April 1. By May coal was so scarce that the steel industry cut production by one-half, and many auto plants were forced to close for lack of steel. According to Dubofsky and Van Tine, "The Office of Defense Transportation clamped a tight embargo on rail freight and reduced passenger service 25 percent. Harry Truman dimmed the lights in the White House, and . . . New York's Great White Way lost its glow." The federal government then seized the mines, as it had done in 1943, and eventually acceded to most of Lewis's demands before handing them back to the coal companies in late May. Besides the establishment of a pension fund, the union won control of what had been a company-run medical and health program. These were important breakthroughs in 1946, when very few workers had pensions or health insurance, but they were overshadowed by virulent public animosity toward Lewis and now toward "monopoly unions" and their Democrat allies as well.

Into this mix stepped two railroad unions with the power to shut down the nation's primary transportation system. With air transport still in its infancy and the beginnings of the interstate highway system still a few years away, the rail strike had an immediate impact on its very first day, May 23, as perishable food began to rot and passengers were stranded all over the country. Little that needed transporting moved, including coal, to the visible delight of John L. Lewis, who had suspended the coal strike by then but did not yet have an agreement. Under these mounting pressures, President Truman had something of a political nervous breakdown. Having entertained the notion of drafting miners up to the age of sixty-five, which would include Lewis, Truman went to the House of Representatives on the second day of the rail strike and requested "temporary emergency" legislation that would allow him to draft the rail strikers into the U.S. Army. By a vote of 306 to 13, the House immediately approved Truman's request. The Engineers and Trainmen then decided to take their chances with an arbitrator rather than with the U.S. Senate, and the strike was settled only forty-eight hours after it had begun. Though some aides were concerned with Truman's emotional stability, the House vote reflected broad public approval. The rail unions' leaders were not public lightning rods like Lewis, but neither were they skilled at public relations, as they projected befuddled incompetence and prideful arrogance in about equal measure. Beyond the bad PR, substantively the Engineers and Trainmen, like the mine workers, wanted more than the 18½-cent standard that had been fought out through the CIO strikes. All the other rail unions did too, but they had agreed to arbitrate their differences. As a result, the Engineers and Trainmen were easy to tag as but "a few selfish men," according to Truman biographer David McCullough.

AFL and Local Strikes

By the summer of 1946, a wage pattern had been set and the big national strikes were over. Most of the 1945–46 strike wave took place in thousands of workplaces and hundreds of localities far from the national stage. In 1946, there were thirty-seven strikes involving 10,000 or more workers. In addition, there were more than 4,900 smaller strikes, some involving thousands of workers, some mere handfuls. In the fall of 1945, these local strikes fueled and shaped the big national events; there was an upsurge in strikes in April and May after the national wage standard had been set and then a final outburst in the fall of 1946. But local strikes were continuous throughout the eighteen months after the war, and the vast majority of them involved unions that were affiliated with the American Federation of Labor, by far the largest federation of unionized American workers.

The Oakland General Strike began on December 1, 1946, sparked by the refusal of streetcar operators and bus drivers to cross police cordons set up to escort scab trucks across the picket lines of 425 striking clerks at Hastings' and Kahn's department stores in downtown Oakland. The next day, angry at having been "scabbed on," Teamsters marched downtown and gathered in front of the two stores, which faced each other across Latham Square. On December 3, 142 unions in the Alameda County American Federation of Labor declared a "work holiday" and about 100,000 workers walked off their jobs. (Photographer: Dan Breault. *Courtesy:* Fred Glass, Communications Director, California Federation of Teachers, and *Oakland's "Work Holiday": A Pictorial History of the 1946 General Strike*, by Gifford Hartman, forthcoming. See Oakland General Strike Archive & Resource Guide at www.FlyingPicket.org.)

By the 1940s AFL unions had industrial organizations within them—that is, workplaces organized "wall to wall" with all occupations in the same union rather than being divided into different unions by craft—but because most of the dues money in an AFL union stays at the local level, most of the bargaining gets done there as well. The CIO unions and the UMWA drove larger and more dramatic strike actions because they organized and bargained industry-wide across the country. Their strikes inevitably drew national attention, including the interference of the president and Congress. AFL strikes, on the other hand, happened locally and usually drew only local attention.

For this reason and because the vast majority of AFL strikes were scattered across a large country over eighteen months, we know little about them. Fortunately, cultural historian George Lipsitz has given us a glimpse into several particularly dramatic struggles in Stamford (Connecticut), Lancaster (Pennsylvania), Rochester, Pittsburgh, and Oakland, which he calls "general strikes." AFL Machinists in Stamford, for example, briefly wildcatted in September 1945, then went out on an authorized strike in November that lasted five months; in the middle of the strike the 3,000 Machinists drew 10,000 other Stamford workers out of work for rallies and picket-line support. In Lancaster, striking trolley and bus drivers in February 1946 were supported by a three-day "labor holiday," during which 14,000 workers from twenty-three AFL unions engaged in sympathy strikes that helped move the transit company to settle.

In Rochester, 489 city workers were fired for forming a chapter of the American Federation of State, County, and Municipal Employees (AFSCME) in May, and got their jobs back only after 30,000 private-sector workers quit work to rally in support of them in downtown Rochester. In September, 2,000 clerks, construction workers, meter readers, and repairmen in an independent union at Duquesne Power & Light in Pittsburgh elicited sympathy stoppages from thousands of Steelworkers at Jones & Laughlin and Electrical Workers at Westinghouse, as well as streetcar operators, bus drivers, and others. And, in November 1946, Teamsters in Oakland refused to cross the somewhat porous picket lines of some 1,000 AFL retail workers striking two department stores; when Oakland police tried to escort scab trucks from Los Angeles past the pickets, a struggle ensued that caused the Alameda County AFL to call a general strike, in which some 100,000 workers participated at its height.

These and many other local strikes involved "labor holidays," "sympathy strikes," and "secondary boycotts" of the sort that would be banned and limited by the Taft-Hartley Act. Local work stoppages that had no claim to being "general strikes" need much more study if we are to properly understand the way the strike wave shaped subsequent labor-management relations and, indeed, postwar America as a whole.

Conclusion

According to historian Barton Bernstein, AFL President William Green, CIO President Phil Murray, and Chamber of Commerce head Eric Johnston arrived at an agreement with the Truman administration's Office of Price Administration (OPA) in September 1945 that probably would have been better than the 18½ cents that became the standard. It involved a 10-cent wage raise and the continuation of both government price controls and the no-strike pledge. Assuming the price controls could have been effectively enforced, this would likely have been a better deal for workers because less of their wage increase would have been eaten up by inflation. Further, the steel settlement in February allowed the companies to pass all or most of their increased labor costs on to consumers via price increases, regardless of any productivity improvements or overall profitability, establishing a precedent for the postwar period that could be (and was) used to pit consumers against workers. What is more, if there had been a happy ending by October 1, there might not have been a strike wave with its polarizing effect on public opinion, and thus no Republican Congress in 1947–48 and no Taft-Hartley Act.

The Green-Murray-Johnston-OPA deal fell apart because of internal disagreements within the Truman administration. But it is hard to imagine that, even if consummated, such an agreement could have held. The U.S. Chamber of Commerce did not reflect business opinion at the time, where the main goal was to do away with government price controls. In fact, many employers, particularly at the local level, were not yet reconciled to living with their unions after the war, and many more were not yet convinced that their unions could actually organize a strike and maintain order among their diverse members.

On the labor side, what Green and Murray failed to realize in September was that the wild congeries of unions that came out of World War II were a genuine social movement. Millions of workers wanted to strike—some simply because they could, some to show the boss their assembled power in the postwar world, and some because they needed release for all the bottled-up anger, the daily indignities of the war years—and millions of these people would strike regardless of any prestrike wage-price deal. The amazing thing was that most Ford, Chrysler, RCA, and Goodyear workers and millions of others did not strike when their leaders asked them not to.

If Murray or Green or Truman—or the Chamber of Commerce, for that matter—had been in charge, a better arrangement for workers might have been achieved in the first few years after the war. But nobody was in charge, none of the contenders knew who had what power, and that in a way was the point of the strikers, particularly those who struck without authorization from their top leadership. In the end, the postwar strike wave demonstrated that union workers would accept leadership to achieve discipline and unity, what Walter Reuther called "power under control," but not without testing their collective power against their employers and not without pushing the political system to see what might be achieved. The immediate result, politically and economically, was disappointing, particularly when contrasted with the mass and scope of worker activity. But the strike wave affected not just the first few years after the war, but the next quarter century (and more). Over time, the results achieved by the American labor movement, for both union members and workers in general, were much more salutary and impressive.

See also: Strikes in the United States Since World War II, 226; Steel on Strike, 360; Unionizing the "Jungle": A Century of Meatpacking Strikes, 375; Automobile Workers' Strikes, 389; Rubber Workers' Strikes, 398; The Redwood Lumber and Sawmill Workers' Strike, 438; Coal Miners on Strike and the Formation of a National Union, 449; Seafarers' Strikes in American History, 534; Strikes on the Port of New York, 1945–1960, 559; Retail Workers' Strikes, 620.

Bibliography

Bernstein, Barton. "The Truman Administration and the Steel Strike of 1946," *The Journal of American History* 52 (March 1966): 791–803.

Dubofsky, Melvyn, and Warren Van Tine. *John L. Lewis: A Biography*. Urbana: University of Illinois Press, 1986.

Harris, Howell John. *The Right to Manage: Industrial Relations Policies of American Business in the 1940s*. Madison: University of Wisconsin Press, 1982.

Lichtenstein, Nelson. *The Most Dangerous Man in Detroit: Walter Reuther and the Fate of American Labor*. New York: Basic Books, 1995.

Lipsitz, George. *"A Rainbow at Midnight": Class and Culture in Cold War America*. South Hadley, MA: Bergin & Garvey, 1982.

Preis, Art. *Labor's Giant Step: Twenty Years of the CIO*. New York: Pathfinder Press, 1964.

Rosenberg, Samuel. *American Economic Development Since 1945*. New York: Palgrave Macmillan, 2003.

Schatz, Ronald W. *The Electrical Workers: A History of Labor at General Electric and Westinghouse 1923–60*. Urbana: University of Illinois Press, 1983.

"Work Stoppages Caused by Labor-Management Disputes in 1945." *Monthly Labor Review* LXII, no. 5 (May 1946): 718–35.

"Work Stoppages Caused by Labor-Management Disputes in 1946." *Monthly Labor Review* LXIV, no. 5 (May 1947): 780–800.

Zieger, Robert H. *The CIO 1935–1955*. Chapel Hill: University of North Carolina Press, 1995.

STRIKES IN THE UNITED STATES SINCE WORLD WAR II

Nicola Pizzolato

During the Second World War, the American Federation of Labor (AFL) and the Congress of Industrial Organizations (CIO) agreed to a "no-strike pledge" committing their members to refrain from any work stoppages for the duration of the conflict and to settle all labor-management disputes through the National War Labor Board (NWLB). The Roosevelt administration instituted the board with the aim to maintain labor peace, which had become critical for war production. The no-strike pledge was both a patriotic and a strategic decision on the part of AFL and CIO. In fact, as the U.S. economy became the "arsenal of democracy," strikes fueled anti-labor sentiments because they could be easily portrayed as undermining the war effort. However, embarrassingly for union leaders, "wildcat" strikes not authorized by union leaders did occur during the war. The disruption caused by these strikes, as well as a major coal strike led by the United Mine Workers (not affiliated to the CIO), prompted the passing of stricter legislation (the Smith-Connally Act in 1943) that gave the federal government the ability to seize industries threatened by strikers. The act also aimed at weakening the ties between labor and the Democratic Party, as it prohibited unions from making contributions in federal elections. Notwithstanding this restriction, the war represented a time of extraordinary growth for the labor movement. By the end of the conflict, union membership had risen to 14.7 million from 8.9 million in 1939, making unions powerful organizations that expected to be actors in the postwar transformation of American society.

The 1946 Strike Wave

The end of the war released unions from their no-strike pledge. There was a rapid increase in the number and length of strikes, culminating in an unparalleled wave of labor protest that shut down not only single plants but entire industries. The statistics are impressive. Consider the number of strike days per month: 4 million in September 1945, 8 million in October, 20 million in January 1946. In that year, 4,985 strikes took place involving 4.6 million workers for a total of 116 million days. Strikes occurred in industries related to war production, such as the automobile, steel, electrical, shipbuilding, and coal industries, which had been affected during the war by a "wage-freeze" policy aimed at containing inflation, and also in telephone, railway, lumber, meatpacking, and other industries. Workers speculated that a renewed depression would follow reconversion to civil activities, and momentary cutbacks and plant closures appeared to confirm their concerns. Workers and union leaders also worried about a repeat of the post–World War I open-shop and wage-cutting drive, and their fears fueled strike participation. In fact, the strike wave pit union leaders who envisioned stronger economic and political power for the labor movement against corporate managers who wished to roll back much of the New Deal legislation and regain the "moral leadership" of the country that they had lost during the Depression.

The longest (November 1945 to March 1946) and most significant of these confrontations, the United Automobile Workers (UAW) strike against General Motors, should be understood within this framework. The 113-day GM strike shut all of the company's plants. Most were concentrated in Detroit, Flint, Toledo, and Cleveland. The UAW demanded a 30 percent wage increase without a rise in the price of cars. Walter Reuther, who was to emerge as one of the leading progressive figures in the labor movement, claimed that thanks to the rise in productivity during the war GM had the ability to pay, and provocatively asked the company to open its books to a panel of government experts to show otherwise. Reuther argued that only a redistribution of income could forestall another depression by sustaining consumers' spending. If wage hikes were passed on to consumers they would undermine sustained growth. He called on the government to maintain price controls and living standards for the working class. President Harry S. Truman, however, refused to assume such a role.

By not giving full support to the UAW, Truman encouraged GM to resist the kind of social ambitions that labor leaders had nurtured during the war. GM manager Charles Wilson, on behalf of the entire business community, upheld the principle that unions should not intrude in management matters such as prices, profits, or organization of work. Therefore, the GM strike was essentially about what sphere organized labor would occupy in the postwar period. Eventually, settlements by the United Steelworkers and United Electrical Workers undermined the UAW's position. With little space for political maneuvering, the UAW had no alternative but to accept the principle that the wage increases would eventually be passed on to the consumer. Although the final settlement did not deliver the promised wage increase to autoworkers, it launched Walter Reuther to the leadership of the UAW and, six years later, of the CIO.

The unprecedented power of unions to coordinate nationwide stoppages of different plants of the same company, as shown in the GM case, intensified calls from conservative legislators, employers, and managers to curb the influence of organized labor. As historian Elizabeth Fones-Wolf recounts, business writer Whiting Williams encapsulated the perception of the business community by arguing that the strike wave was as catastrophic an event as the Civil War. From the business perspective, postwar strikes demonstrated that organized labor had opened a new chapter in its attacks upon managerial prerogatives; equally threatening was its social agenda, which found particular support among industrial workers, based on the welfare state and the social protection of workers' rights. Most alarming for those who fought against labor and the New Deal was the greater legitimacy and support that strikers and unions enjoyed among the general public as well as the networks of solidarity that they created.

The rash of general strikes that took place in cities as far apart as Stamford, Connecticut, and Oakland, California, showed that strikers fighting for the legitimacy of the union movement enjoyed widespread support in the community. A case in point is the Oakland general strike of December 1946, in which more than 100,000 workers in 142 AFL locals stopped work for two days in solidarity with the clerks of Hastings' and Kahn's department stores, who were on strike for union recognition and whose jobs were endangered by the strikebreaking techniques of management and city officials. As the word spread that Hastings' and Kahn's, together with the police, were bringing in strikebreakers, workers shut down all the factories and public transit in the area and effectively halted almost all the commerce. The strike was an inebriating experience for those who took part in it. Many participants in the strike sang and danced in the streets in what they called a "work holiday."

In Stamford, strikers who marched in protest against the attempt of the town's largest employer to revert to a union-free shop carried placards that read: "We will not go back to old days." The slogan graphically conveyed the spirit of this crucial period in American history. The strike wave reacted against business' endeavors to reestablish labor relations according to the tenets of the free enterprise system. But it also consolidated fears that organized labor would gain a prominent position in the society and "dictate" its agenda to the government. Although only a portion of the strikes successfully achieved their aims (especially in terms of wage increases), they demonstrated that the open-shop and union-busting strategy of the 1920s was no longer a viable strategy, at least for a while. Thus, the strike wave played an important part in shaping both postwar industrial relations and the social and economic options available for the labor movement.

The Impact of the Taft-Hartley Act

The strike wave of 1946 acted as a catalyst for changes in labor law, particularly the implementation of curbs on the power of organized labor envisaged by the political alliance of Republicans and Southern conservatives. The reformation of existing labor legislation was the result of intense lobbying from business associations, such as the National Association of Manufacturers (NAM), and corporate leaders. NAM's public relations program exemplified the type of anti-union propaganda that called for an amendment of the too-liberal Wagner Act (1935). The association poured half of its $2.5 million budget into advertising, printed millions of leaflets, and sponsored radio series and motion pictures. Business propaganda labeled opponents as Communist "fellow-travelers" and proved crucial in supporting the passage of the Taft-Hartley Act over President Truman's veto. The AFL asserted that Taft-Hartley constituted a "slave-labor bill."

Finally approved in June 1947, the Taft-Hartley Act restricted in several ways unions' space for maneuvering both at the shop floor and at the national level, and it did so primarily by hitting at their capacity to organize strikes and enlist new members. The act defined strikes as practices that have "the intent or the necessary effect of burdening or obstructing commerce . . . [and] impair the interest of the public in the free flow of such commerce." The act prohibited "secondary boycott" strikes and "common situs" picketing of the type that had been so effective during the general strikes of 1946, thereby crippling working-class solidarity. The ban on "jurisdictional" strikes eliminated the possibility of unions having a say in the assignment of a particular task to a worker or to protest the assignment of a job to a member of another union. Title II of the act allowed the U.S. president to seek an injunction to suspend for sixty days strikes that "imperil[ed] the national health." This clause, although never seriously implemented, was intended to lower public support for unions by portraying them as selfish economic actors who were harmful to the interests of the nation. With a similar intent, Title III facilitated the suability of unions for breaches of contract, as in the case of wildcat strikes.

Other provisions concerned strikes indirectly, but in a no-less-effective manner. The act emphasized the employee's right to refrain from collective activity and allowed states to pass "right-to-work" laws that banned the union shop altogether, making it more difficult for unions to represent workers under the rule of the National Labor Relations Board (NLRB), while under the terms of the law only certified unions could lawfully call a strike. Restricting the possible pool of union members motivated the act's redefinition of the term "employee" in a way that excluded foremen, thereby impeding the efforts of these workers to build a union in the form of the Foremen's Association of America. Organizing a union had brought foremen nearer to the CIO and threatened to deprive management of a fundamental instrument to govern the shop floor. Manufacturers' victory in keeping foremen strictly on management's side represented an insurmountable barrier for the expansion of workers' rights to strike to other categories of employees. Finally, the law required union officials to sign an affidavit declaring that they were not supporters of the Communist Party. The NLRB would not acknowledge unions that did not comply, depriving them of the protection of labor law. This clause opened a period of internal struggle (especially within the CIO) that resulted in the purge of Communist-led unions and Communist officers. While the majority of CIO members were not Communists, in the 1930s Communists did play a significant role in building the organization. Communists occupied key posts in the United Electrical, Radio and Machine Workers (UE); the Food, Tobacco, Agricultural, and Allied Workers (FTA); and the International Longshore and Warehouse Union (ILWU). The purge of Communists took away from organized labor the staunchest strike organizers and recruiters of unskilled workers.

The act was important for the development of organized labor and its subsequent decline in several ways: it curtailed workers' ability to settle disputes outside arbitration and grievance procedures, thereby fixing the character of American industrial relations for the following twenty years; it left employees vulnerable to changes in managers' strategy; and it limited the collaboration among unions and encouraged the pursuit of highly particularistic bargaining strategies in dealings with employers. The postwar decline in strikes demonstrates that the Taft-Hartley Act successfully impaired working-class militancy, deprived unions of the possibility of pursuing a strategy of structural reform of the American political economy, and restricted unionization within a core of industries and states.

Collective Bargaining and Strikes

Despite the restrictions it imposed, the Taft-Hartley Act was not the "vicious piece of Fascist legislation" that UAW's Walter Reuther claimed it to be. However, by undermining unions' ability and ultimately workers' right to strike, it did confine unions into the straitjacket of collective bargaining structures. Collective bargaining pursued economic efficiency and orderly industrial relations by rendering most types of strikes illegal during the life of the contract. It transformed shop stewards into guardians of the rank and file insofar as they had to restrain workers' actions that violated the contract. As early as the late 1940s, radical sociologist C. Wright Mills pointed out that in the new system unions effectively shared management's role in disciplining the personnel.

Collective bargaining also affected the internal structure of unions. Because only full-time officials could administer the complex body of contract rules, unions became complex bureaucratic organizations. Instead of protesting via strikes or other workplace actions, workers' only option was to file a grievance in response to a "speed-up" or a safety hazard. Officials at the local level were responsible for the application of the contract, including keeping workers in line. A precondition for a strike vote was that every step of the grievance procedure had been exhausted. At every stage, union and management negotiated to solve the problem according to the contract. Often grievances were solved with a *quid pro quo* between the two sides. For instance, management could revoke a disciplinary action toward a worker if the union, in exchange, pardoned an increase of the work pace. If the grievance could not be solved at the lower level of the hierarchy it would move higher, until eventually it would be submitted to arbitration by a neutral third party with a binding decision. Only in the instance that this procedure failed to solve the issue could a majority of the local members go on strike. In the case of the UAW, a strike needed further authorization from the International Executive Board. In any case, the sheer volume of grievances meant that only a small proportion was ever submitted to this procedure.

Formally, the rules governing this system committed the union to internal democracy; in reality though, they reinforced the decision-making power of the union hierarchies at the expense of the rank and file. Union officials maneuvered with great skill to allow for the possibility of a strike at the end of a contract period. A brief strike had a cathartic effect on the workforce, functioning as a safety valve—it let out the frustration of working conditions, met the expectations of the membership, and reminded the company of the union's potential power of mobilization. Management adjusted unwillingly to the power held by unions, but from its point of view, collective bargaining functioned well in neutralizing strikes—or at least making them difficult.

In many instances, workers contested this set of constraints on shop-floor activism by engaging in "wildcat" strikes and infringing upon the grievance procedure. By taking part in these illegal activities, they lost the protection of the union and became vulnerable to company reprisals. Technological changes, soon labeled "automation," introduced into several industries automatic transfer machines that moved material between different assembly lines without workers. Labor-saving devices made it easier for management to argue the need to revise well-established work practices. It was the spread of automation that often triggered wildcat strikes against management as well as against unions' policy to trade off the introduction of new technology with higher wages and benefits for those who remained employed. Eventually, the deployment of automation, which often made it more convenient to build a new plant in another location instead of updating old ones, became a formidable deterrent against strikes.

While levels of industrial action moderately declined from the mid-1950s, they remained high in industries where the speeding-up of production meant harsh working conditions. This was the case in the steel industry, which was hit by strikes throughout the decade. These confrontations usually came to an end with the industry handing out wage increases offset by higher prices to the customers. The 1952 steel strike, which lasted fifty-three days, involved a full-scale dispute with the government. President Truman refused to offset the wage increase that the union demanded with higher prices and, in order to avert a new strike that would cripple the economy in the midst of the Korean War, decided to seize the industry and force strikers back to work. The Supreme Court later declared Truman's decision unconstitutional.

A turning point for the steel industry and for the American industrial landscape was the 1959 strike, which lasted an unprecedented 116 days and affected 540,000 union members. The strike originated in U.S. Steel's resolve to curb workers' wages and the size of crews, and to impose a new set of work rules. The United Steel Workers (USW) was equally adamant that it would not give an inch on these issues. After Eisenhower threatened to apply the section of Taft-Hartley Act that allowed the president to suspend the strike, the two parties eventually worked out a contract. However, the big steel corporations against whom the unionized workers fought had lost shares of the market to foreign imports and small, nonunionized mills (the "mini-mills"). This began a disastrous downward spiral that eventually led to a wave of plant shutdowns in the 1980s.

Despite these setbacks, the 1950s was a decade of achievement for the labor movement—in 1954 union membership stood at about 17 million and represented 34.7 percent of nonagricultural workers—but the challenges that it faced prefigured the decline that was to follow. Management only grudgingly accepted the very existence of unions. Historian Nelson Lichtenstein has questioned the traditional idea that a "labor-management accord" in which "big labor" and corporations bargained on equal footing ever existed. Unions also faced challenges from insurgent members who believed that shop-floor bargaining and conflict and not the legalist "contractualism" that regulated the workplace was the way to protect and advance workers' rights.

The 1960s: Strikes and Civil Rights

The most formidable critique of collective bargaining and its effect on the daily life of workers did not come from the relatively small number of disenchanted shop-floor activists who remembered the militant days of the 1930s, but from the new ranks of workers who joined the industrial workforce in the 1960s.

Before the late 1960s, it was skilled white men among mechanics and craftsmen in the IAM, UAW, and USW who created the most trouble for the union leadership by refusing to subscribe to the collective agreements signed by their central representatives and by going on strike to defend their prerogatives and raise their wages. However, the spread of the Civil Rights movement, the escalation of the Vietnam War, and the growth of Black Power and the New Left encouraged the emergence of a new generation of militant workers who did not recall the CIO's organizing days or its postwar battles for social reforms.

Two of the more well-known strikes of the 1960s illustrate the connection between workers' rights and civil rights. In 1965 the National Farm Workers Organization (NFWO, later the United Farm Workers, or UFW) led a five-year strike of migrant grape pickers in Delano, California. Their leaders were two charismatic figures, César Chávez and Dolores Huerta. The Delano strike addressed the issues of hazardous work conditions; wage differentials among *braceros* (Mexican contract workers), Filipinos, and Mexican Americans; and the workers' poor living conditions. However, the goal of the strike went beyond these typical workers' requests to include recognition of these ethnic workers as first-class American citizens. It was a fight for dignity as well as for wages.

Chávez and Huerta used innovative techniques that gained them national and worldwide attention. Inspired by Gandhi (and in concurrence with Martin Luther King, Jr.), they insisted that the strike remain nonviolent, even in face of police assault and intimidation. In several instances, Chávez fasted to call attention to the migrants' cause and to oppose the use of pesticides on grapes and the employment of illegal aliens as strikebreakers. The Delano strike was accompanied by a nationwide call to boycott California grapes. The call was successful, and all over the country activists picketed grocery stores, holding placards with slogans such as "Every Grape You Buy Keeps a Child Hungry." The UFW could call for boycotts because farm workers fell outside the terms of the Taft-Hartley Act. An epic moment of the strike was the grape pickers' march from Delano to the state capital of California in Sacramento, a 350-mile trek that dramatized *La Causa,* as the strikers were calling their endeavor, and elicited a sympathetic response from the public. The campaign ended in 1970; by that time the UFW had signed contracts with major grocers and employers covering about 10,000 workers and their families. The success of the Delano strike seems therefore to suggest that only innovative strike tactics could revitalize the labor movement.

While industrial relations scholars and consultants saw strikes as simple economic disputes, the connection between workers' rights and civil rights showed that they were often struggles for social justice. The 1968 Memphis sanitation workers' strike is another case in point. The walkout started in February 1968 and originated from garbage workers' grievances about working conditions and wage discrimination. Sanitation workers in Memphis were for the most part African-American, while their supervisors were exclusively white. These workers lived below the poverty line and worked in an appallingly dangerous environment. The death of two black workers accidentally crushed by a malfunctioning garbage compactor was one of the issues that fueled the strike.

Dr. Martin Luther King Jr. went to Memphis several times in 1968 to support the strike of African-American sanitation workers. Hard at work launching the Poor People's Movement, he saw the strike as a way to expand the civil rights movement to encompass economic rights. During the strike, he gave some of his most inspiring speeches, insisting that "now is the time for justice." (Photographer unknown, Press Scimitar, Memphis, Tennessee. *Courtesy:* Mississippi Valley Collection, Special Collections, University of Memphis Libraries.)

The strikers demanded the recognition of the American Federation of State, County, and Municipal Employees (AFSCME) Local 1733 (which had no official status because the city of Memphis did not accept bargaining agents for municipal employees) as well as wage increases, overtime pay, and equal treatment in promotion and retirement benefits. From the outset, the strike combined a racial struggle with an economic one. The black community coalesced on the issues of underemployment, job discrimination, and residential segregation that had long divided the city along racial lines. On the other hand, the business community, the city press, and the majority of the white population backed the strikers' opponent, Mayor Henry Loeb, who resisted the strike by employing strikebreakers to continue garbage collection, albeit only partially. Police brutality against strikers and demonstrators on two instances further inflamed the protest of the black community. The protesters' slogan "I AM A MAN" encapsulated the need for recognition of black people's dignity and the basic demand to be treated as citizens with equal rights. This slogan was later reprised in civil rights struggles elsewhere.

As in the Delano campaign, strikers in Memphis adopted a wide range of tactics including mass meetings, boycott of businesses using discriminating labor practices, picketing, and even a mock funeral in front of the municipality (freedom was the symbolic victim). Martin Luther King Jr. supported the strike as part of his Poor People's Campaign. King's speech on March 18 gained national media coverage for the strike, which soon came to symbolize the grievances of the working poor everywhere in the country. King returned to Memphis on March 29 to lead a march that ended with the police attacking the crowd with nightsticks, tear gas, and gunfire. On this occasion, police killed Larry Payne, one of the many high school students who had joined the protest. Events reached an even more dramatic climax when Dr. King returned a third time to support the strike, in defiance of court prohibition to lead other marches. King's "I've Been to the Mountaintop" address delivered to the strikers' rally was to be remembered as his last speech, as he was assassinated the next day. In the aftermath of the national outpouring surrounding King's death, AFSCME became the largest union local in the city.

The assassination of King and the massive riots that ensued all over the United States formed the backdrop for a new, powerful wave of wildcat strikes in those cities where the workplace discontent of black workers mixed with the insurgent protest of the urban riots. In Detroit, African Americans had made major inroads into the car plants during the wartime labor shortage, occasionally as strikebreakers, and in those occupations that white workers would no longer accept at lower pay, such as in the forges or as janitors. The skilled trades, such as the tool and die makers and the electricians, continued to be the reserve of white labor. However, with the boom in car production in the mid-1960s, Detroit's African Americans entered the assembly line. Most of them regarded the UAW as a bureaucratic organization extorting their union dues and disciplining the workforce on the account of the corporation.

In 1968, DRUM (Dodge Revolutionary Union Movement) organized black workers on the assembly line at Chrysler. As they joined the wildcat strikes, these black workers demonstrated that they were in a crucial, though alienating, position in the production process, able to disrupt production in the whole plant with effects that reverberated also in other plants. The strikes spread to other major automobile companies, and the following year different revolutionary groups coalesced in the League of Revolutionary Black Workers. In a language that blended Marxism-Leninism and Black Nationalism, the league demanded better working conditions and more black supervisors and union officers. The league represented a real threat to the UAW because its militant tactics and aggressive rhetoric challenged the status quo of labor relations developed during the postwar period. Unions such as the UAW moved against these groups with all their strength as they undermined labor's principal negotiating resource: the capacity to govern strikes. By 1971, as the league failed to capture a major following and their leaders were evicted from the plant, the dissent subsided, although the issues that had given rise to it did not.

The 1970s: Wildcat Strikes and Recession

The late 1960s and the early 1970s were characterized by a wave of wildcats that challenged both management and unions across America, hitting both the private and public sector. In this period the number of unauthorized stoppages exceeded any other period in American labor history. These stoppages meant that American unions were potentially losing the support of a whole generation of workers. Rank-and-file agitation demonstrated that the labor movement did not always coincide with the union movement. In many cases, what triggered the wildcats were not only unbearable working conditions or low pay, but also the bankruptcy of the grievance procedure and of the contractual system of shop-floor representation that did not address workers' problems at the point of production.

Toward the end of the 1960s, when the productivity push coincided with a slowdown of the economy and a number of union concessions on wages and benefits, rank-and-file rebellion spread outside the revolutionary groups of Black Nationalists. In some cases, the rank and file built organizations at the industry level to challenge the union leadership, such as among miners, truck drivers, and auto workers. The most successful of these groups was Miners for Democracy (MFD). Founded in 1969 after the assassination of Jock Yablonski, opposition candidate for the UMWA presidency, the MFD toppled the corrupt (and murderous) UMWA president Tony Boyle in 1972 and proceeded to dismantle the centralized and authoritarian structure of the union in an effort to return power to the shop floor.

In 1970, several Teamsters locals rejected a contract signed by their president, Frank Fitzsimmons, who settled for a per-hour raise of $1.10 after an original request of $3.00. The pay raise was meant to offset an increase in living costs that had accompanied the Vietnam War. In response, truck drivers in sixteen cities went on strike and formed picket lines. Fitzsimmons's characterization of the wildcatters as "Communists" and the negative description of the strikers by the mainstream media further infuriated the rank and file. Although strikers did not achieve their wage demands, they managed to have the contract wiped away. The strike initiated a national reform organization called Teamsters United Rank and File (TURF).

In the UAW, a union with a more sophisticated and democratic leadership, the United National Caucus—operating after the defeat of the League of Revolutionary Black Workers—was one of the opposition groups behind a series of walkouts that shut Chrysler plants in Detroit in the summer of 1973. The UAW rationalized the accelerated succession of wildcats in that city as the product of pernicious external influence from Black Nationalist or Communist groups. However, their cause was hazardous safety conditions in the aging Detroit plants and the continuous speed-up on the lines necessary to meet the production levels of Chrysler's automated competitors. The wildcat summer of 1973 famously ended with a clash between a UAW "flying squadron" and militant rank and filers on the picket line, in which UAW officers carrying baseball bats broke the strike of their fellow workers. As historian Nelson Lichtenstein wrote, this episode "symbolized to many the distance traveled by even the most progressive unions of the old CIO."

The conclusion of this labor dispute stands in stark contrast with another key strike that occurred at the same time. At Lordstown, Ohio, GM had designed a modern, automated plant for the production of the Chevrolet Vega. According to GM managers, the plant's integration and speed of operation exceeded that of older plants; here the assembly line could run at a speed of 100 cars per hour. When Lordstown workers—who were rural and, unlike in Detroit, white—went on wildcat strike in the middle of the contract period, the national media framed the episode as an instance of rebellious long-haired hippie workers protesting the alienating condition of the automated factory. The Lordstown strike became a symbol of young people's disaffection from work. The new generation of workers who grew up in the 1960s, it was claimed, would not settle for their father's routine job. However, the fight against speed-up and forced overtime was remarkably similar to the one in Detroit, while the UAW's response was only slightly different: partially embracing the struggle, but at the same time diminishing its effect by refusing to authorize a similar strike in another Ohio GM plant led largely by older workers.

In the first half of the 1970s, workers in traditionally unionized sectors of the economy, such as the automobile industry, revealed a new militancy against the accommodating attitude of union bureaucrats toward working conditions. However, concurrently many other workers who did not belong to the mainstream American labor movement and who had long suffered lower wages and benefits came to the fore by winning union contracts in previously unorganized sectors of the economy. Postal workers, schoolteachers, farm workers, sanitation workers, and hotel maids, among others, gained a public voice through claiming their right to strike. Remarkably, in contrast with the declining density of organized labor as a whole, public-sector unions increased their size in the 1970s, with density among government workers rising from 23 percent in 1973 to 37 percent in 1979.

Two examples of public employees' militancy are worth mentioning. The postal workers' strike of 1970 was an instance of workers who were generally considered passive and loyal but turned militant in response to deteriorating wages and job conditions. The strike spread from New York to other cities despite severe penalties (a year and a day in prison and a $1,000 fine, because as federal employees they had taken an oath to stay on the job) for its participants. President Richard Nixon declared a national emergency and called in the National Guard to deliver New York mail. However, the soldiers lacked the necessary knowledge and often sympathized with the strikers, so Nixon was forced into a compromise with the strikers, which delivered substantial improvements in wages and bargaining rights.

The American Federation of Teachers (AFT) is another example of a public employee union that grew in militancy during the 1970s despite legal constraints on their right to strike. In the mid-1970s it was the fastest-growing union within the AFL-CIO, and by the end of the decade the AFT represented the majority of public school teachers. Often under scrutiny during McCarthyism, through strikes and hard-won collective bargaining teachers achieved better workplace conditions, pay increases, and guarantees against unfair dismissal.

For most of the 1970s, workers in traditional sectors of organized labor effectively protected their standard of living in the context of a stagnating American economy, but the effectiveness of strikes was dramatically reduced as managers made clear that any disruption of production could result in the closing of the plant or the transfer of work elsewhere. Likewise, in the public sector, municipal governments responded to the inflation and the fiscal crisis by cutting budgets, stopping recruitment in a time of rising unemployment, and demanding concessions from the recently recognized public-sector unions. The year 1978 saw a wave of strikes among teachers, firefighters, sanitation workers, and even policemen, but the tide had changed. Public opinion, largely fueled by the anti-tax revolt, backed mayors who were determined to resist public employees' demands and approved the anti-labor tactics of permanently replacing strikers.

The 1970s were therefore an ambivalent decade during which the militancy of workers was counterbalanced with the dwindling political significance of organized labor. The economic recession, global competition, a conservative backlash against the demand of social justice put forward in the 1960s, and the loss of credibility of unions among their members all diminished the effectiveness of strikes.

The 1980s: Concession Bargaining

In broad terms, the mid-1970s represented a turning point marking the beginning of a steady decline of strikes over the next twenty-five years. In this context, the election of Ronald Reagan—itself related to the rise of neoliberal conservatism and the restructuring of the economy—gave the signal to the business community that the administration would curb the remnant of labor's influence in the nation. The federal government famously exhibited its anti-labor stance in the Professional Air Traffic Controllers Organization (PATCO) strike. PATCO had organized in the late 1960s, along with other public-sector unions, without the legal right to strike. During the Nixon administration air traffic controllers had staged a "sickout" that wreaked havoc on the traffic of the major flight hubs. Although the disguised strike involved almost 3,000 controllers, the Nixon administration eventually fired only one strike leader and negotiated with PATCO for the return of the others. The grievances of the air traffic controllers accumulated under President Carter and exploded during the first year of the Reagan administration, despite the fact that PATCO had supported Reagan during the presidential election.

PATCO went on strike in August 1981, demanding a pay raise and a shorter work week. A decade after the first PATCO action, Reagan's handling of the strike demonstrated the magnitude of the political shift against labor. Forty-eight hours after the beginning of the strike, Reagan fired the 11,350 air traffic controllers who had not returned to work and drafted the military to keep Americans flying. For the first time since the 1920s, the government directly attacked organized labor and unabashedly discredited unions in the public opinion. Reagan's response showed also that the tactic of replacing strikers, which had been initiated by municipal governments in the late 1970s, had now found legitimization at national level. As this tactic spread to the private sector, union leaders felt that strikes often ended up working to the benefit of the employer. The statistics of the Department of Labor demonstrate the impact of the striker replacement tactic: after 1981 there was a sharp drop in work stoppages involving 1,000 workers or more, from 235 strikes in 1979 to ninety-six in 1982, going down to forty in 1988.

The PATCO defeat opened the way to several manufacturers' "concession drives," which were attempts to lower wages and curtail benefits to workers. Concession demands were behind most of the strikes in the 1980s. These strikes often showed a cleavage between local union officials and the top AFL-CIO leaders. The latter in fact believed concession bargaining to be the lesser evil compared to the tangible threat to job security. For the rank-and-file workers (often backed by their local), concessions instead meant working in more hazardous conditions and abandoning aspirations to a respectable standard of living.

The Hormel strike in Austin, Minnesota, effectively exhibited the dilemma that confronted labor activists, as well as the difficulty in gathering support for strike action in the post-PATCO era. The members of United Food and Commercial Workers (UFCW) Local P-9 initiated a campaign against wage and benefit concessions at Hormel, one of the largest members of the meatpacking industry. In late 1984, Hormel planned to decrease the hourly wage at Austin from $10.69 to $8.25. The 1,500 members of Local P-9 felt betrayed by both the company and the national UFCW, which had created the contractual conditions for this request.

Aware of the high stakes connected to a strike, the Hormel workers at first used the innovative strategy of hiring a public relations consultant firm that embarked on a "corporate campaign" to discredit Hormel among the public. The campaign used publications, newspaper ads, and picketing targeted at the headquarters, the shareholders' meeting of Hormel, and its financial partners (the First Bank), with the aim to expose their unfair practices. However, it failed to elicit a new offer from the company. As a result, in August 1985, Local P-9 members started a strike that stretched through the fall and into the winter. The cause of the Hormel workers acquired nationwide notoriety. Women played a crucial role in sustaining the struggle by organizing the distribution of food and the exchange of clothes, by speaking at public events, and by facilitating fund raising. The strike was broken only when the company decided to reopen the plant using replacement workers. Hormel managed to bring a large number of strikebreakers into the small Austin community. This was done thanks to the help of the National Guard as well as the unsympathetic response of the national UFCW, which eventually cut strike benefits to workers who refused to go back to work and, after the final debacle in 1986, placed the union local in trusteeship.

Concession demands were also the prime motive behind the miners' strike against Pittston in 1989. Pittston withdrew from the main association of coal-mining firms, the Bituminous Coal Operators Association, in order to negotiate a new contract with the UMWA that would introduce subcontracting, more flexible work schedules, and a drastic limitation of health and pension benefits for retired and disabled miners and their families. These proposals threatened to overthrow hard-won work practices and long-held expectations that the company would care for aging miners who had given their health to the company. As the protest turned into a strike, miners realized that under the framework of the national labor law, their actions in support of the strike were classified as illegal. Courts issued huge fines against mass pickets and sit-downs, while the occasional threats to Pittston properties or to replacement workers were picked up by the media in their portrayal of strikers as violent thugs, which obscured the important issue of the company rolling back health insurance and the general nonviolent character of the action. The Pittston episode exemplified the limited space for action that was left to unions during a strike. While the law did not prevent Pittston from using replacement workers or abstaining from bargaining, it severely limited the scope of activity for the workers. However, it was in part workers' readiness to go beyond the frame of the law that increased costs for Pittston to a level that drove the company back to the negotiation table. Notwithstanding the bitter struggle, the final settlement was a compromise: miners retained their benefits for the sick and the elderly, but the contract allowed the company to subcontract and provided for Sunday work and more irregular work schedules.

In the 1980s, many private employers followed the tactics or the threat of hiring replacement workers to gain the upper hand in bargaining concessions in wages and work schedule from the unions. As efforts to alter the law that allowed employers to use striker replacements failed, the spread of this tactic made the threat of strikes less effectives and their use by unions became increasingly rare.

The 1990s: Reversible Destiny?

Strikes in the 1990s and in the first years of the twenty-first century have reached a new minimum. There were on average 34.7 strikes of 1,000 workers or more per year in the 1990s and only 23.6 per year between 2000 and 2005. Compared to the average of 266 in the 1960s or to the frequency of workplace conflict in other advanced capitalist nations, the number of strikes in the United States during this period was low. The number of lost strikes over concession demands has discouraged union members from using this traditional and irreplaceable weapon in contract negotiation.

Notwithstanding the paucity of strikes and the difficult moment for the labor movement, a few work stoppages have captured the imagination of the nation and have shown that strikes are still essential to gain organizational strength and better contracts.

The 1997 Teamsters strike against United Parcel Service (UPS) was one of the most successful work stoppages of recent years and inspired confidence in a revival of the labor movement. In the summer of 1997, the Teamsters waged a nationwide strike—the first in ninety years—against UPS by mobilizing 185,000 workers from coast to coast in virtually every American town and city. The issues at stake were the increasing reliance on part-time workers, the company's pressure to diminish safety on the job, and its attempt to take control of the workers' pension fund away from the union. The strike lasted sixteen days and eventually led to the company settling for terms close to the unions' demands. The strike disrupted national shipping patterns and business in general and, as on other occasions, the media invited the audience to identify with UPS and its customers, yet public opinion supported the strikers over the company by a wide margin. The Teamsters put a lot of effort in organizing public support for the strikers and managed to make good use of public support to pressure UPS to settle the strike. They succeeded in this because the strike exposed the company's position on issues of contracting out and exploitation of part-time workers that were important in the public perception; also, the public empathized with the UPS delivery workers who are familiar figures in American daily life. UPS miscalculated the public attitude and the volume of business that would be lost during the disruption. As many ground service customers switched to its main competitors, the company decided to take a softer approach at the bargaining table.

Many of the contract gains proved to be illusory. UPS did not deliver the promises concerning working conditions and did not change the ratio of full-time workers to part-time workers. However, the workers, the Teamsters, and the labor movement came out stronger from the strike. In 2002, when the 1997 contract expired, the memory of the strike gave the Teamsters great leverage in the negotiations. UPS feared a loss of business as shippers wanted to avoid the potential trouble of another strike. As a result, the 2002 Teamsters contract at UPS was one of richest concerning wages, benefits, preservation of jobs, and pension security. This would have been impossible without a credible strike threat to the UPS volume of business.

Other signs of revival of the labor movement included a new wave of militant organizing in sectors such as the service economy, where employers normally expected they could easily replace strikers. This is the case of the two-decade-long movement of Justice for Janitors, backed by the Service Employees International Union (SEIU), the fastest-growing union in the country. Justice for Janitors has infused strikes with refreshing tactics, such as community picketing and organizing mass demonstration in order to defuse the threat of potential strikebreakers. The style of action adopted by the movement (marching, fasting, sitting in, and generally striving to attract public attention), which is similar to that of the civil rights movement, has won Justice for Janitors important allies among authorities and politicians. More importantly for the effectiveness of the strike, the SEIU adopted the strategy of exploiting the time and spatial nature of the service provided for janitors. Janitorial services are essential to operate an office building and, unlike cars or coal, cannot be stockpiled before a strike or moved from another location. Because of this, contractors are compelled to settle quickly or lose their clients. In 1995, the rise of John Sweeney, formerly president of the SEIU, to the top of the AFL-CIO signaled that within the labor movement more resources would be devoted to recruitment and organizing strikes.

Conclusion

The postwar era started with a great upsurge in strikes. The 1946 strike wave demonstrated the great power of organized labor in the most productive industries of the country, but failed to alter in a fundamental way the structural features of the American political economy. A backlash against the strike wave led to legislation in 1947 that limited the right to strike. Since then, labor law has permitted only a narrow range of strikes, in particular those institutionalized within the collective bargaining system that regulated the renewal of contracts. Ultimately this system proved ineffective in protecting workers' rights and wages and, consequently, between the end of the 1960s and the mid-1970s workers engaged in wildcat strikes. However, since 1975—and especially since 1981—the number of strikes has declined dramatically due to the widespread adoption of striker replacement tactics.

In the context of de-industrialization, outsourcing, and ruthless competition for cheaper labor, strikes are a high-stakes struggle for workers. In the winter of 2004, 59,000 grocery workers in Southern California who went on strike for nineteen weeks against a cartel of supermarket chains settled for a contract that lowered their wages and health benefits to a level close to nonunion companies like Wal-Mart. The supermarket chains gained the upper hand by continuing operations during the strike, although with substantial losses. At the beginning of the twenty-first century, going on strike means something very different than it did after V-J Day. The latest strike campaigns have used a wide range of tactics to overcome the limits of the law and the resolve of companies to cut labor costs. Unions like SEIU have responded to corporate restructuring by organizing an entire workforce within a labor market rather than organizing employer by employer. At the onset of the twenty-first century, the kind of industrial actions that were characteristic of the heyday of collective bargaining are unlikely to be of any consequence. However, the rebirth of the labor movement is still linked to the possibility of organizing strikes, especially ones that can involve categories of workers outside the umbrella of the existing unions and therefore challenge the spread of working poverty and the threat to Social Security.

See also: Civil Rights Strikes, 118; The 1946–1946 Strike Wave, 216; Teachers' Strikes, 252; Postal Workers' Strikes, 266; Automobile Workers' Strikes, 389; Rubber Workers' Strikes, 398; Agricultural Strikes, 415; The Redwood Lumber and Sawmill Workers' Strike, 438; The Rise and Fall of Rank-and-File Miner Militancy, 1964–2007, 471; Strikes in the U.S. Airline Industry, 1919–2004, 577; Aerospace Engineer Strikes, 590; Teamster Strikes and Organizing, 1934–1964, 601; Service Industry Strikes, 620–722.

Bibliography

Fones-Wolf, Elizabeth. *Selling Free Enterprise. The Business Assault on Labor and Liberalism, 1945–60*. Urbana and Chicago: University of Illinois Press, 1994.

Lichtenstein, Nelson. *Labor's War at Home: The CIO in World War II*. Cambridge: Cambridge University Press, 1982.

———. *State of the Union: A Century of American Labor*. Princeton, NJ: Princeton University Press, 2002.

Lipsitz, George. *Rainbow at Midnight. Labor and Culture in the 1940s*. New York: Praeger, 1981.

McCartin, Joseph. "'Fire the Hell Out of Them': Sanitation Workers' Struggles and the Normalization of the Striker Replacement Strategy in the 1970s." *Labor: Studies in Working-Class History of the Americas* 2, no. 3 (2005): 67–92.

Moody, Kim. *An Injury to All: The Decline of American Unionism*. London: Verso, 1988.

Thompson, Heather Ann. *Whose Detroit? Politics, Labor, and Race in a Modern American City*. Ithaca, NY: Cornell University Press, 2001.

PART IV
PUBLIC SECTOR STRIKES

Introduction by Immanuel Ness

Public sector workers have not been as prone to strike as their private sector counterparts, but their strikes have tended toward the dramatic. Postal workers carried out the largest wildcat strike in U.S. history when 200,000 of them hit the streets in 1970. New York City transit workers brought the city to a standstill three times in forty years. In 1968, striking Memphis sanitation workers, most of them African-American, drew inspiration from and expanded the scope of the civil rights movement. In 1919, Boston police went on strike with devastating consequences, immediate in the form of death and destruction and long-term in the form of a backlash against public sector unionism that lasted decades. Less violent but equally consequential, the 1981 Professional Air Traffic Controllers Organization (PATCO) strike was a disastrous defeat for the labor movement, kicking off several decades of anti-union attacks in both the public and private sectors.

All of these strikes were illegal in some form, either because workers left their jobs in violation of an explicit legal prohibition against strikes, as in the case of the postal workers, transit workers, police, and air traffic controllers; or because they continued their walkout in violation of court injunctions, as in the case of the sanitation workers. Very few public sector workers have ever enjoyed the right to strike in the United States. Indeed, only since the 1960s have many of them even won the right to bargain with their government employers.

In the hundred years before the 1960s, unions of public sector workers were limited in how they could represent their members. Prior to the 1912 Lloyd–La Follette Act, federal workers could not belong to unions, though some state and local workers could. These unions, along with those among federal workers after 1912, engaged in lobbying efforts to try to win legislation such as civil service reform, or other government action to improve their wages, benefits, and working conditions. They won modest successes and in some cases became influential in politics, but they could not win the rights to bargain or strike. Their opponents in business and government, most interested in ensuring public order, argued that public sector collective bargaining violated principles of democracy and could lead to destructive strikes, citing the Boston police strike as the prime example. In response, many public sector unions publicly renounced their right to strike, hoping to convince legislators that their promises of labor peace would be rewarded with collective bargaining. Until the 1960s, however, few federal, state, or local governments bargained with their employees. As a result, the few strikes that took place in this period were illegal, small, and short.

After World War II, the expansion of the public sector, particularly at the state and local levels, along with the stabilization of private sector labor relations, encouraged public sector unions to push for collective bargaining rights. New unions were founded in the 1930s, including the American Federation of Government Employees and the American Federation of State, County, and Municipal Employees. They joined older unions such as the National Association of Letter Carriers (founded in 1889) and the National Association of Post Office Clerks (founded in 1906) to press for rights at the state and federal levels. They first won in Wisconsin in 1959. Then in 1962, President John F. Kennedy signed Executive Order 10988, allowing for limited collective bargaining by federal employees. Over the next two decades, a majority of states, along with the federal government, passed laws allowing for some type of collective bargaining by groups of public employees. These laws varied tremendously, as did numerous local ordinances and executive orders. But one thing united the disparate authorities—the vast majority of them prohibited strikes.

Nevertheless, the incidence of strikes by public sector workers increased in the late 1960s and 1970s, which was also a period of rising strike activity among private sector workers. In addition to the Memphis sanitation strike and the postal workers' wildcat, tens of thousands of teachers, firefighters, garbage collectors, and even police defied the law and engaged in walkouts. In quite a few cases, they risked draconian fines, encumbrance of union funds, and even imprisonment. Anger over the disparity between public and private sector wages and working conditions—some full-time postal workers qualified for welfare—drove the public sector strikes, as did the civil rights and women's movements. Governments became more open to hiring African-American and women workers in the post–World War II years. When their movements filtered into government offices, schools, post offices, garbage barns, and other workplaces, militancy increased.

The combination of political clout and workplace militancy, along with the right to bargain, resulted in a huge expansion of public sector unionism. The percentage of public sector workers in unions rose from 12 percent in the early 1960s to 40 percent in 2000. Today, approximately 40 percent of all union members work in the public sector. While the strength of public sector workers within the American labor movement reflects primarily the movement's weakness in the private sector, it is also the legacy of public sector workers' determination to improve their lives by winning and asserting their rights, including the rights to bargain and strike.

LABOR AND THE BOSTON POLICE STRIKE OF 1919

Joseph Slater

When almost all of Boston's police officers went on strike in September 1919, they did so for reasons similar to those that motivated other workers before and since to do the same, but with unique consequences for the history of American labor. Although the strikers were concerned with wages, hours, and working conditions, it was immediately and ominously clear that this event would be like no other job action. As the policemen walked off the job they were attacked by a crowd of more than 1,000 volunteer substitute policemen, and for the following three days many denizens of the city engaged in a variety of criminal acts, including assaults, public gambling (with attendant thefts and violence), robbery, and destruction of property. Parts of the city were frighteningly lawless. Rioters in South Boston stoned a group of reserve park police, chanting "Kill them all!" On the second day of the strike, mounted troopers confronted a crowd of around 15,000. The next day's *Boston Herald* reported: "All Day Fight With Mob in Scollay Square—Cavalry Useless. . . . From 7 last night almost complete anarchy reigned . . . until early in the morning." State guards finally intervened, firing point-blank into the crowds, killing nine and wounding twenty-three others. Hundreds more were injured during the strike. Property damage was estimated in the hundreds of thousands of dollars. The *Herald* explained that the rioting was "suppressed by the rigorous rule of 7,000 patrolling soldiers, their authority backed by loaded rifles, fixed bayonets, [and] mounted machine guns." Ostensibly to prevent further violence or even a general strike, Governor Calvin Coolidge called out the rest of the state guard and told the federal secretaries of war and navy to be prepared to send troops. With peace finally restored, all 1,147 strikers were fired.

Unfortunately for public sector unions, the most searing and enduring image of their history in the first half of the twentieth century was the Boston police strike. The strike was routinely cited by courts and officials through the end of the 1940s. Even in later decades, opponents of public sector unions would invoke the strike as a cautionary tale of the evils of such unions. It provided evidence that strikes by government workers were dangerous and destructive and made it more difficult for officials to see public employees as "workers"—the type of people who should have the right to form unions. Although the Boston police strike was as atypical as it was dramatic, it contributed far more than any other single event to the peculiarly American view that public sector labor relations were something entirely distinct from private sector labor relations.

The Boston police strike can only be understood as part of the larger narrative of the period's labor history. From 1916 to 1922, historian David Montgomery explains in *The Fall of the House of Labor*, "workers' demands became too heady for the AFL [American Federation of Labor] . . . to contain . . . and too menacing for business and the state to tolerate." During and directly after World War I, the union movement was growing in both the public and private sectors. In 1919 police unions were affiliating with the American Federation of Labor (AFL) at an impressive rate. That year, however, management suspended union leaders and announced it would not tolerate an AFL union, pushing the new police local to lead the Boston strike. The underlying issues were common for the day: wages eroded by postwar inflation, long hours, unsanitary conditions, a weak company union, and supervisor favoritism and reprisals. The precipitating event of the strike—the suspension of union leaders—was also typical. The police strike involved over 1,100 workers, led to considerable violence and several deaths, and achieved national notoriety, not unlike other prominent labor actions of that year, such as the Seattle general strike and the steel strikes. Despite all this, the Boston police strike is rarely seen for what it was: a vitally important moment in the history of labor and workers. This is almost certainly because the strike involved public employees, specifically police.

Unionists and their advocates have traditionally been wary of police, in large part because they often broke strikes. Analyzing the place of police in a system of class structure can be complicated. Still, cops on the beat have traditionally been from working-class backgrounds, they perform rigidly disciplined wage labor, and in many other ways they share the identity of "worker." Indeed, the unionization in Boston was part of a national trend of police affiliation with the AFL, which in turn was part of a national boom in the organizing of a broad range of public employees around World War I. In 1919, the AFL extended this vision of worker solidarity to police, chartering thirty-seven locals.

Opposition to police affiliation with the labor movement caused the Boston strike. A central issue debated before, during, and after the strike was whether public employees should even be allowed to organize. Nonetheless, studies of the event, such as those by Francis Russell, Thomas Reppetto, and Jonathan White, have traditionally concentrated on ethnic and political factors specific to Boston and its police department. These studies have contrasted elite Republican Protestants, such as Massachusetts Governor Calvin Coolidge and his appointee, Police Commissioner Edwin Curtis, with the largely Democratic, Irish-Catholic police force and Democratic Mayor Frank Peters. The strike is also well known for launching the national political career of the future President Calvin Coolidge. But the cause of the walkout was Curtis's ban on police affiliating with the AFL, and the broader trend on which contemporaries focused was the nationwide increase in public workers, including police, joining the AFL. In fact, government officials, businessmen, union leaders, and socialists all predicted that public sector unions would shift the balance of power in all labor relations. The AFL maintained that government employees were members of the working class. Opponents insisted that they had nothing in common with labor and that AFL organizing in the public sector would lead to union interests dominating the state.

In early and mid-1919, these debates increasingly centered on police. Would AFL police unions refuse to break strikes? Would they strike themselves? Neither side dealt with these issues successfully. Across the country, government officials ordered police officers to leave the AFL, prompting numerous confrontations, including the Boston strike. Labor leaders never reconciled their support of public sector unions with the alarming possibility of a police strike. The disastrous conclusion of the Boston dispute ended the first, false dawn of public sector unionism, and reverberated for decades. Still, the labor movement in 1919 understood the common interests of public and private sector workers, and historians should do the same.

Public employee unions had a history before the Boston strike. In the United States as well as abroad, some government workers had been unionized and active since at least the 1830s. In the nineteenth century, organized public employees were typically members of predominantly private sector unions—for example, skilled tradesmen working in naval yards. Much of their activity centered on hours legislation. In the twentieth century, public workers began organizing more extensively as government employees. By January 1918, the AFL's *American Federationist* could proudly announce that public employees had "come forward voluntarily in recent years in large numbers" to join the AFL. After fitful starts in the first decade of the century, the movement took off around World War I. In 1906, the AFL created its first national union of government workers, the National Federation of Post Office Clerks. In 1902, the Chicago Teachers Federation had affiliated with the Chicago AFL, and the national AFL directly chartered a teachers' local in San Antonio. After a few abortive attempts to create a national teachers' union, in 1916 the AFL formed the American Federation of Teachers (AFT). In the year before the Boston strike, the AFT grew from 2,000 to 11,000 members. In 1917 the AFL established the National Federation of Federal Employees (NFFE). That same year, the National Association of Letter Carriers (NALC), founded in 1889, affiliated with the AFL, as did the Railway Mail Carriers. The AFL chartered its first firefighters' local in 1903 and created the International Association of Fire Fighters (IAFF) in 1918. The IAFF soon grew from about 5,000 to over 20,000 members. From 1918 to 1919 alone, the number of its locals more than tripled, from 82 to 262, according to historian Philip Kienast.

The overall rate of unionization in the public sector reflected this activity. From 1900 to 1905, union density in government employment was less than 2 percent, increasing to only around 3.5 percent in 1910. Then from 1915 to 1921, density increased from 4.8 to 7.2 percent, an especially impressive increase given that the total number of government employees in these years grew by more than one-quarter, from 1,861,000 to 2,397,000, according to the Bureau of Statistics. Thus, from 1915 to 1921 the total number of public workers in unions nearly doubled. Considering that these unions lacked even the grudgingly bestowed basic rights to organize and exert limited economic pressures that private sector unions had won by this time, these gains are striking.

With the public sector movement in full swing, repeated requests by ordinary officers finally convinced the AFL to accept police unions. Until 1919, the AFL had refused to charter such locals. The 1897 AFL convention rejected an application from a police group in Cleveland, despite the endorsement of the application by the Cleveland Central Labor Union and the AFL's regional organizer. According to the AFL convention proceedings, it was "not within the province of the trade union movement to specially organize policemen, no more than to organize militiamen, as both . . . are too often controlled by forces inimical to the labor movement." In 1917, prompted by more requests from police organizations and a request from the St. Paul, Minnesota, delegation, the AFL convention voted to reexamine the prohibition on police locals, but in May 1918 the AFL Executive Council (EC) let the old rule stand, stating that it was "inexpedient to organize policemen at the present time." A year later, however, faced with yet more applications from police, the EC referred the issue to the June 1919 AFL convention, and that body reversed the prohibition. The resolution doing so simply stated that since police in various cities had organized and requested affiliation, the AFL would go "on record as favoring" the organization of police unions and would grant them charters. The response was immediate. By September 1919 the AFL had received sixty-five requests from police organizations and had chartered thirty-seven locals. Samuel Gompers remarked during the thirty-ninth annual AFL convention that in his thirty-six years as AFL president, in no other trade had he ever seen as many applications in as short a time. The enthusiasm was mutual. According to AFL records, Frank Morrison, secretary of the AFL, instructed organizers to give "particular attention" to police.

Gompers portrayed police as public employees, and public employees as workers. He compared the ban on police affiliation with the AFL by District of Columbia commissioners to President Theodore Roosevelt's repudiated "gag order" of 1902, which had prohibited federal workers from seeking to influence legislation on their own behalf. Arguing that the end of war-related production had hurt public and private workers equally, Gompers stressed that the police officers themselves had chosen to join the AFL to combat low wages and poor working conditions. Emphasizing the fact that all workers should have the right to organize, Gompers argued that if "working people . . . policemen included" had the right to join "any lawful organization" before the war, they should not be denied that right after.

Ominously, however, Gompers's testimony displayed the unresolved tensions between the AFL's declared moderation and the radical prospect of a police strike. He stressed that the AFL was responsible, patriotic, and law-abiding, unlike the Industrial Workers of the World (IWW)—to whom, Gompers implied with no evidence, police might turn if they could not join the AFL. Indeed, the AFL would be a "stabilizing influence." New members were told that the membership "obligation" of a police local contained nothing contrary to police duties. When pressed on the strike issue, he replied that the Lloyd–LaFollette Act barred federal employees from joining groups that imposed a duty to strike.

These assurances implied a distinction in the ability of public and private workers to strike that was clearer in theory than in fact. Formally, the AFL held that the "final remedy" for government employees was legislation, not withholding labor. Yet public sector unions in the AFL had struck, as had unaffiliated police unions in Ithaca, New York, in 1889 and in Cincinnati, Ohio, in 1918. In both cases the striking officers were immediately replaced and the strikes ended quickly and with little disruption, but the issue was not imaginary. The question was whether organization or affiliation with labor increased the chances of strikes. Believing that it did, and foreshadowing the battle in Boston, the mayor of Cincinnati had forbidden police officers to join the AFL after they had voted to do so.

Thus, while Gompers asserted that the police unions in the AFL would bring greater stability and while no AFL police union had struck, when Gompers proclaimed that police wanted the "great mass of four million workers" to support them, nothing in his testimony indicated exactly what that could mean. Such ambiguities would be devastating in Boston, where labor leaders would have to confront the contradiction implicit in Gompers's position: insisting that public workers had the same rights as private sector workers, while at the same time worrying that strikes by certain public employees—notably police—would lead labor into a deeply damaging confrontation in which its demands would be opposed to the public interest.

In addition to fears of police themselves striking, union opponents were also extremely concerned about how police officers in the AFL might act during strikes by other unions. The Washington, DC, commissioners claimed that they welcomed unaffiliated police organizations but had barred AFL organizing to assure the "independence" of the department. They spoke of "divided loyalty" and "charges of favoritism" if police officers who were members of an AFL union were called on to handle strikes by members of other AFL unions. This was a concern voiced later in Boston and elsewhere, often by private sector business interests. Ironically, this concern seemed to assume a greater set of common interests among public and private sector workers than that side of the debate would normally admit. Gompers parried that the AFL merely wanted the police to be neutral and "not throw their full weight" against workers. Unconvinced, the commissioners suggested that AFL-affiliated police would attack strikebreakers and the commissioners insisted that the ban on affiliation was needed to prevent "even the charge of partiality."

The rapid rise of police unions sparked a nationwide spate of attacks by local government employers before the Boston strike. In Portland, Oregon, Mayor George Baker fought unionization, claiming that it would cause divided loyalty in labor disputes. Portland police officers countered that joining the AFL would help them understand the views of workers. Los Angeles Mayor Frederick Woodman raised wages and formed a police relief association to impede union organization. Officials in Terre Haute, Indiana, and Norfolk, Virginia, ordered police officers to leave the AFL or resign; Norfolk's director of public safety threatened to use soldiers to patrol the city if the officers refused both options. Typifying much opinion in Congress, Senator H.L. Myers, a Republican from Montana, proposed that police officers in the District of Columbia who had joined a union be denied pay. In Jersey City, New Jersey, Mayor Frank Hague prohibited police from joining the AFL, alleging it was "subversive of discipline." In no sense, however, were these attacks limited to police unions. Public and private employers opposed other public sector unions as well, focusing on those affiliated with the AFL. The 1919 AFL convention proceedings noted that all the members of a firefighters' local in Cincinnati had been fired to discourage affiliation with the IAFF. In 1918 and 1919, resistance to the IAFF prompted seven strikes in the United States and Canada. Many school boards in this period prohibited schoolteachers from joining the AFT; teachers responded with political campaigns and lawsuits. In August 1919, former Massachusetts Attorney General Albert Pillsbury offered legislation that would have made it illegal for *any* government worker in the state to join a union. "Every . . . public service is now being conducted at the sufferance of organized labor," he complained, according to historian Francis Russell.

The leaders of the AFL (all from private sector unions) tried to resist these attacks, as did local

AFL bodies and the police officer members themselves. The AFL Executive Council advised police that they had the right to organize, and the labor press across the country supported police unions. The New Jersey Central Labor Union declared it would fight for the Jersey City police local. The District of Columbia police local won a temporary restraining order that blocked the commissioners' ban on AFL affiliation on the grounds that the rule was not "needful," and the commissioners' authority extended only to "needful" rules. (The Boston police union would later unsuccessfully make a similar claim.) President Woodrow Wilson then asked that the District of Columbia case be held in abeyance and resolved at an upcoming general labor conference. In the wake of the Boston strike, Congress settled the issue with laws barring strikes and AFL affiliation by police in the District of Columbia.

The Boston Police Union was born in August 1919 amid the increasing controversy over AFL police unions, but also amid increased militancy by public workers in that city. In August 1918 the Boston Firefighters Union, a charter IAFF local, won raises after threatening to resign en masse. In August 1919, hundreds of city engineers and stationary firemen threatened to strike unless they received raises. The Boston Central Labor Union (BCLU) and its newspaper, the *Boston Labor World,* consistently supported public sector unions in general and the police union specifically. In August 1919 the BCLU, which was dominated by private sector unionists, warned Boston Mayor Frank Peters that it supported the demands of city workers. The BCLU also backed the wage requests of a National Federation of Postal Employees (NFPE) local; the *Labor World* claimed that the board of health would close a private business that was in as poor a condition as the main post office. The *Labor World* also championed the AFT locally and nationally. Generally, the BCLU welcomed the new Boston Police Union and cheered rumblings of police organizing in other Massachusetts cities, such as Wellesley and New Bedford.

Massachusetts and Boston had actually faced public sector strikes before. Workers struck over Taylorist management methods in the Watertown arsenal in 1911 and the Charleston navy yard in 1914. Moth workers (exterminators) struck at least four times in Massachusetts between 1907 and 1917, and gravediggers in Milford struck in 1913. The Watertown workers went out again in 1918. Boston carpenters struck army and navy work sites in 1918. Garbage and ash collectors walked out in Springfield in 1917, in Lawrence and Lowell in 1918, and in Newburyport in 1917, 1918, and 1919 (the workers suffered defeats in all but the first action). The Fall River City Employees Union won pay hikes after striking in July 1919. On a larger scale, in April 1919, 20,000 employees of New England Telephone and Telegraph, then under government control, waged a six-day illegal strike and gained significant raises. But, as with the national AFL, the BCLU was concerned about the consequences of public sector strikes and thus seemed to equivocate on the point. Former BCLU president Edward McGrady told a meeting of over 2,000 postal workers that the AFL did not want them to strike "except as a last resort." Indeed, the BCLU was often cautious about strikes of all kinds, reproaching employees of the Bay Street Rail Company for threatening to stop work over dissatisfaction with a War Labor Board award.

In contrast to labor's approach, leaders of the Boston Police Department sharply differentiated their employees from other workers. The conflict began in 1918 when Police Commissioner Steven O'Meara learned that Boston police officers were considering AFL affiliation. O'Meara issued an order stating that even rumors of unionization were "likely to injure the discipline, efficiency and even the good name of the Force." If officers had obligations to an outside organization, he stated, they would be "justly suspected of abandoning their impartial attitude." He claimed that he did not dispute the "wisdom or even necessity" of unions in the private sector. Public sector unions, however, were "of doubtful propriety," and police in particular should not be allowed to organize because they were responsible for impartial law enforcement. On July 29, 1919, in response to more talk of affiliation, the new police commissioner, Edwin Curtis, promulgated Rule 102, which stated that he was "firmly of the opinion that a police officer cannot consistently belong to a union and perform his sworn duty," and that a police officer "should realize that his work is sharply differentiated from that of the worker in private employ."

Undeterred, police in Boston affiliated with the AFL on August 9, 1919. Their complaints were typical of all workers: low wages, long hours, unhealthy conditions, and despotic supervisors. Police were voted a raise in 1898 that was not put into effect until 1913. Over this period, the cost of living had doubled. After that, pay remained at the 1913 level until a small increase was granted in the spring of 1919. At the time of the strike, officers in their second to fifth years earned $1,200 a year; the most any officer could earn was $1,400; and officers had to buy their own uniforms, which cost over $200. "Leaving out all the pretty theories and grandiloquent phrases about their duty to the State," the *Labor World* reasoned, "can a man . . . even live on such a wage? No, he manages to exist, that is all."

Officers worked regular weeks of seventy-three hours (day shift), eighty-three hours (night shift), or even ninety-eight hours (wagon work). They were sometimes required to remain on duty seventeen hours in a single day. Supervisors also limited where they could go on their days off. "Such men are deprived of enjoying the comforts of their home and family," Boston Police Union President John McInnes insisted in the *Labor World*. Station houses were so unsanitary that the men frequently found vermin on their clothes when they went home. "If the board of health made an investigation as they do in the case of private houses and stores . . . there would be court prosecutions," McInnes lamented. He also complained of many indignities caused by authoritarian management, such as supervisors requiring their subordinates to run menial errands unrelated to work.

Patrolmen had received little help from the Boston Social Club, a company union that Police Commissioner O'Meara had organized thirteen years earlier. McInnes called it a "weak-kneed organization, controlled by police officials," according to the *Labor World*. Police supervisors, McInnes explained, had ignored the club's requests and fixed its elections. Further, McInnes charged that the club representatives were "marked men" and were given less desirable assignments. Notably, he listed strike duty as such a penalty. Instead of this hapless organization, the officers wanted a "red-blooded" union to "formulate their own policies and not be subject to the dictates" of management. In frustration with the impotency of the club, its president and vice president, Michael Lynch and John Harney, joined the Police Union before the strike.

Police Commissioner Curtis would not allow a union affiliated with the AFL, and this position, coupled with the refusal of the police officers to leave the AFL, caused the strike. On August 11, two days after the union affiliated, Curtis issued General Order 110, which barred officers from belonging to almost any organization with ties outside the police department. According to the order, a "police officer is not an employee but a State officer" and must be prevented "from coming under the direction and dictation of any organization which represents but one element or class of the community." There was no doubt that this was aimed squarely at the AFL. On August 20, Curtis summoned union leaders to his office to tell them they could not organize an AFL local. On August 21, over 800 officers met and defiantly installed the officers of the local that they had elected the night before. Frank McCarthy, regional organizer for the AFL, announced that the union had been formed to give "assistance within legal lines" to police and to establish "collective bargaining in all matters" affecting their working conditions. The local now claimed over 1,300 members. Leaders of the BCLU met with Governor Coolidge and told him that this was not only a police matter but a fight of organized labor; Coolidge rebuffed them.

On August 26, Curtis tried union president McInnes and seven other policemen for violating Order 110; on August 29 he held a ten-minute hearing for eleven others. Of these nineteen men, seventeen were union leaders, and Curtis mistakenly thought the other two were as well. Further confirming the nature of the dispute, Mayor Peters stated that the question was "clear cut": police did not have the right to affiliate with the AFL.

On September 7, Curtis suspended the nineteen men for violating the anti-union policy. The next day, the union voted to strike by the overwhelming total of 1,134 to 2, and on September 9 more than 1,100 officers walked out, leaving about 400 on duty. Curtis fired the suspended men on September 13. During the strike, police department officials left no doubt about the centrality of the AFL, distributing circulars that stated that the department opposed "Divided Authority" and identifying labor affiliation as "the Real Issue." Well after the event, Curtis maintained that the "sole issue" of the strike was police membership in the AFL.

Curtis claimed to be prepared with substitutes ready, but although he had a day's notice before the strike, no replacements were deployed for over twenty-four hours after the work stoppage. The first two days saw petty crime escalate into looting and violence, especially in South Boston. The state militia eventually restored order using 4,768 troops, but nine people were killed and hundreds injured. Labor blamed Curtis and Coolidge for being unprepared and not reacting properly, but it was the union that was broadly condemned. The striking police were vilified by the press, public officials, and employers. In one of the more temperate responses, the *New York Times* editorialized on September 10 that a "policeman has no more right to belong to a union than a soldier or sailor."

More broadly, the debate over the Boston Police Union turned on a central issue in American labor history: the extent to which government employees could be a part of organized labor. The *Labor World* consistently supported police and other public sector unions throughout the country, affirming that they were part of a public sector movement and a larger struggle for workers' rights. "Theoretically, no injustice is ever perpetrated on servants of the public," the paper editorialized, but police had "grievances just the same as men in other walks of life." All workers should have the right to bargain collectively, and thus Curtis's ban on the AFL was "un-American" and threatened the rights of labor generally. On September 20, BCLU President Michael O'Donnell and AFL organizer Frank McCarthy issued a statement that justified the organization of police in part because they were "among the lowest paid workmen in the city, and the longest worked." They also cited AFL unions in fire, water, and other city agencies that were working well with management. The BCLU pointedly accused local newspapers of "pronounced capitalist tendencies" for one-sided coverage of the strike.

Similarly, opponents of the Police Union made objections that applied to all public sector unions. The heads of many private businesses wrote to Curtis recommending that no government employee of any kind be allowed to join the AFL. Using logic that could be extended to any public worker, Governor Coolidge declared that police were not "employees" or even "holders of a job," because no private concern made a profit from their efforts. Police "are not in any sense labor bodies," the *Buffalo Courier* on September 14 protested, and "their duties do not constitute a trade." Curtis's Orders 102 and 110 similarly asserted that police were public officers, not employees. The *Labor World* rejected this designation on September 20 by focusing on class: "Does a policeman's daughter marry the son of a chief justice or do the sons of a policeman and of a chief justice play on a Harvard football team together?" It added that even "public officers" had to eat. Meanwhile, some opponents of the Police Union ironically imitated the rhetoric of the industrial labor relations they were trying to distinguish. Taking a page from private sector employers, O'Meara and Curtis claimed that "agents of an outside organization" could not help police.

At the August 26 disciplinary hearing, police department representative James Devlin argued that government workers were "not employees in any sense of the word" but rather were "public officers." A public officer "is not employed, he is appointed; he is not discharged, he is dismissed; he holds office, but he does not hold employment." The attorney for the members of the Police Union, James Vahey, replied that the officers had organized for "the same three reasons that actuate and inspire every man who wishes to join a union—to increase wages, to shorten hours, and to improve working conditions." In any job where workers faced "closely knit, powerful corporations," Vahey continued, an employee acting alone would be forced to accept the employer's terms. Increased costs of living had hit policemen as hard as anyone else, yet police pay was half that of a carpenter or mechanic and less than that of a streetcar conductor. Vahey insisted that unionized police would perform their duties during strikes without bias. Just days before the strike, McInnes vowed that the Police Union would not renounce its right to affiliate. On the day of the strike vote, he proclaimed that the AFL "has once and for all come to stay," and in mid-September he declared that the AFL charter would "never leave my hands." Well into the strike, the police officers voted to remain in the AFL.

The two sides also sparred over the legal rules applicable to unions in government employment, an issue that would remain central to public sector labor relations for the rest of century. At the disciplinary hearing, Vahey argued that a Massachusetts state statute prohibited "yellow dog contracts"—agreements not to join unions as a condition of employment—and that this principle should be applied to police. Devlin parried that the U.S. Supreme Court had held such statutes unconstitutional in the 1915 case of *Coppage v. Kansas.*

Despite Vahey's assurances, opponents of the Boston Police Union spotlighted the issue of "divided loyalty." Even before the local affiliated, the *Boston Herald* editorialized that it would be "a long step toward 'Russianizing' ourselves" if police were "the servant of a special interest," meaning the Boston Police Union. Curtis's Order 102 asserted that officers could not be impartial if they were "subject to the direction of an organization existing outside the department." Order 110 admonished that a policeman should not be controlled by "one . . . class" because in attempting "to serve two masters" he would fail either as an officer or "in his obligation to the organization that controls him." Business leaders were even more explicit in their concern that AFL affiliation would mean greater power for organized labor. A statement by the Boston Chamber of Commerce on August 27 raised the specter of sympathy strikes by police to support other AFL locals. The Chamber announced it would make its building available as a recruiting station for strikebreakers if the police walked out. Hundreds of businessmen wrote Curtis to support his policies and express horror at the concept of police joining the AFL. The Boston Bar Association and the Boston Fruit and Produce Exchange, among other organizations, also opposed affiliation well before the strike.

Union advocates, not surprisingly, denied that police had a tradition of impartiality in dealing with labor. The *Labor World* noted on September 17 that the Boston police force had frequently been deployed against strikers. It also described a steel strike in Pennsylvania in which police, "(non-unionized, of course) rode down a crowd of union workers, injured several, and arrested 19 at the behest of the company. Did someone say 'neutral'?" Of course, union supporters understood the anxiety of the complaining employers. The *New York Call,* a socialist newspaper, published a cartoon on September 11 of that year boasting that "a union cop won't club another union worker." The *Call* added that organizing campaigns in police departments and the newspaper industry would, if successful, restrain two of the most significant opponents of labor. Before the Boston strike, the *Call* even claimed that police unionization would cause "a complete reversal" of the positions of capital and labor. "Organized force, for the first time in history," would be aligned with unions, the paper enthused.

In 1919, the year of the "Red Scare" and unprecedented militancy by workers, such radical visions of union power stiffened opposition to the Police Union and placed organized labor in a difficult position. The seemingly socialist Seattle and Winnipeg general strikes earlier in the year had alarmed portions of the nation, including many AFL leaders. Businessmen across the country echoed the New Hampshire Manufacturing Association's appreciative description of Curtis—two weeks before the Boston strike—as "the Ole Hanson of the east" (a reference to the mayor who defeated the Seattle strike). The Boston Police Union and labor in general were denounced as "Bolshevik," much to the chagrin of the AFL and BCLU, both of whom vehemently opposed communism. The prospect of police striking or supporting others who did was a particularly emotional issue in a year that saw 3,600 strikes involving 4 million workers in the United States. Massachusetts alone experienced 396 strikes in 1919, the most since records began being kept in 1887. More broadly, from 1916 to 1922, levels of strike participation were greater than at any previous time. Compounding the bad timing for the Boston Police Union, in August 1919, just as the controversy in Boston was heating up, police in London and Liverpool led highly publicized strikes.

The BCLU soon became trapped between its support for public sector unions and its fear that radical acts such as a police or general strike would end badly. It made threats while simultaneously arguing that the AFL and the Police Union were moderate and responsible. Before the strike, the

Labor World insisted that the AFL preferred peaceful settlements and only struck when employers forced them. McInnes denied that union membership would interfere with police duties. AFL regional organizer McCarthy and BCLU President O'Donnell sent Coolidge and James Jackson Storrow, a prominent Boston investment banker and philanthropist, copies of the AFL's organization manual and constitution to show that affiliation was not inconsistent with police work. On the other hand, in mid-August the BCLU announced that it had named a seventeen-member committee to work with McCarthy to prepare to "fight on aggressive lines if a single policeman is suspended or discharged for his union membership." Moreover, on August 23 the BCLU declared its willingness to call a general strike to back the police. It ultimately would refuse to take this step. This failure to act was partly due to the risks inherent in joining an unpopular and losing strike, but it also resulted from the inability of the BCLU to work out the contradictions between its genuine support for public workers and its legitimate concerns about the results of an actual police strike.

The inconsistencies of the BCLU, particularly on the crucial question of whether to call a general strike in support of the police union, had disastrous consequences. Up to September 20 labor leaders talked tough. On August 23, the *Labor World* reported that the BCLU had "manifested its readiness to call a general strike of all the organized labor in this city" and that three unions had already agreed to this plan. Although the Massachusetts attorney general's office quickly declared sympathy actions illegal, on September 12 the Massachusetts Federation of Labor ordered Boston locals to vote on a general strike, and many unions voted yes. By September 20, various sources had reported that Telephone Operators, Hebrew Trades, Plumbers, Machinists, Boilermakers, Bartenders, Electrical Workers, Cooks & Waiters, Garment Workers, Typographers, Sheet Metal Workers, and Teamsters were prepared to strike in support of the police. McCarthy asserted that the AFL, from Gompers on down, backed the right of police to affiliate, and that nine-tenths of the BCLU unions had voted to support them.

However, on September 21, the BCLU was not ready to undertake what would have been one of the most daring and radical acts in the history of the AFL. At its meeting that day, the BCLU delayed its decision on the general strike and refused to release the results of a vote on the issue. The *Labor News* reported that some felt this was a "tacit confession of defeat." On October 5, the BCLU met again and made a final decision not to stage a mass work stoppage. Remarkably, its leaders barely averted a vote in favor of striking at the October 5 meeting after two Police Union members appealed to labor unity. Policeman Charles McGowan singled out unions involved in the press, asserting it was "high time that newspapers being run by the brains of union men stopped rapping the unions. These men took an oath not to injure union men, but they are doing so every day by writing stories, setting the type and printing the newspapers." But McCarthy, O'Donnell, and BCLU business agent Jennings, while promising support, all spoke against a general strike. Significantly, Stephen Kitchell of the Lithographers Union recounted the manner in which the Winnipeg and Seattle strikes were crushed before advising against a Boston general strike. The *Labor World* explained the BCLU's decision: "With prejudice fanned so astutely by certain anti-union interests, any further demonstration is bound to react on the laboring class as a whole." Showing remarkable faith after the BCLU had been indecisive and misleading, the Police Union still voted confidence in the BCLU at the union's next meeting. Conversely, the AFL's behavior caused historian Frederick Koss to call organized labor "the nearest thing to a villain in the piece."

Nonetheless, locally and nationally, labor exhibited some real solidarity. The Amalgamated Clothing Workers refused to sew uniforms for police replacements. Members of the Theatrical Stage Employees gave free benefit performances for the strikers. Locals of the Carpenters, Railroad Station Employees, Sheet Metal Workers, Bartenders, and Freight Handlers voted financial support, as did the Massachusetts Federation of State, County and Town Employees. The BCLU placed a weekly strike assessment on its members. The Massachusetts AFL called for Curtis's removal and reinstatement of the strikers, and the BCLU also pressed hard for rehiring strikers. Gompers wired Governor Coolidge and Mayor Peters on September 12, offering to end the strike if the matter could be resolved along with the District of Columbia police dispute at President Woodrow Wilson's labor conference. Coolidge countered that only Curtis could make such a decision. Gompers blamed Curtis for the strike and demanded his removal.

The final defeat of the police was their failure to win reinstatement after the strike was over. The *Labor World* strongly advocated rehiring the strikers; it sponsored and publicized a petition drive and quoted the few local leaders who supported the idea. It denounced the mainstream press for urging Curtis "to make the wholesale discharges permanent and to create a new force that shall be spineless as far as organizing for their own protection is concerned." It argued that "the men desire to resume their work at once and nothing stands in the way but violent prejudice and lack of understanding. . . . Put the men back to work!" Early in the strike Mayor Peters had requested an opinion from the state attorney general as to whether he could reinstate officers whom Curtis had removed; the reply was that he could not. Labor briefly took heart when the campaign manager for Democratic gubernatorial candidate Richard Long announced that Long would bring back the strikers if he beat Coolidge. Nearly 100 members of the Police Union campaigned around the state for Long. Trumpeting his leadership during the strike, Coolidge was victorious, although notably he lost in the city of Boston by over 5,000 votes despite support from every mainstream newspaper.

Curtis and Coolidge opposed reinstatement, and their position was widely popular. A letter to Curtis from the Cameron Appliance Company was only slightly more emphatic than average: "Recruit a new force, if it takes twenty years and costs a billion." A fund of $471,758 was collected to pay state guards until replacements were found. Those who favored rehiring, including the Dorchester American Legion (which stressed that many of the strikers were veterans), were an ignored minority. The nineteen men whom Curtis had suspended and discharged tried to regain their jobs through a lawsuit. They alleged that the anti-affiliation rule was not "needful" and thus was beyond Curtis's authority, that yellow dog contracts were impermissible in public employment, and that the rule was unconstitutional. On November 7, 1919, the court ruled for Curtis; the union filed exceptions, but on December 16 the court dismissed the case. In May 1920 McCarthy wrote Gompers that he could "see nothing that would give me the right to believe that there is any chance for the restoration of the strikers to their old jobs." He also noted that all but fifty had found other employment.

Ironically, the strike resulted in wage increases for Boston police. The minimum pay for patrolmen was quickly boosted from $1,100 to $1,400 per year. Neighboring jurisdictions also saw improvements. Melrose, Massachusetts, police received a $200 raise to $1,600 per year. "We hope they will show some appreciation for the work the striking Boston patrolmen did for them," the *Labor World* commented. "If it did nothing else, the much criticized strike improved conditions all over the country." Indeed, in the District of Columbia, New York City, and elsewhere, police were given pay hikes and other benefits soon after the strike. Boston teachers also received a salary increase in the strike's wake. On the other hand, in the 1920s, the new Boston police force developed something of a reputation, at least among unions, for violent treatment of strikers and picketers.

The aftermath of the Boston strike significantly restrained the movement for public sector unions. All police locals affiliated with the AFL were soon destroyed. The Boston Police Union ended as it had begun, with the language of union solidarity. The local's last statement, in mid-October 1919, rejected Coolidge's label of "deserter": "We went out because we were not deserters, because we would not desert the comrades punished for our fault." The police local in Knoxville, Tennessee, which had been the first to affiliate, surrendered its charter soon after the strike. Congress quickly prohibited police and firefighters in the District of Columbia from striking or affiliating with the AFL, and a number of local governments and police departments followed suit. There would be no AFL-affiliated police locals until the 1930s and 1940s, and these too would meet strong opposition. A national AFL-CIO police union would be proposed only in 1969 and not created until 1979.

While other public sector unions tried to avoid association with the Boston disaster by emphasizing or adopting no-strike policies, many were still devastated. In November 1919 the National

Federation of Post Office Clerks voted down a proposal to remove a constitutional ban on strikes. The AFT reaffirmed its no-strike rule in 1920. The number of strikes by IAFF locals decreased sharply after the Boston strike, and the IAFF ratified a no-strike clause in its constitution in 1930. National public sector unions formed in the 1930s, such as the American Federation of State, County and Municipal Employees (AFSCME) and the American Federation of Government Employees (AFGE), adopted similar no-strike rules. Into the 1960s, neither the AFL nor the Congress of Industrial Organizations (CIO) would approve of any strikes by government employees. Despite the moderation, the IAFF lost fifty locals, including its Boston affiliate. The strike also led to losses in the membership of the AFT and other public sector unions.

Thus, the strike stopped the first dawn of public sector organizing in its tracks. After years of increases, the number of unionized government employees fell from 172,000 in 1921 to 171,000 in 1922, despite an increase in total government employment from 2,397,000 to 2,455,000. Such trends continued, and the rate of unionization in the public sector, which had bolted up rapidly in the preceding years, now stagnated, hovering just below the 1921 rate of 7.2 percent for nearly all the 1920s. It finally inched past 8 percent in 1929 and 1930, but the momentum that was once so strong had dissipated. Beyond the numbers, memories of the Boston strike inhibited the growth of public sector unions for decades; it became too easy to equate any form of public sector unionism with the calamitous confrontation. The strike also helped separate government employees from the labor movement. Rules against affiliation with the AFL forced public workers into "associations" that often resembled company unions. The national AFL also took less of an interest. For example, the Boston strike ended attempts by the AFL to form a council of unions of city workers known as the Municipal Employees' Association. One study concludes that the Boston police strike gave public sector unions "a nearly fifty-year set-back."

At the heart of the Boston police strike was the issue of AFL affiliation, whether or not police officers were part of the labor movement. "The policemen, firemen, street cleaners, and other employees of the municipality are part of the working class, with the same interests, the same rights and wrongs, as men in the building trades, the garment industry, or any other field of private employment," the *New York Call* asserted on October 2, 1919. The AFL's Frank McCarthy even predicted that the militia would not act against striking police: "The time when a soldier takes orders to work against his brothers and sisters is past." Such visions may have been idealistic, but they had intriguing implications in the context of contemporary labor militancy and radicalism. At a minimum, police in Boston showed that many public "officers"—even police—were also workers, both in their own minds and in the minds of the labor movement.

See also: Postal Workers' Strikes, 266; Three Strikes Against the New York City Transit System, 277.

Bibliography

The Boston Police Strike: Two Reports. New York: Arno Press, 1971.

Gammage, Allen, and Stanley Sachs. *Police Unions.* Springfield, IL: Charles C. Thomas, 1972.

Kienast, Philip. *Police and Firefighter Employee Organizations.* Ph.D. diss., Michigan State University, 1972.

Koss, Frederick. "The Boston Police Strike of 1919." Ph.D. diss., Boston University, 1966.

McNulty, William. "Boston Killed Police Union, But Then Came Corruption." *Public Safety* (September 1930). Building Service Employees International Union.

Nesbitt, Murray. *Labor Relations in the Federal Government Service.* Washington, DC: BNA, 1976.

O'Neil, Hugh. "The Growth of Municipal Employee Unions." In *Unionization of Municipal Employees,* ed. Robert Connery and William Farr. New York: The Academy of Political Science, 1971.

Reppetto, Thomas. *The Blue Parade.* New York: Free Press, 1978.

Russell, Francis. *A City in Terror: 1919, the Boston Police Strike.* New York: Viking Press, 1975.

Schrag, Zachary. "Nineteen-Nineteen: The Boston Police Strike in the Context of American Labor." A.B. honors thesis, Harvard University, 1992.

Tager, Jack. *Boston Riots: Three Centuries of Social Violence.* Boston: Northeastern University Press, 2001.

White, Jonathan. "A Triumph of Bureaucracy: The Boston Police Strike and the Ideological Origins of the American Police Structure." Ph.D. diss., Michigan State University, 1982.

TEACHERS' STRIKES

John P. Lloyd

The history of teacher strikes in the United States, while not extensively studied in comparison with strikes in other sectors of the economy, is as significant as it is vast. Indeed, the sheer number of teacher strikes in American history is difficult to quantify, but it is safe to say that the number of strikes of at least one day in duration since the beginning of the collective bargaining era in 1960 would be well over 3,000. Therefore, this article will focus on those strikes by K–12 teachers that were the most significant in terms of size, precedence, or issues involved.

Until the mid-twentieth century, teacher strikes were exceedingly rare for a number of reasons. Most teachers were hired by contract and saw themselves not as "workers" but as "professionals." Early professional organizations, such as the National Education Association (NEA), founded in 1857, reinforced this culture of professionalism and as a matter of policy strongly discouraged collective bargaining or striking through most of the twentieth century. As historian Merle Curti once noted, "Hardly an annual meeting of the National Education Association was concluded without an appeal on the part of educators for the help of the teacher in quelling strikes and checking the spread of socialism and anarchism." The culture of professionalism as it applied to teachers centered on the idea that teachers were salaried professionals who engaged in work that required a relatively high degree of education and who had a measure of autonomy over pedagogy and curriculum in their workplace. As such, the theory was that teachers were different from other laborers who needed unions for collective strength in a regimented industrial workplace. As David Selden has written, "Teachers are generally aspiring members of the middle class who become militant only after extreme provocation."

The culture of professionalism could also foster support for unionization and, ultimately, for strikes by teachers when they perceived their status as professionals beginning to erode. As bureaucratization of school systems increased in the first half of the twentieth century, hierarchical control of teachers' work by administrators increasingly took decisions about curriculum, pedagogy, and other matters out of their hands. Teachers' roles increasingly came to be defined and circumscribed by administrators. Historian David Tyack has also noted the correlation between bureaucratization of urban school systems and the feminization of the teaching profession. Women comprised 59 percent of the teachers in urban schools in 1870 and 86 percent by 1920, when the bureaucratization trend was well under way. That proportion had changed little by the end of the century, as the U.S. Census Bureau reported that in 2000, 71 percent of all K–12 teachers, and nearly 80 percent of elementary and middle school teachers, were women. In the early years of public schools, school boards tended to hire women because of what one educational theorist in the nineteenth century termed their "peculiar qualifications for the education of the young." Aside from such crude biological determinism, however, was the widespread assumption that women could be hired for a lower salary than men, as Joel Spring has chronicled. The feminization of the teaching profession had implications for teacher unionism, insofar as teachers' unions have come to represent a significant sector of women workers and have often championed equal pay for equal work provisions in contracts as well as state legislatures.

A strong reluctance to engage in job actions that might inconvenience or hamper the education of young people was also a strong disincentive for teachers to strike. Moreover, until the mid-twentieth century, the NEA leadership consisted primarily of school administrators and higher education leaders—the people against whom teachers would strike. Given the fact that teachers, like other workers who strike, also faced economic hardship and possible loss of career if a strike went badly, the frequency of teachers' strikes was an indication of profound teacher frustration and anger. As one striking teacher in Buffalo, New York, told a reporter during the bitter strike of 1947: "I've always been opposed to strikes. . . . I don't think it's right to keep the children out of school. But it looks as though the city wants it this way. Aren't teachers supposed to be human beings? How long do you think we can be stepped on?"

Despite these barriers, teachers in many cities and states have organized and fought for the right to bargain collectively, and when unified they have won significant improvement in pay and working conditions throughout the years. The story of their strikes is about more than pay raises, however—it is ultimately a story of the struggle over the dignity of work and education in a democratic society.

The earliest attempts to unionize teachers began in response to the increasing bureaucratization and stratification of the educational system in the early twentieth century. As Julia Wrigley has argued, the rise of the American Federation of Teachers (AFT) must be seen in the context of the social struggles of the period, specifically the labor struggles around the turn of the twentieth century. Chicago teachers led by Margaret Haley formed their union in response to school officials' encroachments on teachers' prerogatives in the classroom. Many of the teachers in Chicago's working-class communities identified with the city's labor movement and saw their resistance to bureaucratic impositions as analogous to industrial workers' resistance to managerial control. While Chicago teachers considered striking on a number of occasions, ultimately they did not strike during these early years. However, the Chicago Teachers' Federation (CTF) did support several high-profile student walkouts in protest of deteriorating educational conditions and overcrowded classrooms, as historian Marjorie Murphy has detailed.

Unionized teachers faced another set of hurdles to collective bargaining and striking. Unlike private sector employees, teachers and most other public sector workers lacked substantive collective bargaining rights for much of the twentieth century. A controversial strike by Boston police in 1919 led to the passage of numerous state laws prohibiting strikes by public employees, including teachers. In 1920, Samuel Gompers insisted that any public employee union that wished to affiliate with the AFL must include a "no-strike" clause in its constitution. As a result, the AFT reluctantly included a "no-strike" clause in its constitution in the 1920s.

For its part, the U.S. Congress specifically excluded public sector employees from the landmark National Labor Relations Act (NLRA) passed in 1935, and most state laws did not begin to change until the 1960s. In 1962, President John F. Kennedy signed Executive Order 10988, giving federal employees collective bargaining rights, and this provided momentum for similar changes in state laws. Just as the passage of Depression-era labor legislation resulted from an upsurge in organizing in the early 1930s, public employee organizing brought about a change in state and federal law in the 1960s. The changes that resulted from the attainment of collective bargaining rights for teachers in the 1960s were significant. Teachers who were unionized now had more power to bring school boards to the negotiating table. Prior to the 1960s, when the modern era of collective bargaining began, school boards frequently assumed a "take it or leave it" attitude toward teachers' representatives. "Negotiations" often went something like this, according to Marc Gaswirth and his cowriters:

> A group of teacher representatives appeal to the local school board for a $300 salary increase and an extra $150 for all teachers at or reaching the maximum step on the salary guide. The board first would thank the teacher representatives for their presentations and would express appreciation to its professional staff for dedicated service to the school system. Then the board president would state that financial conditions prevented the school board from granting more than a

> $150 raise and an additional $50 to all teachers on maximum step. The teachers would thank the board for its generosity, and then return to their seats.

By the end of the twentieth century, however, it was still illegal for teachers to strike in many states, and even where legal the strikes often were restricted. Striking teachers not only faced hostility from management, but sometimes from angry parents and students as well. This legal and political context made teacher strikes among the most difficult to win. But despite these disadvantages, public school teachers have made impressive strides since the 1960s in pay, benefits, and workplace rights through collective bargaining and, when necessary, striking.

The formation of the AFT in 1916 did not lead immediately to collective bargaining or strikes. A backlash against teachers' unions during and after World War I, specifically against Margaret Haley and others in the AFT who opposed the war, put the new union on the defensive. In one manifestation of the period's anti-union and anti-left "Red Scare," the American Legion targeted "disloyal" teachers for dismissal and pushed for a school curriculum that inculcated uncritical patriotism. In another manifestation recounted by Murphy, in 1915 Chicago passed the infamous "Loeb Rule." This rule, which prohibited teachers from joining unions, was named for the Chicago School Board President Jacob Loeb, who feared that unionized teachers would bring issues of "class distinction . . . to the attention of immature minds," that they would tend to be "contemptuous and rebellious towards those in authority," and that they would "send forward children who in turn are likely to be dissatisfied, contemptuous and rebellious towards authority, and who have no regard and no respect for law and order."

In the 1920s, school boards sometimes prohibited teachers from joining unions, and some were pressured to quit the AFT, causing membership to fall during the decade. The combination of political repression and the lack of any legal support for the right to strike prevented strike activity until the upsurge of labor radicalism in the 1930s.

During the 1930s, teachers' salaries stagnated and workloads, especially class size, increased as state governments cut budgets to meet the exigencies of the Depression. Teacher strikes were extremely rare, but some teachers began to articulate their grievances collectively, demonstrating against low pay and poor working conditions, as Chicago teachers did when they marched en masse on their board of education to protest the district's default on their salaries in 1936. Demonstrations like "the walk" in Chicago were an important step in teachers' collective articulation of grievances and illustrate a widening gap between the culture of professionalism and the deteriorating working conditions of many teachers. While some labor legislation of the 1930s benefited teachers, the most significant labor law of the decade, the National Labor Relations Act, excluded them. By the end of the decade, teachers still lacked the most basic collective bargaining rights enjoyed by most other workers in the United States. Economic hardships continued during World War II, as wartime inflation eroded teachers' income. As historian Marjorie Murphy has noted, during the war years the average real income of industrial workers rose 80 percent while teachers' real income fell 20 percent. By 1945, the pent-up frustration of teachers burst forth in a brief but notable wave of strikes.

The postwar strike wave began with an eight-day walkout by Norwalk, Connecticut, teachers, who successfully won a pay raise and union recognition. Significantly, the NEA-affiliated union did not call these job actions "strikes," but referred to them as "professional group action by professional methods." Despite some opposition from the NEA, its affiliated teachers in Hawthorne, New Jersey, also staged a short strike in 1946. That same year in Paterson, New Jersey, teachers staged a one-day walkout over low salaries. Probably the largest of the postwar strikes was the St. Paul, Minnesota, strike of November 1946 by a large AFT affiliate. When St. Paul voters defeated a teacher-backed tax increase to raise teacher salaries, teachers struck for five weeks until the board of education agreed to hold another referendum on the question in February 1947. The tax increase was voted down again, but a teacher-led campaign finally won them a pay raise in April of that year.

Later in the 1946–47 school year, the Buffalo teachers' union went on strike, winning concessions after other Buffalo labor unions struck in support. There were also small strikes by NEA affiliates in McMinnville and Shelbyville, Tennessee, and by unaffiliated teachers in Wilkes Barre and Rankin, Pennsylvania. Inspired by the example in St. Paul, teachers in neighboring Minneapolis walked out in May 1948 and won a pay raise despite efforts by the board of education to lock them out. That same year, AFT locals in San Francisco, California, and Jersey City, New Jersey, won pay raises after militant teachers struck. Chicago teachers also voted to strike, but called off the strike when the board of education granted concessions. By 1948, teachers had gone on strike in twelve states, and the reaction of many school boards to the increase in teacher militancy was to grant pay raises, pushing the average teacher salary up by 13 percent since the end of the war.

If the strike wave of 1946–48 had a positive impact on teacher pay nationwide, it also provoked a backlash by state legislatures, who retaliated by passing strict anti-strike laws for public employees. When teachers in Delaware struck for half a day and marched on the state capitol for a pay raise, they were met with a bill calling for a $500 fine and one year in prison for any public employee who struck. New York's Condon-Wadlin Act, passed after the Buffalo strike, was another example of this backlash. Unfortunately, this anti-strike reaction meshed with a growing "Red Scare" of the early Cold War to taint many militant teachers with the charge of "subversion" and the resulting purge of teachers from the ranks of many locals decimated the activist core of those locals during the 1950s. Moreover, the chill of the Cold War effectively discouraged teacher strike activity for much of the rest of the decade.

It is worth noting, however, that while strike activity dropped dramatically in the 1950s, it was never completely absent. As one analysis of teacher strikes in New Jersey noted, there were a total of nine strikes during that decade alone. Most were one-day walkouts protesting low salaries and unpaid extra duties, but the AFT local in Garfield walked out for three days in 1953, as did the NEA and AFT affiliates in Bayonne. Teachers in Providence, Rhode Island, struck for a week in 1950 and won a basic contract, one of the first in the nation for teachers. At the same time, a small group of AFT organizers at the national level led by President Carl Megel, while not attacking the no-strike policy directly, stressed to members the advantages of collective bargaining over the often fruitless alternative of begging school boards for overdue raises. Following their lead, in 1958 the AFT officially called for the repeal of state no-strike laws for teachers. Meanwhile in New York, teachers were laying the groundwork for the formation of a new AFT-affiliated union that would win a strike in 1960 that became the watershed for teacher strikes in the twentieth century.

New York teachers had a long tradition of unionization prior to the 1950s, but a Cold War schism over leftists in the old AFT Local 5 had preoccupied the union for much of the late 1940s and early 1950s. In 1953, a young energetic organizer from Michigan, David Selden, came to New York City and began to organize teachers into a newly rechartered AFT Local 2. The previous year, New York City's high school teachers had staged a boycott of after-school activities until coaches received extra pay for this work, so New York teachers were no strangers to collective action. Within four years, New York City teachers threatened a one-day work stoppage to protest low pay, but it was called off when the board granted a last-minute raise. The following year, New York's evening high school teachers organized a mass resignation followed by picketing. This was done to protest low pay and poor working conditions with the "resignations" being a tactic for circumventing New York's draconian Condon-Wadlin anti-strike law. The success of this action paved the way for the formation of the United Federation of Teachers (UFT), which combined high school and elementary teachers into a single citywide union.

In what can be seen as the beginning of the modern collective bargaining era for K–12 teachers in the United States, the UFT launched a one-day strike on November 7, 1960, to convince the mayor and the board of education to hold an election that would enable teachers to choose a collective bargaining unit. State law forbade public employee strikes and the striking teachers risked dismissal, but almost half went on strike and thousands formed picket lines around the schools. The teachers prevailed and the city agreed to hold a collective bargaining election the following spring. In the subsequent election, the UFT was chosen by the teachers to be its collective bargaining agent and began negotiations with the New York City board of education. The UFT's demands included a pay raise, sick pay for substitutes, a fifty-minute break for lunch, and binding arbitration for enforcement of collective bargaining rights.

During negotiations for its first contract, board intransigence again forced the UFT to strike in April 1962, when negotiations over salary reached an impasse. This second strike lasted only one day, but the willingness of some 25,000 teachers to strike convinced New York governor Nelson Rockefeller to intervene. He found additional funds to cover a raise for the teachers. In the final version of the contract, the board inserted a no-strike clause that was so broadly written as to prohibit any future teacher strike as "contrary to public policy." The UFT faced a dilemma: if it refused to accept the contract, it risked losing the gains it had already won, but if it accepted the no-strike pledge, the union would be in effect renouncing the right to strike. UFT leaders resolved the dilemma by signing the contract while at the same time adopting a "no contract, no work" policy that reserved the right to strike in the absence of a contract. "In a single stroke the union had turned the tables on the board of education," wrote David Selden of the AFT. "Instead of renouncing the right to strike, the union had reasserted that right and strengthened it."

As with the strikes following World War II, teachers made significant gains in New York, but political leaders there again sought to limit the ability of public sector workers to strike. The 1962 strike along with other high-profile public sector strikes led the New York state legislature to pass the so-called Taylor Law, which legalized collective bargaining for public employees but severely limited the conditions under which those employees could strike. Nevertheless, the UFT's militancy grew in the 1960s, and New York teachers successfully struck again in 1967 for increased funding for schools, smaller class sizes, and greater teacher control over curricular decisions. After gaining recognition, the UFT continued to negotiate successive contracts that brought teachers higher salaries, benefits, and a greater voice in district policies and working conditions. The significance of the early UFT strikes is difficult to overestimate, for the UFT had now set the standard for teacher contracts nationwide.

The success of the UFT led to a major organizing effort by AFT locals all over the United States in the 1960s. In a major shift, in 1963 the national convention of the AFT ended its decades-long "no-strike" policy. Selden describes how AFT organizers fanned out across the United States, determined to set up locals and win collective bargaining for teachers in major urban school districts such as Philadelphia and Boston, while the organization added to existing staff in Los Angeles, Chicago, Milwaukee, and Newark. In 1964, Detroit's AFT local won its first contract and, in a harbinger of the growing political power of teachers' unions, backed a slate of candidates for school board. Some of the early strikes took a page from the worker rebellions of the 1930s. For example, in 1965, Hamtramck, Michigan, teachers, like the autoworkers of the 1930s, held a two-week sit-down strike. Pittsburgh teachers, many of whom had a strong connection to the city's blue-collar workforce, went on strike to earn collective bargaining rights in 1967. When police arrested several of the striking teachers, the public outcry convinced a sympathetic judge to release them. Similarly, in Gary, Indiana, the AFT local first won collective bargaining rights in 1967. The union's first major strike in 1970 lasted two weeks, while a second strike lasted an entire month, from mid-April to mid-May in 1972. Gary's first African-American mayor, Richard Hatcher, who had won with the support of Gary's black schoolteachers, finally mediated a settlement, establishing the union as a major player in city politics for the next decade.

The 1960 UFT strike resulted in a jump in AFT membership, and by 1966 membership in the AFT had increased to more than 125,000 teachers nationwide. By 1968, AFT locals had become the collective bargaining agent for teachers in New York, Chicago, Philadelphia, Detroit, Boston, Kansas City, Cleveland, Newark, Toledo, St. Louis, New Orleans, Washington, DC, and many other cities. In many cases, teachers had to strike or threaten to strike in order to win basic collective bargaining contracts. According to the AFT, there were more than 300 teacher strikes during the 1960s, and in 1967 alone there were at least 105 teacher strikes nationwide. David Selden has calculated that at least 1,000 school districts experienced a strike or threatened strike during the hard-fought representation struggles of the 1960s, and another 2,000 to 3,000 districts saw job actions of one kind or another short of a strike.

While nationwide statistics are difficult to come by, some states have compiled statistical records of teacher strikes. A study of public sector strikes in Michigan from 1965 to 1988 documented no less than 622 teacher strikes in that state alone. The impact of the New York strike was felt in the NEA as well. The willingness of teachers to strike for the right to win collective bargaining rights was a major reason the NEA, which had previously been lukewarm to the idea of unionism for teachers, reassessed its policy on collective bargaining in 1962 and adopted policies on collective bargaining that closely resembled the AFT's. As one historian of the NEA, Donald J. Keck, has written, "For over 100 years the NEA had been essentially a professional society. In a single decade it became one of the largest and most powerful unions in the United States."

While the UFT could be seen as an innovator in using strikes to bargain for teachers, the union soon became embroiled in a conflict that pitted the teachers' newly won bargaining power against community control, an idea that emerged from the civil rights movement. The result was the 1968 Ocean Hill–Brownsville (OH-B) strike, which revealed deep schisms between the labor and civil rights constituencies in New York City.

The 1968 Ocean Hill–Brownsville strike had its roots in the deteriorating economic base in many of New York City's communities of color in the decades following World War II. In 1968, the median family income of the community was less than half the federal poverty line and the city had neglected the community's infrastructure. This economic destitution exacerbated other social problems as well. The high school dropout rate hovered around 70 percent, and less than a third of the residents had finished high school. Community leaders felt that these educational problems could be addressed at least in part through greater community control of the schools.

Community groups organized a local school board for Ocean Hill–Brownsville, led by the Reverend C. Herbert Oliver, though there was contention between the local board and central administrators about how much authority the local board actually had over personnel decisions. The local board wanted control over the hiring of teachers and curriculum. Conflict with the union arose when teachers realized that the personnel authority sought by the local board would violate some of the UFT's most hard-won contractual gains. This conflict formed the crux of the 1968 strike. For the UFT the issue was the threat that the local board posed to its professional dignity. For decades teachers had struggled to gain some measure of respect and workplace control, and the local board appeared to be an effort to circumvent the UFT's power altogether. As Albert Shanker, the UFT president, wrote, according to Jerald Podair, at the time: "How would you react if you could be fired without any charges or any procedures to hear your objections? I think you will agree that a union is worth nothing if it fails to defend the rights of its members to their jobs and to a fair procedure for dismissal."

In addition, racial and cultural tensions between teachers and community leaders surfaced during the strike. Historian Jerald Podair argues persuasively that the 1968 teacher strikes in New York City reconfigured the city's political landscape, polarizing white and black citizens at the same time as it heightened class tensions. The Ocean Hill–Brownsville community was overwhelmingly African-American and Puerto Rican, while OH-B teachers were mostly white. For a number of years prior to the 1968 strike, there had been a growing rift over the educational philosophy best suited to the black community. The UFT tended to support a philosophy of "compensatory" education that would bring to bear greater educational resources to prepare students to enter "mainstream" American culture. The assumption behind this philosophy, many felt, was that African-American children were hampered by a "culture of poverty" that manifested itself as a "pathology" and hindered academic achievement and social advancement.

Critics of compensatory education argued that the lack of "achievement" was more a result of institutional racism and an educational hierarchy that lacked any genuine respect for the culture and values of the African-American community.

To many community activists in New York, the predominantly white UFT represented another element of an oppressive power structure that harmed their community.

The rift between white teachers and black parents had grown wider during a two-week UFT strike in September 1967, when the UFT sought among its contract demands a controversial "disruptive child" provision that would give teachers the unilateral power to remove seriously misbehaving students from their classrooms. A number of African-American teachers who were members of a rival association called the African American Teachers' Association (ATA) crossed the picket lines during the September 1967 strike. Later, during the height of the 1968 strike, hostility between the union and the community led some activists to accuse the UFT of "raping" the African-American and Puerto Rican communities.

The racial tension was further exacerbated by the hostility between the city's power structure and the union. A number of the city's elite policy makers, including Mayor John Lindsay, sympathized with the community control experiment and saw in it a means of reining in public employees' unions that he felt were too strong. Board of Education president John Doar, who was appointed by Lindsay, agreed, telling an interviewer in 1968 that he thought the situation reflected a fundamental split between civil rights and labor. "Union concepts of security and seniority were formulated in the period of struggle between company and union," he said. "Now the struggle is between the Negroes and the unions. It is our position that a basic conflict exists between labor union concepts and civil rights concepts."

The OH-B community control advocates found an ally in one of the most influential corporate foundations, the Ford Foundation, which offered financial backing to the activists. The foundation's support heightened the sense among UFT teachers that the community control experiment was a Trojan horse for an anti-union agenda.

A notable exception to the growing racial rancor engendered by the strikes was the position of A. Philip Randolph and Bayard Rustin, two African Americans who had argued for years that the issues of civil rights and labor rights were part of a larger struggle for social democracy. Randolph and Rustin maintained solidarity with the UFT, but they were almost alone among New York's black leadership. In an open letter, quoted by Podair, they argued that the "real issue" was class, not race. "If due process is not won in Ocean Hill–Brownsville," they wrote, "what could prevent white community groups in Queens from firing black teachers?" For its part, the UFT sought an alliance with the city's Central Labor Council, which was dominated by the city's craft and construction unions.

The strike began on May 9, 1968, when the local Ocean Hill board dismissed thirteen teachers as well as six other supervisory personnel from Junior High School 271. The union insisted that the due process rights of the dismissed teachers had been violated and that they be reinstated. On May 14, when the teachers showed up at JHS 271, they were met by a wall of angry community residents and ATA members, who blocked their entry. In firing the teachers, the local board had deliberately singled out a number of prominent UFT members and dispensed with the procedural rights accorded dismissed teachers by the collective bargaining agreement. The chair of the local board's personnel committee considered due process for the teachers as little more than "laws written to protect the white monied power structure of this city," while the UFT saw due process as the bedrock of teacher—and worker—rights.

New York superintendent of schools Bernard Donovan immediately ordered the teachers reinstated, but a local parents' group moved to block their return and UFT president Albert Shanker threatened a strike unless the teachers were reinstated. Angry crowds blocked repeated attempts by the dismissed teachers to return to JHS 271 until Mayor Lindsay ordered them escorted by police. On May 22, 350 UFT members in OH-B struck in support of their ousted colleagues and remained out for the rest of the academic year. By early June, the UFT and the OH-B board had agreed to mediation of the dispute by Theodore Kheel, who suggested that all the teachers should be reinstated unless serious allegations of misconduct could be proven. The UFT agreed to this but the local board did not. The board rejected even the temporary reinstatement of seven of the teachers, and within a week Rhody McCoy, who had been appointed as a local administrator by the OH-B board, sent letters of dismissal to all the striking teachers.

Over the summer, tensions continued to build, as a retired civil court judge brought in by Donovan to mediate the case of the dismissed teachers ruled that the teachers had been illegally fired and were entitled to return to their jobs. Meanwhile, McCoy hired replacement teachers and UFT leaders recommended a strike vote, contending that the community control plan violated the collective bargaining contract of the teachers. When talks over reinstatement of the ten teachers cleared by the judge broke down on September 7, 1968, the UFT voted to strike. Two days later, nearly 95 percent of the teachers in New York City—more than 54,000 teachers—went on strike. A compromise was reached the next day with the central New York City school board and teachers returned to work, but after striking teachers were harassed and threatened at JHS 271 in OH-B, the union walked out a second time on September 13 and held a rally of 15,000 mostly white pro-UFT demonstrators at City Hall. This second strike lasted until September 30, when the central board, after negotiations with the UFT, ordered the local board to reinstate the teachers and station observers to monitor compliance at troubled OH-B schools.

On October 9, after replacement teachers and community members clashed with returning UFT teachers at JHS 271, Superintendent Donovan ordered the school closed. On October 13, the union voted to strike a third time, alleging the central board was not enforcing its original agreement to stand behind the reinstated teachers in OH-B. This time teachers stayed off the job over a month, until November 19. On October 17, a massive rally of over 40,000 in support of the UFT outside City Hall demonstrated to Mayor Lindsay that he would have to settle with the UFT. Ultimately the state stepped in, negotiating a settlement that temporarily suspended the local board and ordered it to be placed under trusteeship after the suspension, reinstated the UFT teachers, and established a state commission to assure the rights and safety of teachers.

The following year, the legislature passed a school decentralization bill that gave the UFT most of what it wanted. The decentralization law of 1969 reduced the power of local boards over personnel, made the central city school board elected rather than appointed and, most importantly for the UFT, protected the job rights of teachers. Unfortunately, despite the UFT's apparent victory on the due process issue, the African-American and Puerto Rican communities, including Ocean Hill–Brownsville, continued to suffer the effects of postindustrial economic malaise. The racially polarized politics of New York City in the 1970s led to a conservative turn among growing numbers of white voters, who cut funding for many of the city's social services, including education.

In the 1960s, New Jersey teachers renewed their own struggle for unionization. Prior to 1936, the New Jersey Education Association (NJEA), an NEA affiliate, represented teachers in some of the largest urban districts in the state. The NJEA, like its national counterpart, saw itself as a professional association and eschewed strikes and other forms of teacher militancy. Beginning in 1936, the Newark Teachers' Union (NTU), an AFT-affiliated local, began to organize teachers in Newark, and the two organizations vied for the loyalty of New Jersey teachers. Activist teachers formed the NTU. They wanted a union and believed that the strike was a legitimate means for teachers to obtain better working conditions when other methods failed. As Esther Tumin, an early NTU activist, told historian Steve Golin, the NJEA "considered [the NTU teachers] radicals, and they considered themselves professionals, and felt that *strike* was a dirty word because professionals don't strike." Another Newark teacher, Harold Moore, characterized the early NJEA as "a big zero. . . . There were no changes as a result of anything they did—anything that I can remember. And the [NTU] was militant, strident, and that was in keeping with the time, I think. Those were strident times in our history."

Despite the NJEA's lukewarm position on strikes prior to the late 1960s, eleven strikes occurred in New Jersey in the eighteen-year period between 1945 and 1963, most lasting one day and the vast majority involving salary issues. By contrast, in the subsequent eighteen-year period between 1963 and 1981, New Jersey teachers were engaged in a total of 160 separate strikes of at least one day in duration. The majority of teachers' strikes during this period occurred in NEA affiliates because, as Gaswirth's study of New Jersey teachers' strikes concludes, competition from the more militant AFT affiliates pressured the NJEA to embrace collective bargaining and the right to strike by the late 1960s.

Not only did teachers' strikes in New Jersey become more common, but the issues over which teachers struck became more varied. After 1965, issues such as working conditions, school supplies and buildings, control over curricular decisions, class size, school budget cuts, grievance procedures, and administrative prerogatives, such as unpaid duties and involuntary reassignment, became issues to strike over. Instead of destroying professionalism, as some in the NEA had alleged, the existence of collective bargaining rights and the right to strike appear to have given teachers in New Jersey an additional means to defend and even expand professional rights and prerogatives.

The Newark Teachers' Union paid attention to the growth of the UFT in neighboring New York. It captured the allegiance of a large cohort of young teachers in 1968 and 1969 and built the organization with a network of school site representatives who listened to teachers' grievances. The NTU won a hotly contested representation election in 1969, becoming the recognized bargaining agent for the Newark teachers and setting the stage for a pair of dramatic teacher strikes in Newark in 1970 and 1971.

Golin has described how Newark teachers in 1970 faced many of the same problems faced by other large urban school districts at that time: overcrowded classrooms and a lack of adequate educational supplies combined with low pay and the gradual loss of control over many curricular decisions. Moreover, rising unemployment and the loss of a stable job base in urban areas like Newark added to the challenges faced by students and teachers alike. The NTU presented an initial set of demands to the school board in 1970 that included smaller class size; the elimination of "nonprofessional chores" (those extra duties like lunch and recess monitoring that teachers were expected to perform without additional compensation); a seniority system for transfers and reassignments; and, perhaps most importantly for Newark teachers, a binding arbitration system for enforcing the contract and resolving teacher grievances. These key issues for Newark teachers were not primarily about money, but sought to increase the teachers' voice in the workplace as well as improve the educational quality of the schools. Binding arbitration was the cornerstone of all these issues because teachers believed it was essential to their ability to enforce their rights in the workplace.

The board negotiating team, led by an experienced negotiator in Newark attorney Jacob Fox, thought teachers' concerns about class size and educational quality were "bunk" and approached the negotiations determined to block any efforts by teachers to infringe on what the board saw as its prerogatives to manage. The board initially offered the NTU more money, but as Newark teacher Hannah Litzky remembered, "The teachers were more concerned with working conditions and the welfare of the pupils, which the board negotiators refused to discuss."

With talks at an impasse, the NTU held a mass strike meeting on February 1, 1970, and with the press assembled, NTU members voted overwhelmingly to strike. The teachers' experience with the board had led them to believe that only a willingness to strike would win teachers the improvements they sought in working conditions and educational quality.

The 1970 Newark strike lasted three weeks, and the board took a hard line. During the first week of the strike, the board asked the Essex County Superior Court to issue arrest orders against seven union leaders. In the second week of the strike, Judge Ward Herbert issued an injunction against rank-and-file picketers, and police went to schools and ordered picketers to disperse. In the course of the strike, a total of 188 teachers were arrested and charged with violating a court order. Among those arrested was AFT president David Selden, who had joined the picket lines. The arrests tightened the battle lines of the strike, as New Jersey labor leaders rallied to the teachers' side and New Jersey judges criminalized the strike. Joseph Weintraub, chief justice of the New Jersey Supreme Court, called the strike "an attack upon the state." Meanwhile, hundreds of striking teachers rallied outside the courthouse, where they held a "funeral for justice," and civil rights leader Bayard Rustin and UFT president Albert Shanker cheered the striking teachers. Throughout the strike, roughly two-thirds of the teachers in Newark stayed out of work, and the solidarity of the teachers, combined with the intervention of Newark mayor Hugh Addonizio, convinced the board to reach a settlement.

As a result of the 1970 strike, the Newark teachers won a modest pay increase and the board promised to hire 252 teachers' aides to take over many of the "nonprofessional duties." The contract included limits on class size and, most significantly, a grievance procedure with binding arbitration that teachers hoped would enable them to enforce the contract provisions and protect their rights. The NTU scored a major victory in 1970, but some aspects of the strike inflamed already simmering racial tensions in Newark. These would boil to the surface a year later during a strike the NTU would later call "the most bitter and savage teacher strike ever seen in the history of this country"—the Newark strike of 1971.

Many of the same race and class issues that shaped the Ocean Hill–Brownsville strike echoed in Newark in 1971, though the echo reverberated somewhat differently as a result of Newark's political and social landscape. As in New York City, Newark's Black Power movement, led by Amiri Baraka, was taking aim at the school system as a bastion of white privilege and cultural dominance, arguing instead for community control and an Afrocentric curriculum. The NTU had also inflamed many in the African-American community when it invited Albert Shanker, whom they saw as a symbol of white teacher power, to speak before the Newark teachers during the strike. Jesse Jacob, an avowed opponent of the NTU, accused "Shanker and his hoods" of destroying the community control experiment in Ocean Hill–Brownsville. During the 1970 strike, black activists had invited Rhody McCoy to speak to black community leaders, urging them to defeat the teachers' union and strike a blow against "white supremacy and racism." Parents in Newark had been split along ominously racial lines, with parents in the predominantly African-American neighborhoods opposing the striking teachers and, in some cases, organizing volunteers to cross picket lines and teach during the strike, while in predominantly Italian-American wards, parents overwhelmingly supported the strikers. These lines, visible during the first strike, would be hardened during the second strike, adding racial tension to the already volatile labor-management conflict.

There were differences between Newark and New York. In Newark it was much more difficult to portray the union's campaign for "teacher power" as a stalking horse for "white power." In New York City, 90 percent of the city's teachers had been white, while in Newark nearly 38 percent of the teachers were African-American. Whereas the UFT leadership had been overwhelmingly white in 1968, the NTU had elected Carole Graves, an African-American teacher and one of the union's heroes during the 1970 strike, as president. Moreover, Graves's slate of leaders included many African Americans as well as women. Despite its "old guard" of white male teachers, the NTU was rapidly changing. Historian Steve Golin has concluded that by 1970–71 the NTU was probably the most racially integrated group in the district. The fact remains, however, that in an era of social unrest and economic stagnation, the educational system in Newark (as in other urban areas) would come in for its share of blame for many of these problems. In Newark, with its history of racism that had exploded in the city's 1967 riots, the grievances of the African-American community clashed with the newfound muscle of the Newark Teachers' Union.

In October 1970, the NTU prepared for negotiations, but the school board refused to negotiate, hoping to break the union. In January, just days before the contract was set to expire, school board president Jesse Jacob refused to meet with NTU president Carole Graves, setting the tone for the confrontation to follow. A state-appointed mediator, Jonas Silver, proposed a settlement on January 25 that would have made some minor modifications to the binding arbitration system and would have required teachers to perform some, though not all, "nonprofessional chores," but the board rejected it. Anticipating a deadlock, Graves lined up support from the Industrial Union Council of New Jersey. Prior to the expiration of the contract on January 31, Newark's newly elected mayor, Ken Gibson, had actually negotiated a tentative settlement with the NTU behind closed doors, which allowed the teachers to maintain binding arbitration, but the board again rejected the offer and seemed determined to push its gambit to break the union.

When the contract expired on January 31, 1971, the board instead issued its list of forty-eight demands, which included concessions on every major issue the union had won during the previous strike. The board proposed the complete elimination of binding arbitration and restoration of all "nonprofessional chores." These concessions were particularly galling considering the fact that in October an arbitrator had ruled in favor of the union on the question of nonprofessional chores, a major victory that resulted from the earlier strike. In addition, as if to twist the knife further, the board proposed that there be no time limit on faculty meetings after school hours, and that teachers henceforth be required to punch a time clock at each school site. Considering the experience of the previous strike, the board's proposals seemed calculated to provoke a second strike. On the evening of January 31, at a mass meeting of the NTU, teachers voted overwhelmingly to strike. For many, there was no alternative. If the teachers did not strike, everything for which they had fought so hard in the previous strike would be lost.

As the strike began, the racial tensions that had simmered during the first strike boiled to the surface almost immediately. Prior to the second strike, some in the African-American community were particularly incensed by the teachers' interpretation of the ban on "nonprofessional chores" and the way in which some teachers, in order to enforce the board's agreement, would refuse to perform such duties as playground supervision or walking children to and from the classrooms. What to the teachers was a demonstration against management was seen by many parents in the African-American community as a racist refusal to support the education of black children.

On the morning of February 2, as fifteen teachers were leaving the downtown office of the NTU preparing to head to the picket lines, they were confronted and attacked by approximately twenty African-American men. Six teachers were hospitalized with injuries and two teachers had to be kept overnight. That night, at a large NTU rally, two of the injured teachers told their story, while television cameras recorded the event. The incident galvanized the teachers, and the number of teachers who stayed out the next day increased dramatically (throughout the second strike approximately 50 percent of the Newark teachers stayed home at any given time, though this number spiked upward in the aftermath of the attack).

As with the first strike, parents and students in the predominantly African-American wards tended to oppose the strike, while the strike's support was much higher in the predominantly Italian-American wards. Teachers, fearing for their safety, began to carry weapons such as screwdrivers or knives for their protection, and verbal confrontations quickly escalated on the front lines of the strike. Carloads of strike opponents often cruised by picket lines in the morning, hurling epithets at strikers, and striking teachers often took their frustration and anger out on those who crossed the picket line. "The picket lines were vicious scenes," remembered NTU president Carole Graves, and the vandalizing of cars—on both sides—became a common occurrence. As if racial tensions were not already at the breaking point, in the aftermath of the February 2 attack, groups of white toughs, led by Tony Imperiale, a voluble figure in Newark's Italian-American community who was notorious in the African-American community for his racist rhetoric, began to prowl the streets as "protection" for teachers on the picket lines.

As the labor dispute began to disintegrate into a racially charged conflict, the school board continued to take a hard line with the teachers. The board refused to budge on its position, and as the strike dragged into its second month, it suspended 347 striking teachers, canceling their benefits, and began proceedings to have them fired. In late March, the Superior Court of Essex County again issued arrest warrants for picketers, and many began to return to work under the threat of dismissal and arrest. Since the state's 1968 law establishing the Public Employment Relations Commission (PERC) provided public employees no mechanism to force good-faith negotiations or determine unfair labor practices, there was little the union could legally do. In the end, approximately 500 hard-core teachers remained on strike the entire time, and many were forced to find new jobs to make ends meet as the strike dragged on.

Mayor Gibson began to intervene by moving negotiations downtown in hopes of insulating the negotiators from community pressure and by appointing Clarence Coggins, a respected figure among community organizers and labor leaders, as advisor to a new state-appointed mediator, Ron Houghton. Houghton, too, had a good relationship with the AFT and was able to reach out to the African-American community by bringing in two liaisons, Dee Watson and Warren Taylor, who had connections in the community. Houghton effectively worked on members of the board who might be willing to compromise and isolated the hard-liners. Meanwhile, the mayor tried to build momentum for compromise, finding allies in both the African-American and Italian-American communities. By early April the two sides had hammered out a compromise settlement that maintained arbitration, but allowed for a tripartite panel of arbitrators (one chosen by the union, one by the board, and one agreeable to both). The compromise on nonprofessional duties required teachers to perform a few minor duties such as walking students to and from the classrooms at the beginning and end of the day, but relieved them of most major nonprofessional chores. The settlement was initially voted down by a one-vote margin at a rancorous April 7 board meeting, but Mayor Gibson's efforts finally resulted in approval of the settlement by April 19.

In the end, nearly 200 teachers were sent to jail for their participation in the strike, but the experience firmly established the NTU as a power in the Newark school system. The NTU conducted a one-week strike in 1976 and a two-day strike in 1980, but neither was as significant or as divisive as the 1971 strike.

Teacher militancy was not limited to the East Coast. On the West Coast, the teacher rebellion of the 1960s also had an impact, and the result was resurgent teacher activism and a number of high-profile strikes. In 1968, the San Francisco Federation of Teachers (SFFT) staged a one-day walkout that won salary increases, improved benefits, smaller class sizes, and the hiring of 300 new teachers under a union-negotiated affirmative action plan. Successful strikes in 1971 and 1974 built on those gains.

The passage of Proposition 13 in 1978 had a devastating impact on California teachers. The San Francisco school board used the budgetary changes wrought by the tax-cutting measure to lay off approximately 1,200 San Francisco teachers, provoking a bitter six-week strike in 1979 that forced the district to rehire the teachers and staff. Berkeley's teachers staged a six-week strike in 1976 that enjoyed the support of a majority of teachers and parents in the district, but ultimately had to settle for less than they had hoped. As Fred Glass has described, neighboring Oakland had a long history of socially active unionism, with the Oakland teachers' unions supporting the downtown general strike of 1946 and being allied with Oakland's labor and civil rights constituencies for decades.

In Southern California, the United Teachers of Los Angeles (UTLA), formed by the merger of an NEA local and an AFT local in 1969, engaged in its own struggle to win a contract and improve both pay and educational conditions in the Los Angeles Unified School District (LAUSD). Los Angeles teachers had been divided between NEA and AFT affiliates prior to 1970, and this lack of unity hampered two short-lived strikes in the late 1960s. In May 1968, AFT Local 1021 called a one-day walkout that was not supported by the NEA local, and the weak turnout hampered the effectiveness of the job action. In September 1969, the two locals agreed to another one-day walkout. However, when Local 1021 wanted a longer strike the NEA-affiliated local was unwilling to support it, and Los Angeles school superintendent Jack Crowther was able to keep the schools open, once more undercutting the strike's effectiveness.

Finally, with a unified front in 1970, teachers in Los Angeles engaged in a twenty-day strike that won them a contract that included a significant pay increase as well as provisions for smaller class sizes and additional funding for inner-city school reading programs. Without collective bargaining rights, however, the contract was negated by Superior Court Judge John L. Cole, an appointee of then-Governor Ronald Reagan, who said that the contract was illegal because teachers lacked collective bargaining rights. UTLA was hampered until California teachers helped to get the legislature to pass a collective bargaining law for K–12 teachers in 1975. Three years later, however, Proposition 13 placed strict limits on property taxes and shifted much decision making over school funding from local school boards to the state. In the early 1980s, the UTLA worked at both the state and local level to secure more funding for Los Angeles schools, and after a one-day walkout in 1983, UTLA won teachers a significant pay raise. Four years later, when it was discovered that locksmiths in the LAUSD made more than starting teachers ($31,000 a year and $20,600, respectively), teachers staged another one-day walkout and won a 10 percent pay increase, followed by an additional 5 percent the following fall.

By 1989, low salaries relative to the high cost of living in Los Angeles again became an issue for UTLA teachers. The union wanted a 12 percent pay increase but the district was only willing to offer a 4.1 percent increase. The union cited a study by the Los Angeles County Office of Education showing that LAUSD teachers ranked twenty-ninth out of forty-three districts in teacher pay. The union began by using job actions short of striking to put pressure on the district. Teachers boycotted duties unrelated to teaching, such as recess duty and completing attendance records. Teachers later refused to turn in grades until a settlement was reached. The UTLA sought a 20 percent raise over two years, and the district countered with an offer of 20 percent over three years. When the two sides reached an impasse, teachers voted to strike, and on May 15, 1989, nearly 25,000 UTLA teachers went on strike.

After more than a week, with student attendance collapsing, State Senator David Roberti and State Assemblywoman Maxine Waters met separately with district and union officials and hammered out a compromise that was acceptable to both sides. Teachers received a 24 percent wage increase over three years, the contract eliminated yard duty for elementary teachers, and the union received an agency fee for each teacher who did not join the union but was nonetheless represented by the union in collective bargaining. Circumstances were much more favorable to teachers in 1989, argues John Donovan. Unlike 1970, in 1989 teachers had collective bargaining rights in California, UTLA was more unified, and the state government was more willing to work with the teachers. The experience of the two major Los Angeles teacher strikes demonstrates that the political climate and union cohesion are two key factors affecting the success of strikes.

In the wake of the teacher rebellions of the 1960s, there was a maturation of teachers' unions in an era of collective bargaining. The nation saw a rise of teacher militancy during the 1970s, as teachers' unions began to push for more of a voice in educational policy. The "teacher power movement" sought to influence issues such as class size and the mentoring of new teachers and to place innovative ideas such as the formation of teacher-controlled committees to counterbalance the power of school boards and principals. The NEA also took a more politically active role with its 1976 endorsement of Jimmy Carter, and began a trend toward the support of candidates by teachers' organizations. The 1980s and 1990s saw the number of strikes decline nationwide, but also saw increased political activism in teachers' unions. During the 1980s, teachers' unions responded to the critics of public education who sought significant changes in the structure of public education through voucher programs, charter school initiatives, and other measures that had the potential to undermine teachers' unions and workplace rights. By the late 1990s, teachers in a number of cities went on strike in protest of skyrocketing health care costs.

Teachers, like other workers, have often found it necessary to organize, bargain collectively, and strike to improve their compensation and the quality of their working conditions. Teachers' unions and organized job actions, which include strikes as well as "work to rule" and other forms of protest, have frequently involved more than issues of pay and job security. They have often reflected teachers' concerns over the erosion of professional prerogatives such as academic freedom, the role of teachers in shaping the curriculum, and the social concerns of teachers about their communities and their society. Moreover, because the ranks of elementary and secondary schoolteachers have historically been overwhelmingly female, concerns over the dignity and professional recognition of teachers have invariably been connected to larger issues of gender as well as class.

As a special edition of *American Teacher,* the AFT's journal, noted in April 1997, Albert Shanker, a math teacher who was president of the UFT from 1964 to 1986, recognized that teachers faced even more resistance when they tried to bargain for issues that gave them a measure of control over their professional lives.

> In addition to the traditional union goals of improvements in wages, hours, and working conditions, teachers wanted to use their collective power to improve schools in ways that would make them work better for kids. . . . But as soon as the words "good for children" were attached to any union proposal, the board would say, "Now you're trying to dictate public policy to us," and that was the end of that proposal.

In short, the history of teachers' strikes is more than a history of teachers engaging in collective action for better pay and benefits. It is also a history of teachers asserting their rights as working people and their dignity as professionals, and fighting to improve the education of their students.

See also: Civil Rights Strikes, 118; Three Strikes Against the New York City Transit System, 277; Social Workers and Strikes, 287.

Bibliography

Altenbaugh, Richard J., ed. *The Teacher's Voice: A Social History of Teaching in Twentieth-Century America.* Washington, DC: Falmer Press, 1992.

Citizens Research Council of Michigan. *Public Sector Strikes in Michigan.* Detroit: Citizens Research Council of Michigan, 1988.

Curti, Merle. *The Social Ideas of American Educators.* Patterson, NJ : Charles Scribner and Sons, 1959.

Donovan, Join. "A Tale of Two Strikes: The Formation of United Teachers—Los Angeles and the Los Angeles Teacher Strikes of 1970 and 1989." *Southern California Quarterly* 81 (Fall 1999): 377–88.

Gaswirth, Marc, William M. Weinberg, and Barbara E. Kemmerer. *Teachers' Strikes in New Jersey. Studies in Industrial Relations and Human Resources, No. 1.* Metuchen, NJ: Scarecrow Press, 1982.

Golin, Steve. *The Newark Teacher Strikes: Hopes on the Line.* New Brunswick, NJ: Rutgers University Press, 2002.

Murphy, Marjorie. *Blackboard Unions: The AFT and the NEA, 1900–1980.* Ithaca, NY: Cornell University Press, 1990.

Podair, Jerald E. *The Strike That Changed New York: Blacks, Whites, and the Ocean Hill–Brownsville Crisis.* New Haven, CT: Yale University Press, 2002.

Selden, David. *The Teacher Rebellion.* Washington, DC: Howard University Press, 1985.

Tyack, David. *The One Best System: A History of American Urban Education.* Cambridge, MA: Harvard University Press, 1974.

Urofsky, Melvin, ed. *Why Teachers Strike: Teachers' Rights and Community Control.* New York: Doubleday, 1970.

Wrigley, Julia. *Class Politics and Public Schools: Chicago, 1900–1950.* New Brunswick, NJ: Rutgers University Press, 1982.

POSTAL WORKERS' STRIKES

Aaron Brenner

The first strike of postal workers took place in 1868, but little is known about the walkout. It took 102 years before there was a second post office strike—but what a strike! It began slowly at 12:01 A.M. on March 18, 1970, when a handful of letter carriers set up a picket line outside the massive General Post Office building in Manhattan. A few of them held makeshift signs demanding higher pay. Most shoved their hands in their pockets to stave off a late winter chill. Hardly anyone noticed. Postal workers, like other government workers, were widely viewed as loyal and passive civil servants. Their unions, lacking real collective bargaining rights, did little more than lobby. Federal law prohibited strikes against the federal government, imposing a $1,000 fine and/or one year and a day in jail against violators. Yet within two days, some 200,000 postal employees joined picket lines in front of post offices throughout the country, making theirs not only the largest strike against the federal government, but also the largest wildcat strike in U.S. history.

Though unprecedented, the 1970 postal strike was not an isolated incident. Rather, it was perhaps the most dramatic example of rank-and-file militancy in a period characterized by widespread labor unrest, and as such it shared many of the same causes and took many of the same forms as agitation by other union workers. Like other groups of workers, postal workers resented the deterioration of their wages, the intransigence of management, and the indolence of their union leaders. These resentments led them to challenge their employers, defy their union leaders, go on strike, and create their own independent rank-and-file organizations. Yet the postal strike also had roots in the unique organization of the Post Office, the specific conditions of postal employment, and the particular social composition of the postal workforce.

Post Office Crisis

The Post Office in the late 1960s was in crisis. Between 1960 and 1970, the amount of mail handled rose by more than one-third, to over 80 billion pieces a year. Simultaneously, the cost of handling all that mail more than doubled. Though the Post Office had almost always operated in the red, by 1969 the deficit was draining more than $1 billion a year from the national treasury—ten times the 1946 amount. Projections indicated the deficit would grow faster if no remedies were sought. As the debt rose, service deteriorated. The number of pickups and deliveries, often two or three a day in busy areas such as New York City, was reduced. The speed of delivery also fell. As M. Brady Mikusko has reported, after president-elect John F. Kennedy named J. Edward Day Postmaster General in 1961, he was asked whether Day intended to restore twice-a-day delivery. Noting that a recent letter of his took eight days to reach Boston, Kennedy replied that he hoped Day "would be able to restore once-a-day delivery." These delays were widespread by the end of the decade, prompting *BusinessWeek* to complain in March 1970 that "a debtor's claim that he did not get a bill [in the mail] is as good today as a note from the doctor." In one dramatic example of how troubles were literally mounting, 10 million pieces of mail sat heaped upon the Chicago Post Office floor for three weeks during October 1966. Summing up the crisis in April 1967, Postmaster General Lawrence F. O'Brien declared, according to the *New*

York Times, that the Post Office was in "a race with catastrophe."

Crisis in the Post Office hit postal workers hard. By most standards, letter carriers, postal clerks, mail handlers, special delivery messengers, and workers in the other postal crafts were drastically underpaid. In 1970, the starting yearly salary of postal workers was $6,176. By comparison, the starting salary for sanitation workers in New York City was $7,870, or 27.4 percent higher. Police and firefighters in the same city earned 53.8 percent more than postal workers, and transit workers received 61.9 percent more. Postal workers in other American cities experienced similar discrepancies.

Though federal employees, postal workers received wages well below those needed to meet federally defined acceptable living standards. A married letter carrier with two children and twenty-three years of experience earned $2,836, or 25.2 percent, less than the amount the federal government calculated workers needed to maintain a moderate standard of living in New York City. A starting postal worker earned $600 less than the federal government's budget estimate for a low standard of living in the same city. Wages were so low that as many as 10 percent of full-time postal workers in New York City applied for and received supplemental city welfare benefits. Many postal workers who did not apply for welfare worked second and third jobs, driving taxis, doing deliveries, pressing clothes, parking cars, and so on. James Troupe, a letter carrier who lived in the Bronx, told the *New York Times* that he would do anything "to make ends meet and keep my family in dignity."

Post Office managers, representatives, senators, and presidential administrations from John F. Kennedy to Richard M. Nixon publicly acknowledged postal workers' substandard pay and promised to do something. Their efforts never matched their rhetoric. In 1962, Kennedy sponsored the Federal Salary Reform Act, which established the right of federal employees, including postal workers, to earn salaries comparable to those in private employment. The act also prescribed procedures for matching government salary schedules with those in the private sector. Since the wage increases necessary to achieve comparability were too expensive to implement immediately, the act stipulated three annual stages, with the first raise on January 1, 1963, and comparability in 1966. Despite the act, postal workers' salaries never matched those of their private sector counterparts. Each year, the Bureau of Labor Statistics, the Civil Service Commission, and the Bureau of the Budget generated the appropriate wage schedules, but President Lyndon B. Johnson, President Nixon, and Congress refused to pass the required raises.

The Post Office crisis also meant deteriorating job conditions for postal workers, especially in the nation's larger cities. In the mid-1960s, management introduced several cost-cutting procedures that intensified the labor process, including the use of letter-sorting machines (LSMs). A July 1967 study sponsored by the Post Office and carried out by a management professor at Southern Methodist University detailed the stress imposed by the new machines and listed various ailments that "could be the grounds for claims against the government as being job induced." It recommended a battery of physical and mental tests for all LSM operators as well as the exclusion of all workers over the age of forty-five. Decrepit postal facilities posed another danger to postal workers. Many local post offices were built during the Great Depression without adequate heating or air conditioning. Workers shivered in the winter and sweltered in the summer. Health and safety conditions were appalling. According to *BusinessWeek,* postal officials "rolled along accepting a steadily mounting accident rate that by early 1969 had climbed to 16 disablements per million man hours, twice the National Safety Council's industry average."

Postal workers also suffered under increasingly arbitrary and tyrannical management authority. Under Executive Order 10988, signed by President Kennedy, federal government unions won the right to represent their members in relations with management for the first time. For postal unions, this representation excluded bargaining over wages, hours, and fringe benefits, which remained in the hands of Congress and post office management. It included other personnel policies and grievance procedures. However, with only an advisory arbitration procedure (as opposed to binding arbitration), postal unions lacked bargaining leverage. Management retained the right to declare any issue nonnegotiable. Strikes were illegal. Indeed, the order prohibited unions from even asserting the right to strike.

Under the executive order, postal unions made early gains, such as the right to negotiate local working conditions. With the growing fiscal crisis, however, Post Office managers consulted postal unions less often, declared more issues nonnegotiable, and unilaterally imposed their will. Two edicts particularly irritated postal workers: the reduction of overtime, an important source of extra income, and the increased use of temporary workers, who were paid less and had fewer rights on the job. Postal workers also complained about capricious supervisors who had them moving from job to job. In testimony before the Senate Committee on Post Office and Civil Service in 1969, Postmaster General Winton Blount openly admitted that existing supervision practices "smack more of a Dickens novel than of intelligent use of fine (and costly) human talents." These and other labor problems led to skyrocketing employee turnover rates, which in turn intensified the post office crisis.

Johnson and Nixon administration officials expressed sympathy with the plight of postal workers and promised to correct the inequities of Post Office labor relations. Rather than address the issue directly, however, they made labor relations part of an ambitious program to solve the general crisis of the Post Office. Originating in a 1967 speech by Postmaster General Lawrence O'Brien, this program for complete reform of the Post Office eventually became Nixon's first major legislative initiative in May 1969.

Nixon's proposal would transform the Post Office Department into a nonprofit corporation owned by the federal government and operated by a board of directors appointed by the president and confirmed by Congress. Daily management would be left to a professional executive appointed by the board without reference to political affiliation. The Post Office Department would be eliminated and the new Postal Service Corporation would no longer be part of the president's cabinet. It would provide services authorized by Congress, but it would no longer depend upon congressional appropriations for its budget. After a transition period, the Postal Service would be a self-financing corporation, able to issue bonds, rent its property, and increase rates to raise revenue. Rate revision would be subject to public hearings and review by an appointed public commission. On the subject of labor relations, Nixon promised in his recommendations to Congress on postal reform that "there will be, for the first time in history, true collective bargaining in the postal system." Congress would no longer control the appointment of postmasters and rural letter carriers, nor would it set postal workers' wages and benefits. The Postal Service would approximate a private corporation and postal workers would approximate private sector workers.

Nixon's legislative proposal sparked a wide-ranging debate about the role of the Post Office in the American economy, whom it should serve, and how it should be run. This contest over the intricacies of Post Office policy often ran along ideological and political fault lines within and between organized labor, the business community, the government, and consumer groups. Though the debates over postal policy often had little to do with postal labor relations, Nixon's proposal put virtually every aspect of postal operations on the table, thereby creating an arena in which postal workers and their unions could express their grievances and seek redress.

Nixon's proposal contributed to an already expanding rights consciousness among postal workers. During congressional hearings and in various public forums, administration officials filled in the details of Nixon's promise of "true collective bargaining." As they did so, they enumerated a list of rights granted in the proposal and compared them favorably to those enjoyed by workers in private industry. Postal workers would now be covered by the Wagner, Taft-Hartley, and Landrum-Griffin acts, which are enforced by the National Labor Relations Board and the federal courts. For the first time, according to Postmaster General Winton Blount in testimony before the Senate, postal workers would "have a statutory right to organize collectively and to bargain collectively with management on all of the matters—including bread-and-butter issues like wages and hours—which their neighbors in private industry have long been able to bargain for." Charges of unfair labor practices would be handled "just as they are in the private sector." Other disputes would be handled by binding third-party arbitration, similar to that provided for during the life of a "normal collective bargaining agreement" in private industry. Grievance procedures would mirror "those that have come to be accepted as a commonplace in the private sector." But there was one right enjoyed by workers in private industry to which postal workers were not entitled: "The present statutory ban on strikes by federal employees would, of course, continue," said Blount.

By calling for the complete overhaul of Post Office labor relations, extending the enumerated rights of postal workers, and continually referring to the rights of private sector workers, the Nixon administration expanded the arena of debate over postal labor relations. Before the proposal, any discussions of postal workers' collective bargaining privileges were abstract and peripheral because postal workers' interests had to be pursued through Congress. Once collective bargaining appeared on the agenda, however, questions about its extent, including the right to strike, moved to the center of debate. Once there, collective bargaining practices in the private sector shaped the contest. The more the administration said they would resemble private employees, the more postal workers felt they should enjoy the right to strike. As David Silvergleid, president of the National Postal Union, told *BusinessWeek*, "Blount wants to bring us under the provisions of the Taft-Hartley and Landrum-Griffin laws without giving us the right to strike that goes with them. . . . If we have to bargain collectively, we have to have the right to strike on money."

Postal workers' contemplation of their rights coincided with their rising anger over stagnating wages and declining conditions. They felt increasingly betrayed by postal management, Congress, the president, and, in several cases, their own union leaders. A series of perceived insults fueled their frustration. The first of these was Nixon's threat to veto any postal wage legislation that did not include his corporation proposal. Just such legislation was pending, in part to compensate for the small raise Nixon had approved earlier in the year. Already angry at the size of the raise, postal workers were irate at being held hostage to Nixon's political project. Their exasperation grew when he and James Rademacher, the president of the National Association of Letter Carriers (NALC), reached a secret agreement on the corporation proposal. Rademacher dropped his opposition to the plan in exchange for a 5.4 percent wage increase. Other postal union leaders denounced Rademacher for breaking ranks. Rank-and-file postal workers were more infuriated by the skimpy raise, the fact that Rademacher had not held out for the right to strike, and the fact that tying wages to the corporation bill would delay the pay increase.

Postal workers' outrage only grew after Nixon's February 1970 budget message. To fight inflation, he delayed an upcoming postal comparability increase by six months. Based on year-old statistics, the comparability raise was already too low. To postpone it further left postal workers even farther behind their counterparts in the private sector and delayed yet again the promise of comparability. Postal workers resented that Nixon was making them pay for his battle against inflation when they were some of its primary victims. They particularly resented that Congress had recently doubled the president's salary and voted itself a 41 percent raise while they—already promised a raise—had to wait.

Feelings of violation reinforced postal workers' willingness to assert, and even exercise, their rights. In a letter to AFL-CIO president George Meany, Steve Parise, a post office clerk from Brooklyn, described the "injustices" that made him consider striking: "Our union and our rank and file feel that the Government has forfeited its immunity to a strike, not only because its open disdain for these men, but also the humility of financial hardships they have forced upon our families; such as seeking welfare to survive."

A more general, even international, politics of rights protest amplified postal workers' grievances and bolstered their militancy. Illegal dissent, such as the civil disobedience of civil rights demonstrators or the strikes of public workers, was particularly apropos, as it mirrored the position of postal workers. In a letter to two New York senators and seven Brooklyn representatives, Ben Zemsky, president of Local 251, the United Federation of Postal Clerks in Brooklyn, described the effect of the larger political context:

> Postal workers have been seeing the City and State workers who were once behind them in wages and fringe benefits go on strike and pull ahead of them in these areas. . . .
>
> Postal workers have been watching as their counterparts in Canada, New Zealand, France, Italy, Israel, Germany and Greece go on strike without going to jail and wondering how in hell we can teach democracy to the rest of the world while denying it to our own citizens.
>
> You'd better find out why "STRIKE" is the most popular word among postal employees and, you'd better find it out NOT from the brass but from us. . . .
>
> We are no longer going to cringe. A lot of good people have gone to jail in recent years to make a point; civil rights leaders, union leaders and a few others. You'd better make the Brooklyn scene now or you may have to visit some of your constituents . . . in jail.

Zemsky's strike warning wasn't the only one. By early March 1970, New York postal union officials were meeting with local congressional representatives and Post Office Department officials to warn them of growing strike sentiment among the rank and file. Moe Biller, then president of the Manhattan-Bronx Postal Union (MBPU), recalled that when he met with a number of New York congressmen, "most of them had a look of blank stares on them. Even Congressman Mario Biaggi, a good friend of mine, made a comment to the effect that postal workers would never strike." Strike warnings came in other forms, too. The White House received tens of thousands of letters supporting a postal wage bill. At least a few of them warned of a possible strike.

The Rank and File Organizes

Rank-and-file letter carriers in New York City were particularly upset—and organized. The proximate source of their anger was a 1969 sick-out in the Bronx. On July 1 and 2, eighty-eight clerks and letter carriers in the Kingsbridge and Throgs Neck post offices called in sick to protest an "insulting" 4.1 percent wage increase granted by President Nixon in an executive order. Their action was the culmination of a series of demonstrations against the size of the raise.

On June 20, postal workers and postal union officials held informational pickets in front of post offices throughout New York City. At the General Post Office in Manhattan, more than 2,000 postal workers paraded, shouting "Strike, strike, strike," and carrying signs reading, "Pay, Not Peanuts," and "Better Pay Means Better Service." Moe Biller warned the *New York Times* that Nixon's raise "hit postal workers like a napalm bomb and they're really burning. . . . The Post Office thinks we're kidding when we warn about possible wildcat strikes. But anything could light the tinderbox." A week later, Letter Carrier president James Rademacher provided the spark that Bronx postal workers needed. He warned that he would call a strike on July 1 if postal workers did not receive a 9 percent pay raise.

By June 30, rumors spread throughout New York post offices that there would be a strike the next day, but no one could confirm them. At the Kingsbridge station, the workers discussed their options, while two of their fellow routemen called the Letter Carriers' office to get more information. Unwilling to talk over the phone (presumably for security reasons), Frank Cumbo, who was vice president in charge of Bronx affairs for NALC Branch 36, told them, "Today the Bronx, tomorrow Manhattan." Unable to decipher the message and unable to agree on a strike, the workers decided to call in sick. Seventy-two of Kingsbridge's seventy-seven nonsupervisory employees failed to report for work the next day, July 1, but workers elsewhere did. Rademacher had decided not to act on his strike threat. Sixteen letter carriers from the Throgs Neck post office were the only other workers to join the sick-out, and they did so on its second—and last—day.

Post Office officials reacted swiftly and severely to the sick-out, placing seventy-two letter carriers and sixteen postal clerks on indefinite suspension, pending disposition of their cases. Only twenty-one letter carriers presented medical certification to legitimize their absence, and they received no punishment. The rest of the workers served suspensions of two or three weeks without pay. Manhattan-Bronx Postal Union officials decided that they could not win the reversal of the penalties and agreed to pay the sixteen suspended clerks their lost wages. The suspended letter carriers were not so fortunate. At a special Branch 36 meeting on August 5, branch leaders mobilized to defeat a member-initiated motion to pay them. Rademacher, who attended the meeting, spoke against the measure, but received applause for promising to lead a real strike should Congress fail to pass a pending postal wage bill.

Despite Rademacher's tough talk, a group of Manhattan letter carriers, including Vincent Sombrotto, Sidney Klein, Morris Rose, Edward Donavan, Mark Roth, and Marty Weinstein, were unhappy that the union would not reimburse the Kingsbridge carriers. Over the next few months, they began to organize support for the reimbursement motion. They spoke with letter carriers at work, on breaks, and at the Branch 36 fall bowling league. To each successive monthly branch meeting they brought more members, but never enough to pass their motion. In December, they picked up the support of a twenty-nine-year-old letter carrier named Thomas Germano.

Germano's youth made him different from the rank and filers previously drawn to the dissident cause. The dissidents had come into the Post Office during the 1930s and 1940s, often with veteran credit. Many had been intermittently active in the ethnic and veteran associations that had served as postal patronage machines before Kennedy's executive order put teeth into the postal union movement. With the help of these groups, these older dissidents had carved out decent, secure positions for themselves. Still, they deeply resented their poor pay, especially the fact that some had not reached the top pay tier despite their long tenure. For this they blamed their union leaders. With the reimbursement motion, they hoped to begin a long-term intervention in branch politics that would ultimately lead them to branch office.

Germano, by contrast, was young and headstrong, which he demonstrated in several confrontations with postal management in the early 1960s. He grew up pro-union but initially had little interest in union politics. He preferred to spend his time socializing and playing sports, often with other postal workers. Through this activity and through working in several post offices, he developed an extensive social network among New York letter carriers and clerks. He was well known, sociable, and popular. Then he returned to college at Queens College, where he studied political sociology and came to know anti-war and civil rights activists. He met H. Rap Brown and Julius Lester, worked with Christian coalitions against the war, and supported the Young Lords. These experiences stimulated a political awareness and encouraged him to think about union activism as part of a larger project of social justice. But he still hesitated to get involved.

In late 1969, Germano was interviewed by postal officials searching for a postal worker who was eligible for welfare but who had not taken it. They hoped to counter the bad publicity they were receiving by demonstrating that postal workers survived adequately on postal wages. Married with five children, Germano was indeed eligible for welfare, though he had not been aware of it nor was he interested in receiving it. However, he believed it was disgraceful that full-time postal workers could be eligible for government support, and he resented that Post Office officials would sugarcoat the plight of its employees. The experience convinced him to join the efforts to get reimbursement for the suspended letter carriers.

In addition to sheer numbers, Germano and his friends brought a new element to the rank-and-file campaign. They were more interested in postal wages and working conditions than union politics. Whereas dissidents like Sombrotto and Klein were interested in running for union office, Germano and his "crowd" wanted to organize against postal management as well as union leaders. With his college experiences and connections to the city's social movements, Germano contributed even more. On a practical level, he used his ties to secure needed resources, including church space for rank-and-file meetings. On another level, he drew upon his social skills and political acumen to become a leader, not only of his associates but of the entire group of dissidents.

Despite the continued opposition of both Branch 36 president Gustave Johnson and Rademacher, the rank-and-file campaign organized enough support to pass its reimbursement motion at the January 1970 monthly branch meeting. Buoyed by their success, Sombrotto, Germano, and others proposed and won a vote to reject the Nixon-Rademacher pay/reform agreement. In its place, they proposed their own platform, including full government payment of pension, hospitalization, and life insurance premiums for both active and retired letter carriers, twenty-year optional retirement, area wage differentials for cost-of-living differences, and the right to strike. Then they committed the branch to strike if the national union did not agree to substitute their platform for the Nixon-Rademacher package. By March, the national union had taken no action on the Branch 36 platform proposal.

Rank-and-file organizing built monthly meetings from fewer than 100 participants in November 1969 to over 800 in March 1970. At successive meetings, strike sentiment grew. At the March 12 meeting, rank-and-file letter carriers took control of the meeting from Branch officers and won a vote for a special strike organization meeting at Manhattan Center on March 17. To derail the strike, branch officials organized a strike vote instead of a meeting. They arranged balloting machines at the center and called in the Honest Ballot Association to count votes. They hoped to defuse strike sentiment with a "No" vote and campaigned heavily in Manhattan and Bronx post offices. Rank and filers learned late that the vote would take place, but campaigned vigorously for a "Yes" vote as the only way to "win our demands."

Disagreement arose when Sombrotto and others began working on a platform of demands for the strike, an effort Germano, speaking in an interview, felt was premature. "When we met, the two different groups, these guys, I thought they were just wasting time sitting around. I'm saying, 'Hey, you can draw up platforms and plans all day long, but if you don't get the vote out it's meaningless. Let's just get the vote out and worry about that later.'" The group around Sombrotto ignored Germano, which turned out to be the right thing to do, as Germano later acknowledged: "Now I'm glad I did what I did because you had to get the vote out, but looking back now I'm glad they did what they did, because when there was a strike they did have a list of demands that they read off right there."

More than 2,500 of the 6,700 branch members turned out to vote on the evening of the 17th. The voting took several hours, but the majority waited for the results. Finally the vote was announced: 1,555 for, 1,055 against. Johnson told the assembled carriers that the strike would begin at 12:01 A.M. Jack Leventhal, president of NALC Brooklyn Branch 41, announced that his members would join the strike and pledged the support of branches in Queens, Jamaica, and Flushing. Moe Biller, MBPU president, announced that his union would have to vote before it could strike. Since MBPU was the largest postal union local in the country, representing 25,000 New York clerks and other postal workers, the letter carriers were disappointed by Biller's unwillingness to call an immediate strike. After they booed his announcement, he admitted that "good union people don't cross picket lines," implying that his members would honor letter carrier picket lines. This was met with cheers and the strike was on.

The Strike Spreads

The first picket lines went up when a few night carriers and clerks walked out of several New York post offices at midnight, but "by the next morning, the nation awoke to a wildfire strike that spread swiftly through most of New York, New Jersey and Connecticut," according to *Newsweek*. By Saturday, postal workers in Chicago, Cleveland, Los Angeles, Detroit, San Francisco, Boston, Denver, Pittsburgh, Minneapolis, Philadelphia, and dozens of other cities and towns had walked off the job. They did so of their own volition. There was no national strike coordination, since national postal union officials actively opposed the strike. Local union officers were ambivalent. Most followed their leaders in active opposition. Some, including Johnson, arranged strike votes, but then retreated from the scene once postal workers set up picket lines. A few, including Biller and Zemsky, led pickets. For the most part, rank-and-file workers organized the strike, post office by post office. Despite their lack of coordination, they paralyzed mail delivery with devastating effect. No mail moved in the country's major cities. The strike lasted eight days in New York but was briefer in other cities; close to 200,000 workers participated.

Though opinion polls indicated public sympathy for the strikers, a formidable collection of people and institutions arrayed themselves against the strike. Postal workers faced their own union leaders, the federal court system, the president, Congress, the press, and eventually the National Guard.

Postal union officials launched a verbal barrage against their striking members. They issued telegrams, distributed flyers, sent letters, held meetings, and made speeches commanding postal workers to return to their jobs. When this failed, Rademacher, on national television, falsely denounced rank-and-file leaders in New York as radicals and members of Students for a Democratic Society. Gustave Johnson, other local leaders, and members of Congress made similar public statements.

On the strike's first day, federal courts in New York and Brooklyn issued temporary injunctions against the strike. A few days later, they were made permanent. Strikers ignored the injunctions, leading one federal judge to declare Branch 36 and its officers in contempt of court. He imposed ever-increasing fines that the union officers would have to pay even if they actively opposed the strike, but he granted a twenty-four-hour extension on payment. The strike ended before the fines were due, but not before postal union officials, obeying the court, visited picket lines to demand a return to work.

Newspaper editorials condemned the strike in harsh terms, but usually granted the reasonableness of postal workers' demands. Similarly, congressional leaders sympathized with the strikers' demands, but vowed not to pass any legislation while the strike continued.

President Nixon demanded a tough stance toward the strike and immediate action. H.R. Haldeman, Assistant to the President, recorded the following notes on March 20, 1970: The president "wants something much tougher[.] examine law—Get Mitchell[.] if people can be fired fire them[.] if troops can be moved move them[.] want to do something—this morning[.] not going to tolerate Fed employees strike[.] Suspend if can't fire[.] all out attack[.] hit square on the nose[.] it's the principle[.]" In public, Nixon was less strident, but no less firm. In a statement, he appealed to postal workers' patriotism: "The men who work in the United States postal service have taken the same oath to uphold and defend the Constitution of the United States as I have taken. Further, their proud tradition—that the mails must go through—dates to the earliest days of our Republic. I expect that both the oath and the tradition will be honored. . . ." He resolved to meet his constitutional obligation to move the mails and refused to negotiate while the strike continued. He then worried about the damage the strike could cause. The *New York Times* reported that brokerage houses, banks, lawyers, and department stores were the hardest hit by the strike, but when he described the strike's threat to national interest, Nixon invoked the images of welfare recipients, veterans, and Social Security recipients awaiting their checks.

Opponents of the strike were unanimous in condemning its illegality. They worried about the example it set and about the contribution the strike made to the very politics of protest it drew upon for inspiration. A *New York Times* editorial expressed fears that "the nation will henceforth be at the mercy of every employe [*sic*] group with control over a strategic public operation." This anxiety was not misplaced. Other federal employees pressed to join the postal workers on the picket lines: air traffic controllers engaged in an effective sick-out, and at the end of the month, 50,000 Teamsters held a wildcat strike of their own. The *Times* also cited more ominous possibilities:

> Even more dismaying is the encouragement the postal workers' defiance gives to the lawlessness already so rampant in many sectors of society that it is beginning to undermine national stability. What hope can there be for fostering respect for law and democratic processes among all the disaffected elements in the ghetto, on campus and elsewhere if Federal employees disregard their oath to stay on the job or if public administrators fail to invoke the full legal penalties?

Nixon summarized strike opponents' thinking best. "What is at issue then is the survival of a government based upon law."

When asked about the illegality of their actions, strikers were defiant. One group of older postal workers told the *New York Daily News*, "We haven't got anything now. So, what can we lose?" James Warden, a New York letter carrier, told *Newsweek*, "Of course, I realize that a strike is illegal and that we could be jailed for this. I'm prepared for that if it comes. I think it'd be well worth going to jail for." Another letter carrier told the *Times*, "Everybody else strikes and gets a big pay increase. The teachers, the sanitation and transit workers all struck [in violation of the law]. . . . Why shouldn't we? We've been nice far too long."

In striking, postal workers asserted an identity they felt had long been denied by the Post Office, Congress, and successive presidents. Despite a growing number of women in the Post Office, the workers generally described themselves as American men who provided for spouses and children. The corollary to this family responsibility was the right to a decent wage. Poor pay made it difficult to support a family, which made it impossible to fulfill the responsibilities of manhood. One postal worker felt shame when his wife admitted in print that she was married to a postal worker who earned only $7,000 a year. His fellow workers couldn't believe she would admit such a marriage in public. To do so was to admit his failure, a great sin for any man, as they saw it. Masculinity was also at stake in Post Office labor relations. Without collective bargaining rights, postal workers believed themselves trapped in a state of dependency, forced to go to Congress, "hat in hand, and beg." And with few workplace rights, they could not defend themselves against management. They suffered what one group of workers in Cleveland called, in a letter to George Meany, "tyranny in its most odious form, psychological and social economic castration."

Postal workers also demanded rights as citizens. As Herman Sandbank, a vice president of Branch 36, said, the strikers would not return to work until they had become "first-class citizens." Closely related to their sense of citizenship was postal workers' vision of themselves as public employees. Both involved a set of responsibilities to the nation and a set of reciprocal rights. Postal workers usually expressed these themes in patriotic appeals, such as that of Steve Parise in his letter to George Meany. Writing just before the strike in defense of 135 disciplined Brooklyn postal workers, he pointed out that they had "a total of 3000 years of service to their Government, which includes years of fighting in World War II and the Korean conflict for the preservation of liberty which they themselves are being denied." He went on to observe that postal workers had never struck because they chose not to defy "the Government which we have fought to preserve, and dedicated our lives to." Parise and other postal workers believed that they had lived up to their responsibilities—it was now up to the government to meet its responsibilities and implement their rights.

After postal workers defied the federal court's injunctions, Nixon, through his secretary of labor George Shultz, offered to negotiate with postal union leaders as soon as strikers returned to work. The offer was unprecedented, as postal unions had never been allowed to negotiate wage and benefit issues with the government. Shultz began his meeting with Rademacher and other postal leaders with the government's keynote: "There's only one thing worse than a wildcat strike—a wildcat strike that succeeds." Rademacher quickly got the hint. Rank-and-file success would undermine his power within the union. As *Newsweek* understood, Shultz's offer to negotiate upon the end of the strike "was aimed at restoring control by driving the wildcatters back into the arms of their leaders." In return, all Rademacher had to do was press for the end of the strike. Postal workers rejected the Shultz-Rademacher deal immediately. It granted none of their demands, and just made more promises. Rademacher's credibility, already low, evaporated.

The failure of the Shultz-Rademacher agreement led Nixon to declare a national emergency and mobilize 30,000 unarmed National Guard and Reserve troops to work the post offices in New York City. They occupied the city's larger post offices early on the sixth day of the strike. Lacking the necessary skills, the soldiers moved little mail. Many fraternized with the strikers. In an ironic twist, some actually were strikers, reservists called up under the mobilization order. The troops failed to intimidate New York City strikers, who urged the guardsmen to "gum up the works," but in other parts of the country Nixon's resolve had impact. The back-to-work movement, just a trickle before Nixon's declaration, began to flow.

Despite their growing isolation, New York City postal workers remained on the picket lines for three more days after the arrival of the troops. Their initiative and resolve differentiated them from other postal workers. Just why New York postal workers were more determined than others is not entirely clear, but some reasons stand out. New York was a heavily unionized city, with a tradition of "militant and socially conscious" unionism, according to union officials interviewed by the *New York Times* during the strike. Local union stalwarts of this tradition included Branch 36 and MBPU. Postal workers in New York also faced the worst working conditions in the country and the highest cost of living, and they had watched their relative pay fall faster than those elsewhere. "When I first came on the job in the thirties," said one New York City postal worker, "we used to get almost as much as a cop and more than the street cleaners. Now where are we? At the bottom." The gap grew after a series of strikes by city public workers, including teachers, police, sanitation, and transport workers, whose walkouts were illegal but still quite successful. There were so many strikes, in fact, that the *Economist* dubbed New York the "City of Strikes." While all these developments motivated New York postal workers' militancy, the local leadership of the letter carriers' union lacked both experience and the respect of the membership, providing dissidents with the space to organize strike sentiment. Finally, rank-and-file activists in New York City were committed and well organized.

New York postal workers ended their strike only after an apparent compromise on the part of the government. Letter carrier union officials and congressional representatives announced that the Nixon administration had agreed to a 12 percent pay increase retroactive to October 1969, fully paid health benefits, top pay after eight years instead of twenty-one (compression), area wage differentials, provisions for collective bargaining and binding arbitration of deadlocked disputes, and total amnesty for all strikers. At a rally on March 25, 1970, in front of the General Post Office in Manhattan, Moe Biller announced the terms of the settlement and told the thousands of assembled workers that the strike would end immediately. Most rank-and-file activists liked the settlement, but they still argued to continue the strike until the administration presented its proposal in writing. Without access to the platform, controlled by Biller, few at the rally heard the militants' arguments and not all of those who did agreed. With apparent victory in sight, sentiment to end the strike was overwhelming and the activists had no choice but to return to work.

The actual settlement took five months to negotiate through Congress and was not quite so generous, prompting New York City postal workers to threaten several more strikes. Union leaders had exaggerated the administration's commitment to various pieces of the compromise. The Post Office Reorganization and Salary Adjustment Act of 1970 implemented the Nixon corporation plan and some of the promised improvements. It did not include fully paid health benefits or a guarantee of area wage differentials. It delayed implementation of compression, meaning workers with more than eight years on the job were not immediately upgraded. It made only 6 percent of a total 14 percent raise retroactive, and moved the effective date of retroactivity from early October to late December.

Despite these setbacks, Labor Secretary Shultz's fears had, in large part, come to pass. Much to Rademacher's chagrin, the wildcat strike had succeeded. Postal workers won two major improvements—a 14 percent wage increase and compression. They also won substantial collective bargaining rights.

Lingering Dissent

The strike's achievements demonstrated the collective power of rank-and-file postal workers, convincing many of their capacity to organize for change within the postal unions. In New York City, rank-and-file activists drew upon their success to build a massive electoral challenge that quickly swept away the old Branch 36 leadership before the end of 1970. Vincent Sombrotto was elected branch president at the head of a complete rank-and-file slate, which included many of the original Branch 36 dissidents and Thomas Germano. With the help of the New York activists, similar victories took place in Boston, Minneapolis, and Philadelphia.

Using its base in the New York branch, the rank-and-file group began to exert influence on national union politics, and in 1971 helped form the National Rank and File Movement (NRFM). Consisting mostly of newly elected officials, the NRFM acted as a union opposition party, pressuring the incumbent administration during negotiations and running candidates during union elections. Under

NRFM cajoling, the Rademacher administration reformed the constitution to require one-member, one-vote elections for regional and national officers and convention delegates. Through his activity in the NRFM, but even more through his high-profile position as president of the Letter Carriers' largest branch, Sombrotto soon became a national figure inside the union. In 1974, he ran for president of the union on the NRFM slate, but lost to Rademacher. Though the NRFM soon fell apart, Sombrotto continued his rise. After sitting out the 1976 election, in 1978 he beat Rademacher's successor, J. Joseph Vacca, to become NALC president, a position he held until 2002.

The development of rank-and-file organization inside the Letter Carriers contrasted with that inside the American Postal Workers Union. A group of younger postal workers at the world's largest bulk mail facility in Jersey City, New Jersey, formed a group called the Outlaws. Led by radicals with experience in the social movements of the 1960s and working in the most factory-like of all postal facilities, the Outlaws focused more on workplace militancy and less on union politics than the rank-and-file groups among letter carriers. This orientation made them the best fighters on the shop floor and led to the election of one Outlaw leader, Kenneth Leiner, as chief shop steward for the Jersey City facility. Outlaw activities also included occasional demonstrations, quickie strikes, and interventions at union meetings. At the meetings they put pressure on their union officials, including their local president Moe Biller, to be more aggressive in dealing with postal management at the workplace. They also organized opposition to contract proposals.

The Outlaws precipitated two large work stoppages in the 1970s. The first, later nicknamed the "Battle of the Bulk," occurred in 1974 when the Outlaws initiated a protest against an involuntary shift change at the Jersey City facility. Hundreds of workers protested and were backed by the union, leading to a lockout/strike that lasted three days. The brokered settlement reversed the involuntary shift change and gave the Outlaws some credibility. Then, in 1978, they walked out against a proposed contract. This time they were not so successful, despite the fact that workers in Richmond, California, joined their wildcat. Making an example of them, Postmaster General William Bolger ordered Jersey City postal managers to fire 200 of the 4,000 strikers. Union efforts to save their jobs were too little, too late. Within a few years, the Outlaws faded from the scene.

The 1970 Post Office strike was an extraordinary display of rank-and-file militancy on the part of previously passive workers. Even though postal workers and their unions could not sustain the strike's energy and collective activity for very long, they parlayed their militancy into substantial collective bargaining rights, increased wages, and more powerful and democratic unions. That such an improbable group of workers would show so much strength and determination demonstrates how deep the militant impulse ran through the American working class in the late 1960s and early 1970s.

See also: Three Strikes Against the New York City Transit System, 277.

Notes

This essay draws on Aaron Brenner, "Striking Against the State: The 1970 Post Office Wildcat Walkout," *Labor's Heritage* (Spring 1996).

Bibliography

Brenner, Aaron. "Rank-and-File Rebellion, 1967–1976." Ph.D. diss., Columbia University, 1996.

Cullinan, Gerald. *The United States Postal Service.* New York: Praeger, 1973.

Mikusko, M. Brady. *Carriers in a Common Cause: A History of Letter Carriers and the NALC.* Washington, DC: National Association of Letter Carriers, 1982.

Walsh, John, and Garth Mangum. *Labor Struggle in the Post Office: From Selective Lobbying to Collective Bargaining.* Armonk, NY: M.E. Sharpe, 1992.

THREE STRIKES AGAINST THE NEW YORK CITY TRANSIT SYSTEM

Michael Hirsch

Over the course of nearly 130 years, transport workers in New York City struggled for dignity and respect in one of the most onerous jobs in the metropolis. Their struggles arose in response to the brutality of transit system operators, whether private owners of independent lines during the early years of mass transit or administrators of the consolidated public system after 1940. Transit workers' goals hardly varied over the years—better wages, benefits, and working conditions—yet their fights took on many forms. Central, of course, was the battle for unionization and collective bargaining. Early on, craft and industrial unions vied for the allegiance of workers, but eventually, beginning in 1937, Transport Workers Union Local 100 became the main organizational vehicle for workers' mobilization. Throughout this history, transit workers and their unions engaged in workplace agitation, political and community organizing, and, of course, strikes.

In the first twenty years after the American Federation of Labor (AFL) began trying to unionize city transit workers in 1888, there were at least 206 strikes nationally, according to political scientist James J. McGinley. Significant strikes took place among New York City trolley, rail, subway, or bus workers in 1904, 1905, 1916, 1918, 1919, and 1926. These varied considerably in their character. Some included violence against strikers, scabs, and property; others involved inchoate protests, but none were successful. The 1904 strike against the Interborough Rapid Transit (IRT) was broken when AFL President Samuel Gompers and Grand Chief Warren Stone of the Brotherhood of Locomotive Engineers refused to support the craft union locals striking against millionaire August Belmont's IRT. Belmont, head of the National Civic Federation, on whose body sat Gompers and Stone, insisted the strike was a breach of the union's ongoing contract, and the labor tops agreed. An August 1916 strike by an AFL affiliate turned into a general strike in September, which again failed when the building trades unions refused to honor picket lines. The 1926 IRT motormen's strike lasted sixteen days, but was broken by a police action, by scabs from the Brotherhood of Locomotive Engineers, and by the deep pockets of management.

A turning point in the history of transit strikes occurred in 1937. That year, transit workers engaged in a small but successful sit-down strike as part of a larger struggle that led to union recognition for Transport Workers Union (TWU) Local 100 from a number of subway and bus lines in the city. Transit workers then engaged in strikes in 1939, 1941, 1948, and 1957. All but the last of these work stoppages took place against individual transit lines during a period when public transportation remained divided among different systems, and the 1957 strike was confined primarily to subway motormen. The next three transit strikes, in 1966, 1980, and 2005, stand out from the rest because they were general strikes that completely shut down the city's public transportation system, including all of the city's subway lines and most of its bus lines.

From Strike Threat to Strike

After achieving recognition in 1937, Transport Workers Union Local 100 expanded rapidly under the leadership of Michael (Mike) J. Quill, an Irish immigrant who gained the confidence of transit workers through his powerful organizational and oratorical skills. In the early years of the union,

Quill and large segments of both the union's leadership and rank and file were Communists. Some members were activists in the Irish Republican Army's (IRA) U.S. adjunct Clan na Gael, and there was considerable overlap between Communist Party (CP) and IRA membership within the TWU. Quill famously bragged, "I'd rather be a red to the rats than a rat to the reds." Other factions within the union included workers affiliated with Catholic and anti-Communist organizations, such as the American Association of Anti-Communists.

The meaning of Communist Party influence within the union changed over time as CP policies shifted. Nonetheless, CP influence generally put Quill and other TWU leaders on the left of the spectrum of city politics and imbued the union with an ethos of social equality, including a commitment to end racial discrimination. Depression-era civil rights leader and later Harlem congressman Reverend Adam Clayton Powell Jr. credited the union for agreeing to work with African-American activists in 1941 not just to win a twelve-day strike but to end Jim Crow hiring on the largest bus network in Manhattan. After World War II, as the anti-Communist movement gained steam and as the Congress of Industrial Organizations (CIO) moved to the right, Quill broke with the CP. Following passage of the Taft-Hartley Act in 1947, Communist Party members were restricted from positions of union leadership. At the same time, Quill, a radical pragmatist, came out in favor of a fare hike, which the CP opposed. Like the leadership of the CIO, he supported Democratic Party presidential candidate Harry S. Truman, while the CP and much of the labor left supported third-party candidate Henry Wallace. Quill purged the remaining Communist leaders in the late 1940s, though he allowed some of them to return in the 1950s and remained on the left of the political spectrum.

Under Quill, particularly after the city took over all the subway lines and many of the bus lines after 1940, the union improved the wages, benefits, and working conditions of transit workers. It also developed into a political force within the city, especially during the mayoralty of Robert Wagner Jr. in the 1950s. Wagner had close ties to labor unions, including TWU Local 100, and in 1958 he signed Executive Order 49, which gave municipal workers not just de jure collective bargaining rights but mechanisms for securing them. This represented a significant victory for TWU and other city unions. Still, city workers did not enjoy all the rights of their private sector counterparts. Most importantly, strikes by public workers in New York State remained illegal under the 1947 Condon-Wadlin Act.

Despite a public sector strike's illegality, Quill was nothing if not clear in defending the strike as an option, a tactical last resort in an industrial relations environment where public employees were outgunned if not outmanned. As his biographer and second wife Shirley Quill put it, "Mike hated strikes and had called fewer than any other national leader." In a 1961 debate televised on NBC's "The Nation's Future" with former U.S. Representative Fred Hartley, co-author of what President Harry Truman had called the Taft-Hartley "slave labor bill," Quill defended the right of public employees—including police, firefighters, and teachers—"as American citizens"—to strike. But he also insisted that "the strike is unnecessary; I believe that intelligent government on a county, city, state or national basis, can bring about such machinery that thereby the employees can have general and collective bargaining, like the transport workers have in New York City for 30,000 civil service subway workers. . . . and [with that machinery] we have never struck the subways of New York for one hour in the last 30 years." Five years later, Quill's actions would defy his words.

As TWU Local 100 entered into negotiations with the city in late 1965, the union faced considerable internal discontent. According to historian Joshua Freeman, "Quill badly needed a militant fight and a huge victory to reunite a fragmented union, upgrade wages, and ensure his legacy, for by then he was a dying man" with a long history of heart disease. Negotiations were complicated by the fact that they took place during a mayoral transition between Robert Wagner Jr., a Democrat, and John V. Lindsay, a liberal Republican who would take office the same day the transit workers' contract ended, January 1, 1966. As Freeman described it, "Normally, Quill quietly worked out a deal with the mayor while going through a public display of strike threats, theatrics, and last minute agreement. This time, both outgoing Mayor Wagner and Mayor-elect Lindsay avoided participation in the negotiations, not wanting responsibility for a strike or an agreement that might force the Transit Authority (TA) to raise the bus and subway fares." As it turned out, they got both.

The dispute was largely about money. While the union demanded a four-day, thirty-two-hour workweek, improved pensions, longer vacations, and other benefits, a huge wage increase was particularly crucial, because transit workers were clearly underpaid. Many starting subway and bus workers had to work overtime in order to exceed the government's definition of a "modest" income for a family of four. The pay of unskilled new hires barely exceeded the poverty level, and transit workers generally earned less than city employees holding comparable jobs. The Transit Authority, a supposedly self-sustaining, independent agency that received city money only for capital expenditures and not for operations, claimed that the union's demands would cost $680 million and require a large fare increase (a familiar threat in every transit union negotiation). The union disputed this claim and had the evidence to prove it. Nonetheless, there was considerable concern among the politicians about where the money for increased compensation would come from.

To increase the pressure on the Transit Authority, and despite the fact that the contract did not expire until January 1, Quill set a December 15 strike deadline, when a walkout would paralyze the city during the holiday shopping rush. He also demanded that Lindsay participate personally in the negotiations. Quill disliked the mayor-elect, and purposely mispronounced his name as Lindes-ley. Apparently, the feeling was mutual. New York columnist Jimmy Breslin observed, "John Lindsay looked at Quill and saw the past; Quill looked at Lindsay and saw The Church of England." Quill, the working-class tough, and Lindsay, the boyishly handsome patrician, did made for striking and opposing archetypes, and Quill's comment that Lindsay was "more profile than courage" only added to the melodrama.

Lindsay initially refused to join the negotiations, and twenty-one bargaining sessions were held with little progress. Without Lindsay's participation, Transit Authority bargainers could only plead poormouth, unable to talk dollars and cents. Wagner and Lindsay convinced Theodore Kheel, an experienced mediator, to lead a three-person mediation panel, and Quill used this development as reason to delay the strike deadline from December 15 to January 1, when the contract would expire. Still, negotiations stalled, as Lindsay refused to meet formally with TA and union bargainers until four days before the deadline. And even then no agreement was reached. On December 30, as the deadline neared, the TA secured a show-cause order from the State Supreme Court calling on Quill and other TWU leaders to explain why they should not be enjoined from striking. Quill, speaking before TV reporters, tore up the court papers and blamed Lindsay for the impending walkout. The next day, at the behest of Lindsay, the TA convinced the court to issue an injunction against a strike. Retiring three-term Mayor Robert Wagner Jr., son of the Depression-era New York State senator who sponsored the National Labor Relations Act, did not help matters much. He jetted off to Acapulco on December 31, just when negotiations were at their most intense. He told reporters he was going for "a little sun and swimming. This is Lindsay's show now."

The strike began on January 1, 1966, after Quill left discussions with Lindsay at about 2:00 A.M. As a result, the new mayor spent his first day in office confronted with the first general strike of transit workers in New York City's history. The walkout was virtually complete, as 33,000 workers refused to run trains or drive buses. The *New York Times* said on January 3, "The rank and file of transport workers seemed enthusiastic yesterday over the stoppage," despite the fact that they risked dismissal under the state's Condon-Wadlin Act. Thirteen unions pledged support for the strike. Faced with such determination, Lindsay advised all workers to stay home, to which Quill responded, "Working people can't afford to stay home."

On the fourth day of the strike, again at the behest of the Lindsay administration, Quill and eight other union leaders were arrested for ignoring the court-ordered injunction to end the strike. As he was hauled off to jail, Quill said in the thickest of Irish brogues, which had grown steadily broader as the strike deadline approached, "The judge can drop dead in his black robes and we would not call off the strike. We will defy the injunction and go to jail." He then added, "I don't care if I rot in jail.

I will not call off the strike." Lindsay, meanwhile, railed against unspecified "power brokers" and "special interests" who would "dictate to the city" and its duly elected leaders. The *New York Times* editorialized against Quill and the strike. While being processed to enter jail, Quill collapsed and was moved to Bellevue Hospital, where it was determined he had suffered another heart attack.

The jailing of TWU leaders backfired on Lindsay by making them martyrs. It unified rank-and-file transit workers and rallied other workers to their cause. Several mass demonstrations took place. Before going to jail, Quill named Douglas MacMahon, a TWU international vice president and his administrative assistant, as chief negotiator in his stead. MacMahon continued Quill's tough style over the next eight days, even as President Lyndon Johnson sent Secretary of Labor W. Willard Wirtz to participate in the negotiations. As a result, after twelve days on strike, the TWU and the TA agreed to a contract that represented a clear victory for the union. At a cost estimated between $52 million and $70 million, transit workers won a 15 percent wage hike over two years, including a $4.00-an-hour wage for "motormen" (now called train operators). The contract eliminated inequities between transit workers and other city employees, even though it also violated the Johnson administration's wage stabilization guidelines. The workers also won a $500 supplemental pension plan. Perhaps more important, the strike had a demonstration effect that put transit workers in a powerful bargaining position over the next few years. In the eight years after 1965, wages increased annually at an average of 9 percent, and in 1968 workers won the so-called 50/20—retirement at half pay after twenty years of service at age fifty—sparking "a massive exodus of senior workers from the system, including nearly all those who remained from the generation that had organized and nurtured the TWU," according to Freeman. The agreement accelerated the change in the union's social and racial composition, and widened the gap between the elected officials and the rank and file.

The final deal also included a retroactive waiver of the state's punitive Condon-Wadlin Act penalties, a non-negotiable condition Quill demanded to end the strike and something that would not be offered again. Despite enacting the amnesty, state lawmakers in 1966 went on to propose and enact the Taylor Law, which would prohibit strikes by public employees. TWU and other city unions mobilized to try to stop the law, including holding a rally at the old Madison Square Garden. There, an overflow crowd seeping out onto 8th Avenue, but with the building trades unions conspicuously absent, erupted after a Declaration of the Rights of Public Employees was read describing the Taylor Law as the "illegitimate offspring of a diseased bipartisanship" and speakers called on workers to "stand together in defense of one another until this evil law and its promoters are left in the dust of history." The law was called a product of a "diseased bipartisanship" because it was jointly orchestrated by the Republican millionaire governor Nelson Rockefeller and the Democratic Assembly Speaker from Brooklyn Anthony J. Travia. The Taylor Law, which still governs New York State public sector labor relations, was named for the University of Pennsylvania labor-relations expert George W. Taylor, "the father of American arbitration." The unions called it the "RAT" bill after its bipartisan supporters Rockefeller and Travia.

The Rank and File Forces a Strike

As in 1966, the main issue in the 1980 transit strike was wages. Rank-and-file transit workers were angry that their real wages, after inflation, were falling. In 1978, they received a 6 percent raise over two years, but in those two years, between December 1977 and January 1980, the consumer price index rose more than 25 percent. Understandably, transit workers were upset by the deterioration of their standard of living. A few days before the strike, at a rally of 7,000 transit workers and thousands more city employees, including police and firefighters, demonstrators carried signs that read "We're being burned by inflation" and "Our children have to eat, too." Writing about Pedro Ocasio, a subway conductor, veteran *New York Times* labor reporter William Serrin noted,

> When the situation is stripped to its essentials, the strike is about Mr. Ocasio and his fellow subway and bus workers, about the money they

> say they must earn to live in these inflated times and about the sociology of the city's blue-collar workers . . . [F]or blue-collar workers, a strike is often a way of asserting themselves, of standing up to their bosses, of stepping out, for a moment, from their anonymity.

Serrin's last point held especially true for the rapidly growing African-American and Latino portion of the Transit Authority workforce, most of whom had the worst jobs, such as cleaning and maintaining the subway's tracks and trains.

Like Mike Quill, many of the original members of TWU Local 100 were Irish. Even as more African-American and Latino workers signed on with the Transit Authority, Irish workers held onto the best jobs, such as driving buses. By 1980, approximately 51 percent of the workforce was white, 40 percent African-American, and 7 percent Latino, with white workers predominating above ground and workers of color taking most of the jobs underground. Many workers of color felt the union, still run by an Irish man, John Lawe, did not do enough to address the racial disparities on the job by, for example, challenging racist supervisors or providing additional training so that workers of color could move into better jobs. They also felt that more African-American and Latino workers should be included on the union's bargaining committee, which conducted contract negotiations.

In addition to racial division, the union was divided along political lines. John Lawe was elected president in 1977, but he did not receive a majority of the vote, which was split among four candidates. The forty-six-member union executive board was evenly divided between Lawe's supporters and other factions, including many dissidents who demanded a more militant approach toward the Metropolitan Transit Authority (MTA). During negotiations in late March 1980, dissidents, both rank and filers and board members, maintained a presence at the hotel where MTA and union officials met to discuss the contract. The dissidents continually advocated for a large wage increase and warned Lawe and other members of the union's negotiating team against a "sellout" contract. The divisions within the union and the overall agitation of the membership undermined Lawe's control of the situation. As John F. O'Donnell, general counsel to the union, told the *New York Times:* "In almost all prior years, the union was controlled by the leadership. Today, the leadership does not control the membership."

Though it was not revealed publicly until after the strike, in late February or early March, about a month before the contract deadline, Lawe, O'Donnell, and MTA chairman Richard Ravitch attended a dinner meeting arranged and conducted by mediator Theodore Kheel, the same mediator of the 1966 transit strike. At the meeting, which took place at a private club called Boardroom NYC, the men devised a plan to avoid a transit strike, agreeing to the outlines of a contract without the participation of the union's bargaining committee or executive board. The plan collapsed, however, in the face of heavy opposition from dissident local officials and the agitation of the membership. Lawe was forced, against his will, to lead a more militant bargaining effort and, if necessary, to strike.

Under pressure from the restive rank and file, Lawe set out the union's initial wage demand at 30 percent over two years. The union also demanded quarterly cost-of-living adjustments and six weeks of vacation after five years. MTA officials, led by Ravitch, insisted that the MTA could not afford such a large wage increase and hinted that a fare hike would be necessary if they were to concede the workers' demands. Instead of offering his own wage increase, Ravitch insisted that the union agree to forty-one productivity "improvements" that he claimed would save the MTA $150 million per year. These included hiring part-time workers, eliminating breaks, cutting differential pay for nights and weekends, reducing overtime opportunities, and cutting sick pay. The union called the so-called productivity improvements "givebacks" and refused to relinquish the benefits it had won through years of struggle.

Negotiations between the union and the MTA were complicated by politics. New York City, New York State, and the federal government contributed funds to the MTA, so politicians at each level determined the amount of money available to the MTA and, thus, to the workers. New York City mayor Ed Koch and New York governor Hugh Carey agreed before the contract expired that the city, which provided money to the MTA for capital expenditures, not operations, would not be required to increase its contribution. Nevertheless, Koch took a hard line against the transit workers, insisting that a 4 percent increase was all they should get. Despite his protestations to the contrary, most everyone understood that the primary motivation for his hard line was to prevent transit workers from setting the precedent of a large wage increase that the city would have to match in negotiations with nearly 300,000 city workers later in the year. Like Lindsay before him, Koch refused to participate in the negotiations, despite the fact that the city appointed several members of the MTA board. Governor Carey, who appointed the majority of the MTA board, including Chairman Ravitch, took a more accommodating, but still distant, approach to the negotiations. He claimed to support the state legislature's attempt to funnel more money to the MTA, but did little to move a pending bill.

In analyzing the negotiations, William Serrin astutely noted that officials on both sides had reasons to want a strike. For Carey and Ravitch, a strike would facilitate their requests for greater transit funding from Albany and Washington. It would also make a fare hike more palatable. For Lawe, a strike was a necessity because there was little chance he could get the union membership to accept a contract without one. Koch's position was more ambivalent. A large wage increase would undermine his position in negotiations with city unions, but a strike would allow him to hold the line on costs, appear tough in public, and continue his public attack on those same city unions.

As the strike deadline of April 1, 1980, approached, Ravitch refused to make a wage offer as long as the union insisted on a 30 percent increase, but at the last minute he offered 6 percent in each of two years. The union rejected the offer and called the strike. The Amalgamated Transit Union, which represented 2,000 city bus workers in Queens and Staten Island, was also involved in the negotiations and walked out with TWU. Over the next eleven days no Transit Authority subways or buses operated as 33,000 transit authority workers picketed stations, depots, and other workplaces. Workers also rallied around the city, often following Mayor Koch to picket or protest at his events. Union dissidents, including some on the negotiating team, formed the Good Contract Committee, which advocated for a more militant strike, a large wage increase, expanded benefits, and no concessions.

The city tried to reduce the traffic jams by implementing a three-person carpool requirement for cars entering Manhattan during rush hour, but snarls persisted. Many businesses suffered severe revenue declines, while others, such as hotels, saw income skyrocket as commuters stayed overnight in the city. Some of the economic damage was reduced by the fact that the strike coincided with the Passover and Easter holidays. On the first day of the strike, Mayor Koch stood at the foot of the Brooklyn Bridge welcoming "commuters" as they walked to work in Manhattan and asking them what would become his signature phrase, "How am I doin'?" He also initiated a lawsuit against the union, seeking compensation for the strike's damage to the city. The union also faced fines under the Taylor Law, and on the ninth day of the strike a Brooklyn judge fined the union $750,000 for the first eight days of the walkout. Negotiations continued on and off during the strike. Eventually, Mayor Koch and Governor Carey got involved, leading to several heated confrontations between them as Koch resisted any significant wage increase without offsetting productivity increases. With control of a majority of the MTA board, Carey prevailed and, drawing on the President's Emergency Board formula for the Long Island Railroad, the MTA agreed to a 9 percent increase the first year and 8 percent in the second year, plus a cost-of-living adjustment after the first year estimated at 3 percent.

The MTA also promised a $5 million contribution to the union's underfunded health and welfare fund. Koch fumed at the size of the wage increase, stating, "The city won the battle in the streets; the Metropolitan Transportation Authority lost it at the bargaining table." Contradicting his earlier denial of a link between the TWU contract and the upcoming negotiations with the city union, he complained that the transit agreement would raise city workers' expectations too high.

When the union's executive board considered the package it split twenty-two to twenty-two (one member was serving the weekend in the National Guard and one had recently died), but unanimously agreed to put the package to a membership vote. Afterward, there was some confusion among the board, as some dissidents believed the mail ballot would take place while the strike continued, but Lawe announced the end of the strike. Some of the dissidents, including the member serving in the National Guard, sued the union to force another executive board vote on the package, but a judge dismissed the complaint. In the end, the members voted 3-to-1 in favor of the agreement, which also included concessions on breaks, slower wage progression for new hires, and "broad banding"—the practice of having workers in one skill classification do the work of other classifications, which weakened union control over the work process. The agreement did not include amnesty from the Taylor Law, so workers lost an additional day's pay for each of the eleven days they were on strike, which essentially took back the first-year wage hike.

In June 1980, the MTA increased the subway and bus fare to 60 cents from 50 cents.

Striking for the Present and the Future

The 2005 strike had its roots in the contract campaigns of 1999 and 2002, both of which saw significant mass mobilizations. Each time, more than 10,000 transit workers demonstrated outside MTA headquarters and, at mass local meetings, voted overwhelmingly to authorize a strike. They did not hit the bricks, however, as union leaders and management negotiators reached last-minute agreements each time. Although the members voted 2-to-1 in favor of the settlement in both 1999 and 2002, there was considerable disappointment among the ranks. Discontent with the 1999 contract contributed to the electoral defeat in December 2000 of incumbent TWU Local 100 president Willie James and the election of Roger Toussaint, with 60 percent of the vote. Toussaint had developed a following in the track division in the early 1990s and then in 1997 joined New Directions, an increasingly influential rank-and-file caucus within Local 100. Elected at the head of the New Directions slate, Toussaint nonetheless left the group after taking office as local president and the group soon disintegrated. He won reelection in 2003, despite dissatisfaction with the 2002 contract—a dissatisfaction that would emerge full-blown in 2004 and 2005; Toussaint had pledged in 2002 to reduce the number of disciplinary write-ups, but the number actually increased between 2002 and 2004.

Rank-and-file agitation only grew when MTA officials announced months before the contract expiration that the agency had a $1 billion surplus for the year, but none of it would be used for improved wages and benefits. Indeed, the MTA demanded givebacks intended to save money or increase productivity, including the fusing of job classifications, eliminating conductors, and lowering pensions for new employees. MTA demands for givebacks came on top of transit workers' workplace concerns, most of which surfaced in virtually every contract dispute, including those that resulted in earlier strikes in 1966 and 1980.

Subway track work is among the most dangerous and physically demanding of city occupations. Between 1946 and 2007, 238 New York City subway workers were killed on the job and 150 were hit by trains. Bus operators suffered from "driver's stomach," or ulcers. Pulmonary disease above and below ground was common. A 2007 Mount Sinai Hospital study showed transit workers coming into regular contact with creosote, a wood preservative and cancer trigger used to soak railroad ties, and "absorbing significant quantities of the carcinogen through their lungs and skin." Token clerks, train operators, and conductors on graveyard shifts were frequently the targets of harassment and assault. The arbitrariness of supervisors in every division of the Transit Authority also angered the workers, many of whom found themselves under some type of discipline that threatened their pay or even their jobs. Taken together, the low wages, harsh conditions, physical danger, and arbitrary discipline gave transit workers the distinct impression that nobody, especially the administrators and politicians who controlled the Transit Authority, respected their efforts. "Everybody treats us like crap all the time. We're tired of being treated like we're the garbage of the city," one transit worker told *Newsday.*

Significant differentials in pay and benefits between New York City transit workers and those on the region's commuter railroads, which were also run by the MTA, further stoked workers' anger. A majority of city transit workers were African-American, Afro-Caribbean, or Latino, and they served riders who were largely people of color.

On the commuter railroads, a much larger portion of workers and riders were white, so many Local 100 members concluded that their lower pay and benefits, harsh disciplinary treatment, and unsafe working conditions illustrated the MTA's racism.

On December 10, 2005, five days before the contract expired, the union held a mass membership meeting. Toussaint pledged "no givebacks" and won an overwhelming roar of approval when he asked for authorization to call a strike if no settlement had been reached when the contract expired. On the 15th, the MTA presented its "final offer," which included the demands that new workers pay a 2 percent health care premium and that the retirement age and years of service required for a pension be raised from fifty-five and twenty-five, respectively, to sixty-two and thirty. Toussaint and the union's executive board rejected the offer, but did not call a strike, agreeing to postpone the strike deadline until December 19. Toussaint was adamant that there would be no two-tier health care system or pension givebacks: "They have to get away from the notion that in this round of bargaining the T.W.U. will give up its young, will give up its unborn." Over the next few days, the MTA withdrew the retirement age and years of service demands and replaced them with a demand that new hires pay 6 percent, instead of the current 2 percent, of wages to the pension plan, without an increase in pension benefits. The MTA was determined to win givebacks. Local 100 members were equally determined to avoid them. The result: on December 20 the union declared a strike, which was 100 percent effective.

For nearly three days, no subway cars or buses moved in New York City. Internally, however, the union was ill-prepared for a strike, and Toussaint's critics claimed he had resisted calls by rank-and-file activists to plan for a strike. These activists, including former New Directions members who had formed a new group called Rank and File Advocate, proposed that the union develop a clear slogan to unify the membership, line up support from other unions, encourage members to develop their own strike funds by putting money aside each week, identify and train picket captains, and, once the strike started, send pickets to the MTA's commuter railroads. The union rejected all these ideas, leaving members to simply walk picket lines around the city.

Public support for the strike was widespread, with surveys suggesting a slim majority of New Yorkers supporting the workers. The city's labor movement was more ambivalent. Only the other public sector unions offered outspoken support. Among building trades unions, support was nil. TWU International President Michael O'Brien, a political opponent of Toussaint's, openly opposed the strike, and he wrote an open letter to Local 100 members recommending they "cease any and all strike or strike-related activities and . . . report to work at their regularly assigned work hours and work locations." Mayor Michael Bloomberg and Governor George Pataki condemned the strike, the strikers, and the union. Bloomberg said union leaders had "thuggishly turned their backs on New York City," and many transit workers interpreted his reference to "thugs" as a thinly veiled racial epithet.

The strike ended after sixty hours when the union's executive board voted to return to work, *without a contract,* but with a tentative framework for negotiations. To many disgusted members, it appeared that the union had relinquished its greatest weapon at the most crucial moment. Without the strike, the union had lost its leverage. But for Toussaint, the strike had served its purpose. As he later said, "Our members would not accept a contract that was not the product of a strike," leaving his rank-and-file critics to conclude that Toussaint called the strike not to extract concessions from the MTA, but to convince members to accept the contract he would negotiate. Support for this interpretation arrived on December 28 when the parties announced a settlement in which the MTA withdrew its pension demands in exchange for the union's agreement that workers would now pay a 1.5 percent premium for their health care plan. In effect, Toussaint and the executive board, despite their pledge of "no givebacks," had traded one giveback (increased pension contribution) for another (health care premium). The union also conceded to have the contract expire in January, reducing the impact of any potential future strike, since it would not take place during the holiday shopping rush. The wage gains were 3 percent per year, which did not keep pace with the city's inflation rate. On the issue of discipline, the MTA agreed only to hire an independent consultant to improve the system.

Disappointment with the settlement was widespread among Local 100 members. Activists hastily arranged a "vote no" campaign, while Toussaint and other Executive Board members campaigned in support of the proposed contract. The vote, which took place in January, was agonizingly close. Members rejected the contract by a mere seven votes. Divisions representing train operators, track maintenance workers, and station agents rejected the contract by sizable majorities. Workers in these divisions were mostly African-American and Latino, and they had overwhelmingly supported Toussaint before the strike.

After the members rejected the proposed agreement, Toussaint chose not to renew the fight for a better contract. Local 100 leaders then did nothing until March, when Toussaint announced that the union would conduct another contract vote. With all the strike's momentum dissipated and with the union leadership refusing to lead a new contract fight, members acquiesced and overwhelmingly supported the previously rejected contract by a 3-to-1 margin. However, the MTA withdrew its agreement to the proposal, leaving the union without a contract, and further demoralizing the membership. Eventually, the two sides agreed to submit to arbitration, which resulted in a contract essentially the same as the original agreement. Meanwhile, a judge issued a $2.5 million fine against Local 100 for disobeying his injunction against the strike, ordered the MTA to stop deducting dues from members' paychecks after the fine was paid (the union regained the right to collect dues in November 2008), and sentenced Toussaint to ten days in jail for contempt of court (he served four days before receiving time off for good behavior). Additionally, under the Taylor Act against public sector strikes, each Local 100 member lost a day's pay for each day of the strike.

Declining Fortunes

The transit strikes of 1966, 1980, and 2005 had many elements in common. In each, city and state officials were determined to keep a lid on wage increases in order to prevent other municipal unions from ratcheting up their own pay demands. All three were motivated by restive rank-and-file workers who demanded respect from transit officials. In each case, many of these workers distrusted their union leaders' commitment to carry the fight to management. All three strikes had community support, but faced relentless criticism from the media, business officials, and politicians. In each strike, union leaders pursued essentially the same strategy—a simple walkout aimed as much at assuaging members' anger as extracting concessions from management. In all three strikes the union had vocal support from other public sector unions, but active strike support from other unions was nominal, with few or none volunteering to join transit workers on the picket lines.

Despite these similarities, the outcomes of the three strikes differed significantly. The 1966 strike was a clear victory for the union, with long-lasting positive implications for years to come. The victory in 1980 was more ambiguous, since wage gains came with union givebacks. The union achieved even less in the 2005 strike, and it made a significant concession in the form of a health care premium. The long-term deterioration of labor's economic and political power and the increased pressure on government's coffers partly explain the union's difficulties. Additionally, the union did not adjust its strategy to confront a more determined opposition. Indeed, the 2005 strike was the shortest and least militant of the three.

In the New York City transit strikes of 1966, 1980, and 2005, transit workers demonstrated the considerable power they have over the city. Their united refusal to work had enormous impact on the economy of the city and the lives of its residents. Despite the hardship they caused, transit workers won public support for their actions because many New Yorkers recognized their contribution to the city and the universality of their struggles for all workers. Unfortunately, despite transit workers' power, importance, and popularity, they continue to receive lower pay and worse benefits than their counterparts on commuter railroads and still suffer from the arbitrary discipline of management. No doubt, they will continue to struggle to improve their conditions, learning the historical lessons of the successes and failures of their past massive strikes.

See also: Labor and the Boston Police Strike of 1919, 241; Teachers' Strikes, 252; Postal Workers' Strikes, 266; Trolley Wars, 519.

Bibliography

Cannato, Vincent J. *The Ungovernable City: John Lindsay and His Struggle to Save New York.* New York: Basic Books, 2001.

Downs, Steve. "What Happened—and Didn't: Behind New York's Transit Strike." *Against the Current* 124 (September–October 2006).

Downs, Steve, and Tim Schermerhorn. "Hell on Wheels: Organizing Among New York City's Subway and Bus Workers." In *The Transformation of U.S. Unions: Voices, Visions and Strategies from the Grassroots,* ed. Ray M. Tillman and Michael S. Cummings. Boulder, CO: Lynne Rienner, 1999.

Freeman, Joshua B. *In Transit: The Transport Workers Union in New York City, 1933–1966.* New York: Oxford University Press, 1989.

———. *Working-Class New York: Life and Labor Since World War II.* New York: The New Press, 2000.

Marmo, Michael. *More Profile Than Courage: The New York City Transit Strike of 1966.* Albany: State University of New York, 1990.

McGinley, James J. *Labor Relations in the New York Rapid Transit Systems, 1904–1944.* New York: King's Crown/ Columbia University, 1949.

Powell, Adam Clayton, Jr. *Adam by Adam: The Autobiography of Adam Clayton Powell Jr.* Secaucus, NJ: Carol Publishing Group, 1994.

Quill, Shirley. *Mike Quill Himself: A Memoir.* Greenwich, CT: Devin-Adair, 1985.

SOCIAL WORKERS AND STRIKES

Howard Karger

The Bureau of Labor Statistics (BLS) estimated that in 2004 there were 562,000 social workers in the United States, a number that seems high in light of the fact that there are only 442 accredited bachelor's and 148 master's degree programs in social work. The BLS also estimates that 16.5 percent of community and social services occupations are unionized.

Despite BLS estimates, it is impossible to gauge the exact number of unionized social workers in the United States. First, the National Association of Social Workers (NASW) does not compile a count of unionized social workers. Second, most social workers are ensconced in large bargaining units that are rarely broken down into discrete employee classifications. Third, the category of "social worker" itself is vague. For example, many states that license social workers mandate that the title can be used only by licensed social workers. On the other hand, states that license social workers often exempt public sector employees who hold social work–like titles from licensing requirements.

The relationship between the social work profession and labor unions dates back to the late nineteenth century. This connection is marked by three distinct periods. The first dates from the late 1880s until the early 1920s, when social work reformers helped others—notably women—to organize into trade unions. Since social work was predominately a profession of volunteers until the 1920s, there was little impetus for social workers to organize themselves.

Social work became a bona fide profession by the late 1920s, albeit one that was paid poorly. The profession grew rapidly during the late 1920s and early 1930s, when the Great Depression led to the massive hiring of social workers, most of whom were unemployed teachers, technicians, accountants, and insurance and business salespeople. Most had no training in social work. As the Depression wore on, many of these welfare workers saw little hope of returning to their original vocations, and the prospect of organizing for better pay and working conditions became more pressing. This middle phase represented the halcyon period of social work unionism.

The third period—from 1947 to the present—is marked by the formal disengagement of social work from the labor movement. Although a significant number of public and some private sector social workers have been organized since 1947, they were blended into larger bargaining units. Consequently, by the early 1950s the profession of social work had lost any claim to a unique presence in the labor movement.

Social Reformers and the Union Movement

The relationship between social work and organized labor was born in several of the larger settlement houses that dotted America's urban landscape. Witnessing the impact of industrialization, settlement house leaders knew firsthand the misery produced by an unfettered market economy. For example, employers in the 1910 New York garment industry demanded that their women employees work an average of fifty-six hours a week, often requiring them to do work at home after hours. Wages for learners in this industry—about 25 percent of the workforce—were from $3.00 to $4.00 a week. For average operators—about 60 percent of the workforce—salaries ranged from $7.00 to $12.00 weekly.

Women working in Baltimore department stores averaged about fifty-six hours a week, with some working as many as sixty-five hours. During the Christmas rush, the average workweek was seventy hours. According to historian Sarah Eisenstein, 81 percent of women working in these stores earned less than $6.70 per week, the amount considered necessary for a single woman to be self-supporting in the area.

The female workforce exploded between 1870 and 1910. By 1910, 20 percent of all workers were women, and the labor force participation of married women reached 25 percent of the total female workforce, an increase of almost 50 percent from 1890. Despite the large number of women workers, in the late 1890s only 25 percent of states had adopted maximum-hour laws for women—and in only three of those states were the laws effective. Moved by these injustices, many larger settlement houses supported organized labor. For example, labor unions met regularly in Boston's Denison and South End Houses, in New York's Henry Street Settlement, and in Chicago's Hull House, Chicago Commons, and the University of Chicago Settlements.

Among the best known of the settlement leaders was Jane Addams, founder of Chicago's Hull House. According to Mary Anderson, former head of the Federal Women's Bureau, "It was around . . . Miss Addams, in the early days, that the whole movement for the organization of women and the improvement of their working conditions centered."

As an expression of her philosophy, Addams was involved in several strikes in the early 1900s, including the Chicago stockyards strike of 1904, various building trades strikes, a waitress strike, and her most important strike—the 1910 garment workers' strike against Hart, Schaffner, and Marx.

Support for labor unions also came from other settlement quarters. Robert Woods, Head Resident of Boston's South End House, wrote, "The greatest improvement in all the conditions of labor that has been wrought during these recent years, is without all possible question, the result of working class organization." As quoted by historian Allen F. Davis, settlement house leader Ellen Gates Starr believed that "if one must starve, there are compensations in starving in a fight for freedom that are not found in starving for employer's profits." The outrage felt by social workers at the plight of working women translated into their support for labor unions and the right of men and women to bargain collectively. This concern spawned the national Women's Trade Union League (WTUL).

Jane Addams, founder of Chicago's Hull House, was involved in several strikes in the early 1900s, including the Chicago Stockyards Strike of 1904. Her most important strike was the 1910 garment workers strike against Hart, Schaffner, and Marx. (Published ca. 1907. Copyright Ed. D. Waters. *Courtesy:* Library of Congress.)

Perhaps the most compelling example of the position occupied by social work reformers in the movement to unionize women is evidenced by their role in the WTUL. Founded at the 1903 American Federation of Labor (AFL) convention, the WTUL was not an official union, but a quasi-educational organization. Although membership was open to anyone who promised to assist women in their attempts to organize into trade unions, a policy existed to ensure that the majority of the board would be women. The WTUL was a hybrid organization that included both leisure-class activists and trade union members.

Despite lackluster support from the AFL leadership—a problem that would persistently plague the WTUL—by the end of the 1903 AFL convention the new organization had officers and a constitution. It also had, as chronicled by historian Meredith Tax, a program consisting of five demands: (1) the organization of all workers into trade unions, (2) equal pay for equal work, (3) an eight-hour day for all workers, (4) a minimum wage scale, and (5) women's suffrage. Almost immediately, local leagues were set up in Chicago, New York, and Boston.

Although the WTUL was never an official part of the AFL, it was heavily involved in much of the early-twentieth-century strike activity, including the "Uprising of the Twenty Thousand," a 1909 strike called against the Triangle Shirtwaist Factory and Leiserson's, two of the largest garment manufacturers in New York City. In the midst of 20,000 to 30,000 striking workers (the strike had quickly spread to other manufacturers), massive arrests, brutal police actions, and hired thugs, the WTUL organized a volunteer force of 275 "allies" and nine lawyers and furnished almost $30,000 in bail money. The headquarters of the New York WTUL became a strike center where on short notice volunteers could organize a parade of 10,000 workers, according to historian William O'Neill. Moreover, the WTUL was aided by several leisure-class female activists, including Ann Morgan (an heir to the J.P. Morgan fortune) and J. Borden Harriman. In the end the strike cost $100,000, one-fifth of which was raised by the New York WTUL. As a consequence of the "Uprising of the Twenty Thousand," the International Ladies' Garment Workers' Union (ILGWU) became the third-largest union in the AFL.

In 1910, as Tax chronicles, the WTUL was embroiled in Chicago's huge Hart, Schaffner, and Marx clothing strike. By October 1910, 40,000 workers had walked out and the garment district of Chicago was immobilized. Margaret Drier Robbins, the head of the national office of the WTUL, was given a seat on the strike committee. When the strike ended fifty days later, the Chicago WTUL had raised $70,000 for strike relief. By 1911 the WTUL's New York branch had almost doubled in size, the Boston group had grown by one-third, and the Chicago chapter became the largest, with 725 members. Despite the WTUL's growth and influence, the AFL remained largely disinterested in the organization. In fact, the only money the WTUL received from the AFL was $150 per month in 1912, and that was cut off when the league strayed from the AFL's position and supported the Lawrence strike.

During the Progressive Era, social work reformers helped others—particularly women—to organize. While social workers encouraged traditionally exploited groups to become involved in trade union activities, little thought was given to organizing their own nascent profession. That, however, would change with the creation of the large government bureaucracy necessary for dispensing the relief programs of the New Deal.

The Legacy of the Rank and File in Social Work, 1934-47

The Depression of the 1930s devastated the social work profession, as it did most of U.S. society. By 1932 it was obvious that the Depression would not be as ephemeral as some politicians had promised. The social and political volatility of the middle 1930s resulted in massive and often violent strikes, the polarization of Americans into opposing camps, and mounting pressure for massive social change. President Franklin D. Roosevelt understood that to save capitalism he would have to create social remedies, many of which took the form of public welfare.

Roosevelt's social welfare strategy led to the creation of massive public welfare services, which in turn required a virtual army of social workers. The existing supply of trained social workers fell far short of the new demand, and schools of social work did not have the time, money, or resources to train this standing army. Moreover, using professionally trained social workers would cost more than state or federal welfare authorities were willing to spend. Hence, the majority of social workers were untrained, many having been drawn from the ranks of the unemployed. It was this group that would later form the bulk of the rank-and-file movement in public sector social work.

A handful of practitioners—the majority of whom were caseworkers in private Jewish agencies—formed the Social Worker's Discussion Club of New York (SWDC) in the spring of 1931. The SWDC defined itself as an "open forum for the analysis of basic social problems and their relation to social work," according to writer Jacob Fisher. Contact between the New York SWDC and other progressive social workers led to the formation of clubs in Boston, Philadelphia, and Chicago. Unlike its New York counterpart, the Chicago SWDC primarily attracted public welfare workers and stressed workplace concerns—payless vacations, salary cuts, uncompensated overtime, and unsatisfactory working conditions—as well as social issues. Perhaps the most important aspect of the SWDC was their insistence that social workers be defined as "workers," believing that the fate of social workers was strongly tied to the destiny of working people.

In 1931, social work unionization in the private sector emerged in the form of the Association of Federation Workers (AFW), an organization of senior caseworkers employed by agencies of the New York Federation for the Support of Jewish Philanthropic Societies. Spearheaded by the New York SWDC, the AFW emerged in response to the salary cuts imposed by the federation. For the first time, social workers employed trade union tactics, which included picket lines, strike activities, mass meetings, petitions, and collaboration with labor and community groups. The AFW represented the first organized effort by social workers to demand collective bargaining, and on February 5, 1934, the New York AFW staged the first work stoppage in social work history.

The attempt to organize public welfare workers was started by the Chicago SWDC, composed largely of employees of the Cook County Welfare Department and the Unemployment Relief Service. Shortly after the passage of the 1933 National Industrial Recovery Act, the Chicago SWDC announced that the act's standards could be met only by creating a union. The Social Service Workers' Union (SSWU), the first protective union in public social services, was voted into existence on November 6, 1933.

The SSWU's workplace problems were similar to those in other Depression-era relief agencies designed to turn out cheap welfare services. The litany of complaints included the lack of desks, chairs, and stationery; crude sanitary facilities; long hours with uncompensated overtime; nonexistent or inadequate vacations; little or no compensated time for illness or injury; low salaries; arbitrary pay cuts; no job tenure; excessive caseloads; and inadequate or nonexistent training.

Welfare officials responded to the formation of the SSWU by attempting to crush the organization. Charges of Communist domination were hurled at the union by Chicago officials. Strident Cook County anti-union attacks succeeded in driving away all but a handful of the membership, which ensured that the SSWU would never develop beyond the blueprint stage. The lesson of Chicago was burned deep into the consciousness of the social work union movement: When faced with union organization, public relief commissions would employ the same anti-union tactics as industry.

The Chicago setback was partly balanced by a successful union-organizing drive in New York City. In 1933, more than 100 workers of the New York City Emergency Home Relief Bureau (EHRB) became one of the most effective social work unions of the 1930s. While the issues and working conditions were similar to those in Chicago, EHRB employees had one unique grievance—they all came from the welfare rolls and were subject to periodic checkups to reestablish need.

Although social workers were part of the rank-and-file labor movement as far back as 1931, it was not until 1934 that the unionization and organization of social workers under a working-class identity really began to take shape. The event that triggered the growth of the union movement occurred at the 1934 National Conference of Social Work. Social reformer Mary van Kleeck, in two eloquent and powerful papers, swept the national conference off its feet. In "Our Illusions Regarding Government," van Kleeck charged that government was dominated by the strongest interests, and because of capitalism it tended to protect property rather than human rights. Van Kleeck's second paper, "The Common Goals of Labor and Social Work," called on social workers to work with labor to eliminate unemployment and exploitation.

Fired up by van Kleeck's speech and that of Columbia University professor Eduard Lindeman, a group of progressive social workers called on the editors of *Social Work Today,* the organ of the New York City SWDC, to establish a National Coordinating Committee (NCC) to organize the activities of the various rank-and-file groups. To further that pursuit, a call was issued for a national convention. The 1935 convention of the NCC had delegates that represented eighteen protective organizations, six discussion clubs, four practitioner groups, and three miscellaneous organizations. In 1935 and 1936, the NCC was affiliated with eighteen organizations representing more than 12,000 members.

The End of an Illusion

The NCC's weakness lay in its loose-knit structure and the absence of money, paid staff, and office space. The organization functioned more like a clearinghouse than a strong, centralized union capable of providing leadership and direction. To be fair, the NCC was conceived only as a provisional organization that would eventually lead to a national union of social service employees. Despite a brief and frustrating attempt at organizing a national social workers' union under the AFL, by 1936 the NCC recommended that until they could create an autonomous department, the rank and filers should join the American Federation of Government Employees (AFGE).

In 1937 the NCC met for the last time at the National Conference of Social Work and voted to dissolve. It also recommended that *Social Work Today* be incorporated as an independent publication. With the dissolution of the NCC, affiliate groups rushed to the AFL and the newly emerging American Federation of State, County, and Municipal Employees (AFSCME), which had recently separated from the AFGE.

The dream of a social work union did not come to fruition for a number of reasons. Because the NCC did not have the time, money, or paid staff, it could not fully support union organizing. The NCC's lack of resources did not encourage the trust of social service workers facing layoffs and other workplace problems. When confronted with major labor problems, most social service workers turned to AFGE for assistance. Plus, by 1937 several national unions had already claimed workplace jurisdiction over most of the social service field. An application by NCC for national union status would probably have been denied by both the AFL and the Congress of Industrial Organizations (CIO).

Instead, the State, County, and Municipal Workers of America (SCMWA) was formed through a CIO charter in 1937. This charter allowed the union to organize all nonfederal government workers. The CIO also issued a charter in 1937 to the United Office and Professional Workers of America (UOPWA) to organize white-collar workers not claimed by other CIO unions.

Among the earliest subscribers to these two new unions were most of the public welfare locals in the AFL's AFSCME and all of the AFL-chartered social service unions in private agencies. By 1937, SCMWA had signed up 35,000 members, 8,500 of whom were in twenty-eight public welfare locals. By 1940 the UOPWA had negotiated a contract with the National Refugee Service that covered more than 500 employees. These organizing victories climaxed in 1941 when the UOPWA signed a contract with the Jewish Social Service Association, the largest Jewish family agency in the country. By 1948, the Social Service Employees Union (SSEU), an affiliate of the UOPWA, had contracts covering thirty locals representing about 10,000 workers. UOPWA's success in collective bargaining was far less spectacular than its growth, however. By 1942 the union had only about twenty-five contracts, many informal agreements, and union recognition in roughly fifty agencies. Out of that number, most of the formal written contracts were won by Local 19, a New York–based unit.

Social Work Today: A Journal of the Rank and File

From 1937 to 1942, the major connection between the social work profession and the unionization movement occurred through *Social Work Today.* To stabilize the financially shaky journal, fund-raising activities were conducted, including theater and dinner parties, benefit concerts, and the creation of a financial sponsorship system called Social

Work Today Cooperators, which included notables such as Bertha Reynolds, Mary van Kleeck, Grace Marcus, Kenneth Pray, Grace Coyle, Mary Simkhovitch, Ellen Potter, and T. Arnold Hill. Although the fund-raising activities kept the magazine afloat, actual subscriptions never exceeded 6,000.

Social Work Today attracted a wide variety of authors, including faculty members from schools of social work; governmental figures such as Frances Perkins, Katherine Lenroot, and Thomas Parran; and well-known public figures such as Roger Baldwin, John L. Lewis, and A. Philip Randolph. Despite its promising start, the focus of the magazine was predominantly leveled at the adequacy of public relief rather than on the function it performed as a capitalist palliative. By 1938, *Social Work Today*'s critique of the New Deal had turned into a glowing endorsement; and by 1942 the magazine was almost indistinguishable from mainline social work journals. *Social Work Today* abruptly disappeared in May of 1942. The reason for its sudden demise is unclear.

The radical unionization movement in social work ended as quickly as it began. Both UOPWA and SCMWA fell victim to the "red purges" of the CIO and were disbanded in 1947. In the end, most social work locals organized by UOPWA or SCMWA affiliated with AFSCME or AFGE.

The rank-and-file movement exposed large numbers of social workers to the powerful concept of "organization." Thousands of social workers exposed to the NCC, *Social Work Today,* and other rank-and-file activities were provided with a training ground that would prove useful in later public sector organizing. Furthermore, the experience that social workers received in arbitrating grievances, pushing demands, organizing meetings and rallies, and walking a strike line were skills that were later used in labor organizing and in the civil rights and anti-war movements. Through their experiences with the union movement, social workers were trained in confrontation and power—skills that schools of social work were ill prepared to teach.

The later history of labor and social work is uneventful compared to the 1930s and early 1940s. While large numbers of social workers joined AFSCME, the Service Employees International Union (SEIU), AFGE, and the Communications Workers of America, they did so as public sector employees—not as social workers with a unique professional identity.

The Contemporary Scene

Social work's reliance on often-rigid notions of professionalism has historically been an obstacle to unionization. For example, the NASW Code of Ethics contains contradictory messages. On the one hand, the code states that "social workers may engage in organized action, including the formation of and participation in labor unions, to improve services to clients and working conditions." On the other, it states that "the actions of social workers who are involved in labor-management disputes, job actions, or labor strikes should be guided by the profession's values, ethical principles, and ethical standards. . . . Social workers should carefully examine relevant issues and their possible impact on clients before deciding on a course of action."

NASW's admonitions about professionalism stand in sharp contrast to the financial reality experienced by social workers. For example, a 1998 AFSCME salary study found that the pay of social workers with a Bachelor of Arts or Bachelor's in Social Work ranged from $17,597 to $31,000 per year, with most falling into the mid-20,000s. The study points out that in many agencies social workers seldom, if ever, approach the upper end of the salary scale. This salary structure is hardly what most people would associate with a profession that requires a college degree and advanced training.

Despite the mixed messages inherent in the ideals of professionalism, large numbers of social workers have joined and are actively participating in union activities. For example, while the union membership rate in the private sector fell from 25 percent in 1975 to 8.2 percent in 2004, the unionization rate in the public sector increased to more than 35 percent. While we cannot accurately ascertain how many of these union members are social workers, it stands to reason that at least some of them are.

Anti-union sentiments combined with rigid notions of professionalism may partly explain the dearth of reported social work strikes in the

United States. This stands in stark contrast to the relatively frequent strikes by social workers in European industrialized nations. There are, however, some exceptions. In Portland, Oregon, child welfare social workers in SEIU's Local 503 went on strike in 2004 to lower turnover rates, improve staffing ratios and working conditions, and obtain higher wages. Turnover rates for staff who worked with children were about 50 percent. College graduates working with vulnerable children earned $9.28 an hour with little possibility of raises. In contrast, a study by the Northwest Federation of Community Organizations found that a single person living in Oregon must earn $10.17 an hour to meet their basic needs. For those with a child, the minimum necessary salary jumps to $17.60 an hour.

The opposition of social work management to an expanded scope of bargaining may partly explain why some observers view social work bargaining as less developed than teacher bargaining. Teacher workloads, including periods of preparation and relief from extracurricular activities, are accepted as proper subjects for bargaining. Class size, once considered a policy issue, is now accepted as a working condition. Teacher consultation rights provide for a variety of labor management committees. Social service labor agreements, on the other hand, rarely specify maximum caseload size. Instead, workloads are subject to reasonable standards, and if deemed unreasonable, the standard can be challenged in the grievance process. In many agreements, joint labor-management committees are established for the specific purpose of evaluating staff caseloads.

A number of current trends may lead to a stronger relationship between social workers and the labor movement. Primary among them is the proliferation of privatized, for-profit social welfare services. Privatized social services are being promoted as the public sector's answer to escalating costs, and their rapid growth is rooted in the desire of federal and state governments to offload their responsibility for delivering social welfare services. Consequently, the responsibility for service delivery is increasingly being carried by subcontractor firms, most of which provide few or no employee benefits and are hostile to anything resembling a labor union.

Eager to leave the poorly paid and highly restrictive public welfare sector, some of the most qualified social workers are opting for the promise of privatized social services. However, this initial enthusiasm often wanes when they see their higher salaries evaporate through inflation. It also wanes when these social workers come to appreciate how profit dominates the service goals of private providers, and how their hierarchal and bureaucratic structure replicates that of public agencies. These employees are also sobered by the realization that they have less job security than in the public sector. When all of these factors converge, a large and disillusioned group of social workers may be ripe for unionization.

Addressing the challenge of privatization will require that public sector unions pursue a more aggressive policy of recruiting private sector social workers, many of whom are employed in small agencies. Unfortunately, this kind of small-scale organizing is not cost effective and strains the fiscal resources of unions.

Another obstacle facing unionized social workers is that a social work strike is hardly a fearsome weapon. In fact, most social work strikes have been unsuccessful since managers, bureaucrats, and legislators seem not to fear them. Arnold Weber summarizes the dilemma:

> Public management will have little incentive to succumb to sanctions unless the service is "essential" in the sense that its curtailment will mobilize the consumer and impose political "losses" on the executive. . . . [In referring to a 1969 Chicago strike of social workers,] there were no competitors vying for the opportunity to provide funds and services to indigent persons. The strike did not diminish revenue to the agency . . . the department was able to distribute the monthly welfare payments without interruption. . . . The inability of social worker unions to impair a politically sensitive service helps to explain the consistent defeats of strikes by social workers all over the country.

Another obstacle to unionizing social workers is the emphasis on business unionism. Traditional beliefs about trade unionism fail to address many of the concerns of professional social workers. For example, some years ago I had to the opportunity to meet a large group of social workers, all of whom were committed union members. Although concerned about salaries, members of this group seemed more disturbed by their inability to provide high-quality services to clients. The problems discussed in this group centered around unmanageable caseloads, administrative insensitivity to clients, incompetent colleagues, and inadequate resources. When I brought these concerns to the union staff, they responded by pointing out that they had engineered significant raises, better grievance procedures, and so forth. Two themes emerged from this encounter: conventional trade union leaders seemed uncomfortable in usurping the traditional prerogatives of management, and they were deaf to the professional concerns of unionized social workers.

As such, union leadership must recognize that although bread-and-butter issues are important to social workers, this group is also concerned about professional issues that bear directly on their ability to serve clients. To be successful, unions must learn to better fuse traditional union concerns with the professional issues of social workers.

See also: Civil Rights Strikes, 118; Teachers' Strikes, 252; Garment Worker Strikes, 342.

Bibliography

Alexander, Leslie B., and Milton Spiezman. "The Union Movement in Voluntary Social Work." In *The Social Welfare Forum, 1979.* New York: Columbia University Press, 1980.

Bremner, Robert. *From the Depths.* New York: New York University Press, 1964.

Davis, Allen F. *Spearheads for Reform.* New York: Oxford University Press, 1967.

Fisher, Jacob. *The Rank and File Movement in Social Work, 1931–1936.* New York: New York School of Philanthropy, 1936.

———. *The Response of Social Work to the Depression.* Rochester, VT: Schenkman Books, 1980.

Karger, Howard Jacob. *Social Workers and Labor Unions.* Westport, CT: Greenwood Press, 1987.

———. *The Sentinels of Order: Social Control and the Minneapolis Settlement House Movement, 1915–1950.* Latham, MD: University Press of America, 1987.

———. "Reclassification and Social Work: Is There a Future for the Trained Social Worker?" *Social Work* 28 (November–December 1983): 431–39.

Levine, Daniel. *Jane Addams and the Liberal Tradition.* Madison: State Historical Society of Wisconsin, 1971.

O'Neill, William L. *Everyone Was Brave.* Chicago: Quadrangle Books, 1969.

Shaffer, Gary. "Labor Relations and the Unionization of Professional Social Workers." *Journal of Education for Social Work* (Winter 1979): 83–84.

Weber, Arnold R. "Paradise Lost: Or Whatever Happened to the Chicago Social Workers." *Industrial and Labor Relations Review* 22 (1969): 337–56.

Woods, Robert, ed. *The City Wilderness.* Boston: Houghton, Mifflin and Company, 1899.

PART V

STRIKES IN THE PRIVATE SECTOR

Introduction by Immanuel Ness

The private sector has dominated the American economy since the nation's founding. Except for periods of war when the state sector expanded to meet the call to arms, private enterprise has accounted for the bulk of the economy's output. Whether it was textiles in the 1830s, farm implements in the 1850s, railroads in the 1860s, steel in the 1880s, automobiles in the 1920s, fast food in the 1950s, or computers in the 1980s, the vast majority of the nation's goods and services came from the private sector. As a result, the private sector has consistently set the tone for labor relations, and the vast majority of strikes have occurred in the private sector.

The corollary to the preeminence of the private sector has been the relatively weak state sector, especially in terms of the social safety net. Whereas European labor and social movements succeeded in pushing governments to establish job protections, universal health insurance, unemployment insurance, and pensions, workers in the United States had to wrest many of these benefits from their employers, public and private. Strikes played a key role in their struggles.

The supremacy of the private sector shaped the history of strikes in the United States. Private employers were rarely expected to pursue any goal other than their own profits. They faced relatively little regulation, received more extensive government encouragement, and enjoyed greater cultural sanction than private sector employers in Europe. As a result, they had more latitude to fire union activists or replace striking workers with scabs. Federal, state, and local governments took a hands-off approach to labor relations, which usually meant enforcing employers' property rights and supporting their strikebreaking activity. Workers thus faced both powerful employers and hostile governments. Even during periods when state and federal labor relations policy tilted more toward organized labor, private property rights remained paramount. Employers' rights to control their factories and offices trumped workers' rights to their jobs or benefits.

Operating in such a hostile environment, private sector workers had to strike more often and more intensely than their European counterparts just to win union recognition, increase wages, or improve benefits. The history of private sector strikes is a nasty one, particularly in mining, manufacturing, agriculture, and infrastructure industries. Violence was not uncommon on either side, and where violence was absent the conflict could still be extremely harmful. Strikers most often bore the brunt of the conflicts. Employers routinely fired them and then blacklisted them, making it impossible for them to work in the local industry again. Police arrested and jailed them. Prominent citizens often ostracized them. Workers lost their lives, their livelihoods, and their loved ones in strikes.

Sometimes, however, the tables turned: strikers would shut down a business at the right time or for long enough to inflict serious economic pain on its owners and managers. This might involve damaging property or simply winning enough support to make replacement workers impossible. Employers would fail to win the backing of local elites or government officials. Instead, strikers would rally community cooperation and enlist the aid of the authorities. As a result of their superior organization in multiple arenas, strikers would compel their employers to honor their demands.

The variety of private sector strikes was mind-boggling. Construction worker strikes shared little with strikes by agricultural workers, which were light years apart from strikes by autoworkers. The nature and organization of the work, the skill and background of the workers, the size and economic strength of the employer, the political regime, and even the law varied significantly across the economy and over time. Still, workers in almost every private sector industry at some point went on strike—even cartoonists, computer programmers, and lawyers. They each determined that withholding their labor was an appropriate method for achieving their collective aims. Whether they were successful or not was another question.

To make some sense of the diversity of private sector strikes, the essays in this section organize industries into three groups that share some common characteristics. Manufacturing, mining, and agricultural industries are all devoted to the production of goods. Strikes in these industries shared the common goal of reducing or halting the output of those goods. Of course, the diversity of the goods and the methods used to produce them meant workers and their unions had to devise very different strategies to succeed in their strikes. For example, agricultural workers could time their strikes to take advantage of the perishable nature of the goods they produced, while miners developed intense cultures of solidarity to deal with the constant danger of coal mining.

Infrastructure industries support other parts of the economy, mostly by moving people, goods, and information. Without infrastructure, modern economies are impossible. Given this importance, the government often takes a keen interest in the development and maintenance of infrastructure industries and, by extension, their labor relations. To ensure strong infrastructure industries, governments often regulate them—for example, by setting prices and limiting competition in the trucking industry or by allowing, but regulating, the phone company monopoly. Government involvement in an industry usually translates into government intervention in the industry's labor relations. Not surprisingly, government officials have often shaped the outcome of infrastructure strikes.

Service industries are all those businesses that do not produce goods. Instead, they perform services that people and other businesses need. The sheer diversity of these businesses makes it difficult to generalize about them or their strikes. Nurses treat ill people, and their strikes can have profound implications for the lives of their patients. By contrast, the strikes of office workers represent little more than an inconvenience for the wider public. As a result, it has been easier for nurses than for office workers to focus popular attention on their plight. The strength of their connection to the rest of the community created by their work is a crucial element in the success or failure of service workers' strikes.

The sanctity of private property rights in the United States, particularly the relatively unfettered freedom employers have when it comes to labor relations, is one of the main reasons for the comparatively large number of strikes in U.S. history. Federal, state, and local authorities have generally been hostile to organized labor, seeing in it a threat to property. Workers have had to rely on their own collective activity, often in the form of strikes, to advance their interests at work. In doing so, they have often argued that the owners of private property have obligations to the workers who give that property value. At times, they have taken the argument further, pointing out that it is not just workers but the rest of society that makes property worth something. In this way, private sector strikes have often been about much more than simply wages and benefits.

Part V, Section 1

Manufacturing, Mining, and Agriculture Strikes

Introduction by Immanuel Ness

This section examines strikes in U.S. manufacturing, mining, and agriculture from the precolonial era to the first decade of the twenty-first century. During this long history, employment in these sectors rose and fell, the nature and organization of work changed, and the legal framework of labor relations evolved, but each of the three industrial sectors remained crucial to the national economy. In each sector, workers challenged oppressive conditions, miserly wages, and draconian employers.

In agriculture, racial slavery was a primary form of labor organization for several centuries, ending only with the Civil War in the 1860s. African-American agricultural workers did not often engage in traditional strikes, but they did develop many forms of resistance to the tyranny of slavery, including shirking work, running away, and, at times, revolt. In August 1831, in Southampton County, Virginia, fifty slaves and freedmen led by Nat Turner staged a violent insurrection that led to the deaths of more than fifty white people and the hanging of more than fifteen rebels. Smaller uprisings occurred sporadically. Perhaps the largest strike in American history was the strike of African Americans during the Civil War: hundreds of thousands refused to work, left their plantations, reunited with previously sold-off family members, and sought shelter with the Union Army. Their actions helped to end slavery in the United States.

In the postbellum era, agricultural strikes took place periodically, sometimes staged by migrant workers. The 1903 Oxnard, California, sugar-beet strike united 200 Mexican workers with some 800 Japanese workers against the American Sugar Beet Company and farm growers to end labor contracting and improve conditions. Remarkably, these proletarian farmworkers still won despite the American Federation of Labor's disdain for foreign-born workers. Throughout the twentieth century, California remained an epicenter of farmworker strikes. In 1939, John Steinbeck's prizewinning novel, *The Grapes of Wrath,* captured the plight and resistance of farmworkers in the California orchards.

The brutal conditions of mineral mining, both underground and in company towns, made it one of the most strike-prone industries. Workers in virtually every period and in every geographic location waged strikes against mine owners, their hired thugs, and government forces.

Mining strikes occurred frequently in mineral-rich Colorado, where members of the Western Federation of Miners (WFM) and, later, the United Mine Workers (UMW) organized. Mine operators paid low wages and turned a blind eye to unsafe conditions in the mine shafts. Typically, they broke strikes with the assistance of the National Guard, bands of hired mercenaries, and replacement workers, but in 1894 the tables turned. The populist governor refused to authorize the use of state troops to break a strike by WFM gold miners in Cripple Creek, who were protesting a wage cut and a lengthening of the workday. The owners still recruited some 1,300 vigilantes, but the superior organization of the WFM prevailed. After five months, the union forced the owners to restore the eight-hour day and rescind the wage cut.

Twenty years later, a different governor was less sympathetic to 1,200 striking UMW members at a bituminous coal mine owned by the Rockefeller family in Ludlow, Colorado. In what immediately became known as the Ludlow Massacre, on April 20, 1914, National Guard and company troops attacked the strikers' tent village with machine guns and set fire to the town, killing sixteen workers and their families. Violence such as that at Cripple Creek and Ludlow was common in miners' strikes. It resulted in part from the intense solidarity miners built and their willingness to fight the cruelty of mine owners. That solidarity has become a durable element of American culture, portrayed in films such as *Salt of the Earth* and *Harlan County USA,* and in songs such as "Which Side Are You On?"

Strikes by manufacturing workers have tracked the ups and downs of the myriad industries within the sector. The first manufacturing strikes were by cordwainers (shoemakers) and carpenters around the time of the American Revolution. Artisans in these and similar fields continued to strike throughout the nineteenth century as their industries were de-skilled and they turned, in the title of Bruce Laurie's book, *From Artisans to Workers.* The first strikes in mass production industries were by textile workers, many of them women, in New England in the 1830s. Such strikers often fought to establish or preserve a moral economy in which the prices for such essential items as bread and labor were set not by impersonal market forces but democratically by the community.

As the industrial revolution progressed, the number of manufacturing industries multiplied and market relations colonized more of the economy, while ideals of moral economy faded. Manufacturing dominated the economy, creating huge industries that employed millions of workers reconciled to selling their labor power to make a living. From the mid-nineteenth century to the present, manufacturing workers on strike have sought primarily better wages and working conditions, but many of them have also sought broader, even revolutionary, social and political transformation. Manufacturing strikes motivated social reform in the Progressive Era early in the twentieth century, and they led to the New Deal in the 1930s, which established such fundamental rights as unemployment insurance and social security.

In the second half of the twentieth century and into the twenty-first, manufacturing's importance within the economy declined; it accounted for a smaller and smaller portion of the nation's output and employment. The number of union members in these industries decreased, as did the number of strikes. Nonetheless, manufacturing workers continued to strike as part of their effort to win unions, better wages, improved working conditions, and dignity. In 2002, United Auto Workers at three recently organized Johnson Controls auto parts plants walked out in a campaign to win a first contract. They won their strike in two days because their stoppage shut down auto assembly plants—such as the Jeep Liberty plant in Toledo, Ohio—that depended on the parts they made. In addition to better wages, company-paid health insurance, and a company-matched pension plan, their victory included employer neutrality and card-check recognition at twenty-six additional Johnson Controls plants, making their walkout an example of how unions can use the power of a strike to expand their membership.

Today, technological change has reduced the number of workers that the manufacturing, mining, and agriculture sectors need. Furthermore, globalization has meant that businesses in these sectors must compete with low-wage producers in other countries. Nonetheless, these sectors still employ millions of workers and remain crucial to the U.S. economy. For workers and unions in manufacturing, mining, and agriculture these are challenging times. Perhaps the history of their strikes, as the essays in this section describe, holds some lessons for reversing their decline.

STRIKES AND APPRENTICESHIP IN THE UNITED STATES

Daniel Jacoby

Before industrial unions achieved their dominance within the labor movement, skill constituted a central element in the battles between labor and capital. Both sides in these conflicts learned to attach importance to apprenticeship because of the strategic opportunities it offered to alter the production, distribution, and even the definition of skill. Rarely was apprenticeship the immediate cause of strikes; but strikes often turned on attempts by employers and workers to control key aspects of apprenticeship.

The apprenticeship process may be defined as one involving a formal exchange of labor for trade instruction. Over the course of history, the terms of that exchange have been governed to various degrees by individual contract, government regulation, employer associations, and labor organizations.

Theoretical Perspectives on Apprenticeship Strikes

Theoretical models of human capital investment are helpful in defining the costs and risks inherent in skill investments. Firms have a stronger incentive to invest in worker skills when they know they can retain their workers after their investment has been completed. Requiring workers to serve for several years enhances employers' ability to profit from their investments. However, long-term contracts can overprotect employers, enabling employees to be misused during the period they are legally bound to serve. Historically, American employers that were plagued by runaways sought rights to bind their apprentices, while simultaneously avoiding regulations designed to protect their trainees. Unions, on the other hand, placed greater emphasis on employer than on apprentice responsibilities, though they also desired to see indentures completed.

Union regulation of apprenticeship lent itself to charges of monopoly. Limitation of the number of apprentices had two purposes, the first of which was to restrict entry and competition within trade. The second purpose was to improve the quality of craftsmen. Limiting apprentice-to-journeyman ratios, as with class-size limits today, was often regarded as a proxy for quality. In general, higher-quality training required increased investment costs and thus exerted an independent tendency to limit the number of apprentices.

Current understanding of apprenticeship regards cooperation between modern employer associations and organized labor as essential. Positive relations expand the scope of investments in apprentices, minimize incentives to misuse apprentices, and reduce the uncertainties relating to skills investment. Such cooperation, however, depends crucially on the history of particular countries. In the United States, as nineteenth-century craft unions began to fill the void created by weak or nonexistent guilds, they assumed the task of regulating what had previously been matters determined unilaterally by craft masters. Union perspectives often differed from those of their employers. Skilled artisans soon realized that the investments they made in their skills could be jeopardized by new technologies. Confrontations over business decisions that threatened to alter the demand for skilled labor increased as organized labor sought to regulate apprenticeship.

Unions justified their demands as protection for the apprentice or the journeyman. Likewise, regulation might also be justified as quality protection for consumers, though it is often argued that this protection comes at a cost most buyers would prefer not to bear. Thus, observers tended to regard union restrictions as monopolistic restraints on trade. The same charge had been made earlier against guild masters when they had regulated apprenticeship for their own interests. For unions, as for the guilds before them, apprenticeship was a means of controlling craft entry. Craft entry was also particularly important during times of strike.

Whatever nominal interests were involved in strikes fought to regulate or deregulate apprenticeship, the outcome of such conflicts still had an independent strategic value. Similarly, strikes that were not ostensibly about apprenticeship could turn into apprenticeship conflicts as each side necessarily looked for strategies to alter the supply of potential combatants. This strategic value complicated the political posturing by both sides. Employers who justified their combativeness by arguing that unions monopolized their crafts to the detriment of others found that their arguments rang hollow if they were discovered to use strikebreakers to undermine labor standards or training. In contrast, labor had to show not only that its control over apprenticeship was an essential part of workplace justice but also that its restrictions were essential to properly educate craftsmen well and that it did not discriminate against women, minorities, or others who wished to practice a trade.

The Failure of Early Strikes Involving Apprentices

Regulation of apprenticeship played a noteworthy role in several early "cordwainer cases" where striking shoemakers were prosecuted for criminal conspiracy. Sean Wilentz has written about these cases, as has John R. Commons. In the first case in 1806, *Commonwealth v. Pullis* (Mayor's Ct. Phil., 1806) Philadelphia journeymen apparently recognized employers' right to control of their apprentices, but refused to work alongside former apprentices who failed to join their society. The New York case, *People v. Melvin* (1 Yates Sel. Cas. 112; 1809 N.Y. Lexis 257), shows that by 1808 journeymen had stepped up their pressure by striking not only to regulate wages, but also to limit the number of apprentices a master could take. As Paul B. Gilje and Howard B. Rock document, when the strikers were brought to trial for criminal conspiracy, their defense attorney, William Sampson, justified their actions:

> . . . can it be said that the resolution not to work for a master who employed more than two apprentices was unpraiseworthy? The masters were in the habit of crowding their shops with more apprentices than they could instruct. Two was thought as many as one man could do justice by. The journeymen shoemakers therefore determined to set their faces against the rapacity of the masters, and refused to work for those who were so unjust as to delude with the promise of instruction which was impossible they could give.

In 1815, a Pittsburgh case, *Commonwealth v. Morrow,* indicated that although journeymen recognized apprentices' contractual obligations to obey their master, their society still struck to prevent apprentices from completing work they wished to reserve for themselves. Increasingly, journeymen were challenging the right of employers to direct the work of apprentices when that work was considered contrary to their interests.

Journeymen printers also raised apprenticeship issues, but initially stopped short of striking. In 1809 they felt their immediate problem in New York was the burden created by the large number of apprentices who had absconded from their masters before serving their full term. The union asked the masters for aid in enforcing indentures by refusing to hire "halfway" craftsmen. Printers and typographers in Baltimore, Philadelphia, and New York attempted different approaches to limit the number of apprentices, including refusals to instruct learners. Printers' grievances over apprenticeship would generate clashes and strikes for more than a century.

Early apprenticeship strikes must be understood to have occurred in a context different from those that followed. Sean Wilentz, Gordon Wood, Robert Steinfeld, and William Rorabaugh are among the authors who have discussed this topic. In particular, American society was in a process of radical change as employment and social relations shifted from traditional and forced labor to free contract. Democracy took hold of the American imagination by way of a republican ideology that touted virtue and independence as the essential ingredients of self-governance, both in personal and in civic life.

Wage labor, by contrast, was regarded as a kind of vassalage that left a worker dependent upon his master. To be truly independent and capable of exercising virtuous or dispassionate judgment, individuals needed sufficient resources or property so as not to be beholden upon anyone else. For American workers, the independence of property could be gained through the possession of a craft, and the surest way of securing this was through apprenticeship. This understanding of republicanism would never be completely undone, but over the next century, as wage labor became more common and the prospect of attaining independence as a master craftsman became more remote, the appeal to apprenticeship as a basis upon which to foster democratic citizenship became increasingly tenuous.

The concern by early journeymen societies for apprenticeship was fed by their understanding of craft as an alternative form of property. This property was created through the investments workers made in their own apprenticeships—investments they expected would lift them out of degrading wage labor as journeymen and into the status of independent master. Early strikes supported workers' political understanding of artisan republicanism; they aimed to prevent divisions of labor that undermined worker independence. There also emerged a sense of the journeyman as citizen within their crafts. In America, where the guild had failed, craftsmen collectively assumed the duty to regulate the conditions within their trades to achieve real equality. As historian Sean Wilentz has written, "The workshop, a site of collaborative labor, ideally turned out both handicrafts useful to the public and new independent craftsmen to replenish the ranks of the trades."

Craft apprenticeship was the subject of many threats. Not only did individual freedom of contract eat away at the legal status of apprentices, but dynamic technological change altered the boundaries between crafts destabilizing traditions of instruction. Yet when workers sought to stabilize the trades and apprenticeship, they confronted the legal doctrine of criminal conspiracy. It was on this charge that New York's cordwainers were convicted when they struck to prevent employers from hiring apprentices and other men who were not party to their society.

The criminal conspiracy charges were the result of a confusing English legal tradition, one that would eventually be redefined by the new American republic. On the one hand, the law extended English traditions denying workers rights that had been formalized in 1563 with the Statute of Artificers. This servile aspect of labor policy came into to an uneasy marriage with Britain's increasingly liberal tradition, of which Adam Smith was the principal spokesman. Smith, in the first book of *The Wealth of Nations,* argued against collective action saying, "People of the same trade seldom get together to meet, even for merriment and diversion, but that the conversation ends in a conspiracy against the public, or in some contrivance to raise prices." Thus, the strikes of workers involving apprentices—as well as other collective action—became monopolistic infringements upon the liberties of others. It would take more than a century before a clearly defined exemption from monopoly law—the Clayton Act of 1914—was crafted to ensure the rights of workers to organize, bargain, and strike. The early cordwainers' strikes, in which craft journeymen refused to work with any individual who was not a member of their society, constituted forerunners for latter-day closed-shop battles involving apprenticeship.

The court's decision in New York's cordwainer strike would have made it virtually impossible for associations of workingmen to regulate an apprenticeship system to their own satisfaction. Yet despite the persistence of the conspiracy doctrine through the 1830s, apprenticeship did become the subject for occasional strikes and negotiations. Workers could do this because juries often winked at the law, fining guilty workers only trivial amounts. Unions also found ways to pressure employers covertly.

Nevertheless, the failure of labor's first protests placed employers more firmly in control over their own apprenticeships, opening the door to changes that weakened craft traditions. From the time of Britain's Statute of Artificers, the apprenticeship indenture was understood as a long-term contract that bound youths to serve and masters to teach and supervise in loco parentis. There had always been abuses of apprentices, especially when poor or orphan children were bound out without their consent, yet these typically did not undermine the institution itself. In the New World, however, employers seemed to find apprenticeship most desirable when it provided them the advantage of flexible child employment that avoided the parental obligations inherent in traditional indentures. Indeed, by the early 1800s it was common to find advertisements in newspapers offering rewards of only $1.00 for the return of an apprentice. Posting minimal rewards for the capture of their apprentices freed employers of their legal obligations while simultaneously assuring that no one would invest much time or effort searching for the children. The arrangement suggests that apprentices were valued more as cheap labor than as skilled employees who were worth the effort required to find and keep them.

It was the new possibilities for factory or sweated work that increased opportunities to use boy labor as machine tenders or operators requiring no expensive training. Similarly, the growing cash economy encouraged employers to substitute monetary payments for the parental supervision, housing, and care that custom dictated. Apprenticeship became a matter between the employer, the apprentice and, to a lesser extent, the law. Unions were relatively powerless against such arrangements. New indentures often existed outside the law—not illegal, but merely unenforceable. However, even if the law would not enforce them, long-term contracts could be secured if they included incentives for contract compliance. Thus, a parent wishing to bind a child to a trade could provide surety of performance by committing themselves to make good any loss, by allowing the employer to defer compensation until the completion of the task, or simply by paying the master for the right to place their child. The master, on the other hand, seldom provided an explicit bond that could be confiscated for nonperformance (though by the 1860s Massachusetts did attempt to require such double bonding).

The Second Try

Workingmen awoke to these and other challenges in the 1830s. The influence of machinery upon skill and trade was especially keen in the printing trades, where the craft had been divided into pressmen, typographers, and editors. New machinery increased the capital requirements for running printing enterprises. That in turn reduced the prospects that journeymen would ever become independent master printers, which was the cornerstone of artisan republicanism. William Rorabaugh has documented how such issues became elements in an 1835 strike by the Columbia Typographical Society.

Duff Green, owner and editor of the *U.S. Telegraph* and the official printer for the House of Representatives, adroitly seized upon ideas and trends that were already in place and proposed to open an orphanage in Washington, DC, and then have the boys there serve as his apprentices. In this way, Green expanded contemporary practices, thereby making trade "mysteries" less mysterious. Craft knowledge was opened up beyond select initiates to the wider public through publishing books, creating apprentice libraries, and setting up numerous workingmen's or mechanics' institutes in cities like New York and Philadelphia. It was but one more step to go from using institutes to enhance craft knowledge to developing short courses that sidestepped apprenticeship.

Green suggested that the boys, who ranged in age from eleven to fourteen, would work and learn their trade for eight hours a day to help offset the expense of the orphanage. He assumed it was permissible not to pay his help until they graduated at age twenty-one—and even then the wage arrears were only to be loaned back to the boys if they desired to open their own offices in other locales. His competitors, the other master printers in Washington, protested that the arrangement would give Green an unfair competitive advantage inasmuch as the latter stood to benefit from captured boy labor. Yet his critics failed to form an effective employers' guild to defend their notions of apprenticeship, and that task fell to the journeymen printers in the Columbia Typographical Society. The men struck Green's establishments, where he employed forty or fifty boys from the newly created Washington Institute. The boys, boasted Green, would save him over $15,000 as compared with the costs of hiring journeymen. However, Green never saw those profits because one year later the striking journeymen succeeded in closing the Washington Institute. In 1837, continued clashes with labor along with "declining political fortunes" forced Green to also abandon the *U.S. Telegraph*.

The strike illustrates the scale of abuses that long-term contracts might support. Because the value of gaining a craft was real enough, boys could be attracted to such situations with mere promises of future success. However, enforcing an employer's obligations to instruct over the length of a long contract was exceedingly difficult, so there could be no guarantee that boys would learn the entire printing trade. There are suggestions that Green may even have hoped boys would run off before fulfilling their terms, eliminating the necessity of providing them any compensation at all. Although Green hoped to capitalize on the tradition of apprenticing orphans, his relationship with the boys shows that the ideal that masters would care for their charges as they would for their own children was unlikely to be met. Instead, Green declared that sick or disabled boys would be sent home to their families for care and support.

As far as the law was concerned, Green was free to do what he wanted. His was but one more expression of what Morton Horwitz, in *The Transformation of American Law, 1780–1860,* calls the "triumph of contract." The courts were largely indifferent, except insofar as they would not compel boys to complete an invalid indenture. Most notable in this situation was the device that Green used—deferred wages—to ensure that his training investments paid off. Securing an apprentice's services without incurring an immediate wage liability would naturally reduce costs. Deferring wages likely increased the incentive boys had to complete their terms, which again increased the return on employers' investments—unless, as noted earlier, the boys ran off, forfeiting their deferred wages altogether. The employer had multiple motives to abuse the situation through harsh treatment or insufficient training.

Worst of all, those who had already undertaken investments in their training had no guarantee that employers would not continue to apprentice more individuals, and in so doing glut trades. Workingmen's unions had strong reason to aggressively insert themselves into the training process. Duff Green's defeat is particularly notable, especially in contrast to earlier and later employer victories, because fellow printers did not support his actions. The weakness of employer associations or guilds at this time provided workers with opportunities to govern craft entry on their own.

Foreshadowing future arguments, Green contended that workers had no right to this power. For example, in 1887, Colonel Richard T. Auchmuty, hoping to rally public support against union "monopoly," would echo this claim by suggesting, "It is not the province of any body of men, certainly not of any self-constituted organization, to decide who or how many shall be allowed to work. . . . Mechanics did not invent their trades, they have no proprietary rights in them."

Craft, a growing number of employers asserted, was not property and could not be governed collectively by workers. Though risky long-term investments are essential, the regulation and protection of those investments was to be a matter of individual contract. Anything that violated an employer's right to employ or a worker's right to quit would be regarded as an infringement upon individual liberty.

Given ineffectual state apprenticeship enforcement of apprenticeship indentures, the responsibility for ensuring craft standards fell to organized labor. Yet, this was a responsibility for which they were not particularly well suited in light of labor's tenuous legal position. Consequently, while workingmen looked to their organizations in order to restore order and stability in the apprenticeship process, in the 1830s we can document only a few unions—such as New York's bakers—who walked out specifically over apprenticeship issues.

Postbellum Strikes

William Sylvis of the Iron Moulders' International paved the way for more aggressive union defense of apprenticeship. Under his leadership, trade unions reasserted a protective movement, forming the National Labor Union in 1869. The rival Knights of Labor also responded to the training question.

The mid-century growth of the metal trades encouraged unions, once again, to "legislate" their trades. Such legislation typically consisted of advisories telling employers to obey the rules they declared. Enforcement of these rules required that employers be dependent upon union employees, a situation characteristic of the skilled trades. Sylvis began organizing molders in 1859, a time when the trade was increasingly subjected to the standardization of production. Yet, in *Fincher's Trades Review*, Sylvis wrote that the molders' trade had become so prosperous that employers quickly gave in to union wage and apprenticeship demands. Molders also benefited from legal rulings opening new channels by which unions could successfully challenge their employers. By 1866, however, employers banded together to resist the molders. As Commons records, the American National Stove Manufacturers' and Iron Founders' Association declared that they would "resist any and all actions of the Moulders' union to employ as many apprentices as they deemed fit and to exclude shop committees." The new association posted its resolutions in its Troy and Albany shops, where workmen promptly walked out in response. Sylvis agreed to put the International's resources at the disposal of the strikers and after several months the union emerged completely victorious, able to keep its shop committees and to regulate apprenticeship. The Moulders thus set an example: not only highly skilled artisans but also the relatively unskilled shoemakers in the Knights of St. Crispin insisted upon limiting apprentices.

The Knights of St. Crispin was organized explicitly "to protect its members from injurious competition." Don Lescohier is one of its historians. The organization's rules declared, "No member shall . . . teach or aid in teaching any part or parts of boot or shoe making" unless given explicit permission. If ever a trade had been undermined by technology, it was shoemaking. By 1885, more than 200 new machines and gadgets—perhaps the most important of which were leather-stitching machines—had been applied to the cordwainers' trade. The effect was to divide their labor and increase the use of factories. Although shoemakers had already lost a major strike in Lynn, Massachusetts, after becoming organized under the Knights of St. Crispin, they came back in the late 1860s to defend what was still left of their trade. Some historians have regarded the St. Crispin strikes and confrontations over the use of inexperienced workers as peculiar, especially given the de-skilling they had already experienced. Yet it seems likely that their refusal to teach "green hands" their trade—an act virtually indistinguishable from a strike—may have been intended to avoid legal repercussions against their collective actions. Refusals to teach permitted individual laborers to claim they had acted to protect the "capital" that was the Crispin's trade. Surely, they could not be required to train their own replacements? By withdrawing their instruction, they trod a blurred line between "malicious" injury to others and defensive "cooperation." In the 1873 case *Snow v. Wheeler* (113 Mass. 179), at least one court asserted that such cooperation was legal.

Although crafts such as the cordwainers had been undercut by the technology, the industrial revolution also gave rise to new trades while it expanded others. Among scholars, there is now a resurgence of interest in employers' desire to maintain craftsmanship. Historian Phillip Scranton, in particular, has been important in pointing out the ways that many manufacturers valued and secured mechanisms to produce skilled workmen. Such employers did not seek economies of scale but of scope. The capacity of workmen to work independently was particularly important in the machine tools trades, where custom work created new problems to be solved on the shop floor on a daily basis. Thorough training proved vital to many machinist employers.

Employers in problem-solving trades often turned to schools, which, unlike on-the-job training, could not be easily monitored by unions. Of particular note is one institute created by the Worcester Mechanical Association in the 1860s.

Unlike the workingmen's or mechanics' institutes of the 1820s, the Worcester Institute did not stop at providing trade instruction. Its distinguishing feature was the Washburn Workshops where products were produced for the market. At the "Worcester Institute students would for three years learn principles in half-day classes (mechanics, drafting, etc.) while gaining practice in the shops of a real, if captive, business." The workshops bear a marked resemblance to Duff Green's 1835 Washington Institute for orphan apprentices, but

As manufacturing and machining accelerated in the United States in the middle of the nineteenth century, employers needed more skilled workers. Industrial schools arose to teach such subjects as drafting, metallurgy, and mechanics. The Worcester Institute went beyond the education of machinists. Its Washburn Workshops employed apprentices to turn out products that the Institute then sold on the market. (Circa 1880–1899. *Courtesy:* Worcester Polytechnic Institute, Archives and Special Collections, George C. Gordon Library.)

where that experiment failed, this one endured, eventually giving rise to Worcester Polytechnic Institute.

The 1880s and Sustained Conflict

The Worcester Institute's success is particularly notable because it occurred amid the upswing in protective movement in which unions demonstrated their willingness to strike over apprenticeship. This activity ebbed temporarily after 1873. Improvement in the economy in the 1880s once again provided new impetus for protective trade unions, a fact reflected in the 1881 establishment of the Federation of Organized Trades and Labor Unions, the forerunner to the American Federation of Labor (AFL). Secure and enforceable apprenticeships ranked among the Federation's highest priorities. Its competitor, the Knights of Labor, also organized several craft-based District Assemblies, including glassblowing and plumbing. The Knights, too, proved willing to strike over apprenticeship regulations.

Compiling statistics for Minnesota's Bureau of Labor, L.G. Powers (1894) calculated the frequency of U.S. strikes from 1881 to 1892. He found that apprenticeship was particularly important to strike activity in 1883 and 1887. In these years strikes involving apprenticeship affected nearly 8 percent of all industries. Moreover, because apprenticeship was frequently embedded in confrontations involving multiple issues, Powers believed it likely that official statistics were understated.

The apprenticeship strikes of the 1880s gave rise to three enduring developments. First, the modern vocational movement was formed. Second, the conflicts over apprenticeship became an integral element of the labor and capital "open shop" battles. Finally, apprenticeship conflicts catalyzed larger alliances among both business and labor groups.

A Chicago bricklayers' strike in 1883 signaled increasing concern in the building trades over apprenticeship. This strike involving 132 establishments expanded into the apprenticeship arena when the Boss Masons declared the unilateral right to certify the skill levels determining wage rates. Workers feared that, with this power, masters would settle the strike with lower pay rates for workers they determined to be semiskilled. Certification of skill was a matter of apprenticeship, not employer fiat. The settlement to this strike did not endure, and the issue resurfaced when another strike followed in 1887. This strike began with a demand to change the payday, and soon escalated into a lockout of thousands of men across several trades, according to *30,000 Locked Out,* a chronicle of the strike by James C. Beeks. By the time the strike had concluded, Chicago's building trades employers had surrendered their sovereignty to hire apprentices at will.

Shortly after the strike began, building trades employers asserted a set of cardinal principles, including the right of capital to hire and fire as it pleased. Employers wished to exempt themselves from the apprentice regulations that labor, in reciprocal fashion, had unilaterally legislated. As Beeks recounts, the Chicago builders voted not to allow their men to return until each signed an oath "endorsing the rights of individuals to work and hire at will, of employer freedom from the walking delegate," and of "the right of every father to have his son taught, and of every son to learn any lawful trade." This stance resonated positively with employer associations across the country. However, workers resisted for more than a month until the employers quietly agreed to arbitrate principles that they had previously declared could never be compromised.

The arbitration procedures were umpired by Judge Tuley, who concluded, according to Beeks, "The main cause of trouble was in the separate organizations endeavoring to lay down arbitrary rules for the regulation of matters which were of joint interest and concern." Tuley ruled, "It is not a question whether everybody shall have the right to learn a trade, but whether the craft will teach every boy a trade, to its own destruction." The judge's finding explicitly recognized the right of unions to participate in the regulation of apprenticeship. His opinion went down poorly with employers who believed it at odds with prior legal rulings.

Though Chicago gained a moment of calm, employers elsewhere had no intention of letting this be the final word. In New York, Colonel Richard Auchmuty, already known as a spokesman for America's youth (arguing that they had been shut out of the trades), made common cause with employers who chafed at union restrictions. According to *Sanitary Plumber* (a plumbers' journal), Auchmuty told employers, "The public care nothing about wage quarrels, but are greatly interested in the care of the young." Writing in popular and trade journals, Auchmuty became the point man for trade schools. The premises of his argument were that apprenticeship was a thing of the past, that forced indentures constituted a form of slavery, that proper instruction could not be performed on the job, that completion of a fixed term of indenture was a poor proxy by which to measure learning, and that unions dominated by foreign-born craftsmen prevented "American boys" from learning an honest trade. Auchmuty was widely quoted as an authority on apprenticeship and trade schools, though subsequent research would reveal flaws in his arguments. Most notably, it was untrue that American-born youths were shut out of apprenticeships and that, were it not for union resistance, employers were willing to train many more youths.

Auchmuty championed his ideas by subsidizing and managing the New York Trade School. Founded in 1881, he claimed the school had developed a thorough technique by which boys could enter a trade fully prepared after three to six months of instruction, in need only of on-the-job experience to become fully proficient. His ideas were not popular with unions. They insisted his school would be the source of incompetent scabs. Whether they were incompetent or not, the school did supply over 100 students to master plumbers in a strike that began when the union decreed a limit on the number of apprentices and helpers a shop could hire.

The strike was a long affair in which the employers ultimately locked out their journeymen. When arbitration was proposed, here as in Chicago, the Master Plumbers Association responded in *Sanitary Plumber* by stating, "We think that all questions between capital and labor, or in other words, the employer and the employee, might very justly be submitted to arbitration, save one, and that one is the inalienable right for the employers to say who shall or shall not be in his employ. That question is beyond the pale of arbitration."

Auchmuty fanned the strikes' flames by announcing that "the Battle for the Boy" had begun. Writing in *Sanitary Plumber,* he told the employers, "What you do in New York will be done in Chicago, in Philadelphia, in St. Louis, in Cincinnati, and in Boston. A victory here is a victory all along the line." This was no idle prophecy. Already employers in Chicago had been emboldened to pursue a similar course, though they met with less success. In St. Louis, when apprentices surprisingly walked out alongside the journeymen in an eight-hour-day dispute, the master plumbers apparently took their revenge, adopting a rule that prohibited their members from hiring former apprentices without written consent from their previous bosses.

By requiring the consent of former masters, the plumbers were in a better position to enforce their indentures. Although unions agreed boys should fulfill their indentures, this particular device was not satisfactory as it could be used to blacklist strikers as easily as runaways. Indeed, one St. Louis apprentice did take his employer to court for sending out notices that no one should hire him. After two appeals, the Missouri court, in *Lally v. Cantwell* (30

Missouri Appeals 524) ruled in favor of the boy, arguing that the master's indenture was invalid and therefore that the allegation asserting the apprentice had broken faith was libelous.

Employers clearly saw advantages in apprenticeship if they could bind boys to their will through indentures. Even the New York plumbers who worked closely with Auchmuty never abandoned the idea of apprenticeship. Instead, they merely permitted their boys to reduce the term of their apprenticeship by one or two years if they graduated from the New York Trade School. As the bosses in St. Louis had done, New York's masters attempted to control their boys through the power of compulsory references.

The strikes and skirmishes over apprenticeship in the 1880s and early 1890s left a visible trail from the establishment of trade schools to the open-shop battles that would soon follow. In St. Louis, Colonel Auchmuty gave $1,500 to the president of the National Association of Builders, Anthony Ittner. Ittner later became chair of the National Association of Manufacturers (NAM) Industrial Education Committee. The issue had gone dormant in the building trades. Then in 1904, Ittner used his new position to oppose apprenticeship regulation and advance the role of trade schools. The NAM, the Citizens' Industrial Association, and other business groups became stalwarts of the open-shop movement, all invoking principles earlier proclaimed by employers' associations of bricklayers, plumbers, and builders. Trade schools became a positive program by which employers advanced their goal to achieve the open shop.

While relatively little is written of J.P. Morgan's attitude toward labor, the financier's gift of $500,000 to the New York Trade School in 1893 tells its own story. As will be noted, Morgan, who personally sat on the board of the school, would later become associated with the open-shop movement in the metal trades. At the same time, Morgan's partner, Anthony Drexel, endowed the creation of Drexel College in Philadelphia. Auchmuty also reached out to Philadelphians, supporting another school at the local builders' exchange that inspired resistance from building trades workers. Philadelphia and New York became hotspots in the next wave of industrial conflicts involving skills training.

Trade schools played a role in disciplining skilled workforces by providing apprentices who could undermine solidarity. In at least one case, an employer, the jeweler Tiffany & Co., used a potent mix of gender, training, and skill to maintain control over its workforce. Clara Driscoll broke the craft gender barrier at Tiffany after a strike by the glaziers and cutters union in 1892. Having previously faced strikes over apprenticeship in 1887 and 1890, the firm had sent strong signals that it would not tolerate union control over training and had actively sought ways to discipline labor on this issue. Driscol, an 1888 graduate of the Metropolitan Museum's Art School—a program had been developed in close tandem with Auchmuty's New York Trade School—was brought in to direct a new women's glass-cutting unit that eventually produced several notable Tiffany designs. Touted for their patient "nimble fingers," up to forty female artisans skirmished with union men for job rights at Tiffany until they succeeded in winning production rights to Tiffany's fourteen-inch stained glass Wisteria lampshade. Throughout her tenure until 1910, Driscol maintained a personal relationship with Louis Comfort Tiffany, with whose interests she identified. The case shows how apprenticeship strikes could open opportunities for minorities who otherwise were locked out of skilled trades, how the struggle for those opportunities undermined labor solidarity, and how trade schools succeeded in fostering strikebreaking psychologies among their students.

Apprenticeship and Open-Shop Strikes

One conduit by which apprenticeship-related strikes became part of a larger open-shop movement was through the International Association of Bridge and Structural Iron Workers (IABSIW) and its adversary, the National Erectors' Association. At first blush, it is not obvious why a connection between training and the IABSIW existed. The apprenticeship of structural ironworkers typically lasted just one and one-half years compared with three or four in other building trades, which suggests they needed relatively little training. But as Sidney Fine has shown, what was unnecessary in terms of skill was offset by the strength and courage to take risks, such as walking narrow beams on tall structures. The IABSIW's reputation for courage was offset by an equally earned reputation for rough tactics and graft. Founded in 1896, the International consisted of twenty-seven locals and 6,000 members by 1901. Aiding their expansion was the union's propensity for intimidating strikebreakers and bosses that soon earned it the enmity of others in the field. Because many of these firms fabricated the metal they used in their erection work, the expanding influence of the IABSIW was regarded as a threat to the metal trades as well.

Despite this, as the nineteenth century ended there were signs that labor and capital might work to secure mutually satisfactory arrangements. Foremost among these signs was the willingness of industrialists and union leaders to join together in the National Civic Federation at the turn of the century. Still, a series of frustrating strikes and failed negotiations, of which the IABSIW was but one, produced deeper distrust than ever.

In 1900 and 1901, J.P. Morgan, along with other industrialists, appeared to extend a hand of partnership to labor leaders, even in the building trades into which the financier had been drawn by his relationship to the American Bridge Company, a subsidiary of his new U.S. Steel Corporation. The larger steel company also faced strained relations with the Amalgamated Iron and Steel Workers after the union's leaders disavowed a 1901 compact drawn up with Morgan's direct participation. American Bridge, formed in 1901, was immediately targeted for organization by the IABSIW. After a Philadelphia strike, American Bridge settled and indicated it was willing to accept the IASBIW within its erection divisions. The firm, however, held the line against expansion into its steel fabrication divisions, where 35 percent of the nation's supply was hammered out. With IASBIW membership on the rise in 1903, American Bridge sought out other erection companies to form an organization that would eventually lead to the National Erectors' Association. Though this group permitted union restrictions of one apprentice for every journeyman, the organization declared itself in favor of the open shop. The IABSIW responded by striking American Bridge. The union president and Morgan met, but the latter declined to surrender his right to hire nonunion men. Under the settlement reached in May 1903, the union lost its right to supply skilled workers.

As mentioned, the IABSIW was considered a bridgehead that building-trades workers might successfully traverse to organize key positions in the larger metals industry. Specifically, the fear was that the steel fabricated by nonunion divisions of American Bridge might become hot cargo that IASBIW members involved in erection would refuse to handle. That would have given the union leverage back to fabrication shops. This drove metals manufacturers, especially those in the National Founders' Association and the National Metal Trades Association (NMTA) to find common interest with the National Erectors' Association (NEA) in support of its frontline resistance.

The NEA cemented its position as the bulwark of the open-shop movement when the IABSIW entered into yet another strike against American Bridge in 1905. Again, apprenticeship was only a peripheral issue. Union President John Ryan expanded the strike to nonunion subcontractors. By expanding the strike in New York, Ryan's International violated the existing arbitration agreement in the building trades and thereby cut off support from other trade unionists while gaining a reputation among employers as a dishonorable bargaining agent. The widening strike, along with increasing costs of business—much of which was attributed to union restrictions on apprenticeship—pushed the employers toward an open war. It was the NEA that led the troops. As the strike continued on into 1906, connections between the NEA and other employer organizations were made. The NMTA in particular assisted firms by recruiting 650 strikebreakers through their labor bureau.

Apprenticeship was a wedge issue in the dispute, dividing a small number of firms that refused to join others in a settlement because of the unions' insistence upon regulating apprenticeship. More generally, employer actions show they were willing to sacrifice quality training for the strategic advantages of being able to hire without restriction. Unlike other employer organizations, the NEA did not complement recruitment through employment bureaus with its own apprenticeship training.

Outmatched, the IABSIW soon resorted to

outright violence. Dynamite attacks and physical assaults occurred widely, occasionally leading to death. The attacks continued until they became public with the infamous 1910 bombing of the Los Angeles Times Building that killed several workmen. One consequence of the violence was to refuel employers' resolve to destroy the IABSIW by fighting for the open shop.

Apprenticeship issues kept surfacing. They became more important as open-shop strikes moved from relatively unskilled IABSIW to open-shop warfare with more skilled trades, including machinists and molders. The widening circle of strikes and conflicts would redraw the contour lines that defined the commanding heights of skill.

In the great steel and iron works that David Montgomery has studied, the principal trades—rollers, puddlers, heaters, and nailers—were generally learned without formal apprenticeship. In such fields technical knowledge was typically gained when a youth was employed as a helper to skilled workers. As former puddler James Davis (quoted by Montgomery) said, "We learned the trick by doing it, standing with our faces in the scorching heat while our hands puddle the metal in its glaring bath." Thus, many strikes and conflicts in the steel and iron industries largely sidestepped the question of apprenticeship, even though the cause of unrest frequently owed its origins to new technologies that were undermining the power of skilled workers. However, in the downstream industries involving the foundry work of casting and molding metals and then in machining and engineering them, apprenticeship played a much more significant role.

The open shop became a major point of contention for the International Association of Machinists (IAM) in 1900 when its members went out on strike in Chicago, Cleveland, and Paterson. The Machinists met with officers from the newly formed National Metal Trades Association in New York and signed an accord known as the Murray Hill Agreement. Their primary objective—the nine-hour day—was apparently accepted. The agreement also allowed for one apprentice in each shop and a maximum apprentice ratio of one to five. However, the union did not secure a written promise from the employers that take-home pay would remain the same despite their agreed reduction in hours. When the nine-hour day took effect in May 1901, employers refused to raise the hourly wage, and 40,000 Machinists went out on strike in 1901. The NMTA declared that the union had broken faith with their agreement and decided to pursue an open-shop course rather than deal with the union. The NMTA created its own employment bureau, which provided its mid-sized members with an independent supply of workers that was especially helpful during strikes. The employment bureau challenged union restriction of apprenticeship while simultaneously increasing employers' capacity to enforce their own apprenticeship indentures.

As Howell John Harris has chronicled, effective open-shop campaigns required local employers to have access to adequate supplies of labor. The NMTA secured for them "certificate men": individuals who had already proved their willingness to cross picket lines. When these fell short, the employment bureau screened additional applicants for skill and loyalty. Local employment bureaus in Cincinnati, Worcester, and Philadelphia cooperated with the NMTA. Not incidentally, the employment bureaus established a more efficacious method by which to monitor and enforce apprenticeship contracts.

After the Machinist strike of 1901, employers in Cincinnati looked to the employment bureau as part of a positive program to supply skilled workers with opportunity while undermining union control and influence. Cincinnati metal and tool industry employers collaborated closely with the city's public industrial education system. In addition, the employers created a new model for cooperative education at the University of Cincinnati. The program provided tool, machine, and engineering training for pairs of students who rotated between six months in college and six months on the shop floor, where they applied their school-based learning. The co-op program married theory with hands-on experience, while freeing employers from union control in a way that improved upon prior efforts at places like the Worcester Institute or the New York Trade School.

Vocational education and employment bureaus could not avoid becoming strategic battlegrounds as employers proclaimed their open-shop freedom to hire whom they pleased. These fronts collided with apprenticeship as workers and firms actively vied for control of the shop floor. Locals were often more militant about shop-floor control, including the regulation of apprenticeship, than were their international unions, especially the Machinists. The IAM leadership increasingly came to believe that they should confine themselves to narrow economic goals, such as wages and hours, over which there was broad consensus. Internally, the new divisions of labor increasingly required specialization so that newly hired machinists often tended one machine rather than practicing as all-around craftsmen who engineered the solution of design problems in machine manufacturing. These changes made it harder to find common purposes among employees, outside of wages and hours. IAM leaders also saw that employers generally dug in their heels to maintain their managerial prerogatives more so than they did with regard to wages. Indeed, P.K. Edwards's major study of strikes shows that between 1886 and 1905 strikes over wage issues had about a 50 percent success rate whereas strikes over union rules succeeded less than 40 percent of the time. More tellingly, strikes that challenged employers' hiring prerogatives succeeded less than 25 percent of the time.

In this trail of union defeats, employers sometimes became advocates for apprenticeship. As scholars Phillip Scranton and Howell John Harris have shown, many employers truly depended upon skilled workmen and sought well-apprenticed workers. Others, however, saw indentured apprentices as a way to reduce turnover, secure cheap labor, and sometimes to bully novices into strikebreaking.

Similar patterns played out in the nation's foundries, where molders, core makers, metal polishers, and patternmakers toiled. Compared with the NMTA or the NEA, the employers in the National Founders' Association (NFA) were slower in their decision to fight rather than to compromise with the unions. After the machinists and metals manufacturers' agreement collapsed in 1901, the foundrymen did not rush into warfare, but instead expanded their agreements. In exchange, International Moulders' Union (IMU) President John Frey agreed to give up elements of job control, including "arbitrary limitations" of output. Individual firms under local arrangements still had to contend with union rules and traditions. Of these, the right to limit apprentices was most provocative. In Philadelphia, Howell John Harris explains, foundry owners chafed under the national truce as they "wanted the freedom to dilute the skilled component of the labor force at will, to give themselves a cheap and adequate labor supply in rush times, and to gain an improved bargaining position vis-à-vis their journeymen at all times." Yet the employers waited for the completion of their contracts in 1904.

Harris's account of Philadelphia gives an excellent description of events. Following the lead of militant Cincinnati foundrymen, several Philadelphia members of the NMTA and NFA created an association of their own, the Metal Manufacturers Association (MMA). The first series of open-shop battles between the IMU and the MMA in Philadelphia occurred between 1904 and 1907. This series began with a strike at the Cresson workshop. It was crushed with aid from the MMA's new Labor (employment) Bureau, securing the firms' prerogative to hire and fire at will. By the time the strike was over the city's workshops were staffed by nearly as many apprentices and semiskilled workers as journeymen, with the IMU's regulations on apprenticeship tossed aside.

Increasingly then, the IMU—like many other unions—proved unable to resist skill dilution and employer control over apprenticeship. With each retreat, training slipped further from the control of organized labor and ever-closer to public or private vocational institutions, including large corporate schools. Only a few enclaves remained in which labor successfully called the tune.

It is impossible to document all strikes that occurred before World War I as the open-shop drive by manufacturers collided with apprenticeship regulations. It is from the evidence in places such as Philadelphia, Cincinnati, Chicago, and New York that we must understand how such battles were waged and settled. What we can be certain of is that struggles over the production, distribution, and even the definition of skill became increasingly important. We also know that firms innovated to diminish union control and power. Where possible they set up corporation schools on their own sites, like Philadelphia's Baldwin Locomotive—one of the oldest—or Westinghouse and General Electric. Indeed, a survey by the National Association for Corporation Schools identified over fifty large firms that had done so, including many that formally indentured their trainees.

Yet because only large corporations could typically afford to run such schools, mid-sized firms turned instead to the public sector, or simply attempted to rid themselves of unions while training their own men. When employer associations won their battles against unionists, they invariably left behind an alternative training institution capable of bypassing organized labor, such as the New York Trade School, the Worcester Institute, Cooperative Education at the University of Cincinnati, or the Dunwoody Institute in Minneapolis. Both large and medium-sized firms increasingly employed technologies that reduced reliance upon highly skilled craftsmen while increasing their demands for semiskilled operatives.

Small contractors, whose work centered on custom, niche, or specialized small batch jobs, were most in need of unionists to maintain skilled apprentice or helper arrangements. This was most clearly true in the building trades. They benefited significantly when Congress passed the Smith-Hughes Act of 1917, appropriating funds to underwrite the state systems of vocational education. Local authorities responsible for putting that law into place faced a choice about how closely they would cooperate with labor or management. In the building trades they often chose cooperation with labor. In New York, the benefit to labor was mirrored by complaints from officers in the New York Trade School, who felt that publicly funded extension classes served unions by restricting apprenticeship training to those already employed in the field, and thus normally to unions. In 1937, federal passage of the Fitzgerald Act cemented much of this relationship, setting out a minimum educational requirement for apprenticeship and making explicit the obligations of employers who hired apprentices. Still, the number of jobs to which the act was applied was to remain relatively small, and employers often found it expedient to turn to other sources of supply. However, for highly skilled labor, American firms turned to technical programs located within colleges that maintained relative independence from organized labor.

Aftermath

Strikes involving apprenticeship and skills left their mark on core labor institutions in the United States. Not only have unions been forced to organize by industry because unskilled workers outnumber skilled workers—a situation that favors economic over job- or shop-control unionism—but also, with few exceptions, labor has accepted social arrangements that make it the duty of individuals to prepare themselves for their desired lines of work. The arrangement avoids much contractual rigidity by shifting the risk of training—first to the individual, and second, to the state. It is an arrangement that tends to reproduce social inequalities because poorer families have fewer resources with which to make the investments that can distinguish themselves within a multitiered system of education. Through the 1950s, that tendency was offset by the rising tide of industrial unionization. However, as the percentage of unionized workers began to fall, the extension of the labor movement to women and minorities faltered.

Minorities have been at odds with union traditions that tended to exclude them from skilled work. Their issues made headlines in the late 1960s and 1970s. As so often happened, the apprenticeship issue was usually peripheral in union strikes. One telling exception occurred on July 23, 1969, when Operating Engineers Local 66 struck construction sites in Pittsburgh. The strike set off a wave of reactions that ultimately led to the Pittsburgh Plan, one of the first affirmative action agreements concerning the hire of minorities into the construction trade. The engineers' strike over "hiring hall violations" effectively locked out African Americans who had been trained under a program known as Operation Dig. Civil rights groups immediately protested. Some 3,000 white union construction workers then took to Pittsburgh's streets asserting their "right to work." The situation had come full circle—while employers had earlier asserted the need for open shops in order to protect workers' and managers' freedom of contract, members of the union movement now appropriated their "right to work" language in a divisive struggle. Battles over exclusionary practices in the construction trades, the remaining bastion of apprenticeship, weakened organized labor as minority workers turned away from unions and to the government for protection of their civil rights. Although policies aimed at raising minority participation in apprenticeship through affirmative action have partially succeeded, a legacy of distrust remains among minority communities regarding labor.

Separately, recent strikes by teaching assistants at American colleges and universities may legitimately be considered an extension of earlier apprenticeship conflicts. Some scholars have questioned whether the apprenticeship model is appropriate in this situation because it masks graduate students' labor by overemphasizing their role as "student/professional" in training. Yet, as this essay makes clear, it is precisely the antagonism between work and training that has been responsible for the degradation of apprenticeship at the heart of most conflicts. Specifically, strikes arise because the boundary between instruction and labor is no longer well policed, and because the minimum qualifications necessary to practice trades are not collectively agreed upon.

The expansion of postsecondary education—itself a response to rising vocationalism—creates internal pressure on faculty training in graduate schools. States have typically underfunded colleges and universities relative to the tasks they set for them. This funding crisis creates incentives for universities and their faculty to follow their short-term financial and professional interests. Faculty members want additional graduate students to reduce their teaching responsibilities, assist in their research, and ensure that their graduate programs are adequately enrolled. Within academia, a number of specialized jobs have cropped up, many of which appear not to require completion of the Ph.D. The proportion of faculty holding such degrees typically hovers around 20 percent, with a particularly low proportion in community colleges. Even more telling is the emergence of contingent academic labor, in which faculty members are hired on a short-term or as-needed basis. Faculty lines have come to reside in one of a number of tracks ranging from casual labor to fully tenured positions. Casual or contingent academic work is increasingly centered solely upon teaching divorced from the production of scholarly works. On the other hand, shortages of funds have led more and more universities to increase their reliance upon research overhead, creating a new class of nontenured research professors, who are usually entitled to remain in the employ of their institutions as long as they bring in sufficient grant money. These subdivisions within the ranks of faculty have left doctoral students less certain that the investments they make in a Ph.D. will eventually pay off.

The history of strikes among graduate students begins in 1970 with an action by the Teaching Assistant Association (TAA) at the University of Wisconsin. After eleven months of bargaining, the TAA struck for twenty-four days to obtain a contract that included grievance resolution procedures, class size limits, and health care. The graduate employees' organization at the University of Michigan struck for one month in 1975 while negotiating its first contract. Strikes have escalated sharply as diverse unions including United Electrical, Radio and Machine Workers, the United Auto Workers, the Teamsters, and the more traditional American Association of University Professors and American Federation of Teachers have organized graduate students on campuses across the country—from Yale to Berkeley.

These modern strikes illustrate how strained for training the American institutions are. Because apprenticeship has been relegated to a minor function within the economy, it has become widely regarded as an exclusionary device, much as open-shop proponents said it was. Yet it was the failure of American employers to systematically assume responsibility for building a broad-based system of certification that could accommodate the aspirations of American youth that caused the infighting among working classes over the limited number of opportunities for successful blue-collar training. This was not inevitable, as Germany's experience makes clear. Instead of collaborating to build explicit job structures and accountability, employers battled unions over apprenticeship and reinforced capital's tendency to outsource job training to a disorganized assemblage of trainers that had few common standards. It is perhaps appropriate to end with the irony that the training function among educators is now the new frontier for apprenticeship.

See also: Strikes in the Nineteenth-Century Cotton Textile Industry in the Northeast United States, 314; Steel Strikes Before 1935, 351: Striking the Ivory Tower: Student Employee Strikes at Private Universities, 685.

Bibliography

Commons, John R. *History of Labor in the United States.* Vols. 1–3. New York: Macmillan, 1918–35.

Commons, John R., Ulrich B. Phillips, Eugene A. Gilmore, Helen L. Sumner, and John B. Andrews, eds. *A Documentary History of American Industrial Society.* New York: Russell & Russell, 1958.

Dirnback, Eric, and Susan Chirmonas. "Shutting Down the Academic Factory: Developing Worker Identity in Graduate Employee Unions." In *Cogs in the Classroom Factory,* ed. D. Herman and J. Schmid. Westport, CT: Praeger, 2003.

Edwards, P.K. *Strikes in the United States, 1881–1974.* Oxford: Blackwell, 1981.

Fine, Sidney. *Without Blare of Trumpets: Walter Drew, the National Erectors' Association, and the Open Shop Movement. 1903–1957.* Ann Arbor: University of Michigan Press, 1995.

Gilje, Paul B., and Howard B. Rock, eds. *Keepers of the Revolution.* Ithaca, NY: Cornell University Press, 1992.

Harris, Howell John. *Bloodless Victories The Rise and Fall of the Open Shop in the Philadelphia Metal Trades, 1890–1940.* New York: Cambridge University Press, 2000.

Jacoby, Daniel. "Legal Foundations of Human Capital Markets." *Industrial Relations* 30, no. 2 (Spring 1991): 229–50.

———. "Plumbing the Origins of American Vocationalism. *Labor History* 37, no. 2 (1996): 235–72.

———. "The Transformation of Industrial Apprenticeship in the United States." *Journal of Economic History* 51, no. 4 (December 1991): 887–910.

Lescohier, Don. "The Knights of St. Crispin, 1867–1874. A Study of Industrial Causes of Trade Unionism." *Bulletin of the University of Wisconsin,* no. 355 (1910).

Rorabaugh, William. *The Craft Apprentice: From Franklin to the Machine Age in America.* New York: Oxford University Press, 1986.

Scranton, Philip. *Endless Novelty.* Princeton, NJ: Princeton University Press, 1997.

Wilentz, Sean. *Chants Democratic: New York City and the Rise of the American Working Class, 1788–1850.* New York: Oxford University Press, 1984.

STRIKES IN THE NINETEENTH-CENTURY COTTON TEXTILE INDUSTRY IN THE NORTHEAST UNITED STATES

Mary H. Blewett

Men and women workers from different ethnic cultures with competing ideas about union organization, gender relations, and political ideology—who faced fierce opposition from textile capitalists—shaped the strike experiences in the cotton textile industry in nineteenth-century America. Historians of the nineteenth-century labor movement in textiles have underestimated the impact of English immigrants and the importance of conflicts and coalitions among genders and ethnic groups. Weavers and mule spinners in the Northeast United States (Maine, New Hampshire, Massachusetts, Rhode Island, Connecticut, New York, and New Jersey) hammered out their labor politics during multiple strikes between 1848 and 1894.

American textile industrialization began at Samuel Slater's spinning mill in Pawtucket, Rhode Island, supported by the crafts and metal firms along the Blackstone River. The Rhode Island system of cotton manufacturing used child labor under close supervision to tend Slater's copies of the Arkwright spinning throstle frames. Families in the surrounding countryside then wove the yarn into cloth on handlooms. After 1820, capital from Providence and the New Bedford whaling industry began to develop the village of Fall River in southeastern Massachusetts. Learning how to make cloth from the Pawtucket pioneers, Fall River mills intended to dominate textile production, first taking on local competitors and later textile firms throughout southeastern New England.

Meanwhile in northern Massachusetts, in the early 1820s the Boston Associates invested capital in the much more rapid development of fully integrated and mechanized cotton mills at Waltham and Lowell, equipped with water-powered machinery. The Lowell system provided both integrated production of all spinning and weaving operations and paternalistic boardinghouses for women factory workers from rural New England. By 1830, Lowell had become the big success story, boasting ten of the largest corporations in the United States, capitalized between $600,000 and $1 million. The economic and political power of Boston investors created a model of mass production copied by many mills throughout the Northeast.

The men and women in the rapidly industrializing Northeast, whether working at home producing boots and shoes and woven cloth, in integrated textile factories, or throughout the various construction trades that built the new towns, mills, and central shops, shared many grievances over wages and long working hours. Textile workers in Waltham protested wage cuts as early as 1821 in "turnouts," or work stoppages, which were often spontaneous and hard to sustain. In Lowell, according to historian Thomas Dublin, female operatives struck spontaneously and unsuccessfully in 1834, but during a rising market in 1836 their turnout, prompted by their refusal to become "factory slaves," prevented a reduction in wages and stimulated organization. In the 1840s, the Lowell Female Labor Reform Association (LFLRA) led by Sarah Bagley focused on regional political action, primarily through petitioning the state legislature to limit the working day to ten hours. Most native-born working people shared rural upbringings, Protestant religion, artisan training, and the republican heritage of the American Revolution. But there were many divisions among emerging cities, towns, and rural mill villages, among skilled trades and less skilled occupations, and between mechanized, centralized production or outwork done at home by hand. Differences among men and women workers, native and immigrant, white and "colored," operative and artisan, made unity difficult. These similarities and differences shaped a rich but contentious pre–Civil War heritage of labor activity.

The process of cotton textile production and the hierarchies of skill and gender were well established before the outbreak of the Civil War. The dangerous work of opening cotton bales and preparing the cotton for spinning fell to skilled male pickers and carders. Throstle spinning frames run by native-born Yankee women had been displaced by self-acting mules operated primarily by skilled male immigrants from England and Ireland. Developed in England, the self-actor in the hands of experienced mule spinners could produce a vast range of yarn counts or sizes for a variety of textile products. The huge mule machinery ran back and forth on metal tracks in the mill floor, usually powered by steam. In New England, mule spinners, who manipulated the frame and its spinning bobbins, had to depend on back boys, unskilled and poorly paid youngsters trained to dodge the motions of the machinery while tying up broken ends of yarn. Once spun, the yarn was further prepared for the looms, kept in mechanical repair by skilled and well-paid loom fixers. Every male weaver aspired to become a fixer. Men and women ran looms and were paid at the same piece rates, but no woman was permitted to adjust the machinery. After the Civil War, immigrant women dominated the weaving workforce, but some had chances to learn more skilled and better-paid work, such as drawing-in, the intricate arrangement of yarns for the loom harnesses before the weaving process commenced. In the late nineteenth century, ring spinning machinery with a cleverly designed combination of steel rings and "travelers," which together automatically twisted the yarn into the proper count, began to replace mules. Young immigrant women ring spinners threatened the skills and wages of experienced mule spinners.

English Immigrants Lead Fall River Strike

By the 1850s, immigrant labor from England, Scotland, and Ireland transformed the workforce in many northeastern cotton factories. As historian Roland Berthoff recounts, immigrants from Lancashire in northern England "abounded as nowhere else" in Fall River and New Bedford, Massachusetts, while other British workers crowded textile mills in Rhode Island, New York, New Jersey, and Pennsylvania. Lancashire immigrants brought with them, depending on the timing of their emigration between the 1820s and the 1890s, various strike strategies and tactics that included the rituals of mass demonstrations. English-led activism emerged first in the textile mills of Philadelphia. In February 1848, a strike of textile workers organized and led by English immigrants occurred in Fall River. During their strike, the weavers and other operatives joined the skilled mule spinners and mill mechanics to create a coalition born of discontent and unrest. Native-born Yankees and foreign-born workers combined to protest a surprise wage cut ranging from 5 percent to 17 percent. Introducing English customs and tactics to deal with overbearing employers into the streets of Fall River created patterns of strike activity that prevailed for the rest of the nineteenth century. The mill owners, who decided to crush this uprising by eliminating its leaders, also established policies that they followed consistently thereafter.

Native-born textile workers invited British immigrants to lead the strike, but tensions between the two groups threatened their unity. Yankee workers were suspicious of "the Old Country people" as competitors, and many believed "that they had come to take the bread from the mouths of the Natives." Still, they agreed that if native workers organized the Yankee operatives and the immigrants, their own national groups, they could win the strike. English immigrant Thomas Norris emerged as the main leader, drawing on his experience in "old England." The manufacturers refused to give any reason to justify the wage cut and threatened Norris that unless he stopped his agitation he would become "a marked man" and would be refused employment (blacklisted) throughout New England. Nothing happened until the morning of February 7, according to the *Voice of Industry*, a New England labor newspaper. At a meeting of the assembled strikers, Norris advised the men and women to meet in front of two key mills and when the operatives came out at noon to confront them and follow them home. Strikebreakers were to be labeled "knobsticks," an English term quickly applied to all who refused to join the strike. Norris also advised the strikers to give knobsticks "three British cheers"—Hip, Hip, Hurray!—in derision.

The strike and its aftermath were chronicled in the *Fall River News* (hereafter *News*). *A* crowd of several hundred strikers approached the Troy mill. At first, they let the mill owners know they were there by kicking the door of the countinghouse and knocking on the windows. This was unheard of. The sanctity of the feared countinghouse, where the managers congregated, had been violated. An overseer at the Troy mill told them to go about their business. One female striker from England, who was dancing in defiance in front of the door, refused. A few Yankee women strikers told this "very bold young woman" to stop at once. Tensions were becoming apparent between native-born and immigrant female operatives. Nevertheless, many of the activists, even among those who threw snowballs at nonstriking workers, were native-born workingwomen.

Norris, who was standing in front of the Troy mill carrying his walking stick, began to lose control of the situation. Despite the protests, many of the Troy workers returned to work after their noontime meal. Twenty minutes before noon, Ann Bell came out of the Troy countinghouse door. As an American, she felt no connection with striking immigrants. When she refused to join in, she was snowballed until she reached her boardinghouse but later returned to work. She admitted that she was "some afraid when they followed me." Others who left at noon were yelled at, pelted with snow by young women and boys, and also followed home. In the afternoon, Norris, flourishing his stick, led the crowd to the Annawan mill, where he was arrested.

During the indictment proceedings, strikers repeatedly testified that Norris had not counseled or engaged in violence or snowballing. Ellen Ennis, an unmarried twenty-eight-year-old English immigrant with nine years of experience in the Fall River mills, defended Norris's behavior as actively trying to protect the knobsticks. A number of young female operatives at another Fall River mill reinforced this testimony, though under cross-examination operative Flora Bennett determinedly admitted: "We come for our rights. Yes, to get the wages put back." Norris and two others were indicted, and the trial was set for mid-March.

In court, the prosecution zeroed in on the fears inspired by English behavior in the streets of the city and on Norris's role in creating it. A riot, the prosecutor argued, had taken place. A tumultuous crowd had assembled to prevent the operatives from going to their work. "All this was done to the terror of the people. Actual violence is not necessary to terrorize." Norris was held responsible for all the "evil consequences" that resulted from his speech to the strikers regardless of his intentions. In his charge to the jury, the judge went even further. He insisted that while striking operatives did have the right to meet and combine, they possessed no right to obstruct other operatives from leaving and going to their work. Forcible obstruction constituted riot. Whatever Norris's intentions, "he was answerable for any disturbance" that followed. Endorsing a legal concept of conspiracy to riot and collective guilt for which the strikers were held responsible, the judge insisted that "the act of each bound all." The jury found Norris guilty and jailed him. Many of the participants in the strike who testified for the defense left town, fearing they would be blacklisted.

Sarah Bagley of the LFLRA, defending Norris in the April 7, 1848, issue of the New England labor newspaper *Voice of Industry,* saw no problems with American workers joining with immigrants or using English tactics. She denounced this infamous prosecution of innocent and well-intentioned men as the prostitution of "the law to purposes of selfish oppression. It demonstrated the oppressive and dangerous power of combined capital, in hostile competition with labor." But divisions among native-born and immigrant workers and the repressive tactics of mill owners would continue to plague strikes in the nineteenth-century textile industry.

Defending Manhood Against the Drive

In late 1850, mule spinners in Fall River and New Bedford faced a 10 percent wage cut by managers. They objected bitterly to "numerous petty tyrannies and unjust actions" by the overseers in the Fall River mills. To English mule spinners, an overseer who merely carried out the orders of his superintendent—either for money or out of fear, without any individual sense of just treatment—was something less than a man. During this 1850–51 strike in Fall River, described in the *News*, immigrant mule spinners used the term "the masters" in published letters when referring to superintendents or mill owners. No white American male in pre–Civil War New England would voluntarily use the word "master," although many spoke derisively of their working conditions as wage slavery and often complained about their overseers as slave drivers. The word "master" applied to an American overseer would place a white worker on a level with black slaves. But "master" was the commonplace word for "employer" among Lancashire textile workers, often indicating expectations of obligations between the master and his "hands": the operatives, according to the *Oxford English Dictionary*. English workers were offended by the New England term "help" for operatives. This reference to experienced workers as servile was demeaning.

Immigrant mule spinners also pointed out the special liabilities of the wage cut. English workers, unused to the bitter winters of New England, had already bought coal, staples, and warm clothing. If the reduction had been announced for the spring or summer, the immigrants would have had alternatives: go to another town or return home. The wage cut seemed timed to keep them in Fall River throughout the winter to work at reduced wages or lose money. This was a damning charge, suggesting a conspiracy by the mills to coerce the men and their families. The spinners' organization also questioned the employers' figures on their profits and the costs of production. Strikers asked the superintendents to compare calculations by opening their books to public scrutiny to seek reconciliation, as in Lancashire. This request to open the mill accounts was a far more potent act than pounding on the door of the countinghouse during the strike of 1848. The employers absolutely refused to comment and continued the policy of disclosing nothing to the public.

During the 1850–51 strike, the mule spinners raised issues about working conditions and class power that underlay their opposition to the wage reduction. The mills utilized self-acting mule spinning machines that allowed their agents to claim that one spinner could do the work without the assistance of a "piecer," or apprentice spinner, as in Lancashire mule spinning. The spinner would in effect do the work of two. Inexperienced "back boys," between eight and twelve years old, became common in New England mills as helpers to "piece up" or repair the multiple strands of flimsy yarn spun from cheap cotton during the back-and-forth motions of the huge frames. These pressures produced a Fall River–style walk, brisk and quick. This change undermined both the mule spinners' authority as men who supervised other adults and weakened their claim that spinning was fit work only for strong, experienced men. Furthermore, the new machinery ran faster and faster. In the *News*, one spinner complained that while more wages are earned and more yarn spun by the spinner, less money is paid to him. "O, my God! What a life is ours. It is emphatically, 'drive, drive, drive,' from early morning till night." The mills could not claim they paid higher wages when a man was doing the work of two but getting the pay of one. Mill agents insisted that the increase in productivity of the self-acting mule allowed them to pay their spinners 10–15 percent more than the average New England mill for the same number of hours and days worked. Who, after all, should reap the benefit? Not the spinners, but the capitalists who paid for the new machinery. The spinners' organization protested that in fact they earned less than other mule spinners in Massachusetts, New Hampshire, and Rhode Island, indicating an informational network operating throughout New England.

The work stoppage of the Fall River mule spinners halted all mill operations. The strikers numbered 1,300, the total workforce of seven small cotton mills. Carders who prepared the cotton for spinning had no work and the weavers had no yarn, while both faced even deeper wage cuts. In January 1851, an organization representing men and women weavers and carders formed to raise a strike fund. One female weaver joined a delegation of male strikers to New York City to raise money, according to the *News*. Other women workers agreed to board in rural farm homes in exchange for housework to sustain the strike, while weavers raised strike funds in nearby Massachusetts and Rhode Island cities, towns, and mill villages.

The weavers, many also English immigrants, rejected the manufacturers' arguments about costs, profits, and arrogance. They regarded periodic wage cuts as a calculated plan to reduce labor costs without cause. The mill owners could pay but would not, said the *News*, "believing that it is a humiliation to comply with a request from their workpeople." Weavers argued based on Lancashire experience that well-conducted strikes were not injurious but defended the legitimate interests of workers. Submission to repeated wage reductions would prove much worse. The weavers created a potent ideological mix of a Yankee working-class belief in the creation of all wealth by the laborers with Lancashire traditions of needful defiance, including of masters who worshipped "mammon" or false idols. Like the mule spinners, the weavers expressed their contempt. The employers should learn to respect their workers, and "treat them as men and as women." Along with respect for manliness, the Fall River strikers began to express the idea of independent and respectable working-class womanliness—in contrast to the mill owners' earlier paternalistic treatment of dependent Yankee "mill girls." This rhetoric of respectability recalled the defiant testimony of the female defense witnesses in the 1848 trial that convicted Norris and reached further back to Sarah Bagley and the LFLRA activists. Distrusting the local press, the weavers organized the short-lived *Trade Union and Fall River Weavers' Journal* with an Irish-born, Lancashire-trained editor. While the mule spinners returned to work in April, the weavers stayed out for two more months. The *Fall River Monitor* (hereafter *Monitor*) reported that many families and individuals found work in other northeastern textile centers.

Fall River Mills Dominate

The defeat of the 1848 and 1850–51 strikes meant textile workers in the Fall River mills remained unorganized. Still, immigrant mule spinners donated to the 1853–54 Preston, Lancashire, strike fund, thus maintaining transatlantic ties and hoping some day to create throughout New England spinners' unions that were strong enough to counter strikebreaking and blacklisting. In 1858, mule spinners led by Irish-born, Lancashire-trained leaders reorganized their movement. These men and many like them had learned mule spinning, weaving, and other skills in English mills before immigrating to the United States. When they prepared a petition asking for increased wages, none wished to sign at the top and risk the blacklist, so they signed in circles rather than a list to prevent employers from identifying the leaders and exacting retribution. To their surprise, the Fall River manufacturers in 1858 agreed to one-third of this wage request, but only for the mule spinners. After the Civil War, the employers developed many more tactics to divide competing ethnic, gender, and skill groups to undercut class unity.

The cotton textile workforce in Fall River quadrupled between 1865 and 1875. By 1880, Fall River boasted thirty-three corporations running 150 mills, in comparison with eleven corporations in Lowell. Fall River investors dominated this mill expansion in contrast to the dependence of Lowell and Lawrence on Boston capital. Growth during the 1870s stimulated rapid construction in Rhode Island and eastern Connecticut as well as in New Bedford. By 1880, 57 percent of the printed cotton cloth produced in the United States was made in southeastern New England textile centers, with well over half made in Fall River mills. Unprinted cloth or "grey goods" were sent to New York and Philadelphia printers. Mills from Maine to Pennsylvania produced the remaining 43 percent, but Fall River dominated post–Civil War production and set the price of print cloth and wages paid to operatives.

No city in New England grew as fast as Fall River, which more than doubled its population between 1860 and 1870, according to Massachusetts census data. By 1875, the city's residents nearly doubled again to 45,260, with 38 percent foreign-born. The workforce in Fall River in the mid-1870s consisted of one-quarter native-born (25 percent); one-third English immigrants (34 percent); one-fifth Irish immigrants (21 percent); and less than one-fifth French-Canadian immigrants (17 percent). Fall River had the highest proportion of foreign-born workers in Massachusetts, 53 percent; Holyoke the next highest at 52 percent; then Lawrence with 45 percent; Lowell with 36 percent; and New Bedford with 23 percent. Among the female workforce, more wives worked in the Fall River mills than in Lowell or Lawrence.

For the Ten-Hour Day

In 1867, the mule spinners throughout New England struck for a ten-hour day. This regional movement included spinners in Fall River, New Bedford, Lawrence, and Lowell, Massachusetts; Manchester, Salmon Falls, and Great Falls, New Hampshire; and Lewiston and Biddeford, Maine. After the failure of moral suasion to pressure the mill owners or the legislature to act, a strike seemed the logical means of protest. The Fall River strike committee insisted on the "right to a voice in the fixing of these things [hours and wages], or are we mere machines . . . ?" They drew their rallying cry from the Preston, Lancashire, strike, "Ten Per Cent and No Surrender," changing it to "Ten Hours and No Surrender." The mills in Lawrence fired the leaders of the spinners' strike to prevent a feared general uprising of the operatives. As the mule spinners were leaving the mill yards on April 1, large portions of the Lawrence "female help" left with them and were evicted from corporation housing. According to the *Boston Daily Evening Voice*, the strike committee responded:

> They turn the daughters and sisters of the men who shed their blood [in the Civil War] and left their bones to whiten on a southern soil [,] into the streets, because they will not allow themselves to be ground down to the same object—slavery. . . . This, fellow-citizens . . . is your reward for fighting the enemies of your country while they sat home in opulence and ease.

In 1867, the mule spinners brewed a rich mixture of Lancashire rights, Civil War sacrifice, suffering womanhood, and hostility to those who bought themselves out of the draft.

The Fall River mills fell silent while Rhode Island mills quickly moved into the lucrative print cloth market. The strike and competitive pressures yielded results. The mill agents in Fall River experimented with the ten-hour day beginning in 1868, fully capable of speeding up machinery or withdrawing the privilege whenever they chose. Mills in Lawrence and New Bedford also adopted ten hours. Then, after only one month, the agent of the Wamsutta mills in New Bedford abruptly returned to eleven hours. The textile operatives struck the mill immediately, as described in the *New Bedford Standard*. The Wamsutta mills produced fine shirting and sheeting, which required skilled mule spinners from Lancashire. Many weavers were Irish immigrants and native-born workers, but no members of the African-American community, who usually worked as shipwrights, mariners, and whalers, were employed. The strikers crossed skill, gender, and ethnic lines. Opponents claimed that only "a hundred Englishmen," were "behind" the strike: "a few bullies with the aid of a few natives." English and American names dominated the leadership, but the strikers were a mix of nationalities. Women strikers with American, German, English, and Irish names canvassed as a committee for strike funds. Refusing to compromise, the agent arrogantly announced that Wamsutta would reopen on March 1 with an eleven-hour day. The strikers voted unanimously to hold out, but first the weavers and then the mule spinners returned to work. Still, English immigrants were accustomed to such defeats. "A Working Man" insisted that ten hours works well in England. We will ". . . wait our time, agitate, work and wait." The Massachusetts ten-hour law finally passed in 1874, later followed by similar laws throughout the Northeast.

Women Overcome Immigrant/ Native Divisions

In 1869, the Lancashire mill owners cut wages by 10 percent. The union weavers and spinners of Preston, Blackburn, and other Lancashire mill centers organized to promote the emigration of 2,000 weavers and mule spinners to the United States. Reinforcements of skilled, experienced Lancashire workers were on their way. However, in 1872 there were 3,646 French Canadians living in Fall River; by 1874, 4,000 rural migrants worked in the mills, but experienced mule spinners from Montreal could not get jobs in New England, according to the Fall River newspaper *L'Echo du Canada*. Mule spinners opposed French Canadians in their trade, and many others feared a post–Civil War tide of non–English-speaking, inexperienced Quebecois who, as a "race," everyone believed would gladly work an eleven-hour day: man, woman, and child. Thus, a racialized Quebec people became a pawn used by employers against operatives.

Historians have ignored the regional power struggle among British immigrant mule spinners and weavers in the Northeast over strategy, tactics, ideology, and objectives. Many historians, such as Charlotte Erickson, view English immigrants as "invisible" or easily acculturated into American society. Historian Isaac Cohen regarded mule spinner Robert Howard's career as the leader of the National Mule Spinners' Union in the American Federation of Labor as typical. However, the majority of immigrant weavers and many other workers opposed Howard's exclusive trade unionism based on his experiences in Lancashire. They defended their own alternate heritage of popular radicalism, including the ideal of a moral economy and an amalgamation of all skill groups. As historian Neville Kirk argued, both divisions and communities among working people detail the ways that unity and fragmentation interact "at specific points of time and over time." Two Fall River strikes in 1875 and their regional impact provide immediate examples.

During the 1870s, Fall River capitalists were attempting both to dominate the American domestic market for print cloth in the West, South, and urban East and to purge their English workers of "their chronic insubordination." From the moment that Lancashire workers landed, the mill agents, regarding them with contempt, systematically challenged their customary measures of skill and strength. Fall River mills used the cheapest raw cotton and the best machinery, paid the lowest wages in the region, and demanded increasingly intense physical exertions from their operatives—especially from mule spinners—to produce massive quantities of inferior fabric, relying on the cloth-printing process to conceal defects. They controlled the domestic market for print cloth by having the capacity to glut it with the cheapest possible goods. In turn, English workers held the agents of New England mills in contempt for making "shoddy" (flimsy cloth) using "shoddyite morality." Lancashire immigrants organized community associations reflecting their working-class culture. Consumer cooperatives and friendly societies, including fraternal organizations, dotted towns in the Northeast, while large centers of textile production boasted music halls, fish-and-chip shops, "pubs" or saloons, and (for the pious) Primitive Methodist chapels and Catholic churches.

In January 1875, the Fall River mills cut wages by 10 percent and flooded the market to undersell their competitors. The mule spinners and male weavers reluctantly accepted the reduction but faced a revolt among female weavers and some Quebec-born operatives, according to the *Boston Globe*. The rebels organized all-female meetings to shame their male coworkers into the only successful weavers' strike in nineteenth-century Fall River. During two regional strikes in 1875, the first in January and the second in August, New England labor politics focused on the differences among mule spinners and weavers over the nature and direction of strikes. The successful challenge of activist women to male leadership and the conflicting emphasis on amalgamations of all operatives by the weavers and on local trade unions by mule spinners produced intraclass conflict over the meaning of working-class manhood and the desirability of female activism. The transnational culture of Lancashire provided the framework.

In 1875 there were approximately 8,000 weavers and 2,000 mule spinners in the Fall River workforce. Women represented one-third of the striking weavers and half of the weaving workforce. As the *Providence Sun* reported, female operatives organized themselves in early 1875 across skill and ethnic lines, insisting that "all national differences" end to preserve the general rights of operatives. Lancashire immigrants provided the leadership, but the women's meetings included native-born Americans and Irish and French-Canadian immigrants. The leaders demanded action to prevent recurrent wage cuts, denouncing conciliation and deference as cowardly and unmanly. Using their heritage of nineteenth-century popular radicalism, the Lancashire women leaders cited examples of the effectiveness of resistance—win, lose, or draw—on the relationship between labor and capital. Women strikers directly challenged working-class manhood, reported the *Boston Globe*, shouting: "Come on, you cowards! You were [be] got in fear, though you were born in England." According to the *News*, a manufacturer told an overseer after a number of Lancashire operatives had landed in New York, "Well, we shall have a lot of greenhorns here to-morrow." The overseer replied: "Yes, but you'll find that they have brought their horns with them." Women strikers wanted the men to use those aggressive "horns" in bold action and imaginative strategy.

The initial issue of supporting the women's strike in January and thereby tolerating their independent activism created dissension among Lancashire men. Some criticized the female rebels as "babbling Amazons," according to the *Boston Globe.* Careful men soberly weighed the possibilities of strike action, not misguided by emotional, rebellious "Eves." But other Lancashire men agreed with the women strikers on the lessons of history, especially a sense of manhood with a satisfying, if unruly, physical core. Wrote the *News*, "If a man cannot knock down his oppressor, you at least like to see him try; and if you cannot knock the tyrant down who would oppress you, you can at least give him a welter [punch]!" Before 1875, male weavers deferred to the leadership of the mule spinners, but they quickly joined the women's strike, followed by the mule spinners and other operatives.

The strike spread to New Bedford and to English immigrants among the working people of Rhode Island's Blackstone Valley: Valley Falls, Central Falls, Lonsdale, Berkeley, Ashton, Pawtucket, and Woonsocket. Support for the strike spread to Lawrence, Newburyport, Lowell, and Taunton, Massachusetts. Reports of the strike appeared in the *Boston Herald*, the *Lawrence Journal*, the *Lowell Courier*, the *News*, and the *Providence Sun*. Prospects for a settlement brightened. The mule spinners of Lowell struck in March, while the print cloth mills of Lawrence promised their workers no wage cut. Operatives in Lonsdale, a center of print cloth operations, were notified of a wage increase in April, while the agents in New Bedford and in Newburyport reversed wage cuts. Contemplated wage cuts were stopped or rescinded throughout the region.

The activities of the women weavers during the 1875 strikes significantly expanded their participation in labor protest. Many wives worked in the Fall River mills, providing mature leadership for the women's meetings as well as connections among working-class families. Single women were also prominent, especially Irish immigrant Cassie O'Neill. Women appeared regularly on public platforms with men, agitating at strike meetings and traveling to other textile centers to raise money. O'Neill spoke at strike meetings in Lowell, urging the men of both Fall River and Lowell to organize young women recruited by the mills to operate the first, very primitive ring spinning frames. The new technology would begin to replace mules by 1879. Weaver activism also encouraged 400 male and female French-Canadian operatives to organize to support the strike. They also supported 600 French-Canadian strikers involved with other nationalities in a similar walkout in Taftville, Connecticut. The reputation of French-Canadian immigrants as docile, submissive, and faithful only to their own proved false in 1875.

On March 12, the weavers offered a compromise; within four days the strike was over. All strikers were rehired. Only Lancashire immigrant George Gunton, the leader for regionwide amalgamation, was blacklisted. Despite the misgivings about female activism, once the battle was over, the weavers controlled local labor politics. Their aggressiveness and unexpected success had defeated the arrogant employers. Fall River wages became the standard for print cloth production in the Northeast. Quickly the weavers began to organize a regional association of textile operatives for a standard list of wages and to agitate for additional ten-hour laws, making New England the Lancashire of America. The *News* reported that at their convention on May 11, the weavers announced their goal: ". . . to establish a union in every village where the spindles revolve or the click of the busy shuttle is heard."

Asserting a Moral Economy

In July, the mill owners challenged the weavers' ambitions by cutting wages to glut the print market with cheaper cloth. Angry weavers and mule spinners met and agreed to deny their employers the power to set wages based on the prospects of the market. In doing so, they were resurrecting the Lancashire tradition of a moral economy documented by historians Edward P. Thompson and William Reddy. That tradition rejected their employers' definition of the rules of the marketplace and the ideology of supply and demand. Instead, textile operatives would influence the price of cloth by withholding their labor and taking an English-style "long vacation" in late summer. It made no sense, they said, to flood an already depressed market with huge amounts of goods. The best solution would be a work stoppage, not a pay cut. The operatives seized control of the timing of the stoppage for late summer when their living costs were low. This defiant act denied the validity of a morally neutral market run by natural economic laws, which masked the dominant position of the mill agents.

By early August, thirty-four mills and nearly 15,000 operatives squared off. The *Boston Globe*, the *New York Herald*, the *New York Times*, the *Providence Journal*, and the *News* told the story. The mill owners were absolutely determined to crush this unprecedented threat to their power at all costs. The ferocity of the "vacation strike" in 1875 exposed the mule spinners and the male weavers to charges of "unmanly" recklessness and irresponsibility. Hundreds of French operatives chose to return by rail to Montreal or left town for other New England mill centers. This became the common pattern for French-Canadian workers during late nineteenth-century strikes. After four weeks of no work and no price increase in the cloth market, the operatives abandoned their "vacation," accepting the wage cut. But the mill agents were eager to demolish any hope for an American Lancashire. Fearing that secret unions would flourish despite the anti-union contracts operatives were forced to sign, mill owners particularly wished to destroy Lancashire-style union discipline: "Up goes a hand and out goes the help!" They decided to lock out their employees for another month, threaten more wage cuts, and starve them into giving up their unions.

On September 27, when the mills reopened, the operatives flocked to the mill yards. They were willing to work but refused to sign the anti-union contracts. Hunger and the knowledge that the mills would employ only the utterly defeated produced a response by angry Lancashire operatives that recalled the late eighteenth-century bread riots. Historian John Bohstedt is correct that food riots acted as responses to changing economic and political contexts. This response, shared only by Lancashire people, threatened to alienate them from other ethnic communities. Thousands of

In late September 1875, hundreds of angry mill workers in Fall River, Massachusetts, marched to demand food relief from the mayor. For a month, mill owners had refused to let the operatives back to work unless they signed anti-union contracts. Many of the demonstrators had emigrated from Lancashire, England, where traditions of moral economy and collective protest had deep roots. They carried an American flag upside down, which was a sign of distress, and a placard that read: "15,000 white slaves for sale at auction." Their conflict with the militia alienated other operatives who did not understand their protest traditions, leading to divisions among the workforce and the disintegration of the fledgling amalgamated union.

disappointed workers marched to a nearby city park. A delegation asking for relief from the mayor returned unsuccessful. Hundreds of men and women strikers marched to City Hall, cheering and yelling "Bread!" and "Tyranny!" Boys held symbolic poles on which were impaled loaves of bread. An American flag upside down as a distress signal preceded a sign that read "15,000 white slaves for auction," topped with a loaf of bread. Lancashire workers were incensed at American pretensions to freedom in contrast with the servility thrust on them. One angry woman striker hit the mayor on the head with a loaf of bread.

The historic significance of the food riot rituals that gave direction to the angry turmoil was clear to Lancashire people but baffling to many others. Only the Boston and Providence press recognized the revolutionary implications of Manchester-style bread riots in New England, while labor reformer

Jennie Collins appreciated the "extraordinary proof of English cool-headed control" that indicated disciplined crowd action. Others saw only mayhem. Showers of stones, bread, and brickbats fell on arresting police. The violent spectacle of the ritualized demonstration split the textile operatives into confused, hostile camps. To the uninitiated, these customs appeared to be "hideous" and "incendiary" conduct by a riotous "mob."

These divisions and the crushing defeat of the vacation strategy convinced the mule spinners that the weavers' union with its contingent of "vulgar" female rebels and agitators had led the strikers into disaster. Begging city authorities for bread backed with threats of violence was no manly way to deal with their employers. Mill owners used the disorderly conduct of bread rioters to demean the spinners and weavers as Lancashire brutes. Female weavers' activism had challenged the authority of spinners in labor protest and undercut the respectable manliness of mule spinners by association with public riot. The struggle shattered the fledgling amalgamated union and its regional vision. Worst of all, mule spinners signed away their union memberships, while the local weavers' organization disintegrated. With the Lancashire past rendered too passionate and perilous in 1875, the spinners recaptured the leadership of union organization in the New England print cloth industry.

Competing Visions of Labor Power

After lost strikes in 1876, 1877, and 1878 over wage cuts in Lonsdale, New Bedford, and Fall River, mill agents shaped a consistent policy to undermine regional labor protest. They divided the nationalities and skills through preferential treatment, unequal wages, general denunciation of English radicals, or demonstrations of arbitrary power through wage cuts. The announcement of unspecified wage cuts demonstrated their power to manipulate through fear and uncertainty while dangling advances if the market improved. An informal network of agents and owners in New England, bound together in the late nineteenth century by low prices, worked together to crush regional labor protest.

George Gunton, editor of the Fall River *Labor Standard,* believed that amalgamations of the weavers in the Northeast in all textile operations, including the print cloth mills of Cohoes, New York, and the silk mills of Paterson, New Jersey, offered a counterbalance. Organized resistance operating in the broadest possible arena seemed the key to obtaining power in any single community and essential to preventing the cultural fragmentation inherent in American industrial life. Gunton believed that Lancashire experience spoke to all textile workers. The silk weavers of Paterson, like the Lancashire immigrants, were seasoned industrial workers eager to assert their rights, but the vitality and success of the labor movement in Paterson contrasted sharply with the disarray in Fall River.

Unlike Gunton, Secretary Robert Howard of the Fall River Mule Spinners' Association saw no future for Lancashire-style protest in American trade unionism or for a political coalition between spinners and weavers. Howard believed that trade unions with ample strike funds and regionwide locals offered a better chance to deal with mill agents. According to the *Boston Globe,* he won acceptance as a union leader whose goal was to make his members "as obedient and docile and harmonious as the parts of a mule frame." Howard counted on Fall River agents' stubbornness to contrast with his strategy of patience, forbearance, and moderation. Out of a local workforce of 14,000, 1,000 spinners adopted exclusive policies that attempted to restore their proper sense of respectable manhood: recognition of their union by the managers and higher wages based on calculations of costs and profits. But these efforts could not address their employers' power to refuse to negotiate, hire strikebreakers, or set wages and working conditions. Even as the new technology of ring spinning began to threaten their craft, the mule spinners refused to organize young female and male ring spinners. Instead the mule spinners wanted a family wage paid to skilled men to support dependents. In the *Fall River Herald,* Howard insisted that his organization represented only the mule spinners. Any wage increase advances would go to "males and heads of families . . ." to shield them from the shame of an empty pay envelope, considered "a disgrace in the eyes of their fellowmen."

In May 1879, the spinners' union struck against a 15 percent wage cut, while Howard traveled to Massachusetts and Rhode Island mill towns to organize support. The *Boston Globe*, the *Boston Herald*, the *Fall River Herald*, the *Labor Standard*, and the *News* wrote about the strike. The spinners' union wished to avoid a lockout and urged the weavers not to strike. Howard wished to prevent any militant weavers' uprising, but the mill agents rejected conciliation and arbitration. The spinners' respectable manhood would be tested by their endurance and handling of strikebreakers, while male and female weavers remained at work.

Mill agents became tougher and used the divisions within the workforce. They withheld the monthly pay of those who lived in corporation tenements and fired and evicted all relatives of striking spinners—men, women, and children. The mills remained open and running in part, but soon filling yarn would be used up and the weavers would have to stop. The agents called for strikebreakers and gave them pistols. By mid-July, the situation had become nightmarish. After the workday ended, the strikebreakers housed at five mills used their revolvers for target practice in the mill yards in violation of city ordinance. No one was arrested. The mill agents, it was rumored, supplied the knobsticks with beer and whiskey, fearing to let them walk the streets. Gunton called it "rum and revolver rule."

When a strikers' delegation sought to negotiate a truce as an "honorable end," the agents insisted on an unconditional surrender. The issue was no longer wages or profits but a struggle over power. Most of the strikers held out, but the sight of eight French-Canadian families, sixty people in all, being taken in wagons on September 16 to housing provided by the mills, drove some of the striking spinners wild. Many strikers believed that French Canadians provided the core of the knobsticks, but most had Irish, English, and Yankee names. When the families walked through the streets, a crowd of about 200 men, women, and children hooted and stoned them. These were not armed knobsticks. Anguished strikers had abandoned respectable manhood.

Facing defeat and the failure of his policies of caution and moderation, Howard lost control of the situation. The mill agents paid whatever it cost to beat the union, including the expenses of unruly, defiant strikebreakers, to exercise power over the workforce. They hired virtually any adult male who showed up. They built barracks, provided meals or board, and furnished handguns, beer, and whiskey. The knobsticks knew their worth to the mills and shirked work. As the strike collapsed with no wage concessions, the knobsticks either took off or went on their own short strikes. The lost strike proved to Robert Howard the desperate need for a regional organization for mule spinners to prevent strikebreaking.

The Rise of Craft Unionism

When the market rose in 1880, the Fall River mills reversed the 15 percent wage cut. A chain reaction of strikes throughout New England and New York textile centers indicated that Fall River set the wages for the cloth industry. In fifteen different locations, operatives in Connecticut, Rhode Island, New York, and Massachusetts demanded wage hikes. Initially refused or shortchanged by Fall River standards, strikes erupted in Valley Falls, Rhode Island; at the Harmony print cloth mills in Cohoes, New York; and at the Lancaster gingham mills in Clinton, Massachusetts. Young women weavers led the way. To prevent a mass uprising, Rhode Island mills announced an immediate statewide wage increase. The supervisor of the Harmony Mills at Cohoes used as many Fall River tricks as possible: withholding wages, firing relatives, and importing strikebreakers. Finally giving in, he negotiated only with the mule spinners "as men," while firing two "insolent," "impertinent," (and female) leaders of the weavers. Historian Daniel Walkowitz assumed that only skilled men were militants, but when another woman was blacklisted, the *Labor Standard* reported that 4,000 operatives, the majority of women weavers, shut down the mills in less than an hour using the 1854 Lancashire slogan: "ten per cent and no surrender." Women weavers, as in Fall River in 1875, proved both militant and aggressive.

For George Gunton, it was time to form an amalgamation of textile operatives from the mills of New Jersey and New York to Maine and New Hampshire to demand a national ten-hour day and a regional wage list. In Cohoes and in Valley Falls, the mule spinners eagerly supported the weavers. Gunton made room for them in his Amalgamated Cotton and Woolen Operatives, challenging Howard's Mule Spinners' Association. According to the *Labor Standard*, Gunton's regional organization included all textile operatives from spinners and weavers to "crossing [floor] sweepers," the lowest-paid job in the mills. The enthusiasm of the weavers in 1880 and their inclusive unionism of all skills and nationalities became vital to a strong, regional organization. This inclusiveness characterized the successful 1880 strikes and Paterson leaders supported it, but in Fall River only the spinners were organized.

During the early 1880s, the print cloth mills in the Northeast enjoyed high dividends, rising stock prices, huge production, and large salaries for their managers. Gunton observed in the *Labor Standard*: "When trade is dull they cannot afford to pay and when trade is good they can afford *not* to pay." Targeting the spinners' union leadership, they fired, harassed, and blacklisted spinners. Ignoring the weavers, Howard reached out to other labor organizations to sustain his National Mule Spinners' Association, representing four states in May 1881. The fledgling Federation of Organized Trades and Labor Unions, headquartered in New York City, provided his best allies. By 1883, Howard was treasurer of the federation with Samuel Gompers, an English immigrant from London, as president. Howard's organizational efforts were halted by the strikes of 1884.

The *Fall River Herald* described the events. When the 1884 strikes began, many operatives returned to the more settled labor conditions of Lancashire or to Quebec. Fall River mule spinners believed that French-Canadian operatives refused to strike and undercut working standards, but most were weavers. Local spinners would not train Quebec boys or accept experienced French-Canadian spinners from Montreal, Connecticut, or western Massachusetts. Two French-Canadian mule spinners from New Bedford found jobs, and others appeared in groups, always a threat to the union. Some French-Canadian weavers ignored the 1884 strike, but others joined in, angry at weave room brutalities. In small numbers, Howard's union men and the 300 nonunion spinners in the city became knobsticks, perhaps seeking promotion to "second hands" or bosses. These "renegades" undermined strikers' morale, but Howard counted on the depressed market to rise. As the market sagged, desperate union spinners began, as they had in 1879, to attack knobsticks. Beatings, stonings, and exchanges of gunfire again became common on Saturday nights. Two unusually violent acts against knobsticks eroded public sympathy. Union men beat one sixty-year-old impoverished spinner so badly that he died. Three weeks later, an insulting exchange between knobsticks and union men resulted in mill arson. Full of flame from tower to basement, it was gone in an hour, illuminating the whole city. The striking spinners and weavers trickled back to work in June. The cloth market remained severely depressed.

Howard supported the development of Gompers's American Federation of Labor (AFL) and its preference for exclusive trade-based unions, thereby dividing spinners and weavers. Still, the weavers had skills, numbers, experience in labor protest, and a tradition of adversarial strikes. They and other operatives reorganized unions in the late 1880s. Union mule spinners lost strikes and faced the threat of technological improvements in ring spinning, which Howard discounted, ignoring the young ring spinners. Where some weavers saw opportunity for organization, Howard feared for his union of respectable men. The national mule spinners' organization, like other trade unions in the AFL, adopted policies to benefit skilled white-male workers. To Howard this seemed politically wise and potentially empowering, but too many allies in the textile mills were left out. The weavers, the women, the French Canadians, the loom fixers, the less skilled men, the ring spinners, the back boys—all their grievances and interconnecting interests and the potential of their united power—were either briefly used or ignored.

The Limits of Craft Unionism

During the decade following the 1884 strike, Howard and the national mule spinners' union negotiated a special deal with mill agents eager to control labor strife. Recognizing him as a bargaining agent, in 1887, managers offered a sliding scale of wages. Earnings for the spinners would rise and fall based on a formula that involved the price of baled cotton, the market price of print cloth, and an assured margin of profit. The first year, spinners' wages did not budge. Howard feared he had been lulled into a special position that assured conservative unionism but failed to raise wages to offset past reductions. In early 1888, the manufacturers' granted a 9.5 percent increase for the spinners but only 4.5 percent for the other operatives. The late 1880s and early 1890s brought great prosperity to the print cloth mills and high dividends to their shareholders. Wages lagged far behind, especially for the weavers, while union spinners could not escape the speeding of the mules, one of their most common grievances. High speed and fatigue produced injured feet and hands from splinters and crushed bones. The "sick spinners" continued to relieve exhausted or injured men. Faced with continual complaints about cheating, speeding, and overtime, Howard often intervened personally to resolve grievances.

Angered by the differential wages granted in 1888 to the small but well-financed spinners' union, thousands of weavers began again to organize. But the weavers' union represented only 14 percent of the 7,000 weavers. Response to a strike call depended on the weavers' shop committees organized in the mills, some with their own unions. The market was rising, and profits were high. When the weavers asked for an increase equal to that of the spinners, the mill interests advertised for 5,000 weavers in Lancashire through the *Cotton Factory Times* of Manchester. The outraged weavers went on strike. According to the *Fall River Herald*, which described the strike, the agents regarded the weavers' union as "only a handful of men . . ." easily ignored. The strike that began on March 11, 1889, surprised many.

Support was widespread and deep. Nearly 6,500 from a workforce of 7,000 men and women walked out. Many nonunion French Canadians struck and some joined the union. Fancy weavers struck even though they had no quarrel over wages. Overseers fired loom fixers who refused to weave, and the weave rooms fell silent. The manufacturers knew that the new union's treasury could not last more than a few weeks. One agent insisted that even the lure of high profits and the demands of large contracts would carry no weight.

Beneath a show of unity, boisterous mass rallies, and the solid front of the seventeen-day strike lay conflicting styles of labor protest. The weavers responded out of a sense of deep injustice, unlike the spinners who calculated the direction of the cloth market. The spring trade was over; the fall trade not begun: the manufacturers could easily stop a few weeks to exhaust the weavers' treasury. The spinners continued to work, filling yarn sold for high prices in Philadelphia and throughout Rhode Island. Sympathetic spinners with relatives who were weavers objected, while one with eight weavers in his family was ordered to bring them in or be fired. These family connections had brought the trades together during the strikes of the 1870s.

After a week of impressive unity, the new union, unable to support 6,000 strikers, offered to compromise. The mill agents demanded that the weavers return at the old wage scale. But the mills did not threaten a lockout as long as filling yarn sold well, for this might lead to action from the spinners. We propose, said one agent to "let [the strike] die out unnoticed." Compromise would mean union recognition, a privilege reserved for the mule spinners. The strikers hoped to keep their union going after the inevitable return to work; until then, they would enjoy an early, warm spring and "hang hard."

Unity, Division, and the Triumph of Craft Unionism

The aftermath of the 1889 weavers' strike would reshape the future of unionization in the Northeast. The involvement of women workers in union activities diminished. With women and boys crowding the ring spinning rooms, the number of men in weaving grew to half the workforce. The language of the strikers reflected the rising position of family men among the weavers. But to exclude women weavers from the union's leadership created a large, potentially uncontrollable group that might operate independently. Women weavers were increasingly viewed as separate and uncontrollable. Tensions grew among weavers, reflecting the wishes of male weavers to imitate the mule spinners and demand a family wage, excluding women.

The prosperous years of the late 1880s ended

with a cloth market slump in 1891 caused by overproduction, which halted wage agitation from both the spinners and the weavers. When the business depression began in the fall of 1893, the mills cut wages 15 percent. Print cloth production continued at lower wages, flooding a market with little demand. By August 1894, the Fall River mills decided to try another 10 percent; this resulted in a strike chronicled by the *Fall River Globe* and the *Fall River Herald*. Unexpected combinations and divisions, haunting memories, and resurrected traditions shaped the course of events. When the mills announced the wage cut, both the weavers' and the mule spinners' leaders acquiesced. The weavers' union claimed about 3,000 members, less than half of the 7,500 weavers, including some Portuguese immigrants. But the deeply alienated rank-and-file weavers disagreed, and the spinners would follow their lead. It was 1875 again—Robert Howard's worst nightmare.

The weavers' grievances included more than the wage cut. In 1892, Massachusetts law had forced textile mills to specify in writing the length of a "cut" or cloth piece, prohibiting changes profitable to the mills. The agents in Fall River and New Bedford had evaded this by paying by the pound, weighing the cloth in secret. One weaver felt that next they would pay by the quart.

As in 1875, the weavers and spinners took a two-week August vacation to raise the market price of cloth. The strike united all skill groups, fancy and plain weavers, men and women, organized and unorganized, and the various nationalities. Following the strike vote, the weavers gave ". . . an outpouring of shouts that would have drowned out the noise of a battery of guns at short range." The old spirit of protest echoed, haunting everyone. Most strikers had some savings, but not a berry or a clam would escape their foraging. Each ethnic community served its version of strike rations: porridge or fish and chips, boiled salted meat and cabbage, or pea soup with bread. The agents, astonished at the breadth and depth of the walkout, watched the market reports. Their old fears of losing control over the workforce and the market unified agents in a lockout. The market slowly crept up, but never high enough for the Fall River agents. The issue was beating down wages, the operatives, and their unions. Some mills with huge, secret inventories unloaded them for considerable profit, although supporting the lockout. The "vacation" ended on September 15 in a rising market, but confrontation continued. Even the spinners who managed the union treasury were in "a fighting mood," provoked by cloth prices.

When Howard returned from traveling in Lancashire, he offered a compromise on behalf of the spinners. The weavers refused to let him speak for them or consider anything less than the restoration of 10 percent. They denounced him for ignoring the amalgamation, but Howard shrugged it off. The print market began to fall; the depression years were setting in. Compromise talks with the agents got nowhere. If the mule spinners wished to exhaust their treasury, so be it. The mill agents wanted unconditional surrender on their terms: accept the 10 percent cut, then we will see. This offered nothing, while in a slightly up market inventories sold briskly. Meanwhile the New Bedford spinners and weavers settled for a 5 percent cut.

Howard gave "the speech of his life" on October 12, 1894, to get the spinners to accept terms many considered unworthy. His arguments rested on his reputation and the depressed market, using pathos and threats. His men had been angry, even outraged, but would be reasonable under his guidance. Ten years ago, Howard pointed out, we had mules in every mill but—for the first time in public—he insisted that ring spinning threatened all warp and some filling mules. The strike must end to preserve the craft and the treasury, and prevent general starvation. Union spinners supported their leader, but the weavers refused to return to work when the mills reopened.

With folded overalls and working skirts over their arms, the weavers held a spontaneous march through the central mill district. For thirteen days, over 4,000, perhaps more, refused to tend their looms. One weaver pointed out that the American flag they carried was made of silk, not print cloth. Other marchers held up their tools Lancashire-style: reed hooks and bobbins. They waved handkerchiefs, sang songs, and jeered, hooted, and shook doubled fists as they marched past the mill agents' mansions. More parades followed, some primarily of women weavers. Banners, echoing traditional Lancashire defiance, read: "We Are Willing to Starve but Not at the Looms." "Weavers want 5 per cent or no surrender." Music from bands or single instruments kept up the pace. One tall, grey, thin woman weaver of about sixty danced happily around in circles to the music as she marched, a symbol of spirit and perseverance.

The weavers held out, organizing parade after parade, as the weather turned windy and colder, keeping more than half of the mills' looms silent. Then they returned to work. The weavers had their vacation, relived some of the old-time spirit of defiance, felt the power of united action, and the market had risen. These last, seemingly futile parades were important gestures of courage and spirit, demonstrating that the striking weavers were neither beaten nor starved, but remained men and women worthy of their honor. But by 1894, more male weavers had a different vision of working-class manhood and womanhood. Ignoring the importance of women weavers in the strike and demonstrations, the male weavers began to insist on the same bargain as the mule spinners. "We are men as the spinners are. We have families as the spinners have. Why can't we get the same treatment?" If their union only had a treasury as the spinners did and leadership as firm, they too would gain recognition as union men. The family wage and craft union idea seemed the answer. The Lancashire traditions of the weavers' union were abandoned. In 1905, with new nationalities flooding the workforce, the Fall River weavers' union voted to join the American Federation of Labor.

Conclusion

The strikes that occurred, locally and regionally, in these nineteenth-century textile communities, especially during the post–Civil War years, contributed to the rise of small, conservative, and exclusionary trade unions for skilled male textile workers within the emerging national American Federation of Labor. Nineteenth-century textile workers in the Northeast disagreed over what constituted effective class power. A federation of craft unions would never represent the majority of textile workers but might provide a means during strikes to shut down production centers if strong regional organization prevented strikebreaking. Craft unions depended not only on regional organization but on maintaining control over specific skills, while textile capitalists feverishly developed new technology, most important, ring spinning, to replace the skilled male workforce. Furthermore, a defensive position adopted by craft unions to protect certain groups of skilled men meant an inflexible approach to ongoing changes in the gender and ethnic makeup of the workforce of ring spinners.

The idea of an amalgamated union for all textile workers promoted by weavers was based on transnational cultural and political legacies of popular radicalism brought from Lancashire to the Northeast in recurrent waves throughout the nineteenth century. Amalgamation meant an inclusionary strategy for union members regardless of skill, gender, religion, or nationality, and a determined commitment to resist capitalist domination, whatever the consequences, backed by the faith that resistance itself—win, lose, or draw—demonstrated worker power. But deep cultural and ideological differences among the waves of new immigrant workers in the industry had to be overcome to achieve a transcultural class unity.

Determined employers manipulated divisions among nationalities and religions, pitted women against men, and consistently sought to lower wages and break unions. By the late nineteenth century, the ideology of the family wage for male weavers assumed dominance. Amalgamated textile unionism diminished during a prolonged series of struggles with craft unions and industrial capitalists. At the beginning of the twentieth century, the vast majority of multiethnic textile workers remained unorganized. Still, successive waves of new immigrants with radical traditions from Italy, Belgium, and Eastern Europe joined with American socialists to keep the dream of transcultural class unity alive for textile workers during the first two decades of the twentieth century. In contrast, the powerful but conservative mule spinners' trade unions of the Northeast, dominated by English and Irish immigrant men, became leaders in the American Federation of Labor. They increasingly distanced themselves from other operatives, lent themselves to the emerging monopoly power of textile capitalism at the turn of the century, and embraced American partisan politics.

See also: North Carolina Women on Strike, 154; Strikes and Apprenticeship in the United States, 299; Twentieth-Century Textile Strikes, 330.

Bibliography

Blewett, Mary H. *Constant Turmoil: The Politics of Industrial Life in Nineteenth-Century New England*. Amherst: University of Massachusetts Press, 2000.

Berthoff, Roland T. *British Immigrants in Industrial America, 1790–1950*. Cambridge, MA: Harvard University Press, 1953.

Bohstedt, John. "The Moral Economy and the Discipline of Historical Context," *Journal of Social History* 26 (Winter 1992): 265–84.

Cohen, Isaac. *American Management and British Labor: A Comparative Study of the Cotton Spinning Industry*. Westport, CT: Greenwood Press, 1990.

Connecticut Bureau of Labor Statistics. "The Strike At Taftville." In *Second Annual Report*, May 1875. Hartford: Author, 127–31.

Dublin, Thomas. *Women At Work: The Transformation of Work and Community in Lowell, Massachusetts, 1826–1860*. New York: Columbia University Press, 1979.

Erickson, Charlotte. *Invisible Immigrants: The Adaptation of English and Scottish Immigrants in 19th Century America*. Ithaca, NY: Cornell University Press, 1990.

Kirk, Neville. *Labour and Society in Britain and the USA*. 2 vols. Aldershot, UK: Scholar Press, 1994.

Reddy, William. "The Textile Trade and the Language of the Crowd at Rouen, 1752–1871," *Past and Present*, 74 (February 1977): 62–89.

Ten Hour Association of Fall River. "To the Operatives and Working Classes of Massachusetts." May 8, 1869.

Thompson, Edward P. "The Moral Economy of the English Crowd in the Eighteenth Century," *Past and Present* 50 (February 1971): 76–136.

Walkowitz, Daniel. *Worker City, Company Town*. Urbana: University of Illinois Press, 1978.

Weavers' Union. "A Workingman." In *History of the Fall River Strike*. Fall River, 1875.

TWENTIETH-CENTURY TEXTILE STRIKES

David J. Goldberg

The textile industry is the oldest mass production industry in the United States, and machine production has been used in the making of cloth since the 1820s. It has employed roughly equal numbers of men and women, with female employees often playing a prominent role in strikes. By the early twentieth century, it had become a highly complex industry, since the manufacture of cotton cloth, woolens and worsteds, and silk each comprised a distinct sector, and a number of other specialty branches produced products such as carpets, hosiery, and knit goods. The textile industry has historically been a highly competitive industry, and labor costs comprised a high percentage of total costs. Initial startup costs were low compared with other mass production industries, and employers often transferred operations to new locations in order to escape labor strife.

Workers employed in the textile industry conducted numerous mass strikes. Participants in the walkouts often did not belong to labor unions and sought to win improvements in working conditions and increased wages as well as union recognition. Employees continued to conduct strikes even though the majority of work stoppages in the textile industry ended in defeat and resulted in the dismissal of activists.

Strikes in the textile industry varied considerably. Some walkouts sought to win improvements and could be described as "offensive," while others sought to prevent a wage cut or an increase in loom assignments (known as the stretch-out in the textile industry) and could be considered as "defensive." In some northern strikes, the vast majority of participants came from immigrant backgrounds, while native-born whites comprised the vast majority of strikers in the South. Many walkouts were led by leftists or radicals and others were led by an American Federation of Labor (AFL) union, the United Textile Workers (UTW), a Congress of Industrial Organizations (CIO) union, the Textile Workers Union of America (TWUA), or conducted by independent organizations. Many of the strikes led to violence and the local police and National Guard frequently intervened on the side of employers. Besides the mass strikes, skilled workers such as loom fixers, wool sorters, and mule spinners conducted numerous walkouts that rarely extended beyond a single craft or sector. These received limited publicity and only affected a small number of workers.

IWW-Led Immigrant Strikers

The era of mass immigrant strikes in the textile industry began in 1912 and 1913, when the Industrial Workers of the World (IWW) led walkouts in Lawrence, Massachusetts, and Paterson, New Jersey. Because of the IWW's involvement, historians have tended to lump these two walkouts together but, because these two textile centers differed considerably, the issues, tactics, and outcomes also differed.

The Lawrence walkout, which became known as the Bread and Roses Strike, is one of the most famous strikes in American labor history. It began in January 1912, when female employees of the Everett Mill, upon discovering that their pay had been cut, pulled the switch on their machines and left the plant. Soon, they were joined by over 20,000 employees of Lawrence's other large mills: the American Woolen Company, the Pacific, and the Arlington. The pay reduction had resulted from a Massachusetts law that cut the maximum

Elizabeth Gurley Flynn, 1890–1964, grew up a Socialist and became a leading organizer for the Industrial Workers of the World at age seventeen. She led dozens of strikes, including the 1912 Bread and Roses Strike in Lawrence, Massachusetts, and the Paterson, New Jersey, Silk Strike in 1913. As a feminist, she criticized the sexism of the male-dominated leadership of the labor movement, but she nonetheless remained a vocal and militant supporter of workers of all kinds throughout her life. She fought for birth control, women's suffrage, and women's rights and was a founder of the American Civil Liberties Union and member of the Communist Party. (*Courtesy:* George Grantham Bain Collection, Library of Congress.)

hours that women could be employed from fifty-six to fifty-four per week. Employees demanded a pay increase to make up for the two lost hours. Other demands sought abolition of a premium pay system that affected weavers at the giant American Woolen Company mills and double pay for any overtime work.

It is surprising that such modest demands led to a walkout fought with revolutionary élan. Some of the spirit that infused the strike came from charismatic IWW leaders such as Big Bill Haywood, Elizabeth Gurley Flynn, and Carlo Tresca. But much of the enthusiasm came from within Lawrence's varied immigrant communities, which included Italians, Franco-Belgians, Lithuanians, Poles, Syrians, and many other nationalities. On the other hand, many English, Irish, and French-Canadian workers opposed the strike, and their hostility, in turn, angered the strikers, who were determined to keep strikebreakers out of the mills. Those who opposed the walkout often had higher-paying or more skilled jobs or were devout Catholics who wanted no part of a walkout led by the IWW.

The Lawrence strike established the model for subsequent mass immigrant strikes in the textile industry. Though the walkout occurred in the dead of winter, daily picket lines prevented workers opposed to the strike from entering the mills. A constant round of mass meetings and rallies maintained spirits. Female strikers, making use of community-based networks, did much to build support for the work stoppage in Lawrence's dismal tenement district. Ethnically based soup kitchens fed many of those who needed assistance, and, based on workers' nationality, the IWW developed a form of organization that proved highly effective. Mass arrests, the killing of one striker, Anna LoPizzo, and the imprisonment of IWW leaders Arturo Giovannitti and Joseph Ettor after they were indicted for conspiracy to commit murder only stiffened the determination of the participants.

Financial support provided by members of the Socialist Party also helped sustain the strike. Many Socialist Party members in the Northeast also began to take in the children of the strikers so as to provide them with sustenance during the walkout. The success of this tactic so annoyed city officials that on February 24, 1912, police attacked a group of children and their supporters who were about to embark for Philadelphia. The brutal assault served only to garner additional support for the immigrant workers and led to congressional hearings that further publicized the employees' cause.

Since many of the Lawrence mills produced woolens and worsteds, the goal of the workers had been to tie up the mills when the busy season began in March. And just as they anticipated, by the second week of March the Lawrence mills believed they had no choice but to give in or risk losing orders. Workers won wage increases and American Woolen weavers won a significant modification in the premium payment system. So astonishing was this triumph by immigrant workers over the nation's largest textile firm (the American Woolen Company) and the other large Lawrence mills that it sparked strikes in other textile centers such as New Bedford, Massachusetts; Little Falls, New York; and Passaic, New Jersey.

Despite the victory, workers were not able to sustain a permanent organization. In October 1912, employers unleashed a massive "For God and Country" campaign that proved highly effective. More significantly, an economic downturn in 1913 and 1914 enabled the companies to dismiss activists, so that by 1915 the IWW had practically disappeared from Lawrence, though ethnic organizations continued to harbor activists.

On the surface, the IWW-led Paterson silk strike of 1913 resembled the Lawrence walkout, but the two strikes differed considerably. Paterson had been the center of the nation's silk industry since the middle of the nineteenth century. Highly skilled workers, predominantly from English, German, Jewish, and Italian backgrounds, wove ribbons and broad silks in Paterson's numerous small shops. The less skilled employees worked in the dyehouses. Ribbon and broad-silk weavers had conducted numerous shop strikes stemming from concerns over working conditions. Broad-silk employees had also become concerned that mill owners had transferred some operations to the anthracite district of Pennsylvania, where the daughters of coal miners could find employment. In 1907, the UTW had tried to organize these employees, but a walkout led by the AFL union ended in failure. Adding to Paterson's complexity, Italian anarchists had gained a following and participated in a violent 1902 dyehouse strike.

Throughout the history of the United States, strikes have triggered the mobilization of troops. This strike in Lawrence, Massachusetts, sometime between 1910 and 1915, was no different. Here the troops provide a path to the mills for scabs. (*Courtesy:* George Grantham Bain Collection, Library of Congress.)

The IWW also gained a following in Paterson in 1909, after the UTW signed an agreement with the Henry Doherty Company, Paterson's largest silk firm, allowing it to operate on a four-loom-per-weaver basis. The UTW acquiesced to the stretch-out because it feared the competition provided by the Pennsylvania mills might cause other firms to leave the city. The Wobblies' organizing efforts paid off in January 1913 when the Doherty weavers struck against the four-loom system. They were soon joined by Paterson's other broad-silk weavers, ribbon weavers, and dyehouse employees in what became the only general textile strike in Paterson's strife-torn history.

The unified response of more than 25,000 silk workers came about, in part, due to the effectiveness of the same IWW leaders who had rallied workers in Lawrence. The unified response also resulted from the workers' determination to win the eight-hour day, since weavers often complained of stress and eyestrain, and dyehouse employees resented the fact that they still worked a twelve-hour day. In addition, broad-silk and ribbon weavers framed demands peculiar to their jobs.

The tactics used by the IWW resembled those in Lawrence, but workers in Paterson faced much harsher repression. Close to 2,000 strikers were arrested during the seven-month walkout and, when local authorities closed down their meeting halls, the IWW was forced to schedule their weekly Sunday mass meetings in the neighboring town of Haledon, which had a Socialist mayor.

As the strike dragged on into its sixth month, the IWW decided that it could raise needed funds and boost morale by staging a strike pageant in New York City's Madison Square Garden. John Reed, a young Greenwich Village radical, took on much of the responsibility for organizing the spectacle. After rehearsing for days, 7,000 Paterson workers participated in this unique event, during which they reenacted scenes from the strike. Melvyn Dubofsky argues in *We Shall Be All* that the pageant gravely damaged the walkout because it failed

During the 1913 strike of silk workers in Paterson, New Jersey, the Industrial Workers of the World adopted a tactic similar to the one used in Lawrence the year before, when they sent strikers' children to live with sympathetic families in larger cities. Here they sent the children to participate in New York City's May Day parade. (*Courtesy:* George Grantham Bain Collection, Library of Congress.)

to raise the needed funds, distracted workers from the daily picketing, and created jealousies between participants and nonparticipants. On the other hand, Steve Golin, in *A Fragile Bridge,* has argued that the pageant represented a highly successful collaboration between workers and intellectuals, and the strike ultimately failed because hostility to the IWW created unity among Paterson's previously divided employers.

By July, the strike movement had collapsed. In part, this occurred because the outside IWW leaders did not understand how much Paterson differed from Lawrence, and they continued to insist that workers act as a unified body. But the more-skilled ribbon weavers had always acted on their own, and they split away to accept separate shop settlements. By the end of July, all workers had returned to their looms and vats, having gained little for their efforts.

From Offense to Defense in the Northeast

The 1913–15 depression put a damper on labor activity in textiles. But the buildup for the war that began in 1916 and the accelerated production schedules of 1917 and 1918 created great resentment on the part of workers, who felt victimized by speedups and runaway inflation and who accused employers of wartime profiteering. Emboldened by the full employment of wartime, shortly after the Armistice the UTW launched a nationwide campaign for the eight-hour day. (In reality, they sought a standard forty-eight-hour week with a Saturday half-holiday.) The UTW established February 3, 1919, as the date when they expected employers to implement their demand. On that day, many northern mills announced that they would henceforth operate on a forty-eight-hour schedule, though they did not increase employees' pay for the lost hours. The UTW accepted the arrangement, but in two textile communities, Passaic and Lawrence, the UTW demand reignited the mass immigrant strike fervor of 1912 and 1913.

In Passaic, most of the city's 15,000 workers labored in the two large woolen and worsted mills, the Botany and the Forstmann & Huffmann. Slavic immigrants (Poles, Slovaks, and Ukrainians) comprised the bulk of the labor force, though a considerable number of Hungarians and Italians also worked in the mills, which often had German supervisors as well as German owners. Workers had conducted shop strikes in 1912 and 1916 and, after employees won some of their demands in 1916, Passaic employers had formed the Industrial Council of Passaic Wool Manufacturers (generally referred to as the Wool Council) in order to screen all workers before hiring them and to cooperate on all labor-related issues.

When February 3, 1919, arrived, almost all of the Passaic employees left the mills and started the city's first general textile strike. Workers demanded that they be granted the forty-eight-hour week with the same pay as for the old fifty-five-hour schedule. The 48/55 demand proved to be a unifying element in the walkout. The ethnic homogeneity of the workforce and anger at the Wool Council, which workers accused of spying on employees, also help to explain the unified response.

Upon leaving the mills, Passaic workers, distrustful of national organizations, formed their own union, which they called the Independent Union of General Workers of the Textile Industries of Passaic and Vicinity. They chose Matthew Pluhar, a skilled weaver and a Socialist from Passaic's small Czech community, as their leader. The 12,000 striking employees received considerable support from local shop owners and priests and had their cause bolstered by walkouts of local handkerchief and rubber workers. Besides seeking 48/55, Passaic workers also demanded employers' recognition for their union, a goal that reflected workers' concerns about the overweening power of the Wool Council.

After six weeks of parading and picketing, mill owners lured workers back to the plants by promising to grant 48/55 and recognition to shop committees. When employees returned, they discovered that a number of activists had been fired and employers had no intention of dealing with shop committees. Some militants staged a short-lived second walkout, but the achievement of reduced hours and a significant wage increase discouraged any continuation of the walkout. At the end of the strike, organizers from the New York–based Amalgamated Clothing Workers of America (ACWA) arrived to aid the workers and the strike established hopes that a permanent union could still be formed in Passaic.

The 1919 strike in Lawrence demonstrated that the city remained a center of militancy and radicalism. On February 3, 1919, the Lawrence mills also announced that they would begin operating on a forty-eight-hour basis, but, as in Passaic, they did not grant a wage increase. In response, immigrant workers at the American Woolen, Pacific, and Arlington mills struck, as they had in 1912, though once again English, Irish, and French-Canadian workers proved reluctant to join them.

Just as in 1912, local militants emerged from the various immigrant communities to provide leadership for the strike, and once again Lawrence workers welcomed outside supporters. In 1919, the outside leadership came from a group of young ministers and intellectuals, including A.J. Muste, who subsequently went on to a long career in the American labor and pacifist movements.

In many ways, the 1919 Lawrence battle resembled the 1912 strike, and workers employed many of the same tactics that had previously proved effective. The local police, though, took a much harsher attitude toward picketers, and hundreds of workers ended up being arrested. But, just as in 1912, the employees' ability to stay out until the busy season began paying dividends. When in mid-May employers announced a 15 percent increase effective June 2, jubilant employees returned to the mills. As in Passaic, the ACWA provided assistance at the end of the strike, and workers hoped that a new union that emerged from the two walkouts, the Amalgamated Textile Workers of America (ATWA), would enable them to win further gains.

Quite notably, northern cotton textile employees had not participated in the mass immigrant strikes, which had stretched between 1912 and 1919, though wartime prosperity had provided some respite for an industry that faced stiff southern competition. However, once a postwar depression began, in January 1921 New England employers cut their employees' wages by 22.5 percent. This wage slash evoked little protest. However, in January 1922, when many cotton textile manufacturers reduced their employees' wages by an additional 20 percent, and New Hampshire and Rhode Island employers increased their employees' hours from forty-eight to fifty-four per week, close to 70,000 New England textile workers struck in a desperate effort to preserve their hard-won gains and their slender standard of living.

Anger at the increase in hours added an extra level of desperation to the struggle in Rhode Island and New Hampshire. In Rhode Island's Pawtuxet Valley, the ATWA led most of the striking workers, while the UTW provided the leadership in the Blackstone Valley. In both areas of Rhode Island, workers made use of flying squadrons, mobile automobile units that went from mill to mill exhorting workers to leave their machines. Considerable violence and frequent clashes with police occurred throughout the nine-month struggle. Portuguese, Polish, Italian, and French-Canadian ethnic organizations rallied in support of the strike, and young women, the daughters of immigrants, displayed considerable militancy on picket lines.

The New Hampshire walkout spread to smaller textile centers, such as Nashua and Dover, but strike activity centered on Manchester's giant Amoskeag mills. Tamara K. Hareven has provided a framework for understanding the 1922 events. According to Hareven, before the walkout, Amoskeag's paternalistic labor policies had created a degree of trust between workers and management. But after the war, due to southern competition, management made increased use of speedups and the stretch-out. The deteriorating working conditions led many workers to believe that management had betrayed them and explains why French-Canadian workers, who had previously been loyal to management, joined others in a UTW-led walkout that saw parades, picketing, and arrests, though not the violence of Rhode Island.

In Massachusetts, the large Fall River and New Bedford mills did not cut their employees' wages, and Lowell workers, already battered by southern competition, proved reluctant to strike. Therefore, Lawrence once again became the center of attention, which focused on the Pacific Mills, a major producer of cotton fabric. At the Pacific, the UTW and a new radical union, the One Big Union, competed with one another for workers' support, while both organizations called upon employees to resist the wage cuts.

The 1922 textile strikes had an ambiguous conclusion. In Lawrence, workers won a clear-cut victory when the Pacific Mills announced in late August that it would rescind the cut. In Rhode Island, the strike lasted until September, and workers also won a rescission of the cut, though some employees returned on a fifty-four-hour-per-week basis and many activists lost their jobs. In New Hampshire, mill owners also agreed to forgo the wage cut, but hours were increased and, according to Hareven, workers became deeply disillusioned with the UTW and the strike also destroyed the "spirit of the Amoskeag." On the other hand, the UTW in many localities had displayed renewed vigor, though the 1922 strikes signaled the start of an era when New England textile workers would mainly be fighting defensive battles.

Regardless of whether they were employed in cottons, woolens, or silk, northern textile workers encountered difficult times throughout the decade of the 1920s. Faced with southern competition, increased use of synthetics, and fashions dictating shorter hemlines, mill owners in a desperate effort to maintain profits sought either to cut wages or to adjust working conditions. Workers often resisted these efforts. In Paterson, for example, broad-silk weavers, led by an independent union known as the Associated Silk Workers, conducted a partially successful strike in 1924 to prevent imposition of the four-loom system. But the big battles in Passaic in 1926 and New Bedford in 1928, during which the Communist Party became involved in strikes for the first time, demonstrated the desperate and defensive character of northern textile walkouts.

The Passaic strike began in January 1926, when the Botany Company fired a committee that had demanded cancellation of a pay cut announced in September 1925. In response to these firings, workers immediately shut down the Botany and a number of smaller mills. Albert Weisbord, a recent graduate of Harvard Law School who had joined the Communists (then known as the Workers Party), had been active in Passaic since fall 1925 and had developed close ties to Gustav Deak, a Hungarian worker, and a number of other local militants. As soon as the workers left the mills, the Communists organized them in a United Front Committee.

Even though their pay had not been cut, Forstmann & Huffmann employees encountering massive picket lines in front of their mills also joined the walkout (the Forstmann & Huffmann Company had left the Wool Council in 1925). The central goal of the strike became union recognition along with rescission of the cut and a pay increase. All of Passaic's immigrant communities rallied around the strikers, and priests and ethnic shopkeepers proved very supportive of the walkout. The Communist Party members took the lead in organizing numerous mass demonstrations, arranging legal and medical help for those who suffered arrests and beatings, holding special meetings for women workers, publishing a weekly newspaper, and producing a motion picture about the strike. Support also poured in from other liberal and radical organizations, especially since the walkout represented one of the few manifestations of labor militancy in the midst of so-called Coolidge Prosperity.

The 15,000 strikers displayed remarkable solidarity even when faced with the use of fire hoses in the middle of winter. Weisbord refused any offer of a settlement in March and April (the normal time for settling woolen textile strikes) because he hoped the walkout would spread to Paterson and Lawrence. This meant the walkout continued right through the summer. As it dragged on, the Workers Party leadership ordered Weisbord to hand the strike over to the UTW, which had never had a presence in Passaic. The Communist Party leaders made this decision because at this time they favored working within the AFL rather than forming dual unions. The strategy proved disheartening to Passaic workers. After holding firm for ten months, they drifted back to the mills between November 1926 and February 1927. Though they won a cancellation of the pay cut where it had been made, they had lost a year's wages and continued to be denied the much-sought-after goal of union recognition. Passaic workers, believing the unprecedented yearlong walkout had been for naught, never conducted such a mass strike again.

The 1928 New Bedford strike began in April when the local Cotton Manufacturers Association announced a 10 percent pay cut. Many of the New Bedford mills produced fine cotton cloth and had not suffered as much from southern competition as some other New England mills, which produced coarser cloth. The most skilled employees in New Bedford had long belonged to craft unions, which had been affiliated with a locally based Textile Council. Although for many years the Textile Council had belonged to an independent textile workers union, it had rejoined the UTW. Outside Communist Party organizers, many of whom had been active in Passaic, stepped in to organize Portuguese and Polish employees whom the more skilled workers had scorned. Thus, two rival organizations aided New Bedford's 20,000 mill employees in their fight against the pay cut, though the Communist-led Textile Mill Committees also sought a number of other improvements.

The less skilled workers engaged in daily picketing, sponsored numerous rallies and meetings, and established neighborhood-based soup kitchens, forms of activity not seen in New Bedford since an 1898 walkout. Over 1,000 workers were arrested during the strike. But the Communist Party leadership failed in their effort to convince neighboring Fall River cotton textile workers, who had also suffered a pay cut but who had not forgotten a bitter 1904–5 strike defeat, to join them. After six months, the seven craft unions that belonged to the Textile Council decided on a compromise and accepted a 5 percent cut. The Textile Mill Committees failed in their effort to keep the mills closed, though they had succeeded in giving voice to workers who had never had any representation in New Bedford.

Southern Workers vs. the Stretch-Out

Before World War I, southern textile mill employees had only occasionally participated in walkouts. Many southern textile mill employees only worked part of the year in the mills and often returned to their farms in the summer. Laboring in hundreds of small mill villages that dotted the Piedmont (a region stretching from Virginia through Alabama), employees had not expressed much overt dissatisfaction with the paternalistic policies of southern mill owners, whose operations were often located in unincorporated communities where management owned the workers' housing, schools, and even the churches.

World War I proved to be a turning point in the history of southern textile workers' strikes. Faced with glutted markets, after the war employers began to pressure workers to produce more without increasing their pay. As a result, a series of strikes, some of which involved the UTW, broke out in the South between 1919 and 1921. In 1921 alone, walkouts occurred in Huntsville, Alabama; Rock Hill, South Carolina; and Charlotte, Concord, and Kannapolis, North Carolina. In many of these work stoppages, the state militia intervened on the side of employers and none of them resulted in any permanent gains for workers.

During the 1920s, mill managers subjected southern textile workers to stricter discipline by introducing new machinery and using efficiency experts in an effort to rationalize and modernize their operations. Laboring in states that lacked laws to protect workers, southern mill employees often worked sixty-hour weeks and earned wages 30–40 percent below those of the North. Piecework began to replace weekly wage systems, and employers often substituted women for men believing they would work for less. Many women worked night shifts, since this was the only way they could care for their families. Scorned as "lintheads" and "white trash" by the local middle class, southern mill workers still suffered from pellagra, a vitamin deficiency, and lived in homes that lacked modern conveniences, though some significant improvement had been made in their diets and living conditions during the 1920s.

In 1929 and 1930, southern textile workers

revolted against these increased work pressures. Four work stoppages in particular, in Elizabethton, Tennessee; Gastonia and Marion, North Carolina; and Danville, Virginia, focused national attention on their plight. As in almost all subsequent textile strikes, workers rebelled against the stretch-out, the term they used for the speedups imposed by mill managers. Many of the participants no longer spent part of the year on farms and now considered themselves permanent mill employees. Historian Jacquelyn Dowd Hall has also argued that during the 1920s, many young women in the mill villages had been exposed to new fashions, radio, films, and the automobile, and that the new consumer culture had heightened their expectations for the future.

The Piedmont revolt began in 1929 in the east Tennessee community of Elizabethton, where women employees led strikes against the sparkling new, German-owned Bemberg and Glanzstoff rayon plants. More than 3,000 employees participated in the UTW-led walkout. But as so often occurred in the South, use of court injunctions, the state militia, and kidnappings of UTW organizers allowed employers to crush the walkout and blacklist over 1,000 employees while eliminating any union presence.

The 1929 Gastonia strike attracted the most national attention. The walkout centered on the Loray Mill, the largest textile mill in the South, which produced fabric for automobile tires. Gastonia and Gaston County had numerous other textile plants, and workers did not live in an isolated mill village, though many resided in company housing. But, unlike in the North, they received no support from the local middle class, who often expressed contempt for the "hands," and even many of the local preachers failed to side with their parishioners.

The strike had been encouraged by Fred Beal, a Communist Party organizer and veteran of Lawrence, Passaic, and New Bedford. Numerous other Communist organizers came to Gastonia to aid the walkout. Workers welcomed their support, though advocacy of racial equality by some of the organizers angered them. (Almost no African Americans worked in the southern textile mills due to racially discriminatory hiring policies.) Loray Mill employees made a number of demands, including abolishment of the stretch-out, adoption of a standard wage scale, a cut in hours, improvement in sanitary conditions, and elimination of the hated "hank-clock," which monitored their looms.

Vigilante violence during the walkout exceeded even the southern norm, and after a few weeks, mill owners crushed the strike and evicted participants from company housing, forcing them to live in a tent colony. The strike would have been forgotten except for two subsequent incidents. In the first of these two events, Gastonia police chief Orville Aderholt was killed in a shootout. Thirteen male and three female Communist organizers eventually faced trial, and a number of them fled to the Soviet Union (when out on a bail) after having received long sentences in a blatantly unfair trial. Also, after the walkout's conclusion, Ella May Wiggins, "the minstrel of the strike," was gunned down, though no one ever faced a trial for the cold-blooded murder. Ella May had borne eight children, four of whom had died, and her "Mill Mother's Lament" and many of her other ballads spoke of the travails and hardships of southern female textile workers. The two shootings and Communist involvement led numerous authors, including Mary Heaton Vorse and Sherwood Anderson, to write novels about the strike, but the Communist Party had failed in its effort to establish a beachhead in the South and conditions in the Loray Mill remained essentially unchanged.

Violence also focused national attention on the Marion strike. In this small town, 2,000 employees at the Clinchfield and Baldwin cotton mills walked out in July 1929, protesting the stretch-out, unsanitary working conditions, and excessive charges at the company store. The UTW became involved and, despite an injunction, evictions from company housing, and deployment of the National Guard, they won a reduction in the workweek from sixty hours to fifty-five hours, but with no increase in pay to make up for the lost time. When workers returned, they discovered that many strikers had been blacklisted and they began another walkout, during which sheriff's deputies killed six strikers, shooting them in the back. The shootings ended the UTW's organizing campaign in Marion.

Groundwork for the Danville walkout had begun at the 1929 AFL convention, which encouraged the UTW to focus more of its efforts on the southern textile industry. The UTW decided to pinpoint the Dan River and Riverside cotton mills, which employed more than 4,000 workers producing ginghams and cotton cloth, the largest such complex in the South. The Danville mills had earned a reputation for enlightened management and had instituted many welfare capitalist programs. But with the onset of the Depression, the company had cut its employees' wages by 10 percent.

The UTW-led walkout began in September 1930 and the UTW's chief organizer, Francis Gorman, worked closely with Matilda Lindsey of the Women's Trade Union League in coordinating the strike. Partly because many local residents disliked the mill's owner, workers received considerable community assistance, including support from the local chapter of the Ku Klux Klan. But inadequate aid from the national UTW and the usual combination of injunctions and the militia drove workers back to the mills and doomed one of the UTW's most concerted efforts to organize in the South, a region many veteran textile unionists considered a "foreign land."

The Last Mass Strike

The only victories in 1929 and 1930 were won by workers in South Carolina mill villages, who utilized a "homegrown" strategy in winning some modification of the stretch-out. Of course, once the full force of the Great Depression began to be felt, it became almost impossible for workers to consider striking, though some Lawrence employees under Communist Party leadership conducted a forlorn walkout in 1931. But the election of Franklin Roosevelt and the passage of the National Industrial Recovery Act (NIRA) in 1933 aroused new hopes among textile workers.

The NIRA promised a real New Deal for textile workers, especially those who labored in the southern cotton textile industry. The Cotton Textile Code established a $12 weekly minimum in the South ($13 in the North), along with the forty-hour week and the prohibition of child labor. Section 7(a) also guaranteed workers the right to join labor unions and to engage in collective bargaining. Spurred on by this provision, thousands of southern textile workers rushed to enroll in the UTW, though the union was not prepared for the onslaught of new members.

Southern textile mills sought to evade the code provisions. They began to cut workers' hours, curtail production, and, most seriously, increase the stretch-out to force more work out of their employees. Complaints began to pour into the Cotton Textile Code Authority, which lacked the means and the will to act on them.

Northern Alabama textile workers took the initiative in staging walkouts demanding that the new federal law be enforced. Spurred on by these workers and by spreading discontent in the North and the South, a special UTW convention in July 1934 voted to authorize a general cotton textile strike to begin on September 1, and granted authorization to woolen, silk, and other textile workers to stage their own walkouts. On that date, 350,000 mill employees refused to work and began the most extensive strike ever in the United States.

Despite the impressive numbers, support for the walkout varied from locality to locality. Nevertheless, the 1934 strike stands out as unique in the history of textile strikes in the number of workers and localities involved. From a national perspective, it illustrated that the New Deal had raised expectations and that workers now demanded the federal government live up to commitments it had made in adopting the National Industrial Recovery Act.

The UTW demanded weekly rates of $13–14 (depending on the job), the elimination of the stretch-out, union recognition, and that employers not discriminate against participants. In an effort to convince workers to leave the mills, union supporters made use of flying squadrons that went from mill to mill in states as far flung as Rhode Island and Georgia. UTW vice president Francis Gorman, who took charge of the walkout, also made effective use of the radio in urging textile workers to join the strike. Due to the success of these tactics and workers' anger at the manufacturers' defiance of the federal government, the strike received strong support in southern mill centers such as Charlotte, Columbia, and Spartanburg, South Carolina; Dalton, Georgia; and Huntsville, Alabama. But workers in some other communities opposed the strike and resented efforts by the flying squadrons and pickets to keep them from reporting to work.

Fourteen workers lost their lives during the two-week work stoppage. In the most serious incident, special deputies killed six workers who had been on strike at the Chiquola Mills in the tiny town of Honea Path, South Carolina. In North Carolina and South Carolina, governors declared martial law and called out the National Guard. In Georgia, Governor Eugene Talmadge waited until he had defeated his opponent in a hotly contested primary election before using the state militia to suppress the strike.

Northern textile workers in communities such as Sacco and Biddeford, Maine, and Hazelton, Pennsylvania, displayed considerable militancy during the walkout. Rhode Island, though, became the focal point of the strike in the North. Use of flying squadrons led to numerous confrontations with police and clashes between strikers and nonstrikers in Saylesville and throughout the Blackstone Valley. Rioting workers looted and destroyed property in downtown Woonsocket. In both Rhode Island and Maine, governors called out the National Guard. Wherever it occurred, the violence indicated that the national UTW leadership lacked control over workers in a walkout that, despite appearances, should not be thought of as a coordinated national event. In part, the walkout also clearly reflected frustrations and anger among workers that had been building up ever since the Great Depression began and that also made 1934 a memorable year due to general strikes in Toledo, Minneapolis, and San Francisco.

By the end of the second week of the strike, employers, especially in the South, regained control of the situation, and the UTW became overwhelmed by the scale of a walkout, which it could not manage. Searching for a way out, the union hoped that a Special Board of Inquiry for the Cotton Textile Industry (known as the Winant Board) appointed by President Roosevelt on September 5 would offer recommendations favorable to textile workers. But on September 20, the board offered only vague promises of improvements in the future. Nevertheless, the UTW, welcoming the recommendations, called off the strike and declared it one of the most significant victories in the annals of the A. F. of L. Gorman's grandiose language did not fool workers who knew the strike had failed. The defeat had long-term implications. Historians Janet Irons and John A. Salmond have emphasized that southern textile workers never forgot the 1934 debacle and the UTW's abandonment of them. After 1934, these memories proved a formidable obstacle whenever northern-based organizers tried to convince southern workers to join textile unions. In addition, Salmond has interpreted the 1934 walkout as a "last stand" of northern textile workers whose militancy would be sapped by the continuing decline of the industry.

New Tactics, Same Results

The year 1934 marked the last time a mass strike occurred in the textile industry. Most notably, textiles did not experience the wave of strikes that affected practically all of America's mass production industries between 1935 and 1941. In 1937, supporters of the CIO formed the Textile Workers' Organizing Committee (TWOC) and this organization conducted some successful walkouts in August 1937 in silk and rayon plants in the Northeast, including a sitdown strike at the Apex Hosiery Company in Philadelphia. In 1939, the UTW and the TWOC joined together to form the Textile Workers Union of America, which was affiliated with the CIO, but the new union lost a bitter eighteen-week strike at the Crown Mill in Dalton, Georgia, and on the eve of World War II, only about 5 percent of the South's 100,000 cotton textile workers were covered by union contracts, a marked contrast to developments in the northern automobile, steel, electrical, and meatpacking industries.

During World War II, no major walkouts occurred in the textile industry. Almost immediately upon the end of hostilities, the CIO, with much ballyhoo, launched Operation Dixie, an all-out effort to bring unionization to the South. Textiles represented the CIO's principal southern target, especially since the north/south wage differential in cotton textiles limited the TWUA's ability to win higher wages and benefits for the northern textile workers it now represented. But despite pouring considerable resources into the effort, Operation Dixie did not lead to any major gains for textile unionization in the South.

A disastrous 1951 strike that centered on the huge Dan River Mills did more damage to the cause of southern textile unionism than the failure of Operation Dixie. According to historian Timothy J. Minchin, the TWUA pushed the walkout as part of an effort to bring the southern mills, where it had signed contracts, up to the standards of the North. Along with requesting a wage increase and cost-of-living escalator clause, the union sought employer-paid pensions, a minimum of eight paid holidays per year, and a company-paid medical insurance plan—the kinds of benefits that unionized automobile and steel workers had been winning in their contracts.

The strike began on April 1, 1951, in the midst of the Korean War, and involved 45,000 southern workers employed at plants that the TWUA had under contract. Dan River, the largest textile mill in the world, was by far the most important of these mills and had served as a model of the gains the TWUA had hoped to win for workers in the South. But the company surprised the union by their determined resistance to the demands and by their use of strikebreakers. In addition, workers who had taken out loans on their homes, cars, televisions, and home appliances feared risking all they had gained in the prosperous post–World War II era. On May 5, 1951, the union called off the strike in the hope that a government panel would grant some of their demands. The union's disguised surrender resembled the 1934 events and the dismal outcome destroyed all hope that Dan River could be a pattern-setter for contracts in the South. The strike left the TWUA in a far weaker position in the region.

After the Korean War, the northern textile industry practically disappeared, as more and more manufacturers either shut down their operations or moved to the South. In the 1960s, the TWUA launched a new southern campaign that focused on the mills operated by J.P. Stevens, the South's second-largest producer of textile products. Having realized that a mass walkout could not be effective against Stevens, the TWUA complemented a massive organizing drive directed at the company with a "corporate campaign" seeking to expose the corporation's defiance of the National Labor Relations Board and failure to correct conditions causing byssinosis (brown lung disease). Rather than relying on a strike or a threat of a strike, the union also organized a nationwide boycott of the company's products.

To aid the effort to organize Stevens, in 1976 the TWUA merged with the ACWA to form the Amalgamated Clothing and Textile Workers Union (ACTWU). In 1980, ACTWU ended the campaign against Stevens after winning a contract that contained some very limited gains for workers. But by the 1980s, the South faced intensified competition from overseas manufacturers, and it became even more difficult for organizers to consider using the strike as a weapon. In the 1990s, plant after plant closed as southern workers became victims of the same process that had cost northern workers their jobs.

In retrospect, mass strikes took place only in the first third of the twentieth century. By the mid-1930s, workers and unions had become leery of using this tactic, since they knew they had little chance of winning victories. Certainly, many sectoral strikes occurred throughout the twentieth century, but these rarely reached beyond a single craft or department. Strikes had won some gains for employees, but workers in the textile industry faced formidable barriers they could rarely overcome.

See also: North Carolina Women on Strike, 154; Strikes in the Nineteenth-Century Cotton Textile Industry in the Northeast United States, 314.

Bibliography

Cameron, Ardis. *Radicals of the Worst Sort: Laboring Women in Lawrence, Massachusetts, 1860–1912.* Urbana: University of Illinois Press, 1993.

Dubofksy, Melvyn. *We Shall Be All: A History of the Industrial Workers of the World.* Chicago: Quadrangle, 1969.

Georgianna, Daniel, with Roberta Hazen Aronson. *The Strike of '28.* New Bedford, CT: Spinner, 1993.

Goldberg, David J. *A Tale of Three Cities: Labor Organization and Protest in Paterson, Passaic and Lawrence, 1916–1921.* New Brunswick, NJ: Rutgers University Press, 1989.

Golin, Steve. *The Fragile Bridge: Paterson Silk Strike, 1913.* Philadelphia: Temple University Press, 1988.

Hall, Jacquelyn Dowd, et al. *Like a Family: The Making of a Southern Cotton Mill World.* Chapel Hill: University of North Carolina Press, 1987.

Hareven, Tamara K. *Family Time and Industrial Time:*

The Relationship Between the Family and Work in a New England Industrial Community. New York: Cambridge University Press, 1982.

Irons, Janet. *Testing the New Deal: The General Textile Strike of 1934 in the American South*. Urbana: University of Illinois Press, 2000.

Minchin, Timothy J. *"Don't Sleep with Stevens!" The J.P. Stevens Campaign and the Struggle to Organize the South*. Gainesville: University Press of Florida, 2005.

———. *What Do We Need a Union For? The TWUA in the South, 1945–1955*. Chapel Hill: University of North Carolina Press, 1997.

Salmond, John A. *Gastonia 1929: The Story of the Loray Mill Strike*. Chapel Hill: University of North Carolina Press, 1995.

———. *The General Textile Strike of 1934: From Maine to Alabama*. Columbia: University of Missouri Press, 2002.

Watson, Bruce. *Bread and Roses: Mills, Migrants and the Struggle for the American Dream*. New York: Viking, 2005.

GARMENT WORKER STRIKES

Paul Le Blanc

Founded in 1900, the International Ladies Garment Workers Union (ILGWU) was one of the most radical and colorful labor organizations in the early decades of the twentieth century. Major strikes of the union had a profound impact that went well beyond its own multiethnic membership. Especially important in the union's founding and evolution were dedicated socialists and anarchists who articulated a vision of a better world to be achieved through the collective struggle of workers against their own oppression. Nonetheless, the ILGWU's trajectory (and that of the U.S. labor movement in the twentieth century) took it in a far less radical direction, a story reflected in the strikes conducted by the union in New York City, the center of its power.

Industry and Union

At the time of the union's founding, much of the work in the garment industry was done in the home, with contractors providing raw materials to and gathering finished products from workers laboring in small, poorly lit, and poorly ventilated apartments in the tenement buildings of urban slums. Increasingly, however, the work was done in small garment shops set up by ambitious entrepreneurs who had contracts with larger manufacturers to produce clothing goods. The small shops required a relatively small outlay of capital. Space could be rented in tenement buildings and apartments converted into miniature factories. Sewing machines were cheap and could be bought on an installment plan or even rented, and they were small enough to be easily installed in the room of a tenement house. Immigrants who were flooding into the cities served as a source of cheap labor. Contractors found them through makeshift labor exchanges. Their foot movements powered the sewing machines.

The survival of employers often depended on paying the garment workers in these cramped and unsanitary "sweatshops" as little as possible (ranging from $3.00 to $12.00 per week); making them work as long and intensively as possible (generally eighty-four hours per week); and compelling them to buy or rent their own machines, supply their own needles and thread, and even pay a fee for the privilege of securing a job in the shop. The larger manufacturers played these "sweatshop" contractors off against each other. They used the inferior pay and conditions of the sweatshop workers to erode wages and conditions and increase the hours of work prevailing in the industry (which tended to fluctuate around sixty hours per week).

The garment industry has historically been marked by instability, mobility, and volatility. In addition to dramatic market fluctuations that come with the fickleness of fashion, this labor-intensive industry with relatively light capital outlays generates cutthroat competitiveness among entrepreneurs, many of whom are often on the edge of bankruptcy. Under such conditions, employers almost always seek to increase profit margins by subjecting their workers to intensified exploitation and innumerable indignities.

The ILGWU embraced all workers in the women's garment industry, regardless of specific occupation or skill level, organizing on an industrial rather than craft basis. The workforce was largely immigrant, increasingly shifting after 1880 from Irish and German to East European Jewish, as well as Italian, Bohemian, Polish, Russian, Syrian, and others. The female composition of the work-

To identify themselves and win support, these striking cloakmakers dressed well, wore union pins, and carried American flags. The quote on the picket sign is from Jacob H. Schiff, a very wealthy banker who supported labor-management harmony, Jewish organizations, and liberal causes. (*Courtesy:* George Grantham Bain Collection, Library of Congress.)

force was large, although increasing numbers of men and many children also found employment in this industry.

The occupational structure in the women's garment industry of this period was complex. There were cloakmakers, dressmakers, waistmakers, hatmakers, those making underwear, knit-goods workers, those engaged in embroidery, and more. The four basic occupational divisions that came to dominate the industry were seen as constituting four basic crafts. The cloakmakers made outerwear such as overcoats and capes (requiring somewhat greater skill than other clothing). This workforce was predominantly male and tended to be among the most volatile, radical, and militant of the workers in the industry. The cutters, also predominantly male, were the most highly paid and highly skilled, with a reputation for being the practical-minded elite of the industry's labor force. A significant number of cutters were native-born Americans or Americanized Irishmen, Germans, and Jews. The pressers were especially muscular, owing to the strength needed to handle the heavy irons used to press the various garments, and they were commonly seen as being interested in more down-to-earth matters. The great majority of women workers in the industry were concentrated among the dressmakers. Many viewed them as the most idealistic and radical element in the workforce.

The earliest unionizing efforts among "modern" garment workers were loosely affiliated with the Knights of Labor in the 1880s, but these hit-or-miss organizational efforts did not yield any permanent organization. The United Garment Workers, an affiliate of the American Federation of Labor (AFL), was a relatively conservative and, in many areas, corrupt organization, focusing mainly on skilled workers such as tailors and cutters. By the end of the 1880s, clusters of socialist and anarchist activists were forming cadres that would lead to a broader and more sustained effort to "educate, agitate, and organize" around the trade union idea. A number of militant strikes and vibrant local unions resulted, particularly among the cloakmakers.

From the beginning, the ILGWU represented a curious blend of conservatism and radicalism, reflected in different ways in all of its leaders. Among its earliest leaders were Secretary-Treasurer John A. Dyche, a former socialist favoring "pure and simple" unionism and known as "the Jewish Gompers," and the ideologically compatible Abraham Rosenberg, who served as president from 1907 to 1914. They were challenged not only by the left wing in their own union but also by insurgents from the rival Industrial Workers of the World (IWW), led from 1905 to 1907 by Morris Sigman, who subsequently rejoined the ILGWU, becoming its secretary-treasurer in 1914 and serving as a relatively conservative president in 1923. Benjamin Schlesinger, prominent first in the Socialist Labor Party and then the Socialist Party of America, served as the union's president in 1903–4, 1914–23, and 1928–32.

Schlesinger helped facilitate a transition to the leadership of a young Socialist trade unionist named David Dubinsky who, while championing industrial unionism (in helping to launch the Congress of Industrial Organizations in the 1930s), also embraced the Democratic Party, maintaining little more than a nostalgic attachment to shreds of Socialist rhetoric.

The ILGWU became a force to be reckoned with in the garment industry through audacious, militant, hard-fought strikes in its earlier years. The nature of the garment industry—in which larger and more substantial manufacturers were supplemented by smaller sweatshops whose low wages and abysmal working conditions naturally undermined the conditions of all workers—made the union's initial gains difficult to sustain and also led to explosive struggles, including the "rising of the 20,000" in 1909 and "the great revolt" of 1910.

Rising and Revolt

An accumulation of grievances—cuts in wages and piece rates, charging workers for supplies needed in producing garments, subcontracting—generated a crescendo of protests, strikes, and lockouts in 1909. On November 22, Samuel Gompers, president of the American Federation of Labor, joined with Socialist lawyer Meyer London, Mary Drier of the Women's Trade Union League, and other prominent speakers to address a protest meeting of 3,000 shirtwaistmakers at New York City's Cooper Union. Exasperated with the overabundance of words, a young radical worker named Clara Lemlich, as quoted by historian Philip Foner, challenged the assembly: "I have listened to all the speakers, and I have no further patience for talk. I am one who feels and suffers from the things pictured. I move we go on a general strike!" The electrified crowd voted to strike and raised their hands in the Hebrew oath: "If I turn traitor to the cause I now pledge, may this hand wither from the arm I now raise."

The demands included a union shop, a fifty-two-hour workweek, limitations on forced overtime, a uniform price scale for piecework, the elimination of unfair penalties, no additional charges for equipment and materials, and the end of the subcontracting system.

The ILGWU could count on the support of the AFL as well as the Socialist Party, the Women's Trade Union League, and an impressive array of social reformers, feminists, and intellectuals. There were also many who denounced the strike, and hired thugs along with unsympathetic police introduced the element of violence and intimidation. The strikers held firm. The newly formed employers association was finally prepared to accept many of the union's demands (bargaining with the union's all-male negotiating team), but not the union shop or the elimination of nonunion subcontractors. The breakdown of negotiations with the employers' association and the erosion of AFL support caused the ILGWU leadership to end the strike in February 1910. Only weak contracts could be signed with individual shops, but 339 of the 353 firms belonging to the employers' association signed union contracts.

While many of the problems that generated the strike remained unresolved, there was now an upsurge in ILGWU membership and a new vitality in the union. Out of this struggle, a number of female figures became prominently visible (if not necessarily powerful) in the ILGWU: in addition to Clara Lemlich, among the best known were Pauline Newman, Rose Schneiderman, and Fannia Cohn. In this struggle and the strike to follow, a number of men also distinguished themselves. One of these was the former IWW dissident and tough-minded street fighter, Morris Sigman, whose later conservatism never prevented him from maintaining a powerful base of support especially among anarchist currents within the ILGWU.

The struggle was resumed, with less spontaneity and more careful organization, with the "great revolt" of the cloakmakers on July 7, 1910. Here, men were in the forefront, and the ranks of the strikers swelled to 60,000. "Many of our devoted workers wept tears of joy seeing their long years of work and sacrifice crowned with success," recalled ILGWU president Abraham Rosenberg, according to historian Irving Howe. "To me it seemed that such a spectacle had happened before only when the Jews were led out of Egypt. . . ." Union ranks soared from about 20,000 to almost 75,000.

Establishing a forty-hour workweek, hiking the minimum wage, ending charges for equipment and materials, eliminating the subcontracting system, and employing only union members were among the demands. It was a solid and massively effective strike, with scores of newly trained union cadres mobilizing thousands of workplace shutdowns, pickets, rallies, and mass meetings, and it won widespread community support.

While more than 300 smaller manufacturers caved in, the larger firms in the Cloak, Suit, and Skirt Manufacturers' Protective Association held firm. They mobilized their considerable resources to win court injunctions and mass arrests of workers. "We offer no apology for the general strike," proclaimed Socialist orator Meyer London, who was also a union lawyer and negotiator. "If at all we should apologize to the tens of thousands of the exploited men and women for not having aroused them before." As Leon Stein recounts, he added: "This general strike is greater than any union. It is an irresistible movement of the people. It is a protest against conditions that can no longer be tolerated."

Upper-class progressives intervened in order to mediate the conflict, foremost among them the future Supreme Court Justice Louis D. Brandeis, who enjoyed a significant degree of confidence from both sides. Largely through his efforts, a "Protocol of Peace" was negotiated that brought an end to the strike on September 2.

Replacing Strikes?

There were immediate and longer-range components of the Protocol, which, as the name implied, sought to eliminate strikes from garment industry labor relations. Employers agreed to a fifty-hour workweek, ten paid legal holidays, payment of time and a half for overtime, an increased minimum wage, mechanisms to oversee prices for piecework, and the abolition of inside contracting. They also accepted a union shop, with some restrictions. The Protocol established the Union Health Center, which provided health care to union members who could not afford to buy it individually.

The longer-range components of the Protocol involved the establishment of three new institutions. A Joint Board of Sanitary Control, with representatives of union and industry, was to wipe out the remnants of the sweatshop by seeing that shops established a sanitary work environment. A Board of Grievances, also with representatives of both sides, "replaces the strike," as ILGWU secretary-treasurer John Dyche put it bluntly, according to Stein. All disputes that it could not resolve would be passed on to the third institution—the Board of Arbitration, chaired by Brandeis and made up of representatives of the "public" who were accepted by both sides.

As Stein notes, according to Brandeis, "It was the purpose of the Protocol to introduce into the relations of the employer and the employee a whole new element; that is the element of industrial democracy." By this, however, he did not mean the socialist notion of "rule by the people" over the industries, but instead "a joint control" of industry by the employers' association (representing the handful of wealthy owners) and the union (speaking in the name of the masses of workers), functioning as equal partners, and "with joint control a joint responsibility for the conduct of the industry." This would eliminate those conditions "which prevented the employers and the employee alike from attaining that satisfactory living within the industry which it must be the aim of all effort in business to secure." A comment by Samuel Gompers that future wage increases would come as "adjustments on a scientific basis" suggested that there would be a common union–employer interest in the productivity and profitability of the garment industry.

While the Protocol brought great public acclaim and some obvious improvements for the workers, it did not directly address a myriad of problems and tensions that continued to divide workers and bosses, despite all the "industrial democracy" and "social harmony" rhetoric. It also contained profound ambiguities—especially for the more militant trade unionists, socialists, and anarchists in the union's ranks who dominated the powerful Cloakmakers' Joint Board in New York City. Many grievances began to pile up, and not everything could be arbitrated quickly or, from the workers' standpoint, appropriately. Powerful ILGWU leader John Dyche was a devoted supporter of the Protocol and fully prepared to help enforce Protocol provisions designed to control the union ranks. In the name of supporting the Protocol, he would help to break up strikes of union members rendered illegal by the agreement.

The Joint Board brought in from Chicago the practical-minded but principled radical Abraham Bisno to head its dealings with employers. Bisno's efforts to interpret the Protocol in ways that would enhance the position and power of the workers soon ran into dogged opposition from both the employers' association and ILGWU president Dyche. He was soon replaced by Dr. Isaac Hourwich, a highly respected academic long associated with the union, whose socialism was widely known to be of the most moderate variety. Yet Hourwich also generated antagonism from the employers and from some sectors in the union as he insisted on his own authority to interpret and redesign the Protocol on a more rational and equitable basis. Hourwich finally went the way of Bisno.

In 1911, a disaster hit the Triangle Shirtwaist Company that had been one of the focal points of the 1909 "uprising." Unsafe conditions had persisted, resulting in workers being trapped (and many leaping to their deaths) when a fire broke out—the death toll was 146 women and men. "I can't talk fellowship to you who are gathered here," said Rose Schneiderman at a memorial meeting, according to Foner. "Too much blood has been spilled." She spoke the feelings of many workers as she added: "I know from my experience it is up to the working people to save themselves. The only way they can save themselves is by a strong working-class movement." There was no mention of the Protocol here, and a rising tide of anger, frustration, and militancy ultimately culminated in the 1914 replacement of Rosenberg and Dyche with Socialist Benjamin Schlesinger as president and militant strike leader Morris Sigman as secretary-treasurer.

Despite the dramatic role of women in the militant struggles of the ILGWU, however, the central leadership of the organization continued to be male. And despite the militancy of the union's traditions and rhetoric, what some militants called the conciliatory "class-collaborationist" approach reflected in the Protocol of Peace remained dominant in ILGWU policies.

Communists vs. Anti-Communists

Not everyone in the ILGWU was inclined to embrace the underlying philosophy of the Protocol. Many garment workers were drawn to the revolutionary idealism reflected in the Russian Revolution of 1917, identifying with Soviet Russia's "Workers' Republic" of Lenin and Trotsky. When a unified Communist Party was established in the United States in 1921, after ragged splits in the Socialist Party, a number of the more radical garment workers and ILGWU members could be found among the Communist ranks. Even more joined the left-wing Trade Union Educational League (TUEL), which from 1921 to 1923 began to play a significant radicalizing role in many affiliates of the AFL. A flare-up of Communist Party sectarianism in 1923–24, however, turned many one-time allies against it, facilitating an alliance of conservative, "progressive," and moderate-Socialist forces whose intention was to suppress the TUEL and destroy the radical influence of the Communists and their allies in the AFL.

Within the ILGWU, however, the Communists maintained a powerful following, building an influential left-wing caucus led by Louis Hyman, Joseph Boruchowitz, and Charles (Sasha) Zimmerman, and including popular female militants such as Rose Wortis and Sylvia Bleeker. By 1925, the left-wing caucus had won control of the influential New York Joint Board. The left wing represented a sharp divergence from the "Protocol of Peace" orientation, launching a campaign to organize more workers and to press forward struggles to secure greater power and benefits for workers throughout the garment industry. At least initially, however, employer resistance to what were seen as entirely legitimate worker demands (for better pay and conditions, and more secure employment) generated a broad consensus within the ILGWU and the larger labor movement in favor of a cloakmakers' strike, which was called on July 1, 1926, with 40,000 workers walking off the job.

The left-wing leadership of the New York Joint Board initially had broad support as it organized mass picketing, with as many as 20,000 picketers standing up to thugs and police. By mid-September, employers were able to secure injunctions against picketing, but strikers violated the injunctions. Despite 600 arrests per day, the ILGWU strike endured, with substantial material support coming from other unions. Early on, the smaller manufacturers had given way—but the three strongest employers held tough. For many years after, there was controversy among historians regarding what happened next. Anti-

Communist critics argue that there were several opportunities to settle the strike on terms relatively favorable to the workers as early as September, but that thanks to Communist Party influence these were squandered by the left-wing leadership. Some have suggested that it was in part a competition to occupy the militant "high ground" within the Communist Party between rival leaders Jay Lovestone and William Z. Foster that dragged the strike out for six long months—neither side wanting to be accused of sanctioning too much moderation in the class struggle. In addition, it was alleged that there was significant mismanagement of strike funds.

Communists such as William Z. Foster responded with accusations of their own against "the socialist leaders" who were alleged to be "unscrupulous in their strike-breaking tactics" and "sabotaged the collection of strike funds, spread defeatism among the strikers, . . . used their official positions generally to paralyze the strike, . . . informed the bosses of the union's plans and exposed the workers' weaknesses," and so on.

By December the national leadership of the ILGWU, backed by a broad conservative–socialist alliance, moved against a left-wing strike leadership whose base of support was dramatically eroding. By January 1927, leadership of the strike had been taken over by the national ILGWU, and the dispute was settled on highly compromised terms. At the same time, union President Morris Sigman launched a far-reaching and in some ways damaging campaign to purge Communists from the organization. A year later, when Benjamin Schlesinger returned to the presidency of the ILGWU, an effort was made to moderate the left/right conflict in the union, but by that time the Communist Party had made a decision to abandon the ILGWU and other AFL organizations in order to establish a rival, ill-fated Trade Union Unity League. This wiped out any significant Communist Party influence in the ILGWU. Angry Communist militants would sing songs such as:

> The Cloakmakers Union is a no-good union,
> It's a company union by the bosses.
> The right-wing cloakmakers
> And the Socialist fakers
> Are making by the workers double-crosses.

As Irving Howe has recounted, Morris Hillquit, the grand old man of Jewish-American socialism and a longtime attorney for the union, commented on the erosion of the radicalism that had animated the early ILGWU. "In the years of spiritual indifference that had taken hold of the whole country and all movements [in the 1920s], your union . . . began to conduct itself too much as a business enterprise," he warned at the 1928 ILGWU convention. "There was not enough soul in it." The union's formidable bureaucratic machine was led by men who, according to Howe, "sometimes found themselves using methods and making alliances within the unions that they would have felt ashamed of a few years earlier. . . . Many had been badly shaken by the years of poisonous factionalism, shaken out of complacence but also out of idealism. . . . Some grew bitter, others cynical. A rigid anti-Communism became a reigning passion."

Bitter divisions among the organized garment workers, as well as the disappointed hopes and failed struggles of 1926, were not the only problems facing the ILGWU. There was a general anti-union onslaught by the employers in the conservative political atmosphere of the 1920s, which broke many labor organizations and certainly took a terrible toll on the membership of the ILGWU. The union's numbers collapsed from 120,000 members in the early 1920s to about 32,000 by 1929. The fact that the charismatic Sasha Zimmerman and others associated with Jay Lovestone split with the Communist Party mainstream in 1929 and returned to ILGWU ranks in 1931, while not insignificant, was in itself hardly enough to repair the damage. Communist Party garment workers later filtered back into the union, maintaining some influence among ILGWU dissidents before becoming entirely marginalized through negative reactions of many Jewish workers to the 1939 Nazi–Soviet Pact.

As Schlesinger and his supporters labored to rebuild the shattered union, they blended elements of the old Protocol of Peace with elements of "class struggle." In a 1929 report quoted by Stein, Schlesinger explained his strategy as involving an effort "to stabilize the industry" by seeking "to control and guard the conditions of all the workers in all the shops" while at the same time helping employers to rationalize business practices, working to "enlist the cooperation of reputable retailers in the effort to eliminate substandard shops which are detrimental to the industry." At the same time, "it required a general strike of the 30,000 cloakmakers of New York [in 1928] to convince the employers that we were alive again. . . . It was a short strike, two weeks only, but it was productive of results." As his lieutenant David Dubinsky commented, "It was the shortest general strike in the history of the union," but it "revived the spirit of the workers" while securing agreement from the employers to enter into the cooperative relationship outlined by Schlesinger.

The Turbulent Thirties

With Schlesinger's death in 1932, leadership of the ILGWU passed to Dubinsky, who headed the organization for thirty-four years. The new president faced an immense challenge as the Great Depression stimulated a new antiunion offensive on the part of those employers not driven out of business. Among workers, hard times generated contradictory waves of fear-induced submissiveness toward remaining employers and combative anger toward a seemingly failed capitalism. While by no means abandoning his earlier moderation, Dubinsky drew on his union's tradition of working-class militancy through a series of organizing drives and strikes that resulted in dramatic growth in ILGWU membership.

As it grew, a serious problem that the union had to address involved the influence of gangsterism both in the garment industry and in some ILGWU locals. The most dramatic flare-up of the problem had occurred during the 1926 strike, when employers utilized the Legs Diamond mob and elements in the union counterattacked by employing the mob of "Little Augie" (Jacob Orgen), both controlled by mobster kingpin Arnold Rothstein. The notorious "Murder Incorporated," run by Louis Lepke and Jake Gurrah, maintained a foothold in some ILGWU locals until the mid-1930s, when their influence was broken through the concerted efforts of Dubinsky, Zimmerman, and others.

A key aspect of the struggle to build the ILGWU involved counteracting efforts by employers to move increasing segments of the garment industry outside of New York City to smaller cities and towns in New York State and nearby regions. This was dramatically demonstrated on August 16, 1933, by a strike of 60,000 dressmakers from both union and nonunion shops embracing not only New York City but also the out-of-town area stretching from Camden, New Jersey, to New Haven, Connecticut. Employer resistance collapsed almost immediately.

New layers among garment workers were drawn into the union, including a substantial number of Italian Americans in Luigi Antonini's dressmakers' Local 89, which became the largest local in the union, and significant numbers of African Americans and Puerto Ricans, particularly in Zimmerman's militant dressmakers' Local 22. In the same year, new locals were established and old ones revived in many cities, with successful strikes in Philadelphia, Chicago, Los Angeles, Boston, and elsewhere consolidating the union's power and membership. By 1934, the ILGWU's ranks had swelled to 200,000, making it the largest affiliate of the AFL. It was 300,000 strong by the end of the Depression decade.

In 1935, the ILGWU joined with the United Mine Workers of America (led by John L. Lewis), the Amalgamated Clothing Workers of America (led by Sidney Hillman), and several other AFL affiliates to launch a Committee for Industrial Organization (CIO). They were determined to challenge the AFL leadership's bureaucratic-conservative adherence to craft unionism and disinclination to organize industrial unions among increasingly militant semiskilled and unskilled mass production workers. ILGWU resources and support contributed mightily to organizing drives and strike waves that brought millions of industrial workers into vibrant new unions of the CIO.

The industrial conflicts and the growth of union power were best represented by a remarkable 1937 musical comedy, *Pins and Needles*, composed by Harold J. Rome, Arthur Arent, Marc Blitzstein, and others. Partly financed by the ILGWU, an exuberant cast of dressmakers, cloakmakers, and others from the shops sang, danced, and joked their way into a theatrical hit that ran for three and a half years. A 1938 command performance for Franklin and Eleanor Roosevelt in the White House (at which the president "roared with laughter" as a high-society matron insisted that "It's Not Cricket to Picket" in the face of the buoyant militancy of "Picket-line Priscilla") reflected the extent to which the strike actions of

ILGWU members had inserted themselves deeply into the popular culture.

President Roosevelt's pro-ILGWU sympathies were by no means of recent vintage. As governor of New York during the union's difficult days in the late 1920s, he had used his influence to pressure garment manufacturers to sign contracts with the ILGWU, and his lieutenant-governor, Herbert Lehman, had joined three prominent bankers in lending the union $100,000. The rationale for these patrician-capitalists' coming to the aid of organized labor was rooted in their concern to help secure stability in the garment industry that was so important for New York's economic health—an idea at the core of the old Protocol of Peace.

Indeed, the spirit of the Protocol of Peace persisted in the attitude of Dubinsky and other labor leaders during the 1930s. It can be found in such legislation as the National Labor Relations Act (NLRA) of 1935, which placed the authority of the U.S. government behind guarantees of union recognition by employers, compelled union enforcement of workers' contractual obligations and industrial peace, and inserted the government as central arbiter representing the interests of the "public." Dubinsky himself resigned from the Socialist Party in order to work for the election of Franklin D. Roosevelt and other Democrats, and the ILGWU became a pillar of support for Roosevelt's New Deal. Almost the entire labor movement of the 1930s—both the AFL and CIO—moved into the Roosevelt camp, viewing the Democratic Party (with its reform-capitalist program) as the U.S. alternative to the socialist-oriented labor parties that had developed in most industrialized countries.

Similar electoral orientations of the AFL and CIO and the growing acceptance of industrial unionism by the AFL leadership did little to ease the intense rivalry that was termed "labor's civil war." Even though the AFL had moved to expel CIO dissidents, Dubinsky and other ILGWU leaders argued that eventually the AFL and CIO should reunite. In 1938, the union's leadership balked when John L. Lewis led the CIO majority onto a path of sharpened organizational rivalry. In reaction to this, and also because of discomfort over the important role and influence of Communists in some of the CIO unions, Dubinsky led his union out of the CIO—and in 1940 back into the AFL.

Years of Moderation

In the 1940s, foreign policy dramatically shaped the ILGWU. In 1941, when the United States entered World War II, Dubinsky joined with other leaders of the AFL and CIO in supporting the war effort and agreeing to a "no-strike pledge" for the duration of the conflict. The far-reaching alliance of business, labor, and government on the home front was reminiscent of the old Protocol of Peace. This approach continued, to a significant degree, as the Cold War crystallized around the capitalist–Communist confrontation between the United States and the Soviet Union. The ILGWU became a pillar of American anti-Communist foreign policy. While Dubinsky and his union identified with an expansive social liberalism, the former Socialist now insisted, according to Sidney Lens, that "trade unionism needs capitalism like a fish needs water."

In the spirit of the Protocol, while unions were accepted under the modified structure of the NLRA, the ILGWU (and its sister organizations in the AFL-CIO, reunified in 1955) would work to safeguard the profit margins and productivity of the employers, with workers' wage increases and other benefits "scientifically" linked to the success of the capitalist enterprise. A working-class commitment to a regulated capitalist economy—a capitalist "welfare state" initiated in the 1930s and destined to endure through the 1970s—that would provide decent living standards with extensive health and social services led naturally to diminishing militancy and strikes. While there were still some strikes, the old period of "industrial conflict" had seemed to give way, at long last, to a new era of durable "industrial maturity." In addition, the ILGWU provided numerous benefits for its rank and file, such as ambitious educational and cultural activities, low-income housing projects for members in New York City, a generous scholarship program for members' children to go to colleges and universities, a vacation resort (Camp Unity) in the Poconos, union-administered retirement, health and welfare programs, and more.

Inseparable from this well-enforced commitment to social harmony, however, was a deeply ingrained paternalism that fit poorly with the ILGWU's self-image as a paragon of democratic trade unionism. But as Dubinsky, according to Bert Cochran, once commented to Victor Reuther while observing a rough-and-tumble convention of the United Auto Workers in 1937: "In my union we have democracy too, but everyone knows who is boss!" According to Irving Howe's insightful characterization, the union chieftain's "leadership was characterized by a blend, not at all unknown in American unions, of democracy and 'Bonapartism,' a reasonably firm adherence to rules and a stringent domination from the top. . . . Within the union he became a rampaging 'papa,' quick to lose his temper and indulge his generosity."

Dubinsky retired from the presidency in 1966. To all appearances, the union was in better shape than ever before financially. The union treasury, crushed with debt in 1932, was bulging with half a billion dollars in union, pension, and welfare funds. More than this, Dubinsky, according to Stein, had helped to carry out what he himself termed "a revolution in the American labor movement" (although left-wing critics might have called it a counterrevolution): "In the old days it used to be 'we' and 'they.' Now it is all 'we.'" He elaborated: "Thirty years ago the important thing for a union leader was how to organize economic strength. Organize! Strike! Settle! That was labor-management relations. But today, with laws and labor boards, almost all of our problems are settled at the conference table through negotiations. Now it is diplomacy instead of the big stick."

Yet this triumph of the "Protocol of Peace" spirit did not enable the union's succeeding presidents—Louis Stulberg, Sol Chaikin, and Jay Mazur—to overcome new challenges that increasingly threatened the existence of the ILGWU. From 1968 to the early 1990s, the union lost more than 300,000 workers. Socialists, Communists, and anarchists of an earlier day might have explained this as being related to the inexorable need for capitalist employers to be guided by "the bottom line"—the maximization of profits—at the expense of the needs and dignity of the workers. Later analysts would refer to the underlying cause as "globalization," involving a shift of garment manufacturing to low-wage portions of the country that used "right to work" laws to block unions, and finally to low-wage portions of the world where authoritarian regimes supported by the U.S. government even more brutally repressed union organization. Unprepared for what one labor leader called this "one-sided class-warfare," the ILGWU was unable to prevent the erosion and collapse of the Protocol principles.

By 1995 the ILGWU, with only 125,000 members, felt compelled to merge with the 175,000-member Amalgamated Clothing and Textile Workers' Union (itself a result of a merger between two unions), forming the Union of Needletrades, Industrial and Textile Employees (UNITE). In 2004, UNITE merged with the Hotel Employees and Restaurant Employees International Union (HERE). The new organization, UNITE HERE, claimed an active membership of more than 440,000. The future of the industry and the union, and the role of strikes in helping to shape this future, remain to be seen.

See also: Strikes Led by the Trade Union Unity League, 1929–1934, 166.

Bibliography

Bernstein, Irving. *The Lean Years: A History of the American Worker 1920–1933*. Boston: Houghton Mifflin, 1966.

———. *The Turbulent Years: A History of the American Worker, 1933–1941*. Boston: Houghton Mifflin, 1969.

Buhle, Paul. *Taking Care of Business: Samuel Gompers, George Meany, Lane Kirkland and the Tragedy of American Labor*. New York: Monthly Review Press, 1999.

Cochran, Bert. *Labor and Communism: The Conflict that Shaped American Unions*. Princeton, NJ: Princeton University Press, 1977.

Foner, Philip S. *History of the Labor Movement in the United States*. Vols. 5 and 10. New York: International, 1980, 1994.

Foster, William Z. *Misleaders of Labor*. New York: Trade Union Educational League, 1927.

Howe, Irving. *World of Our Fathers*. New York: Harcourt Brace and Jovanovich, 1976.

Kessler-Harris, Alice. "Organizing the Unorganizable: Three Jewish Women and Their Union." In *The Labor History Reader*, ed. Daniel J. Leab. Urbana: University of Illinois Press, 1985.

Lens, Sidney. *Working Men*. New York: Putnam, 1960.

Lovell, Frank. "Sylvia Bleeker (1901–1988): Union Organizer, Socialist Agitator, and Lifelong Trotskyist." In *Revolutionary Labor Socialist: The Life, Ideas and Comrades of Frank Lovell*, ed. Paul Le Blanc and Thomas Barrett. Union City, NJ: Smyrna Press, 2000.

Stein, Leon, ed. *Out of the Sweatshop: The Struggle for Industrial Democracy*. New York: Quadrangle/New York Times, 1977.

STEEL STRIKES BEFORE 1935

John Hinshaw

Before the 1860s, the iron and steel industry primarily involved the manufacture of iron, which was relatively brittle and expensive. In 1856, Henry Bessemer invented an inexpensive technique for making steel. Steel is essentially iron that has been reheated and worked to remove impurities and make it more supple. In the Bessemer process, compressed air was blown through molten iron, causing many of the impurities to burn away. The process used coal instead of charcoal, allowing the molten iron to reach higher temperatures. This breakthrough launched a series of technological advances in metalmaking, but it did not eliminate the skill required to handle and shape the molten metal. Over time, however, the iron and steel industry relied more on science than tradition to transform iron ore into metal.

Beginning in the 1860s, the steel industry grew increasingly technologically advanced and more capital intensive, and its ownership more concentrated. Larger and larger steel mills owned by bigger and bigger corporations produced more and more of the building blocks of the industrial revolution, ending up in machines, nails, railways, steamships, skyscrapers, and weapons. With each decade, the trend toward economic concentration became increasingly pronounced, and by 1901, U.S. Steel controlled almost 60 percent of American steel production. Steel corporations had greatly limited the power of free markets to lower prices or profit margins, buying their raw materials from captive companies and setting the prices for the consumer; corporations also determined the dynamics within industrial labor markets. At this point, unions nearly disappeared and for the next thirty-five years, strikes became desperate attempts to alter the unbearable.

The history of steel reveals that the organization of business exceeded that of labor by decades, and between the 1860s and the 1930s big business and its allies in government denied workers the ability to organize openly and with legal protections. As one trade unionist observed in the *National Labor Tribune* in 1881, "Consolidation and centralization of wealth is all the rage, and a very bad rage it is . . . to meet it is a simple problem in theory: Workmen must concentrate more closely in union." But steelworkers rarely overcame their vast differences in skill, ethnicity, or race, or the considerable economic and political power of employers.

Until the 1860s, metallurgical labor organizations, to the extent they existed, were based in localities or regions and were organized along craft lines. When strikes broke out, they were at individual firms. For instance, in 1848, puddlers (skilled workers who melted and worked iron in furnaces that predated Bessemer) struck against the Tredegar Iron Works, in Richmond, Virginia, to keep the company from using slave labor. The company evicted workers from company housing, the strike failed, and the company became a major employer of enslaved as well as free workers. Employers in the North also relied on tactics such as the blacklist (firing suspected agitators) to prevent unions. The Sons of Vulcan, a craft union of puddlers, despite being a secret society, was forced to disband in 1858. Its members re-formed in 1862.

Ironworkers needed the cover of full employment engendered by the Civil War to build durable unions organized along craft lines. Throughout the 1860s and 1870s, workers struck during boom times and by 1865 had forced employers throughout the country to pay workers a share of the market price of iron based on a "sliding scale." When prices rose, so did workers' wages; when prices went below a certain level, however, the union maintained a floor for workers' pay. Consequently, when iron prices plummeted during the depression that began in 1873, employers locked out workers to lower their costs and nearly destroyed the union. As was common practice, they hired black strikebreakers from the South, although strikers claimed this was done to provoke a riot so the militia could crush the strike. According to one white trade unionist speaking in the *National Labor Tribune* in 1875, "The firm [is] very anxious to get only one 'nigger' killed so they can call it a riot and call in the militia, and arrest a few puddlers, to demoralize the rest." The puddlers lost their national sliding scale, but maintained regional ones in a "dearly bought victory of labor over avarice." But it made little sense for local or regional unions to bargain with nationally organized companies. So in 1876, workers responded by amalgamating the various craft organizations, notably that of the puddlers and the rollers, who reshaped hot iron into shapes. The resulting union was called the Amalgamated Association of Iron and Steel Workers, or the Amalgamated for short.

Despite the new national labor organization, many strikes remained local affairs. For instance, iron- and steelworkers supported the massive rail workers' strike in 1877, joining the crowds that rioted and burned railroad cars and drove militias from their cities. Following that conflagration, a strike broke out at Jones and Laughlin's Pittsburgh works. While skilled workers did not join it, they apparently helped the unskilled increase their wages from 80 cents to a dollar a day.

Employers still relied on the skills of puddlers to manufacture iron and rollers to shape iron and steel. Skilled workers were thus often able to stop short of strikes to win concessions, but workers proved capable of waging bitter strikes, largely throughout the industrial North, to defend wage scales and work rules. The unionized craft workers who had mastered the secrets of iron making demanded and received a large measure of respect from employers. One indication of this was that in the iron industry in the 1880s, the pay of some skilled workers sometimes exceeded the pay of managers. Until the 1880s, skilled ironworkers resembled subcontractors who were paid a certain amount per ton of metal that they produced. Furthermore, these craft workers had the power to hire and fire members of their crew. Their union regulated wages, working conditions, and access to the craft. In steel towns and cities, the tastes of skilled workers dominated the social and cultural landscape in what historian Francis Couvares described as a "craftsmen's empire." Employers relied upon suasion, recruiting craft workers into management, and coercion, bringing in scabs protected by private or public police, to defeat strikes.

Unionists vacillated between embracing the exclusivist logic of craft unionism, mocking black and especially immigrant workers, or building solidarity with different workers, a particularly important point as mechanization reduced the leverage of the skilled over employers. But solidarity in the Amalgamated had its clear limits. Not until 1881 did the Amalgamated allow blacks to join racially segregated, or Jim Crow, lodges. That same year, when black puddlers went on strike, the strikers simply secured work at another union shop. That event led the *National Labor Tribune* to exult that "the [white] members of the A.A. [Amalgamated] are getting their eyes opened to the fact that the color line is being used against them, and the objection to working alongside a colored man is fast fading away." However, racial prejudice remained strong. Sometimes, when black workers tried to join the Amalgamated, they were rebuffed. In 1890, 400 white unionists walked off the job to protest the hiring of black workers who then represented between 2 percent and 3 percent of all iron- and steelworkers in Pennsylvania. These problems were not simply a product of racial prejudice, but also the craft-mindedness of many workers. Not until 1889 could lodges (or locals of the Amalgamated) admit common laborers. (In the 1880s, many unskilled workers had joined the Knights of Labor.) Craft rivalries plagued the Amalgamated and skilled workers sometimes scabbed on each others' strikes. Although the Amalgamated evolved toward greater solidarity, it only partially overcame the hierarchies of the workplace.

Technological change was another potent challenge. The Bessemer furnace promised employers a means to make larger amounts of metal without puddlers. Whereas puddlers could make no more than 600 pounds of iron per batch, Bessemers could produce five times that much steel. In Pittsburgh, industrialists used new technology to weaken craft unions, lower costs, and raise productivity. In 1877, Andrew Carnegie shut down the Edgar Thomson mill to install Bessemers. Afterward, men could return to work only if they renounced the union. Renounce they did, and although they later rebuilt their union, wages of puddlers fell by about 40 percent. By the 1890s, Bessemers were outproducing puddling furnaces by ten to one. In the 1880s, most of the Amalgamated's strikes failed, and by 1885 the union had just 5,000 members. The union recovered and entered the 1890s with 20,000 members, but had to confront ever larger and stronger companies.

As in many industries, managers used ethnic diversity to challenge the solidarity of unions. Amid the constant mechanization of iron and steel making, the number of iron- and steelworkers increased dramatically, and employers increasingly sought workers from a wider variety of backgrounds. As quoted by James Howard Bridge, one of Andrew Carnegie's managers explained that the most tractable workforce was a "judiciously mixed" group of "Germans and Irish, Swedes and what I denominate 'Buckwheats' (young American country boys)." But the increasingly heterogeneous workforce favored by employers threatened the social cohesion of the Amalgamated, where native-born and North European rollers and puddlers had built a union tradition based on their technical skills and a cultural solidarity based on white manliness. From the perspective of many unionists, foreign-born common laborers possessed neither the requisite technical skill nor the proper social identity to join craft unions. As more immigrants from Southern and Eastern Europe joined the workforce in the mills, the social distance between skilled and unskilled workers widened still further. The president of the Amalgamated, speaking before the 1883 Senate Committee Upon the Relations Between and Labor and Capital, saw cultural differences as a direct threat to union scales, arguing that Slavic workers did not know "the difference between light work and heavy work or between good wages and bad wages . . . these people can live where I think decent men would die; they can live on almost any kind of food, food that other men would not touch, and in houses that other men would not live in at all."

Yet despite the ethnic chauvinism of many in the Amalgamated, craft workers in Homestead, Pennsylvania, developed a culture of solidarity so strong that most immigrant workers, the unskilled, and Bessemer workers joined their picket lines and barricades. In 1882, despite the presence of the National Guard, armed scabs, private police, and deputy sheriffs, unionists' organization and solidarity held solid during a strike by the Amalgamated at Homestead. Strikebreakers unfamiliar with the mill's unique equipment produced shoddy goods and caused the company to lose orders. Unionists' threats to extend the strike to other mills owned by the company forced the company to sign a contract. A year later, the company sold the mill to Carnegie, who relied on technology and incentives to managers and skilled workers to improve productivity dramatically. For the next ten years, Carnegie sparred, skirmished, and battled with members of the Amalgamated for complete control over the pace of production. The stakes were enormous—between 1891 and 1892, tonnage at Homestead's various departments increased between 17.5 percent and 52 percent.

In 1892, Carnegie finally found the means to destroy the Amalgamated in Homestead. Homestead remained the last major stronghold of trade unionism in steel, and the showdown was viewed by journalists and politicians then, and by historians since, as a turning point for the post–Civil War labor movement. Technology alone had proved insufficient to break the union, since Amalgamated activists had proved themselves flexible enough to incorporate Bessemer workers into the union. Management had hired a far more diverse workforce, but prejudice did not cripple Homestead's unionists. They had successfully extended a culture of solidarity to Slavic immigrants, although not to African Americans. Workers controlled the local government, and even the county's sheriff refused to authorize the use of deputy sheriffs to escort scabs into the mill. When Carnegie and his partner Henry Clay Frick finally resorted to the use of hundreds of heavily armed Pinkerton guards, the workers forced them to surrender after a lengthy gun battle. However, at this point, the company convinced the state's governor to send in

With this print commemorating the "Great Battle of Homestead," the printing firm Kurz & Allison sought to profit from the fame of the Homestead strike. The images glorify the workers and vilify the "Pinkerton invaders," suggesting that Kurz & Allison believed the public sided with the strikers. (*Courtesy:* Library of Congress.)

the National Guard, who finally ensured that the company could operate the mill with nonunion workers.

When the conflict was over, the union was finished in steel. In 1897, the last Amalgamated contract at a major mill expired. The new techniques provided by university-trained engineers, scientists, and chemists further increased managers' knowledge and control over the workplace. Every worker became replaceable. By the early 1900s, employers boasted that with eight weeks of training a green hand could replace even the most highly skilled worker in the mill.

However, technology was less critical to the power of employers than their extensive spy system to identify and punish activists. In 1895, 1899, and 1901, workers attempted to rebuild the union at Homestead. In response, as historian John Fitch noted, "The company let the newly made union men know that it was cognizant of every move that had been made." Some leaders were "invited" to spy on their comrades—and hundreds who refused to spy were fired. Once out of a job, even highly skilled workers frequently found it impossible to find work in the same firm or industry. In many towns, workers knew that "if you want to talk . . . you talk to yourself." One Homestead worker put it this way: "They own us body and soul; our bread and butter depends on our silence." Given the pervasive company presence, Fitch asked, "Is it any wonder, therefore, that [steelworkers] suspect each other and guard their tongues?" The effects of the spy system reached far beyond the mill gate. In 1906, steelworkers at another mill in Pittsburgh called a public meeting to protest having to work on Sunday, but "a foreman, with several mill policemen, stationed themselves where they could see every man who went into the hall. As a result, no one attempted to go to the meeting." The blacklist bled the workplace of its natural leaders and deterred other would-be unionists.

U.S. Steel, formed in 1901 out of Carnegie's and other mills, offered no quarter to unions. At its formation, "the Corporation," as U.S. Steel was called, acquired several rolling mills that had contracts with the Amalgamated. Against the advice of other unionists, the Amalgamated's leaders led a strike against the Corporation with the goal of unionizing all of the company's hoop, sheet, and tin mills. Workers at nonunion mills such as the Duquesne Works and National Tube in McKeesport, Pennsylvania, were blacklisted if they answered the Amalgamated's call and joined the 35,000 strikers. The Amalgamated offered no support; as researcher Robert Asher chronicles, one worker recalled that he had never abandoned the union but that "the union left us." Racial bigotry compounded incompetence. When black strikers from the Lafayette Lodge sought temporary work at another union mill, white unionists refused to work alongside them.

In 1909, another steel strike eliminated the last Amalgamated lodges at U.S. Steel and the company announced its adherence to the principles of the open shop. Despite calls for unity among white workers ("forget you are English, Irish, Welsh, Slavish [*sic*]"), the Amalgamated remained hostile to black workers. One skilled union man told the *Amalgamated Journal* in 1909 that he had briefly worked in a nonunion mill, but quit because "no self-respecting American" could work alongside the "great, dirty crowd of Negroes and Syrians. . . . It is no place for a man with a white man's heart to be." In the following years, unions in the corporation's coalfields, on its ships, and even those members of the building trades who erected the corporation's skyscrapers were wiped out. The Amalgamated retreated to the wrought iron industry, where puddlers' skills were still indispensable. The puddlers revolted against the Amalgamated and reestablished the Sons of Vulcan on a lily-white basis. In 1910, Amalgamated members scabbed on one of their strikes. The Amalgamated "won" this contest, but the union was a hollow shell, with no resources, strategy, or will to organize steel.

Immigrant steelworkers did not always wait for the Amalgamated to organize them; sometimes they acted on their own. In 1909, the Pressed Steel Car Company in McKees Rocks, Pennsylvania, unilaterally reduced workers' wages. The largely immigrant workforce convinced American workers to go on strike, but the company soon encouraged native-born skilled workers to cross picket lines. Ethnicity was also the alibi for repression: when "American" workers claimed that intimidation from immigrant strikers prevented them from going to work, the company called upon the State Police. Troopers rode their horses into armed pickets, a riot broke out, and about a dozen strikers and two troopers were killed. More State Police were called in, and they conducted house-to-house searches for weapons, but only in immigrant neighborhoods. Even the staid *Amalgamated Journal* observed that "there is no stronger proof that the power of government is allied against the working men in their effort to resist the despotism of capitalists than the existence of the state constabulary." The company helped to organize a company union, and the disarmed strikers were unable to prevent the subsequent back-to-work movement led by newly "unionized" Americans.

Faced with these tactics, the immigrants called upon organizers from the radical Industrial Workers of the World (IWW). The IWW, or Wobblies, promised to kill a trooper for every striker killed, and the union was as good as its word. The Wobblies did not shy away from violence, but understood that workers could not win their strike with guns. Workers' solidarity soon forced Pressed Steel Car to rehire all the strikers. But back in the plant, the antagonism between the immigrant and American unions remained fierce. In 1910, as John Ingham chronicles, the American union went out on strike and called up the IWW to support them. The IWW offered this bitter reply: "What for? Do you want us to take the Hunkies up on the hill again, make us do the picketing and offer ourselves as targets for the Cossacks [a common nickname for the State Police] . . . and then you will take your flag and march back to work as you have done before? . . . Nothing Doing!" With only the support of American workers, the strike failed. With a base at Pressed Steel Car, the Wobblies spread their organization to nearby plants. By 1912, the IWW had led several partially successful strikes in the region and claimed 4,000 members. Nonetheless, within a few years, just a handful of die-hard Wobblies remained as dues-paying members. While internal disputes and the IWW's refusal to sign contracts with employers weakened the union, the Wobblies, according to historian Charles H. McCormick, complained that the Pressed Steel Car spy system "made the Russian police look like amateurs."

World War I changed the circumstances of metalworkers. Economic prosperity and minimal federal government protection for unions buoyed their confidence. At the end of the war, however, steel company managers sought to reestablish their control over wages and shop-floor conditions, setting up a showdown. In 1919, the militancy of unskilled immigrant steelworkers throughout the country forced the leadership of the Amalgamated to call a general strike of the industry. The leadership of William Z. Foster, a former IWW member, led to charges that the strikers were radicals bent on revolution. The 1927 Biennial Report of the Pennsylvania State Police justified its role in the strike on the basis that "this appeared to be an industrial war in which the leaders were radical, social and industrial revolutionaries while their followers . . . were . . . chiefly of the foreign element, steeped in the doctrines of class struggle." Employers once again relied on thousands of their "Cossacks," the Coal and Iron Police, deputy sheriffs (5,000 in one county alone), and state troopers. One union organizer grimly observed in a statement recorded in the *Amalgamated Journal* that "the fourth day of the great steel strike, presents all the aspects of war, with the exception that only one side is equipped to fight it." Machine guns were mounted in front of some mills. In one mill town, the mayor disarmed strikebreakers. Most resembled the "czar-like attitude" of one town's chief executive who told the *Amalgamated Journal* that "Jesus Christ himself can't hold a [union] meeting." After the strike, a state trooper defended his methods to a group of U.S. senators, recorded in the Interchurch World Movement Report on the Steel Strike: "I would not say I hurt any of them, I just clubbed a few of them."

Once again, the Amalgamated and the American Federation of Labor (AFL) had let steelworkers down. The twenty-four craft unions that formed the "National Committee for Organizing Iron and Steel Workers" failed to provide the necessary funds or leadership. Much of the money came from left-wing (and non-AFL) unions in textile and the needle trades. While the Amalgamated took the dues money of strikers, it later claimed that it only represented men in lodges with contracts. During the strike, it sent some union men back to work to protect the "sanctity" of its contracts. Similarly, some railroad workers offered to strike, but their union urged them to honor their contracts. As recorded in the Interchurch World Movement report, one worker bitterly observed that "if the railwaymen in the steel plant yards had struck, this strike would have been won." The unions "made them strikebreakers." Although 100,000 strikers stayed out, the Amalgamated's leaders called off the strike. Much of the strike fund donated by other unions remained unspent, as did much of the dues collected from immigrants. Whether the Amalgamated spent the money on investments in real estate or a lackluster organizing drive in 1923 was immaterial. The Amalgamated and the AFL had utterly failed to provide leadership to steelworkers. It would be another decade before steelworkers attempted to unionize again.

Workers' inability to overcome potent ethnic and racial divisions bolstered management's hand during the 1919 strike. Numerous native-born workers believed that the strike was a mere "hunky strike." In the Pittsburgh district, the Amalgamated failed even to try to organize black workers into the union. Amalgamated activist John N. Grajciar later recalled in an interview with Arthur S. Weinberg stored in the papers of the United Steelworkers of America (USWA) at Penn State University that "Negroes were never a question . . . you never even heard it mentioned." Thus numerous American workers, black and white, crossed the picket lines throughout the country. (There were exceptions: in Cleveland, black workers strongly supported the union.) In some places, skilled whites joined supervisors as deputy sheriffs; in other areas, black workers were deputized. Some white Americans struck one mill only to scab in another town. Other white Americans remained true until the union called off the strike. As in the past, black workers' labor solidarity was no guarantee that unions would respond in kind; Grajciar noted, "At Youngstown, for example, one lone [black] machinist striker, who struck to the end, was never admitted to the striking machinists' local."

The racial and ethnic dimensions of the strike set the tone for the "100 percent Americanism" of the 1920s. The crucial role that skilled whites played in defeating the strike has been largely forgotten, in part because many employers argued that their victory was because "the niggers did it." The racial animus was so strong by the end of the strike that some employers fired or downgraded black workers in order to regain the loyalty of white strikers who were rehired. But most employers hired even more black workers in the 1920s because, as labor economist Abram Lincoln Harris observed in 1924, they viewed them as "more individualistic, does not like to group and does not follow a leader as readily as some foreigners do." Industrialists believed that "the Negro . . . shows little susceptibility to radical doctrine." Indeed, at least one black worker, F. J. Amormes, a strikebreaker in 1919, took out his frustrations on immigrant workers in the 1920s. He told the Pittsburgh Urban League in an interview, "The foreigners are worse than the true Americans," in part because a gang of them had opposed his promotion to foreman. He bided his time until "it was my job to weed the men out"; the leader of the immigrants "was the first to go." As in the past, managers stoked the fires of hatred, fear, and resentment to smother class organization.

During the Great Depression, increasingly desperate steelworkers adopted desperate measures. The most dramatic measure, which some thought a portent of things to come, was a strike led by radicalized coal miners that led to a strike at a major steel mill in Clairton, Pennsylvania. Clairton supplied the fuel for all of U.S. Steel's mills in the Monongahela Valley, and a successful strike there would have effectively shut down the Corporation. Although the strike had been called by the United Mine Workers of America (UMWA), or at least its left wing, many rank-and-file Amalgamated members such as Francis DiCola answered its call for solidarity. His analysis of the strike is recorded in the papers of the USWA: "If everybody would have come out, they would have got the union." At a mass meeting in Clairton, 3,000 Amalgamated members voted to strike. But half of those "union men" ended up crossing the picket lines of the miners, and most of those steelworkers who struck were blacklisted. "I knew a lot of cranemen . . . they never got their jobs back." Years later, many steelworkers claimed that the company organized the strike in order to fire Clairton's activists. More likely, trade unionists were embarrassed that they had not joined the strike.

The coal strike was salvaged by the timely intervention of the state's first pro-labor government in decades. Several months later, in January 1934, U.S. Steel signed an agreement that bound them to bargain with whomever their employees elected to represent them. The company insisted that this agreement preserved the "liberty" of their employees to bargain on their own behalf. Most miners chose the UMWA. The radical journalist Harvey O'Connor observed that when the miners returned to work "there was no jubilation. As a final gesture of defiance they marched in columns, headed by the American flag, and marched, sullen, silent but united back into industrial feudalism." Nonetheless, the miners had breached the ramparts of the steel trust.

Radical organizations, including the Communist Party, also tried to organize steelworkers, and, like most previous union organizers, failed. By the 1920s and 1930s, they confronted steel companies who had perfected their methods of labor control over decades. Steel firms organized their jobs to offer opportunities to politically reliable workers and ethnic groups. Big steel had state, county, and local politicians and police forces, in their pocket. Steel companies also retained their own police force and extensive spy network. Communists and other radicals hurled themselves against this formidable fortress. It is hardly surprising that their efforts failed; what is surprising is how many workers joined them in their crusade.

For several years in the 1920s and 1930s, the Communists had sought to organize steel through the Steel and Metal Workers Industrial Union (SMWIU). It peaked in strength in the year of the Clairton strike (1933), but its membership was modest, at most 3,000 members in the Pittsburgh region with two to four times that number throughout the country. Its appeal was strongest among immigrant and black laborers, the most vulnerable workers in the industry. Most native-born white workers joined company unions, the Amalgamated, or nothing at all. The SMWIU was strongest in smaller shops, although nuclei existed at bigger mills.

The union and its members often fell short of the Communist Party's expectations because the organization of the union stressed "rank and file control" that in practice allowed union locals a high degree of autonomy. Communists dominated the national leadership of the union, although most union members were not party members. Some Communists lamented that there were not even party units in some union locals. In contrast to the party's view that the global depression had deeply radicalized industrial workers, just a dozen unionists joined the party from the SMWIU. In the wake of one SMWIU strike in which several thousand workers participated, one journalist found that most unionists were completely unaware of any connection to communism. According to journalist Harvey O'Connor, in the workers' view, the SMWIU was "just a union, our union." Just because a leader of the SMWIU was a Communist was of no importance. He "never talked communism" in the town of Ambridge. Communist steelworkers often refused to sell the *Daily Worker* or to campaign openly on behalf of the party. Rather than acknowledging the real limits that the spy system imposed on activists in steel towns, party officials preferred to view cautious Communists as "party comrades . . . capitulating before the red scare." In numerical terms, the results were meager; one leader of the SMWIU, James Matles, later admitted in an interview with Ron Filippelli stored at Penn State University that it was a "skeleton organization." A non-Communist assessment of the SMWIU by Horace R. Cayton and George S. Mitchell in 1939 concluded that it had "no organizational integration, no funds, and suffered from a lack of competent personnel; but these inadequacies were more than compensated by the tremendous courage and energy of the union's leaders." The SMWIU was nothing if not militant. The Communist Party's view that conditions were ripe for a revolutionary upsurge among workers led the SMWIU into numerous strikes; in some instances they were pulled along by events. A few strikes were successful, others less so. In 1933, the SMWIU succeeded in leading 500 workers off the job at the Pressed Steel Car plant in McKees Rocks and getting dozens of union members rehired. But a harsh fate awaited most workers who ventured onto the picket line. Organizers were run out of many towns, and members were frequently blacklisted. For instance, a month after 1,100 SMWIU members in Greensburg, Pennsylvania, struck the Walworth Company, 300 of them were blacklisted. One terse organizing report in *Steel and Metal Worker* laid out the difficulties that industrial unionists confronted: "The SMWIU was going along fine until the bosses shot and clubbed the workers." According to a 1934 report by the Commission of Special Policing in Industry of the Pennsylvania Department of Labor and Industry, 200 deputy sheriffs (many were private guards) used "four tear gas guns, twenty buckshot guns, two machine guns, revolvers and riot sticks" to drive strikers away from the plant gates and then "fired unnecessarily at the fleeing men." One bystander was killed and several pickets were wounded.

Although the SMWIU dreamed of a large-scale uprising, they could never overcome their lack of leadership, membership, and effective strategy to confront steel companies. By 1934, Communists rejoined the Amalgamated, where a "rank-and-file movement" threatened to lead to another walkout, as in 1919.

With little or no encouragement from the national leadership of the Amalgamated, steelworkers joined its locals in 1934. National membership surged from about 5,000 to at least 80,000. One steelworker later recalled that "the Amalgamated made some effort to organize steel, but [it was] a rather feeble effort." Some employers viewed the Amalgamated as a lesser evil than the SMWIU, but the different attitude that the government took was more important. John Fitch, a longtime observer of the steelworkers, noted in a 1936 issue of *Survey Graphic* that U.S. Steel executives who admitted that "a few years ago we would have fired" unionists "like that" now feared the repercussions from a liberal state governor if they penalized unionists. In 1934, Secretary of

Labor Frances Perkins met with steel unionists in Homestead over the strenuous objections of local Republican politicians. Perkins's reported assessment of Homestead's Mayor Cavanaugh ("he's a very nervous man") suggested the strain that the spy system and its agents were under.

By 1934, many rank and filers in the Amalgamated dreamed of a large strike that would shatter the power of steel companies. While this was also the ambition of the SMWIU, most leaders in the Amalgamated rejected open collaboration with the SMWIU because they would have been smeared immediately as Communists. Instead, rank and filers lobbied for federal intervention. But Roosevelt dreaded a replay of the earlier coal strike and New Deal administrators did little more than stall unionists with promises of investigations and legislation. The experience helped the National Recovery Administration (NRA) earn the epithet "National Run Around" among radical workers. Without political support, few were willing to carry out their threat to strike in June 1934. (Few rank and filers believed that the willingness of the SMWIU to support their strike outweighed the antipathy of their own union and Roosevelt to the strike.) The Amalgamated's national leadership remained as timid and inept as it had been in 1919; however, excelling in political infighting, it expelled many rank-and-file locals. Membership in the union plunged. At this point, Communists were ordered by the party to abandon the SMWIU for the Amalgamated. Small in number but highly disciplined, Communists played a key role in maintaining an Amalgamated presence in the mills and consolidating the rank-and-file members' opposition to the leadership of the Amalgamated.

This was the prehistory of labor organization in steel before the Steel Workers Organizing Committee (SWOC), which later became the United Steelworkers of America (USWA). In the pre-SWOC period, steelworkers attempted nearly every form of labor organization: craft unions, amalgamated craft unionism, revolutionary syndicalism, Communist industrial unionism, and company unionism. It was not for lack of trying that these organizations failed. They tackled the task of organizing a diverse workforce increasingly employed by large, well-organized, highly profitable, and politically powerful firms. Strikers contended with efficient and ruthless labor spies, company police, pro-business local police, National Guard troops, and state police. The strikes against the steel companies indicate workers' desperation and desire for a better life. These pre-SWOC labor organizations failed to organize steel, but arguably laid the groundwork for the rise of the SWOC. Ironically, when the SWOC finally organized the largest firm in the country, U.S. Steel, it won without taking the workers out on strike.

See also: Business Community's Mercenaries, 52; Corporate Strike Strategy, 66; Polish Workers and Strikes, 138; World War I Era Strikes, 191; Steel on Strike: From 1936 to the Present, 360.

Bibliography

Asher, Robert. "Painful Memories: The Historical Consciousness of Steel Workers and the Steel Strike of 1919." *Pennsylvania History* 45 (January 1978): 81.

Bridge, James Howard. *The Inside History of the Carnegie Steel Company: A Romance of Millions*. 1903; reprint, Pittsburgh: University of Pittsburgh Press, 1991.

Brody, David. *Steelworkers in America: The Nonunion Era*. Cambridge, MA: Harvard University Press, 1960.

Cayton, Horace R., and George S. Mitchell. *Black Workers and the New Unions*. Durham: University of North Carolina Press, 1939.

Couvares, Francis G. *The Remaking of Pittsburgh: Class and Culture in an Industrializing City, 1877–1919*. Albany: State University of New York Press, 1984.

Fitch, John A. *The Steel Workers*. Pittsburgh: University of Pittsburgh Press, 1989.

Harris, Abram Lincoln. "The Negro Worker in Pittsburgh." Master's thesis, University of Pittsburgh, 1924.

Hinshaw, John. *Steel and Steelworkers: Race and Class Struggle in 20th Century Pittsburgh*. Albany: State University of New York Press, 2002.

Ingham, John N. "A Strike in the Progressive Era: McKees Rocks, 1909." *Pennsylvania Magazine of History and Biography* 90 (July 1966): 373–74.

McCormick, Charles H. *Seeing Reds: Federal Surveillance of Radicals in the Pittsburgh Mill District, 1917–1921*. Pittsburgh: University of Pittsburgh Press, 1997.

O'Connor, Harvey. *Steel-Dictator*. New York: John Day, 1935.

STEEL ON STRIKE: FROM 1936 TO THE PRESENT

Robert Bruno

The 1930s represented a turbulent period of great economic hardship for millions of Americans. Working people, reduced to standing on long bread lines and victimized by housing evictions, became the spark for tremendous social and political upheaval. The nation's most serious confrontations arose over the grievances of millions of workers denied their rights under laws passed during the New Deal, including the National Labor Relations Act, popularly referred to as the Wagner Act. Workers across the country engaged in the highest level of strike activity in American history. Between May 1933 and July 1937, 10,000 strikes took place involving some 5.6 million workers. The Wagner Act created elaborate state-regulated machinery for the protection of workers desiring union organization. The nation's steelworkers were among the first to begin organizing under this new law.

Once organized, the steelworkers' union was regularly enmeshed in conflict with the steelmakers. In 1937, the union was thrust into a titanic struggle against corporate entities determined to disavow the federal government's legal monopoly on the use of violence and coercion. Striking workers again took to the streets in 1941 against the nation's second-largest steel company and throughout World War II staged hundreds of episodic local walkouts. Even after a modern postwar liberal labor accord was established, work stoppages in the steel industry were as consistent as the seasons. National strikes occurred triennially from 1943 to 1952 and then again in 1955 and 1956. Three years later in 1959, the decade was capped when a record-setting 116-day strike erupted in the nation's steel mills. It was to be the industry's last national shutdown.

Following the 1959 conflict, labor peace became the norm for a little more than two decades until a major steel company was struck in 1985. Two years later the nation's largest steel concern USX (U.S. Steel) locked out its union employees. Struggles in the steel industry flared up again in the 1990s and early in the twenty-first century with nasty fights against Bayou Steel, Wheeling Pitt, Colorado Fuel and Iron, and Warren Consolidated.

While violent strikes in the revolutionary milieu of the 1930s differed significantly from the more bureaucratic, circumscribed, and peaceful postwar walkouts, steelworker militancy has always factored largely in the collective bargaining regime permitted under American labor law. United Steelworkers (USW) vice president and Basic Steel Industry Conference Director Tom Conway has said of the union's historical approach to management abuse, "When necessary, we have sat down on the steel as easily as we made it."

But strikes have also been part of a unique strategic tripartite bargaining relationship involving the union, steel companies, and the federal government. Strikes in the 1940s and 1950s were not triggered or settled simply between private bargaining partners but were strategically influenced by governmental and presidential involvement. Ultimately the terms of cessation would be significant to establishing how the right to strike would be conceived as an instrument to advance collective bargaining goals. In the 1980s and 1990s, the American steel industry underwent severe economic dislocation and thousands of workers were permanently unemployed. But during these times of terrific corporate pressure to erode the value of collective bargaining, the union waged a number of heroic defensive strikes that preserved the dignity and value of a steelworker's job.

The Memorial Day Massacre

Prior to the 1930s, steelworkers had endured nearly half a century of failed efforts to establish a viable national union organization. While daily wages had crept upward from $1.50 in 1910 to between $4.00 and $5.00 in the late 1920s, most steelworkers were living under substandard conditions as the Great Depression hit. The need for a new workers' organization that could overcome the limitations of narrowly drawn craft-based approaches to unionizing was conceived as an answer to the plight of thousands of industrial steel hands. Organizing workers into an industrial union structure was promoted by the Committee for Industrial Organization (CIO), a group of unions that defied the craft orientation of the American Federation of Labor (AFL) in November 1935. The CIO strategy called for all steelworkers regardless of craft to join one union and bargain collectively as a group. Decades of suppressed organizing efforts in the steel industry and memories of the brutalization of steelworker communities during the 1919 national strike gave birth to a near-messianic worker commitment to organize under the CIO's industry-wide banner.

In June 1936, the Steel Workers Organizing Committee (SWOC) was set up in Pittsburgh, Pennsylvania, by the CIO. Its chairman was Philip Murray, a vice president of the United Mine Workers. Murray, along with CIO president John L. Lewis and a cadre of Communist Party organizers, spread out across the country's industrial heartland. SWOC's newspaper, *Steel Labor,* began to report the progress of the drive to organize. The nation's economy had begun to improve and the steel industry was running at almost 90 percent of capacity, employing about 800,000 men. It was within this framework of hot furnaces and mounting profits that the CIO began to organize. By the middle of 1937, the union had formed more than 750 union lodges.

While there were numerous companies producing steel, one firm dominated the industry. Dubbed "Big Steel," the U.S. Steel Corporation controlled nearly 60 percent of the market and since the turn of the century had routinely set the price of steel. In 1936, the company reported $55,501,787 in profits; in the first three months of 1937 the company recorded a net gain of $28,561,533. SWOC initially exerted most of its early efforts toward organizing the sprawling U.S. Steel mills. In an effort to undermine the union's growing strength, in November 1936 the company granted a wage increase to its employees, but the move failed to stem the tide of new SWOC enrollees. Sensing the ultimate unionization of the company and wanting to avoid the cost of violent disruptions, in January 1937 a personal meeting occurred in Washington, DC, between CIO head Lewis and U.S. Steel's chairman of the board, Myron Taylor. The cordial dinner meeting in Taylor's suite commenced a series of secret negotiations that culminated on March 1, 1937, with the signing of a labor contract recognizing SWOC as the bargaining agent for its members only. At the time of the agreement, SWOC represented less than 20 percent of U.S. Steel's employees.

Nonetheless, the contract established a grievance procedure with binding arbitration and confirmed a base wage rate of 52 cents an hour. The deal also provided for an eight-hour day with time-and-a-half pay for overtime work, a forty-hour week, three holidays, a one-week paid vacation after five years, and departmental seniority rights. U.S. Steel's surprising capitulation to SWOC, shortly after the United Auto Workers forced General Motors to sign a labor deal in 1937, created a powerful national foundation for the spread of industrial democracy. SWOC gained instant credibility among the rank-and-file steelworkers and membership cards poured into its Pittsburgh headquarters. Organizing success was rapid. By May 1937, there were 110 steel firms under a SWOC contract. Some companies resisted signing a labor agreement. In response, SWOC called its first strike involving 25,000 workmen against the Jones and Laughlin Steel Corporation. However, thirty-six hours later, the corporation agreed to a federally supervised election, which the union won handily 17,028 to 7,207.

SWOC then turned its attention to the rest of the steel industry, fully expecting the "Little Steel" companies (i.e., Bethlehem Steel, Republic Steel, Youngstown Sheet and Tube, National Steel, Inland Steel, and American Rolling Mill) to follow Big Steel's lead. All together, these firms employed almost 200,000 workers and accounted for almost

40 percent of the steel produced in America. One of the "Little" companies, Republic Steel, had earned $4,000,000 in 1935 and $9.5 million in 1936. But to SWOC chairman Phil Murray's disappointment, the rest of the industry rejected U.S. Steel's less confrontational approach to labor relations.

The remainder of the steel industry did match the wage and hour provisions of the U.S. Steel agreement, but refused to sign a contract or recognize SWOC. The "Little Steel" companies were headed by leaders who saw unionization as a deadly infringement upon their management prerogatives, and one corporate boss's antiunion vehemence foreshadowed the carnage to come. Tom M. Girdler of Cleveland-based Republic Steel personified the rough-hewn steel magnate who had transformed America's nineteenth-century craft-based iron industry into the twentieth century's most technologically advanced center for steel production. Girdler had previously managed the Jones and Laughlin Steel Company's mill in Aliquippa, Pennsylvania. His tyrannical reign was so absolute that Aliquippa's Slavic residents referred to Girdler as the "czar" of "America's Siberia."

In 1930, Girdler was named chairman of the board of the newly formed Republic Steel Corporation. He had nothing but contempt for unions. In an attempt to subvert genuinely independent unionization at Republic, Girdler formed an Employee Representation Plan (ERP), or company union. The ERP, however, did not divert workers from pursuing a powerful countervailing force to the company's shop-floor control. In response to continued SWOC agitation, Girdler elevated his level of union resistance to a frightening degree. The company resorted to industrial espionage, firing of union men, and hiring of strikebreakers to intimidate workers. Republic and the other Little Steel firms went as far as to stockpile industrial munitions, including guns, teargas, and clubs in their various plants. An invoice entered on the books of Federal Laboratories, dated September 30, 1933, noted the following shipment to Bethlehem Steel: 100 blast type billies, 24 Jumbo CN grenades lot No. X820, 24 military bouchons, 48 1½" cal. projectile shells (CN), 24 1½" cal. short range shells (CN), 4 1½" cal. riot guns, style 201 sr. No. 337, 386, 390, 403, and 4 riot gun cases.

Bethlehem's armament was sizable, but Youngstown Sheet and Tube acquired enough deadly firepower to stage a war against a small country. On June 6, 1934, the firm was billed for the following: 10 1½" cal. riot guns 201 ($60 ea), 10 riot gun cases 211 ($7.50 ea), 60 1½" cal. long range projectiles ($7.50 ea), 60 1½" cal. short range projectiles ($4.50 ea), 60 M-39 billies, std. barrel no disc ($22.50 ea), 600 M-39 billy cartridges ($1.50 ea), 200 grenades 106 M (10% disc., $12 ea). And Republic's police force was equally prepared to use deadly force. They purchased 7,855 tear and sickening gas grenades and shells, 105 guns for firing gas shells, 247 revolvers, 142 shotguns, 75,650 rounds of ammunition, and 400 magazines for rifles. In addition, a corps of "4 special men" was stationed in select plants and equipped with Thompson machine guns. As president of Republic, Girdler became nationally known for his favorite antiunion manifesto. "We won't sign a contract. I have a little farm with a few apple trees and before spending the rest of my life dealing with unions I [will] raise apples and potatoes," he said, according to Benjamin Blake. The company anticipated that SWOC would call a strike and Girdler relished an opportunity to squash it and the fledgling union by any means necessary.

Girdler acted first. Over 1,000 union supporters were expelled from Republic's Canton and Massillon, Ohio, mills. Facing similar company actions at plants in Chicago and Cleveland and recognizing the unwillingness of the other Little Steel firms to diverge from Girdler's recklessness, Philip Murray called a "war board" meeting of the union's 200 Little Steel representatives on May 26, 1937. Before midnight on that day, SWOC delegates had committed the organization to striking three of the Little Steel companies (i.e., Republic, Youngstown Sheet and Tube, and Inland). As union delegates communicated word of the strike call, 85,000 steelworkers walked off their jobs. At the strike's inception, Republic Steel hurriedly mailed off a pamphlet to its 55,000 workers that reiterated the company's traditional support for an "open shop." The pamphlet, *The Real Issues*, argued that SWOC's ultimate goal was a "closed shop" and a dues check-off system in which all workers would be required to join the union and the company would deduct union dues from workers' paychecks. Absent from the pamphlet, among other items, was any acknowledgment that Republic's phalanx of lawyers were in court raising a legal challenge to SWOC's petition for a federally supervised election to determine the workers' interest in union representation.

Less eager to engage in industrial warfare and all too willing to allow Girdler to take on the fight, both Inland and Youngstown Sheet and Tube closed their plants and prepared to wait out the strike. Mass picket lines were quickly set up by SWOC at closed Republic Steel plants, but a few undaunted ones remained open. One of these plants was the Republic Steel South Chicago plant.

At the Chicago plant the walkout began shortly after 3:00 P.M. on Wednesday, May 26. To ensure continued production, Republic housed approximately 200–300 workers who opposed the strike in a recently completed wire mill and brought in food and cots. Plant management was in close contact with Chicago police officials in an effort to ensure uninterrupted production. Whereas police in other strike cities did not interfere initially with picketing, Chicago's finest acted differently. As the walkout began, the strikers gathered outside the plant gate and formed a picket line. Despite the facts that no disturbance had yet taken place and any legal opinion granting the police the right to interfere with peaceful picketing was absent, the police forcefully broke up the picket line. Republic also provided extra pay for a contingent of fifty Chicago police, who were permanently stationed inside the mill. These actions by the police were properly seen by the strikers as converting the city's law enforcement officers into agents of Republic Steel.

On the basis of newspaper reports that Mayor Edward J. Kelly had said that peaceful picketing would be permitted, the strikers made repeated attempts to march to the gate to reinforce the picket line. Saturday, May 29 was quiet at the plant with only limited picketing. As a protest against the actions of the police, however, SWOC District Director Nick Fontecchio called for a mass meeting at Sam's Place for, May 30. Sam's had been a "ten-cent" dance hall, but it was now serving as the workers' strike headquarters, kitchen, and infirmary. On Saturday, the police received an anonymous report that an attempt would be made the next day to invade the plant and drive out the nonunion workers. An additional 264 policemen were ordered to be on duty at Republic Steel on Sunday afternoon. The stage was set for the tragic events of Memorial Day.

The *Chicago Tribune* reported that May 30, 1937, was a sunny, hot day. By mid-afternoon, a shirt-sleeved crowd of approximately 1,500 strikers, wives, children, and sympathizers had gathered to participate in a protest march to Republic's main gate. After a motion was approved to send a resolution to government officials protesting police conduct at Republic Steel's South Chicago plant, a loose formation of marchers fell in behind two American flags and began to march across a marshy prairie chanting "CIO, CIO!" Some of the strikers carried placards with simple slogans like, "REPUBLIC STEEL VIOLATES LABOR DISPUTES ACT," "WIN WITH THE C.I.O.," "NO FASCISM IN AMERICA," and "REPUBLIC STEEL SHALL SIGN A UNION CONTRACT." No fewer than 200 policemen aligned in double file were waiting for the marchers. They waited with nonregulation clubs obtained from Republic Steel and teargas from Republic stockpiles. The marchers bravely approached the police line to within a tantalizing three feet and implored the officers to let them through to set up their picket line.

A standoff lasted for several minutes. Then, a rash toss of sticks and stones turned into a massacre of bullets and billy clubs. Frustrated by police recalcitrance, some marchers picked up sticks and began to throw them near the police line. Almost simultaneously, teargas bombs were thrown by police into the marchers and then, inexplicably, policemen drew their revolvers and fired "point blank" into the wildly panicked retreating crowd. Approximately 200 shots rang out. Within fifteen seconds the shooting had ended, but the violence did not stop. Police began to wield their billy clubs indiscriminately against any human body floundering on the marshy prairie ground. The beatings lasted for several minutes, after which numerous arrests were made. Patrol wagons were teeming with seriously wounded men and women who were detained without any attempt to treat or dress their wounds. Following the assault, a subcommittee of the United States Senate Committee on Education and Labor investigated the incident and characterized the treatment of the wounded as callous indifference and declared that "wounded prisoners of war might have expected greater solicitude."

The final casualty list included ten people mortally wounded, thirty others with gunshot wounds, twenty-eight hospitalized for lacerations and contusions, and another thirty who received some sort of emergency medical treatment. Thirty-five policemen reported minor injuries with no gunshot wounds and only three policemen required overnight hospital care. Reactions to the "massacre" ranged from angry strikers ready to proclaim war against the police to the anti-union *Chicago Tribune* accusing the marchers of being Communists who had attacked the police with clubs, bricks, and guns in a plan to storm the plant. However, the Senate subcommittee investigating the event came to the conclusion that the Chicago police and Republic Steel Company had coordinated a premeditated violent attack on peaceful protestors. The Senate hearing featured exhibits of still photographs along with a morbid chart of gunshot wounds suffered by the victims, known as "Exhibit 1463." Despite additional third-party investigations finding fault with the police and company, no single officer was ever indicted for any action taken that sun-drenched, bloody Memorial Day. The deaths, company arranged back-to-work movements, and anti-union propaganda combined to demoralize the striking steelworkers. The strike was subsequently called off.

The slaughter in Chicago was only a part of the much larger carnage associated with the Little Steel Strike. The nationwide death toll in the strike reached sixteen as six other strikers lost their lives on picket lines in Ohio. Two of them were killed outside the Republic Steel Lansingville Plant in Youngstown, Ohio. Youngstown police opened fire on a crowd of women gathered at the plant as part of a "Women's Day" on the picket line. Several union supporters were wounded, but despite a chaotically unfolding scene, surprisingly, the crowd did not disperse. A violent battle ensued throughout the night; eventually two strikers were killed. While the steelworkers fought the police to a standoff, it was a pyrrhic victory. While sympathy for the strikers remained high within Ohio's steel communities, management's claim that SWOC was actually a violent organization gained credibility in other areas of the state. Republic and the other Little Steel firms increased their lobbying of the governor for National Guard intervention to reopen the mills.

Democratic governor Martin Davey immediately mobilized 5,000 Ohio guardsmen, justifying his action by declaring that the National Guard was needed "in order to prevent riots, bloodshed, and possible loss of life," according to Blake. The legal impact of the decision was to place Youngstown under martial law. Guardsmen acting as local law enforcement arrested at least 160 unionists and conducted night raids on the homes of union supporters, resulting in the jailing of whole families. As martial law began to thin out the mill presence of union pickets and supporters, Little Steel management withdrew from federal mediation efforts. With chances for a settlement nearly exhausted, Governor Davey took a decisively anti-union step. On June 24, he ordered the reopening of the mills under National Guard protection. Davey justified his action in official orders to the National Guard: "Government must not abdicate its sovereign powers and responsibilities to any who challenge its existence. The right to work is sacred. Those who want to return to their employment shall enjoy that privilege without being molested. . . . The safeguarding of our liberties individually and collectively is a priceless heritage for our children and the millions of future Americans yet unborn." His edict served to break the strike and temporarily defeat the union drive.

Four years later, World War II broke out in Europe. Under intense government pressure to maintain war production, Little Steel management surrendered to SWOC without the formality of a representative election. Republic was even forced to pay more than $20 million in back pay for workers it had blacklisted in 1937 as part of a National Labor Relations Board (NLRB) judgment. The NLRB also provided for a process of secret-ballot elections that later established bargaining rights for SWOC. One year later, in 1942, the Little Steel companies signed their first contracts with the newly formed United Steelworkers of America (USWA). The Little Steel Strike is surpassed by few twentieth-century economic conflicts in the areas of corporate viciousness, press distortion, state suppression of rights, and police brutality.

Steel Strikes and the Liberal State Era, 1941–1959

The Little Steel Strike had only delayed the march of steel unionism. The nation's million-plus steelworkers were nearly entirely unionized five years later. At a 1942 convention in Pittsburgh, SWOC transformed itself into the United Steelworkers of America. A major national industrial steel union was born and conflict with "Big Capital" was forthcoming. But conflicts now would be highly regulated by a modern executive state tightly policing strike policy within a pure-and-simple union framework. No longer would private companies be allowed to use unrestrained deadly force against striking workers or would governors be permitted to turn state militias loose on peaceful picketers. Mediators, arbitrators, labor boards, and NLRB machinery would now be available to navigate labor–management conflicts to a safe harbor. But even good ship captains sometimes run aground in raging storms.

The outbreak of war in Europe generated a government need to ensure war production and a way to peacefully settle industrial disputes. Rising war-driven employment and a surge in union numbers emboldened the steelworkers (still SWOC) in 1941 to demand their first pay increases since 1937. The famous "Little Steel Formula," adopted by the National War Labor Board in 1942, established a process for hiking wages 5½ cents, granting exclusive bargaining rights and, more important, a "maintenance of membership" clause securing union membership in labor agreements. But within one year the now-USWA was pressuring the industry to break out of the limited Little Steel Formula. In December 1943 the union demanded a 17-cents-an hour wage boost. When the War Labor Board reacted hesitantly to approving a formula-busting pay increase and to granting retroactive pay to any settlement, the union called a pre–Christmas Day strike. On the first day of the strike, approximately 150,000 workers walked out and with each passing day the numbers rose by the thousands. The speed and solidarity of the steelworkers' action convinced President Franklin D. Roosevelt to intervene and to promise that "full retroactivity within the Little Steel Formula" would apply. In short order, the War Labor Board assigned the case to a review panel, but then delayed acting until after Roosevelt's reelection in 1944. Eventually the steelworkers were granted a wage increase, improved shift differential pay, and additional vacation days. The new labor agreement would be in effect until 1946 with the possibility of a wage reopener if national wage policy was altered.

The steelworkers' brief Christmas strike in 1943 was not the only one taken during the war. Despite agreeing to a "no-strike pledge," the USWA participated in over 1,000 episodic local work stoppages before Armistice Day. However, short-term walkouts over shop-floor or managerial abuse proved to be just a warm-up for pent-up worker discontent, when industrial production on the home front returned to domestic items. In January 1946, 750,000 steelworkers joined 4 million other workers in the largest strike wave in the country's history. Steelworkers, like other manufacturing employees, experienced an economic shock caused by a dramatic drop-off in industrial production after the war. The average steelworker saw his/her overtime earnings drastically curtailed, reducing their monthly income by as much as $52. In defense-related plants, weekly wages dropped by 20 percent and after V-E day unemployment jumped by 25 percent. Falling worker incomes contrasted starkly with manufacturing employer profits that ballooned to $24 billion in 1944.

At the same time that workers' economic and job security was plummeting, the government lifted its wartime price controls, causing the cost of basic foodstuffs and housing to skyrocket. The USWA demanded an increase of 18½ cents an hour, and after the workers cooled down the blast furnaces for twenty-eight days the steelmakers capitulated. Despite, or perhaps because of, the massive and disciplined nature of the strike, there were few reported violent demonstrations. Acceptance of the state's narrow protection of a worker's right to strike for commercial reasons restrained the steelmakers from recruiting strikebreakers or trying to smash picket lines. Market leaders such as U.S. Steel were also placated by a presidential executive order granting the industry a $5.00-per-ton increase in the price of carbon steel. The increase would easily allow the companies to recoup the additional spike in labor costs. Linking wage increases to steel prices settled the strike but also forced the Truman administration to repudiate its postwar, inflation-sensitive stabilization policy.

In April 1947, the union negotiated an improved compensation package with U.S. Steel amounting to 15 cents an hour. The pact was approved by the other large steel producers a few months later. Immediately after the wage settlement the industry raised product prices across the board. While the deal included a two-year contract, the next year the union asked the industry to reopen the wage package. U.S. Steel initially resisted, but with steel output rising to nearly 66 million tons and manpower shortages reported in major production centers such as Youngstown and Chicago-Gary, it agreed to another 13-cent hike. Once again, despite government criticism, the industry lifted the per-ton price of steel an average of 9.6 percent. For two years, wages and prices moved upward together, forestalling any work stoppage. Since 1945, worker output had increased annually and company profits had nearly quadrupled. But in 1949 the union wanted something more than hourly pay increases and a half-million steelworkers had to strike against the industry's thirty-seven largest companies to bring about a resolution.

The key issues sparking this stoppage were company-financed social insurance and pension benefits. Different "health and welfare" plans existed throughout the industry, but most required employee contributions. U.S. Steel offered to pay 50 percent of social insurance costs but rejected making any pension contributions. Angered by the companies' opposition to pensions, the USWA signaled its readiness to strike but agreed to postpone it to allow a presidential fact-finding board to investigate the matter. The board, which was principally interested in avoiding a strike, recommended that company-financed pensions and insurance programs be provided. Unfortunately, the industry's chief executives disagreed with the board findings and publicly complained about "government dictated" terms. To no one's surprise, on October 1, yet another nationwide steel strike began. By the end of the strike's first week, 90 percent of the country's steelmaking capacity was shut down and Secretary of Commerce Charles Sawyer was predicting that the steelworkers' action would cause 5 million people to lose their jobs by December 1.

It appears that by refusing to accept the board's conditions, the companies had hoped to precipitate a walkout, thereby leaving President Truman with little alternative but to invoke the emergency powers of the Taft-Hartley Act, which authorized the president to request that the Supreme Court enjoin a work stoppage deemed a threat to the nation. But the *New York Times* reported that Truman "was firm and emphatic in his views . . . that he would not use the Taft-Hartley Law's emergency dispute provisions unless and until there was an emergency." The strike lasted forty-two days before agreement on the principle of employer-paid pensions was reached with Bethlehem. For nearly a week USWA President Murray and Bethlehem President Eugene Grace bartered over settlement terms. The company, which for twenty-six years had provided employees with free pensions of $50 a month, agreed to increase the payment to $100 a month. The employer contribution (an estimated 7 cents an hour) was actually better then the fact-finders' proposal (6 cents). In exchange, Murray agreed to have Bethlehem's 80,000 workers pay half the cost of a new 5-cents-an-hour insurance and hospitalization program. By November 11, all the companies had settled and the USWA had successfully extended the scope of industry-wide collective bargaining to include pensions.

One year later the steel contracts were reopened on wages and the union negotiated a raise of 16 cents per hour. The industry promptly hiked steel prices by about 5½ per ton. In the winter of 1951, however, the government reinstituted wage and price controls. In January 1951, the consumer price index had already climbed 10.3 points from just before the outbreak of the Korean War in November 1950. Reestablishment of the Wage Stabilization Board (WSB) meant that the government would have wide-ranging powers to intervene in any labor–management conflict that might threaten national defense. As the steel contracts expired on December 31, 1951, a long list of potentially contentious issues confronted the government's conflict-resolution machinery. Among them were union wage and fringe benefit demands totaling more than 30 cents an hour, and a provision to extend union coverage to every production worker while conditioning employment on union membership. The steel companies summarily rejected the "closed shop" and refused to even consider a wage offer. Steelmaker intransigence pushed the union to announce that they would strike on the date of contract expiration. But with the Korean War unfolding and American rearmament under way as part of a muscular foreign policy doctrine committed to Communist containment, President Truman urged both parties to submit their issues to the WSB.

Hearings on the steel dispute dragged on past the contract expiration date and repeatedly delayed the strike action. As the USWA set a new strike date for midnight April 8, on March 20, the WSB finally put forward its recommendations. Over the dissent of its industry representatives, the board recommended a two-year contract providing the most generous offer ever made to or negotiated by a CIO union. The total package included a wage hike of 17 cents per hour, an increase in shift differential pay, double-time pay for six holidays, and other fringe benefit improvements. In addition, it endorsed a union shop clause. The USWA immediately accepted the board's plan and Truman added his enthusiastic support for the settlement terms. Industry response was initially partially favorable to the wage and benefit increases, believing that the government would allow prices to rise, but adamantly opposed the union shop. However, once the Office of Price Stabilization rejected the companies' demand for a $7.00-per-ton price increase, the industry walked away from the bargaining table. Knowing that they had the president's endorsement for the entire board's recommendation and seeing no chance of brokering a deal directly with the companies, the union ordered a national walkout on April 9.

Facing the reality of a looming steel shutdown just hours away, on April 8, President Truman took one of the county's strongest assertions of presidential authority and ordered that the nation's mills be seized. Truman's actions were predicated on his belief that the Constitution granted the president inherent powers to protect the nation's health. As political scientists Chong-do Hah and Robert M. Lindquist have recorded, he announced that his seizure decision was "by virtue of authority vested in me by the Constitution" and placed Secretary of Commerce Charles Sawyer in charge of the seized mills. To support the national emergency nature of his order temporarily halting the walkout and to maintain the country's steel production for the time being, Truman observed that "steel is a key material in our entire defense effort . . . [it] is essential in order to meet urgent demands for steel—steel for weapons, for highways, and hospitals and schools." While the USWA cooperated with the president's order and kept its members at work, the companies, according to political scientists Frederick H. Harbison and Robert Spence, characterized the move "as a step toward nationalization of industries by a socialist-minded Administration."

Industry heads saw the brazen grab of their assets as part of a government strategy to keep workers on the job, while allowing political pressure to build for a settlement on the WSB's recommendation. Neither Congress nor the courts supported the seizure, and when a U.S district judged ruled the president's action illegal on April 29, the steelworkers struck. But Truman appealed the decision to the Supreme Court and restored government operation of the mills. The steelworkers subsequently went back to work. Finally, on June 2, by a margin of six to three, the Supreme Court found Truman's seizure to be unconstitutional. Upon hearing the decision, the USWA went on strike for second time.

At that point, encouraged by the industry, Truman considered invoking the Taft-Hartley procedures, but after being informed that the workers would respond by waging a wildcat (unofficial) strike he declined the option. However, shortly after the strike commenced, progress on the wage package was made as the companies won assurance that they would be granted the price relief they sought. The breaking point was the union's demand for a union shop. More specifically, the industry was determined to resist the imposition of "compulsory unionism" at the hands of the federal government. Not withstanding the industry's fierce opposition to the union shop, Bethlehem Steel negotiated a modified union shop agreement. But the agreement had no practical impact on industry talks and the strike dragged on. After weeks of fruitless two-way bargaining, on July 24, union and industry representatives agreed to conduct a bargaining session at the White House. The session proved to be critical because an agreement was reached to end the fifty-five-day standoff. Final terms of the agreement closely resembled the union's initial twenty-two demands, minus the principle of a union shop. However, the Bethlehem formula was incorporated into the labor deal. The union security provision required all new employees to sign application cards for union membership to take effect within thirty days, unless revoked by such employees. In practice, few employees took advantage of this "out" and the net effect was to secure nearly 100 percent union membership in the nation's steel mils. The strike, while peaceful and lacking any of the plant gate drama of the 1930s, foreshadowed a bigger fight on job security lurking just over the horizon.

The 1952 strike did not bring about conflict-free labor relations in the steel industry. Three years later, in the first industry-coordinated bargaining round (Inland Steel the lone exception), talks over a wage reopener broke down and, to signal their unhappiness, the union "sat on the steel" for one symbolic day. Workers were granted a general wage increase of $0.115, but were rebuffed on their demand for a "Guaranteed Annual Wage" (GAW). The one-day walkout was, by historic standards, insignificant, but what marked this dispute and settlement as unique was that for the first time the federal government played no substantive role in the negotiations. One year later, however, the government returned to its more interventionist posture.

In 1956, the USWA shut down the industry for a little more than one month (July 1 to August 3). Walking a peaceful, event-free picket line proved beneficial to workers' winning substantial contract improvements. In addition to general and premium wage increases, for the first time the contract featured company recognition of the union shop, supplemental unemployment benefits, and cost-of-living adjustments. In exchange, the union settled on a three-year deal with no wage reopeners. The agreement was once again brokered by a federal government playing a behind-the-scenes pressuring role. In retrospect, the end of the strike proved to be the apex point of union bargaining accomplishments. The union's wage policy committee considered the settlement the union's crowning achievement in its twenty-six-year history. In *Striking Steel*, historian Jack Metzgar underscored the value of the 1956 dispute by summing up the success of steelworker militancy: "From 1946 to 1956, the companies resisted every improvement the Steelworkers sought, but each time they yielded bit by bit until, in 1956, they finally gave the union everything it had wanted, even the union shop." While steelworker compensation was steadily improving, the companies' near-total wage and benefit capitulation hid a growing industry frustration with the USWA's ability to use contract language to inhibit job reductions. As the three-year deal wound down, the industry finally decided to make a stand against a provision it had handed to the steelworkers a decade earlier.

In 1947, the U.S. Steel Corporation agreed to include a little-noticed clause in the contract that placed limits on when and how the company could reduce work crews. Known as "Section 2-B," according to business historian James Rose, the six-paragraph clause concretely limited "management's right to cut staffing levels and reorganize jobs without a corresponding introduction of new equipment or technology." Metzgar describes the companies' perspective on 2-B as a "universal right to featherbedding" that kept "them from achieving maximum efficiency." Steelworkers saw it very differently. Recalling the pre-1942 tyrannical control management once held over working conditions and staffing, the USWA had ingeniously and assertively maneuvered to limit unilateral management changes. By 1959, Section 2-B had become a rigid set of work rules that protected steelworker jobs against company efforts to lower production costs by simply dumping labor. USWA general counsel Lee Pressman boasted, according to Rose, that 2-B protected "everything that pertains to a man's job by way of conditions of work." As Metzgar notes, to undo what U.S. Steel labor relations head R. Conrad Cooper provocatively called "mistakes of the past eighteen years," was understood by steelworkers as an attempt "to turn the clock" back to an ugly workplace servility.

In the run-up to the 1959 contract talks, the industry demanded the right to control the number and content of all jobs while denying the union recourse to the contract grievance and arbitration procedures. Large layoffs (1953–54 and 1957–58) and job elimination programs had hurt plant-level labor relations throughout the 1950s, and the union liberally used 2-B to oppose such cuts. By 1952 over half of the union's grievances involved 2-B, and by the end of the decade they amounted to 60 percent of disputes at some U.S. Steel plants. Each time management insisted that they had the right to eliminate a person's job solely on the basis of economic factors, the union pushed back and insisted that changes in technology or the production process were needed first. But doing so was costly and the industry preferred a much cheaper "rounding out" of production by making piecemeal add-ons to existing facilities. In the 1952 negotiations, according to Rose, the industry unsuccessfully attempted to excise 2-B by including the contract right to "have complete freedom to rearrange duties and assign the work, and to establish, change, or terminate jobs." USWA president Philip Murray incredulously responded to the industry by referring to the "the Soviet-like, the imperialistic-like, the totalitarian-like nature of their dirty, rotten, reprehensible proposal. . . . [T]he acceptance [of which] would [mean] our people would no longer be free." In 1952, the union refused to give ground on local work rules. Management licked its wounds and plotted another assault.

Early contract talks in 1959 did not focus on work rules but, with less than a month remaining before the contract expired, the companies proposed an eight-point plan that would eviscerate "the workplace rule of law," according to Metzgar. The industry offered a modest wage increase in exchange for the union's accepting the work rule changes involving scheduling, seniority, staffing, and work standards. As Metzgar noted, however, the industry's ploy was to force the union to strike and then offer a settlement whereby they would drop all but one of the eight proposals—Section 2-B. On July 15, the union complied with the industry's strike plan by shutting down 90 percent of the country's steelmaking capacity. More than 500,000 workers stayed home, and it would take President Eisenhower and a Supreme Court order to get them back into their steel-toed shoes.

The strike lasted for 116 days, the longest in the industry's history. Eventually, Eisenhower invoked Taft-Hartley's eighty-day cooling-off period and the Supreme Court ruled that the strike was a clear threat to the nation's security. These actions broke the strike, but they did not stimulate productive bargaining between the parties. Eventually, Kaiser Steel broke ranks with the industry and agreed to a modest pay pact minus the intolerable 2-B changes. However, hard bargaining with the rest of the major producers continued until January 5, when a settlement was announced. Facing the likelihood that union members would vote down any follow-up industry proposal that included work-rule changes and subsequently would be able legally to strike again, President Eisenhower directed Vice President Nixon to convince U.S. Steel chairman Roger Blough to make a deal. The final contract provided for a wage increase of 39 cents an hour spread over thirty months, and reduced Section 2-B to an agreement to form a joint committee to study the issue. In announcing the joint committee, union president David McDonald derisively noted, according to Rose, "Of course, you know what that will amount to. It won't amount to a hill of beans." Once again, the industry had picked a fight about costs and managerial prerogatives and, according to Metzgar, the union had scored a "decisive knockout that left the companies flat on their industrial relations backs."

However, the importance of the 1959 steel strike went beyond hourly monetary measurements of dollars and cents and shop-floor control. Many steel historians, including Paul Tiffany, have come to label the 1959 strike as a "watershed" in the eventual decline of the American steel industry. Numerous postwar strikes produced an unintended negative consequence. Prior to predicted walkouts, steel users began buying and stockpiling steel. Following a brief stoppage, demand for steel would drop off as users drew down their supplies. The anticipated shutdown stimulated a destructive boom-and-bust cycle. In anticipation of a long struggle with the union in 1959, the steelmakers juiced up steel buyers' stockpiling in the first half of the year, gambling that they would earn sufficient prestrike profits to easily weather a shutdown. But buyers also had other options. They could and did, in record numbers, purchase steel from foreign producers. With national mills closed for four months in 1959, steel imports exceeded exports for the first time since the turn of the century. "Practically every year thereafter saw a rise in imports," lamented business writer John

Hoerr. As I have noted elsewhere, the flood of less expensive foreign steel was to figure significantly in the industry's and union's misfortunes in the "crisis" of the late 1970s and mid-1980s.

Steelworker Militancy After the "Crisis"

As the casualties of the early 1980s' recession began to mount, Donald Barnett, chief economist at the American Iron and Steel Institute (AISI), made the prediction (in a book written with Louis Schorsch) that the U.S. integrated steel industry, which processes its own raw materials (i.e., coke ovens and blast furnaces), makes steel (i.e., open hearths, basic oxygen or electric furnaces), and rolls semifinished products (i.e., slabs, billets, and blooms) in primary mills and finished products (i.e., flat rolled sheets, wired rod, and bars) in finishing mills, would either "continue to perform poorly, with bankruptcies and facility closures, or it will restructure radically, boosting productivity in order to regain international competitiveness." The crisis in steel was alternately described as a failure of corporate investment strategy, labor relations, and government policy. Whatever the real source of decay, the result of this failure was a growing import sector and the expansion of efficient, largely nonunion, domestic mini-mill operators. Where in 1960 major integrated firms had controlled 95 percent of the U.S. steel market, by 1982, their market share was reduced to 60 percent.

In the center of this tempest the USWA still had labor contracts to negotiate. But along with negotiating over typical items, the union also made a decision to try to use the bargaining process to save the basic steel industry. Struggling steelmakers, like the nation's seventh largest, Willing-Pittsburgh (W-P), had been given multiple wage concessions in the early 1980s. But in 1985, the union embarked on a plan that Hoerr noted "seemed suicidal." Despite W-P's large mounting losses and $450 million in accumulated debt, the union struck the company's holdings in West Virginia, western Pennsylvania, and southeastern Ohio.

Shutting down work at W-P was a novel and risky strategy for the union. In April 1985, W-P filed for Chapter 11 bankruptcy protection, and a work stoppage could force it into liquidation. Nonetheless, union officials were angry that the company petitioned the bankruptcy judge to allow it to cancel the existing labor agreement. USWA leaders understood that granting the company unilateral power to impose a new deal would, in Hoerr's words, "break the back of the union." W-P demanded a 28 percent reduction in wages and near unassailable rights to contract work out to nonunion employees. The union decided it could not capitulate to dictatorial terms and also believed that it could pressure the company's board of directors into an agreement that would salvage the asset value of the firm.

The strike commenced on July 21, 1985, and ended nearly three months later on October 15. The settlement was made possible when W-P's chief executive officer and union villain, Dennis Carney, and five board members resigned. Carney's departure removed a major negotiating roadblock, but it was a unique bargaining provision that made an agreement possible. Under pressure from W-P lenders, the company and the union agreed to terminate the employer's $470 million underfunded pension plan and to allow the government's Pension Benefit Guarantee Corporation to assume the retiree obligations. The deal dramatically lowered W-P's labor costs and also significantly reduced the hourly wage concession that workers would have to make. In addition, notes Hoerr, the company agreed to pay a "price escalation bonus" of $1.00 per hour depending on how steel prices were adjusted upward.

Labor peace at W-P was only temporary. In 1990, the union authorized a strike vote, but managed to reach a deal without a stoppage. However, continued slack in steel markets and rising foreign imports brought the company and union back into conflict four years later. Facing demands for further reductions in wages, health care, funding for retiree health care, and changes in work rules, 4,700 union workers struck W-P on March 1, 1994. Two days later the strike was over. Critical to the union's willingness to end the strike was the company's agreement to triple its contribution into a voluntary employee benefits association (i.e., VEBA) and to considerably increase employee health care and life insurance benefits. Unfortunately, this time harmonious labor relations lasted less than three years. Frustrated with management's insistence on maintaining an inferior pension plan, W-P workers returned to the picket lines on October 1, 1996. Unlike the 1994 stoppage, this struggle would not be quickly resolved.

Union members at all eight W-P plants celebrated the 1996 Christmas holiday by sharing strike duty and living off of USWA local donations. As one day after another passed with no settlement, the strike became a national cause for the entire labor movement. In April 1997, the union's *Steel Labor* noted that AFL-CIO President John Sweeney pledged the national federation's support. "Your fight is our fight," Sweeney announced and stressed that "the outcome of this battle will affect every working person." Union hopes for a settlement were further raised when the NLRB accused W-P of bad faith bargaining that both "caused and prolonged" the strike. Armed with the NLRB's complaint, the steelworkers pressed major shareholders of W-P to encourage the company to bargain a fair contract. Finally, ten months after the strike had begun, a new labor agreement was reached. When USW members put down their picket signs in Ohio, Pennsylvania, and West Virginia, they had established a new record for union militancy, widely eclipsing the 116-day national steel stoppage in 1959.

The union's extended difficulties with W-P were mirrored by its struggle with industry leader U.S. Steel. In the summer of 1986, the two parties were locked into a fierce standoff over total employment costs and contracting out. The union demanded that the company fully disclose its financial conditions, as other steel firms had done, but U.S. Steel refused. Instead, while keeping more than 20,000 workers on layoff and assigning 11 percent of the workforce to overtime, the company stockpiled over 1 million tons of steel. In negotiations, U.S. Steel demanded a wage cut of $7.00 an hour and the unilateral rights to eliminate jobs, change crew compositions, and compress job classifications. According to Hoerr, USWA official and lead negotiator James McGeehan decried that "the company has put on the table contract changes that would turn back the clock on worker's rights more than fifty years." To make matters worse, in the midst of heated contract talks the company announced a name change and reorganization. Signaling the decreased value of its steel production, U.S. Steel was turned into a subsidiary of USX. Steelworkers mockingly wondered if the "X" stood for ex-workers. Not surprisingly the union's 22,000 U.S. Steel members voted "unanimously" to shut down the company if necessary.

Apparently prepared to "take" a strike, the company rejected a union offer to extend the old agreement and to keep working while negotiations continued. USX then put some teeth behind its rejection by initiating, on July 31, a national lockout of its unionized employees. The company labeled the work stoppage a strike, while union pickets arrived at plant gates in twenty-five locations with signs that read "locked out." Whether strike or lockout, union workers were fighting against USX's plans to "whittle down" the workforce. "Occurring in the midst of scarcity and decline," noted Hoerr, the "USX stoppage was a defensive strike." At root "it was a matter of job ownership."

The lockout/strike lasted for six months and ended in February 1987. Workers survived the 184-day ordeal on $60.00 a week in strike benefits as well as unemployment compensation in those states where locked-out employees were eligible for assistance. While USX managed to ship steel out of its stockpile, it lost $3–5 million a day during the stoppage. The final four-year settlement included hourly wage and benefit cuts between $2.52 and $2.07, as well as the elimination of 1,346 jobs. The union won comprehensive contracting-out language, as well as a company-financed job retraining fund, recall rights for laid-off workers equal to the number of workers displaced, and a profit-sharing fund. The deal was painful for the union but was approved by 19,621 members and opposed by 4,045. Unfortunately, the pain of a concessionary contract was rubbed raw by USX's announcement, shortly after member ratification of the agreement, that it would close three mills. The news of the unexpected permanent shutdowns angered the union and ensured that labor–management relations would remain strained at USX for the foreseeable future.

Tense labor relations did not however dampen a strengthening market for domestically produced steel. The industry saw a recovery in the early 1990s. But higher profit margins only invited opportunities for exploitation. On March 21, 1993, approximately 300 members of USWA Local 9121 began walking a picket line at the Bayou Steel firm in Louisiana. The workers shut down the plant when negotiations over a new contact stalled. The union accused Bayou of not bargaining in good faith and charged the company with numerous unfair labor practices. By a margin of 286 to 6, the union membership voted to strike after rejecting a company offer to eviscerate employee wages and medical insurance. As the strike dragged into its fifth month, the union widened its resistance by deploying a strategic campaign to pressure Bayou investors, creditors, customers, and government officials. International Union vice president George Becker announced the start of the campaign by declaring in *Steel Labor* that "labor disputes no longer are restricted to the picket line." The union specifically targeted the company's $44 million in state and parish tax waivers and bondholder fears that their company paper would lose its value if the strike went on any longer.

In the ninth month of the strike, the union's pressure began to pay dividends. The St. John Parish Council (home to the LaPlace steel plant) voted to urge state officials to revoke Bayou's state tax exemption. According to *Steel Labor* the Council also condemned the company for hiring out-of-state individuals to "replace workers who live and pay taxes in the parish." The striking workers at Bayou were also buoyed by the women of the "Hearts of Steel," who raised funds to donate 250 Thanksgiving turkeys to striking families and cooked more than 1,300 meals. The union got more good news in February 1994 when the company was found guilty of eight labor law violations and ordered by the National Labor Relations Board to settle the strike. On another front, the union's pressure campaign had moved to Manhattan. A delegation of union officials and striking workers attended a meeting held by Bayou's underwriter, Chemical Securities, to warn investors against buying $75 million in new bonds issued by the steel firm.

With the union's corporate strategy beginning to raise critical concerns about the company's senior management, Bayou agreed to attend contact talks mediated by Louisiana's governor, Democrat Edwin Edwards. The meeting—a fourteen-hour session—proved fruitful and a tentative agreement was reached. However, once the governor's intervention ended, the company added additional conditions to the settlement and the union membership rejected the offer. The strike stretched beyond its one-year anniversary, as did the company's bad news. In the spring of 1994, the Occupational Safety and Health Administration fined the steelmaker $35,000 for "failure to provide medical and lead-exposure records" requested by the union, according to *Steel Labor.* A few months later one member of the company's board of directors, Alan J. Patricof, resigned his seat, citing Bayou's unlawful behavior. Patricof's resignation along with a lawsuit filed by the union against Bayou convinced the shareholders to allow a steelworker delegation to speak for twenty minutes at a New York meeting about the unfair labor practices. At that meeting, union secretary-treasurer Leo Gerard pointed out that while other steel companies were making money, Bayou had suffered three straight years of losses and its stock had plunged from $13.00 a share to just under $4.00.

Despite the union's dogged uncovering of company environmental problems, including a citizen lawsuit for alleged violations of the Clean Air Act, financial mismanagement, and mounting charges of labor law violations, Bayou refused to come back to the bargaining table. Strikers remained on the picket line throughout 1995 and for most of the next year. Finally on September 26, 1996, the union and the company signed a six-year deal that ended the forty-two-month work stoppage. All union employees were returned to their jobs without loss of seniority.

The year 1995 was a particularly contentious time for steel industry labor relations. Along with the W-P and Bayou struggles, steelworkers at Warren Consolidated Industries (WCI) in Warren, Ohio, braved a seven-week strike reminiscent of those in the 1930s. Characterized by physical engagements with company security, county police, and replacement workers, 1,650 striking USWA members from two locals waged a constant twenty-four-hour street battle against company plans to scrap vital contract language. In early September, just three days after the previous contract expired, a police-estimated crowd of more than 7,000 attended a USWA-organized demonstration. The size and noise of the crowd convinced the company to send second-shift workers home and later to refuse to let those reporting for the third shift enter the plant. At the same time, the company bussed into the plant hundreds of non-union workers and security guards, together with makeshift sleeping and eating facilities—actions that recalled the 1937 Little Steel Strike. In fact, the lockout marked the first time since 1937 that anyone had attempted to run an integrated steel mill in the United States with "scabs."

WCI had earned $114 million since 1988 and was the second-most-profitable company in the steel industry in the second quarter of 1995. The union saw WCI's actions as exploitive, provocative, and heavy-handed. The company seemed determined to crush the century-long history of union activity in the Warren, Ohio, community. WCI invested in a series of intimidating tactics in an attempt to break the unity of the strikers. Instead, the workers' resolve produced a four-year agreement that provided a wage increase, a new defined-benefit pension plan, medical insurance improvements, and a much-needed successorship clause (i.e., the workforce would remain unionized) if the company was sold. The deal also included assurances that the company would not discharge or discipline any employee for any activity related to the work stoppage.

Jubilation, however, over a local victory at WCI was short-lived. Two years later a second "crisis" in steel erupted. By 2003, thirty-seven steel companies would file for bankruptcy, including the second and third largest. The industry was now operating at a fourteen-year low of less than 65 percent of capacity and steelworker job loss exceeded 75,000. Between 1999 and 2003, roughly one-fifth of the nation's steelmaking capacity with the means to produce 25 million raw tons of steel would be idled. The causes of this dislocation were divided between low-cost competition from foreign producers and an indifferent U.S. economic policy toward manufacturing.

On the cusp of this brutal decline in steel markets, the union attempted to reconstruct a form of pattern bargaining that had been loosened during the tumultuous crisis years of the 1980s. But while contracts at a number of national steel firms had been successfully negotiated, some firms appeared to welcome a struggle. One such company was Colorado Fuel and Iron (CF&I) Steel. Located in Pueblo, Colorado, the firm was once owned by John D. Rockefeller and was now operated by Oregon Steel. On October 3, 1997, more than 1,100 USWA members went on strike refusing to accept the company's demands for draconian cutbacks in wages, benefits, and pensions. In response to the shutdown, CF&I operated the plant with replacement workers. In *Steel Labor,* International Union secretary-treasurer Leo Gerard resolved to spend "every damn cent" of the union's $200 million Defense Fund to "be here one day longer than Oregon Steel." Part of that expenditure went to pressuring Wells Fargo Bank, the lead partner in a consortium of banks providing credit to Oregon Steel, to withhold financing from the steel firm. At a Wells Fargo Bank demonstration in Portland, approximately 150 people rallied and 21 steelworker supporters were arrested.

As the strike stretched into its third month, the union altered its strategy and made an unconditional offer to return to work while continuing to bargain. In response, the company notified the union that its members had been permanently replaced. At that juncture the Colorado Department of Labor and Employment began to award unemployment compensation to CF&I workers. But the union, according to *Steel Labor*, warned that failing to "fire all the scabs they've hired and recall the striking workers" could cost Oregon $600,000 a week in back-pay liabilities. At the end of 1997, the company had reinstated only 117 former workers and had hired more than 200 replacements. That warning proved prescient when on February 27, 1998, the NLRB issued a complaint against the company for violating the law by not rehiring approximately 690 additional union members. The board's ruling also set the actual back-pay liability for the company at $1 million a week. Reinforced with the government complaint, a large delegation of steelworkers calling themselves the "Pueblo Posse" raided the company's annual shareholders' meeting to demand justice for the CF&I workers. A few days earlier, steelworkers romped into San Francisco and stationed a horse-drawn stagecoach labeled "Wells Fargo Anti-Worker Wagon" at the headquarters of Wells Fargo. The wagon was draped with old leather money bags representing the bank's $125 million investment in Oregon Steel.

Despite the union's strategic campaign, which included politically mobilizing union workers throughout Pueblo's 125 voting precincts, bargaining was at a standstill until the USWA offered the company a compromise package at a summer 1998 negotiation session. At that point, Oregon had become the target of community and religious-based opposition and Wells Fargo had lost $1.3 billion in accounts as a result of a steelworker boycott. Remarkably, Oregon not only rejected the union's latest offer but refused to bargain any further. The dispute then turned into a form of trench warfare. It lingered on until March 2004, when the CF&I (now Rocky Mountain Steel) workers approved a settlement. More than six years since they had set up twenty-four-hour pickets, the Pueblo-based workers had won the right to take their "rightful place" in the mill and to do so with pension improvements, a wage increase, back-pay awards, a profit-sharing plan, and language prohibiting the sale of the company to any new firm without the buyer recognizing the union agreement. CF&I workers also now held the distinction of having participated in the longest strike in steel union history.

Conclusion

Much has changed in America's steel industry. Where once dozens of firms produced steel, now there are only three major producers. Where once there were nearly a million steelworkers, now there are less than 50,000. Where once the industry was considered a bellwether of the nation's economic fortunes, it is no longer determinant of economic forecasts. But some things have not changed. From the 1930s cauldron of union formation to the early twenty-first-century opposition of union-busting firms, the USW has shown an implacable willingness to "sit on the steel." The union's survival and continued relevance as a labor organization has been nourished by the militancy of thousands of steelworkers from Gary, Indiana, to Pueblo, Colorado. While many labor-relations commentators have called the labor strike a dead tactic, the USW has proved that it is very much a live weapon to be wielded for America's working class.

See also: Corporate Strike Strategy, 66; The 1945–1946 Strike Wave, 216; Strikes in the United States Since World World II, 226; Steel Strikes Before 1935, 351.

Bibliography

Barnett, Donald, and Louis Schorsch. *Steel: Upheaval in a Basic Industry.* Cambridge, MA: Ballinger, 1983.

Baughman, James. "Little Steel Strike in Three Ohio Communities." Master's thesis, Columbia University, 1975.

Blake, Benjamin. "Ohio's Steel Mill War: The Little Steel Strike of 1937." Western Reserve Historical Society. Available at academic.csuohio.edu/clevelandhistory/Issue3/articles/steelpage2content.htm.

Bruno, Robert. "USWA-Bargained and State-Oriented Responses to the Recurrent Steel Crisis." *Labor Studies Journal* 30, no. 1 (Spring 2005): 67–91.

Hah, Chong-do, and Robert M. Lindquist. "The 1952 Steel Seizure Revisited: A Systematic Study in Presidential Decision-Making." *Administrative Science Quarterly* 20, no. 4 (December 1975): 587–605.

Harbison, Frederick H., and Robert Spence. "The Politics of Collective Bargaining: The Postwar Record in Steel." *American Political Science Review* 48, no. 3 (September 1954): 715.

Hoerr, John P. *And The Wolf Finally Came: The Decline of the American Steel Industry.* Pittsburgh: Pittsburgh University Press, 1988.

Metzgar, Jack. *Striking Steel, Solidarity Remembered.* Philadelphia: Temple University Press, 2000.

Rose, James D. "The Struggle over Management Rights at US Steel, 1946–1960: A Reassessment of Section 2-B of the Collective Bargaining Contract." *Business History Review* 72, no. 3 (Autumn 1998): 446–77.

United Steelworkers of America. *Steel Labor.* Various issues, 1993–2000.

Stein, Judith. *Running Steel, Running America: Race, Economic Policy and the Decline of Liberalism.* Chapel Hill: University of North Carolina Press, 1998.

Tiffany, Paul. *The Decline of American Steel: How Management, Labor and Government Went Wrong.* New York: Oxford University Press, 1988.

UNIONIZING THE "JUNGLE": A CENTURY OF MEATPACKING STRIKES

Jackie S. Gabriel

The last couple of decades of the nineteenth century were marked by dramatic labor conflicts in the American meatpacking industry. Labor historian James R. Barrett explains that "meat packing was the most strike-prone of all U.S. industries in the years between 1881 and 1905." Chicago became the epicenter of these labor conflicts because its Union Stock Yards employed more than a third of the total national meatpacking labor force, and its labor relations set industry standards. In the summer of 1877, as a general strike swept across the city, packinghouse workers took to the streets demanding a wage increase of $2.00 per day. When the Chicago police ordered them to disperse and go back to work, they remained and subsequently the police fired into their ranks. By the time the battle ended, nearly three dozen workers were killed and over 200 injured, according to Barrett. Ultimately, the workers won a wage increase and secured labor agreements with the packers (owners). Just two years later, in December 1879, labor unrest again erupted as 5,000 to 6,000 packinghouse workers struck, demanding a closed shop. Once again, violence broke out and the police were called in. The strike was short-lived as workers began to break ranks and return to work within barely a month of walking off the job.

A series of additional meatpacking strikes punctuated the 1880s. The most notable one occurred in May 1886, when a national strike of an estimated 400,000 workers broke out for an eight-hour day in answer to a call issued by the Federation of Organized Trades and Labor Unions, the predecessor of the American Federation of Labor (AFL). On May 3, 1886, headed by leading cattle butcher John T. Joyce and with no formal organization, Chicago packinghouse workers joined the strike. The packers quickly capitulated to the workers' demands, granting them ten hours' pay for eight hours of work. This victory for over 35,000 Chicago packinghouse workers represented the largest number of workers in a single industry to receive the eight-hour day. However, their victory was also short-lived. Within five months the packers, led by Philip Armour, organized an employers' association—the National Independent Meatpackers Association—that reneged on their agreement and announced a return to the ten-hour day. On October 8, when packers posted notices of the reintroduction of the ten-hour day, a strike erupted among hog butchers at an independent plant and quickly spread throughout the stockyards. The strike was soon called off by the Knights of Labor leadership. However, the leadership could not contain the workers' militancy for long and a second strike broke out in early November. Once again the workers were forced back to work, as Grand Master Workman of the Knights Terrence Powderly unilaterally ended the strike and threatened to revoke the charter of any local that did not comply with his instructions. When the workers returned to their jobs, they were confronted with a contract that forced them to renounce all unions.

Throughout the 1890s, minor spontaneous strikes erupted in meatpacking, reflecting workers' continued dissatisfaction with wages and working conditions in the industry. The next major labor conflict, however, occurred in the summer of 1894 when Eugene V. Debs's American Railway Union called for a sympathy strike during its historic dispute with the Pullman Company in Chicago. On the morning of July 13, 1894, between 1,000 and 2,000 packinghouse workers in Chicago walked off their jobs in sympathy with the railroad workers and also in demand of a wage increase of their own. The strike soon spread to Omaha, Kansas City, East St. Louis, and other meatpacking centers. However, the strikers were no match for the packers, who were able to maintain production by utilizing foremen and superintendents to perform the skilled work and recruiting hundreds of immigrant and African-American workers to fill the unskilled jobs. Polish immigrants were the first strikebreakers to come to the packers' assistance. They were soon joined by African Americans and other recent immigrants from Eastern Europe. Historian Walter Fogel explains that African-American workers—who were barred from membership in the American Railway Union—did not feel compelled to honor the packinghouse workers' strike, which supported a union that actively discriminated against them. As the conflict dragged on, the striking workers sought vengeance against the strikebreakers, and even though the majority of them were white, African Americans became the targets of most of the strikers' hostility. African Americans were attacked and burned in effigy. The strike dragged on for nine weeks before it was abandoned in failure. The packinghouse workers' struggle was ill-timed given the depressed economy and the army of unemployed workers readily available to replace them. In the aftermath, organizing activity in the industry declined as activist workers were blacklisted and effectively shut out of the industry.

At the close of the nineteenth century, the industry was virtually unorganized. By 1896 the AFL carried on its rolls just five packinghouse local unions and five retail butchers' local unions nationwide. That same year, Samuel Gompers, head of the AFL, invited these local unions to send delegates to the Federation's national convention in an effort to organize an international union for meatpacking workers. As a result, the delegates who attended the convention founded a new union—the Amalgamated Meat Cutters and Butcher Workmen of North America, commonly referred to as "the Amalgamated." With the newly formed union came a renewed effort to organize the packinghouse workers nationally. The union immediately began to make progress in the industry, chartering twenty-eight local unions during its first year. Over the following few years, the union continued to grow, and by August 1901, it had organized twenty different local unions in Chicago alone. As the Amalgamated expanded its organizing efforts, workers flocked to the union, swelling its membership to 56,000 in a labor force estimated at 74,000 by 1904.

The 1904 National Strike

The Amalgamated managed to negotiate labor contracts for its skilled workers, but without a floor on unskilled workers' wages, union officials realized all wages could be lowered. At the union's national convention in the summer of 1904, union members proposed an industry-wide wage standard and increase. Union leadership, specifically Amalgamated President Michael Donnelly, was reluctant to demand a wage increase during a depression, with unemployment high. Nevertheless, Donnelly took the membership's demands to representatives of the so-called Big Seven packers (Armour, Swift, Morris, National Packing, Schwarzschild and Sulzberger, Cudahy, and Libby, McNeill and Libby). He asked for a uniform wage scale for all meatpacking plants based on the rate that prevailed in the Chicago plants and an increase in the minimum wage from 18½ cents to 20 cents per hour for all classes of unskilled workers. The "Big Seven," bargaining together as a single unit, rejected the union's demands. They objected to an increase in wages during a depression and refused to negotiate over an unskilled rate, which they claimed was determined by supply and demand. After compromises from both sides, the packers eventually offered a minimum wage of 16½ cents an hour. The union countered with an offer that would have made the Chicago rate of 18½ cents an hour standard for the industry. But the packers again rejected the union's offer and negotiations came to an impasse.

On July 12, the workers struck. Barrett explains the scene in Chicago: "Precisely at noon on July 12, twenty-eight thousand packinghouse workers finished the killing which they had in hand, wrapped up their tools, cleaned their workplaces, and marched out of the plants. Thousands of others in packing centers throughout the country joined them." On the first day of the strike, approximately 50,000 packinghouse workers in Chicago, New

York, Kansas City, Omaha, East St. Louis, St. Joseph, Sioux City, St. Paul, and Fort Worth walked off the job. The packers immediately responded by hiring replacements found among the thousands of unemployed workers. Fogel reports: "The packers contended that even at the prevailing rate of 16.5 cents an hour, 3,000 to 5,000 transient laborers sought work each morning in the Union Stock Yards, and that jobs were available for less than one-tenth of them. Within days the packers resumed operations, proving that they could run their plants without the unionized workers.

Eight days into the strike, and under the threat of a sympathy strike among the allied trades, the packers agreed to resume negotiations. The two sides quickly reached an agreement that allowed the packers to retain the strikebreakers that wished to remain on the job, while reinstating the strikers on an individual basis as jobs became available and without discrimination. On July 22, the strikers returned to work. However, when foremen at the Armour plant in Chicago refused to rehire returning cattle butchers, who were some of the most prominent strike leaders, other returning strikers refused to work, which renewed the strike. By the time the Amalgamated's leadership arrived, the strike was widespread and the leadership saw no option but to declare the strike and send out word to other packing centers. During this second phase of the strike, according to David Brody, the Amalgamated demanded, under the threat of a sympathy strike among the allied trades, "that *all* employees be hired back within *ten days*. . . . That *all* killing, cutting and casing department men be reinstated to their former positions within *forty eight* hours after the resumption of work . . ." The packers rejected the union's demands and on the following Monday the allied trades joined the strike. Both the packinghouse workers and the allied trade workers were quickly replaced by strikebreakers. The packers were able to easily recruit workers from among the locally unemployed. They also imported a significant number of African Americans from the South. Fogel explains that trainloads of several hundred African-American workers, accompanied by law enforcement, arrived in Chicago each day. Between the foremen and the strikebreakers, the packers were able to resume near-normal production.

As the weeks dragged on, the packers refused to bargain with the union because they were confident they could defeat the strike. A delegation of social reformers including Jane Addams and Mary McDowell pleaded with J. Ogden Armour to meet with the union. Armour consented and offered to take back the striking workers as needed and give skilled workers their prestrike wages. On September 6, the union membership rejected Armour's offer. Within just two days, however, Amalgamated leadership called off the strike in total defeat. Over the next several weeks, strikers drifted back into the plants, with the exception of many union activists who were blacklisted and driven out of the industry, similar to previous strike efforts. The strike defeat was devastating for the Amalgamated. Within just a year, the number of Amalgamated locals in Chicago fell from twenty-one to six, and the union's national membership dropped from an estimated 34,000 to 6,200, according to Barrett. After their defeat, the Amalgamated retreated from the packinghouses, choosing to concentrate its organizing efforts on the skilled butchers of the retail meat trade.

World War I and Renewed Unionism in Meatpacking

What unionism remained in the packing centers after the 1904 union defeat not only tended to be concentrated among the skilled butchers but also remained relatively ineffective until the economic and political context of World War I once again facilitated labor organization. Wartime demand for meat, coupled with a shortage of labor, created unrest throughout the industry, and a series of spontaneous strikes erupted in 1916 and 1917 across the major packing centers including Sioux City, East St. Louis, and Omaha. In Omaha, the strike began on September 1, 1917, when fifty truck drivers walked off the job at the Armour meatpacking plant. Over the next few days more than 4,000 packinghouse workers at the Cudahy, Morris, and Swift plants joined the Armour strikers. The packers quickly settled on terms that favored the striking workers.

Realizing that the packinghouse workers were ripe for organization, the Amalgamated and the AFL seized the opportunity. In Chicago, they created the Stockyards Labor Council (SLC), which consisted of a number of local unions with jurisdiction in the meatpacking industry. Shortly after it was established in September 1917, the SLC initiated an aggressive organizing campaign. Within a couple of months it had successfully organized the majority of Chicago's packinghouse workers. Historian Alma Herbst reports that by November, "the union, which boasted 100 percent organization of the skilled workers, 90 percent of all workers and a membership between 35,000 and 40,000 in Chicago, felt itself firmly entrenched in the industry." Confident in its organizational strength, in mid-November the Amalgamated presented the "Big Five" packers, which at the time were Armour, Swift, Cudahy, Morris, and Wilson, with a list of demands, including union recognition, wage increases, overtime pay, and equal pay for men and women. When the packers resisted the union's demands, packinghouse workers in the major packing centers voted overwhelmingly to strike.

Fearing that a strike would disrupt essential wartime production, the federal government intervened in the packinghouse dispute. President Woodrow Wilson's President's Mediation Commission set up an arbitration board, headed by federal judge Samuel S. Alschuler. On Christmas Day 1917, the Big Five packers and the Amalgamated signed an agreement with the Mediation Commission prohibiting strikes in the major packing centers for the duration of the war. Approximately three months later, Judge Alschuler granted packinghouse workers an eight-hour day to replace the ten-hour day, a forty-eight-hour week, time and a quarter for overtime, seven paid holidays, paid lunches, and equal pay for men and women doing the same class of work. This award boosted the union cause and within a ten-month period, the Amalgamated doubled its national membership.

During a second round of arbitrations in April 1919, the Big Five packers requested to extend the existing labor agreement for one year after peace had been signed with Germany. However, with the onset of an economic depression in 1920, declining meat prices meant declining profits for the packers, who now perceived the agreement as a hindrance and therefore tried to withdraw from it. In November 1920, Judge Alschuler rejected the Big Five packers' request for concessions. Then in February 1921, the packers notified the federal government that they would no longer abide by the agreement and in the following month announced a reduction in wages and reintroduced the ten-hour day. The Amalgamated appealed to the government and a compromise was reached in March 1921 in which the union accepted a wage reduction in exchange for maintenance of an eight-hour day and an extension of the arbitration agreement for six more months.

Both the packers and the union knew that a confrontation was inevitable at the expiration of the agreement in September 1921. Therefore, both sides began to prepare for the conflict. While the Amalgamated tried to build its strength in the packinghouse, the packers turned to employee representative plans, or so-called company unionism. These representation plans were designed to minimize workers' grievances and gain workers' allegiance to the company. Barrett explains that the packers used the period between signing the last arbitration agreement and the following September to set up organizations parallel to the unions, which could compete directly with the Amalgamated for workers' loyalties. Although Armour took the lead, all of the major packers established such company unions, which were given names such as Employees' Representation Plan at Armour, the Joint Representation Committee at Wilson, and the Employees' Benefit Association at Swift. Upon expiration of the arbitration agreement, the packers submitted a request for wage cuts to these company unions, where they were approved in mid-November.

Meanwhile, the Amalgamated asked for negotiations and demanded a continuation of the wages and working conditions that prevailed under the arbitration agreement. When the Big Five packers refused negotiations and arbitration, the Amalgamated called a national strike, which began December 5, 1921. The strike lasted just nine weeks and ended in complete defeat for the union. At the time it was called, America was in a deep economic depression, with the national unemployment rate over 20 percent. The number of packinghouse workers in Chicago alone declined 40 percent from 45,000 in 1919 to 27,000 in 1921. Given these labor market conditions and the newly established employee representation plans, many packinghouse workers decided that devotion to their employers was more likely to lead to job security than walking out with the union. For instance, according to historian Alma Herbst, many African-American workers who came into the industry during the war remained at work during the strike rather than joining the union that "had not admitted them whole-heartedly or even on the basis of equality." Labor historian Rick Halpern explains, "The majority of black workers stayed on the job rather than cast their lot with the 'white man's union.'" Moreover, he suggests that the strike was ineffective, with less than a third of the packinghouse workers heeding the Amalgamated's initial strike call.

As it became evident that the packers could operate near normal production without the striking workers, the Amalgamated once again appealed to the federal government for help. Yet the federal mediators urged the union to abandon its strike. When the union's leadership presented the idea of ending the strike to the membership on January 26, 1922, a majority of the members voted to continue the struggle. Nevertheless, the Amalgamated's leadership called off the strike on February 1, 1922, and the striking workers began to return to their jobs. In the aftermath of the strike, the Amalgamated's membership dropped to 5,000, according to researchers Charles R. Perry and Delwyn Kegley. The union had lost virtually all the members it had gained during its tremendous wartime organizing effort. As in 1904, the Amalgamated once again retreated from packinghouses and clung to the more secure ground of the retail meat trade.

Throughout the 1920s, welfare capitalism in the form of employee representation plans, or company unions, flourished in the meatpacking industry, which effectively undermined genuine labor organization among the packinghouse workers. It was not until the 1930s that unionism resurfaced in the industry, encouraged by New Deal labor policies and the newly formed Congress of Industrial Organizations (CIO).

The New Deal and the CIO

The Roosevelt Administration's National Industrial Recovery Act (NIRA) of 1933 established workers' rights to organize and bargain collectively through representatives of their own choosing and free from coercion by their employers. This legislation evoked an immediate response among the packinghouse workers, and the Amalgamated's membership once again began to expand. In the last two months of 1933 alone, labor historian David Brody reports that 50,000 packinghouse workers joined the Amalgamated. However, the Amalgamated's organizing success was short-lived as packers refused to recognize or negotiate with the union, maintaining that collective bargaining was already in effect at their plants through employee representation plans or company unions. The problem for the union was that Section 7(a) of the NIRA did not prohibit company unions. This problem was soon resolved with the passage of the National Labor Relations Act of 1935 (the Wagner Act).The NIRA period also witnessed the emergence of a number of new packinghouse unions that were independent of both the Amalgamated and the AFL. Perhaps the most dynamic of these independent unions was at the George A. Hormel & Company packing plant in Austin, Minnesota. In the summer of 1933, Frank Ellis and a group of hog kill workers began organizing workers at the plant around a number of unresolved grievances, especially the company's new insurance plan and payroll deductions. Subsequently, these workers formed the Independent Union of All Workers (IUAW), which was modeled after the Industrial Workers of the World (IWW or "Wobblies") and its strategy of organizing all workers into "one big union." In September 1933, Hormel signed an agreement with the IUAW granting the union recognition. Just a few weeks later, frustrated over negotiations for a wage increase, on November 10, 1933, the union struck the plant. "For the next three days, in what some labor historians consider to have been the first sit-down strike of the 1930s, the IUAW maintained control of the plant," according to labor historian Peter Rachleff. Charles R. Perry and Delwyn H. Kegley report: "Armed with clubs, the workers took possession of the plant and forced officers of the company to leave the general offices of the building . . . National Guard units were mobilized, but Governor Floyd B. Olson was able to avoid a crisis by persuading the parties to refer the wage issue to arbitration by the Minnesota

Industrial Commission." The strike ended after the three-day takeover, when the Commission granted workers a wage increase of 2 to 4 cents per hour and instituted a grievance procedure. Thereafter, Hormel and the union entered into an unusually fruitful relationship, which resulted in relatively peaceful labor relations at the plant for the next fifty-two years.

From its base in Austin, between 1933 and 1937, the IUAW spread to a number of other packing communities throughout the upper Midwest, including Alert Lea, Faribault, Thief River Falls, Bemidji, Owatonna, Mankota, and South St. Paul, Minnesota; Mitchell and Madison, South Dakota; Fargo, North Dakota; Alma, Wisconsin; and Mason City, Waterloo, Algona, Ottumwa, Fort Dodge, and Estherville, Iowa. Labor historian Roger Horowitz notes that other notable independent unions to emerge during this period were the Midwest Union of All Packing House Workers at the Wilson plant in Cedar Rapids, Iowa, and a number of independents in Chicago, including the Packing House Workers Industrial Union (PHWIU), which consisted primarily of African-American workers from the killing floors at Armour plants; the Stockyards Labor Council, which represented mostly white ethnic butchers in small packing plants; and a small independent union at the Hygrade plant. Eventually, many of these independent unions joined the Congress of Industrial Organizations, a new union federation formed by a split of several unions from the AFL in late 1936.

When the Amalgamated refused to leave the AFL and join the more militant CIO, the new federation set out to organize the meatpacking industry itself. It launched the Packinghouse Workers Organizing Committee (PWOC) in October 1937, and its first target was Armour's huge Chicago plant. The PWOC chose the plant because it had more than 7,000 workers and because union organizers had already developed a group of supporters.

Within a year the PWOC had won a decisive union election, and within another year it had organized seventeen of Armour's twenty-nine plants. With the onset of World War II, the PWOC was able to utilize the defense economy and the newly established National Defense Mediation Board to pressure the major packers into collective bargaining and signing master agreements covering the industry. As Brody reports, "On September 6, 1941, Armour & Co. and the PWOC signed the first master contract in the annals of the packing industry. This historic achievement was extended to Cudahy on November 1, 1941, and on April 2, 1942, Swift unexpectedly informed the PWOC of its willingness to enter negotiations for a master agreement." Wilson was the last of the major packers to submit to a master agreement and only did so under the direct compulsion of the federal government. By 1943, the PWOC—renamed that year the United Packinghouse Workers of America (UPWA)—represented more than 60 percent of the nation's packinghouse workers.

In October 1945, the executive board of the UPWA decided to demand a wage hike of 25 cents and petitioned the government for a strike vote, in accordance with the War Labor Dispute Act. The UPWA set a strike date for January 16, 1946, and began to prepare for a conflict. It initiated a drive to recruit nonunion workers and appointed additional organizers to plants that were represented by relatively weak local unions. The union established a National Strike Strategy Committee to oversee all aspects of the strike from negotiations to picket-line instructions. In addition, committees within each local union and from each metropolitan council were set up to organize mass pickets around the plants, food commissaries, and community support. The Amalgamated eventually joined the UPWA's effort to secure a wage increase in the industry and went along with the UPWA's demands. The packers responded to the strike threat by offering a wage increase of 7½ cents, but the UPWA rejected their offer and subsequently reduced its demand to 17½ cents. After several rounds, the negotiations reached an impasse and local unions voted by a ratio of 20 to 1 to authorize the strike.

On January 16, 1946, the industry effectively shut down, as both the UPWA and Amalgamated struck. In Chicago and across the country, packinghouses sat idle, curtailing meat production by as much as 50 percent and threatening widespread consumer shortages. This prompted the federal government to move quickly to end the strike. Just ten days into the strike, after receiving assurance from the Amalgamated leadership that they would order their members back to work for a settlement of 15 cents, President Harry S. Truman used his power under the War Labor Disputes Act to seize the plants and ordered both the Amalgamated and the UPWA to end their strike and instruct their members to return to work. "The Amalgamated dutifully responded, calling off the action and accepting a settlement of fifteen cents," reports Halpern, but the UPWA defied the president: "Gathering in special session the day after Truman's order went into effect, local union representatives condemned the industry seizure as a 'strikebreaking' action and voted overwhelmingly to defy the order to return to work."

As part of the government's seizure, a presidential fact-finding commission was established and charged with investigating the labor dispute. The UPWA decided to wait for the commission's findings and recommendations. When the secretary of agriculture Clinton Anderson informed the UPWA that the law provided criminal penalties for impeding the return of strikers to seized plants, the union reaffirmed its decision to hold out until the government guaranteed that the packers would be bound by the fact-finding commission's recommendations. Eventually, when Anderson assured the UPWA that the National Wage Stabilization Board would implement the commission's recommendations, the UPWA ordered its members to return to work pending the commission's findings. Within a few weeks the commission awarded the UPWA a 16-cent wage increase, just 1 cent more than the Amalgamated settlement. Horowitz reports, "Although many local unions approved the agreement under protest, arguing that they deserved a 25 cent raise, it was still the greatest single increase ever won in the packing industry and the first successful national meatpacking strike."

The 1948 National Strike

The next round of major labor conflict in the industry occurred with the reopening of contract negotiations in 1948. This time around, the UPWA asked for a 29-cent wage increase, which the packers rejected and subsequently countered with an offer of a 9-cent increase. On January 29, 1948, the Amalgamated accepted the offer from Armour and Swift. The UPWA, however, rejected the offer and the membership voted overwhelmingly in favor of another national strike. The UPWA established March 16, 1948, as its strike deadline. On the eve of March 16, President Truman asked the UPWA to postpone its strike pending a presidential inquiry into the conditions surrounding the conflict. The UPWA rejected Truman's request and, as scheduled, at 12:01 A.M. on March 16 the union struck Swift, Armour, Cudahy, Wilson, Morrell, and Rath plants across the country. According to historian Bruce Fehn, "As many as 100,000 UPWA packinghouse workers forced 140 plants in twenty states to shut down." Without the cooperation of the Amalgamated, however, the UPWA was unable to shut down the entire industry, which severely reduced the strike's effectiveness. The UPWA was able to completely halt production in just Omaha and Sioux City, while reducing production in Iowa, Minnesota, and Kansas City by about 50 percent, and in Chicago by as much as 30 percent. Continued production at the Amalgamated plants allowed the packers to alleviate the worst effects of the strike and avoid a sharp decline in the meat supply.

Also hindering the effectiveness of the strike was the recently passed Taft-Hartley Act of 1947, which placed new restrictions on union strike activities. Specifically, this new legislation required a sixty-day strike notice and outlawed a number of strike activities, such as mass picketing and secondary boycotts. The mandatory sixty-day strike notice, which the UPWA filed in mid-December, allowed the packers time to prepare for the strike by increasing their inventories and recruiting strikebreakers. As the strike commenced, the courts began serving the UPWA with injunctions restraining union picketing and other strike activities. Halpern explains: "By May, the union had been served with over fifty court orders restricting mass picketing and other activities. . . . In some packing centers, the courts effectively opened the plants by barring virtually all picketing. . . . Defiance of these injunctions resulted in the arrest of more than two thousand strikers and National Guard intervention in Minnesota and Iowa." These Taft-Hartley injunctions allowed the packers to continue production and resist the union's strike actions and demands. Ultimately, the new legislation hampered the union's ability to wage an effective strike, especially without the support of the Amalgamated.

As the strike dragged on and the packers recruited strikebreakers, violence erupted at a number of plants. Historian William Pratt reports, "On April 5, 1948, [in Omaha] pickets converged on a strikebreaker's car and one of the strikers was shot. . . . A few days after the shooting, strikers allegedly beat an Armour truck driver. The following day, two trucks ran into four pickets at an entrance to the Cudahy plant." A similar incident in Waterloo, Iowa, resulting in the death of a striker, was followed by a riot. Fehn explains that angry picketers halted African-American Fred Lee Roberts's car as he tried to drive through a crowd of picketers to enter a Rath plant. As strikers began to rock his car from side to side, he waved a pistol and fatally shot white unionist Chuck Farrell. By the end of the strike, hundreds of strikers were injured and three had lost their lives.

Although the strike remained solid for the first several weeks, by late April a growing number of union members began returning to work. Then, nearly six weeks into the strike, the major packers announced that they would implement a 9-cent raise and encouraged striking workers to return to work or forfeit their seniority rights. As a result, back-to-work movements began taking shape at key plants in Chicago, such as Swift's and Armour's flagship plants. As Horowitz explains, "Within a few days, 1,500 workers crossed the picket lines at the Chicago Swift plant, along with six hundred at nearby Armour." At the Chicago Armour plant, union members received telegrams from the company notifying them that they would forfeit all seniority rights unless they returned to work by May 10, which prompted several hundred to return to work. Not just in Chicago, but across the country, the strike was rapidly collapsing. As a result, on May 18, 1948, the UPWA's National Strike Strategy Committee voted to accept the packers' offer of 9 cents and end the strike with the stipulation that the packers rehire all of the discharged union members. In the days that followed, the strikers returned to work en masse. The UPWA eventually negotiated the reinstatement of most of the discharged workers, 541 out of 591, at Swift, Armour, Cudahy, Morrell, and Rath. At the Wilson plants, however, the strike lasted an additional two weeks and ended without a contract.

Although the strike defeat severely reduced the UPWA's membership and left the union in serious debt, the defeat did not destroy the union. As Brody points out, "For the first time, the industry experienced 'a lost strike that did not mean a lost union.'" Remarkably, the UPWA was able to recover quickly from its weakened position. Within a few months of the defeat "American UPWA membership grew by 50 percent, from its poststrike low of sixty thousand back to ninety thousand" according to Horowitz. By the end of 1948, the UPWA had signed one-year contracts with Swift and Armour providing an additional wage increase of 4 cents.

In the aftermath of the strike, the UPWA's leadership believed that interracial cooperation was essential to the union's survival and therefore adopted an anti-discrimination program and established an anti-discrimination department. These measures were aimed at eliminating segregation and discrimination both inside the plants and in the larger meatpacking communities. According to geographer Brian Page, " . . . as a result, significant progress toward racial equality was made, including increased participation in leadership by minorities, the elimination of discriminatory hiring practices and departmental segregation, the elimination of segregated dressing and eating facilities in plants throughout the nation, and the narrowing of the wage differential between Northern and Southern plants."

The strike defeat also demonstrated the need for greater cooperation between the UPWA and the Amalgamated, which both unions recognized. After several years of cooperation and disagreement, on June 23, 1953, the two unions signed a memo of understanding in which they agreed to seek joint bargaining with common employers, exchange information on contracts and wages, eliminate raids, and strike in tandem. By the early 1960s, unionism was firmly established in the meatpacking industry, with the UPWA and the Amalgamated representing more than 95 percent of the industry's workforce outside of the South. However, a "new breed" of packers, including the Iowa Beef Packers (IBP), emerged beginning in the 1960s, transforming the industry and altering the terrain of labor relations.

Industry Transformation

In 1960, two former Swift employees, Currier Holman and Andy Anderson, founded Iowa Beef Packers (IBP). In March 1961 they opened their first plant in Denison, Iowa. This highly mechanized single-story plant revolutionized the industry. As Michael Broadway explains, "Previously, cattle had been shipped by rail from producing areas to terminal locations such as Chicago, Kansas City, and St. Paul, where they were sold and slaughtered in multistory packinghouses. The Denison plant, by contrast, was located in the center of a large cattle-producing area. This enabled the company to purchase cattle directly from the farmer, eliminating the need for middlemen and reducing transportation costs and shrinkage and bruising associated with transporting animals long distances." The new plant allowed for greater automation and the development of a disassembly line whereby individual workers would be responsible for one standardized task in the preparation of the carcass. This de-skilling of the production process not only reduced labor costs by eliminating the need for highly skilled butchers, but also allowed the company to justify its low wages and avoid industry-wide master agreements.

In 1967, IBP opened an additional plant in Dakota City, Nebraska, and produced a new product—boxed beef. As Broadway describes, "Instead of shipping carcasses, the company prepared vacuum-packaged portions of beef according to retail specifications at its facilities, thereby reducing shipping costs and retaining valuable waste materials for sale, such as entrails for pet food. The product appealed to meat wholesalers and supermarkets, since it enabled them to lower their own labor costs by eliminating many of their skilled butchers, while vacuum packaging added to the product's shelf life and reduced shrinkage from exposure to air." These cost-cutting strategies resulted in an increased demand for boxed beef, and the company responded to this demand by constructing additional packing plants throughout the Midwest and High Plains. Boxed beef quickly grew to be the preeminent method for marketing and distributing beef. By 1985, IBP had become the world's largest meatpacking company.

To compete with IBP and other "new breed" packers, the Big Four—Armour, Swift, Wilson, and Cudahy—shut their old, obsolete plants in urban centers and opened new, modern, technologically advanced plants in rural areas. Armour moved first. It eliminated 12,000 jobs by shutting plants in Chicago, Kansas City, Fort Worth, and Sioux City. Its new plants, in places such as Worthington, Minnesota, employed fewer workers. These plant closures and relocations struck at the core of the UPWA. By 1968, with its membership down to 68,000, the UPWA merged into the Amalgamated.

At the time of the merger, the Amalgamated understood the necessity to organize IBP and the new breed of packers because they threatened to undermine industry-wide wage rates set at Armour and Swift. With a major organizing effort at IBP's flagship plant in Dakota City the union won a certification election in 1969, but negotiations reached an impasse over union demands to increase wages to the master agreement level, which was $3.53 per hour. The company insisted the union was trying to win skilled wages for unskilled workers. The workers walked out on August 24, 1969, and IBP immediately brought in strikebreakers. The move provoked extensive violence, including "one death, 56 bombings, over 20 shootings, death threats, and the fire bombing of an IBP vice president's home," according to Broadway. Despite the violence, IBP kept its plant running.

During the IBP strike, the Amalgamated opened negotiations with the Big Four packers and in April 1970 they reached an agreement that preserved the industry's master agreements and increased wages and benefits. Shortly after, Amalgamated officials instructed Dakota City local union leaders to settle their strike at IBP. They agreed to a three-year contract that provided a wage increase of 58 cents, followed by increases of 15 cents in the second and third years, and retained the slaughter/processing wage differential, which the company had sought. Horowitz describes the mixed results of the nine-week strike: "The union secured the first contract with IBP at the critical Dakota City plant, and helped maintain the master agreements with major meatpacking companies. However, the settlement also allowed IBP to keep its pay rates far beneath the master agreement levels; by 1972, the gap ranged from 91 cents to $1.52

under the base master agreement rate of $4.71." Over the next twelve years, IBP's Dakota City plant would experience a strike or lockout at the conclusion of nearly every contract. Each time the union sought industry-wide wages and each time the company refused. As Perry and Kegley note, the 1973 lockout ended in binding arbitration, with the arbitrator concluding that "there should be a significant narrowing of the gap between the master agreement rates and the IBP rates." However, in subsequent bargaining rounds, IBP defeated the union and widened its wage gap with the Big Four. The keys to victory for the company were hiring replacement workers, closing unionized plants, and spreading boxed-beef operations beyond Dakota City. IBP built new plants in Texas and Kansas to supplement its flagship plant, which soon became the only unionized plant in the company. Each time the union went on strike at Dakota City, the company hired replacements to keep the plant operating, even at reduced capacity, and shifted production to the nonunion plants. This is precisely what happened in June 1982. The union, now called the United Food and Commercial Workers after the Amalgamated's 1979 merger with the Retail Clerks International Union, walked out to preserve wage rates. They shut the plant for nearly two weeks, until IBP hired approximately 1,400 replacement workers, about half the prestrike workforce. Violence began the first day the plant reopened, as replacement and nonstriking workers crossed the union's picket line. Twenty-nine people were injured and dozens of vehicles were damaged. The National Guard quelled the violence and protected the plant. In October, the union acceded to the company's terms, including a 12 percent pay cut.

The union-busting success of IBP forced the Big Four to follow suit. A number of them closed plants and threatened to close even more unless the UCFW granted concessions. In late 1981, the UFCW agreed to a forty-four-month hourly wage freeze at $10.69. In exchange for the concessions, the companies agreed not to close any plants for eighteen months and to recognize the UFCW at any new plants they opened in which a majority of the workers signed union authorization cards. In the end, threats of plant closures persuaded the UFCW to grant mid-contract concessions at five major packing companies with an estimated 30,000 workers.

The UFCW's concessions did not stem the tide of wage cuts, job losses, and union-busting that flooded over the entire industry. Indeed, union-busting only accelerated in the early 1980s, often in creative fashion. Swift, for instance, closed a number of plants and sold them to a new company called Swift Independent (SIPCO), which reopened them as nonunion plants with wages $3.00 an hour below the master agreement. Armour closed twenty plants and sold them to Con-Agra, which reopened them as nonunion plants with wages ranging from $5.50 to $6.50 an hour, versus the master agreement's $10.69. And, in 1983, Wilson filed Chapter 11 bankruptcy, which unilaterally terminated the company's master agreement and reduced hourly wages to $6.50. In what was dubbed a "controlled retreat" by the union's International president William Wynn, the UFCW responded to the onslaught by granting even more concessions. It accepted a $2.44 hourly wage cut at three SIPCO plants and averted a threatened shutdown at Morrell's Sioux Falls by agreeing to a similar reduction. As a result, master agreements virtually disappeared from the industry. Indeed, by the mid-1980s, most of the gains achieved by meatpacking unions over the previous fifty years had disappeared.

The P-9 Strike of 1985–1986

Dozens of strikes broke out throughout the 1980s in response to packer's concessionary demands. Perhaps the most dramatic and widely publicized of these struggles involved Local P-9 of the UFCW and the Hormel Company's flagship plant in Austin, Minnesota. The strike captured the nation's attention and inspired Barbara Kopple's 1991 Academy Award–winning documentary *American Dream,* as well as a handful of books.

The strike began in August 1985 and lasted approximately ten months. It marked an end to nearly fifty years of relatively peaceful labor relations at the plant, which was originally organized in 1933 by the IUAW. The strike was triggered when Hormel unilaterally cut hourly wages at the plant from $10.69 to $8.25. However, the struggle between Hormel and P-9 had been simmering since 1978, when the union made a number of concessions to induce the company to build its new plant in Austin. P-9 agreed to freeze wages for seven years, eliminate incentive pay, raise productivity standards, and ban all strikes for three years after the new plant opened in August 1982. In September 1984, the UFCW and Hormel reached an agreement covering six of the company's other packing plants, which lowered hourly wages from $10.69 to $9.00, eventually increasing to $10.00 in September 1985. P-9, however, refused to accept further concessions, maintaining that since Hormel was a profitable company such concessions were unnecessary. As Perry and Kegley record, P-9 president James Guyette stated, "If concessions are going to stop, they'll have to stop with the most profitable plant of the most profitable company." Nevertheless, on October 8, 1984, Hormel exercised its right under its contract with P-9 to reduce the hourly base wage by 23 percent. As a result, P-9 began to gear up for a strike when the contract expired in August 1985.

In late 1984, P-9 hired Ray Rogers and Corporate Campaign, Inc., of New York to analyze the situation at Hormel and help the union in their struggle against the company. Over the next several months, P-9 engaged in a number of strategies to pressure the company to restore workers' wages and benefits, all of which failed. In May 1985, Hormel announced that it would not extend its labor agreement with P-9 beyond its August expiration date. Late in June, however, the two parties began negotiating. After more than a dozen fruitless bargaining sessions, in early August the company put forth its final contract offer, which included: an hourly base wage of $9.00 that would increase to $10.00 on September 1, 1985; a two-tier wage system with new employees starting at $8.00 an hour; the elimination of the plant's guaranteed annual wage, seniority job assignments, and fifty-two-week layoff notice; and other benefit reductions. P-9's negotiating committee unanimously recommended rejecting the company's proposal to the membership, which voted 93 percent to strike.

An estimated 1,500 workers walked out of the Austin Hormel plant on August 17, 1985. Hormel immediately shifted production to its other facilities and contracted some of its production to a big Iowa-based meatpacker, FDL Foods, Inc. Although most of these facilities were unionized, they continued working, severely weakening P-9's strike. In fact, writers Dave Hage and Paul Klauda show that for the entire year of 1985, Hormel's "sales rose 3.3 percent to $1.5 billion, and profits were up almost one third, to $36.6 million. For the three months that ended October 26, total sales grew by 7 percent, even though the giant Austin plant had been shut down for all but three weeks of the quarter."

Nearly five months into the strike, Hormel announced it would reopen the Austin plant on January 13, and indicated that any striker who did not return to the plant would be permanently replaced. On the morning of January 13, nearly 350 strikers gathered at the plant to discourage strikebreakers and union members from entering. P-9 leadership reported that only about a dozen cars crossed the picket line and just seven union members went to work. In the days that followed, however, more and more cars arrived at the plant. Author Neala Schleuning reports, "Men and women flooded into Austin from Iowa—where, rumor had it, welfare recipients from Mason City were being told to go to Austin to apply for work or lose their benefits—and from farming communities surrounding Austin." The number of union members retuning to work also increased. Five days after the plant reopened, according to Hage and Klauda, nearly fifty union members had abandoned the strike and crossed the picket line.

To stop the flood of cars entering the plant, on January 20, P-9 members and supporters drove their vehicles onto the plant's perimeter road and turned off their engines, creating a traffic jam that blocked all access. The Minnesota governor sent more than 500 National Guardsmen to escort strikebreakers into the plant. As the Guard provided unfettered access to the plant and the number of replacement workers continued to grow, a group of P-9 dissenters—which came to be known as the "P-10ers"—began organizing a back-to-work movement among the strikers. By January 24, 1986, Hormel had hired some 300 nonunion replacements, adding 50 more each day, and more than 100 P-9 members had returned to work.

In late January, just after the National Guard took up its position in Austin, P-9 began dispatching pickets to a number of other packing plants, including Hormel's two key slaughtering plants in Ottumwa, Iowa, and Fremont, Nebraska; the FDL Foods, Inc., plant in Dubuque, Iowa; and small plants in Dallas and Houston, Texas, and Algona, Iowa. Without the sanction of the international union, when P-9 strikers arrived at these plants hoping to establish picket lines and halt production, their efforts were largely rebuffed, with the exception of workers at the Dallas and Ottumwa plants. At Hormel's pepperoni plant in Algona, Iowa, most of the plant's first-shift employees ignored P-9's picket line after they had been told by their union steward that they were obligated to cross the line and report to work. In Fremont, Nebraska, after being warned by their local union leaders that they would be in breach of their labor contact if they honored P-9's picket line, only 65 out of 850 workers refused to cross. P-9's roving pickets had greater success in Dallas, Texas, where an entire 52-person workforce refused to cross the picket line, closing down operations In Ottumwa, P-9 picketers shut down production several times in late January and early February by convincing some 750 union workers to join their picket lines. The company invoked the no-strike provision in its labor contact and dismissed over 500 of the Ottumwa workers who honored P-9's picket line and began hiring permanent replacements. Under this pressure, P-9 officials chose to end their roving picket at Ottumwa after four days. In the end, "up to three fourths of Hormel's union workers had ignored P-9's call," according to Hage and Klauda.

In mid-February, the picket line in Austin no longer prevented workers from entering the plant and the company announced that it had reached its hiring goal of 1,025 workers, which included some 460 P-9 members. The following month, the UFCW's international leadership declared the strike a lost cause and withdrew its authorization. It also ordered P-9 to call off the strike and inform Hormel that its members were willing to return to work. At a meeting on March 16, more than 800 P-9 members voted overwhelmingly to ignore the order and in the next few days the UFCW began proceedings to place the local union into trusteeship. P-9 tried to mount a legal challenge to the trusteeship but failed, and by mid-September the UFCW had taken over the local and negotiated a concessionary four-year contract that eliminated the guaranteed annual wage and fifty-two-week layoff notice that Hormel workers in Austin had enjoyed since 1940. The agreement contained no provision for the rehire of the 850 remaining P-9 strikers, fewer than 100 of whom ever regained their jobs. A year later, when the UFCW refused additional concessions, Hormel outsourced its slaughter operations, thereby eliminating hundreds of jobs.

Of the many ways the P-9 strike has been interpreted, Hage and Klauda suggest, "The showdown at Hormel can be read as a tragedy—a failure of collective bargaining and unemployment for more than a thousand workers. . . . Or it can be read as a mystery—the puzzle of workers who felt so aggrieved that they martyred themselves in a labor dispute everyone else told them to give up on."

IBP's 1986–1987 Lockout at Dakota City

On December 13, 1986—just months after P-9's strike defeat at Hormel—IBP locked out 2,500 workers at its Dakota City plant, continuing the recent history of labor conflict at the company. The company took its action when UFCW members voted to reject the company's concessionary contract offer but keep working. By not striking, the workers hoped to avoid replacement and continue their struggle on the job—but the company had other ideas. It used the lockout to renovate the plant without having to pay the unemployment benefits that would have accompanied layoffs during a routine renovation. After completing the renovation, IBP began hiring replacement workers.

The UFCW filed charges with the Occupational Health and Safety Administration (OSHA), claiming that the company had falsified its safety records. The union managed to spark congressional hearings on the issue in March. The Department of Labor (DOL) also filed charges against the company for allegedly violating the overtime provision of the Fair Labor Standards Act. The combination of OSHA and DOL scrutiny pushed the company back to the bargaining table. The result was a settlement in July 1987 that some observers labeled a sweetheart deal. All the workers won their jobs back, and the union accepted a three-year wage freeze and a two-tier wage scale. Mysteriously, however, the company agreed to voluntarily recognize the union at its new 1,700-employee plant in Joslin, Illinois. According to one UFCW Dakota City local official quoted by Horowitz, "[The] UFCW sold its soul to the devil and got a bad deal in the bargain." Horowitz adds that others believed that IBP's willingness to "voluntarily let the union in is inherently suspicious."

Return to the "Jungle"

Since the 1980s, organized labor's power in the meatpacking industry has declined dramatically. Less than half the workers at the three biggest companies (IBP, Cargill, and ConAgra) are unionized, and wages and working conditions at unionized plants are not much better than those at nonunion plants. The main source of union decline was the industrial restructuring that began with IBP in the early 1960s. The combination of automation, the introduction of boxed beef, and union-busting has taken its toll. The industry's unions, too, bear some responsibility for their powerlessness. Concessionary bargaining and the unwillingness to mobilize workers on an industry-wide scale have allowed the companies to take the upper hand in labor relations. Wages and working conditions in the industry have deteriorated significantly. Real hourly wages were $10.30 in 1980, but only $6.46 in 2002. Once characterized as a relatively high-wage industry, meatpacking wages "fell below the average U.S. manufacturing wage for the first time" in the early 1980s, according to labor lawyer Lance Compa. "Since then, the decline has accelerated—15 percent lower in 1985, 18 percent lower in 1990, 24 percent lower in 2002."

Workplace health and safety in the industry have similarly deteriorated. As Compa reports, "Since the breakdown of national bargaining agreements, meatpacking has become the most dangerous factory job in America, with injury rates more than twice the national average." About one-third of the industry's workers are injured each year.

The decline in meatpacking wages and working conditions has caused an increase in labor turnover, which now averages between 80 percent and 100 percent per year. As a result, the industry requires a constant and steady stream of new workers. To find those workers, meatpacking companies began to aggressively recruit immigrant workers from Latin America and Southeast Asia. In a recent report to Congress, William Whittaker claims that "by the late 1990s, it had become standard industry practice to import workers through border-state labor recruiters." The result is a demographic shift that has transformed the meatpacking workforce from mostly white and native-born to immigrants of color.

Thus, as it was at the turn of the nineteenth century, meatpacking today is characterized by low wages, poor and dangerous working conditions, and a predominantly immigrant labor force. And as they did a century ago, unions are fighting to expand their power—only this time they have a century of struggle to draw upon.

See also: Corporate Strike Strategy, 66; Polish Workers and Strikes, 138; World War I Era Strikes, 191; Strikes in the United States Since World War II, 226; Labor Upheaval on the Nation's Railroads, 1877–1922, 483.

Bibliography

Barrett, James R. *Work and Community in the Jungle: Chicago's Packinghouse Workers 1894–1922.* Urbana: University of Illinois Press, 1987.

Broadway, Michael J. "Following the Leader: IBP and the Restructuring of Canada's Meatpacking Industry." *Culture & Agriculture* 18, no. 1 (Spring 1996): 3–8.

———. "From City to Countryside: Recent Changes in the Structure and Location of the Meat- and Fish-Processing Industries." In *Any Way You Cut It: Meat Processing and Small-Town America,* ed. Donald D. Stull, Michael J. Broadway, and David Griffith. Lawrence: University Press of Kansas, 1995.

Brody, David. *The Butcher Workman: A Study of Unionization.* Cambridge, MA: Harvard University Press, 1964.

Compa, Lance. *Blood, Sweat, and Fear: Workers' Rights in U.S. Meat and Poultry Plants.* New York: Human Rights Watch, 2004.

Fehn, Bruce. "'Chickens Come Home To Roost': Industrial Reorganization, Seniority, and Gender Conflict in the United Packinghouse Workers of America, 1956–1966." *Labor History* 43, no. 2–3 (Summer 1993): 324–41.

———. "'The Only Hope We Had': United Packinghouse Workers Local 46 and the Struggle for Racial Equality in Waterloo, Iowa, 1948–1960." In *Unionizing the Jungle: Labor and Community in the Twentieth Century Meatpacking Industry,* ed. Shelton Stromquist and Marvin Bergman. Iowa City: University of Iowa Press, 1997.

Fogel, Walter A. *The Negro in the Meat Industry.* Philadelphia: University of Pennsylvania Press, 1970.

Hage, Dave, and Paul Klauda. *No Retreat, No Surrender: Labor's War at Hormel.* New York: William Morrow, 1989.

Halpern, Rick. *Down on the Killing Floor: Black and White Workers in Chicago's Packinghouses, 1904–54.* Champaign: University of Illinois Press, 1997.

———. "The Iron Fist and the Velvet Glove: Welfare Capitalism in Chicago's Packinghouses, 1921–1933." *Journal of American Studies* 26, no. 2 (August 1992): 159–83.

Herbst, Alma. *The Negro in the Slaughtering and Meatpacking Industry in Chicago.* New York: Arno and New York Times, 1971.

Horowitz, Roger. "The Decline of Unionism in America's Meatpacking Industry." *Social Policy* 32, no. 3 (Spring 2002): 32–36.

———. *"Negro and White, Unite and Fight!" A Social History of Industrial Unionism in Meatpacking, 1930–90.* Urbana: University of Illinois Press, 1997.

Page, Brian. "Rival Unionism and the Geography of the Meat Packing Industry." In *Organizing the Landscape: Geographical Perspectives on Labor Unionism*, ed. Andrew Herod. Minneapolis: University of Minnesota Press, 1998.

Perry, Charles R., and Delwyn Kegley. *Disintegration and Change: Labor Relations in the Meat Packing Industry.* Philadelphia: Industrial Research Unit, Wharton School, University of Pennsylvania, 1989.

Rachleff, Peter. *Hard-Pressed in the Heartland: The Hormel Strike and the Future of the Labor Movement.* Boston: South End Press, 1993.

———. "Organizing 'Wall-to-Wall': The Independent Union of All Workers." In *Unionizing the Jungles: Labor and Community in the Twentieth Century*, ed. Shelton Stromquist and Marvin Bergman. Iowa City: University of Iowa Press, 1997.

Schleuning, Neala. *Women, Community, and the Hormel Strike of 1985–86.* Westport, CT: Greenwood Press, 1994.

Whittaker, William G. "Labor Practices in the Meatpacking and Poultry Industry: An Overview." Washington, DC: Library of Congress, Congressional Research Service, Report for Congress, June 20, 2005.

AUTOMOBILE WORKERS' STRIKES

Ian Collin Greer

Automobile workers' strikes occurred in essentially four eras: the lost strikes by the industry's craft unions in the early twentieth century, the dramatic sit-down victories of the 1930s, the mixture of wildcat and authorized strikes during the postwar economic boom from the 1940s through the 1970s, and the decline of strikes that accompanied the policy of "jointness" between company and union after 1980.

Autoworkers' strike strategies reflected, in part, the particular structure of the industry, which took shape in the 1920s. Auto production is a complex process of interdependent operations to produce parts and assemble vehicles, each containing tens of thousands of parts. These parts are either produced or bought by the original equipment manufacturers (OEMs), who assemble and market vehicles. Due to the diversity of the operations and materials required to create a car, no single company carries out the whole process in one single location. The result is a networked production organization, with parts flowing through an interdependent chain of operations. Stoppages in one part of the chain within an OEM or at a supplier can result in disruptions to the overall flow of production and financial pain for the company, with implications for the national economy as a whole.

The industry in the United States has been highly concentrated, with three companies dominating production before the 1970s. General Motors was and still is the largest; at one point in the 1970s it was the nation's largest employer. Ford was the second-largest seller of cars, followed by Chrysler, which was until recently a distant third. Together, these automakers are known as the Big Three, and their blue-collar workforce is almost entirely unionized. Since the 1970s, however, a handful of foreign OEMs have made major inroads, first through sales of imported cars and then, since the 1980s, through domestic auto production. In order of 2005 sales in the United States, these foreign competitors include Toyota, Honda, Nissan, BMW, Mitsubishi, Isuzu, and Subaru. Toyota surpassed Chrysler to take over the number three spot in 2006 and may soon pass Ford. Excluding their joint ventures with the Big Three (such as the NUMMI joint venture between General Motors and Toyota in Fremont, California), foreign-owned assembly plants are completely nonunion. The growth of imports and the rise of nonunion transplants have put pressure on the unionized Big Three to cut costs and improve quality. This change has corresponded with the rise of labor–management partnership and the decline of strikes.

Despite the growth of employment in the Southeast, around 70 percent of auto employment is still located in the Midwest, mainly in Michigan. The Midwest still benefits from its first-mover advantage of the early twentieth century, when local companies developed internal combustion engines (while other regions were still working with steam power) and then perfected mass production processes. Since the 1970s, companies have been closing plants in California and the eastern seaboard and opening new plants in the Southeast, first with the "southern strategy" of General Motors and then with the foreign transplants of the 1990s. This movement is partly due to right-to-work laws, anti-union attitudes, and subsidies from southern state and local governments, and partly due to the expansion of the demand for vehicles in the region. Nevertheless, much of the industry retains its midwestern identity—the Big Three as well as a wide range of supplier firms are based in the Detroit area and carry out the bulk of their production in the Great Lakes states.

The most important union in the industry was and is the United Automobile, Aerospace and Agricultural Implement Workers of America International Union (UAW). Founded in 1935, the UAW grew to a peak of 1.5 million members in 1979, immediately before the domestic industry began its long decline. Though founded as an affiliate of the Congress of Industrial Organizations (CIO) to represent workers in heavy industry, the membership of the UAW has become quite diverse. The UAW has organized workers in the public sector, health care, universities, and a wide range of other sectors in order to make up for some of the jobs lost in the automotive industry. The union has repeatedly attempted and failed to organize workers at nonunion transplants. Between 1983 and 2005, union density in the motor vehicle manufacturing sector declined from above 58 percent to below 30 percent. Other important unions in the industry, particularly at independent supplier plants, include the International Union of Electrical Workers (part of the Communications Workers of America), UNITE HERE, and the United Steel Workers.

The Defeat of Craft Strikes

The automobile industry was born around 1900, at first heavily dependent on the skills of native-born craftsmen recruited from horse-and-buggy and bicycle manufacture. Labor productivity was about 1.6 cars per year per worker. Work methods were experimental, firms small, and production manual. Craft unions affiliated with the American Federation of Labor (AFL), such as the International Association of Machinists, organized the workforce.

The situation began to change as firms discovered the mass production methods first associated with Henry Ford. Ford divided the process into dozens of components using new machines that were highly productive, and he reduced the company's reliance on craftsmen and worker knowledge. He introduced the assembly line and created a much more vertically integrated process by purchasing a wide range of supplier businesses. The Rouge Plant, for example, not only assembled vehicles but also produced a wide range of parts and even contained a steel mill.

Unions of skilled crafts resisted the changes to the work process, which allowed the companies to hire migrant and unskilled workers at lower wages. In 1907, nearly all of Detroit's organized crafts—the boilermakers, machinists, molders, patternmakers, metal polishers, painters, and upholsterers—went on strike to protect their organizations. This strike movement was a bitter defeat for organized labor and revealed splits built into the occupational structure of unionism at the time. A boilermakers' strike, for example, degenerated into fighting between native-born unionists and Italian strikebreakers; the metal polishers were broken in an eight-week strike and replaced by Hungarian workers. To break the unions, employers used injunctions, police patrolling, and a citywide "Labor Bureau" with files detailing the union activities of 40,000 workers—nearly half of the city's workforce.

Until the 1930s, unionism and striking were rare in the auto industry, although a few attempts were made. In the 1920s, a British immigrant organized the United Automobile Aircraft and Vehicle Workers of America, which, after collapsing, was reorganized as the Auto Workers Union (AWU). These organizations were modeled on the British shop-steward system and led department-level strikes, mainly at auto body plants. Although these unions at first had difficulties uniting skilled and unskilled workers, they managed in 1933 to organize a successful strike of nearly 1,500 workers against a pay cut at the Motor Products firm. This inspired a series of strikes, not all successful, accounting for 15,000 workers in Detroit, mainly led by skilled-trades workers at body plants. The largest of these strikes, a strike of 10,000 workers at Briggs, failed due to the tactical mistakes of the Communist strike leadership, and led to the collapse of the AWU a few months into the strike wave.

Sit-Down Strikes, Skilled Trades, and the Rise of the UAW

During the 1930s, autoworkers fought pitched battles with companies and public authorities in their efforts to establish collective bargaining.

The most famous of these efforts were the sit-down strikes of 1936–38, which coincided with the organization of the UAW at General Motors. Along with subsequent strikes and the union's cooperation with the government in World War II, these strikes led to industry-wide coordinated bargaining with the UAW.

In the early 1930s, the Mechanics Educational Society (MESA), with organizers in Detroit, Pontiac, and Flint, emerged to organize skilled tool and die workers in the auto industry. In the fall of 1933, MESA led a six-week strike that spread throughout these cities and closed more than 100 shops and included 14,000 participants. Although the strike failed to impose sectoral bargaining, it did bring plant-level agreements to fifty-one plants, including a few large "captive shops" like Fisher Body. These agreements included union recognition, an end to precarious contract work, and some wage increases. By early 1934, MESA claimed 21,000 members in Detroit. Eventually, the organization split over the issue of whether to amalgamate with the UAW, and several key local organizations became militant, democratic UAW locals.

The Auto-Lite strike of April and May 1934 was another important event, involving not only workers but also the unemployed. An AFL local organized the strike, but only 50 percent of the workforce joined the walkout. The company kept the plant running with strikebreakers. A local organization of unemployed people, affiliated with the American Workers Party led by A.J. Muste, supported the strike and mobilized pickets. In defiance of a court injunction won by the company, unemployed workers continued to block the plant's gates. When leaders were arrested for contempt of court, thousands more citizens gathered to disrupt the proceedings; rallies escalated and included up to 10,000 workers at the plant. After the sheriff began arresting demonstrators, a battle broke out between law enforcement authorities (including "special deputies" paid by the company) and demonstrators. Deputies attacked protesters with fire hoses, guns, and tear gas, while demonstrators used stones to smash factory windows. On the second day of unrest, 900 National Guard troops arrived with bayonets and machine guns. The troops fired on protesters, killing two, but were still unsuccessful in quelling the protest. Eventually,

Although Governor Frank Murphy authorized the mobilization of the National Guard during the 1936–37 General Motors sit-down strikes in Flint, Michigan, he refused to allow the Guard to use force to remove the strikers from the plants. His decision—a rare one in American labor history—essentially allowed the workers to stay in the plants and gave them tremendous leverage in negotiations with the company. (*Courtesy:* Walter P. Reuther Library, Wayne State University.)

management agreed to close the plant, allowing protest to die down, and with a threatened general strike involving eighty-five additional local unions, management finally recognized the union, rehired strikers, and granted a wage increase.

The most important episode of the period came in 1937–38, with the sit-down strikes at General Motors (GM) in Flint. In 1934, the AFL had discredited itself in a failed effort to win concessions from GM. After the union threatened to strike over a wide range of worker grievances, President Roosevelt agreed to arbitrate the matter, prompting the AFL to back down. The president's decision conceded nothing to the workers and the AFL locals collapsed. The following year, the UAW emerged and affiliated with a new breakaway confederation, the CIO. Using the sit-down method developed by rubber workers in Akron, the UAW supported spontaneous in-plant efforts to resist speedups and pay cuts. In 1936, local UAW affiliates supported sit-downs in Atlanta, South Bend, Detroit, Cleveland, and Kansas City. By the end of the year, strikers had crippled Fisher Body, a crucial plant in Flint. Workers shut down production, took over the plant, and ceased production. The strike spread throughout the GM system, bringing January 1937 production down from 224,000 cars and trucks to 60,000.

The company fought back with an injunction (from a judge who was also a major shareholder in the company) and a community petition, and using the police, the National Guard, and private guards to starve out the strikers. When police attempted to block supporters from bringing supplies to the strikers, workers used fire hoses and threw heavy objects to drive them away. Local leaders spread the strike to another large local GM plant on February 1, prompting a new injunction and an influx of thousands of union supporters into the city. GM management and the governor asked local authorities to demobilize and agreed on February 11 to negotiate with the UAW as the sole representative of workers. During negotiations, local strikes continued without UAW authorization, and sit-downs spread to other companies, especially Chrysler. The Bureau of Labor Statistics estimated that during 1937 nearly 400,000 workers engaged in sit-down strikes lasting a day or longer.

In 1939, the union expanded its victory of 1936–37 through a strike of tool and die workers. The union was still numerically weak in the workforce as a whole. Among GM's 200,000 workers, only 3 percent were in the skilled trades. The tool and die workers, however, represented a UAW stronghold. These workers were mainly foreign-born, from Great Britain or Northern Ireland. As the strike wore on, the company faced the problem of how to introduce its 1940 models, and its attempts to bring dies from outside of Michigan to the Detroit area merely had the effect of spreading the strike. Competitive pressures along with urging from federal and Michigan government officials, including the new National Labor Relations Board (NLRB), forced the company to settle after a month. The agreement foreshadowed several features of auto unionism to come: GM made the UAW the exclusive representative of workers at all plants where it did not face a contending AFL group and accepted coordinated bargaining across all plants; in return, the UAW agreed to oppose strikes of its members outside of established dispute resolution procedures. As Steve Babson chronicles, this strike brought Walter Reuther to prominence, and he continued promoting these policies in the postwar decades as UAW president. This struggle built momentum for NLRB elections in 1940, which solidified the UAW's exclusive right to represent 227,000 workers in 110 plants.

Sit-down strikes gradually went out of favor with union leadership, which over time imposed more and more discipline over the rank and file in its use of strikes. While the UAW won recognition from GM management as the bargaining agent of workers, workers continued to strike over workplace problems, although the union had agreed to end strikes. Top UAW and CIO leaders blamed Communist influence, while ironically the Communist Party also denounced the unruly behavior of strikers. Given the no-strike clauses that spread throughout the workplaces represented by the CIO, unions were poised to take on a new role—not only as worker representatives, but as a moderating force over a strike-prone industrial workforce. The centralization of union power, the ban on sit-downs by the U.S. Supreme Court, and the growing role of government-sponsored dispute-resolution machinery led to a transformation of how strikes in industry would take place.

Wildcat and Sanctioned Strikes

For four decades after the establishment of the UAW in the Big Three, a tension existed between national officials seeking to contain strikes and militant local union stewards pushing for immediate solutions to workplace problems. During this period, substantial numbers of worker hours were lost to both sanctioned and wildcat strikes, but the cause and outcome of each type of strike could be considerably different.

Sanctioned Strikes

In the years after World War II, the UAW organized strikes that played an important role in shaping the industry's institutional organization but did not have the profound impact of the earlier sit-down strikes. Perhaps the most important official strike was the 113-day walkout at General Motors in 1945–46. With the no-strike pact in the past,

Taft-Hartley still in the future, and a strike wave involving 3 million workers ongoing, it was arguably the all-time high-water mark of the U.S. labor movement. With demands for a 30 percent wage increase, access to corporate financial data, and no increase in the price of cars, the UAW embarked on a strike at GM that was to last from November 1945 to March 1946. Some 320,000 workers walked picket lines.

As Nelson Lichtenstein describes it, the strike was part of a broader CIO strategy, spearheaded by UAW leader Walter Reuther, to compensate for the large increases in the cost of living that took place during the war, which were calculated at between 30 percent and 45 percent. The union demanded access to GM's books, with the goal of forcing the company to prove its claim that it could not afford a large wage increase. The union also insisted that GM hold the price of its cars steady, so consumers would not suffer from the workers' wage gains. These demands gave the strike a broad significance. They demonstrated that the union was fighting beyond its membership, for Americans as consumers as well as workers. The strike's outcome would determine not just workers' wages, but whether or not unions would play a role in corporate decisions usually left exclusively to management, such as the price of a company's products. A victory would transform the relationship between company and union, giving the union heretofore unheard of power.

The strategy was to strike the company while allowing its competitors to continue producing, potentially threatening its market share (at one point, the strike leadership considered allowing GM parts plants supplying the company's competitors to reopen). While the company put out advertisements in newspapers criticizing the union, it agreed to shut down production, thereby limiting the potential for violent conflict at plant gates between strikers and scabs. The union responded with a steady stream of press releases and public speeches using the language of anti-fascism, workplace democracy, and "a larger pie" (to divide between worker pay and profits). Reuther created a coalition involving the National Association for the Advancement of Colored People, Eleanor Roosevelt, and other celebrities to support the strikers and their goals, emphasizing the broad social import of the conflict for postwar American society. Despite the strength of this coalition and the determination of the workers to stay out, under pressure from a presidential fact-finding board, the UAW settled the strike for a raise of just 18½ cents, or about 15 percent. The union won no access to the company's books and no guarantee that the company would hold car prices steady. For Reuther, the strike was a success, as it consolidated his leadership of the UAW.

Inflation soon wiped out the 1946 wage increase at GM, and the UAW determined to eliminate the impact of inflation in the 1950 bargaining round. It negotiated the so-called 1950 Treaty of Detroit without a strike, taking advantage of the company's desire for labor peace and wage stabilization in a period of prosperity. The agreement set wage increases to match the cost of living plus an "annual improvement factor" of 2 percent that would distribute part of GM's productivity increase to the workforce.

From then on, sanctioned autoworker strikes were mostly staid affairs. A 104-day Chrysler strike in 1950 revolved around the union's demand for stringent actuarial standards for the firms' pension plan, but ended merely in the company following the industry-wide pattern. The GM strike of 1964 did not include all plants; under pressure from Democratic allies in the White House, Reuther agreed to keep the parts plants open and prodded militant locals into settling plant-level contracts before the presidential election. Neither the company nor the UAW declared victory. The forty-seven-day Ford strike of 1968 further ratcheted up wages and payments to laid-off workers in the context of Vietnam-era inflation, but once again was a far cry from the militant energy of the 1930s.

A more frequent but smaller kind of sanctioned strike occurred at the plant level. James Zetka calls these "bureaucratic strikes" for their highly regulated character. These strikes were especially frequent from the mid-1950s through the early 1970s. Under the terms of collective bargaining, local unions were allowed to go on strike over a wide range of issues not covered by the master contract, but, in practice, most of the strikes were over job control issues. These strikes, however, happened in such a predictable form that management had the ability to control their timing and outcomes to avoid strikes that would harm the company's bottom line.

Wildcat Strikes

During World War II, the national UAW signed the same no-strike pledge as several other national unions. In a special convention, the union passed a resolution not only banning strikes during wartime but also eliminating special payments for Saturday, Sunday, and holiday work in order to keep plants running twenty-four hours a day, seven days a week. (Auto plants were covered, because they had been largely converted to war production.) Although this limited what workers could demand and how they could win it, tight labor markets, cost-plus government contracting practices, and a focus on quality (as opposed to low cost and high quantity) all served to strengthen workers' bargaining power in the workplace. Despite opposition at high levels within the union, there were numerous walkouts, especially at Chrysler, over management demands for changed work organization and hiring practices. In 1943, a walkout of more than 27,000 workers on the day of a War Labor Board hearing led to a stronger grievance procedure; new work standards in February 1945 led to an eleven-day strike of 19,000 workers, also resulting in a victory for workers. As Steve Jefferys has shown, both of these strikes and the many other wartime wildcats were important blows to the authority of management and showed how difficult the national union's task of containing conflict was.

In Detroit, the UAW faced an especially volatile racial mix in the plants. The recruitment and promotion of black workers in formerly segregated plants prompted "hate strikes." Not only did white workers walk off the job, but some supervisors and managers used hate strikes as an argument against racial integration in the workplace. At Packard, for example, hundreds of white workers walked off the job when the company promoted three black workers. This strike reflected a company strategy to split the local union. However, it prompted action from the War Labor Board and the national UAW president R.J. Thomas, which led to the firing of thirty of the strike's ringleaders, according to historians August Meier and Elliott Rudwick. As racial conflict continued through the postwar decades, the national UAW faced the difficult task of dealing with the racism of its white members.

Throughout the 1940s and 1950s, as James Zetka shows, unauthorized strikes were more frequent than authorized ones. During the 1930s and 1940s, workers had developed the camaraderie, confidence, and workplace organization with which to take on management. In 1955 there were sixty wildcat strikes reported in the news media; in 1958 there were eighty (in more normal years, the number would be between twenty and thirty). Wildcat strikes, however, declined in frequency during the 1960s and early 1970s, never getting above fifteen per year. Wildcats in this period generally concerned speedups, unfair treatment by supervisors, health and safety, heat, and other workplace issues.

In the late 1960s and early 1970s, wildcat strikes, though infrequent, took on a new meaning. As activist chroniclers Dan Georgakas and Marvin Surkin have described, they became a way to articulate demands for racial equality and worker control. Marxist parties dispatched activists to Detroit, which seemed to be turning into the cradle of a second American revolution, and dozens of radical university students went to work in auto plants to organize the workers' uprising. After the urban riots of 1967, the League of Revolutionary Black Workers established organizations—usually small—in several of Detroit's auto plants. These local activists criticized the indifference of local union officialdom to racism and speedup and the bureaucratic conservatism of the UAW. The first walkout, in May 1968, involved 4,000 workers at Dodge Main. It was the first wildcat strike there in fourteen years and was led by a group called the Dodge Revolutionary Union Movement (DRUM). DRUM activists followed this with a walkout three years later, this time including a march to the local union hall and a public hearing of grievances.

An analogous group at Chrysler's Eldon Avenue gear and axle plant staged a brief wildcat strike in 1970 over the company's threat to arbitrarily fire a worker. In the summer of 1973, walkouts idled three of Chrysler's plants. At Chrysler's Jefferson Avenue assembly plant, for example, two workers in their twenties shut down the assembly line by taking over a portion of it and locking themselves in a cage in order to protest the racist behavior of a foreman. After thirteen hours, during which the two men were protected by a large group of supporters, the company agreed to fire the foreman and grant the protesters amnesty. Two other strikes by in-plant revolutionary groups took place to protest severe health and safety problems.

The Lordstown, Ohio, strike of 1972 similarly became a fixture of left-wing discourse, and had very similar causes and goals, although the strikers were predominately white. Rather than becoming linked to urban revolution, Lordstown was associated with a revolt of young workers against the alienation of factory life, according to Stanley Aronowitz. However, a similar strike at Norwood, Ohio, was led by older workers, suggesting that alienation and the effects of speedup were hardly limited to young workers.

1980 and After

The U.S. auto industry faced increasing competition from foreign imports in the 1970s and 1980s. Union leaders responded by offering to work with management at the Big Three U.S. auto companies. The era of cooperation did not bring the complete disappearance of strikes—a 1998 strike against a GM parts plant in Flint, for example, brought most production to a standstill throughout North America and resulted in billions of lost dollars. Curiously, this strike strengthened the hand of advocates of labor–management partnership in corporate management, who argued that provoking strikes was expensive. For the UAW, this strike was highly exceptional, and the union has shown itself less and less willing to exercise the strike threat out of its interest in retaining jobs and maintaining its influence in company policies. As a result, since the late 1970s, strikes in the U.S. auto industry have become rare.

Chrysler's 1979 bankruptcy sent a signal across American industry that chronic problems with quality and price needed to be solved, and that contentious labor relations were part of the problem. The U.S. Congress passed a special act that year allowing $1.5 billion in loan guarantees in exchange for concessions from the UAW, suppliers, and lenders. With 40,000 out of 64,000 workers on layoff, workers—including the UAW, other unions, and nonunion workers—took pay concessions of $627 million, suppliers froze prices, lenders forgave debts, and state governments extended loans. Top UAW leaders argued that these concessions were preferable to the alternative—a complete collapse of the industry. Similar concessionary pacts were reached at GM and Ford, and labor–management partnership efforts began to develop at all three companies. At first, "jointness" was carried out primarily on an experimental level. By the mid-1980s, however, bureaucracies had developed, with in-plant appointed officials and separate office buildings in Detroit, to spread the message of constructive labor relations. Meanwhile, with political support from the union hierarchy and technical support from the joint training infrastructures, the companies implemented lean production techniques to ratchet up pressure on employees to work more efficiently, as Mike Parker and Jane Slaughter have shown.

The most important strike of this period came in 1998. It began in Flint at a GM stamping plant employing 3,400 UAW members and a Delphi components plant making spark plugs, fuel filters, and speedometers. The former was a key supplier for the new generation of pickup trucks and SUVs, on strike over management demands to reduce job classifications, while the latter, the only plant making a number of key components, was locked in a dispute over outsourcing. Because of GM's "lean" production system, dependent on quick deliveries and made vulnerable by low inventories, the effects of the strike quickly spread. The strike began on June 8, and by July 23, 193,517 workers at GM assembly plants and suppliers throughout North America were idled. This dispute did not lead to an upsurge in militancy; in fact, it was the end of a long string of local strikes at GM over in-plant issues. After this strike, there were very few strikes at GM, as managers struggled to compensate for billions of dollars of lost revenues and top UAW officials scrambled to avoid any implication that a seemingly "local" strike might really be a mid-contract "national" strike, banned by the national collective bargaining agreement.

Other strikes at suppliers involved the Big Three in various ways. During a 1997 recognition strike at Johnson Controls in Oberlin, Ohio, and Plymouth, Michigan, for example, Ford refused to accept parts from the struck companies. This led to the first major victories in the UAW's attempt to force parts makers—mainly just-in-time suppliers carrying out work outsourced from the Big Three—to renounce union-busting through card-check neutrality agreements.

In another case, management at American Axle, a firm controlling five former GM axle plants, used a strike to strengthen its bargaining position with its former corporate parent. In 2003, American Axle was the last spun-off supplier to negotiate two-tier wages. It was well known to union officials that the supplier was negotiating simultaneously with GM's purchasing agents and the union. A show of resolve by the UAW demonstrated that squeezing prices might result in late deliveries to GM, which remained heavily reliant on the company for axles. In a system of just-in-time inventory, an extended strike would have been as damaging as the Flint strike of 1998. Unlike the Flint strike, however, the strike was ended after a day, with the acceptance in principle of the same two-tier wage structure agreed at other former Big Three suppliers. The outcome and process of striking at this independent company was, in fact, bound with a pattern of concessions and the employer's relationship with the assembly company.

In a third case, Visteon, a firm consisting of Ford's spun-off parts plants, forced non–UAW members on strike over deep pay cuts. At the Bedford, Indiana, plant, workers were represented by the manufacturing arm of the Communication Workers of America. Managers threatened to shift half of the plant's 1,100 jobs to Mexico and proposed a pay cut from $16.00 an hour to $10.00 an hour. When the company began removing equipment from the plant, workers went on strike. The strike had all the markings of American class struggle: bussed-in African-American strikebreakers to spark racist reactions among the mostly white workforce, private security guards assaulting pickets, and a pair of overturned burning cars in front of the plant gate. When workers discovered through an internal Web site that the machines were being moved not to Mexico but to a UAW-represented plant in Michigan, UAW local leadership announced that it would not accept the work. Despite this show of solidarity, the local union in Bedford agreed to management's demands, according to *Labor Notes*.

Conclusion

The UAW rose and fell with its ability and willingness to strike. The sit-down and skilled trades' strikes in the 1930s midwifed the union's birth. From the beginning of World War II until the Chrysler bankruptcy, the national union leadership took increasing responsibility for controlling autoworkers' strike weapon. Strikes became increasingly rule based, governed not only by labor law but also at the local level by master agreements. Wildcat strikes became important, especially because they sought to solve local workplace issues that union officials often ignored, including in-plant race relations and worker alienation.

After 1980, the environment for autoworkers' strikes changed radically. Economic competition and poor management brought a crisis to the Big Three automakers. Labor–management partnership became the union's primary response, and the emergence of a "jointness" infrastructure created large numbers of union positions to work full-time in cooperation with management. The UAW failed to organize the Big Three's competition or win a reform of pensions and health care that would have shifted the costs of the in-firm retirement system more broadly across society or industry. Strikes became shorter and localized, and the intensifying relations of interdependence, information exchange, and cooperation made the whole issue of striking an uncomfortable one for the union. Meanwhile, an immense nonunion sector grew, not only in the Southeast but also in union strongholds like Ohio and Indiana, where striking was completely absent. As the union lost its will or ability to strike, union density declined and unionized employers became increasingly vulnerable to nonunion competition. At the beginning of the twenty-first century, the UAW faces a crisis threatening its very existence in the auto industry.

See also: The Decline of Strikes, 72; World War II Hate Strikes, 126; The Rise and Fall of the Sit-Down Strike, 204; Strikes in the United States Since World War II, 226; Rubber Workers' Strikes, 398.

Bibliography

Aronowitz, Stanley. *False Promises: The Shaping of American Working Class Consciousness.* Durham, NC: Duke University Press, 1992.

Babson, Steve. *Building the Union: Skilled Workers and Anglo-Gaelic Immigrants in the Rise of UAW.* New Brunswick, NJ: Rutgers University Press, 1991.

Brecher, Jeremy. *Strike!* Boston: South End Press, 1997.

Daily Labor Report. Washington, DC: BNA, various issues.

Dollinger, Sol, and Genora J. Dollinger. *Not Automatic: Women and the Left in the Forging of the Auto Workers' Union.* New York: Monthly Review Press, 2000.

Fine, Sidney. *Sit-Down: The General Motors Strike of 1936–1937.* Ann Arbor: University of Michigan Press, 1969.

Georgakas, Dan, and Marvin Surkin. *Detroit, I Do Mind Dying: A Study in Urban Revolution.* New York: St. Martin's Press, 1975.

Jefferys, Steve. *Management and Managed: Fifty Years of Crisis at Chrysler.* New York: Cambridge University Press, 1986.

Labor Notes. Detroit. Various issues.

Lichtenstein, Nelson. *The Most Dangerous Man in Detroit: Walter Reuther and the Fate of American Labor.* New York: Basic Books, 1995.

Meier, August, and Elliott Rudwick. *Black Detroit and the Rise of the UAW.* New York: Oxford University Press, 1979.

Parker, M., and J. Slaughter. *Working Smart: A Union Guide to Participation Programs and Reengineering.* Detroit: Labor Notes, 1994.

Zetka, James R. "Bureaucratic Strikes and the Rationalization of Factory Conflict: The Case of the U.S. Automobile Industry, 1962–1979." *Social Problems* 43, no. 1 (February 1996): 39–56.

———. *Militancy, Market Dynamics, and Workplace Authority: The Struggle Over Labor Process Outcomes in the U.S. Automobile Industry, 1946 to 1973.* Albany: State University of New York Press, 1995.

RUBBER WORKERS' STRIKES

John L. Woods

The rubber industry had its origins in the production of rubber-coated consumer goods such as shoes, boots, raincoats, and gloves. Prior to exponential growth accompanying tire production, manufacturers were typically small, local concerns that catered to the needs of nearby markets. Through the revolutionary process of vulcanization, discovered accidentally by the hapless Charles Goodyear, modern rubber products came into existence and spearheaded the move toward mass production.

By the 1890s, major manufacturing concerns were beginning to develop. The first came about when wholesale rubber merchant Charles R. Flint merged nine boot and shoe companies to form the United States Rubber Company. By the end of the decade, U.S. Rubber controlled nearly 50 percent of the domestic market with the remainder being divided between Akron's B.F. Goodrich and a group of Trenton, New Jersey, producers.

For rubber workers in the early days of the industry, strength, skill, and dexterity were the hallmarks of success, especially in the skilled trades. Once raw rubber was processed and calendared into sheets, it moved to the cutting room where the cutter would pull a sharp knife around a tin pattern, producing the various parts for assembly. Makers, mostly women, would then glue or sew the myriad parts together to produce the final product. By the middle of the nineteenth century, the task of bootmaking was increasingly dominated by men, as manufacturers believed that the task required not only dexterity but also strength. Most other jobs in the industry were considered unskilled. Regardless, the typical workday ranged anywhere from eight to fourteen hours depending on job and ability.

The earliest boot and shoe manufacturers centered on the textile regions of New England and were similar in structure and operation. The Goodyear Metallic Rubber Shoe Company headquartered in Naugatuck, Connecticut, engaged in an industrial paternalism very similar to that employed in the mill works of nearby Lowell, Massachusetts. In addition to providing local housing for its workforce, the company also implemented programs that encouraged regular church attendance and discouraged drinking. As in Lowell, the male workforce consisted of mostly part-time farmers who relied on the piecework wage as a supplemental income source, while the female workforce typically consisted of the unmarried adult daughters of nearby families who also relied on their wages as a supplemental source of income.

Early Unions and Strikes

Except for the Knights of Labor era, unionization within the early rubber industry could best be characterized as local and isolated. The evanescent organizing efforts of the Knights of Labor during the 1880s saw the only national union movement to emerge within the rubber industry during the nineteenth century. Though no lasting organization survived, unions or union organizing efforts were responsible for thirteen of the fifty-six strikes that occurred in the industry between 1881 and 1900.

As the turn of the twentieth century approached, towns or cities with a history of strong labor movement sentiment saw the organizing pattern of local, isolated unions evolve toward the American Federation of Labor's (AFL) federal system. Nationally, in 1902, seven independent locals sought affiliation with the Allied Metal Mechanics, reflecting both the continued perception of rubber work as a metals trade and a desire for greater strength. By that fall, rubber workers petitioned the AFL for an international charter of their own and formed the Amalgamated Rubber Workers Union of North America. By 1903, the Amalgamated had fourteen locals, the largest being Trenton's Local 4, which claimed between 800 and 900 members.

As the unions grew, so too did their militancy. Between 1901 and 1905, nineteen strikes were called by the Amalgamated unions. In January 1903, workers at U.S. Rubber's Morgan and Wright facility struck for and won a seniority plan. In June, workers at Trenton's Whitehead Brothers called for a walkout after a union member was fired for asking for a raise. A settlement was quickly negotiated and the workers returned. As an indication of the growing militancy and power of rubber workers, makers at the nonunion L. Candee and Company struck when a new line of shoes was introduced because they feared a speedup. The plant superintendent, fearful that workers would take this opportunity to organize, quickly raised rates and then called the makers into his office, where he served them ice cream and cake. Not all walkouts, however, were successful. A ten-week strike by Maple Leaf Rubber employees near Toronto ended when their request for a wage increase and union recognition was rejected out of hand and they were forced to return to work.

Trenton Strike

The Amalgamated enjoyed considerable organizing success as it rode the wave of AFL expansion at the turn of the twentieth century. But as with the exponential gains of the Federation during this period, this success would be short-lived. Trenton's Local 4, the largest of the Amalgamated unions, saw its struggle for employer recognition end with the destruction of the first national union of rubber workers.

Although Trenton's Local 4 called for a strike on January 25, 1904, the origins of the strike could be traced to late December 1903. Committees from Local 4 approached the nine Trenton rubber manufacturers to request the use of the union label on their products. They were summarily rejected. The manufacturers, having held a meeting to discuss the matter, feared that use of the union label would imply recognition of the union. Later that month, the local submitted to the same employers a written list of demands asking for recognition of the union as the bargaining agent for rubber workers in Trenton; adoption of the union label on all products; and adoption of a wage scale that increased wages by 10 percent. These demands were once again rejected, and the manufacturers responded by posting notice that the 1903 wage scale would continue through 1904. Despite the affront, the union again tried to meet with the employers to press their demands, this time sending a committee to each employer to request a meeting. This request was simply ignored by the employers. In an attempt to display their determination, Local 4 publicly called for a strike vote to be held and a strike deadline of January 25 was set.

As the strike deadline approached, the Federation made preparations to support the strike. AFL President Samuel Gompers arrived to address the workers. During the strike, benefits were paid to the workers and boycotts were implemented. Violence erupted at the Grieb Rubber Company when strikebreakers were brought in. On March 20, the nine manufacturers issued a statement in which they sought to quell rumors that they had met with the union and were trying to settle the strike, asserting instead that their plants were operating without incident.

By April, it appeared that the cause was lost. A special vote was called on April 13 and the remaining strikers voted eighty-three to fifty-eight to return to work. The strike had been an abject failure. In the aftermath, the union's secretary-treasurer blamed the AFL and claimed that the lack of financial support by the Federation was the determining factor in the strike's failure. According to Local 4 Secretary-Treasurer James O'Donovan, requests for financial assistance to the Federation went unanswered; instead, each time a request was made Gompers responded by sending an additional organizer. Other critics of the strike cited employer intransigence, police interference, and a large and ready labor pool as significant factors in the failure of the strike. When workers returned to the plants not all found jobs waiting for them—nearly 100 were unable to find work.

The Akron Strike of 1913

The Akron Strike of 1913 proved the most divisive and contentious of all the early tire-era strikes and marked the first major conflict in what had become the "Rubber Capital of the World." Competition between the Industrial Workers of the World (IWW) and the AFL contributed to the failure of the strike and demonstrated the difficulties associated with organizing industrial workers. Expansion of the rubber industry, especially due to the development of tire manufacturing, signaled a change in direction for much of the industry. Where the bicycle craze of the 1880s created the tire market, it was the rapidly growing automobile industry that drove its expansion. Compared to footwear manufacture, the production of automobile tires required a greater investment in specialized machinery and a stronger workforce. Thus this era of transition elevated the physically elite tire builder to a place of importance. Initially built entirely by hand on a circular mold, a finished tire and mold could weigh as much as 175 pounds. In an effort to ensure an adequately staffed building room, manufacturers offered high wages to the young, strong, and predominantly male workforce that was needed to produce automobile tires.

The origins of the strike can be found in the ever-increasing demand for automobile tires, which led manufacturers to look for ways to increase production. The greatest advance in tire-building technology was the development of the State tire-building machine. Designed in 1909 by Goodyear master mechanic William State and heralding the age of mass production, this colossal machine, which still required the same level of strength and stamina from the builder, improved quality and output by over 500 percent.

During the transition from hand- to machine-built tires, wage levels were in considerable flux as manufacturers and workers tried to negotiate a level that each believed reflected an equitable scale. In early 1913, Firestone won the contract to provide original equipment tires to the Ford Motor Company for that model year by underbidding its competitors. To ensure that they maintained profitability, the company began to ruthlessly cut costs. The new tire-building machines presented their own set of problems in that the company had virtually no experience setting the rates for machine-built tires. In early February, the company posted a new piecework scale that divided the difference between the rate for machine operators and those workers who still built tires on stands by hand. After requesting that the original rate be restored, 150 workers were sent home by the foreman but instructed to return the next day. On February 11, 1913, the workers returned and again requested that they be paid at the old rate. When the foreman again refused, a large group left and the department closed. As a number of the workers gathered around the gate, someone threw a hat in the air and shouted "Hurrah! We're out." A meeting was hastily called at the nearby Socialist Hall, where a group of IWW leaders gave speeches, encouraged the workers to reject violence, and called on them to establish a strike organization and leadership.

By the next day, the walkout had become a full-blown strike with pickets gathering at the Firestone gate. As word spread, more and more rubber workers left the factories, and it was reported that on February 15 nearly 12,000 workers were on strike throughout Akron.

As the employers waited for a list of demands from strikers, the mayor of Akron closed all the saloons and asked state authorities for National Guard troops to police the strike. One of the major problems with the strike from its inception was its lack of leadership. IWW organizers seemed more interested in promoting their cause and filling their ranks than in finding a settlement for the strike. The governor of Ohio ignored the mayor's request for troops and instead sent arbitrators to try to work out a deal to end the strike. Nearly a week after the strike began, a committee of strikers produced a detailed set of wage demands and presented them to the employers. The proposal was ignored and the manufacturers announced that they would reopen the plants the following week. The strike fell into a stalemate.

By mid-March, the six-week strike would collapse for a number of reasons, the most important being the employers' unwillingness to deal with the strikers or their representatives. Contributing to this was the strikers' lack of any realistic goal or plan around which their fellow strikers could rally. One example was the detailed wage scale presented to the manufacturers. The proposal not only created significant disunity among strikers, who quarreled among themselves over the various rates and job classifications, but it also demonstrated the complete lack of knowledge among the strike leadership about the negotiating process.

The behavior of the two labor organizations that professed to be there to assist the strikers also contributed to their ultimate failure. The IWW with its radical doctrines created a large and effective target for the manufacturers and other antistrike forces. Said historian Harold Roberts, "The principles and philosophy of the IWW . . . tended to obscure the real issues involved in the strike." The AFL, which had arrived shortly after the strike began, engaged in a series of attacks on the IWW that did little to help the cause of the strikers and much to turn public opinion against the strike. The strike officially ended on March 30, when the remaining 200 strikers voted to return to work. The strike would be the last significant labor action in Akron for the next twenty years.

The World War I Era

According to historian Daniel Nelson, "The best known organizing efforts and strikes of the war period occurred in the eastern plants." He found that "of all the rubber workers, the New England footwear employees most closely fit the model of the rebellious war worker." The year 1915 saw Trenton workers form a federal labor union and Boston raincoat makers calling a strike. U.S. Rubber walked out in 1916 after a dispute over a wage increase; the company fired the strikers and gave the remaining workers a raise. Strikes in the state of Rhode Island were among the longest—lasting nearly two months—and the most contentious, with federal agents arresting or harassing strikers for not taking their problems before the War Labor Board. Also during this time, some of the most dramatic inroads among rubber industry workers were made by the metal trades. The International Association of Machinists experienced dramatic growth while also experiencing an increase in militancy among its membership. This militancy translated into considerable unrest in the industry and was the source of at least three different strikes in Akron alone. But as war production came to an end, so too did the union's strength and organizing efforts.

The 1920s and Company Unionism

The postwar recession had a considerable effect on the rubber industry, and many of the major manufacturers found themselves in dire financial situations. The most notable of these was Goodyear Tire and Rubber Company. Goodyear's founder, Frank Seiberling, and his brother were forced to resign when the company found itself insolvent and nearly bankrupt. Paul W. Litchfield, who had served as factory manager during Seiberling's tenure, took the reins of the company and implemented various austerity programs that kept the company afloat during the recession and returned it to profitability afterward.

For rubber workers, the postwar recession brought with it a new form of unionism—company unionism. Goodyear's company union, known as the Industrial Assembly, was established as part of Litchfield's Industrial Relations Plan. This plan was Litchfield's response to the 1913 strike as well as to other strikes of the war era, and served as a counterpoint to AFL and other adversarial union attempts to organize the industry. It also served as an excellent example of welfare capitalism or worker welfare, which had its foundations in paternalism and developed after World War I to repress trade unionism. At the same time, U.S. Rubber introduced its own form of paternalism, known as the Factory Council, but management resistance confined the plan to a handful of plants. Goodyear's Industrial Assembly copied the structure of the U.S. government, with a bicameral legislature consisting of elected plant employees and an executive branch with veto powers headed by President Litchfield.

In late 1925 and early 1926, the first and only recorded industrial union "strike" took place when the House branch of the Goodyear Industrial Assembly called a two-week forced adjournment. The primary cause of the "strike" was Litchfield's attempt to rein in assembly costs by limiting the number of compensable hours for representatives. In 1919, assembly representatives were devoting an average of 900 hours each month to assembly business; by 1925, assembly business was consuming 2,860 hours per month. Historian Bruce Meyer found that "Litchfield showed how the Goodyear assembly was not a real union in the truest sense when he declared he would not pay for more than 1,500 hours a month toward assembly work." In retaliation, the assembly passed a bill calling for a 12.5 percent wage increase, which was promptly vetoed by Litchfield. The adjournment ended when the company assured representatives that assembly activities would not be restricted and that wages would increase once rubber prices stabilized. The lasting effects of the "strike" became evident later, when several members left the assembly to establish an independent union. This union, known as the Ameliorate Club, had little effect on the operation of the plant—it published an occasional newsletter, and membership was reported at somewhere between 3,000 and 6,000—and seems to have been more a stepping stone for the ambitions of its leadership than an industrial union of rubber workers. Competing ambitions ultimately resulted in the club's demise.

The 1930s and the Great Depression

While the Great Depression had a devastating impact on most manufacturing sectors, with the exception of Goodrich and U.S. Rubber, most of the rubber manufacturers remained economically strong, relying on replacement tire sales to keep them afloat. And, while layoffs did hit the industry, the manufacturers for the most part tried their best to keep as many people working as possible. As Daniel Nelson has documented, Goodyear's Litchfield believed that "the problem of unemployment [was] underlying all other ills," and in response, implemented a plan to "rotate employment." The six-hour day became the standard throughout much of the industry as manufacturers embraced the Hoover administration's "share-the-work" policy. But, for those rubber workers lucky enough to keep their jobs, these share-the-work programs severely cut their incomes. Nelson found that among Akron rubber workers, annual wages declined by 37 percent from a high in 1928 of $1,672 to $1,046 in 1933. In addition, not all workers were happy with the six-hour day, as some came to believe that companies were using the shorter day to "rawhide" workers and speed up production.

U.S. Rubber's Mishawaka, Indiana, footwear operation was the site of the only major labor unrest to occur during the early years of the Depression. In 1930, management at the Mishawaka operation implemented time studies and an incentive wage scale in an attempt to create more competition between workers. As the Depression deepened and the footwear market collapsed, management responded as the tire manufacturers had by reducing hours instead of laying off workers. Some of the workers blamed this reduction on the incentive plan, and seeds of dissent began to grow within the plant. This dissent culminated in the spring of 1931 with the establishment of an independent union for the plant. The company responded by firing the union's most active members. In response, seventy cutting room workers walked out. By May 19, 2,400 employees were on strike and the plant closed.

The strike continued for three weeks, with the company trying to reach a settlement with the workers. Soon, an agent from the Federal Mediation and Conciliation Service (FMCS) arrived and began talks with both sides of the dispute. The agent tried to convince the striking workers to accept the original settlement offer, which called for the rehiring of all striking workers, retention of the incentive plan, and the implementation of a Factory Council in the plant. AFL organizer Paul Smith, in town to help establish the union, worked with the conciliator to win acceptance of the settlement, which was approved by a margin of five to one. But, while the settlement returned the employees to the plant, the unrest and distrust that had been building among the workers remained. As historian Daniel Nelson recounts, the FMCS agent reported that the company was "sitting on a powder keg." Finally, in July of 1932, nine hundred workers walked out for a disastrous three-day strike. In the wake of this failure, the union disappeared.

The New Deal Era

Labor actions in the rubber industry during the New Deal era tended to center more on the idea of exercising worker rights and autonomy than on wage concerns or specific grievances. For example, the General Tire strike of 1934 was very similar to the Akron strike of 1913. However, the General Tire strike had a very different outcome and demonstrated to the strikers the value of established goals and effective leadership. The Goodyear strike of 1935, fought during the zenith of the National Industrial Recovery Act (NIRA), was yet another labor action that served as a mechanism for the newly established United Rubber Workers (URW) to exercise its autonomy by challenging the legitimacy of the Industrial Assembly. The sit-down era provides further evidence of this new reality of rubber worker organization. A variety of sit-down actions took place during 1935 and 1936 and proved surprisingly effective in demonstrating to management and nonunion workers the developing power of industrial unionism and the Congress of Industrial Organizations (CIO).

The intervention of the U.S. government in the affairs of labor, especially through the New Deal and the Wagner Act, marked a turning point in collective bargaining. For Akron workers, the acceptance of unionism by their employers was relatively easy. Most employers already had experience with employee representation plans and held a more informed view of employee relations. Other rubber companies were not so enlightened, and many engaged in more traditional responses to unionization movements.

As part of the strike wave of 1934, the Federal Labor Union at Akron's General Tire plant called a strike that would be known as much for its bitter nature as for its role as a harbinger of future labor actions. Called as the result of two relatively minor grievances—General's relatively low wage rate when compared with the Big Three tire companies and management's insistence that the company union was the sole representative of General workers—the strike, according to Daniel Nelson, proved "the most important strike in the industry since 1913." Unlike the 1913 strike, however, this time strike leaders had in place a set of realistic goals and demands. The strike is notable too because it is the first recorded instance of the use of the sit-down tactic. In this instance, the sit-down strike was used only until management agreed to meet with the union to negotiate a settlement. Nevertheless, it proved prescient as unions in numerous other industries began to use the sit-down tactic as well. Ultimately, the true value of the strike was that it demonstrated the viability of a rubber workers' union to both workers and the company.

During 1935, a number of strikes took place among outlying and non-tire rubber manufacturers in Ohio. A strike at Ohio Rubber turned violent as the company employed spies to infiltrate the union and hired thugs to beat organizers and strikers. The strike was finally settled after the county prosecutor put pressure on both the company and the union to find a settlement and customers threatened to find new suppliers unless a settlement was reached.

The Goodyear strike of 1936 was the first of its kind for the fledgling United Rubber Workers union, which formed during the summer of 1935. Although the economy had started to show signs of recovery, tire manufacturers found themselves locked in a price war that kept profits at their lowest level since the 1920s. These low profits would fuel labor unrest throughout much of 1936. Among the hardest hit by the profit wars was Goodyear, which also found itself embroiled in a tense labor situation, with roots leading back to the "tea-cup" agreement of 1935. The "tea-cup" agreement was a settlement brokered by Secretary of Labor Frances Perkins after it was determined that unrest in the rubber industry threatened to stall the fragile recovery of 1935. It was called the "tea-cup" agreement because Perkins served tea to both sides during negotiations, which were held in separate rooms adjacent to her Washington, DC, office. The defining feature of the "tea-cup" accord was that it was reached without any face-to-face contact between the manufacturers and the union, thus preventing the manufacturers from recognizing the union as the legitimate bargaining agent for the workers. The tense situation at Goodyear could also be traced to the company's failure to live up to provisions of the "tea-cup" settlement and continued insistence by Litchfield that the company would only deal with workers individually.

One event that precipitated the walkout and further agitated the already tense situation in the plants was a rate cut that the company imposed without first notifying the union—a direct abrogation of the "tea-cup" accord. Litchfield had determined that the best way for the company to regain profitability and overcome the price war was to cut wages and increase hours. Because of the Depression, the company had been sharing the work among a greater number of employees by working a four-shift, six-hour day. Litchfield's plan called for a three-shift, eight-hour day which would ultimately result in layoffs for a large number of fourth-shift workers. Layoffs among fourth-shift workers were what finally brought the Goodyear strikers out. As Meyer describes, on February 18, 1936, behind a rallying cry of "come on boys, let's go," 500 workers walked out of Goodyear Plant 2. Within hours, all of Goodyear's Akron operation was shut down and workers began to walk an eleven-mile picket line, the longest in U.S. history, surrounding the whole of the Goodyear facility. This strike is often considered to be the first CIO strike, and evidence supports this assertion. Litchfield tried in vain to maintain at least some production by using supervisors and other non-striking personnel; Litchfield himself even went so far as to live in the plant for the first twelve days of the strike, sleeping on a couch in his office. He also tried to influence local authorities to side with the company. However, his efforts were rebuffed by Akron's mayor, Lee D. Schroy. Unlike numerous other strikes during the period, the 1936 Goodyear strike was marked by a lack of violence; in fact, the local police moved in to protect strikers against a planned attack by vigilantes led by Summit County Sheriff Jim Flower. On March 16, at the urging of Secretary of Labor Perkins, Litchfield entered negotiations with the union and this time was willing to compromise. In the end, the settlement provided few economic gains for workers. The company and union agreed to a thirty- to forty-hour workweek in non-tire departments and to hold an employee referendum vote before implementing any workweek change in tire and non-tire departments. In return, the union dropped its call for the dismantling of the Industrial Assembly and withdrew its demand for a wage adjustment and signed a contract. In the end, it was the union that profited the most from the strike. As a result of the strike, membership in the URW skyrocketed. Furthermore, workers began to see the Industrial Assembly as moribund and the URW as a new venue for demonstrating their militancy.

The Sit-Down Strike

As word of its effectiveness spread among Akron unionists, the sit-down strike found widespread use in area rubber plants. Between March and December 1936, no less than sixty-five sit-down actions took place within Akron rubber plants. But, unlike the sit-down strikes of the auto industry, for rubber workers the tactic served more as an arbitration tool than an organizing strategy. For the most part, sit-downs in Akron were of relatively short duration, often lasting only a few hours, with the longest lasting only days. For example, the General Tire sit-down of 1934 was conducted just long enough for the union to get the company's attention and arrange negotiations with management; then a traditional strike was called. Further evidence can be found in the fact that by 1936, the sit-down strike was the preferred method among pro-union workers of protesting the presence of nonunion employees in the plant.

Whereas the 1936 Goodyear strike transpired with almost no violence, another strike at Goodyear in 1938 "erupted quickly into . . . the bloodiest battle in Akron labor history," according to Meyer. Initiated by the militant faction of the Goodyear local, which charged favoritism after the company transferred a large number of employees to a new tire line in violation of seniority, the walkout came as the Local 2 president left town to join other union leaders trying to negotiate a nationwide contract with the company. Lasting less than a week, the strike was punctuated on the second day by a massive street battle between local police and nearly 1,000 strikers who had gathered to prevent a shipment of tires from leaving the plant. Company and local police attacked the crowd with tear gas and nightsticks and later laid siege to the local union headquarters. Local 2 President John House returned to Akron upon hearing of the attack and, fearing another attack, hastily called together the membership, which overwhelmingly voted to return to work.

The World War II Era

Despite no-strike pledges, a small number of walkouts occurred in the rubber industry during World War II. Most of these centered on wage-control arrangements negotiated between government and labor. The largest sticking point and cause of the most unrest during the period were the guaranteed profits that companies received on war contracts. Workers were particularly angered by these arrangements, since inflation continually cut into the purchasing power of their frozen wages. In Akron, the most active local was General Tire Local 9, which staged twenty-four wildcat strikes between August 1943 and January 1944. The International responded to these unauthorized labor actions by expelling, over the vehement protests of the membership, a number of workers who participated in these illegal work stoppages. By and large, workers in the rubber industry engaged in fewer illegal strikes than their CIO counterparts, but they were not immune to the contentious issues faced by workers during the war.

The remaining years of the 1940s were relatively peaceful for American rubber workers, but the same could not be said for Canadian unions. Ontario rubber workers struck in 1946 in an effort to win an industry-wide bargaining agreement. The strike, lasting four months and involving nearly 10,000 rubber workers, completely shut down the Ontario rubber industry, which was comparable in size to that of Akron. For the union, the strike proved less significant in its economic gains and more significant for the recognition and power that the union and its leadership attained.

The 1950s Era

During the 1950s, workers in the rubber industry enjoyed the benefits of the social accord reached by representatives of labor and management. Rubber industry labor relations during this period can best be described as both productive and peaceful. However, this labor peace would fall into decline by the middle of the 1960s, as the American economic landscape began to suffer the ravages of double-digit inflation. For rubber workers, the 1960s became a watershed era with the election of Peter Bommarito to the presidency of the International union. Bommarito, a former marine who served in the Pacific theater during World War II, would bring his strong, assertive personality to bear on the manufacturers and help rubber workers achieve unprecedented economic and shop-floor gains.

The 1960s

Bommarito took the reins of the union in 1966 and developed the industry-wide strike into an effective tool for negotiating significant gains from manufacturers for most of the next two decades. The impetus for the development of the industry-wide strike tactic was an economic assistance agreement among the manufacturers that served to cripple the effects of the union's targeted negotiating strategy. Bommarito labeled this agreement an "unholy alliance" during negotiations in 1967. According to the terms of the agreement, firms that were not targeted with strikes by the URW would provide tires to customers of struck firms with payment for those tires going to the struck firm. The overall goal of this agreement was to ensure that manufacturers did not lose market share as the result of a strike. For example, during the 1967 strike, which the union hoped to make industry-wide, Goodyear continued to produce tires for the customers of Firestone, Goodrich, General, and Uniroyal until it too was struck by the URW, with payments going directly to the company holding the original contract. While similar arrangements had been made by manufacturers in the past, 1967 marked the first time that cash payments were made to the struck firms.

Unfortunately, this first attempt by Bommarito to call an industry-wide strike failed because tire production continued throughout most of the strike. While the strike itself was fairly unremarkable, the walkout helped establish Bommarito's reputation as an aggressive and effective negotiator. As a result, Bommarito won a substantial economic package for the membership, but the real victory of the 1967 strike was the Supplemental Unemployment Benefits (SUB) package that was negotiated into the contract. The SUB ensured that laid-off employees would continue to receive 80 percent of their regular weekly straight-time pay for as long as four years. Unfortunately, the 1967 strike would also become a harbinger of conflicts to come, as the "unholy alliance" would come to play a major role in later negotiations between the manufacturers and the URW.

The 1970s

Continuing the URW tradition of using the strike as a negotiating tool and in comparison with both past and future strikes, the 1970 strike against Goodyear and Goodrich was relatively uneventful. The settlement included an 8 percent across-the-board wage increase for workers in the rubber plants, exceeding that won during the 1967 strike by nearly three percentage points. In fact, the most significant aspect of the 1970 strike was Bommarito's insistence on including health and safety issues as part of the contract negotiations. This reflected his long-held concerns about the ill effects of the numerous and often toxic chemicals that rubbers workers encountered as a regular part of their workday. Historian Bruce Meyer summed up Bommarito's intentions best, declaring "Bommarito wants to cure cancer."

The 1976 strike between the URW and the Big Four—as the dominant tire manufacturers Firestone, Goodyear, Uniroyal, and B.F. Goodrich were known at the time—was long, polemic, and fruitful, while at the same time presaging the growing danger of an increasingly global industry. Negotiations opened on January 28, 1976, in Cincinnati, Ohio. The bargaining issues that made up the bulk of the union's initial proposal had roots that went back as far as 1967. Particularly galling, however, was the settlement of 1973. Negotiated under the wage and price controls of the Nixon administration, the union settled for a 5.5 percent increase, the maximum allowed by the government. Soon after the agreement was finalized the government lifted its sanctions and inflation soared, quickly eroding the meager increase. The URW was the only major union to be hamstrung by wage and price controls. President Bommarito entered the 1976 negotiations looking to "catch up" from the losses of 1973, with a cost-of-living allowance (COLA) increase near the top of the negotiating list. The URW, like the United Auto Workers and other major unions at the time, engaged in industry-wide pattern bargaining.

With the contract set to expire on April 20, 1976, representatives of the union and the companies met in early April to begin serious negotiations. As the deadline approached, it became apparent that Firestone, as the most financially viable of the Big Four tire producers, would be the target company. As an additional incentive, the URW had been trying to organize two of Firestone's southern plants, and the Akron *Beacon Journal* reported that union leaders were "fed up with the nature of Firestone's arguments." In years past, the URW had chosen to strike only the target company, but in 1976 the union decided to conduct an industry-wide strike. The impetus for this decision could again be found in the 1967 Mutual Assistance Pact (MAP) or "unholy alliance" between the major tiremakers. The first attempt to call an industry-wide strike in 1967 had failed, but by 1976 the union was better prepared and this time was able to strike each operation at the end of its contract period.

As April came to a close, negotiations began in earnest with the union firing the first salvo. In May, the union announced that it would undertake a boycott against Firestone products. In addition to a domestic boycott, *Industry Week* reported that, in keeping with their promised support, overseas trade unions had implemented "an inventory watch . . . to determine if loss of production in U.S. plants is being compensated for by shipments from foreign factories." Meanwhile, letters of support poured in from around the world as members of the World Rubber Council of the International Federation of Chemical and General Workers Unions (ICF) of Geneva, Switzerland, implemented a show of solidarity arranged by ICF secretary-general Charles "Chip" Levinson. As the Memorial Day holiday approached, Bommarito filed charges with the U.S. Department of Transportation alleging that tires produced in struck plants by untrained white-collar workers were unsafe. In June, *Industry Week* reported that the Ford administration would take "a hands-off posture toward the deadlock."

As the nation celebrated its bicentennial that July, URW and Big Four negotiators met at the insistence of U.S. Secretary of Labor William J. Usery. Unfortunately, after what appeared to be a good start, the negotiations reached a stalemate. Usery tried once again in July to find a settlement to the dispute and called both parties to Washington, DC, on July 27 for another round of talks. With neither side willing to give, talks broke down three days later. This time Usery was not ready to give up and instead decided to reconvene the negotiations. On the evening of August 5, he sent a telegram informing each side to meet in his office at 10 A.M. August 7, informing the parties to "come fully prepared to take the actions required to reach an agreement. Come prepared to remain in continuous bargaining." And they did; in the early morning hours of August 12, 1976, the two sides came to an agreement. In the end, the union got much of what it had gone on strike for, with the agreement providing for the coveted cost-of-living adjustment. The URW had negotiated the largest compensation package of 1976. According to reports, the package exceeded by three percentage points the agreement signed by the Teamsters that April.

The 1980s

The 1980s saw not only a change in leadership but also a change in tactics. With Bommarito gone, having served as president of the union for fifteen years, URW leadership fell to his successor Milan "Mike" Stone. Stone, who entered the rubber industry at the U.S. Rubber plant in Eau Claire, Wisconsin, in 1946, would inherit from Bommarito the unenviable task of presiding over the painful contraction of the American rubber industry and its concomitant concessions and plant closings. With job security as a primary goal, the URW entered industry-wide pattern bargaining in the spring of 1988. Prior to the 1988 negotiating period, B.F. Goodrich and Uniroyal had merged their ailing tire production lines and formed Uniroyal Goodrich Tire Company. The merger forced a renegotiation of the contracts each party held with the URW. This took place outside the normal contract cycle and, as a result, Uniroyal Goodrich already had a three-year agreement in place as the 1988 negotiations began. This left Goodyear and Firestone as pattern-bargaining targets. Since Firestone was in the process of being acquired by the Japanese firm Bridgestone at the time, the URW chose Goodyear to negotiate the pattern agreement.

In light of the volatile nature of the rubber industry at the time, Goodyear and the URW reached a tentative settlement rather quickly. While the Goodyear locals were contemplating the agreement, 4,800 hundred Firestone workers walked off the job after the company failed to make a comparable offer. As the Goodyear locals rejected the initial agreement and voted to approve a strike, company and union negotiators returned to the bargaining table and hammered out an agreement. Firestone officials signed on to this second agreement and the striking workers returned to their jobs. Gone were the long, contentious strikes of the Bommarito era. The union and the industry were no longer in any position to engage in the kind of adversarial bargaining that had come to characterize their earlier meetings. The rubber industry as a whole was in a state of flux and it was unclear at the time which direction it would take.

The 1990s

As the rubber industry entered the 1990s, the uncertainty that began in the 1980s continued to influence the labor relations milieu between rubber manufacturers and the URW. The upcoming contract cycle in 1994 proved no exception. This round would become known as the "War of '94" and would signal the beginning of the end of the United Rubber Workers as an independent union. The Bridgestone/Firestone strike of 1994 could trace its roots back to the late 1980s, when Japanese tire manufacturer Bridgestone, which had long been looking for a way to break into U.S. manufacturing, purchased Firestone. Initially, the union and company developed and maintained good labor relations, but that period quickly came to an end in the early 1990s as Bridgestone/Firestone found itself hemorrhaging money from its American operations. Following a management shake-up, Bridgestone/Firestone began making overtures to the union that it was interested in making sweeping changes to the collective bargaining agreement between the company and its workers. Believing that Firestone management had failed to reflect the current state of the industry in its negotiations with the union, Bridgestone management set out to enter 1994 negotiations with a plan that would, according to Meyer, "turnaround" the old agreement and replace it with a new one that would "fix the things that it thought needed to be fixed."

The URW, on the other hand, viewed the Bridgestone/Firestone proposal as an attempt to break the union. As if to reinforce this view, just as pattern-bargaining agreement negotiations were starting, URW president Kenneth Coss received a tip from a representative of another tire company warning him that Bridgestone/Firestone hoped to "declare war in '94" on the union. As negotiations began, company executives visited various locals trying to sell the company's proposal to the membership. Negotiations between Bridgestone/Firestone and URW coordinators began well in advance of the existing contract expiration date, but it became apparent early on to union negotiators that company representatives were interested only in getting the union to accept the proposal in its entirety, not in bargaining on its various aspects. Attempts by coordinators to negotiate separate sections of the proposal were met with roadblocks. As the contract expiration deadline loomed, it was apparent that the union would have to call a strike. And, since industry-wide negotiations take place with all manufacturers each contract cycle, 1994 was no exception.

Once the URW wrapped up its negotiations with the other companies, it hoped that this development would inspire Bridgestone/Firestone to negotiate a contract and reach a settlement. However, the company refused to move from its earlier position and the union called a strike. On July 12, 1994, 4,200 workers at five Bridgestone/Firestone plants in the United States walked off the job. The Bridgestone/Firestone strike of 1994 would forever change the URW. The strike would continue without resolution for nearly a year, with the company simply implementing the proposed contract and hiring permanent replacement workers to continue production in the plants. The URW fought a noble battle for most of that year, but in the end the strikers were forced to return to work unconditionally in order to avert an NLRB decertification election. More significant for the URW was the toll that the strike took on the International union. Shortly after the Bridgestone/Firestone strikers returned to work, the URW leadership began talks with the United Steelworkers of America (USWA) about the possibility of a merger. In the end, at a special convention called to consider the merger, two-thirds of the delegates elected to represent the URW local unions would vote to merge with the USWA and become steelworkers. Nearly two years after the lengthy and contentious strike between the URW and Bridgestone/Firestone, USWA Rubber/Plastic Industry Council representatives negotiated an agreement with the company that not only got workers out from under the company-imposed terms under which they were forced to work following their surrender but also saw them gain improvements in health care coverage and a general wage increase.

The first to be conducted under the leadership of the USWA, the Continental-General strike would last almost one year. The union, active well before the contract deadline, demonstrated its seriousness during the negotiations by bargaining more than the URW ever had in the past. Following a change in company management, the union succeeded in negotiating the first general wage increases that workers at the company's Charlotte, North Carolina, plant had received since 1989. The union also established pattern bargaining by negotiating contracts at Continental-General's other two U.S. plants.

The Future of Labor in the Rubber Industry

As workers in the rubber industry enter the twenty-first century, their fate appears far from certain. With more and more multinational corporations moving greater and greater numbers of U.S. manufacturing jobs overseas, unions and workers find themselves struggling to maintain their fragile place in the American economy. The rubber industry is no exception. For example, the battle between the rubber workers' union and Bridgestone/Firestone continues with the USWA running an informational picketing and petition campaign as part of its contract negotiations strategy. The campaign, part of which took place during the 2005 Indianapolis 500, was an attempt to raise public awareness of the issues facing rubber industry workers and their desire to negotiate a fair contract. At the heart of this campaign is the union's concern that Bridgestone/Firestone has not shown enough interest in reinvesting in its U.S. operations and may move its tire production overseas sometime in the future. According to a longtime Bridgestone/Firestone worker quoted in *USWA News*, "Union workers would like to concentrate on making top quality tires, but we're not going to watch more and more of our jobs be exported overseas without a fight." Shortly after the campaign ended, the USWA and Bridgestone/

Firestone reached an agreement in their 2005 contract negotiations.

See also: The Rise and Fall of the Sit-Down Strike, 204; Automobile Workers' Strikes, 389.

Bibliography

Babcock, Glenn D. *History of the United States Rubber Company: A Case Study in Corporate Management.* Bloomington: Indiana University Press, 1966.

Chandler, Alfred D. Jr. *The Visible Hand: The Managerial Revolution in American Business.* Cambridge, MA: Harvard University Press, 1977.

Meyer, Bruce M. *The Once and Future Union: The Rise and Fall of the United Rubber Workers, 1935–1995.* Akron, OH: Akron University Press, 2002.

Nelson, Daniel. *American Rubber Workers & Organized Labor 1900–1941.* Princeton, NJ: Princeton University Press, 1988.

———. *Managers and Workers: Origins of the New Factory System in the United States, 1880–1920.* Madison: University of Wisconsin Press, 1975.

Norton, Nancy Paine. "Industrial Pioneer: The Goodyear Metallic Rubber Shoe Company." Ph.D. diss., Radcliffe College, 1950.

Roberts, Harold S. *The Rubber Workers: Labor Organization and Collective Bargaining in the Rubber Industry.* New York: Harper, 1944.

Woods, John L. "High Stakes and Last Stands: Global Unionism in the 1976 Rubber Industry Strike." Paper presented at the North American Labor History Conference, Wayne State University, Detroit, MI, October 21–23, 2004.

PLUMBING STRIKES

Kim Phillips-Fein

The labor history of the sanitary potting industry—a subsection of the broader pottery industry, focusing on the production of bathtubs, sinks, and toilets—is complex far beyond the relatively small size of the industry as a whole. Episodes of intense strife and conflict have alternated with long periods of labor peace, and strikes in the industry have played a disproportionately important role in American labor history. In particular, the decade-long strike of the United Auto Workers at the Kohler Company of Sheboygan, Wisconsin, in the 1950s and early 1960s became a focal point for the political energies of businessmen frustrated by the limitations they faced under the labor relations regime inaugurated during the New Deal.

Crockery and pottery manufacturers were scarce in the antebellum United States. Most pottery in the country was imported from England. But in the 1830s and 1840s, declining wages, accelerating competition, and attacks on customary rights in English ceramics shops led potters to immigrate to America. The city of Trenton, New Jersey, became the center of American pottery production in the late 1850s, when several immigrant potters established new shops.

It was a fortuitous time to start a pottery, for the depreciation of the dollar during the Civil War gave domestically produced goods a sharp advantage over imports. By 1863, the number of potteries in Trenton had grown from three to seven; by the 1870s many shops employed 200–300 workers, and were easily able to compete with English potters. Production in the potteries was organized along traditional craft principles. Skilled journeymen oversaw the various steps of the multistage production process (wedging, molding, and firing), each one hiring a small staff of poorly paid helpers (more than a quarter of whom were children). English and Irish immigrants and their descendants continued to dominate the pottery industry into the early part of the twentieth century. Most pottery workers were men; women made up about 20 percent of the workforce in the late nineteenth century. The workforce as a whole was young, in part a result of the hazardous nature of the occupation, in which accidents were common and industrial illnesses such as silicosis (known colloquially as "potters' rot") affected many.

The journeymen potters exercised a great deal of power over the production process. Rather than using a mechanized process of continuous production, workers produced pieces in small-scale batches, often working to fill particular orders. Yet at the same time, their control should not be overestimated. The pottery operatives were wage workers who depended upon their employers for machines and the material they needed to deploy their craft, and they never had any expectation of graduating to become master craftsmen.

Unionism grew with the expansion of the industry, at least among the skilled operatives. Workers established their first union, the Operative Pottery Union (OPU), in 1862. After accumulating a defense fund for two years, the OPU struck in 1864, demanding a 10 percent wage increase to come out of the wartime profits of the manufacturers in order to rectify inflation and the high cost of the helpers (which came out of operatives' wages). The workers won the higher wages, but their union was largely wiped out by the financial strain of the strike. The formation of the union, however, helped to spur the manufacturers to create their own Manufacturing Potters' Association (MPA), which was able to effectively stop further efforts at organization by the OPU (for example, when nine workers walked out in 1866, the MPA orchestrated a lockout of the entire trade until the workers gave in). In the 1870s, the pottery operatives—still excluding unskilled men, women, and children—organized once again as the Operative Potters' Beneficial Association. When the Trenton manufacturers announced rate cuts of 10 percent to 25 percent on New Year's Day 1877, the pottery workers again struck. The Trenton community rallied to their support, extending credit, attending benefit balls, and donating money to the strike fund. But after three months, the operatives, who had anticipated support from English potters that failed to materialize, admitted failure and returned to work.

In the 1880s, pottery operatives were able to organize once again, this time with the Knights of Labor. Because pottery operatives could capitalize upon divisions among manufacturers, these unions were initially more successful. During their association with the Knights, the pottery unions expanded to include some apprentices, although the helpers remained outside of the organization. Intensifying competition in the early 1890s from nonunion potteries in the West gave Eastern manufacturers new impetus to break the unions, which they were able to do.

Relations between workers and owners finally stabilized in the early years of the twentieth century. Consolidation within the industry made it possible for owners to raise wages, eliminating the tensions over wage cuts that had driven much of the conflict between owners and operatives in the late nineteenth century. A new employers' association formed, which made a concerted effort to find ways to negotiate with the operatives. Strikes became much rarer, in part because the National Brotherhood of Operative Potters (the new union representing the pottery operatives; NBOP) required a very high majority vote (initially 90 percent, dropping to 75 percent) to call a walkout. Throughout the period, the union remained primarily a union for skilled workers only.

The period of labor peace ended with World War I. Employers began to introduce new technologies of casting, which made it easy to replace skilled workers with cheaper immigrant labor. Trenton's potteries started to face increased competition from nonunion firms outside of the employers' association. In November 1922, after employers threatened stiff wage cuts, several thousand NBOP members struck to protect their jobs. The company hired strikebreakers, effectively ending unionism among sanitary potters for a generation. Shortly thereafter, the Justice Department found the employers' association guilty of violating antitrust law. It was disbanded, and many of the Trenton potters closed. An era of the industry's history had ended. What had begun as a skilled craft had been transformed into industrial labor.

The Kohler Company of Sheboygan, Wisconsin, emerged out of the industrial chaos of the 1920s as one of the most important plumbing manufacturers in the nation (indeed, Kohler bought out one of Trenton's old potteries in the late 1920s). Founded in 1873 by John Michael Kohler Jr., who was born in the Austrian Tyrol and immigrated to the United States at age ten, the Kohler Company began as a general machine shop manufacturing agricultural implements. It began to specialize in the production of enameled bathtubs and kitchenware in the late 1880s. The company grew steadily over the years, until in the 1950s it employed about 4,000 people and was the second-largest plumbing manufacturer in the United States.

Aside from one short-lived strike in 1897, labor relations at the company were paternalistic and free of overt conflict. The founder of the company passed ownership on to his sons, the eldest of whom, Walter, oversaw the construction of a "model village" for Kohler workers (most of the residents of the village were management and office workers, but several hundred factory hands lived in it as well). The employees received life insurance benefits; they could join a benefits association; and the Kohlers provided them with a recreation club. In contrast to the skilled operatives of Trenton, many of Kohler's employees had little previous experience with ceramics. Many new immigrants, almost all of whom had come from agricultural regions in Germany or from the Wisconsin countryside, worked at the company, living in a dormitory-style building dubbed the American Club. Walter Kohler took a special interest in these new immigrants, bringing them down to the courthouse on company time so that they could take—and hopefully pass—their citizenship tests.

Labor conflict first arrived at Kohler during the Great Depression. Inspired by Section 7(a) of the National Industrial Recovery Act, Kohler workers began to talk about forming a union. One of their grievances was that National Recovery Act codes had reduced the wages of semiskilled workers, grouping them with "common labor"; Walter Kohler was part of the plumbing code authority that set the wages. In August 1933, the Kohler workers applied for and received a charter from the American Federation of Labor, as Federal Labor Union No. 18545 (the union was not affiliated with any national organization). In response, Kohler helped to sponsor a company union, the Kohler Workers Association (KWA). The company evaded calls for a representation election.

In July 1934, the Kohler workers went out on strike. While it is unclear whether or not they saw themselves as part of the strike wave sweeping the nation that summer, it is hard to imagine that the Kohler workers were entirely unaware of the uprisings erupting elsewhere in the country. Their strike lasted two weeks before violence broke out. In late July, company deputies fired upon a crowd of workers who had been throwing stones at the factory and breaking windows. Two strikers died and forty-seven were injured. At this point, most workers returned to the company, or else gave up entirely and left Kohler to seek new jobs. In September 1934, the National Labor Relations Board (NLRB; established under the National Industrial Recovery Act; a weaker precursor to the NLRB of the 1935 National Labor Relations [Wagner] Act) ruled that even though the company had founded the KWA, the Board was unwilling to order the dissolution of the company union. Instead the Board insisted that a union election be held at Kohler, in which workers could choose between the KWA and Federal Labor Union No. 18545. The election was held at the end of September, and the KWA won a resounding victory. Yet sporadic picketing continued at the company, and Federal Labor Union No. 18545 attempted to orchestrate a boycott of Kohler. The strike officially ended only in 1941.

But in the early 1950s, the workers active in the KWA began to grow frustrated with the relative impotence of their company union. They had no way of compelling the company to negotiate on issues they deemed important, and if the company did not want to sign a contract, it would simply refuse to do so. The workers began to research joining a new national union. Some unions, such as the International Association of Machinists, were not interested in the Kohler workers, fearing that a protracted fight against the company's management would prove too expensive and difficult (it was estimated that it would cost millions of dollars). But District 10 of the United Auto Workers (UAW), which was seeking to expand its power in the region, was interested. From the standpoint of the Kohler workers, the size and power of the UAW seemed attractive. As one KWA member put it, "If we're going to affiliate with a national union, let's get into the biggest one."

In early 1952, the leaders of the KWA began a movement to affiliate with the UAW. As the leadership of KWA activists suggests, most of the Kohler activists were the company's longtime employees who had been accustomed to seeking out leadership roles. Most workers at Kohler were second-generation immigrants, descendants of people who had come to the United States from Germany, Austria, and other European countries. Very few migrants from Appalachia worked in the Kohler Company, and as of the 1950s, the company had never hired an African-American person.

The UAW won a representation election at Kohler and successfully bargained a first contract with the company. But when the time came to bargain a second contract, the Kohler Company sought to make significant alterations in the agreement. Most important, the company wanted to weaken the position of the union at the company by eliminating third-party arbitration, refusing to have dues check-off or a union shop agreement, and seeking revisions to seniority that would reduce its role in promotions (which the union feared would lead ultimately to the demotion of its activists). While the two sides also differed on wages and other issues (for example, the amount of time allotted for lunch breaks and job security for pregnant women), the real issues at stake were the questions of union security. For the UAW, the Kohler Company's dismissal of arbitration, seniority, and the union shop, especially in light of the company's previous history of anti-union violence, reflected an attack on the very principles of collective bargaining, a throwback to an earlier age of labor feudalism. In the context of the postwar economy, in which industrial unions like the UAW had won a variety of security provisions that gave them the ability to bargain with major corporate employers, the Kohler Company's demands seemed out of step with the times, a dramatic divergence from the overall development of labor relations. For the company, the union's insistence on modern contract language seemed an intolerable assault on management authority. The two sides were unable to reach an agreement, and the union struck beginning April 5, 1954.

The strike would become one of the longest in American labor history. It started well for the union: in the early days of the strike, mass picket lines, dozens of people deep, surrounded the company and prevented strikebreakers from entering the plant. But the company appealed to the Wisconsin Employee Relations Board, which found the mass picketing an illegal incitement to violence. At this point, the company began to appeal to strikers to return to work, and also to hire strikebreakers, many from the farms that surrounded the city of Sheboygan. Over time, production at the company resumed. In many ways, the legal dissolution of the mass pickets was the turning point for Kohler workers. Episodes of violence erupted in the town, as angry strikers turned on neighbors who were crossing the picket line while people who had gone back to work or started working at the company reacted angrily to those on strike.

Once the company had broken the picket line, there was little that the union could do to stop production. Facing defeat after the strike had been ongoing for two years, the UAW called a nationwide boycott of Kohler products, asking the Teamsters union and construction unions not to work on jobs where Kohler products were used and urging local governments to boycott Kohler for public construction products. Local religious leaders and political officials (including the governor of Wisconsin, himself the nephew of the Kohler company president) entreated the company to return to the bargaining table and settle the strike.

Despite these efforts, the Kohler Company was entirely intransigent. Management was outraged by the boycott. Herbert V. Kohler (the younger brother of Walter) and other company officials began their own publicity campaign, traveling around the nation and speaking to business audiences about the lawless violence of the UAW. Kohler's speeches brought him into the developing world of conservative politics. He was among the early faithful donors to the conservative journal *National Review.* He appeared on Clarence Manion's radio program, *The Manion Forum,* to discuss the strike; when various networks refused to air the show, citing fear of libel, the case became within conservative networks an example of liberalism's tyrannical power. Kohler opened a new plant in Spartanburg, South Carolina, where his friend Roger Milliken (a militantly anti-union textile manufacturer who closed a factory after his workers voted to unionize) had his plants. Arizona senator Barry Goldwater, one of the members of the Senate Committee for the Investigation of Improper Activities of Labor or Management, brought the UAW to Washington, DC, to testify about the many allegations of violence in Sheboygan, implying that there was a pattern of violence and abuse in UAW strikes. Kohler enthusiastically supported Goldwater's presidential bid, agreeing to purchase advance copies of *The Conscience of a Conservative* and helping to fund the short-lived 1960 campaign. For businessmen concerned with labor power in the 1950s, the Kohler Company seemed to be an example of a brave little business standing up to the all-powerful UAW.

The outcome of the Kohler strike was ultimately determined by the National Labor Relations Board and the U.S. Court of Appeals. In 1960, the NLRB ruled that the company had committed unfair labor practices, and ordered the two parties to bargain. The company refused. In 1961, the U.S. Court of Appeals upheld the NLRB decision. Kohler tried to appeal the ruling to the Supreme Court, but the Court would not hear the case. In 1965, the company finally agreed to a back-pay settlement of $4.5 million for the Kohler strikers, many of whom had long since left Sheboygan and moved on with their lives. The company agreed to recognize the union, and negotiations resumed at last. Local 833 of the UAW is the representative of workers at Kohler to this day.

But despite the positive NLRB and court rulings, the question of who won the Kohler strike is harder to decide. Throughout the strike, union leaders portrayed the Kohler Company as a retrograde throwback to the pre–New Deal past, a small family-owned business that was out of the mainstream of American industry. One union leader said that the $13 million the union had spent on the strike was worth it because "this was fighting the 'open shop' movement." It is true that at a larger, publicly held company, there might have been less support for such a protracted strike, and certainly Kohler was willing to undertake a vigorous campaign against the union for ideological reasons that larger companies would likely have eschewed. Yet the role of the strike in the burgeoning conservative movement, and the support Kohler attracted from other companies and business associations, suggests that perhaps the Kohler strike, far from being a remnant of the past—the holdout of one small, paternalistic, privately held family corporation against the new regime of law and industrial democracy—was in fact a vision of the future. For the movement that the Kohler family helped to build, and the politicians, magazines, and political groups that helped make Kohler a cause célèbre, saw too-powerful unions as illegitimate in and of themselves and sought to weaken the labor movement as a whole. The rollback of union power, not simply labor relations at one small firm, was at stake in the Kohler strike, from the standpoint of its supporters. Just as the craft workers had sought to preserve their power and their trade in the late nineteenth and early twentieth centuries against the forces of mechanization and low-wage competition, so too the industrial unions that had organized Kohler in the mid-1950s would ultimately find themselves on the defensive as well, fighting an employer onslaught and industrial transformations that would ultimately weaken the labor movement as a whole.

See also: Corporate Strike Strategy, 66; Automobile Workers' Strikes, 389.

Bibliography

Petro, Sylvester. *The Kohler Strike: Union Violence and Administrative Law*. Chicago: Regnery, 1961.

Phillips-Fein, Kim. "Top-Down Revolution: Businessmen, Intellectuals, and Politicians Against the New Deal, 1945–1964." Ph.D. diss., Columbia University, 2005.

Stern, Marc Jeffrey. *The Pottery Industry of Trenton: A Skilled Trade in Transition, 1850–1929*. New Brunswick, NJ: Rutgers University Press, 1994.

Uphoff, Walter. *The Kohler Strike: Its Socio-Economic Causes and Effects*. Milwaukee, WI: Cuneo Press, 1935.

———. *Kohler on Strike: Thirty Years of Conflict*. Boston: Beacon Press, 1966.

AGRICULTURAL STRIKES

Dan La Botz

Agricultural workers have engaged in hundreds of strikes during the nearly 150 years since the Civil War, but with a few exceptions, they did not manage to sustain labor organizations that could win and defend workplace gains. The structure of the agricultural labor market, the changing demographics of farm workers, and the roles of politics, the law, and the government generally retarded their collective action. It is remarkable that despite such barriers as racial discrimination, debt peonage, government violence, and inept leadership, agricultural workers repeatedly laid down their tools and left the fields to strike. In doing so, they often won temporary improvements and sometimes won union recognition and legislative changes that improved their lives. Since strikes by themselves often proved incapable of bringing employers to the bargaining table, union groups such as the United Farm Workers, the Farm Labor Organizing Committee, and the Coalition of Immokalee Workers combined strikes with boycotts. Because agricultural unions were generally weak, other organizations, such as the Socialist Party, the Communist Party, the Mexican Consulate, and the Catholic Church, often played a significant role in organizing farm workers to carry out strikes. The weakness of farm labor organizing meant that strikes, boycotts, and political protest tended to take place in short periods of upsurge, notably in the late nineteenth century, the 1910s, the 1930s, and the late 1960s and early 1970s.

With the evolution of agriculture as an industry, conditions generally inhibited farm workers' collective action and organization. Unlike industrial workers, agricultural workers were not protected by labor legislation at the federal level, such as the National Labor Relations Act; they did not have the positive right to organize, bargain collectively, or strike. By contrast, farm employers tended to form powerful economic organizations and political blocs. They often cooperated with national, state, and local governments to deprive agricultural workers of labor rights and civil liberties, and they frequently turned to vigilantism and terror to quash workers' movements. In the South, a history of slavery, sharecropping, debt peonage, Jim Crow discrimination, disfranchisement, and lynching held workers in general and farm workers in particular in a state of subjugation. Farm workers in the South and West were often nonwhite workers without citizenship and civil rights. As nonwhite workers they faced racial discrimination and disfranchisement, and as noncitizens (or citizens denied their citizenship rights) they could not exercise civil rights, vote, or otherwise engage in the political process. Undocumented immigrant agricultural workers faced the additional threat of deportation.

Farm workers often lived and worked in rural areas in relative isolation from towns and cities, from the communications media, and from other workers, making it more difficult to win support for their struggles. Agricultural labor camps reinforced the isolation, social exclusion, and social control of employers. Farm laborers were often ethnically and culturally heterogeneous, and even in one area there might be groups from many different nations and cultures speaking a variety of languages; in the West the existence of European, Asian, and Latin American workers made organization more difficult.

The very nature of agricultural work inhibited collective action. It is largely unskilled work, making replacements easy to find. It is seasonal, often migratory, and usually impermanent, making for a transitory workforce. It has been increasingly capital intensive as technology has eliminated workers. Labor contractors have played important roles, complicating the employment relationship and making it more difficult to hold employers responsible for wages and conditions.

Workers' organizations often failed to provide the leadership, resources, and inspiration for successful organization and strikes. The American Federation of Labor (AFL) and its local unions were often unwilling to organize farm workers because they were unskilled, foreign, or nonwhite.

Although many aspects of agricultural development impeded workers' collective activity, some conditions facilitated their organization and strikes. Possession of a valuable skill or trade, such as that of sheep shearers, gave some workers economic power. Belonging to a common ethnic and/or cultural group often instilled in workers a sense of cohesion and solidarity. Labor camps may have isolated agricultural workers from other possibly sympathetic groups, but they concentrated workers together—facilitating communication, fostering a sense of shared conditions, helping them develop a feeling of shared purpose, and easing barriers to their organization. Likewise, the seasonal nature of agriculture may have made for a transitory workforce, but it also created moments of maximum leverage; farm workers could time their strikes to coincide with the harvest, threatening employers with the loss of their perishable crops.

Political and economic developments at times lowered the obstacles to strikes and organization among farm workers. A tight labor market, due to such things as war, immigration policy, or industrialization, could give them greater economic leverage. Likewise, belief that there was a sympathetic political administration at the local, state, or federal level sometimes encouraged farm workers to take more risks. Labor organizations dedicated to organizing farm workers, such as the Industrial Workers of the World (IWW), the Communist Party's Trade Union Education/Unity League (TUEL/TUUL), or the United Farm Workers, offered leadership and resources to agricultural workers, increasing their willingness to face down employers. In general, the more centralized the organization (whether bureaucratically, democratically, or administratively), the more successful the strike. A secular ideology that emphasized the value of labor and the importance of the working class at times inspired farm workers' strikes, as did religious or nationalist ideologies. Finally, support from outside governmental, political, or other organizations, such as the Mexican Consulate or a New Deal relief organization, enhanced farm workers' power and confidence.

Not surprisingly, agricultural strikes tended to occur in periods when conditions were more favorable. Because there were rarely preexisting workers' organizations, periods of agricultural labor militancy appear spontaneous at first glance. But, contrary to popular view, strikes are almost never spontaneous. Even when a strike appears to be spontaneous, there are usually networks of activists who have been discussing issues, building informal organizations, planning, and waiting for an opportune moment. This was the case during the main periods of farm worker strike activity. In the 1910s, when Industrial Workers of the World sent activists to the fields and onto soapboxes, the number of strikes increased. The same occurred again in the 1930s, when strikes were inspired in large part by New Deal politics and Communist Party activists. In the late 1960s and early 1970s, the key organization was the United Farm Workers.

Agriculture in the United States

Two forms of organization typified agriculture in colonial America and the early American republic. One was the family farm, owned by free white men who often engaged in subsistence farming in conjunction with some commercial agriculture. This family farm holds a special place in U.S. history, but from the late eighteenth century on, agriculture experienced what economic historian Charles Sellers has characterized as a "rolling crisis" as family farms focused on subsistence were transformed into commercial farms that sold their crops on the open market. Commercial farmers often employed hired hands, and as their farms expanded some employed large numbers of wage laborers. By the late nineteenth century, these workers had become a sizable agricultural proletariat. Only then did they turn to the strike as a weapon in their struggle for a living wage, decent working conditions, and respect from their employers.

The second form of agriculture during colonial times and before the Civil War was the Southern plantation based on slave labor. In the South's slave system, on both plantations and farms, law, religion, and social practice combined to oppress and exploit African-American workers, making the strike impossible. Instead, as historians such as Eugene Genovese and Peter Kolchin have shown, African Americans resisted oppressive working conditions through "silent sabotage," "day-to-day resistance," flight to the North, and occasional rebellion. Strikes never figured in the slaves' resistance—until the very end.

In *Black Reconstruction in America, 1860–1880* W.E.B. DuBois argued, in a chapter titled "The General Strike," that with the coming of the Civil War and the presence of Union troops in the South, African Americans engaged in the largest, most powerful, and most successful agricultural strike in U.S. history. As he writes:

> As soon, however, as it became clear that the Union armies would not or could not return fugitive slaves, and that the masters with all their fume and fury were uncertain of victory, the slave entered upon a general strike against slavery by the same methods that he had used during the period of the fugitive slave. He ran away to the first place of safety and offered his services to the Federal Army. So that in this way it was really true that he served his former masters and served the emancipating army; and it was also true that this withdrawal and bestowal of labor decided the war.

If striking means leaving work in order to pressure employers and the government to change conditions, this was a strike on a massive scale. If one accepts DuBois's characterization, then this was a mass political strike with profound military, economic, and political implications: it helped defeat the Confederacy, end slavery, and replace one economic and political system with another. There has been no other mass agricultural walkout of such proportions and significance in U.S. history.

In the late nineteenth and early twentieth centuries, speaking very broadly, the growth of industrial capitalism and finance transformed American agriculture. Developments were distinct in different regions. In the South, tenant farming, sharecropping, and debt peonage expanded among both African-American and white farmers in the cotton belt. In the Northeast and upper Midwest, dairy farming and diversified agriculture predominated. In the Midwest, among dairy and diversified farmers, and in the Great Plains, among corn and wheat producers, there was an increasing concentration and industrialization of agriculture, with the introduction of horse-drawn and then steam-powered harvesting equipment accompanied by the employment of large numbers of seasonal workers. In the Far West, particularly in California and Texas, the dominant agricultural units were large-scale industrial farms (often called ranches) based on enormous tracts of land, huge irrigation systems, and the employment of massive numbers of both permanent and migrant workers. Immigrants from Europe, Asia, and Latin America made up a large proportion of these farm laborers in the Southwest and West. Many tenant farmers, sharecroppers, and especially permanent and seasonal wage laborers adopted the agricultural strike as a weapon at one time or another.

In response to the Great Depression and the crisis of the Dust Bowl, President Franklin D. Roosevelt's New Deal agricultural programs led to the elimination of many tenant farmers, sharecroppers, and small farmers, as well as the consolidation of many former family farms into large-scale farms owned and operated by corporations. Many of these farms had few permanent employees and most used large numbers of seasonal, often migratory, workers. Today, according to analyst Sherry L. Baron, less than 2 percent of the U.S. population, or about 6 million people, are farmers, while there are also about 2.5 million hired farm laborers, about 1.8 million of them crop workers. Of these, 84 percent are Hispanic, 79 percent were born in Mexico, and 42 percent are migratory workers. A large percentage of these workers are undocumented immigrants, and many of the most recent migrant farm laborers are indigenous people from southern Mexico. Agricultural unions represent less than 1 percent of all of these workers, and for decades there have been no large-scale strikes.

First Strikes

The first successful agricultural strikes took place among livestock workers, particularly sheep shearers and cowboys. Sheep shearers, highly skilled workers whose union owned the patent to the shear, created a strong craft union exerting job and wage control that lasted almost fifty years, controlling all work in the Northern Plains states. The craft union model, however, was not readily applicable to the mass of agricultural crop workers, most of whom were unskilled or at best semiskilled.

During the late nineteenth century, immigrant farm workers in California organized on an ethnic basis to get jobs, raise wages, improve conditions, and sometimes engage in strikes. Chinese contractors and workers in the 1860s and 1870s, and then Japanese contractors and workers in the 1880s and 1890s, organized to drive other workers out of various crops by underbidding the work. Then, once in control of the jobs, they sometimes struck for higher wages. While not labor organizations, dominated as they were by the contractors—who were in some cases quite corrupt—these ethnic contractor-worker organizations on occasion proved effective in using the strike to discipline employers and win higher wages.

The success of these boss-worker combinations in competing for work and wages was one reason white employers and white workers joined together to exclude Chinese and Japanese labor from the United States. Threatened by the success of Chinese ethnic labor organization, white workers organized on a racial basis against the "Yellow Peril"—the perceived threat of a massive invasion of Asian immigrant workers who would drive down the wages of American workers and introduce the vice of opium. Japanese workers, who organized in a similar fashion, faced similar discrimination and anti-immigrant campaigns. American employers were also antagonized by the fact that, although successful in having won jobs and saved their wages, these Chinese and Japanese workers bought farms themselves and became economic competitors. The U.S.-organized labor movement proved incapable of incorporating these Asian workers. Chinese and Japanese workers were not permitted to join the American Federation of Labor and most found the IWW with its call to overthrow capitalism too radical.

The American Federation of Labor did at various times in the nineteenth and twentieth centuries make attempts to organize farm workers. However, its attempts were hampered by several factors: (1) the AFL's craft union model applied to few farm workers; (2) the AFL's racial exclusion and its refusal to accept Japanese, Chinese, and African-American workers limited membership; (3) the AFL unions' initiation fees and dues were too high for farm workers' low wages and insecure employment; (4) the AFL was unwilling to modify its organizational structure to incorporate temporary and migratory workers; (5) AFL organizers refused to share the working and living conditions of migrant workers on farms and ranches; (6) the AFL was unwilling to challenge the Democratic Party, Jim Crow segregation, and disfranchisement in the South. Hamstrung by conservative attitudes, biases, and organizational rigidities, the AFL's few organizing efforts in agriculture in the early 1900s failed, leaving the field open to other organizations.

The Industrial Workers of the World in the 1910s

Founded in 1905 by radical labor unionists, revolutionary syndicalists, and socialists, the Industrial Workers of the World (IWW) sought to organize farm workers starting in 1906. Unlike the AFL, the IWW welcomed workers of all races and nationalities, and it organized largely through singlejacking, or one worker recruiting another on the job. IWW halls served as social centers for resident and migrant workers. IWW members, who were known as Wobblies, used songs and newspapers edited and written by workers, published in five languages (including two in Spanish) to win fellow workers to their views. The union's popular songs, often set to familiar church hymns, formed a central part of its propaganda work. The IWW advocated the use of direct action, particularly the slowdown and the strike, but it sometimes disdained and often neglected the negotiation of union contracts. The IWW began its campaign to organize farm workers in California in 1906 not at the workplace, but by soapboxing and signing up workers into mixed locals (of various industries) in Los Angeles and San Francisco. Two years later, the IWW altered its strategy. It emphasized opposition to labor contractors, fought for year-round jobs, and established IWW locals throughout the agricultural valleys of California. By 1910, IWW offices and volunteer organizers existed in Holtville, Brawley, Redlands, Tulare, Sacramento, and Bakersfield.

When, as part of their organizing campaign and general propaganda, the Wobblies in Local 66, led by Frank Little, criticized a local labor contractor and discouraged workers from signing up with that contractor, the police began to jail Wobbly speakers. This sparked a series of famous Wobbly free speech fights that spread from Fresno to San Diego. The Wobbly strategy was to refuse bail, demand a trial, and fill up the jails. Wobblies came from all over the West to Fresno and San Diego to speak and be jailed. The repression was severe. Police and vigilantes beat hundreds of Wobblies and killed at least two of them, but the free speech fight won support from civil libertarians and made the organization famous among workers all over the West. In 1913 the IWW created "camp delegates." Carrying membership cards, dues books, and IWW pamphlets and newspapers, they began to jump on boxcars, enter labor camps, and take up residence in the hobo jungles. Camp delegates brought IWW literature advocating sabotage as a tactic for disciplining employers—with detailed instructions on how to implement it. The camp delegates not only cleaned up and policed the camps and jungles to protect them from stick-up men, but they also organized slowdowns and strikes over wages and conditions.

IWW organizing suddenly erupted in August 1913 into an aborted strike that became known as the Wheatland Riot. The events took place on the Durst hop ranch in Wheatland, at the time the largest employer of agricultural labor in California. The Durst family needed 1,500 hands to harvest their crops that summer, but advertised throughout California and Nevada for 2,700 workers. In late July, some 2,800 men, women, and children appeared at the ranch and camped on a treeless hill. While many came from towns and cities throughout California and others from the Sierra foothills, about a third of the workers were "fruit tramps" who followed the crops, among them Japanese, Hindus, and Puerto Ricans. Some rented tents from Durst for 75 cents a week, but others simply slept on piles of straw or lay down in the fields.

The workers, including 200 or 300 children, began work at four o'clock in the morning and worked on through the heat of the day (temperatures reached as high as 105 degrees Fahrenheit) until late afternoon. They were paid between 78 cents and $1.00 a day, but those who left before the end of the season forfeited 10 percent of their pay. Those who stayed could purchase their necessities only from Durst's concession store. While about 1,500 workers found work at the ranch, another 1,000 or more remained idle, hoping for a chance in the fields. The water supply was inadequate, perhaps because the owner's brother sold the workers lemonade at a nickel a glass. For the nearly 3,000 workers there were nine outdoor toilets. The poor sanitary conditions led to dysentery throughout the camp, causing vomiting and diarrhea among the workers.

Among the workers on the Durst ranch were some 100 card-carrying IWW members, plus another 400 sympathizers. Some were veterans of the Fresno and San Diego free speech fight, and two of them, Richard "Blackie" Ford and Herman Suhr, began to call for a job action or strike. On August 3, the Wobblies called a mass meeting at which Blackie Ford urged workers to strike. Taking a sick baby from its mother's arms, he held the child up, saying, "It's for the kids we are doing this."

As the meeting ended with a singing of the Wobbly song "Mr. Block," the Yuba County district attorney, the sheriff, and a posse arrived to arrest Blackie Ford. One of the deputies fired a shot in the air—"to sober the mob," he said later—but it provoked a riot. In the course of the fighting, the district attorney and the sheriff were killed, as were two workers. Several others were wounded or badly beaten. The posse, encountering stiff resistance and fearing for their lives, fled the scene, and soon afterward most of the workers also left. The governor immediately dispatched four companies of the National Guard to Wheatland, where, together with the local police, they arrested about a hundred workers.

In the following weeks, after Durst hired the notoriously anti-union Burns Detective Agency, a period that writer Carey McWilliams called "one of the most amazing reigns of terror that California has ever witnessed" took place. Throughout the state, private detectives, local authorities, and vigilantes rounded up hundreds of IWW members and other workers, holding some of them incommunicado for as along as eighty days. Some of the prisoners were beaten and tortured, one went insane, and another committed suicide. Suhr was found in Arizona, put in a boxcar, and brought back to California with no extradition papers or other legalities. Eight months later, Ford and Suhr were convicted of murder and sentenced to life imprisonment, their convictions sustained on appeal. The Wheatland Riot led to an investigation by the California Commission on Immigration and Housing led by Simon J. Lubin, the state's leading progressive reformer, but it did nothing to guarantee the right of farm workers to organize. Nevertheless, it did attract migratory farm workers to the IWW, whose membership rose to 5,000 organized in forty local unions in 1914.

After 1914 the IWW shifted the center of its activities to the grain farms in the Midwest and Great Plains states. Walter Nef headed the Agricultural Workers' Organization (AWO) in Minneapolis, and under his highly centralized direction IWW organizers had success in fields throughout the upper Midwest in 1915 and 1916. The AWO demanded a $3.00 minimum for ten hours' work, good food, a clean place to sleep, blankets, and no discrimination against union members. The IWW had enough members to begin pressuring farmers to make moderate wage increases, and farmers in the prewar prosperity had enough money to pay them. During this period the IWW had at least 20,000 members in the AWO, perhaps more. The AWO organizers and members used militant tactics to take control of the freight trains that transported workers, using weapons to keep the trains free from criminals and to demand that workers join the union. The Wobblies led several strikes in this period, some involving thousands of workers, but the union's success was based more on the combination of union density and employer prosperity. According to Greg Hall, historian of the Wobbly agricultural drive, " . . . the AWO harvest organizing drive of 1916 netted a measure of success unlike anything that had ever taken place in American agricultural labor up to this time."

The Woodrow Wilson administration's repression during World War I, combined with similar campaigns at the state and local level, destroyed the national organizations of Industrial Workers of the World and severely weakened the IWW role in the fields. The federal government indicted, convicted, and jailed IWW leaders, as did state and local governments, while the American Legion and other vigilante groups destroyed IWW offices and beat or even murdered IWW leaders. During the war and afterward the IWW remained a factor in the fields, but the peak of its organizing strength among agricultural workers had passed.

The California Strikes of the 1930s

From 1900 to 1930, Mexicans fleeing the Mexican Revolution (1910–20) and the Cristero Rebellion (1926–34) poured into the United States, about one million in each period. Most sought work and settled in the Southwest, and many worked in agriculture in California, Arizona, and Texas. Mexicans became the dominant ethnic group in the fields, working alongside Filipinos and Japanese, as well as European immigrants and some African Americans.

The Great Depression of 1929–39 led local and state governments to pressure Mexicans to return to Mexico, and 500,000 were driven from the country in the 1930s. During the early 1930s, with a brief economic recovery and with the expulsion of many Mexicans creating a tighter labor market, an opportunity for agricultural labor organizing arose. For the first time in decades, California farm labor meant white workers and workers who were citizens. The Communist Party entered the fields to take advantage of that window of opportunity. The Communists created the Cannery and Agricultural Workers Industrial Union (CAWIU), operating almost entirely in California under the general direction of Communist organizer Sam Darcy. The real leaders of the CAWIU, however, were Pat Chambers and Caroline Decker, who were dedicated, talented, and courageous organizers. Chambers and Decker directed several Communist Party members who formed the cadres of the CAWIU.

They in turn often based their organizing efforts on existing independent unions, ethnic unions of Mexicans and Filipinos, and networks of informal organization among farm workers. While CAWIU leaders and local union leaders tended to focus on immediate economic demands, the Communist Party leadership constantly pressured the union leaders to put forward the party's revolutionary program.

The Communists were initially drawn into farm worker organizing by a large strike of 5,000 workers under the leadership of the Mexican Mutual Aid Society in the Imperial Valley. The CAWIU launched its organizing campaign in 1930, struggling with other unions for leadership of the workers. The CAWIU led many strikes of hundreds and sometimes thousands workers from 1930 to 1932, gradually becoming the dominant labor organization for California agricultural workers by 1933. Writing in 1940, activist historian McWilliams put the number of Communist Party–led strikes in these years at twenty-four, involving a total of 37,500 workers. *Labor Unionism in American Agriculture*, a 1945 report by Stuart Marshall Jamieson for the Bureau of Labor Statistics, counted sixty-one strikes led by the Communist Party involving a total of 57,000. Then, in the great upheaval of 1933, the Communist Party led strikes involving tens of thousands of workers. Jamieson called these "the largest strikes in the history of American agriculture" and they are still among the largest.

The most important of the strikes in 1933 was the cotton strike in the San Joaquin Valley in October. "Elaborate planning and intricate organizational structure lay behind this movement," wrote Jamieson. Before the strikes began, the CAWIU conducted a study of wages and working conditions and organized its work on the basis of that study. The CAWIU leadership, headquartered in San Jose, also created a skeleton organization of sections, subsections, and union locals. The district organizers called mass meetings that elected "farm committees" or "camp committees," so that workers chose leaders from their own ranks. Through its strikes over the previous three years the CAWIU had recruited a core of white, African-American, and Mexican organizers who now functioned as leaders in nineteen new local unions in the San Joaquin Valley. Tulare, where the CAWIU had led a strike at the Tagus Ranch, became the local organizing center. In September, as the growers were meeting, the CAWIU had called a conference of delegates from the cotton fields. The delegates' conference had come up with standard demands including $1.00 per hundredweight (up from 40 cents), abolition of labor contractors, and union hiring without discrimination. To spread the word, the union printed up literature, held mass meetings and parades, and distributed union membership cards.

The strike began in October. The cotton fields were not compact; there were over 1,000 ranches spread over 100 miles across three counties. To overcome this logistical problem, the union used a combination of mass picketing and flying squads. Employers responded by evicting strikers from ranch housing. The CAWIU then gathered the evicted strikers into what were called "concentration camps," tent cities set up in the towns of Corcoran, McFarland, Porterville, Tulare, and Wasco. The camps functioned not only as tent-city communities for the strikers, but also as union centers where mass meetings were held and from which flying squads were dispatched. "The leadership in the camps and on the picket lines came from Mexican workers," writes Devra Weber in *Dark Sweat, White Gold: California Farm Workers, Cotton and the New Deal*. "Mexican leaders acted as conduits between CAWIU organizers and workers, organized strikers' camps, directed picketing, and dealt with workers on a day-to-day basis. When the strike began, Mexican leaders emerged from recognized chains of authority within the community; they were contractors, ex-officers of the Mexican army, members of the small merchant class, leftists, and workers experienced in earlier strikes." And women, Weber points out, often took leading roles on the picket line in calling out scabs.

The growers responded by organizing their own mass meetings and parades to win public support. The pro-grower press berated the CAWIU organizers as Communist agitators, calling for them to be rounded up and run out of town. The local authorities arrested and jail strike leaders, and vigilante groups attacked and attempted to destroy the camps. There were many violent conflicts, and many people were injured and several strikers killed in the course of the strike.

The growers refused to bargain with the CAWIU and called upon workers to repudiate their Communist leaders. They also went to the Mexican consul, asking him to organize Mexican workers into separate unions to deal directly with the employers. Nevertheless, the strike grew in numbers, unity prevailed, and the CAWIU remained in the leadership. The CAWIU's leadership depended in good measure upon the Communist Party and its various organizations, particularly the Workers' International Relief, which raised a considerable amount of money from supporters in large cities. Most important, the California Emergency Relief Administration, a federal New Deal agency, ruled that strikers were entitled to relief payments. Wrote Jamieson, "Probably for the first time in labor history in the United States, a public agency under Federal direction provided public relief to workers actively involved in a large scale strike." Attempts by the State Department of Industrial Relations to mediate the strike were rejected by the employers.

The strike was finally settled by Edward J. Fitzgerald, Conciliator of the U.S. Department of Labor. Avoiding dealings with the CAWIU in order to appease the growers, Fitzgerald brought in Mexican consul Enrique Bravo, and the two officials then picked representative cotton pickers from the camps to give testimony to a fact-finding board appointed by the governor of California. After hearing the testimony, the board, headed by Dr. Ira B. Cross of the University of California, recommended a compromise rate of 75 cents per hundredweight. Federal and state agencies, including the agricultural credit bank, brought pressure on the growers and in effect made the rate mandatory. The growers finally accepted the 75-cent rate.

With the settlement of the strike, state relief to the strikers ended, the state highway patrol imposed law and order, and employers blacklisted union members. At the same time, farm workers refused to work for some egregious employers. While it had won a significant victory, the union had not won recognition or a contract. When the harvest ended, workers moved on, leaving the CAWIU with little more than its headquarters in Tulare.

After 1933, there were still a great many strikes of thousands of workers, yet the farm worker movement in California declined for a variety of reasons. First, the CAWIU had lost the element of surprise, and the employers were better prepared for the next wave of organizing. Second, an influx of Dust Bowl refugees from Oklahoma (Okies) and Arkansas (Arkies) in 1937 and 1938 created a labor surplus that made organizing extremely difficult. Third, the California authorities indicted and succeeded in convicting the CAWIU leaders under the state 1919 Criminal Syndicalism Act. Eight CAWIU leaders and activists—five men and three women—were convicted and sentenced to prison for from one to fourteen years, including Pat Chambers and Caroline Decker, the two principal leaders of the CAWIU. The courts reversed the decision in 1937 and the eight were freed. Finally, the Communist Party, whose leadership had been decisive in the organization of the great strikes of 1933, changed its line in 1935 on orders from the Communist International in the Soviet Union. Communists were now to cooperate with reformist labor unions and labor parties, and even with capitalist parties, in the new period of the Popular Front. This meant folding up the CAWIU and the TUUL, as Communists entered the AFL.

Alabama Share Croppers' Union

Before the turn to the Popular Front, the Communist Party created the Alabama Share Croppers' Union (SCU), which it led through a series of agricultural strikes in the 1930s in spite of the most terrible repression by employers, vigilantes, and government officials. The SCU grew directly out of the Communists' "Third Period" organizing strategy of independent unions and the prioritization of work with African Americans. "Our line, projecting the question of U.S. Blacks as essentially that of an oppressed nation, called for making the South the 'center of gravity' for our work among them," wrote Harry Haywood, a Communist organizer. The Communist Party's leading role in the defense of the "Scottsboro boys" won it respect among African Americans in the South, as did the presidential campaign of William Z. Foster and African-American vice-presidential candidate James W. Ford of Alabama on the Communist Party ticket. Most important for the future of agricultural organizing, the Communist Party organized steelworkers in Birmingham into the United Steel Workers of the Congress of Industrial Organizations (CIO). The first Communist organizer dispatched to the sharecroppers was Mack Coad, a black steelworker from Birmingham. He then contacted two local leaders, Ralph and Tom Gray in Talapoosa County in 1931. Estelle Milner, schoolteacher and daughter of a black sharecropper, acted as liaison between the party and the local farmers. Later, Capitola Tasker organized and headed the SCU Women's auxiliary, which was often organized in sewing circles.

In the fall of 1934, the SCU called its first strike of 500 cotton pickers in Tallapoosa County, demanding 75 cents per hundredweight. The union reported that it won its demands in the local area. Other strikes were also called, but many were broken by the combination of vigilante and official violence. By 1935, the SCU, claiming 10,000 members (probably an exaggerated figure), led 1,500 members out on strike in five counties to demand a wage of $1.00 per day. Despite severe repression, the union won compromise wage increases in several areas. Also in 1935, the SCU led strikes of dairy workers, shrimp fishermen, and other agricultural laborers, winning some gains. The union claimed 12,000 members (an exaggeration) at its peak in 1935, with 2,500 in the states of Louisiana, Mississippi, Georgia, and North Carolina. A strike in Lowndes County, Alabama, in August 1935 became a "miniature civil war," with the sheriff organizing gangs of vigilantes. The union claimed twenty strikers were beaten or flogged and six killed, among them three union members.

In 1936, the Communists briefly led the SCU into the AFL Farm Laborers and Cotton Field Workers Union (FLCFWU) No. 20471, and from there into the United Cannery, Agricultural, Packing and Allied Workers of America (UCAPAWA), an affiliate of the Congress of Industrial Organizations. By 1938, union organizing and strikes had mostly died out in the region.

The Southern Tenant Farmers' Union (STFU) in Arkansas

The most important sharecroppers' movement of the twentieth century took place in Arkansas. Many of the Arkansas Delta plantations, which had only been developed since 1900, were owned by absentee landlords, such as insurance companies, urban companies, and private investors, and there was little of the personal and paternalistic relations found elsewhere in the South. Sharecropping had become a form of debt peonage in which both black and white tenants and croppers were held in conditions of virtual slavery. The Great Depression and the policies of the New Deal's Agricultural Adjustment Administration (AAA) aggravated the already miserable conditions of sharecropping. The AAA programs tended to protect landlords, not croppers. The "plow up" program of 1933 and the reduction program of 1934 was intended to reduce cotton production and increase prices but also ruined many small producers. The AAA was supposed to make payments to landlords, tenants, and sharecroppers, but usually only landlords got paid. Tenant and sharecropper incomes suffered. One authority estimated that Arkansas sharecroppers earned $210 per year in 1933. Many sharecroppers were dispossessed and forced to become day laborers at even lower rates of pay.

In the town of Tyronza, Martha Johnson, the Socialist Party organizer; H.L. Mitchell, owner of a dry-cleaning business; and Clay East, owner of the filling station next door, felt that something should be done about the sharecroppers' situation. Mitchell had been involved in organizing an Unemployed League, which had helped tenants. Now Mitchell, East, and a socialist professor William Amberson decided to conduct a survey of eviction patterns among Arkansas sharecroppers and tenants. The study found that as part of a scheme to collect their payments, landlords were evicting the tenants. The results were published in a pamphlet, *The Plight of the Sharecropper.* Martha Johnson wrote to invite Socialist Party leader Norman Thomas to come and see the conditions there. Thomas spoke to an overflow crowd at the Tyronza schoolhouse and denounced the system of semi-slavery. In a meeting with Mitchell and East, he told the men that, while it was good to recruit more socialists, what was needed was a sharecroppers' union.

Mitchell and East then set about organizing the union. In July 1934, twenty-seven white and black men came together in the town of Tyronza and formed an integrated sharecroppers' union to fight for their share of the benefits denied them by the AAA. The men elected a white sharecropper, Alvin Nunally, chairman, and chose a black minister, C.H. Smith, as vice chairman. The formation of an integrated organization in the South at that time was a radical and dangerous step. Mitchell needed assistance and wrote to friends and acquaintances for help. J.R. Butler, an ex-schoolteacher and sometime sawmill hand and farmer influenced by the Populists and the IWW, wrote the group's Constitution. It called for "one big union" to fight for occupant-ownership and eventually "a cooperative order of society." Unlike the Grange, the Wheel, and the Alliance, the Southern Tenant Farmers' Union (STFU) was to be a workers' organization. E.B. McKinney, a charismatic African-American man influenced by Marcus Garvey, organized the black sharecroppers in the town of Marked Tree. Two ministers, Ward H. Rodgers and C.H. Smith, traveled the countryside spreading the gospel of the union. Smith was beaten and jailed. A lawyer who had represented some factory workers, C.T. Carpenter, took up Smith's case and got him out of jail. The union's amazing victory inspired others to join.

Tenant farmers and sharecroppers, members of the United Cannery, Agricultural, Packing, and Allied Workers of America, met in Bristow, Oklahoma, probably in 1940. Farmers like these formed a number of regional organizations in the 1930s, including the Southern Tenant Farmers Union and the Sharecroppers Union, and went on strike several times. They had some success in California and Arkansas. (Photograph by Russell Lee. *Courtesy:* Library of Congress.)

The union adopted a strategy of "nonviolent resistance" combined with legal and political action. It fought a legal case against planter Hiram Norcross's evictions of the founders of the union and lost. Nevertheless, the lawsuit gave the union publicity and a reputation for fighting for sharecroppers. The union sent delegates to Washington, DC, who came back to report on their meetings with federal authorities, but the meeting was broken up and the speakers jailed. Norman Thomas came back to Tyronza to encourage the sharecroppers, and at a national level he publicized the STFU and fought to win support from the AFL. Thomas and the Socialist Party provided indispensable connections for the STFU: financial assistance from the party's Workers' Defense League, connections to liberal Protestant denominations such as the Presbyterians, and connections to liberal lawyers and journalists. The union grew in a few months to seventy-five locals with 15,000 members throughout the state of Arkansas. Later, at its 1935 convention, the AFL endorsed the STFU.

The STFU began to call strikes in the fall of 1935, during the peak of the cotton-picking season. The union's situation was complicated because, while defined as a workers' organization, the tenants and croppers also sometimes employed laborers as choppers and pickers. The strike was defined as a "stay-in," or a labor boycott in which the day laborers collectively refused to pick cotton while the sharecroppers picked their own cotton in order to force the supervisors to stay in the fields. The union claimed that 11,186 voted in support of the strike with 450 against, and that 4,000 day laborers struck. To counteract the strike's impact, the authorities in Shelby, Tennessee, cut 4,500 people from the relief rolls, forcing them to pick cotton. The union claimed that the strike forced some raises in wage rates in some counties, though that claim was disputed and seems unlikely.

Despite the strike's failure, the STFU continued to grow, reporting a membership of 25,000 at its January 1936 convention in Little Rock. The union also spread to Oklahoma and west Texas, drawing in white, black, and some Mexican workers. The STFU joined with the Sharecroppers' Union of Alabama to win a better cotton contract, as announced by the federal government in 1936.

Sharecroppers were to receive higher payments that would be paid directly to them. This, however, gave the landlords a motive to get rid of the sharecroppers and replace them with day laborers, leading to a new wave of evictions in 1936.

The STFU called a general strike of all cotton choppers—tenants, sharecroppers, and day laborers—in May of 1936. Choppers were being paid 75 cents per day and the union demanded $1.50 (though it later lowered the demand to $1.00) for ten hours. The strike spread from Arkansas to Mississippi and Missouri, and strikers received aid from the Workers' Alliance of Memphis, Tennessee. While the union claimed 4,000 were on strike, others reported 2,000 and some claimed only a few hundred. The strike was met with great violence in some areas, with many workers beaten and one African-American worker, Frank Weems, beaten to death. When ex-preacher and STFU vice president Claude Williams and a woman social worker from Memphis with whom he was traveling went to investigate Weems's death, they were flogged by a group of planters. After several weeks, the union declared the strike ended and claimed a victory with wages as high as $1.25, but others reported that no wages were over $1.00 and that some worked for as little as 50 cents per day. "The cotton choppers' strike of 1936 was a failure as an instrument of collective bargaining with planters," writes Jamieson. But, he adds, the publicity that attended it did help to end the terror in Arkansas after 1936.

The STFU grew rapidly, claiming 328 locals with 30,827 members in seven southern states by January 1937. The influx of small farmers from Oklahoma and Texas led to internal differences over the nature of the organization. The new members wanted to amend the constitution to include farmers, while the founders wanted to keep it a workers' organization. By 1937, the STFU and other farm organizations had begun to move toward the new Congress of Industrial Organizations (CIO), and in July 1937 the STFU became part of the UCAPAWA. Now a part of the CIO, the STFU called a general strike of cotton pickers in 1938, with a demand of $1.00 per hundredweight. The union claimed that 6,500 union members and nonunion workers joined the strike for a period of a week to ten days, and claimed a victory with employers now paying the requested dollar per hundredweight.

During 1939, the STFU came into conflict with UCAPAWA over issues of local autonomy. The STFU wanted to run their own organization and they accused the UCAPAWA of stifling them. Moreover, Mitchell and the socialists of the STFU came into conflict with Donald Henderson and the Communist leadership of the UCAPAWA. When the STFU voted to withdraw, the UCAPAWA then set up its own rival STFU. In the end, the farm workers' movement was weakened by the split and declined.

Braceros, Operation Wetback, Cold War, and the NFLU Strike of 1947

The period between 1940 and the 1960s saw a much lower level of agricultural organization and strikes, largely as a result of the Bracero Program. During World War II, the Mexican and U.S. governments agreed to establish what Manuel García y Griego characterizes as "a program unprecedented in the history of both nations; the large-scale, sustained recruitment and contracting of temporary migrant workers under the aegis of an international agreement." The Bracero Program, as it came to be known, was eventually extended, with various modifications, from 1943 through 1964. Altogether some 4.2 million Mexican migrant workers, virtually all men, entered the United States under the program, the majority working in agriculture, though some also worked for the railroad industry. Between 1943 and 1946, about 49,000 workers came each year; between 1947 and 1954, about 116,000 came per year, and between 1955 and 1964, about 333,000 entered annually. The year of highest immigration was 1956, when 445,197 workers were issued contracts.

At its height in the 1950s, the Bracero Program coincided with "Operation Wetback," which was organized by the border patrol under the leadership of retired Army General and Immigration and Naturalization Service Commissioner Joseph Swing, a friend of President Dwight D. Eisenhower. During Operation Wetback, the Border Patrol conducted "military-style" operations that caught 865,318 "deportable Mexicans" in 1953 and 1,075,168 in 1954. The roundups created an atmosphere of quasi-military repression in immigrant farm labor communities that had a chilling effect on organizing efforts.

While the Bracero Program, parallel illegal immigration, and Operation Wetback were the principal obstacles to labor organization from the 1940s to the 1960s, the Cold War and anti-communism also created an a conservative political climate that made union organizing and strikes more difficult. Nevertheless, union organizing activities and strikes did take place. On October 1, 1947, some 800 workers of Local 218 of the National Farm Labor Union (NFLU), under the leadership of Henry "Hank" Hasiwar, Ernesto Galarza, Bob Whatley, and James Price, put up a picket line and struck DiGiorgio Farms, a multi-million-dollar family-owned corporation in California.

DiGiorgio used a variety of traditional tactics to defeat the union: eviction of strikers, vigilante violence, and legal charges against workers. However, the firm also exerted pressure on Congress that led the House Committee on Un-American Activities (HUAC) to investigate the strike in 1948. No evidence of Communist involvement in the NFLU or the strike was ever given. In response to the employer's maneuvers, the NFLU produced a film entitled *Poverty in the Valley of Plenty*, but the corporation brought a libel suit and won in court, forcing the union to suspend showings. The NFLU Local 218 strike was ended on May 8, 1950, at the order of the union head H.L. Mitchell.

When the Bracero Program ended in 1964, the U.S. government created the H-2 Guest Worker program to continue to provide Mexican workers for U.S. agribusiness. This was "essentially a unilateral *bracero* program," notes García y Griego. But illegal immigration by undocumented workers—often tolerated by authorities—became the main substitute for the Bracero Program.

César Chávez and the United Farm Workers in the 1960s and 1970s

California would once again be the stage for big farm worker strikes in the 1960s and 1970s under the leadership of César Chávez, founder of the United Farm Workers (UFW). Chávez, inspired by Catholic social teaching and using the symbols of Catholicism, especially the Virgin of Guadalupe, and of Mexican nationalism, such as the Mexican flag, won mostly Mexican-American workers to the UFW. The union carried out some of the longest-lasting agricultural strikes in U.S. history, involving thousands of workers, and organized national and international boycotts. Working closely with liberal union leaders such as Walter Reuther of the United Auto Workers and with liberal Democrats such as Robert Kennedy and Jerry Brown, Chávez succeeded for a time in creating a farm workers' union, winning employer recognition and contracts that raised wages and increased benefits as no other agricultural union in the continental United States had ever done.

Chávez, a Mexican American, a former farm worker, and a longtime community organizer, began to organize Mexican-American workers in California in the early 1960s, traveling through the towns of the central valley to talk with workers. He did not trust the AFL-CIO, the Teamsters, or any other existing labor union to organize farm workers, believing that he knew best how to build a farm workers' union. He decided to create a new, independent union, with a volunteer organizing staff, and focused on the settled Mexican-American workers. During the summer of 1962, he recruited some 1,000 farm workers to his union. On September 30, 1962, the National Farm Workers' Association (NFWA) held its founding convention, attended by about 200 farm workers, mostly Mexicans, though also some Filipinos, Anglos, and African Americans came. The convention, mostly conducted in Spanish, displayed posters of Mexican heroes like Emiliano Zapata and adopted Mexican symbols. Chávez, influenced by both Catholic social teaching and Mahatma Gandhi, was committed to building a nonviolent movement. The NFWA adopted a constitution creating a highly centralized organization with power vested in the president and executive board. The union's staff would be paid $5.00 per week for 80 to 100 hours of work.

The NFWA began organizing slowly, operating more as a mutual aid organization than a union, attracting members by offering them such services as cheap gas, a cooperative grocery store, legal aid, and a credit union. By 1965, the union was engaging in small-scale strikes as well as tenant organizing and rent strikes in company housing.

Chávez planned to spend several more years in such slow organizing to lay a foundation for his union. Then in September 1965, Filipino workers in the AFL-CIO's Agricultural Workers' Organizing Committee (AWOC) struck a grape farm in Delano for higher wages, forcing the NFWA to take a stand. The NFWA voted to join the AWOC strike, and the strike soon spread to 5,000 workers over an area of 400 square miles. By 1966, the two unions would merge into the United Farm Workers' Organizing Committee (UFWOC), affiliated with the AFL-CIO and led by Chávez. The grape strike would last five years, involve thousands of strikers, and bring millions to honor the national grape boycott.

Chávez felt that farm workers could only win if they could create alliances with others outside of the agricultural valleys of California, where growers held all the power. He first took the union to the university campuses of California, where he told students about the agricultural workers' issues, collected money, won volunteers, and built up a network of urban supporters. Chávez also helped to inspire the Chicano civil rights movement. Throughout the heroic period of the UFW from 1965 to 1975, the farm workers' movement was buoyed by what activists of the time called "the movement"—that is, the upsurge of social activists formed by the civil rights and anti-war movements. "The movement" provided the UFW with inspiration, strategies, cadres, troops, and financial support. Very often movement activists came to support the strike and stayed.

The strike alone, however, was not winning, and in 1965 the UFWOC decided to supplement the strike with a national grape boycott. Chávez believed that the farm workers themselves would be the best organizers of the boycott, and hundreds of farm workers were dispatched to cities throughout the United States and Canada. UFWOC's boycott organizers were supported at the local level by Students for a Democratic Society (SDS) and the Student Nonviolent Coordinating Committee (SNCC), as well as by labor unions and churches. The UFWOC boycott confronted millions of Americans with a choice to support the union by refusing to buy grapes or to support the employers by buying them. The boycott not only served as economic pressure, but also educated millions about farm worker issues, informed them about the existence of the union and the strike, and projected Chávez as the leader of the union and the best-known spokesman for Mexican Americans.

The strike and boycott brought the union support from Walter Reuther of the United Auto Workers (UAW) and then from Robert Kennedy, a leading liberal figure in the Democratic Party. The administration of Lyndon B. Johnson in Washington provided funds for union-related projects. Protestant churches and liberal foundations also began to provide funds to the union, as did the UAW and other labor unions.

In order to dramatize the farm worker strike, Chávez organized a pilgrimage through the state by farm workers. The 300-mile march from Delano to Sacramento, led by banners of the Virgin of Guadalupe and American and Mexican flags, eventually culminated in a rally by 500 at the state capital. There, on April 7, 1966, Chávez announced that the union had won its first contract in grapes with the Schenley Corporation.

The strike continued through 1966, complicated by competition from the Teamsters union, which offered itself to DiGiorgio and other employers as the less-militant alternative that would accepted a lower wage. Though Chávez called for tactics of nonviolent resistance in the tradition of Gandhi, the strike became increasingly violent. Employers, vigilantes, and police attacked UFWOC picket lines, and the farm workers fought back. Chávez, feeling that he was losing control of the strike, decided to carry out a fast in an attempt to redirect the strike along more disciplined and peaceful lines. A twenty-five-day fast, covered on a daily basis by the state and national media, ended with Robert Kennedy joining Chávez to break the fast. The union and the boycott were stronger at that point than they had ever been, a strength based on broad national support from labor unions, churches, and the liberals of the middle class. Employers began to sign contracts with the union.

By the end of the 1960s Chávez had succeeded in building a new labor union, the United Farm Workers' Organizing Committee, in bringing about 95 percent of the table grape growers under union contract, and in establishing a national reputation as a spokesman for the Mexican Americans of the

Southwest. *Time* magazine put him on its cover on July 4, 1969. The UFWOC contracts signed in 1970 raised field workers' wages by 40 percent. Farm workers' wages, which had been 50 percent of those of manufacturing workers in 1965, rose to 60 percent of factory workers' wages in 1970.

During the 1970s the employers, state and local authorities, and the Teamsters fought the union, now called the United Farm Workers, for control of the fields. The violence peaked in 1973, when the Teamsters brought in thugs to beat up UFW pickets. During this period, the police or vigilantes killed two UFW members. The growers succeeded temporarily in stopping the UFW's drive to organize farm workers. The UFW lost 90 percent of its contracts, and union members under contract plummeted from 50,000 (30,000 of them full-time, year-long members) to just 6,500, with about 12,000 members altogether.

Because of the violence, for periods of time the UFW virtually gave up the strike in the fields and relied on the boycott to pressure employers. The union's public support was remarkable. A Louis Harris Poll conducted in 1975 indicated that 12 percent of the adult population (17 million people) had stopped buying grapes because of the boycott, while 11 percent (14 million people) had stopped buying lettuce; and 8 percent (or 11 million people) had stopped buying Gallo wine. Some 45 percent of those surveyed supported the UFW, and only 7 percent supported the Teamsters.

While the boycott continued, Chávez worked with California governor Jerry Brown, a liberal Democrat, to create a California collective bargaining law for agricultural workers. With support from labor and liberals, in May 1975 California adopted the Agricultural Labor Relations Act (ALRA). Brown then appointed a state agricultural labor relations board sympathetic to the union. For the first time in history, California farm workers had the right to vote for a union. Altogether during 1975, there was an average of five elections a day, and the UFW won 55 percent of the elections on over 400 farms, while the Teamsters won about 33 percent. In the other 12 percent, the growers won when workers voted for no union. Union victories meant improved lives for farm workers in California, as UFW and Teamster contracts raised wages by as much as 30 to 50 percent, and for the first time workers also won benefits such as health insurance and pensions. Most importantly, the UFW had become the dominant union in the fields.

Altogether between 1975 and 1979 the Agricultural Labor Relations Board conducted 824 elections, with union victories (either the UFW or the Teamsters) in 584 of them. By 1980, the UFW claimed 100,000 members, and represented between 40,000 and 50,000 members under contract on hundreds of farms throughout the state. Farm wages in California in 1964 had averaged $1.10 per hour, but by 1980 union lettuce workers were making over $5.00 per hour. Finally, Chávez seemed to have established the long-dreamed-of farm workers' union as a secure institution in California agriculture. Yet, while no one saw it at the time, 1980 represented the union's high tide. During the 1980s, the UFW faced hostile Republican leadership in both the California and federal governments, extensive changes in crops and methods, and a transformation of the demography of farm workers with the immigration of hundreds of thousands of new immigrants, often Amerindian indigenous workers from southern Mexico. The impact of these changes in politics, economic organization, and immigration was profound, and the union's power declined dramatically. In the years between 1980 and 1984, there were only 125 elections, and unions won just 94. Between 1985 and 1989 the numbers fell again; in 116 elections unions won only 53. From 1990 to 1994 there were 86 elections and just 43 union victories. Finally, between 1995 and 1999 there were 21 elections and a mere 12 union victories.

César Chávez died on April 23, 1993, as his union declined. By the1990s, the UFW was virtually eliminated as a factor in the fields of California. In the mid-1990s, California had 25,000 growers who hired about 900,000 farm workers each year, many of them undocumented immigrants from Mexico. Several thousand farm labor contractors and crew bosses actually did most of the hiring. Among those 25,000 employers and 900,000 workers, the UFW had only twenty collective bargaining agreements and only 20,000 workers under contract (though it claimed 26,000 members total). After about thirty-five years of organizing, the UFW represented about 2.2 percent of all farm workers in California, and almost none anywhere else. Farm workers' wages, which had risen during the 1970s to almost 60 percent of nonfarm wages, declined during the 1980s and 1990s to the historic average of about 50 percent of nonfarm levels. Workers' wages tended to hover around the minimum wage of $4.75 per hour in the mid-1990s, though some farm workers made more if they had special skills.

The FLOC and the Coalition of Immokalee Workers

The example of César Chávez and the United Farm Workers inspired other farm workers in the United States and led to organizing drives, the formation of unions, and strikes. In 1967, Baldemar Velásquez created the Farm Labor Organizing Committee (FLOC) in Ohio. FLOC engaged in several small strikes in its first decade, but its largest strike took place in 1978, when 2,300 workers struck some 500 farmers producing tomatoes for Campbell's Soup and Libby's. Faced with the strike, Campbell's ordered ninety farms to mechanize their harvest. FLOC, which existed informally for a decade, held a founding convention in 1979 in the midst of the conflict with Campbell's. At that convention, the union decided to carry out a boycott against Campbell's products.

The FLOC strike and boycott of Campbell's proved difficult to win because both the soup company and local farmers claimed that they did not have the power to resolve the issue. The soup company said the union should deal with the farmers, and the farmers said they had no power because Campbell's made all the decisions. The FLOC mounted a national boycott, forming alliances with labor unions, churches, and civic organizations throughout Ohio and the nation. Campbell's profits suffered, and in January 1985, Campbell's and FLOC began meeting and reached an agreement on May 13 to suspend the boycott while a representation election was held. The FLOC won by a big margin among the 3,100 farm workers voting. In February 1986, the FLOC signed an historic agreement with Campbell's covering both Campbell's Soup tomato growers and Vlasic pickle growers. The contracts provided for wage gains, benefits, holidays, and grievance procedures.

In 1993, a group of Mexican, Guatemalan, Haitian, and African-American workers in Immokalee, Florida, came together to create the Coalition of Immokalee Workers (CIW). The CIW called itself "a community union" rather than a labor union. It argued that, despite the experience of the UFW and FLOC, labor union organization of a traditional sort was impossible among farm workers because such workers had no collective bargaining rights. The CIW called three general crop strikes of several hundred workers in Florida in the mid-1990s. Six of its members engaged in a month-long hunger strike, and the organization carried out a 230-mile march from Ft. Myers to Orlando in 2000. With some of its workers in actual slave labor conditions, the group carried out an anti-slavery campaign. "From 1997–2000, we helped bring three modern-day slavery operations to justice, resulting in freedom for over 500 workers from debt bondage," according to the union's Web site. From 2001 to 2005, the CIW carried out a boycott against Taco Bell, eventually forcing the company to agree to make its suppliers improve wages and conditions on tomato farms. Interestingly, the CIW won no union recognition or contracts.

See also: The Catholic Church and Strikes, 162; Strikes Led by the TUUL, 1929–1934, 166; Labor and the Transformation of the Hawaiian Sugar Industry, 431; The Watsonville Cannery Strike, 1985–1987, 444.

Bibliography

Barger, W. K. and Reza, Ernesto M. *The Farm Labor Movement in the Midwest: Social Change and Adaptation Among Migrant Farmworkers*. Austin: University of Texas Press, 1994.

Baron, Sherry L. Baron. "Agricultural Workers." In *Occupational and Environmental Health*, ed. Barry S. Levy, et al. Philadelphia: Lippincott Williams & Wilkins, 2006.

Daniel, Cletus E. *Bitter Harvest: A History of California Farmworkers, 1870–1941*. Berkeley: University of California Press, 1981.

Ferriss, Susan, and Sandoval, Ricardo. *The Fight in the Fields: César Chávez and the Farm Workers Union*. San Diego: Harcourt Brace, 1997.

García y Griego, Manuel. "The Importation of Mexican Contract Laborers into the United States, 1942–1965." In *Between Two Worlds: Mexican Immigrants in the United States*, ed. David G. Gutíerrez. Wilmington, DE: Scholarly Resources, 1996.

Genovese, Eugene D. *From Rebellion to Revolution: Afro-American Slave Revolts in the Making of the Modern World*. Baton Rouge: Louisiana State University Press, 1992.

Gonzalez, Gilbert G. "Company Unions, the Mexican Consulate, and the Imperial Valley Agricultural Strikes, 1928–1934." *Western Historical Quarterly*, 27, no. 1 (Spring 1996): 53–73.

Griswold del Castillo, Richard, and García, Richard A. *César Chávez: A Triumph of Spirit*. Norman: University of Oklahoma Press, 1995.

Grubbs, Donald H. *Cry from the Cotton: The Southern Tenant Farmers' Union and the New Deal*. Chapel Hill: University of North Carolina Press, 1971.

Hall, Greg. *Harvest Wobblies: The Industrial Workers of the World and Agricultural Laborers in the American West, 1905–1930*. Corvallis: Oregon State University Press, 2001.

Jamieson, Stuart Marshall. *Labor Unionism in American Agriculture*. Washington, DC: U.S. Department of Labor, Bureau of Labor Statistics, 1945.

Kelley, Robin D.G. *Hammer and Hoe: Alabama Communists During the Great Depression*. Chapel Hill: University of North Carolina Press, 1990.

Kolchin, Peter. *American Slavery: 1619–1877*. New York: Hill and Wang, 1993.

McWilliams, Carey. *Factories in the Field: The Story of Migratory Farm Labor in California*. Boston: Little, Brown, 1940.

Meister, Dick, and Loftis, Anne. *The Struggle to Unionize America's Farm Workers*. New York: Macmillan, 1977.

Morin, Alexander. *The Organizability of Farm Labor in the United States*. Cambridge, MA: Harvard University Press, 1952.

Sellers, Charles. *The Market Revolution: Jacksonian America, 1815–1846*. New York: Oxford University Press, 1991.

Street, Richard Steven. *Beasts of the Field: A Narrative History of California Farmworkers, 1769–1913*. Stanford, CA: Stanford University Press, 2004.

Weber, Devra. *Dark Sweat, White Gold: California Farm Workers, Cotton and the New Deal*. Berkeley: University of California Press, 1994.

LABOR AND THE TRANSFORMATION OF THE HAWAIIAN SUGAR INDUSTRY

Edward D. Beechert

From a rudimentary beginning in 1835, the Hawaiian sugar industry began to produce a crude raw sugar for the California market. The first plantation was developed on Kauai, using native Hawaiians supplied by the local Hawaiian chief at Koloa, Kauai, who utilized his traditional power to command the obedience of the local male population.

The workers were paid 12½ cents per day in scrip redeemable only in the company store. The poor conditions led the workers to strike in 1841, demanding a pay increase to 25 cents per day, in cash. The workers failed to win their demands, but the strike produced what came to be a persistent topic of discussion: the "labor question." Management claimed that the Hawaiian workers were "lazy" and "idle," that "they spend their days in idleness and therefore their lands are grown over with weeds." Caught between exploiting chiefs and a patronizing missionary class, the Hawaiians preferred to withdraw into their subsistence economy or were drawn to the port communities where work opportunities at higher wages were available. In addition, plagues and Western diseases were decimating the native population.

The Hawaiian chiefs promulgated the Laws of 1842 to establish that the traditional contributions of produce and labor required under the old Hawaiian system be paid in cash. Finally, in 1850, the Hawaiian legislature gave the category of "wage laborer" legal sanction in the Masters and Servants Act, fashioned after the apprenticeship and orphan laws of New York and Massachusetts. Work no longer had a cultural bond to the tasks of the community. A final paragraph provided for contract labor and, by implication, imported labor. Unlike other contract labor systems of plantation labor, Hawaii's law was more liberal in extending protection of the workers' civil liberties as though the immigrant were a citizen. This permitted the expired contract worker to either leave Hawaii or move to another plantation or occupation.

The disruptions of the Civil War increased the market for Hawaiian sugar and led to an urgent need for labor. The improved market conditions permitted the plantations to expand their mill technology, adding steam power to the mill and modern grinding and boiling equipment from Scotland.

In 1860, China was the world source of plantation labor. Chinese laborers were sufficiently numerous, supposedly docile, and inexpensive, and the "coolie" trade was a thriving industry. Imported in groups, the Chinese workers were housed in hastily built structures next to newly planted fields. This process continued with each wave of immigrant labor until cane field railways permitted large base camps. Isolated as the plantations were, workers, contrary to their supposed reputation, tended to react to unfavorable treatment with violence, either individually or in small groups. This type of response quickly earned the Chinese a reputation as being prone to violence. This same isolation reinforced ethnic identity and resulted in the development of a language of work communication. Beginning as a mixture of English, Chinese, and Hawaiian words, *hapa haole* speech eventually developed into a creole language, commonly termed "pidgin," adding words from the Japanese and the Filipinos.

The signing of a Reciprocity Treaty with the United States in 1876 admitted Hawaiian sugar duty-free into the U.S. market in return for U.S. access to and control of Pearl Harbor. The subsidy touched off a frenzy of investment in new plantations, creating a renewed pressure to provide an ample labor supply. In 1873, English agitation against the Chinese "coolie" trade resulted in a prohibition against shipping signed contract workers from Chinese ports when the Chinese government acted to follow the British example in Hong Kong. Chinese immigrants to Hawaii often preferred to go to Chinese employers, particularly those in rice, rather than the new sugar plantations largely owned by American and British businessmen.

Opposition to the Reciprocity Treaty from mainland sugar producers and protectionists resulted in a barrage of publicity about the Hawaiian labor system as a form of slavery. The fine line between discipline and abuse of gang labor was a constant problem wherever plantation-type labor was used. Despite the growing opposition to imported labor, the principal sources of imported labor were sufficiently impressed with the opportunity for a cash wage that they came in large numbers.

In 1885, Hawaii was able to negotiate an agreement with Japan to import Japanese workers. Planters and the Hawaiian government hoped to overcome the opposition to Asian labor at home and on the U.S. mainland by evolving a theory that the Japanese were a "cognate race" with the Hawaiians, a rather popular concept of the day. This would "solve" the problem of an adequate labor supply and boost the Hawaiian population through intermarriage.

An important condition of the Japanese immigration was that the process be overseen by the Japanese government. Payment of wages was to be in cash and 15 percent of the wages were to be withheld and paid at the end of the contract. After 1887, these sums were paid in gold to the Japanese consul-general in Honolulu. Physicians were appointed by the Japanese government to oversee the health of the workers. Complaints of abuse were to be investigated by inspectors for the consul-general. Twenty-nine thousand workers came from Japan until the government turned the process over to private banks and immigration companies in 1894. Abandoning careful recruiting, these immigration companies had imported more than 68,000 workers by 1904. Approximately one-third of these moved to the mainland and a similar number returned to Japan.

After the overthrow of the Hawaiian monarchy in 1893, actions by the governing council of the republic dramatically worsened the contract system. In March 1899, the Bureau of Immigration reported both an upsurge in Japanese labor importation and a rise in Japanese desertion of contracts and warned of "strikes and other labor difficulties." The basic cause of the Japanese unrest was the 15 percent withholding of wages until the end of the contract. The refusal of the plantations to comply with the law or to consult the Japanese consul led to numerous strikes and, eventually, to the formation of the Central Japanese League to represent Japanese workers. The law was ambiguous as to when and who was to pay the withheld wages. These individual, unorganized protests met with little or no success. Threats of eviction from plantation housing usually sufficed to end the walkouts. They did create a widespread sense of injury and unfair treatment.

Annexation by the United States effectively put an end to the system of contract labor. Of the twenty strikes recorded in 1900, the list of causes reads like a short history of bound labor and its problems: fines, brutal overseers, retention of withheld wages, poor sanitation and water supply in the camps, unfair task systems, and requests for employment of Japanese overseers. By 1909, out of approximately 180,000 Japanese imported to Hawaii, only 54,000 remained. The Japanese workers who tended to remain in Hawaii were those who came after 1898, when the emigration companies recruited primarily urban Japanese with no experience in agriculture.

A highly organized group of Japanese sugar workers on Oahu caused a considerable conflict in 1909. Led by urban Japanese professionals—a lawyer and a newspaper publisher—the workers demanded better pay and working conditions through the Higher Wages Association. Four broad demands were presented:

1. An increase of $8.00 per month in the basic wage for field work, $2.50 for mill workers, and an end to all racial pay scales.
2. An increase of 10 cents per ton for cane-cutting and cane-loading contractors.

3. A reduction of the workday to ten hours with all Sunday work at double time.
4. Improvements in housing for families with immediate improvement in camp sanitation.

The demands, accompanied by voluminous documentation, were presented to the Hawaiian Sugar Planters' Association (HSPA) board of directors in January 1909. The directors adopted a policy of complete silence. No reply was forthcoming. Tired of waiting, the workers began walking off the job in May.

As the walkout gradually spread to the more remote plantations on Oahu, the planters were confronted with the possibility of an island-wide strike, if not an industry-wide strike. To meet this threat, the HSPA adopted a loss-sharing agreement in May 1909 that would spread the damage over all the member plantations. Plantations were to submit claims of loss, which would be compared to their production record. The planters announced that workers who did not return to work would be evicted from plantation housing immediately, beginning on May 22. Workers and their families were accommodated in a variety of makeshift camps around Honolulu and Waipahu. Neither the workers nor their leaders had any experience in strike organization. The leadership was arrested and charged with conspiracy to harm the industry. In an atmosphere tainted by hysterical newspaper stories about plots to seize control of the industry and/or Hawaii itself, the leaders were convicted and sentenced to prison. The HSPA hired strikebreakers, mainly Hawaiian, Chinese, and Portuguese urban workers, at the higher rate of $1.50 per day. The common rate of pay was 75 cents per day or $18.00 per month. The Higher Wage Association demanded a raise to $22.50 per month. Since there were a limited number of workers who could be summoned up for short periods of time, the tactic was of little use. Many of the so-called strikebreakers were actually strikers from other plantations. Managers, desperate to maintain production, blinked at the practice, despite the unity demanded by the HSPA.

Drained of financial resources, the Japanese strikers called an end to the strike on August 5. The arrests of the strike leaders were designed to convince the workers of the futility of labor organization and strikes. Two newspaper editors and two strike leaders were convicted of conspiring to obstruct plantation business.

Following the collapse of the strike, the HSPA met in November to deal with its impact. Most of the strikers' pay demands were met. Bonuses were to be paid to day workers based on a twenty-six-day month. Contract workers were to earn no less than $22.00 per month and extensive camp renovations were undertaken. A greater emphasis was put on cultivating and harvesting contracts to lessen the need for day labor. The strike established a pattern that would be followed in subsequent disputes until 1924.

One important result of the strike was the strengthening of the role of the HSPA. In times of labor unrest, the HSPA assumed complete control of labor policies for the individual plantations. However, the workers had demonstrated an ability to force changes in the industry. Another important outcome of the 1909 strike was the decision to increase the number of Filipinos in sugar production. The Philippines had been pacified by 1906, and the legal definition of Filipinos as American nationals meant they could be recruited with no restrictions. However, recruitment was slow. Filipino employment increased for a few years after 1910, but leveled off at slightly more than 8,000 per year in 1921.

Wartime inflation in both plantation profits and the cost of living produced another crisis in 1920. Urban workers began to organize in 1919. There were six nonplantation strikes in 1919 (longshore, carpenters, and transit workers) and two minor plantation disputes. The Japanese plantation workers organized a new Japanese Federation of Labor, modeled on the American Federation of Labor, with units on a majority of the territorial plantations. Workers elected delegates to a central council and carefully excluded nonplantation workers from participating. Buddhist temples in plantation communities provided the opportunity for young workers to discuss their situation and the basic issues of wages, hours, working conditions, and, above all, the question of dignity. Workers again presented a list of demands to the HSPA and, again, the response was total silence. Evictions began at once, flooding the makeshift camps set up in urban areas.

At the same time, the fledgling Filipino workforce formed a loose organization, the Filipino Federation of Labor. This organization existed without significant plantation organization, but emphasized Filipino ethnicity and the region from which they came. The dual unions, however, presented the growers with the prospect of ethnic labor cooperation, which would end the standing practice of playing one ethnic group against the others. The less-experienced Filipino workers and their charismatic leader, Pablo Manlapit, struck Oahu plantations on January 21, 1920, upsetting Japanese plans to strike at the peak of the harvest season in late spring or early summer. Pushed by events, the Japanese workers decided to strike on February 1. The Japanese had planned to strike only five Oahu plantations, using the remainder of the industry to provide support for the Oahu strikers. Faced with rising resentment among hungry Filipino workers and the lack of adequate support from the Japanese Federation, Manlapit called off his strike February 9, causing more confusion.

The planters were confounded by the solidarity of Japanese workers. An estimated 97 percent of Japanese workers walked off the Oahu plantations. An outbreak of influenza hastened efforts to end the walkout. Business leaders and government officials began in March to seek a compromise end to the strike. The planned hiring of strikebreakers foundered on the solidarity of the Japanese workers. The HSPA was able to find only 2,206 strikebreakers (primarily Caucasian, Korean, and Filipino) at the peak of the walkout on March 27, compared to the 5,442 regular Japanese workers. The daily average number of strikebreakers was 1,739. On July 1, the leadership capitulated and ended the 165-day strike. Beyond scattered, individual instances, there was none of the organized violence that the HSPA leaders had freely predicted. Fifteen of the leaders of the strike were convicted of an alleged conspiracy to dynamite the home of a Hawaiian plantation official. Other cases against the leaders were thrown out of court. Again, as in 1909, the scheme of prorating the losses of the struck plantations to be paid by a tax on the production of sugar and a close examination of expenses incurred in dealing with the strike worked reasonably well. However, the HSPA was surprised to find that production losses on some of the nonstriking plantations exceeded those of the struck plantations.

For the HSPA, the strikes of 1909 and 1920 combined to produce a monolithic, efficient, and ruthless organization able to manipulate the full power of government to control the workforce. Subsequent events would further reduce the ability of the individual plantation to pursue independent policies, whether with regard to labor policies or production policies. In 1923, the legislature enacted an anti-picketing statute with the active support of the HSPA.

The fact that many of the organizers and leaders of the Japanese Federation of Labor were Hawaii-born Japanese presented new problems for the HSPA. Imported workers were always threatened with deportation. Citizens could claim protection under the Bill of Rights. The case of the Filipinos was different. As American nationals, they had free movement between the Philippines, Hawaii, and the mainland. They did not enjoy the full civil liberties of the citizen, however. The goal of the HSPA was to convert Japanese workers to contractors for planting, harvesting, and irrigation, freeing them from immediate supervision but carefully controlling their earnings and production. The Filipinos would be used as day labor for the more onerous tasks of clearing land, new plantings, and casual labor.

The possibility of Japanese and Filipino workers cooperating persuaded the planters that a drastic change was necessary. A massive social welfare program was instituted aimed at creating viable plantation communities. A Welfare Department was set up under a newly hired official who oversaw the building of better family homes, community centers, and improved bathing facilities and sanitation. The reforms were far-reaching and seemed to ensure that tranquility would be the order of the day. The HSPA was confident of its control of territorial government and the effectiveness of the punitive anti-strike legislation enacted after the 1920 strike.

The Filipino strike of 1924 was a complete shock and something of a mystery to the industry. The strike began on Kauai when a McBryde Sugar Company foreman lost his temper, causing about one-half of the Filipino workforce to strike on January 22. The HSPA did not consider the strike a serious matter until a clash on Kauai resulted in the deaths of sixteen strikers and four deputies. The Higher Wages Movement's demands were submitted to the HSPA on January 17, 1924. As usual, the demands were met with silence. As historian John Reinecke observed, "No other major strike was so haphazardly planned and conducted or failed so completely." On the standard American model of a strike in which the demands of the strikers are measured against the outcome, it was indeed a failure. As the HSPA report on the strike concluded:

> Contrary to the situation of 1909 and 1920 we find that in 1924 many of the plantations which did not have a strike actually suffered more on account of labor shortages than those that had strikes. The reason for this is because . . . while the striking plantations have received incoming Filipinos, plantations not suffering on account of the strike received no allotments of the same.

Yet this strike produced some of the most significant changes in the structure and operation of the sugar industry. Despite the length of the strike, from April through November 1924, and its extent, reaching all but a few plantations in turn, on each island, none of the immediate demands were met by the HSPA. The planters followed the strategy laid down in 1909, confident that the welfare changes and tight control of the individual plantations would again defeat the strikers. This expectation was partially defeated by the widespread support for the strike from the Japanese long-term contract cultivators and by the uneven distribution of newly imported workers. Since the 1920 plan called for the Filipinos to assume the day labor tasks and the Japanese to become long-term contract workers, the rhythm of production was broken.

At the conclusion of the strike, the HSPA began to assess the costs of the strike. The "cost-sharing strategy" of 1909, 1920, and 1924 had proved to be a failure. The HSPA hired the firm of Curtis, Fosdick, and Belknap of New York City to investigate the causes for unrest and make recommendations for change. The resulting survey laid much of the blame for poor labor relations on the haphazard methods of hiring supervisors and the lack of training for such positions. A training program for both field supervision and plantation management was begun and continued until 1984. An overhaul of the long-term contract system was undertaken and extended to Filipino workers. A comprehensive medical plan for workers earning at least $100 per month was established. Satisfied that they had resolved the difficulties revealed by the strike, the planters returned to their plans for expansion.

In 1928, expressions of resentment in Congress against Filipino immigration to the mainland clearly signaled to the HSPA that its supply of plentiful and cheap labor was threatened. This spurred efforts to develop mechanical means of cultivation and harvesting to reduce the need for labor replacement. Another important development was the arrival of the National Labor Relations Board and the fledgling Congress of Industrial Organizations (CIO) in Honolulu.

All of these factors came together when the new Filipino labor organization, the Vibora Luviminda Union, a semi-secret organization led by Antonio Fagel, struck Puunene Plantation on Maui in 1937. The name selected for the union reflected the Filipino concern over the U.S. occupation and the Filipino attachment to the home locality: Vibora means "snake," the nickname of Filipino war hero General Artemio Ricarte, who was renowned for his ability to strike the U.S. Army without warning, and Luviminda refers to the island groups of the Philippines—Luzon, Visayas, and Mindanao.

Fagel was slowly organizing his union when the strike was precipitated by an ad hoc decision by a foreman to drastically reduce the rate of pay for cutting cane. Coupled with rising discontent over other issues, workers demanded the managers' presence. The dark mood of the workers frightened the manager and he dismissed the strikers and evicted them from plantation housing. The strike slowly spread until it involved 1,500 men at Puunene Plantation.

Fagel appealed to the newly formed CIO in Honolulu at a time when the National Labor Relations Board (NLRB) was investigating a complaint against Castle and Cooke stevedoring operations. The newly appointed, unpaid Hawaii CIO director sent two experienced maritime organizers, Bill Bailey and Jack Hall, to Maui. This exposure stimulated the nascent labor movement and spurred the HSPA to return to the 1925 report and initiate the suggested reforms. From that point forward, the Hawaii labor movement developed an increasing contact and reliance on mainland U.S. labor developments.

Six of the Vibora Luviminda leaders were convicted of a variety of charges, as in previous ethnic strikes. This time, however, the International Labor Defense (ILD), at the suggestion of the International Longshore and Warehouse Union (ILWU), provided a labor lawyer for the trial in Maui. The lawyer challenged the nature of the proceedings, including the selection of jurors from a list made up of non-Filipinos and company executives. Worried that the Filipino workforce would be encouraged by the challenges to the legal system mounted by the ILD lawyer, the trial was moved to Honolulu, where the six were quickly found guilty. Five were given the option of thirteen months' probation in lieu of four months in prison if they refrained from any "labor organizing." Antonio Fagel refused the offer and served his four months, promising to continue his organizing activities.

Perhaps the most significant outcome of the events of 1937 was the NLRB's issuance of their investigator's report on the Maui strike and general labor conditions in Hawaii. The Eagen Report, as it came to be known, was the first thorough critique of labor conditions in Hawaii. From this point forward, Hawaiian labor had good access to mainland labor organizations. The ILWU granted charters to Honolulu and Hilo locals in 1937. These locals in turn began organizing sugar plantation workers in 1944. The National Labor Relations Act excluded agricultural workers from its protections, but in 1945 the ILWU was able to secure passage of the Hawaii Employee Relations Act—the "Little Wagner Act"—which extended bargaining rights to all workers.

All this activity came to a head in 1946 when the ILWU called the first industry-wide sugar strike. This was also the first strike to include all eligible plantation workers, in contrast to the purely ethnic strikes of the past. Ostensibly about wages and working conditions, the strike solidified the union and changed the basic structure of the industry. The perquisite system of housing and medical care was abolished. A standardized housing classification system established fair rents for worker housing. In turn, through strike camps and soup kitchens that served ethnic foods, a widespread community support system was established. The territory-wide strike deprived the planters of their old weapon—eviction from plantation housing.

The union won a job classification system, a forty-hour week, and a ban on discrimination by race, creed, color, or political activity. When the strike ended on November 14, 1946, the union won on all counts. More importantly, the union demonstrated the importance of ethnic solidarity and careful organization. The next question was how would the HSPA respond to this defeat? The answer was not long in coming.

In November 1947, a disgruntled longshoreman published a pamphlet entitled "The Truth About Communism," attacking the leadership of the union and claiming Communists dominated the union and its decisions. The attack continued with congressional hearings and culminated in the indictment and arrest of six individuals, including the division director of the ILWU, Jack Hall. Throughout the attacks on the local leadership and the attempts to deport ILWU president Harry Bridges, the membership remained loyal and supported their union vigorously. The charges were easily refuted by the consistent democratic structure of the union. Five of the six had no connection with the organization of the ILWU but were sympathizers. The conviction of the six in 1951 was overturned on an appeal in 1953.

The planters were confronted once again by the need to take advantage of mechanical improvements in new agricultural machines. The labor shortages of the 1930s and the wartime dislocations had spurred the use of mechanized agricultural tools. Elsewhere in the sugar world, new machines had been developed to cut costs. For both the union and management, the negotiations for the sugar contract of 1958 were critical. The industry made one last effort to promote a paternalistic image to the workers, suggesting that the union was "irresponsible" and controlled from the mainland. For the union, the issue was the transition from hand-work to the highly mechanized, intensive techniques of modern sugar production. The impasse resulted in the Aloha Strike of 1958, so called because of the union strategy of sending pickets out into the community to work on parks, schools, and churches.

The experience of previous strikes had produced a good number of highly successful organizers in each of the sugar communities. The Strike Strategy Committee put members to work repairing churches, cleaning parks, and generally being very visible while improving the public appearance of their communities. Others worked for farmers for a share of the produce to supply the strike kitchens. As a final touch, the union put some members to work irrigating the sugarcane to prevent losses to the crop. These workers donated one-fourth of their earnings to the strike fund. After 128 days, the strike was settled essentially on the terms offered by the union at the outset.

The Aloha Strike of 1958 resulted in a mechanization and modernization agreement. Older workers were retired with adequate pensions. Training programs for younger workers were established and significant pay increases characterized the settlement. The ILWU literally brought white-collar benefits to agricultural workers. In addition to the fringe benefits, the union managed to maintain the year-round employment that had always characterized Hawaiian sugar plantations. In subsequent years, the union continued to improve the contract, strong community ties, and political action, despite rising costs and declining sugar production.

Finally, beginning in the 1980s, plantations began to close. Changes in the support prices of sugar, extra-low worldwide sugar prices, and rising labor costs put an end to the once-thriving Hawaiian industry.

See also: Agricultural Strikes, 415; Longshoremen's Strikes, 1900–1920, 547.

Bibliography

Aller, Curtis. *Labor Relations in the Hawaiian Sugar Industry.* Berkeley: Institute of Industrial Relations, University of California, 1957.

Beechert, Edward. *Working in Hawaii: A Labor History.* Honolulu: University of Hawaii Press, 1985.

Hawaiian Sugar Planters' Association Plantation Archive, Hamilton Library, University of Hawaii, available at www2.hawaii.edu/~speccoll/hawaiihspa.html.

Kuykendal, Ralph. *The Hawaiian Kingdom: Twenty Critical Years, 1854–1874.* Honolulu: University of Hawaii Press, 1963.

Larsen, J.D. "Man-Day Performance in Relation to Agricultural Methods and Implements." *Hawaiian Planters' Record* 36 (1932): 21–30.

Mollett, J.A. "Capital in Hawaiian Sugar: Its Formation and Relation to Labor and Output, 1870–1957." *Agricultural Economics Bulletin* 21. Hawaii Agricultural Experiment Station, University of Hawaii, Manoa, 1961.

Rainholt, Eiler. "The Politics of Sugar: Sugar's Iron Triangle." Center for Responsive Politics, 2002.

Reinecke, John. *The Tragic Filipino Piecemeal Sugar Strike of 1924–1925.* Honolulu: Social Science Research Institute, University of Hawaii, 1996.

Tinker, Hugh. *A New System of Slavery*. Oxford: Oxford University Press, 1974.

Taylor, William. "The Hawaiian Sugar Industry," Ph.D. diss., University of California, 1935.

U.S. Congress, House of Representatives, Committee on Immigration and Naturalization, "Labor Problems in Hawaii," 57th Cong., 1st sess.

Zalberg, Sanford. *A Spark Is Struck: Jack Hall and the ILWU in Hawaii.* Honolulu: University of Hawaii Press, 1979.

THE REDWOOD LUMBER AND SAWMILL WORKERS' STRIKE

Calvin Winslow

The Redwood strike began January 14, 1946, when 4,200 lumber and sawmill workers shut down eight of the nine major redwood producers in Northern California: Arcata Redwood Company, Caspar Lumber Company, Dolbeer and Carson Lumber Company, the Hammond Lumber Company, Holmes Eureka Lumber Company, Northern Redwood Company, the Rockport Lumber Company, and the Union Lumber Company. Four days later, hundreds of pickets led by strikers at the Union Lumber Company's Fort Bragg mill shut down the only mill still operating: Pacific Lumber in Scotia. In 1945, these nine mills were responsible for 85 percent of the redwood lumber produced in the world.

The Redwood strike was a big strike in a year of big strikes. World War II brought an end to the Depression, but it did not resolve the outstanding issues of the 1930s and it created problems of its own, particularly inflation. Workers greeted the peace with an astonishing strike wave—in the twelve months following the end of the war there were 4,630 work stoppages, involving 5 million workers and 120 million days of idleness. The Redwood strike was the single longest strike in this wave.

The California redwood timber workers were members of the Lumber and Sawmill Workers' Union, regionally organized in the Redwood District Council, an affiliate of the United Brotherhood of Carpenters. In 1945, the council formulated a series of demands anticipating the removal of wartime regulations, including the end of the no-strike pledge. These included a minimum wage of $1.05 an hour; shift differentials; bonuses; a guaranteed forty-eight-hour week; equal pay for women; vacation pay; rest periods; and, importantly, the union shop in all operations. The prestrike vote was 90 percent in favor of striking.

There was great enthusiasm for the strike. The *Humboldt Times* reported "a huge crowd of striking redwood workers assembled at the Eureka Municipal Auditorium." The union held regular strike rallies. On May 10, another Eureka rally ended with a unanimous vote to continue the strike. The union leaders pledged, "Never again will we submit to the forms of slavery heretofore imposed upon us by the Redwood Lumber Barons."

Picketing stopped all production for six months. Then, in July, the companies began a counteroffensive—the operators decided to reopen the mills and, one by one, they succeeded. The companies first relied on token contingents from management, then increasingly on strikebreakers. Soon they were shipping significant quantities of redwood lumber. At the same time, the companies began evicting strikers from company housing.

Strike Support

The unions responded by calling sympathy strikes, or more precisely, a secondary boycott. The California Carpenters ordered all union members to refuse to handle struck goods: "No member will use, handle, install or erect any material produced or manufactured from wood not made by the United Brotherhood." All union-made lumber would be stamped "AFL-8." Interestingly, company spokesmen pointed out that this could include "CIO lumber," made by members of the Congress of Industrial Organizations (CIO). The union then began picketing lumberyards and construction jobs statewide. The national leadership of the Carpenters pledged its commitment to the strike; in a letter to all carpenters, William Hutcheson, the president, pledged, "This is not a strike we are going to see lost." The national union appointed a full-time organizer, Carl Chapman, a veteran of strikes in the Pacific Northwest, to direct the strike and establish a strike fund. By November, according to D.H. Ryan, state secretary of the Carpenters, the strike was costing $50,000 a month. Twenty thousand Bay Area carpenters were contributing $1.00 a month.

As the production of redwood lumber increased, strikers attempted to physically stop the shipments, and this led to violence. Confrontations in Mendocino County resulted in exchanges of gunfire and arrests. Rockport strikebreakers, under the eye of sheriffs' deputies, began reporting for work armed. In Eureka, Fort Bragg, and Crescent City, CIO longshoremen stopped shipments from the harbors; timber would never be shipped again from Fort Bragg or Crescent City. Similarly, lumber hauled by train was stopped. Strikers pulled the train crews off the company-owned Arcata and Mad River Railroad. Trains were stopped in South Fork, in Humboldt County. In Fort Bragg, the company ordered its crews to break through picket lines, even when they included women and children. In Santa Rosa, for four days mass pickets stopped traffic on the Northwestern Pacific Railroad; freight cars were backed up from Santa Rosa to Ukiah, sixty miles to the north. Inevitably, there were arrests followed by court injunctions. The blockades stopped.

The trade unions in the northwestern counties supported the strike, though their contributions were often token and, aside from the longshoremen, there were no walkouts in other industries. The vice president of the Humboldt County District of the American Federation of Labor (AFL), Albin Gruhn, reported to the convention of the California AFL that affiliated unions in Humboldt supported the strike "financially and morally." Sympathetic AFL unions operated a strike commissary, "which supplied strikers and their families with such essentials as groceries, meats, shoes, clothing, etc." Gruhn appealed to "all AFL affiliates to support this strike against the leading open-shoppers in Northern California."

There was some public support for the strike, too. In San Francisco, a "Citizens' Committee for Civil Rights and Rent Control in the Redwood Area" organized; the group's first meeting brought ten people to the St. Francis Hotel, where they agreed to send a delegation to Fort Bragg to investigate the housing situation. In Eureka, the Social Action Committee of First Congregational Church backed the strikers. These organizations were denounced as Communist by the owners.

There were negotiations throughout these months, some involving federal mediators. The companies appeared to be willing to compromise on wages; they claimed to consider the other sixteen demands to be insignificant. They would not compromise on the union shop. The union, reported the *Humboldt Standard,* responded with this statement:

> When we went up against the powerful Redwood association, we knew it meant quite a fight. What is this fight really about? Wages? Yes. Vacations and certain other conditions? Yes. But it is really a fight by this powerful group of employers to crush the union and to have open shop conditions so that they can exploit their workers in any way which they see fit. Over the years this has made them extremely rich and powerful. We, the lumber and sawmill workers, therefore renew our determination to fight for our rights . . . we are determined never again to submit to the Association [that] in past times have [*sic*] been able to destroy our union. Make no mistake about it, this is a fight to the finish, an economic war and we want the union shop.

The employers were well prepared for the confrontation. They were represented by two organizations, the California Redwood Association and the Redwood Industrial Relations Committee (IRIC), as well as by the San Francisco law firm of Littler, Coakley & Lauritzen. Their strategy was to present the union with a united front. S.L. Gregory, director of the IRIC, Kenneth Smith of the Redwood Association, and the companies' lawyer, Thomas Coakley, ran a highly organized campaign. Gregory advised each company president to phone him at least twice daily. As a team, they placed ads in newspapers, published fact sheets about the strike, and developed a network of sympathetic businessmen, politicians, and veterans' organizations.

They opposed arbitration in any form and agreed from the start that the demand for the union shop was the key issue. This position, a mirror reflection of the union's, hardened as the strike continued. San Francisco banker Fentress Hill, president of Northern Redwood Company, speaking before the Taft-Hartley hearings in the U.S. House Labor Committee thirteen months into the strike, testified, "The one thing most needed to restore health to the management-labor relations is to outlaw any and every form of compulsory union membership as a condition of employment."

United Front of the Employers

The companies insisted on "an industry-wide contract," as did the union. The companies took the position that a strike against one is a strike against all, believing an industry-wide strike was preferable to allowing the union to strike one mill at a time. "There is a genuine fear here," Gregory wrote to Coakley, "that the union, after failing in the present strike to get a union shop on an industry-wide basis, will set forth to get it plant by plant." Moreover, they believed opposing the union shop was their best case to win support. According to Fred Holmes, president of Holmes-Eureka: "Our main case is against the union shop and it is to our advantage to keep the spotlight on that issue."

Company strategy rested on an assessment of the relative strengths of labor and management. They ran anti-strike advertisements in the rural press but not in Bay Area papers: "These metropolitan communities being so strongly unionized may result in all labor uniting to beat the redwood operators in their fight." Citing decisions of the National Labor Relations Board (NLRB), they advised that evictions be undertaken only with great caution, sometimes to the owners' dismay. Fentress Hill had flatly declared: "If they don't work for me, they don't live in my house. . . ."

The companies focused on the huge demand for lumber in Southern California. The Rockport manager advised against shipping lumber by sea to the south: "The harbor district in Los Angeles is a pretty 'tough' one . . . all the lumber companies in that district are closed union shop." However, in the rest of the city, "many cars of redwood from the struck mills are being received by retail and wholesale yards and . . . [there is] no trouble about carpenters using it."

The companies were increasingly successful in luring strikers back to the mills. On August 25, Hill told his colleagues, "We cannot put on any more men at the present time, simply because our hotel is completely filled and we not only have no vacant company-owed houses but have a waiting list." They also worked to divide the strike leaders, such as Abe Muir, head of the West Coast Carpenters union; Martin Balke, the Carpenters union international representative in Eureka; and Oscar Erickson, a local Lumber and Sawmill Workers organizer. In July, Gregory reported: "I met Balke on Market Street last week . . . I tried to persuade [him] . . . that he was fighting a losing cause and the best thing that could happen to him and his union (before it breaks apart) was to make a contract on the basis of maintenance of membership with an escape clause." In the same month, Coakley suggested "Muir and Balke are not getting along . . . Balke . . . disgusted with the length of the strike . . . Muir in awkward position. Takes orders from Hutchinson." Otis Johnson of the Union Lumber Company, in handwritten notes, called Balke "a good fellow, a fairly good organizer," but referred to Erickson as "that communist."

The managers also kept an eye on the owners. Kenneth Smith of the Redwood Association, in a confidential memo, worried that Hammond was going to sell out to Weyerhaeuser, the Pacific Northwest giant with a history of union recognition. He also worried because Fentress Hill was "a banker not a lumberman and will be the first to say he has to protect the interests of his stockholders. . . ."

Managers offered interesting advice concerning Communists. They advised the owners to refrain from red baiting because others would do it. This was true. In Mendocino County, a union strike bulletin regularly denounced "Communists." In Humboldt, Albin Gruhn reported that "the 'Commies' and their fellow travelers have used every possible means to infiltrate into key positions of the local labor movement [but] . . . thanks to the alertness and cooperation of various Lumber Workers' union officials, we were fortunate in stopping the 'Commie' invasion before it got too strong a foothold." When Otis Johnson objected to the activities of a Mr. Wagner, an officer in the San Francisco Pile Drivers Union, the lawyers responded: "He is the man . . . who was working actively with [Oscar] Erickson in publicizing the boycott . . . Erickson in fact is working out of Wagner's San Francisco office . . . there is no question but that he is a communist. The difficulty, as in the case of most communists, is proving that they are such." The lawyers believed that

> Mr. Wagner's real reason in injecting himself into the redwood situation is to open the door for the CIO and the communists. This may seem strange in view of the fact Mr. Wagner is an officer of an AFL union . . . but my information, nevertheless, is that he believes the AFL to be much too conservative and works far more closely with the CIO and the communists . . . it may not appear particularly significant, yet it must be watched carefully. It would be a catastrophe if in winning the fight against the union shop we were to split the ranks of labor in the redwood area so badly as to open the door for the CIO and the communists under the leadership of Erickson . . . that is the very worst thing that could happen to our companies. . . .

Oscar Erickson was a Finn and a lumberjack raised on a collective east of Fort Bragg. He joined the Communist Party in the 1920s. In 1945, he was hired by the Lumber and Sawmill Workers and became an important local strike leader. He urged the union leaders to continue the strike. On September 5, returning from the Bay Area, he gave the strike committee a highly optimistic report: "All unions in northern California [are] now aroused. We still can and will win. All other unions think so."

By late summer, the mills were operating nearly at full strength. They reported employment at more than 70 percent of prestrike levels. Holmes reported, "We now hear from both sides that the union is licked." Hill believed, "There never was so good a prospect of winning as now. . . ." The strike was not settled yet, however. On January 15, 1948, the *San Francisco Chronicle* reported that "the longest major strike in the nation's history begins its third year today . . . the struggle has been costly and bloody . . . it has cost the union more than a million dollars." The employers' costs remained unknown. The report, written from Fort Bragg, continued:

> Drive up Highway 1 and you pass the company towns and small communities dominated by the smoking stacks of the mills . . . step into the woods and the ring of axes sounds through the 250-foot trees. . . . Lumber from the eight struck mills is rolling down the highway . . . with most of the strikers now working in the wildcats or in other industries, only token picket lines continue around the gates. . . .

The only victory for the strikers came in February 1947, when after more than a year on strike, the Hammond Lumber Company broke ranks, accepting a "modified" union-shop agreement. The others held firm until the end, which came in April 1948.

Why was the strike broken? This was a powerful strike—one of the great strikes of the postwar strike wave. It was led by a strong national union, the United Brotherhood of Carpenters. The end of the war did not bring a return to the 1930s, which was the great fear of the country's workers. And while poverty—sometimes extreme poverty—persisted in the redwood region, predictions that wartime prosperity would collapse into renewed depression proved unfounded. In fact, the long years of postwar economic growth and prosperity began almost at once. There were no new bread lines. There was no return to vigilantes and gun thugs, no mass unemployment and hunger, at least not for those white workers who formed the core of the organized labor movement. Still, workers believed they had sacrificed, both during the Depression and in the war, and they had a very long list of grievances. The strikes of 1946 were the result.

The 1946 strikes reflected deep changes in the system of industrial relations in the United States. In 1950, the historian Arthur Schlesinger, listing ten events that shaped history, placed the rise of labor second only to the two world wars. In the same year, industrial relations specialist Sumner Slichter reflected that the United States "was shifting from a capitalist community to a laboristic one—that is, to a community in which employees rather than businessmen are the strongest single influences."

The Carpenters' Union

This, of course, was not true, but in 1945 the unions felt powerful. The United Brotherhood of Carpenters with which the Redwood strikers were affiliated, certainly believed it could win. This union, one of the oldest and entrenched among the skilled workers of the building trades, had grown dramatically since the mid-1930s, in particular in the period of wartime regulation. It had not supported the organizing drives of that period but had taken advantage of them.

The Carpenters' strategy was to let others do the organizing, then to claim jurisdiction. They claimed jurisdiction over any worker who had anything whatsoever to do with wood. They established themselves in the Pacific Northwest this way, then in Northern California. In the early thirties, the California timber workers were organized by small groups of radicals, including Communists, centered in Eureka and Fort Bragg. They sought affiliation with the AFL, which granted them "federal" charters, but then turned jurisdiction over to the Carpenters.

The leader of the West Coast carpenters was Abe Muir, son-in-law of the Carpenters' president, William "Big Bill" Hutcheson. "Big Bill's" son, Maurice Hutcheson, the first vice president of the union, supervised the Redwood strike and visited the picket lines. All were Republicans. The union was plagued with corruption and unethical activities. Muir had ordered the ill-fated 1935 strike—against, it seems, rank-and-file opinion—then weathered the storm. He disbanded the defeated local unions, isolated the radicals, and then reconstituted new locals, all in keeping with the top-down traditions of the Carpenters. It seems quite likely that the company spokesmen were correct to believe that the Carpenters' leaders called the strike, however justified, and prolonged it for purposes of their own.

The CIO had considered an organizing drive in the redwoods. It had an affiliate in the region, the Woodworkers. It hoped to use longshoremen and the prestige of their 1934 victory to organize timber workers. Although nothing came of the CIO scheme—the result, no doubt, of the demise of shipping by sea—it undoubtedly strengthened the determination of the Carpenters to establish themselves alone as the union in the redwoods. This was a period of intense factionalism in the unions: Albin Gruhn's reports to the state AFL routinely referred to the conflict with the CIO. Concerning CIO efforts to organize local fishermen, Gruhn assured fellow unionists that "effective counter-measures are being developed to offset any further C.I.O. activities."

The Lumber and Sawmill Workers were well-positioned to take advantage of the new wartime conditions. In exchange for the no-strike pledge and guarantees of productivity, they secured dramatic improvements for the timber workers during the war years. With increasing production, hours were shortened, grievance procedures were introduced, and pay was improved—all under the supervision of the War Labor Board. As a result, the union emerged from the war representing workers in all the major producers: in just months in 1942–43, union election victories at Pacific Lumber, Hammond, Holmes Eureka, Northern, Dolbeer Carson, and the Union Lumber Company in Fort Bragg were certified by the NLRB. The Caspar Lumber Company, the smallest of these firms, signed in 1944.

The Carpenters' strategy was based on outlasting the companies—effectively winning representation in the industry by defeating the dominant producers. This strategy had been successful in the 1930s. There were two problems. First, the companies were determined not to concede the union shop, and, in a period of Republican resurgence, the tide had turned in their favor. Second, the Taft-Hartley Act, passed in 1947, severely limited union security by banning the closed shop and restricting the union shop.

The Carpenters intended to stop the flow of redwood lumber by shutting down the main producers; this had worked in the past. In 1945, there were at most fifty mills in the Redwood region and the majority of these were small operations. The big mills produced nearly all the redwood lumber. But in less than two years, there were 250 mills employing thousands, including significant numbers of the strikers. The *San Francisco Chronicle* reported that the region was being "overrun by sawmills" and that Humboldt had become the center of the boom in "the state's last great stand of commercial timber." The report continued:

"The great stands of Oregon and Washington are depleted . . . the small operator wants to cut and sell now, so he has moved to northern California and changed his shipping address from Portland to San Francisco and Los Angeles. . . . Foresters estimated that 500,000,000 board feet are cut each year—at the 1945 rate the forest would last about 90 years . . . but that was before the boom."

Union spokesmen actually referred to the boom as a "god-send." "The most hopeful thing that has happened to help the workers has been the unabated influx of small mills into this territory." But in fact, small operators armed with chain saws and shipping by truck filled the gap and took pressure off the big mills to increase the supply of redwood lumber. The union's strategy backfired. Solidarity, never the watchword of the Carpenters, was further undone by other new developments, including the explosion of the trucking industry and the rise of the Teamsters, another union led by Republicans and committed to nothing but its own fortunes. Strike committee minutes abound with complaints of Teamster drivers carrying struck lumber. There was lumber for the market; there were jobs for workers. The local economy was not unduly depressed. In such circumstances, even the Carpenters were unlikely to prevail—certainly not on their own.

One other issue weighed on the strike. Workers emerged from the war greatly strengthened, but also de-radicalized. In the 1930s, radicals often led strikes, which frequently involved direct action, mass participation, and wide solidarity. This was not the case following the war.

The Redwood strike was militant and the union involved a core of strikers who remained loyal to the union until the end. But it was a top-down strike, typical of the Carpenters and increasingly typical of most unions in the postwar period. What remained of the radical tradition was undermined by anti-communism; the small Communist groups themselves in Humboldt and Mendocino counties had all but gone underground. The party's leading organizer, Oscar Erickson, in line with party policy, had discontinued his membership and gone to work full time for the union. Hence, there were no independent voices, no alternatives, no critiques of the strike—only, here and there, violence, never sanctioned by the union, but as an expression of frustration and defeat.

On April 12, 1948, in a letter to members, the Redwood District Council of the Lumber and Sawmill Workers announced that it was impossible to carry on the strike. The union survived only in the Hammond mill, though in the course of the strike it had won representation in a number of the new small mills as well. The letter ordered that all local unions, "after an affirmative vote," remove their picket lines.

See also: The 1945–1946 Strike Wave, 216; Agricultural Strikes, 415.

Bibliography

Christie, Robert. *Empire in Wood.* Ithaca: New York State School of Industrial and Labor Relations, 1956.

Cornford, Daniel A. *Workers and Dissent in the Redwood Empire.* Philadelphia: Temple University Press, 1987.

Jensen, Vernon. *Lumber and Labor.* New York: Farrar and Rinehart, 1945.

Lembcke, Jerry, and William M. Tattam. *One Union in Wood.* New York: International Publishers, 1984.

THE WATSONVILLE CANNERY STRIKE, 1985–1987

Myrna Cherkoss Donahoe

From 1985 to 1987, 1,000 cannery workers in Watsonville, California, were on strike. "It was a deep lesson in the power of unified action," wrote Frank Bardacke, a Watsonville community activist and longtime agricultural union organizer. Overcoming great economic hardships, the Latino workforce saved their union, preserved wages and benefits, won a voice in the political structure, and gained social respect.

Agricultural work includes those laboring in the fields and those employed in the processing plants, such as canneries. It can also include those who are involved in the shipping of the products. In his pioneering 1937 analysis of the agricultural industry, *Factories in the Fields,* Carey McWilliams understood that union organizing drives in this setting were more difficult because the majority of workers were Mexican nationals, whose fate was tied to the state of the U.S. economy. McWilliams compared U.S. policy on Mexican immigration to a revolving door. When the economy is robust and labor in short supply, Mexican nationals are welcomed through farm labor programs, such as the Bracero Program (Helping Hands) of 1942–64. When the economy enters a downward cycle and unemployment rises, Mexican labor is less welcome and workers are denigrated as "wetbacks" and illegals. During good times or bad, growers and food processors have threatened to deport Mexican workers when they sought to establish unions. Union organizers had to overcome this before a stable labor organization could be established.

Both the fields and processing plants employed large numbers of women, but the canneries were predominantly a female, or Latina, workforce. Conditions were appalling in all areas due to low wages, seasonal work, and the vulnerability of the workforce. Despite the challenges, a number of unions sought to organize the workforce in all agricultural-related work. The workers themselves proved to be courageous and militant in the face of adversity.

Organizing Campaigns

Cannery and Agricultural Workers' Industrial Union (CAWIU)

One of the earliest attempts to organize agricultural work occurred in the throes of the Great Depression. The Cannery and Agricultural Workers' Industrial Union (CAWIU) was a Communist-led union involved in thirty-seven major strikes throughout the Southwest between 1930 and 1933. One of the most successful campaigns was against the Southern Pecan Shelling Company in San Antonio, Texas. Three important Latina leaders were Manuela Solis Sager, Emma Tenayuca, and Luisa Moreno, all of whom sought to bring Mexican workers into the labor movement. The growers and processors retaliated by enlisting the government to conduct large-scale deportations of workers and by charging union leaders with criminal syndicalism. Criminal syndicalism laws were designed to punish people who advocated violence as a means of accomplishing industrial or political reform, but were more often used to punish union leaders who advocated peaceful civil disobedience, such as picketing. Criminal syndicalism laws were declared unconstitutional in the 1960s as an infringement on free speech, but were used effectively against labor unions until then. The legal battles depleted the union's resources and led to their demise, but in the short course of its existence, the CAWIU won millions of dollars in wage gains and gave workers an education in trade unionism, laying the basis for future organizing campaigns in the industry.

United Cannery, Agricultural, Packing and Allied Workers of America (UCAPAWA)

After the demise of CAWIU, agricultural workers reorganized into the United Cannery, Agricultural, Packing and Allied Workers of America (UCAPAWA) in 1938. UCAPAWA became one of the largest Congress of Industrial Organizations (CIO) affiliates. The CIO was a newly organized and more militant union federation that split from the more conservative American Federation of Labor (AFL).

Recognizing that Latinas were the dominant group in the processing plants, UCAPAWA dedicated itself to developing women leaders. Luisa Moreno, who had long-term and extensive organizing experience in agricultural industries, was one of the founders. Moreno was a Guatemalan immigrant and served as vice president of UCAPAWA for many years. She recognized the interrelation between trade unionism, civil rights, and social justice and helped create El Congreso de los Pueblos de Habla Español, the Congress of Spanish Speaking People, in 1938. This organization, which included academics, students, workers, and artists, sought to improve the socioeconomic life of Mexican people, promote understanding between Anglo Americans and Mexicans, and organize democratic trade unions to give workers a voice. Moreno traveled all over the United States publicizing how agribusiness dominated the fields and how Mexican labor was utilized as a cheap workforce and subject to deportation.

Food, Tobacco, Agricultural, and Allied Workers (FTA)

By 1944, UCAPAWA had changed its name to Food, Tobacco, Agricultural, and Allied Workers (FTA), since it had found considerable success organizing tobacco workers. The union aimed to build strong cannery units, mostly by developing leadership among female and immigrant workers. Women recruiting women was a key factor in the FTA's successful organizing campaign. In 1945, as a CIO affiliate, FTA began making inroads into organizing cannery workers. One challenge came from an AFL union, the International Brotherhood of Teamsters (IBT).

The Teamsters were more conservative than the FTA. IBT leaders cared little about incorporating women and immigrant workers into their union, fighting for wage increases, or promoting union democracy and social justice. Their goal was to preserve the status quo, which meant leaving the power of the growers and processors unchallenged and allowing Teamster union leaders to receive their share of the industry's spoils. Naturally the California processors and growers preferred the more conservative union, which began to sign "sweetheart" contracts favorable to the companies.

To further undermine the efforts of the FTA, in 1947 the Taft-Hartley Act eroded many of labor's gains won through the 1935 National Labor Relations Act. After a fierce battle that included virulent red baiting, eleven left-led and largely democratic unions, including the FTA, were expelled from the CIO in 1950. Losing government sanction weakened these unions considerably, and their more conservative rivals began to defeat them in the battle for workers' allegiance. During this repressive era, some foreign-born activists and union organizers, such as Moreno, were deported. In this vein, the Teamsters became firmly entrenched among cannery workers in California for over two decades.

In the 1970s, Teamsters for a Democratic Union (TDU), a rank-and-file faction dedicated to democratizing the Teamsters, was born. The TDU's goals were to wrest control from the conservative leadership and reestablish a union dedicated to democracy, rank-and-file leadership, militancy, and social justice. One area where the TDU was active was Watsonville, California.

Watsonville Canning Company Strike, 1985–1987

Watsonville is a small blue-collar town mainly populated by Latinos. It is located in the Pajaro Valley of

Santa Cruz County, California. Watsonville stands in sharp contrast to its more affluent neighbors, Santa Cruz and the Silicon Valley to the north and the Monterey Peninsula to the south. In Watsonville there was a long history of struggle between agribusiness and the workforce. The region, which is adjacent to California's Salinas Valley, has been called the "frozen food capital of the world." It is a prime example of California's agribusiness industry. The Teamsters defeated the FTA in 1950, after the union's expulsion from the CIO, and Teamster Local 912 held firm control of this area's cannery workers for thirty years. Similar to many Teamster locals, Local 912 was controlled by a corrupt leadership and not responsive to the needs of the workforce, especially immigrants and women.

By the latter part of the twentieth century, the workforce in Watsonville had become more permanent. Generations of families had worked in the fields or the various processing plants for years. There was a strong sense of community as people socialized together through their children's schools, the Catholic Church, and sports activities such as soccer. This sense of community would enable the workers to endure the many hardships and challenges in the struggle that began to unfold in the mid-1980s.

Among the ingredients for a successful strike are full participation of the workforce, leadership development of the rank and file, cooperation and support of merchants and landlords through the establishment of labor/community coalitions, bringing production to a halt, and a consumer boycott. Another important ingredient, often missing in the modern, disconnected urban world, is a sense of community among the strikers. All these ingredients were present in the eighteen-month-long Watsonville strike.

The strikers developed a spirit similar to the CIO organizing strikes of the 1930s. The predominantly immigrant workforce brought to the battle renewed militancy and creative strategy and tactics, which was a decided break with the business unionism that had been entrenched for decades. The workers were predominantly immigrant women. Despite repeated attempts to intimidate and harass them, Mexican women workers had been at the forefront of the struggle to organize the food production sector for decades.

In 1985, workers at Watsonville Canning Company were told that they were to increase the number of broccoli heads cut from fourteen to twenty per minute, in violation of a union agreement. Supervisors began to time the workers with stopwatches. Many workers who could not keep up were disciplined and fired. Then, the company forbid workers to use restroom facilities between breaks. Next, the company returned each worker's union dues and informed them they were no longer represented. Finally, the company announced a wage reduction from $6.66 per hour to $4.25. Although leaders of Teamster Local 912 refused to launch a counterattack, the women workers refused to accept the gross violations of their contract.

Since 1980, a small group of workers within the Teamsters had been struggling to form a viable chapter of the TDU in Watsonville. They hoped to regain control of the union and reestablish union democracy. Although Local 912's leadership had no interest in a strike, the workers, mainly women like Esperanza Torres and her sister, Anita Contreras Mendoza, took matters into their own hands. They had developed rank-and-file organization and leadership and led the workers in a strike with the help of the fledgling TDU caucus in Watsonville. Faced with this walkout and the militancy exhibited by the workers, Local 912 and the Teamster International were forced to sanction the strike.

Watsonville Canning Company, one of eight canneries in the town, employed 1,000 workers. Despite overwhelming hardships, not one worker crossed the line for eighteen months. The strong sense of community bound them together; none was willing to cross the line and face the future ostracism of their fellow workers and community members. As a result, the company could never recruit enough stable replacement workers, and the supervisory personnel could never get the plant into working order without a significant minority of experienced workers. Watsonville Canning could not continue production.

Despite the use of injunctions and other forms of harassment, the strikers held firm. The TDU organized a Solidarity Day on which over 3,000 labor activists and supporters from other regions participated. The workers themselves coordinated a strike committee and organized twenty-four-hour picket lines, a speakers' bureau, food distribution, newsletters, and the distribution of other necessities. Several hundred workers regularly walked the lines and attended strike-coordinating meetings to discuss strike strategy and tactics.

The sense of community helped the strikers endure the eighteen-month struggle. They not only worked together, but socialized together through various activities, such as soccer games, church events, and their children's schools. They helped each other with child care. They understood how to rely on one another to survive. Although the TDU leaders were supportive and involved, workers took initiative on their own. At the onset of the strike, the women strikers immediately organized a bimonthly food bank and provided meals for thousands of strikers and supporters. The workers were not hesitant to go to church leaders, their children's schools, grocery merchants, and landlords asking for support.

The workers' decision to hold firm entailed great sacrifice. Many lost their homes, cars, and other possessions. Many had to move in with relatives in already crowded residences. Some had to secure employment in other areas, since they could not survive on the union's $55.00 weekly strike benefits. Especially hard hit were the 40 percent of the strikers who were single mothers. All had to rely on each other, food banks, and other supportive organizations.

By 1987 the owners of Watsonville Canning Company, recognizing the staying power of the strikers and the magnitude of public support for the workers, agreed to negotiate a new contract. The owners offered an hourly wage of $5.85, which was still below their initial pay of $6.66, and withheld their health package. The workers, most of whom were sympathetic to or actual members of the TDU, rejected this contract. The rejection of the contract displeased the national Teamster leadership, which refused to continue sanctioning the strike. The strike became a wildcat, and workers proceeded to set up headquarters in the Torres home. They also set up a camp at the plant gates, resumed picketing and all strike activities, and seven workers began a hunger strike. Finally, in March 1987, Watsonville Canning agreed to return the workers' health benefits. Although they would not receive the wages with which they had begun the strike, the workers ratified the contract. The workers had saved their union, ousted the worst of the corrupt Teamster leadership and replaced them with TDU leaders, and kept their health benefits.

The strike strengthened the Watsonville Latino community and bolstered its confidence. The workers next took on their political exclusion from the city's political leadership. Several Latino residents filed a voting rights lawsuit to win representation on the City Council. The suit went all the way to the U.S. Supreme Court, which ruled in their favor. For the first time in Watsonville history, a Latino was elected to the City Council in 1988.

Conclusion

Frank Bardacke has written extensively on Watsonville and the strike. He has repeatedly stressed the strong sense of community that enabled the strikers to maintain the long struggle until they achieved their goals. According to Bardacke, "In Watsonville it was Mexican women, documented and undocumented, who emerged from the obscurity of the frozen food plants and took center stage. It was their solidarity, which was primarily responsible for all that was won."

See also: The Catholic Church and Strikes, 162; Agricultural Strikes, 415; Labor and the Transformation of the Hawaiian Sugar Industry, 431.

Bibliography

Bardacke, Frank. *Good Liberals and Great Blue Herons: Labor, Land and Politics in the Pajaro Valley.* Santa Cruz, CA: Center For Political Ecology, 1994.

———. "Watsonville: A Mexican Community on Strike." In *Reshaping the U.S. Left: Popular Struggles in the 1980s,* ed. Mike Davis and Michael Sprinker. London: Verso Press, 1988.

Camarillo, Albert. *Chicanos in California.* San Francisco: Boyd & Fraser, 1984.

Donahoe, Myrna Cherkoss. "Cannery Workers Movement." In *Encyclopedia of American Social Movements,* vol. 2, ed. Immanuel Ness. Armonk, NY: M.E. Sharpe, 2004.

Gonzalez, Gilbert. *Labor and Community: Mexican Citrus Worker Villages in a Southern California County, 1900–1950.* Urbana: University of Illinois Press, 1994.

———. *Mexican Consuls and Labor Organizing.* Austin: University of Texas Press, 1999.

La Botz, Dan. *Rank and File Rebellion: Teamsters for a Democratic Union.* London: Verso Press, 1990.

Martinez, Elizabeth, ed. *500 Años del Pueblo Chicano: 500 Years of Chicano History in Pictures.* Albuquerque: SouthWest Organizing Project, 1991.

McWilliams, Carey. *Factories in the Fields: The Story of Migratory Farm Labor in California.* 1939. Santa Barbara, CA: Peregrine Press, 1971 (reprint).

———. *North from Mexico: The Spanish-Speaking People of the United States.* 1948. Westport, CT: Greenwood Press, 1968 (reprint).

Moody, Kim. *An Injury to All: The Decline of American Unionism.* London: Verso Press, 1988.

Ruiz, Vicki L. *Cannery Women/Cannery Lives: Mexican Women, Unionization, and the California Food Processing Industry, 1930–1950.* Albuquerque: University of New Mexico Press, 1987.

COAL MINERS ON STRIKE AND THE FORMATION OF A NATIONAL UNION

Jon Amsden and Stephen Brier

Strikes represent an important index of social conflict either on the economic or on the political level, and sometimes on both levels at once. The economic effects of strike action are first felt by the employer and then by the community at large as the workers interrupt their regular pattern of labor and refuse to produce. In an attempt to further their aims, workers also inflict economic hardships on themselves. The political consequences of strike activity find expression in the heightened class consciousness from their concerted action against the employer and often from a direct confrontation with the power of the state.

A meaningful approach to strike analysis in historical writing therefore necessitates an awareness of both the economic and political aspects of strike activity. For this study we analyze strikes in a single industry over a relatively short but crucially important period of time. We argue that strikes in coal mining between 1881 and 1894 reflect both the changing economic position of coal in a burgeoning capitalist economy and the quality of the mine worker's life in and around the pits. The coal industry in this period showed all of the tensions created by the vast expansion of production, the emergence of a national market, and incessant competition and consolidation of ownership and control. The stringent financial constraints faced by most coal operators formed the boundaries for the daily confrontation with mine workers. The grievances of the latter grew out of a particular occupational structure and network of rules and practices that governed the work process and the system of payment.

Our theory of strike activity is based in part on these aspects of class struggle in the coal industry. The necessity of constant conflict with the employers over a broad range of work and related problems resulted in the creation of a trade union organization that did not rest exclusively on the narrow base of craft skill. This organizational form represented an advance in working-class consciousness and is reflected in the changes in the form and content of miners' strikes.

In 1888, the *Engineering and Mining Journal* (the principal trade paper in the industry) editorialized that "the industrial condition of the country is more accurately measured by the consumption of coal than by any other item." The railroads, directly and indirectly, were the biggest consumers of bituminous coal in the late nineteenth century. Of the 71.7 million tons of bituminous coal consumed in 1885, 42 percent was burned in railroad locomotives, 13 percent was used for coke (largely destined for steel production), and the remainder went into various industrial and domestic uses.

The figures in Table 1 reflect the incessant growth of an intensely competitive national market for coal during the 1880s and 1890s in which local differentials in price and production began systematically to disappear. The emergence of the national market and intense competition during this period ultimately gave rise to the creation of larger and larger economic units in the industry. The situation resulted, on the one hand, from the increased size and economic hegemony of the railroads and, on the other, from the persistent expansion of new coalfields and the consolidation of the ownership and marketing of coal output.

The development of the rail empires led to economic consolidation in three ways: (1) by uniting producers and retailers throughout the country with an improved transportation network, thus undercutting the competitive advantage enjoyed by the smaller operator in the local market; (2)

Table 1

Production and Average Value of Bituminous and Anthracite Coal, 1880–1895

	Bituminous			Anthracite		
Year	Annual U.S. Production (1,000 net tons)	% Change from Previous Year	Average Value per Ton at Mine	Annual U.S. Production (1,000 net tons)	% Change from Previous Year	Average Value per Ton at Mine
1880	50,757		$1.25	28,650		$1.47
1881	51,945	+2.1	1.12	31,920	+11.5	2.01
1882	58,917	+13.5	1.12	35,121	+10.0	2.01
1883	64,860	+10.2	1.07	38,457	+9.4	2.01
1884	71,737	+10.5	.94	37,157	–3.1	1.79
1885	71,773	0	1.13	38,336	+3.0	2.00
1886	74,645	+4.0	1.05	39,035	+1.8	1.95
1887	88,562	+18.8	1.11	42,088	+7.9	2.01
1888	102,040	+15.1	1.00	46,620	+10.7	1.91
1889	95,685	–6.2	.99	45,547	–2.4	1.44
1890	111,302	+16.3	.99	46,469	+2.0	1.43
1891	117,901	+5.9	.99	50,665	+9.3	1.46
1892	126,857	+7.6	.99	52,473	+3.6	1.57
1893	128,385	+1.2	.96	53,968	+2.9	1.59
1894	118,820	–7.5	.91	51,921	–3.9	1.51
1895	135,118	+13.7	.86	57,999	+11.7	1.41

Source: Historical Statistics of Minerals in the United States (Washington, DC: Resources for the Future, Inc., 1960), 8, 9, 11, 12.

by making possible the application of economic power against the smaller operator whose profit rates and production levels were effectively decided by the railroad companies upon whom the operators were dependent for haulage; and (3) by creating marketing agreements and pooling schemes dominated by the railroads.

The consolidation of the coal industry was also driven forward by factors outside the direct control of the railroads. What would later be called the "overdevelopment" of coal production caused operators to engage in intense competition during the upswing of the business cycle and to band together for mutual protection in periods of decline. Whatever the impetus for consolidation in any particular case, the effect on mine workers was the same: consolidation gave the forces allied against the miners a degree of concentration and coordination never previously achieved.

Business depressions were a recurrent phenomenon in this period. A long run of falling prices following the financial panic of 1873 resulted in a sharp contraction of economic activity and a severe depression lasting to 1878. The following year marked the beginning of a short but intense period of expanded industrial activity in which prices and wages also rose. The reversal of this trend came in 1882, when another contraction of business activity led to a general depression. The decline lasted into early 1886, reaching its low point in 1884–85 when an estimated 7.5 percent of all U.S. factories and mines were idled.

The widespread labor agitation and social upheaval that took place in 1886 occurred in the context of a reviving economy. The events of that year brought about a heightened awareness of class issues among American workers, an awareness expressed in an aggressive and widespread strike wave. As we show, 1886 also constitutes a turning point in the pattern of coal miners' struggles with the operators.

Between 1886 and 1890 total existing rail mileage increased by an estimated 30 percent following financial reorganization of the industry. In the same period, production of pig iron and steel rose 62 percent. The production of coal paralleled railroad growth and steel production in every year save 1889. In that year the first decline in annual coal output since 1874 resulted from a series of factors internal to the industry, although business remained healthy in other sectors of the American economy. A short depression in the United States then followed in 1890, but good harvests led to a brief recovery in late 1891. A gradual decline in prices and monetary instability began in 1892, which eventually culminated in the panic and subsequent depression of 1893–96.

Figure 1, which shows the yearly incidence of strikes from 1881 to 1894, suggests the absence of a simple and direct correlation of coal-mining strikes with the general movement of the business cycle. The number of strikes between 1882 and 1884 decreases relatively so that if the mine workers experienced increasing misery during the depression of those years, they did not respond by employing the strike weapon. The next period of relative decline in strike activity between 1886 and 1888 occurs in the midst of general economic prosperity and expansion. If in 1888 mine workers had rising expectations resulting from the business upswing, they did not at that time try to increase their share of the growing national income by striking as frequently as they did two years earlier. It should be recognized, however, that two of the relative peaks of strike activity (1886 and 1891) came at moments of economic recovery. These facts, taken together, suggest that it is not possible to make a direct correlation between strike activity in the coal industry and the level of general business prosperity.

Figure 1 **Number of Coal Strikes,[a] 1881–1894**

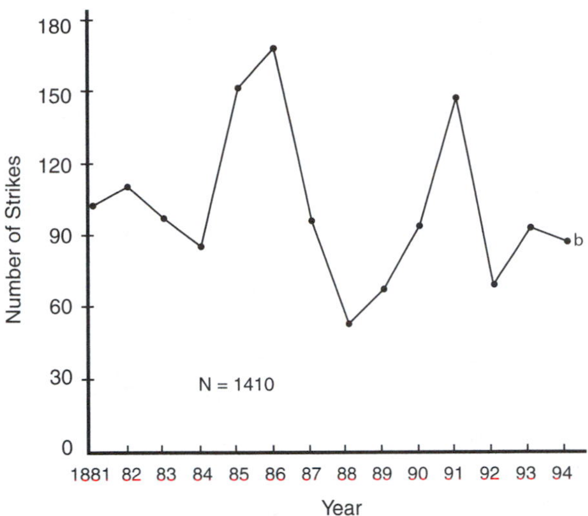

[a] Lockouts are not included in these figures because of their relative insignificance in the coal industry. In the 1881–1886 period, a total of eleven lockouts occurred in all mining industries, including metals. In the 1887–1894 period, there were a total of sixteen lockouts in the coal and coke industries.

[b] The number of strikes in 1894 includes strikes recorded in the Commissioner of Labor's Report between January 1 and June 30 only.

We propose to overcome the difficulties inherent in the narrow economic interpretation of coal strikes by looking more closely at strike demands. The analysis of strike demands, however, necessitates an understanding of the techniques of mining and the organization of production in the industry. As many of the strikes that took place in our period were not only occasioned by wage issues but also by questions of control of the productive relations in the pit, it is necessary to precede an analysis of the causes of strikes with a certain amount of description of the mining process.

Throughout the 1880s and 1890s the "practical miner" who dug the coal from the seam's vertical "face" dominated the coal industry's occupational structure. The pit workforce generally was divided between surface and underground workers. Underground workers averaged between 85 and 90 percent of the total number of workers. The miner worked with an assistant or "buddy" in his own individual "room" at the coal face. The miner's

Table 2

Structure of the Bituminous[a] Coal Mining Labor Force, by State

State	Total Number of Coal Mine Workers (1889)	Underground Workers/Total Coal Mine Workers (%)	Miners[b]/Total Coal Mine Workers (%)	Miners[b]/Total Underground Workers (%)	Underground Supervisors/ Underground Workers (%)
Pennsylvania (bitum.)	53,132	90.6	75.5	83.3	1.3
(Allegheny Cty.)	(9,314)	(90.2)	(80.4)	(89.1)	(1.0)
(Westmoreland Cty.)	(8,962)	(90.2)	(73.5)	(81.5)	(1.4)
Ohio	19,343	89.4	76.2	85.2	1.3
West Virginia	9,778	84.1	65.1	77.4	1.4
Alabama	6,864	85.2	59.9	70.3	1.2
Tennessee	4,031	85.9	63.0	73.3	1.6
Maryland	3,702	91.3	72.6	79.5	0.7
Illinois	23,934	89.2	64.3	72.1	1.4
Indiana	6,448	89.7	73.5	81.9	2.3
Iowa	9,244	88.4	71.3	80.6	1.7
Colorado	94,904	83.5	69.1	82.7	1.1

Source: U.S. Census Office, *11th Census* (1890*)*, *Report on the Mineral Industries in the United States* (Washington, D.C.: G.P.O., 1892), 349–350. The data included in the *11th Census* is for the 1889 fiscal year.

[a] States listed represent the major geological coal seams in the United States: Appalachian, Central, Western, and Rocky Mountain. Anthracite was not included in this table because the size and structure of the labor force, as well as methods of production and geographical concentration are markedly different from bituminous coal production.

[b] The term "miner," as used by the Census, denotes a mine worker engaged in removing coal from the seam. The miners' helpers were aggregated with other underground workers, such as trappers, tracklayers, etc., in a "laborers" category. If the miners' helpers could be aggregated with miners, the face workers' domination of the occupational structure would be even more marked.

basic work at the coal face consisted of making an undercut with a hand pick at the bottom of the coal seam, drilling the holes for the introduction of blasting powder, and firing the shot. The force of the explosion broke off several tons of coal in pieces of varying size, and the miner and his helper then loaded the coal with shovels onto mine cars. The pace of the work and the methods employed were decided upon by the miner. Miners also determined the length of their own working day. Face workers generally came to work when they pleased and went home when they were ready. The face teams were supported by a small force of auxiliary workers, which included blacksmiths, carpenters, ventilation workers, and hoisting engineers (all working on the surface). Also working underground, in addition to the face teams, were coal car drivers, timbermen, track layers, and "trappers" (who watched and regulated the ventilation doors). The support workers were usually hired directly by the coal operator and paid a daily wage, whereas the miners were paid on a tonnage rate for coal sent to the surface.

Despite the large number of different occupations in the industry, coal mining in the late nineteenth century was almost wholly the domain of the coal miner and his helper. Table 2, adapted from the 1890 census, indicates the extent of the miner's domination; it was a dominance that was to have important consequences for the form that trade union organization would take among mine workers.

The miner's commanding position in the occupational hierarchy was reinforced by a contracting system in which each miner was permanently assigned his place or "room" in a particular pit. The miner usually hired and paid his helper.

Because of the ways in which miners functioned as individual contractors under this system and because of the relatively high degree of autonomy that they enjoyed in their normal day-to-day work activities, it is tempting to ascribe to them the sort of craft exclusiveness and preoccupation with job control that characterized other skilled workers in the nineteenth century. However, several factors worked against the creation of craft consciousness among coal miners. The most important of these factors probably was the miners' numerical weight in the industry's occupational structure. Craft exclusiveness in other industries developed out of the needs of a relatively small craft group to protect its work skills and methods from managerial encroachment and from the technological dilution that usually followed. In the iron and steel industry, for example, the rationalization and mechanization in the 1890s resulted in opposition by skilled craft workers to the loss of their strategic position in the productive process. Nineteenth-century coal miners, however, hardly felt the pressures engendered by mechanization or rationalization through supervision. The number of confrontations between miners and operators over these issues was minimal, and miners did not articulate an ideology of craft control over production as, for example, did the iron puddlers.

Table 2 suggests the relatively minor role played by managerial supervision in coal mining in 1890. Mechanization of production to 1894 was halting at best; the transfer of skill from miner to machine did not occur until well into the twentieth century. The first form of power equipment to be introduced was the mechanical undercutter, which was operated initially with compressed air and later with electric power. By 1891, only 6.6 percent of U.S. coal output had been undercut by machine, although the incidence of mechanical undercutting in certain geographical regions was higher than the national average would suggest. The southern Illinois field and the Hocking Valley in Ohio, for example, had both experienced the sharp impact of the coal undercutter by the mid-1880s. By 1888 three-fifths of the coal produced in southern Illinois for the St. Louis market had been undercut by machine. Similarly, in the Hocking Valley machines had almost totally replaced the pick by the mid-1890s.

A number of different factors impeded the early introduction of mining machinery in most places. For one thing the narrow headings and crooked passageways of the older coal workings made the operation of new machinery difficult. Most important, however, was the resistance of the miners themselves, who consistently fought hard to blunt the economizing power of the machines by insisting that machine miners, runners, and pick miners be paid at comparable rates. Installation of the coal undercutter was initiated in the 1880s more for its "moral effect" in combating the organization of pick miners than for its value as an "expense reducer." A prominent coal operator, William N. Page, writing in the mid-1890s, argued that the machine was introduced

> . . . not so much for its saving in direct cost as for the indirect economy in having to control a fewer number of men for the same output. It is a weapon with which to meet organized skilled labor and their unreasonable demands. . . . As the machine does the mining, the proportion of skilled labor is largely reduced, and the result is found in less belligerence and conflict; a sufficient inducement though the direct costs be the same.

It was only in exceptional circumstances where the potential short-term economies were sufficiently great that the operators undertook the introduction of coal undercutters. In the Hocking Valley, where the seams were ten feet thick, introduction of the undercutter had a great profit potential. This motivated the operators to prepare a careful campaign to introduce the machine in 1884, deliberately forcing the miners to engage in a bitter and violent strike shortly thereafter.

One explanation for the relative absence of craft exclusiveness among miners can be found in their pragmatic awareness of the need to control the potential power of certain categories of day workers (drivers being the most important example). Such workers could throw the vast majority of miners out of work by undertaking independent strike action. Throughout the 1880s various groups of day workers refused on occasions to support strike demands put forward by the "tonnage" men while at the same time being prepared to shut down the entire operation in support of their own demands. Although coal miners and their leaders initially were ambivalent about permitting other categories of mine workers to join their organization, by 1890 and the founding of the United Mine Workers of America, they had come to accept the need for inclusive trade union forms in order to wage coordinated struggles. The need to wage strikes over the general and inclusive demands of all grades of mine workers had, by this time, raised the industrial form of union organization to the level of basic necessity.

In general, during this period questions involving the pace, the methods of labor, and the length of the working day were decided by the individual miner, and his control over these matters generally went unchallenged by the operators. What then were the sources of conflict between the operators and the miners? Not surprisingly, questions of remuneration predominated. The number and range of disputes under this heading, however, varied greatly. The wealth of contentious questions between worker and employer derived in large part from the particular economic pressures to which the coal operator was being subjected. The individual operator increasingly was obliged to meet competition in a national market. Second, labor costs, representing an astonishingly high proportion of total costs, generally could not be reduced through intensified managerial supervision or by the replacement of man by machine. The coal operators, unable to reduce their rather high labor costs, had only limited means by which they could directly extract increased amounts of surplus value from the miners' labor. They were impelled, therefore, to rely on a wide variety of methods through which the mine workers contributed indirectly to the company's profits.

Writing about the period of the 1880s and 1890s, labor relations analyst Arthur E. Suffern listed the various forms of "audacious robbery" to which the miners were subject. Competition and overproduction, Suffern held, caused the operators to engage in the following illicit practices: shortweighing; the abuse of the "dockage" system (where the miners were penalized for slate and clay sent up with the coal); abuse of the coal screening system (by which the large "lump" coal was separated from the less desirable "slack"); nonpayment of the miners for so-called "deadwork" (which included all sorts of necessary maintenance); gouging through the company store; the coercion and exploitation associated with company housing; and, finally, a number of different abuses in payment systems (e.g., payment in "scrip," irregular payment, and payment at long intervals).

Coal screens allegedly were introduced by the operators in order to separate the larger and more marketable pieces of coal from the smaller pieces of slack. As it happened, the operators were able to sell the smaller pieces anyway, often as coking coal, and sometimes as "nut" coal, which had a good domestic market. Since the miner received no payment whatsoever for this slack, it came to represent virtually pure profit for his employer. Accordingly, the operators often responded to competitive pressures (as well as to their own greedy impulses) by increasing the gauge of the coal screen when they could get away with it. Miners in Ohio estimated that every increase of one-quarter of an inch over the standard one-inch gauge cost them 10 percent of their output.

In mines where screens were not introduced, coal operators often maximized profits by refusing to weigh the mine workers' daily output. Miners testified that they might be forced to load a "one-ton" coal car with as much as 3,500 or 4,000 pounds of coal. Since underpayment for tonnage was endemic, the disputed amount of the miners' daily output in many pits often provided the first occasion for organization. The principal object of such efforts was the employment of a check-weighman (paid for by the miners). In mining operations where no check-weighman existed, miners might be cheated by as much as 50 percent of their output.

The company store, known to the mine workers as the "pluck me," commonly enjoyed a monopoly position either because the miners were strongly pressured to trade there or because there were no other stores in the area. The store represented an important source of profit for the company and could yield as much as a 15 percent return on capital investment. In some instances the operation of the company store was the only thing that kept a company in the black during a bad year. One operator, while admitting that the "pluck-me" was a "dishonest imposition," argued that it was employed "largely as a means of reduction where the organized miners would resist an open and honest reduction in wages." He concluded by saying that the abolition of the company store". . . would take from capital one of the best means for reconciling labor to necessary reductions, by reducing its cost of living at the same time."

The method and form of payment also were contentious questions during the 1880s and 1890s. Payment in company paper or "scrip" had as its principal aim forcing the miner to use the company store. In addition, it probably helped the operator to solve his cash flow problems. That the operator had such problems is illustrated by the fact that during periods of economic decline some operators were willing to offer their workers a choice of either a wage reduction or the acceptance of payment on a monthly basis.

Given the multiplicity of indirect means by which operators were able to reduce the miners' pay, the control exercised by face workers at the point of production provided an insufficient basis from which to fight back against these abuses. This fact impelled all categories of mine workers toward a common struggle against the employers.

The pattern of strike activity that developed during the period of our study reflected the drive to build a national industrial organization. This pattern emerges clearly when these strikes are separated and classified by the nature of the specific demands put forward.

As is obvious from Figure 2, strikes concerning organization and conditions demonstrate a very different development from those undertaken to secure wage increases ("offensive wage strikes") and those undertaken to resist pay cuts ("defensive wage strikes"). It should be noted that the lines that describe the incidence of the latter two types of strikes move against one another during most periods. In a period of depression (e.g., 1883–84) these curves move apart, and then as the economy turns into a period of prosperity (1886–90), there is a "scissors-effect" as they reverse position. Thus, offensive and defensive wage strikes are best seen

Figure 2 **Strike Causes, 1881–1894**
(as percentage of total annual strikes)

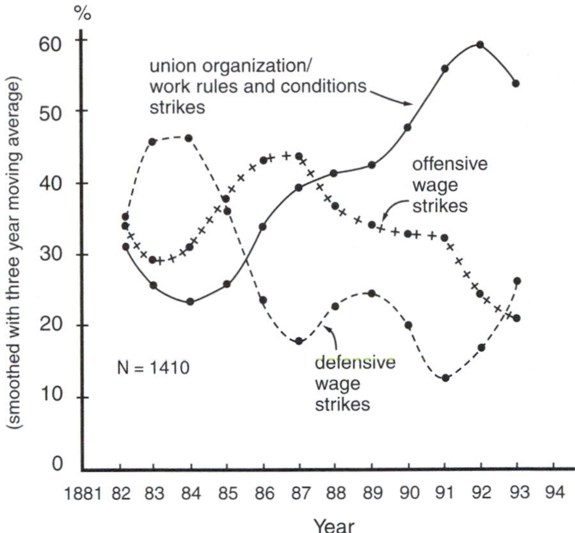

as immediate and short-term responses to direct economic pressures.

In sharp contrast to this scissors-like progress is the line describing strikes over organization and conditions. This curve seems to follow a logic of its own. These strikes reflected the struggle to order productive relations in the industry. The productive relations category amalgamates three basic types of strike causes: (1) those over work rules and conditions including questions of the form and regularity of payment and the conditions of life in the mining community; (2) those involving questions of union organization and worker solidarity; and (3) those over the employment of particular workers, including strikes to rehire a victimized worker and strikes to fire an obnoxious foreman. These types of strikes are regarded as efforts to reorder productive relations because in each case they represent an attempt to confront directly the coal operators' economic and social control in and around the mines. The dramatic increase in these strikes shown in Figure 2 is a direct reflection of the miners' increasing determination to challenge this control in a period of intensified consolidation and conflict in the industry. The increase in strikes to reorder productive relations represented the whole complex of relationships among the miners,

Figure 3 **Strikes Called by Unions, 1881–1894**

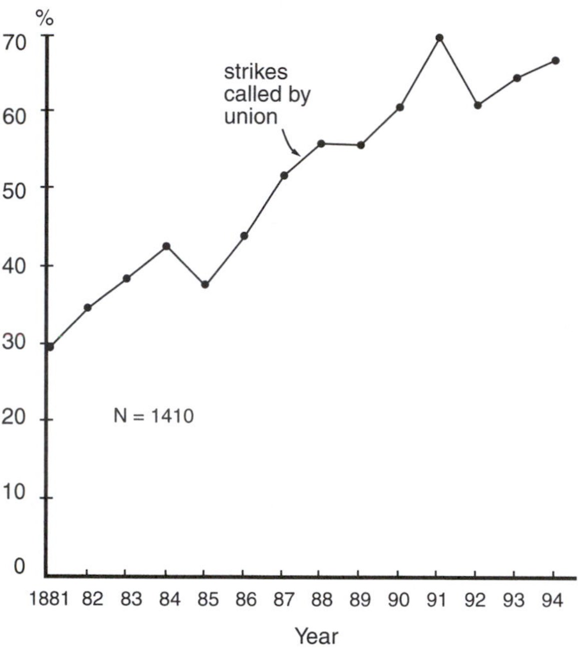

the operators, and nationwide economic forces out of which a national union of mine workers was beginning to emerge.

As the following figure shows, the miners increasingly confronted the operators as trade unionists, or at the call of a trade union organization. Figure 3 demonstrates the steady increase in the number of strikes called by labor organizations, which suggests the steady growth of the miners' awareness of the need for a formal organization upon which to base strike activity. Union-called strikes in the coal industry reached a majority in 1886 and attained a peak of 70 percent in 1891.

The miners' efforts to build a national union were prolonged both by the economic vicissitudes that characterized the times and by organizational competition among the early labor organizations in the industry. The initial attempts to organize nationally after the Civil War were smashed during the depression of 1873–78. At the beginning of the 1880s, "secret" local assemblies of the Knights of Labor had replaced "open" miners' unions in many localities. Many of the Knights' local assemblies in the coal districts consisted almost entirely of mine workers and functioned as local trade unions. In this way they simultaneously propagated the political ideas of the Knights of Labor and acted as the practical centers of organized strike activity.

Before 1886, strikes were local, or at the most districtwide. In many coal fields during the depression of 1882–85, for example, miners carried out limited and defensive strikes in response to the operators' attempts to cut wages as orders declined. The data indicate that in addition to being relatively limited geographically, these defensive strikes were of comparatively long duration (54 percent of the defensive wage strikes undertaken in this period lasted one month or more). For many miners, therefore, the idea of a national union came to represent the prospect of overcoming the isolation and defeat of the lengthy local struggles. The preamble to the Constitution of the National Federation of Miners and Mine Laborers, written near the end of this depression period (September 1885) and quoted by George McNeil, reflects the miners' recognition of the need for a national organization.

> As miners and mine laborers, our troubles are everywhere of a similar character. The inexorable law of supply and demand determines the point where our interests unite. The increased shipping facilities of the last few years have made all coal-producing districts competitors in the markets of this country. This has led to indiscriminate cutting of market prices and unnecessary reductions in our wages, which for some time have been far below a living rate. . . . Our failure to act in concert when contesting for principles and rights brought has brought about the demoralization and degradation of our craft. Local, district and State organizations have done much towards ameliorating the condition of our craft in the past, but to-day neither district nor State unions can regulate the markets to which their coal is shipped. . . . Hence, while approving of local organizations, whether secret or open in character, we are convinced that by federating under one general head our powers for good would be increased and a speedy betterment of our common condition follow. In a federation of all lodges and branches of miners' unions lies our only hope.

The economic upswing that began in 1886 provided the miners with the opportunity to fight for their aims. They did so by undertaking offensive pay strikes to restore wage rates that had been forced down during the depression and by undertaking numerous strikes over work rules and conditions and union organization (strikes over these matters during 1885–86 exceeded those during 1883–84 by 75 percent). The National Trades Assembly #135 of the Knights of Labor was established in May 1886 as an organizational rival to the more open trade unionism of the National Federation. By this point the mine workers had developed two national organizations with which to wage offensive struggles against the operators.

The standard view of these two organizations has stressed the vigorous and sometimes even bitter competition between them. The organizational rivalry that did exist, however, was considerably less important than the traditional view suggests. More significant than the occasional fistfight between members of the rival organizations was the fact that the National Federation and NTA #135 were committed to similar programs. Both sought to build up powerful district and state organizations, both preferred arbitration and conciliation despite an increasing reliance on strike action, and both undertook extensive political and legislative action to secure gains for mine workers.

The traditional interpretation of the American labor movement has tended to counterpose pragmatic job action and third-party political agitation in describing the rivalry between the Knights of Labor and the other labor organizations of the period. As far as the two major mine workers' organizations in the 1880s were concerned, however, political and strike action certainly were not opposing strategies. On the contrary, miners in both NTA #135 and the National Federation frequently challenged the operators' political power through vigorous efforts to secure legislation to guarantee fair and frequent payment and regular safety inspection of mines and equipment. Furthermore, legislative campaigns and strike action were frequently tied together when miners walked out to ensure the enforcement of state mining laws. The direct local challenge to the operators' control, the fight to build a national union of mine workers, and the campaign to pass and to enforce protective state legislation were, therefore, inextricably bound together in the miners' struggles.

There is evidence to suggest the existence of legislative and organizational cooperation between the NTA #135 and the National Federation after 1887. For example, the common desire to employ arbitration and conciliation mechanisms led these organizations to attempt to cooperate in joint-scale agreements between 1887 and 1889. Moreover, rank-and-file demands to disregard the antagonisms engendered in the early 1880s pressured the leaders of the two organizations to overcome their differences. These contacts and pressures would eventually culminate in the merger of NTA #135 with the National Federation (renamed the National Progressive Union in 1889) to form the United Mine Workers of America (UMW) in January 1890. The creation of the UMW represented the final amalgamation of the organizational and political orientations present in its antecedents.

At the time of its founding, the UMW could claim only 17,000 "paid up" members out of the total labor force in bituminous mining of nearly 200,000 workers. Nevertheless, large numbers of miners were influenced by the national organization, whether or not they were actually members. By the end of the period under examination (1894), the UMW could call for a series of massive strikes across the country to defend wage levels and bring out one 125,000 miners, although only 13,000 were members of the union at the time. The union was clearly influential beyond the confines of its formal membership.

Figure 4 indicates that both union and nonunion miners increasingly utilized the strike to reorder productive relations in the pits. This suggests the possibility that trade union consciousness preceded rather than followed formal organization. Once the union became established, however, miners were better able to carry on strikes once they had begun, to extend the strike to more than a single establishment, and to involve consistently higher proportions of the workforce in each pit.

As with many of the results presented earlier, Figure 5 indicates the way in which 1886 marks an important turning point in the nature of strike experience in the coal-mining industry. Our evidence indicates that there is an important qualitative different between the long strikes of the early 1880s

Figure 4 **Productive Relations Strikes, 1881–1894**
(comparing union and nonunion establishments)

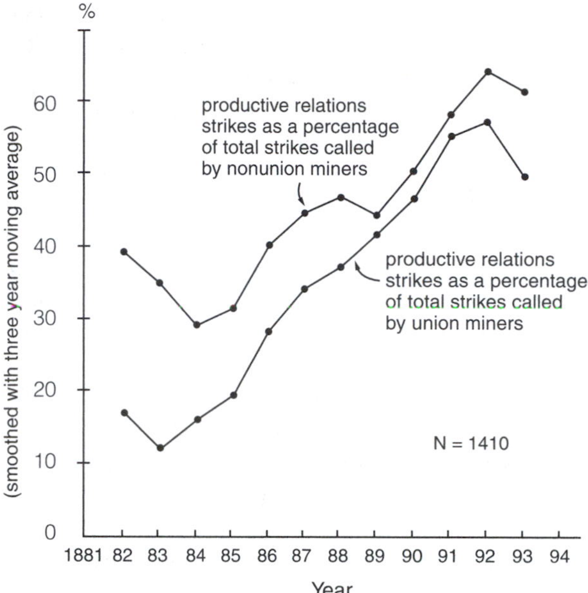

(many of which were desperate and unsuccessful struggles against pay cuts imposed by employers during the 1882–85 depression) and the strikes of relatively long duration that occurred during the period of economic upswing following 1886. As Figure 5 dramatically demonstrates, it was the unionized miners who were able to mount strikes of longer-than-average duration. After 1886 it can be seen that the curves representing the mean duration of union and nonunion strikes move apart, suggesting that the unionized mine workers were able to take advantage of the prosperity of the late 1880s to press their demands on employers with strikes of greater duration. Nonunion miners appear much less able to do this as indicated by the strike duration figures recorded on the lower line in Figure 5.

Another indication of the growing aggressiveness of coal strikes in the late 1880s and early 1890s is suggested by the number of mining establishments affected by a particular strike. An increasing ability to mount multi-establishment strikes demonstrates the mine workers' ability to carry out strikes over greater geographical areas. Between 1881 and 1894, two-thirds of all multi-establishment strikes in coal were called by unions. Further, although 42 percent of all union-called strikes were multi-establishment in scope, only 20.4 percent of nonunion strikes extended beyond a single pit.

When the growth in the number of mining operations involved in multi-establishment strikes is considered over time, a marked upward trend is noticeable. The mine workers' increased ability to undertake multi-establishment strikes after the mid-1880s is related positively to the crucial role played by the national union: more than half of the strikes called by trade unions between 1886 and 1894 were multi-establishment in scope, whereas in the same period only 17 percent of all nonunion strikes were of this character.

Finally, in addition to the usual parameters of strike activity (duration and geographical dispersion), we show the impact of union organization on the miners' ability to achieve strike solidarity. To do this we compared the categories of "strikers" and "number of employees" (i.e., total employment figures for each mine) as the basis of an index of solidarity for strikes in coal mining. By taking those who had actively involved themselves as a portion of the entire mine workforce (as opposed to those who had merely been "thrown out of work"), we developed a measure of solidarity by which to

Figure 5 **Mean Duration of Union and Nonunion Strikes, 1881–1894**

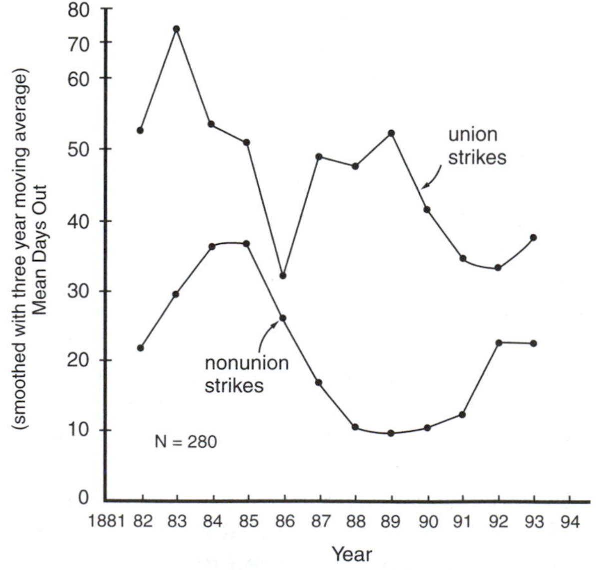

compare the experience of the union and non-union miners. The index numbers listed in Table 3 represent the number of strikers as a proportion of the total number of employees:

Strikers / Total Employees = Level of Solidarity

Solidarity increases as the index number approaches 1.00.

As Table 3 indicates, unionized miners consistently were able to involve a higher percentage of the mine workforce in their strikes. We would attribute this fact to the ability of the miners' unions to mount strikes that involved a greater number of the occupational categories in each pit. It will also be noted that there is significantly less variation from the norm among the union-called strikes (i.e., standard deviations are much lower), indicating fewer numbers of cases that did not conform to the general pattern among union-called strikes.

Our data have suggested a consistent relationship between the growth and impact of trade unionism among the American mine workers between 1881 and 1894 and the pattern of strikes in the coal industry during the same period. We have contended that the evolution of the strike in coal is reflected in the changing pattern of strike demands. Specifically, strikes over the reordering of productive relations in mining increase as a proportion of the total despite the fluctuations in business activity that characterized the times. In response to the attempts of coal operators to enhance their economic control over their employees, coal miners increasingly relied on strike activity that had as its object not only the elimination of imme-

Table 3

Index of Strike Solidarity

	Union-Called Strikes		Nonunion Strikes	
Year	Index of Solidarity[a]	Standard Deviation[b]	Index of Solidarity[a]	Standard Deviation[b]
1881	.946	.076	.833	.251
1882	.893	.097	.789	.305
1883	.920	.091	.711	.384
1884	.965	.085	.809	.324
1885	.801	.224	.736	.332
1886	.867	.119	.793	.310
1887	.825	.265	.590	.320
1888	.912	.101	.682	.299
1889	.816	.178	.614	.349
1890	.883	.113	.873	.130
1891	.810	.252	.589	.384
1892	.846	.077	.641	.373
1893	.848	.146	.757	.200
1894	.905	.097	.636	.397
mean	.863[c]	.169	.731[c]	.316

[a] mean solidarity index for all sample strikes = .795
[b] mean standard deviation for all sample strikes = .264
[c] analysis of variance F Test = 18.0824, T Test = 4.2523

diate grievances but also the creation and extension of a permanent institution of self-defense.

The ability of formal trade union organization to increase the impact and solidarity of the strike was an important lesson carried by mine workers through the severe depression that followed the defeat of the 1894 strike. Even though their union was nearly destroyed, formally speaking, between 1894 and 1896, mine workers were able and willing to rally to the UMW's strike call with the economic upturn of 1897. That year marked the beginning of a string of strike victories for the UMW, which would ultimately make it the largest and one of the most militant of all American trade unions before World War I. It was in the formative years between 1881 and 1894, however, that the miners transformed the strike into an aggressive and more broadly class-conscious tactic in their struggle to reorder the productive relationships within individual coal pits and in the industry as a whole.

See also: "Better Than a Hundred Speeches": The Strike Song, 103; Mesabi Iron Miners' Strikes, 461; The Rise and Fall of Rank-and-File Miner Militancy, 1964–2007, 471.

Note

This essay is excerpted from the authors' essay "Coal Miners on Strike: The Transformation of Strike Demands and the Formation of a National Union." *Journal of Interdisciplinary History* 7, no. 4 (Spring 1977): 583–616.

Bibliography

Cartlidge, Oscar. *Fifty Years of Coal Mining*. Charleston, WV: Rose City Press, 1936.

Harvey, Katherine. *The Best Dressed Miners*. Ithaca, NY: Cornell University Press, 1969.

Page, William N. "The Economics of Coal Mining." In *The Mineral Industry: Statistical Supplement of the Engineering and Mining Journal*. Vol. 3. New York: Western & Co., 1894.

Roy, Andrew. *History of the Coal Miners in the United States*. Columbus, OH: J. L. Trauger, 1903.

Suffern, Arthur E. *Conciliation and Arbitration in the Coal Industry of America*. Boston: Houghton Mifflin, 1915.

MESABI IRON MINERS' STRIKES

Gerald Ronning

Organizing the steel industry had proven to be a seemingly impossible task for unionists in the late nineteenth and early twentieth centuries. The owners and managers of the Steel Trust had committed themselves to the nonunion "open shop" and for the most part had been successful at keeping organizers away from the blast furnaces and rolling mills. The industrial map of the steel industry did not consist solely of the large factories in steelmaking cities like Pittsburgh and Gary, however. While labor organizers seemed unable to make significant progress at the heart of the industry, they did attempt to influence events at the core from the industry's vital extremities. On two occasions, in 1907 and 1916, miners working the rich iron deposits of northern Minnesota took the lead in the attempt to wrest control of their working lives from mine owners and steel companies. On guard against attacks from within and without, on both occasions the steel industry fought back with all of the resources at its command. Though both strikes ultimately failed and the steel companies were able to forestall these attempts at closing the open shop, as a result of their second effort Minnesota's miners gained significant concessions from the otherwise resistant mining corporations and, perhaps more importantly, played a central role in forging a new working-class identity among miners that would transform the region's social and political order.

Corporations and Immigrants Create the Iron Range

Northern Minnesota presented a howling wilderness to the entrepreneurs who first stumbled across iron ore there in the 1860s. A U.S. government surveyor discovered the ore of the Vermillion Range in 1865 and convinced Jay Cooke to finance a railroad to develop the region. Historian Rudolph Pinola has told the story. In 1874 the government of Minnesota provided an incentive for development, giving the railroad ten sections of land for each mile of road built in iron country. Little came of this early venture as the quantity and quality of the ore did not warrant significant development and steel companies and investors seemed hesitant to make the financial commitment to develop the region. Entrepreneurs and prospectors continued to search the North Country for iron, however, convinced that more significant finds lay hidden in the vast woods.

In 1890 prospectors discovered the first Mesabi Iron Range ores, and this time speculators descended on the region with a vengeance—the rich and seemingly endless supply of ore provoked a frenzy of development. From December 1, 1890, to September 1, 1892, investors incorporated 127 mining companies, according to historian Harlan Hatcher. Would-be captains of industry brought the first of a long line of steam shovels to the Range in 1894, its thirty-five tons transported in the dead of winter over frozen ground because the railroad could not handle the weight, and within six years miners had pulled over 31,389,888 tons of ore out of the ground. By 1902 the Mesabi Iron Range provided the bulk of the iron ore for the American steel industry.

Few of the many companies founded in the opening decade of development survived the first flush of growth, however. The enormous capital outlays required for developing the raw frontier and the dampening effect of the economic depression drove most of the small operators into the waiting arms of Big Steel. Henry W. Oliver followed this pattern, turning to a friend from Pittsburgh, Carnegie Steel's Henry Frick, to save his operation from bankruptcy, and in 1892 Frick and Oliver opened the Oliver Mining Company. Taking advantage of the economic downturn, the two quickly bought up claims and expanded. In 1901, U.S. Steel inherited the Oliver Mining Company and its sixty-five mines (out of a total of 104 mines that shipped ore that year) as well as five railroads and 112 vessels that could carry two-thirds of the ore required by its mills.

Mine owners required a workforce in addition to capital, and town building began quickly after the discovery of iron. Historian Arnold R. Alanen has described these small "locations," not quite towns but somewhat more substantial than encampments, hastily built in the wilderness of northern Minnesota at the start of the 1890s. They lent to the region an ad hoc appearance and character. Mining companies founded the communities of Tower, Hibbing, Biwabik, Chisolm, and Mountain Iron, all within the first year of the discovery. Towns sprang up on top of iron deposits almost overnight as prospectors and speculators rushed to house legions of immigrant workers who opened up the newly found mineral resources, and within the next two decades companies brought most of the other Range settlements into existence, almost seventy-five in total.

An abundance of cheap immigrant labor filled the locations and allowed iron production on the Mesabi Range to expand quickly. The demand for labor, in turn, caused a rapid growth in population across the region. St. Louis County, encompassing most of the ore-bearing deposits on the Mesabi Range as well as providing a home to the region's largest city, Duluth, almost tripled in population in a mere ten years, jumping from 19,000 to over 52,000 people in the decade after 1895. Native-born American, Cornish, French-Canadian, Irish, Swedish, Italian, Polish, Slovenian, Croatian, Serbian, Montenegrin, Bulgarian, and Greek settlers all moved into the region, though most residents were recent European arrivals. In 1905, for example, 55 percent of the residents living in the twelve principal Iron Range towns had emigrated from Europe; in the first decade of the twentieth century, two-thirds of all the Range miners were foreign-born, according to Carl Ross, a historian of immigrant Finns.

However, Finnish immigrants seemed to be the most numerous in the mines by 1900. *Amerikan tauti* (American disease) and *Amerikan kuume* (American fever) took hold among Finns in the second half of the nineteenth century. Large-scale immigration of Finns to the United States began in 1864 when a labor recruiter convinced Finns from Norway to work in Michigan's copper mines. Once the connection with copper had been established, the lure of employment and available land exerted a powerful pull on Finns.

Economic and social change in Finland also pushed Finns into the Upper Midwest. A decline in agricultural productivity, the depletion of forest resources, and increases in the rural population and the ranks of the landless all served to motivate Finns to search for alternate means of making their living, including away from their homeland. Compounding the demographic shift, industrial change swept over the rural areas of Finland, undermining traditional methods of agriculture and severing the people's connection to the land. The inability of Finland's small industrial cities to employ the rural population, coupled with the increasingly oppressive Russian control of Finland, prompted Finns to leave their homes in significant numbers. In the five decades after their initial arrival, some 350,000 Finns, one-ninth of the total population of Finland in 1900, left for America; the majority, some 215,000, arrived between the years 1900 and 1914. Though the Finns had initially concentrated themselves in the copper-mining country of Michigan's Upper Peninsula, the development of Minnesota's Iron Range drew large numbers of Finns to northern Minnesota from Michigan and directly from Finland. Within a short time, most Iron Range communities possessed "Finntowns," often dismissed as "Pig Towns" or "Finn Hells" by native-born neighbors.

In the first decade of the twentieth century Finns dominated the Iron Range, comprising the single largest group of immigrants to the area and, according to an early chronicler of the area, Stewart H. Holbrook, setting "a pattern of life on the range" that subsequent groups of migrants followed. Over one-half of all the Finns in the United States lived in Minnesota, Michigan, and Wisconsin by 1905, and over one-third of the population of the Minnesota Iron Range had immigrated directly from Finland. In some towns Finns made up over 80 percent of the population. Range towns like Embarrass, Minnesota, owed their very existence to Finns. In 1895 Embarrass, "Minnesota Arrowhead's Finland," consisted of only a couple of settlers. By 1905 Finns had moved to the township, drained swamps, and established farms in the dense forests of pine. Embarrass, according to a Works Projects Administration study of Arrowhead County, "naturally took on many characteristics of Finland," and the unique "gumdrop" haystacks that the Finns constructed on their farms "gave the [Embarrass] valley a foreign appearance."

Militant Unionism Emerges

During the first years of intensive development, the Iron Range's miners remained unorganized, overlooked by a Minnesota Federation of Labor more interested in organizing skilled workers than the thousands of relatively unskilled immigrant miners. In 1905, however, having recognized the connections between the fortunes of western hard-rock miners and the iron miners of the Upper Midwest, the Western Federation of Miners (WFM) began to send organizers to the Iron Range, according to historian Carl Chrislock. Initially the union sent Anglo-American organizers, but in 1906 it changed its tactics and sent Teofilo Petriella, an Italian socialist, who strengthened the efforts of the union by hiring local immigrant miners as organizers and dividing their efforts between the Italian, Slavic, and Finnish miners. Several grievances pushed the miners to organize in 1907, among them a significant wage differential between native-born and immigrant miners, materials costs deducted from pay, the short work season that forced them into lumber camps over the winter, the high cost of living in northern Minnesota, and the inability of immigrants to rise above the position of a common miner. On top of these factors, mine safety was abysmal: the fatality rate of 7.5 per thousand employees in 1905–6 did not include the numbers of those injured or maimed in the commonplace accidents of daily mine life. By June 1907, a sizable organization had taken shape, with 2,500 members divided into fourteen federated locals.

The WFM had not anticipated a walkout in the summer of 1907, but that June a sawmill strike spread to dockworkers in Superior, Wisconsin, and Duluth, Minnesota, as well as to the Duluth, Missabe and Northern Railway, bringing shipping to a halt by mid-July. The miners grew increasingly restive, but the WFM realized the weak position they were in given the stockpiles of ore on the docks. After the Oliver Mining Company laid off 100 union miners, the WFM bowed to the wishes of its membership and brought a list of demands to the Oliver Mining Company superintendent. The WFM called for an eight-hour day, an end to the system of bonuses and petty bribes, and a daily minimum wage of $2.50 for open-pit workers and $3.00 for underground workers. Oliver immediately fired 300 of the most active members of the union, and the WFM proclaimed a strike on July 20, 1907. As many as 16,000 miners walked out of the mines that summer, few of them with any experience of strikes or unions. A majority of the strikers, perhaps three-fourths, were Finns, with the rest coming from Austria-Hungary and Italy, according to historian Neil Betten. Working-class luminaries like Mother Jones and a very young Industrial Workers of the World (IWW) organizer Elizabeth Gurley Flynn toured the Range and buoyed the spirits of the striking miners. Their efforts and the energy of the miners' families helped the strikers to maintain their discipline in the first weeks of the strike—strikers even obeyed the local sheriff's ban on mass marches.

The mine owners reacted swiftly to the strike, reporting to the governor that "state troops must be hurried to the iron range if you would prevent bloodshed and destruction of property," a claim that they repeated frequently over the first month in phone calls, telegrams, and letters to the state capitol, according to Pinola. In the absence of violence, the governor refused to send state troops, and the mine owners started to hire their own gunmen, recruiting over 1,000 strikebreakers by August—primarily Montenegrins and Croatians—in order to take advantage of any possible ethnic rivalries. In addition to intimidation, mine owners also hoped to starve the striking miners into submission, pressuring local merchants to cut off their credit. Local newspapers also allied them-

Mary Jones Harris, known popularly as Mother Jones, was a labor organizer and Socialist who helped found the Industrial Workers of the World. She was an organizer for the United Mine Workers and toured the Mesabi Range during a strike of miners in 1907. To build support for strikes, she often organized protests by the women and children of the strikers' community. (Copyright by Bertha Howell. *Courtesy:* Library of Congress.)

selves with mine owners, reporting that the WFM and the striking miners were attempting to bring about anarchy on the Mesabi. By early August the dockworkers' strike ended in defeat and the docks were again open for shipping. At that point, determined to end the walkout, mine owners began to import thousands of strikebreakers. Hungry iron miners began to drift back to work, and the strike effectively ended that September.

In the aftermath of the strike, the mining companies increased their level of vigilance and fired and blacklisted hundreds of workers, a majority of them Finns. These blacklists excluded large numbers of workers from both the mines and the docks and resulted in a forced migration either to western mines or lumber camps or to midwestern farm communities—an action that spread radicalized Finns to mines in Montana and Arizona, among other states. Mining companies had concluded that Finnish miners had formed the majority of the strike leadership and were the most militant; even before the end of the strike Oliver was making plans to rid itself of these undesirable employees. "A great many of the Finns employed here have quit," reported one of the company's superintendents quoted by historian Robert M. Eleff. "In my judgment they should not be re-employed and I have given instructions to our Mining Captains to this effect." The prestrike percentage of Finns in the mines, roughly 18 percent of all miners, dropped to 8 percent.

In addition to blacklists, the mining companies attempted to have several radical Finns deported as nonwhites, supposedly prohibited from staying in the United States by the Chinese Exclusion Act. The racial character of Finns tended to cause no small amount of debate among native-born Americans, debate that usually ended with, at the very least, radical Finns residing in a gray area between white and nonwhite. According to one Progressive Era tract on the origins of Finnish immigrants, they, like Indians, could trace their racial heritage to Mongolian stock, specifically the "Finno-Tartar branch of the Mongolian race." Adding to this racial confusion, some nineteenth-century philologists traced the Finnish language to an indeterminate category they called "Turanian," a linguistic ancestor to Turkish, Mongolian, Basque, Tamil, and the languages of the American Indians. In the end, according to historian Michael Gary Karni, St. Paul's district attorney held up the immigration papers of sixteen striking Finnish miners because of their radicalism during the 1907 strike, claiming that their Mongol origins excluded them from citizenship.

In spite of the best efforts of the mining companies, immigrant radicalism did not disappear from the Iron Range. Rather than acknowledge defeat, the Finns formed cooperative stores to protect themselves in the event of future walkouts, and joined the Socialist Party and the IWW in ever-increasing numbers. Now facing the harsh realities of life in the mines, the immigrants brought in to replace the strikers in 1907 began to see past their ethnic and national differences and drift toward the Finns, who began to take leadership roles in the budding radical movement while opening up their ubiquitous Finn Halls for organizing efforts.

Spontaneous Strikers Organize

In the summer of 1916, independent action on the part of immigrant miners on Minnesota's Mesabi Iron Range, now the taproot of the powerful Steel Trust, once again resulted in a walkout. This time the Industrial Workers of the World (aka Wobblies) assisted in the conflict with the nation's most powerful corporation—the WFM had turned its back on radicalism and the Range's industrial workers had affiliated with the American Federation of Labor. That year the acute demand for iron ore caused by the Great War, the curtailment of European immigration, and an increasingly radical Range workforce seemed to bode well for the Wobblies' chances. The existence of a vibrant socialist movement among the immigrants who lived and worked on the Mesabi Range, especially among radical Finns, offered an additional ray of hope that IWW organizers simply could not pass up.

The grievances of the miners remained much the same. Housing on the Range continued to be expensive and prices for food and household necessities remained high, at times fifty or even 100 percent higher than prices for the same goods in Duluth or the Twin Cities of Minneapolis and St. Paul. Typical hours in 1916 for a miner still stood at ten, pay remained low, and the contract system, subject to the vagaries of favoritism and changing rates of pay, persisted across the Range, according to Betten. By the summer of 1916, conditions had become unbearable and the miners of Minnesota's Mesabi Iron Range walked off the job and began feverishly organizing their ranks. The exact origins of the strike remain obscure, though most accounts suggest that the Mesabi strike represented what labor historians call a "spontaneous" action. George West, writing in the September 1916 issue of the *International Socialist Review,* commented that the strike "started without any organization of any sort, and spread almost instantaneously through the iron range before any outside labor organization had participated." Historian Melvyn Dubofsky, in his classic *We Shall Be All,* also calls the strike spontaneous, though curiously he also details a flurry of organizational activity on the Range prior to the strike. The most detailed accounts seem to agree that on June 2 an Italian miner, Joe Greeni, angered over his short pay—a result of variations consequent to the hated and capricious contract system—threw down his pick and walked off the job. As the story goes, Greeni's act of frustration quickly escalated from one shift's "wildcat" walkout to a strike encompassing the whole Iron Range that involved anywhere from 10,000 to 20,000 miners.

Though the Finns did not dominate the strike numerically to the extent they had in the 1907 Range strike—blacklists and new waves of immigrants had diluted their ranks—they nevertheless provided much of the leadership, opened their Finn Halls for strikers to use as meeting places, and infused their radical sentiment into the rhetoric and ideology of the 1916 strike. After the failure of the WFM in 1907 and 1913, the Finns of northern Minnesota, rather than rejecting unionism, embraced the far more radical IWW in increasing numbers. Weeks prior to Greeni's precipitate action, Finnish organizers had sensed the restiveness of the Range's miners and had wired IWW headquarters in Chicago for Italian and Slavic organizers. Elizabeth Gurley Flynn had also toured the Range just prior to the strike, lecturing to enthusiastic crowds of radical Wobblies and industrial unionists across the Range in Finnish Industrial Union Halls.

After the strike began, word quickly made it to the IWW office in Duluth, where an active Marine Transport Workers' Union affiliated with the IWW made its headquarters. Wobbly organizer Arthur Boose wired Chicago with news of the strike and left immediately for the Range town of Aurora to stage what he hoped would be some "hot" meetings. In less than a week, the IWW sent a group of their most experienced organizers to the Range, prompting the Chisholm *Tribune-Herald,* which had been bought in January 1916 by a retired executive of the Oliver Mining Company, to caution citizens to "remain calm under the invasion of the I.W.W. agitators, who would commit rape upon the progress and tranquility of the [Range]." The organizers sent from Chicago were joined by a formidable contingent of locals, and by the end of June the IWW and its local organizers had set up five locals of the Metal Mine Workers' Industrial Union 490 with a membership numbering in the thousands. The miners' union had also drawn up a list of demands: the abolition of the contract system, the eight-hour day, bimonthly paychecks, a raise in pay, and immediate payment upon termination. Significantly, the miners' demands did not include the recognition of the IWW-affiliated union.

Employer and State Repression

In their battle against the miners, the owners and their allies once again possessed overwhelming economic might, the blessing of the state's government, a legion of armed mine guards, and control over the police. They also counted on their ability to whip up anti-radical chauvinisms in order to de-legitimize the strikers and justify their quick and brutal suppression. Of course, Minnesota's employers emphasized the foreignness and un-American qualities of the immigrant miners, as well.

Predictably, employers and authorities responded to the strike with overwhelming force. Minnesota Governor Joseph Burnquist granted the Oliver Mining Company the authority to deputize its private mine guards to help keep order and, by the end of June, the owners had augmented this force with some 1,000 additional guards recruited from outside of the Range and equipped them with riot sticks, guns, and deputies' badges. According to *Survey* journalist Marion B. Cothren, guards fanned out across the Range, "stationed at frequent intervals along the roads, silhouetted against the sky as they [stood], gun in hand, on the tops of the surrounding hills, stationed at the very doors of the miners' cottages," and patrolling the rural roads in armored cars. The Duluth sheriff, the symbol of state authority on the Range and widely regarded as an instrument of corporate and state anti-union sentiment, boasted that he deliberately did not look too deeply into the backgrounds of his recruits. According to newspapers, including the *New Republic, Survey,* and the IWW's *Solidarity,* the guards represented the "worst elements of society," from the gutters of Duluth, Minneapolis, and St. Paul, "any place where men could be found willing to go to the [R]ange, strap on guns, grasp riot sticks, pin deputy sheriff's badges on their shirts, and go forth to attack picket lines, menace strikers' parades, and brow-beat strikers wherever they should be met, singly or alone." These "Burly Booze Tanks" were, according to the Hibbing, Minnesota, strike paper, irritable, prone to violence, and almost instinctively hostile to the foreign striking miners.

In conjunction with the company's demonstration of brute force, newspapers sympathetic to the mine owners played on the nativist sentiments of some Range residents by invoking the threat of alien subversion. "The trail of the I.W.W.," asserted a letter writer in the Chisholm *Tribune-Herald,* "is one of blood" that would persist "as long as a single follower of their red emblem" remained on the Range. *Tribune-Herald* reporters accused the IWW of an "invasion" in order to "commit rape upon the progress and tranquility of the village," gravely warning that "rioting and violation of law and order must cease if it is necessary to place under arrest every deluded foreigner who has pledged allegiance to the I.W.W."

Critics reserved their most venomous denunciations for the Finnish miners, a "temperamentally morose, suspicious, sullen, self-centered and obstinate" group, according to one U.S. Army military intelligence operative, a people who "made ideal recruits for any ultra-radical labor agitation." The Finns, the agent continued, seemed to be "dissatisfied with any and all conditions and against the established order of things in general." Though estimates of Finnish participation in radical activities on the Range varied wildly, from a low of 15 percent to as high as 50 percent of the adult population of Range Finns, they formed a distinct and visible ethnic presence at the forefront of most organized radical agitations on the Range from the 1907 strike forward. At the same time that agents for employers working for the Department of Justice or military intelligence claimed that the Finns "were always ready to stir up trouble among the workmen" and that the Finns were "trouble breeders and a class not to be trusted," IWW reporters and organizers noted that the Finns seemed "easier to reach with industrial unionism than other . . . races," some claiming that if "the American Wobblies was as catty as the Finns, we would have some fighting union."

Empowered and encouraged to arrest strikers

on the slightest pretext and transport them to Duluth to face justice in company-dominated courts, the hired gunmen carried out their instructions immediately upon their arrival, selectively enforcing the law and harassing strikers' parades to provoke and intimidate the miners. On June 21, gunmen equipped with armored cars and rifles harassed parading strikers in Hibbing, causing a riot. The next day in the town of Virginia, gunmen followed the same strategy. When the parading miners resisted, this time the gunmen opened fire, killing a striking miner. The most significant single act of violence occurred as a result of selective law enforcement in Virginia, Minnesota, and though it was caused by neither Finns nor Wobblies, the disturbance was ultimately blamed on both. When gunmen pursuing complaints of "blind pigging," or bootlegging, raided the home of Nick Masonovich and his family in early July, Masonovich and his family resisted the invasion. In the pitched battle that followed, deputies killed Masonovich. One of his assailants, allegedly an ex-bouncer at a "house of ill-fame," was shot twice through the thigh.

Authorities arrested four Montenegrin miners and Mrs. Masonovich at the scene on charges of first-degree murder and sent them in chains to Duluth to await trial. Officials also decided to use Masonovich's murder as a pretext to round up the IWW organizers and remove them from the region. The next morning, sheriff's deputies—without warrants—pulled Wobbly organizers Carlo Tresca, Sam Scarlett, and Joseph Schmidt from their beds in a Virginia hotel, placed them under arrest, and sent them to the county jail in Duluth as accessories to murder. One hour later, five deputies woke a third Wobbly, Frank Little, in his hotel room and sent him in chains to Duluth on the same charge. Though none of the IWW organizers had been present at the shootings, prosecutors accused them all of first-degree murder, claiming that their speeches had caused the violence at Masonovich's house. Though many felt that the state likely could not successfully convict the Wobblies, authorities had nevertheless succeeded in removing their most able organizers.

The raid on Masonovich's blind pig was not a singular event, however. Rather, it represented one incident in a broader offensive that used liquor as a pretext for authorities to attack striking miners. The ubiquitous presence of saloons on the Range and the wide use of alcohol among the striking miners offered proof of barbarism to mine owners, who used temperance and prohibition as a means of policing miners' behavior, enforcing industrial discipline, and undermining the strike. Recently, historians have pointed out that that the saloon served many purposes for immigrant workers and that, while always a place to get drunk, the saloon ought to be viewed as having played a vital role that transcended its nominal function. According to historian Madelon Powers in *Faces Along the Bar,* the saloon "served as both shelter and staging ground" for its immigrant clientele. A "masculine domain" where workers could reinforce their sense of gender and group identity, the saloon buttressed ethnic identity in a foreign land, allowing workers to preserve a sense of their uniqueness in the corrosive landscape of American industry. As Finnish miner Matti Pelto recalled, after "experiencing the life of a tramp," the saloon was the place where Finnish immigrants "extinguished their longing for Finland." Saloons also played banker, post office, information exchange, and union hall. Saloons dotted the Iron Range—350 of them in the principal villages and towns of the region in 1912, run by native-born Americans, Poles, Scandinavians, Italians, Croatians, Slovenians, and Finns. Some of the earliest legitimate businesses Finns established on the Range in independent towns were saloons. Even when companies banned saloons on their locations and in the towns that they controlled, Finns defied regulations and bootlegged.

Liquor's critics, especially national crusaders for temperance and prohibition, believed saloons harbored vice and corruption and fostered the most debased and primitive instincts in men. The attitudes of the Women's Christian Temperance Union, for example, reflected common ideas concerning the evils of drink, especially in relation to work, criticizing as well the ways that saloons insulated workers from Americanizing influences. To them alcohol represented a constant temptation and distraction to the working class, hindered the functioning of a democratic government, corrupted youth, contributed to domestic violence, promoted other vices like gambling and prostitution, and, according to a letter by one Range schoolmaster, Burton O. Greening, spawned "swarm[s] of degenerate children" that would burden future generations. Prohibition sentiment also motivated employers who believed that temperance increased the efficiency of industry, the rationalization of production, and the successful control and scientific management—measured by the degree of political, social, and cultural subordination—of immigrant workers. Continually frustrated by working-class resistance to their efforts to promote prohibition on the Range, temperance advocates resorted to a curious instrument to achieve their ends and banish the alcohol trade: an almost half-century-old treaty imposed by the U.S. government on the Anishinaabeg (Ojibwe Indians) that prohibited the sale or use of alcohol on Indian lands.

During the 1916 miners' strike, alcohol and the so-called "Indian Lid" functioned as a tool that helped suppress radicalism. Immigrants' alcohol usage allowed Indian Bureau agents to patrol Range towns to ensure that no alcohol would make its way onto any Indian reservations and to break up blind pigs, hauling suspects, Indian and immigrant, to Duluth to face federal charges. Indian Bureau agents employed force as well as subterfuge to track down and arrest violators both on and off of Indian land, searching suspicious-looking residents on the slightest pretext and employing Indian decoys to shut down saloons. In fact, a frequent complaint leveled against the Indian Bureau bulls was the difficulty in telling the difference between the decoys and legal, non-Indian, drinking customers.

Opposed by an alliance of corporate, local, state, and federal authorities, by mid-summer the strike settled into something of a stalemate, with strikers' wives and children (less likely to be shot at though still subject to harassment and arrest) holding parades, and employers and mine guards conducting periodic raids and arrests of immigrant miners. At the end of July, Duluth's district attorney released several of the IWW organizers who had been arrested in the wake of the Masonovich killing for lack of evidence, and they rejoined the parading strikers who were now led by Elizabeth Gurley Flynn. Two IWW organizers along with eight others implicated by authorities in the incident, including Mrs. Masonovich, remained under arrest.

Making and Breaking the Working Class

By August, the miners' persistent struggle began to gain the sympathy and support of many Range politicians and national figures, among them Helen Keller. Several Range mayors called for federal mediation, a request likened by one hostile Duluth paper to asking the Mexican government to intervene on behalf of the villainous bandit Pancho Villa. Mediators did, in fact, visit the Range, though their efforts came to naught. Sensing the exhaustion of the miners, the companies rejected all overtures from the miners, the IWW, and local, state, and federal officials. By the end of the summer of 1916 miners began to drift back to work, pressured by a lack of funds, the imprisonment of key organizers, and threats and assaults from mining company gunmen. With winter fast approaching, several of the strike's leaders still in jail, and hunger stalking their families, the miners officially called off the strike on September 17, 1916.

Their efforts did not end in complete failure, however. The striking miners did win a 10 percent pay raise and, more importantly, the strike had forged a new regional working-class identity among the miners. The IWW locals also remained and the union had gained what seemed to be a more permanent foothold in the region. Moreover, though they experienced defeat in both the 1907 and 1916 strikes, the miners' labor radicalism had helped to galvanize the working-class population of the Iron Range and assisted some local politicians in leveraging significant concessions from the companies by other means. By the 1910s, increasing numbers of immigrants began to exercise their political power over the towns they lived in, and while they could not change the conditions of labor in the mines, they could use their civic power to tax to help improve their living conditions at home. Between 1913 and the onset of the Great Depression, the towns of the Iron Range used levies against the iron companies to finance road-building projects; electric improvements; the construction of heating plants, parks, schools, libraries, and extensive sanitation systems; and even a zoo. While radical miners challenged the companies at its gates, their elected officials and neighbors exacted a price for corporate intransigence on tax day.

Fearing renewed struggle the next spring, the Oliver Mining Company began to set up an elaborate—and costly—spy network to head off future conflicts. Minnesota's newspapers quickly picked up on the failure of the Steel Trust to discourage Range radicalism, especially among the Finns. In February 1917, in spite of the Steel Trust's best efforts to ferret out radicalism, one journalist writing in the *Mesabi Ore and Hibbing News* could still speculate that the "wonder of it all is that there has been no bloody revolution in Minnesota long before this." "Notwithstanding all the noise made by the Steel corporation and its subsidized newspaper," a Hibbing reporter noted that same month, the IWW "is gaining a following, in membership and sympathizers, that is fairly carrying the Big Fellows off their feet." Throughout the spring and summer of 1917, a continuous flurry of reports from corporate and government agents indicated the continued presence of radical activities.

In May, one government agent reported that "Finnish persons" in Biwabik, Minnesota, claimed that the IWW would soon "run this part of the country." In June, an agent for the vice president of operations of James J. Hill's Great Northern Railway indicated that the IWW had been giving the company trouble all summer, advising that "militia be retained at [the] head of [Lake Superior], especially on the Wisconsin side where the laws are more favorable to the IWW element, who have rented a building in . . . Superior [Wisconsin]." One Great Northern agent reiterated a preference for military action one month later, opining that "the soldier is the best antidote" for the IWW. In July as well, government agents sniffed out a possible alliance between the Non-Partisan League and the IWW Agricultural Workers' Organization in the fields of the Dakotas and Minnesota. Rather than receding after their supposedly disastrous defeat at the hands of the steel corporations, the Wobblies came roaring back, borne on the shoulders of Finnish immigrants. These immigrants joined the IWW in record numbers, adding 5,000 new members in summer of 1917 despite the network of corporation spies and government committees created to suppress their radicalism.

In spite of this efflorescence of radicalism on the Range, ultimately the Wobblies became the target of a sweeping federal dragnet during World War I. Rather than relying on the piecemeal efforts of corporations and local and state authorities, the federal government used the war and the Espionage and Sedition Acts of 1917 and 1918 to toss the IWW's organizers into jail across the nation. In the two years after the declaration of war, the Justice Department effectively silenced the last vestiges of the union, though they did not succeed in erasing the IWW entirely. While a significant portion of the miners on the Range maintained their radical beliefs and preserved the solidarity of the 1916 strike as best they could, they remained unorganized until the 1930s. Nevertheless, their struggles against the mining companies in 1907 and 1916 did accomplish a small but significant portion of what they had hoped to gain. While they did not bring about the industrial democracy that they struck for, they did transform their communities from rough, ethnically and racially segmented frontier mining settlements into modern towns that exhibited pride and a strong sense of a working-class American regional identity.

See also: Steel Strikes Before 1935, 351; Steel on Strike: From 1936 to the Present, 360.

Bibliography

Alanen, Arnold R. "The Locations: Company Communities on Minnesota's Iron Ranges." *Minnesota History* 48 (Fall 1982): 94–107.

Betten, Neil. "The Origins of Ethnic Radicalism in Northern Minnesota, 1900–1920." *International Migration Review* 2 (1970): 44–56.

———. "Riot, Revolution, Repression in the Iron Range Strike of 1916." *Minnesota History* 41 (Summer 1968): 82–94.

———. "Strike on the Mesabi—1907." *Minnesota History* 40 (Fall 1967): 340–47.

Chrislock, Carl H. *The Progressive Era in Minnesota 1899–1918.* St. Paul: Minnesota Historical Society, 1971.

Eleff, Robert M. "The 1916 Minnesota Miners' Strike Against U.S. Steel." *Minnesota History* 51 (Summer 1988): 63–74.

Hatcher, Harlan. *A Century of Iron and Men.* New York: Bobbs-Merrill, 1950.

Holbrook, Stewart H. *Iron Brew: A Century of American Ore and Steel.* New York: Macmillan, 1939.

Karni, Michael Gary. "Yhteishyvä—or, For the Common Good: Finnish Radicalism in the Western Great Lakes Region." Ph.D. diss., University of Minnesota, 1975.

Kivisto, Peter John. "Immigrant Socialists in the United States: The Case of Finns and the Left." Ph.D. diss., New School for Social Research, 1982.

Pinola, Rudolph. "Labor Politics on the Iron Range of Northern Minnesota." Ph.D. diss., University of Wisconsin, Madison, 1957.

Ross, Carl. *The Finn Factor in American Labor, Culture and Society.* New York Mills, MN: Parta Printers, 1977.

Syrjamaki, John. "Mesabi Communities: A Study of Their Development." Ph.D. diss., Yale University, 1940.

THE RISE AND FALL OF RANK-AND-FILE MINER MILITANCY, 1964–2007

Paul J. Nyden

> *There is never peace in West Virginia because there is never justice. Injunctions and guns, like morphia, produce a temporary quiet. Then the pain, agonizing and more severe, comes again. So it is with West Virginia. The strike was broken. But the next year the miners gathered their breath for another struggle. Medieval West Virginia! With its tent colonies on the bleak hills! With its grim men and women! When I get to the other side, I shall tell God Almighty about West Virginia.*
>
> —Mother Jones

Rank-and-file rebellions began rumbling in the coalfields from Pittsburgh and down the Ohio River after 1964, when dissident miners first challenged incumbents in international and district United Mine Workers (UMW) elections. Concern and anger also seethed through the coalfields of southern West Virginia during those years, particularly over black lung, or pneumoconiosis, a painful and often-fatal occupational disease. Doctors Isadore E. Buff and Donald Rasmussen helped spark those rumblings with speeches in union halls, schools, and churches.

A tragic spark ignited the growing resistance. Before dawn on November 20, 1968, a methane and coal dust explosion ripped through Consol No. 9, located between Mannington and Farmington in West Virginia's northern coalfields. The blast killed seventy-eight miners. People living in Fairmont, ten miles away, felt the tremors. The tragedy captured national attention.

Reactions from political and union leaders were telling and typical. Hulett C. Smith, governor of West Virginia, offered these words of comfort: "We must recognize that this is a hazardous business, and what has occurred here is one of the hazards of being a miner." Assistant Interior Secretary Jay Cordell was baffled: "The company here has done all in its power to make this a safe mine. Unfortunately, we don't understand why these things happen, but they do happen." United Mine Workers president W.A. "Tony" Boyle traveled to Mannington. With the still-smoking mine portal in the background, Boyle announced: "As long as we mine coal, there is always this inherent danger of explosion. . . . This happens to be one of the better companies as far as cooperation with our union and safety is concerned."

What a contrast to John L. Lewis, who visited Central Coal's No. 5 Mine in Centralia, Illinois, after an explosion killed 111 miners there on March 19, 1947. With coal dust on his face, preserved in a nationally famous photograph, Lewis said, "Coal is already saturated with the blood of too many men and drenched with the tears of too many surviving widows and orphans."

The 1969 Black Lung Strike

I.E. Buff, a Charleston heart specialist, launched a one-man crusade against coal operators for doing little or nothing to control coal dust inside their mines. Continuous mining machines, introduced in the 1950s, usually increased the density of dust in the air underground. In 1968, Buff told Governor Smith that only four coal miners in the history of West Virginia had ever received compensation for getting black lung. In November, Buff participated in a television program about black lung, which fatally afflicted miners as young as their early thirties. Charles Andrews, Provost of Health Sciences at West Virginia University, responded, "Coal dust may add to the difficulty, but cigarette smoking is perhaps the most important factor." UMW leaders in Charleston and Beckley showed little concern. Buff continued his speaking tour. The Consol No. 9 tragedy propelled his lonely crusade into a national issue. Some county physicians' groups also criticized Buff. The Cabell County Medical Society proclaimed pneumoconiosis was "a condition compatible with reasonable health." The Kanawha County Medical Society passed a resolution condemning "the activities of those in the medical profession who have unduly alarmed and have incited a number of those employed in the coal industry without first having presented scientific documentation of their findings."

On January 26, 1969, thousands of miners, their families, and supporters gathered in the Charleston Civic Auditorium. Miners proposed a new bill to the state legislature to control coal dust and compensate black lung victims. Tony Boyle was invited to the rally. He didn't show up. Three days later, R.R. Humphreys, president of UMW District 17 in Charleston, sent a letter to all local unions in his district ordering them not to donate money to the Black Lung Association (BLA), which working and retired miners and their spouses had formed in late 1968. Any miner joining the "dual association," Humphries warned, could be expelled from the union.

Dr. Rowland Burns, who engineered the Cabell County Medical Society's resolution about black lung, testified during legislative hearings in February. State Senator Warren McGraw, who came from a coal-mining family in Wyoming County, asked Burns how much coal operators were paying him to testify. To the surprise and amusement of many, Burns replied, "I have not been paid near enough. I can't tell you exactly what I've been paid, but I've been paid for my opinion and my time." The hearings dragged on.

Then, on February 18, a local dispute erupted at Westmoreland Coal's East Gulf Mine near the little town of Rhodell. As the day shift was about to go underground, one miner dumped water out of his lunch pail, the traditional signal of a strike. All the miners walked off the job. Asked why, they said they wanted the legislature to pass the black lung bill. The next day, fourteen nearby mines shut down. By the end of the week, 12,000 men were on strike. The next Monday, dozens of miners arrived in Charleston and jammed galleries inside the state capitol building, carrying signs that said, "No Law. No Coal." By Tuesday, 30,000 miners were out on strike.

Some blamed "Reds" and "Communists" for inciting the strike. Buff blamed the "sick Legislature" for refusing to act. A legislative committee reported out a very diluted black lung bill on February 26. Two days later, an amended bill that included a series of changes demanded by the miners passed the House of Delegates, ninety-four to one. The lone dissenter switched his vote. When the state Senate began debating the bill on March 5, 40,000 of West Virginia's 43,000 miners were on strike—illegally. The Senate passed a much weaker bill than the House did, and legislative arguments continued. On March 8, the final day of the regular legislative session, both houses approved a bill very much like the original House bill. Miners met the next day in Beckley and pledged not to return to work until Republican Governor Arch Moore signed the bill. Under pressure, Moore signed it on March 12 and miners returned to work. The new law created tough dust control standards and a state fund to compensate miners suffering from pneumoconiosis.

No one could ever explain exactly how the strike began and grew. Its spontaneity was helped by an ironclad principle of union coal miners never to cross picket lines or go to work after a fellow miner dumped his water. Robert Payne, a disabled African-American miner who was president of the Disabled Miners and Widows, described strike spontaneity during a 1972 interview. "The strike's the onliest weapon the rank and file has. . . . There wasn't no one person responsible for what happened in 1969. Everybody was responsible for it. It was all the miners and disabled miners striking to get this Black Lung law passed." Later that year, Congress passed the Coal Mine Health and Safety Act of 1969, a major advance over earlier mine safety laws.

West Virginia's twenty-three-day Black Lung Strike had three clear results. For the first time in history, the West Virginia Legislature recognized black lung as a compensable disease. Second, the threat of another wildcat strike, a much bigger one that would spread to several states, helped convince Congress to pass a new federal Coal Mine Health and Safety Bill, which became law on December 30. And third, the strike was the key factor convincing longtime UMW leader Jock Yablonski to run against Tony Boyle, the first major challenge to the union hierarchy in forty-three years. The West Virginia Black Lung strike was the longest and most successful political strike in modern U.S. labor history.

Joseph A. "Jock" Yablonski

Seven weeks after the Black Lung Strike ended, Joseph A. Yablonski, a member of the UMW's International Executive Board from western Pennsylvania, spoke at a Students for a Democratic Society rally at the University of Pittsburgh. Yablonski still publicly backed Boyle, who had become UMW president in 1963, three years after John L. Lewis retired. Speaking on May Day, Yablonksi said, the day was "labor's day to take stock of what is accomplished and what is yet to be accomplished and what is to be done in the interest of society." After talking about what coal miners and other workers needed, Yablonski paused. Students thought his speech was over.

Then, in his gravelly voice, he added, "There's one more thing we need to do in this country, and that's to get the hell out of Vietnam." Jock praised the militancy of young people in the 1960s. "Nothing was ever achieved in the world without getting militant. Young people in America today, if they are to cope with the wealth that is milking our country, better get militant or they are going to pay a terrible price in the future."

On May 30, 1969, Jock opened a press conference in Washington, DC, by quoting John L. Lewis, "When ye be an anvil, lay ye very still. But when ye be a hammer, strike with all thy will." Announcing his candidacy for UMW president, Yablonski said, "Today is the day I cease being an anvil." For more than six months, Yablonski waged a campaign that played a critical role in building a movement to democratize the union. But when the votes were counted, he lost 80,577 to 46,073—Boyle stole the election (two years later, U.S. District Judge William B. Bryant would order the UMW to conduct a new election to be supervised by the U.S. Department of Labor). At the end of December 1969, Yablonski, his wife, and daughter were murdered in their Washington, Pennsylvania, home. The three gunmen later went to prison. So did the man who hired them—Tony Boyle, the president of the United Mine Workers. At Yablonski's funeral, Miners for Democracy was born.

Rank-and-File Groups

The Black Lung Association (BLA), formed shortly before the Black Lung Strike, allied itself with Miners for Democracy. Charles Brooks, a black miner who worked thirty-two years in Kanawha County mines, was the BLA's first president. When Arnold Miller became the association's president in June 1970, he began publishing *The Black Lung Bulletin* with help from other miners and Volunteers In Service To America (VISTA) volunteers. By late 1971, the BLA had nearly twenty chapters in West Virginia, Kentucky, Virginia, and Tennessee. Many were politically active, and all chapters worked to help miners with pneumoconiosis apply for state and federal compensation benefits. Robert Payne, a miner for twenty-seven years before he was badly burned in a 1967 accident, had been one of Yablonski's strongest supporters in southern West Virginia. Payne remembered Yablonski's words at a Logan rally: "One thing I want you all boys to do is to keep the fight up. Now I'm going to win this election. But it is going to be stolen away from me. And I won't be able to prove it."

After Yablonski's death, Payne helped organize a meeting in Beckley in May 1970, inviting Boyle to meet with disabled miners. Boyle refused to come. Payne's new group, the Disabled Miners and Widows of Southern West Virginia, called for another wildcat strike in June against coal companies as well as the UMW for failing to help disabled miners. After it spread to neighboring coalfields in Ohio and Pennsylvania, this strike involved more than 40,000 miners. Payne believed the June 1970 strike helped keep the miners' rank-and-file movement alive and growing. In June 1972, Payne predicted Arnold Miller would defeat Boyle in the election for UMW president later that year—Miller did. Payne kept his organization alive after the election. It was always the most militant of the three coalfield reform groups, never giving up its commitment to direct action, protests, and strikes.

Hyden and Buffalo Creek

Two other mine tragedies—an explosion and a flood—increased the drive for coalfield reforms. On December 30, 1970, the first anniversary of the Coal Mine Health and Safety Act, thirty-eight miners died in an explosion in Hyden, Kentucky. At the instruction of company owners, miners used an illegal fuse to trigger a blast of between 100 and 200 sticks of dynamite. Mining laws prohibited the use of more than ten sticks in any underground detonation. Elburt Osborn, from the U.S. Bureau of Mines, said, "This disaster was not unexpected. We've had two good years since Farmington, and I think we can almost expect one of these a year."

On February 26, 1972, three Pittston Coal Co. slate dams collapsed near the head of Buffalo Hollow in Logan County. At 8:00 A.M., more than 120 million gallons of black water began surging down the narrow hollow in waves up to thirty feet high. Moving thirty miles an hour, the murky waters demolished most of sixteen mining towns before reaching the Guyandotte River, killing 125 and leaving 4,000 homeless. An eerily similar tragedy had struck the mining town of Aberfan, Wales, on October 21, 1966. After days of heavy rains, a slate dump collapsed, rolled down a mountainside and buried Pantglas Junior School, killing 116 children and twenty-eight adults, five of whom were teachers. The Aberfan tragedy sparked studies of dangerous slate dumps and impoundments in Great Britain and the United States.

But despite warnings from these studies—some specifically citing the Buffalo Hollow dam—coal companies like Pittston did nothing. In the wake of the Buffalo Creek disaster, Pittston Coal Vice President Francis J. Palamara said, "We're investigating the damage which was caused by the flood which we believe, of course, was an act of God." Palmara said there was nothing wrong with the dam, which was simply "incapable of holding the water God poured into it." During a citizen's protest meeting in the Buffalo Grade School in Accoville a month later, one older woman said, "I've lived at the top of the hollow for a long time. And I ain't never seen God up there driving no bulldozer dumping slate on the dam." Not to be outdone, Governor Arch Moore said, "The only real sad part about it [the news coverage] is that the state of West Virginia took a terrible beating which far overshadowed the beating which the individuals that lost their lives took, and I consider this an even greater tragedy than the accident itself."

Before Moore left office in January 1977, he settled a state lawsuit against Pittston Coal for $1 million, far less than the damage company negligence cost the state in reclamation and rebuilding expenses. Moore was accused of taking bribes from coal companies during his first two terms as governor between 1969 and 1977, but was never formally charged. In 1984, after eight years out of office, Moore again ran for governor and won. On May 8, 1990, Moore pleaded guilty to five federal felony counts of extortion, tax fraud, mail fraud, and obstruction of justice. Shortly after finishing his third term, on August 7, 1990, Moore began serving a two-year term at Maxwell Air Force Base in Montgomery, Alabama, where he helped prepare food for fellow inmates.

Beckley coal operator H. Paul Kizer played a major role in those indictments. Kizer told federal authorities he paid more than $723,000 in extortion money to Moore in 1985 and 1989 to receive black lung refunds and to qualify for lucrative "super tax credits."

The 1972 United Mine Workers' Election

In 1970, Lou Antal headed the first Miners for Democracy (MFD) ticket. He ran for president of District 5, which included coal counties near Pittsburgh. All the top three MFD candidates won. But pro-Boyle election officials tossed out ballots from three of the district's largest locals and counted illegal absentee ballots. Rank-and-file miners challenged the results of both the 1969 International and 1970 District 5 elections in federal court. In May 1972, three federal court rulings threw out the results of both those elections, ordering new ones. The rulings also ordered elections to be held in seven other UMW districts.

Later that month, 463 delegates from coal towns from Alabama to Nova Scotia gathered at Wheeling College (now Wheeling-Jesuit College).

Miners for Democracy, the Black Lung Association, and the Disabled Miners and Widows met to choose candidates and to write an election platform. There was still back-room dealing. On Saturday night, "pragmatism" convinced many that one principle in choosing the top MFD candidate should be, "No hunkies, no blacks," meaning no miners of Central or Eastern European heritage and no African-American miners. Antal, who had already run twice for District 5 president, quipped, "With this kind of an attitude, the only man truly eligible to run for UMW president would be a Native American Indian." Payne was also disturbed, but said, "During the campaign, I've been trying to get this thing ["No hunkies, no blacks"] squashed down. . . . But we want to get rid of Tony Boyle for good this time." On Sunday, the MFD convention nominated Arnold Miller, a disabled miner from Cabin Creek, near Charleston, West Virginia. Mike Trbovich, from western Pennsylvania (but whose father was born in Serbia) was nominated for vice president. Harry Patrick, from northern West Virginia, was nominated for secretary-treasurer.

The MFD platform reflected Yablonski's platform, identifying mine safety as the "foremost issue." The platform also demanded an overhaul of the union administration, democratic elections in all districts, moving the union headquarters back to the coalfields, a new contract increasing pensions and health benefits, and a six-hour workday. In December 1972, Miller beat Boyle 70,337 to 56,334, winning 55.5 percent of the vote. For the first time in the union's eighty-three-year history, a slate of rank-and-file candidates won. Miller's victory was followed by MFD victories in most district elections held in 1973.

Arnold Miller: A Disappointment

After Arnold Miller won election in December 1972, many UMW members no longer saw a need for independent rank-and-file groups. Miners for Democracy disbanded. The Disabled Miners and Widows met sporadically. Only the Black Lung Association remained active. In 1974, when Miller began negotiating a new contract, he worked behind the scenes, just like Boyle. A new contract was approved in December, but 44 percent of the miners voted against it. Distrust of Miller spread and a new wave of wildcat strikes protested company safety policies. In the summer of 1975, one strike involved 80,000 miners. The next summer, 120,000 miners walked off their jobs—nearly every union miner east of the Mississippi River. Smaller wildcat strikes, often shutting down just one mine, were common occurrences everywhere. Miller won reelection in June 1977 with just 39.8 percent of the vote. UMW Secretary-Treasurer Harry Patrick, backed by younger and more militant miners, got 24.9 percent. Lee Roy Patterson, a Boyle supporter from western Kentucky, received 35.3 percent.

After the election, Miller drifted further away from rank-and-file unionism. In November, he proposed expelling all "Communists" from the UMW and deporting them from the country. When Miller began negotiating a new labor contract in 1978, the union's thirty-nine-member Bargaining Council voted down his first draft on February 12. A second proposed contract went to UMW members for a vote. They rejected it on March 6. President Jimmy Carter then invoked anti-strike provisions of the Taft-Hartley Act. But after miners routinely ignored Carter's Taft-Hartley sanctions, a federal judge withdrew them one week later. The miners approved a third version of the contract, with 57 percent of the vote. The new version eliminated proposed repressive workplace disciplinary measures, increased wages slightly, increased pension benefits significantly, but reduced health benefits. *New York Times* reporter Ben A. Franklin summarized the bitter 110-day strike:

> Looming through the gritty Appalachian mist was one stirring fact. Although its leadership and its reputation and its treasury have been ruined, the rank and file of the United Mine Workers have emerged as unexpectedly, stubbornly, even heroically strong men and women. They overcame their own inept hierarchy and, to an extent that Mr. Miller obviously never believed possible, humbled the operators.

During the strike, union, church, community, and professional leaders set up Miners' Support Committees in cities like Pittsburgh, Cincinnati, Chicago, and New York. In Beckley, West Virginia, several doctors and health care professionals set up a free clinic to donate services to striking miners.

Miller openly discouraged the formation of these committees and blocked the distribution of strike relief funds until the miners returned to work. Ill from black lung, Miller retired in November 1979 and died in July 1985 at age at sixty-two.

Growing Assaults on Union Miners After 1980

McDowell County epitomizes the history of West Virginia's coalfields over the last thirty-five years. McDowell has produced more coal than any West Virginia county and at one time was the nation's leading coal-producing county. In 1970, coal mines generated 68.3 percent of all jobs and 78.9 percent of all wages there. McDowell County had the highest percentage of African-American miners in the Central Appalachian coalfields, many of them sons of miners who migrated from Alabama. Today, only a handful of African-American miners have jobs anywhere in West Virginia. McDowell was home to many model coal towns, like Gary, built by U.S. Steel. Welch, the county seat, was a bustling center. Stores, restaurants, and movie theaters packed Main Street.

Today, McDowell is the state's thirteenth-largest coal-producing county. Main Street is desolate. Hardly any African-American miners have jobs. Movie theaters are gone. Stores are boarded up. Office buildings are closed. A couple of restaurants still serve lunch, near the courthouse steps where Baldwin-Felts gunmen shot Sid Hatfield and Ed Chambers in January 1921. (In 1920, Hatfield and Chambers, police officers in Matewan, Mingo County, encouraged striking miners to arm themselves to stop company Baldwin-Felts guards from evicting them. In the fight that ensued, seven guards and four local residents died. The deaths of Hatfield and Chambers sparked the famous 1921 Armed March on Blair Mountain, the largest armed labor protest in U.S. labor history.) By 1980, coal employment began to decline throughout West Virginia, but coal production continued to increase.

A.T. Massey's Anti-Union Crusade

In the early 1980s, A.T. Massey Coal began a major crusade to keep the UMW out of new mines and bust the union at existing operations. The battle continued in 2007 at the Cannelton mining complex near Charleston, a mining operation that opened in 1871 near Smithers. Massey Energy, the new name of the company based in Richmond, Virginia, bought Cannelton after a Kentucky bankruptcy judge nullified a UMW contract signed by Horizon Natural Resources, the bankrupt company. His August 2004 ruling terminated all health care benefits the union contract promised miners and their spouses for the rest of their lives. Massey is now reopening the mining complex with non-union workers, the latest of its anti-union drives.

Massey began concentrating its coal acquisitions and operations in southern West Virginia twenty-five years ago because low-sulfur coal reserves help electric-power plants comply with Clean Air Act standards. Massey's first major battle came in 1981, when the UMW tried to organize the new Elk Run mining complex in Boone County. This strike signaled a turning point in a half-century of union strength in the Central Appalachian coalfields. Massey kept the UMW out of Elk Run after a long and bitter organizing effort that included the arrests of dozens of miners, including Cecil Roberts, now the union's president. The second major battle came when the UMW called a "selective strike" on October 1, 1984, against several Massey subsidiaries in southern West Virginia and eastern Kentucky. Unlike Elk Run, these mines were already operating with union workers. In 1984, Massey refused to sign a new union contract at subsidiaries including Rawl Coal Sales, Rocky Hollow Coal Co., and Sprouse Creek Processing. Today, Massey Energy is the largest coal producer in West Virginia and the fourth-largest coal company in the country. Just 170 of the company's more than 5,500 employees are UMW members, most of who work in coal preparation plants.

Donald L. Blankenship, a young company accountant in 1984, played a major role in leading strikebreaking efforts in 1984–85, when E. Morgan Massey still headed the company. In early 1985, scores of miners were arrested. Tensions increased in late May when a sniper killed a truck driver hauling coal for non-union Massey operations in eastern Kentucky. Massey used barbed wire, German shepherd dogs, armed guards, and video cameras to intimidate miners from entering company property during protests. The fifteen-month strike, the longest authorized strike in UMW history, ended in December 1985. Some union miners began working alongside strikebreakers hired by Massey. But Massey fired UMW strike leaders and refused to sign new union contracts.

Richard Trumka, who became UMW president in 1982, coordinated the 1984–85 strike, focusing on legal efforts rather than direct action. Trumka, now secretary-treasurer of the AFL-CIO, opposed mass demonstrations, marches, and sit-ins to block roads near Massey mining operations. The UMW lost.

The 1989 Pittston Strike Brings Victory

Things turned out differently in 1989, when Pittston Coal tried to eliminate the union from its Central Appalachian mines. Pittston wanted to force miners to work weekend shifts, change work rules, subcontract work to nonunion companies, and cancel health benefits. On April 5, 1989, 1,200 miners in Virginia and 500 in West Virginia walked out on strike. (In a very unusual move, Massey allowed Pittston to send its strikebreakers to work weekend shifts at Massey's Elk Run mining complex, helping Pittston fill its coal contracts.) But this time, the union ran things differently. Led by former UMW organizer Eddie Burke and then-UMW vice president Cecil Roberts, massive demonstrations blocked roads near Pittston mines. One march involved 20,000 union, religious, and community leaders in southwestern Virginia. The Pittston strike climaxed in mid-September when union miners took over the Moss No. 3 Preparation Plant in Russell County, Virginia, and shut down coal production for a week.

The union won a new contract, though it was not perfect. "But the terms of the agreement were vastly more favorable to the union than anyone dreamed would be possible when Pittston first set out to break the union, to drop all health care obligations to retirees, and to bust up the BCOA [Bituminous Coal Operators' Association]," wrote Jim Sessions, a strike leader quoted by Stephen L. Fisher. Pittston executives admitted they were caught off guard by the ability of the union to organize massive and peaceful resistance.

Coalfield Changes in the 1990s and Beyond

During the 1990s, the coal industry and coal town life continued changing. First, increasing numbers of mountaintop removal mines hurt union organizing efforts. Surface miners more resemble construction workers than underground miners, and tend to be less militant. In 2004, nearly 37 percent of the 151.7 million tons mined in West Virginia came from mountaintop removal and other surface operations. Mountaintop removal mines typically level mountains and remove up to a dozen coal seams. These operations drove wedges between the union and local residents angered by the total destruction of nearby mountains. They also caused conflicts between the union and environmentalists.

Second, steel companies began selling their captive mines throughout Central Appalachia. Historically, steel companies were the industry's best employers. They built the nicest towns and had the best safety records, and hired more African-American miners. When steel companies—faced with economic difficulties of their own from cheap foreign steel imports—sold mines and high-quality metallurgical coal reserves, Massey stepped in to buy them. Today, Massey owns more than 75 percent of all U.S. metallurgical coal reserves.

Third, classic coal company towns continued disappearing as employment declined and people moved. In the early 1900s, people traveling to coal towns had to ride railroad trains. Early coal companies built their own towns, since most areas with major coal reserves were basically uninhabited. By the 1950s, most people owned cars and drove on the growing public highway system in Central Appalachia. But classic coal towns still existed and thrived. In earlier years, coal companies reigned supreme in company towns. They owned all the homes. They owned company stores and paid miners in company-issued scrip to make purchases. They owned the schools, the churches, and the meeting halls.

U.S. Steel, Bethlehem Steel, Wheeling-Pittsburgh Steel, Eastern Associated Coal, Pittston Coal, and Consolidation Coal built scores of mining towns in Appalachia over the years. Massey Energy and Arch Coal never built coal towns. Between the 1920s and 1950s, nearly every industrial town throughout Appalachia and the Deep South had a baseball team—towns from the chemical cities lining the Kanawha Valley to coal towns scattered throughout West Virginia's mountains, down to the tobacco and textile mill towns in the Piedmont region of the Carolinas. Coal operators and factory owners often gave special vacation and traveling privileges to their best baseball players during those summers. Coal companies could evict striking miners from their homes and often did. But company towns also created social ties between miners and mining families. Residents of company towns knew each other and felt a real solidarity.

Fourth, increasing geographical mobility helped companies like Massey push the gradual decline of coal towns a step further. Declining employment made it harder to find mining jobs. So did the increasing number of people available to work at any given mine, since they could drive 100 miles or more to go to work every day. By 1980, companies could afford to fire local union workers, in part because they could attract replacements so easily. Geographic dispersal also discouraged social interaction. After an eight-hour shift, miners rarely join their fellow workers for a quick beer at a local bar on their way home.

Fifth, the character of the coalfields also changed as some major companies began hiring "contract mine operators," small companies that operate mines on land owned or controlled by the major companies. A.T. Massey and Island Creek Coal led this trend, hiring 750 contract mine operators between 1977 and 1993. Massey used nearly 500 contractors, including 247 in West Virginia and 176 in Kentucky. Island Creek used at least 250 contractors, including 177 in West Virginia and 84 in Kentucky.

Most of these contract operators disappeared or went bankrupt by the end of 1993, typically owing millions of dollars in wages and benefits, unpaid Workers' Compensation Fund premiums, and a variety of federal and state taxes. Between 1980 and 1993, Massey and Island Creek produced the majority of their coal from mines they operated directly. But the majority of fatalities occurred in small mines operated by contractors. During those years, thirty-eight miners died in mines affiliated with Massey or Island Creek in West Virginia. Of those, twenty-seven died in contract mines. In Kentucky, thirty-two miners died in mines producing coal for Massey or Island Creek, twenty-three of them in contract mines.

Production also shifted to Wyoming's nonunion coalfields during these years. In 2003, the nation produced nearly 1.1 billion tons of coal. The top three states were Wyoming with 376.3 million tons (35 percent of the total); West Virginia, 145.9 million tons; and Kentucky, 112.7 million tons.

In 1969, when the Black Lung Strike erupted, 41,941 miners produced 139.3 million tons of coal. About 95 percent of West Virginia's miners were union. In 2003, the state had 17,014 miners who produced 145.9 million tons of coal. Perhaps one-third of those miners were union members.

The Personal Impact of Tragedy

Under constant pressure from large companies to produce more coal for less money, many coal contractors took shortcuts. The day before his fifth birthday, a boy named Eddie turned the pages of his little scrapbook, looking at pictures of the father he never knew: his dad cradling him the day he was born in a Logan hospital and his dad holding him at home when he was an infant. Eddie Walter Bailey Sr., his father, died on March 8, 1990, the day he turned thirty. Little Eddie was fifteen months old. At 8:25 that morning, just after the day shift began, Bailey's "head was crushed like a grape between the canopy [of a mine shuttle car] and a roof bolt," the legal papers said. Bleeding from his mouth and nose, Bailey reached the surface, where he stopped breathing.

"Eddie never had a daddy to love him. Nothing but pictures," said Bailey's widow, Beulah. "All my baby has is pictures." Eddie Walter Bailey Sr. worked at Brandy No. 3, a small contract operation mine near Holden operated by Carey Cline for Island Creek. Bailey ran a shuttle buggy, a machine twenty-eight feet long that hauled coal from the continuous miner to a conveyor belt that hauled it outside. Cline altered that shuttle buggy, designed for mines with higher seams, so it could fit into his mine because it could haul more coal than smaller models designed for smaller mines like Brandy No. 3. Cline's mechanics sheared six inches off posts that supported the steel canopy over the operator's head, then welded the canopy back.

Lowering the canopy left a space just four inches high for Bailey to see while driving his shuttle buggy. Crammed inside the operator's compartment that morning, Bailey stuck his head outside to see where he was going. When he did, his head struck a block of wood bolted into the mine roof. Bailey probably knew he was in danger. But miners, especially those working in small contract mines, take chances. "The fear of losing your job is sometimes greater than the fear of losing your life," said Stephen Webber, then the director of the West Virginia Office of Miner's Health, Safety and Training.

Coalfield Politics Today

Coal operators have always been involved in politics, trying to elect sympathetic state and federal officials. In 2004, Massey President Donald L. Blankenship took coal's political involvement to a new level. For years, Blankenship, like many operators, contributed thousands of dollars to pro-industry candidates. But in 2004, Blankenship spent more than $3.1 million of his own money to defeat pro-labor West Virginia State Supreme Court Judge Warren McGraw. McGraw's defeat is already making it more difficult for plaintiffs to win favorable rulings from the five-member court. (In November 2006, a similar attempt by Blankenship turned out very differently. In West Virginia House of Delegates elections, Blankenship spent $3.7 million of his own money buying television, radio, and mail ads attacking Democratic candidates and backing Republicans—a total amount nearly as much as all election committees for all House candidates put together spent. But on Election Day, just one of the forty-two Democrats Blankenship targeted lost and Democrats increased their majority from sixty-eight to seventy-two in the 100-member House.)

In addition to broad political issues, Blankenship had one personal compelling reason to defeat McGraw. Hugh Caperton, owner of Harman Mining, sold high-quality metallurgical coal from his mines in Grundy, Virginia, to steel mills operated by LTV Corp. through United Coal in Boone County. After Massey bought United in 1997, Blankenship took over Harman's ten-year coal supply contract and bankrupted Harman. Caperton sued Massey in Virginia and won $6 million. Caperton then sued Massey in West Virginia and won $50 million, almost all of it in compensatory damages, in an August 2002 Boone County verdict. With interest, that verdict is now worth more than $70 million. In 2008, the case was on appeal to the United States Supreme Court.

Blankenship's contributions to the 2004 West Virginia Supreme Court race included:

- $2.5 million of the $3.5 million raised by a group he set up called "And For The Sake of the Kids"—the largest 527 group in any state Supreme Court race in the country. The group's negative television ads used questionable information to attack McGraw for being "soft" on sex and drug offenders.
- $515,708 to buy radio, newspaper, and television ads supporting Brent Benjamin, the Republican who defeated McGraw.
- $100,000 to Citizens for Quality Health Care, another 527 political organization attacking McGraw.
- About $50,000 to "West Virginia Wants to Know," a group that ran ads against McGraw and his brother, Attorney General Darrell McGraw.

Robert Rupp, a political scientist at West Virginia Wesleyan College, believes the ongoing population shift out of the overwhelmingly Democratic coalfields and the demise of local businesses both help Republicans. "Wal-Marts have taken over the state. Big is better. We have gone from retail [the local hardware store] to wholesale [Wal-Mart]. Television ads are wholesale politics," Rupp told the *Charleston Gazette* in October 2005. "The old age of retail politics is gone. . . . Now you can beat somebody [Warren McGraw] with nobody [Brent Benjamin]."

A Third World

Ronald D. Eller compared Appalachia's mountain counties to third world nations in his 1982 book *Miners, Millhands and Mountaineers: Industrialization of the Appalachian South, 1880–1930.* "Without local or regional markets, the economic structure of the mountains was solely dependent upon exterior demand. . . . This condition of growth without development placed the mountains in a highly vulnerable relationship to the larger market system. . . . Despite the vast natural wealth within its borders, the southern mountains remained comparatively poor—not because it was backward, but because its wealth enriched the modernizing centers in other parts of the country." In 1884, the West Virginia Tax Commission published a remarkable study warning West Virginians their state would soon "be despoiled of her wealth" in coal, oil, natural gas, and timber. "The question is whether this vast wealth shall belong to persons who live here and who are permanently identified with the future of West Virginia, or whether it shall pass into the hands of persons who do not live here and who care nothing for our State except to pocket the treasures which lie buried in our hills."

In 1974, I closed my doctoral dissertation with these words: "Today, thousands of railroad cars leave the mountains every day, overflowing with coal. When they return, they are empty. The people of Appalachia have nothing to say about how that coal is used, nor about who reaps the harvest of riches from their mines." Today, in 2007, all these statements remain true.

See also: Strikes in the United States Since World War II, 226; Steel on Strike: From 1936 to the Present, 360; Coal Miners on Strike and the Formation of a National Union, 449; Mesabi Iron Miner's Strike, 461.

Note

Originally published as Paul Nyden, "Rank-and-File Rebellions in the Coalfields, 1964–80," *Monthly Review* 58, no. 10 (March 2007).

Bibliography

Eller, Ronald D. *Miners, Millhands and Mountaineers: Industrialization of the Appalachian South, 1880–1930.* Knoxville: University of Tennessee Press, 1982.

Fisher, Stephen L., ed. *Fighting Back in Appalachia: Traditions of Resistance and Change.* Philadelphia: Temple University Press, 1993.

Nyden, Paul. "Coalfield Contracts: Mining at What Price?" Ten-article series, *The Sunday Gazette-Mail* and *The Charleston Gazette* (November 7–December 26, 1993).

———. "Miners for Democracy: Struggle in the Coal Fields." Ph.D. diss., Columbia University, 1974.

———. "Rank-and-File Organizations and the United Mine Workers of America." *Insurgent Sociologist* 8, no. 2/3 (Fall 1978): 25–39.

Part V, Section 2

Infrastructure Industry Strikes

Introduction by Benjamin Day

Infrastructure industries—those sectors that support a broader economy and culture, whether local, national, or global—are the foundation of a modern society. The development of new infrastructure industries, particularly in the fields of communication and transportation, transform entire economies and create pressures that alter the nature of work. The introduction of the telegraph, telephone, radio, and, more recently, digital and satellite-based wireless communication have had a dramatic impact on a wide range of industries; as have the introduction of railways, urban trolley systems, national roadways supporting a national trucking industry, and airplanes; and the spread of electricity-based energy through coal, natural gas, or nuclear power. Over the years, older infrastructure industries such as shipping have undergone changes so fundamental that they amount to the emergence of new infrastructure.

Virtually all infrastructure industries are established with some type of large-scale government intervention. These "connective institutions" are developed in the name of and imbued with a public interest. However, in the United States many basic infrastructure industries have never been properly public, but rather developed as private enterprises regulated by the state to a greater or lesser degree. Depending on the outcome of political contests, government regulation took a stronger or weaker form. Where legislators deemed infrastructural goods and services unsuitable for market competition, they established regulatory bodies that limited the market access of private entities, established entry barriers, set up industry standards, and implemented price controls. The reach of such regulation could be extensive, as in the case of the Bell System's monopoly in the telephone industry; or it could be more limited, as in the regulation of urban trolley systems.

Given the nature of infrastructure industries and their regulation, workers have faced a unique set of common restraints as well as opportunities, and have shared a similar historical trajectory distinct from their counterparts in the public and private sectors. The essays in this section illustrate the shared characteristics of infrastructure strikes.

The first common characteristic of industrial conflict across infrastructure industries is that disruptions in services quickly led to the immobilization of vast portions of the economy, up- and downstream from the industrial action, as well as the incidental disruption of cultural and social routines. For this reason strikes within infrastructure industries were quickly politicized and infrastructure workers often faced restrictive or exceptional legal constraints. Many infrastructure workers are not covered by the National Labor Relations Act (NLRA), do not enjoy an official right to strike, or may be ordered back to work as a perceived breach of national security. This pivotal position in the economic and social supply chain, however, also means that infrastructure workers have been uniquely situated to give and receive solidarity. For this reason, class consciousness and relations with other unions and working-class organizations are exceptionally important in the history of infrastructure industry class conflict.

Secondly, infrastructure industries were regularly revolutionized, and particular employers were vulnerable to competition from new technologies. The dominant institutions of communication, transportation, and energy for one generation have rarely been the dominant institutions of the next generation. This means that every infrastructure industry must be organized anew, and that displacement is a constant threat for almost every generation of workers. The implications of industrial reinvention for working-class militancy, particularly the willingness of workers to go on strike, have been profound. This theme recurs throughout the essays in this section, a number of which describe dead or dying industries.

Lastly, in the United States many infrastructure industries that were regulated during the New Deal era in the 1930s and 1940s were deregulated over the 1970s and 1980s by a coalition of free-market conservatives opposing market regulation and left liberals opposed to the consolidated power of regulated big business. As a consequence, industries such as airlines, trucking, and telecommunications fragmented, with new players entering the market, undercutting the incumbent companies, and sparking massive restructuring. Following this initial fragmentation, each of these industries saw a rapid sequence of bankruptcies and reconsolidation through mergers and acquisitions. The result was the emergence of a new class of unregulated oligopolies governing the country's infrastructure, with sweeping consequences for labor and consumers. At the same time, many of these same companies have become leading players in a growing global infrastructure, supporting transnational supply chains and communications. Globalization has played a dramatic role in restructuring and in many cases relocating the global telecommunications, shipping, and aerospace industries. Again, the consequences for strike activity have been far-reaching.

The unique characteristics of infrastructure industries have made for many dramatic walkouts. Knowing full well that they work in crucial industries, infrastructure workers have used the power of their position to wage strikes. Knowing, too, that their actions could have adverse impacts on the public, these same workers have reached out to their fellow citizens to argue that it is their employers and not their strikes that represent the real threat to the community. In many cases, these arguments have carried the day, inspired vigorous solidarity, and helped to win strikes. At other times, infrastructure workers have failed to arouse public sympathy, making it that much easier for state authorities, whether in the form of the police or the judiciary, to crush their strikes.

The essays in this section also illustrate some of the distinctions between infrastructure industry strikes. These differences often rested on the particular form of regulation for each industry. For example, regulation in the trucking industry allowed for the continued survival of small local firms, making it easy for the Teamsters to wage and win local and even national strikes into the 1970s. By contrast, telephone and telegraph workers faced large monopoly employers with virtually unlimited resources and considerable political power; winning strikes against such employers was extremely difficult.

Other distinctions arose from the nature of the job. For example, with few differences in skill and a history of shared exploitation, longshore workers built extensive and consistent solidarity, making it possible for them to win many strikes. Conversely, airline workers were divided into different unions by skill and found it very difficult to build the joint efforts necessary to defeat their large airline employers.

During the late nineteenth and much of the twentieth century, infrastructure workers were some of the most consistently militant and class-conscious workers. Even as their industries grew and changed, they built and maintained some of the most powerful unions in the country. Now, as their industries are restructured by deregulation and globalization, it remains to be seen if they will create new tools for building solidarity.

LABOR UPHEAVAL ON THE NATION'S RAILROADS, 1877–1922

Theresa Ann Case

In 1902, before a convention of the Brotherhood of Locomotive Firemen, President Theodore Roosevelt, in a passage quoted by historian Paul Michel Taillon, praised the attributes of railway workers:

> There is in modern life with the growth of civilization, with the growth of luxury, a special tendency to the softening of the national fiber. . . . It is a good thing that there should be a large body of our fellow citizens in whom the exercise of the old, old qualities of courage and daring resolution and unflinching willingness to meet danger. . . . A man is not going to be a fireman or an engineer or serve in any other capacity well on a railroad long unless he is a man.

The reminiscences of railroad men Henry Clay French, Charles B. George, and J.J. Thomas in some ways struck this same chord. They recalled the heavy risks of railroad employment, but also celebrated the occupation as, in Taillon's words, "a heroic confrontation with the task." The "task" involved performing one's job well, toughing out even the worst conditions, and doing everything possible to avert disaster. The startling statistics on railway accidents—one in twelve killed or injured in Kansas in 1885, for example—also confirm Roosevelt's notion that railroaders of this era were vigorous, rough-and-tumble men of character and integrity. These traits are not accessible to everyone, he suggests—individuals either possess them or do not.

Roosevelt's portrait of railroaders as rugged individualists ignores, however, the frequency and intensity of their collective approaches to improving safety, wages, hours, and work rules. In the nearly half century of railway expansion and consolidation between 1877 and 1922, railroaders launched multiple strikes that extended over hundreds and sometimes thousands of miles of track and attracted the active support of their neighbors, wives, children, and elected officials. In examining the pattern of nineteenth-century railroad strikes, historian Shelton Stromquist called this period the "audacious era." It is a different story of daring railroaders than the one that Roosevelt told.

The term "railroaders" conceals far more than it reveals. Deep fault lines existed among railroad workers on the basis of skill, race, and ethnicity. Engineers, firemen, and conductors were skilled workers who typically belonged to railroad brotherhoods—the Brotherhood of Locomotive Engineers (BLE), the Brotherhood of Locomotive Firemen (BLF), and the Order of Railway Conductors (ORC). These unions began as fraternal or mutual aid societies but eventually pursued trade unionism, albeit cautiously and with the aim of fostering cooperation between themselves and railroad officials. Skilled shopmen, such as boilermakers, machinists, and blacksmiths; semiskilled brakemen and switchmen; and unskilled trackmen and laborers stood outside the major brotherhoods, held less leverage in the workplace, and tended to sympathize with industrial unionism. Switchmen and shopmen were especially prone to an inclusive approach, because in the course of their workday they had regular contact with railroad men of various skill levels.

Much less permeable than the line between skilled and less-skilled, brotherhood and nonbrotherhood, was the racial and ethnic divide on the railways. Brotherhood members were white, usually native-born, and generally saw the unskilled as degraded, dependent, and unmanly, in part because they associated common labor with African Americans, Mexicans, European immigrants, and the Chinese. The ranks of the unskilled were mixed racially and ethnically, but native- and foreign-born white workers invariably dominated the positions (e.g., braking, apprenticing in shops) that were traditionally paths to skilled work.

The Great Strike of 1877, the 1885–86 Gould System strikes, the 1894 Pullman strike, and the 1922 Shop Workers strike represent major labor upheavals on the nation's roads. They have a number of themes in common. First, a tension persisted between the federal government and local sources of authority over how to approach the strikers. The federal judiciary influenced the parameters of this debate by increasingly ruling against strikers and limiting the available courses of action. A second pattern involves the declining fortunes of less-skilled western railway workers, particularly shopmen, brakemen, and switchmen, all of whom played a progressively more important role in organizing and spreading strike activity and who often found themselves in direct conflict with brotherhood leadership or members. Finally, in protesting railway policies, these workers at times made alliances across racial, ethnic, and skill lines and rejected nonrailroader participation or attention.

The Great Strike of 1877

The Great Strike began as a railway conflict but quickly took on the character of a broad-based, class-wide revolt against railroad monopolists and managers. Railroad workers generally sought to discourage violence and were underrepresented in the strike's riotous crowds. On the one hand, the Great Strike was not simply a railroad strike, as it involved other occupations and a wide array of issues. On the other hand, the strike held special significance for railroaders, who suffered particularly repressive measures in its wake. These measures contributed to a growing rift among railroaders over industrial versus craft-based approaches to the "labor question."

The roots of the Great Strike lay in the deepest economic crisis in United States history to that point—the depression of 1873–79, which sent thousands of businesses into bankruptcy. Historian Alexander Keyssar has found that during the most severe period of the crisis almost one-third of workers in Massachusetts were employed only four months out of the year. In the year of the Great Strike itself, as many as 3 million Americans lacked work entirely and more than four-fifths of those working were underemployed.

The desperation that many workers experienced produced a shift in labor activists' view of the relationship between employers and employed. Free-labor ideology, with its emphasis on cooperation between capital and labor, had attracted most postwar Americans. But in the wake of the Panic of 1873, historian Eric Foner argues, "Labor increasingly abandoned older free labor shibboleths in favor of a more forthright recognition of the permanence of the wage system and the reality of conflict between employer and employee." Across the country—from Tompkins Square in New York City to eastern Pennsylvania coal mines—wage cuts, layoffs, anti-union tactics, and the lack of relief galvanized both the unemployed and the employed to action. The railroad industry was likewise restive, as the *Railroad Gazette,* an industry journal, warned its readers in 1874: "Strikes are no longer accidents but are as much a disease of the body politic as the measles or indigestion are of our physical organization." Indeed, from 1872 to 1874, railroaders on eighteen different railroads participated in walkouts in response to demands for longer hours at increasingly lower wages, crew reductions that left equipment and roads neglected, and ironclad (anti-union) contracts. These same issues sparked the Great Strike in July 1877.

On July 16, 1877, firemen and brakemen on the Baltimore & Ohio Railroad in Martinsburg, West Virginia, immediately decided to strike upon learning that their wages were to be cut by 10 percent. In little more than a week, the walkout had spread to Baltimore, Pittsburgh, Columbus, Chicago, Terre Haute, Kansas City, and San Francisco. In Baltimore, Pittsburgh, and other cities and towns, discontented nonrailroaders and the unemployed joined crowds that destroyed railroad property, often with the clear sympathy of police or militia. In some areas, large crowds attacked federal troops brought in to crush the strike. According to contemporary estimates, the Great Strike involved at its apex upwards of 80,000 railroad workers and over 500,000 others. Most of the affected lines were east of the Mississippi River, but western roads such as the Missouri Pacific were also struck.

Historian Shelton Stromquist reveals how the strike unfolded in one locale—Hornellsville, New York. There, a strike committee formed after the Erie Railroad fired a group of men for contacting management about employee grievances. Upon receiving news that a strike in Martinsburg was extending west, the committee organized their own strike. Participants began with the traditional strategy of placing coupling pins in secret locations, thereby preventing the movement of trains through the town, which because it was a central switching site on the Erie, affected traffic on the railroad generally. Strikers and their supporters and families also physically blocked trains, soaped the rails to slow the trains and then uncoupled their cars, and attempted to shame engineers and firemen who continued to work. They boycotted shop- and innkeepers who they believed undermined the strike and asked saloons in town to suspend business during the conflict. Although strikers enjoyed the support of the town's leading citizens even after state troops arrived in town, once troops took over the switching yards and began to arrest strikers en masse, support for the effort withered and railroad officials succeeded in imposing most of their terms.

In St. Louis, the strike precipitated a general strike, the "first truly general strike in history," according to historian Philip S. Foner. After strikers successfully blockaded freight traffic, unskilled workers as well as skilled ones (coopers, molders, and mechanics) walked off their jobs, shutting down about sixty factories in the city. Many had demands of their own for higher wages and shorter working hours, such as employees of a beef cannery, who sought more than double their current wages. But broader labor demands captured the strike's participants as well: marchers 10,000 strong assembled in Lucas Market and adopted resolutions calling for an eight-hour day and child labor laws.

St. Louis was spared serious violence, but riots and bloodshed marked the conflict in a host of other areas across the nation. Philadelphia mobs set fire to railroad property after militia shot into a crowd of strikers and their supporters. The fire spread and was not extinguished until the next day, leaving thirty-nine railroad buildings, over 100 engines, forty-five passenger cars, and more than 1,200 freight cars destroyed. Pittsburgh for a time came under the control of crowds, which overcame local police and state militia and then looted stores and freight cars, eventually doing somewhere between $5 million and $7 million worth of damage. Anti-railroad feeling there was strong due to the heavy-handed policies of the Pennsylvania Railroad. Street fights broke out between strikers and police in Chicago, killing forty to fifty people, and in East St. Louis, police fired into a hostile crowd, taking eleven lives. All told, over 100 mostly innocent onlookers died in clashes with militia, police, and federal troops. This was the first time that federal troops intervened on a national scale to crush labor unrest. A total of nine governors called upon President Hayes for federal troops. These troops played the role of strikebreaker as well as peacekeeper.

In his study of Buffalo, Albany, and Syracuse, New York, historian David Stowell discovered that a significant aspect of the violence involved not labor issues but community concerns that railroad companies had long ignored or frustrated. Specifically, many working-class and poor neighborhoods had for years endured the pollution, noise, and danger that came with railroad expansion. Railway tracks cut across busy public intersections, damaging or ruining nearby small shops and businesses, and railroad accidents killed and injured more nonrailroaders than railroaders. To little avail, citizens had petitioned their local leaders to force railroad companies to provide flagmen and rescind plans for laying more track. Railroad workers' walkout and commitment to stopping freight traffic unleashed a flood of resentment among working-class, unemployed, and middle-class nonrailroaders, who often came into conflict with striking railroaders over the strike's main goals and strategies. While, as Stowell points out, the composition of riotous crowds remains a historical mystery, the limited evidence available suggests that participants in the Great Strike represented a mix, and sometimes a clash, of interests and ideals.

The mainstream press's perception of the Great Strike was that an undifferentiated working-class mass, rather than the usual suspects—immigrants and radicals—was responsible for the violence and destruction. As historian Eugene Leach has observed, the strike "confounded the crucial distinction between riotous workers and law-abiding ones" that had dominated elite understandings of crowd action. "The riots seemed to spill across divisions of occupation, ethnicity, geography, and even gender, expressing resentments widely shared in the working class." A number of commentators worried that the events of 1877 were a harbinger of a class-based revolution. Viewed in this light, strikes threatened not merely economic chaos, but also widespread violence, social disarray, and class hatred.

Authorities responded to the strike with a number of policies that limited independent working-class organization on the railroads and elsewhere. First, while the push for an expanded federal army (to suppress future labor unrest) failed, state governments established National Guard units that gained favor among business owners, and Chicago and other major cities invested more money in local police forces. Second, striking railroad workers in 1877 and thereafter faced special legal impediments. During the strike, United States District Judge Walter Q. Gresham declared any striker who obstructed the movement of trains on a road in receivership in contempt of court and not entitled to a jury trial. Receivership involved a federal equity court's management of a bankrupt railway in the public interest. The federal judiciary's view of its duty in such cases was that it should build the economic integrity of a railway and saw strikes as a threat to this authority and purpose. Gresham's ruling laid the basis for the courts' exercise of much broader injunctive powers in railroad strikes in the following decades, when judges extended their protective authority to railway companies in general, since unimpeded freight and passenger traffic were critical to the nation's commerce. With a similar appeal to the public interest the federal government held strikers legally responsible for disrupting the delivery of the mail.

Another consequence of the 1877 strike was reconfigured labor relations on the railways. Managers used the blacklist and ironclad contracts to purge unionists. In this climate and under the pressure of economic duress, railroaders' industrial unions disintegrated (they had initially attracted members across lines of skill and craft to engage in walkouts during the 1873–74 crisis years). Craft-based unions such as the Machinists' and Blacksmiths' Union and the Brotherhood of Locomotive Firemen barely survived. Only the Brotherhood of Locomotive Engineers (BLE) quickly regained its footing. It led the way among the brotherhoods in rejecting alliances with other unions, expelling members who had joined the 1877 strike, distancing itself from the unskilled "rabble," and seeking the favor of railroad officials. During the economic upswing of the early 1880s, the BLE's conservative strategy paid off in the form of signed agreements with railway officials regulating wage rates and work rules.

While conservative craft unions survived the strike, industrial unionism likely went underground. Stromquist contends that many participants in the 1873–77 strike joined the Knights of Labor. This organization had its start in a number of secret societies formed among Philadelphia artisans following the Civil War. Unlike previous major industrial unions among railroaders, such as the Brakemen's Brotherhood, it opened its doors to all wage workers (with the significant exception of the Chinese): blacks and whites, native-born and immigrant, the skilled and unskilled, sympathetic shopkeepers and business owners, and, beginning in 1881, women. As railroad men followed opportunities for work further west, Stromquist writes, many "packed away with their belongings their knowledge and experience with industrial organization."

Despite the threat of blacklists and dismissals, the Knights of Labor rejected secrecy in 1878 and began to openly organize on a national scale as part of a growing political movement that took from the 1877 strike the lesson that reform was essential. Independent political parties such as the Greenback-Labor Party, the Labor Reform Party, and the Workingmen's Party formed. In some major American cities and numerous small towns, reform tickets emerged victorious. Even when these parties lost, they often succeeded in pushing the dominant political parties to adopt some of their demands, such as railroad regulation. What many of these reform groups shared with the Knights was an anti-monopolist ideology that saw economic concentration as a fundamental danger to the health of the Republic. Monopolists, they charged, held excessive political and economic influence and always seemed to be groping for more, while the traditional safeguard against the threat of tyranny, an independent citizenry, was fast disappearing. These ideas resonated increasingly with railroaders in the mid-1880s, when railroad companies consolidated into large concerns and began again to cut labor costs in the midst of an economic downturn.

The 1885-1886 Gould System Strikes

The strikes that shook the Gould System in 1885 and 1886 are often called the "Southwest Strikes" because they took place in Kansas, Missouri, Arkansas, Illinois, and central and eastern Texas on Jay Gould's "Southwest System" of railroads. This system included the Missouri Pacific, Texas and Pacific, International and Great Northern, the Cotton Belt, and finally the Missouri, Kansas, and Texas, or KATY. The railroad that linked the Southwest System to the northeast via Illinois, the Wabash, St. Louis & Pacific, was also under Gould's control. Gould, an infamous Wall Street tycoon and "railroad king" of the Gilded Age, had built up his empire as part of a war of expansion against economic rivals. According to his most recent biographer, Maury Klein, Gould's ambition was a transcontinental system. However, by 1884 the Wabash and the Texas & Pacific, roads that connected the Missouri & Pacific to the East and West, were mired in financial difficulties.

Gould's system managers faced the same problems and concocted the same solutions as many other western railway officials. Despite massive public and private financial backing, railroad expansion was a risky business in the 1870s and 1880s due to the speculative nature of much of the industry's investment, the need to maintain and service roads in remote or yet unsettled areas that produced little revenue, the intense competition among roads in overbuilt areas, and high overhead. One portion of railroad companies' high overhead was the relatively high wages and favorable work rules that railroaders, skilled workers especially, received in the West, where labor was initially scarce. As the available pool of labor grew with settlement, western railroad managers pushed, little by little, to reduce operating costs by cutting wages and work crews, avoiding extra incentives for overtime work, placing trainmen on irregular schedules, and hiring "extras" rather than full-time men, and, finally, instituting promotion from within. With this latter policy, railroad companies, rather than the brotherhoods, controlled who moved up into skilled positions. Its purpose was to diminish the leverage of skilled workers by increasing their numbers.

Many western railroaders were "boomers," or, in the words of economist Victor Clark, "train hands who drift about the country, working for first one road, and then another." On the labor-scarce frontier, they had come to expect and prize the relatively good wages and conditions on western roads, but they increasingly faced the same deteriorating conditions as eastern railroaders. Company cost-cutting measures also disrupted the fraternal bonds that made railroad work more tolerable and survivable. Depressed wages hampered workers' ability to search elsewhere for work, contribute to funds for injured men, or to build savings. Experienced men took unskilled or semiskilled work in order to make ends meet. Moreover, reductions in work crews pushed to the limit workers in an already hazardous occupation. One St. Louis trackman, M.J. Reed, told the congressional committee that investigated the 1886 Southwest Strike that his hours repairing track had been cut to only a few days per week, despite the dangers associated with understaffed maintenance crews:

> There was work enough for a hundred right along, let alone the six men that was on. They could work twice as many men and have just as much as they could do . . . because there was breaking down every day, and the track was . . . in bad repair, and there wasn't men enough to do it in the few minutes they was on; they couldn't do it.

Charles Maier worked for the Missouri Pacific during these years and later recalled his humiliation. He contrasted his own situation to the hired man on his family farm who had "enjoyed every comfort that the family had." He felt "confused and troubled to find that what had promised so much to me . . . had placed me in the position of a man without a chance to preserve his self-respect and at the same time provide bread for himself and his family."

The building tension between railroad management and workers such as Maier helps explain how a series of specific measures between September 1884 and February 1885 sparked the first systemwide general strike on Gould's Southwest System. During those months, Wabash railway and Missouri Pacific railway shopmen saw their pay cut and their hours extended, and various classes of general laborers on both roads faced reductions in pay and hours. The first sign of protest emerged at a meeting of Wabash men on February 25, 1885, in Springfield, Illinois. Their decision to strike was endorsed by fellow Wabash men in Indiana, Illinois, and Galveston, Texas. On March 1, Texas & Pacific shopmen joined the walkout and within a matter of days had paralyzed freight traffic on the Gould system in much of Texas. Then, around 400 Missouri Pacific and KATY shopmen in Sedalia, Missouri, quit work in unison at the sound of the whistle on March 7. By March 11, about 4,500 employees, mainly shop- and yardmen, had walked off their jobs. Trackmen and other unskilled laborers swelled strikers' ranks soon after.

The Gould system strike had a special focus beyond railroaders' growing fears of economic and social dependence—Jay Gould himself, who had a reputation for financial trickery stretching back to 1869 when he and his partner Jim Fisk sought a monopoly of the gold market. Newspapers across the country had vilified him for this as well as his penchant for speculating in, rather than building up, the companies under his control. Strikers often assumed that the Gould system's financial woes were due to similar maneuvering, a sentiment that was widely shared in their communities, where anti-monopoly movements had long influenced local and state politics. Indeed, the walkout won the support of many townspeople, farmers, and local press editors. In some towns, local boardinghouses refused service to strikebreakers, and merchants extended strikers credit. One participant reported that public support was so strong that few men even attempted to fill strikers' positions.

Public opinion sustained the strike for other reasons. First, strikers turned to moral suasion rather than intimidation and violence in stopping freight traffic. Typically, crowds of strikers and their sympathizers gathered at public crossings to block approaching trains and appeal to trainmen to abandon their posts. Their appeal usually gained trainmen's sympathy, despite the fact that the engineers' brotherhood had not endorsed the strike and had renounced labor alliances. Second, railroaders remained connected to community sympathizers through the daily mass meetings that were held in numerous strike towns. Third, and most importantly, the walkout did not overly tax the resources of local communities. The suspension of most freight traffic lasted little over a week.

With traffic tied up in Sedalia, Marshall, Fort Worth, Palestine, Denison, Parsons, Atchison, and other small towns, representatives from the Missouri Pacific and Texas Pacific railway companies, surprised by the depth of strike sympathy, met with state leaders in St. Louis on March 15. They agreed to most of the strikers' demands, including the stipulation that strikers retain their old positions without discrimination and receive overtime pay and the wage rates of September 1884 (before the major cuts). The railways further promised to offer thirty days' notice of any change in wage rates. Significantly, engineers signed a separate agreement on March 24, 1885. It promised relief on a number of issues, especially the use of "extras." Engineers were reluctant to jeopardize this compact in 1886 when strikers once again immobilized the Gould system.

In the wake of the March 1885 agreements, thousands of workers along the Gould system lines organized Knights of Labor assemblies. Railroaders were especially enthusiastic supporters of the Order. Many surely felt that only increased organization would prevent the railroads from violating the settlement. No major organization had coordinated strike activity that spring. The Knights held promise, because the Order had won a major victory on the Union Pacific in August 1884. Also, many clearly identified with the Order's emphasis on the nobility of labor. "Producers," the Knights contended, were due a just share of the nation's wealth. Participants in the 1885 strike found these ideas compelling, as they had argued that the Gould system sought to reduce them to "wage-slavery."

As railroaders feared, violations of the March 1885 agreement quickly multiplied. Wabash employees were particularly vulnerable to judicial repression of strike activity, since the Wabash was in receivership. When bad weather disrupted traffic, the road's managers cut wages and replaced its Knights shopmen with nonunion men. To make matters worse, when the locked-out Knights appealed to the Order's national leader, Terence Powderly, he at first refused to give them aid. The union's rapid growth had weakened his ability to respond quickly and substantively to local and even regional emergencies. Beyond this, Powderly adamantly opposed strikes. When Powderly finally attempted to intervene, the Wabash's general manager declined to meet with him. Faced with this intransigence, the Knights' General Executive Board threatened Gould with not only a strike on the Wabash but also a sympathy strike of Knights on the Union Pacific, the "Southwest System," and any other railway that dealt with Wabash cars. Gould responded by sending Wabash officials to meet with Powderly in St. Louis on September 3, 1885—here, a national labor organization negotiated with a major industrial concern for the first time. Under the agreement, the railway pledged to reinstate locked-out and striking Wabash men and not to discriminate against Knights. For his part Powderly committed to hold a conference with railroad officials before calling another strike. The Knights' victory brought in yet another explosion in membership. By spring of 1886, the Order's numbers had grown sevenfold to almost 730,000.

Still, the historic March and September 1885 agreements failed to protect many Gould system railroaders. Locked-out Wabash Knights wrote Powderly in late September that the railway had reemployed only one-fifth of their number. In numerous places, men received neither restored wages nor overtime pay. Missouri Pacific roundhouse and shop laborers in Kansas City and elsewhere testified that they regularly put in thirteen hours a day but were only credited for ten. Several Knights later reported that managers exhibited prejudice against them by, for example, only honoring agreements with nonunion men, disproportionately assigning Knights to part-time rather than full-time work, or blacklisting them. When bridge, section, and roundhouse men protested violations of the March accord, company officials argued that it applied only to shopmen, which was clearly not the case. For fear of losing their jobs, most men did not voice their concerns to officials but instead turned to the local grievance committees organized by District Assemblies 93 and 101, the Knights' district assemblies of Wabash and Southwest System employees, respectively. In February 1886, Martin Irons, chair of District Assembly 101's executive committee, asked local assemblies to vote on whether they would support the demands that railway officials negotiate with the assembly's board to raise the wages of unskilled laborers to $1.50 a day. Though historian Ruth Allen questioned the authenticity of the vote, the evidence suggests that the majority voted in favor of the proposal.

The spark that set the 1886 strike in motion involved termination of a local Knights leader by a Texas & Pacific foreman in Marshall, Texas. On March 6, 1886, District Assembly 101 called a systemwide strike in order to protect its membership from further discrimination. It needed Gould employees to participate because the Texas & Pacific had come under receivership and so its strikers were, like Wabash employees, legally compromised. District Assembly 101 took this action without alerting the national office of its grievances or plans and with little in the way of strike funds in its treasury. The district's leaders probably ignored the national Knights because local leaders had been largely left out of the high-level discussions and pacts of 1885. Those contracts had not set in place any sort of institutional mechanism for resolving labor troubles. Thus, when faced with contract violations, Gould system Knights in 1886 looked not to their national leadership but to themselves. Nor did they rely on engineers or firemen. The main spectacle of the 1886 strike was not moral suasion of trainmen but, in each major strike town, the immediate occupation of shops and roundhouses by hundreds of strikers, who "killed" or disabled locomotive engines and hid pins and links as the chief means of stopping freight traffic.

Over one-third of the Missouri Pacific's 13,000 railroad workers participated in the 1886 strike, along with about 1,000 from the Texas & Pacific. The walkout drew both black and white Knights, who had organized racially separate local assemblies in the preceding months. In part this biracial alliance rested on anti-Chinese sentiment. One of the strikers' central demands was the abolition of Chinese labor on the system. The Knights' cross-racial organizing was not its most controversial feature in the public's eye, however. In fact, it drew little comment, in part because Knights conformed to the prevailing racial hierarchy by forming racially separate assemblies.

The independent course that District Assembly 101 set for itself played the most important role in the strike's demise. Strike leaders had not kept the public or press well informed about the railroads' violations of the 1885 contracts, so when the railroads charged that the Knights had struck in blind obedience to the order of Martin Irons, the leader of District Assembly 101, or on the account of the discharge of only one man (the Knights leader discharged in Marshall), those charges quickly won credence with a public eager to see a cessation of the difficulties. The walkout's long interruption of commerce tried the patience of merchants, farmers, and shop owners, leaving them less willing to support the strikers' cause. Widespread acts of sabotage also undermined public support and brought local, state, and finally national authorities in to protect railroad property and to issue injunctions against strikers, even strikers who merely had engaged in moral suasion of engineers and firemen. On the Texas & Pacific, state and federal troops crushed most of the remaining resistance. Railroad managers soon began employing new men and some returning strikers in the shops and yards. On March 26, Powderly dealt the walkout another blow by issuing a strongly worded anti-strike circular—a move that many perceived was aimed at District Assembly 101.

A large number of trainmen sympathized with the Knights but refused to abandon their positions. The railroads had held up their part of the 1885 bargain with engineers. To strike in sympathy with District Assembly 101 would jeopardize that gain. Also, the BLE's chief, Peter M. Arthur, specifically ordered engineers to remain at their posts. Any engineer who violated this order endangered his membership in the brotherhood. With the engineers' and firemen's refusal to cooperate, crowds of railroaders, their families, and friends turned to blocking freight trains with their bodies and to cajoling, harassing, intimidating, and physically attacking trainmen and returning strikers. In East St. Louis, these tense confrontations escalated into violence when crowds of railroad men and their supporters, some armed, vastly outnumbered deputies, who in a panic fired into the assembly, and a deadly exchange ensued in which several deputies and strikers lost their lives. By April the strike had crumbled. In the 1886 walkout's aftermath, the Knights of Labor entered a period of rapid decline on the Gould system. In the public's eye, Martin Irons replaced Jay Gould as the main instigator of labor trouble on the railroads. In May 1886, public attention turned to the Haymarket Affair during which a bomb was thrown at police breaking up a strike rally in Chicago, after which eight anarchists were tried for the murder. This incident and the wave of anti-radicalism that followed, along with major defeats on the western railroads and elsewhere, undid the Knights. In 1890, its ranks numbered only 100,000.

The Pullman Strike

The Pullman strike is unique among the major railway strikes in that it began not on the railroads but in the small community of Pullman, located several miles south of Chicago. There, industrialist George Pullman had built a model town, one that he hoped would revolutionize relations between labor and capital. On a more practical level he envisioned that it would serve as a central locale for the production and repair of the Pullman Company's sleeping cars and also realize a tidy profit. Instead, he and the town's residents came to symbolize for many railroad workers the dangers of monopoly and dependence.

The streets in Pullman were lighted, paved, tree-lined, and spacious. It boasted a ready water supply and state-of-the-art sewage system, terraced grounds, parks and playgrounds, and richly decorated public buildings, including a well-stocked library and a lush theater. Pullman workers found their homes far less roomy, convenient, and attractive than those occupied by Pullman officials, but far more modern, clean, and livable than those in the slums of industrial cities. Paternalism, then, was Pullman's answer to the "labor question." For a time Pullman workers acquiesced. As historian Janice L. Reiff has noted in her contribution to *The Pullman Strike and the Crisis of the 1890s: Essays on Labor and Politics*, they traded their dissatisfaction with Pullman's control over church, politics, housing, and land for "the wages and the kind of lifestyle and opportunity for families that Pullman also provided," one in which wives remained in the home and families saved money for their children's education. Their ambivalent acceptance of life in Pullman gave way to anger and bitterness when in 1894 the company implemented a series of wage cuts but refused to lower rents or utilities. Four thousand Pullman workers joined the American Railway Union and in May 1894 declared a strike.

The American Railway Union (ARU) was a fledgling organization in 1894. Eugene Victor Debs, who came to national prominence during the Pullman strike, had helped to establish it only the year before. Debs was an Indiana-born ex-railroad worker who had served as the editor of the Brotherhood of Locomotive Firemen's journal and as a state legislator during the 1880s. Like the Knights, the ARU welcomed railroaders, regardless of skill, into a broad-based organization that promised to protect them from the tyrannical control of monopolistic railways. This strategy represented a departure from Debs's previous position that the natural relationship between labor and capital was harmonious and cooperative. Harmony could only be achieved, he argued in the ARU's Declaration of Principles, when "the great body of railroad men" unionized. He hoped that such a unified front would supplant the brotherhoods, which were undemocratic, vulnerable to their employers' recruitment of the unorganized during strikes (as an 1888 strike on the Burlington railroad had amply demonstrated), and unmindful of the inefficiency of the grievance system for even its own members. The ARU attracted shopmen and laborers but also firemen and brakemen. Eastern railway workers were the least represented in the ARU's ranks, as railroaders of all skill levels in this region faced stiff labor competition and, since the 1870s, a history of lost struggles over wages and work rules. Western workers proved the ARU's most ardent supporters. This was even true of a significant number of skilled trainmen who had become disenchanted with the brotherhoods' conservative course.

One month after the Pullman walkout began, strike committee members sought the aid of the ARU, which called a convention to address the crisis. There, strikers reported that starvation and hopelessness threatened strikers and their families, despite funds and supplies sent from supporters in Chicago and elsewhere. One daughter of a railroader made an impassioned appeal to the principle of labor solidarity. After the ARU's efforts to arbitrate met with the Pullman Company's rebuff, delegates voted to refuse to handle Pullman cars until the corporation agreed to come to the bargaining table. The boycott began on June 26. When railroad companies dismissed railroad workers who respected the boycott, a wave of railroad strikes followed. Within two days, 18,000 men had struck. By July 5, the ARU's effort had shut down freight traffic on all but three of the twenty-six railroad lines that ran through Chicago.

Like the Knights of Labor's national leadership, ARU leaders saw strikes as a weapon of last resort. Why then did the union vote to defend a few thousand strikers whose only relationship to the railroads was that the Pullman Company was invested in a small section of railway line? Even more to the point, why had its members waged a strike in the middle of a deep depression that had thrown nearly 22,000 miles of railway into the hands of receivers and put tens of thousands of Americans out of work? There were several interrelated reasons for these actions. Many railroaders, especially the unskilled, had their own grievances that echoed those of the Pullman strikers—reduced wages, company spies, prejudice against union members, extended hours, blacklisting, and the capricious policies of foremen. To many ARU members the situation in Pullman epitomized the evils of monopoly. They pointed to the General Managers' Association, an organization of railroad companies formed in 1886 in Chicago after the Gould system strikes to address labor troubles on the railroads. Reactivated in 1892, its twenty-four member railroads, representing 41,000 miles of track, coordinated their activity, including mobilization of strikebreakers, refusal to negotiate, and lobbying of city and state officials. To many railroaders the ARU seemed an answer to this threat. In the spring of 1894 it led and won a strike against the Great Northern Railroad, attracting thousands of nonbrotherhood men into its ranks. The Pullman boycott also came on the heels of other dramatic demonstrations of labor unrest—the journey of "Coxey's Army," a march of the unemployed on Washington, DC, to demand federal intervention in the economic crisis, and a massive United Mine Workers strike involving 180,000 workers.

Fear of unrest quickly led to actions on the part of the federal government and the railroads that seriously undermined the strike. U.S. Attorney General Richard Olney, in particular, played a critical role. He was, according to historian Almont Lindsey, hostile to railroad strikes and placed no faith in the ability of local or state officials to contain the crisis militarily, given lax enforcement of court orders against sectors of the Coxey movement that had commandeered trains. The chief justification for federal intervention was the disruption of mail service during the strike. The ARU worked to avoid this, but the Department of Justice accepted the railroads' argument that their contracts with the Pullman Company required that they refuse to detach Pullman cars from mail cars. Moreover, Olney pushed for and won prosecution of the ARU under the Sherman Anti-Trust Act, which Congress passed in 1890 to combat "every contract, combination in the form of trust or otherwise, or conspiracy, in restraint of trade or commerce among the several states, or with foreign nations." Federal judges had applied the law to a railway labor union in 1893, reasoning that workers who sought to induce others to strike with the aim of disrupting business engaged in conspiracy. On this basis courts issued blanket injunctions against Pullman strikers and their leaders, banning a wide variety of strike activity, including the use of peaceful persuasion to convince potential strikebreakers to respect the strike.

By July 10, nearly 2,000 troops were in Chicago to aid the railroads in restoring freight traffic. This was in addition to 5,000 deputy marshals recruited to serve in the city, two-thirds of whom were paid railroad employees. Soldiers were also sent to Los Angeles, Raton (New Mexico), Trinidad (Colorado), and many other towns to enforce the approximately 100 orders against the ARU and other unions engaged in the strike. Debs and many other union leaders were arrested and charged with contempt of court for unlawfully combining in restraint of interstate trade and the U.S. Mail. The effect of the arrest of union leaders in the midst of the strike was extremely dispiriting and disruptive.

In part, the media drove the fear of violence. In contrast to press coverage of the 1886 Southwest strike, most reports on the Pullman strike were hostile to the strikers from the very beginning. Depictions of the boycott in Chicago gave the impression that civil war had erupted—illustrations showed railroad property in flames, standoffs between determined troops and anarchic crowds, looting, and destructive strike supporters. Newspaper headlines screamed, "MOB IS IN CONTROL"; "WILD RIOT IN CHICAGO"; and "GUNS AWE THEM NOT." The *New York Times* cast Debs as a madman and "an enemy of the human race," while the *Chicago Tribune* falsely charged that he had traveled on a Pullman sleeper during the strike. More to the point, *Harper's Weekly*, as historian Almont Lindsey recounts, represented the boycott as "blackmail on the largest scale" and the ARU as an insurrectionary organization. In fact, little violence occurred in Pullman.

Most of the disorderliness elsewhere followed rather than preceded the arrival of federal troops on July 3. Prior to July 3, sabotage was the chief difficulty facing Chicago authorities. The major exception to this was in Blue Island, a suburb of Chicago, where riotous elements dominated. The governors of seven states protested the federal government's involvement, insisting that the state militia and municipal forces were in control. Governor Altgeld of Illinois was particularly vocal. In a telegram to President Cleveland, he pointed to his record of calling in troops when and where the situation required it, but no local law enforcement person, he claimed, had given him the impression that such federal intervention was justified. The presence of soldiers seriously aggravated circumstances. In Chicago on the evening of July 4, they dispersed (with some trouble) a mob 10,000 strong, and on July 6 the fire department was overwhelmed by a series of fires set to railroad property. The damage was alarming—700 cars destroyed in one part of town and $340,000 worth of railroad property in another. Still, Lindsey has noted, no hard evidence linked this incendiary activity to the strikers.

In the end, the strike involved twenty-seven mostly western and midwestern states and territories and the use of 16,000 federal troops. Traffic came to a standstill on all but one transcontinental railroad. Switchmen and shopmen, especially, honored the boycott. In California, where the Southern Pacific operated as a hated monopoly, strikers enjoyed broad support. Indeed, railroad towns in western states such as Nebraska, Wyoming, Utah, Montana, and New Mexico were particularly disposed to back the ARU. Some areas saw peaceful conditions while others experienced violence. Acts of terrorism in the form of dynamited bridges and deadly rail damage emerged in Oklahoma, for example. In several places, including Hammond, Indiana, soldiers fired into restless crowds, sparking the outrage of community members and local officials.

By July 18 the ARU's defeat seemed imminent. Trains ran according to schedule in Chicago and other points with the aid of federal troops and court orders that granted those troops the power to suppress any resistance. Railroad companies had little trouble securing replacement labor in a context of not only massive economic crisis but, as Stromquist has observed, also a general context of labor surplus that the railroads increasingly enjoyed in the West. The major railroad brotherhoods condemned the boycott, primarily because the ARU's industrial strategy threatened their very existence, though many of their members lent it support. With the ARU leadership under arrest and the federal government's strong anti-labor stance in mind, otherwise sympathetic delegates to an American Federation of Labor (AFL) meeting voted against a general strike and issued a statement denouncing sympathy strikes as a perilous strategy. Labor unions in Chicago representing about 150,000 workers pledged a general strike, but most of its membership ignored the pledge, probably because the Pullman boycott appeared all but lost. As strike activity declined, workers in Pullman applied for work with the Pullman Company. Some were hired back but on the condition that they sign an ironclad oath to sunder any ties that they held with labor unions. The following May, the Supreme Court unanimously sustained the blanket injunctions issued by federal courts and the charges against Debs, who served a six-month jail term.

Debs emerged radicalized from his experience with the Pullman strike and prison. He rejected the idea that workers could find justice under capitalism and ran as a Socialist candidate for president five times between 1900 and 1920. Arguably, the major significance of the Pullman strike does not lie here, as Debs never attracted more than 6 percent of American voters. Its importance has more to do with the degree to which railroad workers and their communities sympathized with the strike and the aggressiveness with which the federal government pursued an anti-strike policy. Debs and others were prosecuted in both criminal and equity courts. The latter courts, which did not require jury trials, had issued the blanket injunctions that ultimately undermined a widely supported strike. This hard reality convinced Debs to embrace a socialist solution. For Samuel Gompers of the AFL, it confirmed his faith in the opposite tack, an approach historians call "voluntarism." This required that trade unions eschew broad, industrial, and political strategies because history had demonstrated that the state had no positive role to play in reforming labor conditions. Gompers believed that the state had dramatized again and again its business bias and thus the necessity of relying on the economic power of skilled workers rather than legislative action in affecting meaningful change.

Legal historian William Forbath has echoed Gompers's emphasis on the role of the state in determining events. With the Pullman strike, says Forbath, the government's hostility to strikes reached its highest point:

> By the eve of the Pullman Strike the main elements that composed the federal judicial role in that strike were also in place. Built up over sixteen years of judicial experience, they included the enjoining of strike and boycotts on non-receivership lines; the long experience of collaboration with railroad management and attorneys; the precedents for summoning troops over the heads and against the will of state authorities; the preference for summary proceedings over jury trials; and the transformation of the federal courtroom into 'a kind of police court,' in Judge Taft's words, when railway workers went on strike.

Contributors to *The Pullman Strike and the Crisis of the 1890s: Essays on Labor and Politics* have questioned Forbath's interpretation, pointing to, for example, the cultural sanction that judges' rulings against Pullman strikers enjoyed. One of those contributors, Melvyn Dubofsky, has observed that "judges, elected officials, and the citizens they claimed to represent shared a common commitment to principles of what might be termed *civic republicanism* . . . [which] assumed that the community (public interest) had rights (interest) that must be protected against the selfish claims of organized private interest groups, whether composed of business people or working people."

Though many saw the Pullman boycott as a just cause, many others saw it as a threat to the public peace and public good. Dubofsky views the strike as a pivotal event in the shift from anti-strike to reform sentiment within the government. In the face of rising class tensions, some judges, such as John Marshall Harlan and Oliver Wendell Holmes Jr., began to accept the arguments of labor leaders and lawyers that strikes and even the effort to press others nonviolently to strike were legal. Opinions among public officials began to change, too. Ironically, Attorney General Olney became an avid supporter of reforms that ultimately were codified in the Erdman Act of 1898. This act recognized the collective bargaining rights of the brotherhoods representing operating railroad employees, established a mechanism for mediating disputes between these workers and railroad companies engaged in interstate commerce, and banned the yellow-dog contract (forbidding employees from joining labor unions) at Interstate Commerce Commission–governed companies. This legislation passed in large part because the public opinion favored some method of arbitration to avoid future large-scale disturbances on the railroads.

The 1922 Shop Workers' Strike

The Erdman Act severed the remaining links of solidarity between on-train and off-train railroaders by granting only the former collective bargaining rights. Ironically, then, the history of the 1922 shop workers' strike is partly rooted in the differential treatment railroaders received under the legislation. Operating workers' unions (firemen, conductors, engineers, brakemen, etc.) did not join this walkout, since they did not want to jeopardize their special relationship with the federal government. As a result, the strike did not paralyze large sections of railway as the Pullman, Southwest, and 1877 strikes did.

The exclusion of shopmen's unions from federal protection left shop workers' wages and work rules vulnerable to employer attack and intimidation. Railroad companies routinely used spies and the blacklist to root out union sentiment in the shops. A major movement developed among shopmen to organize system federations. A system federation sought to unify workers of diverse skills within an industrial union but without disrupting craft lines. This strategy was especially advantageous for shop workers, given the diversity of their skills. In 1909, the AFL, under pressure from the three major shopcraft unions, created a national organization, the Railway Employees' Department (RED), but a strike on the Illinois Central and Harriman railroads from 1911 to 1915 demonstrated the federation's weaknesses. Federal judges bankrupted strikers' unions with sweeping injunctions. Shopmen across the country treated the fight as localized and did little to support it, and black workers, whom most shop workers' unions excluded, took strikers' places in large numbers.

These trying circumstances changed dramatically with the election of Woodrow Wilson and the coming of World War I. The Wilson administration advocated a regulatory state that would mediate labor conflicts and encourage collective bargaining as means to avoid strikes. Wilson's conciliatory approach became a matter of national interest during the war when economic and military demands necessitated cooperation between labor and industry. The federal government took over the nation's railways and created an arbitration board (the United States Railroad Administration) that limited shopmen's workdays to eight hours and banned the controversial piece rate system and discrimination against union members. The protection of the federal government was a mixed blessing to many shop worker unionists. On the one hand, they gained a number of agreements with railroad companies even before the war, and membership in shopmen's unions soared to 420,000 due to government backing. In 1920, shopmen obtained their first national agreement. On the other hand, federal control meant the loss of local officials' influence. It also came at an economic price. Shopmen agreed to wage rates that rising wartime prices quickly undercut. Despite these problems, the overwhelming majority of organized shopmen pushed for continued federal control after the war in the hope of preserving the federation system. Reform-minded farmers and trade unionists across the nation, as well as the four major railroad brotherhoods, concurred.

However, by 1920 the ground under shop workers' feet had shifted again. Railroad companies, many of which had protested federal intervention during the war, aggressively sought a return to prewar labor relations. Their anti-union stance gained popularity with the public after a series of massive strikes in 1919 involving one-fifth of the workforce. Indeed, a number of Americans drew parallels between postwar labor unrest and the Bolshevik revolution in Russia in 1917. Finally, Republicans commanded the Congress and the presidency.

The more conservative political environment forced a number of unwelcome changes for shop unionists. Congress rejected continued government ownership of the railroads in favor of the Transportation Act, which set up a Railroad Labor Board (RLB). The RLB's decisions were not mandatory, and President Harding further weakened the board in the eyes of labor by appointing two pro-management members. The following year, the RLB threw out the ban against piecework and some conditions mandating overtime pay. Between 1920 and 1922, major railroad companies laid off tens of thousands of shop workers, contracted out a good deal of shop work, and cut the wages of most classes of railroad labor, moves that historian Colin J. Davis argues had more to do with management's desire to reassert control over the workforce than economic imperatives. The RLB confirmed shopmen's growing distrust of federal agencies when it approved the railroad industry's recommendations to cut the wages of shop and maintenance-of-way workers (but not of brotherhood men).

On July 1, almost 400,000 men launched a nationwide strike under the leadership of the RED. More than 80 percent of railway shop workers participated in the strike. Most were white workers, but African Americans participated in significant numbers. Black workers were not as universally excluded from the organizations that launched the 1922 strike, as had been the case in 1911 (and 1894). Some were members of segregated locals of shopmen's unions. Others had belonged to the AFL's federal unions. Railroaders of Japanese and Mexican heritage also walked out with their white counterparts. Still, Davis concludes, the multiethnic alliance was mostly one of convenience.

Railroad officials responded with equal boldness, employing a massive number of guards to protect railroad grounds, recruiting and importing strikebreakers, and going to great lengths to house, feed, and protect these new employees. Managers placed tremendous economic pressure on local merchants and authorities who publicly supported the strike. In one case, they threatened to move the company's division point elsewhere and, in another, to hold municipalities responsible for any damage done to railway property during the conflict. A major blow to strikers came when the RLB accepted the railroads' argument that the new employees were not strikebreakers, and, therefore, striking shopmen were no longer railway employees and had forfeited any privileges seniority accorded them. This in effect defined the walkout as an outlaw strike.

The strike was not immediately felt by the railroads. This was the primary weakness of a shop workers' strike; it affected train repair rather than train operation. While rolling stock (all of the vehicles moving on the railway) remained in good condition, which it could for months, shop workers held little leverage. Nevertheless, the nearly total support for the strike among shopmen, radical and conservative, and the sustenance that local communities gave the effort convinced participants that the walkout would succeed. Police forces and store owners often demonstrated their sympathy for strikers, and women formed auxiliaries that played an active role on the picket lines. Citizens of small railroad towns saw the railroads' new employees as a kind of invading army and naturally hoped to defend railroaders, who sometimes comprised the majority of the local population. Unlike the 1877, 1885–86, and 1894 strikes, the 1922 walkout was truly national in scope, extending from New York to California and deep into the Midwest, Southeast, and Southwest. Significantly, major sites of the conflict in 1922 were also strike towns in 1886 (St. Joseph and Hannibal, Missouri; Fort Worth, Marshall, Denison, and Sherman, Texas; Parsons and Topeka, Kansas; and Little Rock, Arkansas), suggesting the powerful, long-term tradition of anti-railroad sentiment that existed in many small American towns.

The strike began in an orderly fashion—workers left their posts in unison, often bringing their tools to underline the seriousness of their effort, and paraded through town to the local labor hall, where leaders urged a peaceful and legal strategy—but violence quickly became a key feature of the conflict. This occurred despite the counsels of shopcraft union leaders, who correctly recognized that disorder would inevitably encourage government repression. Davis has gone so far as to characterize the strike as a "rebellion," pointing to the propensity of townspeople to engage in or tacitly support crowd actions against guards, strikebreakers, and troops with tactics that included stoning of trains, taking over railroad shops and yards, and beating of men who sought work. Strikers, too, faced violence. Guards with little experience or credentials fired into masses of people, killing and maiming participants and onlookers. On several occasions railroad detectives were culpable for needless bloodshed.

The injunction once again demonstrated its usefulness to the federal government and the railroads. Most court orders were broadly conceived and interpreted, prohibiting not only trespassing on railroad property and physical intimidation but also freedom of speech. In one famous case, a Kansas man faced charges when he displayed a pro-strike sign in the window of his business establishment. No federal troops intervened in 1922, but U.S. marshals and National Guardsmen restored order on the railroad companies' terms at the behest of U.S. Attorney General Harry M. Daugherty, who, like Richard Olney, expressed acute hostility towards strikers, casting them as pro-communist and anti-American. In the context of the postwar Red Scare, these were serious charges that helped to sway a large segment of public opinion against the strike, particularly populations in large cities. Public opinion in these areas also reacted negatively to the escalation in violence that accompanied state involvement.

Vigilante action multiplied in communities that troops occupied. "Auto-raiders" used all available means to terrorize replacement labor, including drive-by shootings, vandalism, kidnapping, whipping, and stripping. Track was dynamited and rail lines sabotaged. These tactics were desperate ones, as by September the strike was faltering. Railroads found replacements for striking men among white and nonwhite college students, adventurers, and hobos and tramps. A significant number were strikers themselves who clandestinely sought the employ of railroads other than their own. The main enemy of the railroads at this point was time, as mainly small, inexpert crews of strikebreakers failed to maintain and repair rolling stock.

Though initially President Harding considered a conciliatory approach, a number of conditions convinced him and his administration to adopt a hard-line policy: the railroads' refusal to negotiate; the risk of a sympathy strike by operating workers who identified with shopmen's plight and who opposed running broken-down or ill-repaired equipment; and an impending national shortage of coal due to both the shop workers' strike and a major coal miners' strike. Daugherty pushed the railroad brotherhoods from the brink of striking by associating labor unrest on the railroads with radicalism and by forcefully pursuing legal cases against local pro-strike leaders. Harding characterized picketing and pro-strike arguments as the work of mobs. Most importantly, federal judge James H. Wilkerson granted Daugherty's request for a federal injunction against the strike. According to historian Colin J. Davis, Wilkerson's injunction charged the strikers with conspiracy to disrupt interstate commerce and to violate the right of replacement workers to freely choose their employers. It prohibited a wide range of activities, including strikers' attempts to persuade workers to join them "in any manner by letters, printed or other circulars, telegrams, telephones, word of mouth, oral persuasion, or suggestion" and leaders' efforts to "promote or encourage" the walkout. While the injunction against Pullman strikers enjoined a boycott or secondary strike, the 1922 injunction challenged the right of railroaders to strike at all, or more precisely, as Davis notes, the right to unionize shop workers.

Panicked strike leaders searched for a way out. Their solution further fractured the shopcraft workers' movement. When the president of the Baltimore and Ohio railway offered a settlement that preserved strikers' seniority rights, RED officials urged signing separate agreements with willing roads in the unrealistic hope of softening the mood of intransigent managers. Rank-and-file shop workers expressed strong disapproval. Davis recounts that one embittered delegate invoked the sacrifices made by jailed unionists and wounded and killed strikers, who "went out for the principle of a National settlement." Others favored the RED's attempts to salvage what they could from the debacle, which in the end was not much compared to the gains that walkout participants had so doggedly sought. Strikers able to return to work on the roads found few mechanisms to redress their grievances. Company unions dominated and not the RED, which along with the AFL drew the lesson that, in the absence of federal support for labor rights, cooperation with management was essential.

Conclusion

When railroader Harry French took up a collection for the widow of a fellow "rail," from men working on the Hannibal & St. Joe, the Kansas City, Fort Scott & Gulf, and the Kansas Belt Line, he obtained generous contributions from the train crew, yard crew, and office employees—basically "anyone who would listen." French recalled that no one refused to donate some amount, since "one never knew when [the hat] would be going around for him or his widow." His description suggests that the dangers of railroad work encouraged not an individualistic ethic among railroaders but collective action and fraternal protection. Recurring labor unrest on the roads between 1877 and 1922 in part grew out of such forms of cooperation. Cooperation also helped to sustain non-brotherhood men whose organizations were decimated in the wake of the failed strikes of 1877, 1886, 1894, and 1922.

See also: The Strike Wave of 1877, 177; World War I Era Strikes, 191; Coal Miners on Strike and the Formation of a National Union, 449.

Bibliography

Case, Theresa A. "Free Labor on the Southwestern Railroads: The 1885–1886 Gould System Strikes." Ph.D. diss., University of Texas at Austin, 2002.

Davis, Colin J. *Power At Odds: The 1922 National Railroad Shopmen's Strike.* Urbana and Chicago: University of Illinois Press, 1997.

Dubofsky, Melvin and Warren Van Tine, eds. *Labor Leaders in America.* Urbana: University of Illinois Press, 1987.

Foner, Eric. *Reconstruction: America's Unfinished Revolution, 1863–1877.* New York: Harper & Row, 1988.

Foner, Philip S. *The Great Labor Uprising of 1877.* New York: Monad Press, 1977.

Forbath, William E. *Law and the Shaping of the American Labor Movement.* Cambridge, MA: Harvard University Press, 1991.

French, Chauncey Del. *Railroadman.* Norwood, MA: Macmillan Company, 1938.

Leach, Eugene E. "Chaining the Tiger: The Mob Stigma and the Working Class, 1863–1894." *Labor History* 35 (Spring 1994).

Lindsey, Almont. *The Pullman Strike: The Story of a Unique Experiment and of a Great Labor Upheaval.* Chicago: University of Chicago Press, 1964.

Schneirov, Richard, Shelton Stromquist, and Nick Salvatore, eds. *The Pullman Strike and the Crisis of the 1890s: Essays on Labor and Politics.* Urbana: University of Illinois Press, 1999.

Stromquist, Shelton. A. *Generation of Boomers: the Pattern of Railroad Labor Conflict in Nineteenth-Century America.* Urbana: University of Illinois Press, 1987.

Taillon, Paul Michel. "Culture, Politics, and the Making of the Railroad Brotherhoods, 1863–1916." Ph.D. diss., University of Wisconsin at Madison, 1997.

_____. "'To Make Men out of Crude Material': Work, Culture, Manhood, and Unionism in the Railroad Running Trades, c. 1870–1900." In *Boys and Their Toys? Masculinity, Technology, and Class in America,* ed. Roger Horowitz. New York: Routledge, 2001.

STRIKES BY TELEGRAPH WORKERS

Anthony J. Silva

The telegraph industry emerged from the first successful test of a telegraph system in the United States. On January 6, 1838, in Morristown, New Jersey, Samuel F.B. Morse used a crude device to send electrical impulses along a two-mile circuit, activating a pencil that recorded a series of dots and dashes on a paper tape at the other end. Six years later, on May 24, 1844, Morse transmitted the well-known first message, "What Hath God Wrought?" from Washington, DC, to his assistant Alfred P. Vail forty miles away in Baltimore, over wires erected with a federal grant of $30,000.

Morse's success inspired the construction of dozens of new lines. By 1851 over fifty telegraph businesses had been formed. One of these was the Mississippi Valley Printing Telegraph Company, launched on April 1, 1851. Five years later, it merged with Ezra Cornell's New York and Western Union Telegraph Company. Cornell had worked with Morse in 1844 on the construction of the Washington–Baltimore line, built several other telegraph lines, and founded Cornell University in 1865. The name "The Western Union," favored by Cornell, was given by the New York Legislature, and the new enterprise was chartered as The Western Union Telegraph Company on April 4, 1856. Henry S. Potter, president of the former Mississippi Valley Printing Telegraph Company, became Western Union's first president. The telegraph brought quick communication into a society that had depended on sailing ships and stagecoaches for its mail and news, and it soon revolutionized the nation's business practices.

Western Union grew rapidly by buying its rivals or driving them from the industry with its predatory pricing. It moved east by merging with the American Telegraph Company and the United States Telegraph Company in 1866, went west by absorbing the Overland Telegraph Company the same year, and reached the Pacific Coast by acquiring the California State Telegraph Company in 1867, becoming the nation's first near-monopoly business. With the completion of a transatlantic cable in 1866, Western Union gained access to the international telegraph network as well. New acquisitions often resulted in redundant lines between cities that lowered revenue per mile of wire, prompting the company to cut wages and tighten discipline in the operating rooms, conditions which led to the first signs of labor unrest at Western Union and the strike of 1870.

Telegraphers have been referred to as Morse telegraphers, Morse operators, or simply as operators. For decades, they used an electro-mechanical instrument devised by Samuel Morse and Alfred Vail known as a key and sounder to send and receive messages between the offices of the various telegraph companies. The text of each message was transmitted in Morse code, a system in which clicks and pauses are used for numerals and each letter of the alphabet. The instrument used by the operator to make or break an electric current was the "key." The key was used to activate an electric magnet at the other end of the line that attracted the "sounder," a spring-loaded metal armature that produced the audible clicks of the Morse code. In 1904, Horace G. Martin patented a mechanical semi-automatic key, which he called a Vibroplex, that used a lever on a vertical pivot as a key. Moving the lever to the right caused a spring-mounted contact on the other end of the lever to vibrate against a stationary contact, making strings of dots. Dashes were made manually by pushing the lever to the left and releasing it. The Vibroplex was popularly known as a "bug" and soon became the favorite instrument of telegraphers because it not only increased the speed of sending, but also reduced "glass arm," a cramp or paralysis in the arm caused by long periods at the key, a common ailment among telegraphers who sometimes worked ten or more hours a day.

Telegraphers were thought to be more talented and better educated than the average industrial worker, and telegraphy was often looked upon as a profession or a "genteel" vocation rather than a trade. Prior to the 1890s, most telegraphers were young, native-born, and largely of Irish and German descent. They closed their craft to nonwhites and immigrants. Most labor unions, including some commercial and railroad telegraphers' unions, included all-white hiring clauses in their constitutions, although some sources suggest that a few African-American men were employed as telegraphers in the South during the 1860s. In general, white workers held all but menial jobs in all departments until after World War II. Then, beginning in the 1960s when civil rights legislation increased opportunity, African Americans and other previously excluded workers began to fill clerical, technical, and managerial positions in greater numbers.

Despite social restrictions that barred women from many jobs and professions, women gradually entered the telegraph business. Sarah Bagley became the first female telegrapher when she assumed the duties of operator at the Lowell, Massachusetts, depot for the New York and Boston Magnetic Telegraph Company in 1846. Emma Hunter worked the wire in Westchester, Pennsylvania, near Philadelphia, for the Atlantic and Ohio Telegraph Company in 1851, and Ellen Laughton managed the same company's office at Dover, New Hampshire, in 1852. When male telegraphers were drafted for military service during the Civil War, women took their places in hundreds of civilian telegraph offices at salaries lower than those usually earned by men. However, women were not allowed to work as messengers—the lowest-paid telegraph job—because company managers worried about who might meet them at the door, or that they might be required to deliver messages to saloons and other undesirable locations of the city. The fledgling National Telegraphic Union barred women from full membership, but succeeding telegraphers' unions began to accept them and added "equal pay for equal work" to their bargaining agendas. As a result, women became enthusiastic members and dedicated participants in the various strikes by telegraph workers over the years.

By the late 1870s, Western Union had 7,672 offices with 12,224 workers and 199,022 miles of wire. The Baltimore & Ohio (B&O) with 136 offices, 341 employees, and 1,409 miles of wire was its largest competitor, until it was absorbed by Western Union in 1887. The small, one-person office in which a lone male or female operator served the public, transmitted and received Morse-coded messages, maintained the equipment, and swept the office remained the norm in small towns and railroad way stations. But as the company grew, its offices in large cities consisted of Western Union's three main departments: Commercial, Traffic, and Plant. The Commercial Department operated the company's public offices, which were staffed by bookkeepers, cashiers, clerks, messengers, operators, sales and service representatives, stenographers, supervisors, and office managers. Traffic Department employees handled the flow of messages between offices and included operators, clerks, and supervisors. The Plant Department employed clerks, draftsmen, engineers, and managers, and the various blue-collar workers who installed, maintained, and repaired the company's physical plant, such as cable splicers, linemen, equipment installers, technicians, and foremen.

One of the earliest reported telegraph strikes occurred during the Civil War, when a group of telegraphers formed the Southern Telegraph Association in 1863 and struck the Southern Telegraph Company, seeking a reduction of hours and an increase in pay. Dr. William Morris, president of the company, immediately threatened to dismiss any worker who was a member of the union. After a week's standoff, the union called off the strike and most of the operators returned to work.

Western Union's hostility toward unions began soon after the company was founded. When nascent telegraphers' unions attempted to improve their extremely bad working conditions—low pay, long hours, and overbearing management—the company adamantly refused to deal with them. One of the earliest unions, the National Telegraphic Union, began as a mutual aid society in 1863, admitting only telegraphers to membership, excluding clerks and women, and remaining timidly conservative in its relations with the telegraph companies. When disgruntled members demanded a more militant stand against employers, Western Union retaliated with layoffs, pay cuts, and the threat of discharge against operators who joined the union. The company steadfastly refused to deal with any outside organization that sought to improve or regulate wages and working conditions, forcing the young union to disband in 1867. An enmity toward "outside organizations," as the house organ *Western Union News* dubbed unions, characterized the company's decades-long labor policy.

To protect themselves from the wage reductions that followed each Western Union acquisition, operators formed a new Telegraphers Protective League in 1868, electing Ralph W. Pope as Grand Chief Operator. The league was a secret organization, but it led the first general strike in the telegraph industry. The strike of 1870 began after the Protective League's local in San Francisco failed to negotiate the reinstatement of operators who had been discharged for protesting pay by walking off the job. The league, anticipating the company's plan for a general reduction in wages despite its handsome profits, stood by its San Francisco local and began a nationwide strike against Western Union on January 3, 1870. Knowing that the league lacked funds to support a prolonged strike and determined to reduce wages, Western Union general superintendent Thomas Eckert—an implacable anti-labor foe—stood fast. Resorting to espionage and hiring replacements from the large number of unemployed telegraphers, he broke the strike. The defeated strikers returned to the working conditions they had failed to improve and took cuts in pay to keep from being replaced by telegraphers idled by a lagging economy. The failed strike of 1870 brought an ebb in the push for unionism among telegraphers and the decline and eventual disappearance of the Protective League in the 1880s.

There were no improvements in working conditions for telegraphers during the depression years following the strike of 1870. Western Union expected operators to process up to 125 messages a day, and by 1883 the requirement rose to over 300 per day. Condemning the ever-increasing workload and the disparity between their declining wages and the growing prosperity of the company, operators formed the Brotherhood of Telegraphers in March 1882 as District 45 of the Knights of Labor. Reflecting the philosophy of the Knights, the brotherhood welcomed all who worked for the telegraph companies, men and women, "whether smartly dressed operators who manipulated delicate and temperamental instruments or rough-hewn linemen shod with muck-encrusted climbing boots," according to telegrapher historian Edwin Gabler.

On July 19, 1883, the brotherhood, led by District Master Workman John Campbell, struck Western Union seeking eight-hour day tours, seven-hour night shifts, a minimum of $65 per month for linemen, $75 per month for operators, a 15 percent wage increase, equal pay for men and women, the elimination of compulsory Sunday work, and other improvements. The young union was no match for the power of Western Union, now controlled by Jay Gould and managed by Eckert. The press condemned the strike and denounced the occasional acts of violence. Charges of poor leadership within the brotherhood and disagreements between telegraphers and the more militant linemen members divided the membership. The Great Strike of 1883 collapsed on August 17, 1883, and the brotherhood, like the Knights, soon faded away. Returning strikers faced layoffs, blacklists, surveillance by company spies, and yellow-dog (anti-union) contracts. These "contracts" required workers to abandon membership in any group that sought to deal with wages and working conditions and to pledge not to join one while in the employ of the company. Those who did not sign were put on blacklists, ensuring that union sympathizers would not be hired by other employers in the industry.

There followed a period of relative calm in union activity among telegraphers. Although there was growing discontent over long hours and low pay, the large number of jobless operators made it difficult to organize protest. A group of telegraphers joined Eugene Debs's American Railway Union, but disbanded after the depression of 1892–94, reemerging in 1902 as the Order of Commercial Telegraphers.

The Order of Commercial Telegraphers and the Commercial Telegraphers Union, both organized in 1902, merged in 1903 to form the Commercial Telegraphers' Union of America (CTU). It received its charter from the American Federation of Labor on July 19, 1903, the twentieth anniversary of the Great Strike of 1883, and soon began an ambitious campaign to organize telegraphers in the industry. President Theodore Roosevelt gave the union's newly elected officers a reception and wished them success.

In May 1903, CTU Local 3 in St. Louis sought an injunction to restrain Western Union from firing telegraphers who joined the union. But on August 18, 1903, the union was rebuffed when Judge John Rogers sided with Western Union and denied the injunction. On November 17, 1903, in a protest over the discharge of four members, the young union conducted its first strike, a four-hour walkout against the Canadian Pacific Telegraph Company in Winnipeg that crippled the company's operations and forced it to reinstate the men. In April 1904, CTU struck the Great Northwestern Telegraph Company after five of its members were dismissed in Toronto and won their reinstatement. These short strikes succeeded because all of the operators left their jobs, causing a complete shutdown of telegraph service.

In 1905 the CTU succeeded in obtaining wage agreements for press telegraphers employed by the Hearst News Service and the Scripps-McRae Press Association without strike action, but the union failed to win at the Associated Press. In 1906 the CTU negotiated wage agreements with a number of brokerage firms, and won an agreement from Postal Telegraph that provided a day tour of nine hours, an early night tour of eight and one-half hours, seven hours on the midnight to morning tour, and a pay scale up to $90.00 per month. Early in 1907, the CTU pressured the Associated Press for an increase of $2.00, giving its operators a pay scale between $26.50 and $52 per week depending upon skill level, but Western Union telegraphers' pay remained at an average $42.50 per week, while the company was earning large profits and paying an average annual dividend of 5.3 percent. Although the CTU negotiated pay increases with some employers and pressured others to do the same, none of these "wage agreements" constituted formal recognition of the union.

In April of 1907, CTU president Samuel J. Small announced that "organization of Western Union operators is nearly complete," according to the *New York Times.* The dismissals of dozens of telegraphers confirmed that many were joining the union, but not all Western Union workers were flocking to the CTU, as Small claimed, because many hesitated to join for fear of losing their jobs. Still, the union continued to protest against the discharge of union members and issued ultimatums to Western Union and Postal Telegraph demanding their reinstatement under threat of a strike. While walkouts were occurring in Chicago, New Orleans, San Francisco, Oakland, Kansas City, and Los Angeles, Western Union managers met in New York to prepare for a strike, and cots were delivered for strikebreakers at various offices. Business leaders looked to President Theodore Roosevelt to prevent the pending work stoppage, and the president directed Labor Commissioner Charles Neill to handle the matter. Neill met with company officials and union leaders in unsuccessful efforts to mediate the dispute, and although business groups continued to press Roosevelt to intervene, the president repeatedly refused to become involved.

On August 7, 1907, Western Union telegraphers in Los Angeles walked off the job to protest the dismissal of five union members who had protested the firing of a union operator. The worker had discovered that the woman operator on the other end of the line in San Francisco had been a strikebreaker and accused her of being a scab and a woman of loose morals. She complained to supervisors who verified her accusations and fired the accuser. When other operators learned of the dismissal, a nationwide walkout began in support of the Los Angeles strikers, including most of the women operators who sympathized with the union and joined the strike. On August 11, members of the Order of Railroad Telegraphers stopped handling Western Union traffic, and the *New York Times* reported that thousands of Postal Telegraph and Western Union workers joined the strike as it spread across the nation. On August 12, operators at the Montreal office of the Great Northwestern Telegraph Company walked out in support of their striking union brothers and sisters in the United States, prompting the union to consider extending the strike in Canada. On August 15, according to the *New York Times,* the CTU General Executive board called out "all telegraphers employed by the commercial companies, Associated Press, private and leased wires, not working under a union agreement."

The union's agenda included many of the improvements sought by the brotherhood in 1883: a 15 percent increase in the prevailing pay scale of $65.00 per month, a slightly greater increase for operators in the Oakland-San Francisco area who were enduring the results of the 1906 earthquake, eight-hour day shifts, seven-hour night tours, company-furnished Morse keys, overtime pay at time-and-one-half, the elimination of split shifts, scheduled lunch periods, and the important demand of equal pay for men and women. The telegraph companies were unyielding in their rejection of the union's demands, and thus began the disastrous strike of 1907. During the eighty-nine-day strike CTU received the support of many other unions. The largest contributions came from the United Mine Workers, which gave about $140,000; the Order of Railroad Telegraphers donated $34,500; the American Federation of Labor sent $30,000; and the Brotherhood of Trainmen gave $5,000. Various other unions contributed an additional $24,000, and Thomas A. Edison, a former Western Union telegrapher, reportedly gave several hundred dollars to the cause.

Despite this support, the strike did not go well. The union did not have a majority of working telegraphers as members and lacked the funds to support a prolonged strike. The strike was badly managed by inexperienced CTU leaders who, as the walkout continued, eventually lost the support of strikers. To avoid violence and enhance its public image, the union did not prevent the company from hiring strikebreakers. Although the strike seemed doomed, many of the strikers continued to hope for victory. Others knew that failure was certain, but would not admit defeat. Women made up some 30 percent of the company's workforce and, because of the union's goal of equal pay, joined the strike. When Small took steps to end the strike, conflict developed between his supporters and those who wished to continue striking. The rift led to Small's replacement by W.W. Beattie at a special convention in Milwaukee on October 23, 1907, and the suspension of the strike on November 9. Western Union and Postal Telegraph again resorted to blacklists, espionage, and yellow-dog contracts. After the strike, Postal Telegraph abandoned its previous wage agreement with the CTU. Instead, it established an employee association, which provided sickness and death payments to members, for which they had to submit applications and a pledge not to join a union.

Unlike earlier telegraphers' unions that disappeared after disastrous strikes, the CTU did not disband following its defeat in 1907. Instead, it maintained its memberships in brokers' offices and newswire services in Canada and the United States, and planned new campaigns among operators at Western Union and Postal Telegraph.

After the United States entered World War I in April 1917, President Woodrow Wilson established the twelve-member National War Labor Board (NWLB), with former U.S. President William Howard Taft and Frank P. Walsh as joint chairmen. The NWLB sought to maintain the uninterrupted production of war materiel by providing for the resolution of wartime labor-management disputes. To achieve that goal, the board declared that there be no strikes or lockouts during the war period; that workers should not be discharged for joining unions; that there be equal pay for equal work for men and women; that wage scales meet the prevailing local rates; that all workers should be entitled to a living wage; and that a basic eight-hour day be recognized. Despite the board's authority, most employers, including Western Union, refused to recognize and bargain with unions.

CTU president S.J. Konenkamp warned that a strike scheduled for April 22, 1918, would take place unless operators who had been discharged for joining the union were reinstated. According to the *New York Times,* Secretary of Labor William B. Wilson, attempting to avert a wartime strike, informed Konenkamp that telegraph service was "absolutely necessary for the conduct of the war . . ." On April 29, 1918, the CTU Seattle local held a meeting for Western Union and Postal Telegraph members, many of them young women. When the next day they displayed ribbons in the colors of the CTU at work—red, white, and blue—both companies discharged them and locked out more than 350 workers. Konenkamp delayed the call for a nationwide strike pending a decision by the NWLB. On May 18, Board co-chairman Taft proposed to Western Union president Newcomb Carlton that if Western Union took back the operators who had been discharged the company could then bargain with its own employees and not be required to deal with or recognize the CTU.

The union agreed to the terms, but Carlton refused to reinstate the workers and rejected the plan. Instead, on May 22, he offered to let Western Union workers choose between joining the CTU or forming a separate organization whose membership and officers would be confined to Western Union workers. On June 11, after being apprised of the situation, President Wilson interceded on behalf of the Board and wrote to Carlton and Clarence Mackay, the president of Postal Telegraph, asking for their cooperation and compliance with the board's rulings.

Mackay replied on June 12 and agreed to "waive, during the war, our right to discharge employees who join a union, and you may rely upon our doing so," according to historian Valerie Jean Conner. However, as reported in *Western Union News,* on June 17 Carlton refused to accept the decision of the NWLB and informed the president that, in accordance with the company's long-standing policy, his employees would not be allowed to join a union, and that "today there are no members of such organization in our employ." Carlton was wrong. Telegraphers were joining the union secretly, some under assumed names, many not discovered by company spies. In pursuing its anti-union policy, Western Union had developed an espionage system that employed special agents to join CTU local unions throughout the country. The agents were paid to discover and report to management the names of workers who were union members. Western Union also used some of its own amenable employees to spy on their fellow workers.

The union scheduled a protest strike for July 8, but postponed it at the request of Labor Secretary William Wilson and American Federation of Labor (AFL) president Samuel Gompers. On July 10, 1918, Western Union further defied both President Wilson and the National War Labor Board by establishing its own company union, the Association Western Union Employees (AWUE), which did not use "of" in its name. President Wilson's reaction to Carlton's defiance and the threat of a strike was to seize all telegraph and telephone facilities at midnight on July 31, 1918, and place them under the control of Postmaster General Albert S. Burleson. Because of Burleson's anti-labor views, labor leaders urged Wilson to replace Burleson with "a progressive man more in line with modern government policies," and cited a report that he had informed Carlton that "if the telegraph and telephone lines are taken over, the employees should not be affiliated with any outside organization," according to historian Philip Foner.

The nation's communications facilities were managed by a Wire Control Board made up of three government officials, and an Operating Board composed of telephone and telegraph company executives. According to Alexander Bing, an official in two government agencies during the war, "telegraph and telephone workers had hoped that government control would result in the removal of grievances; instead, its only effect was that company officials who had been fighting the demands of the workers were thereby changed into officers of the government whose decisions it was much harder to oppose."

Fueled by Burleson's broken promises that discharged operators would be given back their jobs, discontent among union telegraph and telephone workers erupted into walkouts and strikes. On April 15, 1919, more than 8,000 telephone operators struck at telephone companies throughout New England. The actions were led by Julia O'Connor, president of the telephone operators' department of the International Brotherhood of Electrical Workers (IBEW), who had resigned from the Wage Commission of the Wire Control Board in protest of Burleson's "hostility to the organized telephone and telegraph workers." The *Commercial Telegraphers' Journal* issued a call for every person employed by Western Union, Postal Telegraph, AT&T, Associated Press, United Press, International News Service, newswires, and brokers to attend CTU meetings on April 28. The telegraph companies and AT&T continued to fire workers who joined a union. With no settlement in sight, on June 11 the CTU and the IBEW expanded the strike by calling out thousands of their members who worked for Western Union, Postal Telegraph, and AT&T. To divert support from the walkout, Western Union announced that it was preparing a distribution of $1 million in back pay to its "loyal operators."

In addition to the reinstatement of the discharged workers, the unions demanded the right to belong to a union; the right of collective bargaining; standardized wage scales; a pay increase; and rules governing working conditions. While company officials disparaged the strike, police made preparations to meet possible disturbances at Western Union offices. The *Commercial Telegraphers' Journal* of June 1919 carried strike bulletins from around the country. One from First International vice president L.J. Marshall reported the strike's early effect in CTU's Western Division:

> My reports from Montana indicate a complete tie-up of the lines; Idaho presents nearly a like situation. In Washington the Postal, like in the balance of the Western Division (west of Denver) is a badly crippled telegraph company, over 90 percent of the forces having walked out. The Western Union workers in most of the smaller offices throughout the district have struck. In Portland, Ore., 50 percent of the force quit. In Seattle, San Francisco and Los Angeles, where propaganda from the Employees' Association has had full swing, the initial walkout resulted in a reduction of approximately 20 percent for the three cities.

Sit Tight Boys And Girls—We Are Out To Win!

According to the *Commercial Telegraphers' Journal,* Operations at Santa Barbara were suspended; Postal Telegraph members in Boston said there were no more than fifteen workers in their offices and that Western Union was badly crippled. In Philadelphia, all postal linemen and burglar alarm men were walking and 90 percent of Western Union was out with no desertions. Washington, DC, claimed that ninety-eight workers were out at Postal Telegraph and only three in the office, "two operators and one wire chief from New York (scabs)," and "79 out at Western Union." Fort Worth was 90 percent out. Oklahoma City was "locked up; not a dynamo running nor a tick on the wire." And from Cairo, Illinois, "We will be out in Cairo until we win. Our wives here are very loyal and say they will take in washing before they would allow us to go back to work."

Despite these encouraging reports, the strike turned for the worse when operators in brokerage houses declined to strike and the IBEW cut short its walkout after Postmaster Burleson acceded to its demands, "the first decisive victory for telephone workers under the Burleson Wire Administration," according to historian Stephen Norwood. The Order of Railroad Telegraphers continued its refusal to handle Western Union and Postal Telegraph traffic, but the strike was lost. On July 2, 1919, CTU president Konenkamp surrendered with a final strike bulletin:

> We realized that in order to make this protest effective it would be necessary to make the strike sufficiently acute to compel action. This does not seem possible now either through our efforts or the efforts of others we relied upon to help us. . . . I hereby declare the strike at an end, and you are instructed to return to work without further delay. . . . The future, however, is not without hope. The principles for which we contend are going to prevail in the end.

Once again telegraph workers failed to win union representation. Over the next decade, Western Union expanded the AWUE. In 1923, the company instructed its managers to give each new worker a copy of the AWUE's "Welcome to New Employees" folder, which included literature describing the activities of the AWUE, an invitation to join, and a membership application. In 1925 the roster still listed only 24,000 names, but by 1926 *Telegraph World* reported a noticeable increase to 32,727 members. However, the same report showed a pocket of resistance in the company's New York Metropolitan Division, where only 4,100 had joined, a showing of about 60 percent of the Division's 6,869 workers. Company pressure and discrimination against nonmembers drove AWUE membership to a peak of 37,683 in 1930, almost 76 percent of the company's 49,824 eligible employees, according to the AWUE's *Telegraph World.*

For decades, transactions at brokerage firms

and at stock exchanges, as well as their interoffice communications, had traditionally been relayed by telegraphers using a key and sounder. In May 1930, when C.F. Childs & Co. decided to replace the keys with teleprinters, fifty telegraphers, members of the Commercial Telegraphers Union, walked out to protest against being moved to the new Teletype machines at a reduction in pay. On the second day of the dispute, the Childs Company supplanted the striking Morse operators with teleprinter operators. At its 1930 convention in September, the CTU adopted a resolution that Morse operators be given the work when automatic printers replace Morse equipment.

On June 1, 1933, Roy B. White, president of the Central Railroad of New Jersey, succeeded Newcomb Carlton as president of Western Union. The change did not alter the company's anti-union policies. In 1935 and 1936 White expanded the company's espionage system by hiring additional special agents and using cooperative employees to report on the increasing union activity of fellow workers, especially among increasingly discontented messengers.

Long excluded from the AWUE, messengers were turning to the CTU for help in improving their pay and working conditions, and in some cities were forming their own unions and threatening to strike the telegraph companies. On April 19, 1934, at a meeting called by the Independent Messengers Union in New York City, some 200 messengers discussed possible strike action against Postal Telegraph and Western Union, seeking a minimum weekly pay of $15 and a forty-hour work week. When company officials promised double pay for those who stayed at their jobs and warned that strikers would be fired, instead of a strike the boys voted to appoint a committee to meet with the companies. Meetings with both companies proved fruitless, and the messengers canceled their strike plans.

Increasing unrest among messengers led to a threatened-strike in 1935 in Flemington, New Jersey, and to messenger strikes in 1936 in Reading, Pennsylvania, and in 1937 in Toledo, Cleveland, Chicago, Gary, and other cities throughout the Midwest. Seattle messengers struck on June 9, 1937, when Western Union refused to bargain with the newly formed CTU Messengers Local 40 and denied the union's demand for a pay raise. On June 17, the company agreed to bargain and the strikers returned to work with full pay from the strike date, but the company's promise to bargain was short-lived.

In 1933, the National Industrial Recovery Act (NIRA) established the National Recovery Administration, which imposed Codes of Fair Competition on many industries, including telegraph. Postal Telegraph abided by the telegraph code, but Western Union resisted. The AWUE backed Western Union, because the code's reduction in hours meant a loss in pay and might encourage the company to revoke an earlier wage increase. The AWUE also worried that the NRA would use the code to prohibit company unionism. The Supreme Court ruled the NIRA unconstitutional in *Schechter v. United States* in May 1935, but Congress passed the National Labor Relations (Wagner) Act in July. One provision of the Wagner Act outlawed company-dominated employee associations, such as the AWUE. Again, Western Union and the AWUE resisted the attempt to democratize the company's labor relations. It took four years and the intervention of the National Labor Relations Board (NLRB), created by the Wagner Act, to finally free telegraph workers from the AWUE.

On January 12, 1938, the young American Communications Association (ACA) filed unfair labor practice charges against Western Union with the NLRB. The ACA, an affiliate of the Congress of Industrial Organizations that changed its name from the American Radio Telegraphists Association in 1937, already represented workers at Postal Telegraph and in Western Union's New York City area. In *NLRB v. Western Union* (1939), the Board found significant evidence that the company had in fact dominated and supported the AWUE since its formation on July 10, 1918, and rejected Western Union's appeals. On November 1, 1939, the NLRB ordered Western Union to cease and desist from controlling the Association Western Union Employees, and emphatically named the only remedy that would cure the situation: "Nothing short of disestablishment can effectively eradicate the effects of twenty years of interference and domination."

Western Union workers, no longer constrained by the AWUE, began to join existing unions and to form dozens of independent unions. By 1943, Western Union had signed some 100 contracts nationwide, eighty-five with AFL affiliates, four with CIO affiliates, and a number with independent unions. In addition, under the terms of the Merger Act (which brought Western Union and Postal Telegraph together), it agreed to honor Postal Telegraph's existing contracts with the ACA. However, not all telegraph workers rushed to join a union. In an NLRB election held on January 31, 1940, Western Union workers in Indianapolis rejected CTU Local 7 by a vote of 152 to 87.

Additionally, the disestablishment of the AWUE did not eliminate the culture it had created. Former AWUE leaders lingered on as CTU officers at all levels, many retaining their pro-company leanings. While it preferred no union at all, when it became clear that a union was inevitable, Western Union officials encouraged former AWUE leaders to become active in the CTU and in the newly formed AFL federal unions, because it perceived these to be more conservative and manageable than the more militant and left-leaning CIO-affiliated ACA, which vied with the CTU for the right to represent Western Union workers. Some former AWUE officers later became effective local and national leaders of the CTU, but many continued doing business as they had in the days of the AWUE, opposing strikes and walkouts, or any other "radical" activity against Western Union, even when the company was found to be in serious violation of its contract with the union.

The new CTU locals and the various independent unions executed dozens of local agreements with Western Union. The company's idea of collective bargaining was to have a contract prepared by company lawyers, present it to the local union's bargaining committee, and insist that it was the only agreement it would sign, forcing the small unions to accept weak contracts. This practice prevailed until national bargaining began in 1946. Four AFL unions joined the CTU in a coalition that petitioned the NLRB for a nationwide representation election, which was held in January of 1945. On May 13, 1945, the CTU was certified to represent some 53,000 Western Union workers in six of the company's seven divisions, while 7,000 workers in the company's New York Metropolitan Division chose the American Communications Association. Both unions then proceeded to negotiate contracts with the company—those negotiations stalled.

In October 1945, during one of the greatest strike waves in U.S. history, the ACA called hundreds of Western Union workers in New York City from their jobs to attend mass meetings to protest the company's delay in granting an 18-cent-per-hour wage increase authorized by the War Labor Board (WLB). Likewise, CTU locals planned a nationwide work stoppage demanding a similar pay raise. ACA members quickly approved strike action to force compliance with the WLB award. But on December 31, the Board reversed its position and ordered a 12-cent-per-hour pay increase for both groups, in effect reducing the increase previously granted to other New York workers. Western Union president J.L. Egan agreed to the Board's award and refused Mayor O'Dwyer's offer to arbitrate the dispute. ACA president Joseph P. Selly scorned the decision and on January 9, 1946, proceeded with the strike, calling 7,000 Western Union workers from their jobs in the New York City metropolitan area. CTU president W.L. Allen urged his members to accept the new award, canceled the national strike planned for January 7, 1946, and rejected ACA appeals for cooperation.

The ACA pledged not to interfere with government and overseas military traffic not transmitted from Western Union facilities, as did other CIO unions representing telegraph workers at cable and radiotelegraph companies. Nevertheless, the strike disrupted all other overseas cable and radio traffic; caused airlines, newspapers, and stock exchanges to rely on telephone service; and picket line violence led to arrests and injunctions. In February 1946, the long strike was settled when both sides agreed to accept the WLB award, and ACA Local 40 approved a new contract with Western Union.

CTU avoided a strike when renewing its contract with Western Union in April 1947 and again when it negotiated a wage reopener in December of that year with the help of a government fact-finding committee. The next year, the ACA was not so lucky.

The ACA sought a huge 30 percent wage increase for radio telegraphers employed by All-America Cables, Commercial Cables, Mackay Radio, and Western Union Cables, which the companies adamantly refused to grant. To force the issue, 2,600 ACA members walked off their jobs on January 2, 1948, striking the cable companies on both coasts. Technological advances allowed supervisory personnel and workers who had not struck to keep business moving. The prolonged strike prompted the companies to invoke the recently passed Taft-Hartley law. After a series of court orders and injunctions, the ninety-day strike was called off on March 31, 1948, with no new contract or a pay increase for the 2,200 workers at All-America Cables, Commercial Cable, and Mackay Radio. A meager contract was secured with Western Union Cables, providing nothing more than a few changes in its pension plan but no improvement in wages for its 400 cable workers. It was a clear victory for the cable companies, who now planned to cut their workforces by 20 percent or more, selectively preserving the jobs of those who had not struck or who had abandoned the strike and returned to work.

In April 1952, after several months of fruitless contract negotiations, 31,000 CTU members went on strike at Western Union. It was the first nationwide telegraph strike since 1919. The union's principal demands included the long-sought-after forty-hour workweek with forty-eight hours pay, and a 16-cent wage increase. It also sought to improve pension and sickness benefits, allow the closing of public offices only by mutual agreement between the company and the union, extend the existing severance pay provisions to all cases of layoffs except for resignations and terminations for just cause, eliminate reduced-time tours, and other improvements.

CTU president Adolph Brungs claimed that the strike closed some 2,000 Western Union offices. The company said that it temporarily shut down telegraph and money order services, while Western Union vice president J.L. Wilcox maintained that the company's offer was "still zero." In the New York Metropolitan Division, Western Union workers represented by the ACA crossed CTU picket lines as they reported for their midnight shifts.

The strike continued amid charges and countercharges. The company said that many of its offices were reopening and accused the union of using "goon squads," which the CTU denied. The union claimed that thousands of its members were still out maintaining twenty-four-hour picket lines. It accused Western Union of sending strikebreakers from New York to other areas, and charged the company with unfair labor practices. On May 3, as the strike reached its sixth week, Cyrus S. Ching, director of the Federal Mediation and Conciliation Service, invited company and union representatives to meet with a special panel in an effort to settle the stalemate. Western Union initially refused, but the parties finally met on May 7, but recessed on May 9 without agreement.

On May 19 the parties resumed talks, and on May 24 a tentative agreement was reached that provided for a uniform forty-hour workweek with forty-eight hours' pay, and a general wage increase of 10 cents per hour. When the company tried to dictate the order in which workers would return to their jobs, more than 90 percent of the strikers across the country insisted, "We all came out together—We will all go back together." Reflecting similar occurrences nationwide, some 300 members of Oakland Local 208 stayed out an extra day, until company officials backed down and allowed them to return together. The fifty-three-day strike of 1952 is noteworthy because it finally brought Western Union into compliance with the Fair Labor Standards Act of 1938, which set a basic forty-hour workweek. Months later, the forty-hour week was extended to Western Union workers in the New York City area covered by the ACA contract.

After the strike of 1952, the renewal of each two-year contract between Western Union and its two unions occasionally required the threat of strike action and, in a few cases, a short strike. In 1956, the ACA agreed to a day-to-day contract extension after expiration. The CTU delayed its planned nationwide strike pending further negotiations, and reduced its wage demand from 16 to 15 cents per hour, while the company offered 10 cents. The lack of progress produced restlessness among telegraph workers throughout the country, resulting in walkouts for mass meetings and short strikes. In New York, some 3,500 ACA members attended a three-hour union meeting at the Diplomat Hotel and voted to return to work while negotiations continued. In Philadelphia, several hundred CTU members left work to attend a meeting, while nearly 450 telegraph workers walked out for several hours in Cleveland to protest the lack of a timely agreement. Mass meetings were also being held in Washington, Chicago, New Orleans, Kansas City, and other cities. The sporadic walkouts effected business at the stock exchanges and caused delays in public service nationwide. Finally on June 6, 1956, Western Union and the two unions agreed on a two-year settlement that provided for a general wage increase of 13 cents per hour, retroactive to June 1; an additional 5 cents an hour for needed improvements in job classification; increased allowances for messengers; and an increase in the minimum pension payment to $100, while the company continued to deduct half the amount of the worker's Social Security.

On June 1, 1966, the CTU, by then reduced to 20,000 members, resorted to a four-hour walkout when no agreement was reached before its contract with Western Union expired at midnight. When further negotiations failed to produce an agreement, the union ordered a strike for June 8, the first nationwide strike since 1952. By this time, the ACA had merged with the Communications Workers of America (CWA), and Western Union workers who were members of the CWA Local 1177 continued to cross CTU picket lines in New York. An agreement was reached on the afternoon of June 9, 1966, and CTU members were instructed to return to work. The next year, at the union's 1967 convention in San Francisco, International president E.L. Hageman reported that "our difficulties in the 1966 negotiations were greatly increased by the doublecross we were given by the officers of the Communications Workers of America which represents about 3,500 Western Union Employees in the New York City Metropolitan area. Although CWA officers at the top level had agreed to meet with us and coordinate our bargaining with Western Union, we found that these promises were worthless." Hageman pointed out that the CTU had rejected an unsatisfactory offer from Western Union and was preparing to strike when CWA agreed to a slightly better settlement (but still much less than what the CTU was seeking), and that "after CWA agreed to this cheap settlement," Western Union tried to force an agreement upon the CTU in the pattern set by CWA. After the CTU won its best contract in years, CWA resumed bargaining and was given much the same.

In 1971, the Commercial Telegraphers' Union changed its name to the United Telegraph Workers (UTW). By then Western Union's bargaining unit had been reduced to slightly more than 20,000 workers, including teletype operators, clerical workers, and installation and repair technicians. The new name reflected the end of the era when telegrams were transmitted by a telegrapher at a key and sounder. The UTW represented 17,000 telegraph workers nationwide, while CWA Local 1177 bargained for its 3,100 members in the New York City and New Jersey area.

On March 22, 1971, the UTW presented Western Union with its agenda for the upcoming contract negotiations. Its major demands included a 16 percent general wage increase; refusal of the company's proposal to establish two unequal pension plan tracks; all mailgram messages to be prepared, transmitted, and mailed by Western Union workers; that mailgram equipment be installed and maintained by Western Union technicians; pension and vacation improvements; and a two-year contract.

On June 1, 1971, after negotiations failed, 20,000 members of the UTW and CWA struck Western Union. On June 4, federal mediator Nicholas Fidandis met with both parties in an attempt to resolve the dispute. Company officials refused to bargain on their plans to contract work historically performed by Western Union workers to other individuals and firms, refused to negotiate on a proposal to split the pension plan, and offered no more than previously proposed. The meeting adjourned with no other meetings scheduled. On June 23, UTW president E.L. Hageman gratefully accepted a contribution of $100,000 from CWA executive vice president Gus Cramer to the UTW's dwindling strike assistance fund, a generous donation to aid smaller UTW locals that had little or no funds. Some of the larger UTW local unions that had established strike funds were able to survive without assistance.

On July 1, the UTW bargaining committee resumed negotiations with Western Union and obtained a commitment that the company would not proceed with its intention to split the pension plan to provide separate pension systems for management and workers. The company jettisoned language that would have allowed its board of directors to suspend or terminate the pension plan at any time, which the union feared would weaken or even do away with the existing plan. The company also agreed to continue its partial funding of the pension plan.

The strike continued with the unions claiming 100 percent support nationwide. The prolonged strike was not without an occasional confrontation. The most serious occurred on the picket line in Washington, DC, when a supervisor opened a door by repeatedly kicking it so forcefully that it struck a picket in the back several times, and then kicked the picket in the rear as he departed the scene.

Finally, on the evening of July 26, 1971, the UTW and Western Union signed a two-year contract ending the fifty-seven-day strike, although the agreement did not apply to the New York area workers covered by CWA Local 1177. The new agreement provided for a wage increase of 10 percent on July 28, 1971; another 9 percent raise on July 28, 1972; five weeks of vacation with pay after twenty-five years of service; improvements in the medical and life insurance plans; changes in job security and severance pay for those subject to force reduction; a new Article 56 that made it the policy of the company "to preserve for its own employees all work normally and historically performed by them"; and other changes and improvements.

While the new contract awaited ratification by the members, UTW president Hageman obtained a ruling that the ninety-day wage freeze imposed by President Richard Nixon would not apply to wage increases and benefits that were effective as of July 28, 1971. CWA Local 1177 and Western Union reached a tentative settlement on September 1, which was ratified by the members on September 11, both sides agreeing there would be no wage increase during the government's ninety-day wage-price freeze. Subsequent three-year contracts were executed in 1973, 1976, and 1979 without strike action.

By 1985, Western Union was reporting losses of millions of dollars each quarter. Some observers blamed the company's plight on poor management that could not cope with a fast-changing communications industry. To help the financially troubled company, UTW and CWA members agreed to cut their pay by 10 percent for the six months remaining in the contract that would expire on July 27, saving Western Union $10 million a year. Continuing losses forced the sinking company to throw additional workers overboard and to refinance its debt with lending banks. Under these circumstances, negotiations proved difficult when union and company representatives met in April 1985 to forge a new agreement.

When the contract expired on July 27, 1985, the number of Western Union workers stood at approximately 7,100, with about 6,500 represented by the UTW and the rest by CWA. The UTW settled for wage increases of 2 to 3 percent instead of the 4 to 5 percent it had sought and accepted reduced vacations, while the company agreed to cut the number of executive positions. However, according to UTW president Richard Brockert, negotiators "remained far apart on several major points." The sticking points included the company's intention to contract out work, reduce its workforce by between 1,500 and 2,000 workers, cut severance payments, hire part-time employees, and reduce health benefits. When contract talks broke down at midnight, UTW members struck the company nationwide. New York CWA Local 1177 continued to bargain and its members worked until July 31, when they joined the strike. On August 6, the UTW and Western Union settled on a two-year contract that included important concessions by the union that it hoped would bring stability to the company.

The ten-day strike produced an agreement that restored the temporary cut in wages previously agreed to; no pay raise the first year; a 3 percent wage increase the second year; a two-year "wage-investment" plan funded by a percentage of the company's pretax profits each year; the elimination of a "comparable job" clause that gave workers with five or more years of service whose jobs became redundant the right to remain on the payroll if a comparable job was not available; the elimination of certain job classifications; the creation of a ten-member labor-management advisory board; permission for the company to hire part-time workers; changes in the severance pay schedule; and other minor benefits and concessions.

UTW President Brockert summed up the difficult negotiations by stating that "we preserved as much as we could, yet we gave the company flexibility." According to Western Union chairman Robert Leventhal, "Tough decisions had to be made, and both sides had to face up to them." On September 4, the UTW announced the ratification of the new contract and Western Union proceeded with its plan to further reduce its workforce. Western Union workers in the New York area, members of CWA Local 1177 that had walked out on July 31, remained on strike until mid-November. They finally settled for an agreement essentially the same as the two-year contract that the UTW had negotiated in August.

Western Union continued to close public offices, and the company's declining workforce had reduced the membership of the UTW to a level that threatened its viability. In 1986 the UTW merged with CWA, an affiliation that provided for a CWA/UTW General Bargaining Council to protect the interests of its remaining members. Several UTW locals remained intact as CWA locals, while many of the UTW's small locals merged with existing CWA locals or disbanded. The General Bargaining Council, chaired by former UTW president Dan Beckstead, continued to negotiate new agreements covering the remaining Western Union workers until the mid-1990s, when CWA assumed the duties of contract administration.

In 1987, Western Union underwent a major financial restructuring that temporarily solved the company's financial problems through the sale of $500 million in high-yield, five-year notes, and established a new wholly owned subsidiary, Western Union Financial Services, Inc., to handle its money transfer services. On April 18, 1991, at its annual meeting, the Western Union Corporation was renamed the New Valley Corporation, after the New Valley Telegraph Company of 1851. On September 19, 1994, a bankruptcy court approved the New Valley Reorganization Plan, which included the sale of WU Financial Services to First Financial Management Corporation for $1.9 billion, including the Western Union name, trademark, and public identity, and on January 18, 1995, New Valley emerged from bankruptcy.

The name "Western Union," reminiscent of miles of wire strung from poles across the country, of telegraphers seated at clicking keys and sounders, of the bearer of good and bad tidings, today is applied to much of the money order business of the First Data Corporation. The communications business, once highly unionized, has become one of mixed cellular and traditional telephones, of computerized data transfer, and satellite transmissions, an industry that, except for telephone workers, is largely nonunion.

See also: Telegraph Messenger Strikes and Their Impact on Telegraph Unionization, 511.

Bibliography

Barbash, Jack. *Unions and Telephones: The Story of the Communications Workers of America.* New York: Harper & Brothers, 1952.

Bing, Alexander M. *War-Time Strikes and Their Adjustment.* New York: Dutton, 1921; reprint, New York: Arno & *The New York Times*, 1971.

Brooks, Thomas R. *Communications Workers of America: The Story of a Union* New York: Mason/Charter, 1977.

Coe, Lewis. *The Telegraph: A History of Morse's Invention and Its Predecessors in the United States.* Jefferson, NC: McFarland & Company, Inc., 1993.

Conner, Valerie Jean. *The War Labor Board, Stability, Social Justice and the Voluntary State in World War I.* Chapel Hill: University of North Carolina Press, 1983.

Gabler, Edwin. *The American Telegrapher: A Social History, 1860–1900.* New Brunswick, NJ: Rutgers University Press, 1988.

Jepsen, Thomas C. *My Sisters Telegraphic: Women in the Telegraph Office, 1846–1950.* Athens: Ohio University Press, 2000.

Norwood, Stephen H. *Labor's Flaming Youth: Telephone Operators and Worker Militancy, 1878–1923.* Urbana: University of Illinois Press, 1990.

Thompson, Robert Luther. *Wiring a Continent: The History of the Telegraph Industry in the United States, 1832–1866.* Princeton, NJ: Princeton University Press, 1947.

Ulriksson, Vidkunn. *The Telegraphers: Their Craft and Their Unions.* Washington, DC: Public Affairs Press, 1953.

TELEGRAPH MESSENGER STRIKES AND THEIR IMPACT ON TELEGRAPH UNIONIZATION

Greg Downey

During the first half century of telegraph expansion in the United States, telegraph operators attempted to form unions several times, and each attempt ended in failure. Western Union (WU), the main telegraph company in the country, was largely to blame for the unions' failures. When confronted with a new organizing attempt, it offered comparable union benefits to undermine the incentives for joining a union. When confronted with a strike, the company used its contractual links to the railroad and press companies to call in replacement telegraphers. Yet the unions—the National Telegraphic Union, the Telegraphers Protective League, and the Knights of Labor's (KofL) Brotherhood of Telegraphers—shared some of the blame for their failures. Until the Great Depression, telegraphers and their unions ignored the organizing goals and strategic potential of their youngest coworkers, the telegraph messengers. Although WU assistant vice president T.B. Gittings declared to the Senate Committee on Education and Labor as late as 1945 that "there has never been, we believe, a single instance in history of a strike caused or threatened by the employment in commerce of messengers under sixteen," the messengers had a long history of labor militancy. In fact, only after the adult, skilled telegraph workers began to ally with their youthful, unskilled counterparts in the 1930s would the unionization movement in telegraphy have any real success.

Despite the lack of attention from the operators' unions, the messengers began to grow their own form of labor militancy. They were often employed not by WU but by subcontracted "district telegraph" companies, including franchises of the American District Telegraph (ADT) company. Messenger strikes increased in frequency, size, geographic extent, effectiveness, and union involvement, all the way to the turn of the century. For example, in 1874, ADT boys in New York City struck over an increase in daily hours from eight to ten with no raise in their $4-per-week pay. The strike resulted in four boys being fired and sixteen being fined for "leaving their posts." Similar small, unsuccessful strikes occurred in other places as well, but failed, according to the National Telegrapher Union's journal, *Telegrapher,* due to "the superabundance of labor, especially of juvenile labor, in our large cities."

Yet the messengers had the power to paralyze the entire telegraph system, if only they would all strike together. The New York City ADT boys tried this in August 1880 when around 100 ADT messengers walked out for a wage increase. The strike grew until half of ADT's entire 700-strong New York City messenger force was out, affecting nearly all city offices. However, by bringing in strikebreakers from other companies and arresting any boys who interfered, the company broke the strike within a week. Other strikes, though, were more successful. A May 1882 WU messenger strike in Boston over a proposed pay decrease from 2½ cents to 1¼ cents per message was victorious. Tactics of the striking "trotters" included posting signs all over town warning other boys to stay away from WU and harassing anyone hired to break the strike. WU was forced to use linemen, clerks, and other employees to deliver messages. Some local businessmen sided with the messengers, writing letters to the telegraph managers. After three days, the company agreed to keep the current pay rate. This success hinged on the very resources that made messengers valuable in the first place: urban mobility, the sympathy of the local business contacts they served every day, and youthful energy. But victory was still rare in the larger messenger market of New York City. Even when 660 ADT messengers went on strike there a month later over the threatened loss of a 57-cent Sunday holiday, forcing the company to back down on the rule, the twenty-five boys who organized the strike were fired.

While the boys might have exerted their right to protest, they still hadn't earned the right to organize. In early 1887, the still-popular KofL became involved in a New York City messenger strike, the first union to do so. This was also the first time that messengers from both ADT and WU all joined in a single, citywide strike, and it revealed the difficulty that children faced when using adult tactics to demand adult wages. According to Foster R. Dulles and Melvyn Dubofsky, when the ADT manager found out that 150 of his employees had been meeting with the KofL to list grievances, he sent a letter to all the parents of the messengers, warning them of the dangers of unions:

> We send you a notice that we are well informed from reliable sources that your son is in danger of falling into the hands of agents who are trying to bind together the honest working boys of this city and lead them to commit acts against the laws of peace, good order, and honest industry. We wish to warn him through you to be on his guard, to keep away from such influences, and avoid serious results.

The fact that over seventy parents called to thank him for this letter shows that the failure of this strike could not be attributed to company hostility alone.

Later messenger strikes would be trivialized by the media. By 1899, *Telegraph Age* painted messenger strikes as the absurd actions of lazy boys who "refuse to allow, if strikes can prevent it, any arrogant and money-bloated corporation to compel them to hurry." By 1910, the *New York Times* wrote of "Wall Street's annual strike of messenger boys" and quoted an ADT manager as saying, "It is a sign of Spring, this strike talk among the messenger boys. It comes every year and nobody takes it seriously." Even large messenger strikes were lampooned. In November 1910, after 600 messengers attended a meeting with union representatives from the Central Federated Union, 500 ADT boys from forty offices around New York City went on strike. They were soon joined by Postal Telegraph (PT) boys as well. But within a week and a half, the strike had been broken because ADT and PT were willing to pay bonuses to the abundant strikebreakers. Still, the strike gained national press in the social work journal *Survey* and the attention of a major labor group. Messenger boys in Philadelphia, Pittsburgh, and Los Angeles went on strike as well, apparently inspired by the New York City boys. But the *New York Times* poked fun at the strikers in cartoons (portraying a messenger being spanked by his mother) and caricatured their public speeches as uneducated.

These messenger strikes, although increasing in frequency and effectiveness, were of little concern to WU for two reasons. First, messenger labor actions were constrained in space. Unlike operators' strikes (which could be signaled nationwide over the telegraph), messenger actions were inevitably confined to a single city (if not a single neighborhood or office). Second, messenger labor actions were constrained in time. Unlike operators, who could plan on a relatively stable career with time to build a union over several years, messengers moved through the telegraph company in a revolving door, rarely remaining for more than a year. These circumstances frustrated the development of a shared memory of struggle within the messenger population and thwarted the maintenance of long-term workplace gains. By the turn of the twentieth century, enough new operators felt the need for a union to make a fourth attempt at organization. In 1903 the Commercial Telegraphers' Union of America (CTU) was formed, comprising sixty locals and 8,010 members, with separate divisions for press, brokerage, and commercial operators. The new union affiliated with the American Federation of Labor (AFL).

Messengers were excluded from the CTU; however, the union mouthpiece, the *Commercial Telegraphers' Journal (CTJ)*, talked of messengers regularly. By 1903, messengers were now striking not just in big cities like New York, but in smaller cities from Butte, Montana, to Memphis, Tennessee. The CTU took notice after fifty-three messenger boys in Portland, Oregon, set up a "Messenger Boy's

Protective Union" affiliated with the AFL in order to "keep the lads off the streets and amused during leisure hours" with a club room, gymnasium, and reading room. "Some of these little fellows are beginning to realize that the only way to redress their grievances lies in organization. They are to be congratulated." The *CTJ* lamented the fact that "men with the intelligence of the average telegrapher of today" did not themselves organize: "You are not doing even as much as the poorly paid messengers."

Most telegraph operators were wary of messengers rather than celebratory. This reflected in part the deteriorating workplace conditions for operators after the turn of the century: salaries dwindled; operators had to supply their own "mills" (typewriters); the companies hired greater numbers of women at lower wages; and more and more "ham" (poorly prepared) operators graduated from the "plug schools" (small, private, and often transient, telegraph operator training schools of varying quality). CTU operators feared that messenger boys trained by the telegraph companies would be offered existing operator jobs at lower salaries, dropping operator wages from $60.00 to $70.00 per month to $35.00 to $40.00 per month. In the *CTJ*, they advised: "Discourage these would-be 'knights of the key' and tell them that the 'telegraph profession' is a thing of the past."

Such fears were ironic since messengers were still striking all over the United States. The year 1907 brought an economic crisis, with nonfarm unemployment rising to 16 percent, and messengers struck in Chicago and Omaha. Operators walked out as well, and the strike quickly spread to nearly 100 cities and involved nearly 10,000 commercial operators, with support coming from railway and press operators as well. This was not an official CTU strike, as the union "had made no headway worth mentioning in its efforts to organize Western Union employees." But dissent had grown among WU operators over punishments for union involvement and a promised 10 percent pay raise that never materialized. The CTU, which had not been prepared for a strike, ran out of money as the strike lasted eighty-nine days, a waiting game that WU won.

The 1907 strike failed, but it motivated Congress to call for an investigation of the telegraph industry. The 500-page report, "Investigation of Western Union and Postal Telegraph-Cable Companies" (Senate document 725), released in 1909, revealed that after the strike, WU stepped up its efforts to replace skilled, male Morse Code operators using keys and sounders with (supposedly) unskilled female "Automatic" operators using printing typewriters. According to historian Charles Craypo, the number of so-called "extra" or part-time operators increased while full-time operators decreased. And even without an actual blacklist, the few big telegraph companies led by WU could simply fire all union operators and agree not to hire new operators without (union-free) letters of recommendation.

These aggressive tactics shifted somewhat in 1909, when AT&T, led by Theodore Vail, purchased a controlling interest in WU. AT&T was fighting unionization just as WU was, but under Vail the two companies began to promote the "welfare capitalism" tactics of the corporate-backed National Civic Federation, as historian Stephen H. Norwood has chronicled. Even though he still fired operators for union activities, Vail began to improve conditions in telegraph offices. He increased WU wages 50 percent between 1910 and 1913 and instituted both a pension fund and a loan program. Even the CTU journal hailed his "broad mind and liberal views." The Vail years were brief—in 1914, AT&T gave up its stake in WU over antitrust fears—but Vail's groomed successor, Newcomb Carlton, continued Vail's reforms. Under Carlton, operators could receive bonuses of up to 7 percent of their annual pay, and even messengers could receive up to a $25.00 bonus.

Such reforms foreshadowed a new labor strategy for WU: creating an in-house labor organization for its employees to compete against independent labor unions. By 1917 only twelve company unions existed in the entire United States, but then the country entered World War I. Nearly 4,500 strikes broke out, involving over 1 million workers, due to the rise in wartime prices without a corresponding increase in wages. At the same time, unemployment fell to less than 2 percent and factories experienced heavy job turnover as workers moved through many jobs looking for better wages. Wary of the recent Bolshevik Revolution in Russia and eager to avoid a general economic

Striking telegraph messenger boys in New York City, circa 1918. Despite their youth and only intermittent support from other telegraph workers and their organizations, messengers engaged in numerous strikes from the 1870s to the 1940s. The strikes were mostly local, usually short, and sometimes successful. (*Courtesy:* George Gratham Bain Collection, Library of Congress.)

upheaval, the U.S. government acted to safeguard key infrastructure industries. In December 1917, the government took control of the railroads. WU executives feared that communications were next in line—and they were right.

WU president Carlton accelerated the government's takeover by attacking the unions in *WU News:* "We know that more than ninety five percent of our employees aim to give the company a square deal. But less than five percent are Bolsheviki who would, if they could, do to the Western Union what has been done to Russia." Among Carlton's "Bolsheviki" would have been the New York City messengers. A messenger strike that began in February 1918 quickly grew to 300 boys—25 percent of the city total at the time. The boys demanded a piece wage increase to 3 cents a message from 2½ cents, an increase from 15 cents per hour to 20 cents per hour for "temp" work, and a ten-hour day. WU responded by increasing telephone deliveries, substituting telegraph clerks and linemen for messengers, and even by hiring messenger girls. Though WU succeeded in breaking the strike after a few days, the messengers gained both union and government involvement at a critical time and place. Over 400 messengers attended a meeting at New York's Yorkville Forum, known as "the Socialist headquarters of the upper east side." The AFL was one of the sponsors of the meeting, and a special representative from the State Department of Labor attended as well. Carlton certainly would have taken notice of this.

Perhaps also noting such widespread unrest, President Wilson's National War Labor Board ordered WU to cease discriminating against employees who joined unions. But Carlton refused and instead unveiled his own company union. Like his mentor Vail, Carlton thought of WU as a public utility, entitled to receive the same protection against strikes as the Post Office. Of course, Carlton, like his predecessors, fought fiercely to keep WU as a private corporation, immune from democratic public control. Carlton's argument against the unions backfired, and the government took over both the telegraph and the telephone industries, putting the telegraph under the control of the Post from August 1918 to August 1919. But government control did not put an end to the company union.

The Association Western Union Employees (AWUE), which did not use "of" in its name, was "neither a trade union, nor a workers union" but a "voluntary association of individuals in the employ of the Western Union Telegraph Company." A grievance procedure existed, but employees who were members of the AFL were not eligible to join the AWUE, and strikes were disallowed—the AWUE's journal, *Telegraph World,* advised "most collective effort is based upon some form of conspiracy instead of being the expression of the spirit of co-operation."

Even though the AWUE was clearly an anti-union organization, it signed up nearly half of WU's 40,000 employees during its first year. The CTU was heartbroken; its president resigned in shame. The CTU's failure mirrored that of the AFL at large—with the "Red Scare" in full force after the end of the war, kicked off by the notorious "Palmer Raids," the AFL began to purge itself of "radicals" in the 1920s, and its membership shrank from about 5 million to 3 million in the first few years the decade. Meanwhile, company unions prospered in the 1920s. AWUE continued to grow until by 1930 it included almost all WU employees—advertising itself to members as "Your Friend—Counselor and Advisor."

The AWUE, though born in the midst of a widely publicized messenger strike, at first did not cater at all to messengers. When WU demonstrated the AWUE's effectiveness by distributing over $3 million to employees in 1920 in a new profit-sharing plan, this money was divided among only 28,676 of the 60,500 total WU employees—messengers and temporary workers were excluded. AWUE rules allowed any employee aged eighteen or above who had been with WU over three months to join, thus excluding all but the oldest messengers on the basis of age and job tenure. During the AWUE's first year, not even a New York City strike of nearly 2,000 WU boys—a strike so serious that state mediators were called in—bothered the new organization.

The prosperity of the 1920s ended for much of the nation in 1929, with the Great Depression bringing a change in labor markets and a rise in union activity. Boys with jobs held on to them into their early adult years, and men who ordinarily would not think to apply for "boys' jobs" sought out such positions in earnest. Thus, the average age in the messenger service began to rise in the early 1930s, causing messenger work to be viewed differently by employers, unions, and government regulators. This change came just as the AWUE had signed up nearly all of its target audience, some 36,603 adult employees. But the independent union threat was returning—overall union membership would rise from 3 million to 9 million in the 1930s. Thus, in April 1934, at a time when the AWUE only counted 500 messenger members nationwide, the company union began to organize messengers at the request of WU management. This activity, however, was "confined to certain divisional offices where disturbing influences might arise," especially when new messengers demanded cancellation of their uniform rentals.

The AWUE had for some time allowed messengers to become "associate" members who paid dues but lacked voting rights. By June 1934, AWUE bylaws allowed all messengers to become voting members, and the organization proclaimed in *Telegraph World,* "thousands of Messengers are affiliating with our Organization throughout the United States." In November 1934 the AWUE claimed that it had signed up 3,000 of the estimated 20,000 WU messengers across the United States, imploring to its members, "Let's make it 100% strong—Every messenger a member!"

Ironically, it was the messengers who struck the first blows against the AWUE. In March 1937, the Toledo WU messengers affiliated with the CTU and went on strike. The WU division president, in a move similar to ADT management decades before, sent telegrams to the parents of the messengers, warning them of the outside union and encouraging their sons to return to work under the AWUE instead. The strike was broken, but it had an important consequence behind the scenes. WU vice president J.C. Willever, fearing efforts of "outsiders to stir up discontent among our messengers," wrote to all AWUE division heads: "I suggest that you keep your ear close to the ground and arrange to get the Association in promptly on any sign of dissatisfaction or unrest." The letter, revealed in a National Labor Relations Board (NLRB) case, documented the fact that WU controlled AWUE policies at the highest levels.

Close on the heels of the failed Toledo strike, a Seattle messenger strike in June 1937 closed that city's main Western Union office and all nineteen branch offices when 116 boys demanded higher wages. Some 400 workers were idled by the closings, but the effects did not end there. The messengers again affiliated with a CTU local, and they filed unfair labor practice charges against WU on July 26. WU responded that it only recognized the AWUE as a proper bargaining unit, not the CTU.

The Seattle messenger strike was the first time the NLRB scrutinized WU practices. Newcomb Carlton, now no longer WU president but chairman of the board, traveled from New York City to testify at the hearing. Nonetheless, the NLRB sided with the messengers' union. It ordered the Seattle WU office to cease encouraging membership in the AWUE and to recognize the CTU instead. The messengers had finally demonstrated a role in winning telegraph unionization, partly through their willingness to act and partly through their sheer numbers, especially in urban offices. Mike Rivise, a WU manager, later wrote, "It was inevitable . . . that the backbone of the unionizing movement would be the messenger, the man from below."

The union that learned the most from these events was neither the CTU nor the AWUE, but a new telegraph union formed in the 1930s. Originally organized as the American Radio Telegraphists' Association (ARTA) in 1931, it soon developed a broader agenda of uniting all communications workers. In 1937, it affiliated with the Committee for Industrial Organization (CIO), expanded its target to land telegraphs, and began to organize New York telegraphers. The CIO was the right place for the ARTA, because after less than a year the upstart telegraph union had organized the second-largest U.S. telegraph company, Postal Telegraph, ousting the CTU in the process. After it won, the ARTA changed its name to the American Communications Association (ACA), reflecting its enlarged mandate. While the ACA set its sights on Western Union, all the CTU could do in response was to accuse the ACA of communism.

In its first move against WU, the ACA filed unfair labor practice charges with the National Labor Relations Board, charging WU with discrimination against the ACA in favor of the AWUE—just as the Seattle messengers' union had done successfully a few years earlier.

The ACA used the AWUE's haphazard approach to organizing the messengers as part of its evidence that the AWUE was a company union, demonstrating that the AWUE only tried to organize messengers when ordered to by WU managers—citing J.C. Willever's order to the AWUE after the 1937 messenger strikes. For example, in response to this order by WU, the president of the AWUE Gulf Division had told his local officers, according to court documents, to "select from six to twelve boys of the highest type; high school graduates, clean cut, intelligent, good personality" and to "Sell these boys on the fact that the A.W.U.E. is the parent organization that deals for all employees in all matters pertaining to the welfare of Western Union employees." He also warned, "Mass meetings of all the boys must be avoided as only demands and more demands will be made upon you."

The ACA pushed messenger issues not only in the courts but at the bargaining table as well, so much so that *BusinessWeek* mistakenly referred to them as a "messengers' union." In October 1938 the Fair Labor Standards Act, introduced by FDR a year earlier, instituted a 25-cents-per-hour minimum wage, rising to 40 cents in seven years. Western Union immediately objected, seeking a special exemption from Congress, saying that it could not possibly afford to pay messengers that rate. But the ACA fought for the messenger minimum, secretly delighted that Western Union disregarded the law: "I think a hearing on the messengers, provided we can pin it on WU, would give us a chance for some publicity and make the messengers good and restless everywhere," wrote one organizer. ACA locals made direct appeals to messengers in large cities: "Only the ACA has a program and is making a stiff fight to win the $11 [weekly] minimum for messengers, and to defeat any merger except on terms which will fully protect the jobs, wages and working conditions of all employees." When the Senate Committee on Interstate Commerce held hearings on whether or not to investigate the telegraph industry, the ACA was there, not the CTU, and the ACA brought messengers to testify on their own behalf.

Using the messengers made sense for the ACA. For example, they began to organize San Francisco WU messengers in May 1939, and by September they were ready to strike. With the messengers out, the San Francisco office closed down. Non-messenger ACA members joined their young colleagues a few days later. The strike was serious enough that the Secretary of Labor intervened, calling WU president Roy White and ACA president Melvyn Rathborne to Washington to settle in November 1939. WU boycotted the meeting, again arguing that the AWUE was the only union they recognized, but a month later they accepted the Secretary of Labor's recommendation that the strike end with all employees returning to their jobs—and with the ACA as the new union in the San Francisco office. The ACA's focus on messenger boys worked. By late 1939 the AWUE admitted that "an increasing amount of conference time is being utilized in the solution of messenger working condition problems." That year the NLRB trial examiner ruled that the AWUE was dominated by WU and could no longer be recognized as the bargaining agent of the employees. WU appealed, especially on the question of whether the AWUE only tried to organize messengers to keep WU strike-free. The AWUE now argued that organizing messengers had never made sense in the first place because such employees did not deserve a union vote when they only paid dues once and then quit a month later. But the appeal failed, and in June 1940 the AWUE's *Telegraph World* folded. By using the messenger boys as a point of leverage, the ACA had broken WU's twenty-year-old company union.

The passing of the AWUE left a power vacuum and nearly all of the nation's WU employees without union representation. The federal government was close to finalizing a merger between the ailing but ACA-dominated Postal Telegraph and the powerful but unionless Western Union. One company would result, and only one union could represent its workers. By 1940, elections for telegraph union representation had been held in most major cities, and a pattern was set that would last for the next decade. The ACA and the CTU were forced to share bargaining power within Western Union, but unevenly: CTU power was spread out among the states and ACA power was concentrated in New York City. As the nation's center of telegraphic communication and the site of WU headquarters, New York City in 1940 was where over 2,000 of the industry's 14,000 messengers worked—more than anywhere else.

Having captured New York, the ACA continued to press for the messengers in the other large urban telegraph markets. When 400 Chicago messengers struck in May 1941, a settlement was negotiated with ACA mediators, including seniority assurances, a lunch period after four hours of duty, no more fines for tardiness, a company promise to keep uniforms in good condition, and an elimination of speedup. The election held in July 1941 to decide which union would represent the 1,000 Detroit WU employees was won by ACA, in part due to the votes of 200 eligible messengers, even though 150 other messengers were declared ineligible to vote because they had started with WU only a month earlier. The ACA bragged that the CTU could not match its messenger organizing tactics: "The CTU-AFL stooped to a new low when they tried to capture the 200 eligible messenger votes by feeding whiskey to seventeen-year-old messengers and by passing out 'courtesy police cards' which were supposed to grant immunity to the bearers from prosecution by the police for traffic violations." The ACA also followed through in its courting of the Detroit messengers by remembering them in the new contract with WU, proposing free bicycle maintenance, full tours (shifts) with lunch hours, and time-and-a-half for the big telegram holidays, such as Christmas.

When World War II began, the landscape of telegraph unionism was uneven and contested. Congress pushed telegraph consolidation forward, fearing that disarray at Western Union and Postal Telegraph would endanger the efforts of the military. Only one union could prevail and suddenly the ACA was at a disadvantage, in part because of its reliance on the messengers. The government's main fear concerning the merger was mass layoffs, not wages or working conditions. In this context, the high endemic messenger turnover rate was a hidden asset; messengers, the biggest single category of employees, could be expected to quit with such regularity (especially during a wartime industrial boom where higher-paying jobs were plentiful) that they represented no layoff concern at all. ACA arguments about the plight of the messengers fell on deaf ears.

Finally, in 1943, Congress amended the Communications Act of 1934 to provide for a merger of Western Union and Postal Telegraph. New union elections were necessary for all 50,000 telegraph employees, including the 12,000 messengers.

Although the ACA was still more aggressive than the CTU in targeting messengers in the new organizing campaign, the boys were losing their strategic appeal. In August 1944, ACA president Joseph Selly urged the NLRB to "eliminate from the election those who came on the payroll after October 8 [1943]," because between the date of the merger and the date of the election, "approximately 5,000 messengers" had "gone out of the industry in the course of the usual turnover . . ." In other words, even though on the day of the merger the ACA represented 15,000 employees, on the day of the election they only represented some 6,000 employees. Even though the ACA argued publicly that increasing messenger wages would directly "improve the delivery service rendered the public by the company," behind the scenes new ACA organizers were warned, "work should be concentrated among non-messenger employees . . . since the turnover among messengers is so great that the number eligible to vote (that is, on the payroll long enough) will be negligible."

The NLRB-sponsored election was finally held in January 1945, and the geography of labor had an important effect on the results. Although the nationwide vote was roughly 20,000 to 11,000 in favor of the CTU, the ACA prevailed in one division: New York City. This ACA victory was due in part to the still-substantial messenger numbers in the city. But telegraphy was made up of more than just urban messengers, and in the end the CTU controlled around 50,000 of the 60,000 WU workers. The ACA controlled only 8,000. For the messengers, though, a larger battle was lost. Once their wages were brought in line with national legal minimums, WU opted to increase mechanization and subcontract to the Post Office and taxi services to carry its telegrams instead of keeping a large messenger force of its own. The success of the unions (and the government) in making messengers into "men" instead of boys thus marked the end of the messengers' tale.

See also: Strikes by Telegraph Workers, 498.

Bibliography

Craypo, Charles. "The Impact of Changing Corporate Structure and Technology on Telegraph Labor, 1870–1978." *Labor Studies Journal* 3 (1979): 283–307.

Downey, Gregory J. *Telegraph Messenger Boys: Labor, Technology, and Geography, 1850–1950.* New York: Routledge, 2002.

Dulles, Foster R., and Melvyn Dubofsky. *Labor in America: A History.* Wheeling, IL: Harlan Davidson, 1993.

Gabler, Edwin. *The American Telegrapher.* New Brunswick, NJ: Rutgers University Press, 1988.

Norwood, Stephen H. *Labor's Flaming Youth: Telephone Operators and Worker Militancy, 1878–1923.* Urbana: University of Illinois Press, 1990.

Oslin, George P. *The Story of Telecommunications.* Macon, GA: Mercer University Press, 1992.

Rivise, Mike J. *Inside Western Union.* New York: Sterling, 1950.

Thompson, Robert L. *Wiring a Continent: The History of the Telegraph Industry in the United States 1832–1866.* Princeton, NJ: Princeton University Press, 1947.

Ulriksson, Vidkunn. *The Telegraphers: Their Craft and Their Unions.* Washington, DC: Public Affairs Press, 1953.

TROLLEY WARS

Scott Molloy

Many bus lines in older metropolitan areas of the United States follow the same routes as earlier electric streetcars. In many cases the trolley traveled the identical thoroughfares as more primitive forms of public transportation such as horsecars, omnibuses, and even stagecoaches. The lineage of these routes reaches back into the eighteenth century. Behind the technology stood generations of transit workers.

Historian George Rogers Taylor detailed the development and impact of all forms of mechanical transit in a seminal work: *The Transportation Revolution, 1815–1860.* He outlined the changes in the superstructure that created a modern transit grid: turnpikes, public roads, and tracks. The impact was indeed relentless and far-reaching for travelers, employees, and society.

As historians such as Alfred D. Chandler Jr., Sidney Harring, David Nye, Shelton Stromquist, and John Stover have illustrated, the steam railroad, more than any other form of public transportation, crisscrossed the nation with passengers and freight like blood veins carrying nutrients through a body. From humble beginnings in the late 1820s, trackage reached a staggering 250,000 miles by 1917, serving urban centers and rural outposts. As the country's first big business, transportation companies as well as other industries witnessed the railroad experience and copied its organizational arrangements. In the arena of personnel relations, labor-management disagreements exploded on the rails into some of the greatest conflicts in American history. Trainmen launched the first national strike in 1877; fought railroad tycoon Jay Gould in several epic railroad battles in the 1880s; and capped the walkouts with the famous Pullman strike in 1894. Although intermittent friction plagued these carriers well into the twentieth century, a mature and sophisticated personnel system finally took root in the federal Erdman Act in 1898.

By the time the railroad industry reached uneasy agreements with its employees—represented by some of the strongest labor unions in the nation—a parallel, urban transit matrix developed in the United States. If the steam railroad served as the country's long distance transportation artery, horsecars and electric streetcars became America's metropolitan capillaries. The economic successes of the steam railroad rubbed off on the trolley business, but the earlier problems in personnel and political relations plagued streetcar companies in even greater fashion. Commentators dubbed ensuing battles between employers and employees as "car wars." Collectively they outstripped any mayhem on the railroads. However, because of the local nature of these outbursts, they seldom garnered the national attention of a major train tie-up or an industrial slugfest.

Horsecars

New York City hosted the nation's first omnibus—a kind of urban stagecoach—in the 1820s. The following decade the city sported the country's initial horsecar system, a major step forward in urban mass transportation. Municipal service, although still tied to the horse, now rolled by city blocks on iron rails. At five to six miles per hour, the new "animal railway" was not rapid transit but an important predecessor to the coming electric revolution. Horsecars accommodated the middle class, professionals, and some upper-crust patrons. When the new railway replaced the lumbering omnibuses in one New England community, a distraught patron beseeched the crew from his porch to wait a few minutes while he finished breakfast. The horsecar conductor informed him that the system worked on a fixed schedule unlike the more accommodating but slower primitive omnibus. He would have to wait for the next car.

While blue-collar riders occasionally took a jaunt with the family on Sundays or holidays, most Gilded Age toilers lived near their work. Passengers used the sobriquet "people's carriages" to describe the horsecars more for their potential as mass transit than any immediate reality. Some wealthy homeowners opposed the installation of rails, fearing a decline in property values as well as an influx of day-trippers and working people into exclusive neighborhoods. This invasion was postponed until the development of electric propulsion. Real estate adjacent to horsecar lines actually appreciated. As slow as the animal railway may seem today, the horses moved faster than anyone could walk. Boston claimed twenty competing enterprises in 1860 and the nation hosted more than 500 lines in 300 towns by 1886.

An intense battle between proprietors in the horsecar industry provoked early political involvement. Companies influenced mayors and city councils, governors and general assemblies. Such action paralleled the fierce, high-stakes interference in state and federal arenas by steam railroad interests. Owners sought franchises, subsidies, and lower taxes while staving off rules and regulations that required municipal compensation, restrictions of any kind, or shorter hours for employees. Before the Gilded Age played midwife to the Progressive Era, machinations by transit interests already irritated civic sensibilities as public transportation became ever more public.

Similarly, personnel relations, especially in larger cities, provided a preview of the mayhem that would accompany the electrification of mass transportation. Although the majority of horsecar drivers and conductors (fare collectors) toiled long hours, the compensation, skill, and chance to work in a vocation that interacted pleasantly with the public made the job a desirable one in most locales. In big city venues unaccustomed to such civility, the Knights of Labor harnessed anger about impersonal, cutthroat management practices, low wages, and long hours as adroitly as the crews harnessed their steeds. During the Knights' Great Upheaval in the mid-1880s, violent strikes rocked transit operations in New York City, Chicago, and elsewhere. These outbursts centered around the usual complaints of Gilded Age workers in almost any industry—salary and working conditions—although as with most sectors, transit operations had problems peculiar to that line of work. Still, in most municipalities crews joined mutual benefit associations, not unions, for a slice of protection. The rapport between employer and employee seemed as genuine as the affection between drivers and their horses in the more amicable, medium-sized operations.

Electricity

The clipitty-clap of the horsecars barely changed over a half-century. To be sure, the vehicles improved, routes expanded, and the nickel fare remained in effect. However, after the Civil War inventors and entrepreneurs tinkered with ways to accelerate urban travel as new technologies became available. Experimental horsecars—without the horses—employing primitive naphtha (petroleum) engines, large chargeable batteries, or overhead electric wires for motive power startled passersby, who searched futilely for the suddenly invisible animals. By the late 1880s the trolley pole extended from the top of a streetcar, punctuated the sky, and downloaded electric current from overhead wires to motors beneath the body of the vehicle. Electrification transformed the urban landscape with a cobweb of wires and gadgets.

This new applied science influenced the social sciences as much as the physical world. As this author has written in *Trolley Wars*, "The trolley created a new mobility and speed in everyday life. Urban, suburban, and rural geography were telescoped into one another. Housing patterns, real estate speculation, consumerism, and entertainment all felt the occult impact." These technological changes upset the utopian world of animal-powered travel more than the upheaval caused by the Knights of Labor in the realm of personnel relations.

The upfront costs of electrification overwhelmed most horsecar operators, but speculators saw the potential bonanza. Capital investment skyrocketed from $150 million in equestrian transportation in 1882 to $2 billion in electric streetcars a generation later. Street railway financiers brushed aside startup costs and salivated at the geometric increase in riders lured by rapid transit that could reach fifty miles per hour on suburban rights-of-way. Between 1890 and 1902, track length almost tripled, from 8,123 to 22,576 miles. The number of employees doubled to 140,000. By 1902 the American trolley provided an incredible 1 billion miles of car service and carried an astounding 4,774,211,904 passengers annually (the number being inflated by repeat riders who commuted to work), seven times as many carried by the steam railroad. In the North Atlantic region, the average person rode a streetcar a staggering 124 times a year, according to an 1896 study by Edward E. Higgins. But the ripple effect of revolutionary technology created havoc among the workforce. They operated the latest vehicles in a mix of burgeoning utility inventions that invited mergers and included the telephone, gas power, and electricity for the home.

The trolley, a small grooved wheel at the end of a pole that gave its name to the streetcar, carried electric current from an overhead wire to the vehicle. It also served as a lightning rod for the growing hostility against transit carriers in some big cities. The proliferation of new personnel and political and social problems caused by electric transportation became a rallying point in the emerging Progressive Era and coincided with the establishment of electric railway service in almost every major city in the 1890s. Shifting alliances of passengers, taxpayers, investors, and politicians (sometimes on different sides of the issue) battled streetcar companies about fares, franchises, taxes, and transfer tickets among other issues.

The new technology supplanted the old locally owned animal railways with regional and national trolley networks owned by magnates who often trampled local sensibilities with controversial policies hatched in distant corporate headquarters. The muckrakers and reform journals like *McClure's* eventually exposed this lower layer of robber barons. Similarly, utility company executives merged services into even larger monopolies in a financial paper shuffle that rivaled the betting in a high-stakes poker game. These captains of industry worshipped at the altar of rationalization and emulated the practices of the steam railroad. Organizational structures became complex, management split between line and staff, and auditing methods became as precise as the new, tighter timetables. Efficiency controls emerged from the gospel of scientific management as accountants reveled in the minutiae of railway finances as well as freight and passenger schedules, work patterns, and the interplay between fares and transfers.

The Amalgamated

The activism of the Amalgamated Association of Street and Electric Railway Employees of America triggered more than 200 strikes from 1895 to 1920, according to legal historian Sidney Harring. Transit workers felt the changes in the industry more keenly than anyone else. The rapid pace of electric power caused a proliferation of accidents, injuries, and deaths. Vehicles became as large as steam coaches, "standing room only" replaced open seating, and the number of trips increased as dramatically as the speed. Horsecar crews had practiced a vanishing civility with passengers even at the hurried pace of industrial life. Just as the animal railway obliterated the doting service of omnibuses, electrification eliminated most of the remaining genteel kindnesses between crews and riders. Time became money in the eyes of managers, who pasted together ever-tighter schedules. Rationalization mandated that the conductor ignore stragglers not at a designated stop, one of the popular courtesies that anchored the employee-passenger alliance but also slowed service.

Ironically, electric power actually de-skilled horsecar drivers, who once reined teams of horses with rare dexterity. Electricity also threw out of work legions of stable hands that cared for the expensive herd of horses that easily outnumbered the crews. Despite the addition of skilled electricians who tended miles of wire that overarched the tracks and mechanics who fine-tuned the new motors on the trolleys, the workforce numbers probably did not vary greatly between one mode of transportation and the other. Rather, the increased frequency and speed of service actually swelled employment and patronage with the advent of electricity more than anything else. The industrialized world provided craft workers—electricians, sheet metal workers, and machinists—for the new jobs in the garages that replaced the farm skills of hostlers and grooms in the barns. Horsecar drivers, regardless of habit, morphed into motormen. Most made the transition with the simple push of a control arm on a trolley and a week's training, despite an ever-present danger from the new technology. At times, they also longed for their beloved steeds and the disappearing slower pace of life. Conductors, on the other hand, still patrolled the body of a car, regardless of horsepower or voltage, collecting fares with a clipped smile and abbreviated humor. The quickened pace curbed their once freewheeling personalities and introduced a new element of danger. They now risked life and limb scrambling alongside the running boards of the trolley. Sideswiping a tree or pole at twenty-five miles per hour on an electric streetcar proved more perilous than the diminutive speed of a lumbering horsecar. Despite this risk, the motormen and conductors remained the public face of mass transportation. They maintained a close rapport with patrons regardless of the pace of the new vehicles or the alacrity of industrial society itself.

Transit crews spent entire careers in the transit system, evolving with the changes in technology. Workers served the profession with legendary dedication, sometimes on the same route spanning several modes of transportation. They lived close to the car barns and walked to work in the early morning hours. Drivers and conductors knew their passengers, as well as their extended families from personal service that sometimes stretched a half-century on the same line. They kept an eye on the neighborhoods they lived in themselves as they traversed the same streets year after year. Such familiarity informally turned these transit employees into social police: the eyes and ears of the community. A local newspaper, *The Providence Star,* on August 9, 1885, penned a truism that probably applied throughout the nation for this vocation: "What a car conductor don't know about every regular patron of the line isn't worth knowing." They became purveyors of news and gossip and performed favors and kindnesses, such as selling single tickets rather than a more expensive booklet as required by the company. These native-born Yankee crews grew up on farms, worshipped in Protestant churches, and belonged to supportive fraternal groups. In Gilded Age Rhode Island, for example, about 70 percent owned their own homes and rented flats to colleagues. They used their personalities as a vocational skill.

Passengers reciprocated accordingly. They provided hot meals and drinks, presented gifts on holidays, attended fundraisers for the carmen's beneficial association, and joined the festivities at a retirement party. Regular patrons willingly signed witness cards to protect the "blue uniform men," a popular moniker for the nattily attired motormen and conductors. An occasional malcontent on a trolley trip usually faced the wrath of these daily riders. Only the solidarity among employees surpassed the passenger-crew alliance. Transit workers formed ironclad friendships, sometimes serving together on the same route for decades. They spent further time bantering during the innumerable split shifts that characterized the industry. Transit families socialized during precious leisure time that had to be carefully planned in an occupation that covered 365 days a year.

When local transit owners managed animal railways, they kept a close eye on public relations and thought twice before tampering with the solid wages paid to popular, senior employees. As these concerns electrified or sold out to larger, out-of-state conglomerates, the emphasis slowly changed from courtesy and service to the inevitable bottom line. Wages fell and novel two-tier wage systems were introduced that rewarded Yankee veterans of horsecar days with better wages, while new hires, often Irish Americans, received less for the same work. The Amalgamated exploited the deterioration in wages and working conditions while forging an unusual alliance among their own members, the riding public, middle-class progressives, and wealthy reformers. The union offered arbitration and advocated municipal control. Tight-fisted management refused to take the bait for any sort of bicameral negotiations, fearing that all such bargaining was a labor ploy to garner greater control over the workplace, its practices, and eventually the company's coffers. The fight was on.

Transit brawls ignited mayhem in city after city: more than a hundred deaths and ten times as many injuries. Only the period's coal conflicts caused greater casualties. Local historians often chronicled the trolley wars as the most uproarious in a town's history. The walkout in St. Louis in 1900 took sixteen lives and injured hundreds. The 1901 strike in Albany sparked mayhem and the mobilization of thousands of militiamen. Even Terre Haute, Indiana, home to Socialist Party presidential candidate Eugene Victor Debs, witnessed a transit imbroglio in 1902 that ripped the community apart. A number of factors, some measurable, others more impressionistic, determined the actual outcome of these episodes.

The strikes seemed to follow the rails in no discernible design, rocking big cities, small towns, and metropolitan areas on both coasts and points in between. Just when a pattern seemed to emerge, walkouts would occur in areas around earlier hot spots or reignite in the same cities. Southern systems experienced their share of outbreaks, but an animus against unions tempered these strikes. Although beyond the scope of this analysis, similar railway troubles appeared in Canada, South America, and Europe.

Although a local management team might camouflage or moderate the outside control of a transit syndicate, the ethos of the Progressive Era seemed to condemn most proprietors as intrinsically corrupt. Public knowledge of "foreign" control from an out-of-state corporate boardroom also inflamed opinions, as did the involvement of some politicians, usually Republicans, who served the local railway in some paid capacity. On the other hand, populist officials—usually Democrats at the city or state level—championed strikers and passengers against transit monopolies and provided respectability and political assistance.

Crusading newspapers and muckraking magazines, particularly abundant during this period, printed innumerable exposés about corrupt and substandard service. These frequent screeds scorched public emotions. A highly charged progressive mind-set meant a chorus of support for the popular streetcar workers, who could count on unusual allies countenancing a labor demonstration, such as religious figures, professionals, small and large businesses that resented the railways' arrogance, and other reformists, even within the Republican Party.

The electrification of service drew thousands of new riders who flocked to faster service for the bargain of a nickel fare. Yet the new working conditions that bedeviled motormen and conductors also adversely affected passengers. Congested vehicles, poorly heated cars, accidents, and a lack of free transfers between intersecting lines provoked intense resentment. The spirit of the age transformed everyday hassles into the larger battle cry against the period's cartels. During the walkouts, patrons formed a reliable phalanx of militant supporters for the strikers, especially when police, militia, and strikebreakers appeared. Riders, at least according to arrest figures, stood at the front of these tumults, influenced by a personal rapport with the strikers and a gut-level hatred of railway ownership. A majority of these walkouts featured boycotts and "we walk" campaigns.

Motormen and conductors employed their personalities as occupational skills. Their bond with the community served them well during strikes, when riders and other supporters sponsored a cornucopia of fundraising events while even some businesses slipped much-needed funds to the carmen.

Only a generational splice among the carmen softened their own fraternal solidarity. Horsecar workers, whose skills and life experience came from a more agricultural and conservative background, seemed to resent the up-tempo pace of life they helped to promote. Their popularity and years of service gave pause to owners who often exempted them from the wage cuts or lower pay scales for other electric employees who possessed no seniority or goodwill reservoir from horsecar days. Old-timers, as susceptible to the union message as newcomers despite the salary difference, sometimes wavered in their labor solidarity. A strike could mean termination at an age too close to retirement, while younger colleagues could still start another career if necessary. Beside the difference in age, transit veterans usually came from old-stock, Yankee backgrounds, while new employees usually represented more recently arrived ethnic groups, depending on the region.

The Amalgamated, despite its youth, employed a sophisticated strategy against the owners, notwithstanding a depleted treasury from so many strikes so early in its existence. William Mahon, the president of the organization, was an avowed evolutionary socialist who sat on the executive board of the American Federation of Labor (AFL) and was close friends with Samuel Gompers and Eugene Debs. He built the Association into a remarkable organization over a fifty-year career. The union employed public relations to champion any kind of arbitration, a popular concept in the Progressive Era but not one likely to find support from a management team opposed to collective bargaining in any form. On the other hand, the Amalgamated used arbitration and even municipal ownership of the means of public transportation as a tactical maneuver to build public support for its position. Mahon commanded employers' attention with a scorched-earth policy championed more by militant public supporters than union members themselves. The aggressiveness of the Amalgamated attracted other unions to support its cause, especially the AFL's influential, decentralized labor councils that honeycombed the nation's cities. As chronicled in the Amalgamated's monthly journal, *Motorman and Conductor,* the unyielding mayhem, an army of willing shock troops, and the progressive spirit of the times produced the urban chaos that at times frightened owners and politicians into a negotiated settlement.

There is no better insight into the other side of the labor-management chasm in this time period than the willingness of owners to "take" a strike, notwithstanding the immediate, grave consequences and long-term damage to the carrier's bottom line. Despite some of the Amalgamated's vaunted public resources, the proprietors still held the upper hand and seemed compelled to employ it regardless of the outcome. In most instances, influential owners had easy access to the halls of power. Police and military authorities often coordinated strategy with management before a walkout, although local working-class soldiers and cops sometimes took the side of the union, leading to the mobilization of out-of-town forces. However, in larger cities professionally trained police forces eschewed any outward sign of sympathy. Furthermore, regional transit monopolies could always outwait a strike while income poured in from other properties. In fact, the longer a transit struggle lasted, the greater the chance of a management victory, as public support wavered after several months. Some companies, up to the challenge of class struggle, called upon the services of several battle-hardened strikebreaking firms that could field a considerable force of scabs with street railway experience despite such actions creating further tension. The Amalgamated could sustain its members for a time, but once the initial rush of popular excitement and pandemonium waned the authorities seized control. Union victories had to be won within the short-term parameters of an urban maelstrom, although Mahon's organizers returned repeatedly to the scenes of chaos, sometimes for a generation, to finally secure representation. In fact the national union worked hard to squelch wildcat strikes by local activists until a representative of the Amalgamated arrived on the scene to coordinate strategy. Unsanctioned walkouts scuttled the $5.00-a-week strike pay from national headquarters but did little to harness spontaneous job actions initially.

The cavalcade of transit strikes during the era of electrification has a familiar quality. However, each one contains a few different elements, disparate forces, or variables that contrast with other walkouts over time and place, but the similarities usually trump anything unique.

Brooklyn, 1895

A city unto itself, Brooklyn witnessed the transportation revolution firsthand as animal railways stapled down tracks in the early 1850s. Thirty years later elevated railways eclipsed the plodding horses in the 1880s. Street-level electric surface completed the transit revolution beginning in 1892 and helped the city annex other, smaller towns now connected by trolleys. As mass transportation developed technologically, powerful competitors devoured some smaller lines and opened the way for costly electrical investment. While politicians from both major parties usually applauded the expansion of travel opportunities, subsequent labor problems caused a divergence in opinion. The corporate boardrooms of New York ordinarily controlled the industrial and transit fortunes of distant states but in many instances also dominated the same kind of ventures outside their own office windows. The element of "foreign" control, at least in Brooklyn, was measured in city blocks, not in interurban distances. The proximity of corporate capital only added another emotional element to the strike of 1895, as its historian, Sarah Henry, has shown.

The introduction of electricity and the manifold changes in work practices and grievances triggered the Brooklyn walkout as was almost always the case in the transition from horsepower to electricity. In fact, carmen at the largest railway there had organized an assembly of the Knights of Labor during a successful horsecar strike in 1886 and 1889 that provided decent wages and working conditions. A New York state law in 1887 enhanced the union's position by limiting a day's work for railway employees to ten hours in a twelve-hour framework. The Knights flourished in the area despite a downward turn of fortunes for the union nationally. With more than a decade of progressive organizing and achievement, the Knights fended off any feelers by the AFL's fledgling, craft-oriented Amalgamated. They probably saw little advantage to fracturing workforce solidarity at a time when motormen and conductors still ruled the union's roost and enjoyed professional equality in the field.

The Panic of 1893 and the upfront capital to electrify the lines strained the railways' bottom line by the inauguration of the new service in 1894. Crews had their own gripes that, if remedied, further cost the enterprise: speed, more trips in a ten-hour period, congested vehicles, and the spiraling stress of railway operations. Local citizens, in a preview of coming attractions and civic activism, bristled at fraudulent franchises, tax evasion, financial shenanigans, and brutal trolley accidents.

Organizationally, the Knights represented employees on all six of Brooklyn's railways. When the common contracts expired in 1894, the Order asked for a 25-cent daily raise, more full-time employees, and fewer trips to observe the ten-hour law. The owners of the largest three lines, under financial constraints, decided to chance a walkout in hopes of breaking the Knights and ensuring cost savings. The railways quickly advertised for experienced transit strikebreakers in other large cities. Within a few years unscrupulous companies formed to provide these services on a mammoth scale. At this early juncture of employer-employee conflict, the railways acted on their own, although tough economic times drew in individual recruits.

The intermittent running of trolleys during the strike caused commercial chaos among small businesses, especially in dry goods enterprises and entertainment outlets. Several merchants actually sued the railways for loss of profit. Although the inconvenience of the strike irritated passengers and businessmen, the appearance of scabs infuriated the community, which maintained a close relationship with drivers, motormen, and conductors. Merchants refused services and supplies to scabs, religious figures supported strikers, and public sentiment eventually endorsed a general boycott of the trolleys—a standard tactic in almost every subsequent transit upheaval. Ethnic groups, fraternal organizations, and political societies took a stand with the Knights and held solidarity fundraisers.

Electric service offered greater opportunities for sabotage due to miles of vulnerable electric wire, an estimated 16,000 miles of it in Brooklyn alone. Union supporters waged an early manifestation of "guerrilla progressivism" when some of the better segments of society opted for immediate gratification against the hated traction companies rather than patiently wait for a legislative or political solution. Waves of protestors (including thrill seekers) confronted strikebreakers and created mayhem. As in most of the upcoming Progressive Era walkouts, few strikers went to jail. On the other hand, neighbors, passengers, and working-class colleagues made up the bulk of the arrests, an occurrence repeated in most other episodes. In fact, the union preached peaceful confrontation and even assisted scabs to return home by paying travel costs.

Despite the emotional and powerful cross-class coalition, the Knights, and later the Amalgamated, faced formidable odds against entrenched protectors of property and civil order. The Republican mayor of Brooklyn, who also served as the town's chief magistrate, ran interference for the street railways by ordering out the police, mobilizing local troops, and vetoing any curbs on the companies. Significant politicians, mostly Democrats but some Republicans too, championed the strikers but lacked the power to trump the mayor's military orders. Despite some outward sympathy for the employees, police officers rode two to a car to protect strikebreakers during the upheaval. In the face of continued community activism, the mayor engaged the city's militia for the first time to guard railway property. Unlike some upcoming transit battles where troops looked the other way during incidents, in Brooklyn the soldiers did not actively sympathize with the rioters or the Knights who tried to curry favor with the militia. New York City's National Guard joined the fray a few days later, bringing the number of troops to 7,500, a massive show of force that resulted in several deaths and the bayoneting of protestors.

In the end, the streetcar companies simply waited out the strikers. The Knights called off the walkout in February 1896, a year after the original campaign, but the railway rehired only a small percentage of strikers. However, a small labor victory came later in the year when another public boycott forced the companies to bring back many of the popular, dismissed veterans. The financial savings realized by outlasting the union failed to materialize, as several of the larger railways reorganized financially, a common development after such events. The Knights managed to protect its transit empire for almost another decade until the AFL's street carmen's union finally replaced the Order in many geographic regions. Interestingly, despite the AFL affiliation, the Amalgamated often organized across crafts, preferring to pack all the trades in a trolley garage into one division rather than separating motormen, conductors, electricians, and mechanics. The costs of a management victory would be pyrrhic in almost every instance, while the union enjoyed a Phoenix-like recovery as poor working conditions triggered multiple organizing drives.

Houston: 1897, 1904

The electric street railway strikes that began in Brooklyn in 1895 careened into areas not usually associated with labor strife. Although the American South never proved hospitable to trade unions in general, Richmond, Virginia, hosted the nation's first functioning electric railway in 1887 and a walkout in 1903. Houston, Texas, faced strikes by the Amalgamated in 1897 and 1904.

According to strike historian Robert Zieger, despite company hostility the Amalgamated formed a small local division of forty-seven members in the burgeoning port city of Houston in March 1897. In July a one-day strike forced recognition after a show of support by other unions, widespread sympathy by the riding public, and editorial backing from a major newspaper. In March 1898, the railway company and the fledgling division tangled again over the same issue of recognition. This subsequent walkout lasted twenty-six days. Local unions in Houston and surrounding areas pledged financial aid, while participants in a public demonstration voted to initiate a boycott.

The railway, under outside proprietorship, fired all the strikers but unwittingly raised the issue of control by Boston capitalists. Ownership of local railway operations by out-of-town corporations was another pressure point in the era's list of public concerns that seemed to galvanize citizens to support trolley strikers. Financial holdings in the South by northern interests still seemed to conjure up the ghost of carpetbaggers three decades after the Civil War. Management hired untrained strikebreakers, which aroused strike sympathizers who physically prevented the movement of some trolleys. This led to some minor violence—or at least minor compared to the Brooklyn affair. Public officials declined to provide police protection despite a rowdy gathering of 3,000 that stopped service once again. A further melee featured gunshots from strike sympathizers and forced the hand of the authorities to take some action. In the interim, a group of prominent citizens worked out an agreement between the two parties, including a partial arbitration panel to decide some working conditions, a remarkable union achievement given the temper of the times, especially in this geographical location. Both sides compromised, but the question of public violence in a Southern municipality clouded future relations and local union support.

Further financial difficulties for the company resulted in total receivership by a Boston syndicate. The union's pay scale was moderate and played no apparent role in the railway's difficulties. In 1902, both sides squared off once more over recognition and the red herring of wages: recurrent issues despite earlier agreements. Changes in ownership, management, and finances meant that union security was always at risk on almost any railway property in the United States. In this case another short strike, featuring alternate transportation by the union, ended in a labor victory. The Amalgamated gained a nine-hour workday, arbitration, and a union shop. This agreement lasted two years, and the union showed willingness to compromise during the contract. However, in 1904 when management fired sixteen employees, an arbitration decision went against the union. As relations deteriorated, a strike seemed imminent, especially after the dismissal of the union's president for speaking to the press.

The company, no longer willing to negotiate equitable contracts, took a hard line, but local solidarity once again backed the strikers with $15,000 in donations and loans. The railway hired outside strikebreakers. Local advocates stopped scabs in a demonstration that featured some violence. Strikers actually pleaded with supporters not to block the trolleys or engage in obstructions. The company then outraged local sentiment by encouraging black passengers to ride during the boycott and took down Jim Crow partitions that separated the races in the cars. The union symbolically seemed to remain at the controls until the formation of a larger anti-union Citizen's Alliance that had its genesis in an earlier transit strike in Beaumont in 1903 and was part of a larger, national group and ideology that took a different tack than eastern interests. The president of the Alliance in Houston was a streetcar official.

In July 1904, several instances of dynamiting strengthened the belief, in some quarters, that unions harbored a tendency toward lawlessness and anarchy. The turn in public opinion, sustained by the Citizen's Alliance propaganda, weakened labor's cause and led to a cave-in by the Amalgamated after five months on strike. The organized opposition to unionism in general and the Houston strike in particular combined with the rail bombings to sour local union support. The length of the walkout and the endless hostilities helped weaken the boycott. A new management team, buoyed by a wave of public support and city officials who now felt the heat from a conservative direction, created a different dynamic. Although Progressivism ruled the political roost in much of the country, the fear of anarchy and disorder clashed with the tradition of law and order and even vigilantism, especially in the southern region.

Providence, Rhode Island, 1902

Before the Civil War, Rhode Island hosted a web of omnibus lines within its diminutive borders. Several horsecar lines replaced the primitive omnibus by the end of the rebellion. A politically influential family united the competing animal railways into a single entity, not uncommon in smaller metropolitan areas. In this instance the owners installed a crackerjack manager who practiced progressive personnel relations. Solid wages, lifetime employment, seniority, and even cold lemonade on the Fourth of July—with a dose of ginger to prevent stomach cramps—made the job enjoyable. A comfortable atmosphere prevailed between labor and management and even the Knights of Labor, powerfully situated in Rhode Island's textile empire, could not break the bond in the 1880s. Instead workers settled for an independent mutual benefit association with the railway's assistance. Accidents and incidents were few and far between in these Gilded Age neighborhoods.

When electrification came to Providence in the early 1890s on the heels of the departure of the respected manager, things changed dramatically. A new set of outside owners, represented by the state's senior United States senator, transformed the operation from horse power to electricity between 1892 and 1894. The system expanded statewide, legions of new commuters stepped on board, and life's tempo jumped. But the same problems appeared in Rhode Island as in every other electrified system. The city council and state legislature granted lucrative franchises that insured long-term monopoly control of city streets at a fraction of the value. Taxes lagged. Then a New York syndicate purchased the hometown system, unleashing a firestorm of protest. The local senator who arranged the buyout stayed on as president, but had little to fear from public protests since state legislatures elected U.S. senators at the time. The high cost of electrification was offset by greater efficiencies and rationalization from the economy of scale of increased patronage and the replacement of expensive horses with cheaper, dependable electric motors.

Although passengers marveled at the speed and new destinations of the trolley, the same headaches that appeared elsewhere caused migraines here as well. Businesses and towns clamored for new routes. Massive electric streetcars replaced petite horsecars. Standing "freight" could accommodate more than 100 riders in a single vehicle. Accidents, injuries, and deaths spiraled. During the last two years of animal power there were only a dozen minor mishaps and no deaths. In the first twelve months of electric service in 1894, nine riders perished in local trolley crashes. The year before the 1902 strike, the railway counted 140 accidents and a dozen deaths; 1,218 died nationally including 122 employees.

The trigger for the strike was, as usual, an attack on the work standards of the employees. Newspapers carried the rumors of threatened wage reductions and other deleterious changes. The Amalgamated sniffed the insecurity of these takeovers among veteran crews and organized several nearby local divisions in New England only a few years after the national union's formation in 1892. The changeover in Rhode Island brought organizers to Providence as hundreds of transit workers joined Division 39 of the Amalgamated. (The union developed a successful habit of following a positive effort in one town by moving on to other nearby localities: Providence was finally organized in 1913, less than a year after the national chartered the Boston local and sent a wave of activists to Rhode Island.) Local groups, minor politicians, merchants, and others applauded the initial unionization effort.

Management acted quickly. Salaries would be reduced, but only for the new hires (usually Irish) needed for the expanded service that now approached twenty-four hours a day. Veterans would enjoy the older, higher pay scale until retirement. Furthermore, the company provided an employer-controlled mutual benefit association that offered minimal perks but shrewdly hired the union's business agent to direct it. Although most employees joined the Amalgamated, the lingering impact of the Panic of 1893, fear of losing a job near the end of a long career, and the defeat of the Brooklyn strikers in January 1895 dampened and finally ended the brief and initial flirtation with the union.

Another phenomenon, a withering attack on the syndicate from a myriad of local sources, sounded a popular and progressive assault against corporate government. The trolley company and its endless machinations became the object of intense dislike. Management's two-tier wage system eventually became a sore point as more newcomers came aboard. While electrification enhanced travel, new problems arose in a framework of unease at the changing nature of industrial life in America at the turn of the century. The railway always seemed to alienate passengers as new complaints targeted novel problems: the lack of transfer tickets to intersecting lines, frequency of service, and a crescendo of trolley accidents. One such accident in 1901 killed six and seriously injured Rhode Island's lieutenant governor.

Meanwhile, as horsecar veterans retired to the accolades of the riding public, new employees replaced them but at a lower wage to do the same job. Management also tightened discipline by hiring "spotters," detectives, and more supervisors to prevent wayward activities, especially stealing fares. As conditions worsened, the railway had difficulty replacing the once-vaunted workforce with quality candidates willing to tolerate long, stressful workdays. Crews still managed smiles and small favors that endeared them to several generations of riders, even if their banter sported the lilt of an Irish brogue. Both passengers and crews lamented the loss of time for civility and placed the problem at the company's doorstop.

While good-government groups and local newspapers continued to assail the railway, employees were dying in a spate of accidents. Motormen and conductors discussed grievances at baseball games between garages in different towns in the state. To head off the latest drive, management presented a new eye-popping pension plan, one of the best in the nation. Once again, the owners hired the union president to run it. Labor advocates rebounded and talked up the ten-hour work day and a plan to legislatively mandate it as in some other states such as New York. Surprisingly, given Republican control in Rhode Island, the general assembly authorized a ten-hour limit in April 1902, probably because so many of the popular and influential crews registered to vote that year as part of a larger labor offensive. Then the company announced a plan to merge most of the state's public utilities—gas, water, electricity, and railways—into one highly profitable entity. Critics now interpreted the railway's failure to attack the shorter workday as a ploy to deflect attention from the new corporate power grab. Public anger reached a fever pitch, so the railway refused to recognize the ten-hour law and stalled the enabling legislation by appealing the provisions to the state Supreme Court. The strike was on but before the Amalgamated sanctioned it.

The newly rechristened Providence local, Division 200, inaugurated a walkout that detonated the worst riot in the capital city's history. On the second day of the strike, an estimated crowd of 20,000 attacked trolleys in the downtown area after a march by motormen and conductors. The mayhem lasted until midnight. The company canceled all service, despite having hired 300 strikebreakers to augment some of the old-timers who feared termination in the twilight of a career. At the headquarters of the highly corrupt Republican political machine in Providence, authorities mobilized the experienced police force, judges, and ever more scabs. Although vandalism and violence punctuated the evening hours for the next month, the popular uprising lasted only one evening under the withering clamp of law and order.

Pawtucket, Rhode Island, 1902

Unexpectedly, the action moved across the city's northern border to nearby Pawtucket, cradle of the American industrial revolution. There, the changes in the state's demographic profile ensured the election of a young, militant Irish-Catholic lawyer in 1900. Mayor John Fitzgerald engaged the state Republican machine on a wide series of fronts, including an action that ripped up an unauthorized stretch of railway tracks to the cheers of citizens around the state. During the strike, nightly riots went unpunished by the local police force; in fact the mayor actually deputized some of the carmen. When the state sheriff sent in deputies, primarily political operatives, demonstrators pummeled them unmercifully. The Republican governor mustered the militia for the first time in sixty years, but the guard was honeycombed with working-class soldiers, including some railway strikers. Upon arrival in Pawtucket on June 12, 1902, the militia virtually mutinied, harassing strikebreakers and company officials, and generally siding with strike sympathizers. The governor had to call in reinforcements from Newport who lived too far away to be associated with local union members. Military discipline prevailed, but uneasily. When the troops finally left Pawtucket two weeks later, they took a steam train rather than a scab trolley as a final gesture of camaraderie with the strikers. Not a single militiaman suffered any injuries as the crowds carefully targeted only Republican operatives. The class makeup of the soldiers and the nature of the political situation in any particular strike made a big difference in the enforcement of law and order by rank-and-file officers.

Fitzgerald's Irish-Catholic championship of the strike included a strong civic, religious, and ethnic element against the reigning Yankee, Republican machine. Strikers and supporters boycotted the railway with a proliferation of ribbons proclaiming, "We Walk." A cross-class alliance embraced the action and even participated in widespread violence as a reaction to the importation of hated, professional strikebreakers who suffered serious injuries just as the GOP sheriffs had. In late June, the State Supreme Court belatedly declared the ten-hour law constitutional, but the strike fizzled outside the explosive corridors of Pawtucket, where several demonstrators took bullets and dozens suffered wounds and injuries. Although the strikers in Pawtucket prevailed into July, the police crackdown in Providence doomed the walkout from the beginning. Furthermore, the spontaneous nature of the action, before the arrival of Amalgamated officials, deprived the militant but untested local of valuable leadership and strike pay. Significantly, the Democrats won a huge political victory in the fall elections, including a rare gubernatorial triumph, as a direct result of a backlash against Republican support of the railway company.

The years after 1900 included some of the most devastating trolley strikes in U.S. history, including several that triggered wider labor revolt. The 1909 Philadelphia transit walkout spawned a general strike and labor unrest along the entire Eastern seaboard. Others remained local but explosive, such as the actions in Chicago, St. Louis (again), New Orleans, New York, Buffalo, Columbus, and Los Angeles, among many others. The Wilkes-

Between 1900 and 1915, some of the most devastating trolley strikes occurred in American history. Some spawned a general strike and labor unrest along the entire eastern seaboard. Depicted here are Brooklyn police on trolley car strike duty. During the strike, trolley car passengers used other means to get around town. (Circa 1910. *Courtesy:* George Grantham Bain Collection, Library of Congress.)

Barre conflict in 1915 was something of an anomaly because of an existing, equitable contract that fell apart over a penny-an-hour dispute and a two-tier wage system.

Wilkes-Barre, Pennsylvania, 1915

The Wilkes-Barre Railway Company and the Amalgamated had a sophisticated collective bargaining agreement, one of about 200 the union administered at the time, almost all of which featured arbitration clauses. According to historian Harold Cox, when the contract expired in 1915, both sides agreed to the provisions of a union shop, working conditions, and mediation of any discharges. However, neither side could agree on wages. The company, citing a decline in riders, offered a 1-cent raise, to 25 cents an hour. The union invoked the mandatory arbitration clause to send the issue before a panel of arbitrators, one each chosen by labor and management. The two arbitrators would then select a third party to join them in any decision. Unable to find an acceptable industrial umpire, the two respective mediators unsuccessfully tried to reach an amicable conclusion. The company authorized a 2-cent raise, but the union demanded more and struck for nine days before political interests pressured both sides to accept the state's labor commissioner as the neutral third party in an attempt to forge an acceptable wage package.

The commissioner and the company representative agreed to an increase of 2¾ cents for those employees with five years' seniority. The railway immediately paid the wages retroactively. Although the union negotiator demurred, the rank and file seemed content with the decision. The union representative, a national officer, continued to agitate against the agreement fearing that a sliding scale would eventually divide the local union between veterans and newcomers with different wages for equal work. The Amalgamated official finally convinced the commissioner of labor to reopen the decision even though the contract contained no such provision once the arbitration ended. The company refused to participate, but the two negotiators agreed on a flat wage increase to 27 cents an hour for all employees regardless of seniority. Two wealthy railway board members pledged to hold the line and promised to spend their own fortunes to overcome a threatened strike.

Both sides called each other's bluff in October 1915 in an area of the state that was heavily unionized. Service unions, the mine workers, some key politicians, and the local labor council formed a credible support group. A subsequent boycott, which lasted an incredible fourteen months in the mass transit sector, severely cut trolley patronage. Simultaneously, a national development provided alternative transportation, a solution that eventually bedeviled both the Amalgamated and the railways. In this case jitneys—private automobiles acting as taxis—raided trolley stops and provided a more personal ride for the same price. Although the Amalgamated inadvertently solved the issue of substitute transit, the competition of the jitney and private buses threatened future union security. In this immediate case, jitney operators wisely donated funds to the strikers, augmenting a very liberal $5.00 a week in strike pay from the Amalgamated, which by this time enjoyed discretionary funds unavailable during earlier, leaner organizing drives. Such largesse maintained internal solidarity and kept strikebreakers to a minimum. Several attempts to mediate the conflict and clarify the original rounds of arbitration failed.

At this juncture the railway turned to a professional strikebreaking outfit led by James Waddell from New York. Several hundred scabs, with extensive transit experience, directed the Wilkes-Barre streetcars. The replacement firm systematically reopened the lines one at a time and trained local, permanent recruits, who supplanted the hated out-of-state crews. This unusual, almost liberal approach by Waddell secured a well-trained force of denizens to completely operate the system by March 1916. The company also aggressively attacked the legality of jitney service, slowly forcing a cessation of such transportation. Simultaneously, the company hired a public relations expert in an early example of a sophisticated campaign to discredit the Amalgamated as a violent organization through advertising and court proceedings, as opposed to the extralegal efforts in Texas a decade earlier. The judiciary issued an injunction against the union.

Despite a mass rally headed by Samuel Gompers, president of the American Federation of Labor, the strikers had their backs to the wall. Union sympathizers now turned to violence, but at the end of the walkout rather than its usual placement at the beginning of a conflict. The Amalgamated eventually sued for peace and tried to have all strikers reinstated. Ironically, the mine workers union intervened with the carmen to accept a compromise because the anti-labor feeling now generated by the company's shrewd offensive was taking a toll on the miners' reputation as they prepared for a strike of their own. The railway agreed to rehire about one half of the original strikers immediately but kept many of the scabs on the job as well. Surprisingly, both sides agreed to a new, three-year contract with a sliding scale that reached 28½ cents, close to the original bargain. The company, however, never recouped lost revenue or the costs of strikebreakers, legal action, and public relations—and eventually had to be reorganized. The labor movement suffered a black eye but remained the representative of the employees at the property. The cost of the fourteen months of hostility hardly seemed worth it in this rare instance when the national union, rather than rank-and-file militants, fanned the fires and seemed to outsmart itself.

End of the Strike Wave

By the end of World War I, a quarter century of street railway conflicts was almost over. Battles against the union cost the traction companies dearly, in lost revenues and soured public relations, even in the sophisticated Wilkes-Barre situation. The Amalgamated returned, time and again, to organize railways where they suffered earlier defeats. With the advent of war in Europe in 1914, the costly materials required to run a transit operation—rails, machinery, and parts—went into the inflationary global conflict long before U.S. troops mobilized.

The government instituted a War Labor Board during this era to mediate industrial disputes in order to avoid disruptions in production or travel. The board took a liberal policy toward wages and working conditions that gave unions like the Amalgamated a new opening in the assault on management and set a final precedent for arbitration that still marks that union's current negotiating policy. Strikes tapered off dramatically once the government forcibly pushed the owners to the negotiating table. During this difficult period, simultaneous competition from a proliferating fleet of private automobiles and public jitneys further strained the railways' bottom line. A spate of bankruptcies and reorganizations followed the war, weakening management's will and capacity to deflect the unstinting efforts of the Amalgamated. Antipathy from the trolley wars seared the popular conscience, so much so that required reforms and legitimate municipal assistance to a declining industry got sidetracked for decades. The union suffered as well when carriers switched to streetcars and buses operated by a single employee who did the work of a motorman and conductor as a cost-saving measure.

The Amalgamated organized approximately 960 local divisions from its inception in 1892 through the end of 1919, although only about 300 survived intact. Some merged, paralleling the consolidation in the industry itself. In other railway systems, the parent union issued more than one charter over the years as a local disbanded or lost a strike. Providence, for example, held numbers 39 (1894), 201 (1901), 504 (1908), and the final division number 618 in 1913 after a generational effort to organize the Ocean State.

The union issued only forty new charters during the entire decade of the 1920s, a reflection of a solid organizing effort through the war years as well as the changing, more hostile political atmosphere for labor during the Roaring Twenties. William Mahon, the Amalgamated's president almost from its inception in 1892 until his retirement in 1946 (he died three years later at age eighty-eight), purportedly was the longest-serving labor chief in U.S. history. At the end of three decades of intense, blistering drives, he said, according to historian Emerson Schmidt, "I would sooner face the world with an organization of 10,000 men with $1,000,000 in their treasury than I would with an organization of 10,000,000 men and $10,000 in their treasury." He and the Amalgamated had accomplished the goal the hard way. A few stalled unionization efforts reignited during and after the Great Depression. The radical Transport Workers Union (TWU) assaulted some of the last bastions of anti-union properties in the same period, especially in New York, Philadelphia, and the West Coast. The TWU also organized other transportation employees outside the confines of street railways, as historian Joshua Freeman has chronicled.

The road to union dominance of the industry seemed as long as any interurban journey, and by the end of World War I it was possible to go from one end of the country to the other on a trolley if a passenger had enough nickels and time. With its opportunistic use of strikes and arbitration, the Amalgamated employed, in the words of legal historian Sidney Harring, an approach "that reflected a deep understanding of the legal and political complexities of union organizing in a period of intense class violence."

Harring recognized the emerging contours of a new body of labor law that the Amalgamated helped institute and which, in turn, benefited all unions. The requisites of labor peace in wartime cemented this approach even in a once-hostile federal government. The Amalgamated was still using the War Labor Board a year after hostilities ended.

Guerrilla Progressivism

Just as the union helped shape its own destiny by changing the country's personnel laws, the Progressive Era created an atmosphere conducive to such alterations by the Amalgamated and other reform groups. In this period wealth grappled with commonwealth. Traditional interpretations of this situation often depict a frightened middle class determined to end industrial warfare at the voting booth or through legislation. Other historians detected pockets of resistance and support for workers across several time periods and regions, especially against the bullying of "big business." Some academics went further to suggest workers played a more active role in the reform.

Yet the working class practiced a more militant style of resolution: guerrilla progressivism. "In a way, control and use of the nation's streets became a metaphor for control of society, and the combatants often chose to fight it out on the very thoroughfares in question," this author has written in *Trolley Wars*. Strike supporters displayed a medley of frustrations during the only game in town—the visible and highly charged atmosphere of a transit strike. A temporary breakdown in law and order in the face of these mammoth outbursts allowed a collective response by local citizens dappled with white and blue collars. Demonstrators, some well dressed, joined working-class crowds to yell an insult, curse the railway, or even toss a rock or two at a moving target. Usually more comfortable pulling the lever in a polling booth, these middle-class participants became part of guerrilla progressivism, if only briefly. The psychic relief of bombarding a trolley controlled by a scab and a sheriff provided greater redress than the more traditional but much slower method of voting for change.

The transit industry, under the auspices of the American Street Railway Association, understood the situation but refused to plead guilty. *Street Railway Journal* wrote in February 1900, "Some wonder has been expressed at the prevalence and extent of strikes on street railroads during the present time of prosperity, the sympathy of the public, either by countenancing acts of violence, by boycotting the cars or by supporting retaliatory measures in the Municipal Court. This tendency indicates a serious condition in municipal and industrial affairs being a direct attack on order and the rights of property and in favor of confiscation." Obviously the owners feared the trolley strike but seemed even more afraid of a local government takeover, although that alternative was rare and served more as a union straw man in public relations battles.

The traction question highlighted the Progressive Era and served as a magnet for different classes and groups to come together in common battle against the ubiquitous symbol of the era's urban malaise. Ironically, the trolley itself, as a simple technological instrument, stood as an emblem of the new century's progress in the realm of mobility and speed. But even here, society seemed to resent the new pace of life almost as much as they enjoyed it. While the Amalgamated garnered tremendous and unusual support for its strikes, partisans mobilized partially out of hatred for the despised owners. The spirit of the times raised the traditional labor-management discord in the transit industry to an entirely different level. Trolley wars reflected the inner turmoil of the period and, at the same time, served as a gauge to measure the population's frustration with wayward corporate rule.

See also: The Business Community's Mercenaries: Strikebreakers and Union Busters, 52; World War I Era Strikes, 191; Three Strikes Against the New York City Transit System, 277.

Bibliography

Amalgamated Transit Union. *A History of the Amalgamated Transit Union.* Washington, DC: Amalgamated Transit Union, 1992.

Burran, James A. "Labor Conflict in Urban Appalachia: The Knoxville Streetcar Strike of 1919." *Tennessee Historical Quarterly* 38 (1979): 62–78.

Cox, Harold E. "The Wilkes-Barre Street Railway Strike of 1915." *Pennsylvania Magazine of History and Biography* 94 (1970): 75–94.

Freeman, Joshua B. *In Transit: The Transport Workers Union in New York City, 1933–1966.* New York: Oxford University Press, 1989.

Harring, Sidney L. "Car Wars: Strikes, Arbitration, and Class Struggle in the Making of Labor Law." *Review of Law and Social Change* XIV (1986): 849–72.

Headlee Jr., Thomas J. "The Richmond Streetcar Strike of 1903." *Virginia Cavalcade* 25 (Spring 1976): 176–83.

Henry, Sarah M. "The Strikers and Their Sympathizers: Brooklyn in the Trolley Strike of 1895." *Labor History* 32 (Summer 1991): 329–53.

Leonard, Stephen J. "Bloody August: The Denver Tramway Strike of 1920." *Colorado Heritage* (Summer 1995): 18–31.

Molloy, Scott. *Division 618: Streetcar Workers Fight for a Union in Rhode Island.* Providence: Division 618, 1977.

———. *Trolley Wars: Streetcar Workers on the Line.* Washington, DC: Smithsonian Institution, 1996.

Olson, Bruce A., and Jack L. Howard. "Armed Elites Confront Labor: The Texas Militia and the Houston Strikes of 1880 & 1898." *Labor's Heritage* 7 (Summer 1995): 52–63.

Rogers, Bruce. "The Street Car War at Indianapolis." *International Socialist Review* 14 (December 1913): 340–42.

Scharnau, Ralph. "Dubuque Walks: The Streetcar Strike of 1903." *Labor's Heritage* 6 (Winter 1995): 58–77.

Taylor, George Rogers. *The Transportation Revolution, 1815–1860.* New York: Holt, Rinehart and Winston, 1951; reprint, Armonk, NY: M.E. Sharpe, 1977.

Turner, Walter. "Streetcars of Charlotte." Charlotte: North Carolina Transportation Museum, 2003: 1–10.

SEAFARERS' STRIKES IN AMERICAN HISTORY

Nathan Lillie

The Nature of Seafaring Strikes

Sailors originated the term "strike" in the eighteenth century. Since that time, their strike history has been shaped by their industry's unique conditions, including the unusual and casualized method of hiring, the quasi-military nature of workplace discipline, links to other transport industries, direct international competition, highly specific skills, and the political and military importance of the industry. Seafarers are usually hired for a particular time period or voyage, which makes union control over the hiring process crucial to union power. Maritime traditions and practical necessity dictate that seafarers cannot strike except at certain times, such as when a ship is in port. While employers have frequently abused shipboard discipline to stifle unions, there are nonetheless objective reasons for this discipline. Conversely, sailors often have a high degree of leverage when they strike. Seafaring work is time sensitive and cargo is frequently perishable. Furthermore, there are natural linkages to workers in other parts of the transportation chain. If seamen strike, longshore workers, truckers, and others can support them by honoring their picket lines, so even if the employer is able to hire strikebreakers, it may still be impossible to move cargo.

The skilled craft nature of many shipboard tasks makes it possible for unions to control the labor market, forcing employers to come to the union for workers. Then again, the division of seafaring labor into many small crafts splits the maritime labor movement. "Licensed" seafarers, or officers, have separate unions from "unlicensed" seafarers, or ratings, and even within these categories there are subdivisions. This has undermined unity on many occasions.

Seafarers are also constantly in competition with workers from other countries, particularly in international trades. In modern times, this is seen most dramatically in the "flagging out" of shipping to "flags of convenience," whereby ships are registered in countries with the poorest regulation and lowest costs of operation. Historically, shipowners have hired crew from a variety of locations, a practice made easier because ships move from country to country. The industry also has strategic and military importance, making it easy for shipping companies and unions to lobby the government for subsidies. During the two World Wars, seafaring unions consolidated their positions by participating in wartime production planning; in each case after the war, employers tried to roll back these gains, resulting in major strikes.

Four Phases of Seafaring Union Development

The characteristics of seafaring—including the methods of hiring and discipline, skill control, transport chain linkages, international competition, and the strategic nature of the industry—were important to union strategy when the first enduring seamen's union, the Coastal Seamen's Union, was founded in San Francisco in 1885, and they are still important today, even if their relative importance has shifted over time. The early history of maritime unionism was defined by the struggle to establish that seafarers had the same rights as other men (sailors were all men at that time, and even today there are very few women in the industry). In the United States, this was not established in law until the Seamen's Act of 1915. In the second phase of maritime unionism, seafarers sought to establish stable union representation, which given the nature of seafaring work and hiring, meant establishing a union hiring hall system. This occurred primarily as an outcome of labor struggles in the 1930s. The third phase involved improving the wages and conditions of seafarers during major strikes in 1946, 1962, and 1965, and through numerous workplace actions and negotiations. The fourth and current phase is the fight to establish control over flag of convenience (FOC) shipping. As a result of the FOC system, seafaring labor markets, employers, and unions have globalized, so that the important industrial relations actors are global and transnational union associations and employers.

Phase 1: Birth of Seafaring Unionism

From the Coastal Seamen's Union to the ISU

According to Peter Linebaugh and Marcus Rediker, the term "strike" originated from eighteenth-century sailors "striking" (or lowering) their sails to show they were unwilling to work. Early seafaring strikes took place while ships were in port, because any refusals to work at sea were considered mutiny, punishable by imprisonment or death. Confined to the periods when seafarers were in port, early strikes were episodic. They were also often violent and met with violence. At sea, discipline was harsh. Officers could flog seafarers to keep discipline, and there were few effective restrictions to the discretion of officers in deciding what merited flogging. "Jumping ship" in port was desertion, so sailors were prohibited from quitting until their voyage had finished. Hiring took place via crimps and boardinghouse masters, who recruited seafarers in exchange for fees paid by the shipowner but deducted from the seafarers' wages. Occasionally, seamen would be "shanghaied," or kidnapped, put aboard a ship, and forced to work, effectively enslaved for the length of a voyage. Victims of shanghaiing were not always seamen, but men picked by crimps as targets of opportunity. Nineteenth-century seamen saw abusive officers and crimps as major grievances and union hiring halls and the legal right to quit work as the most workable remedies.

Unionism emerged earliest and most forcefully in the western coastal trade, although conditions were actually worse on the deep-sea ships. Deep-sea sailors frequently ended up working as strikebreakers in early coastal strikes. Stable union organization in seafaring began with the founding of the Coastal Seamen's Union (CSU) and the Steamship Sailors Protective Association in 1885 and 1886, respectively, in San Francisco. While seamen had set up a Seamen's Friendly Union in 1866 and a Seamen's Protective Union in 1878, these left no enduring institutions. The impetus for the new unions came from a wage decline caused by the 1885 depression. To force the cooperation of employers, the coastal seafarers exploited a loophole in the California desertion law. To be considered bound by the desertion law, a seaman had to be hired in the presence of a shipping commissioner. Since this took time, it was often not done. Using a tactic called "the oracle," a crew would strike just before a ship was scheduled to set sail. In this way, coastal sailors quickly achieved concessions from many employers.

Shipowners responded by persuading the police to harass union organizers. This resulted in some minor violence, but did not stem the tide of organizing. So in 1886, the shipowners set up the Shipowners' Association of the Pacific Coast to fight the union. The association announced that union members would have to give up their union books to work and instead take employer books. This fight over books was an early example of an enduring conflict in seafaring industrial relations. Seamen have long carried books recording their voyages, with space for employers to make remarks. Who controls the books and what goes in them has been a crucial issue, since employer-controlled books (sometimes referred to by seafarers as "fink books") can be used to blacklist union activists. In this first conflict with the association, the union lost when the association successfully recruited strikebreakers from deepwater ships. However, in subsequent years, the CSU recovered by recruiting the scabs, and making its way back onto ships using the oracle. Following closely on the growth of the CSU was the Steamship Sailors' Union, which merged with the CSU in 1891 to form the Sailors' Union of the Pacific (SUP).

Union organization in the rest of the country

was slower to take hold. Great Lakes sailors successfully organized the Lake Seamen's Benevolent Association in 1878. In 1886 this group affiliated with the Knights of Labor, but according to historian Richard Schneirov, this organization was weak. In 1889, with the help of American Federation of Labor (AFL) leader Samuel Gompers, the CSU founded an Atlantic Coast Seamen's Union. These seamen's unions met in Chicago in 1892 and formed the National Seamen's Union, which the following year changed its name to the International Seamen's Union (ISU) and affiliated with the AFL.

In 1892, the California State Legislature closed the loophole in the desertion law with a new law making sailors liable for damages if they did not show up for work. This, combined with an economic depression, gave West Coast shipowners the resolve they needed for a new open-shop offensive. They began to hire scabs off deepwater vessels instead of hiring union sailors from the SUP. Employing an agent with the alias C.G. Williams, the employers orchestrated a campaign of dirty tricks and negative publicity against the union. The SUP survived the campaign, but was obliged to reduce its wage rates during the 1893–94 depression.

The ISU pushed for national legislative changes to regain the right to strike, resulting in the passage of the Maguire Act in Congress in 1895. The act intended to give seamen the right to quit a ship, but in the 1897 case of *Robertson v. Baldwin* (165 U.S. 275), the Supreme Court invalidated the law. The case involved four seamen who quit the *Arago,* a barkentine (three-or-more-masted ship), in 1895, were arrested, jailed until the ship was ready to sail, and forced back to the ship. The court (over the dissent of Justice John Marshall Harlan) ruled that sailors were "deficient in that full and intelligent responsibility for their acts which is accredited to ordinary adults," that they were "wards of admiralty," in the way children are wards of their parents. Further, the court ruled that the Thirteenth Amendment abolishing involuntary servitude did not apply to seafarers' contracts. Seamen surrendered their rights as workers and as human beings when they "signed their articles" ("shipping articles" was another term for the contract between sailors and shipowners).

The failure of the Maguire Act to grant seamen the same rights as other workers does not seem to have prevented the SUP from participating fully in the San Francisco General Strike of 1901. In July of that year, San Francisco waterfront unions, unified under the City Front Federation, defended themselves against an employer offensive sparked by an attack on the newly formed local Teamsters union. The dispute quickly became a general open-shop offensive by organized employers, who refused to negotiate with the unions or do business with unionized employers. The mayor and police backed the employers by escorting scabs to work. The strike lasted until October 2, 1901, when California's Governor Gage ended it by arbitrating a compromise and threatening to put San Francisco under martial law if the parties did not abide by the agreement.

The Rise and Fall of Early Seamen's Unions

The next two decades saw little strike activity on the West Coast, but major defensive strikes on the Great Lakes and Atlantic Ocean. ISU president Andrew Furuseth lobbied actively in Washington, DC, for improvements to seamen's legal status. This eventually resulted in the passage of the Seamen's Act of 1915, establishing that seamen could quit their jobs. It also made ship masters and owners liable for brutality against their crew, established safety and catering standards, forbade wage allotments except to relatives, established that 75 percent of ships' crew should be able to understand English, and protected the right of foreign seamen to quit in U.S. ports.

In the Great Lakes in 1900, the ISU launched a union-organizing drive, and in 1903 obtained recognition from the employers organized in the Lakes Carriers Association (LCA). In 1908, the LCA launched an open-shop offensive, refusing to sign contracts with the unions, which went on strike in April 1909, as the *New York Times* reported. The employers were prepared to bring in scabs and the strike failed after a three-year struggle. On the Atlantic, a similar open-shop offensive precipitated a major strike in 1912. The strike failed amid divisions between Spanish- and English-speaking seamen, operation of the government-owned Panama

Line by U.S. Navy crew, and faltering support from longshore workers.

Dramatic losses in the Great Lakes and Atlantic Coast represented temporary rollbacks rather than crushing defeats, while steady union gains accumulated from smaller actions. Unlicensed, or nonofficer, union membership on the East Coast expanded from 3,600 in 1915 to 81,700 in 1921, according to labor economist Leonard A. Rapping. Employers became increasingly dissatisfied with the growing strength of the seamen's unions and, in 1921, saw the opportunity to return to the open shop. In cooperation with the U.S. Shipping Board, they planned to break the power of the ISU.

At that time, the U.S. Shipping Board still had wartime powers to regulate maritime wages. In January 1921, the board asked the ISU for a reduction in wages and a move from the three-watch system to the two-watch system. The three-watch system (eight-hour day) allowed for better sleep than the two-watch system (twelve-hour day) and was preferred by seafarers. In the context of high shipping profits, the union saw this as unreasonable, despite there being large numbers of unemployed seamen as a result of wartime training programs. When the Shipping Board and the ISU failed to reach agreement, the Shipping Board imposed its new rules, and in April 1921 the Steamship Owners' Association locked out ISU members from coast to coast. Where they were not locked out, ISU members went on strike. Employers began a massive scab recruitment drive, and by July the union was defeated. Employers introduced their own hiring halls, called "fink halls" by unionists, wages sank, and the ISU would virtually disappear as a force until its resurgence in 1934.

Leftists criticized the ISU for the strike loss, and the perceived weakness of the ISU leadership attracted seamen to the militant Industrial Workers of the World (IWW), or "Wobblies." As Stephen Schwartz chronicles, the growth of the IWW and decline of the ISU was helped along by the conciliatory attitude ISU president Furuseth took toward the shipowners. Instead of rebuilding his union, Furuseth focused his energies on attacking the Wobblies and other perceived radicals, on the misguided assumption that this would make the ISU more respectable in the eyes of shipowners.

Much of the IWW leadership was in jail, having been sent there during World War I or during the "red scares" in its aftermath. On many occasions Wobblies incited strikes with the goal of getting other Wobblies out of jail, although the strikers also generally had workplace-related demands as well. In the wake of the ISU's 1921 defeat, the IWW built momentum through a series of small job actions reminiscent of the nineteenth-century "oracle" tactic. Frequently, they forced employers to grant their demands for a return to the three-watch system and overtime pay. These job actions culminated in a major work stoppage at Atlantic, Gulf, and Pacific coast ports on May 1, 1923, in combination with IWW actions in other industries. According to Schwartz, despite some successes, IWW actions made little headway against larger employers and had little lasting impact.

Phase 2: Maritime Union Rebirth in the 1930s

Depression and the Strike of 1934

The history of the resurgence of the SUP, the birth of the National Maritime Union (NMU) on the East and Gulf coasts, and the death of the ISU are tied to the simultaneous resurgence of longshore unionism. Like the ISU, the International Longshoremen's Association (ILA) had been battered by a series of lost strikes, in San Francisco in 1919, Seattle in 1920, Portland in 1922, and San Pedro in 1923. By the 1930s, the "fink halls" had essentially replaced union hiring halls as places for seafarers and longshoremen to get jobs. For both seamen and longshoremen, fink halls served to help employers blacklist union agitators and allowed corrupt foremen to sell jobs, as Ottilie Markholt has detailed. Weak union organization allowed employers to drive wages and conditions down to the bare minimum. Licensed officers also found their organizations, such as the Masters, Mates and Pilots (MMP), and the Marine Engineers Beneficial Association (MEBA), under attack, as employers demanded they join company unions instead. Officers, too, were obliged to work harder for lower wages.

With the arrival of the mass unemployment of the Great Depression, wages and conditions deteriorated even further and work intensified even more. The ISU, still run by Furuseth out of offices on the East Coast, did little to organize seamen and improve conditions. Some seamen supported the IWW Marine Transport Workers 510, which was strongest in Gulf ports, but with the exception of the Gulf, the IWW as an organization played little role in the strikes of the 1930s. The Communist Party and its Marine Workers Industrial Union (MWUI) competed for the support of seamen, with more success on the East Coast than on the West.

Union resurgence began on the West Coast, with the locus in San Francisco, following the passage of the National Industrial Recovery Act (NIRA) in 1933, which asserted employees' right to organize and bargain collectively. This emboldened longshoremen, many of whom were MWUI members, to begin an ambitious West Coast organizing program under the auspices of the ILA, which in the 1920s had been virtually wiped out in the West, except in Tacoma. The NIRA established that each industry would set down National Recovery Administration (NRA) codes to regulated maximum hours and minimum wages, which participating employers would then observe. Nothing compelled employers to sign NRA codes, however, so many unions began struggles to force employers to sign and abide by them.

As shipowners stalled on the codes issue, West Coast longshoremen spent the first months of 1934 debating strategy and preparing to strike. The strikes of the 1920s had taught the longshoremen that if they wanted to win a strike, they needed to close all the ports at once. The SUP watched these developments, and resolved that if the ILA West Coast longshoremen went out, so would the sailors. On May 9, 1934, around 12,000 longshoremen struck Pacific Coast ports. Teamsters pledged support, and the ILA set up pickets along the waterfront. As ships came into port, seamen, both organized and unorganized, joined the strike. Almost immediately, employers tried to put scabs to work on the docks, resulting in some violence, with some strikers killed and many injuries on both sides. In Portland, the port remained shut, but in San Francisco and Seattle the shipowners moved some cargo for a short while, though they were not able to sustain the movement. San Pedro remained open throughout because it was difficult for strikers to patrol the entirety of the Los Angeles port area. Licensed officers also struck, sensing that their members' relations with the ratings (nonofficers) would suffer greatly if they did not. Although relatively fewer in number, the licensed officers' strike was strategically important because of the limited supply of scabs with the officers' specialized skills.

With the ports for the most part effectively shut down, both employers and the unions dug in for the long haul. The SUP issued "strike cards" to striking nonmembers, which allowed them to participate in strike-related union activities. The unions set up relief kitchens and allowed strikers to sleep in the union halls. When the federal government threatened to set up its own service to ship supplies to Alaska, the unions negotiated an agreement to free up some ships for the Alaska trade. The unions set up a Joint Maritime Strike Committee (JMSC) to coordinate strike strategy, including representatives of all the seafaring and longshoring unions. The JMSC resolved that no unions would return to work unless all obtained their demands. Both the longshoremen and the seamen had hiring halls and closed shops as core demands.

On May 26, ILA president Joseph Ryan arrived in San Francisco from the East Coast to negotiate an end to the strike. The West Coast longshore leadership was skeptical of Ryan's motives, since he was perceived as conservative and corrupt. Furthermore, he was dismissive of the Pacific Coast ILA's solidaristic stand with the seafaring unions. On June 16, Ryan and the employers' representative negotiated an agreement giving the longshoremen their most important demands, including a hiring hall, leaving out the other maritime crafts entirely. The longshoremen overwhelmingly rejected Ryan's contract and resolved to remain on strike until the other unions obtained their demands as well.

In late June and early July, employers attempted to reopen the major ports. In Seattle, clashes between police and strikers occurred when police escorted scabs to the docks. In Tacoma, an attempt to open the port failed when police cooperated with strikers to disarm the employers' "special deputies." Seattle unions tried to retaliate against the employer attempt to open the ports by withdrawing their agreement to operate Alaska-bound ships, but federal pressure forced them to reopen this agreement on July 6. From June 20 to July 11, police and employer "special deputies" in Portland battled to reopen the port, resulting in police shooting at strikers on July 11, wounding several, one fatally.

In San Francisco, Ryan drafted another agreement, similar to the last, but conditional on the seamen receiving an (unspecified) agreement. This time, it was the employers who rejected the agreement. Following this, on July 3, union pickets and police battled in San Francisco, as police opened the port. Street clashes continued on July 5, until eventually police opened fire on strikers, killing two unionists, a longshoreman named Howard Sperry, and a Communist cook named Nickolas Bordoise, and injuring more. Later that day, California governor Frank Merriam sent in the National Guard. The killings galvanized the labor movement. Thousands marched at the funerals of Sperry and Bordoise, showing widespread support in the labor movement for the struggles of the maritime unions. The fifth of July became known as "Bloody Thursday" and is now an International Longshore and Warehouse Union contractual holiday.

In June, the Roosevelt administration set up a National Longshoremen's Board to arbitrate the strike. In July, under the threat of a general strike, the Board held public hearings. For both the seamen and the longshoremen, the closed shop and union-controlled hiring halls were central to their demands, and in broad terms they presented these as non-negotiable. While the employers proposed to settle the contested issues through federal arbitration, the unions insisted that there would be no end to the strike while those demands were not met.

As hearings dragged on, the San Francisco Labor Council declared a general strike beginning July 16. Oakland struck as well, and according to Markholt there were over 100,000 workers on strike in the Bay Area. Over the next four days, however, the general strike's momentum weakened, and on July 19, San Francisco unions returned to work. This left the marine unions alone again, since the Teamsters, who had previously not worked the ports during the strike, began to haul cargo. This shook the morale of the strikers, and the longshoremen began to consider a return to work. With guarantees from the employers of nondiscrimination for strikers and union recognition, the ILA voted on July 22 to submit to arbitration. The seafaring unions were in a difficult position because they could not return to work with the fink hall system intact, even though the employers stated they would recognize the ISU. ISU President Furuseth arrived at an innovative solution to this dilemma: the ISU returned to work, but before doing so the seamen held a dramatic ceremony to burn their fink books.

The unsettled issues went to arbitration, which was precisely what the unions did not want. However, the strike had displayed the power of the Pacific Coast maritime unions, creating a situation where the arbitration outcomes had to be perceived as fair if the government and shipowners did not want to precipitate another strike. Perhaps more importantly, the unions had created the structures with which they could systematically pressure employers within the workplace to accede to their demands, and this is what they set about doing over the next two years.

Consolidating the Victory

Seamen forced employers to fire their scabs and hire from the union hall through numerous minor job actions in the months and years following the 1934 strike. Federally supervised elections established the ISU overwhelmingly as the representative union for most West Coast shipping (the MWUI and in some cases company unions received small minorities of the votes, and some tankers remained unorganized). Federal arbitration awards legitimated the union hiring hall, but the ISU had already taken control and forced employers to come to the hall, simply by ensuring that they had a difficult time finding enough seamen anywhere else and could expect trouble from the maritime unions if they tried. Licensed officers also did well out of the elections, although in a few cases company unions, and sometimes no union at all, won the vote.

Tanker operators, most notably Standard Oil, resisted unionization, prompting ISU Pacific Coast district representative Paul Scharrenburg to call a tanker strike on March 9, 1935, without polling the West Coast membership. The union failed to keep scabs off the tankers. In Portland, as Markholt decribes, police arrested several union officials and prosecuted them for "reckless and malicious possession of dynamite on a public highway," in what became known as the "Modesto Frame-up." The strike ended with the ISU embarrassed and Standard Oil unorganized. SUP rising star Harry Lundeberg accused Scharrenburg of planning the disaster and deliberately working against the interests of the union. A coastwide membership vote expelled Scharrenburg, to the dismay of the International leadership on the East Coast. In April 1935, Lundeberg was elected SUP president.

The Maritime Federation of the Pacific and the Demise of the ISU

In the meantime, West Coast longshore and seamen's unions joined together to form the Maritime Federation of the Pacific. The goal of the federation was to continue the solidarity exhibited in the 1934 strike by coordinating strike policy. Tensions within the Maritime Federation quickly became apparent around the issue of Communist influence. The Communist movement was a strong force within the West Coast longshore organization but was marginal within the SUP. In order to sail on the West Coast, MWUI members had to give up their MWUI affiliation and become SUP members. The SUP was suspicious that the MWUI would try to infiltrate via the longshoremen.

Consolidation of unionism on the West Coast set the stage for the demise of the ISU and the consequent growth of the NMU in the East, as the SUP rose in power dramatically and the ISU proved unable to maintain control of its supposedly constituent organization. Matters came to a head with the 1936 passage of the Merchant Marine Act, which established the federally regulated Copeland Continuous Discharge Book. Although not specifically an employer book, it appeared to the SUP to be quite similar to the one they had just eliminated in the 1934 strike. The ISU, however, wanted the SUP to accept it.

In January 1936, at a meeting where SUP representatives were not present, the ISU voted to expel the SUP, which had the additional effect of ejecting the SUP from the AFL. Apparently, ISU officials thought they could simply assume control themselves. SUP members rallied to defend their regional leadership, however, and SUP leaders refused to leave their posts, asserting that the expulsion had been illegal. Although the ISU seized some SUP funds through the courts, the SUP quickly issued new membership books and took an emergency levee to keep operating.

The Rise of the NMU and the 1936-1937 Strikes

At the same time, the ISU was also challenged in the East by a rank-and-file movement associated with the Communist MWUI. Many seamen perceived the Atlantic and Gulf Coast ISU as corrupt and autocratic. They saw the gains made by seamen on the Pacific and wanted to match their militancy. On March 26, 1936, against the wishes of the ISU, East Coast seamen struck, led by Joseph Curran and the rank-and-file Seamen's Defense Committee. ISU officials labeled these seamen as "rebels," and neither the Teamsters nor the East Coast ILA provided support or respected their picket lines. Without the sanction of the rank and file, ISU heads negotiated a contract with Eastern shipowners at West Coast rates ($62.50 a month), but without the West Coast working conditions or overtime pay. During the strike, ISU leadership continued to provide crews for shipowners and refused to submit the contracts they negotiated to a vote of their membership. With ships sailing regardless of the strike, the insurgent seamen called it off on May 29, with the explicit intention of regrouping to try again in the autumn, when they presumed the West Coast Maritime Federation unions would also be on strike.

On October 29, 1936, the Maritime Federation unions struck. This time the strike was much more complete than in 1934. Employers could not find scabs and did not make a concerted effort to move cargo. No U.S. shipping moved at all on the Pacific Coast except for unorganized tankers and a few vessels released by the unions for specific emergencies. Employers made clear that their objective in the strike was to end the closed shop, while the unions struck to maintain the closed shop. With the West Coast shut down, the weakness of waterfront unionism in British Columbia became apparent. Goods diverted from U.S. ports moved through Vancouver without interference. Unions had to track goods moving south and refuse to handle them when they arrived. Vancouver would continue to be a problem until the Canadian longshoremen joined the ILWU in the 1940s.

Immediately following the West Coast strike, the Seamen's Defense Committee chaired by Curran voted for an East Coast "sit-down strike" in sympathy with the West Coast seamen. This strike spread quickly down the Atlantic coast and proved much more effective than the one earlier in the year. As the *New York Times* reported in November, ISU officials labeled the strike illegal and sought to undermine it, citing Communist backing and maintaining that the seamen must abide by ISU contracts signed in May. The strikers responded that ISU contracts had not been negotiated with the consent of the membership, were arrived at in "corrupt and secret negotiations," and hence were illegal.

The Pacific Coast ILA, seeking support for their cause as well as for Curran's, asked Ryan and then appealed directly to the East Coast ILA rank and file for a hot cargo boycott. When they heard reports that the Atlantic ILA continued to work hot cargo, Harry Bridges of the ILA San Francisco local, who had earned Ryan's resentment during the 1934 strike, visited the East Coast to determine the real situation and, if possible, organize solidarity. According to Markholt, Bridges discovered that "in Philadelphia 'gangsters' beat up rank-and-file longshoremen and stuffed the ballot box to defeat a strike vote." In response to Bridges' accusation, Ryan stopped his salary as ILA Pacific Coast international organizer.

The East Coast strike proved much less peaceful than the West Coast one, and also less effective at totally shutting down shipping. ISU thugs joined police and employers in trying to intimidate and divide the Atlantic Coast seamen. Without official longshore or teamster support, ships could sail and expect to move cargo if they found enough scabs. Nonetheless, the strike did succeed in tying up many ships.

The West Coast strike dragged on amid accusations from shipowners that Bridges was prolonging the strike by waiting for a favorable settlement on the East Coast. This was likely true, as many of the same employers operated on both the East and West coasts. A union defeat in the East would have allowed shipowners to hire cheaper seafarers there, weakening the position of the SUP and undermining Curran, who was Bridges's political ally. East Coast seamen returned to work in late January 1937 without gaining their demands. They did, however, obtain a promise from the National Labor Relations Board (NLRB) to hold elections on all shipping lines. On January 30, 1937, the West Coast unions agreed to submit a contract to their memberships. The settlements were a mixed bag, but the unions retained the gains of 1934 and made modest advances.

Labor Infighting and the Collapse of the Maritime Federation

For the ISU insurgents, however, victory over the ISU old guard was probably just as important as victory over the shipowners. Unable to seize power from within ISU because the NLRB would not supervise internal elections, Curran's faction set up a new union, the NMU. In NLRB supervised elections, the NMU won representation elections for Atlantic and Gulf Coast seamen on most shipping lines. A few stayed with the ISU. The organizational strength the NMU had built up during the strike now allowed the NMU seamen to obtain their demands by taking on shipowners one by one.

Maritime labor's newfound power immediately brought about a series of fratricidal disputes, with unions setting up picket lines against each other rather than against employers and then taking sides based on political affiliation. The SUP refused the new Copeland "fink books" and pulled intercoastal sailors who carried them off of ships, including sailors affiliated to the NMU. The NMU was in no position to refuse the books, however, since there were still ISU officials who were more than willing to furnish employers with seafarers carrying Copeland books. SUP sailors picketed ships for "West Coast" status, arguing that the SUP had fought for the right to man these ships in the 1934 strike. The NMU also began to take SUP sailors off ships in eastern ports, prompting the SUP to align with the ILA in a crusade against the NMU.

Disenchanted with the role of the AFL in propping up the ISU old guard, and probably influenced by Communist Party strategy, the NMU moved to join the Congress of Industrial Organizations (CIO). The SUP, freed up by its expulsion from the ISU, also considered the issue of affiliation. At this point, the CIO had not yet coalesced into a full-fledged alternative national center, so it was unclear whether the industrial union idea behind the CIO mandated combining the two unions into a unified organization. The NMU was several times as large, and anti-Communist SUP seamen imagined that if they joined the CIO they would become an extension of a Communist-dominated national union. The Pacific Coast District of the ILA, however, went to the CIO, and in doing so disaffiliated from the ILA. It renamed itself the International Longshore and Warehouse Union (ILWU) and, learning from the SUP's experience, hid its assets to prevent their seizure by the ILA. Harry Bridges became the new union's president. A few locals, the only important one being Tacoma, voted to remain with the ILA. Of the smaller maritime unions, the MMP remained in the AFL, the Marine Firemen remained independent, and the Inland Boatsman's Union, MEBA, and the Marine Cooks and Stewards joined the CIO.

Tensions grew between the ILWU and SUP, fueled by the support of the former for the NMU. In practical terms, this meant that the ILWU did not respect SUP picket lines when these were directed at expanding SUP jurisdiction vis-à-vis the NMU, resulting in many broken noses and breeding animosity between the unions. When the Maritime Federation met in 1938, it was ready to break up. The matter nominally under dispute was whether to seat Tacoma ILA delegates, whom the ILWU wanted to exclude. The ILA, including the Tacoma local, was still affiliated with AFL. The SUP and the AFL unions perceived this as an effort to use the Maritime Federation to pressure unions into the CIO, so they withdrew from the federation in protest. Since its main purpose had been to coordinate ILWU and SUP strategy, the SUP's withdrawal meant the end of the federation's usefulness.

The SUP accepted an AFL offer to join in 1938 and took a charter to set up the Seafarers' International Union (SIU), later called the Seafarers' International Union of North America (SIUNA). Within SIUNA, the SUP preserved its regional autonomy, while a new Atlantic and Gulf Coast section took in the remnants of the ISU, keeping an AFL presence among ratings on East Coast shipping.

During the months and years following the 1936–37 strike, the NMU consolidated its position by small strikes against individual ships and companies, forcing shipowner recognition. To stabilize the situation and prevent the job actions, shipowners organized to bargain a general agreement with the NMU in 1938. Between 1933 and 1939, membership in unlicensed unions expanded from about 5,000 to 51,300, and by 1939, according to Leonard A. Rapping, "both the National Maritime Union and the Seafarers' International Union had achieved substantial control over the supply of labor by means of the union controlled hiring hall with union preference."

Phase 3: Pork Chop Unionism

World War II and the Postwar Accord

All the maritime unions enthusiastically supported the U.S. role in World War II, taking "no-strike pledges" and participating in wartime production planning. Unlike most production workers, seamen worked in combat zones. Their role as unrecognized war veterans, combined with wage restraint during the war, meant that when hostilities ceased in 1945, seamen were ready for a raise and felt they had earned it. Employers eliminated war bonuses as soon as they could, so that instead of raises seamen saw pay cuts.

Shipowners figured out ways to use "flags of convenience" (FOCs) to register their vessels in countries with weak regulatory systems. In the immediate post–World War II period, this would remain a minor irritant to the unions, although FOCs grew steadily in importance. The growth of passenger air travel also began to reduce the need for passenger shipping, reducing the number of service jobs in the industry. Although world trade grew significantly in the postwar period and world shipping grew with it, the number of ships under U.S. flag and the number of American crew members fell steadily.

Despite the short-term disruption caused by the transfer of many vessels to foreign flags, a stable core of U.S. shipping remained as a result of government policy. The 1920 Jones Act restricted cabotage (within a single country) routes to U.S.-flag vessels and mandated that 75 percent of seamen on U.S.-flag ships must be citizens. Great Lakes, coastwise, intercoastal, and shipping to Hawaii, Alaska, and U.S. island territories remained the preserve of U.S. seafarers. The 1936 Merchant Marine Act provided for subsidies to preserve a merchant marine for national defense and military cargo reservation for U.S.-flag shipping. The federal government played an active role in promoting settlements, becoming an arbitrator for the "national interest," which generally meant keeping industrial peace and ensuring that ships were available for war-related transport.

Government regulatory and foreign policy provided room for maritime unions to improve wages and working conditions as long as they agreed not to challenge the underlying precepts system. Accepting the postwar framework, however, meant that maritime unions were powerless to act against the growing threat of FOCs. Very quickly, acceptance of "pork chop" unionism eroded the militancy and democracy on which the 1930s revival of union strength had been based. The often violent and criminal methods used to suppress "Communist" dissent brought in corrupt and anti-democratic elements, which continued to control the NMU and the SIU for decades.

The Committee for Maritime Unity and the Red Scare

When World War II ended in 1945, a major maritime strike seemed inevitable. To prepare for the strike, Harry Bridges called all maritime unions to a "Committee for Maritime Unity" (CMU) in February 1946. The CIO and independent unions attended, while the AFL unions stayed away, coordinating their own activities in the AFL's Maritime Trades Department. President Truman, recently having broken a railroad strike, threatened to use the Navy to crew ships if unions struck. Despite concerns that they might share the fate of the railroad unions, the CMU made strike plans and preparations. According to *Time* magazine, numerous foreign dock unions pledged not to handle cargo from ships run by strikebreakers, which restrained Truman from using the military to run the industry. In June 1946, both AFL and CMU unions struck at the same time, but only for a few hours, winning a return to wartime pay rates. Although enough to stop the strike, the unions were not happy with it. Immediately following the June strike, the CMU prepared for the expiration of contracts in September by raising a "negotiation fund." It was clear to everyone involved that the June strike had only been a show of strength; the real contest would be in the fall.

In August, the NMU jumped the gun by beginning its strike before the contracts expired, presumably, according to *Time*, to have a head start on the SIU in organizing Great Lakes seafarers, many of whom were still nonunion. The shipowners and government quickly settled with the CIO unions for a $17.50 per month wage increase. The SUP, dealing with private shipping companies, bargained a $22.50 increase, while the SIU managed $27.50. This caused much consternation at the Truman Administration's Wage Stabilization Board, entrusted with controlling postwar inflation. The board attempted to "rescind" the AFL union's differential, with no success, according to Stephen Schwartz. Predictably, the NMU walked out again in the interest of "equity." In the end, the government was unable to control the wage increases, and the NMU brought its pay up to par.

In the wake of the 1946 strike, the CMU fell apart amid accusations from the NMU and the Marine Firemen that Bridges was trying to use the CMU as a weapon against the AFL. Probably, the rupture had more to do with political infighting in the NMU. Curran may have wanted to distance himself from Bridges, since Bridges was under attack as a Communist, and since Curran was now looking to establish himself as an anti-Communist. During the NMU's formative years, Curran had been a close ally of the Communists, exploiting their efficient organization. The NMU was a very open and democratic organization, with a substantial regressive faction as well. Now, Curran switched sides, allying himself with the regressive forces to violently purge Communists from leadership positions. In sharp contrast to the "lily white" SUP, in the 1930s and 1940s the NMU was at the forefront of racial integration in the workplace. African-American members occupied prominent leadership positions, including the union's second-highest post, as Gerald Horne has shown. This alliance between the civil rights movement and Communists, though very successful in strengthening the NMU in its formative stages, provided a basis for racists to link up with anti-Communists during the Cold War period, particularly in ports in the South. According to Horne, these purges weakened the NMU, initiating its decline from one of the most powerful, democratic, and militant labor organizations in the world to the tiny, undemocratic, ineffectual, and corrupt affiliate of SIUNA it is today.

Juridisdictional Struggles

Having expanded to organize the whole U.S.-flag labor force but constrained by its declining size, seafaring unions fought over members by raiding each other. In 1953, the SUP struck Pacific Coast shipping for sixty-three days. The strike was probably at least in part an effort to raid the Marine Cooks and Stewards Union, which was trying to retain its independence because it was a mainly African-American union, while the SUP was perceived as racist.

In 1949, the SIU took advantage of an opportunity to expand into Canadian shipping, which was tied up by a strike of the allegedly Communist-led Canadian Seamen's Union (CSU). SIU president Paul Hall sent Hal Banks, a goon from California, to head the SIU's new Canadian section and expand the SIU's presence on Canadian shipping. Banks used openly violent methods to break through CSU pickets and expand his union at the expense of the CSU and later at the expense of other Canadian unions. The SIU Canadian District became the main union for Canadian-flag shipping. In the end in 1964, the Canadian Labor Congress expelled the SIU as a "hoodlum empire," and Banks returned to the United States to escape a five-year prison sentence for ordering the murder of an organizer from a rival union. Presumably because the murder was committed in the name of the global struggle against communism, the United States never extradited Banks back to Canada to serve his sentence.

Phase 4: Flagging Out, Stagnation, and Decline

A bargaining system began to develop whereby all unions would partake in gains that any one of them made. The complexity of maritime agreements made this somewhat like dividing a cake between two small children: the pieces are never quite equal, disputes result, and the only resolution is to find the resources to give everyone bigger and bigger pieces. In many cases, federal subsidies covered increased labor costs, so shipowners found it easier to give in to union demands than to risk expensive strikes. Those ships not on domestic routes, or for which shipowners could not get a subsidy, flagged out to avoid the higher wage costs. In this way, the unions faced increasing unemployment at the same time as pay increased.

However, it was clear to maritime union leaders that in the long run they needed to find a way to stem the tide of flagging out. At a meeting of seafaring unions in Oslo in 1948, the International Transport Workers' Federation (ITF), a global association of transport unions with affiliates around the world, launched the flag of convenience campaign. For the most part the FOC campaign was an American-led effort, with marginal non-U.S. participation, although this would change in 1971–72, as European and Australian unions took leading roles.

In the early 1950s, as part of the action against FOCs, the SUP helped some FOC crews to strike and obtain better contracts. However, the campaign soon ran into legal barriers. In September 1952, the crew of a Greek-owned, Liberian-registered ship, the *Riviera,* struck in Portland, Oregon, and the SUP and MMP set up pickets. The Greek owners sued the unions and eventually won in a case that went all the way to the Supreme Court, effectively restricting U.S. unions from organizing foreign-flag ships. In 1958, the ITF organized a worldwide boycott action against FOC shipping, which tied up at least 130 ships for four days but had no permanent impact.

On June 15, 1961, the U.S. maritime unions

struck over a range of economic issues, as well as over FOCs. A day before the strike, the *New York Times* reported that the unions believed they could use industrial muscle to "force employer action in the legislative and administrative fields," to resolve the FOC problem. While employers were willing to make concessions on wages, they were quite clearly not willing to make any concessions on their right to flag out. The NMU settled quickly, apparently only using the FOC issue as a bargaining chip for a substantial wage hike, but the officers' union kept shipping tied up for a bit longer. Political pressure from President Kennedy and the threat of a Taft-Hartley injunction soon forced the officers back to work. The strike showed that maritime unions had lost the ability to shut down significant parts of the U.S. economy; unlike with previous strikes, enough cargo still moved freely under foreign flags. Maritime unions could no longer apply the kind of political pressure needed to bring about fundamental policy changes.

The last major strike on U.S.-flag shipping occurred in the summer of 1965, when the unions struck for seventy-seven days. Although the 1961 strike clearly had not settled the FOC issue in the unions' favor, FOCs do not appear to have played a major role in the unions' demands in 1965, according to the *New York Times*. This may have been because the Vietnam War was just beginning and there was a temporary upswing in U.S.-flag shipping needs, making the FOC issue less pressing. Employers claimed that interunion rivalries prolonged the strike, since it was very difficult to ensure that each union received equal benefits.

The End of National Unions

In the 1970s, seafaring unions focused their efforts more and more on political action, and major strikes ceased. Without subsidies and cabotage restrictions, U.S. maritime unions would soon disappear, so it is not surprising that they have become major political donors. Through the 1970s and 1980s, the FOC fleet continued to increase in size at the expense of the U.S.-flag fleet, so that in 1976 only 5 percent of U.S. trade was carried in U.S.-flag ships. By the 1980s, employer commitment to subsidy programs and Jones Act shipping was on the decline. The union bargaining position had seriously eroded, and unions began to bargain concessions, according to Clifford B. Donn.

Today, American ratings unions are marginal, although officer unions have some prospect for survival in the new global environment. The NMU as well as some of the officers unions have been absorbed into SIUNA. America's maritime unions are quite far from the militant and progressive organizations of the 1930s. They no longer even have the industrial clout and "pork chop" attitude of the 1950s and 1960s. Rather, they appear to be just trying to preserve their organizations and have no real strategy or prospect for revitalization.

Shipping is now manned by seafarers from India, the Philippines, Russia, the Ukraine, and other places with relatively low pay expectations, hired through a global manning infrastructure. Unions bargain globally over conditions on about one third of the FOC fleet in the context of the ITF flag of convenience campaign. ITF contracts, though providing for good pay by developing world standards, do not come anywhere near the standards once achieved by unions in the U.S. For the nonunion majority of the FOC fleet, conditions range from ITF standard to extremely poor. U.S. seafaring unions play a role in the negotiation of ITF agreements, but overall they are probably more of a liability to the campaign than an asset. As discussed elsewhere, while SIUNA is involved in ITF FOC campaign decision making at a high level, it is not clear how this benefits the campaign other than ensuring the continued support of SIUNA. SIUNA receives significant dues payments from administering ITF contracts. These are paid into an offshore account in the Cayman islands through a "dummy" union, the Union of International Seafarers (UIS). UIS, though, provides no services to its members and is apparently only a vehicle for political side payments to SIUNA. Longshore unions provide the campaign's industrial muscle by boycotting ships without contracts. U.S. longshore unions are active in this, although their ability to act is restricted by industrial legislation. The ITF FOC campaign system marks a return to old traditions of seafaring-longshoring solidarity, but organized on a network model at the global level. Eventually, the new global unionism may make the United States and other national seafaring unions irrelevant, as the locus of union activity shifts to a new level.

See also: Longshoremen's Strikes, 1900–1920, 547; Strikes on the Port of New York, 1945–1960, 559.

Bibliography

Donn, Clifford B. "Concession Bargaining in the Ocean-going Maritime Industry." *Industrial and Labor Relations Review* 42, no. 2 (January 1989): 18.

Horne, Gerald. *Red Seas: Ferdinand Smith and the Radical Black Sailors in the United States and Jamaica.* New York: New York University Press, 2005.

Lillie, Nathan. *A Global Union for Global Workers: Collective Bargaining and Regulation in Maritime Shipping.* New York: Routledge, 2006.

———. "Union Networks and Global Unionism in Maritime Shipping," *Relations Industrielles/Industrial Relations* 60, no. 1 (Winter 2005): 88–111.

Linebaugh, Peter, and Marcus Rediker. "The Many-Headed Hydra: Sailors, Slaves, and the Atlantic Working Class in the Eighteenth Century." *Journal of Historical Sociology* 3 (1990): 225–52.

Markholt, Ottilie. *Maritime Solidarity: Pacific Coast Unionism 1929–1938.* Tacoma, WA: Pacific Coast Maritime History Committee, 1998.

Rapping, Leonard A. "The Impact of Atlantic-Gulf Unionism on the Relative Earnings of Unlicensed Merchant Seamen." *Industrial and Labor Relations Review* 17, no. 1 (1963): 75–95.

Schneirov, Richard. *Labor and Urban Politics: Class Conflict and the Origins of Modern Liberalism in Chicago, 1864–97.* Urbana: University of Illinois Press, 1998.

Schwartz, Stephen. *Brotherhood of the Sea: History of the Sailors' Union of the Pacific 1885–1985.* New Brunswick, NJ: Transaction Books, 1986.

Sailors' Union of the Pacific (SUP). Photo album, available at www.sailors.org/photoalbum/1897men.html, downloaded October 25, 2005.

LONGSHOREMEN'S STRIKES, 1900–1920

Calvin Winslow

The New York longshoremen's strikes of 1907 and 1919 were harborwide general strikes. They each involved tens of thousands of workers and shut down the port for more than a month. In these strikes, rank-and-file longshoremen moved in the direction of multiracial, industrial unionism, reflecting patterns of waterfront trade unionism internationally, as well as "the new unionism" then transforming the American labor movement.

The strikes fit in an era of dramatic confrontations on the world's waterfronts when longshoremen, in the words of E.J. Hobsbawm, were known for "raw power" and when their strikes were feared "from Santos to San Francisco, from Sydney to Liverpool." The New York strikes were also part of the national upsurge in class consciousness and radical trade unionism prior to and during World War I. In these years, the most basic disputes, often spontaneous, could quickly become movements, characterized by audacious strikes, the use of direct action, and working-class solidarity. Industrial unionism became a near universal demand, reaching far beyond the Industrial Workers of the World (IWW) and its supporters. This was the case in New York, where even local craft unionists became caught up the movement. The strikes were led by immigrants. They were simultaneously classwide strikes and alliances of the waterfront's ethnic populations—Irish, Italian, German, African American—in which ethnic and class consciousness merged in the movement for an industrial unionism.

May Day Walkout

The strike began on May Day: May 1, 1907. Longshoremen went on strike, tying up the port for six weeks. The strike began in Brooklyn, spread to the East River, then the Hudson River piers, and on to Hoboken and Staten Island. It involved tens of thousands of workers in a confrontation with the shippers, as well as with the railroads, the civil authorities of New York and New Jersey, and armies of strikebreakers. This army of the rank-and-file longshoremen, according to the writer Ernest Poole, "made only one demand. . . . Give us higher pay!"

The New York dailies paid some attention to May Day events in 1907, reporting demonstrations by workers in New York and in cities and countries around the world. The May 1st edition of the *New York World* noted that "all records for the number of immigrants arriving in the port in one day were broken yesterday when more than 15,000 [migrants] . . . got their first view of the city." The paper predicted 150,000 more would arrive within the month.

The New York papers, however, did not include accounts of Italian longshoremen, carrying red flags, marching in Brooklyn and Lower Manhattan. But the *Brooklyn Daily Eagle* did. The May Day marchers were demanding higher wages and their numbers grew as longshoremen quit work and joined the demonstrations. In one such action, a crowd of Italians marched though Brooklyn's Atlantic docks carrying flags, only to be driven from the Union Stores warehouses by armed superintendents. Then several hundred striking Italian longshoremen from Brooklyn crossed the bridge to Battery Park in Manhattan. Again, carrying red flags and the flags of various nations, they marched up West Street, bringing out the longshoremen on the Hudson River in a sympathy strike. The *Eagle* reported more marchers on May 2—hundreds of

Italians marching along the Clinton Street Wharf in Brooklyn demanding that all work be stopped.

The result was more than a strike; it was a demonstration of immigrant laborers, and a May Day appeal for working-class solidarity. "There is a general impression along the waterfront," reported the *Eagle,* "that there will be serious trouble before this strike is settled." Furthermore, "a peculiar feature," had already emerged, the reporter continued, "the Irishmen are joining issue with the Italians."

There was widespread dissatisfaction with wages in the spring of 1907, and this created disputes in all parts of the harbor. With unemployment low and work plentiful, there were strikes and "all sorts of rumors of strikes," reported the *Eagle.* Longshoremen attempted to push up their wages on the job, one dock at a time. Black longshoremen on the Ward and Mallory lines were already on strike by May Day, despite attempts to replace them with white strikebreakers. They demanded an increase in wages from 25 to 30 cents an hour for day work and 45 cents for overtime and holidays. This demand itself indicated the complexity of industrial relations on the waterfront. Black workers were paid less than others; when Italians walked out at the Bush Stores warehouses in Brooklyn's Sunset Park district they demanded 40 cents an hour and 60 cents for overtime.

There is evidence of temporary settlements of these disputes due to pressure to move ships, but the May Day marches changed this. Inspired by the Italians from Brooklyn, longshoremen throughout the harbor joined in a strike that soon became, according to the *New York Evening Journal,* "the largest strike of any single trade ever in New York." Within days the strike was 10,000 strong, and on May 6, 4,000 Hoboken longshoremen struck in support of the New York longshoremen. This constituted an unprecedented degree of solidarity, ultimately uniting an enormous number of men, workers of all classifications, nationalities, and races, from every region in the huge port.

At the end of the second week of the strike the *World* summarized: 30,000 on strike; Manhattan 10,000; Brooklyn, 12,000; Hoboken, 6,000; Staten Island, 2,000; 1,000,000 tons of unmoved freight on the piers; business losses, $2,000,000; and 1,000 strikebreakers arriving in the city each day. Fully four weeks into the strike, the longshoremen and their union, the Longshoremen's Union Protective Association (LUPA), were, according to the well-informed writers of the *Brooklyn Eagle,* "in control of the situation." The socialist *Daily People* was not alone with its June prediction that "Victory is at Hand!"

Race, Ethnicity, and Class

The strikers challenged not just the economic interests of the shippers, but also the occupational, racial, and ethnic hierarchies that prevailed on the waterfront. At the same time, the strike provided a dramatic illustration of the difficulties of forging an industrial union in this highly fragmented workforce. In New York, workers who were already separated by occupation and locality were further divided by the presence of dozens of racial and ethnic groups competing for work.

The New York longshoremen in 1907 were overwhelmingly immigrants and the children of immigrants. The Irish still constituted a majority of longshoremen; they were concentrated in Chelsea on Manhattan's West Side, the center of a band of neighborhoods that stretched from Chambers Street toward midtown. They lived there, cramped in narrow streets between warehouses and factories, in neighborhoods known for big families and saloons. These streets gave the longshoremen a reputation as "loafers, drinkers, and brawlers." The neighborhood was "the most hopeless in the city," social worker Mary Oakly Bay told the Commission on Industrial Relations.

The majority of Italians lived in South Brooklyn—"the Italian Quarter"—adjacent to where they worked on Red Hook's Erie and Atlantic basins, and southward along the waterfront to the Bush Terminal piers and Bay Ridge. The Italians first came to the Harbor as strikebreakers in the time of the "big strike," the revolt of the longshoremen led by the Knights of Labor in 1887. Their numbers grew through the 1890s and into the twentieth century, until by the time of Charles Barnes's classic 1915 study, *The Longshoremen,* they constituted half the longshoremen in the city.

E. Franklin Frazier, the sociologist who wrote the pioneering study of black longshoremen, visited his subjects in the Columbus Hill neighborhood on the West Side of Manhattan, where he found them living in "dilapidated" four-room flats, with "rusty mail boxes, broken bells, ruined tiles, disfigured walls and general dirtiness . . ." He discovered that 50 percent of the men he questioned were unemployed three months of each year or more. The result was desperately low incomes despite relatively high wages, especially compared to the average wage of black workers.

Most New York longshoremen lived in poverty in segregated ethnic neighborhoods. They tended to be employed on separate piers, to work in separate gangs, and to belong to separate local unions. On the docks and in the unions, this was not exactly "Jim Crow"; there were too many exceptions, too much variety in the patterns. Moreover, there was a voluntary component in ethnic organization. In the face of exclusion from the Irish-dominated West Side "deep-sea" docks, and in the context of New York's hierarchy of racial-nativism, Italians often organized their own local unions and worked on "Italian docks," where companies such as the Kerr Line hired only Italians. Germans did the same in New Jersey. African Americans organized their own unions but were less successful in monopolizing work on specific docks.

On the New York waterfront, therefore, racial and ethnic division generated great barriers to working-class unity, particularly for workers facing united, powerful employers such as Cunard and North German Lloyd, but above all J.P. Morgan's shipping trust. Yet in the course of this strike, racial and ethnic identities came to play highly contradictory roles: potential sources of weakness became sources of strength; indeed, they transformed racial and ethnic division into a moment of working-class solidarity and internationalism. The ethnic mobilizations of 1907 began within the separate groups of longshoremen and proceeded through them. In this strike, independent (that is, separate racially and ethnically distinct) mobilization and organization, far from impeding solidarity, was an indispensable component in the movement for industrial unionism. Consequently, racial, ethnic, and class consciousness were intertwined.

Early in the strike, the leaders of a small trade union, the Longshoremen's Union Protective Association (LUPA), emerged to speak for the strikers. "We strike for our families," LUPA president Patrick Connors, an obscure West Side trade unionist, told reporters from the *New York Evening Journal*. "They say we can live comfortably on our present wages. My answer is this . . . Let them—the capitalists—go down in the holds of ships and work eighteen hours a day." Connors also made the wage demand universal and, apparently, non-negotiable: raise wages for all longshoremen to 40 cents an hour, with 60 cents for overtime and 80 cents for holidays and Sundays. In 1907, trade unionism existed on the New York waterfront, though it was weak and fragmented. Reporters searched for leaders in the first days of the strike, but could find none, or so they claimed. Nevertheless, trade unionism had a long, if troubled, history on the waterfront. There were significant strikes in 1874 and 1887, as Barnes described. Each ended in defeat. There was an attempt to organize the port in the 1890s, led and financed by British longshoremen. They attempted to organize the American Longshoremen's Union, most often referred to as the McHugh Organization after Edward McHugh, a Liverpool longshoreman. McHugh came to New York in the mid-1890s and by 1897 was the leader of an organization estimated at 15,000 members, including 1,500 Italian longshoremen. McHugh was a follower of Henry George, the single taxer; the union motto was "all men are brothers," and it made no distinction "of race creed, color or nativity," according to Maud Russell.

The American Longshoreman's Union was succeeded by the Longshoremen's Union Protective Association (LUPA), led by Irish longshoremen who took their name from an organization of the 1860s. Barnes wrote the only account of this union and he was contemptuous of it. His account has shaped most subsequent writing. According to Barnes, by the end of 1906, when the Italian locals withdrew after failing to get an Italian walking delegate, LUPA's membership was only about 3,000. LUPA's leaders seem to have been caught unprepared by the strike, though spokesmen later denied this. Nevertheless, formal leadership of the strike quickly passed to the Irish longshoremen of LUPA in Chelsea.

This, however, did not diminish Italian participation. On May 14, the *New York World* reported that all 8,000 Italian coal heavers were on strike and that they had been joined by the tidewater coal handlers, also Italians. These workers brought coal to the coaling stations from Perth Amboy in barges. Together with the coal heavers, they caused havoc even for those shippers who managed to load their ships. Without coal the ships could not sail. Moreover, the Italian longshoremen joined LUPA en masse, allying with the other longshoremen on class lines, even when this led to bitter disputes within the Italian communities, chiefly concerning the massive use of Italian strikebreakers.

Pressure on Patrick Connors, the LUPA president, mounted as New York's elite demanded the union retreat on its wage demands as the way to settle the strike. Ralph Easley, the chairman of the National Civic Federation, joined with Tammany mayor George McClellan and leaders of the New York Central Federated Union (the affiliate of the American Federation of Labor, AFL) in pressing for a conciliation commission. Reverend Father Flannery of St. Veronique's Roman Catholic Church on Christopher Street claimed ". . . the utmost sympathy for the men" and urged the LUPA to take part in a conference, according to the *World*. Samuel Gompers, the president of the AFL, personally called on the longshoremen to settle. He sent his New York organizer, Herman Robinson, to mediate. Connors, however, refused to participate in a conference, stood by the wage demands, and even declined Gompers's offer of mediation.

War

This was no ordinary strike; certainly it was not the kind organized by affiliates of the city's Central Federated Union. It was far from a simple walkout over 10 cents an hour. On the contrary; it was an explosion of anger built up over years, a rebellion against a system of work and a way of life: the shape-up; exhausting toil; days without work; life in crowded, disease-ridden tenements; and a level of competition for work that went well beyond the normal experience of "ethnic rivalry."

Other trade union leaders demanded what Connors could not deliver—a settlement. But it was a settlement that would primarily benefit the most regular and best-paid Irish longshoremen, at the expense of all the others. The strike began over wages, but the wage demand had become highly symbolic. The shipping executives recognized this, hence their stubborn refusal to agree to the union's demands. There was an "all or nothing" spirit among the strikers. And there was tremendous pressure on Connors and the LUPA leadership from below, including from the rank-and-file Irish longshoremen, to win a major victory against the shippers. Connors did not lead the men out, nor did he choose the demands. How could he simply order them back? This was probably a situation unfamiliar to the condescending leaders of the New York labor movement. Connors's only real base was small and centered in Chelsea. The Brooklyn Italians and the longshoremen in Hoboken were, in effect, autonomous, as were a considerable number of the Irish.

Moreover, on the piers and in the working-class neighborhoods, the strike had become a movement, with mass picketing—even picketing by sea with strikers patrolling the harbor in picket boats. There were marches and rallies and the inevitable violent clashes with strikebreakers—clashes frequently involving the longshoremen's neighbors and families.

At times, observers called the strike a "war." There was violence almost from the beginning of the strike—between strikers, between the police and strikebreakers, at the gates of the piers, and even on the water when strikers fought to stop barges ferrying strikebreakers to and from the strikebound ships. The fighting spilled over into working-class neighborhoods adjacent to the docks and even to places well removed from the immediate conflict.

Strikebreakers were often the immediate target of the strikers' anger, and as the scale of strikebreaking was enormous so the extent of violence was widespread. In the Williamsburg section of Brooklyn, for example, longshoremen attempted to close down the waterfront with pickets. But this escalated into "savage rioting," according to the press, when on May 7 2,000 sugar workers at the sugar trust's American Sugar Refining Company walked out in a wildcat strike. The company brought in hundreds of Italian strikebreakers. The two strikes merged in the streets, and by the end of the day the *New York World* reported "fifty wounded in a pitched battle" as longshoremen and refinery workers "rioted from daylight until dark."

"The strikers," the report continued, "were armed with monkey-wrenches, iron bars and big sticks and lay in wait in doorways for the hundreds of strikebreakers . . . Ten thousand sympathizers with the strikers looked on." On May 11 in Manhattan, audacious strikers seized a ship and attacked the strikebreakers working on it, again Italians. The *New York Times* reported that the strikers "rushed the gates" of the Thirty-Fourth Street Pier, stormed the liner *Campagnia,* and "took control of the ship" for a time, only to be driven off by police and armed company men. There were regular mass meetings, including a "monster mass meeting" on May 9 at Hudson Street in Manhattan that was addressed by Connors and other union leaders. But the largest meeting was in Brooklyn, where the police estimated 7,000 Italian longshoremen gathered in Prospect Hall, overflowing into the streets. "For three hours," reported the *Brooklyn Eagle,* "they were harangued by Italian orators . . . Not a word of English was spoken." The strike leaders' speeches were greeted with "the wildest kind of cheering and howling, waving of banners and tossing of hats in the air." Connors announced at one meeting that he had received requests for 650 additional union badges for Hoboken and an order for 10,300 from Brooklyn, reported the *New York Evening Journal.* Certainly this was significant, and an indication of enthusiasm for the union, whatever it may have indicated about the actual level of commitment to the organization on the part of the new members.

The longshoremen's strike rapidly propelled LUPA in the direction of industrial unionism quite in keeping with the "One Big Union" sentiment. The strikers' single demand, one wage increase for all longshoremen, bonded workers from all the crafts and specializations in the industry, including the checkers. The union's multiracial organizing and the strike's immigrant leadership were also characteristic of the times, as was the direct action and involvement of large numbers of sympathizers.

There is reason to believe that there were significant numbers of longshoremen who believed in multiracial industrial unionism. James Connolly, the Irish revolutionary, worked for the IWW in the aftermath of the strike. According to Connolly, writing in the *Industrial Union Bulletin* of the 12,000 members of the "independent" union that survived the strike, "Many of the present members were once in the Knights of Labor and they are conversant with the fact partly gained by actual experience in their fights against the employers that the American Federation of Labor is a scab-herding capitalist institution."

There were also Wobblies (IWW members), Italian syndicalists, German socialists, Irish nationalists, and black militants from both the United States and the West Indies. This may help explain the failure of the IWW to effectively intervene in the strike. The fact was that IWW members were not the only players in the field. LUPA filled the vacuum left on the New York waterfront by the skilled workers of the Central Federated Union. LUPA provided leadership for the strike, which was a militant, industrial strike with rank-and-file support that included all major ethnic groups. The IWW supported the strike, and the socialist *Daily People,* which at that point supported the IWW, was uncritical of the union leadership during the course of the strike. It reported IWW meetings, paper sales, and recruitment, but offered little tactical advice to the strikers and nothing on alternative forms of trade union organization. In February 1908, nearly a year after the strike, Connolly, writing in *Industrial Union Bulletin,* described this union and its 12,000 members as "industrial and progressive . . . free from the ordinary grafting and corruption elements."

The shippers were united in opposing the wage demands from the very beginning; their "solid front" never cracked. In the end, the strikers were overwhelmed. The companies were willing to take staggering losses. Moreover, the existence of an apparently limitless supply of strikebreakers must have demoralized the strikers. The violence of the conflict must have exhausted them. Also, the calculated policy of fueling race hatred must have severely strained the strikers' unity.

In early June, the strike began to disintegrate. The *New York Times* reported Irish women were making desperate appeals to the charity societies and settlement houses. The *Daily People* called it the "old, old story, empty stomachs . . . against concentrated capital." Connors offered a compromise: 35 cents an hour for day work, 50 cents an hour for nights and 60 cents on Sundays and holidays.

The press reported that the Italians opposed it. The *Times* announced—correctly it turned out—that this was "the death knell of the strike." The shippers refused to consider the offer.

The ILA and the Shape-Up

The strike defeated, LUPA sank back into obscurity. James Connolly's vision of a progressive, industrial union failed to materialize. Its place was taken by the International Longshoremen's Association (ILA). The ILA originated on the Great Lakes and arrived in New York in the first years of the century but restricted its activities to a number of crafts on a few docks. In 1913, however, the ILA absorbed LUPA, and then in the course of the war, in collaboration with the shipping companies and the U.S. Shipping Board, organized the majority of longshoremen in the harbor. This imposed a form of unity in the waterfront labor movement, though it was done strictly from the top down, according to historian John R. Commons.

From the start, the ILA was aggressive. It grew rapidly in the first years of the century, including in Southern and Gulf Coast ports, winning the closed shop by guaranteeing employers a steady labor supply and ruthlessly crushing wildcat strikes. The ILA leaders insisted on the sanctity of contracts and believed in the absolute authority of trade-union leaders. One unique aspect of the ILA was its policy of recruiting African Americans, and this it did in large numbers, especially in the Gulf ports. By the time of the war, the ILA could boast of black vice presidents, scores of black delegates at its conventions, and thousands of black members. While this makes the ILA interesting, it was always a Jim Crow union, though with important local and regional variations, according to social scientists Sterling Spero and Abram Harris.

In 1919, New York Harbor was the world's largest port with more than 700 miles of industrial waterfront, a vast complex of piers, warehouses, railroad terminals and neighborhoods clustered on both sides of the Hudson River, on the Manhattan side of the East River, and all along the Brooklyn waterfront from Greenpoint to Bay Ridge. The Atlantic "deep-sea" shippers were concentrated in Chelsea and Hoboken; the coastal trade prevailed on the East River and in South Brooklyn. There were coaling stations in Jersey City and the Bronx, lumberyards in Newtown Creek, and brick yards in Midtown. Tens of thousands were employed in the harbor: marine transport workers, teamsters, sailors, railway workers, warehouse workers, and small armies of day laborers. There were perhaps 60,000 longshoremen.

The industry of the harbor was both archaic and advanced. The great liners that arrived at the piers of the Cunard, North German Lloyd, and White Star lines represented the highest levels of technology. The shippers demanded piers be extended farther and farther into the river to accommodate ever-larger liners, but on the docks work was primitive. On the eve of the war, the piers were old-fashioned with improvements overdue and mechanization rare. Coal heaving in Perth Amboy on the Jersey side of the harbor was still done with hand baskets. As late as 1914, there was still not a moving crane on the New York waterfront, according to historian David Montgomery. The war effort brought change, but grinding toil remained the lot of the longshoremen.

Casual labor was the norm for the harbor's labor market, and the "shape-up" was the method of hiring. While the shape was never directly an issue in the strikes, it was crucial to the companies and the union. According to the shippers and the leaders of the I LA, this system was dictated by the harbor itself and the nature of the industry. Shippers' profits depended on a fast turnaround, but the sea, the tides, and the traffic made planning impossible. The industry compensated with casual labor—the more the better. "The ship must sail on time," and the shape gave the foreman discretion over whom to hire, when, and for how long, and it all but guaranteed his authority.

While the shape-up often divided the longshoremen, literally setting them against each another, it was also a key element in their common experience, as important in many ways as their work. When a ship arrived at a pier, the longshoremen gathered, usually in a semicircle at the head of the pier. There the foreman looked for and then hired the "best men," the "good gangs," though never too regularly, lest the others become discouraged and the surplus disappear. The cruelty of this system was always apparent. On the relatively well-organized Chelsea piers, John Riley, an ILA officer, estimated for the Commission on Industrial Relations that 2,500 men might be hired on a "normal day," but "twice that number would shape-up." Those not chosen would wait for another shape, or a third, and again the next day if the work continued. Some might be taken on for an hour or two, then "knocked off" to wait again.

The work of the longshoremen was heavy and dangerous, accompanied with long, uninterrupted stretches of toil. Work on the piers varied, of course, but the typical longshoremen did heavy, monotonous hauling in and out of the holds of ships: 220-pound sacks of potatoes, 280-pound sacks of sugar, lumber, machinery, or bananas. They were "human machines," according to Montgomery, often "the piers' only machines." Sometimes, according to Charles Kiern, a New Jersey longshoreman who testified to the Commission on Industrial Relations, "men work 20, 30, I have seen them work over 40 hours in a stretch . . . One day he will almost work his life out, and the next two or three days have nothing to do, except when he has a few spare coins to go to the saloon and spend it." On the White Star lines docks, according to Kiern, the work is so "Taylored that they work a man's life out of him in ten years."

The Ranks Spark the Strike

President Woodrow Wilson's administration made wage restraint the central feature of its postwar labor policy in an attempt to contain inflation and "the high cost of living," as consumer prices had doubled during the war. It instructed those wartime labor boards not already disbanded to resist concessions to the unions. This was the goal of the U.S. Shipping Board's National Adjustment Commission (NAC), which oversaw industrial relations on the nation's waterfronts and piers; it sought to maintain wartime wage rates. The employers favored this shift and set out to increase the productivity of labor, which they claimed had fallen sharply during the war.

On the New York waterfront, it was the wage award of the NAC that sparked the great strike. The fall of 1919 marked the expiration of the wartime waterfront wage agreements. The U.S. Shipping Board reconstituted its NAC in midsummer to consider the future of longshoremen's wages and working conditions. The top leaders of the ILA, T.V. O'Connor, the International president, and Joseph Ryan, the New York District leader, were members of the Commission. They were joined by William Z. Ripley, a Harvard economist who chaired the Commission, and two shipping company executives, Frederick Toppin and Oakley Wood. The Commission issued its "award" on October 6, 1919, after lengthy hearings. The Commissioners awarded an increase in the "deep-sea" rate of 5 cents per hour for day work and 10 cents an hour for overtime work, effective from October 1, 1919. O'Connor and Ryan dissented on the specifics of the wage award but signed the agreement. The longshoremen had wanted $1.00 an hour for an eight-hour day and $2.00 an hour for overtime. The award was greeted with anger; longshoremen called it the "'Woolworth Award'-five and ten," said the *New York Call.*

The 1919 longshoremen's strike began in Brooklyn early on October 7. The strike spread to the Chelsea piers in Manhattan, then engulfed the Harbor, ultimately stranding 650 ships. Sixty thousand longshoremen, perhaps more, struck; it was impossible accurately to estimate the size of this vast waterfront workforce. The longshoremen were then joined by tens of thousands of others, workers from dozens of harbor trades; by the week's end, 150,000 workers were idled in what was perhaps the largest harbor strike ever.

The Italian longshoremen in Brooklyn anticipated the strike, stopping work on October 5, returned to work, then struck again, this time taking picket lines to Chelsea, the stronghold of the Irish dockers and the center of the union in New York. There they found support. When John Riley, an ILA district leader, waded into a crowd of strikers on a Chelsea pier and ordered them back to work, he was beaten bloody and left unconscious in a mud puddle. "Mobs," reported the *New York Times,* "now rule the waterfront." The strike was a remarkable display of industrial power. It involved virtually every longshoreman who worked in the Harbor, uniting Irish and Italians, blacks, Hungarians, Swedes, Russians. It effectively stopped shipping for nearly one month; traffic was not back to normal for six weeks. At the end of October, the *Times* reported "more than 600 vessels tied up in the Harbor—the largest number of ships ever known to be here at one time—540 steamships, fifty passenger liners . . . More than 100 ships anchored along Red Hook." William Ripley, the chair of the National Adjustment Commission, estimated the cost of the strike at more than "one million dollars a day."

T.V. O'Connor immediately ordered the strikers back to work. "This is not a strike," he insisted; it was the work of "the Italian element, aided by German sympathizers," and men from "166 Sackett Street in Brooklyn" (the headquarters of the IWW), he told the *Times*. Samuel Gompers, president of the AFL, wired O'Connor that the strike was in violation of "the fundamental principle of the American Federation of Labor. The agreement to abide by the award is a sacred contract." The press discovered a "Bolshevik conspiracy," led by foreign-born members of the IWW, chiefly Italians. Its partisanship was extreme, as each day it condemned the strikers, listed names and addresses of alleged IWW members, and announced the strike broken.

George Speed, a member of the IWW's executive board, spoke for the Wobblies in New York during the first chaotic days of the strike. Speed arrived in the city just before the strike began. He had just been released from Leavenworth, the federal penitentiary where he had been imprisoned with William Haywood and the 100 IWW leaders convicted in Chicago. The longshoremen's strike, he told the *Call*, was spontaneous: "The men tumbled out over the heads of their union officials."

Strikers themselves came forward to make the same point. John Gunlach, a Hoboken longshoreman, spoke to the NAC, which had reconvened in emergency session in New York. He criticized the International officers for "shoving the award down their throats." "The men rebelled against that. . . . They are out for justice." How could the press, he asked, "vilify the men who have been out for only one purpose, to get a decent living . . . to make it possible for them to live a decent life, as well as for their families." Walter Bell, the black leader of Local 968, pleaded with the Commissioners: "You cannot question the loyalty of the men of my race (colored) . . . I wish you would consider this, that the five and ten cents you have offered to these men, is more an insult than it is justice."

The black longshoremen were prominent among the strikers, despite large numbers of African-American strikebreakers. According to a hiring stevedore on the Ward Line piers, African-American longshoremen had been profoundly "affected by the wave of radicalism during the war." Certainly a significant section of the black longshoremen were militant supporters of the strike and were willing to ally with whites, yet they pressed their own demands against discrimination and for a black organizer, for black local unions, and for more work. Class consciousness and black consciousness converged—also evidence of the impact the Harlem Renaissance and the "New Negro" had on black longshoremen.

When Mayor John Hylan established a "Conciliation Committee" to settle the strike, the longshoremen came with demands that local officers and rank-and-file longshoremen appear to have formulated. The mayor's committee met with this grievance committee, which also presented an "addendum" from "the Brooklyn longshoremen." The grievance committee, which included Italians and blacks as well as Irish, presented a list demanding an eight-hour day, a forty-four-hour week, overtime on Saturday afternoons, and no Sunday work whatsoever. They demanded that all men who handled coal receive 10 cents per hour extra and that "there shall be at all times a basket or box to take out of the ship's hold all men who may be hurt, immediately, so that he may get first aid." The grievance committee specifically included the demand of "the delegates representing the Brooklyn locals" that "their conditions be exactly the same as in New York." Moreover, they demanded that "every working man on a ship, whether he be Coastwise or Deep Sea, be considered as longshore workers." The committee concluded by stating that "no man will return to work until every local, no matter what the craft is, is satisfied."

The rank-and-file character of the strike, and the degree to which the conflict was changing the consciousness of the strikers, was illustrated by a series of mass meetings. On October 9, the ILA called a meeting at Tammany Hall, with the purpose of organizing the men back to work. But the thousands of longshoremen attending overwhelmed the officers in a tumultuous show of support for the strike. On October 12, the officers called another meeting; they presented a series of influential speakers with the hope of regaining control of, or at least dividing, the workers. But this meeting, attended by an overflow crowd of 3,000 at the Cooper Union, "became from the outset, a wild repudiation of all union leadership," reported the *Call.* The rally got off to a bad start when the chairman was heckled by strikers who "wanted a real longshoreman in the chair." A telegram from Samuel Gompers was received with catcalls and then ignored. When O'Connor then appeared, the strikers "booed and hissed . . . until his plight was pitiable." "You double-crossed us. You called us IWWs," they shouted. "Now listen," O'Connor tried to explain, "there is an element here that doesn't want this strike settled, an element of agitators . . . an Italian element." "Why pick on the Italians," interrupted a striker. The jeering lasted five minutes. O'Connor continued in vain "to beg, plead, cajole and threaten" the strikers until, at midnight, he turned the meeting over to Joseph Ryan, the District leader, whose motion that the men immediately return to work was drowned in opposition.

Red-Baiting

There were scores of local meetings, such as "the enthusiastic meeting" of Local 838, held at its headquarters on Union Street in Brooklyn, where 150 members "voted unanimously to back up the dock strike after listening to speeches by Salvatore Mangiamale, president of the local, and other officers. The speeches were all in Italian." A meeting of 1,200 New Jersey longshoremen at St. Mary's Hall in Hoboken became a brawl when O'Connor, Ryan, and a group of armed bodyguards forced their way in, refusing to show their credentials to the men at the door. When a fight ensued and the bodyguards began attacking the strikers, shots were fired and the intruders were chased from the area. Some were arrested by Hoboken police, the *Call* reported.

Perhaps the most remarkable rally was held in Brooklyn on October 18, in Pilgrim Hall on Court Street. There, 3,000 members of Locals 37, 346, 903, 923, and 929 "howled down all mention of ILA leaders," according to the *Eagle* reporter present, "and roundly cheered speakers who have been identified by union men as IWW highlights among the Brooklyn longshoremen." The reporter, who called this rally an "ugly turn of events," estimated that the locals represented there involved 17,000 longshoremen and that only three Brooklyn locals were absent. "The speakers," according to the *Eagle,* charged the officials of the ILA with "forcing the members of local 808 to go back to work at the point of a pistol." They also attacked "the capitalist press" for reporting that 20,000 Brooklyn dockmen had gone back to work. The strikers voted to "stay out on the streets until their demands were met" and then "cheered at the top of their lungs." The meeting was conducted in Italian, with an interpreter for those present who spoke only English. The *Eagle* report also noted that "IWW agitation was clearly the purpose of the speakers . . . and their agents circulated through the audience."

This meeting reflected the growing influence of the Wobblies in Brooklyn. When an *Eagle* reporter investigated the Brooklyn IWW, he had no difficulty locating its headquarters. "It does not attempt to hide itself. It is in a congested Italian neighborhood. In a window above an Italian fruit and vegetable store is a large colored sign reading 'Industrial Workers of the World'." The Wobblies "laughed" at O'Connor's charge that they led the strike: "I wish it were," said one. A subsequent *Eagle* report described times when there would be "thousands of Italian longshoremen" surrounding the little Sackett Street IWW hall in apparently spontaneous, informal strike rallies.

The IWW did not lead the strike; the denials were true. The IWW in 1919 was still the target of fierce repression and the chief victim of the government's "red scare." It had in most places been reduced to an organization that was forced to concentrate on the defense of its own members; George Speed was in New York to help raise support for "class war prisoners," reported the IWW publication *One Big Union.* IWW leader Fred Thompson remembered that in 1919 few New York branches were in a position to do more than "offer moral support . . . [and] cheer workers on. Leadership was out of the question."

Nevertheless, the press exaggerated IWW involvement until the end. The Bureau of Investigation, a predecessor to the Federal Bureau of Investigation or FBI, relentlessly pursued signs of the IWW on the waterfront, even though its final report was somewhat skeptical of the IWW leadership theory. The War Department's military intelligence also attributed the strike to the IWW. An officer, Mayor H.A. Strauss, offered a more sophisticated, though equally wrong, version of this: "The fight in the longshoremen's union is between O'Connor and conservative labor against the IWW element, the same as the steel strike is a fight between Gompers on the one hand and Foster and Fitzpatrick on the other." Another Strauss report warned of collaboration between the IWW and the editors of the *Messenger* magazine, the journal of black radicals. Strauss was concerned with "the radical element" in Hoboken, whose members "are to a great extent German, but as yet it is impossible for me to state whether German interests and money are behind the strike."

The truth is that it was the absence of the left that was a factor in the strike. As J.B.S. Hardman noted in assessing the 1919 strikes, a great weakness of the workers' movements was that "there was no radical political party in the field which would seek to give the movement centralized and sustained political guidance." The IWW in New York, with all its weaknesses, attempted to fill this vacuum. While its press and its strike circulars were often vague and remote, its members and sympathizers pressed the strike in the streets. They criticized corrupt labor politicians and consistently championed industrial unionism. They played an important role among the Italian strikers, and this was a significant achievement. In November, they reported having recruited 1,200 longshoremen during the strike.

Breaking the Strike

Once it was clear that neither O'Connor nor a "red scare" would get the longshoremen back to work, the authorities set about breaking the strike in three ways. First, secretary of labor William B. Wilson announced the appointment of the Special Conciliation Commission, led by New York City mayor John Hylan. Second, the federal government made a show of force, sending soldiers into the Harbor, though chiefly to the army docks. The *New York Call* reported that the first soldiers involved in the strike were "regulars," who unloaded the army transport, *Northern Pacific*, at Hoboken. "Thousands of striking longshoremen stood by and silently watched the uniformed men unload the vessel," according to the *Call*. The striking longshoremen were no doubt angered and discouraged. Third, the shippers increasingly resorted to using strikebreakers, chiefly along the East River and in South Brooklyn but also in New Jersey—though rarely in Manhattan, presumably because that is where the union was strongest.

In Brooklyn, the use of strikebreakers, plus the attempts of small groups of workers to return, led to a series of street confrontations. On October 14, for example, the *Eagle* reported that the South Brooklyn waterfront was "tight as a drum" but only after a "crowd of 1,000 strikers gathered at the docks and marched up 13th Street to stop strikebreakers." The *Call* reported on October 15, "When some members of Local 808 appeared at the foot of 1st Avenue to go to work, more than 1,000 strikers were there to make a street protest." The following day there was "a violent disorder on the East River," during which four men were shot and another man stabbed in a confrontation between strikers, strikebreakers, and police. According to the *Eagle*, "Along the Greenpoint docks, so serious is the danger of riots, strong-arm men have been imported to protect workers. There are 800 stevedores keeping in operation six of the twelve docks there and they are being protected by a delegation of ex-service men recruited in Oklahoma . . . These men have guns and ammunition and are excellent rifle and pistol shots."

Questioned about the violence, T.V. O'Connor responded that, as there was no strike, he didn't consider "strikebreaking" to be an issue. "The violence," he said, "was further evidence of intimidation by 'reds.' These men are mostly Italian," he told the *Call*, "the foreign element . . ." On October 22, "large groups of longshoremen were on the waterfront," the *Times* reported, with "raiding parties" attacking the United Fruit piers, "which operate on the open-shop principle" and have been working "right along in spite of the strike." This time "1,000 or more Italian longshoremen" attacked strikebreakers and the police, many of them calling for "a war to the finish on the waterfront."

The Irish locals in Chelsea refused as stubbornly, though not as violently, as did the New Jersey longshoremen. It is impossible to say just why the strike broke in the first days of November. There were increasing reports of longshoremen, in fear of starving, searching the city in desperation for work. Certainly strikers must have been exhausted. The government and the shippers remained enormously confident, never blinking. Mayor Hylan, though often discouraged, kept his door open, still hoping to claim a victory. On November 5, at a meeting called by the mayor, the Chelsea longshoremen voted to return to work; the Brooklyn and New Jersey locals followed, though there were scattered disruptions in the port for two weeks. The vote followed the mayor's "final" plea. The longshoremen, however, remained defiant, insisting they were not accepting the NAC award; they returned "on the basis of the pre-award wages and conditions."

The great strikes of 1919 were nearly all lost, and there is little point in speculating about alternative outcomes to the longshoremen's strike. Still, there is a difference worth noting. Other workers would achieve industrial unionism a generation later, in the turbulence of the 1930s. The New York longshoremen never would. There was not another major strike on the waterfront for twenty-six years. In the 1950s the shape-up, favoritism, and casual work continued, "every man is hired fresh every day," and Joseph Ryan was still in charge—the "president for life of the International Longshoremen's Association."

The rank-and-file New York longshoremen in 1919 showed a great capacity to organize and to struggle in an effort to overcome staggering obstacles. In the face of this, the officers of the ILA, led by O'Connor and Ryan, clung tenaciously to their control of the union, despite the overwhelming opposition of the New York members. In doing this they were supported, even praised, by the shipping companies, by their colleagues on the National Adjustment Commission and the Shipping Board, and by the leaders of the American Federation of Labor (AFL). Moreover, they reaped great rewards. O'Connor went on to become chairman of the U.S. Shipping Board, though he maintained the title "Honorary President" of the ILA. Ryan, in addition to being "President for Life," also served as vice president of the New York State Federation of Labor, AFL, for more than twenty years. He was president of the Central Labor Council of Greater New York City from 1929 to 1938.

The "small-time criminals" of the prewar waterfront faded away; in their place came crime and corruption on a grand scale. Irish gangsters would dominate the West Side piers and the International union for decades to come. Brooklyn was awarded to the Anastasia brothers and "Murder, Inc." Marlon Brando's character in *On the Waterfront* became the stereotypical image of the New York longshoreman, a victim of trade union corruption and gangsterism. There have been many explanations of why the mob came to be so deeply entrenched in the Harbor and of how the longshoremen's union came to be so corrupt. That is not the subject here. One can say, however, that its triumph must not be seen as inevitable. The rank-and-file longshoremen fought heroically in 1907 and again in 1919 for a kind of unionism which would have presented enormous obstacles to the criminals and the shippers, as well as to corruption in the trade union movement itself. The stillbirth of industrial unionism on the waterfront in New York was a great tragedy in a time of working-class defeat.

See also: World War I Era Strikes, 191; Strikes on the Port of New York, 1945–1960, 559.

Bibliography

Barnes, Charles. *The Longshoremen.* New York: Survey Associates, 1915.

Commons, John R. "The Longshoremen of the Great Lakes." *Labor and Administration* (1913): 267–68.

Frazier, E. Franklin. "The Negro Longshoremen." Unpublished manuscript, 1921, Russell Sage Foundation, 40–45.

Hardman, J.B.S. "Postscript to Ten Years of the Labor Movement." *American Labor Dynamics.* New York: Harcourt, Brace and Company, 1928.

Hobsbawm, E.J. "National Unions on the Waterside." In *Labouring Men,* ed. E.J. Hobsbawm. New York: Anchor Books, 1967, 241.

Montgomery, David. "The New Unionism and the Transformation of Workers' Consciousness in America." In *Workers Control in America,* ed. David Montgomery. New York: Cambridge University Press, 1980, 91–112.

Poole, Ernest. "The Ship Must Sail on Time." *Everybody's Magazine* 19 (August 1908): 176–86.

Russell, Maud. *Men Along the Shore.* New York: Brussel and Brussel, 1966.

Spero, Sterling, and Abram Harris. *The Black Worker*. New York: Columbia University Press, 1931.

Winslow, Calvin. "Italian Workers on the Waterfront." In *The Lost World of Italian American Radicalism*, ed. Philip Cannistraro and Gerald Meyer. Westport, CT: Praeger, 2003, 99–112.

———. "On the Waterfront: Black, Italian and Irish Longshoremen in the New York Harbor Strike of 1919." In *Protest and Survival: Essays for E.P. Thompson*, ed. John Rule and Robert Malcolmson. New York: New Press, 1993, 355–93.

STRIKES ON THE PORT OF NEW YORK, 1945–1960

William Mello

From 1945 to almost 1975, the Port of New York was the site of intense class conflict. Striking longshoremen frequently battled the shipping companies, the police, federal and state political authorities, and their own union leadership. Through a series of strikes and protests, New York's dockworkers paralyzed the transportation of goods, both domestically and abroad, imposing financial losses of billions of dollars on U.S. business. Driving the strikes was the longshoremen's claim for a greater role in the decision-making process and control of the dock labor process. An important feature of longshoremen's strikes during this period was that, although their demands were largely economic, the methods used by the rank and file often advanced a claim for greater internal democracy in their union and a greater say in collective bargaining. The labor process on the waterfront was transformed over these years by rapidly changing technology and the reorganization of work, which turned even basic economic demands into highly charged political conflicts. The strikers faced ideological, judicial, economic, and political opposition and in the end the interests of business elites and political authorities usually prevailed.

The Rank and File

The dockworkers' rank-and-file movement drew on formal and informal labor organizations active in waterfront politics to organize and lead strikes. The informal organizations were made up of myriad politically distinct groups of labor activists. These groups eventually coalesced into an informal, alternative organization for contesting the formal collective bargaining institutions that regulated the waterfront labor process through the International Longshoreman's Association (ILA) and the New York Shipping Association (NYSA).

The Dockers News group was the most enduring of longshore associations on the waterfront. Organized by the Communist Party in the late 1940s, with support on various piers throughout the port, the group's influence was greatest on the Brooklyn docks. The group became a nucleus for the organization of radical longshoremen, and their presence on the waterfront was both respected and contested by other rank-and-file organizations. Dockers News was an informal organization of radical longshoremen active in the principal waterfront conflicts of the 1950s, 1960s, and 1970s. The newsletter survived and circulated throughout the Port of New York, in spite of opposition from the union, the employers, and the political authorities that dominated waterfront politics. It reflected the culture of independent action that predominated among longshoremen. In interviews with the author, Dockers News activists Gus Johnson (not his real name) and Servio Mello described their work; Johnson stated:

> When there was a hot issue and something had to be done, we would sit down and discuss how we could tap the anger of the men into a constructive way. The guys who put out *Dockers News* were all longshoremen, influenced by the left-wing longshoremen on the West Coast and the trade union movement. In the period 1953–54, with the red scare, it began to be distributed underground. The way it was done was to get the newsletter, use two or three cars, and hit the different boroughs at two, three o'clock in the morning. Each time at a different time, putting the newsletter on the floor on certain street corners, or luncheonettes.

> What the average longshoremen would do was collect them and carry them down to the pier. The union officials never knew who was putting it out because everyone was reading it and everyone was holding it. It was a very well-respected paper because it nailed down the issues. Through different means the men knew that the guys who were writing *Dockers News* were longshoremen.

Servio added:

> At times of crisis we would go right to the shape-up . . . and you go in and hand out bundles to men and they would give out the bundles. They realized that you couldn't stay too long . . . that you had a message that wasn't welcomed by the union. At most places it was well received, but in some places where the leadership was real rotten, where the guys were really oppressed and scared, they were afraid to pick it up. It went by different piers; on some the guys were very receptive. The union leadership used to say that it was the work of Communists trying to take over the waterfront, agents of Harry Bridges, parrots of Moscow, etc.

In Manhattan, ILA Local 791, led by Gene Sampson, was another highly influential group. Located on the Chelsea piers, its participation in the reform movement is a good example of how the movement combined formal organization with informal methods of collective action. While they belonged to a formal organization of the ILA, it was the dockworkers of Local 791 who were the first to walk off the ships, spurring the first port-wide wildcat strike of 1945. Gene Sampson's leadership of the local union reflected conflicting interests, both individual and collective, within the rank-and-file movement. The participation of Local 791 in the waterfront rebellion reflected Sampson's individual interests; he was a frequent contender for the presidency of the ILA and the brother of Frank Sampson, an ex-Tammany leader with strong ties to New York's political elite. As the movement for reform of the waterfront grew, Sampson rode the anti-communist hysteria of the McCarthy era and associated his demands for reform with strong anti-communist rhetoric, thus disassociating himself from the left-led Dockers News group.

An additional group that comprised the growing reform movement came from Local 968 in Brooklyn, which held a charter from the ILA since 1917. Known as the "Black Local," Local 968 was a Jim Crow union set up by the ILA, comprised solely of African-American longshoremen. Unlike other ILA locals that assigned pier jurisdiction to different local unions, Local 968 had no pier jurisdiction, forcing them to seek work with other local unions along the port. Counting a comparatively small membership of 500 dockworkers, only 100 of the local's members were able to find regular employment on the waterfront, according to the New York State Crime Commission in June 1953. Led by Cleophas Jacobs, the actions of Local 968 were restricted not only because of its limited possibilities of gaining employment for its members, but also due to long-standing racial divisions within the waterfront labor force.

With the rise of the rank-and-file reform movement, the Catholic Church also sought to influence the rebellious dockworkers. Led by Father John Corridan, director of the Xavier School for Labor Studies, the Catholic Church aspired to inform and direct the mobilization for reform, mainly among the predominantly Irish longshoremen on the West Side of Manhattan. The church sought to expose the evils of the waterfront labor process, and it staunchly opposed the increasing influence of Communists on the docks and the struggle for waterfront reform. In spite of the growing presence of the church in waterfront affairs, up until 1948 the Communists and their allies took the lead in organizing opposition to the ILA leadership.

The brutal conditions of waterfront work and the violence that defined the relationship between dockworkers and their union were essential aspects upon which rank-and-file activists built a common culture of solidarity outside of the formal union structure, allowing activists to build informal organizations that served as the catalyst for the strikes. The dockworkers' culture of solidarity was guided by the notion that the only recourse to the injustice and exploitation of waterfront work was through independent action, either individually or collectively. Corrupt union officials dominated the waterfront local unions under control of Joseph Ryan, president of the ILA. A tight network of relations among the union leaders, political elites, and employers distanced the union from its membership. The ILA leadership thwarted the participation of the rank and file. In his early study of the waterfront labor process, Edward Swanstrom wrote: "In various sections of the country the important decisions for the union are made by the officers without much regard for or questioning the opinion of the rank and file of the men."

Joseph Ryan ran the ILA and the waterfront with bare-knuckled brutality. Since the early years of Ryan's tenure as president, the ILA had an "anti-communist fighting fund" (that he often used for personal expenses) from which he paid organizers to guard the docks and repress rank-and-file opposition, which in Ryan's rhetoric was always "communist inspired." Violence was used to instill fear, intimidate rank-and-file activists, and eliminate opposition to the ILA leadership and policies. The union assumed the role of strong arm for the employers' control of the workforce, relying on ex-convicts hired as "union organizers" to dominate the docks, as historian Howard Kimmeldorf has chronicled. Similarly, the casual nature of waterfront employment and the hiring of dock labor through a process known as the "shape-up," where longshoremen would wrangle for work on a daily basis, became fundamental to guarantee the predominance of racketeers in the leadership of the ILA. The casual labor process served the interests of the shipping companies and racketeers alike. By creating a large surplus of labor, the employers were able to meet the need for a large workforce during the periods of the industry's peak demand while keeping labor costs low. The ILA's control of the hiring bosses guaranteed that the men would work to capacity. It also served as a means of extracting kickbacks from the men and a deterrent for any eventual worker revolt. In exchange, employers did not intervene in the pier rackets controlled by mobsters disguised as labor leaders.

The central demands that united the rank-and-file activists were greater safety regulations (such as weight limits on large loads lifted in nets or 'slings'), higher wages, and greater democracy in the ILA's decision-making process. Demands for reform escalated to one of labor's most explosive moments in the post–World War II period. As dock activist Sam Madell pointed out to Kimmeldorf, "The men would go along with all of these terrible things for a period of time, and then there would be an explosion, and the docks would be all tied up."

The Resurgence of Rank-and-File Mobilization, 1945

As economic historian Richard Franklin Bensel has described, the New York waterfront at mid-century played a particularly major role in the nation's politics and economy: "New York clearly stood apart as the primary entrepot linking the European and American economies. The dominance of the Port in the import/export trade of the United States conferred on the city's financial markets a dominant role in managing domestic and foreign investment. . . . [A]mong the leading trade centers, New York City alone was responsible for almost half of the (380 of 840) financial capital addresses in the cable directory." The Port of New York employed a large part of the city's workforce (both directly and indirectly) and generated much of New York's economic activity. The waterfront's position in the world market gave New York's elites greater influence in national politics and less dependency on the regional development common in other American industrial cities.

In October 1945, just five months after the end of World War II, New York's dockworkers staged a wildcat strike, a harbinger for a highly politicized and contentious movement to reform the waterfront labor process. Challenging the ILA leadership and demanding greater democracy in the decision-making process, rank-and-file dockworkers staked a claim for greater control of the waterfront labor process. Even though Local 791 on the Chelsea piers of Manhattan initiated the movement, informal rank-and-file organizations led by left-wing dockworkers quickly expanded their role and gained leadership of the strike, according to historian Colin Davis. The growing contention on the docks was a signal that the traditional alliances of local political elites with the ILA leadership would not survive.

The complex waterfront labor process that emerged after World War II was shaped by four distinct factors: first, the shifting alliances of economic groups embedded within the local political structure; second, the antagonistic relations between dockworkers and their unions; third, competing forces within the national labor movement that disputed control of New York's waterfront unions; and finally, the emergence of state and federal authorities as a political force on the waterfront.

"No Contract—No Work!"

In October 1945, just five months after receiving commendations for their productivity and vital support for the war effort, New York's longshoremen staged the first in a long series of wildcat strikes. Striking dockworkers systematically attempted to shift the center of the contract negotiations out from under the close-knit relations between the ILA and the NYSA and to win inclusion of the rank and file.

After ILA president Joseph Ryan announced a tentative agreement between the ILA and the NYSA, the longshoremen of Local 791 walked off the six piers under its jurisdiction. They protested the failure of the ILA and its Wage and Scale Committee to negotiate a reduction in the weight limits on sling loads by refusing to handle loads heavier than 2,240 pounds. In response to the walkout, Ryan, with the support of the ILA district council, called for an end to the work stoppage, which further enraged the rebellious dockworkers, according to historian Vernon Jensen. The following day, the entire Port of New York was paralyzed. Rank-and-file groups in Brooklyn and Manhattan rapidly organized meetings along the waterfront and increased the number of their demands, forcing Ryan to place more grievances before the bargaining committee. As the *New York Times* reported: "The strike spread from its starting point in Manhattan, it took in the long Brooklyn waterfront including the huge Bush Terminal . . . it took in the Jersey shoreline from Bayonne to the Hoboken piers . . . it spread to Staten Island, Newark Bay, the Army's Caven Point Terminal to the naval base at Leonardo, NJ." (All remaining quotes are from the *Times* unless otherwise stated.) Approximately 350 ships remained idle. Although the newspapers estimated that there were approximately 30,000 striking workers, according to Jack Gerst, secretary treasurer of Local 791, the number was closer to 60,000: 46,000 longshoremen and 14,000 ancillary port workers such as checkers and carpenters. The demands of the striking workers were reduction of the duration of collective bargaining agreements to one year; reduction in the number of shape-ups from three to two per day; four hours guaranteed pay for hired longshoremen; and time-and-one-half pay when working through the lunch period. The strikers also demanded a reduction in the limit of the sling load to 2,240 pounds (one "long" or "imperial" ton). The rebellious dockworkers claimed that the unlimited sling load often went as high as 7,000 pounds.

The demands of the strike quickly shifted from the initial grievances to include greater control of the ILA by demanding the resignation of "King Joe Ryan." By the third day of the strike, the Department of Labor issued a statement declaring that "the strike had reached dangerous proportions" and Captain Hewlett Bishop, Atlantic Coast Director for the War Shipping Administration (WSA) added, "The situation was growing more serious." The impact of the strike on domestic and foreign trade was almost immediate. By the tenth day of the strike, the NYSA reported that 110,000 tons of European relief cargo and U.S. military supplies were sitting idle on the port. This included 37,000 tons of Army cargo, of which 8,000 tons were meat. Moreover approximately 13,000 U.S. troops stationed in Europe were awaiting redeployment to the United States because seventeen cargo liberty ships were held up by the strike.

The West Coast Longshoremen of the ILWU quickly gave their support to the insurgents, as did the National Maritime Union (NMU), by donating $2,500 and distributing leaflets supporting the striking dockworkers. Ryan dismissed the endorsements for the insurgent workers as a Communist attempt to control the waterfront and the ILA, a diatribe he would frequently use over the following years to explain the enduring and vocal opposition to his leadership of the union.

The rebellious longshoremen's movement contested the autocratic structure of the ILA organization and its alliance with the shipping companies. That is, while the demands of the wildcat strike were predominantly economic, the method the rank and file employed of mass assemblies along the waterfront advanced the claim for greater internal democracy in the decision-making process. On October 10, in a mass meeting held in a vacant lot near the Brooklyn waterfront, 2,500 dockworkers formalized the rank-and-file committee and elected William Warren as chairman and a steering committee comprised of Sal Barone (Local 338), Eurico Ceccarelli (Local 1199), Joseph Alanpi (Local 338–1), Fred Cerutti and John Susino (Local 338).

Even if the steering committee was able to paralyze large sectors of the waterfront, their capacity to influence the contract negotiation process was limited. The ILA leadership and the waterfront employers remained steadfast in their alliance against the rank and file. Defining the conflict along ideological lines as a struggle between patriotic Americans and "evil communists," Ryan set out to isolate the rebellious movement and force the longshoremen to return to work, always insisting that the strike was the result of "communistic influence." Ryan rallied the support of conservative trade-union organizations in what was called the "Back to Work" movement. His action received support from labor organizations such as the Seafarers International Union (SIU) led by Harry Lundeberg, as well as the New York Central Labor Council and the New York State American Federation of Labor (AFL). Ryan's "Back to Work" movement combined high levels of red-baiting with physical coercion and began taking its toll on the piers where the rank and file was less organized, according to Jensen. By October 17 the local newspapers wrote that approximately 11,500 longshoremen, reinforced by ILA-sanctioned strikebreakers, were returning to work. The main holdouts continued to be in Brooklyn and New Jersey. In spite of the growing return to work, 3,000 striking dockworkers marched through the center of Manhattan from 34th Street to Chelsea along the waterfront chanting "Down with Ryan—Down with the Finks" in reference to the returning workers. In Brooklyn, where the rank-and-file resistance was greatest, the ILA recruited Army veterans as strikebreakers. Some wore their Army coats with ILA badges pinned on them. According to Jensen, they broke through the pickets, claiming: "You guys made plenty of dough while we were in the Army; now we're going to get some of it."

Striking workers clashed with hired goons and strikebreakers, as well as the local police, organized by Ryan to remove the picket lines and reopen the docks. On October 18, the fledgling Rank-and-File Committee, unable to sustain the escalating battle with no apparent solution in sight, admitted that the strike had been broken and advised all to return to work. In a statement to the press, strike committee chair Warren declared that the return to work was "to preserve the unity of the longshoremen that had developed during the strike and to continue to build the unity to achieve our economic demands and a clean and democratic union . . . we make this recommendation because the continuance of the strike at this time in the face of Ryan's gangsterism, the strike breaking of Harry Lundenberg [president of SIU], and the lies in the anti-labor press, the active collusion of the ship owners with Ryan and Lundeberg convinces me that the unity of the ILA rank-and-file may suffer."

However, Warren and Barone quickly switched loyalties in the aftermath of the strike. Just three days after making these declarations, they were physically beaten by gangsters in Brooklyn and expelled from the ILA. Warren almost immediately turned on his fellow insurgents and gave his support to Ryan. In a later statement, he declared that they had been "misled," that they had been "wrongly steered into the communist camp," and that in fact they were "just a couple of plain, ordinary longshoremen who wanted a good, strong, honest union . . . and were just being used as dupes" by Rank-and-File Committee lawyers Nathan Witt and Harold Cammers. Witt responded that it was the beatings Warren suffered that must have "convinced him to work for Ryan." The Rank-and-File Committee quickly replaced Warren and Barone, appointing John Berg as chairman, Charles Andersen as secretary, and James Glasgow as treasurer. When Ryan was informed of the new leadership, it was reported that he declared Berg and Andersen were "part of a small group that had been boring from within for the communists in the ILA for the past five years."

Even though the rank and file failed to achieve their demands, the strikers forced the ILA leadership to allow local unions to vote on the contract proposals. In spite of high levels of physical and ideological coercion, the organized strikebreaking movement, and the haphazard return to work, the membership voted to reject the ILA's contract proposal. The NYSA responded that they would make no further concessions. The ILA, allied with the employers, successfully bypassed the rank and file's claim for port-wide votes to decide a new contract by submitting their proposals to arbitration. As the Rank-and-File Committee's newsletter argued, "We do not oppose to arbitration as such. We do oppose to any attempt to settle the longshore situation without giving the longshoremen an opportunity to decide democratically and free from coercion what steps shall be taken on our behalf [*sic*]." Despite the dockworkers' claims, the arbitrator quickly approved the proposals submitted by the shipping companies and the ILA; the contract negotiations were over. If Ryan won the battle, however, the conflict was far from over. The 1945 wildcat strike was just the beginning of a reform movement that intermittently paralyzed the Port of New York in future years.

The backdrop for the 1947 waterfront contract negotiations was a back-pay campaign waged by the Rank-and-File Committee. Rank-and-file activists argued that the agreement between the ILA and the NYSA violated the 1938 Fair Labor Standards Act of 1938 when shipping employers failed to pay overtime to longshoremen who worked through the evening. The movement resulted in a lawsuit representing approximately 3,000 dockworkers requesting $5 million in unpaid wages. The dockworkers of Local 791 once again paralyzed the port between Canal Street and Chelsea in Manhattan. On August 19, 1947, a tentative contract agreement was reached between the ILA and the NYSA that provided for nothing more than a 10-cent hourly wage increase. In reality the ILA and the NYSA were attempting to preempt the Taft-Hartley Act ban on preferential hiring practices by signing the agreement before the legislation was enacted. Informed of what was happening, Sampson of Local 791 held an "unscheduled meeting" at which the members rejected the ILA's contract scheme (before the agreement was even officially announced). In a move similar to what had occurred less than two years before, 4,000 longshoremen walked off the piers in Manhattan. Sampson initially denied any knowledge of the wildcat strike, stating, "The men just aren't around for work." However, he ended by declaring that he "supported their actions 100 percent." The demands of the rebellious workers were a 25-cent-per hour wage increase, eight hours of guaranteed pay when hired, two weeks of paid vacation, and a reduction of the sling load.

Compared to the strike of 1945, there was not widespread support for the job action. The strike received the support of dockworkers from Locals 895 and 1258, also in Manhattan. In Brooklyn, half the piers were paralyzed on the second day of the strike, only to return to work the following day. After six days on strike, the longshoremen of Manhattan's West Side returned to work. Significantly, the limited support for the strike suggests that conflicts were brewing within the leadership of the rank-and-file movement, between Sampson and the left-led Rank-and-File Committee. Whatever their differences they would not impede the resurgence of the movement in the renewed contract negotiations the following year.

On August 17, 1948, just four days before the contract was to expire, President Truman, informed of the growing tension on the Port of New York, invoked the recently passed Taft-Hartley Act and ordered a halt to any strike activity for eighty days. Truman's decision postponed the formal strike date to November 9. On November 10, as the ILA announced that it would sign the agreement with the NYSA, the rebellious dockworkers once again walked off the ships. More than just a protest against unresolved grievances between employers and employees, it became increasingly evident that the ILA leadership was unable to represent the collective claims of New York's longshoremen. In contrast, the rank-and-file movement allowed dockworkers to exert a larger influence in the decision-making process, filling the vacuum where the institutional means of representation were highly exclusionary.

Sensing that the rank-and-file movement had expanded in scope and scale since the 1945 wildcat strike, Ryan shifted strategy. Three days after the wildcat started, Ryan reversed his previous position and sanctioned the rebellious job action. This move paralyzed dockworkers from Portland, Maine, to Hampton Road, Virginia. He also instructed affiliated dockworkers in Montreal, Halifax, and on the Gulf Coast not to work on ships diverted from New York. The proposed settlement endorsed by both the ILA and the NYSA had been rejected almost unanimously. The employers responded that they would make no further offer. The ILA's strategy was twofold: first, it attempted to gain control of the rebellious movement by sanctioning the strike; second, it sought to weaken the Rank-and-File Committee's claim to representation by limiting strike activities, such as picket lines and demonstrations. This strategy kept the bulk of the membership disorganized and uninformed. To reverse the ILA's attempt at co-opting the strike movement, the Rank-and-File Committee called for a general meeting on November 16 at the ILA's Manhattan Center. Ryan responded with his usual red-baiting tactics, claiming that the meeting was "communist inspired" and declaring to the *New York World Telegram,* "If the communists interfere with this, our men will throw them in the river." The rank-and-file activists outnumbered Ryan loyalists and expelled them from the meeting. The meeting then outlined the dockworkers' main demands: a 25-cent-per hour wage increase, $3.00 per hour additional pay for work performed at night and on weekends, an employer-financed welfare fund, two weeks of paid vacation, lighter sling loads, and payment for the past years of unpaid overtime. They then closed the meeting with a minute of silence in memory of rank-and-file activist Pete Panto, who had been slain in 1939 by gangsters linked to the ILA leadership.

While the Rank-and-File Committee had a significantly high level of political legitimacy among the striking workers (confirmed by its ability to immobilize the port), it had little if any influence in the institutional sphere. On November 25, the ILA and the NYSA signed an agreement that allowed for a 13-cent-per hour wage increase, two weeks paid vacation after 1,350 hours work, and the organization of the ILA Welfare Fund. Ryan quickly announced that a majority of longshoremen had voted to accept the agreement and return to work.

In response, dockworkers organized a meeting at St. Stephens Hall in Brooklyn. They decided to wait for the complete election results to decide whether or not to return to work. In their initial polling, a majority of Brooklyn's dockworkers had voted against the proposed contract, as did the longshoremen of Local 1249 in Jersey City. Speaking at the meeting, activist Mitchell Berensen declared: "Joe Ryan didn't call this strike and we have no faith in his announcement tonight." Paul O'Dwyer (the brother of the mayor and ex-Brooklyn district attorney William O'Dwyer) stated: "[The meeting] was to take whatever action necessary on the outcome of the voting . . . [and] if the majority votes for it we will accept it." The continued exclusion of the Rank-and-File Committee from the negotiation process reflected the limits of informal organization in an industry that was increasingly under the scrutiny of the federal authorities.

The burgeoning rank-and-file movement continued to challenge the ILA leadership. In 1951, yet another wildcat strike gripped the Port of New York when rebellious dockworkers refused to accept a two-year agreement that had been negotiated between the ILA leadership and the NYSA. The longshoremen questioned the validity of the ILA-sponsored contract ratification election. Approximately 25 percent of the estimated 40,000 dockworkers participated in the vote. The contract was approved two to one in a highly suspicious plebiscite. The rebellious movement, however, continued to demand radical changes in the antidemocratic nature of the union's decision-making process as well as a 25-cent-per hour wage increase, a guaranteed day's pay with only one shape-up, and increased contributions to the union's welfare benefits.

The employers' counterproposal offered an 11-cent wage increase, a 16.5-cent wage increase for overtime pay, and the promise that improvements to the welfare fund would be submitted to a joint committee for further study. The proposals of the union and the NYSA continued to be very different in spite of Ryan's "confidence" that a new accord would be reached. The ratification vote, however, would not suffice to gain the longshoremen's acquiescence to the new labor accord.

On October 15, one week after the ILA-sponsored ratification election in which Ryan had boasted of the two to one margin approving the new contract, a wildcat strike slowly began to immobilize the Port of New York. Strikers protested the vote and demanded that Ryan reopen contract negotiations with the NYSA. Members of ILA Local 791 on the Hudson River initiated the strike, but the movement quickly spread to Brooklyn. The dockworkers argued that the ILA voting process was, at best, highly suspicious, and that "ballot box stuffing," repeat voting, and a vote-tally system that relied solely on local ILA officials to call in the results after the votes were counted was no guarantee of a fair tally. The rebellious longshoremen demanded a new ratification election supervised by an independent third party.

Hoping to convince striking longshoremen to return to work, Ryan went to the Chelsea Pier, but was immediately rebuffed by the strikers. "They won't listen to me," Ryan stated. "They feel they have a grievance but they have no leader I can deal with." However, when questioned about the fact that the strike had spread to Brooklyn, Ryan's answer was completely different. Hoping to drive a wedge between Manhattan and Brooklyn longshoremen, he replied, "As for the Brooklyn walkout that's strictly communist inspired. They're riding around Brooklyn in cars now prevailing on the men to walk out. You know [Harry] Bridges was in town last week." Ryan tried to deflect his own incapacity to convince striking longshoremen to return to work and the growing discontent of dockworkers with the ILA leadership by continuously reinventing a supposed communist plot to dominate the Port of New York, and the following day he announced a campaign to rid the port of communist influence. "They [Ryan loyalists] will be armed with circulars explaining how the Commies are seeking to break-up our union and they will try to talk to the boys in Brooklyn into returning to work [*sic*]. If there is any violence it will be Bridges' fault," Ryan declared. The ILA leadership's red-baiting attempt to portray striking dockworkers in Brooklyn as "un-American" was intensified by the fact that the workers had paralyzed the activities of the Brooklyn Army Base Embarkation pier. The ILA leadership continuously tried to link the Communist Party's position against the war in Korea to the Brooklyn job action.

Particularly in Brooklyn, ILA Local 1814 president Anthony "Tough Tony" Anastasia was making little headway at deterring striking longshoremen, although the ideological pressure placed on rebellious dockworkers by the union leadership did obtain some results. In an attempt to break the strike, Anastasia appeared at the Brooklyn Army Base. Appealing to striking longshoremen, he shouted, "I am Anastasia, one of the foremen on the waterfront. This is one place you gotta work. If you don't I supply the men. This army base is controlled by the United States Army. I was here yesterday and I'm back today as a good American citizen." Even though the dockworkers initially ignored Anastasia's orders, when he ordered approximately seventy-five strikebreakers to move in toward the pier, the climate changed. Fearing for their jobs, Pier 4 hatch boss Salvatore Brocco climbed up on a truck and responded, "Anyone who calls us Commies is a damned liar. We are patriotic; we have worked this base since before the war. Gene Sampson [Local 791 business agent] is our man and a better leader than Joe Ryan." Then, turning toward Anastasia, Brocco declared, "Get those stooges out of there and we'll go in." Anastasia called off the strikebreakers and the dockworkers filed back onto the pier. If "Tough Tony" was able to force rebellious longshoremen to return to work at the army base, he and his brother Gerardo Anastasio were not so successful on other piers in the Port of Brooklyn. The piers of Brooklyn for the most part remained paralyzed.

The strike was the initiative of local ILA leaders who had grown disenchanted with Ryan's control of the ILA. Left-wing dockworkers, however, were strong supporters of the movement. By the end of the first week, local ILA leaders appointed Gene Sampson the "strike leader." The political implications of Sampson's appointment as spokesman for the striking longshoremen were twofold. First, it was a logical move because his local union had initiated the movement on the first day. His appointment, however, also reflected a deep ideological conflict that was growing among different rank-and-file groups along the waterfront. For example, one strike bulletin carried a picture of the American flag and the caption, "This is not a commy [*sic*] paper." Second, by appointing Sampson, the conservative rank-and-file leaders sought to diminish the capacity of the left to gain influence over the direction of the strike through pier activism as they had done in the 1945 wildcat movement.

With the job action gaining momentum, striking dockworkers showed little inclination towards immediately returning to work. At the beginning of the second week of the strike, ninety piers were paralyzed on the Port of New York; by the end of the week 138 piers and 104 ships were immobilized on the port. Moreover, longshoremen in Boston and Baltimore joined the strike. As the *Dockers News* wrote, "Boston is out solid along with the New York-New Jersey region. Philadelphia and Baltimore may join us at any moment. The start of mass picketing at the docks yesterday makes our strike tighter and stronger than ever." Approximately 20,000 longshoremen were actively participating in the job action, and with no solution in sight the American Railroad Association embargoed all cargo headed for the Port of New York. The Commerce and Industry Association estimated that cargo valued at $250 million was piled up on the port and growing at a rate of $25 million per day. This prompted the executive committee of the Chamber of Commerce of the State of New York to request that Governor Dewey appoint a special district attorney "for a complete investigation of the New York waterfront situation."

The strikebreaking tactics of the ILA leadership coincided with employers' legal action seeking to restrict the striking longshoremen. Despite the dockworkers' resistance, after four weeks on strike, Ryan's "back to work" movement, aided by political and legal pressures, was taking its toll on the rebellious movement. On November 5, the U.S. Customs House reported that 3,000 dockworkers had reported for work on nineteen piers along the Port of New York. Four days later, Sampson advised all dockworkers through a press release to return to work despite the fact that a day earlier the National Labor Relations Board (NLRB) had dismissed the unfair labor practice charges filed by the NYSA.

Even though the 1951 wildcat strike had negligible results, the dockworkers' claim for greater democracy in the ILA's decision-making process continued to mobilize the waterfront, and rebellions against "King Joe" gathered momentum. The movement was a strong indicator of the mounting disaffection for Ryan among local ILA leaders and their increasing capacity to act independently of the ILA president and respond to the claims of dockworkers. Ryan's diminishing capacity to command the dock union would subsequently lead to his removal as "President for Life" of the ILA under a barrage of accusations over the misuse of union funds.

Waterfront Wars

On September 25, 1953, as contract negotiations between the ILA and the NYSA were under way, the AFL, at its national convention in St. Louis, expelled the ILA and chartered a new dock union on the Port of New York. The reason for the new organization, the AFL declared, was the inability of the ILA to adhere to its previous promises to "clean house" and remove the criminal elements from its organization. The creation of the new union, the ILA-AFL, set the stage for liberal waterfront reformers to abandon the ILA and join a new union being formed under the auspices of the AFL, the International Brotherhood of Teamsters (IBT), and the Seafarers International Union (SIU). The new waterfront labor organization also received the support of waterfront priest John Corriden, who viewed the gangsters of the ILA and the radical rank-and-file activists as being equally evil for longshoremen. He argued: "As everybody knows, one of the reasons I am in the work that I am doing is to fight communist penetration in labor unions. I have plenty of sources of information about what the communists are doing anytime they are active on the waterfront." The three-year jurisdictional dispute that ensued between the AFL and the ILA redefined the nature of the growing conflict for control of the waterfront labor process. The newly organized ILA-AFL represented in large part those who viewed favorably the increasing federal and state control of the New York waterfront labor process, which forced the reconfiguration of the political alliances within both the ILA and the rank-and-file movement. As longshoremen on both sides of the fray went to battle, wage and contract negotiations came to a halt, while political elites under the direction of Governor Dewey (in close touch with the president) moved to expand their influence over the newly chartered union.

Purporting to represent the desire of New York's longshoremen for "honest and democratic trade unionism," the AFL executive board appointed IBT president Dave Beck and Paul Hall, secretary-treasurer for the Atlantic and Gulf Coast division of the Seafarers International Union, to lead a five-man trusteeship of the newly chartered AFL organization. The ILA-AFL also counted on the participation of four ILA vice presidents who had abandoned the old union and a war chest of $200,000. If the rampant corruption and abuse of the old ILA had since become widespread public knowledge, the composition of the "honest and democratic" AFL union was not much better. Head trustee Beck, much like his ILA adversary Ryan, was soon to be the topic of a congressional investigation for the misuse of union funds. It was discovered that he "borrowed" over $250,000 from the IBT's Western Conference treasury for personal use and made payments to a Seattle building contractor to the sum of $146,678, a significant part of which was for the construction of a pool at his home and work done on the homes of other IBT officials. The ILA-AFL received at the same time the support of longtime waterfront reformers and gangsters alike. For example, the union was readily supported by longtime waterfront reformers Gene Sampson of the rebellious Local 791 and John Dwyer of Local 895, both on Manhattan's Hudson River. Even though the membership of Local 791 voted overwhelmingly to remain in the old ILA, the members of Local 895 voted to affiliate with the ILA-AFL.

In contrast, the AFL dockworkers union also received the immediate adherence of John and Vincent Erato, union officials of Local 1199–1 in Brooklyn, who years earlier were responsible for leading the persecution and demise of the Brooklyn Rank-and-File Committee led by Pete Panto. There were few ideological differences (if any at all) between the ILA and the newly organized AFL dock union. Both unions were highly conservative. The AFL dock union likewise readily embraced Cold War rhetoric. At first it was used to distance the ILA-AFL from the Communist Party-led rank-and-file movement that remained particularly influential on the Brooklyn waterfront.

The importance of the 1953 contract negotiations was twofold. First, the demands presented by the ILA sought to compensate for the minimal wage increases of past contracts negotiated under Ryan's leadership. Second, the 1953 contract negotiations were also a race against the growing movement led by the AFL with the support of state and federal political authorities to replace the ILA. That is, if the ILA could renew its agreement with the NYSA it would retain its right for exclusive representation of New York's dockworkers for another year and thus ward off any pressure by the AFL for a representation election.

Up to this time, mobilization was not a part of the ILA's traditional political repertoire. As the dock union came increasingly under attack by the AFL and the state and federal governments, however, its campaign for legitimacy would include massive public demonstrations appealing for public support. In the first of such actions, on October 26, 1953, protesting the interference of state and federal authorities into the waterfront labor process, the ILA paralyzed port activity by staging a massive march and rally in Madison Square Garden. Starting at Pier 74 and 34th Street, approximately 15,000 people marched down Twelfth Avenue in support of the ILA. While Ryan made a quick appearance at the rally, for the most part the event was led by "Packy" Conelly.

The AFL, Governor Dewey, and sectors of New York's political elite all reinforced the demand that shipping employers not enter into an agreement with the ILA, no matter how acceptable or lucrative, and even in the event of a strike, the Taft-Hartley law could always be invoked if the situation became uncontrollable. After a meeting between Beck and Dewey, the topic of which was their mutual interest that the NYSA not sign an agreement with the ILA, the ILA-AFL general organizer John Dwyer (formerly of ILA Local 895) sent a telegram to the NYSA urging them not to sign. Their argument to convince the shipping companies was also expressed in a news conference held by George Meany, who noted that given the present division between unions on the waterfront, signing an agreement might not avert a strike, since doing so could lead opposing factions within the ILA to rebel against the ILA leadership. The position of Dewey and the AFL was reinforced by sectors outside of the conflict such as the New York City Crime Committee led by Spruille Braden. In a statement to the shipping association, Braden urged the employers "not to deal directly or indirectly" with the "mobsters or their puppets in control of the union." Finally, even federal and state mediators involved in the contract negotiations appeared sympathetic with the idea that the NYSA refrain from renewing its contract with the ILA. A newspaper covering the negotiation wrote: "Federal and State mediators had all but given up their efforts to promote a direct wage agreement, in the apparent belief that a strike would be less harmful than a contract that would anchor the racket ridden union to the Port of New York and Atlantic Coast for another year."

State political and economic elites had more in their arsenal to control rebellious dockworkers. The Bi-State Waterfront Commission was created in December 1953 as a result of recommendations made to then-Governor Dewey by the New York State Crime Commission hearings and was signed into law by President Eisenhower in August of the same year. Its official task was to reorganize hiring practices and end labor racketeering on the waterfront. The Commission's annual report for 1956–57 stated, "The Commission was charged with re-establishing the dignity of longshoremen by freeing them from discrimination in hiring and from kick-backs, usury and other forms of oppression; with restoring ethical practices on the part of both management and labor representatives by eliminating bribery and extortion." One of the first activities of the commission was to organize employment centers where dockworkers were assigned work by seniority, thus ending the infamous shape-up. While the commission did make progress toward the decasualization of hiring practices, it was also a political implement used to control worker activism. If American political life in the 1950s was marked by the infamous witch hunts of McCarthyism, on the docks things were not different. Political control of dockworkers was an important factor given the importance of the New York waterfront to the U.S. economy. Furthermore, control of the waterfront labor process was also fundamental for the development and support of postwar U.S. foreign policy in Europe, such as the Marshall Plan and later the Korean War. Working in conjunction with the Waterfront Commission, the U.S. Coast Guard would investigate active trade unionists and attempt to remove them from the waterfront by denying them a waterfront pass or Coast Guard pass, which gave the workers access to the pier. The Coast Guard intimidated workers by sending interrogatory letters that stated: "There has come to our attention information of such nature as to warrant inquiry into your eligibility to hold a valid United States Merchant Mariners document . . . requests that you answer the interrogatories attached hereto." What followed was the infamous question "Are you now or have you ever been an officer, or official, or a member of, or affiliated or associated with in any way, any of the organizations set forth below?" What ensued was a list in alphabetical order containing the names of almost 300 organizations. The final part of the interrogatory dedicated two pages to questions regarding activity in the Communist Party. Servio, a longtime activist on the waterfront, recalled:

> They would call you down, they held hearings . . . in an inquisition type of fishing expedition, so if you didn't answer right they could take your pass away . . . they tried with me, asking me if I was a member of the American Labor Party (ALP), whether I was a member of the Peace Committee, I had a whole damn hearing. Anybody who didn't face them out, who got scared, they would take your pass away.

The CIO, then in the middle of the process of expelling Communists from its ranks, worked from within the labor movement and added to the waterfront witch hunt. Within the climate of political witch hunts and red-baiting, the Waterfront Commission eliminated many rank-and-file activists. It screened out dockworkers based on their political beliefs, taking advantage of the anti-communist sentiment stirred up by McCarthyism. While relatively effective in persecuting rank-and-file longshoremen, the commission did not seem to have the same efficiency at controlling labor racketeering. The real criminals it was supposed to screen out went virtually untouched. Approximately one-third of the ILA had criminal records, according to the NYS Crime Commission investigation of 1953.

As expected, on October 1, 1953, approximately 50,000 longshoremen walked off the ships. In response, the NYSA stepped up their efforts, pressuring the governors of New York and New Jersey to intercede, and demanding that the federal government impose the Taft-Hartley Act. Just twelve hours after the strike began, President Eisenhower, in response to the demands of the shipping companies and state political officials and in compliance with the Taft-Hartley laws, requested an immediate Board of Inquiry into the waterfront labor crisis with the purpose of issuing an injunction against the striking dockworkers. With a speed never before witnessed in other cases, the Board of Inquiry met and by October 4, Eisenhower issued an eighty-day injunction against the ILA.

The issuance of the Taft-Hartley injunction on the striking dockworkers, however, was not the traditional "cooling-off" period between employers and workers, which was supposedly the original intent of the law. In fact, state political authorities had little, if any, intention to come to terms with the ILA. Rather, political authorities hoped that the injunction would reinforce the campaign of the AFL to dislodge the ILA from the New York waterfront. In a press conference held after meeting with Dave Beck and Paul Hall, Governor Dewey made it public that at no time was the state interested in reaching an agreement with the striking workers represented by the ILA. "I am greatly interested," he stated, "that the ship owners do not sign with the old racket controlled union. It would make our job much more difficult: our job is to clean out the racketeers and gangsters from the waterfront."

Fear of a strike on December 24 fueled the NLRB's decision for a quick election. The elections, it was decided, would be held on December 22 and 23, 1953, thus giving both sides little (if any) time to prepare for the upcoming battle. Even though he predicted a victory for the AFL slate, George Meany severely criticized the NLRB's decision, calling it "a moral disgrace" and stating "the NLRB deserves public castigation for succumbing to pressure from the NYSA in deciding conditions of the election." In spite of all the pressures, the ILA emerged victorious from the highly disputed representation election that ensued on the Port of New York amid mutual accusations of coercion and promoting violence.

Ultimately, a report submitted by NLRB regional director Charles T. Doud to the Labor Board's general counsel in Washington, reinforced the claims of the AFL and the state and federal political authorities that coercion by ILA activists had played a significant role in the waterfront election and warranted examining the possibility of setting the election aside. Dewey reacted enthusiastically to the regional director's report. If during the first election Dewey and the NLRB were at odds, the NLRB's new position demonstrated that the federal and state authorities were now closing ranks.

By March 1954, however, the growing conflict between the AFL and the ILA was coming close to shutting down the port. The conflict erupted when ILA dockworkers on the West Side of Manhattan refused to handle cargo transported on trucks driven by Teamster drivers of IBT Local 807. The job action quickly spread to New Jersey and the employers declared that the port was rapidly coming to a standstill. In response to the boycott by ILA dockworkers, Teamster truck drivers set up pickets to impede other truckers from entering the port.

In spite of mounting political and legal pressure against the ILA and the striking longshoremen, the job action continued to gain strength. Even though the government viewed the ILA as primarily responsible for the strike, the ILA kept denying it. Shortly into the second week of the job action, a strike committee appeared assuming responsibility for the port-wide work stoppage. The organization of the strike committee resembled that of the rank-and-file activists of years past that the ILA leadership had so strongly persecuted, only this time the identity of the committee members was kept secret for fear of reprisals from the Waterfront Commission. A committee spokesman summed up the tension and frustration that had been growing over the past six months: "For six months we have been working without a contract, waiting for the Labor Board to certify our union . . . we won an election and waited out an eighty day injunction under the Taft-Hartley Act. Now we are being told that we have to wait months and months more while the Board investigates? If the AFL is so strong, why can't it work the port now? It told the longshoremen to work but no one is working."

The strike had met a stalemate; there would be no resolution to the conflict that did not include a solution to the union representation struggle. On April 1, 1954, the NLRB decided to set aside the December dock election and proposed new elections within the next six weeks. It stipulated the condition that the ILA could participate in the ballot provided the dock union ended the twenty-nine day strike, which was considered the most costly and violent dock strike ever at the Port of New

York. The ILA's response to the NLRB was similarly quick. The strike committee quickly convened and decided to return to work immediately.

In the days preceding the election, the ILWU and Communist Party rank-and-file activists became increasingly vocal in their support for the ILA. Harry Bridges wrote in the ILWU's *The Dispatcher*, "[We back the ILA] because it is the union which the majority of the longshoremen want . . . it led the fight against the jurisdictional raiders, the union busters, the scab herders, and the politicians—it led the fight to get a union contract from the employers." The ILWU's support for the ILA provoked a reaction from both political authorities as well as the AFL. Even though the ILA continued to make rhetorical denunciations against communism, linking the ILA to left-wing activity had become the centerpiece of the AFL's waterfront campaign.

The results of the second ballot were almost as close as the results of first, held only months before: the ILA received 9,110 votes, the ILA-AFL received 8,791, with 49 votes void, 51 votes for no union, and 1,797 votes contested by the competing unions. It became clear, however, that the ILA had won the second election and significant sectors of the ILA-AFL began the slow but steady return to the ranks of the ILA. The chief ILA-AFL organizer in Jersey City, Willie DeNobile, announced shortly after the results were known: "98 percent of the AFL members are ready to return to the ILA . . . they say the ILA won two elections and they want no more of this bickering. The rank and file longshoremen are the real sufferers from all these contests, all he wants is a strong union and a chance to work." In the final tally the ILA continued to hold the lead even if the difference between the two dock unions had diminished—the ILA received 9,407 votes and the ILA-AFL received 9,144 votes. By July the ILA was certified as the bargaining agent of New York's dockworkers.

With the election decided, the ILA turned to negotiating the new contract that had expired over a year before. By October 1, 1954, however, still no agreement had been reached. By October 3, with no solution in sight, for the second time in six months, dockworkers abandoned the piers of Brooklyn, Manhattan, and New Jersey. The strike, however, was short-lived; within two days the ILA and the NYSA reached a tentative agreement that paid wage increases retroactively but made no contributions to the Welfare Fund. The agreement also included a thirty-day truce to resolve remaining differences, at the end of which the ILA had signed a two-year collective bargaining agreement that extended to October 1, 1956.

"We Won't Be Back for a Month!"

Since the mid-1950s, new forms of handling cargo began to be used in the shipping industry, such as the use of conveyor belts, the construction of ships with side-port entries, "piggy-backing" (hoisting the entire truck trailer onto the ship), and containerized cargo. This last form of automated cargo handling increasingly became the dominant form of waterborne cargo transportation. Even though the amount of containerized cargo was minimal during the late 1950s, its appearance on the port signaled a radical transformation of the maritime cargo transportation industry and placed significant limits on the control exercised by dockworkers over the waterfront labor process.

Before containerization, the average dock gang comprised of twenty longshoremen could move twenty tons of cargo in eight hours. With the use of modern containerized cargo, ten dockworkers could move forty tons of cargo in a matter of minutes. Currently, container ships carry an average of 75,000 tons of cargo. The shipping industry continues to be the most economically competitive form of cargo transportation available and some have even ventured to define it as a "cornerstone of the global economy." In the 1956 contract negotiations, however, neither the diverse rank-and-file groups nor the ILA fully realized the impact that containerization would subsequently have. In spite of this, the topic of port automation quickly came to the forefront of the dockworkers' claims. One shipping executive declared: "Everything we do is to do it faster and cheaper, I don't know where it is going to end." In 1956, neither did New York's longshoremen.

On August 1, 1956, negotiations between the ILA and the NYSA began for the collective bargaining agreement set to expire on September 30. The demands presented by the dockworkers' union included a wage increase of 32 cents per hour, twelve paid holidays, increased welfare benefits, eight hours guaranteed wages when hired, wage differentials for dangerous work, severance pay, an employer-financed workers' compensation fund, double-time pay for work performed during holidays, and the expansion of the bargaining unit. The ILA proposed a master contract for all longshoremen on the East and Gulf Coast ports, covering the docks from Portland, Maine, to Brownsville, Texas. In the union's proposal a coastwide contract would stipulate wages, vacation, welfare, and pensions, leaving aside port practices and rules for local ancillary agreements. In spite of the extensive economic claims proposed by the longshoremen, the negotiations and ensuing battle focused on the demand for a single coastwide collective bargaining agreement, obfuscating all other demands made by the ILA Wage and Scale Committee.

The demand for a master contract was more than just a negotiating expediency; it reflected the long-standing struggle for control over the waterfront labor process. The ILA argued that the shipping companies that operated in the various ports along the East and Gulf coasts were the same as those that comprised the NYSA. In this sense, the other ports would be represented in their negotiations with the New York shipping employers. A coastwide agreement would expand the capacity of the ILA to influence the waterfront labor process on the entire East Coast. Since the Port of New York was the most organized and was far more readily mobilized compared to the Southern and Gulf ports, it would remain the center from which the ILA could intercede in all of the Atlantic and Gulf Coast ports. A master contract would allow the ILA, through its bargaining process on the Port of New York where conditions were more favorable for the union, to exercise influence on ports where the union's organization and mobilization capacity were limited. Moreover, a coastwide agreement would safeguard the ILA leadership against future challenges to their representation rights. By expanding the bargaining unit to all ports on the East and Gulf coasts, it would be much more difficult for competing rank-and-file groups to mount opposition, because they would have to include the dockworkers of those ports in any future representation challenge.

The ILWU and Harry Bridges immediately came out in support of the ILA's demands. In the union's newspaper, *The Dispatcher*, the West Coast union applauded the ILA's position, noting that the claim for a coastwide agreement would strengthen the bargaining power of West Coast longshoremen. Bridges viewed the movement for an East Coast master contract as a means of advancing his own claim toward achieving a single contract expiration date for both the ILA and the ILWU.

By mid-October, newly elected ILA president Captain William Bradley had notified all ILA locals on the East Coast that the demand for coastwide bargaining was a strike issue and that if employers wished to avert a strike they would have to address the matter. The following day, the ILWU informed officials of the federal government that if the ILA went on strike, similar action could be expected on the West Coast. The circumstances were heading rapidly toward a situation that the federal government and employers alike had long sought to avert—a national dock strike. On October 24, the NYSA entered a complaint of unfair labor practices against the ILA to the NLRB charging that by demanding a coastwide negotiation the ILA was refusing to bargain a contract for New York's longshoremen. By turning coastwide bargaining into a nonnegotiable issue, the NYSA would force the longshoremen into bargaining on their terms. In this way, if the NLRB ruled in favor of the employers' charge, the ILA could once again be enjoined in federal court, making it illegal for the ILA to raise the demand for a coastwide contract.

Insofar as the economic demands of the dockworkers were concerned, the NYSA had presented the ILA with a substantial wage and benefit proposal, which included a 32-cent increase in hourly wages over a three-year period, an increase in the welfare benefit contribution from 9 to 12 cents per hour per employee, two paid holidays—Labor Day and Christmas (up until then longshoremen had no paid holidays)—and an increase in the vacation benefit. Even though both sides agreed to the new contract expiration date of November 15, the employers refused to consider the dockworkers' claim for coastwide contract negotiations. This left the ILA little alternative because, as it had stated earlier, the demand for a master contract was a strike issue, and on November 16, approximately

70,000 dockworkers from Portland, Maine, to Brownsville, Texas, walked off the piers, paralyzing all East Coast maritime cargo transportation. In a show of force in response to the appearance of ILA pickets along the Port of New York, the New York Police Department assigned 3,000 police officers to the task of harbor patrol.

The striking dockworkers immediately received the support of the National Maritime Union, which ordered all deck crews off the strike-bound ships. Similarly, ILA officials in Montreal announced that Canadian longshoremen would not work on ships diverted from the East Coast. The ILA also received the support of the ILWU and Harry Bridges, who advised all West Coast ILWU locals to schedule "stop-work meetings" to discuss the ILA strike. The largest dock strike in the history of the U.S. waterfront had begun, paralyzing all of the Atlantic and Gulf coast ports, with the mounting possibility of the West Coast longshoremen entering into the fray. In addition to their claim for a master contract, the striking longshoremen demanded eight hours guaranteed pay when hired and a limited sling-load weight. During the negotiations employers had demanded a reduction in the gang size from twenty to sixteen dockworkers on palletized cargo, a demand that was quickly rejected by the union's Wage and Scale Committee. The fundamental issues of the strike were not those involving economic claims, but questions regarding the waterfront labor process. The conflict was over who controlled the waterfront.

On November 19, the fourth day of the East Coast work stoppage, West Coast dockworkers joined the striking Atlantic and Gulf Coast longshoremen, paralyzing every port in the United States. Even though it was only twenty-four hours, the biggest fear of American shipping employers had become reality: work on all U.S. ports had come to a standstill. The federal government quickly warned striking dockworkers on both coasts that the job actions were creating "repercussions that spread far beyond the maritime industry." By striking together, the East and West Coast longshoremen increased the financial losses caused by the strike by approximately $20 million, and by the fifth day of the strike the accumulated total losses were estimated at over $100 million.

After nine days on strike and under the force of two federal injunctions, East Coast dockworkers returned to the ports along the Atlantic and Gulf coasts when President Eisenhower requested that the Taft-Hartley Act be set in motion, claiming that a continued dock strike "would imperil the national health and safety." The total cost of the strike was estimated at $180 million. Even though the Taft-Hartley injunction barred any future strike before February 12, 1957, the enjoined dockworkers continued to press their demands for a coast-wide collective bargaining agreement.

As soon as the longshoremen returned to the cargo-laden docks, employers began reporting that a work slowdown was spreading throughout the Port of New York. They claimed that longshoremen were taking up to four times the usual amount of time necessary to perform their work. The shipping companies declared that the movement had reached "serious proportions" and that many workers were refusing to show up for work on a daily basis. One Lower Manhattan pier reported that 100 trucks had to be turned away so that the ships could keep their schedule, another ship left 6,000 bags of mail behind so that it could sail on time, and the *Queen Mary* reported that it left the port with only twenty of the 300 tons it was supposed to carry. Even though the ILA denied any "direct involvement" in the movement, they voiced support for the actions. ILA national organizer Teddy Gleason stated: "It's a natural thing for the men to resent the way the union has been treated, what did they expect these guys to do—kiss them? . . . All the law did was enjoin us from striking—it did not say how many tons an hour the men must give the employers." Localized disputes erupted, plaguing the port. For example, forklift operators at the John W. McGrath Shipping Company on Pier 10, located on the lower end of the Hudson River, refused to handle twenty-eight bags of potatoes, each weighing 100 pounds, on a single lift. They argued that only twenty-four bags could be lifted safely, to which the company supervisor responded that if they did not do as they were told, they could "check-out; within two hours the entire pier was idle."

As soon as the eighty-day injunction expired, dockworkers on the North Atlantic ports returned to the picket lines, as they had done so many times before over the past years. From Portland, Maine, to Hampton Road, Virginia, an estimated 45,000 dockworkers abandoned the ports. In Chelsea, it was reported that many longshoremen anticipated the evening deadline, calling out to pier supervisors "we won't be back for a month," leaving 790 passengers on an American Export Line luxury ship stranded to carry their own luggage. Immediately, 150 cargo ships lay paralyzed and the American Railroad Association renewed its embargo on all cargo trains headed for the strikebound ports.

The NYSA had little alternative but to acquiesce to the demand for a coastwide collective bargaining agreement for the longshoremen that worked the North Atlantic ports. In spite of last-minute dissent from the three major Manhattan ILA locals at the Wage and Scale Committee meeting, after almost seven months of negotiations, two strikes, two federal injunctions, and a twenty-four hour national strike that paralyzed all U.S. ports, on February 18, the NYSA and the ILA reached an agreement.

The terms of the new collective bargaining agreement between the ILA and the NYSA stipulated that they were based on a master contract that included all ports of the North Atlantic coast, regulating wages, hours, and pension and welfare contributions. Local working conditions and the administration of pension and welfare benefits, however, would continue to be negotiated locally. In addition, the dockworkers would receive a 32-cent-per-hour wage increase, retroactive to October 1, 1956, paid holidays, an additional week's paid vacation, a seniority hiring system, and automatic dues check-off of all ILA members working the port.

Automation: Who Controls the Docks?

As the 1956 ILA collective bargaining agreement was to expire, the increasing use of automated methods of stowage set the framework for upcoming port-wide conflicts. On November 18, 1958, the ILA organized a mass "stop work" rally at Madison Square Garden to discuss the growing process of port mechanization and the subsequent loss of employment. At noon approximately 17,500 dockworkers descended from the ships along the port and marched through the streets of Manhattan. At the meeting, local newspapers reported the longshoremen "cheered when the shipping industry was warned that they would have to 'share the benefits' of automation with those who would be displaced." The main thrust of the ILA at the meeting alerted longshoremen to the threat that port mechanization posed to waterfront employment. Reading a statement by Teddy Gleason, ILA District Council president Fred Fields warned that the impact of automation was already being felt. Over the last two years dockworkers had lost approximately 4 million work hours and container operations could manage twelve tons of freight in four minutes, "fifteen times faster than the normal stowage."

The conflict reflected competing strategies with regard to port mechanization. On the one side, the ILA sought to decelerate the introduction of new technology, if only momentarily, so as to gain more information on its subsequent impact on the longshore industry and allow for greater mobilization of the workers. On the other side, the strategy of the shipping association, according to Alexander Chopin, was to introduce the changes first and discuss them with the union at some later date.

By September 1, 1959, a little over two years since the signing of the master contract for the North Atlantic ports, rapid technological transformation of maritime cargo transportation served as a fast-acting catalyst for a renewed revolt on the Port of New York. For longshoremen, the increasing mechanization of waterborne cargo transportation not only raised questions regarding the intrinsic value of dock labor, reflected in their wages, but it also caused workers concern about how they could continue to influence the waterfront labor process, if at all.

Four days before the September 30 contract deadline, longshoremen on the Port of New York began refusing to check cargo off the piers during the weekend. The longshore union maintained that this was a normal practice, even though by doing so most cargo that was unloaded in the days preceding the strike would wind up staying on the port. In spite of the escalating strike preparations, the NYSA made a final offer to the dockworkers' union. The employers proposed a wage increase of 20 cents for the first year and

5 cents for the following two years in the hourly wages of longshoremen. But the employers placed a condition on their proposal: the proposed wage increase would be valid only if the ILA allowed "us to determine certain work rules." Among the rules the NYSA demanded was the vaguely stipulated "right of the employer to operate his operation in a manner deemed desirable." In fact, the NYSA was demanding that workers relinquish any claim for control of the waterfront labor process.

In proposing flexible regulations over the waterfront labor process, the NYSA sought to introduce the mechanization of maritime cargo transportation without assuming the responsibility for the loss of jobs that the new technology would create. It is important to remember that in 1959 containerization was still in its infancy and only slowly being implemented. While the dockworkers realized that port mechanization would lead to the massive loss of jobs, neither the ILA nor the longshoremen had fully grasped the scale and scope of just how quickly the process of port mechanization would occur. Even though the NYSA appeared reluctant to recognize the growing impact of containerization in the longshore industry, the truth is that early on employers realized that the future of waterborne cargo transportation was linked to expanding container technology, and their plans for such had long been set in motion.

In what had become a pattern, on October 1, 1959, dockworkers on the East and Gulf coasts, from Maine to Texas, walked off the piers. Surprisingly, this time the strike was initiated by the dockworkers of New Orleans and spread rapidly along the entire Eastern seaboard. More surprising was the fact that the ILA had already signed a fifteen-day extension to the existing contract only two days before it was to expire, even though it had faced significant internal resistance to signing the agreement. Local 791 declared that they would not accept the contract extension and threatened to call a wildcat strike. This position was also supported by the left-wing rank-and-file *Dockers News*. The quick resolve with which New York's longshoremen paralyzed the port in spite of the ILA having signed a fifteen-day extension was also a reflection of the incapacity of the ILA's top leadership to control competing factions that dominated individual piers. Southern shipping employers refused to agree to retroactivity of wages and benefits based on any future agreement. The ILA viewed the Southern shipping companies as regional representatives of New York shipping concerns and perceived that by refusing to agree with retroactivity on the Southern ports the NYSA was attempting to weaken the coastwide bargaining process, which did not include the South. The ILA leadership quickly claimed that the New York job action was their own doing even though the Manhattan locals that initially called for the walkout had needed to put significant pressure on them to do so. In total, approximately 70,000 dockworkers participated in the strike. Once again the federal government moved to invoke the Taft-Hartley emergency measures. In less than twenty-four hours after his decision, President Eisenhower instructed Attorney General William P. Rogers to seek an injunction and end the longshore strike.

The main issue raised by the strike was not wages but rather the NYSA's demand to implement automation technology "at will" and the implications of new technologies for control over the waterfront labor process. At the onset of the strike, as soon as the ILA and the NYSA returned to the bargaining table, they rapidly reached agreement on the economic questions, but continued to wrangle over technology. The longshoremen's claims concerning automation were only partially assuaged when the NYSA agreed not to reduce the gang size of those working containerized cargo and thus to continue hiring twenty longshoremen per work gang. To offset the loss of employment due to the introduction of mechanization, the employers offered a severance package that was quickly rejected by the ILA, since the concept of severance pay was linked to permanent job loss by closing and the reduction of man hours. The ILA reasoned that not only would automation reduce the waterfront workforce, it would also reduce the number of hours worked for those that remained.

The ILA proposed that employers contribute to a fund based on the tonnage of containerized cargo handled by dockworkers. The employers eventually dropped their proposal for severance pay in favor of the union's container royalty scheme, but the amount to be paid remained unresolved. The standard that was ultimately devised determined contributions to the container royalty fund based on three classifications: (a) 35 cents per ton for containers unloaded from traditional freighters, (b) 70 cents per ton for cargo unloaded in partially automated ships, and (c) $1.00 per ton for work done on completely containerized ships.

By December 1959, with the Port of New York seeing record growth primarily in the sector of international commerce, it is easy to see why the economic demands of the dockworkers were easily resolved, and why those that revolved around the question of automation persisted. According to reports published by the Port Authority of New York and New Jersey, New York's docks handled 4,261,972 tons more in 1959 than in 1958. Compared to the same period during the previous year, the volume of bulk and general cargo handled on the Port of New York had increased by 23.5 percent. Some of the main products that passed through the port were vehicles, sulfur, liquor, wood pulp, bananas, coffee, cocoa, lumber, and rubber.

On December 10, 1959, dockworkers from Maine to Virginia overwhelmingly approved the proposed agreement. In New York, longshoremen voted four to one in favor of the new master contract for the North Atlantic ports. On the Southern and Gulf ports employers held out, with the threat of a renewed walkout on December 27, first Gulf and subsequently Southern shipping employers agreed to terms similar to those signed in the North Atlantic master contract.

By the end of the year, Captain Bradley of the ISA and Alexander Chopin of the NYSA stood side by side, gold-plated shovels in hand, in the groundbreaking ceremony for the new ILA Manhattan Medical Clinic. In spite of appearances, however, it was not the return to "business as usual" on the highly contentious docks of New York. If originally the shipping employers had imagined that resolving the question of representation and the master contract would bring labor peace to the port, they were very mistaken. Rapidly expanding port automation would increasingly reintroduce the struggle for control of the waterfront labor process in the most basic terms. The question of who controlled the waterfront would continue to prime the contentious process of labor politics on the docks in the years to come.

See also: The Catholic Church and Strikes, 162; Longshoremen's Strikes, 1900–1920, 547.

Bibliography

Bensel, Richard Franklin. *The Political Economy of American Industrialization, 1877–1900.* Cambridge: Cambridge University Press, 2000.

Davis, Colin. "All I Got's a Hook." In *Waterfront Workers, New Perspectives in Race and Class,* ed. Calvin Winslow. Urbana: University of Illinois Press, 1998.

Jensen, Vernon. *Strife on the Waterfront: The Port of New York Since 1945.* Ithaca, NY: Cornell University Press, 1974.

Kimmeldorf, Howard. *Reds or Rackets? The Making of Radical and Conservative Unionism on the Waterfront.* Berkeley: University of California Press, 1988.

Mello, William. "Reforming the Waterfront. Rank-and-File Activism and Politics on the Port of New York, 1945–1970." Ph.D. diss., New School University, 2004.

Raymond, Allen. *Waterfront Priest.* New York: Henry Holt, 1955.

Swanstrom, Edward. *The Waterfront Labor Problem.* New York: Fordham University Press, 1938.

STRIKES IN THE U.S. AIRLINE INDUSTRY, 1919–2004

David J. Walsh

This essay traces strikes in the U.S. airline industry from 1919 to 2004. According to airline labor relations expert Mark Kahn, "Considering the variety of bargaining units and the large numbers of airline contracts to be periodically negotiated . . . strikes have been relatively infrequent, although costly to the parties and troublesome to the affected public when they did occur." There is no single authoritative source for the number of strikes in the airline industry. The National Mediation Board (NMB), the federal agency charged with administering the Railway Labor Act that governs labor relations in the railroad and airline industries, has listed strikes in its annual report since 1950, but only those arising out of contract negotiations and lasting more than twenty-four hours. NMB annual reports from 1950 to 2000 list approximately 157 strikes in the airline industry (the total varies somewhat depending on how sympathy strikes are counted). Donald Cullen, citing a variety of sources including Bureau of Labor Statistics (BLS) data on work stoppages, counted 173 airline strikes between 1926 and 1975. Combining the NMB data and Cullen's suggests that there were some 175 to 230 strikes in the U.S. airline industry between 1919 and 2004. This amounts to two or three strikes per year, albeit with considerable annual variation. Relatively few strikes occurred in the airline industry prior to 1950. Airline strikes were most frequent from the 1950s through the 1970s. Strikes have become increasingly rare events since deregulation of the airline industry in 1978; this decline coincides with a withering of strikes generally.

The history of strikes in the airline industry can be divided into three periods. The first period cuts the widest swath, reaching from 1919 until airline industry deregulation in 1978. The starting point is 1919 because that year saw the first recorded strike in the fledgling industry. While considerable change occurred over the next sixty years, the pre-deregulatory period can be broadly characterized as a time when the hand of government touched all aspects of the industry; unions formed and gradually took the initiative in bargaining; and carriers had limited economic incentives to confront labor. Deregulation fundamentally altered the economics of the airline industry; government assumed a more hands-off role, particularly with respect to labor relations; and airlines seized the initiative in bargaining, pressing unions for concessions and in some cases attempting to provoke strikes. The end point of this period of initial adjustment to deregulation is the conclusion in early 1991 of the Eastern Airlines strike that began in 1989. This momentous struggle ended with no clear winner, but demonstrated that a confrontational labor relations policy could be prohibitively costly. Since the Eastern Airlines strike, economic conditions in the industry have varied widely, government intervention has resurfaced, safety issues—including terrorism—have emerged, and many established airlines have faced life-threatening crises. Strikes provide a useful vantage point from which to view the airline industry and its labor relations. The issues that are important enough to "go to war" over and the ways in which those wars are fought tell us a great deal. The history of airline strikes clearly demonstrates the effects on collective bargaining of technological change, evolving industry economics, employer business strategies, the centrality of government action or inaction, and the importance of union tactics and solidarity.

Strikes Prior to Deregulation (1919–1978)

In 1919, the airline industry was in its infancy. The Post Office inaugurated regular airmail flights in 1918 and directly employed the industry's first pilots. Not surprisingly, the work was dangerous. Post Office administrators placed considerable pressure on pilots to fly regardless of weather conditions. When two pilots refused to fly under conditions of extreme fog following a two-week period in which there were fifteen crashes and two deaths, the pilots were fired by Assistant Postmaster General Otto Praeger. A group of their fellow pilots sent a telegram threatening to strike unless the pilots were reinstated, declaring it was not a conspiracy "to avoid killing oneself for the sake of a two-cent stamp," according to labor relations analyst George Hopkins's 1971 study.

Initially contemptuous of the strikers, Praeger agreed to discussions with a group of pilots after a four-day strike in which the pilots received much favorable press coverage and congressmen began to push for investigation of the Post Office. The pilots ended up with a partial victory. They received a raise, reinstatement of one of the fired pilots, and an agreement that disputes over flying conditions would be resolved in the novel fashion of having a field manager go aloft to demonstrate that it was safe to fly. However, the striking pilots failed to persuade the Post Office to improve their equipment, defer to pilots' judgments about flight safety, or reinstate their other comrade. The nascent organization that arose to deal with this dispute spawned the creation in 1920 of the Air Mail Pilots of America. However, it would be more than a decade later before a lasting pilots' union would take hold.

The Kelly Act of 1925 authorized private contractors, rather than the Post Office itself, to haul mail. Numerous private air carriers sprang up, supported primarily by government airmail subsidies. Century Airlines was one of these new private air carriers, although it existed at the periphery of the industry and did not enjoy a profitable airmail contract. The Century Airlines strike of 1932 occurred only one year after the formation of the Air Line Pilots Association (ALPA), the principal union representing pilots at commercial air carriers. Undertaken in the teeth of the Depression, this strike was a seminal event in the union's history. Errett Lobban Cord, the owner of Century Air Lines, had determined that pilot pay should be cut by 40 percent so that Century could carry mail at far lower cost than the carriers with postal contracts. Cord went so far as to promise that if Congress would open up air mail delivery to competitive bidding, Century Air Lines would deliver the mail for half the rates paid to other carriers.

Pilots arriving for work on February 9, 1932, were greeted by armed guards and company officials who demanded that the pilots resign and reapply for their jobs at the drastically lower pay. The pilots declined to do so and marched to ALPA headquarters in Chicago. The strike lasted a little less than two months. Given the economic circumstances, replacement pilots were easy to come by. But, as it would on numerous occasions in the future, adroit political maneuvering by ALPA won the day. Proceedings before Congress and the Chicago City Council resulted in condemnation of the carrier's tactics, pressure to settle, and denial of a postal subsidy. The political heat was sufficiently uncomfortable to convince Cord to bail out. On April 2, 1932, he sold the company to American Airlines. As documented by Isaac Cohen, the strike did not produce an unequivocal victory, since the pilots lost their jobs and Cord eventually became majority owner of American Airlines, albeit remaining distant from management of the carrier. However, the ability of the fledgling ALPA to fend off a formidable adversary under unfavorable economic conditions served notice of the potency of airline labor.

The Century Airlines strike was atypical in that struck carriers most often ceased operations rather than attempt to operate with replacements prior to deregulation. In a regulated industry where (after 1940) routes were allocated by the Civil Aeronautics Board (CAB), carriers had little fear that strikes would result in long-term loss of passengers or markets. Nor was there great advantage to be had by holding out for the most advantageous terms, since the CAB set fares based on average costs for the industry. But there was another factor accounting for carriers' inclination not to operate during strikes. With the CAB's blessing, carriers devised a Mutual Aid Pact (MAP) in 1958. Under the terms of the MAP, member airlines would partially subsidize other carriers experiencing strikes. The MAP was revised three times, with each revision providing successively more generous subsidies to struck carriers. Northwest Airlines and National Airlines experienced the most frequent strikes and were far and away the prime beneficiaries of the MAP between 1958 and 1978. Comparing strike duration to the generosity of the MAP benefits offered at different points in time, industry analysts Herbert Unterberger and Edward Koziara concluded that the MAP was associated with longer strikes. Although Pierre-Yves Cremiux documented some empirical evidence that the MAP might not have had a large effect on the relative bargaining power of the parties, eradication of the MAP was a major aim of airline unions for two decades. The legislation enacting airline deregulation effectively eliminated the MAP by invalidating existing agreements and imposing such onerous terms on any future MAPs as to render them undesirable.

Airline employees are represented on a craft basis. Most carriers deal with a number of different unions representing particular crafts or classifications, such as pilots, flight attendants, mechanics, dispatchers, and office and clerical workers. One of the ramifications of the industry's craft organization is that it can greatly complicate technological change, throwing the existence of entire crafts into question. One of the major changes occurring in the airline industry in the late 1950s was the widespread introduction of jet aircraft. Disputes arose over who would occupy the third seat in this new generation of aircraft: trained pilots represented by ALPA or flight engineers trained principally as mechanics and represented by the Flight Engineers International Association (FEIA).

The FEIA struck United Airlines in 1955, Eastern Airlines in 1958, and Continental Airlines in 1959 over this issue. United and Continental were successful in pressing ahead with their plans to switch to pilot-qualified flight engineers, while the FEIA's greater success in grounding Eastern (with the assistance of Eastern's mechanics) resulted in the implementation of a four-person crew (three pilots and a flight engineer), an expedient but costly solution that several other carriers had also adopted. Matters came to a head in 1961 when the FEIA launched a six-day strike against seven carriers. The strike ended when the Secretary of Labor intervened and promised a special commission to study the problem. This commission, headed by Nathan P. Feinsinger, reported its findings to President Kennedy on May 24, 1961. The Feinsinger Commission maintained that "neither peace nor safety on the airlines will be fully assured as long as there are two unions in the cockpit." It recommended a transition process in which the third seat in the cockpit would eventually be occupied by a pilot, but existing flight engineers would not be required to surrender their positions. While tensions between ALPA and the FEIA festered for years afterward, the commission's report ratified the inevitable and largely resolved the matter.

Government intervention in airline strikes varied considerably prior to deregulation. Congress included the airline industry under the Railway Labor Act (RLA) in 1936, making negotiations subject to the RLA's extensive dispute resolution machinery, including mandatory mediation of indefinite duration, proffers of arbitration, thirty-day cooling-off periods, and Presidential Emergency Boards (PEBs) that engage in fact finding and forestall strikes for at least an additional sixty days. From 1936 through 1945, no airline strikes were deemed to meet the statutory criterion of threatening to deprive an area of the country of essential transportation, warranting creation of an emergency board. However, between 1946 and 1966, thirty-three emergency boards were created in response to airline strikes (in approximately one out of every three airline strikes that occurred during this period). According to Donald E. Cullen, the factors in this change of policy appear to be the precedent established by a 1946 emergency board created to deal with pilot pay and working conditions issues on newly introduced four-engine aircraft; reaction to the general tide of strike activity following World War II that included passage of the Taft-Hartley Act of 1947, with its own national emergency strike provisions; and the growing importance of the airline industry as a means of transportation (and not just shipping mail). However, while the appointment of emergency boards delays strikes, it does not necessarily dispose of them. Labor analyst Charles Rehmus points out that at least eight strikes, some quite lengthy, occurred during this period, after the RLA's procedures had been exhausted.

A 1966 strike by the International Association of Machinists and Aerospace Workers (IAM) against five carriers helped prompt a change in thinking about the impact of airline strikes and the appropriate governmental response to them. Interestingly, this was one of only a very few instances of multi-carrier bargaining in the history of the industry. Typically, airline unions bargain for particular crafts on a carrier-by-carrier basis. In the bargaining that led up to the 1966 strike, the IAM was engaged in individual and joint negotiations with United Airlines, Eastern Airlines, National Airlines, Northwest Airlines, and Trans World Airlines. At the time, these carriers accounted for over 60 percent of the passenger miles flown by U.S. airlines. The issues were conventional ones, centering on pay and benefits. When the negotiations broke down and RLA procedures, including an emergency board, were exhausted, a strike was called against all five carriers. The strike directly involved over 35,000 workers and lasted forty-three days in the summer of 1966.

The U.S. Senate considered legislation (Joint Resolution 181) that would have ordered the employees back to work for at least 180 days, with the further threat that Congress would impose a settlement if none was forthcoming from the parties themselves. The impact of the strike was the central focus of hearings in 1966 on the Senate resolution. William J. Curtin, chief negotiator for the carriers, sought to portray the strike's effects as devastating, resulting in loss of air service to communities, disruption of military personnel transport services, "staggering" economic impact, loss of tax dollars, interference with cargo shipments, and even further deterioration in the nation's balance of payments with other countries. IAM International president Roy Siemiller testified that the strike, although undeniably an inconvenience, did not warrant congressional intervention that would undermine the collective bargaining process. Willard Wirtz, Secretary of Labor, attempted to walk a thin line between the interests of labor and the clamor for government action when he testified that "we are confronted with a serious, substantial adverse impact on the national interest, an impact which, however, has not yet brought the country to an emergency stage. However, any prolongation of the current strike, by increasing the strain on existing services, and by multiplying the current delays and inconveniences may well bring the nation to that crisis, emergency stage." Before further action could be taken by Congress, the parties took Wirtz's thinly veiled threat seriously and settled the strike. The strikers ended up with a wage increase larger than what the Presidential Emergency Board had recommended.

Even though extraordinary congressional action had been contemplated, the 1966 strike by the IAM proved to be a watershed event in the government's handling of airline strikes. If a strike of this magnitude could be weathered, the typical single-carrier strike certainly did not pose a significant threat. Subsequent policy makers, particularly George P. Schulz, who took over as secretary of labor in the Nixon administration, strongly discouraged the practice of establishing Presidential Emergency Boards in airline strikes. Deregulation of the airline industry in 1978 reinforced the notion that the airline industry is a business like any other and that government intervention in strikes is generally unnecessary. No additional Presidential Emergency Boards were sought by the NMB during this period. Ironically, the Airline Deregulation Act of 1978 itself included a provision creating an emergency board to deal with a 620-day long strike by ALPA against Wein Air Alaska. The parties eventually accepted the emergency board's recommendations, ending the strike.

As Congress contemplated airline deregulation, some labor leaders feared an industry regime where new carriers were free to form and enter established markets, lower labor costs could confer a distinct competitive advantage, established carriers would be allowed to fail, and strikes could cause a permanent loss of passengers. Under such a regime, labor would face many more pressures. However, labor opposition to deregulation was relatively muted and restricted to political activity rather than strikes or other forms of direct action. In part, this was because most carriers were themselves on record as being opposed to deregulation. Hopkins suggests that the essential conservatism of most pilots predisposed them to believe that deregulation would be in their interests. Also, labor was tossed a few bones to lessen its opposition, including provisions effectively ending the carriers' Mutual Aid Pact and "employee protective provisions" for workers harmed by deregulation (an utterly empty promise, as it turned out). Sometimes, the lack of strikes or other action by workers is as significant as their occurrence. Whether airline unions could have done anything about deregulation had they taken more forceful action at the time is very questionable, but the effects of deregulation would certainly be seen in the strikes that occurred in its aftermath.

Strikes in the Immediate Post-Deregulation Period (1979-1990)

In the summer of 1981, airline unions sat out another conflict with major ramifications, the strike by PATCO (Professional Air Traffic Controllers Organization). PATCO's ill-fated strike early in the Reagan administration resulted in the firing of over 11,000 air traffic controllers, the decertification of a formerly powerful union, and arguably a major symbolic victory for employers over labor that encouraged employers of all types to "get tough" with their unionized workers. The real issues in the strike and the motivations of the parties continue to be debated.

Government administrators attempted to reduce the conflict to a question of higher pay. Labor economist Herbert Northrup attributed the strike primarily to a desire on the part of PATCO to obtain broader collective bargaining rights than other federal employees. Other accounts more sympathetic to PATCO and the controllers emphasize improvements in work hours and the retirement plan, as well as autocratic management, as core issues. There is little disagreement that relations between the Federal Aviation Administration (FAA) and PATCO controllers were abysmal in the years leading up to the strike. It is also clear that PATCO received only tepid and belated support from other labor organizations (with the exception of Canadian air traffic controllers). Reasons for PATCO's isolation include the failure of PATCO leader Robert Poli to cultivate good relations with airline unions (as his predecessor John F. Leyden had done with ALPA), the arrogant assumption that support from airline unions was not strategically important, legal constraints on unions striking in support of PATCO, and concern that airline workers' jobs could be endangered by a shutdown of the air traffic system.

While ALPA never contemplated striking in sympathy with PATCO, it had seriously considered an industry-wide "suspension of service" ("SOS") earlier in the year. The action, dubbed "Operation USA" ("unity for safe air travel"), was planned for late February 1981 to protest adverse decisions by the FAA and the exclusion of ALPA from the process of certifying new aircraft. Once again, technological change, this time the introduction of a new generation of two-engine jets, raised questions about who should be in the cockpit. ALPA favored retaining three pilots in the cockpit, while the airline industry and the FAA took the position that only two pilots were now necessary. About two weeks before the planned SOS, Secretary of Transportation Drew Lewis reached an agreement with ALPA to examine its concerns and appoint a presidential commission to study the crew complement issue. ALPA cancelled the SOS. The commission later found that two pilots were sufficient for the new generation of jets, although pilots were given an official role in the aircraft certification process. The capacity of ALPA to execute an industry-wide withdrawal from service remained untested and unknown. ALPA International president Henry A. Duffy stated in 1989 that "the possibility of using an SOS to settle a strike raises hopes and expectations in the minds of the striking pilots. The issue needs to be dealt with once and for all, for the tension has come close to tearing this association apart. Either an SOS is something that a striking pilot group can expect to be able to use as a weapon in a strike, or it isn't." Several striking pilot groups would turn to ALPA during the 1980s seeking to have their struggles supported by an industry-wide SOS only to be rebuffed.

Following deregulation, carriers took the initiative in negotiations, demanding substantial concessions aimed at lowering labor costs to counter the threats presumably posed by new entrants and other lower-cost carriers. Unions were thrust into the position of fending off or minimizing concessions. As the pressure for concessions continued, several strikes occurred. In general, airline unions did not fare well in strikes during the 1980s. In contrast to the period before deregulation, carriers usually attempted to operate during strikes and sometimes actively provoked them. Permanent replacements were frequently threatened and sometimes used. A key factor affecting the outcomes of strikes was the degree of interunion support available.

Several spectacularly unsuccessful strikes at Continental Airlines in 1983 set the tone for the decade. Continental had been acquired by Texas Air Corporation in 1981. The head of Texas Air, Frank Lorenzo, has been compared to E.L. Cord of Century Airlines. As with Cord in 1932, Lorenzo sought to impose drastically reduced pay rates and working conditions. A strike in August 1983 by IAM mechanics in response to the carrier's concession demands was not supported by other crafts—or, for that matter, by many of the union's own members. The carrier took the opportunity to eliminate or contract out hundreds of maintenance and service jobs. On September 24, 1983, Continental filed for bankruptcy under Chapter 11 and announced "emergency work rules" that included steep pay cuts and large increases in work hours. The Air Line Pilots Association and the Union of Flight Attendants (UFA) began their own strikes. The strikes occurred during a period of high unemployment, including a glut of qualified pilots. The strikes limped to a close by the end of 1985, with the pilots and mechanics no longer represented (they had previously been "voluntarily" recognized by the carrier and the recognitions were withdrawn), most of the former workers replaced, and the UFA hanging on with little leverage. Although Congress subsequently acted to tighten up bankruptcy laws and make it more difficult for employers to use bankruptcy filings to abrogate labor contracts, the strike was undeniably a low point for airline labor.

The Continental debacle was followed by union defeats in strikes at Alaska Airlines in 1985. The IAM struck on March 4, 1985, largely in response to the carrier's demands for a two-tier wage structure and increased use of part-time workers. David Walsh describes the two-tier wage structure, introduced to the airline industry in the early 1980s, as a type of wage concession in which pay rates are lowered only for those employees hired after a specific date, usually the ratification date of the new agreement. As concessions go, two-tier wage structures have the particularly insidious quality that they place the burden of labor cost reduction on the backs of faceless future coworkers, thus making such a plan more difficult to resist, while at the same time sowing the seeds of division within unions. That demands for two-tier wage structures figured in a number of strikes during the 1980s shows that unions were not blind to the threat they posed, although most carriers that wanted two-tier wage structures were ultimately able to obtain some version of them. Most often, pay rates for the more recently hired employees (the "B-scale") equalize with existing pay rates (the "A-scale") after a specified number of years on the job, but sometimes two-tier wage structures are "permanent" and do not provide for eventual equalization of rates. The two-tier wage structure demanded and eventually obtained by Alaska Airlines was permanent.

The IAM mechanics were initially joined on strike by office and clerical workers who were also IAM members, but it was later determined that the broad no-strike clause in the office and clerical workers' contract precluded a sympathy strike. The Association of Flight Attendants (AFA) also joined the strike, although it was disputed whether they were striking in sympathy with the IAM or attempting to further their own negotiation goals. The pilots crossed picket lines and permanent replacements were successfully enlisted, causing both strikes to collapse fairly quickly.

The Independent Federation of Flight Attendants (IFFA) was similarly unsuccessful in a strike at TWA in 1986. The strike began on March 7, 1986, after lengthy negotiations related to acquisition of the carrier by financier Carl Icahn. The IFFA believed that it was being asked to provide concessions far in excess of those obtained from ALPA and the IAM. ALPA pilots crossed picket lines and IAM mechanics, some of whom initially supported the flight attendants' strike, ceased their sympathy strike when confronted with an injunction ordering them back to work. TWA hired replacement flight attendants and the strike ended after two months with an unconditional offer to return to work. Compounding the defeat was an adverse legal ruling by the U.S. Supreme Court holding that the carrier did not violate the Railway Labor Act by allowing strikers who chose to go back to work while the strike was still ongoing ("cross-overs") to retain their jobs despite the fact that more senior employees sought reinstatement at the end of the strike (*Trans World Airlines v. Independent Federation of Flight Attendants,* 489 U.S. 426).

Somewhat more successful from labor's perspective was a 1985 strike at Pan Am by the Transport Workers' Union (TWU). The strike by mechanics and other ground personnel began on February 28, 1985, and was sparked by several issues, including the carrier's failure to adequately fund its pension plan. Other crafts initially respected the TWU's picket lines and the carrier was effectively shut down. Pilots and flight engineers went back to work on March 8, 1985, largely due to their concern that a prolonged strike could drive the financially troubled carrier into bankruptcy. Along with withdrawal of the pilot's support, sale of the carrier's commissary operation shortly after the strike began and a threat to do the same with building maintenance and fleet service operations placed considerable pressure on the TWU to settle. The Independent Union of Flight Attendants (IUFA) stayed the course, remaining out in sympathy with the TWU until shortly before a settlement was reached on March 23, 1985. The settlement included a 20 percent wage increase over three years, transfers or cash settlements for displaced commissary workers, a two-tier wage structure, increased use of part-time workers, and changes in job classifications. On the whole, the TWU avoided the worst-case scenario of permanent replacement and made a few gains to offset its concessions. Yet its ability to strike successfully was hampered by limited labor solidarity from other unions and the realization that an effective, prolonged strike could lead to the demise of the carrier and render every other issue moot.

A strike by ALPA pilots against United Airlines in 1985 was widely pointed to as a rare successful strike in the aftermath of deregulation, although its "success" was relative to the disastrous strikes that had preceded it. Again, this was a case of a carrier seeking concessions from its pilots, including a two-tier wage structure that would consign newly hired pilots to lower pay rates until they reached captain status, which typically takes eighteen to twenty years. The strike began on May 17, 1985. United planned to continue operating during the strike, in part by utilizing some 570 pilot trainees that it had enlisted and trained prior to the strike. However, to the dismay of the carrier, virtually all of the trainees honored the picket lines, as did the vast majority of pilots and flight attendants.

The strong support from the flight attendants is noteworthy. Georgia Nielsen has described relations between pilots and flight attendants, and the unions that represent them, as historically problematic. Although some change has occurred, both crafts remain heavily sex-segregated. Predominantly male pilots have authority over largely female flight attendants during flights. Most flight attendant unions were initially affiliated with ALPA or the TWU, struggled for autonomy within these male-dominated unions, and eventually broke away in the 1970s. However, on this occasion the pilots recognized the symbolic value of labor unity and its ability to counter efforts to paint them as rich men in a squabble with other rich men. The pilots went further than usual in looking out for the interests of the flight attendants during the United strike, although in the end they settled before an acceptable back-to-work agreement was obtained by the Association of Flight Attendents (AFA). United was largely shut down and a settlement was reached after about a month on strike. ALPA successfully resisted the carrier's more extreme concession demands and demonstrated that it could engineer an effective strike. On the other hand, it still submitted to some concessions, including a two-tier wage structure, albeit one that merged new hire and previous hire pay scales much more quickly. Issues regarding treatment of the trainees were left for the courts to decide, and the strike was very costly to ALPA (estimated at $8 million–$10 million).

If the United Airlines strike of 1985 had served notice that airline labor would not stand quietly by as carriers sought to impose a new regime, Frank Lorenzo was not listening. After his triumph over the unions at Continental Airlines, Lorenzo's Texas Air went on to acquire Frontier Airlines and People's Express. In February 1986, Eastern Airlines was added to the portfolio, in a lopsided deal that left Eastern footing much of the bill for its own acquisition. This gave Texas Air control over about a fifth of the U.S. airline industry. Lorenzo immediately began to demand substantial wage and work rule concessions from Eastern's unions. He placed pressure on the unions by selling, or attempting to sell, various Eastern assets, using intricate contracting arrangements to benefit Texas Air at the expense of Eastern, and carrying out large numbers of layoffs and disciplinary actions. The threat posed by Lorenzo to the wages and working conditions of not just Eastern's workers, but unionized employees throughout the industry, is difficult to overstate. IAM International president George Kourpias envisioned even broader impact: "Frank Lorenzo's style of employee relations is a cancer that must be stopped at Eastern or it will spread to virtually every industry in the nation."

The contract covering IAM represented workers at Eastern was the first to become amendable (in December 1987) and Lorenzo pressed for over $150 million in concessions. Despite frantic efforts by Lorenzo to get the National Mediation Board (NMB) to release the parties from mediation so that the IAM would be forced to strike (and be replaced) or capitulate to his demands, the NMB kept the parties in mediation for over a year. Ultimately, the NMB concluded that further negotiation would be fruitless. It released the parties from mediation on February 2, 1989. The NMB then recommended creation of a Presidential Emergency Board. President George H.W. Bush took the historically unprecedented step of ignoring this recommendation and declined to appoint a PEB.

Over 8,000 IAM members, including mechanics, ramp service workers, cleaners, and stock clerks, went on strike on March 4, 1989. Significantly, and in contrast to the Continental Airlines experience, Eastern's ALPA pilots and TWU flight attendants voted to conduct sympathy strikes. The extent of interunion support, including from the AFL-CIO and even international labor federations, was unprecedented for an airline industry strike. Borrowing from the Continental Airlines playbook, Eastern filed for bankruptcy under Chapter 11 on March 10, 1989. Support for the strike was strong for months, but a dizzying array of efforts to locate buyers for the airline and to outmaneuver Lorenzo in bankruptcy court were ultimately unsuccessful. The pilots and flight attendants continued their sympathy strikes until November 22, 1989. The IAM continued its strike until January 18, 1991, when Eastern Airlines permanently ceased operations and was liquidated. By that point, Frank Lorenzo had already been removed by the bankruptcy court as head of Eastern and had stepped down as CEO of Continental.

The Eastern strikers' rallying cry of "one day longer" was not hollow. Eastern's workers had fought the good fight and outlasted a formidable adversary, but the price that they paid was steep. Former Eastern Airlines pilot Don Huckabee wrote that "time dulls the memory, and in time it will be said that 'we' prevailed, that 'we' drove Lorenzo from the industry and showed management that labor is still a force to be reckoned with . . . But what of those whose flying careers abruptly ended? What say we of the casualties on the Eastern Front—the destroyed careers, the impoverished pilots, the divorces, the dependents' education plans suddenly derailed, and the deaths by suicide?" The airline industry and its labor relations would look very different now if Lorenzo had prevailed and continued to operate Texas Air as an effectively non-union carrier. Instead, the smoldering wreckage of Eastern Airlines made it clear that something other than a frontal assault on labor was needed and left both carriers and airline unions more circumspect about entering into all-out conflict. Yet, the fundamental economic problems of the industry remained.

Strikes in the Later Post-Deregulation Period (1991-2004)

In the early 1990s, the economic woes of the airline industry seemed intractable. The Gulf War of 1991 and a recession had contributed to losses in the first half of the 1990s that were said to be greater than the total profits generated by the airline industry since its inception. A National Commission to Ensure a Strong Competitive Airline Industry was created in 1993. The commission's proceedings lost some of their urgency when the industry quite unexpectedly entered the most profitable period in its history in the second half of the 1990s. During this period, airline unions attempted to recoup some of the many concessions that had been granted and provide their members with a share in the carriers' newfound prosperity. Airlines were content to drag out negotiations. Workers turned to a variety of extra strike pressure tactics, including sickouts and refusals to accept overtime work. The industry returned to more familiar footing with the economic downturn that began in 2001 and was thrown into an unprecedented tailspin by the disastrous events of September 11, 2001. An Air Transportation Stabilization Board was created by the federal government in the wake of 9/11 and granted loan guarantees to a number of carriers. While air traffic slowly returned to more normal levels, bankruptcy filings (e.g., United, U.S. Airways) and threatened filings (e.g., American, Delta) by several major carriers made it clear that the industry, or at least the "legacy carrier" portion of it, remained far from healthy.

Two strikes by flight attendants in 1993 demonstrated the increasing tactical sophistication of airline unions. Finding ways to put pressure on carriers while avoiding permanent replacement in strikes is especially important for flight attendant unions, whose members are more susceptible to replacement and who rarely enjoy the benefit of sympathy strikes by other crafts. After being released from mediation and authorized to engage in self-help in June 1993, Alaska Airlines exercised its right to impose new pay rates and work rules on its AFA-represented flight attendants. Rather than undertake a conventional strike, the AFA responded with a CHAOS ("creating havoc around our system") campaign.

The campaign involved unannounced, short-duration work stoppages targeting specific flights. Shortly before a flight was ready to board passengers, flight attendants would inform their supervisors and AFA would notify the airline that they were engaging in a strike. Within an hour or so the flight attendants would inform their supervisors that they were ready to return to work. Twenty-four flight attendants working on seven different flights employed this tactic, which was quite sufficient to disrupt the workings of an intricately timed, hub-and-spoke route system. A judge enjoined Alaska Airlines from indefinitely suspending, disciplining, or threatening to discipline CHAOS participants, ordered reinstatement of flight attendants who had been suspended, and ruled that permanent replacement could only occur while a work stoppage was under way (and not after an offer to return to work had been made) (*Association of Flight Attendants v. Alaska Airlines,* 847 F.Supp 832). The tactic led to negotiation of a new contract that was overwhelmingly ratified in March 1994. Numerous other flight attendant groups, including those at United, U.S. Airways, and America West, have since used or threatened to use CHAOS campaigns during their negotiations.

Creative tactics were also evident in the strike by the Association of Professional Flight Attendants (APFA) at American Airlines in 1993. Issues in the strike included wages, staffing levels, scheduling, and health benefits for retirees. On November 18, 1993, APFA commenced a strike against American. The union timed the strike to occur over the busy Thanksgiving holiday and announced that it would last for eleven days. The explicit, brief duration of the strike was intended to lessen the chance of permanent replacement, since FAA regulations require safety training prior to placing new flight attendants into service. While the effectiveness of a strike is almost always disputed by the parties, it is clear that the strike had an adverse effect on the carrier. On November 23, 1993, five days into the strike, President Bill Clinton intervened by getting the parties to agree to submit their remaining disputed issues to arbitration. This action signaled an inclination on the part of the Clinton administration to break with almost three decades of a more hands-off approach to airline labor relations. The arbitration award was issued in October 1995 and was generally favorable to the flight attendants. They received a 17 percent pay increase over six years (three of the years were retroactive), retained their vacation time, and kept most of the work rules that the carrier had sought to change.

In the 1990s, pilots at American Airlines had their own problems with carriers. Negotiations between American and the Allied Pilots Association (APA) began in 1994. In January 1997, the membership rejected a tentative agreement. Key issues in the dispute included wages, stock options, and most centrally, the question of which pilots would fly the new regional jets that American was ordering. Once again, technological changes, in this case the introduction of faster, larger regional jets replacing turbo-prop commuter planes, would affect airline collective bargaining. The conflict was especially sharp in this instance, because the carrier wanted the new regional jets to be flown by its subsidiary American Eagle, whose pilots were represented by ALPA rather than APA.

This was also the first of a series of negotiations to take place when airlines were beginning to see sizable profits. After prior concessionary contracts, workers were ready for substantial wage gains. This was one of the factors leading to an unusually high number of contract rejections in the latter half of the 1990s (one-third of the tentative contracts negotiated in the airline industry from 1996 through 1999 were rejected). Rejection of American's offer led to a thirty-day cooling-off period and a strike on February 15, 1997. Just minutes into the strike, President Clinton invoked his authority to create a Presidential Emergency Board, thereby putting off the strike for at least sixty days. While President Clinton had also been directly involved in the flight attendants strike in 1993, his decision to dust off the PEB option (unused since the 1966 IAM strike) was somewhat surprising. Commentators were hard-pressed to explain why this strike and not numerous previous ones, including the Eastern Airlines strike, merited creation of a PEB. In the end, a political calculus seemed most likely. As the *New York Times* explained in February 1997, "So, even if the Transportation Department's math isn't solid, Mr. Clinton's calculations are: 9,300 American Airlines pilots versus thousands of stranded passengers and millions of armchair quarterbacks. No contest." With the strike in abeyance, the parties went back to negotiations and a new agreement was approved in May 1997 providing for a 9 percent raise, stock options, the phasing out of a two-tier wage structure (American's pilots had been among the first groups to accept this arrangement in 1983 and had caught considerable flak over the years from rival unions for doing so), and a creative compromise on the regional jet question: American Eagle pilots would fly them, but less-senior American pilots facing layoffs would have a right of transfer to American Eagle, and American Eagle pilots would be hired for one out of every two new positions at American.

The 1997 agreement did not spell the end of trouble between American Airlines and its pilots. The company acquired the much smaller regional carrier Reno Air in late 1998. American stated its intention to gradually integrate Reno into American's system, but the pilots pressed for immediate integration of the carriers and bringing Reno pilots up to American's pay scale. The pilots were so adamant because they viewed this as one of many actions taken by the carrier aimed at undermining the "scope language" in their contract. Scope language is a basic source of protection for pilots because it defines who can fly a carrier's planes and routes. The American pilots saw the acquisition of Reno Air as a ploy by the carrier to outsource flights away from the higher-paid American pilots.

An unannounced "sickout" began on February 6, 1999, and severely disrupted American's operations for over a week. A federal district court judge issued a temporary restraining order (TRO) on February 11. Upon finding that APA did not go far enough in ordering its members to cease and desist from their sickout, since the number of pilots calling in sick actually increased immediately following issuance of the TRO, the judge found the union and two of its officers to be in contempt of court. An appeals court upheld the $45.5 million in compensatory damages assessed against APA and its officers for violating the court order. An agreement on integration of the Reno Air pilots was reached in late October 1999. The Reno Air pilots would receive a large, retroactive pay increase and an additional 300 American pilots (matching the number of Reno pilots added) would receive "no layoff" guarantees.

The strike that perhaps best exemplified the dynamics of airline labor relations in the late 1990s took place at Northwest Airlines. After extracting major concessions from its unions in 1993 in exchange for stock and seats on the board of directors, Northwest realized record profits in the years that followed. Negotiations for a new contract started in 1996. In addition to wages, the pilots were particularly concerned about Northwest's desire to purchase regional jets for use by its commuter airline affiliates. ALPA's strike began on August 29, 1998, and lasted two weeks. The carrier did not make a serious effort to continue flying. Once again, presidential intervention figured prominently in the outcome. The carrier pressed the Clinton administration to follow the precedent it had set in the 1997 American Airlines strike and appoint a PEB. A board was not created, but administration officials made it clear that the president would do so if a settlement was not immediately forthcoming. A settlement was reached that included a 12 percent increase over four years, a lump sum payment, profit sharing, stock options, and gradual elimination of an existing two-tier wage scale.

Interestingly, the regional jet issue was resolved by creation of a formula linking the number of regional jets used by Northwest's commuter airline partners to the number of wide-body jets maintained by the carrier. Increases in the use of regional jets would be allowed, but they would not come at the expense of job opportunities for Northwest pilots. The union's concern for finding a way to reconcile the interests of its members at Northwest with those of the pilots at Mesaba Express and other Northwest-affiliated commuter lines, whose members are also represented by ALPA, was rewarded by the commuter pilots' promise not to perform any struck work during the Northwest strike. The strike was also notable for the degree of support provided by pilots based in other countries, particularly pilots at the Dutch airline KLM. At the corporate level, Northwest and KLM had close ties, including a KLM equity stake in Northwest and extensive "code-sharing" agreements providing for joint marketing, shared flights, and linking of route systems. While the KLM pilots were enjoined by a Dutch court from engaging in a sympathy strike, they contributed funds and promised not to operate any flights that would have been flown by Northwest pilots. In the face of advancing globalization in the airline industry, unions, particularly pilots' unions, will increasingly find that they need the support of their international counterparts in order to conduct effective strikes.

As commuter or regional carriers have grown to occupy a more prominent place in the airline industry, the wages and working conditions of their employees have become objects of contention. ALPA, which also represents many of the pilots at regional or commuter carriers, is concerned both with the threat to their members at major carriers posed by the shift of flights to lower-paid personnel and with the wages and working conditions of their members at regional and commuter carriers. Bringing the latter closer to parity with pilots at the larger carriers lessens the incentive to substitute one for the other. It is not surprising then, that a major strike in 2001 involved pilots at Comair, a subsidiary of Delta Airlines that uses regional jets to serve cities that cannot be profitably served using Delta's larger planes and feeds traffic from those smaller cities into Delta's route system. Negotiations foundered over the issues of compensation, scheduling, job security, and retirement benefits. The carrier conceded that major improvements would have to be made; the dispute was over how large those improvements would be and how close they would come to bringing Comair's pilots to the wages and working conditions of other large carriers. After rejecting a contract offer that had not been endorsed by the union leadership, Comair's 1,350 pilots went on strike on March 26, 2001. A second offer was rejected in May 2001. The strike was effective in shutting the carrier down, but it still took eighty-one days to reach an agreement. The agreement included an employer-financed retirement plan and "the best pay in the regional airline industry," according to the *New York Times*.

The run-up to the Comair strike included a work slowdown by Comair pilots (exercising their authority to not fly planes with mechanical defects that the airline regarded as minor). Comair went to court to seek an order to stop the slowdown, which the court granted. The GAO documented ten instances since 1998 in which carriers were granted injunctions to halt sickouts, concerted overtime refusals, and other forms of work slowdowns. This total does not include the TRO granted to Comair and a refusal of overtime engaged in with considerable effect by United's pilots in the summer of 2000. Airline workers have employed a variety of pressure tactics in their disputes with carriers over the years, particularly when confronted with troublesome supervisors or management policies, but the frequency of work slowdowns to support negotiation demands in recent years is notable. For their part, carriers have increasingly turned to the courts to enjoin such activities. Nor have the courts been the only source of governmental constraint. Continuing the interventionist approach of the Clinton administration, President George W. Bush ordered the creation of Presidential Emergency Boards to deal with impending strikes by mechanics at Northwest Airlines in March 2001 and by mechanics at United Airlines in January 2002. Following implementation of the PEB at Northwest, President Bush sweepingly declared that "I intend to take necessary steps to prevent airline strikes from happening this year." Both disputes were settled in subsequent negotiations.

An understanding of the history of strikes in the airline industry and of the forces currently shaping the industry permits a few educated guesses about the future. In the short term, as the older, highly unionized carriers struggle to lower their costs and devise workable business models, relatively few strikes are likely. Established carriers derive considerable leverage from threatened or actual bankruptcy filings in pushing for concessions. It may take more than an upturn in the economy and air travel to bring carriers back to financial health, but if that occurs, an increase in strikes and other forms of militancy can be expected. The trend toward a reassertion of government involvement in the airline industry and its labor relations is likely to continue, especially when it would benefit carriers. Deregulation not withstanding, this remains an industry in which the government has a large interest (indeed, through the workings of the Air Transportation Stabilization Board it now holds an ownership stake in U.S. Airways) and from which it cannot easily extricate itself. The airline industry is vital to the economy. Concerns over homeland security and terrorism necessitate close government scrutiny. The industry is predicated on a finite public infrastructure of airports and an air traffic control system. If a carrier is large enough and intervening would be politically advantageous, emergency boards will likely be utilized.

Although their bargaining power is compromised by the prospects of either permanent replacement or, if a strike is successful, the financial destruction of a carrier, airline unions remain powerful. They will continue to use the more sophisticated and varied pressure tactics developed in recent years. As the past two decades have shown, the extent of labor solidarity will be a major factor in determining the outcomes of struggles. Increasingly, that solidarity must come not only from other crafts, but also from workers at those foreign and regional carriers with which an airline is interconnected. Ultimately, airline labor will remain in a defensive posture until it is able to do a better job of equalizing labor costs across carriers. This will require new organizing at currently nonunion low-cost carriers, such as JetBlue, and militant action to bring the wages and working conditions of airline workers up to a common level rather than down to the level of the latest competitive threat.

See also: Strikes in the United States Since World War II, 226; Aerospace Engineer Strikes, 590.

Bibliography

Cohen, Isaac. "Political Climate and Two Airline Strikes: Century Air in 1932 and Continental Airlines in 1983–1985." *Industrial & Labor Relations Review* 43, no. 2 (1990): 308–23.

Cremiux, Pierre-Yves. "Does Strike Insurance Matter? Evidence From the Airline Industry's Mutual Aid Pact." *Journal of Labor Research* 17, no. 2 (1996): 201–18.

Cullen, Donald E. "Emergency Boards Under the Railway Labor Act." In *The Railway Labor Act at Fifty*, ed. Charles M. Rehmus. Washington, DC: National Mediation Board, 1977.

______. "Strike Experience Under the Railway Labor Act." *The Railway Labor Act at Fifty*, ed. Charles M. Rehmus. Washington, DC: National Mediation Board, 1977.

Hopkins, George E. *The Airline Pilots: A Study in Elite Unionization.* Cambridge, MA: Harvard University Press, 1971.

———. *Flying the Line: The First Half Century of the Air Line Pilots Association.* Washington, DC: Air Line Pilots Association, 1982.

Kahn, Mark L. "Airlines." In *Collective Bargaining: Contemporary American Experience*, ed. Gerald G. Somers Madison, WI: Industrial Relations Research Association, 1980.

Nielsen, Georgia Panter. *From Sky Girl to Flight Attendant.* Ithaca, NY: ILR Press, 1982.

Northrup, Herbert R. "The Rise and Demise of PATCO." *Industrial & Labor Relations Review* 37, no. 2 (1984): 167–85.

Rehmus, Charles M. "Emergency Strikes Revisited." *Industrial & Labor Relations Review* 43, no. 2 (1990): 175–91.

Shostak, Arthur B., and David Skocik. *The Air Controllers' Controversy: Lessons from the PATCO Strike.* New York: Human Sciences Press, 1986.

Unterberger, Herbert S., and Edward C. Koziara. "The Demise of Airline Strike Insurance." *Industrial & Labor Relations Review* 34, no. 1 (1980): 82–89.

Walsh, David J. "Accounting for the Proliferation of Two-Tier Wage Settlements in the U.S. Airline Industry, 1983–1986." *Industrial & Labor Relations Review* 42, no. 1 (1988): 50–62.

———. "Continuity and Change in the Structure of Union Representation in the U.S. Airline Industry, 1969–1999." In *New Research on Labor Relations and the Performance of University HR/IR Programs*, ed. David Lewin and Bruce E. Kaufman. New York: JAI, 2000.

———. *On Different Planes: An Organizational Analysis of Cooperation and Conflict among Airline unions.* Ithaca, NY: ILR Press, 1994.

AEROSPACE ENGINEER STRIKES

Stan Sorscher

In February 2000, AFL-CIO president John Sweeney stood quietly at the picket site at 6th Street and Logan Avenue in Renton, Washington, just outside the huge Boeing factory where 737 and 757 airplanes were assembled. His overcoat and hat slowly darkened in the light rain, while a tall middle-aged engineer jabbed his finger toward Sweeney, who listened patiently. The engineer earnestly explained how this strike had challenged his lifelong identity as a Republican and brought him a new appreciation of the value of the American labor movement.

The Society of Professional Engineering Employees in Aerospace (SPEEA) was formed in 1945. In 2000, SPEEA represented over 20,000 engineers, scientists, and technical workers at Boeing locations in seven states. On February 9, 2000, 17,000 SPEEA-represented employees went on strike at Boeing facilities in Washington, Oregon, Utah, Florida, and California. The contractual issues were wages and benefits, but the sound bite heard repeatedly was "respect."

Cultural Context

In the 1980s and early 1990s, the "quality culture" swept through U.S. manufacturing industries in response to the stunningly rapid success of Japanese manufacturing companies, who had increased productivity, reduced costs, and come to dominate a number of important industries. Under the original guidance of engineering consultant W. Edwards Deming in the decades after World War II, Japanese companies and workers demonstrated that process control, statistical analysis, and continuous improvement could outperform traditional industrial engineering methods popularized by Henry Ford.

American versions of this manufacturing culture went by many names, Total Quality Management (TQM), Six Sigma, Statistical Process Control (SPC), and others. At Boeing, the initiative took years to establish and underwent several incarnations. Nevertheless, the new culture did largely displace the conventional industrial engineering approach, which featured hierarchical authority, trained industrial engineers providing work rules, and the practice of shop-floor employees following the rules as directed by management. In the conventional manufacturing culture, the goal was to reduce cost. Lower cost was associated with lower quality, but a minimum threshold of quality was maintained by identifying and rejecting defective products.

In the quality culture, workers at every level would analyze the system around them, looking for the "root cause" of inefficiency or failure. In this culture, the presumption was that improving the process would improve quality and simultaneously reduce cost. This perspective broke any number of conventional industrial principles, not the least of which was the shift in control and authority from managers to workers on the shop floor. The behavioral principles honored in the quality culture were facts-and-data, root cause analysis, looking "upstream and downstream" for cause-and-effect behavior, and granting authority to workplace teams for analyzing and solving problems. Several assumptions went into this perspective. Employees were assumed to possess valuable knowledge, or at least the potential to develop and apply valuable knowledge about the production process. The employees had to assume that when they actively contributed their specialized knowledge, they would share in whatever advantage they created. Said differently, a reciprocal obligation was assumed, where companies drew on contributions from individuals, who willingly took risks and made special effort, anticipating they would share in the fortunes of the company. The Japanese example was significant, as manufacturing success was credited with raising its standard of living and creating the circumstances for shared prosperity.

By applying these "quality" methods, U.S. firms sought to convert the Japanese competitive threat into an opportunity for U.S. domestic workers. The aerospace industry already enjoyed competitive advantages. Quality initiatives promised a steady stream of productivity improvements, lower cost, and higher quality. By improving productivity through the quality methods, the aerospace industry's competitive position would improve. Employees would help create that outcome and would share in the reward. For this to work, employees and managers had to share a strong common interest, keeping their eyes on overall group goals. Narrow interests and short-range goals would lead to suboptimization. To get full value from this culture, commitment to common interest must be cultivated and reinforced by leadership example many times over.

In sound-bite form, "Employees are our most valuable resource." Engineers, technical employees, and workers on the shop floor were ideally situated to this industrial model, since they directly controlled design and manufacturing processes.

A variety of overlapping programs constituted the quality movement at Boeing. Over a period of years, workers witnessed re-engineering, Hoshin, House of Quality, kanban, ken, continuous improvement, just-in-time, Accelerated Improvement Workshops, Shingijutsu, win-win, fishbone diagrams, the Zen-like 5 S program, design of experiments, and a blizzard of more or less comprehensible products and programs to improve productivity. The company created an umbrella initiative called World Class Competitiveness (WCC). WCC would "become a way of life at Boeing," even as the specific programs came and went.

No company transforms itself to a quality culture without some backsliding. Managers would feel threatened and individuals would experience rejection as the social roles adapted to the new culture. Continuous improvement meant constant change. Change brought risk. Workers would not take risk or participate in reorganizing their work processes without trust in company leaders. Deming spoke of "constancy of purpose," meaning leaders had to maintain their focus to overcome skepticism and mistrust. Until they saw otherwise, workers would assume that new initiatives were the "flavor of the day" and any commitment they made or trust they might place in leaders would turn sour as the next business fad replaced the last.

First Test Case: The 1992 Strike

Collective bargaining is a clear opportunity for leaders to demonstrate commitment to their stated principles. What better test of management's "constancy of purpose" than watching how top leaders treat the engineering community and how they respect workers' interests in collective bargaining? In other words, collective bargaining could be an opportunity to hold managers accountable for their stated principles. If contract talks demonstrated "win-win" principles, then credibility, trust, and constancy of purpose will be reinforced in workplace situations generally.

In the 1990s SPEEA had three large bargaining units. Engineers and scientists in California, Florida, Utah, Oregon, and Washington were in the Professional Unit, and the Technical Unit was made up of drafters, planners, laboratory technicians, and other technical employees. These two units were centered in the Puget Sound region in the Pacific Northwest. A third, smaller bargaining unit covered Boeing engineers in Wichita, Kansas. The two Puget Sound units conducted coordinated bargaining with Boeing. The Wichita Engineering Unit contract expired a few days after the Puget Sound contracts, and the Puget Sound professional contract set the pattern for the Wichita unit.

In the 1992 negotiations, SPEEA and Boeing management teams publicly affirmed "interest-based bargaining" in contract negotiations. The teams would listen to each other's interests and look for solutions rather than entering talks with positions that would be pursued through power tactics. The negotiating teams managed to apply interest-based bargaining to noneconomic issues, but management walked out of talks over compensation, declared impasse, and implemented the terms of their last offer. A major sticking point was an improved cost-of-living formula.

SPEEA members were infuriated by this outcome and put the union negotiators under intense pressure. In January 1993, SPEEA called a one-day strike, announcing in advance that a settlement was possible without increasing the compensation package. Management refused to reopen talks or accept mediation. A tag line at the time was, "only Boeing engineers would strike for no more money, and only Boeing management would refuse to discuss it." About 70 percent of the bargaining unit, both members and nonmembers, participated in the one-day strike.

The strike had two consequences. First, it nearly killed SPEEA. At the time, dues-paying SPEEA membership was 55 to 60 percent in the two bargaining units. After the one-day strike, the previous offers were re-voted and accepted, and membership in SPEEA plunged by about a third. The second consequence was to question the entire culture of quality. Problem solving is good only if you have the power to implement your desired solution. Interest-based win-win behavior works if the stakes in the conflict are low, but when the stakes are high parties revert to power-based solutions.

The next round of negotiations took place in 1995. Exceptional preparation by both sides emphasized the principles of common goals, facts-and-data, open sharing of information, clearly expressing your interests, and "no surprises."

Second Test Case: 1995 Contract

The International Association of Machinists and Aerospace Workers (IAM-AW) represented Boeing hourly workers in the Puget Sound region. IAM Local 751, based in Seattle, Washington, was one of the most powerful locals in the country. Many SPEEA members worked side by side with Machinists and a small number of individuals transferred between the units as assignments changed. The Machinists' contracts expired in the fall, a few months before the SPEEA contracts. Historically, the IAM settlement set the pattern for pension and medical benefits in the SPEEA contracts, although the compensation, work rules, and layoff provisions were not linked.

In 1995, the Machinists struck for sixty-nine days, staying on strike through the SPEEA negotiations in November. In discussions with both the IAM and SPEEA, management gave high priority to the introduction of medical managed care plans. Management proposed large monthly premiums for employees who stayed in the traditional medical plan, but anyone moving to a managed care plan would pay no monthly premiums.

During the IAM strike, SPEEA proposed a modest continuing financial incentive for employees who voluntarily switched from the traditional plan to managed care, and no premiums for either plan. This would serve Boeing's interest of establishing managed care as the preferred choice of medical plans through a positive incentive rather than by punishing those who would not give up fee-for-service medical coverage. Boeing repackaged this idea as lump-sum payments, phased over three years, paid to employees electing managed care. This shift in position helped settle the IAM strike, and the incentives were included in the SPEEA contracts as well. Over 80 percent of the voting members accepted the 1995 SPEEA, even though they had weaker compensation packages than the contentious 1992 contracts.

Process Improvement vs. Shareholder Value

The quality culture had shifted its identity often, borrowing slogans and methods from various Japanese and domestic consultants. Workplace experience varied, as would be expected, but the clear drift of activity was to accept the premises and methods of process improvement and to grant authority to employees. The positive effect was probably strongest in shops and manufacturing areas. However, engineers, technicians, scientists, and other professional groups also participated actively in workplace process improvement teams. Managers were expected to become coaches who encouraged employees to take responsibility. Managers would provide resources and protection from bureaucratic challenge. This stood in contrast to the old culture where managers made decisions, gave orders, and expected obedience.

Some managers became strong advocates, and some managers who could not adjust retired. One retiring mid-level manager said, "I used to get up in the morning and look forward to coming into work and kicking someone's ass. This just isn't fun anymore."

By the late 1990s, many employees could sense that executives' ardor for process improvement was fading. Ron Woodard, president of the Commercial Airplanes business unit, spoke of airplanes as approaching theoretical perfection. To the extent that products had been seen as performance-driven, process improvement was relatively attractive. If the products were now commodities far along on their learning curves, then cost cutting had more appeal.

Boeing merged with McDonnell Douglas on August 1, 1997, and the merger marked a profound shift in leadership direction, particularly with regard to quality programs and process improvement. McDonnell Douglas directors transformed the Boeing board of directors, and McDonnell Douglas executives took key leadership roles. In the 1980s and 1990s, McDonnell Douglas had set a standard of sorts for failing to handle cultural challenges. Friction after the merger between McDonnell and Douglas Aircraft was notorious, and their fumbling of TQM was legendary. TQM requires a certain level of investment, but McDonnell Douglas management had not made the necessary commitments. After the merger in 1997, management studied the possibility of setting up 737 airplane production lines in McDonnell Douglas factories, but the cost of upgrading would be so expensive that the facilities would not be economically competitive. As a result, Boeing wrote off over $3 billion in value associated with McDonnell Douglas commercial airplane facilities.

Harry Stonecipher, a former McDonnell Douglas CEO, took control of operations at the merged company. His new management direction placed highest priority on shareholder value and he solidified the tentative shift, signaled by Ron Woodard and others, seen just prior to the merger. Under this new direction, short-term financial performance and share price became the measure of success. A management team can increase return on investment by increasing return or decreasing investment. In the new cost-cutting approach, reducing investment would be a more reliable means to increase return on financial performance than increasing productivity. Specifically, Boeing cut budgets for capital expenditures and research and development.

In the quality culture, most workplace process improvement teams do not worry about shareholder value. The primary goal is making products customers want to buy. Products, processes, and productivity are the primary goal, and profits are a consequence. The shareholder value culture reverses that relationship. A profit margin is set as an overall constraint, and budgets are realigned to produce that outcome. This is guaranteed to work in the short term, but becomes a death spiral in the longer term.

The example of McDonnell Douglas was an immediate case in point. Boeing employees were well aware that McDonnell Douglas had been driven from its military, space, and commercial airplane markets. The employees believed McDonnell Douglas failed to invest in the future. Compromised products, inefficient processes, and inadequate resources were consistent with making money every year, but competitors beat them back from their markets. With the merger, the slow shift from process improvement to cost cutting became a steady march at Boeing. Some executives resisted the new direction. Three high-level Boeing engineering executives were forced out, which helped establish the authority of the new leadership team. A high-profile chief financial officer left in what many saw as a clash of personalities.

As budgets and resources dried up, it was clear Boeing would no longer compete on World Class Competitiveness. In the early and middle 1990s, Boeing had talked of manufacturing as a strategic weapon, meaning that internal efficiencies and a valuable body of knowledge would serve as a sustainable competitive advantage. Engineers, technicians, and hourly workers played a key role in that business model.

In a cost-cutting business model, global suppliers are regarded as equivalent and interchangeable in quality and performance. Decisions can be made on cost rather than performance or strategic value. Within that view, employees at one supplier are equivalent to employees elsewhere. Employees are no longer "our most valuable resource," but rather a commodity interchangeable with workforces in many other locations.

Figures 1, 2, and 3 show trends in capital investment for the years before and after the strike in 2000. The 777 airplane program was completed in the mid-1990s, with deliveries starting in 1995. The 787 airplane program was launched in April 2004, and picked up in activity during 2005. Boeing's cost cutting pleased shareholders, but workers paid the price.

Over the years prior to 1990, Boeing built considerable human capital, retained as a body of knowledge in its engineering community. After 1990, Boeing was not able to attract or retain new knowledge workers, and many of the existing engineers and scientists quit, retired, left the profession, or were laid off. The population aged steadily and shrank significantly, as shown in Figure 4. Eligibility for early retirement started at age fifty-five.

To a large extent, the engineering community stores human capital in the form of social networks. By working on many programs, individuals learn whom they can trust and who depends on them for important and timely information. Communication and coordination are extremely valuable, and the network of personal relationships carries a great deal of information on a tacit or informal basis. Studies of major program failures throughout the aerospace industry have verified this feature of the industry.

While cutting financial investment and allowing human capital to erode, Boeing also embarked on a stock repurchase program that would ultimately consume $10 billion—roughly the cost to develop a new airplane model. As with any stock repurchase, the Boeing board of directors concluded that no investment in the future is more valuable than immediate rewards to shareholders, as illustrated in Figure 5.

From the employee's perspective, shareholder value also breaks the implicit social contract based on shared goals and common interests. If employees are interchangeable, and

Figure 1 **Capital Expenditures**

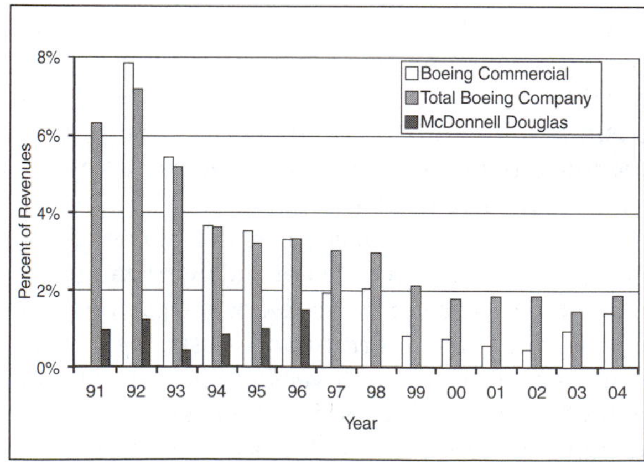

Source: Annual Reports.

Figure 2 **Internally Funded R&D**

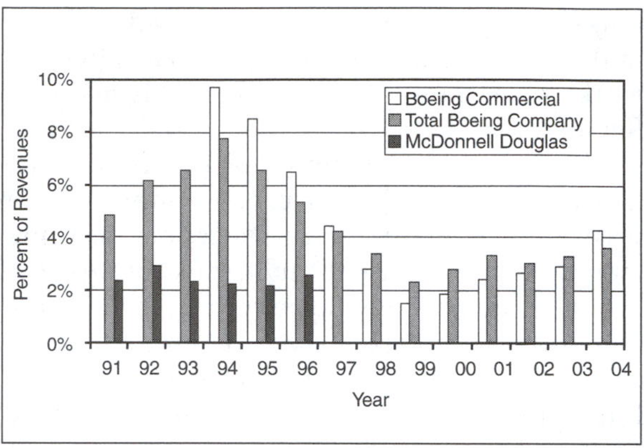

Source: Annual Reports.

Figure 3 **Corporate Investment**
(5-year average, 1999–2003)

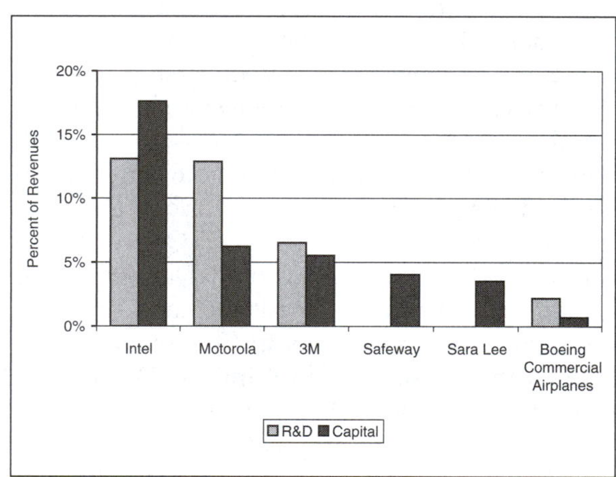

Source: Annual Reports.

Figure 4 **Boeing Engineers and Scientists in the Pacific Northwest**

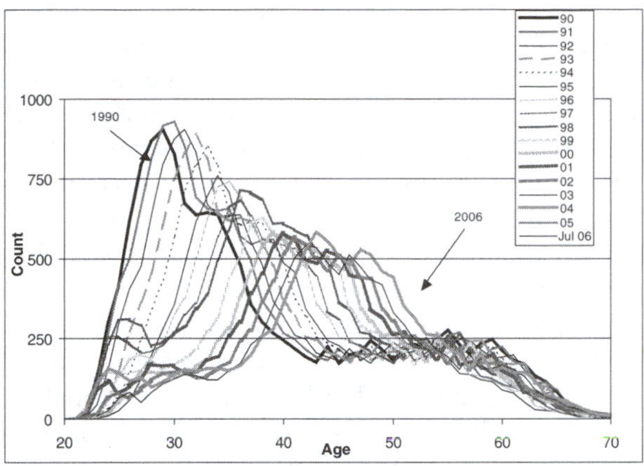

Source: SPEEA tracks employment and attrition through data supplied by Boeing on a regular basis.

Figure 5 **Boeing Shares Outstanding**

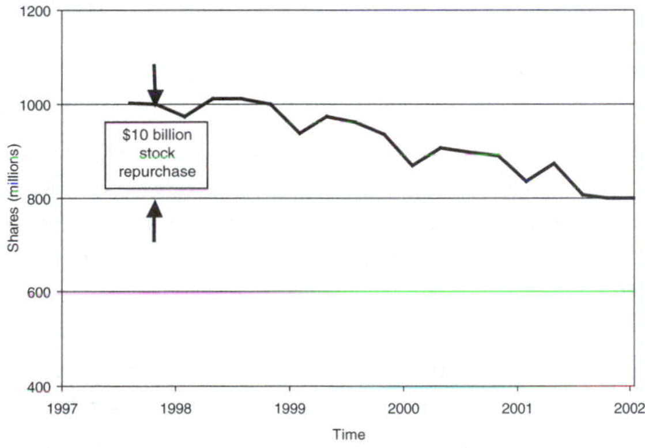

Source: Boeing 10-K and 10-Q reports.

if global suppliers will assume expanding roles, then current employees should expect plant closures, divestitures, layoffs and limited career opportunities.

The shift from common interest to divided interest can be seen in an exchange between an employee and Boeing CEO Phil Condit at the annual shareholders' meeting on May 1, 2000, in Huntsville, Alabama. According to the transcript, the employee asked about Harry Stonecipher's troubles at McDonnell Douglas. She said, "It's perceived that Mr. Stonecipher's mentality didn't work very well at McDonnell Douglas. Why do you think it will work here . . . ?" Condit replied, "One needs to deal with the truth. The truth is that under his guidance share prices at McDonnell Douglas I think quadrupled." The employee was looking at long-term value to all stakeholders—employees, shareholders, and customers. She knew McDonnell Douglas lost a series of critical military program competitions, and its commercial products were being run out of their markets, as shown in Figure 6. However, Boeing executives measured success by share price, not long-term strategic position or appeal of products to their customers. Even if the company's products failed miserably and workers lost their jobs and saw their benefits cut, the shareholders might still do well, and that was the "truth" that mattered to executives.

The new management approach embodied in the merger also shaped labor relations. For decades prior to the merger, Boeing and SPEEA maintained businesslike and productive relations. For almost forty years, SPEEA contracts were settled without strikes or serious confrontation. Boeing saw itself as an "engineering company" and CEOs alternated between engineers and businessmen. T.A. Wilson led Boeing during the drastic downturn in the early 1970s. He came to prominence as an engineer in

Figure 6 **Boeing/Airbus/MDC—Commercial Airplane Deliveries**

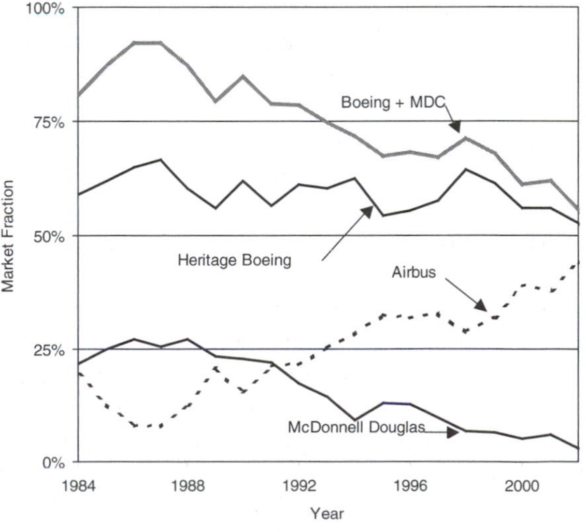

Source: For Boeing, see http://active.boeing.com/commercial/orders/. For Airbus, see http://www.airbus.com/en/corporate/orders_and_deliveries/.

missile programs and had helped create SPEEA in the late 1940s. Frank Shrontz, with a background in law, contracts, and government service, followed Wilson. Phil Condit, who came after Shrontz, had also been a SPEEA member early in his career. Ron Woodard and Alan Mulally each served as president of the Commercial Airplane Group and had been SPEEA members. Many other high-level Boeing executives had been members or activists in SPEEA before going into management.

With the merger, however, an adversarial mood characterized labor relations. Boeing modified its corporate vision materials to remove "working together with unions." The board of directors introduced a cash bonus system for nonrepresented employees, which became an increasing irritant and wedge dividing represented from nonrepresented employees. Starting in 2000, Boeing responded to organizing campaigns by holding captive audience meetings, hosting anti-union Web sites and bringing in anti-union law firms to campaign actively against SPEEA. After the Wichita employees voted to organize almost all the salaried employees at the facility, Boeing management backed a series of decertification campaigns. These provocative actions set the stage for confrontation.

1999 Contracts

Taking a lesson from the botched merger of McDonnell and Douglas, the new Boeing leadership team wanted to consolidate the diverse systems and organizations from the premerger companies into a unified new company. An important premerger business practice at Boeing had been to negotiate new working conditions and terms of employment with the unions and implement those terms for nonrepresented employees. The new postmerger practice would be to develop new terms, impose them on nonrepresented populations, then try to force the unions to accept them.

In the fall of 1999, the Machinists negotiated a good contract. Condit called it the best in the industry. It included a pension increase, no cost shifting in medical premiums, and a large signing bonus. At about that time, SPEEA affiliated with the International Federation of Professional and Technical Employees (IFPTE), which placed SPEEA in the House of Labor for the first time in over fifty years.

SPEEA members held considerable respect for the IAM, which they thought of as a "real union." SPEEA members had a range of expectations about their union. As a professional association, SPEEA fell within the comfort zone of most SPEEA members, who drew a line between trade unions and their identity as professionals. Nevertheless, affiliation with the AFL-CIO in 1999 was widely accepted by the membership.

Negotiations in 1992 and 1995 were seen as barometers of leadership commitment to the future. One lesson from 1992 and 1995 was that culture is imperfect and inconsistent and must be reinforced by example. In the fall of 1999, SPEEA negotiators presented their proposal to members at a large meeting in the Seattle Center. At the meeting, a *Seattle Times* reporter asked a group of engineers how they would know if the contract offer was a good one. One said the contract would show whether Boeing was committed to the future. The reporter asked where in the contract that information would be. The engineers looked at each other and nodded. "We'll know," they said.

The 1999 Boeing and SPEEA negotiating teams were familiar with interest-based bargaining and made reasonable efforts to understand each other in the months before the contract expired. However, Boeing had announced a new benefits package for nonrepresented employees, which they called "Total Compensation." It featured a cash-balance pension plan, large monthly premiums for medical care, and the loss of early retiree medical for employees hired in the future. Negotiations moved through the noneconomic issues, coming to the compensation and benefits packages in the last few days, which was customary. However, at the last moment the Boeing team suddenly shifted direction, withdrew the heritage benefits package, and substituted the Total Compensation benefits package as a whole—take it or leave it.

The SPEEA team reacted harshly for two reasons. First, the company's provocative behavior stood in stark contrast to the deference shown by Boeing to the Machinists. Boeing had conceded the best contract in the industry to the IAM. The Machinists kept their pension, had no medical premiums, and held onto early retiree medical. In the early 1990s, McDonnell Douglas took a strike by the UAW to eliminate early retiree medical for active and future employees, and the Total Compensation package was seen as a mortal blow in the battle over early retiree medical at Boeing.

Second, the management team provoked the engineering community by using power tactics. Engineers and technical workers regard themselves as problem solvers. The prior decade had honored that identity, and the new cost-cutting "company killers" from McDonnell Douglas put it at risk. This new labor relations challenge was a clear line in the sand. The SPEEA Engineering and Technical unit negotiating teams both recommended rejection in late November. SPEEA members voted on contracts by mail over several days, and the results for both units were 98 and 99 percent to reject the offers.

In the workplace, conversation by e-mail and face-to-face was heated. Engineers work to a plan, and all over the region employees started diagramming how an immediate strike would play through the Christmas holidays—a week of paid holiday from Christmas to New Year's Day. SPEEA had rejected contracts before. In the past, after a strong statement from the members, the SPEEA and management teams would return to the tables, and perhaps better judgment would prevail. In this case, many SPEEA members assumed that management was deliberately provoking them into a second strike—one that would finish the job started in 1993. If Boeing could provoke a strike and then break it, SPEEA would be weakened and vulnerable to a decertification election.

The Christmas break came and went, and then the teams met with federal mediators in early January. Hostile e-mail statements from employees at the time argued that the IAM offer was far superior to the offers made to SPEEA. In the mediated talks, Boeing management turned those statements around, saying in effect, if you like the IAM deal so much, here it is. They presented a half-baked package of benefits patterned on the hourly employees' benefits package. Sick leave, bereavement pay, life insurance, disability, and other programs were cobbled together, with some serious loopholes involving disparate pay scales, grade levels, and seniority issues.

Perhaps the most visceral shortcoming of the benefits package was the elimination of employer-paid life insurance, provided to all other salaried employees. Again, the proposal was voted by mail over several days. As the voting period went on, the members' anger steadily rose. Each day, at large meetings in the workplace, the negotiating teams stressed that these were "50 percent-plus-one" votes and that solidarity—accept or reject—was the only course of action. It was also made clear that if one or both of the units rejected their contract(s), a strike would follow.

Many members voted early, but sentiment for rejection built up steadily as mail ballots were cast over the week of voting. Both the Professional and Technical units narrowly rejected the second offer, the engineers by a few dozen votes out of 7,000 eligible voters. A strike was called for early February.

At this point, the situation was brought before the AFL-CIO Executive Council, which counseled SPEEA's negotiating teams and elected officials to exercise restraint. SPEEA agreed to delay the strike for three days, to give the director of the Federal Mediation and Conciliation Service (FMCS) a chance to sort things out. The members howled, but waited three more days. Richard Barnes, director of the FMCS, mediated a round of talks without effect.

Strike

Most industry observers assumed that engineers would need to stay on strike for many months to have any effect on production. In previous strikes, Boeing managers and scabs would try to keep production going. A measure of success in this respect was finishing a few airplanes near the end of the production line and delivering them. Failure would be to finish an airplane, then have the escape slide deploy accidentally and fall into Lake Washington on a test flight, or to have a container of toxic material boil over in a factory, sending workers to the hospital and prompting evacuation of the plant, as happened several years later.

The SPEEA strike was remarkable in many respects. Participation was beyond expectations. Dues-paying membership climbed to about 60 percent prior to the strike, but about 70 to 75 percent of the two Puget Sound bargaining units walked out on February 9, 2000. The Wichita Engineering Unit continued to work as their talks were put

Like so many strikes before it, the 2000 strike of the Society of Professional Engineering Employees in Aerospace against Boeing involved many of the strikers' family members. To keep warm and cook on the picket line, the strikers invented the "SPEEA stove," a burn barrel with vents and an exhaust stack that adheres to Environmental Protection Agency smoke regulations. (Photos courtesy of the author.)

on hold pending resolution of negotiations with the Puget Sound units. The strike became a work project, managed by the union members. Local teams set up picket assignments, built shelters, and provided food, furniture, electric generators, lights, and music, varying by site and conditions. The "SPEEA stove" was invented—a burn barrel with vents and exhaust stack that met EPA smoke regulations and burned noticeably hotter and more efficiently than a simple oil drum burn barrel. Strikers brought their families to the picket sites, and at least one marriage resulted from a relationship started on the picket line.

The strikers organized large events for Valentine's Day, a march on the Boeing headquarters building, a pancake lunch, and a rock concert. AFL-CIO secretary-treasurer Rich Trumka spoke at two rallies in Seattle. The Service Employees International Union provided a phone bank system for calling members at home. The Teamsters, International Longshore and Warehouse Union, IAM, other unions, and local labor councils provided invaluable support. A food bank was used actively by striking members and an emergency fund helped many people pay utility bills and cover other costs. Neighbors and local residents donated firewood, food, and other supplies in enormous quantities as tokens of support for the strikers.

The economic leverage of the strike was much greater than anticipated. Commercial airplane production slowed and deliveries largely stopped. Some customers deferred taking delivery until the strike was settled. The Joint Strike fighter program was in a critical developmental phase and on a tight timeline. Military launches from Cape Canaveral stopped. The Sea Launch commercial satellite program suffered a launch failure, according to the *Seattle Times,* and launches were delayed. Airline customers around the world relied on Boeing for maintenance, repair, training, spares, and other technical support. As time went on, delays and grounded airplanes became a significant cost and operational irritant to customers, who pointedly asserted that future airplane purchases would depend on reliability of needed technical services.

As the strike progressed, it was clear that several specific engineering functions could choke off production and revenue for Boeing. Airplanes could not be delivered without Federal Aviation Administration (FAA) approval. The FAA delegated much of this authority to selected Boeing engineers, roughly 400 in number. Almost all of those engineers were SPEEA-represented, and the great majority of them participated in the strike. Also, FAA certification relies on stable processes and the support work of test and design engineers. That support system was seriously disrupted by the strike. The FAA took back some of the delegated authority and could easily have suspended the regulatory authority for Boeing to build and deliver airplanes. Flight test and nondestructive testing of manufactured parts also became choke points.

In the years before the strike, it became clear that Boeing executives were responding more directly to the financial and investment community. As a result, SPEEA made a special effort to build informal relationships with financial analysts and industry observers. The message from SPEEA was that aerospace products are different from other manufactured goods or retail products. Business models that might be well-suited to running shoes, cell phones, and ladies garments would be ill-suited to complex, heavily engineered aerospace products with life spans measured in decades, enormous unit costs, low production rates, spectacular learning curves, and very high expectations by the public and customers regarding performance and reliability. If ever an American manufacturing industry was dependent on human capital, aerospace was it. In a sense then, the strike could be interpreted partly as a vote of no confidence in the shareholder value business model.

In the first week of March, Boeing hosted a conference for financial analysts at a resort in Napa, California. SPEEA sent a small delegation and took that opportunity to speak in business terms to some of the attendees about the strike and the common interest between employees and shareholders. Near the end of one discussion, Charles Bofferding, SPEEA executive director, asked one of the investor analysts, "What do you think is more important—higher productivity or lower labor unit costs?" The analyst paused and thought for moment. "Lower [labor unit] costs." One influential investor asked, "What would it take to settle the strike?" He was surprised to hear the very low cost in dollars of an acceptable offer, but he wrote down the details, snapped his notebook shut, thanked the union delegation, and left.

Days later, negotiators settled the strike with terms more or less favorable to the striking workers. The heritage benefits package was restored, with retirement improvements corresponding to those of the IAM settlement. A three-part compensation bonus and significant wage increases were included.

Pressure to settle the strike came from several directions. First, the engineers, scientists, and technical workers stopped production of commercial airplanes. Workers in flight test, inspection, quality assurance, and certification had much more leverage on deliveries than many people realized. Some SPEEA-represented engineers serve in dual roles as Boeing employees and as designees of the FAA. With intimate knowledge of airplane systems and structures, the SPEEA-represented engineers watched manufacturing and certification of airplanes during the strike and were able to point FAA specialists to problems that needed attention. On the military side, the Joint Strike fighter development program was already under pressure without the strike, and delays in that program compressed that tight schedule even further. The F-22 program was also affected.

SPEEA contacted university placement centers and encouraged strikers to write to their alma maters to share their concerns about the future of the aerospace industry. By mid-March, it was clear that experienced workers were quitting. *Aviation Week & Space Technology*, an influential trade weekly, printed a harsh assessment of this trend by an unnamed "cerebral longtime observer." "Boeing is performing a lobotomy on itself. To make an object lesson of the talent on which the Company's future depends, management has chosen to potentially cripple itself for life."

Pressure also came from airline customers, who normally make about 10,000 service requests each year for help maintaining aircraft. Over the first five weeks of the strike, a large backlog of unresolved service requests accumulated. Some of the requests involved idled airplanes, costing airlines tens of millions of dollars and lending urgency to the company's need to settle the strike.

Finally, direct communication by SPEEA with the financial community probably helped everyone see a path to settlement.

Poster Child for Globalization

The Boeing engineering strike of 2000 marked the end of aerospace as a characteristically American industry. Up to that point, the engineering community held the view that aerospace was part of the new economy, which the United States would inevitably dominate. This was in line with the mantra of globalization. Knowledge work would become more valuable and knowledge workers would enjoy respect and economic benefits. The specialized body of knowledge held within the design and manufacturing communities was high enough on the value chain to secure a strong future. The engineering community had a keen appreciation for what it took to build an airplane or a space vehicle or a military fighter. But since the strike, Boeing has been more explicit about concentrating on project management and system integration. In that respect, Boeing will rely more and more on global suppliers for design and manufacturing of components and major assemblies.

When the strike was settled and people returned to work, it became clear that management paid no attention to the strategic message of the strike. The vote of no confidence fell on deaf ears, and the dismantling of the engineering community picked up where it left off. One measure of the discouragement felt by engineers was the large attrition rate following the strike. In 2000, approximately 900 engineers quit and another 1,000 retired, a large jump from previous years. In 1999 and 2000, most employees could only imagine what it meant to concentrate on system integration and program management. Starting in 2004, Boeing converted those concepts into reality in the 787 airplane program. This program will be the first big test for this new business model in the aerospace industry. Suppliers in Japan, Italy, China, and elsewhere are responsible for unprecedented amounts of structure and content for the new airplane. To some degree, lines of responsibility are still shifting around as the design, manufacturing processes, and tooling become more clearly defined. In any event, Boeing's vision of its future includes fewer engineers and technicians doing less and less of the detailed technical design and manufacturing work—and the SPEEA faces a continuing challenge.

See also: Strikes in the United States Since World War II, 226; Strikes in the U.S. Airline Industry, 1919–2004, 577.

Bibliography

Cappelli, Peter. *The New Deal at Work.* Boston, MA: Harvard Business School Press, 1999.

Newhouse, John. *Boeing Versus Airbus: The Inside Story of the Greatest International Competition in Business.* New York: Knopf, 2007.

Pfeffer, Jeffrey. *The Human Equation.* Boston: Harvard Business School Press, 1998.

Uchitelle, Louis. *The Disposable American.* New York: Knopf, 2006.

TEAMSTER STRIKES AND ORGANIZING, 1934–1964

Dan La Botz

In 1933 the International Brotherhood of Teamsters (IBT) was a small, weak union with fewer than 75,000 members, principally local cartage drivers and warehouse dock workers in large cities in the Upper Midwest and the Northeast. Some wondered if the union could survive the layoffs, wage cuts, and outright union busting of the 1920s and early 1930s. But by 1964, the IBT had grown to represent about 1.5 million members in trucking and related industries throughout the country. By then the word *Teamster* had become synonymous with working-class power to disrupt business as usual. The vast expansion in the size, power, and political influence of the IBT resulted from the longest sustained union organizing drives in U.S. history, carried out through a series of local and regional strikes.

From 1934 to 1964, the IBT carried out strikes and organizing campaigns that transformed the union, the trucking and warehousing industry, and labor relations and society at large. These strikes, which first organized tens and eventually hundreds of thousands of workers not only in trucking and warehousing but also in food processing and agriculture, arose out of a series of economic, social, and political changes in American society. Foremost among these were the rise of the interstate trucking industry and the Great Depression, accompanied by government regulation and the labor upheaval of the 1930s.

The Teamster strikes and organizing drives began haphazardly out of the economic desperation of the Depression, some led by traditional business unionists, others by militant unions leaders, and some by revolutionary socialists. Soon, however, the union systematized an organizing strategy that broke the links in the transportation and warehousing chain and forced the industry's small employers to the bargaining table. Once it organized transportation and warehousing in one city, the IBT moved on to the next by breaking the links between the unionized and non-unionized cities. This "leapfrog" strategy was so powerful the union could gradually extend its power not only across East, North and West, but even into the fiercely anti-union South. By 1964, the IBT was a genuine continent-spanning industrial union that conducted national bargaining for entire transportation industries.

The leapfrog strategy was based on breaking the links in the transportation and warehousing chain through strikes and "hot cargo" boycotts. The tactics used in preventing employers from operating involved mass picket lines, flying squads, occasional destruction of property such as trucks, diverting and tying up freight, and the use of force to stop scabs and to resist private guards and police. As the Teamsters grew in size, by the 1950s the mere threat of a strike would bring most employers to the table.

Strikes during the period of its expansion made the Teamsters the most powerful union in the country. Moreover, they gave the Teamsters a presence in the national consciousness such as no other union had. The CIO unions, such as the auto and steel workers, dominated the big cities of the Great Lakes industrial region, but the IBT had a presence not only there but in every city and town as well as rural areas throughout the country.

Background: The Industry and Government Regulation

The economic setting for the Teamster strikes developed during the 1920s with the growth of the automobile industry, the introduction of and rapid improvements in the motorized truck, and the construction of state and national highways, all of which made truck transportation an important national industry. The Great Depression caused an already highly competitive industry to become even more aggressive and cutthroat. In response to the industry's chaotic conditions, Congress passed the Motor Carrier Act in 1935. The Act gave to the Interstate Commerce Commission (ICC) authority to regulate motor carriers and drivers involved in interstate commerce by issuing permits to operate, approving trucking routes, and setting tariff rates. The Act reduced competition, helped to stabilize the industry, and made it possible to unionize trucking companies without fear that they would be threatened with competition from new entrants opening new routes or charging lower rates.

The strikes and boycotts of the 1930s proved effective because interstate trucking companies were regional, not national. The ICC did not permit any trucking company to have coast-to-coast or border-to-border routes. Consequently, regional trucking companies operated through inter-lining, where one freight line would take freight from A to B, and a second freight line would take it from B to C. This inter-lining system of nodes and links was vulnerable to disruption by breaking the inter-line link. Such disruption became the heart of the Teamsters' strategy. The regional character of the trucking industry also made the companies less capable of strategic coordination than the Teamsters union, which was national in scope. Finally, government rate regulation made it possible for carriers to pass increased labor costs on to their customers, which reduced employers' willingness to oppose the union.

This political economy of trucking—the combination of a regulated industry that did not permit new entrants or route and rate competition and a shipping system based on inter-lining freight—established the contours of the terrain on which the struggle between the companies and the union took place. For the union to get the power to take on the trucking companies, it needed a base of strength somewhere first. The union had to control at least one of the freight nodes—one city's transportation center—before it could begin to break the links of the regional systems.

Building a Local Power Base

How Teamsters built that local power base differed. Sometimes revolutionary socialists led the movement. In other cases, trade union militants took the lead, while in yet other instances traditional conservative AFL bureaucrats led the way. Under such varied leaderships the Teamsters built power bases simultaneously in several major cities: Seattle, Minneapolis, Chicago, Detroit, and Boston. In the 1930s and 1940s, each of those cities became a hub from which the union, through a series of strategic strikes, gradually extended more-or-less uniform wages and conditions to the surrounding industrial regions through pattern bargaining.

The energy that propelled the initial organizing drives of the 1930s came from the conditions of the Depression and the labor upsurge it generated. Unemployment nationally reached 25 percent. Many employers reduced workers' hours, so that even those with jobs suffered from underemployment. Other employers increased hours and cut wages, squeezing as much out of the remaining workforce as possible. Bosses also took advantage of the Depression to break unions, tear up contracts, and to fire and blacklist union activists.

Workers gradually began to organize to deal with unemployment and to resist employers' stretch-outs and wage cuts. The election of Franklin D. Roosevelt in 1932, his proclamation of a New Deal, and Congress's 1933 adoption of the National Industrial Recovery Act (NIRA), which permitted workers to organize under its Section 7(a), opened political space for unions. Among the many groups of workers that began to organize and to strike were Teamsters.

Minneapolis 1934

The Minneapolis Teamsters strikes were led by a small group of revolutionary socialists, followers of Leon Trotsky, belonging to the Communist League of America (CLA), which later became the Socialist Workers Party. One of the Trotskyists, Farrell Dobbs, a new recruit, emerged as a key leader of the strikes. Others were veterans of the Industrial Workers of the World (IWW), the Communist Party, and various labor union struggles. A few of these radicals were members of Teamster Local 574, a small union with about 75 members and four or five closed-shop contracts. The socialists first organized a strike among the men who shoveled coal and drove coal trucks in February 1934. They mobilized hundreds of workers to shut down dozens of coal yards and formed mobile "flying squads" to stop scab coal delivery trucks. Within a few days the workers won a uniform contract with shorter hours and a small wage increase. The victory and the broader power base of several hundred new members provided momentum for radical, rank-and-file union organizers. Working with sympathetic local union leaders, they began organizing all workers involved in the city's trucking business.

The organizers sent teams to visit all trucking workplaces in the city. They spoke at other local union meetings to raise support and made alliances with unemployed workers councils and with the Farm Holiday Association. To launch the campaign, Local 574 held a mass meeting at which a representative of Minnesota governor Floyd Olson of the Farmer-Labor Party read a letter from the governor urging the men to join the union. After that meeting the union had 3,000 members. It voted to seek a contract with the city's trucking employers and to set a deadline for a strike. Meanwhile, the Citizens Alliance organized employers to resist the union and what it called "the Communist take-over of the city." Attempts to reach agreement failed due to the bosses' resistance. At a mass meeting of thousands on May 15, 1934, the workers voted to strike.

Local 574 approached the strike as if it were a military campaign. Organizers established a strike headquarters with telephones, a commissary, a first aid station, a field hospital staffed by a physician and two interns, and a repair department with a score of auto mechanics. The union's women's auxiliary served as cooks, waitresses, nurses, and office workers. Local grocers and supporters provided food. At its peak, the headquarters, with 100 volunteers working in two 12-hour shifts, served coffee, sandwiches, and meals to as many as 5,000 strikers and supporters. From the headquarters, pickets and flying squads could be dispatched throughout the city. Local 574's leadership created a 75-member strike committee, later expanded to 100, elected by the union members. This committee held a general assembly each night to provide information, hear statements of support from invited guests, and provide entertainment from other unions. The union published a newspaper, *The Organizer*, which reached a circulation of 10,000 and became self-financing. At its peak the union was capable of mobilizing 7,500 pickets, 450 cars, 16 motorcycles, and even 2 biplanes.

The Minneapolis Teamster strike of 1934—really two separate strikes separated by a brief interlude—was a complicated affair that lasted from mid-May to late August 1934. During the strike, Local 574 mobilized thousands of Teamsters and supporters in what became, at times, pitched battles with scabs, police, and the Citizens Alliance. The union's tactics of mass mobilization, strategic deployment of pickets, and use of force to stop scabs, was met with violent repression by the police and the Citizens Alliance. Employers, police, and strikebreakers killed two Teamsters and caused many others serious injuries. Under pressure from the employers, Governor Olson sent in 4,000 National Guard troops, who suppressed Teamster picketing and jailed union activists. A Teamster-organized rally of 40,000 people called for the release of Teamsters held by the Guard in the stockade. As a result of its persistent, exhausting, and courageous fight, all accompanied by complex political maneuvering with the Citizens Alliance and the Farmer-Labor state government, as well as with International Teamster President Daniel Tobin, Local 574 finally succeeded in winning a government-supervised representation election through the mediation of the governor on August 21.

In that election, Local 574 won in 50 of 166 companies, becoming the collective bargaining agent for 61 percent of the workers. After the election, the union negotiated for workers in all 166 companies and within two years the union had contracts with some 500 companies. The initial contract and subsequent arbitrations gave workers significant wage increases and improvements in hours and conditions. Instead of dividing the newly organized drivers by craft into several local unions, all workers became members of Local 574, which transformed from a craft union into an industrial union.

While the Trotskyists were busy organizing in Minneapolis, other Teamster locals also built local power bases that would later make it possible for them to undertake regional organizing campaigns in the trucking industry. In Boston's Teamster Local 25, John M. Sullivan led an organizing campaign between 1933 and 1938 that brought thousands of new members into the union, won contracts with scores of employers, and raised wages for workers. In Detroit's Local 299, R.J. Bennett and his young assistant James R. Hoffa led a city-wide Teamster strike in April 1937 that after three days won a contract and wage gains for workers. Hoffa then went on to organize the carhaulers, truck drivers who hauled automobiles from Detroit to dealerships around the country. In Chicago's Local 710, Sandy O'Brien of the meat drivers union succeeded in organizing all of the over-the-road drivers based in the city. In Seattle's Local 566 it was Dave Beck, a quite conservative union official, and his ally Frank Brewster of Local 174, who by the mid-1930s had, through a series of strikes and organizing campaigns, built up a local power base in the most important city of the Pacific Northwest.

Teamster organizers found that workers' power had to be supplemented by political alliances in order to break the employers' stranglehold. In Minneapolis, the radical leaders built an alliance with the unemployed, other unions, and with farmers. In Detroit and Cleveland, some Teamster leaders turned to the Mafia for support. While the workers' organization, strikes, and boycotts were at the center of the organizing drive, the power of the union's allies also proved to be a factor in breaking the bosses' grip. The kind of alliances the Teamsters leaders established had profound implications for the future of the union.

Local union leaders mobilized union members in strikes that used force against scabs and, though they faced repression from police and local employers' associations, they eventually won contracts and raised union membership. These cities, each with a core of a few thousand battle-tested union activists, became the fulcrums for leveraging union power to break the links in the employers' freight shipping systems and eventually unionize entire regions. The leaders of the key locals established regional organizations: from Seattle down the West Coast, from Boston throughout the Northeast, from Minneapolis across the Upper Midwest, and from Chicago and Detroit throughout the rest of the Midwest. Only the South was not represented in this first stage of regional organizing.

Regional Organizing

To expand its reach throughout the upper Midwest, Minneapolis Local 574 built a staff that grew in the mid-1930s to 14 full-time organizers under the direction of Dobbs. On January 10, 1937, the local hosted a conference that created the North Central District Drivers Council (NCDDC), representing Teamster drivers from North and South Dakota, Iowa, Minnesota, Wisconsin, and Michigan. The idea to form a regional organization was a radical innovation in union-management relations. The NCDDC later expanded, incorporating Sandy O'Brien's Local 710 in Chicago and R.J. Bennett's Local 299 in Detroit. Farrell Dobbs, the lead organizer of the Minneapolis strike, found himself supervising and mentoring the young Jimmy Hoffa of Detroit.

By the late 1930s, the NCDDC was able to send an ultimatum to 1,200 employers telling them that it would no longer accept the "chaotic conditions" in the industry and would not "be sidetracked into a maze of regional and individual city negotiations." The Teamsters threatened to strike Minneapolis, Chicago, and Detroit, and in Colorado, Texas, and Kentucky. The threat alone brought the employers to the table and resulted in a closed-shop contract covering 125,000 workers. When Omaha, Nebraska's trucking employers attempted to resist, the union struck and, despite police repression and the jailing of many Teamster pickets, the union crushed the bosses by shutting off transportation coming into the state from union-organized terminals in other states.

Just as the Teamsters did in the Midwest, so did Sullivan in the Northeast and Beck in the Northwest. Sullivan spread the union from Massachusetts to Connecticut, Vermont, New Hampshire, Rhode Island, and Maine, and by 1938 he was in a position to demand that employers sign a common contract covering truck transportation workers in the entire area. When the bosses refused, the union called a general strike of the whole region, shutting down truck terminals and warehouse and keeping all trucks off the highway. The 11-day strike led to a contract with a small improvement in wages. A second strike in March 1939 was a total union victory, resulting in a uniform contract for all locals in southern New England.

Dave Beck led the expansion of the Teamsters in the West, from Washington, to Oregon and California, and then to all the Western states. Already in the early 1930s Beck had sent his associate "Whitey" Dahlager to strengthen Portland Local 162. By the mid-1930s, Beck was holding joint meetings of Washington Teamsters Joint Council 28 and Oregon Teamsters Joint Council 37 to coordinate organizing and bargaining efforts. The union required drivers coming up from California to join the union or face exclusion.

Meanwhile, Harry Bridges, an activist in the Pacific Coast Division of the International Longshoremen's Association, the stevedores union, led a general strike for union recognition in the Pacific ports on May 9, 1934. While the Bay Area Teamsters leadership had been reluctant to support the strike, local unions of draymen voted sympathy strikes and rank-and-file Teamsters joined in the longshoremen's picket lines and confrontations with police and National Guard troops. After "Bloody Thursday" when two strikers were killed and 67 injured, the Bay Area labor unions, including the big Teamster locals, voted a general strike, which finally forced the employers to recognize and negotiate with the longshoremen's union.

The ILA victory in October 1934 weakened the employers and strengthened the union movement in the West. Labor gained additional strength with passage in July 1935 of the National Labor Relations Act, or Wagner Act, the first Federal law granting workers the right to organize, strike, and bargain collectively. While the Act was an attempt to structure, limit, and control the explosion of labor organizing and strikes, it also reflected an important pro-labor shift in national politics. Within this new favorable climate, the Teamsters continued to roll down the West coast.

With Beck's backing in January 1935, Mike Casey, a Teamster leader in the Golden State, called a meeting of all California Teamsters and formed the Highway Drivers Council (HDC) of California. The union signed up hundreds of new members and began to enforce union jurisdiction, beating scab drivers and destroying trucks. Many new members were recruited and distributed among locals on the basis of the driver's domicile, with San Francisco Local 85 and Oakland Local 70 growing rapidly. As the southern march continued, the union won an important strike in 1935 by Local 431 in Fresno. With Beck's Teamsters in control of Seattle, San Francisco, Oakland, and Fresno, the union was able to force many trucking industry employers to accept the union and its contract or be denied access to those cities.

In May 1937, Beck took over the leadership of the Highway Drivers Council, which had by then expanded to include Denver, Phoenix, and Salt Lake City, and he began to plot the organization of Los Angeles, long an anti-union stronghold. The Merchants and Manufacturers Association (M&M) had for twenty years kept most unions out of the city. In 1932, the Teamsters had only 800 members in the huge city, though after passage of the NIRA membership had grown to 2,000 by 1936, most in Los Angeles Local 208 and Los Angeles Harbor Local 692. Beck's target was Pacific Freight Lines (PFL), which dominated the Motor Truck Association of California (MTA). When PFL refused to accede to the union's demands, Beck struck the company, leading to confrontations between thousands of Teamsters and hundreds of police officers, both sides using clubs, knives, and guns in what was one of the bloodiest strikes in the union's history.

The strike in Los Angeles was accompanied by a boycott of PFL's "hot cargo" and diversions and tie-ups of its freight in terminals in California, Oregon, and Washington. After nine weeks, the company capitulated on June 2, 1937. On November 2, 1937, the MTA reached agreement with the Teamsters on a master contract bringing all truck drivers in California into the union at once. By the end of 1937, 95 percent of all truck drivers in Los Angeles worked in union shops and 75 percent were actually signed up as members of the union. By 1938, 12,000 drivers were signed up and divided into several trade locals. By 1939 the Southern California Joint Council 42 reached 25,000 members and by 1949 it had 84,000, making it the largest council in the IBT. Workers won shorter hours, a wage increase, and improvements in working conditions. Beck used the union's success to create the Western Conference of Teamsters.

Throughout the 1930s and 1940s, the Teamsters often fought aggressive Congress of Industrial Organizations (CIO) unions, and sometimes other AFL unions, for control of workers in warehouses, bottling plants, factories, and agricultural packing sheds, and often won. By 1941, the Teamsters had organized approximately 450,000 new members, growing from 97,632 members in 1929 to 544,247 in 1941. During this same period, the work week for drivers was reduced—in some cases by half—while wages rose by as much as 25 percent, and conditions and job security improved significantly. By the end of World War II the union had 595,200 members; its domination of the trucking industry in all regions of the country except the South had been consolidated.

A Change in the Political Context

With the beginning of the Cold War, the political climate became more conservative. In this new climate, Congress passed the Taft-Hartley Act in 1947 and the Landrum-Griffin Act in 1959. These laws restricted secondary boycotts, "hot cargo" strikes, and picketing for union recognition, which weakened the Teamsters' ability to affect employers and required the union to find new ways to pressure the bosses. Leadership of the international union passed first from Daniel Tobin, to Dave Beck in 1952, and then to Jimmy Hoffa in 1957. Hoffa, the former student of Farrell Dobbs, was determined to bring all the country's trucking industry workers into the union.

Hoffa founded and headed the Michigan Council of Teamsters during World War II, and expanded organizing into Ohio after the war. He then established the Central States Drivers Council, and moved into the South. While secondary boycotts, "hot cargo" strikes, and some forms of picketing had either been outlawed by the Taft-Hartley Act or by NLRB decisions, the union was still capable of devastating strikes against local and regional employers. Moreover, Hoffa found other ways to break the inter-lines and force recalcitrant employers to recognize the union. One of these was the negotiation of simultaneous contract expiration dates. Another tactic was the use of a clause in the Teamster contract which allowed the union to strike over grievances. In other cases, union members acting informally and sometimes illegally simply tied up the cargo of struck companies. The union's domination of the Midwestern companies allowed it to extend its power into the South in the 1950s by threatening to cut off the access of southern companies to union-organized northern cities.

By 1960 the Central States Drivers Council freight contract had been extended to twenty-five states, thirteen of which were in anti-union Southern states. In 1963, Hoffa announced that the union had achieved 85 percent uniformity in all of its trucking contracts. The next year, he signed the first National Master Freight Agreement, covering 2,000 employers with 500,000 drivers and warehouse workers. By that time the union had approximately 1.5 million members, making it the largest labor union. Of all AFL-CIO unions, only the Teamsters proved capable of successful organizing in the South. While the United Auto Workers (UAW) and other CIO unions are often portrayed as leading the transformation of American labor and creating an American middle class, the Teamsters union played a similar role.

Under Beck and Hoffa, and later under Frank Fitzsimmons, Jackie Presser, and Roy Williams, the Teamsters union turned in the direction of conservatism and corruption, and the concept of strategic strikes, organizing, and bargaining was lost. The deregulation of the trucking industry pushed by Senator Ted Kennedy and President Jimmy Carter destroyed the political economic terrain that had made such strikes, organizing, and bargaining possible, returning the industry in the 1970s and 1980s to conditions that resembled the chaos of the early 1930s and leading subsequently to the growth of monopoly carriers and an increase in non-union owner-operators. Despite a brief stint of union reform under the leadership of President Ron Carey in the 1990s, who led a brilliant national strike against United Parcel Service in 1997, the union's ability to dominate the trucking industry has been lost. Jimmy Hoffa, Jr. has not proven capable of reviving the strategies his father learned from the leader of the great Teamster strikes of the 1930s, Farrell Dobbs.

See also: Strike Lessons from the Last Twenty-Five Years, 81; The Watsonville Cannery Strike, 444; Longshoremen's Strikes, 547; Strikes on the Port of New York, 559.

Bibliography

Dobbs, Farrell. *Teamster Power*. New York: Pathfinder Press, 1973.

———. *Teamster Rebellion*. New York: Pathfinder Press, 1972.

Garnel, Donald. *The Rise of Teamster Power in the West*. Berkeley: University of California Press, 1972.

James, Ralph C. and Estelle D. James. *Hoffa and the Teamsters: A Study of Union Power*. Princeton, NJ: D. Van Nostrand Company, Inc., 1965.

Korth, Philip A. *The Minneapolis Teamster Strike of 1934*. East Lansing: Michigan State University Press, 1995.

La Botz, Dan. *Rank-and-File Rebellion: Teamsters for a Democratic Union*. New York: Verso, 1990.

Leiter, Robert D. *The Teamsters Union: A Study of its Economic Impact*. New York: Bookman Associates, Inc., 1957.

Russell, Thaddeus. *Out of the Jungle: Jimmy Hoffa and the Remaking of the American Working Class*. New York: Alfred A. Knopf, 2001.

Walker, Charles. *American City*. New York: Farrar & Rinehart, Inc., 1937.

Witwer, David. *Corruption and Reform in the Teamster Union*. Urbana: University of Illinois Press, 2003.

Part V, Section 3

Service Industry Strikes

Introduction by Benjamin Day

The service sector is a vast and varied part of the American economy, including such disparate occupations as professional athlete, nurse, waiter, bank teller, professor, musician, gardener, and librarian. Generally speaking, service sector workers came later to unionization than those in manufacturing and infrastructure. Exceptions include musicians, motion picture workers, and restaurant workers, whose unions go back almost a century. Mass numbers of service workers joined unions during the upsurge of working-class militancy in the 1930s and 1940s, particularly office workers and retail workers, such as department store workers, grocery clerks, and janitors. As with other service workers before them, these workers often had to strike to win union recognition; in some cases, they adopted strike tactics from manufacturing unions, most famously the Woolworth sit-ins in 1937. Their unionization reflected in part the fact that their workplaces had become much more like mines, mills, and manufacturing plants: large sites with dozens, and even hundreds, of workers concentrated into semiskilled, routine jobs subject to the discipline of systematic corporate management intent on increasing productivity and profit.

More recently, service sector workers have moved to the forefront of the union movement. The Service Employees International Union is now the largest private sector union in the country, followed by the United Food and Commercial Workers. Their growth reflects the changing employment patterns of the U.S. economy. While the service sector has always constituted a large portion of the U.S. economy, the relative decline of manufacturing in the second half of the twentieth century has magnified its importance in terms of jobs and output. Service work has become ubiquitous today, accounting for over 80 percent of all American jobs and just below 80 percent of the country's gross domestic product. Many service jobs, especially those in the fastest-growing occupations, such as personal care, retail sales, janitorial, and health care, cannot be exported, making it much harder for employers to move elsewhere when workers express a desire for unionization. This is one reason why service sector unionization has stabilized and even grown, while manufacturing union density has declined precipitously. Still, the obstacles to unionization of service workers remain considerable.

The nature of service work alters the content of labor relations in service industries. Control over the workplace often involves the social management of employees, how they express themselves on the job, how they look, what they wear, and, most important, how they interact with customers. Thus, service workers' bodies and their social identities are contested at the workplace. The employers' drive for efficiency often clashes with the customers' desire for service and the workers' desire for a humane encounter. Consequently, service sector strikes can have a very particular character. Whereas the work stoppages of mining, manufacturing, agricultural, and infrastructure workers primarily halt the production or movement of goods, strikes by service sector workers interfere with the provision of services to customers, whether they are hospital patients, drugstore customers, or sports fans. Winning public support, particularly the backing of those consumers directly affected by the work stoppage, becomes paramount. Public involvement can be even more intense when personal care is involved. Nurses, for example, often strike to demand greater staffing levels so they can provide better care for their patients. Legal aid lawyers went on strike several times to demand more resources for their impoverished clients. These strikes, like so many by service sector employees, reflect the dedication of service workers to their jobs and their "customers." Beyond some of the unique workplace challenges faced by service workers, they face distinct industry institutions as well. Professional service workers, such as lawyers, professors, information technology experts, actors, and musicians, face social challenges to their right to organize. Their professional associations often discourage unionization, forcing these workers to reconcile their individual professional identities, built over years through education, training, and effort, with their desire for collective struggle to win economic security and dignity commensurate with their social status.

Meanwhile, lower-status service workers have faced a dramatic recomposition of their work, particularly the spread of contingent work—part-time, temporary, or temp-agency-mediated work—along with the abolition of benefits, an increase in short hours, and high turnover characteristic of contingent labor markets. These labor markets are often carved out for socially segregated populations; young adults, who have seen the sharpest decline in union density and some of the steepest declines in economic well-being, fill many of these gutted service industries. Immigrants, who statistically work as many hours on average as native citizens, are disproportionately represented in contingent work situations in agriculture, construction, and services. Likewise, women, filtered out of good jobs, are selected for service work, particularly for interacting with male customers. As the variety of strikes portrayed in this section illustrate, the particular challenges of these populations shaped their strikes.

The geography of service industries is also of great importance. Unlike manufacturing, some of the largest service industries are distributed according to residential concentration. Few service workers live in "union towns" in which their workplaces dominate the local economy. Retail work has, since the early twentieth century, migrated increasingly to the suburbs with the advent of strip malls and metropolitan beltways. Even traditional "downtown" industries, such as hotels, office work, and entertainment, have recently gone the way of retail, moving increasingly to suburban settings. Downtown workers rarely live near where they work, driven to distant neighborhoods by real estate prices. The challenge of building solidarity between workers and their community is a recurring theme in this section's essays, one remarkably different from the histories of solidarity in mill towns or factory cities.

NEWSBOY STRIKES

Jon Bekken

Newsboys long enjoyed a contradictory image in American popular culture—commonly depicted as either plucky entrepreneurs turning an easy buck or two before or after school or exploited child workers needing to be saved from the corrupting influences of the street. The teenage (or younger) boy peddling newspapers on street corners is now a relic of the distant past, eliminated by changing publishing and residential patterns, competition from radio and television news programs, and a society no longer prepared to accept ragged urchins peddling newspapers (although adult street hawkers are now a common sight in many cities, bolstering circulation in a troubled market and handing out the growing numbers of free dailies to commuters). Children continue to play a vital role in newspaper distribution, accounting for about half of all deliveries, but the need to distribute morning newspapers over ever-larger territories has led many papers to turn to adult carriers who use automobiles for their deliveries.

Despite popular images of little merchants or hapless street urchins, newsboys have engaged in a wide range of formal and informal struggles over their wages and working conditions for more than 200 years. Since newsboys typically sold several competing newspapers, they were often able to push the sales of the paper that gave the best terms. By playing publishers off against each other, they sought better pay, the right to return unsold copies, and an end to coercion from circulation agents who bullied them into taking more papers than they needed or giving preferential treatment to one title. The resulting struggles could take the form of boycotts or strikes, where newsboys refused to handle papers that would not meet their terms, or less formal resistance such as not displaying the offending title. In these struggles, newsboys looked for support from the general public—their customers—and from other newspaper workers, with whom they repeatedly tried to make common cause.

Newsboys have from their origins been a diverse lot, ranging in age from children as young as five or six years old to elderly men, although the average newsboy probably began the work as a young teenager. Although women and girls have worked as "newsboys" for more than a century, outside of newsstands the labor force has always been predominately male. The newsboy force has combined home delivery and street sales since at least the 1830s (with the same person often performing both functions in the nineteenth century) and has always employed a mix of children and adults. Street selling and delivery were largely separate by the end of the nineteenth century, with adult carriers delivering papers to subscribers' homes and working-class youths selling papers on the streets. However, in the 1920s, publishers began recruiting children in large numbers to deliver papers in suburban communities—a practice that quickly expanded to cities.

Apprentices might deliver colonial-era newspapers to local subscribers, while the post office handled much of the subscription list. But as early as 1799, a fired adult carrier who delivered newspapers to rural subscribers by horseback arranged with a publisher from a nearby town to distribute that paper to his route instead. As boys could be hired cheaper than grown men, they were pressed into service where rural routes or great distances did not require adults on horseback. While adults always worked on the margins of the newsboy force, children came to play the dominant role in newspaper distribution by the late 1800s. This quickly drew controversy, as social reformers seized on the newsboy as a symbol of the exploitation of children and campaigned to outlaw or at least severely regulate the practice. These campaigns rarely involved the newsboys themselves, who often saw themselves as exploited but sought to redress the situation by negotiating for better terms.

Publishers largely succeeded in turning back the attack of social reformers. Even if many states did pass laws restricting the employment of very young children, most newsboys (whether adults or children) have been barred from coverage under minimum wage, unemployment, and workers' compensation laws—exclusions that have broadened in recent decades, as legal historian Marc Linder has illustrated. But while publishers' portrayal of newsboys as "little merchants" dominates the courts and legislatures, newsboys suffered steady erosion in their earnings over the past century and lost much of the limited control they once had over their working conditions. As a result, publishers save millions of dollars each year by avoiding minimum wage and social insurance payments—offloading these costs onto some of the most vulnerable workers in our society.

The typical street seller bought papers on a cash basis—either directly from the newspaper office or a regional distribution center or, especially for younger children, from a "corner man" who operated a newsstand—making their living off the difference between the price they paid and the price at which they sold the papers to readers. In larger cities, publishers issued several editions a day, resulting in frequent struggles over whether newsboys would be permitted to return unsold copies for credit. While publishers insisted that the newsboys were independent operators, they routinely fixed the price at which papers could be sold, assigned territories and street corners, and—if they had the power to do so—required newsboys to take more papers than they could readily sell (newsboys called this "eating papers").

The share of newspapers' sales prices going to newsboys has dropped sharply over the past 100 years as a result of constant chiseling at newsboys' margins. Fifty/fifty splits were common in the 1890s, and most newsboys received 40 percent in the early decades of this century. Seattle Newsboys' Union members still got 50 percent, fully returnable, in October 1935, according to journalism historian Roger Simpson. In Chicago in the 1920s, however, unionized newsboys made only 27–30 percent. Newsboys only occasionally received hourly or daily pay rates, usually when publishers were trying to promote sales of a particular edition or develop a new territory. More recently, free dailies have had to pay their hawkers an hourly wage, as there is no cover price from which the hawker can derive his living.

Today, youth carriers receive between 20 percent and 30 percent of the retail price of a newspaper. Some adult carriers get as much as 40 percent, but must provide a vehicle and pay for their own fuel. More typical is California's *Santa Rosa Press Democrat,* which in 1971 paid its adult carriers $2.35 per month per subscriber (29 percent of the subscription rate) and estimated that carriers delivered an average of 225 papers in two hours, which would require folding, wrapping, and delivering 1.8 papers a minute to suburban and rural homes (not counting time spent picking the papers up and getting to the route). While the absolute dollar amount has of course increased in the intervening decades, the carriers' relative position has not, with the result that this workforce is composed almost entirely of marginal workers—immigrants, retired workers, and others who have difficulty securing more desirable employment.

Newsboys worked in an industry that historically has been, and continues to be, relatively highly unionized, at least in its production departments. The perishable nature of news and (until recently) highly competitive newspaper markets often gave unions the upper hand in labor disputes. Newsboys, too, sought to benefit from these conditions to secure the best possible terms from publishers. Where informal negotiations were insufficient, newsboys often struck by refusing to handle newspapers that offered substandard terms. When all publishers offered identical terms, they selected the newspaper they thought most vulnerable and then whipsawed competing papers into line. This tactic was particularly effective in highly competitive markets—as the number of competing publishers declined, newspapers were increasingly able to dictate terms and to turn to the courts for relief if newsboys struck or took other industrial action.

A Legacy of Resistance

Documented newsboy strikes took place in Boston (1901, 1908); Chicago (1912); Cleveland (1934); Des Moines (1922); Detroit (1877); Kansas City, Kansas (1947); Lexington, Kentucky (1899); Minneapolis (1918); Mobile (1942); New York City (1886, 1890, 1893, 1898, 1899, 1908, 1918, 1922, 1941, 1948); Oakland (1928); Portland, Oregon (1914); St. Louis (1945); San Jose, California (2000); and Seattle (1917). In other cities, including in recent decades San Francisco, Pittsburgh, and Wilkes-Barre, newsboys have walked out as part of broader newspaper strikes in which they had less of a direct interest. Certainly a great many other newsboy strikes have taken place of which no record survives, as these workers were often too marginalized to establish permanent organizations or secure coverage from a press with a direct material interest in seeing their efforts fail.

Newsboy strikes typically followed publishers' decisions to unilaterally undermine established working conditions. What is undoubtedly the best-known newsboy strike—the 1899 New York City newsboys strike immortalized in the Disney movie musical *Newsies*—was in many ways typical, seemingly flaring up overnight to sweep the city, if either contemporary or historians' accounts are to be believed. But in reality there was a long tradition of unrest, dating back at least to 1883, when Brooklyn newsboys organized a series of mass meetings to protest the *New York Herald*'s terms and announced that they would strike against the paper if their demands were not met. One such meeting began with a parade of newsboys through the Brooklyn streets to the Music Hall, where luminaries, including labor journalist John Swinton and the local congressman, addressed the crowd, pledging their support.

The Brooklyn newsboys, who delivered New York papers to home subscribers and sold single copies on the streets, noted that the *Herald* was the only major daily to deliver its papers unfolded, and yet offered newsboys less margin than any of its competitors. The *Herald* was offering $^1/_3$ of a cent per 2-cent paper, the *Times* and the *World* both offered ½ cent; the *Star, Sun,* and *Tribune* offered two-thirds to a full cent per copy. Even then, the publishers tried to portray the newsboys as independent merchants, an argument Swinton rejected as the "deviltry of power," according to the *Brooklyn Eagle*:

> The revenue of a newsdealer is not properly profit, but largely in the nature of wages. If this man flung his imperfect sheets into the streets of New York they would not be marketable; but you reduce them to salable shape. . . . I say you can beat the *Herald* if you want to. You will be cut down to a tenth of a cent if you will stand it.

Three years later, newsboys struck against the *Brooklyn Times,* demanding that the publisher extend throughout the city the 50 percent margin it was allowing in the city's Western District in order to encourage newsboys to push the paper more aggressively. The strike lasted three days, with the *Times* practically driven from the streets before a compromise was reached under which the newsboys agreed to resume work at the 40 percent rate and the publisher announced that "as a recognition of the manner in which the adult news dealers stood by them" the margin would be unilaterally increased to 50 percent in a week's time. Finally, in 1890, newsboys struck the *New York Evening World* to protest a new scale, resulting in a number of clashes with scabbing newsboys and several arrests of strikers.

During the Spanish-American War of 1898, Pulitzer's *New York Evening World* and Hearst's *Morning Journal* took advantage of the heightened demand for newspapers to cut newsboys' margin from 50 cents per hundred to 40 cents. There was a short-lived strike in May 1898 in which newsboys continued regular deliveries but refused to handle war extras. In the end newsboys were willing to endure the pay cut as long as extras and war news kept sales high. But as the news grew tamer and incomes fell, they grew increasingly restless. After an altercation in Long Island on July 18, 1899, where newsboys tipped over a delivery wagon, they decided to make a fight to restore the 50-cent price. On July 19, Manhattan newsboys announced they would strike the next day unless the old price was restored. Aggressive picketing shut down distribution points throughout the city. The *New York Times* wrote that "Cries of 'Scab! scab!' followed the few who dared to handle the forbidden papers, and before long few of them were to be found on the streets." The strike spread quickly with devastating impact on the newspapers' advertising and circulation and met with widespread public support. Historian David Nasaw reports that the strike spread throughout New Jersey and New York, and sparked similar actions as far north as Fall River, Massachusetts, and Providence, Rhode Island. It later spread to messenger boys as far away as Boston.

Some 2,000 newsboys packed the New Irving Hall on July 24 for a mass meeting called by the nascent Newsboys' Union, while another 3,000 clustered outside. Representatives of the Newsdealers' Association (newsstand operators) attended to express their support (as did several local politicians), while a union committee reported on the unsuccessful negotiations. One speaker, identified in the *New York Times* as Kid Blink, told the assembled throng: "Just stick together and we'll win. If we did it in '93, we can do it in '99." The 1893 strike is otherwise lost to history. But in 1899, the strikers received widespread public support, bolstered by newsboys' circulars inserted into non-struck papers, parades, and mass meetings.

While the *Times*'s report on the strike was generally sympathetic, it was immediately followed with another entitled, "Violent Scenes During Day"—a report of how hundreds of newsboys had blocked efforts to hire a force of 700 men to break the strike and had forced the struck papers off the street throughout the city. While the newsboys did not win the old price, after two weeks the newspapers did concede the right to return unsold papers—a right that was still in force thirteen years later—and the newsboys resumed selling the struck papers on August 2. The New York City newsboys' union did not survive the strike that gave it birth.

Strikes were hardly confined to New York City and its surroundings. Detroit newsboys briefly struck against the *Evening News* in 1877, demanding that the paper increase their margin from ¾ cent to a full penny per copy sold (half the cover price). Two editions went unsold before a handful of younger newsboys broke ranks; without organization or broader support the strike quickly crumbled. Few newsboy strikes were drawn-out affairs; either the publishers or the newsboys typically came to terms within a few days, leaving scant record of the dispute.

Undone by Rats: The 1908 Boston Newsboys' Strike

The Boston Newsboys' Protective Union was organized in 1901, when newsboys tired of publishers' efforts to force them into ruthless competition with each other. Publishers gave extra discounts to early buyers, encouraging newsboys to skip school to get higher earnings, and they refused to accept returns of unsold papers, forcing newsies to work late into the night to sell their papers or "eat" the unsold copies. The union began by approaching one publisher to ask that unsold papers be returnable at 10 percent of the cover price, which still would have entailed a substantial loss on unsold papers for the newsboys. When the publisher refused the proposal and ridiculed the notion of a newsboys' union, the newsies refused to carry the offending paper. Circulation plummeted, and the publisher quickly agreed to full refunds on unsold papers. The threat of similar action soon brought other publishers into line, and the union moved on to restrict the hours of sale, standardize discount terms, and establish a variety of educational and social activities, including an endowed scholarship for union members wishing to enroll at Harvard University.

Membership in the Newsboys' Protective Union was originally restricted to newsboys fourteen years of age or older, but during the course of the 1908 strike the union amended its constitution to allow any licensed newsboy to join, adding many younger newsies. Boston's newsboys took their union seriously, affiliating to the American Federation of Labor (AFL) as a federal labor union and actively participating in the AFL's local and state federations as well as sending delegates to national AFL conventions. But while the union was one of relatively few to survive the initial dispute that inspired its organization, it was not nearly as long-lived as newsboys unions in Chicago, Philadelphia, or Seattle.

Like their brethren in other cities, Boston newsboys worked long hours for meager wages under conditions few adults (with their greater employment possibilities) would have tolerated. After several years of efforts by the union and social welfare organizations, in 1910—shortly after their union was broken in a bitter fight against the *Boston American*—Boston newsboys averaged only about 25 cents a day for five hours' work. Boston newsboys launched their ill-fated campaign against the *American* on January 8, 1908, after the paper refused repeated requests to negotiate its decision to cut newsboys' margins from 50 percent (50 cents for 100 of the penny papers) to 40 percent and cease accepting returns. At a mass meeting, hundreds of newsboys decided on a selective strike—refusing to sell the *American* while continuing to sell other papers, and appealing to the Boston Central Labor Union for support. While not formally endorsing the boycott (which would have aggravated tensions with the Boston Typographical Union and other unions that had contracts with the *American*), the Central Labor Union instructed union members to buy papers only from union newsboys. City officials, meanwhile, weighed in against the newsboys by prohibiting newspaper sales on the Boston Common as a "public nuisance."

In the pages of the *Boston American,* the strike was originally visible only in the Allied Printing Trades Council labels that began heading nearly every column in the paper, and in a cryptic January 16, page-one boxed notice offering home delivery of the paper to those unable to find it on the streets. Virtually all newsboys—even those not belonging to the union—refused to carry the *American* during the dispute, and the paper was available only from salaried agents hired to keep it on the streets. The *American* first openly acknowledged the dispute in its January 22, 1908, issue—two weeks into the strike. The paper simultaneously cut back its use of the union label, but prominently incorporated it into the nameplate (the label originally appeared only atop the paper's daily labor column). Instead, the editors featured news of the handful of labor figures backing its fight against the newsboys—most notably the Boston Typographical Union, which feared that reduced sales would cost them jobs—and reprinted favorable editorials from the *Brockton Enterprise, Northampton Herald,* and other papers.

Boston's newsboys received consistent support from the local labor movement throughout the dispute, ranging from formal endorsements and legal assistance, to labor officials' speaking at newsboy meetings and rallies, to an incident where Hebrew Bakers Union Local 45 refused a $100-a-week donation from the *American* to finance its free bread distribution program to the poor. Competing newspapers offered sympathetic coverage, though they did not make an issue of the *American*'s hiring of thugs to intimidate union newsboys, even when one was arrested in the Hearst offices, where he had fled after assaulting union member Alexander Cohen.

More damaging to the strike in the long run was the building enmity between the newsboys and the printing trades' unions—enmity that spilled over into a heated Central Labor Union meeting where the typographers were called "rats" and "scabs" in debate. The Boston Typographical Union (BTU), in particular, vigorously attacked the newsboys' union, insisting that the newsboys were merchants, not workers, and not entitled to labor support. The newsboys were indignant, condemning the Typographical Union's actions in a resolution insisting that the BTU had frequently called on them for support in its disputes over the years and had always received it. While the newsies did not seek overt support from the union in their dispute, they could ill afford the typographers' active opposition.

Despite solid support for the newsboys in the Boston Central Labor Union (CLU), the typographers were ultimately able to call upon the American Federation of Labor's executive council to step in, ordering a halt to CLU support for the boycott and suggesting that the Newsboys' Protective Union's actions were unauthorized. The *American* hailed the AFL action on its front page; other papers carried the news in their labor columns—subsumed within reports of the union's determination to continue its campaign. The CLU reasserted its support to the newsies, but the AFL ruling hindered efforts to build active support and the strike appears to have gradually petered out.

While the newsboys were defeated in 1908, sporadic efforts at unionization continued at least into the 1930s. In 1920, 175 newsgirls employed by the Hotel and Railroad News Company organized a union to protest low pay and split shifts, which had some working as many as sixteen hours a day. More typically, these newsgirls—employed in the subways and on elevated platforms—worked three hours in the morning and six hours at night one day, and seven hours without relief the next. Wages (they were on straight pay) ranged from $12.00 to

$18.00 a week. The 1920 campaign was the second at the company, which busted it and an earlier 1913 effort by firing union activists and raising wages. In the 1930s, the *American* hired its own newsboy force at $3.00 a week when newsboys began organizing against another cut in their margins, protecting themselves against a repeat of the 1908 strike.

Fighting the Chicago Newspaper Trust

Although Chicago was in many ways a fiercely competitive newspaper market, the city's publishers formed a tight-knit association to set the terms under which newsboys labored—disciplining any publisher tempted to offer better terms—as part of an array of agreements designed to control the costs of competition. When newsboys sought to pressure a publisher to offer better terms by refusing to handle its papers, the Daily Newspaper Publishers Association took a firm stand, notifying them via letter that "you must sell *all* the newspapers in this association . . . or you cannot sell *any* of them." The publishers took advantage of their close cooperation to whittle away at newsboys' earnings, while newsboys seized upon interludes of heightened competition to try to restore some of what they had lost. In 1896, Chicago newsboys earned 50 cents per 100 on penny papers (75 cents per 100 on 2-cent papers), but in 1898 the evening papers agreed to a common margin of 40 percent, prohibited returns or exchanges for later editions, and banned rebates, prizes, or bonuses paid out to newsboys in an attempt to encourage preferential treatment. Such agreements often broke down during periods of intense circulation competition, but were reinstated once publishers tired of spending money countering each other's promotional campaigns.

Chicago newsboys did not passively accept their lot. In 1902, they organized the Chicago Newsboys' Protective Association as a mutual aid association to lobby for better conditions for the trade and assist newsboys prevented from working by sickness or other causes. When the Association proved inadequate to meet their needs, the newsboys organized a union in 1909. The AFL-affiliated Newsboys' Protective Union played a key role in the 1912 newspaper strike, in which newsboys joined a citywide strike by pressmen and stereotypers, refusing to carry the city's leading dailies but continuing to sell newspapers (such as the socialist daily and Scripps's advertising-free *Day Book*) produced under union conditions. The newsboys struck in solidarity with other newspaper workers, but also in hopes of resolving long-standing grievances of their own. When Hearst's *Chicago American* entered the market in 1900, newsboys seized upon the competitive situation to reclaim the right to return unsold papers for credit, set their own hours and working conditions, and restore margins eroded by decades of publisher collusion. But when Hearst's papers became entrenched themselves, the Hearst organization reached an accommodation with other publishers, and newsboys soon found themselves even worse off than they had been before Hearst's entry. While publishers slashed newsboys' margins and abolished the right to return unsold papers, circulation agents forced newsboys to work sixteen-hour days and buy more papers than they could hope to sell, under threat of having their papers cut off.

Hundreds of newsboys were arrested during the strike. Circulation men, many with criminal records, were sworn in as special deputies, harassing, beating, and in some cases killing newsboys and other strike supporters with impunity. Even the publishers, while refusing to negotiate with the newsboys' union, privately agreed that the newsboys had legitimate grievances. When local Hearst executives proved intransigent, Newspaper Publishers Association president Victor Lawson wrote William Randolph Hearst asking him to intercede:

> The newsboys struck in sympathy with the drivers—and, in a way, the drivers struck in sympathy with the newsboys. They both have a common grievance. It is referred to in the inclosed (*sic*) circular distributed by the newsboys, and is technically known as being compelled to "eat papers." . . . I cannot conceive that there can be any two opinions about the right or wrong of this method. I believe you will agree with me that it is wholly indefensible. . . . Resenting this imposition, both the drivers and the newsboys were easy material for the striking pressmen to work on when they went out. I trust you will recognize the importance of co-operating in eliminating

> this abuse in the Chicago newspaper field. . . . Should we . . . fail to cure this evil at this time, I am sure that we shall be leaving seed for a new crop of strike trouble on the part of drivers and newsboys in the future.

Despite this, Lawson and the other publishers refused to discuss newsboys' grievances until they abandoned the strike, instead making supplemental payments to scab newsboys to break the strike. Several weeks into the strike, the *Daily News* was running less than half its presses and allowing nonunion newsboys unlimited returns, in a desperate attempt to keep the newspapers on the streets. Two months after the strike began, newsboys began drifting back to the struck newspapers (though many refused to handle Hearst's *American*, where the strike had begun). Still, the union did not abandon the strike for several more weeks, long after the publishers pledged an end to eating papers. Hearst executives proved incorrigible. In September 1912, Hearst circulation men opened fire against a newsboy who had returned to work but refused to carry the *American* and Hearst's morning *Examiner.* Fortunately, all five bullets were wide of the mark. However, ten weeks later the *American* was making newsboys eat papers, and its circulation agents were destroying copies of the *Journal* and the *Daily News.*

While the union's power declined sharply in the wake of that defeat, the union survived at least through 1931—though it had difficulty maintaining dues payments and rarely represented more than a few hundred of the thousands of newsboys working in metropolitan Chicago. Although the newsboys paid a heavy price during the strike, in many ways they emerged from it stronger than before. Publishers did not formally concede any of the newsboys' demands, but they did begin meeting with representatives of the newsboys' union. While no publisher agreed in principle to allow returns of unsold papers, newsboys were often able to insist upon returns in exchange for increasing their order or giving a paper better display. While drivers and circulation men continued to try to force newsboys to eat papers, and beat them when they objected, other publishers interceded on their behalf in hopes of averting the kind of industrial strife that had cost them so dearly.

The publishers refused formal negotiations with the newsboys, but they did meet with union committees. In 1919, for example, publishers offered a formal grievance procedure (albeit one wholly under their control), agreed to replace papers damaged in handling, and promised according to a letter from the secretary of the local publishers association that "no driver shall require any newsboy to purchase more newspapers at any time than can be sold at his stand by reasonable effort." But publishers' and newsboys' views as to what constituted oversupply differed sharply. In 1925, when the *Daily News* circulation department found that one newsboy usually sold his entire stock of papers, they insisted on increasing his order. One election night they left 100 copies of election extras, and refused to credit him for returns of twenty-five unsold copies. When he refused to pay for the papers he had neither ordered nor been able to sell, the *Daily News* was firm—either he paid for all papers delivered, whether or not he ordered them, or he would be cut off. The *News* circulation department was contemptuous of the newsboy's claim that he was being forced to eat papers, claiming that on average the newsboy had been able to sell 97 percent of the papers delivered (this, of course, ignores the loss on the unsold papers and the additional hours needed on the job to hold the number of "eaten" papers below disastrous levels).

In 1923, when *Daily News* business manager (soon to become publisher) Walter Strong met with a committee from the Newsboys' Union, which included a local AFL organizer, he made it clear that they did not recognize the union and viewed the newsboys as independent merchants. Strong told them, according to a letter he later wrote to Victor Lawson, it was a mistake to try to earn a living as a newsboy: "When a boy grew to the point where his financial needs were greater than the possibility of earning the amount at the corner he should get out of the business and give it to a younger man."

"Will You Help the Newspapers Starve the Newsboys?"

Newsboys sometimes were able to turn reformers' efforts to their advantage. The Portland (Oregon)

Newsboys' Association had its own clubhouse, which had been donated by a local philanthropist as part of social reformers' work with newsboys. But when the reformers proposed to merge the "poorly supervised" clubhouse with a nearby facility, the newsboys refused. And when circulation departments forced newsboys to take more papers than they could sell, in August 1914, the newsboys met among themselves to develop a solution. As newsboy Manly Labby later recalled, according to historian Steve Lowenstein, they decided to take on the Portland newspapers one at a time:

> We took a strike vote and every one of us agreed that we were not going to let a newspaper out of the (*Oregonian*) building, whether it was by mail—many of the papers were mailed to subscribers—whether by truck or by street circulation. We wouldn't let the trucks back up; the trucks brought the papers out to various areas away from downtown, where the circulators distributed them to the route boys. When newspapers came out of the basement in bundles, we immediately shredded them to pieces. . . .
>
> The strike lasted for two days. No papers were going into circulation and people were clamoring for the news. . . . Finally the employers at the four papers agreed to meet with us. It was decided that the circulators would take back any newspapers that were unsold by 6 P.M., and would give us back the money we had paid for those papers. We had won our case.

Minneapolis newsboys struck twice in 1918, after local dailies cut their margin on papers from 50 percent to 30 percent (and raised the cover price from 1 to 2 cents, so that newsboys paid $1.40 for 100 copies instead of the 50 cents they had been paying). The *Tribune* was the first to make the change, and, in response, 300 newsboys elected a committee and declared that they would refuse to handle the paper unless it returned to the original terms. A compromise was soon struck (37.5 percent) pending the publisher's return from abroad for further negotiations. After six months, the newsboys struck the *Tribune, Journal,* and *Daily News,* demanding a return to the full 50 percent and the right to return unsold papers. Publishers refused to meet the Newsboys' Union despite a request from the Typographical Union, and so hundreds of newsboys launched a strike with a march behind a banner asking readers, "Will You Help the Newspapers Starve the Newsboys?" After a few days of sharply reduced sales, local advertisers prevailed upon the publishers to compromise at a 45 percent margin (nonreturnable) for evening papers and establish a grievance procedure. Far from assisting the newsboys in their effort to improve conditions, social reformers seized upon the dispute as proof that "the effects of street life upon growing boys are such as imperil their development into future good citizens."

In Search of Solidarity

While newsboys' unions generally sought affiliation with the American Federation of Labor in hopes that solidarity from other newspaper unions and the broader labor movement would help them win their demands, such support was not always forthcoming. Newsboys occupied an ambiguous position in relation to the publishers, and many in the labor movement shared the publishers' contention that they were more akin to small merchants than to workers.

Thus, when AFL Federal Labor Union No. 22371 called a strike against eight New York City newspapers in 1941 (the *Brooklyn Eagle* and *PM* were exempted from the strike because they had an agreement with the union; the *Post* settled soon afterward), the American Newspaper Publishers Association appealed to AFL vice president (and Teamsters president) Daniel Tobin to ensure that no solidarity would be forthcoming from other newspaper unions. Tobin replied, according to AFL records, that he "owe[d] nothing to the news publishers of New York, who have maintained an independent union of drivers," but nonetheless requested an investigation. Typographical Union officials agreed that the news vendors were merchants and suggested that the union was a cloak for racketeering. The local had been organized a year previously and represented operators of small newsstands. After the local insisted on continuing its selective strike, the AFL's representative wrote AFL secretary-treasurer George Meany: "We would recommend the cancellation of this charter, excepting it would make a hero out of this present president, and time will eliminate the Union entirely. Our recommendation is that no more per capita tax be accepted." Although the Newspaper Guild of New York and the CIO Greater New York Industrial Union Council stood by the AFL news dealers, officials of the AFL Allied Printing Trades Council (who held a much narrower sense of who was entitled to union protection and traditionally sought labor–management cooperation) denounced them in the press.

Many of the union's demands had a familiar sound: full credit on returns of unsold papers, the right to determine how many papers the dealers would take, 40 cents on the dollar margin, elimination of delivery charges (which were running 3–5 percent), an end to coercion by circulation departments, and interest on news dealers' bonds. Some 1,700 news dealers joined the strike, which began as a selective strike against the *World Telegram* on October 11, 1941, and quickly spread as other papers refused to make deliveries to dealers who joined the strike. The strike was suspended from October 22 through November 19, when Mayor La Guardia intervened, but resumed when publishers refused to modify their pay scales. Publishers then secured an injunction against the strike under state antitrust laws after the judge hearing the case ruled that the news dealers were not employees and the newsies were forced to capitulate, though publishers did announce several concessions.

Across the continent, the San Francisco News Vendors Union was more successful. First organized in 1921, the union lasted only a few days when small corner men undercut its strike against pay cuts. However, the union reorganized in 1937, won union recognition, and negotiated a series of contracts limiting hours, reestablishing 40 percent margins and return privileges, requiring publishers to assemble papers before delivering them to be sold, guaranteeing a minimum wage, and providing for arbitration of grievances. The contract did specify that the newsboys were not employees, a provision the union unsuccessfully fought the next year in an effort to secure their rights to Social Security, workmen's compensation, and other benefits. San Francisco publishers then went to Congress to secure a legislative victory, writing the newsboys' independent contractor status into federal law. No newsboys were heard from before their legal rights were stripped away, although the publishers falsely testified that they had always considered themselves "independent businessmen." Decades later, San Francisco's surviving newsboys still resented that legislation.

San Francisco newsboys were still under contract in the mid-1990s as Vendors Local 468, although the handful of remaining (and aging) members worked solely in newsstands. As a member of the Conference of Newspaper Unions, the newsies participated in a strike against the two surviving dailies in 1994 and lamented the decline of their trade: "They would like to get rid of us, because you don't have to pay a machine any wages," said one striker, Bill Ledger, in an oral history.

In the 1940s, the International Printing Pressmen and Assistants Union (IPPAU) attempted to organize newsboys across the country and vigorously protested the invasion of its jurisdiction when other AFL unions—notably the International Alliance of Bill Posters, Billers, and Distributors—sought to organize newsboys under their own auspices. IPPAU-affiliated newsboy unions waged several strikes, often with the support of union pressmen. In Kansas City, pressmen honored a newsboy picket line for sixteen days in 1947 after the *Kansas City Star* refused to recognize their union. The strike ended when the *Star* granted a pay increase to the pressmen and agreed to "study" whether the newsboys were employees or independent contractors. The National Labor Relations Board (NLRB) ultimately ruled they were independent contractors under the Taft-Hartley Act's terms, reversing an earlier string of rulings in which newsboys had generally been held to be employees. In St. Louis, pressmen honored a picket line after local newspapers refused to bargain with their NLRB-certified newsboy union. The publishers insisted the newsboys were merchants, and pointed to the fact that they had bought their routes, sometimes for thousands of dollars. These disputes demonstrated both the power and the limitations of Pressmen affiliation. When newsboys and printers acted together, they could shut down any paper—but the union tended to grant strike authorization only when the pressmen had strong interests at stake.

The labor movement that once welcomed newsboy unions, at least on the local level, was reluctant to challenge a series of NLRB rulings denying collective bargaining rights to newsboys. A 1949 New York City strike ended with an NLRB ruling that the vendors were independent contractors legally barred from collective bargaining. During the dispute, several AFL printing trades unions intervened with the NLRB on behalf of the publishers. While a few newsboy unions continued for decades, most collapsed by the mid-1950s. For example, Philadelphia Newscarriers Union Local 504 survived from 1937 to 1952 despite losing union recognition after its second contract expired in 1945. But it was unable to persuade the parent pressmen's union to take industrial action and eventually faded away.

Newsboys have continued to play key roles in supporting other unions' strikes. In 1978, they crippled the Wilkes-Barre (Pennsylvania) *Times-Leader* by distributing the union-published strike daily rather than carry the struck newspaper. The newsboys stuck with the production unions and distributed their *Citizens' Voice* even after management offered a pay raise and threatened to fire any carrier who did not return. Newsboys have played similar roles in some other recent newspaper strikes, and have also been deployed as rhetorical icons by unionized delivery managers seeking to preserve their jobs (and the jobs of the youth carriers they service) against management reorganization schemes that rely on car-driving adult carriers who require less supervision, fewer distribution points, and perhaps even less pay.

More recently, some newsboys have launched new organizing efforts as their conditions continue to deteriorate. Canadian news carriers (mostly adults) unionized in a number of cities in the 1990s, although the effort largely collapsed with the defeat of a bitter three-week strike in Toronto in April 2001. In October 2000, 600 Vietnamese immigrants—a majority of the 1,100 carriers who delivered the paper to subscribers each morning—struck the *San Jose Mercury News,* winning a pay hike to compensate for higher gas prices and an end to the requirement that they accept responsibility for collecting bills from nonpaying customers. Workers were also protesting long waits for newspapers to be delivered to distribution centers and being required to purchase supplies to assemble the paper. The year before, Cleveland carriers launched an organizing campaign to fight a direct-payment plan that they feared would cut into the tips they rely upon for their profits. Adult carriers in Baltimore and Newark, New Jersey, also had union representation in the 1960s and 1970s. Even youth carriers sometimes organize, as in the unsuccessful six-year struggle (1987–93) by the Rhode Island Carrier Association to negotiate better compensation and work conditions with the Providence Journal Company.

Conclusion

American popular culture has long embraced the myth of the plucky newsboy, pulling himself out of dire poverty by dint of his individual efforts. But newsboys themselves knew better and repeatedly tried to organize to wrest better conditions from the publishers through collective action. These efforts were undermined by the newsboys' uncertain legal status as minors, by their marginalization as casual laborers explicitly excluded from many of the protections other workers take for granted, and by their inability to gain effective support for their struggles. As a result, newsboys continue to earn less than minimum wage and are forced to absorb the risks of their employment themselves, saving publishers tens of millions of dollars a year. Rather than look to the business acumen of publishers and editors in building the great newspaper empires of the modern age, we might do better to turn our attention to the newsboys whose underpaid labor brought those newspapers to the public and provided publishers with the profits that fueled their enterprises.

See also: The News Media and Strikes, 44.

Bibliography

Bekken, Jon. "Crumbs from the Publishers' Golden Tables: The Plight of the Chicago Newsboy." *Media History* 6, no. 1 (June 2000): 45–47.

———. "'The Most Vindictive and Most Vengeful Power': Labor Confronts the Chicago Newspaper Trust." *Journalism History* 18 (1992): 11–17.

———. "Newsboys: The Exploitation of 'Little Merchants' by the Newspaper Industry." In *Newsworkers: Towards A History of the Rank and File,* ed. Bonnie Brennen and Hanno Hardt. Minneapolis: University of Minnesota, 1995.

———. "Undone by Rats: The Boston Newsboys Strike of 1908." Paper presented at the Northeastern Regional Journalism Historians' Conference, New York, March 1998.

Linder, Marc. "What's Black and White and Red All Over? The Blood Tax on Newspapers—or, How Publishers Exclude Newscarriers from Workers' Compensation." *Loyola Poverty Law Journal* 3 (1997): 57–111.

Lowenstein, Steve. *The Jews of Oregon, 1850–1950.* Portland: Jewish Historical Society of Oregon, 1987.

Nasaw, David. *Children of the City: At Work and At Play.* Garden City, NY: Anchor Press, 1985.

———. "Dirty-Faced Davids and The Twin Goliaths." *American Heritage* 36, no. 3 (1985): 42–47.

Simpson, Roger. "Seattle Newsboys: How Hustler Democracy Lost to the Power of Property." *Journalism History* 18 (1992): 18–25.

RETAIL WORKERS' STRIKES

Daniel J. Opler

Perhaps the most remarkable thing about the history of retail workers' strikes in America is the remarkably small amount of research done on these events. No recent studies have addressed retail workers' strikes outside of the Congress of Industrial Organizations (CIO) era (1935–55), and only a handful of works (all but one of them focusing on New York City) discuss retail workers' strikes even during the CIO era. Because of this scarcity of secondary work on this subject, any comments on the overall history of retail workers' strikes in America are necessarily preliminary. However, if the details of individual strikes, as well as the larger picture of this history, still need to be examined further, enough secondary work has been done to provide a very general picture of what such a history might look like.

From the beginning of the history of retail workers' strikes in America until the end of the CIO era, retail workers struck for recognition and to win better working conditions, hours, and pay. Before the 1910s, there were few recorded retail workers' strikes in America. As other industries erupted in strikes around World War I, retail workers followed suit, and there was a series of major retail workers' strikes between 1913 and 1919. While many of these strikes took place in department stores, it was in the grocery industry where retail workers' unions were most powerful. Not until the Great Depression, however, did retail workers' strikes lead to the formation of powerful retail workers' unions, as the strikes became increasingly dramatic and militant. Throughout the era of the CIO, there was a steady stream of strikes by retail workers.

These strikes for better conditions came to an end in the late 1940s and early 1950s. In the early years of the Cold War, the struggles between radicals and liberals for control of the CIO's retail workers' union, the Retail Wholesale and Department Store Union (RWDSU), became more and more heated. The RWDSU collapsed as a result; after 1955, strikes by retail workers again became relatively rare events in American working-class life. When retail workers' strikes did take place in the decades after the 1940s, they were most often about trying to preserve the victories won during the CIO era.

Early Years

Retailing in the United States at the beginning of the twentieth century was a very different practice from today's. In most retailing establishments, customers had no direct access to goods. Goods were stored behind counters so that customers could access them only with the assistance of store employees. In this way, every customer received workers' full attention, helping store managers create an atmosphere of luxury and service in many stores, even in those establishments that did not cater primarily to the wealthy. The practice was also extremely labor intensive and required a highly skilled retail labor force, workers who not only knew the stock the store possessed on hand but also could actively assist customers in their shopping. In upscale department stores, managers compounded this service-oriented method of retailing by offering customers luxuries from parades to petting zoos, telephones, free gift wrapping, and a whole host of other services.

There were relatively few exceptions to the practice of indirect access to goods within retail establishments in the early twentieth century. Supermarkets were by far the most important exceptions; even before World War II, many grocery chain stores offered customers the chance to enter the store, make their selections, and carry their merchandise to the cash register. A few clothing stores used similar practices, but these stores were notoriously cheap, and shopping in them was a mark of poverty that many customers rejected.

The workers within these stores were as diverse as the stores themselves. While little work has yet been done examining grocery store workers, at other low-end retail stores in the early twentieth century, workers and customers alike tended to be the children of new immigrants. More upscale department and clothing stores had more diverse workforces, where children of immigrants worked alongside internal migrants who moved from the countryside to cities. This diversity along the lines of nativity was compounded by gender, ethnic, and racial diversity. Women and men alike worked in the stores in large numbers, although men were generally dominant in the better-paying jobs in furniture and toy departments, with relatively large commissions and salaries, while women worked in most of the lower-paying departments. In addition, white people of all ethnicities worked in department stores, often segregated by departments. Finally, African-American men and women likewise worked in the stores, although, especially before World War II, their job choices were extremely limited; African-American store workers were strictly relegated to cleaning and operating the passenger elevators, the lowest-paying jobs available in the stores.

There were relatively few strikes in retail establishments before the CIO era. Although very little research has been done on the early years of retail workers and their unions, at least two factors might explain the scarcity of retail workers' strikes. First, retail workers were white-collar workers, somewhat removed from the mainstream of the American labor movement. These workers, who often carefully regulated their appearance in order to impress customers and make sales, may well have viewed themselves as somewhat separate from the blue-collar workers who most frequently conducted strikes.

Second, unionization in the retail industry may have helped to minimize the number of strikes. The only major union to organize retail workers before the 1930s was the Retail Clerks International Protection Association (RCIPA), an affiliate of the American Federation of Labor. Founded in 1890, the RCIPA in its early years represented the worst aspects of the AFL. RCIPA organizers received bonuses for every union local that was formed. Because of this practice, RCIPA organizers frequently granted charters to company unions. These chartered company unions, controlled as they were by management, were unlikely to lead strikes.

The first reference to a retail workers' strike in the United States took place long before the RCIPA's founding. In 1835, salesmen and clerks in Philadelphia announced a meeting to plan a strike for the ten-hour workday. Only a few days later, employers in Philadelphia granted retail workers the ten-hour day, and there is no evidence that a strike took place. After this single mention of a strike, there is no evidence of American retail workers' strikes for the remainder of the nineteenth century.

Instead of workers' strikes, in the nineteenth and very early twentieth centuries it was more often customers' actions that dominated the labor movement in the retail industry. It was customers who worked to ensure that stores closed earlier, and, occasionally, it was even customers who were the strongest supporters of unionization. In New York, for instance, in 1913, relatively wealthy women customers joined with suffrage and labor activists for a rally outside Gimbels department store, calling on workers there to join the RCIPA. At least some department store workers apparently joined, but the union did not last, perhaps because of the high employee turnover that has almost always been a factor in American department stores.

That same year was the year of the first major retail workers' strike in America. Like many other retail workers' strikes, the department store workers' strike of 1913, which took place in Buffalo, New York, began in the aftermath of other workers' job actions. In April 1913, streetcar workers in Buffalo staged a six-day strike, demanding union recognition and wage increases. Employers responded by importing strikebreakers and violence ensued. Other workers discussed various means of aiding the streetcar workers, even raising briefly the possibility of a general strike. With the possibility of a general strike on the table, streetcar owners rushed to make a settlement, but the end of that one strike did not bring industrial peace in Buffalo. In May, telephone repairmen, switchboard operators, delivery company employees, and 4,000 department store workers went on strike. As with the streetcar workers, support for the department store workers was quickly forthcoming. The Buffalo United Trades and Labor Council, the organization that had called for a general strike, quickly moved to take leadership of the department store workers' strike. Delivery workers in Buffalo went out on a simultaneous strike against the stores, and as a result the city's retail industry was effectively shut down.

The strike was a violent one. On May 1, the strikers staged a parade on Main Street (presumably in honor of May Day), and mounted police charged the parade. Throughout the ensuing weeks, anyone who crossed the picket line and entered the stores was subject to mob violence. On May 16, store managers settled, offering workers a one-year open-shop contract, as well as a $12.00 weekly minimum wage for men and a $6.00 weekly minimum wage for women.

The late 1910s saw two other major strikes of retail workers. In 1917, the RCIPA demanded that employers at several stores in Memphis, Tennessee, begin paying women workers the same $6.00 weekly minimum wage that the Buffalo workers had won. The union began strike preparations, and Memphis store owners took preemptive action, closing their stores for a few days before customer complaints forced them to reopen. The union postponed the strike in favor of a boycott of the stores, and management responded by firing all union members. With nothing left to lose, the union declared a strike against the stores, and eventually won the $6.00 weekly minimum wage, although store management pointed out that relatively few workers had received less than $6.00 a week even before the strike.

The next major retail strike of the World War I era was less successful. In February 1918, RCIPA workers in St. Louis, Missouri, went on strike against several different department stores simultaneously, demanding wage hikes and union recognition. At first, the strike was extremely impressive, with 5,000 workers walking the picket lines in the first days of the strike. The St. Louis Central Trades and Labor Council and the local chapter of the Women's Trade Union League both moved to support the strike, but neither was able to force store managers to back down. In subsequent days, the number of picketers dwindled, and the strikers fell back on their most powerful weapon, their allies. In the most dramatic moment of the strike, construction workers issued a formal statement that they would go on strike in support of the retail workers' demands. Store managers, however, called the bluff, and the construction workers quickly backed down. The union settled the strike; store managers promised only that they would hire back most (but not all) of the strikers.

If the RCIPA found a few victories in organizing workers in department stores, organizers met with far more success in organizing unions of grocery clerks. There are several possible reasons for the relative strength of workers in this sector of the retail industry. Unlike department stores, which catered primarily to wealthy customers, many grocery stores catered to working people, making it easier for grocery store workers to garner strike support. At least on some occasions, grocery store workers first announced their plans to strike at tenants' meetings in working-class neighborhoods rather than at official union meetings. Additionally, grocery store clerks were almost exclusively men, and because of this they may have had an easier time getting support from the union. Unfortunately, no published history of grocery store workers' unions exists, and the records on grocery workers' strikes are even poorer than the records of strikes in department stores. There are, however, a few indications of the greater militancy of grocery store workers. In 1916, workers in New York went on strike against several different grocery store chains, including A&P stores, demanding and winning union recognition as well as a weekly minimum wage of $15.00. New York's grocery store workers became even more ambitious in the strike-ridden year of 1919, going on strike (this time apparently unsuccessfully) demanding a nine-hour day and a $30.00 weekly minimum wage.

The 1920s saw fewer retail workers' strikes than the previous decade, but there were still a number of important strikes in grocery stores, particularly in New York, due to the success of the unionization campaigns of the previous decade. Unlike the managers of chain stores, the independent store managers in New York had no central organization and no real means to coordinate their efforts to combat the strikers. Despite these employers' weakness, they paid lower wages and demanded longer hours from their employees than did the chain stores. The union demanded that these employers begin offering shorter hours and wage hikes that would make pay rates comparable to workers in chain stores, and when independent store managers failed to comply, in 1926 the union staged a simultaneous strike against hundreds of independent grocery store owners. Unfortunately, records from the 1926 grocery store workers' strike are so poor that there is no clear indication of how the strike ended.

Whatever the outcome of the 1926 strike, by the end of that decade, what strength the RCIPA had was in the grocery stores. The largest locals in the RCIPA, such as New York City's grocery workers' Local 338, were grocery workers' locals, while almost no lasting unions existed outside the grocery stores. The CIO era would see the pattern of unionization in retailing become far more complicated and a comparative explosion of retail workers' strikes.

The CIO Era, 1934-1955

At no time in American history were retail strikes more dramatic or more important than during the CIO era of the 1930s to 1950s. Many of these strikes took place either at the same time as or in the immediate aftermath of strikes by workers outside the retail industry. In 1934–35, for instance, when strikes took place throughout the country following the passage of the National Industrial Recovery Act, there were several interesting retail workers' strikes. Most of these strikes were unsuccessful.

The RCIPA led a brief but important strike against all the A&P stores in Cleveland in October 1934, picketing the warehouses to prevent deliveries and effectively shutting the stores. One of the most important aspects of the A&P strike was the response from store managers. When the strike did not immediately collapse, managers closed all the A&P stores in Cleveland. It was a chilling and important demonstration of the dangers of organizing unions against national chain stores: owners of these businesses could afford to close down individual branches, leaving the strikers with the unwelcome choice of either picketing empty buildings or simply surrendering. The Cleveland strikers immediately withdrew the picket lines and submitted their demands to arbitration, and the stores reopened.

The Boston store strike in Milwaukee, Wisconsin, serves as another example of the sorts of failures the RCIPA encountered in the early and mid-1930s. The Boston strike may well have been the most carefully planned strike of all the retail workers' strikes in 1934–35. The strikers coordinated their efforts with the unionized maintenance and truck drivers at the Boston store. They chose their moment very carefully, beginning the strike in late November, just as the Christmas shopping season began. The union had massive support, since Milwaukee was a strong center of union activism in this era. Despite these important steps, the strike at the Boston store was a disaster. The weather turned bitterly cold, and picketers frequently found themselves in bed with frostbite and colds. The strikers made their situation even worse when they refused aid from some quarters. At one point during the strike, unemployed workers offered to help run the picket line, but strikers refused, believing (according to George Kirstein, a former department store manager and one of the earliest historians of retail workers' unions) that accepting this assistance might lead to violence. Nonetheless, workers stayed on strike throughout December and early January, returning to their jobs on January 10, having failed to win any of their demands.

While both the A&P and Boston defeats were devastating, neither came close to the momentary shock that accompanied the February 1935 strike against the R.A. Freed stores in the Bronx, New York. In this strike, managers asked for and received an antipicketing injunction. The RCIPA challenged the injunction through the courts and received an unfavorable decision from New York State Supreme Court Justice Salvatore A. Cotillo, who declared that any picketing of stores by retail workers' unions was illegal. The shock must have been severe, but it was brief. Two days later the Cotillo ruling had been struck down by the Court of Appeals, whose ruling allowed retail workers to picket as long as they refrained from shouting or interfering with the stores' business in any way. Although the Cotillo ruling was struck down, his decision was only the first of many occasions when the courts would place limits on retail workers' strikes.

Like the RCIPA, radical union organizers also began leading retail workers' strikes in this era, but they had only slightly more success than the American Federation of Labor (AFL) affiliate. The November 1934 strikes against the Klein's and Ohrbach's stores in New York City's Union Square, led by the Office Workers Union, an affiliate of the Communist-led Trade Union Unity League, were two of the most impressive retail workers' strikes of the era. As in the Freed strike, the courts issued antipicketing injunctions against the strikers at both stores. But unlike in the Freed strike, workers at Klein's and Ohrbach's sought to break the injunction not through the courts, but through mass picketing and mass arrests. To conduct this campaign, the Klein's-Ohrbach's strikers successfully assembled an impressive array of allies, including novelists Leane Zugsmith, James T. Farrell, and Nathanael West, all of whom went to jail for breaking the antipicketing injunctions. Strikers also garnered support by linking their strike to the struggles of other working-class people under communist leadership, and often participants in unemployment demonstrations would march the picket line alongside the strikers.

The Klein's-Ohrbach's strike was also uniquely creative. Between November 1934 and April 1935, strikers held weekly parades in Union Square, and they would do whatever they could to convince customers not to shop in the stores—etching the store windows' glass with strike slogans, decorating statues in Union Square as strikers, and giving shoppers' children balloons reading "Don't Buy At Ohrbach's." Strikers also extended their actions far beyond the picket lines, with two strikers going so far as to chain themselves to a balcony in protest when Nathan Ohrbach made a speech. Despite all the creativity that went into the Klein's-Ohrbach's strikes, the two strikes received relatively little attention from the national press or other sectors of the labor movement, and the strikers were not particularly successful. At Klein's, workers got back pay and reinstatement; at Ohrbach's, strikers received a verbal contract guaranteeing a decrease in hours. Managers at both stores refused to recognize the union as the workers' collective bargaining agent, a central demand in both strikes. In the aftermath of the strikes, managers at both stores fired many of the former strikers.

There was certainly an increase in the number of retail workers' strikes in 1934–35, as there was in almost every other industry in the country. But the strikes in the retail industry had little effect: they were small, unsuccessful, and for the most part easily ignored, confined as they generally were to the back pages of newspapers.

It was not until 1937 that retail workers began to stage strikes that were more successful and more important. The sit-down strikes at five-and-dime chain stores in February and March 1937 forced all observers to acknowledge that retail workers had an important role to play in the burgeoning labor movement. Prior to 1937, the CIO had done no significant organizing in the retail field. The few organized retail workers were organized within the RCIPA, which had no connection to the CIO. But by 1937, the RCIPA was splitting apart, as some New York City locals rejected the national policies of the union. It was these dissidents from the RCIPA as well as organizers from other unions that led the 1937 sit-downs.

The sit-down strikes at chain stores began in Detroit. Early in 1937, inspired by the Flint sit-down strikes in late 1936, Detroit workers staged sit-downs throughout the city—at auto plants, seed companies, lunch delivery companies, golf ball manufacturers, and laundries. On February 27, 1937, workers at a large Woolworth's store in downtown Detroit staged a sit-down strike. Led by organizers from the Hotel Employees and Restaurant Employees, the workers demanded union recognition, time and a half for overtime after a forty-eight-hour workweek, free uniforms, seniority rights, and a union hiring hall. The store manager rushed in to demand that workers vacate the store but the workers refused; the Woolworth's district superintendent for Detroit came in and workers repeated their demands, but again refused to leave.

The Woolworth sit-down strikers had important allies. Other local unions sent in mattresses and blankets, and volunteers from the cook's union set up a kitchen. When Woolworth's managers began to threaten to close all stores in Detroit in response to the strike, workers at a second Woolworth's store in the city defied the managers' threat by staging their own sit-down. Members of other unions in the city set up picket lines around the Detroit Woolworth stores as a show of solidarity.

The Woolworth's sit-down strikers also proved remarkably resourceful at getting the attention of the media. The first way they did this was by setting up leisure activities: they smuggled in cigarettes, began playing cards and checkers, and sang union songs, occasionally changing the lyrics to fit their situation. Then they began inviting print journalists and even a newsreel crew into the store to write stories and take pictures of the strikers at play. Although they were not portraying themselves as serious labor activists, but as young women at leisure, the media found this depiction of a sit-down strike fascinating and the strikers' ploy worked. Articles on the "girl strikers" singing and having a good time filled the media, and many of these articles captured the front pages of national newspapers.

On March 5, managers in Detroit finally agreed to negotiate. The company gave workers virtually everything they had demanded: pay raises, time and a half for overtime (after a forty-eight-hour workweek), free uniforms, and a union hiring hall. It was a contract like none before in the history of retail workers' unions.

With this sort of success, the sit-down strikes quickly spread to other stores. Workers in New York, under the leadership of dissident union organizers from the RCIPA (some of whom had helped organize the strikes at Klein's and Ohrbach's a few years earlier), were watching the Detroit strikes carefully. When Woolworth's managers made their threat to close all their Detroit stores, New York workers threatened to initiate a national boycott against Woolworth's. And when the Woolworth's workers won in Detroit, five-and-dime store workers in New York declared their own sit-down strike, first at the H.L. Green store and then at New York Woolworth's stores. The Woolworth's workers in New York found still more opportunities to attract the attention of the media and the public. When store managers refused to allow food into the store for the strikers, the strikers promptly declared themselves on a hunger strike and won more national headlines for their cause.

Sit-down strikes like this one at Woolworth's in New York City in 1937 inspired a high level of camaraderie as workers stayed together for days or even weeks at a time. Despite the levity displayed here, the sit-down strikes were serious business. When store managers refused to allow food into the store, the strikers promptly declared themselves on a hunger strike and won more media coverage and public support. (*Courtesy:* New York World-Telegram and the Sun Newspaper Photograph Collection, Library of Congress.)

As in Detroit, customers stayed away, and supporters quickly emerged in the New York strikes. Not only did other unions and the communist International Workers Order (an ethnic fraternal society) immediately voice formal support for the Woolworth's workers, but crowds of working people gathered outside the stores to demonstrate their support for the sit-down strikers inside. Hours after the sit-down strikers had declared themselves on a hunger strike, these supporters swarmed past the police guard and passed food and cots to the workers inside. The police evicted the workers, placing them under arrest, and were met with huge protests not only at the stores but also at the police precincts. When the workers were freed, they went back to the store, sat down again, were arrested again, and another round of protests took place at the precincts and stores. Faced with this massive opposition that was increasingly difficult to control, New York City mayor Fiorello La Guardia immediately stepped in to negotiate, forcing managers to grant a one-year contract to workers at the stores where strikes had taken place. Due to the rapid turnover at Woolworth's in this era, however, almost no workers who had participated in the sit-down strikes remained at the stores by the end of the year, and the unions at Woolworth's quickly disappeared in both New York and Detroit.

In addition to the innovative ways the strikers used the media, there are several reasons why the sit-down strikes at chain stores gained such massive attention in 1937. Chain stores in general were the subject of tremendous public scrutiny in the mid-1930s. Beginning in the early years of the Depression with a 1931 Supreme Court decision legalizing prohibitive taxes on large chain stores, some politicians began to argue that large chains like Woolworth's were damaging small retailers and therefore bad for the country's economy as a whole. This debate over chain stores reached its height in the mid-1930s, when Representative Wright Patman of Texas led a congressional committee to investigate chain store management and the ways in which chain stores attempted to manipulate the public and damage fair competition with smaller establishments. During the 1937 sit-down strikes, workers were able to use this national suspicion of big retailing to garner immense support.

These strikes also allowed workers to take advantage of the fame of Woolworth heiress Barbara Hutton, one of the wealthiest people in the world in the mid-1930s. Although she owned little Woolworth stock by 1937, Hutton was a powerful symbol of the ruling class. Additionally, she was a powerful negative image in other respects: she had publicly stated that she hated traveling in America and lived almost exclusively abroad; she had already been divorced once, and was married to a count in 1937. Hutton was the perfect nemesis for the strikers: incredibly wealthy, titled, anti-American, and female at a time when the nation was celebrating the rugged masculinity of its unemployed men. Strikers, most of them women as well, did not hesitate to use Hutton's wealth and privilege to make a contrast with their own poverty, using Hutton's name in their songs and chants: "Barbara Hutton, she gets mutton! Woolworth workers, they get nothin'!" The contrast between Hutton and the workers was also very popular in media coverage of the strike. Radical papers such as the *Daily Worker* ran stories attacking Hutton, and liberal newspapers ran stories about the strike directly next to stories about Barbara Hutton relaxing on beaches in Europe. The contrast was unmistakable, and gained the strikers even greater sympathy and support.

If the sit-down strikes at the five-and-dime chain stores captured popular attention in ways that few retail strikes have ever done, they were not isolated. Other sit-down strikes took place in larger retail establishments in 1937. Many of these strikes took place in Detroit as a direct result of the five-and-dime sit-downs. In the weeks following the five-and-dime sit-downs, Detroit workers staged sit-down strikes against Federal department stores, Lerner's, the Crowley Milner department store, and Allen's Shoe Stores. In most cases, these strikes lasted only a few hours or at maximum a few days before managers backed down, and there was relatively little police presence. In fact, at one point during the rash of sit-downs in Detroit, police refused a request by managers to enter the store during a sit-down strike to guard the store's stock, holding that the strike did not constitute a disturbance and therefore police presence would be unwarranted.

Strikes spread far beyond Detroit and New York. Workers at all the major department stores in Providence, Rhode Island, launched a non-sit-down strike to demand union recognition, time and a third for overtime, and seniority. The governor of Rhode Island called for continuous negotiations until the stores were reopened, and the stores in Providence immediately granted workers most of what they had demanded, including union recognition. In the sit-down strikes' aftermath, successful strikes (some sit-downs, some not) also took place at chain stores and department stores in East St. Louis, Illinois; Akron, Ohio; St. Paul, Minnesota; Superior, Wisconsin; Centralia, Washington; and Seattle, where 3,000 store workers went on strike simultaneously and won huge pay raises and the forty-hour week.

One of the most important of the non-sit-down strikes of the late 1930s, however, was the less successful 1938 department store strike in San Francisco. San Francisco store managers had formed the San Francisco Retailers' Council, an organization primarily designed to conduct joint negotiations with employees. In the summer of 1937, following the sit-down strikes in other parts of the country, store managers in San Francisco quickly signed a one-year open-shop contract with RCIPA Local 1100. In the summer of 1938, when the first contract expired, the union began demanding a union shop, as well as a thirty-five-hour workweek and storewide seniority. After lengthy negotiations failed, in September 1938 the union called a strike against all the department stores in San Francisco. The strikers had certain important advantages, most important, the support of the Teamsters, who refused to make deliveries to any store on strike. If worker solidarity was impressive during the San Francisco strike, managerial solidarity was even more so. The union tried to get shoppers to make their purchases at those few stores that were not on strike, only to find managers at these stores willing to refuse Teamsters' deliveries until the Teamsters agreed to cross the picket lines and make deliveries to the stores where workers were on strike. And when the union began to complain that their wages and benefits were not on par with those of other retail workers, managers were able to point out that when the contract had been signed, the union had boasted to its members that it was the best contract for retail workers in the country.

There was one occasion of violence during the San Francisco strike, but like the Klein's-Ohrbach's strikes, the San Francisco strike was primarily notable as an opportunity for workers to get creative with their picket lines. On one day, strikers' children were invited to the picket line, and they marched bearing chalkboards reading "Union kiddies / want to eat / Take our mothers / Off the street," and "Hickory Dickory Dock / My school books are in hock / and now I cannot concentrate / Because the boss won't arbitrate." On another day, workers dressed in costumes from the nineteenth century, bearing signs that said, "These costumes are more than 100 years old. So are the ideas of our employers." Unfortunately, the excitement and pageantry surrounding the San Francisco strike did little to ensure the strike's success. After nearly two months of striking, the mayor agreed to host negotiations in which the union failed miserably, winning back nothing but jobs for the striking workers.

The victorious sit-down strikes greatly outweighed the defeat in San Francisco. Retail workers won not only their demands but also greater legitimacy within the labor movement of the day. In the aftermath of these strikes, the CIO finally set up a retail workers' union, the United Retail Employees of America, later renamed the Retail Wholesale and Department Store Union (RWDSU). Store managers, having no wish to see the events of March 1937 repeated, frequently moved to sign contracts. But unlike many other workers who conducted sit-down strikes in 1936–37, workers in the retail industry were generally exempt from the federal government's Fair Labor Standards Act, meaning that retail workers got neither the eight-hour day nor the minimum wage provisions that the act established. This set the stage for more strikes, most notably the New York Gimbels strike of September 1941.

Samuel Wolchok, president of the RWDSU, was generally opposed to strikes. A longtime activist in New York City's grocery store unions, Wolchok supported policies of moderation and compromise, choosing whenever possible to negotiate with managers rather than lead strikes. At some stores, this tactic was highly successful. At Gimbels, for instance, manager Louis Broido agreed to sign a union contract in the hopes that Wolchok would exert some control over the communist leaders of the local union. As a result, Broido insisted upon negotiating with Wolchok rather than the local leaders. This turned out to be a serious tactical error for Broido. At Gimbels, when Wolchok tentatively agreed to a contract that granted workers a small raise but did not grant them the coveted forty-hour week, local leaders rejected the contract and called for a strike.

The Gimbels strike was a bitter one, a far cry from the celebratory atmosphere within the stores during the five-and-dime sit-down strikes. Workers at Gimbels spent little time trying to convince the wealthy customers of the justice of the strike; they held only one meeting with interested customers. For the most part strikers attacked the store, scabs, and customers with equal ferocity. Strikers let flocks of pigeons and white mice loose in the store, threw red paint at customers who attempted to cross the picket lines, and on one occasion someone (although it may well have been an agent provocateur rather than a striker) let a swarm of bees into the store. Eventually, the workers won, establishing the forty-hour week as a standard for retail workers, but the local union faced New York State investigations as well as condemnation from the national RWDSU leaders for the radical tactics used during the strike.

Neither the conflict within the union nor the series of retail workers' strikes ended with the beginning of World War II. In fact, retail workers conducted one of the more unusual strikes of World War II: the Montgomery Ward strike of 1943 in Chicago. This strike was one of the few wartime strikes that had the full support of not only union leaders but also the federal government. During the war, most unions gave up their right to strike in exchange for the federal government's guarantee of the closed shop. Sewell Avery, the vice president of mail-order house Montgomery Ward, refused to abide by this wartime compromise, demanding new union elections and refusing to negotiate with the union until the elections were held. Union leaders and the government alike tried to get Avery to compromise, but Avery adamantly refused, and union leaders reluctantly authorized a strike, which ended only when the federal government sent soldiers into the Chicago offices of Montgomery Ward to forcefully remove Sewell Avery from his office. Montgomery Ward was run with close government supervision for the remainder of the war.

The Montgomery Ward strike was even more unusual in its aftermath. While liberals supported the strike and hailed the victory as a victory for workers everywhere, communists, due to their strong support for the war, condemned the strike as an unnecessary economic disruption. Despite the supposed alliance between communists and liberals during the war, in the aftermath of the Montgomery Ward strike, vitriolic attacks passed back and forth, both within the RWDSU (Wolchok in particular attacked the communists within his union as traitors who did nothing but follow the latest Russian policy) and in other unions.

As the war drew to an end, the nation's industries exploded in huge and disruptive strikes. Retail workers played an important role in at least one of these postwar strikes. In 1946, retail workers in Oakland, California, under RCIPA leadership struck, demanding union recognition. The stores struck in Oakland did not use Teamsters for deliveries, so deliveries, protected by local police, went uninterrupted. The Teamsters, learning that nonunion truck drivers were being used to break a picket line with the support of the local police, called for a general strike in Oakland. As a result, the city was shut down for two full days until the city government promised that police would cease guarding the nonunion trucks. The RCIPA union that had begun the strike eventually brought it to a successful conclusion.

It was the government's passage of the Taft-Hartley Act, intended to end the disruptive postwar strike wave, that brought about the next major retail workers' strike. With the passage of Taft-Hartley and the necessity for union leaders to sign affidavits stating that they were not communists, those union leaders who were communists, including many of New York City local leaders, found themselves in an extremely difficult situation. In the retail unions, communists sought to solve this situation by declaring that unions had no need for the National Labor Relations Board (NLRB). To prove the NLRB's irrelevance, they refused to sign the affidavits and began renegotiating their contract at the Oppenheim Collins store in New York, despite the fact that they were no longer recognized by the NLRB. Oppenheim Collins managers refused to bargain and called for an NLRB election at the store; and without NLRB recognition, the communists' RWDSU local did not appear on the ballot. As a result, workers voted to be represented by a competing RCIPA local, and those workers who refused to accept this result went out on strike against Oppenheim Collins. In perhaps the most controversial strike in retail workers' history, workers stayed out on the picket line for weeks on end without result, and the mainstream press responded with vicious attacks that were largely false: the strike, the *Daily News* reported, was the work of outside communist agitators rather than retail workers themselves, and all the supporters of the strike were communists.

Faced with these sorts of attacks, the Oppenheim Collins strike quickly came to an end. In its aftermath, the federal government opened hearings on communism in American retail unions, and the communist-led locals eventually left the RWDSU and the CIO altogether. In the aftermath of the communists' decision to leave the RWDSU, Samuel Wolchok was forced into retirement for allowing his union to disintegrate in such a manner, and the RWDSU collapsed for several years.

Besides being the moment of destruction of the RWDSU, the postwar era was also a time of rapid changes in the retail industry. As more and more Americans moved to the suburbs in the late 1940s and early 1950s, store managers responded by opening branch stores in suburban shopping malls, and—even more important for retail workers—restructuring the city stores to allow customers direct access to goods and reduce their workforces. As a result, managers laid off many workers, and the ones who were retained increasingly found themselves paid to be friendly and courteous to customers rather than to have the sort of detailed knowledge of merchandise that had once been requisite for working in most retail establishments.

The New York locals that had deserted the RWDSU were the first to respond to managerial restructuring. After leaving the CIO, these locals united with other left-wing unions to form District 65 of the Distributive Processing and Office Workers Union (DPOWU). In 1953, they led a massive strike against the Hearn's store when managers there tried to cut jobs and restructure the store.

Like many retail workers' strikes, a massive public relations contest surrounded the Hearn's strike. Taking a leaf from the Oppenheim Collins strike, Hearn's managers took out advertisements in the city's newspapers accusing the strikers of being communists. Workers responded by denouncing Hearn's as an "un-American store," where managers fired veterans and mothers of veterans. Other organizations and prominent individuals quickly moved to get involved in the strikers' defense. Local politicians such as Senator Herbert Lehman and city mayoral candidate Robert Wagner also officially endorsed the strike. The well-respected anticommunist coalition Americans for Democratic Action announced that the union had no affiliation with the Communist Party (indeed, the DPOWU had split with the communists in the early 1950s); and the New York chapter of the National Association for the Advancement of Colored People condemned the company and called on African-American workers to honor the Hearn's picket lines. Despite the rift between these unions and the CIO, the CIO also endorsed the strike, and raised thousands of dollars to support it.

Perhaps due to this impressive array of allies, the mainstream media regarded the Hearn's strike with tremendous respect. The *New York Post* actually ran an editorial condemning Hearn's managers for their verbal attacks on the strikers (Hearn's briefly withdrew all advertisement from the *Post* in response). The strikers also produced a fifteen-minute television program that was broadcast on WABC, *The Story Behind the Hearn's Strike*.

But positive media coverage and powerful allies did the strikers little good, perhaps because the union's anticommunist credentials were simply too newly minted. The National Labor Relations Board held a hearing on the union's claim that the firings and restructuring at Hearn's constituted unfair labor practices, and the NLRB ruled that none of the union's accusations held any merit and called for a new union election at Hearn's. Furthermore, a federal appellate court issued an anti-picketing injunction against the strikers at Hearn's. With accusations that they were communists already being leveled against them, the strikers decided not to break the injunction, instead abandoning the picket line. By the end of 1953, the Hearn's strike had ended in defeat.

The defeat at Hearn's was a disaster for retail workers' unions. Restructuring was now a manager's privilege, regardless of its effects on the lives of workers. And retail workers' unions would suffer the consequences in the post-CIO era. But another strike, against five major department stores in Pittsburgh, was an even more telling sign of things to come. Unlike most of the major retail strikes during the CIO era, the 1954 Pittsburgh strike was conducted by truck drivers represented by the Teamsters Union. Workers began the strike in response to an attempt by management to take away the right of every truck driver to travel with a helper, someone to assist in the lifting and carrying. The Pittsburgh strike was notable for its length (it was at the time the longest retail workers' strike in American history, lasting over a year) and also for the lack of solidarity around the strike. Truck drivers struck, but many other workers employed in the five stores, office workers as well as sales workers, remained on the job. Eventually, the union accepted a small raise, gave up their helpers, and ended the strike.

The Pittsburgh strike, both in the lack of solidarity among workers and in the fact that truck drivers rather than sales workers were now the most effectively unionized workers in the retail industry, marked the end of the CIO era of retail unionism. Even with grocery workers, many of whom were unionized across the country, retailing became overwhelmingly a nonunion field. In 1953, as the Hearn's strike ended in defeat and the CIO era drew to a close, the percentage of retail workers who were unionized sat at a dismal 9.5 percent, as opposed to 42.4 percent for manufacturing workers. For all their important successes during the CIO era, workers and union organizers had failed in their efforts to unionize the retail industry.

Toward the Twenty-First Century

The CIO era had, it turned out, been exceptional in its rapid series of retail workers' strikes. However, even after 1955, occasional strikes at major retail stores continued. Several grocery store chains had fairly frequent labor troubles from the late 1950s through the 1980s. As in the Pittsburgh strike, the strikes against these chains were frequently led by the Teamsters Union. In Washington, DC, for instance, the Teamsters struck against Safeway in 1972 and 1984, and came close to striking on numerous other occasions. Safeway was not alone; a 1959 Teamsters strike against A&P shut down 400 grocery stores in the New York City metropolitan area for forty-two days. Usually, the Teamsters struck for reasons similar to those that began the Pittsburgh strike: over questions of work rules and—in the case of the A&P strike—questions of which union local would get what work.

Store clerks were far less likely to strike than were delivery workers after the end of the CIO era. When these workers did strike, they were far less likely to be successful. In 1980, grocery workers struck at five major chains in the Washington and Baltimore area to demand better wages. But even here one could see the shift in power away from store clerks and toward delivery workers: the workers abandoned the strike after only five days, when the clerks found that the Teamsters would not back their picket line. "There really wasn't much choice when the Teamsters wouldn't support us," one grocery store worker told the *Washington Post* in perhaps the best summary of the weakness of retail workers' unions in these years.

It was not until the early years of the twenty-first century that retail workers resumed massive strikes. Like the workers in the 1954 Pittsburgh strike, they struck in order to defend rights that they had already won. Over the late 1990s and the early 2000s, the retail industry began to change yet again. First and foremost among these changes was the rise of ever more massive stores, especially those owned by Wal-Mart. Wal-Mart, the largest retail chain in the country, established a new standard for retailing. Their numbers were staggering. Wal-Mart could undercut market prices by as much as 14 percent to drive out competition, and paid 30 percent less for its employees' health benefits. Wal-Mart also successfully resisted unionization time and again. When meat cutters at one Wal-Mart store voted to unionize, store managers eliminated the meat-cutting department, laying off the workers in the process. "The choice for unions," one editorial from the *St. Louis Post-Dispatch* observed in 2003, "is stark. Go head-to-kneecap with the behemoth Wal-Mart, or hang on by their fingernails as their members' standard of living erodes."

Managers whose stores were already unionized pushed the union to start organizing at Wal-Mart as well, but the AFL-CIO retail workers' union, named the United Food and Commercial Workers (UFCW), avoided Wal-Mart whenever possible, instead attempting to maintain standards of living in those stores where unions had already formed. In the St. Louis area in October 2003, the union reached a tentative contract agreement with three chains, Schnucks, Dierbergs, and Shop 'n Save, with a total of ninety-seven different stores. In the tentative agreement, the union traded a number of cuts to workers' health care plans for a raise of 75 cents per hour for most workers. However, when the union took the contract to the workers, they rejected it, refusing to give up their health care benefits. The union reversed its position and called on workers at the three chains to strike, which they did on October 7.

Public support for the strike was immediate and strong. In the strike's early days, United Auto Workers (UAW) members walked the picket line alongside the strikers, customers stayed away from the stores, and people driving by the stores honked their car horns as a show of support. Perhaps the most important support for the St. Louis strike, however, came from grocery workers in other parts of the country, who went on strike for similar reasons while workers in St. Louis were on strike. Grocery workers in West Virginia, Kentucky, and Ohio all went on strike when managers at stores in those states demanded give-backs similar to those demanded in St. Louis. Most impressive of all was the news from Southern California. On October 11, four days after the workers in St. Louis began their strike, workers struck against Vons and Pavilion stores in Southern California when employers at these stores demanded that unionized workers give back benefits to match the Wal-Mart stores threatening to open in the region. When the strike was declared, managers at Albertsons and Ralphs stores in Southern California locked out their union workers in solidarity with the other store managers. In all, 70,000 workers were on strike or were locked out at 859 different locations in Southern California, and well over 100,000 grocery workers were on strike across the country.

The strikes were long and difficult. St. Louis workers were the first to reach a settlement in late October, with workers there agreeing to pay somewhat more for their health care than they had under previous contracts, but still not giving back as much as managers had demanded at the beginning of negotiations. At best, it was a compromise, one that made workers' health care only slightly more expensive.

The strikes in West Virginia, Kentucky, and Ohio all ended in December 2003 in a similar way, when the stores agreed to pay slightly more toward employee health care than the original contract proposal had promised. Two stores in Ohio and one store in West Virginia permanently closed, due to the loss of income during the strike, the company claimed.

The strike in Southern California, however, dragged on, as both sides absolutely refused to back down. To the managers, the equation was simple: they would defeat the workers or Wal-Mart might well defeat them. To the workers, the stakes were somewhat more complicated. To many workers, employers' proposals meant a shift from a permanent job to one that would not allow a worker to support his or her family. At least one union leader described the struggle by arguing that these had been middle-class jobs but that would no longer be the case if the strikers were defeated.

There were some bright spots in the California strike. The national AFL-CIO openly stated that the strike was one of the most important in recent memory, and local clergy exhorted their congregations to support the strike in whatever ways they could.

But as the weeks dragged on, the situation of the Southern California strikers became increasingly desperate. In late October, the workers withdrew the picket lines from Ralphs in order to concentrate their efforts on the other three stores and to allow customers a place to shop. The decision may have helped customers, but it did little for workers. In December, with no end in sight, there were occasional outbursts of violence against customers crossing the picket lines. The Teamsters, who had initially honored the strike, decided that two months was long enough and returned to work. The UFCW, which had not expected the strike to last this long, began cutting benefits. Negotiations, when they resumed, were not promising: the employers returned to the bargaining table with an offer even worse than the one that had prompted the strike.

To make matters worse, as 2003 ended, workers' savings increasingly began to run out. The emergency fund for the strike was $1.5 million, but the union was able to give funds only to those strikers actually on the verge of eviction. By February, it became evident that the UFCW's international strike fund would not last through May, when a number of other grocery store workers' contracts would have to be renegotiated.

In late February 2004, the union gave up. The stores offered a two-tier wage and benefit system in which veteran workers would keep most of their benefits, but incoming workers would receive far less. The union urged the workers to accept the contract, warning some workers that if they did not accept it, the next offer might well be even worse. Workers agreed and the contract was ratified.

The largest retail workers' strike in American history had ended in defeat.

Conclusion

The history of retail workers' strikes in America serves to emphasize just how exceptional and important the CIO era was in American labor history. Before this era began, retail workers were mostly nonunion, and those who were unionized were unlikely to strike. It was only as part of the CIO in that movement's heyday that large numbers of retail workers were able to win major struggles against management, in part because of the solidarity and support workers outside the retail industry gave to retail workers' strikes in this era. In the 1950s, as the AFL-CIO began its long decline, the fortunes of retail workers' unions similarly declined.

It is uncertain whether retail workers' unions will ever return to those successful struggles of the 1930s and 1940s. A number of factors make further successes unlikely. The rise of Wal-Mart, the increasing centralization of retail chains (the chains that participated in the Southern California strike, for instance, were owned by national grocery companies) as well as the increasing use of mechanization in the retail industry, with more self-checkout machines appearing in retail stores every year, all indicate that retail workers' unions are in a period of crisis. The next few years may well bring about developments critical to the survival of retail workers' unions and to the history of retail workers' strikes in America.

See also: The Rise and Fall of the Sit-Down Strike, 204; The 1945–1946 Strike Wave, 216; Trolley Wars, 519; Waitress Strikes, 633.

Bibliography

Benson, Susan Porter. *Counter Cultures: Saleswomen, Managers, and Customers in American Department Stores, 1890–1940*. Urbana: University of Illinois Press, 1988.

Estey, Marten. "Early Closing: Employer-Organized Origin of the Retail Labor Movement." Labor History 13, no. 4 (Fall 1972): 560–70.

Frank, Dana. "Girl Strikers Occupy Chain Store, Win Big: The Detroit Woolworth's Strike of 1937." In *Three Strikes: Miners, Musicians, Salesgirls, and the Fighting Spirit of Labor's Last Century*, ed. Howard Zinn, Dana Frank, and Robin D.G. Kelley, 57–118. Boston: Beacon Press, 2001.

Kirstein, George. *Stores and Unions: A Study of the Growth of Unionism in Dry Goods and Department Stores*. New York: Fairchild, 1950.

Opler, Daniel J. "'For All White-Collar Workers': The Possibilities of Radicalism in New York City's Department Store Unions, 1934–1954." Ph.D. diss., New York University, 2003.

———. "Monkey Business in Union Square: A Cultural Analysis of the Klein's-Ohrbach's Strikes of 1934–5." *Journal of Social History* (Fall 2002): 149–64.

Philips, Lisa A.W. "The Labor Movement and Black Economic Equality in New York City: District 65, 1934–1954." Ph.D. diss., Rutgers University, 2002.

Ziskind, Minna P. "Citizenship, Consumerism, and Gender: A Study of District 65, 1945–1960." Ph.D. diss., University of Pennsylvania, 2001.

———. "Labor Conflict in the Suburbs: Organizing Retail in Metropolitan New York, 1954–1958." *International Labor and Working-Class History* 64 (Fall 2003): 55–73.

WAITRESS STRIKES

Dorothy Sue Cobble

Most waitress strikes took place in the first half of the twentieth century. These strikes came primarily in a few concentrated strike waves associated with city-based union organizing attempts in the first years of the century and during the New Deal era. Their success depended first and foremost on their own self-organization. On many occasions, waitresses were able to achieve 100 percent participation in their strikes, making it virtually impossible for their restaurant-keeper employers to maintain operations. The strength of such organization illustrated the solidarity that waitresses were able to build despite harsh working conditions and hostile employers.

Waitresses also drew strength from male workers, inside and outside their industry. Interestingly, male workers outside the restaurant industry, such as teamsters, longshoremen, and loggers, were often more forthcoming with their support than male culinary workers, and this support sometimes made the difference between success and failure. Male cooks, bartenders, and waiters were often ambivalent about the unionization of their sister workers. Where men dominated employment, such as in high-class restaurants in New York, they could be downright hostile to the entry of women workers. Where women constituted a larger portion of the workforce, male workers were more willing to support waitress unionization. Still, it took significant organizing work on the part of waitresses to convince their male coworkers. When they succeeded, however, as in San Francisco and Detroit, the culinary unions could be extremely powerful.

Formation of Waitress Unions

In the first decade of the twentieth century, several waitress locals formed to advance the interests of women workers. Neglect among fellow male unionists was a significant factor in their organizing. These first waitress locals encountered considerable obstacles in sustaining their fledgling organizations. In addition to the ambivalence of their own culinary brothers, they faced bitter feuds with employers, condescension from middle-class "uplift" or moral reform groups, and divisions in their own ranks. Nevertheless, many locals weathered these trials and established themselves permanently in the industry.

Women's Militancy on the Job

Typically, female locals faced their greatest battles with employers after they demonstrated significant bargaining power. Employers often underestimated the organizational potential of their female employees and, taken by surprise, were forced to grant concessions. These initial union victories, however, sparked employer counterorganization and open-shop campaigns. Employers in Seattle took the offensive after waitresses won wage and hour concessions in 1908. The restaurant keepers refused to abide by the union's work rules and proposed a return to the seven-day week. Local 240 "did not think the same, so . . . everyone voted to go out." With only one "black sheep" scabbing, the restaurant owners capitulated after twelve hours.

Chicago waitresses also maintained the upper hand with employers in their early years. With the assistance of the milk wagon drivers' union and the Chicago Federation of Labor, forty-one waitresses formed their own organization in March 1902. Within a few months, a majority of their trade—some 1,500—had enrolled. On an appointed day, all union members appeared in their restaurants wearing union badges and demanding a reduction of hours and increase in wages. Taken by surprise, the employers, almost without exception, yielded. Guided by the fiery oratory and "fervent heart" of Irish-born Elizabeth Maloney, who officered the local from 1902 until her death in 1921, Local 424 secured signed agreements with numerous Chicago restaurants, expanded its membership, and moved into its own headquarters in the Chicago Labor Temple. Their success was evident in the Chicago Labor Day parade of 1905. The organizer from the international waitresses' union assigned to Chicago reported that of all the Chicago culinary locals, only Local 484 had participated in the parade. "Over 60 members rode in automobiles with flags flying and a magnificent banner. The girls got the greatest reception along the line of march I ever saw; they certainly did credit to themselves and our organization," he added.

Fierce Employer Opposition

Except for a few isolated strikes and picketing at individual restaurants, the local experienced relative peace until confronted with a major employer backlash against unionism in 1913. Angered by their concession of "one day's rest in seven" or the six-day week, some 100 employers formed the Chicago Restaurant Keepers Association and demanded a return to the seven-day week. The waitresses responded by striking all association restaurants. For the next year and a half, Local 484 and restaurant owners locked horns. The waitress local received little help from its weaker brother culinary locals, but it did receive aid from "the society women who have appointed committees and are assisting us in their own way"; the Hull House settlement workers who held protest meetings, picketed alongside the striking waitresses, and appointed a committee to call on the mayor and police chief; and the bakers and the bakery wagon drivers who honored the waitresses' picket line.

In defense, the Restaurant Keepers Association marshaled its own formidable arsonal of weapons. They brought in black female strikebreakers and hired picketers to harass the union marchers and advertise the employers' point of view. They employed labor spies and gunmen to intimidate the strikers, and they obtained sweeping court injunctions against the union that prohibited "striking, picketing, organizing, boycotting, conspiring, resigning [from work], or in any way interfering with their [the employer's] business." The employers also set up a rival employer-dominated waitress association modeled on the waitress union with clubrooms and job referral services. After more than 200 arrests, the employers prevailed. They broke the waitresses' control over the labor supply and reinstituted the seven-day week in some restaurants. The Chicago local continued to represent some 30 percent of the trade, but they did not regain their former dominance until the 1930s.

Waves of Waitress Strikes in the Early Twentieth Century

In their first two decades, the San Francisco waitresses experienced similar cycles of advance followed by employer backlash and defeat. After the union began pressing for the ten-hour day in 1901, the local Restaurant Keepers Association gained the backing of the San Francisco Employer Association and precipitated a strike. After enjoining union picketing, the owners held out for six months, operating their restaurants with scab labor. The union lost considerable membership—union waitresses had trouble getting jobs and some were forced to leave town or assume false names—but the local followed the strike defeat with a remarkable period of rebuilding. In part, the unprecedented surge in membership resulted from the waitresses' decision to pursue "more subtle means than direct action," according to one early authority on the union.

The waitress union dedicated itself to an educational campaign that brought results both in working conditions and increased membership. Although many restaurants refused to bargain or sign agreements, by May 1902, a handful of establishments instituted working conditions in conformity with the standard 1902 Waitress Wage Scales and Working Agreement: employment of union members only; a six-day week; and $8.00 a week for day work, $9.00 for night work. In December 1903, the waitresses survived a second open-shop campaign and lockout by the employers. With the assistance of Mayor Eugene Schmitz, recently elected by San Francisco's Union Labor party, they emerged victorious with a new one-year agreement that reduced hours to nine a day.

Sit-Ins and Sip-Ins: Detroit Sisters Take Over

By the mid-1930s, mixed-gender culinary locals began aggressive organizing as well. Few matched the 100 percent organization achieved in San Francisco, but in a large number of cities, locals secured contracts with a majority of hotel owners, extended their inroads among independent eating and drinking establishments, and opened their ranks to women for the first time. In fact, during the New Deal and after, the majority of new Hotel Employees and Restaurant Employees (HERE) female members entered sexually mixed units: hotel service worker locals (miscellaneous locals composed of cooks, waiters, waitresses, and bartenders) or mixed-craft organizations of waiters and waitresses.

Next to San Francisco, Detroit culinary unionists came closest to achieving the thorough organization of a large heterogeneous community, building an organization with the help of the local labor movement that by the early 1940s was the second-largest local on the International union roster. Unlike San Francisco, however, no separate local for waitresses existed by the 1930s: the few organized female servers belonged to Waiters' Local 705. The lack of a separate organization and the ambivalence among waiters toward organizing women slowed the growth of waitress unionism in the early 1930s. But the desire for organization among Detroit's female servers was not to be contained.

Myra Wolfgang: Strike Organizer in Detroit

Local 705, led by Louis Koenig, an Austrian waiter who claimed to have been fired from one lucrative job "because of my sober face," reached out first to male cooks, waiters, and bartenders. The dominant sentiment among the waiters was that "the girls were their competition," and as such should be eliminated from the industry (or at least contained) rather than brought in on an equal footing with the men. In 1932, however, Myra Wolfgang (nee Mira Komaroff), an outspoken young dynamo of an organizer, committed her energy to rebuilding the local, and the sexual balance began to change. Wolfgang, born into an upwardly mobile Russian-Jewish immigrant family, spent a few years in college pursuing art studies before being drawn ineluctably into the political and intellectual currents surrounding her. She quickly moved from being Koenig's office assistant to taking on full-time organizing and bargaining responsibilities. Male members reacted, complaining of the "new emphasis placed on recruiting women" and the "dominant role young Mira was assuming." The old-timers in particular protested "what they called 'the sisters' taking over their domain."

Yet as the sit-down fever spread through Detroit, Local 705 jumped in to organize women as well as men. In the fall and winter of 1936 and 1937, after nearly five years of bitter unemployment punctuated by marches, demonstrations, and clashes with police, Detroit's workplaces blazed up under the spark of this new confrontational tactic. In February and March 1937, sit-down strikes in Detroit involved close to 35,000 workers. "Sit-downs have replaced baseball as the national pastime," one Detroit news reporter quipped. The eruption in the hotel and restaurant industry commenced when twenty-three-year-old organizer Wolfgang strode to the center of Detroit's Woolworth store and blew her strike whistle, the union's prearranged signal for workers to sit down. After Woolworth capitulated, signing an agreement covering 1,400 employees, the union toppled department stores, candy and soda shops, and eateries of every description "like nine pins in a bowling alley." Union inroads into the hotel sector began with a "terrific uproar" at the Barlum Hotel: two days after serving the Woolworth strikers a victory dinner, the hotel's coffee shop waitresses occupied their own workplace. After union activists barricaded themselves inside other key hotels, the Detroit Hotel Association granted union recognition and raises of 10–15 percent.

Detroit waitresses responded en masse to the strike actions called by Local 705. They also initiated job actions independently of the local. "I'd be in the local union office," Wolfgang once disclosed "and a girl would call up suddenly, saying, 'Is this Mira? Someone told me to call you. I'm Mamie,

The February and March 1937 sit-down strikes in Detroit, Michigan, involved nearly 35,000 workers, from GM workers to these Woolworth waitresses at a lunch counter. Woolworth signed an agreement with the union covering 1,400 of its employees. (*Courtesy:* Walter P. Reuther Library, Wayne State University.)

over at Liggett's Drug Store. We threw out the manager and . . . are sitting in. What should we do now?'"

By 1941 Detroit culinary unions had obtained collective bargaining agreements with most first-class restaurants, at least forty Woolworth stores, the Stouffer chain, numerous cafeterias and lunch counters, and all leading department stores and hotels. The union membership quadrupled, with women making up the preponderance of new members. Although these victories rested on the militancy and enthusiasm of the food service workers themselves, the inclusive organizing posture of Local 705 by 1937, the openness of the International to unorthodox organizing tactics, and the support of the surrounding labor community all proved critical.

Once Local 705 committed to organizing all workers regardless of sex, race, or craft, they proceeded aggressively, using the latest techniques pioneered by the CIO. Strikes and sit-downs were rehearsed, planned in advance, and showily executed. "We walked in there right at 12 o'clock," organizer and cook Charles Paulsen recalled, "blew the whistle, and the waiters and waitresses and the rest of the help had been geared to answer . . . they all stopped and walked out." At the Woolworth stores and other retail outlets where the local chose the sit-down tactic, the challenge was to buoy the spirits of the sit-downers.

Since the premises were shut down from within, the customer's decision to shop or not became irrelevant. The women inside were assigned committee responsibilities—food, finance, entertainment, and security—with an equal number of unionists setting up parallel support groups on the outside. From morning to night, the organizers scheduled meetings, singing, and calisthenics for the strikers. At the main Woolworth store, guest musicians visited for special evening concerts; a Victrola was smuggled in for late-night dancing; and several women set up a beauty parlor where strikers received hairwaves and manicures. Workers occupying the Crowley-Milner Department Store danced to the music of two orchestras after viewing a floor show staged by the Woolworth strikers. Not all the needs of the sit-downers could be met, however. During one department store siege, two pregnant women were taken out of the store just before going into labor.

The culinary local in Detroit also maintained a close cooperative relationship with the Detroit CIO affiliates, notably the United Auto Workers (UAW) and key unions such as the Teamsters (IBT). Auto workers joined HERE-called "sip-ins" or "customer strikes" in which union sympathizers would keep out better-paying customers by ordering a single cup of coffee and remaining through lunch or the dinner rush. In some cases, Local 705 looked to Teamster muscle in applying economic pressure. The IBT refusal to deliver linens, fresh bread, vegetables, and other catering essentials to wayward employers usually brought quick resolutions to disputes. Although some initial joint ventures turned sour, by the late 1940s, Wolfgang and Jimmy Hoffa of the Teamsters settled into a fruitful working partnership.

The International defended Local 705's militant actions even when criticism came from William Green, president of the American Federation of Labor (AFL). Green publicly disavowed the sit-down and sip-in tactics during a Detroit rally in Cadillac Square and later wrote HERE President Flore complaining of Local 705's adoption of these confrontational methods. Responding, Flore bluntly declared that if such tactics were necessary to break the open-shop hold in Detroit, they were good enough for him. Rather than disciplining Local 705's officers as Green suggested, Flore concluded his letter by praising them: "God bless 'em and full speed ahead."

The Heyday of Waitress Unionism: The 1940s and 1950s

With the advent of World War II, women's position within the labor force and the union changed significantly. Their rosters swelled by the rapid feminization of the workforce, the older established waitress locals in San Francisco, Chicago, Seattle, and Portland moved ahead of all other crafts in size and influence. San Francisco's union doubled its ranks during World War II and by 1946 was the fourth-largest local on the International roster, claiming more than 6,000 members. In contrast, the San Francisco waiters' local dropped to less than 4,000. Female locals, eager for increased membership, negotiated jurisdiction over department store and variety store workers and asserted claims to female cashiers and checkers in hotels and cafeteria employees in schools and hospitals.

In some cases, large, mixed locals experienced a similar surge in female membership during the 1940s. Local 6 in New York, the largest local in the International by the end of the war, had close to 7,000 women, one-third of its total. Detroit's 705, claiming 60 percent female membership, targeted carhops and drive-ins as well as workers in plants and school cafeterias, and expanded their membership among drugstore food servers. By 1947, after weathering a strike against the Restaurant Guild, which involved some sixty restaurants, they reported a membership of 11,000. Hotel locals feminized as they organized cloak and hat checkers, female cashiers, and other white-collar employees.

Unionization in smaller communities, particularly in the West where women service workers now thoroughly dominated the industry, reached a saturation point. Tacoma, Washington, Pittsburgh, California, and other scattered towns across the western region reported 100 percent organization. The union secretary in Watsonville, California, sent a typical account: "This week in Santa Cruz County, we have placed cards in six restaurants, and believe me there are others asking to . . . sign them up, but I don't have enough cards." In Butte, Montana, Lena Mattausch complained that, having organized janitors and other nonfood service women, "no more women could be found." The Women's Protective Union turned its attention to bargaining conducting a model strike in 1948 with the support of the Teamsters, building trades, musicians, and virtually the entire citizenry. The strike secured labor peace and union control over wages and working conditions—a situation that lasted for the next twenty-five years.

Waitresses' Local 639 in Los Angeles leapt into prominence by adding 3,000 new members between 1941 and 1948. Established in the World War I era, Local 639 barely sustained its charter in the face of the open-shop, antiunion drives by Los Angeles employers in the 1920s. As late as 1939, the local told of "almost complete cessation of organizing activity" in part because of the city ordinance limiting strikes, picketing, and other concerted actions. Los Angeles waitresses also confronted organized opposition from consumer groups, such as the Women of the Pacific financed by anti-labor employees. These women picketed stores displaying the union card and campaigned against union organization.

During the war years, however, with 900 or more restaurants on the verge of closing because of the shortage of help, desperate employers agreed to union standards for the first time. Sustained by staunch activists such as Bee Tumber, Nora Saxton, and Mae Stoneman, Local 639 pressed its advantage, organizing house after house. Oklahoma-born Stoneman began her waitress career at thirteen and, following in her mother's footsteps, acceded to union office shortly thereafter. Stoneman was elected vice president of Denver's Local 14 in 1921; six years later she moved into the top position in Local 639, a perch she maintained until the 1950s. The War Labor Board also helped boost the union's prestige by granting substantial wage increases during wartime. By 1945, Class A houses were almost completely organized with new wage scales of 50 cents to $1.00 an hour. From this base, the union moved to organize table, counter, and cafeteria servers; hotel waitresses, hostesses, cashiers, and busgirls; carhops at the drive-ins; and commissary employees in the large Hollywood movie studios.

Buoyed by the example of the Los Angeles local, culinary workers in Southern California cities such as San Diego, Long Beach, San Pedro, San Bernardino, and Bakersfield joined the fray, pressuring countless new houses into union agreements. And although many of the locals were short-lived, unionism also blossomed in communities across the Southwest and South—communities such as Kingman, Arizona; Chattanooga, Tennessee; New Orleans; and Houston. In 1944, the culinary local in Kingman reported 100 percent organization when the last nonunion café succumbed after three years of picketing—the employer finding it impossible to locate workers who were not "either union members or union-minded."

In this era, culinary locals also achieved notable successes among minority workers. During the 1930s, for example, Detroit's 705 had set up separate "colored sections" within the local and hired black organizers. But by the end of the 1940s, the colored divisions were gone, and black workers and white had picketed together successfully on behalf of black waiters in Detroit's Athletic Club, black cocktail waitresses serving in Detroit's East Side nightclubs, and black hotel maids, bellboys, and food handlers. When Hugo Ernst, a long-term socialist with firm ties to interracial equality, acceded to the International presidency in 1945, the union even appointed its first black organizer for the Deep South. In contrast to their success elsewhere, however, HERE made few inroads among southern minority workers. The notable exception was in Miami Beach, where by the late 1950s, the entire strip of oceanfront hotels had unionized.

A few western locals even expanded their organizing among Chinese and Filipino workers. Before the war, locals organizing Asian workers usually set up separate "Oriental locals," and those that bargained with Asian employers usually insisted on white workers being hired. Although these traditions remained in many locals, others opened their doors to both Asian employers and workers. The San Francisco Local Joint Executive Board initiated its first negotiations with the Downtown Chinese Restaurant Association in the early 1940s, adding a large number of unionized Chinese workers.

End of Strikes in the 1950s

By the early 1950s, the flood of strikes and organizing victories had subsided. The union's proportion of hotel and restaurant workers began a slow decline from which it never recovered. Although organizing victories among hotel workers in Miami Beach and other cities were still to come, these gains were offset by losses among culinary workers outside of hotels. In 1953, HERE claimed a quarter of the workforce, and by the mid-1970s less than one worker in ten had the protection of a union contract. The burgeoning new food service workforce of the 1960s and 1970s remained resolutely outside the union field.

Conclusion

For women food service workers, high levels of organization depended not only on a general climate receptive to unionism but also on the support of allies. Of course, in certain circumstances—notably in those few towns, generally in the West and Midwest, where the numerical dominance of female servers and their separate organizational structure allowed them to control the supply of labor through their own self-organization—waitresses could organize relying on their own strength. But these situations were rare. In most circumstances, the extent of unionism among waitresses was determined by the attitudes and actions of supporters outside the waitress community.

In New York, Washington, and other eastern cities, waitresses enjoyed the enthusiastic backing of the Women's Trade Union League and middle-class women's groups. These female allies provided critical support in many campaigns and their work certainly helped extend union organization. Nonetheless, the most effective economic allies proved to be working-class men, not sympathetic middle-class women. Elite women often lacked the economic leverage possessed by working-class men such as teamsters or longshoremen. When the aid of working-class men was forthcoming, such as in San Francisco and Detroit, waitresses achieved close to 100 percent organization of their trade. Working-class men, then—often depicted as universally hostile or indifferent to female organization by feminist scholars—proved instrumental in extending unionization among female food servers.

Significantly, waitresses found that their own union brothers responded in a more ambiguous fashion than did male workers outside their union. Male cooks, bartenders, and waiters organized waitresses only after pressure from waitresses themselves or from interested women's groups. Even then, the men were often more committed to reducing the competitive threat from women than to thoroughly organizing the trade. In New York and Washington, for example, where waitresses were in a minority position within their union, the organization of female food servers lagged behind that of their male coworkers, especially in the female-dominated sectors of the industry that seemingly posed little threat to male standards.

Men outside the culinary industry, however, saw female servers in a different light. Men from many different well-organized trades—longshoremen, logging, and mining—for example, frequented local cafés and restaurants, knew the waitresses personally, and saw the unionization of the eating establishments they patronized as a logical extension of the organizing of their own workplaces. Others, like the teamsters, delivered such daily necessities as fresh bread, milk, and vegetables to restaurants. These men—men for whom the enhanced power of waitresses would threaten their male privilege neither in the workplace nor in the union—proved reliable and quite effective allies, especially in the 1930s and 1940s. In short, the cross-craft, cross-sex ties between waitresses and male workers in other trades proved more crucial organizing support than did either same-sex or same-craft bonds.

Note

This article is an edited excerpt from Dorothy Sue Cobble, *Dishing It Out: Waitresses and Their Unions in the Twentieth Century* (Urbana: University of Illinois Press, 1991).

See Also: The Rise and Fall of the Sit-Down Strike, 204; Retail Workers' Strikes, 620.

Bibliography

Babson, Steve, with Ron Alpern, Dave Elsila, and John Revitte. *Working Detroit: The Making of a Union Town.* Detroit: Wayne State University Press, 1986.

Franklin, S.M. "Elizabeth Maloney and the High Calling of the Waitress." *Life and Labor* 3 (February 1913), 36–40.

Henderson, John P. *Labor Market Institutions and Wages in the Lodging Industry.* East Lansing: Division of Research, Bureau of Business and Economic Research, Graduate School of Business Administration, Michigan State University, 1965.

Josephson, Matthew. *Union House, Union Bar: The History of the Hotel and Restaurant Employees and Bartenders International Union, AFL-CIO.* New York: Random House, 1956.

Matthews, Lillian Ruth. *Women in Trade Unions in San Francisco.* New York: Johnson Reprint Corp., 1966.

Pitrone, Jean Madden. *Myra: The Life and Times of Myra Wolfgang, Trade Union Leader*. Wyandotte, MI: Calibre Books, 1980.

Schwantes, Carlos A. "We've Got 'Em on the Run, Brothers: The 1937 Non-Automotive Sit Down Strikes in Detroit." *Michigan History* 55 (Fall 1972): 179–99.

OFFICE WORKERS' STRIKES

Vernon Mogensen

During the industrial age, the typical office worker was probably white and male; middle class in prestige, education, and salary; and opposed to joining a union or going on strike. Today's information-age office worker is more likely to be female, nonwhite, and have less prestige and salary, but is more willing to join a union and go on strike.

The changing situation of office workers raises a number of questions for investigation. Office workers have had their share of grievances against management, including low wages, lack of career opportunities, discrimination, and job security, but why have they historically been more reluctant to organize and strike than their blue-collar counterparts? Why have office workers been more willing to walk out since the 1970s? Given the fact that white-collar workers have outnumbered blue-collar workers in the workforce since 1956, why have unions not given office workers more strike support? Why did organized labor ignore women office workers for so long, and what role has the women's movement played in addressing this problem?

Nonmanagerial office and clerical workers—white-collar workers—are distinguished from blue-collar workers in that they perform salaried, nonmanual labor that does not require them to wear uniforms and protective gear, such as a hard hat. The word *clerical* derives from the scholarly, recordkeeping work performed by clerics during the Middle Ages, when most people were illiterate. At the onset of the Industrial Revolution, clerks held positions of higher social status and compensation than blue-collar workers, but the gap between the two groups narrowed during the twentieth century when the automation of office work made white-collar workers more expendable while blue-collar workers formed unions.

Efforts by office and clerical workers to organize and strike can be divided into four eras that parallel the organizational history of the labor movement from the 1880s to the present. During the first period (1880s to 1930s) clerks in transportation and retail organized, but the craft-oriented American Federation of Labor (AFL) unions had little interest in capitalizing on these early successes. The second period (1930s to 1950s), which coincides with the birth and rise of the Congress of Industrial Organizations (CIO), saw more energetic efforts to organize white-collar workers and support their strikes around the CIO's broader philosophy of inclusiveness of noncraft workers. The third period (1950s to 1970s) begins with the merger of the AFL and CIO and is characterized by organizing inertia despite the shift from manufacturing to a postindustrial information and service-based economy. The fourth period, from the 1970s to the present, is characterized by the feminist movement's influence on the labor movement and the tremendous influx of women and minority workers into the growing number of back-office, white-collar jobs.

Early Efforts at Organizing and Striking: The AFL Era

From the 1880s to the 1930s, the AFL was primarily interested in organizing skilled blue-collar workers, but it did grant charters to two white-collar unions: the Retail Clerks in 1890, and the Brotherhood of Railway and Steamship Clerks in 1899. The latter became the largest union representing clerical workers in the early years of the twentieth century, but it did not parlay its success into organizing white-collar workers outside the railroad industry. According to sociologist C. Wright Mills, in 1900 only 8.2 percent of blue-collar workers and 2.5 percent of white-collar workers were organized. By 1920, the numbers had risen on the wave of World War I–era organizing to 21.5 percent and 8.1 percent, respectively.

The male-dominated AFL largely ignored women workers. Women's groups such as the Women's Trade Union League ventured to fill the gap. In Chicago, for example, the Stenographers' and Typewriters' Union organized young women and provided support services for them until its demise in 1912. The AFL's failure to nurture the organization of white-collar workers is best exemplified by the fate of the Bookkeepers, Stenographers and Accountants Union (BSAU). The BSAU began as a series of isolated locals with an estimated 3,000 members in the early 1920s and grew to thirty-four locals by the early 1930s. Despite repeated requests for a charter to start a national union, the AFL refused; it would only issue federal charters to individual BSAU locals, which served to isolate the scattered locals and other unions in the labor federation. In keeping with its narrow, skilled-trade orientation, the AFL considered office workers to be unskilled labor like mass production workers, and hence not worth organizing. To make matters worse, the anti-union atmosphere of the 1920s and the high unemployment of the Depression of the early 1930s reduced the blue-collar unionization rate to 12.1 percent and the white-collar rate to 5 percent, according to Mills.

The CIO Era: Industry-wide Organizing

The economic hardship of the Great Depression increased interest in organizing, and membership growth resumed with the pro-labor atmosphere resulting from the passage of the National Labor Relations (Wagner) Act in 1935. In addition, Supreme Court decisions that established a supportive New Deal political environment for organizing and the desire to maintain labor peace during World War II contributed to growth. By 1948, 44.1 percent of wage workers and 16.2 percent of white-collar workers were organized.

Frustrated with delay, twenty-three BSAU locals held a convention in 1937 where they resolved to join the Committee of Industrial Organizations (CIO), which had just been expelled from the AFL. It praised the CIO's more aggressive, industry-wide approach to organizing and John L. Lewis was quick to grant them a charter in the newly formed Congress of Industrial Organizations as the United Office and Professional Workers of America (UOPWA). The industrial unions' charters gave them first right to organize white-collar employees in their jurisdiction, so UOPWA focused its efforts primarily on nonmanufacturing industries, such as banking, insurance, and social work.

Although it had accumulated about 150 white-collar locals, the AFL was slow to adjust, but the CIO's actions forced it to act. In 1942, the AFL's executive council established the International Council of Office Employee Unions to compete with the CIO's UOPWA, and three years later it was chartered as the Office Employees International Union (OEIU), now known as the Office and Professional Employees International Union (OPEIU). While both unions competed to organize office workers, they took different approaches reflecting their respective labor federations' philosophies. OEIU's appeals to office workers stressed the AFL's relatively conservative philosophy of business unionism and also stressed the uniqueness of white-collar workers' interests from those of blue-collar workers. By contrast, UOPWA's approach reflected the CIO's more liberal view of the commonality of interests of all workers and downplayed socioeconomic differences.

Both unions faced the same dilemma when it came to organizing. Wearing white collars, many office workers traditionally identified with management and saw themselves as professionals who did not need the collective protection that unions provided. Moreover, employers fiercely fought efforts to organize white-collar workers, whom they considered to be an appendage of management. These factors made white-collar workers more difficult to organize. Since organizers had to be discreet in their outreach efforts, meetings had to be held in secret, and homes, taverns, meeting halls, garages, and even back alleys became locales for union meetings.

The CIO's industry-wide approach encouraged its unions to organize the white-collar employees who worked in the front offices of industrial corporations where manual laborers were being organized. Indeed, this represented the most successful model for organizing office workers of the era, though musicians, actors, stagehands, and postal and government workers also organized. The United Auto Workers (UAW) began organizing office workers at Chrysler in the winter of 1940. By July 1941, the UAW's efforts resulted in the chartering of its first white-collar local, the Industrial Office Workers Local 889, composed of office workers and nurses from nine employers, including Packard, Dodge, Chrysler, and Westinghouse. In 1951, the UAW had organized enough white-collar workers to warrant the formation of the Office Workers Department. As a sign of its seriousness about organizing office workers, in 1953 UAW president Walter Reuther addressed its first conference of office and technical workers. The Office Workers Department was renamed the Technical, Office, and Professional Department in 1962 to reflect the broader scope of the UAW's organizing drives. For example, the UAW branched out in 1972 to organize striking clerical workers at Michigan's Wayne County Community College, who represented the first higher education employees to join the union. From there, it was a short step to organizing teaching assistants and lecturers.

The Cold War wave of anti-communist attacks on the left and the labor movement produced the passage of the Taft-Hartley Act in 1947. One of its more controversial provisions required that all union leaders sign affidavits swearing that they were not communists. When UOPWA's leaders refused to sign, they were suspected of being communists. The Taft-Hartley Act further stipulated that the National Labor Relations Board (NLRB) would not certify union election candidates who refused to sign the loyalty oaths, and many employers discontinued bargaining once the current contract expired. Faced with the loss of bargaining power and membership, UOPWA's leaders reluctantly signed the affidavits in November 1948, but it was too little, too late. The union, which bucked the CIO's endorsement of Harry Truman for president in 1948 in favor of Henry Wallace, was expelled from the labor federation in 1950.

The Merger Era

During the 1940s, UOPWA gained a foothold in the staunchly anti-union insurance industry, organizing 40,000 workers—90 percent were insurance agents—so its expulsion from the CIO left the playing field open for the AFL's OEIU. In April 1950, the CIO endeavored to fill the void by chartering the Insurance and Allied Workers Organizing Committee (IAWOC); three years later it had grown to the point where it was officially chartered as the Insurance Workers Union (IWU). In March 1951, after conducting a series of strikes, it won the right to represent 6,000 John Hancock agents and Metropolitan Life Insurance agents in New Jersey, New York, and Pennsylvania. It also fought bitter jurisdictional battles with its AFL rival, the Insurance Agents International Union (IAIU), over who had the right to organize the former UOPWA members. In a stunning repudiation of the IAWOC, 9,000 Prudential Insurance Company agents left the CIO for the IAIU. While strikes were relatively rare occurrences, two were noteworthy: the strike against Boston Mutual Life Insurance Company in 1955, and a 119-day strike against Home Life Insurance Company the following year, the longest and most successful strike ever waged against an insurance company. Although the AFL and CIO merged in 1955, the IWU and IAIU did not merge to form the Insurance Workers International Union until 1959.

In 1951, C. Wright Mills wrote: "Whatever their aspirations, white collar people have been pushed by twentieth-century facts toward the wage-worker kind of organized economic life, and slowly their illusions have been moving into closer harmony with the terms of their existence. . . . Now alongside unions of steel workers and coal miners, there are unions of office workers and musicians, salesgirls and insurance men." Perhaps the postwar boom in organizing gave Mills reason to believe this trend would continue, but white-collar workers were increasingly trapped in the middle, identifying with management, but unable to face the reality that they were slipping downward in class mobility and had more in common with wage workers. While many white-collar workers felt like cogs in the corporate wheel, their ideological instincts told them that the best way to get along was to go along, not go on strike.

In 1956, the United States passed an important milestone when, for the first time in American history, white-collar workers surpassed blue-collar workers as the largest group in the workforce. However, like generals who prepare to fight the last war, most labor leaders failed to understand the significance of this event that would radically reshape the composition of the U.S. workforce and pose one of the greatest challenges to the survival of the labor movement. Labor leaders can be forgiven for not understanding the implications of this statistical turning point from their vantage point in 1956. After all, the labor movement had just reached what appeared to be the apex of its organizational strength with the merger of the AFL and the CIO in 1955. The newly combined AFL-CIO hoped, and many employers feared, that organized labor would parlay its enlarged organizational capacity into increasing the organized percentage of the workforce. But the labor movement continued to organize and support strikes by blue-collar workers, and generally ignored the needs of white-collar workers.

From White Collar to Pink Collar

Until the last quarter of the nineteenth century, office work was a man's domain. The industrialization of the U.S. economy during the 1870s and 1880s also fueled growth in the service and information sectors of the economy. Industrial corporations needed front office personnel to keep production records, market and ship products, track sales, and meet payrolls; banks and real estate and insurance companies needed additional personnel as these industries grew. But the carnage of the Civil War, combined with the rapid increase of industrial jobs, made it more difficult to recruit male clerical workers.

Starting in the 1880s, employers found the answer to their shortage by hiring increasing numbers of young women into marginal white-collar occupations, characterized by lower pay, non-career-path, and routinized work. The job of secretary was originally a male-dominated field with management opportunities, but diminished in importance when the typewriter was introduced and employers hired women to operate them. The educational system trained men to be managers and administrators and young women to be clerical workers and secretaries, and sex-typing in education continues to steer many women into clerical positions. Like typewriter work, computer terminal work is now sex-typed as women's work.

Like employers, many labor leaders viewed working women as being marginal to the labor force. In addition, organizing drives were made more difficult because office workers were encouraged to identify with management and its antiunion values, rather than industrial workers. In the few instances where white-collar workers were organized, it was not uncommon to find locals established along gender lines. In the insurance industry, there were separate locals for the male-dominated sales force and the predominately female clerical workforce. In sum, writes Alice Kessler-Harris: "Limited labor-force opportunities, protective labor legislation and virtual exclusion from labor unions institutionalized women's isolation from the mainstream of labor. Not accidentally, these tendencies confirmed traditional women's roles, already nurtured by many ethnic groups and sustained by prevailing American norms."

Well into the post–World War II period, many labor unions viewed women office workers as unworthy of organizing. The unions assumed that women would not strike, would become homemakers as soon as they married, and that their lower wages would not generate enough union dues to make an organizing drive worthwhile. Women have made advances in low- and mid-level leadership positions since the 1960s, but few have reached the level of union president. As a result, the labor movement had little or no structure of support for working women's issues when the issue of organizing women workers arose in the 1970s.

During the 1970s and 1980s, the information and service sectors experienced tremendous growth in employment while the industrial sector shrank. The transformation from industrial to postindustrial economy eroded labor's traditional organizing base, resulted in the loss of tens of thousands of members from its industrial unions, and put the labor movement on the defensive. Membership declined from a high point of 35 percent of the workforce in 1954 to only 13.8 percent in 2004. A more telling indicator of organized labor's weakness is that only 10.9 percent of private sector employees were union members.

The decline in labor's membership has been paralleled by its weakening influence in the political arena. Deindustrialization and the globalization of capital combined to create a post–New Deal, postindustrial political economic order where Democrats recast themselves as a more conservative, pro-business party under the two terms of President Bill Clinton and the Democratic Leadership Council. Since the 1970s, unions have been unable to persuade Congress to pass key pieces of labor/consumer legislation, or stop pro-business measures such as the North American Free Trade Agreement.

Although women's groups such as the National Organization of Working Women (9to5) and the Coalition of Labor Union Women (CLUW) have called for an organizing drive of the female-dominated clerical workforce since the 1970s, the AFL-CIO did not take up the issue until the mid-1980s. In 1984, Secretary-Treasurer Thomas Donahue stressed the need to organize white-collar workers, especially women, and was instrumental in organizing a conference on professional employees. In 1985, this produced the first major AFL-CIO statement on the topic, *The Changing Situation of Workers and Their Unions*.

Unions have had their greatest success organizing white-collar workers in the public sector, but this success was due in large part to factors not prevalent in the private sector. These factors included a tradition of employee associations that served as a ready-made base for the transition to unionization, President John F. Kennedy's 1962 executive order permitting federal employees to organize, and similar reforms at the state and local levels of government. In the process of organizing public sector workers, many women, especially blacks and Latinos, were organized. Also, the passage of the Equal Employment Opportunity Act opened the door to address women's issues such as pay equity, child care, and computer safety. By 1994, 38.7 percent of government employees were organized. However, the public sector experience is not a good model for organizing the private sector, where employer resistance to unions is much stronger.

Unions such as the International Association of Machinists, International Brotherhood of Electrical Workers, International Brotherhood of Teamsters, the United Steel Workers of America (USWA), and the UAW all launched campaigns during the late 1970s and 1980s to organize office workers and push for collective bargaining agreements that included computer safety and health provisions. They joined unions such as the American Federation of State, County, and Municipal Employees (AFSCME), the Communications Workers of America (CWA), the OPEIU, and the Service Employees International Union (SEIU), which had traditionally represented office and service sector workers. In 1981, 9to5 joined forces with the SEIU to form District 925, a union affiliate established to organize office workers. For the first time, traditional unionists and women's rights activists came together to organize women clerical workers, a group that conventional labor wisdom had regarded as unorganizable.

However, workers in other industrialized countries have had greater success than their counterparts in the United States at gaining protective measures. This is due, in part, to the presence in other industrialized nations of labor/left parties, higher rates of unionization (especially among white-collar workers), and a stronger tradition of state intervention in the economy.

Organizing Women Office Workers Around Issues with Computer Technology

The rise of safety and health issues related to the rapid influx of computer terminals into the office workplace gave the U.S. labor movement a golden opportunity to organize new members in two interrelated areas where it was poorly represented: office workers and women workers. At the start of organized labor's computer safety campaign in 1979, only 6.5 percent of the nation's office workers were organized. Since 80 percent of office workers are women, championing safety and health regulations for workers using computers provided organized labor with an excellent opportunity to increase its membership among this underrepresented group. Women constituted 46 percent of the labor force in 2005, up from only 33 percent in 1960. The Bureau of Labor Statistics estimated that 65 percent of the new entrants into the labor pool between 1985 and 2000 were women, many of them minorities. Many women are, and will continue to be, employed in low-wage clerical and service occupations where computer terminals are used. For example, in 2004 women comprised 97.3 percent of secretaries and administrative assistants, 95 percent of word processors and typists, and 92.4 percent of receptionists and information clerks.

During the mid- to late 1970s, unions began to press employers for collective bargaining language that included periodic eye exams; regularly scheduled rest breaks; daily work-time limits on computer terminal use; ergonomically designed furniture and equipment; and glare-reducing screens and lighting. The first union to actively address computer-related safety and health problems experienced by its members was The Newspaper Guild (TNG). This was a reaction to the newspaper industry's pioneering switch to computers in 1970, and the resultant workplace problems. The most commonly cited problems among workers using computers, also known as video display terminals (VDTs), were vision impairment and musculoskeletal strain. Screen glare from lighting and windows and fuzzy characters created eyestrain and headaches. Straining to read the characters on the screen in turn produced neck and arm pains. In 1977, the National Institute of Occupational Safety and Health (NIOSH) reported that "complaints of eyestrain . . . often are voiced. And, with the many VDTs in use, the number of complaints could be quite large."

By 1980, TNG had used the strike threat to negotiate deals with seventeen newspapers for paid eye exams, with seven others for paid eyeglass prescriptions, and with four Minneapolis/St. Paul dailies for rest breaks. Strike threats, as much as management's concern, were the reasons for many of these safety and health gains.

By 1979, the growing volume of worker complaints reached the point where TNG and OPEIU asked NIOSH to investigate computer terminal working conditions at the *San Francisco Chronicle, San Francisco Examiner, Oakland Tribune,* and Blue Cross/Blue Shield of California. NIOSH issued its report in June 1980, finding that clerical workers using computer terminals suffered from the highest levels of workplace stress they had ever recorded: blurred vision, loss of color perception, musculoskeletal ailments, and numbness in hands and loss of strength in their arms. However, the employers were not impressed by NIOSH's report. By the beginning of 1981, working conditions at Blue Cross/Blue Shield worsened to the point that OPEIU workers went out on strike.

In November 1979, the Newspaper Guild and OPIEU formed organized labor's first VDT coalition and were soon joined by seven other unions: the CWA, the Graphic Arts International Union, the International Association of Machinists, the International Typographical Union, the National Association of Broadcast Employees and Technicians, the Transport Workers Union, and AFSCME. The coalition's plan was to publicize the problems surrounding the workplace use of computers, promote the inclusion of safety and health provisions in collective bargaining agreements, and launch a national campaign for federal enactment of regulations.

Women's Groups Organize Office Workers

The women's movement profoundly altered the way many women viewed their jobs. Emphasizing equality with men, it gave female clerical workers the conceptual basis around which to organize and protest their subservience in the office hierarchy. Discriminatory practices, such as paying women less than men for the same work, sexual harassment, and racism, were institutionalized management practices in many offices. Moreover, women had to fight the stereotype of the secretary as office wife/mother, who was expected to fetch coffee and run domestic errands, as well as type and take dictation. These injustices gave rise to support groups that strove to educate, organize, and empower women office workers in order to overcome their disadvantaged situation compared with that of management and male employees.

Some of the more important support groups formed during the 1970s are the Municipal Women's Project in Boston, Women Employed in Chicago, Women Organized for Employment in San Francisco, Women Office Workers and the Women's Action Alliance in New York City, and Working Women in Cleveland. The National Organization for Women (NOW) established a Committee on Women in Office Work to help coordinate these

Dubbed the "Willmar 8," these eight women went on strike against the Citizens National Bank in freezing weather during December 1977 in Willmar, Minnesota. They were protesting gender discrimination, low pay, lack of respect, and a glass ceiling that prevented them from moving up the bank's career ladder. Their strike inspired national media attention, because they seemed to symbolize the plight of women workers everywhere. (*Courtesy:* Minnesota Historical Society.)

efforts on a nationwide basis. CLUW, organized in 1974, and Union WAGE were also instrumental in raising women's issues in labor circles. In 1984, CLUW broadened its role by establishing a task force to address VDT-related safety and health and worker retraining issues.

The most important labor group to emerge from the women's movement was 9to5, the National Association of Working Women. Founded in Boston in 1973, Boston 9to5 later merged with Working Women of Cleveland to form a national organization, "9to5, the National Association of Working Women," with 13,000 members in twenty-five chapters. 9to5 took a leading role in educating women office workers about the safety and health hazards associated with computer terminal use. It published a book and numerous reports on VDTs, ranging from its health effects to the employment prospects in face of computer automation, and it established a "VDT hotline" for working women concerned about their safety and health. On National Secretaries' Day, when managers are encouraged to give flowers to their secretaries, 9to5 held demonstrations and letter-writing campaigns to emphasize the point that working women want "Raises and Roses!" They also drew up a "Bill of Rights for the Safe Use of VDTs," which called for giving workers a greater say in decisions on how new technologies are introduced and used in the workplace, fifteen-minute rest breaks every two hours (once an hour for intense work), a limit of four consecutive hours per day of VDT work, the elimination of stress-creating keystroke pacing and computer monitoring, alternative work for pregnant employees, shielding of terminals to protect operators from nonionizing radiation, and ergonomically designed computer terminal work environments. Karen Nussbaum, cofounder and former executive director, became the leading spokesperson on the VDT issue, writing articles, giving interviews and press conferences to the media, and speaking at demonstrations and academic conferences. In 1985, the *Wall Street Journal* cited her as "part of a small but growing nucleus of women wielding real power" in the labor movement.

The impact of the women's rights movement on the labor movement is also illustrated by the fate of eight small-town women in Willmar, Minnesota, who conducted the country's first bank strike. Dubbed the "Willmar 8," they walked out of the Citizens National Bank in freezing weather in December 1977 over issues of gender discrimination, low pay, lack of respect, and career opportunities. Formed in May, the Willmar Bank Employees' Association Local 1 negotiated without success from June to December. Their strike received intermittent support from organized labor, although the UAW organized several rallies on their behalf. The Willmar 8 quickly became a cause célèbre symbolizing the situation of women workers everywhere. They also received support from NOW members, who joined them on the picket line. The strike received national media attention. Although they were initially suspicious of NOW, the strikers developed a rapport with the group after realizing their common cause. For many of the town's 14,000 residents, the strike boiled down to the question of "Which side are you on?" The bank put financial pressure on a gas station owner who allowed the striking women to use his restroom. Other employers in town refused to hire the strikers, who were finding it difficult to make ends meet. A lawyer who represented the women lost his position as county chair of the Republican Party, but stayed with the case to the end. Many residents boycotted the bank in solidarity with the strikers, severely cutting into the bank's profit margin; others ignored the strikers. Despite the hardship they faced, the Willmar 8 held out for nearly two years. When the NLRB finally heard the Willmar 8's complaints in the summer of 1979, they agreed that bank management had committed unfair labor practices, but inexplicably said that it did not cause the strike. Instead, the NLRB ruled that the strike was "economic" in nature, and therefore the Willmar 8 were ineligible for back pay and reemployment; only one was rehired.

The Challenges of Private Sector Strikes in the Postindustrial Economy

Two of the most significant clerical workers' strikes of the 1980s, the Blue Cross/Blue Shield strike in San Francisco and the Equitable strike in Syracuse, took place in the private sector. The former ended in failure; the latter was a Pyrrhic victory. Both strikes illustrate the hurdles and hardships of conducting private sector strikes in the postindustrial economic environment where information-based work can easily be outsourced to other cites, states, and countries; and in a legal environment that fails to punish employers who engage in unfair labor practices, fail to bargain in good faith, and use replacement workers with impunity.

District 925 faced its biggest challenge when it received a call from some workers at the Equitable Life Assurance Company's claims office in Syracuse, New York, who said they wanted to form a union. Working conditions at Equitable's Syracuse office made it a prime candidate for an organizing drive. One office worker told Congress it "looks and operates like a factory." Except for a fifteen-minute morning break and the lunch hour, workers were confined to their computer screens for eight to ten hours a day processing medical and dental insurance claims. Management ignored their complaints of glare-induced headaches, musculoskeletal aches, and skin rashes. In addition, Equitable used computer monitoring to keep track of every keystroke, set the pace of work, and determine wages (which averaged only $12,000 in 1984). Wages were determined according to management's assessment of each employee's productivity and "attitude" toward the job.

Like many employers, Equitable introduced computer terminals to the office without consideration of the social costs that accompany the computerization of office work. As one of the VDT workers, Rebecca Alford, told a House subcommittee on health and safety: "We were left to master it ourselves. Made to work on a system that determined the pace and content of our work, we were stripped of any autonomy or job satisfaction. We asked for information on safety and health risks and were assured there were none."

When its employees petitioned the NLRB for

a union representation election in February 1982, Equitable responded by bringing in Ray Mickus Associates, a union-busting consulting firm. Management threatened to close the Syracuse office, lay off employees, and electronically reroute work to other locations. Regina Canuso, a District 925 organizer, told the House subcommittee: "We can't strike Equitable. . . . With this technology, they could flick a switch, and the work could be in Kansas City. This changes the whole nature of organizing." The union won the election, but Equitable dragged its feet by challenging the validity of the results before the NLRB. Despite the NLRB's conclusion that the election had been fairly won and that Equitable had filed a frivolous challenge, the insurance giant refused to bargain with District 925. The NLRB failed to compel Equitable to negotiate with the union in a timely manner. Vice President John H. Goddard defended Equitable's stalling tactics, telling *BusinessWeek* that the company was "merely following a course set by hundreds of employers."

The SEIU responded to Equitable's intransigence by calling for a national boycott. NOW endorsed the boycott, as did the AFL-CIO, whose member unions were urged not to invest their $1 billion worth of pension funds with Equitable. Boycotts thrive on publicity and District 925's effort to get Equitable's attention was no exception. It succeeded in focusing public attention—including a congressional hearing—on the conflict. Embarrassed by the negative publicity (its advertising campaign portrayed Equitable as an insurer that cared about women's issues), Equitable agreed to enter into collective bargaining negotiations with the union in September 1983. It took fourteen months to reach a settlement that called for rest breaks every two hours, eye exams, and anti-glare screens. It gave pregnant employees a limited right to alternative work, established a grievance procedure for soliciting employee input on the extent of computer monitoring, included a wage increase, and guaranteed that the office would remain open for the duration of the three-year contract.

Union observers saw the Equitable victory as a major breakthrough, although only fifty-four workers were covered by the contract. Charles McDonald, the AFL-CIO's assistant director of organizing, hailed it as "a tremendous step for unions." District 925's success marked the first time that office workers at any insurance company in the United States had been organized around the issues of monotonous work, speed-ups, computer monitoring, and safety and health hazards. Historically, the insurance industry has been an anti-union stronghold with only 3 percent of its workers (mostly salesmen) organized.

Resistance at Blue Cross

Unions failed to generate and maintain a consistent organizing effort after the Syracuse victory. Nor did the Syracuse victory attract the major commitment from the AFL-CIO that the organizers expected. Although the occupational shift from industrial to service sector was well established by 1984, the year the drive for VDT protection was in full swing, and the advantages of organizing white-collar workers were well known—labor's success rate was 52 percent compared with only 40 percent among industrial workers—only 25 percent of all organizing efforts were directed toward white-collar workers. As *BusinessWeek* commented in 1984, "Only about ten percent of service-industry and office workers have been organized, in part because major unions have not concentrated on signing them up." Despite a sizable war chest and the favorable publicity generated by its victory at Equitable, District 925 organized only 6,000 workers from 1981 to 1986.

Inspired by the success at Equitable the year before, AFL-CIO president Lane Kirkland announced an ambitious plan to organize the nearly 40,000 eligible Blue Cross/Blue Shield workers in 1985. After years of neglect, it seemed as though the AFL-CIO was ready to commit the necessary time and resources to organize private sector clerical workers. The AFL-CIO established a special office to help the lead unions—CWA, OPEIU, SEIU, UAW, and the United Food and Commercial Workers—pool their resources and coordinate organizing activities. Following their lead were AFSCME, the International Union of Electrical Workers, and USWA.

However, the AFL-CIO's one broadly coordinated attempt to organize clerical workers resulted in failure. Union activity was uncoordinated: even with the help of the AFL-CIO's advisory office, it took nearly a year to resolve jurisdictional disputes over which union would organize which workers. The campaign relied on traditional organizing tactics when a new approach was needed: male organizers used traditional tactics more familiar to the male-dominated industrial workplace than to female clerical workers. The campaign lacked a maximum effort by the participating unions: although the campaign was chaired by the SEIU's John J. Sweeney, his union continued to place much of its organizing emphasis elsewhere. The campaign also relied on public relations and a top-down organizing approach rather than a grassroots effort focused around specific employee grievances. When the campaign was met by corporate intransigence, the unions failed to counter with additional rank-and-file organizing attempts. Moreover, organized labor, which had its medical plans with Blue Cross for many years, underestimated the degree of resistance its organizers would meet. To be sure, this was labor's most ambitious effort to organize office workers. There was no guarantee of success. However, the lessons learned from the initial failure have not been incorporated into a follow-up campaign.

Given the difficulties of organizing contingent workers, the labor movement should make greater use of associational unionism that provides services, benefits, and professional support for its members, encourages more flexible work rules and greater workers' participation in the labor process, but does not collectively bargain for workers. Associational unionism might be better applied to the unique characteristics of white-collar workers who are less likely than their blue-collar counterparts to be receptive to the concept of unions—and also more mobile. Based on the concept of mutual aid, groups like the Freelancers Union and the National Writers Union—affiliated with the UAW—have sprung up to provide health care and other benefits for white-collar workers who are employed on a contingent basis. As Charles C. Heckscher writes: "The problem of worker representation extends far beyond . . . [the domain of traditional unionism to] . . . issues faced by all levels of employees—and especially by the white collar and professional employees who are increasingly seen as the leading edge of economic growth." Moreover, associations often prove to be breeding grounds for the development of unions. The presence of employee associations in state and local governments provides a favorable environment that helps unions organize white-collar workers.

Private sector office workers tend to be more suspicious of organizing campaigns and more reluctant to strike than their public sector counterparts. Richard Hurd and Adrienne McElwain found that environmental factors influenced clerical workers' decisions whether or not to join a union. Clerical workers were more likely to support union representation in pro-union states, but awareness of strikes in their state tended to discourage support. Also, clerical workers in industries experiencing growing employment may be more likely to vote for union representation. Not surprisingly, management hostility to union organizing had a negative impact on support for union-organizing campaigns. Clerical workers are more likely to be concerned about losing their jobs, afraid of striking, and afraid of being ostracized by management with whom they interact on a more frequent basis than do blue-collar workers. For these reasons, more time is needed for organizing campaigns. Office workers who are familiar with unions tend to be more supportive of organizing campaigns, while those who are not tend to be less supportive.

Undoubtedly, there would be more work stoppages and the strikers could put greater pressure on management if labor laws did not place severe restrictions on a union's ability to use the strike weapon. California's Public Employment Relations Board, which arbitrates disputes between management and labor, ruled that sympathy strikes are an unfair labor practice and that the unions are as liable to penalties and punishment as the original strikers. When the Coalition of University Employees (CUE) considered walking out in sympathy with striking AFSCME clerical workers at the University of California in 2005, management said that this would be in violation of the state's Higher Education Employer-Employee Relations Act. Many states impose harsh penalties on public employees that strike. New York's Taylor Law limits the leverage that public employee unions have in negotiating with management. It forbids strikes outright and includes jail time for union leaders as well as fines that are twice the workers' daily wages for each day the strike lasts.

Despite the restrictions, office workers have used creative tactics to help them conduct strikes. In Santa Cruz, California, clerical workers affiliated with the SEIU prepared for a strike well in advance, setting up committees to do research, education, and handle strike support. They deliberately left an inspirational leader off the bargaining committee so that she could lead mass support rallies while the negotiations went on behind closed doors. In order to define the agenda, striking Madison County, Missouri, clerical workers, represented by AFSCME, asked residents to demand the full level of services they were normally provided from the skeletal staff on duty to illustrate the importance of the work they perform.

Colleges and universities have been the hot spots in recent years. It is not unusual to find adjuncts, lecturers, and teaching assistants teaching most of the course load on a contingent basis for low pay and limited benefits. Among the public universities where strikes by staff and faculty have occurred in recent years are the universities of California, Minnesota, and Tennessee, Youngstown State University, and the City University of New York. AFSCME clerical workers at the University of Minnesota conducted the first strike there in fifty years over issues of low pay, high health care costs, and job security. In 2002, 1,900 clerical workers belonging to CUE conducted a strike at the University of California, Berkeley, timed to coincide with the first day of classes. It was the biggest strike at Berkeley since 1972. Noting the university's $2 billion endowment, the CUE called for wage increases and an end to the management's overreliance on contingent workers. Refusing to cross the picket line were 2,500 graduate teaching assistants, members of the UAW. CUE workers were also supported by 600 lecturers responsible for teaching nearly half of the campus's classes; they lent their support by educating their students about the issues involved, and they also went on a one-day strike for better pay. Management claimed that the workers could be fired for striking illegally, since negotiations were still ongoing. But CUE countered that management's take-it-or-leave-it offer effectively ended negotiations. Private universities, such as Columbia, Miami University of Ohio, New York University, Pennsylvania, Stanford, and Yale, have also had strikes over similar issues.

Some of the most bitter strikes have been fought over the issues of social justice and respect. Yale University symbolizes the pinnacle of power in the United States, but it is situated in and draws much of its workforce from New Haven, one of America's poorest cities. In 1971, 1984–85, and 2003, Yale fought tooth and nail against its employees over wages, benefits, discrimination, and lack of respect. The Hotel Employees and Restaurant Employees Union's (HERE) clerical, technical, service, and maintenance workers, Graduate Employee Students Organization's (GESO) graduate students, and the SEIU-1199's food service workers have all fought bitter strikes against an intransigent administration. The 2003 strike by all three unions saw acts of civil disobedience, marches, and massive rallies of over 1,000 supporters, many from the local community. HERE alone has gone on strike seven times since 1965. Founded in 1987, GESO has tenaciously fought several strikes, most notably the "grade strike" of 1995–96 when a majority of teaching assistants in the humanities and social sciences withheld final grades as a bargaining chip. In 2005, the GESO struck again over the right to collectively bargain. Yale continues to refuse to recognize GESO, but its strikes have forced the university to make improvements in pay and benefits.

In 2000, the NLRB ruled that graduate teaching assistants were workers, not management. As a result, New York University (NYU) graduate students organized a union and began the process of negotiating a contract with management, the first private sector university to negotiate a collective bargaining agreement with a graduate student union. Over 1,000 graduate students went out on strike in November 2005 when NYU refused to bargain with them, citing the Republican-dominated NLRB's recent reversal of the earlier ruling recognizing graduate teaching assistants as workers.

The U.S. labor movement is more isolated from white-collar workers and political parties than is the case for their European counterparts. In the Scandinavian countries, 95 percent of finance and insurance workers are organized, and the majority of them are organized in many African, Asian, European, and Latin American countries, and 2.5 million bank and insurance workers belong to the

International Federation of Commercial, Clerical, Professional and Technical Employees.

Conclusion

Office workers have not gone on strike as often as their blue-collar counterparts, but that should not be taken as a sign that they are more content with their lot. Office workers have not been nearly as organized, nor have they enjoyed the same level of support by the labor movement as their blue-collar brethren, and therefore the use of the strike to achieve collective goals has not been as successful. Historically, the fate of office workers depended on the organizing fortunes of blue-collar unions. After decades of neglect by the AFL, the most successful efforts to organize office workers have been conducted by the CIO's unions that branched out from workplaces where industrial workers were already organized. However, this dependency relationship has shown signs of changing since the structural transformation from an industrial to a postindustrial economy, and the infusion of energy and ideas from the women's movement in the 1970s.

Today only 5 percent of clerical workers are organized. An organizing campaign among office workers on the scale of the CIO's efforts to organize industrial workers during the 1930s is needed if the labor movement is to reverse its decline. Fifty-one percent of certification elections occur in male-dominated, blue-collar industries, but they account for only 42 percent of new workers organized. Although only 34 percent of elections are held in female-dominated service sector industries, they account for 51 percent of new workers organized. The present era raises the question of whether or not the labor movement has the institutional capacity and the overarching vision to embark on a new era of organizing that—unlike the first three eras—puts the concerns of office workers first.

See also: Retail Workers' Strikes, 620; Waitress Strikes, 633.

Bibliography

Cassedy, Ellen, and Karen Nussbaum. *9to5: The Working Woman's Guide to Office Survival.* New York: Penguin Books, 1983.

"Dynamic Trio: Three Labor Activists Lead a Growing Drive to Sign Up Women." *Wall Street Journal,* January 29, 1985.

Fine, Lisa M. *The Souls of the Skyscraper: Female Clerical Workers in Chicago.* Philadelphia: Temple University Press, 1990.

Gilpin, Toni, et al. *On Strike for Respect: The Clerical and Technical Workers' Strike at Yale University, 1984–85.* Chicago: Charles H. Kerr, 1988.

Heckscher, Charles C. *The New Unionism: Employee Involvement in the Changing Corporation.* New York: Basic Books, 1988.

Hurd, Richard W., and Adrienne McElwain. "Organizing Clerical Workers: Determinants of Success." *Industrial and Labor Relations Review* 41, no. 3 (April 1988): 360–73.

Kessler-Harris, Alice. "'Where Are the Organized Workers?'" In *A Heritage of Her Own: Toward a New Social History of American Women,* ed. Nancy F. Cott and Elizabeth H. Pleck. New York: Simon & Schuster, 1979.

"Labor Gets a Little Toe in the Office Door." *BusinessWeek,* December 3, 1984.

Mills, C. Wright Mills. *White Collar: The American Middle Classes.* New York: Oxford University Press, 1951.

Snyder, Carl Dean. *White-Collar Workers and the UAW.* Urbana: University of Illinois Press, 1973.

Tepperman, Jean. *Not Servants, Not Machines: Office Workers Speak Out.* Boston: Beacon Press, 1976.

U.S. Congress, House Committee on Education and Labor. *OSHA Oversight—Video Display Terminals in the Workplace: Hearings Before the Subcommittee on Health and Safety.* 98th Cong., 2nd sess., February 28, 1984.

U.S. Department of Health, Education, and Welfare, National Institute of Occupational Safety and Health. *A Report on Electromagnetic Radiation Surveys of Video Display Terminals.* Cincinnati, 1977.

Valli, Linda. *Becoming Clerical Workers.* Boston: Routledge & Kegan Paul, 1986.

"Why Clerical Workers Resist the Unions." *BusinessWeek,* May 2, 1983.

STRIKES IN THE MOTION PICTURE INDUSTRY

Andrew Dawson

The U.S. motion picture industry is now more than a century old. Movies began in 1896 and production scattered throughout the eastern United States before migrating westward to Los Angeles on the eve of World War I. Today, the industry is centered in Los Angeles and, to a lesser extent, New York City, where production companies make feature films, television programs, made-for-TV movies, music videos, and commercials. Much of the industry's output reaches world markets and it is the country's second-largest export industry after aerospace. Motion pictures are dominated by seven major producers, employing large numbers of people, but there are also a mass of small and medium-sized specialist filmmakers. It is one of the most heavily unionized industries in the private sector, with many studio employees willing to defend their working conditions through industrial action.

The labor relations of the motion picture industry fall into two equal halves. In the first period, ending in 1950, "below-the-line" workers (an industry term that includes stagehands, camera operators, studio technicians, carpenters, painters, electricians, laboratory workers, and office workers) led the way in confronting studio bosses, while "above-the-line" employees (actors, directors, and screenwriters) were either relatively content with their lot or, when they did organize, unsure of their own strength. Strikes could be extremely violent in this first period, especially in the late 1930s and in 1944 to 1946. In part this was caused by the studios' hostility to unionism, but it was also due to constant jurisdictional disputes where worker confronted worker. At the same time, the Great Depression of the 1930s polarized the studio labor movement. On one side stood a group of local studio unions and rank-and-file "progressives" who were dissatisfied with what they saw as the supine attitude of their international union leaders in the face of studio demands for wage reduction. Some of these local leaders were inspired by the radical industrial unionism of the Congress of Industrial Organizations (CIO). A smaller group was influenced by the Communist Party. On the other side were conservative union leaders and their supporters who periodically took direct control of studio unions and formed alliances with criminal gangs behind a smokescreen of bellicose and indiscriminate anti-communism.

In the second period, after 1950, roles reversed: above-the-line workers, especially screen actors, took the lead in battling with the studios, while below-the-line employees felt weak and unable to challenge their employers. Jurisdictional disputes and political schism, such prominent features of the first period, while they did not disappear altogether, were no longer major animating forces during labor disputes. Compared with the rest of American labor, post-1950 movie unionism is also distinctively different because it escaped substantial long-term decline in membership and today it is one of the best-organized industries. In addition, militancy is much higher than in other sectors as talent workers lead the fight for repeat-performance fees.

I. 1896-1950

Looking more closely at the first fifty years of the movie industry, it is possible to identify three subperiods, each with its own particular characteristics: Back East, 1896–1915; Drive for Recognition, 1915–1930; and Depression and Radical Unionism, 1930–1950.

Back East, 1896-1915

We know very little about the activities of studio workers in the days before the emergence of Hollywood. This "pre-historical" era has, so far, revealed no evidence of any collective action by studio workers, theater projectionists, or film laboratory workers. This inactivity is not particularly surprising as workers from diverse social backgrounds in a new and unformed industry needed time to get to know each other. More important, at this early stage, production was carried out by small, semi-itinerant companies in cities such as Chicago and New York. Departmental structure was crude, while the division of labor was limited and in a state of flux, with crew members performing several tasks. One person could be director, scene painter, property man, photo-playwright, and stage carpenter, while another might be camera operator, bookkeeper, business manager, and wardrobe assistant. At Biograph, for example, the camera operator assumed the creative lead over the director; later on, roles reversed and today's more familiar hierarchy asserted itself, according to Michael Nielsen. Only when workers congregated in large factory-like studios in one location did collective self-identity emerge and industrial action begin.

Drive for Recognition, 1915-1930

When the industry settled in Hollywood, a suburb of Los Angeles, women and men flocked to the new and exciting center of production. The fame-struck beauty queen boarding a train in Kansas City and heading west has some basis in fact: most arrivals in the city were native-born Americans, many from the Mississippi Valley and Mountain states and, unlike previous waves of westward migrants, disproportionately women. During the 1920s, motion pictures and the oil industry provided the major stimulus to the city's population growth.

The Los Angeles business elite, keen to see the city overtake rival San Francisco, welcomed migrants. Still, fearing the importation of eastern social unrest, leaders insisted on racial and class hierarchy. Native-born white Americans and immigrants from Northern Europe were at the apex of the social order; further down were Mexican Americans, African Americans, and East European immigrants. Well-paid jobs in the new movie studios went to American-born white workers and immigrants from Northern and Western Europe, who settled in a racially and socially homogenous Hollywood and its surrounding communities. Racist housing covenants forbidding sale to nonwhites and the vigilance of the Ku Klux Klan in the 1920s effectively barred African Americans and Mexican Americans from all but a handful of studio jobs for the next half century. Familiar with the vagaries of wage labor and economic uncertainty and without the support of welfare agencies, migrants were attracted to Hollywood by the prospect of economic independence and home ownership. Ironically, while cheap tract homes no doubt freed workers from some of the boss's enveloping tentacles, they also diluted collective action as suburban living isolated and individualized workers and their families.

"The production of a sound film is a very complicated process," observed economist Murray Ross, "requiring the active participation of many minds and hands."

> Once a story is chosen from the thousands that reach the readers' desks or an original is written by a trained scenarist, it must be fitted to a cast or a cast fitted to it. Research assistants and librarians check every detail in the scenario. The property department studies the script and gathers the required props down to the minutest detail. The wardrobe department designs the costumes. Architects, art directors, set directors, carpenters, and painters go to work on the necessary sets. Eventually the stage is set and the cameras go into action. Then come the job of sound recording, the scoring of music for the picture, and finally the editing of the film.

Film laboratories made film prints, which were distributed and exhibited in theaters across the world.

The movies, unlike many other early twentieth-century mass-production industries, created a large number of occupations, many demanding specialist skills, in an assemblage of separate departments. A 1942 federal survey listed 545 separate jobs. While studio employees worked cooperatively with each other, they often felt the need to be represented by a union that understood their particular experiences. Wage differentials reflected finely graded hierarchies of esteem. During the era of the studio system from 1920 to 1950, many occupations had strict entry and training requirements, elaborate work rules, and clearly delineated responsibilities and procedures for promotion. This, combined with the fact that multiple unions claimed some trades, led to friction between unions and constant jurisdictional skirmishes. Especially before 1950, strikes were not only battles between employees and studio heads but could also be parallel conflicts between fellow workers.

The arrival of movies in Hollywood heralded the creation of a small number of large studios each employing in excess of 1,000 workers. Pay was often good, but hours were long as studios tried to minimize time spent filming, especially on location. Work was never certain and often irregular. As in other industries, general business conditions led to fluctuations in employment: the early years and most of the 1920s were prosperous; the Great Depression of the 1930s created a deep but short-lived crisis; movies did well in World War II, only to go through serious changes in the 1950s and 1960s; and, more recently, "New Hollywood" has seen more job opportunities for talent workers as the industry has re-created itself as part of multimedia entertainment. Employment also fluctuated seasonally as studios produced films during the summer months for peak winter audiences (in the days before air conditioning). Many studios adopted a core-periphery system whereby a small group of insiders or "family" found regular employment, while the remainder, especially in the early days, were forced to appear outside studio gates looking for work. Under such a casual labor system, favoritism and blacklisting were common. Because studios were unwilling to allow interruption of their film schedule, they paid wages that supported a labor supply sufficient to meet peak demand. As a result, for much of the time, a large pool of unemployed waited to be called upon.

In her study of the Ince Studios (Inceville) in the 1910s, film historian Janet Staiger demonstrates the early impact of managerial control. Bedeviled by separate departments and a plethora of distinct jobs, with a complicated and multiple flow of "product" through the studio, executives looked to add order to filmmaking. At Inceville, the studio used the continuity script to trace and orchestrate a film's progress through the studio in the same way that machine shops used blueprints and instruction cards. Such a strategy separated the conception of a task from its execution; managers who had authored the script assumed control of conception, leaving studio employees to carry out instructions via their departmental heads. Moguls might try to emulate Henry Ford's production line, but such direct control of filmmaking was impossible. While it made sense for managers to hold employees to a steady work rhythm, the complexity of filming and the limits to a fully integrated system meant, for example, that a crew might sit around for hours before moving into action.

As Wall Street finance assumed power over Hollywood, so the studios adopted tighter departmental accounting procedures, as a way of achieving greater efficiency as well as demonstrating probity to their new masters. But continuity scripts and budgetary control reveal the limited scope for managerial integration and efficiency. Executives needed other strings to their bows. In the 1920s, they turned to welfare capitalism, but it was not long before they were forced to accept the presence of organized labor inside the studios. Producers soon discovered that a more sophisticated way of maintaining workplace hegemony was to exploit sectional differences between groups of workers and have one group sabotage the strikes of the other. Efforts in the 1930s and 1940s to transcend narrow craft boundaries and present a common front to employers were rightly seen as a serious threat to managerial control.

Despite their best efforts, movie moguls were unable to keep unionism out of the industry, as migrants to the city brought with them long-held customs and traditions. But what form of unionism best suited the needs of studio workers? The International Alliance of Theatrical Stage Employees (IATSE, pronounced "eye-atsee," often shortened to IA or the Alliance) was the first to organize in Hollywood. Founded in 1893 by live theater stagehands in the East, IA organized movie projectionists working in vaudeville before moving up the supply chain to the studios. The Alliance soon claimed jurisdiction over all movie workers, but its structure was a curious mixture of craft and industrial unionism. Hollywood locals might be either craft (e.g., camera operators) or semi-industrial (e.g., laboratory workers). Outside Los Angeles, locals were often a mixture of several occupations. What complicated matters was the arrival of purely craft unions that laid claim to some movie industry jobs. Powerful international unions, such as the Carpenters, Painters, and International Brotherhood of Electrical Workers (IBEW) were, like the IA, affiliated to the craft-oriented American Federation of Labor (AFL). Until mid-century, intense friction created by competing jurisdictional claims had a significant impact on the character of strikes and labor disputes in the industry; more recently, demarcation disputes play a much lesser role in the lives of studio workers.

Even the most selfish and shortsighted union leader agreed that it was better to settle differences between unions in order to present a common front against studio employers. But in a dynamic and changing industry such as motion pictures, agreements made in good faith were often undermined on the quick sands of changing technology and business practice.

Movie projectionists, influenced by the labor traditions of the live theater, were first to unionize Hollywood studios. As early as 1908, Los Angeles projectionists organized Selig Company workers. Three years later, their local union laid claim to all movie industry workers throughout the city and county. In early 1916, Samuel Gompers, president of the AFL, initiated a further organizing campaign in support of all affiliated studio crafts. Faced with hostility from studio bosses, who soon banded together to form the open-shop Motion Picture Producers' Association (MPPA), and the indifference of some employees, it would take ten years, three major strikes, and the threat of a fourth strike before studio heads recognized and bargained with representatives of their production workers. (It is important, but difficult, to keep track of the changing names of producer associations: the MPPA [1917] was succeeded by the Motion Picture Producers and Distributors Association [1922], while the Association of Motion Picture Producers [1924] acted as the MPPDA's labor-relations arm in Hollywood. Later, the Motion Picture Association of America [1945] was followed by the Association of Motion Picture and Television Producers [1964] and the Alliance of Motion Picture and Television Producers [1982]. Not all major studios belonged to an association, and independent studios formed their own group.)

In July 1918, spurred on by galloping wartime inflation and after studios rejected calls for higher wages and union recognition, the Alliance launched an industry-wide strike that lasted two months. At the same time, the union called out projectionists across the country in sympathy strikes. But the IA failed to achieve its goals as the Carpenters filled the places left by the strikers and the U.S. Department of Labor intervened to secure essential wartime production. The U.S. Army even threatened strikers with the draft if they did not return.

Without concerted action by a united workforce, producers easily ignored early calls for formal recognition. In September 1919, the IA launched another strike, accompanied again by strikebreaking from the Carpenters and IBEW and supported by the Los Angeles Building Trades Council, with equally depressing results. In July 1921, both building trade unions and the IA fought against the studios' imposition of wage cuts and longer hours by bringing 1,200 studio workers out on strike. This time it was the IA that undermined solidarity by returning to work the following month. Those still on the picket line might have rightly suspected the IA of concluding a shabby deal with the producers behind their backs.

Nevertheless, in 1926, producers and unions came together to sign the Studio Basic Agreement (SBA), which recognized unions (but not the closed shop) and established machinery for negotiating wages and conditions and settling grievances. What had changed in the intervening five years? In 1925, Hollywood Carpenters and IA locals concluded a workable jurisdictional agreement, which was followed a year later by a similar accord between the IA and the IBEW. Settling such issues made strike action more effective by reducing the likelihood that unions would fill the jobs of rivals during disputes. As a result, the threat of strike action by building crafts and IA studio workers and projectionists was sufficient to bring recognition.

Producers had also gone through a process of change. While they remained hostile to unions, they were realistic enough to understand that union demands could not be resisted indefinitely and that through a program of preemptive reform they could remain the dominant force in the motion picture industry. The SBA was just one of a number of initiatives designed to draw workers and their unions into closer relations with producers in an attempt to achieve industrial harmony and foster loyalty to the studios. The year before signing the SBA, the Motion Picture Producers and Distributors of America (MPPDA) set up Central Casting (CC) and the Mutual Alliance of Studio Employees (MASE) to act as central employment agencies for actors and production workers, respectively, as a way to eliminate the wasteful and degrading wait outside studio gates. CC and MASE were part of the studios' broader managerial strategy to take control of hiring and remove the foreman's prerogative of recruiting family members, friends, or even fellow unionists. In addition, the producers wanted to disperse hordes of young female extras gathered outside studio gates at a time when the public was concerned with the evils of the casting couch and the threat of sexual exploitation. The following year, fearful that talent workers would succumb to the lure of unionism, the producers created the Academy of Motion Picture Arts and Sciences (AMPAS). The Academy, better known today for handing out Oscars, functioned then as a company union.

Union recognition was won at a price. The SBA grievance procedure was cumbersome, and all-important negotiations between union officials and studio heads took place in New York City. While the venue made some sense—the IA headquarters were located there, as were the corporate offices of the movie companies—the distance between Hollywood members and union leaders created considerable conflict and suspicion.

Depression and Radical Unionism, 1930-1950

The producers' hope that welfare capitalism would create a pliant and contented workforce fell apart in the economic and political crisis of the Great Depression. By 1931, falling box office receipts hit studios already saddled with massive debts accumulated as a result of the introduction of sound. With bankruptcy staring them in the face, producers cut wages and lengthened hours. While the conservative IA leadership favored concessions, individual militants and local unions—both within the IA and among the craft unions—advocated a sturdier response to the studios. The split between supporters of the IA leadership and the radicalized elements among studio labor led to a decade and a half of turmoil in Hollywood.

The crisis of the 1930s also enabled labor racketeers to worm their way into the heart of the IA. In fighting exhibitors intent on reducing wages and cutting staff, projectionists looked to support from local urban gangs. Projectionists might have secured allies among other sections of the labor movement, but the nature of their isolated work and City Hall's close ties with theaters through municipal movie regulation encouraged them to turn to machine politicians in Chicago, New York, and elsewhere.

In a series of disputes in 1931 and 1932, projectionists tried to close down cinemas by using stink bombs, hiring loud bands, and infiltrating groups of disrupters into auditoriums; real bombs were also used, and in a number of ugly incidents audience members were injured. Corrupt city governments shielded projectionists from the police and the law, while at the same time gangster elements moved in to take control of the union. In Chicago, William Browne, head of the IA theater stagehands, teamed up with Willie Bioff, a minor local hoodlum. Using violence, they took charge of the projectionists' local and made arrangements with movie exhibitors to forget about restoring members' wage cuts in return for payoffs to them. These two soon fell in with the Nitti gang, which was looking for new business ventures following the lifting of Prohibition. Using its strength in New York City, the gang had Browne elected as IA president at the 1934 convention. Subsequently, Bioff was appointed Browne's personal representative in Hollywood.

While gangsterism proved a minor irritant to studios, corruption turned the IA into an oppressor of its own members. Bioff and Browne's reputation preceded them to Hollywood, and in a deal with the studios that lasted from 1936 to 1941, the two agreed to keep wage demands down in return for substantial payoffs from the moguls. Fake strike levies of members' wages went straight into the hands of Brown and Bioff, who passed most of it on to the Chicago mob. The increasing conservatism of the leadership, combined with the arrival of gangsterism, turned members of Hollywood locals against their own union.

In July 1933, the IA launched an ill-timed strike of all Hollywood members against the studios, demanding recognition for sound crews. The studios were already furious with the IA for its uncharacteristic rejection of wage cuts during the New Deal "bank holiday" and now plotted revenge. Ominously, the introduction of sound had undermined the 1926 jurisdictional agreement between the IA and the IBEW, with both insisting that producers negotiate with them. The IA held a superior claim because it had far more sound crew members, but the studios, wanting to divide and rule, hid behind the letter of the agreement. They declared that the IA had abrogated the terms of the SBA—which prevented a union from negotiating for a new group of workers without the agreement of all other unions—and, as a result, had forfeited membership in the SBA. But the IA was divided: not everyone responded to their leaders' call, and Camera Local 659 refused to join the strike. With the studios inviting the IBEW to fill the places of strikers, the IA members, fearful of losing their jobs in the middle of a depression, stampeded back to work. Within a short space of time, the IA membership fell from 9,000 to 200 and the union was effectively banished from Hollywood.

But the IA's wilderness years were short-lived. With the passage of the 1935 Wagner Act granting employees the right to join unions of their own choosing, moguls were concerned that production and talent workers might turn to the industrial unionism of the CIO. The producers quickly recognized Browne and Bioff, the newly arrived IA leaders, as two stalwart opponents of militant unionism. But how were studio heads to orchestrate the union's return to favor without rivals spotting the maneuver? According to labor historian Mike Nielsen, Browne arranged a token strike of Paramount projectionists at which signal the producers caved in and invited the IA back to the studios, granting a closed-shop agreement covering the trades lost two years earlier.

In response, unions unaffiliated with the IA, concerned at the increasing power of the Browne and Bioff administration, turned for mutual support to a loose alliance known as the Federated Motion Picture Crafts (FMPC), which had formed in 1932. Most of these unions, such as the Painters, Studio Laborers, Scenic Artists, Hair Stylists, and Makeup Artists, were not part of the SBA. In April 1937, the FMPC struck against the studios for recognition. Facing the strikebreaking tactics of the producers, the IA, and the Teamsters—who used imported muscle to cross picket lines—the FMPC hoped for support from the recently formed Screen Actors Guild (SAG). While on the picket line, CIO longshoremen and factory workers aided the FMPC, SAG entered into an opportunistic, short-lived alliance with the IA and continued to report for work. To counter the FMPC, the IA and Teamsters imported their own muscle and the producers turned for support to organized crime. Inevitably there was picket line violence. Surprisingly, the results of the strike were mixed: the IA absorbed some defeated FMPC locals, including the Laborers, but the Painters, who remained resolutely independent of the SBA, were granted recognition and a closed shop.

Opposition to Browne and Bioff also appeared within the IA studio locals. Known as the "IA Progressives," these workers fought the levy on wages and the IA's direct control of their locals. The Progressives encouraged the California legislature to investigate the leadership's racketeering, while Browne and Bioff replied accusing the Progressives of being Communists. In 1939, at Browne's invitation, the U.S. House Un-American Activities Committee visited Hollywood to investigate Communist influence in studio labor—a forerunner of a far more devastating visit after World War II. In June 1939, the Progressives, with support from the CIO, formed the United Studio Technicians Guild (USTG), a short-lived attempt to create a rival to the IA. In a series of maneuvers the IA again allied with SAG, and the USTG was resoundingly defeated in a National Labor Relations Board (NLRB) representative election. Browne and Bioff took their revenge by purging Hollywood locals of all opposition to their rule. Under the IA's closed-shop agreement, loss of union membership also meant loss of job. As a result, many courageous dissidents never worked in Hollywood again.

But the anti-racketeering campaign begun by the IA Progressives eventually bore fruit. Following investigation by SAG, Bioff was forced to return to Illinois to serve a sentence for pimping. Although he reassumed office in Hollywood, his days were numbered when Joseph Schenck, head of Twentieth Century Fox, revealed Browne and Bioff's payoffs when federal authorities charged him with income tax evasion. In 1941, both union leaders were convicted and jailed for racketeering.

Even though Browne and Bioff destroyed internal resistance to their rule, external opposition coalesced under the combative Herb Sorrell of the Painters union. The Painters left the SBA in 1932, frustrated at the time-consuming grievance procedure, and set about organizing other studio workers ignored by the IA. In 1940, the Screen Cartoonist Guild (SCG) received a charter from the Painters. While Schlesinger and Metro-Goldwyn-Mayer cartoon studios recognized the union, Disney was implacably opposed. In a bitter 1941 strike that lasted nine weeks, a settlement was reached only after studio heads dispatched an obstinate Walt Disney to South America. Jubilant at the success of the strike, independent anti-IA forces formed the Conference of Studio Unions (CSU).

Wartime conditions helped create a temporary truce between the warring studio labor groups, but continued expansion of CSU was, sooner or later, bound to create conflict with the IA and the producers. By 1943, dissatisfied Carpenter and IBEW locals had joined CSU and, for a time, so did the IA film laboratory technicians. In October 1944, CSU members briefly walked out in support of set decorators demanding recognition from the producers, only to be hustled back to work by the War Labor Board. In March 1945, when the strike reignited, the dispute turned into the most violent industrial conflict that Hollywood would ever see.

With a deeply divided studio labor force—separated by politics as much as craft jurisdiction—the stage was set for a protracted and violent struggle on the streets of Los Angeles. Stakes were high; with the end of the war in sight, each side knew that a knockout blow now would determine the future pattern of industrial relations. In March, approximately 10,500 CSU members went out on strike and pickets went up around the studios. They also picketed local movie theaters as a way of making an immediate financial impact, but the CSU lacked the ability to call out projectionists who were IA members. All kinds of tactics were used to turn away theater patrons: a group of killjoy picketers even gave away the plot to the Universal thriller *Lady on a Train.*

The CSU had few allies in the early days of the strike. Most other studio unions were either hostile like the IA or determinedly neutral, like SAG and the Screen Writers Guild (SWG). The Communist Party stuck to its wartime no-strike policy and refused support—ironic in light of accusations that the CSU was Communist. Whatever the policy of their union, studio workers were deeply affected by the dispute: many screenwriters and actors crossed picket lines (the CSU kept a list of celebrity scabs) while others stayed away out of sympathy or fear of violence. The IA had no such qualms, and, with cooperation from the studios, made sure its members not only remained at work but also deliberately filled the places of strikers.

Picket line behavior reflected both the strikers' animosity toward the IA and the broader pattern of wartime politics. Strikers sang songs linking IA president Richard Walsh with the discredited gangsterism of Browne and Bioff. Reflecting the Popular Front ideas of the time, picketers chanted, "Labor produced for victory. Now let's produce a victory for Labor," according to historian Gerald Horne. The IA leadership countered with leaflets accusing the CSU of communism and Sorrell of being a card-carrying member of the Communist Party. Neither was true, but this kind of mud-slinging gained ground in the changed political atmosphere of the postwar years. At least for now, a sympathetic New Deal government adhered to the wartime pact between labor and capital and the CSU benefited from NLRB actions, but by the following year it was left fighting with yesterday's ideological weapons.

With no outward sign of producers giving way, the CSU, in a last desperate bid, concentrated its strength on key studios. Warner Brothers in Burbank was selected—partly because many sympathetic IA members in the studio refused to cross CSU picket lines. The "Battle of Warner

Brothers," which took place in the first week of October, consisted of a series of bloody set-piece confrontations between mass CSU pickets, at times numbering 3,000, and an alliance of IA strikebreakers, hoodlums, Teamster drivers, studio police, and heavily armed county police using clubs, chains, hammers, tear gas, and the hoses of Warner Brothers' fire department. Cars were driven at high speed through the picket lines; fighting broke out; cars were overturned and many men and women on both sides were injured and picketers arrested. Once inside, the strikebreakers had the problem of getting out again; many stayed for days, although little work was done. Mass picketing achieved results, and was soon extended to Paramount, RKO, and Columbia. Just as important, though, the Battle of Warner Brothers attracted widespread sympathy: SAG and SWG called for an end to the dispute, and even the Communist Party, recognizing that the Popular Front was ending, belatedly took up the cause. In October 1945, the producers, weakened by losing an earlier NLRB set decorators' vote, grudgingly conceded defeat but insisted that studio unions must settle all outstanding jurisdictional disputes among themselves or have them settled by a committee of the AFL.

Building on the CSU's ostensible victory, Sorrell again called out members in July 1946 in support of a substantial pay claim. With IA laboratory technicians blocking the release of film prints, the producers settled quickly in what became known as the "Treaty of Beverly Hills."

But the CSU's joy was short-lived. The AFL's jurisdictional committee, rather than helping resolve labor conflict simply created a new problem in an obtuse ruling that took away set construction from the Carpenters and awarded it to the IA (a strange decision since set construction had not been an issue in the earlier strike and outstanding jurisdictional issues had been settled locally). In September 1946, the CSU walked out in support of the Carpenters. Even though SAG once again crossed picket lines, Sorrell thought his alliance with the powerful Brotherhood of Carpenters would win the day, but he was overly optimistic. The producers, though they portrayed themselves as caught in the middle of a jurisdictional dispute, were keen to destroy the CSU, while the IA organized replacements for striking lab technicians and the Teamsters drove actors across picket lines. Having no time to recover from earlier battering, strikers returned to work in early 1947.

The obliteration of the CSU took with it the promise of locally accountable democratic unionism. The IA's resounding victory over its labor opponent transformed it into the dominant force in studio labor. Industrial relations experts Hugh Lovell and Tasile Carter optimistically believed that the triumph of the IA and the ending of labor's civil war was a positive outcome of the 1946 dispute: gone would be the constant jurisdictional battles between the IA, the Carpenters, the IBEW, and rival dual-union federations such as the CSU. But the consequence of the IA's postwar supremacy was the creation of a profoundly conservative union incapable of facing up to the technical and organizational changes brought about by the advent of television; nor could the IA adequately comprehend the political and social changes brought about by the arrival of the civil rights and women's movements.

Talent workers were late in forming independent labor organizations. SAG and SWG emerged in 1933, followed three years later by the Directors Guild of America (DGA). It might seem puzzling that talent workers stirred a quarter of a century later than craft workers, stagehands, and technicians. Many below-the-line workers dismissed actors and other talent workers as narcissistic, self-centered individuals, unable to form trade unions and unreliable as allies. While there are elements of truth in this caricature, environment helps explain a good deal of talent behavior. Actors compete for parts against each other in a vastly oversupplied labor market. They sign individual contracts (in the past twenty years some below-the-line trades have also signed individual contracts) and are concerned about film credits, because future employment depends on it. At times, their artistry steers them toward individualism and the admiration of successful stars; at other times, conditions in the profession drive them to the picket line. Producers did all they could to prevent talent unionism, since above-the-line costs are substantially higher than below-the-line costs and because of the crucial artistic and ideological role played by screenwriters in constructing the screenplay.

Nevertheless, shortly after World War I, some

silent movie actors did join the East Coast stage actors' union, Actors' Equity. With the introduction of sound in the late 1920s and the arrival of unionized Broadway stage actors in Hollywood, Equity made renewed efforts to organize, but producers successfully avoided recognition. In the early years of the industry, many actors believed that conditions in Hollywood were far better than those on Broadway and so felt little need to seek protection. In 1927, the MPPDA set up AMPAS for producers, writers, actors, directors, and directors of photography. Only in 1933, following AMPAS's endorsement of wage cuts, did talent workers see through the veil of paternalism and insist on forming their own independent labor organizations.

The creation of SAG altered the dynamics of the studio labor movement. Growing up in the context of a bitter battle between the IA and its rivals, both sides courted SAG. As a fellow outsider, it was torn between sympathy for the FMPC and CSU and a pragmatic belief that an alliance with the more powerful IA would bring greater benefits. In 1937, SAG gained union recognition and a closed shop. Nevertheless, talent unions remained far too weak to contemplate strike action.

II. After 1950: Against the Trend

IA leaders had little time to enjoy their triumph over the CSU before a series of changes exerted a profound impact upon the workforce in the motion picture industry. In 1948, the U.S. Supreme Court ruled in the *Paramount* decision that the studios must divest themselves of ownership of movie theaters, fatally undermining the whole production process upon which the studio had been built for thirty years. Without an assured income from film rentals, a large element of commercial uncertainty was injected into the system as each film needed to sell on its own merits. The arrival of television drew audiences away from cinemas and led to slashed production schedules, unemployed studio workers, and threats to the commercial viability of producers. At the same time, important technological changes affected the way films were made and distributed. Over the next twenty years, the classic Hollywood system disappeared as the studio lost its central place in the production-line system with the switch to independent makers. Many in the industry feared that TV would lead to the rapid demise of Hollywood. Early TV was live and located in New York City; only from the mid-1950s, with increasing use of prerecorded programs, did a significant amount of work migrate back to Los Angeles.

But these changes, important as they are, did not dislodge labor from a position of strength inside the industry. While motion picture union membership fell compared with earlier times, it was still much higher than the national average in the late 1980s. Estimates indicate that about 90 percent of studio workers were organized at the time of World War II; by the late 1980s, above-the-line membership had risen close to 100 percent, while below-the-line membership had fallen to about 60 percent, according to labor relations researchers Lois Gray and Ronald Seeber. A more impressionistic picture of the 1990s suggests that the proportion of below-the-line union members continued to decline, but in more recent years has stabilized as a result of a successful effort by the IA to widen its appeal. But the decline in strength is much less than the national average where union concentration fell from 32.5 percent of the nonfarm workforce in 1953 to 17.5 percent in 1986. At the same time, motion picture workers continued to confront producers, often in lengthy strikes.

Part of the explanation for the relatively high union membership and the continued role of strike action lies in the fact that motion pictures, now embedded within a dynamic and highly profitable entertainment sector, continue to expand. In 1992, 380,700 people were employed in movie production and distribution. Contrast this to the postwar experience of other highly unionized traditional industries, such as steel and automobiles, where membership declined precipitously. Strong studio unions, fighting for a share of a bigger pie, gained tangible benefits. At the same time, difficult conditions intrinsic to the industry—especially irregular work and long hours—encouraged many to seek protection in union membership.

Talent and production workers did not share the same experiences in the postwar decades. Above-the-line workers gained from the industry's economic and technological changes, while the IA and craft unions stagnated and turned their backs on militant traditions. SAG conducted its first strike in 1952. In 1960 and throughout the 1980s, it and the Writers Guild of America (the WGA succeeded the Screen Writers Guild in 1954) confronted producers, demanding payment for members' repeat performances. While strikes throughout the economy declined during the anti-labor Reagan-Bush administrations of the 1980s, labor disputes in motion pictures actually increased. Ironically, President Ronald Reagan was a former head of SAG, which deeply embarrassed union activists.

Changing technology and industrial structure tended to benefit talent workers. The collapse of the star system liberated stars from long-term contractual obligations—which always favored the studios—and allowed them greater freedom to negotiate. This also had a trickle-down effect on lesser actors. At the same time, rapid expansion in new media outlets created fresh sources of income for above-the-line workers.

In contrast, vertical disintegration and the rise of independent producers undermined below-the-line crafts. By 1970, the process was complete as independent production companies replaced studios as the site of filmmaking. Each film was made on a one-off basis by a company, or small group of subcontractors, which assembled the cast and crew only to dissolve once the film had been made. Increasing numbers of these films were made on location away from Hollywood, making union solidarity more difficult. The arrival of lighter, simpler-to-operate film equipment, especially useful on location, encouraged producers to reduce the size of crews. Although the industry continued to expand, the below-the-line job market stagnated not only due to technological change but also because producers insisted that studio workers take on more responsibilities, work through meal breaks, and accept longer hours of work. Regular below-the-line employment disappeared as stagehands and technicians were hired on a project-by-project basis. Although it is clear that the independents were only nominally free from control of the major distributors, legal separation allowed parent companies to jettison the obligations of existing IA contracts.

The *Paramount* decision separating production from exhibition dealt a serious blow to the IA's bargaining strength by removing the threat of a projectionists' strike in support of Hollywood workers. In addition, increasingly irregular work, short-term contracts, and freelance status were not conducive to union membership. To stop the hemorrhaging of jobs, IA locals countered by enforcing work rules and insisting on minimum crew sizes. They also introduced rosters to ration available jobs among current union members. With large numbers of hopefuls looking for work, including well-trained graduates of film and technical schools, the task of controlling entry to an overcrowded labor market was difficult. Without an infusion of new members, the IA studio locals stood out as white and middle-aged in an increasingly diverse Los Angeles labor force; youth, Mexican and African Americans, and women were underrepresented in most studio unions.

As a result, the IA felt weak and vulnerable as its membership base stagnated in the 1980s. Not surprisingly, when producers demanded concessions during the 1982 and 1985 contract talks, the IA buckled. In 1988, the IA split with its three negotiating partners—the Teamsters, Studio Laborers, and the IBEW. The IA favored delaying negotiations with the studios because the National Association of Broadcast Employees and Technicians (NABET, the IA's sister union in radio and TV) had lost an earlier strike against the NBC network. Weakened without the IA beside them and unable to prevent strikebreaking, the other three unions went down to defeat. The following year, a subdued IA agreed to giveback clauses without a strike.

The IA tried to increase its strength in a number of ways. For low-budget producers operating without union contracts outside of Hollywood, it offered more favorable terms, including clauses deferring wages and benefits if the film failed to gross sufficiently. But Hollywood locals, fearing a threat to collective agreements, were suspicious of such generosity. More recently, the IA responded positively to the changing environment by reforming its parochial semi-craft structure along industrial lines. It also tried, albeit unsuccessfully, to merge with NABET. Since the mid-1980s, under pressure from the international office, local unions have been encouraged to admit more members. At the same time, the IA organized in the South, where a growing amount of film production is located, even though it is a region traditionally hostile to unionism. Between 1994 and 2002, IA membership grew from 65,000 to 103,000, with nearly half working in the Los Angeles area. The IA estimates that in 2002, 90 percent of Hollywood productions were under union contract, substantially up from the previous decade.

In contrast to the IA, SAG and the WGA were far more forceful. Membership rose substantially and both engaged in successful strikes. Indeed, after 1950 there was a complete role reversal between SAG and the IA. In the early period, the IA was assertive while SAG crossed picket lines and failed to conduct any strike of its own. After 1950, SAG was militant while the IA was passive. Actors, writers, and directors benefited from the expansion of the media and entertainment industries, particularly new creative jobs and the proliferation of additional outlets for their labor on TV, videocassette, cable, satellite, and the Internet. Not only did SAG negotiate conditions, minimum rates of pay, and individual contracts, like the WGA and the DGA, it fought a successful battle to obtain payments for repeat performances of members' work.

These "residuals," as they are called, have been a major concern for above-the-line employees. Repeat showings of a film mean that an actor, writer, or director is in competition with a cheaper version of themselves; each program slot filled by a repeat is a new film/show/commercial not made. Residuals are now so important that, collectively, actors receive as much in repeat fees (including commercials) as they do from payment for the initial performance. In an occupation plagued by irregular work, income from residuals helps smooth out the troughs of unemployment. In Gray and Seeber's anthology *Under the Stars*, industrial relations experts Alan Paul and Archie Kleingartner argue that talent guilds are now closely identified with management through their administration of residual payments to members and by their assertion of property rights in films in which their members perform. It is difficult to see how fees for repeat performances grant property rights. However, it is certainly ironic that residuals are obtained from producers through strikes, which are familiar tools of those without an equity stake in enterprise.

Since the 1950s, residuals have been the major cause of industrial action by the talent guilds. They first confronted advertising producers over commercial repeats before tackling film reruns. In 1960, SAG and the WGA engaged in lengthy separate strikes against producers over repeat fees for post-1948 movies shown on TV. Subsequently, the guilds successfully extended claims to cable, video, and satellite, but producers are reluctant to grant more concessions: because films make a profit only when overseas sales are included, they do not want to negotiate away income before the film makes a return on capital. With European TV deregulation, the export market's increasing importance encourages guilds to look for a share of foreign TV repeats.

The 2000 actors' strike against commercial producers was a good example of the changed character of industrial conflict in the second half of the twentieth century. The six-month strike, which began in May, was long and bitter largely because commercial producers insisted on ending payments for repeat performances. Although advertising is not the bread and butter of the industry, everyone realized that the dispute was a dress rehearsal for film and TV contract negotiations the following year. As in earlier disputes going back to the 1980s, the 135,000 actors of SAG and the American Federation of Television and Radio Artists (AFTRA) stood together. They were intent on extending repeat payments to cable, but faced with producers' calls to abolish TV payments, SAG and AFTRA had little option but to fight defensively.

Producers mistakenly believed that the unions would soon collapse. They were surprised at the determination of actors, mostly the unknown rank and file, who operated switchboards, picketed and leafleted studios and casting agencies, and attended morale-boosting rallies. It is true that some union members found it difficult to appear on confrontational picket lines, and there was an early dispute over the color of the strike T-shirt—would white suit everyone?—but most overcame the individualism that goes with their jobs. The vast majority of those who crossed picket lines were not union members but inexperienced young hopefuls willing to face picket line hostility for the slight chance of fame and fortune. According to the *Los Angeles Times*, in August, as some arrived for a deodorant commercial audition, they were met by shouts of "Your grandparents died to join a union!" and "Scab, take 50! Scab, take 70!" Much ad shooting takes place on location, often on public property, so pickets formed and reformed across Los Angeles in a constant cat-and-mouse game, with deception and dissembling used on both sides, as unionists tried to pinpoint the next location. On hearing that a shoot was to take place in a quiet Pasadena neighborhood, SAG members quickly volunteered to cut grass free of charge so that they could loudly rev their mower engines. Soon, off-lot shooting in Los Angeles declined by 75 percent.

To create division within employers' ranks, the unions offered producers interim agreements, which allowed them to shoot with experienced union actors in return for accepting union conditions. As the strike progressed, unions targeted advertisers such as McDonald's, General Motors, AT&T, and Procter & Gamble, who they believed were aggressively commissioning new commercials. Actors, with the support of other AFL-CIO unions, picketed General Motors plants across the country and Canada and turned back delivery trucks; the Communications Workers of America and the IBEW held solidarity actions against AT&T; and Procter & Gamble was threatened with consumer boycotts.

Celebrity strikers attracted much public attention, but they were never the key to the strike. Nevertheless, their support was important. Well-known actors refused to cross picket lines: despite the considerable gap in status and income between celebrities and the less well-known, stars needed to maintain good working relations with fellow professionals. Many appeared on picket lines, lobbied politicians, and boosted the cause at Emmy awards and similar celebrity events; and some gave six-figure sums to the strike fund. In contrast, sports personalities (athletes including football and basketball players and golfers), who carried SAG union cards for their product endorsement shoots but had only a peripheral connection with acting, were more willing to cross picket lines.

Surprisingly, the advertisers were less adept at enlisting support. One company's early attempt to poke fun at SAG and lure production to South Africa backfired when it placed an advertisement in *Shoot* magazine showing the drooping breasts of an elderly African woman with the caption, "In South Africa, this is what SAG means." A general outcry forced the company to sack the executives responsible, but the unions not only noted the advertisement's racism, sexism, and general tastelessness but also saw it as an attempt to break their organization. The producers' most effective weapon was economic. Having failed to maintain production in Los Angeles and New York—the two main union centers—they shifted work to nonunion locations and Canada, leaving many actors who relied on ad work to pay their bills as best they could. The unions responded with picketing across the country and abroad, but they were less effective in stopping production outside the union heartlands.

By October, with both sides exhausted, the strike ended. Although actors could claim to have made the most gains—union jurisdiction over Internet ads was recognized, pay rates increased, and TV repeat payments continued—they were unable to extend repeat payments to cable. In the close-knit world of Hollywood acting, the effects of such a lengthy strike were devastating. Just as in any working-class mining camp or gritty steel town after a bitter labor dispute, friendships ended, arguments broke out in restaurants, people avoided the company of others, and lives permanently changed. Such was the raw emotion of the dispute that SAG rejected strikebreakers' applications to join, and members who scabbed were severely disciplined.

The 2007–2008 screenwriters' strike also illustrates the continued evolution of media workers' activities during industrial disputes. As before, conflict between the Writers Guild of America and producers centered on residual payments—this time for Internet content. Feeling that it had concluded a poor deal in relation to video residuals—the then "new media"—following a 153-day strike in 1988, WGA was determined not to be outsmarted by the producers. (The earlier agreement also determined subsequent DVD residual payments.) Beginning in November 2007 the guild and its 12,000 members hunted out film shoots, picketed studios' gates, and invited stars to join the picket line; they also used the Internet in new and imaginative ways to boost morale, and seek out allies among actors, Teamsters, IA members, and the general public. Blogs kept activists in contact, and short video clips on You Tube and other Web sites provided outlets for the creative talents of writers and their actor allies. Hundreds of videos, of variable quality and artistic merit, lasting from under sixty seconds to several minutes provided basic strike information, imaginative propaganda, illuminating commentaries on the current state of the 100-day dispute, and poked fun at producers. The strike, which ended successfully for the writers, is the first industrial dispute anywhere in the world to generate such a substantial body of digital video evidence—offering rich pickings to social commentators, journalists, and subsequent historians.

Today, studio workers face a number of pressing issues that could play a role in determining the pattern of future industrial action. The experience of conducting joint strike action convinced SAG and AFTRA leaders that a merger was imperative, but a merger vote in 2003 failed when SAG's vote did not reach the necessary 60 percent. Another important issue is "runaway production." The increasing number of shoots taking place outside Los Angeles has led to opposition from Hollywood studio workers who point to job losses as producers search out more profitable locations in other parts of the United States, Canada, or farther afield. The studio unions are divided on the best way forward—some favor state or federal tax subsidies, while others urge tariff protection—but it may be only a matter of time before they tackle this aspect of globalization with strike action.

See also: Musician Strikes, 675.

Bibliography

Clark, Danae. *Negotiating Hollywood: The Cultural Politics of Actors' Labor.* Minneapolis: University of Minnesota Press, 1995.

Gray, Lois S., and Ronald L. Seeber, eds. *Under the Stars: Essays on Labor Relations in Arts and Entertainment.* Ithaca, NY: Cornell University Press, 1996.

Horne, Gerald. *Class Struggle in Hollywood, 1930–1950: Moguls, Mobsters, Stars, Reds & Trade Unionists.* Austin: University of Texas Press, 2001.

Lovell, Hugh, and Tasile Carter. *Collective Bargaining in the Motion Picture Industry.* Berkeley: Institute of Industrial Relations, University of California, 1955.

Nielsen, Michael. "Motion Picture Craft Workers and Craft Unions in Hollywood: The Studio Era." Ph.D. diss., University of Illinois-Urbana, 1985.

Nielsen, Mike, and Gene Mailes. *Hollywood's Other Blacklist: Union Struggles in the Studio Era.* London: British Film Institute, 1995.

Perry, Louis B., and Richard S. Perry. *A History of the Los Angeles Labor Movement, 1911–1941.* Berkeley: University of California Press, 1963.

Prindle, David F. *The Politics of Glamour: Ideology and Democracy in the Screen Actors Guild.* Madison: University of Wisconsin Press, 1988.

Ross, Murray. *Stars and Strikes.* New York: Columbia University Press, 1941.

Schwartz, Nancy L. *The Hollywood Writers' Wars.* New York: Knopf, 1982.

Staiger, Janet. "Dividing Labor for Production Control: Thomas Ince and the Rise of the Studio System." *Cinema Journal* 18 (Spring 1979): 16–25.

ATTORNEY STRIKES AT THE LEGAL AID SOCIETY OF NEW YORK CITY

Michael Z. Letwin

In 1970, Legal Aid attorneys in New York City became the first lawyers in the United States to go on strike, and they did so again in 1973, 1974, 1982, and 1994. Despite expectations to the contrary (and for reasons that cannot be fully explored here) few lawyers elsewhere have followed their example.

It is clear, however, that Legal Aid strikes in New York City took place in the wake of *Gideon v. Wainwright* (372 U.S. 335, 1963), in which the U.S. Supreme Court dramatically expanded the right of counsel for indigent criminal defendants. Instead of establishing a public defender office to meet the obligations imposed by *Gideon*, New York City's municipal government contracted with the Legal Aid Society, a privately funded charity established in 1876, as its primary public defense provider. To fulfill its city contract, the Society hired hundreds of public defenders.

Despite *Gideon*, however, New York City's criminal justice system dealt contemptuously with poor defendants. Grossly inadequate city funding for indigent defense meant low salaries and impossible caseloads, turning the attorneys into glorified production workers who could offer only perfunctory representation for an overwhelming number of clients, nearly all of them African American and Latino. This assembly line was epitomized by fragmented representation in which clients were seen by a different attorney on each of many court appearances in the same case.

By the late 1960s, the civil rights movement had condemned such poor-quality indigent defense as just another reflection—alongside police brutality and discriminatory sentencing—of institutional racism throughout the criminal justice system. But despite a series of official reports and mass inmate protests that sharply criticized such representation in New York City, conditions did not change; politicians, judges, Wall Street lawyers, and Legal Aid management simply did not feel compelled to change them.

In 1968–69, these public defenders took matters into their own hands by founding the Association of Legal Aid Attorneys (ALAA), which conducted five major strikes between 1970 and 1994. Although widely decried as "unprofessional" by the city's political, judicial, and corporate elites, these strikes were catalysts for systemic improvement of indigent criminal representation in New York City, including continuity of representation (assignment of the same trial lawyer throughout a given case), retention of experienced attorneys through higher compensation, workload limits, affirmative action, and health and safety.

Thus, for more than three decades, labor relations in New York City's criminal justice system have been characterized by a recurring cycle of accumulated grievances, strikes, and their aftermath.

Industry Background (1876-1966)

In 1876, Der Deutsche-Rechtsschutz-Verein was established to provide free legal assistance to German immigrants, primarily in civil matters. In 1896, under the auspices of leading members of the private bar, it was renamed the Legal Aid Society. In the late nineteenth and early twentieth centuries, criminal defense representation was typically provided by private solo practitioners, often members of immigrant communities, for a fee. During the Progressive Era, however, the legal elite came to regard such attorneys as an impediment to swift and sure deterrence of immigrant crime. Lawyers for the rich were also concerned that poor immigrants felt "that they were being denied redress, protection and equality before the law," particularly in regard to ineffective criminal defense representation. The resulting political radicalization, warned Legal Aid Society president Charles Evans Hughes in a 1920 speech before the American Bar Association, threatened to "open a broad road to Bolshevism" in the United States.

Although initially concerned that the "public defender movement" was a socialist plot designed to undermine private profit, the legal elite ultimately agreed with other reformers "to accept the replacement of private lawyers in indigent [criminal] cases, because they feared that assigned counsel gave the poor legitimate grievances that contributed to social unrest and presented an ongoing impediment to the efficient administration of criminal justice." In 1914, the first such indigent public defender office was established in Los Angeles. Subsequent years witnessed a national shift to such agencies, the public or private character of which depended on the influence of the organized bar in a particular jurisdiction.

These early reformers, the legal elite, and institutional defenders all agreed that public defense institutions should adopt a nonadversarial approach. In the words of one leading public defender advocate, the prosecution and defense worked together to ensure that "no innocent man may suffer or a guilty man escape." Without the financial incentive to prolong a case, it was argued, public defenders would encourage most defendants to plead guilty, if necessary by seeking to withdraw from cases in which "guilty" clients were intransigent. Rather than seeking "technical" defenses or go to trial, public defenders encouraged their clients to testify, thereby ensuring that only an innocent person was acquitted, and appeals were brought only on merit.

Pursuant to this model, the New York Legal Aid Society gradually took on a growing but still limited number of criminal defense assignments. This qualitatively changed only as a result of the U.S. Supreme Court's 1963 decision in *Gideon*, which greatly broadened the right of counsel to criminal defendants, regardless of their ability to hire a lawyer.

Most major cities responded to *Gideon* by establishing or expanding a governmental public defender office. Instead, New York City government contracted with the already-existing Legal Aid Society to serve as its primary public defender organization. To fulfill this contract, the Society hired hundreds of young public defenders, many of them heavily influenced by the civil rights, student, and anti-war movements.

These new defenders were appalled by the contrast between *Gideon*'s lofty promise and the grim reality of daily Legal Aid practice. As Gerald Lefcourt recounted in a 1994 interview with the author, when he joined the Society in 1968:

> I had no training at all. There was no orientation. . . . There were no mock trials. We did arraignments for a month, and then we were thrown into battle. I had no clue as to what the right thing was to do. We had no research tools . . . no real offices, no telephones. We couldn't call witnesses. There was no anything. I never interviewed a defendant except in the prison or on the floor of the hallway right before a hearing or trial. In the back of my mind, I knew that I should do an investigation, but there were only one or two investigators operating out of Manhattan for the whole [Legal Aid] Society.

Moreover, clients (mostly African American or Latino) saw different Legal Aid lawyers (mostly white males) at each court appearance.

Lefcourt and others responded by organizing the Association of Legal Aid Attorneys, an independent union that was certified as the lawyers' exclusive bargaining representative in December 1969. (The Association of Legal Aid Attorneys affiliated with District 65, an independent general union in 1978, and the union became a local of the United Auto Workers [UAW] in 1996.) Several months later, city jail inmates rebelled, in part to protest the poor quality of Legal Aid representation. The Society responded by threatening to terminate its contract with the city to defend criminals unless it received more funding. After briefly toying with the idea of a public defender system, the city provided a small amount of additional money. Regarding this as merely a token gesture, on May 3–6, 1970, amid international protest against the

U.S. invasion of Cambodia, Legal Aid attorneys in Manhattan conducted the first lawyers' strike in the United States.

The legal establishment reacted with hostility. The *New York Law Journal* cited "authoritative sources" who "blame[d] the strike on the increasing number of so-called 'militant' attorneys who have joined the society in recent years . . . [and whose] attitude . . . is that only through action can change be accomplished."

This brief strike yielded mixed results. To counteract favoritism and promote attorney job retention, the union's first contract included a twelve-step salary scale; direct client representation, however, was not significantly improved.

The 1973 Strike

Three years later, Legal Aid attorneys hoped that such conditions would be remedied by the unprecedented federal court decision in *Wallace v. Kern* (392 F. Supp. 834), which ordered a limit on Legal Aid's criminal caseload. On June 27, 1973, however, these hopes were dashed when the federal appellate court overturned the decision on jurisdictional grounds. On July 2, therefore, Legal Aid attorneys voted 178 to 79 to strike for lower caseloads, private client interview facilities, stenographic help, more time for research, better salaries, and, above all, continuity of representation.

The strikers were immediately attacked by the presiding appellate court justices. As reported in the July 6, 1973, *New York Law Journal*, these justices denounced the strikers for "abandoning the responsibility to the indigent which union members assumed upon their employment," recruited private attorney strikebreakers, and threatened that if the strike did not end, "we will be compelled to take such action as is warranted by the circumstances."

Union president Karen Faraguna answered this attack by arguing, as reported in the July 17 *New York Times*, that the inadequate quality of Society representation had been "abandoning [clients] for years," and that, as reported in the July 9 *New York Law Journal*, "we are on strike to implement the very [continuity] recommendations made by the Appellate Divisions' own committee." She also pointed out, reported the July 3 *New York Daily News*, that "in the next five years we will represent one million indigent clients. We are determined to create conditions under which they can be represented justly and effectively. . . . This strike will be won when no longer will you hear a judge ask a defendant: 'Do you want a lawyer or do you want legal aid?'"

Perhaps the most effective answer came from forty-one inmates who refused to leave their cells for court appearances.

The broader legal community was split. As for the mainstream bar, the *New York Times* reported that "from the Wall Street firms and the Association of the Bar of the City of New York—publicly at least—came not a word of support for their overburdened brethren." However, in a July 2 *New York Law Journal* advertisement, the National Lawyers Guild and National Conference of Black Lawyers asked private lawyers to refuse reassignment of the Society's struck work, pointing out that "your acceptance of [strikers'] assignments will decrease the effectiveness of the strike. We ask you to consider seriously the implications of the present crisis and to join us in supporting the Association's action." An advertisement in the July 19 *New York Law* Journal, signed by professors at New York and Hofstra law schools, "urge[d] members of the private Bar to support this important [strike]." Similar statements of support were issued by the New York Civil Liberties Union and the Puerto Rican Legal Defense and Education Fund.

When the strike ended just six days later on July 9, the ALAA had won continuity of representation within the same court, to "the maximum extent feasible," and an experimental program for continuity between misdemeanor and felony courts. *New York Times* columnist Tom Wicker, who had covered the *Gideon* case, wrote approvingly that "the net effect . . . should be to treat a client's case more nearly as *his or her case* rather than as a file folder. That is what the constitutional right to legal counsel is all about."

The 1973 contract also established workload grievance mechanisms, salary increases, eventual "substantial parity" with assistant district attorneys, shorter probationary periods, greater Spanish-language training, confidential interview conditions, greater office space, and the provision of office equipment, such as desks, chairs, and telephones.

In practice, however, the 1973 strike yielded few representational improvements. Although the number of Legal Aid public defenders had tripled since 1970, the agency remained starved for adequate city funding and attorneys still lacked adequate offices, interview space, or workload limits. Moreover, judges undermined the contractually mandated continuity experiment and were increasingly hostile to Legal Aid attorneys' vigorous advocacy.

The 1974 Strike

In response to these conditions, union members set a strike deadline for September 11, 1974. When management nonetheless equivocated on continuity of representation and blamed the city for the Society's refusal to offer meaningful raises, attorneys voted 193 to 144 to walk out.

Echoing their 1973 attack on the union, the presiding appellate justices declared, according to the *New York Daily News,* that Legal Aid strikers were "attorneys, professionals, not day laborers, and should act accordingly," and threatened to bring disciplinary charges, recommendations of dismissal, and replacement by private attorneys.

The same newspaper also reported the union's reply that "we are striking today because the judiciary and the management of The Legal Aid Society have continued to ignore their responsibility to indigent defendants in this state. . . . The Presiding Justices' statement amounts to the ancient practice of strikebreaking." The union filed charges at the National Labor Relations Board (NLRB) against the presiding justices and repeatedly offered to end the strike in exchange for binding arbitration, a proposal rejected by the Society. Speaking to a strike rally, then-House member Edward I. Koch responded to the presiding justices by declaring, as recounted years later in a 1982 *News World* article, that "to threaten a man—any man—be he lawyer or laborer, with loss of employment, loss of the right to earn his living at his chosen occupation for speaking his mind, for striking to improve his lot, is not only uncalled for but repugnant to our law."

But by the end of the nineteen-day strike, about one-third of the attorneys had crossed the picket line because, Faraguna recalled in an interview years later, "many people did not want another strike when improvements were in progress." Thus, the remaining strikers returned to work, even though management remained free to modify, or even to abandon, continuity in order to handle more cases. As the *New York State Bar Journal* later explained,

> When it was over, the strikers returned to work with a lot less than they had at the beginning. They were out 20 days' pay. The future of their five-year-old union—called with proper professional dignity The Association of Legal Aid Attorneys of the City of New York—was in jeopardy. And the two issues over which they walked out in the first place—cost-of-living increases and the right to represent their clients from the start to finish of each case—were still unresolved.

In June 1975, the union sustained another blow, when a committee of the New York County Lawyers Association issued an opinion that the strike had violated professional ethics. Attorneys nonetheless conducted a one-day strike on October 26, 1976, to reinstate a colleague deemed to have been fired for her union activity.

The 1982 Strike

In negotiations over a 1982 contract wage reopener, the union, which by now had affiliated with District 65, UAW, again sought salary comparability with assistant district attorneys. At the same time, Rockefeller drug laws enacted in the mid-1970s had further exacerbated attorney workload, in response to which management increased the pressure on individual attorneys. One of these was Weldon Brewer, an attorney fired in 1982 for having told a judge that he was unable to file a motion due to his high caseload.

Brewer's firing quickly became a symbol for everything that was wrong with Legal Aid representation. Legal ethics specialist Monroe H. Freedman, of Hofstra Law School, writing in an op-ed piece in the November 7, 1982, *New York Times,* declared that Brewer "has taken up the fight where Mr. Gideon left off," and former U.S. Attorney General Ramsey Clark agreed to represent Brewer. On October 22, enraged by the firing, ALAA members rejected management's salary offer and voted by a two-to-one margin to strike.

Staff attorney support for the strike was strong; by the fifth week, only 5 percent had crossed the picked line, compared with 30 percent by the third week of the 1974 strike. Scabs were dealt with harshly, union spokesperson Gary Sloman told the *New York Law Journal,* "because . . . people who are working are stabbing us in the back."

Support staff represented by Local 1199 continued to work, but supported the strike in a wide variety of ways. The strike was endorsed by local criminal bar associations, including the New York Criminal Bar Association, which in a letter appearing in the *New York Law Journal,* "urge[d] our members, and other private lawyers, not to accept court assignments to indigent defendants now represented by a striking Legal Aid attorney."

In the strike's fifth week, nearly a thousand strikers and supporters rallied at City Hall Park. On November 22, UPI reported a speech by Ramsey Clark, who told a rally of 300 strikers and supporters that the strike represented "a struggle for equal justice" in a system that permitted millions of dollars for defense of the rich, but provided only "pennies for [defense of] the poor." On November 26, eighty-one city judges issued a statement citing the crucial role of Society attorneys in both civil and criminal cases and called for the quickest possible resolution of the strike.

Visitors to the picket line included Lt. Governor Mario Cuomo, City Clerk David Dinkins, City Council member Ruth Messinger, Judge Bruce Wright, contingents of court officers and other unionized court employees, and delegations of labor and community leaders. Teamsters employed by United Parcel Service and by heating oil companies refused to cross picket lines at courthouses and Legal Aid offices. In a message of support reported in the union's November 24, 1982, strike bulletin, Coretta Scott King wrote: "Martin Luther King, Jr. [who was assassinated in 1968 while visiting Memphis to support striking sanitation workers] gave his life in a trade union struggle, and if he were with us today, I believe he would also be among your strongest supporters. . . . Together we shall overcome."

Society supervisors, meanwhile, appeared on pending criminal cases without files, and were soon unable to accept new criminal cases at arraignments. The refusal of private attorneys to cross the lines to take struck Legal Aid cases—and the inexperience of many of those who did—caused numerous criminal defendants to be arraigned without counsel. As long trial and sentencing delays piled up, the jails became overcrowded. Commenting on this logjam, the same issue of the union strike bulletin made clear that:

> None of us gloats over the impact of our strike on our clients—we all work at Legal Aid because we believe in our clients' rights to quality representation. . . . Yet we must recognize that our strongest leverage with management is our ability to close down the courts and this necessarily means putting aside the short term needs of our clients for their long term need for experienced, conscientious lawyers. It is management's refusal to agree to our demand for a decent wage increase, and indeed its refusal to bargain at all, which has prolonged the strike, not any action by the union.

The December 21, 1982, strike bulletin reported that 416 Rikers Island inmates signed a petition stating that "the striking attorneys are balking at the very idea of 'Assembly Line justice.' Underlying the demand for salary increase is the less publicized demand for lighter caseloads and a less hectic pace. . . . We, as detainee/defendants, should all support this strike! It is imperative that they win, because in the long run, we win!" Similarly, the November 23, 1982, bulletin reported the comments of one criminal defendant's mother, who declared that "[the strikers] are definitely underpaid, and overworked. . . . I know what's right and what's wrong—and they're right."

Soon, however, the strikers came under fire from the alliance of Legal Aid management, city government, court administration, and the press. Before the strike was even a day old, management threatened to cut off strikers' health benefits and to discipline attorneys, particularly probationers, for "abandoning" clients. In a November 5 statement, the Society's board called the strike "indefensible economically and incompatible with the Society's mission of providing legal representation to the poor of New York City." Management counsel Robert Batterman threatened to seek legislation prohibiting strikes by Legal Aid attorneys and sought a court order restraining union disciplinary proceedings against scabs—who were given free representation by the Wall Street firm of board member Robert Patterson. In late October, the union responded by filing an unfair labor practice charge against management, and in early November filed a federal lawsuit to enjoin administrative judges from coercing strikers into returning to work.

The November 10 *New York Daily News* reported that Mayor Koch, who as congressman had supported the Legal Aid attorneys in their 1974 strike, had now raised the ante by denouncing the strikers as "unethical" and instructing City Criminal Justice Coordinator John Keenan (who, according to the *New York Law Journal,* had already stated publicly that "I don't think they [Legal Aid attorneys] should have the right to strike") to study "replacing" the Society with a governmental public defender agency. *New York Times* editorials labeled the strike "foolish" and urged Koch to "maintain the pressure by getting standby legislation that permits him to replace the society with a public defender system at any time." The union's December 8 strike bulletin publicly challenged this plan to replace the unionized Legal Aid Society, asking, "what, then, distinguishes any City attempt to replace Legal Aid with, for example, the closing of a factory and moving of it to another state solely to avoid unionization? This is the classic runaway shop situation and is illegal under current labor law." On December 21, according to the *New York Law Journal,* Koch's "Keenan Commission" conceded that:

> Creation of a public defender system with simultaneous abandonment of Legal Aid is not the course to take. It involves numerous startup costs and on-going expenses. . . . There would seem to be little point in jettisoning an established organization, well qualified to perform the desired function, equipped as it is with able personnel and fortified by long experience . . . [and] known for its vigorous independent representation of indigents.

The report also found the Society to be of higher quality and more cost effective than private (18-B) representation. The commission, however, called for replacement of the ALAA's right to strike with arbitration binding on the Society and the union, but not on the city—which funded the Society's criminal defense work.

Finally, on January 3, 1983—ten weeks into a strike that had paralyzed the criminal courts—the parties reached a settlement. It included an 11.2 percent salary increase over two years (compared with management's 4.31 percent prestrike offer), establishment of a joint union–management working conditions committee, and selection of caseload arbitrators. Weldon Brewer would remain suspended with pay, pending an arbitrator's decision (which ultimately upheld his dismissal).

These improvements were the result of a long strike that had been characterized by a high degree of democratic rank-and-file control, in which only 46 (or 8.5 percent) of the union's 540 members had crossed the line. As a result, no striker was disciplined by management, the city, the courts, or the bar. And although the strike cost each striker thousands of dollars in salary, they had emerged prouder, more active, and more confident.

Shortly after the strike, however, a committee of the Association of the Bar of the City of New York issued an opinion—at Koch's urging—suggesting that striking Legal Aid attorneys were ethically obliged to continue to represent their criminal clients.

The 1994 Strike

The 1982 strike won eight years of relative labor peace. From 1990 to 1992, however, conflict erupted when, after years of rising attorney workload, due largely to a dramatic increase in prosecution for crack cocaine, management sought to reduce attorney health benefits and other compensation. The ALAA and 1199 support staff, working in unprecedented alliance, conducted a series of escalating protests, one-day strikes, and other actions.

By 1994, however, a strike seemed unlikely. In June, the Society had convinced the city to deal with the costly and poor-quality criminal representation provided by private (18-B) lawyers by increasing Legal Aid's role. As a result of relentless labor strife, the Society's board of directors came under the control of a more union-friendly leadership, which agreed to raise senior attorney salaries, implement more aggressive affirmative action, improve health and safety, and otherwise lift the quality of representation. A settlement was anticipated by October 1, when the union's contract would expire.

In the middle of September, however, the expected agreement was effectively vetoed by Mayor Rudolph Giuliani, who declared it inconsistent with his hardline position in upcoming municipal labor negotiations. Although the Society emphasized that it would self-fund the agreement, the mayor issued an ultimatum: even modest salary increases would provoke his severe displeasure. Fearing retribution from its primary source of funds, the Society agreed.

When the union contract expired on October 1, the mayor personally vowed to cancel Legal Aid's contracts if the attorneys struck; his criminal justice coordinator privately reminded the union that when Giuliani worked for Ronald Reagan he had helped break the 1981 air traffic controller (PATCO) strike.

At a mass meeting on the morning of Monday, October 3, union members weighed their options. Despite the mayor's threats, most would neither accept a net cut in compensation nor surrender their National Labor Relations Act rights, as private sector employees, to strike. Moreover, many believed that Society management would capitulate before Giuliani could actually carry out his threat, or simply felt that they had no choice but to fight back. Thus, attorneys voted overwhelmingly to strike, before marching down the middle of Broadway to join picket lines already erected by striking 1199 support staff.

Within minutes, as reported by the *New York Times*, Giuliani went on live television to declare that "The canon of ethics says that you can't abandon cases, so I don't know where lawyers come off striking. And here they are abandoning cases for an entire city. I'm not going to let them do that." Although Legal Aid supervisors were prepared to fully staff the courts, Giuliani unilaterally terminated all of the Society's city contracts, which, he said, would be replaced by new agreements with other contractors. As a result, he was quoted in the *New York Daily News* saying, "This will be the last time lawyers strike against the public interest."

Although some press reports portrayed the strikers sympathetically, the city elite enthusiastically supported the mayor's hardline position. According to the *Wall Street Journal*, Arthur Liman, a former Legal Aid Society president and onetime Iran-Contra prosecutor, said that Giuliani "had a responsibility" to end the walkout. The *Daily News* editorialized that "while [strikers] have every right to bargain and demand higher wages, their ability to shut down something as vital as the courts gives them too much power . . . they must be held to the same no-strike law as other key city employees. . . . They must never again be permitted to hold the city hostage."

The next day, Tuesday, October 4, the ALAA sought countermomentum with a mass press conference on the City Hall steps. Foreshadowing Giuliani's later restrictions on First Amendment expression, hundreds of police prevented the media from contact with the strikers, who defiantly chanted "Rudy, Rudy is his name, union-busting is his game."

Notably absent, however, were Governor Mario Cuomo or City Council Speaker Peter Vallone, both of whom were leading Democrats. Also missing were leaders of the major municipal unions. On October 5, the *New York Times* reported that Stanley Hill, executive director of the American Federation of State, County and Municipal Employees DC 37, had publicly advised both sides to return to the bargaining table. Six days later the *New York Post* reported that Sonny Hall, president of Transport Workers Union Local 100 (subway and bus workers), said, "The Legal Aid lawyers' strike was indeed a careless act, although they had an excellent case for their demands. . . . Our concern is not why the mayor said no, but how he said it." Privately, the leadership of both DC 37 and the United Federation of Teachers (UFT) assured Giuliani that they were "neutral" about the attorneys' strike, presumably in hopes of softening the mayor's demands for $200 million in cuts in their members' health care benefits. As the *New York Times* explained:

> Whether the Legal Aid workers realized it, they had walked off their jobs at a critical point in

> the city's relationship with its work force. Mr. Giuliani, having just completed a round of budget cuts and staff reductions, has now gone back to the workers, seeking more job cuts and asking them to start contributing toward their health-care benefits. . . . The Giuliani administration seemed to fear that by striking, the lawyers threatened the spirit of collective sacrifice.

Or, as City University of New York professor Stanley Aronowitz pointed out, "Labor's strategy has become Giuliani's strategy. The big fry make their deals."

Similarly, many private lawyers regarded the 1994 strike as an opportunity for enrichment rather than solidarity, as they told *Newsday.* "I've got to make a living," explained attorney William Blasi, who was anxious to pick up struck cases. Mitchell Salloway, another private attorney, rejoiced that, for him, the strike meant: "More cases. More money. More food on the table."

Further emboldened by such support, Giuliani announced that any striking attorney who did not return to work by the following morning would be permanently blacklisted from all future city-funded representation. Under these overwhelming threats, the strikers returned to work on Wednesday morning, and that evening, they voted 544 to 150 to ratify a slightly improved agreement.

This brief but intense battle left attorneys feeling a mixture of bitterness, defiance, and pride. One junior attorney, Young Ran Ra, told the *New York Times* that "when I took this job I knew I wouldn't be paid well, but . . . [a] lot of people are contemplating leaving because of what has happened." Luis Roman said, "if I'm back here tomorrow, the sign on my door will read 'Dump Rudy Headquarters.'" Mary Beth Mullaney spoke for many when she said, in a letter printed in the *New York Times,*

> Seven months ago I left my family and friends in Irmo, S.C. . . . to work as a staff attorney for the Legal Aid Society in New York. It is the job I had most wanted. On Oct. 1, I went on strike with about 800 of my colleagues. . . . I was asking Legal Aid Society management to redistribute funds already within the society. . . . There was nothing unethical about the strike. . . . I am ridiculed by my family and friends for the work I do. But I am proud of it because I am fighting to uphold individual rights for everyone, not just those who can afford it.

However, the *New York Times* praised Giuliani's "firm foundation in fiscal reality" and declared that the strike had been "a foolish challenge." Writing in the *New York Post,* former Mayor Ed Koch praised Giuliani's "courage in taking on the striking Legal Aid attorneys." *Newsday* quoted Lawrence Kudlow, economics editor of the right-wing *National Review* and a chief budget economist in the Reagan administration, who predicted that "Giuliani's action on the Legal Aid lawyers was a very significant development; to some extent it's a New York City version of Reagan's PATCO confrontation. . . . I'm sure it has sent a lot of public union officials scurrying."

Opposition to the mayor's conduct fell to commentators such as writer and former public defender James S. Kunen, who wrote in the *New York Times* that "the strike was fated to fail because these advocates for the indigent were demanding the one form of compensation their fellow citizens are unwilling to give them: respect." In *Newsday*, radical labor analyst Robert Fitch predicted that municipal unions would suffer from their abandonment of the Legal Aid strikers:

> What's surprising is not that Giuliani broke the [ALAA] strike by threatening to fire everybody and is now picking his teeth today with the attorneys' bones. It's that the rest of the city's municipal labor movement—once regarded as the most militant and powerful in America—mostly looked on while the mayor gnawed away on the carcasses of their fellow trade unionists.

The mayor, however, seemed determined to inflict further punishment for the brief strike. According to *Newsday*, he declared that the attorneys "have a hope, not a reality of keeping their jobs," and he vowed that any "new [contract] between the Society and the city . . . [must] prohibit strikes in the future." When blocked by an NLRB investigation from pursuing a permanent ban on Legal Aid strikes, he demanded an immediate $13 million cut in the Society's $79 million city criminal defense funding. This cut led Legal Aid criminal-defense attorneys to surrender a week's compensation in order to prevent the layoff of 1199 support staff and junior attorneys. The *New York Times* applauded these cuts for yielding "cheaper, more efficient defense services."

Mayor Giuliani also announced plans to transfer an additional 25 percent of the Society's city criminal funding to nonunion contractors, thereby ensuring, reported the *New York Times,* that the city would "no longer be at the mercy of one group that could decide in the future to go out on strike, and then all of a sudden you have a massive backup in the criminal justice system."

But strikebreaking was not the mayor's only purpose. The autumn 1995 *City Journal,* a publication of the Manhattan Institute, a Giuliani administration think tank allied with the right-wing Heritage Foundation, charged that the Society was dominated by the union and "leftist" poverty lawyers whose successful representation of public housing tenants, the homeless, and juvenile offenders had interfered with the Giuliani administration's efforts "to improve the city's quality of life." But "with Legal Aid cut down to a more appropriate size," the mayor could "undertake a broad legal and political counterattack against the pernicious consent decrees and court mandates . . . [and] campaign more effectively in the Legislature for needed reforms in such areas as juvenile justice and homeless policy."

Recognizing such motives, Council member Adam Clayton Powell IV, representing East Harlem and the Bronx, was quoted in the *New York Times* as denouncing the transfer of Legal Aid funds to nonunion contractors as "another vicious attack in a long line of vicious attacks on the poor, the African-Americans and Hispanics who get caught up in this system. For [Giuliani] to be taking this type of action simply as retribution for the strike that they undertook last year is really appalling." Similar statements were issued by former mayor David Dinkins and the Central Labor Council. The *Amsterdam News* wrote:

> Giuliani has been more cruel than human, on the cutting edge of the kind of psychosis that he regards poor whites, Blacks and Hispanics as butterflies, whose wings he can tear off with impunity while he has the temporary power of the bully. . . . The Legal Aid Society has taken a bold step [of opposing new Giuliani indigent defense contractors]. It is imperative that they be supported.

The bluntest statement, jointly issued by the Center for Constitutional Rights, the National Conference of Black Lawyers, National Emergency Civil Liberties Committee, and the National Lawyers Guild stated that they "reaffirm our support for The Legal Aid Society and its unions in reversing Mayor Giuliani's attacks, in particular, call for attorneys to withhold any and all aid and comfort to new strikebreaker indigent defense agencies."

By July 1998, the Giuliani administration used such contracts to slash Legal Aid criminal funding by an additional $13 million, without any significant decrease in the Society's overall workload, leading one judicial oversight body to report, according to *Newsday,* that the Society "is obligated to represent almost the same number of clients for substantially fewer dollars," thereby overwhelming Legal Aid attorneys with impossible caseloads, arraignments, and other work. In the process, this poststrike de-funding seriously weakened continuity of representation and other gains long fought for by the ALAA.

Ironically, however, this same period led to dramatic improvement in the Society's internal labor–management relations, including the Legal Aid board's deliberate rejection of the mayor's demand to break the ALAA, and its appointment of new management whose primary mission was to ensure labor peace.

As a result of such changes, ALAA contracts in 1998 and 2000 yielded an average 6 percent compensation increase—by far the greatest in the ALAA's history, and far higher than that negotiated by municipal unions for the same period. Moreover, both the ALAA and 1199 won a unique level of influence over the Society's hiring, promotion, legal practice, budget, and other critical issues. Not until after Giuliani left office in 2001, however, were the Society and its unions able to recoup some of the millions in lost city funds. And Giuliani's nonunion contractors have outlived his administration, thereby posing an ongoing threat to the unionized Society.

Since it was founded in 1876, the Legal Aid Society in New York City—the oldest and largest legal aid agency in the United States—became the national model for small, private nonprofit charities representing indigent clients in civil (and later juvenile) cases. In the 1960s, however, it was largely transformed into the world's largest indigent-criminal defense (or public defender) agency. Within just a few years, this nearly unique transformation led to the first attorney strikes in the United States. Therefore, New York City's Legal Aid strikes, which took place between 1970 and 1994, have been a response to the often-dismal state of indigent criminal defense representation.

See also: Three Strikes Against the New York City Transit System, 277.

Bibliography

Letwin, Michael. "History of The Association of Legal Aid Attorneys UAW Local 2325." Available at www.alaa.org/pages/History.pdf. Revised August 1999.

Lindenauer, Susan E. "Equal Justice: The History of the New York Legal Aid Society." *Update on Law-Related Education* 18, no. 3 (Fall 1994).

"Legal Aid Society." In *The Encyclopedia of New York City*, ed. Kenneth T. Jackson, 661–62. New Haven: Yale University Press, 1995.

Legal Aid Society. *Encyclopedia of Company Histories* (n.d.). Available at www.answers.com/topic/the-legal-aid-society.

Mirsky, Chester L. "The Political Economy and Indigent Defense: New York City, 1917–1998." In *1997 Annual Survey of American Law*, 891–1017.

MUSICIAN STRIKES

Damone Richardson

The music industry has existed in the United States in some form since the sixteenth century and, before the advent of recorded music, it mainly consisted of musical performance. Today, technological advances allow listeners to enjoy music in multiple media and formats from anywhere on the globe. The supply of and demand for music has expanded exponentially and, as a result, music is a multibillion-dollar global industry that feeds other multibillion-dollar industries, such as radio (terrestrial and satellite), sound recordings, concerts, advertising, and consumer electronics. Over time musical styles, instruments, and production technologies have changed in unanticipated ways. Yet, to a large extent, musicianship is still very much based on the individualized talents and abilities of artists.

While unionization clearly signaled that musicians thought of themselves as sellers of labor, there are major differences between most union workers and musicians. First, the vast majority of musicians do not have a single, steady employer. For most musicians, employment ends with the final notes of the "gig." This means that most working musicians are constantly searching for their next job. Second, an overwhelming majority of musicians, both union and nonunion, do not support themselves exclusively through musical performance. Most of the performers who call themselves musicians engage in other forms of work to make ends meet. Between performances, which are often few and far between, most musicians can be more accurately labeled carpenters, autoworkers, teachers, or any number of blue- and white-collar professions. Third, because only a small number of musicians support themselves as musicians, a disproportionate share of earnings is concentrated within a rather exclusive group of performers. Finally, the workplace for musicians varies widely, and each distinct workplace brings a different set of operating principles. Historically, musicians have worked in places as varied as bars and nightclubs, restaurants, orchestra halls, recording studios, radio and TV stations, parades, arenas, and theaters. Each workplace naturally means a different dynamic and power relationship with employers.

Despite the allure associated with musical performers, the work of professional musicians is often afflicted by the same maladies that plague other seemingly less glamorous forms of work. These include boredom, monotony, occupational hazards, and exploitation. Thus, it is not surprising that musicians have adopted the militancy and methods of blue-collar workers. At the same time, the history of American musician unions is replete with rupture and discontinuity resulting from technological change, foreign competition, corporate consolidation, economic vicissitudes, political conflict, and the state of labor relations. These and other factors have influenced the ability of part- and full-time musicians to advance their economic interests.

Unfortunately, racism in the music industry has proven persistent. For example, as with other American Federation of Labor (AFL) unions, the American Federation of Musicians (AFM) practiced segregation. For decades the union admitted black members, but primarily as members of segregated black locals, the first of which, as Donald Spivey has written, was Local 208 established in Chicago in 1902. Historically, black musicians have had to fight to achieve parity with white musicians inside and outside the AFM. Black musicians founded the Clef Club in 1910. This

New York–based "union" was created to promote solidarity among black musicians and provide representation, support, and booking services then largely unavailable to black musicians. In the 1940s, black musicians in New Orleans picketed for more than two weeks to ensure higher pay, respect on the job, and the ability to enter the front door instead of the kitchen of establishments where they performed in the French Quarter. Only in 2006 did the AFM elect its first black vice president in the 110-year history of the union.

Early Musician Unions

The first musicians' unions were created in the late 1850s, and they adopted the structure of craft-based unions, which had as their primary goal the elimination of competition in specific localities. Because the unions were local, each was focused on protecting and promoting opportunities for musicians within a specific town. Often this meant things like ensuring that musicians from Chicago did not perform in Boston or vice versa. The shortcomings of this approach eventually led musicians from Boston, Chicago, New York, Baltimore, and Philadelphia to establish the Musicians National Protective Association (MNPA), which had foreign competition as one of its primary concerns. As business historian James Kraft described, disparate interests ultimately made the MNPA ineffectual and eventually ripped it apart. The next "national" union of musicians, the National League of Musicians (NLM), was chartered in the mid-1880s. The NLM is believed to have executed the first strike by an American musicians' union in 1893, protesting the "importation" of a Danish cellist to play in an American orchestra, according to George Seltzer. The NLM, which refused several invitations to join the American Federation of Labor (AFL), lasted until 1986. As a result of the refusals, AFL president Samuel Gompers chartered the American Federation of Musicians (AFM) in 1896. The AFM quickly overtook the NLM.

Because most establishments that employed musicians at this time were individually owned small businesses, a citywide musicians union held a strong advantage. As there was not yet commercially available recorded music and musicians were the sole source of music, a strike typically meant big losses for an establishment that relied on musical entertainment. The AFM, as Kraft writes, understood and took advantage of this balance of power:

> Like worker organizations in the building trades, the AFM succeeded chiefly because it confronted literally thousands of small, unorganized employers who had neither the resources nor the know-how to unite and resist union demands. Most trade unions at the time, even those of skilled workers, were less fortunate, for they emerged—when they succeeded at all—in the face of monopolistic or relatively unified employers with formidable power in the marketplace and influence in local if not national political councils. The economic power of unified musicians was relatively strong, in contrast, and their unionization campaigns met little effective competition.

For decades, the AFM exercised what Robert D. Leiter has described as "complete control over professional musicians in the United States," and in some places the ability "to impose the terms of employment upon employers without negotiation." When the union did strike, the repercussions for employers could be dire. Such power would also be enlisted in significant acts of solidarity. In 1919, when theater actors sought union recognition from the Producing Managers' Association, a national consortium of theater producers that already recognized the AFM and the International Alliance of Theatrical and Stage Employees (IATSE), the AFM and IATSE engaged in a month-long sympathy strike resulting in the recognition of Actors' Equity Association (AEA). The AEA, formed in 1913, became the exclusive bargaining agent of theater actors. The live-theater industry is now primarily concentrated on Broadway in New York City, but the three unions still work, often in solidarity, to protect the rights of the actors, musicians, stagehands, and other professionals on Broadway and in theaters across the country.

Motion Pictures and "Talkies"

The appearance of silent movies in 1896 ushered in a boom in employment for musicians that would last for nearly thirty years. While the grainy moving images were remarkable in and of themselves, live orchestration helped silent films become a national sensation. By the 1920s there were well over 25,000 theaters in the country screening silent movies and employing musicians to accompany them. The demand for musicians was extraordinarily high, and in many areas exceeded supply. The AFM's dominance over theater owners at this time was beyond question. AFM members enjoyed a closed shop, and the mere threat of a work stoppage was often enough to ensure that the union's demands would be met. When the union did engage in a strike, they were almost uniformly successful as theater owners faced the prospect of unrecoverable financial losses and typically gave in quickly. The demand for musicians was so high that they sometimes struck to reduce their workloads. Some strikes of this nature resulted in a reduction of the theater musicians' work week from seven to six days.

For three decades silent film provided high levels of steady employment to musicians and this sector was the union's power base. However, by the late 1920s new technology paved the way for the appearance of films that did not require musicians. There was the Vitaphone, invented in 1925, which synchronized a phonograph record containing music with images on the screen. The primary short-term purpose of this technology was to break the dominance of musicians over theater owners and to relieve theaters of any dependence on live musicians, according to Preston Hubbard: "When Western Electric . . . and Warner Brothers Pictures jointly announced an agreement concerning the Vitaphone, they made it clear that the sole immediate goal of the movie industry was to replace live music in movie theaters with mechanical recordings. The announcement did not reveal any intentions of recording and reproducing movie dialogue."

Within a few years, the potential of the new technology was fully realized through the invention of the Photophone, which perfectly synchronized video and audio and posed the ultimate threat to movie theater musicians, according to Robin D.G. Kelley. The "talkies" were considered "more lifelike, present, and three dimensional," notes media scholar Robert Spadoni. Musicians struck to block the implementation of the Vitaphone and the "talkies," but to little effect. Management resolve and public acclaim carried the day. Over 20,000 musician jobs quickly disappeared, and in their wake the "talkies" created a few hundred high-paying jobs at Hollywood movie studios. At this point, film music was being swept up in more "centralized and highly mechanized" production methods that relied on economies of scale, according to Kraft. This was the union's first major battle with the implementation of new technology. Next the AFM turned its attention to AM radio, another technology that had become commercially viable in the early 1920s. Radio at this time was primarily a live medium that featured orchestras and provided employment for thousands of musicians. In the next decade, however, changes in corporate strategies and the regulatory environment would make it possible for recorded music to replace musicians on the radio.

Radio and the Perfection of the Strike

In the 1920s and 1930s, new technology spawned a number of additional inventions that threatened to reduce the demand for live music and for musicians. By the late 1920s jukeboxes were commercially available and, with proper amplification, could compete with small orchestras in some establishments. This resulted in the loss of thousands of jobs for musicians. "Wired-music" technology that facilitated the transmission of live performances to other locations via telephone wires also cost musicians jobs. Some establishments even attempted to show filmed orchestra performances as a way of replacing live musicians.

For more than forty years, the AFM was able to balance an uneasy truce with recorded music technology. For the first twenty years after its invention in 1877, recorded music had no real mass-market application. Only at the turn of the century were the first commercial recordings made available to the general public, and they were not viewed as a legitimate threat to musicians. Fidelity was low, and home "record players" were not suitable as public address systems. Recording technology up to that point had only a small negative impact on musicians and actually provided positive promotion for top songs and musicians. Still, as new technologies were insinuating themselves into American culture, the companies that controlled them were consolidating into larger and more powerful conglomerates. Commercial radio stations became radio networks, and two radio networks were affiliated with record labels. Victor Records was associated with the NBC Radio Network, and Columbia Records was owned by CBS. This vertical integration meant that radio now had a vested interest in recorded music. According to sociologist and rock critic Simon Frith, "Music on record [eventually] became the basis of radio programming [and] radio play became the basis of sound recording."

As media corporations became larger, they became more effective in lobbying government for regulatory policies that favored the bottom line. For example, The Radio Act of 1927 forbade commercial radio stations from broadcasting recorded music, unless there was a disclaimer stating that they were broadcasting recorded music. This temporarily aided the AFM by establishing a priority, albeit a tenuous one, on live music. Broadcasters had created the National Association of Broadcasters (NAB) in 1923, and the NAB, which represented radio broadcasters from across the country, quickly developed a strong presence in Washington. Under intense lobbying from the NAB, regulators provided lax enforcement of programming rules regarding recorded music. By 1930, recorded music was regularly played on the radio with little regard for the Radio Act, according to Paul Starr. The Federal Communications Act succeeded the Radio Act in 1934 and essentially continued this policy. Thus the threat of recorded music as a replacement for live musicians continued to grow as broadcasters substituted recordings for musicians wherever feasible.

As these developments transpired, James C. Petrillo, the most notable leader in AFM history, had assumed leadership of AFM Local 10 in Chicago. He took office in 1922 and by the time he assumed the presidency of the AFM International in 1940, he had proven himself dedicated, ultimately to a fault, to protecting members from the impact of all forms of technologically induced competition. As early as 1930, Petrillo was using strikes to prevent the advancement of recorded music in Chicago. By 1940 he had developed a national reputation among radio executives and station managers as a man who would do whatever necessary to promote the employment of AFM members. His ultimate power rested in the union's ability to use the strike so effectively. Unlike other professions where work to rule and slow-downs are effective weapons for union members, in musical performance such methods were not practical and could actually be counterproductive. Only the strike could convey their message without sacrificing professional standards of performance.

In 1935, the Wagner Act greatly expanded the rights of labor and the AFM was learning to use those powers, specifically secondary boycotts, to impose their will on radio networks and their affiliates. A secondary boycott (strike) by musicians occurred when they refused to perform for a company that was doing business with another company where workers (presumably musicians) were on strike or were involved in a labor dispute. In order to be effective, the secondary boycott required high union density and strong solidarity. At the time, virtually every performer in the country who was or aspired to be a musician was a member of the AFM. The power of the secondary boycott was further strengthened because there was near-uniform solidarity among musicians in honoring all strikes called by the AFM.

During the 1930s Petrillo began to exert greater voice and power within the AFM, and the union had begun to openly brandish the threat of a strike in order to blunt the negative impact of radio broadcasts of recorded music. As president of the Chicago local, Petrillo was able to pressure then-AFM president Joseph Weber in 1937 to threaten both the radio and sound recording industries with a strike. In forcing Weber's hand, Petrillo did not believe he could prevent records or prerecorded network programs from being broadcast on local radio stations. However, he was interested in assuring a minimum level of employment for musicians in radio, which was at that time the union's bread and butter. The strike threat persuaded the top radio networks to agree to increase the amount of money that they and their affiliates would spend either hiring more musicians or ensuring minimum employment. This often included standbys—musicians who were paid to show up even though there might not be any work for them. A similar agreement was signed with the hundreds of independent radio stations throughout the country. Ultimately, the agreement was ruled illegal by the Justice Department and expired in 1940. Still, it illustrated the power of the secondary boycott.

A typical situation in which a secondary boycott would be used to overpower a radio network or its affiliate would occur as follows. A dispute would develop between studio musicians and a local AM affiliate of the NBC Radio Network. After doing all that they could to settle the situation to their satisfaction, the local would enlist the support of the AFM headquarters to bolster its bargaining position. At this point, Petrillo would warn executives at the NBC Radio network that if the NBC network affiliate did not resolve the situation to the satisfaction of musicians in the local, the musicians at the NBC network station (in New York) would engage in a work stoppage until the situation was resolved. This would result in a loss of top-name talent and of the advertising revenue generated by top-notch programming. Petrillo could also threaten to call out traveling bands whose performances would be broadcast remotely from concert halls and hotels by local NBC affiliates across the country. The AFM could also depend on sympathy strikes by other unions to put even more pressure on employers.

The power of the AFM strikes was so great that network executives, in their own best interests, actually became a part of the solution in mediating disputes between musicians and their affiliates, often to the advantage of the AFM. In addition, radio stations ended up hiring more musicians than they wanted. In Petrillo's view, this was merely safeguarding the employment and income security of the AFM membership, but to employers this was a classic case of "featherbedding." This victory helped stem the tide of employment loss in radio, but only temporarily. The radio industry was intent on finding ways to reduce its reliance on live musicians through the implementation of new technology.

The Recording Ban

The most significant strike in AFM history began on August 1, 1942, during World War II, when musicians refused to record any music. The union, and specifically James Petrillo, received tremendous negative publicity during the ban. Radio stations and newspapers, often members of the same corporate families, portrayed Petrillo as a "tsar" and a "Caesar." Nonetheless, Petrillo's actions were in step with the membership, which had authorized at consecutive AFM conventions strategies to protect the membership from the menace of "canned music" broadcast on the radio.

The use of recorded music on the radio placed AFM members in a peculiar predicament. Musicians, by participating in the recording process, were employed to produce a lucrative product that was ultimately used to reduce work opportunities for themselves and for fellow musicians in live radio. In order to focus management attention on a workable solution to this dilemma, the AFM initiated a recording ban, which lasted from August 1, 1942, to November 11, 1944. With very few exceptions, new music was not recorded by AFM members during this period, although some recordings did come from Mexico, and the union allowed members to make "V-discs"—intended for military listeners—as part of the members' patriotic contribution to the war effort. Vocalists, who were members of the American Federation of Television and Radio Artists (AFTRA), at first skirted the ban by recording songs that contained vocal accompaniment instead of instrumentalists. Petrillo also banned these recordings, and AFTRA members dutifully honored his wishes.

In addition to relying on solidarity, the AFM was able to exploit divisions among independent labels and conglomerate-owned labels. Columbia, RCA Victor, and Decca along with MGM, Mercury, and Capitol controlled most of the market for recorded music. But, unlike RCA Victor and Columbia, which were part of major media conglomerates, other labels such as Decca were independently owned and relied almost exclusively on music sales. Losses for RCA Victor and Columbia, on the other hand, could be balanced against parts of the conglomerate that were profitable. This meant that RCA Victor and Columbia were more willing and able to withstand a prolonged strike than the independent labels. In September 1943, the AFM negotiated the first settlement with Decca and, shortly thereafter, hundreds of independent labels followed suit. RCA Victor and Columbia, on the other hand, continued to hold out for a better deal. President Franklin Roosevelt sent a telegram to Petrillo requesting that the union offer a special deal to RCA Victor and Columbia in order to end the strike, but the AFM refused to cut a deal that would give these labels an unfair advantage. Eventually, Columbia and RCA Victor agreed to the same deal as the independent labels in November 1944. Under the settlement, musicians received payments whenever their recorded music played on the radio or on jukeboxes.

The most remarkable outcome of the recording ban was that the AFM forced the recording labels to make contributions, based on record sales, to a fund to support musicians that had been displaced by recorded music on the radio. The resulting Music Performance Trust Fund was intended to mitigate "technological unemployment" among musicians. The fund was an extension of Petrillo's philosophy of "spreading the wealth" and benefiting the largest number of members possible. The fund, which still exists today, is a lasting reminder of just how much power Petrillo and the musicians wielded in the early 1940s. Today it is known as the Music Performance Fund, and it is the world's largest sponsor of live music. In the eyes of many, the victories of the AFM against the radio and sound recording industries were too decisive, and severe negative repercussions would be forthcoming. This work stoppage can be considered the most significant in the history of the AFM, because it was the first time that any union had essentially placed a tax on an employer—anywhere from ¼ of a cent to 5 cents per record sold, according to scholar Mary Austin. These developments did not go unnoticed in an increasingly pro-business Washington.

Reaction to the Recording Ban

Petrillo's zeal for mitigating the effects of competition, whether from abroad or from technological change, was legendary. Unfortunately, Petrillo appeared completely tone deaf when it came to public opinion. In 1942, his wrath extended to high school music students at the National Music Camp in Interlochen, Michigan, who for more than a decade had performed on a nationwide broadcast by NBC for several weeks each summer. Petrillo developed the view that the broadcast of these amateurs was a direct affront to AFM members, because it eliminated opportunities for paid employment of musicians. He first requested that NBC discontinue the practice in 1941, but the broadcast aired and the issue went unresolved. Eventually, under threat of a secondary boycott against the network, Petrillo forced the cancellation of the broadcasts in the summer of 1942. Notes the historian Robert Leiter:

> Petrillo's trait of ignoring the attitudes and opinions of the public when undertaking an action on behalf of the musicians was not sensible. In return for the little he could gain by taking school-boys off the radio, he became deeply involved in negative publicity. Congress then passed restrictive labor legislation aimed at the musicians union which served as a harbinger of a more general law curtailing the power of unions.

In 1946 Congress passed the Lea Act, also known as the "Anti-Petrillo Law." The law effectively wiped out advances that the AFM had made through collective bargaining with the radio industry. The Lea Act, actually an amendment to the Federal Communications Act of 1934, was aimed directly "at some of the practices of the musicians union." According to political scientist William Gomberg, the Act made it a crime to "compel a broadcaster to employ more musicians than was necessary to perform actual services," and also made it "unlawful to use coercion to compel a broadcaster to pay more than once for service performed in connection with any broadcast." The act severely constrained the AFM. As Gomberg notes:

> The enactment of legislation such as the Lea Act, curtailing the activities and power of trade unions was inevitable, however, given the temper of Congress in 1946. The practices of featherbedding, of stand-bys and of banning various groups from radio broadcasting had irked many people who were not fully conversant with the issues.

As Kraft has noted, many members of Congress either owned radio stations or had friends and relatives who owned radio stations, so many legislators were acting in their own self-interest when they passed the Lea Act.

The Second Recording Ban (1948)

As a result of the Lea Act, and the broader and more severe Taft-Hartley Act that followed in 1947, the AFM operated from a position of diminished power relative to its media industry counterparts. Many of the AFM's best weapons had been declared unfair labor practices by the business-friendly legislation. The mid-1940s mark a clear turning point for musicians, particularly in electronic media, because it was during this period that the most effective strikes were no longer permissible and demands formerly attained were now not feasible. This was evident in 1948 when the AFM was locked in contentious contract negotiations with broadcasters and the recording industry.

In addition to reducing the AFM's options, Taft-Hartley made the recently attained Recording and Transcription Fund unlawful. This fact largely determined the AFM's negotiating strategy, which amounted to a defense of "the legal existence" of the Music Performance Trust Fund. This resulted in a second recording ban beginning in January 1948 and lasting eleven months. The AFM saved the fund, but the union was clearly weakened. During the work stoppage, records began to arrive from foreign sources; solidarity was less than absolute, as some musicians secretly recorded in Tijuana, Mexico; and record labels acted in greater coordination against the union. In light of these obstacles, the fact that the AFM was able to save the fund is a laudable feat, especially considering that recording labels had no obligation to honor it.

During the second recording ban, Petrillo also threatened TV and radio broadcasters with a strike. However, after the Lea Act, employers were not obliged to respect previously negotiated provisions. Thus a strike would not necessarily have produced the desired outcome. A primary issue was that musicians wanted additional payments for music that aired on AM, but was also rebroadcast on the fledging medium of FM radio. This time, unfortunately for the AFM, the industry dictated terms and the union dropped this demand. The 1948 negotiations revealed just how big a difference the new, regressive labor measures made. Legislation still granted unions the right to strike, but severely limited a strike's power. As a result of these changes, along with employers' greater consolidation and coordination, the AFM would never again exercise overwhelming power over employers.

Hollywood Studio Strikes

In 1958, negotiations with the major Hollywood film studios resulted in a rupture that ultimately divided the AFM against itself and for a time created dual unionism. In response to the studios' refusal to meet AFM demands, but against the wishes of a significant portion of the Los Angeles–based Local 47 that represented members at the studios, Petrillo called a strike that began in February 1958. Members of Local 47 objected to many things, but their main objection was the fact that gains negotiated by the AFM with "telefilm" producers of music for TV and movie soundtracks were not slated to go to the musicians who did the work, but rather to "technologically unemployed" musicians.

Many Local 47 members believed that the AFM failed to represent their interests. As a result, in March 1958, while the union was on strike, a majority of Local 47 voted to leave the AFM and form the Musicians Guild of America (MGA), which existed alongside AFM Local 47. The MGA became the authorized bargaining agent of the studio musicians and reached a settlement with the producers that the AFM considered a major concession. The most important change was that AFM members would no longer record film scores as staff employees of the studios. The deal negotiated by the MGA specified that the work would be done on an "individual, freelance basis." To this day musicians who work on film scores do so through independent producers who assemble orchestras and act as vendors to the studios.

In 1960, the AFM regained jurisdiction as the exclusive bargaining agent for studio musicians by, as MGA leaders claimed, adopting their practices, according to historian Jon Burlingame. Still, this was the first time that there was an open and effective revolt against Petrillo and his ideas of spreading the wealth. When the AFM regained jurisdiction, studio musicians began forming local "player conferences" that represented the interests of recording musicians. These local "player conferences" eventually came together to form the Recording Musicians Association (RMA) in order to have a greater role in collective bargaining. It is likely that the fallout from this work stoppage in combination with changes in the legislative environment led Petrillo to announce his retirement in May 1958. He realized that the methods that had served him so well were no longer effective. For nearly forty years, Petrillo had provided determined and dedicated leadership, and his personality came to dominate the union. He still remains the most feared, respected, and recognized leader the AFM has ever known.

In 1980, musicians went on strike with members of the Screen Actors Guild (SAG) and AFTRA. For the musicians it was a fight for residual payments on music recorded for films and TV shows. Actors represented by SAG and AFTRA already enjoyed this right. Unfortunately, the limits of solidarity were reached in this strike. After nearly three months on strike, actors were able to settle their dispute with producers. With their issues settled, they crossed AFM picket lines. The AFM stayed on strike for three more months, but eventually settled with their demands unmet.

Symphony Musicians

The AFM has also had its share of acrimony with employers outside the electronic media industry. Despite the "genteel" ambiance of their settings, symphony orchestra musicians in some major cities are considered by many to be among "the angriest and most militant group[s] in the whole field of entertainment and the performing arts." This may seem surprising when considering that symphony musicians enjoy significant job security, generous benefits, and six-figure salaries in the top orchestras. One of the major reasons for such animosity is the fact that in the eyes of today's symphony musicians, who view themselves as highly skilled artists, management's bottom-line mentality too often supersedes artistic considerations. This has been exacerbated by the fact that funding from wealthy, "music-loving" donors and other sources has been shrinking for more than three decades. In their place, a corporate mentality that places greater emphasis on "financial viability and cost-containment" as well as popular commercial appeal has taken hold, as Mary Ann Glynn has described.

Similar to RMA musicians, the right of symphony musicians to control their negotiations or call strikes was a result of intense agitation by these artists within the AFM. In the days of James Petrillo, symphony negotiations were settled by local AFM negotiators with little input from the actual musicians. The right to call a strike or even ratify their own agreement was unavailable to symphony musicians, according to Julie Ayer. The creation of the International Conference of Symphony and Opera Musicians (ICSOM) in 1962 helped symphony musicians gain control over future negotiations. From the outset, ICSOM has not been afraid of conflict. ICSOM, which encompasses fifty-one major orchestras, has a strike fund that has paid out over $5 million in benefits to more than forty orchestras that have either struck or been locked out. Symphony musicians also founded the Regional Orchestra Players' Association (ROPA) in 1984. ROPA is the corollary to ICSOM, representing smaller, regional orchestras. In 2003, ROPA included musicians from sixty-three orchestras.

Since the founding of ICSOM, symphony orchestras in many major cities have struck. They include New York, Chicago, San Francisco, Atlanta, Philadelphia, and St. Louis. The San Francisco Symphony has had numerous work stoppages in the past twenty years. In 1996, Philadelphia Orchestra musicians struck for sixty-eight days over wages, benefits, and working conditions and to address what they called "bad management" and "financial mistakes." In 2005, as the *St. Louis Post-Dispatch* reported, the St. Louis Symphony musicians endured a two-month work stoppage that included a vote of "no confidence" in the symphony's president. Interestingly, encroachments from technology have not affected symphony musicians as much as they have musicians in other sectors of the industry. One logical explanation is that for true symphony fans, new technology is no substitute for the splendor of an orchestra.

Musicians vs. the "Virtual Orchestra"

Orchestra musicians on Broadway face a different dilemma from symphony musicians because they are a subordinate part of the performance, which is primarily focused on the actors. As a result, they are susceptible to encroachments from modern technology. In 2003 negotiations, AFM Local 802 was faced with the demands of the League of American Theatres and Producers (the League), which proposed the elimination of minimum orchestra size requirements. Producers also threatened to utilize a technology called the "virtual orchestra" if musicians went out on strike. The "virtual orchestra" refers to a system that plays music from a computer containing prerecorded tracks. After an impasse in negotiations, Local 802 went on strike for the first time since 1975 in protest of the League's demands regarding minimums. The threat of the "virtual orchestra" technology as a replacement for musicians had been in the pipeline for decades. As early as the 1970s, AFM members had been threatened with replacement by the Moog synthesizer.

Faced with imminent job losses, musicians were forced to strike. While the strike only lasted four days, it was significant because of the circumstances in which musicians found themselves and because the fight became a demonstration of the power of solidarity among unions. Without solidarity from other unions on Broadway, a strike by musicians could have been disastrous. Had it not been for the willingness of AEA and IATSE to honor their picket lines, shows might have opened with actors, stagehands, and the "virtual orchestra," as the *New York Times* reported. It would have established a negative precedent for the union and undercut any bargaining leverage that the AFM had. Realizing the resolve of labor, New York City mayor Michael Bloomberg intervened in the talks. The mayor appointed a mediator and sequestered the two sides in the mayor's mansion with the proviso that they would not emerge until they had reached a deal. All told, 325 musicians, 650 actors (AEA), and 350 stagehands (IATSE) walked out to assure that the show would not go on. In the end, the musicians agreed to reduce minimum requirements from twenty-four to twenty-six musicians to eighteen to nineteen musicians, but this was a far cry from the total elimination of minimums. The contract was for four years, but the agreement with regard to minimums stays in effect for ten years.

In 2005, AFM Local 802 musicians staged an ill-advised one-day strike against Radio City Music Hall's Christmas Spectacular, after which they were locked out for two weeks. These negotiations were particularly bitter, because after months of negotiations in which the two sides could not reach agreement Radio City was not only prepared to use a "virtual orchestra," it also attempted to lure AFM musicians from the Hurricane Katrina–ravaged New Orleans area to potentially replace Local 802 members. During the one-day strike before the lockout, solidarity was in evidence as Rockettes, represented by the American Guild of Variety Artists (AGVA), and stagehands in IATSE honored the AFM's picket lines and shows were canceled. The next day the Rockettes and stagehands went back to work, but musicians were locked out. For the next two weeks the show went on with the "virtual orchestra."

Radio City management also employed a global strategy to defeat the AFM. The soundtrack for the virtual orchestra was recorded in Ireland "two weeks before its first use," according to musicians union executive board member Jay Shaffner, writing in the March 2006 edition of the union's journal *Allegro*. It was the first time in the show's seventy-three-year history that the Rockettes performed without live musicians, according to *Newsday*. Again the mayor of New York appointed a mediator to help settle the dispute. The lesson learned was that with the advent of technology that can produce music in place of live instrumentation, power for theater orchestra musicians requires solidarity with other unions in the theater industry. Otherwise, musician strikes can be rendered meaningless as technology continues to find ways to replace live music.

Conclusion

In the first decades of the twentieth century, before the spread of commercial recorded music, musicians in the American Federation of Musicians exercised extraordinary control over their working lives. Their skill and artistry had no substitutes, allowing them to dictate many of the terms of their labor. In the 1920s, however, new technology became an increasingly legitimate threat to working musicians. The AFM, under the growing influence of James Petrillo, demonstrated its solidarity and willingness to engage in open conflict, winning and losing strikes waged to block new technology. The union and its members exploited the structure of the industry and the legal environment by using secondary boycotts to enforce their demands and protect their employment. Their solidarity overcame the threat of technological change.

The ultimate example of technological resistance was the recording ban of 1942. While the musicians won this battle, the fallout from their victory helped turn the tide against their union. Musicians became the first workers to suffer the political backlash against labor in the mid-1940s, as the Lea Act severely limited their power to strike. Without secondary boycotts, musicians had fewer options in their struggle to preserve their livelihoods in the face of technological change. Without the threat of labor unrest, media corporations have been free to introduce new methods for the creation and distribution of music. Some of these they have controlled, such as the compact disc or the music video; others, such as the Internet, have democratized, to some extent, music production and dissemination.

Musicians operate in a much more fragmented industry, one that is also now global. Faced with these challenges, the AFM has shrunk down to 100,000 members from 360,000 in 1967. But as orchestra members and Broadway musicians have shown, solidarity holds the key to changing that fact.

See also: Strikes in the Motion Picture Industry, 652.

Bibliography

Austin, Mary. "Petrillo's War." *The Journal of Popular Culture* 12, no. 1 (1978): 11–18.

Ayer, Julie. *More Than Meets the Ear: How Symphony Musicians Made Labor History.* Minneapolis: Syren Book Company, 2005.

Burlingame, Jon. *For the Record: The Struggle and Ultimate Political Rise of American Recording Musicians Within Their Labor Movement.* Hollywood, CA: Recording Musicians Association, 1997.

Frith, Simon. "Look! Hear! The Uneasy Relationship of Music and Television." *Popular Music* 21, no. 3 (2002): 277–90.

Glynn, Mary Ann. "When Cymbals Become Symbols: Conflict Over Organizational Identity Within a Symphony Orchestra." *Organizational Science* 11, no. 3 (May/June 2000): 285–98.

Gomberg, William. "Featherbedding: An Assertion of Property Rights." *The Annals of the American Academy of Political and Social Science* 333 (1961): 119–29.

Hubbard, Preston. "Synchronized Sound and Movie-House Musicians." *American Music* 3, no. 4 (Winter 1985): 429–41.

Kraft, James P. *Stage to Studio: Musicians and the Sound Revolution, 1880–1950.* Baltimore: Johns Hopkins University Press, 1996.

Leiter, Robert D. *The Musicians and Petrillo.* New York: Bookman Associates, 1953.

Lunde, Anders S. "The American Federation of Musicians and the Recording Ban." *Public Opinion Quarterly* 12, no. 1 (1948): 45–56.

Mnookin, Robert, Gary Friedman, and Joel Cutcher-Gershenfeld. "A New Direction: Transforming Relations Within the San Francisco Symphony." *Harmony* 13 (October 2001).

Seltzer, George. *Music Matters: The Performer and the American Federation of Musicians.* Metuchen, NJ: Scarecrow Press, 1989.

Spadoni, Robert. "The Uncanny Body of Early Sound Film." *The Velvet Light Trap* 51 (Spring 2003): 4–16.

Spivey, Donald. *Union and the Black Musician: The Narrative of William Everett Samuels and Chicago Local 208.* Lanham, MD: University Press of America, 1984.

Starr, Paul. *The Creation of the Media: Political Origins of Modern Communications.* New York: Basic Books, 2004.

STRIKING THE IVORY TOWER: STUDENT EMPLOYEE STRIKES AT PRIVATE UNIVERSITIES

Mandi Isaacs Jackson

The debate over graduate student unionization in the private sector has largely centered around employee status, with university administrations (particularly those at Yale, New York University, Columbia, Tufts, and Brown) arguing that graduate teachers and researchers are primarily students. Meanwhile, unions and graduate employee organizations have argued that these individuals—like their counterparts in the public sector—are also employees entitled to protections under labor law. While no law prevents employers from recognizing any union regardless of legal employee status, private university administrators have persistently cited employee status as a reason to deny union recognition, and on many private university campuses this unionization struggle has led to picket lines.

This question of employee status, and the demand for union recognition among graduate students at private universities, has steadily intensified along with the shift in the organization of higher education to a more corporate model. Under this model, more teaching and research is done by contingent academic labor (part-time instructors, temporary employees, graduate students, and postdoctoral fellows) and the number of tenure-track faculty positions has stagnated alongside an increase in undergraduate enrollment. Although university administrations argue that graduate students are apprentices training to be professors, graduate students are increasingly facing a tighter job market, and one in which the available jobs are less often full-time, permanent, or tenure-track and more often part-time, temporary positions, often called "adjunct" or "lecturer" positions. Additionally, with the demographic shift of the graduate student population, made possible through more generous financial aid packages, stipends, and a more racially and economically diverse pool of applicants, graduate students in private universities are less likely than they had been in the past to be young, white, affluent, and male, making demands for bread-and-butter issues—from living wages to child care—increasingly urgent.

Each of the years from 2001 to 2006 saw graduate student unions on private university campuses strike for union recognition. Organizing unions at Yale, Columbia, and the University of Pennsylvania have gone out on multiple strikes, and in 2006 the graduate union at New York University (NYU)—the Graduate Students Organizing Committee (GSOC/UAW 2110)—went out on the longest recorded strike of graduate employees and the only academic strike to span two semesters.

In 2000, a ruling by the National Labor Relations Board (NLRB) unanimously granted employee status to graduate students, but only one graduate union, GSOC/UAW 2110 at NYU, was recognized following the decision (after it threatened a strike). A 2004 partisan NLRB ruling involving Brown University overturned the 2000 decision, but this only intensified the movement to organize teaching and research assistants in private universities, as evidenced by a series of strikes on private university campuses after the decision.

Public sector higher education has traditionally been more receptive to graduate unions than has the private sector, in part because public universities fall under the jurisdiction of state labor law, while private institutions are governed under federal labor legislation through the NLRB. While graduate teachers and researchers have enjoyed union contracts at public universities since the University of Wisconsin's Teaching Assistants Association (TAA/AFT) won recognition in 1969, no graduate employees in the private sector worked under the protection of a union until New York University's GSOC/UAW Local 2110 signed its first contract in 2001. That contract expired in 2004, at which time the NYU administration refused to negotiate a second contract, citing the 2004 Brown University decision. As a result, no private university officially recognizes a graduate union, although active organizing drives and long-standing organizations exist on a number of private university campuses across the country, most notably at Yale, Columbia, the University of Pennsylvania, and New York University.

Origins of Organizing in Private Universities

A concerted effort to organize graduate teachers at private universities began in 1987 at Yale University when a group of twenty-five teaching assistants, inspired by the recent contract victory of the university's clerical and technical workers, formed a group called TA Solidarity to protest working conditions and pay schedules. After the group threatened to file a pay discrimination lawsuit with the state Department of Labor, the university responded with regular biweekly paychecks. In 1990, following administrative cuts in teaching positions, TA Solidarity voted to affiliate with existing unions on campus, Hotel Employees Restaurant Employees (HERE) Locals 34 and 35, and to organize for union recognition under the name Graduate Employees and Students Organization (GESO). Members of GESO participated in a one-day walkout in December 1991 along with members of Locals 34 and 35, which resulted in meetings with the Yale administration. When these talks broke down, GESO held a three-day strike in February 1992, resulting in pay raises and teacher training, but not recognition.

GESO continued its organizing drive in the years to follow. In the spring of 1994, a majority of graduate students in the humanities and social sciences signed union cards demanding an election, which was held on April 6, 1995, and supervised by the League of Women Voters. Yale's graduate students voted 80 percent in favor of unionization but the university refused to recognize the election results or to negotiate with the union. In the winter of 1995–96, a majority of humanities and social science teaching assistants at Yale withheld semester grades. In response to the grade strike, Yale attempted to expel strike leaders and took other retaliatory actions that prompted both resolutions of censure from professional organizations and legal intervention by the general counsel of the NLRB, who argued in November 1996, after reviewing the Yale case, that graduate students were employees when they served as teachers.

This development ignited organizing campaigns on a number of other private university campuses, including NYU, where a unanimous 2000 NLRB decision ruled that graduate teachers were employees, stating "it is clear that graduate assistants meet the statutory definition of employee. The fact that individuals are learning aspects of their trade or profession is not a basis for an exception to employee status." A government-sponsored election at NYU took place in April 2000, and although the results were impounded pending appeal, the case was settled later that year and the votes were counted. NYU's graduate teacher's union, GSOC, which served as an independent bargaining unit within New York City's UAW Local 2110, won recognition after holding a strike vote in 2001. GSOC settled its first contract in January 2002, which covered more than 1,100 graduate, teaching, and research assistants.

Columbia

Following the NLRB decision, graduate teachers and researchers at Columbia University also decided to affiliate with UAW Local 2110, under the name Graduate Student Employees United (GSEU). As GSEU's organizing drive continued, the Columbia University administration challenged its graduate students' employee status through the NLRB, pushing back the organization's planned representation election until the spring of 2002. After ballots were cast in March of 2002, the NLRB agreed to accept Columbia's request for review of the teachers and researchers' employee status, impounding the election results. In April, GSEU members voted overwhelmingly for a one-day strike. On April 29, 2002, hundreds of graduate employees and support staff walked the picket line. With final exams just around the corner, this one-day walkout illuminated the extent to which the timing of an academic strike, as much as the duration, held significant strategic value. In the course of the one day action, more than 450 demonstrators marched in protest of the administration's appeal to the NLRB. Although the walkout did not result in a change of the administration's position, GSEU did manage to shut down 75 percent of the university's freshman writing courses, demonstrating the efficacy of withholding their labor.

Brown

In the wake of the 2000 NLRB ruling, graduate employees at Brown University also held a union representation election in December 2001. As with the administrations at NYU and Columbia, the Brown administration explored various strategies to block the election, ultimately deciding on a formal appeal of the NLRB decision granting its graduate teachers and researchers employee status. As a result, Brown's ballot box was also impounded pending the appeal.

University of Pennsylvania

The NLRB decision also prompted a campaign at the University of Pennsylvania, where an organization called Graduate Employees Together (GET-UP) was formed in 2000 under the American Federation of Teachers. GET-UP also held a certification election in February 2003, but their votes—like those at NYU and Columbia, as well as Tufts and Brown—were impounded. Nonetheless, the organizing drive at the University of Pennsylvania continued, and cooperation between the campaigns at Yale, the University of Pennsylvania, and Columbia strengthened, setting the foundation for a unique multiunion alliance.

Cornell

By the summer of 2002, the ballot boxes at Brown and Columbia were still under lock and key, and talk of a similar election at the University of Pennsylvania came with the understanding that a similar outcome was a possibility. In July 2002, officials at Cornell University announced that they would agree not to appeal the results of an upcoming October union election on their campus, making Cornell the first private university to agree in advance to recognize the results of such an election.

However, the agreement between Cornell and the graduate union, the Cornell Association of Student Employees (CASE/UAW), did not include many common fair election provisions, and organizers reported "scare tactics" and intimidation on the part of faculty and administrators, including threats that international students would lose their visas. This, along with distrust of or dissatisfaction with the United Auto Workers (UAW) among many graduate students, resulted in a crushing loss of the election by a margin of two to one.

Yale

At Yale, GESO leaders decided that an NLRB election—with its delays and lack of true protections—was not the best strategy for recognition. The organization sought instead to win recognition through a process called "card check neutrality," in which the employer voluntarily (usually after mounting union pressure) agrees to recognize a union if a majority of workers sign union membership cards. GESO achieved majority membership in April 2002, and the alliance between the graduate teachers' union and the other unions on campus was strengthened in September when more than 700 members of GESO, Local 34, Local 35, and SEIU Local 1199 from Yale-New Haven Hospital, along with members of the New Haven community, committed the largest act of civil disobedience in Connecticut history, demanding organizing rights and a new "partnership" for all university workers. This group of organizations became known as the Federation of Hospital and University Employees (FHUE). Later that year, in March 2003, GESO went on strike for one week with members of Yale's other unions. Shortly thereafter, a massive rally in front of Columbia University's main library marked the one-year anniversary of GSEU's election, with Yale's teaching assistants (TAs) and resident assistants (RAs) in attendance.

Following GESO's weeklong strike and Columbia's mass action, the teachers and researchers at Yale published a public petition signed by 1,100 members demanding a fair process to settle the question of union recognition. A few weeks later, GESO held an election sponsored by the League of Women Voters, the results of which the Yale administration made clear from the outset they would not recognize. GESO narrowly lost the vote, but organizing continued—and even intensified.

Toward a National Movement

With increasing militancy and new levels of cross-campus collaboration within the academic labor movement in private universities came intensified anti-union campaigns at the most influential campuses, along with cooperation on the part of university administrations to overturn the employee status of graduate teachers and researchers. On July 13, 2004, the efforts of administrators paid off as the newly appointed Republican majority on the NLRB overturned the unanimous NYU decision, stripping graduate employees of all protections under the National Labor Relations Act. Two weeks later, at the annual meeting of the Coalition of Graduate Employee Unions (CGEU)—an alliance of American and Canadian graduate unions—more than 200 graduate employees from public and private universities across the United States and Canada passed a resolution stating a commitment to continue fighting for the organizing rights of TAs and RAs at private universities, despite the ruling. Later that day they staged a picket line at the regional office of the NLRB in New York City.

With their campaigns reinvigorated by the NLRB decision, GESO/UNITE-HERE at Yale and GSEU/UAW at Columbia both signed up a majority of their bargaining units on membership cards by mid-December of 2004. In March 2005, both organizations called for their respective institutions to voluntarily recognize their majorities and begin contract negotiations, and both began organizing for strike votes. With no word from either administration, strike votes were held in New York and New Haven in mid-April 2005. Both unions set a tentative strike date for the week of April 18, and both bargaining units voted in favor of the strike by more than 80 percent. The one-week action drew national press attention and international support for both unions, including solidarity actions on the campuses of four Australian universities, the presentation of a written delegation in support of the striking teachers to the European Parliament, and a resolution passed at the Interamerican Regional Organization of Laborers (ORIT), which represents 45 million workers.

On April 20, thousands gathered at Columbia University for a rally and march organized jointly by GESO's UNITE-HERE and GSEU's UAW. Although the strike did not end in recognition on either campus, union leaders considered it to be successful, stating that they had not expected a one-week action to end with recognition, but rather that it was intended to call attention to the national trend toward the "casualization" of academic labor and to raise public consciousness about the issues affecting contingent academic workers. In articulating the ways in which the 2005 strike was a success at Yale, organizers cited significant increases in teaching pay and new initiatives on child care and faculty diversity that came in the wake of the strike.

NYU Strike

The first union contract for graduate employees at a private university expired in August 2005. Citing the NLRB's 2004 Brown decision reversing employee status, the New York University administration announced that it would not negotiate a new contract with GSOC/UAW 2110. A number of public actions and town hall meetings ensued, followed by a positive strike vote. On November 9, 2005, hundreds of NYU's teaching and graduate assistants walked off the job on an indefinite strike for their second contract. Hundreds of classes were canceled and hundreds more were moved to off-campus locations out of respect for the picket lines. Before the Thanksgiving break, NYU president John Sexton issued a warning to striking graduate employees, stating that those who did not return to their classrooms by the following Monday, December 5, would lose their teaching assignments and their pay not only for the remainder of the semester, but also for the spring semester.

Such a threat would have been illegal under the National Labor Relations Act, but of course the NLRB had ruled it did not apply to graduate

In 2001, the Graduate Students Organizing Committee (GSOC) became the first union of graduate student faculty to win recognition from a private university, New York University, in the United States. Then, when the National Labor Relations Board reversed an earlier ruling that graduate students are employees, the university withdrew recognition after the union's first contract expired in August 2005. Hoping to force New York University to re-recognize the union, GSOC organized a strike in November, but went back to work in May 2006 without recognition. (*Courtesy:* Local 2110, UAW.)

employees. Despite the threat, most strikers stayed out, and were joined on their picket line by supporters from other graduate employee unions and other labor organizations throughout the region. By early December, more than 5,000 scholars from around the world had signed an open letter to the NYU administration protesting the treatment of the striking graduate employees, many of whom received letters in January informing them that their pay had been cut for the coming year. By February 2006, the local and national press noticed as the strike reached its 100th day. Local and national support for the strikers continued as sanitation workers refused to cross GSOC's picket line, leaving heaps of trash outside Washington Square Village, and graduate employee organizations across the country sent donations to GSOC's strike fund. At the end of the spring 2006 semester, after striking for more than five months, GSOC members voted to suspend their strike and return to work. Along with their counterparts at Yale, Columbia, and the University of Pennsylvania, they continue to organize new members, reach out to the rest of the labor movement, and build relations with the national academic community.

See also: The Boston University Strike of 1979, 690.

Bibliography

Barba, William. "The Unionization Movement: An Analysis of Graduate Student Employee Union Contracts. *Business Officer* (November 1994).

Becker, Arielle Levin. "Cornell Agrees to Graduate Student Union Election." *Yale Daily News,* July 20, 2002.

Cornell University, "Cornell Officials and Students Reach Agreement for Union Recognition," Press Release, July 12, 2002. Available at www.news.cornell.edu/releases/July02/CU.CASE.UAW.hnd.html.

Entin, Joseph. "Books, Bread, and Butter: Reflections on the Graduate Student Unionization Movement." *Radical Teacher* 51 (1997): 26–30.

Leatherman, Courtney. "NLRB Ruling May Demolish the Barriers to T.A. Unions at Private Universities." *The Chronicle of Higher Education* 46 (April 14, 2000): 18–20.

Nelson, Cary. *Will Teach for Food: Academic Labor in Crisis.* Minneapolis: University of Minnesota Press, 1997.

Norlander, Peter. "Graduate Students Prepare for Union Vote." *Cornell Chronicle,* September 27, 2002.

Robin, Corey, and Michelle Stephens. "Against the Grain: Organizing TAs at Yale." *Social Text* 49 (Winter 1996): 43–74.

Samad, Farouk. "Columbia TAs Go on Strike." *Daily Pennsylvanian,* May 10, 2002.

Vaughn, W. "Apprentice or Employee? Graduate Students and their Unions." *Academe* (November/December 1998): 43–49.

THE BOSTON UNIVERSITY STRIKE OF 1979

Gary Zabel

The history of strikes in the United States among tenured and tenure-stream professors at private colleges and universities is exceedingly thin. Faculty unionization in both private and public sector institutions of higher education began only in the late 1960s, and the Supreme Court's *Yeshiva* decision of 1980 (*National Labor Relations Board v. Yeshiva University*, 444 U.S. 672) effectively put an end to unionization efforts among tenured and tenure-stream professors in the private sector by denying them the protection of the National Labor Relations Act. (Faculty members in public institutions fall under the jurisdiction of state labor relations law and so are not subject to the *Yeshiva* decision.)

During the decade-long period in which unionization efforts proceeded among tenured and tenure-stream faculty members in the private sector, only one strike took place at a major institution: the Boston University (BU) strike of 1979. In addition to being the sole instance of its kind, the BU strike was quite an extraordinary event in two other respects. It placed tenured and tenure-stream faculty members in an unusual and ultimately strained alliance with low-paid, largely female librarians and clerical workers, and it involved them in a rancorous public battle with an authoritarian administration, a battle that attracted wide public sympathy from unions, professors, and nonprofessional workers both within and beyond Massachusetts.

On April 5, 1979, the *New York Times* reported that "something like a general strike" had broken out at Boston University. On a campus torn by eight years of controversy and contention, the strike pitted professors, clerical workers, and librarians, each organized by a separate union, against BU's flamboyant right-wing president, John Silber, and his largely hand-picked Board of Trustees. After three weeks on the picket line, the strikers handed Silber one of the few defeats of his long career, each of the unions winning their central demands. The strike and its aftermath, especially by virtue of its connection with the *Yeshiva* decision, had wide significance for the academic labor movement and, more broadly, for the organization of work and distribution of power on America's private sector campuses. However, very few (if any) participants in the strike understood this at the time. Silber's polarizing presence at BU in the 1970s had provoked the strike, but it also gave it the apparent character of a highly specific struggle against an especially abusive employer, and so obscured its larger historical significance.

Ironically, Silber's successful bid in 1971 for the presidency of BU had been sponsored by the academic left at that institution. In particular, an influential Marxist member of the search committee, professor of physics and philosophy Robert Cohen, recruited Silber from the University of Texas at Austin and proved to be an effective advocate of his candidacy. The two men had been graduate students together at Yale University in the 1940s, where they were active in progressive politics, though Silber was then a New Deal liberal and Cohen a member of the Communist Party. A native of San Antonio, Silber got a job teaching philosophy at the University of Texas at Austin in 1955 and became its dean of Arts and Sciences twelve years later. During his stay at Austin, he became active in the Texas Democratic Party, his reputation as a liberal solidifying when he emerged as an advocate of full racial integration, an opponent of capital punishment, and a member of the Washington committee that created the Head Start program.

As dean of Arts and Sciences, however, Silber developed a growing antipathy for the New Left as the campus rebellion of the 1960s spread to Austin. By 1968, he had come to regard the premier organization of campus radicals, Students for a Democratic Society, as a threat to academic freedom because of its willingness to engage in direct action in an effort to shape administrative policy. He was also appalled when his protégé, Larry Caroline, an African-American assistant professor of philosophy, emerged as a vocal radical and a popular speaker at student rallies. Silber would eventually come to see Caroline, whose contract renewal he vetoed, as an archetypal example of the enemy—a left-wing academic of purportedly slight achievement who curried favor with students by telling outrageous lies at mass rallies and in the process got his name in the papers.

Apparently, neither Cohen nor the other radical faculty members and students who had managed to get on the BU search committee were aware of Silber's shift to the right. Against the background of the recent national student strike in response to the Kent State killings, Silber was invited to BU for a series of interviews, where he quickly gained the support of the left. In a typically self-congratulatory article appearing nearly thirty years later in the neo-conservative magazine *The New Criterion*, Silber boasted that his knowledge of "Marxist argot" had been mistaken by the radicals on the committee for political advocacy. As "ideologues," so Silber claimed, the Marxists and other leftists were incapable of "listening carefully," expecting him to create a "People's Republic of BU" as president. According to his account, the only member of the search committee able to decipher the latent meaning behind the manifest text of his interview remarks was the wealthy "cold warrior" and member of the BU Board of Trustees, Arthur Metcalf, who had been sent by the board to make sure that Silber was not a Communist. Over the next several years, Metcalf was to become Silber's most stalwart supporter, the chairman of his Board of Trustees, and promoter of the stock and real estate deals that were to make Silber a multimillionaire.

Silber had good reason to keep his cards close to his vest when interviewed by the search committee. In retrospect it seems obvious that he came to the BU presidency in 1971 with at least the germ of an agenda involving five principal elements. He planned to (1) purge the campus of its student and faculty left as well as principled moderate opposition, (2) expand administrative power while centralizing it in his own hands, (3) create a privileged layer of "star" faculty cloistered in the elite "University Professors Program," (4) turn BU into an expanding corporate enterprise, and (5) enrich himself and some of his friends in the process. By the time he was finally forced out of BU by a new Board of Trustees in 2003, Silber had accomplished each of these goals.

In the first year of his appointment, Silber initiated his attack against the campus left. He baited anti-war students by inviting military recruiters back onto campus after an absence of several years. When students tried to block the entrances to recruitment areas with nonviolent sit-ins, he called in the Boston police. By most accounts, the police used excessive force in clearing the entrances, beating students before arresting them. BU's new president saw this as a "civilizing" use of force on behalf of the right to free expression of the U.S. military and praised the police accordingly.

Within a couple of years, Silber's relations with many faculty members had also soured—and not only those on the left. There was widespread dissatisfaction with his penchant for pressuring departments to hire his friends at inflated salaries at a time when the average pay for a BU professor was well below the national average. In the fall semester of 1973, professor of general education Richard Newman resigned his faculty appointment in protest over the practice, complaining in addition that any disagreement with the president resulted in placement on his "enemies list." Silber also made a habit of vetoing departmental recommendations for tenure, especially when candidates were guilty of holding left-wing political beliefs. In 1976, the fifth year of his reign, a faculty assembly meeting voted 377 to 117 to demand Silber's resignation. At the same time, eight members of the Board of Trustees called on him to leave BU. He survived the faculty vote of no confidence, and within four years had managed to purge the board of his opponents. When trustees Peter Fuller and James Pappas resigned in 1980, they criticized the president for his inability to tolerate dissent and expressed regret that the board had become a rubber stamp for his policies. By this time, there had been a palpable erosion of customary academic free speech protections. In 1979, the Massachusetts branch of the American Civil Liberties Union (ACLU) accused the Silber administration of violating academic freedom as well as fundamental civil liberties, remarking that it had never received such a large and sustained body of complaints about a single institution as in the case of BU under Silber.

Silber's survival of the faculty vote of no confidence and his purge of the Board of Trustees enabled him to consolidate the autocratic power that was to become his trademark. By the second half of the 1970s, he was ruling BU as a kind of absolute monarch, a chief executive officer without constitutional checks or balances. It is true that he was able to establish a small though powerful base of support outside of the administrative apparatus. In particular, his creation of the prestigious and high-paying University Professors Program provided him with some allies among the most elite layer of the faculty (Nobel Prize winner Elie Weisel was perhaps the jewel in that crown). More importantly, though, Silber used his inordinate power to transform BU profoundly, a transformation that was economic as well as academic in character.

A combination of steep increases in student tuition, low faculty and staff salaries, and a quarter of a billion dollars in borrowing gave Silber considerable operating capital, much of which he invested in real estate deals, high-tech ventures, and new campus construction, including the $100 million science center, named for Arthur Metcalf and containing a huge marble plaque with an inscription praising Silber. Hardly a major deal was made that did not profit either Silber himself or members of his reconstituted Board of Trustees. In one notorious example, in 1987 Silber convinced the board to invest $50 million of the university's money in Seragen, a start-up bio-tech company. It did not require much persuasion for Silber to carry the day since ten members of the board had hundreds of thousands of dollars of their own money invested in the company. Two years later, the risky venture had become a continuing drain on university funds; Silber was then spending $16 million a year in borrowed funds to keep the company afloat, which, of course, protected the trustees' private investment. Perhaps that was an expression of gratitude for past acts of kindness. Silber lived rent-free in the university's presidential mansion in Brookline. But in 1981, the board sold Silber a three-story townhouse for $139,000, far below market value, lending him the money to pay for it without interest. Nine years later, the townhouse was worth $441,000. Silber had also acquired stock in Arthur Metcalf's company, Electronics Corporation of America, which he sold in 1986 for $2 million. When he retired from the BU presidency in 2000 (he remained at BU as chancellor for the next three years), Silber was receiving an annual salary of more than $800,000, the highest pay of any university president in the United States at the time.

The motives for faculty unionization at Boston University in the 1970s ought to be obvious by now. There were few institutions at the time where presidents ran roughshod so blatantly over rights of faculty governance, where low pay for professors contrasted so obviously with the use of university resources to enrich president and trustees, where an administration so openly employed political criteria in vetoing recommendations for tenure, and where rights of free expression were guaranteed to military recruiters through the "civilizing" use of force, while the ACLU received a historically unprecedented volume of complaints from faculty, students, and staff about the violation of their civil liberties. In addition, all of this had occurred in the liberal city of Boston, following a decade of campus radicalization, and compressed into a period of eight years identified with the ascension to power of a single individual. For all of these reasons, BU faculty members were especially well positioned in the 1970s to participate in the new wave of faculty unionization that had begun to develop on America's universities and four-year colleges.

Two historical trends intersecting in the 1960s stimulated faculty unionization: an increasing militancy among public school teachers, expressed especially, though not exclusively in rising levels of strike activity, and the development of a radical student movement on college and university campuses. The story of unionization among public school teachers is far older than that among higher education faculty, extending all the way back to the early years of the twentieth century. Still, the decisive breakthrough in teacher unionization did not occur until the 1960s, when rising teacher demands for better pay, job protection, and greater autonomy in the workplace compelled the American Federation of Teachers, already an affiliate of the AFL-CIO, to drop its opposition to strike activity and the National Education Association to abandon its narrow anti-union professionalism and embrace the practice of collective bargaining. At the same time the emergence of Students for a Democratic Society as the largest and most important radical organization of the postwar period, as well as the development of a broad-based movement against the Vietnam War on college and university campuses, helped politicize a segment of existing higher education faculty, and even more importantly, of graduate students who would soon begin the long march to tenure.

These twin strains of public school teacher activism and college and university student militancy comprised the context in which activists among the higher education faculty began to pursue the methods and spirit of militant union struggle. Initially this occurred on a grassroots level, but activism at the base eventually forced the national teacher federations, the American Federation of Teachers (AFT) and National Education Association (NEA), to take notice. In 1967, the first professors' union was recognized as a collective bargaining agent at a bachelor degree–granting institution, the AFT local at Southern Massachusetts University (now U. Mass Dartmouth). The following year, the NEA followed suit by forming a combined local with the AFT at the City University of New York. By 1975, more than seventy-one four-year colleges and universities, public and private, had unionized faculties, while more than 240 two-year institutions were also engaged in collective bargaining. Around 80,000 faculty members were unionized at that time, representing 15 percent of the American professoriate.

By the 1970s, the American Association of University Professors (AAUP) was swept into this new unionization maelstrom. The AAUP had been created in 1915 at a meeting called by the philosophers John Dewey and Arthur O. Lovejoy in response to the increasing incidence of repression of controversial beliefs, especially anti-war and socialist opinions, on college and university campuses. The purpose of the meeting was to establish an organization that would work to protect academic freedom in the increasingly intolerant climate that marked America's involvement in the First World War, especially by establishing institutional procedures and standards that would prevent professors from being dismissed or otherwise punished for expressing beliefs contrary to those of the administrators at their institutions. In the ensuing decades, the AAUP became the foremost American organization devoted to protecting academic freedom and to establishing tenure as the primary institutional instrument of such protection. By securing the eventual collaboration of the Association of American Colleges, the AAUP managed to "write the book" on tenure, as its leaders like to say, in the process shaping higher education policy throughout the United States.

In 1967, the national AAUP was handed a *fait accompli* when its chapter at the two-year institution, Belleville Area College in southern Illinois, announced that it had won collective bargaining rights with its employer. This victory was followed over the next five years by similarly successful unionization drives by AAUP chapters at Adelphi University and Bard College in New York, Ashland College in Ohio, Bloomfield College in New Jersey, and the University of Bridgeport in Connecticut. In 1973, after a rancorous debate that deeply split the national organization, the AAUP finally gave formal approval to its chapters to act as labor unions with its Statement on Collective Bargaining.

Earlier efforts to unionize K-through-12 public school teachers had also been marked by sometimes rancorous battles between labor movement advocates and those who feared that unionization would mean a loss of professional status. However consciousness of status and anxiety about its possible loss were even more pronounced among college and university professors, sometimes amounting to a downright horror of proletarianization. As a result of its decision to permit collective bargaining among its chapters, many old-guard members of the AAUP allowed their memberships to lapse. Combined with inroads made by the AFT and NEA on campuses formerly dominated by the AAUP, the loss of the disaffected stratum of the old guard has left the current AAUP with only half the number of members that it boasted prior to its 1973 decision.

The AAUP chapter at Boston University was one of the first to pursue collective bargaining, winning a representation election supervised by the National Labor Relations Board (NLRB) in May 1975. The Silber administration, however, refused to accept the election results. Instead it hired—and ultimately paid more than $1 million to—the notorious anti-union firm Modern Management Methods, which proceeded to conduct nearly three years of legal challenges to the union's election victory. In April 1978, the First Circuit Court of Appeals of the United States finally ordered BU to begin negotiations with the union. Silber and the trustees filed an appeal with the U.S. Supreme Court, although under the Circuit Court order they were forced to start contract talks while the appeal was pending.

The leadership of the BU chapter began to prepare the faculty for the possibility of a strike at a series of membership meetings. Though there was, of course, opposition to a strike among a number of faculty members, a history of humiliating treatment at the hands of Silber made majority agreement on a militant strategy an easier achievement than it might have otherwise been. In early March 1979, the union membership voted to strike for two days—on March 21 and 22—unless substantial progress was made at the negotiating table. On the morning of March 21, the membership voted at a general meeting to call off the strike when the union's negotiating team reported bargaining progress, though they also voted to begin an indefinite strike on April 4 unless the negotiating team was able to reach an agreement with Silber and the trustees on a proposal that could be presented to the membership for a ratification vote before that date.

On March 31, the negotiating teams for the Board of Trustees and the faculty union reached agreement on a three-year contract proposal that included a 32.4 percent salary increase, tenure protection and faculty governance rights that were essentially in line with national AAUP standards, and an expiration date for the contract that would have left the faculty with the leverage necessary to threaten a strike at the beginning of the academic year. According to their arrangement, each of the bargaining teams would immediately report the terms of the proposal to its constituents for a maximum seventy-two-hour period of deliberation, after which the trustees and the faculty would cast up-or-down votes on ratification. It was obvious that the failure of either side to endorse the proposal would result in an immediate strike. At the conclusion of the final negotiating session, Silber and the union negotiators took part in a public handshaking ceremony, the BU president assuring the members of the union team that the agreement would receive his full support.

At a union membership meeting on April 2, the faculty ratified the contract by a 252-to-17 vote. The same night, Silber hosted a dinner for the more prominent members of the Board of Trustees at Boston's elite Algonquin Club. When the board met the following day, Silber excused himself from the discussion of the contract proposal and the ensuing vote so that, according to him, he would not exercise undue influence on the board's decision. It was apparent to everyone, though, that the decision had already been made behind the closed doors of the Algonquin Club the previous evening. When the board concluded its deliberations, it had neither approved nor rejected the contract. Instead it asked for a series of "clarifications," which, of course, both reneged on the promise to conduct an up-or-down vote, and represented an attempt to renegotiate key contractual provisions. Two of these were central to the agreement. First, the board wanted the expiration date of the contract changed from the beginning of the academic year to its end, thereby depriving the faculty of the strike weapon next time around when the campus was empty. Second, the board wanted committee work to stop counting toward faculty members' service requirement. Committee work is a traditional aspect of faculty governance, but Silber had been arguing for quite some time that governance rights were incompatible with unionization. In essence, the board's objection to the proposed contract language amounted to a refusal to recognize that governance was part of the job description of BU professors.

The board's request for "clarifications" was

met with outrage by the union's executive board. On the evening of April 3, Silber was lecturing at BU's law school. He was defending a Hobbesian conception of power as the authority possessed by a sovereign to force his subjects to conform their wills to his, provided that he gave them his "protection." The AAUP executive board sent its secretary, sociology professor George Psathas, to the lecture. Psathas interrupted the question-and-answer period to announce that the union would begin its strike on the morning of April 5.

Silber and the board made a fateful error when they reneged on their agreement. The vast majority of BU's faculty shared the outrage expressed by the AAUP executive board. Many of the professors who had been sitting on the fence up to this point now jumped decisively in the union's direction. On the morning of April 5, picket lines formed throughout the university. At the end of the day and by the university's own estimation, nearly 100 percent of the faculty in the College of Liberal Arts failed to meet their classes, though the majority of professors continued to teach in the Law School as well as the College of Engineering, a pattern that would continue throughout the strike. According to random sampling by the student newspaper, *The Daily Free Press,* a majority of undergraduates supported the strike, though most did so passively, simply deciding to observe picket lines, while a substantial minority of students indicated their intent to cross them. Graduate teaching fellows, however, were far more enthusiastic in their support of the strike, the most active among them forming the Graduate Employees Organizing Committee (GEOC), which both coordinated graduate student participation on the picket lines and explored the possibility of a unionization drive among their own ranks. The leadership of GEOC included some of the most seasoned militants involved in the strike, including the former director of the Arkansas Project of the famous civil rights organization, the Student Nonviolent Coordinating Committee (SNCC), an organizer with the New York–based hospital workers union, Local 1199, the chairman of the Communist Party of Massachusetts, and several veterans of Third World liberation struggles.

There is no doubt, however, that the development that most firmly strengthened the position of the faculty union in the strike was the decision of the clerical workers and the librarians to join it. The AAUP's victory in the NLRB-sponsored representation election of 1975 created momentum for unionization drives among secretaries and librarians at BU. A group of clerical workers formed BUSOC (Boston University Staff Organizing Committee), started publishing a newsletter named "Coffee Break," and began attending meetings involving clerical workers at Harvard and MIT as well as organizers from District 65 of the Distributive Workers of America. District 65, a New York City–based warehouse workers union, had a radical grassroots tradition that had managed to survive the repression of the McCarthy years. It was also known for the especially comprehensive health plan it offered its members. In part in order to improve its economic condition, District 65 had decided in the mid-1970s to expand its organizing operations and began to explore unionization drives among clerical workers in the Boston area.

In a separate development, in 1973 a group of feminist office workers in Boston had launched the national organization 9to5, National Association of Working Women, devoted to raising awareness about the exploitation of low-wage workers in traditionally female jobs. Two years later, 9to5 joined with the Service Employees International Union to form the labor union Local 925, with the purpose of unionizing "women's work." Though they were independent and to some extent rival unions, District 65 and Local 925 had a generally cooperative relationship. At BU, BUSOC decided to affiliate with District 65 in a drive to unionize the roughly 800-member clerical staff, while an organizing committee that had formed among the twenty-five librarians decided to affiliate with Local 925. By 1979, each union had won NLRB-sponsored representation elections, though the BU administration refused to negotiate with them, challenging the election results in the courts instead. When the faculty walked off the job on April 5, the clerical workers and librarians voted overwhelmingly to join them both as an act of support and an independent demand for recognition.

It was not clear at that point, however, whether the bond of support would prove reciprocal should the AAUP settle with the university in advance of District 65 and Local 925. History professor Fritz Ringer, the president of the AAUP chapter, had indicated in statements to the press that the faculty might refuse to return to work unless the administration met the demands of all three unions. But Ringer, of course, could not decide that unilaterally. There would have to be a discussion among the AAUP executive board and then a vote by the membership. The clerical workers and the librarians were clearly worried that they might be abandoned by the professors. That worry is understandable when we consider the fact that there was not only a status distinction but also a genuine class divide, especially between professors and secretaries. Not only were there large disparities in salaries between the two groups of employees, but the faculty played an executive and supervisory role with respect to the department secretaries. Governance might involve a kind of democratic self-management on the part of tenured academics, but every faculty decision to propose a dean or recommend a new hire took the form of an order to the clerical staff to retrieve the appropriate forms, type up the relevant documents, carry them over to the administrative building, and so on. From the ground-level vantage point of the department secretaries, the professors were their bosses, or at least their managers, and now they were in a labor alliance with them.

After one week, Silber and the trustees recognized the obvious fact that they had been defeated by the faculty and agreed to accept the contract as originally negotiated. They did, however, insist on one "clarification," namely that the provision in the contract against sympathy strikes would bring the faculty back to work even though the demands of the clerical workers and librarians had not been met. The AAUP leadership was in a quandary. It could try to convince the membership to continue to strike in support of District 65 and Local 925. The plain truth was that once the administration had met their demands, there was little enthusiasm for a continuation of the strike among the faculty rank and file. And, in any event, the executive committee was split over continuing the strike, with an influential member, the Marxist philosopher Marx Wartofsky, urging an immediate return to work. The leadership could simply declare the strike at an end and urge its members to return to their jobs, but that would have involved an outright abandonment of their allies.

In the end, the union leadership recommended ratification of the contract, but most argued that the provision against sympathy strikes did not prevent individual members, as a matter of conscience, from refusing to cross clerical and librarian picket lines. All but a handful of professors returned to work. Fritz Ringer and some other members of the executive board continued to refuse to meet classes. Two famous left-wing faculty activists, Howard Zinn and Frances Fox Piven, offered a compromise proposal that they felt would appeal to moderates as well as radicals, in which faculty members would be able to meet their students off campus. Some professors tried that option, but alternative meeting places were so badly organized that the tactic collapsed. When all was said and done, the membership of District 65 and Local 925 were angry with the AAUP for endorsing the contract; they at least understood that the endorsement meant the effective end of the faculty strike.

Still, there was no way that BU could finish out the semester without the clerical workers. District 65 and Local 925 held fast. Silber sent the unions a series of secret messages. Ultimately he promised to recognize the two unions if they would agree to call off their strike provided that the unions promised not to make public the fact that Silber had made the offer. On the recommendation of their leadership, the members of the two unions accepted Silber's terms. They agreed to return to work with the proviso that they would strike again in two days if Silber reneged on his agreement. But BU's absolute sovereign understood enough about the realities of power to make good on his promise. In the end, the faculty won its contracts, and the clerical workers and librarians won recognition for their unions.

Silber had never abandoned his Supreme Court challenge to the AAUP representation election results, even though he was forced to negotiate a contract. The year following the strike, the Supreme Court rendered its decision in the case of *NLRB v. Yeshiva University*. It agreed with the administration at Yeshiva and their amicus supporters that faculty members enjoying governance rights at private institutions have managerial authority and so are not eligible to form unions under the National Labor Relations Act. With the

Yeshiva decision, Silber no longer had any need to pursue a separate Supreme Court challenge. BU observed the negotiated contract until its expiration in 1982 and then forced decertification of the faculty union. Though Silber moved to fire Ringer, Zinn, and three others for refusing to cross District 65 and Local 925 picket lines, a national campaign in support of the "BU 5," organized by Nobel Laureate George Wald, forced him to give up the effort.

If it had not been for Silber's ruthlessness, his unbridled arrogance, and his abusive treatment of all he deemed beneath him, it is highly doubtful that there would have been a faculty strike at BU. But what was at stake in the strike was far more significant than the bullying of a single tyrant. The campus radicalization of the 1960s and early 1970s was followed by a period of reaction in which administrators moved to regain lost ground, in the process bringing their institutions into closer accord with the interests of the corporate sector. Silber's countenance was simply one outrageous mask worn by college and university administrators in general and their corporate-dominated boards of trustees. It was the face behind the mask that ultimately transformed the victory of the BU faculty in the strike of 1979 into a Pyrrhic one.

See also: Striking the Ivory Tower: Student Employee Strikes at Private Universities, 685.

Bibliography

Arnold, Gordon B. *The Politics of Faculty Unionization: The Experience of Three New England Universities.* Westport, CT: Bergin & Garvey, 2000.

Bender, Daniel E. and Dave Kinkela. "Thirty Years of Academic Labor: The Language of Antiunionism." *Radical History Review* 79 (Winter 2001): 7–13.

Berry, Joe. *Reclaiming the Ivory Tower: Organizing Adjuncts to Change Higher Education.* New York: Monthly Review Press, 2005.

Bousquet, Marc. *How the University Works: Higher Education and the Low-Wage Nation.* New York: New York University Press. 2008.

Dixon, Marc, Daniel Tope, and Nella Van Dyke. "'The University Works Because We Do': On the Determinants of Campus Labor Organizing in the1990s." *Sociological Perspectives* 51, no. 2 (Summer 2008): 325–348.

Donoghue, Frank. *The Last Professors: The Corporate University and the Fate of the Humanities.* New York: Fordham University Press, 2008.

Johnson, Benjamin, Patrick Kavanagh, and Kevin Mattson, eds. *Steal This University: The Rise of the Corporate University and the Academic Labor Movement.* New York: Routledge, 2003.

Martin, Randy, ed. *Chalk Lines: The Politics of Work in the Managed University.* Durham, NC: Duke University Press, 1998.

Nelson, Cary. *Will Teach for Food: Academic Labor in Crisis.* Minneapolis: University of Minnesota Press, 1997.

STRIKES BY PROFESSIONAL ATHLETES

Michael Schiavone

Greedy millionaires wanting more money. Selfish individuals who have no idea how ordinary people live. Millionaires in dispute with billionaires, each as self-interested as the other. Apart from 1904, the baseball World Series was played every year in times of war and depression—except in 1994, when the self-serving players destroyed the entire season. Multimillion-dollar contracts were not good enough for them. Likewise, the 2005 National Hockey League (NHL) season was canceled and the Stanley Cup not played due to similar gluttonous beasts. After all, one can never have enough sports cars, Armani suits, and Rolexes. These are the common perceptions of athletes in the United States when they go out on strike. This is also true when the owners lock out the players.

However, as is often the case, the truth is vastly different. As the doyen of sports broadcasting Howard Cosell argued:

> Maybe you don't see a connection between those men and women who risked everything they had to ask for minimum wage, overtime, and safe working conditions, and football players, basketball players, and baseball players, especially given the rather substantial wages some of them receive. The connection is there, however, and it is as real as the Super Bowl, the NBA finals, and the World Series. And I'm telling you it's every bit as important, because what is at stake when professional athletes strike is a principle, and a protection for every working man and woman, a protection once fought for in the streets of our nation, with fists and guns, and lynching and mass arrests.

When it comes to money, certainly athletes receive substantially more than an average American. However, a person working at a factory may be employed for decades. An athlete's career may last only one, two, or five years, and a career-ending injury may happen at any moment. Generally, athletes have very little to fall back on. In the end, a sportsperson has only a limited time in the sun.

A look at the history of strikes by professional athletes in the NHL, the National Basketball Association (NBA), the National Football League (NFL), and Major League Baseball (MLB), demonstrates that athletes generally have not gone out on strike to fatten their wallets, but for matters of principle. While athletes' strikes do involve more money and are higher profile, in the end they are no different from strikes at refineries or hospitals.

Decimation: Strikes in the National Hockey League

There have been three lockouts/strikes in NHL history 1992, 1994–95, and 2004–5. The NHL Players' Association (NHLPA) came into existence in 1957 after players were outraged that a television deal between the league and CBS saw all revenue go to owners. The most notable accomplishment of the union was that it achieved a minimum salary. After a decade of inactivity, the election of Alan Eagleson revitalized the association. However, Eagleson followed a path of business unionism where he and the association adopted a friendly attitude to the owners. This changed in 1992 with the election of Bob Goodenow. It was under his tenure that the players went on strike for the first time.

Compared to later NHL strikes, the 1992 walkout was a minor one that lasted only ten days. Players wanted changes in regards to free agency, while owners wanted to limit salaries as well as receive a share in the trading card revenue earned by the players. The NHLPA actions were generally a success. Paul D. Staudohar noted in 2005 that "the union won concessions such as the right to choose arbitrators in salary disputes, a reduction in the age for unrestricted free agency from thirty-one to thirty, and an increase in the players' postseason revenue share." However, it was only a one-year agreement, which set the stage for the lockout in 1994–95.

The 1993–94 season was played without a collective bargaining agreement in place. The players were happy to have a similar arrangement for the 1994–95 season. However, the owners wanted the union to make concessions in bargaining. After no agreement was reached, the owners locked out the players. During the negotiations the union asked for a no-lockout/strike clause, which the league rejected. However, the major issue during the negotiations was a salary cap. The league proposed that the wealthier teams redistribute some of their wealth to the less well-off teams. Moreover, there would be a salary cap on the amount teams could pay rookies.

The lockout lasted for 104 days, and the regular season was cut from eighty-four games to forty-eight. On the surface, it was not a success for the players. As Staudohar noted in 2005:

> The owners dropped the payroll tax idea, but achieved a salary cap for rookies under the age of 25, who were limited to an $850,000 salary in 1995, with the cap rising annually to $1,075,000 in 2000. Eligibility for free agency was severely limited. Players who completed their first contract were no longer eligible for free agency. Although players aged 25–31 could still become free agents, their movement to other teams was stifled by stiff draft choice penalties that had to be paid by teams signing such players. Unrestricted free agency could be achieved only at age 32 (up from age 30 under the old contract) for the first two seasons of the agreement and at age 31 after that. It was the most restrictive free agency system in sports.

This contract stayed in place for ten years (it was extended twice), almost unheard of in all union-employer agreements.

While the owners wanted to limit salaries, they then went out and paid individual players massive amounts. In the decade following the 1993–94 season, player salaries tripled. Salaries accounted for anywhere between 66 and 76 percent of league revenue, depending on the season. Faced with these escalating salaries, the league was preparing for a lockout. In November 1998 the league sent a memo to the teams asking them to set aside $10 million for a lockout fund. Moreover, it asked the NHLPA to reopen the collective bargaining agreement in June 1999; the NHLPA refused. However, the union was aware that the league was losing millions of dollars. In October 2003, it argued it was willing to accept a 5 percent reduction in existing contracts, as well as reductions in rookie salaries and the luxury tax. However, this was not good enough for the league. Commissioner Gary Bettman (who boasted when he became commissioner that he had never set foot inside a hockey arena) wanted what he called "cost certainty" through a true salary cap. He proposed six different ways that "cost certainty" could be achieved. These ranged from a hard inflexible salary cap, to the league and not the teams negotiating contracts with player agents. Moreover, salaries could not exceed 55 percent of league revenue. The NHLPA rejected all the proposals, as it claimed they were all forms of a salary cap.

On September 15, 2004, one day after the previous collective bargaining agreement expired, the NHL imposed a lockout. During the first few months of the lockout, Goodenow stated that the players were willing to make enormous sacrifices for the season to happen. The players agreed to, among other things, a massive salary reduction of 24 percent, a reduction in rookie salaries, and a luxury tax (beginning at $45 million). This was not good enough for the league owners. As *USA Today* noted: "The league officially reject[ed] the union offer. It counter[ed] with a rollback that affects top-paid players more, scrubs arbitration, eliminates rookie bonuses and caps player pay at 54% of league revenues."

Another potential breakthrough nearly occurred in February 2005. The league agreed that salaries could exceed 55 percent of revenue. The union accepted this and agreed on a form of a salary cap. However, the league proposed a cap of

$42.5 million per team, while the union wanted a cap of $49 million. The two sides could not come to an agreement, and on February 16 the league canceled the season.

During the "off-season," cracks began forming in the unity of both the players and the owners. Bettman insisted that the 2005–6 season would not occur unless an agreement was in place, and he committed to starting the season on time. This pressure eventually led to a settlement on July 13, 2005, after 310 days. It was not a victory for the players. Among the major points was a salary cap of $39 million, with players' salaries limited to 54 percent of league revenues and with rookie salaries capped at $850,000 per season. Players under contract had their pay cut by 24 percent. If teams' salaries were over $39 million, players would either renegotiate their contracts or be fired and received two-thirds of their existing contract minus 24 percent. In one of the few victories for the union, minimum salaries were raised from $175,000 to $450,000 in 2005–6 and eventually to $500,000. It is hard to disagree with Dave Zirin, who argues that a union has never suffered such a humiliating high-profile defeat as the NHLPA since the Professional Air Traffic Controllers Organization debacle of 1981.

In the end, who is to blame? Did the union underestimate the need for financial reform of the league? After all, the league was losing millions of dollars every year, with players' salaries taking a large slice of league revenue. Then again, without the players the league is nothing. Was Goodenow at fault for telling his members that the union would never accept a salary cap and then agreeing to one just before the lockout, which put the union in a weak bargaining position? Or was it Bettman's fault? Zirin argues in "How Owners Destroyed the NHL" that

> Bettman took one look at this blue-collar league built on the backs of hardscrabble French Canadians, toothless grins, and rabid fans, and recoiled. He examined its base in northern deindustrializing cities and shook his head at the absence of revenue streams to suck dry. He saw the future of ice hockey and, unfathomably, saw Dixie. Bettman expanded the league to thirty teams, putting the sport in places like Nashville, Atlanta, Raleigh, Phoenix and Columbus. The NHL owners sat back and collected hundreds of millions of dollars in expansion fees, giving out fat contracts along the way, with no thought to the long-term consequences. Predictably, these new revenue streams were shockingly shallow. The big national TV contract Bettman promised never came and the NHL was left with unknowable new teams like the Hurricanes, Coyotes, and Predators playing in half-empty arenas.

The end result was that revenue decreased dramatically (due in a large part to a decline in attendance, which accounts for 80 percent of league revenue, a much higher percentage than other professional sports).

In the end, the victors were Bettman, who could now rule as a czar, thirty billionaires, and the fans who just wanted to watch hockey and did not care whether their favorite players received an equitable contract (oblivious to the irony that many of them were in industries demanding massive concessions from their workers).

NBA: Looks Can Be Deceiving

It is often assumed that the relationship between the players and the National Basketball Association was relatively harmonious. But this is misleading. Conflict has been common. Nevertheless, it was not until the 1998–99 season that the first major lockout/strike occurred in basketball (there was a brief lockout in 1995).

The National Basketball Players' Association (NBPA) came into existence in 1954. However, it was not until 1964, when the players threatened to boycott the All-Star Game, that the league recognized the union. While there was never a major lockout/strike until 1998, there were a number of lawsuits filed by the players and the owners against each other.

The 1998–99 lockout can be traced back to 1995 when a number of players attempted to decertify the union in the hope that they could bring a successful lawsuit against the league on antitrust grounds (the players lost an earlier ruling because there was a collective bargaining agreement between the league and the union). The players wanted an end to the salary cap and college draft, as well as the establishment of unrestricted free agency. In response, the NBA declared a lockout and restructured the existing collective bargaining agreement to make it more favorable to players and agents (who pushed the dissident players to attempt decertification). As a result, the players voted against decertification and accepted the agreement. Part of the agreement included a provision that allowed the owners to reopen the contract if salaries were more than 51.8 percent of basketball-related income. As a result of the negotiations/decertification attempts, the league realized a lockout could work and the players split over their leadership and eventually replaced Simon Gourdine as NBPA Executive Director with G. William Hunter. New York Knicks center Patrick Ewing (who was one of the players attempting to get the union decertified) became president of the NBPA.

In March 1998, with players' salaries accounting for 57 percent of basketball-related income, the NBA terminated the 1995 collective bargaining agreement. The league demanded that the players' salaries account for no more than 48 percent of basketball-related income (BRI) as well as a hard salary cap, which would effectively eliminate guaranteed contracts. Not surprisingly, the NBPA rejected these demands and on July 1, 1998, the owners locked out the players. One of the main problems that the union faced was that its superstar players received the bulk of the money. For example, in 1997 the top nine players received 15 percent of all player salaries, and 20 percent of the players received the minimum salary. The union accepted that something had to be done about this.

During the lockout, the league continued to receive income. As Staudhor noted in 1999, "The league did much to ensure its cash flow during the lockout by arranging television contracts so that it would be paid even if no games were played. The league, of course, has to repay the networks for lost games, but not for 3 years, and then with no interest. With income security lined up prior to the lockout, once it began, the league moved to limit costs." Conversely, the players did not receive any income from their contracts during the lockout. This obviously favored the owners. Moreover, the earlier rift in the NBPA weakened the players' position. Nearing the cutoff point for the season to go ahead, NBA commissioner David Stern sent the players a nine-page proposal outlining the owners' position. Some players began to break ranks from the union and demanded a secret ballot on the proposal. However, it was likely the proposal would be rejected, which would have led to the cancellation of the season. But the proposal pushed the NBPA and Stern to agree to further talks, leading to an agreement and an end the 191-day lockout on January 9, 1999.

Under terms of the agreement, there was an individual cap on players' salaries. The maximum a player could receive was $14 million per year if he had over ten years' experience. Moreover, the players agreed to an escrow tax of 10 percent of their salaries, to be imposed if total league-wide salaries exceeded 55 percent of basketball-related revenues for the league. This tax kicked in after three years. In an apparent victory for the players, the minimum salary increased on a sliding scale from $287,500 for rookies up to $1 million for players with over ten years' experience. But both the union and the owners wanted this increase, so it is not the great victory it first appears to be.

Overall, the lockout was a defeat for the players, but the long-term consequences were not that bad. Salaries were curtailed, with an individual salary cap, the first in professional sports in America. However, during the 1999–2000 season, players received 62 percent of BRI, and 65 percent in the 2000–1 season, a new record. However, the 2001–2 season witnessed the onset of the salary control mechanisms. As spelled out in the agreement, 10 percent of the players' salaries was withheld in escrow and eventually paid to the league, which distributed some of it to the teams. Nevertheless, players received approximately 57 percent of BRI revenues. For the next three years, players consistently received about 60 percent of BRI. It is important to remember that at the start of the lockout the owners wanted the players to receive a maximum of 48 percent of BRI and eventually settled for 55 percent. Thus, while individual salaries were curtailed, there is now a more equitable distribution among all players, with them consistently achieving salaries well over the 55 percent of BRI as agreed to in the collective bargaining agreement. Thus, the end result is not as bad as it first appeared.

NFL: Victory Through The Legal System

There have been five lockouts/strikes in the NFL. The first strike occurred in 1968, the second in 1970, the third in 1974, the fourth in 1982, and the fifth in 1987.

The National Football League Players' Association (NFLPA) was born in 1956. The NFLPA was successful in its first two years of operation by threatening to take the owners to court over antitrust violations. Through these threats, the players won many of their demands, including a pension plan and health benefits.

The first strike/lockout in NFL history was relatively minor. One of the major problems for the players' association was that, although the American Football League (AFL) and the NFL had merged, the two players' associations had not. Thus, the league was able to play one group against the other. In 1968 the NFLPA proposed a better pension for the players. They were locked out by the owners for a week, and then staged a brief strike. Eventually an agreement was reached, the first in NFL history. However, it was a disappointment, since the NFLPA represented only sixteen of twenty-six teams.

In 1970, following the merger of the NFL and the AFL and the respective player associations, the NFLPA, after filing a petition with the National Labor Relations Board (NLRB), became a certified union. As with the first strike, the second NFL strike was relatively minor and lasted only two days. The players were unhappy that the owners would not negotiate with them in good faith. Indeed, the owners locked out the players for a brief period and this was followed by the strike. However, the owners threatened to cancel the season, and this caused the players to return to work. Eventually, a new four-year collective bargaining agreement was signed. Among the highlights were a minimum salary increase to $12,500 for rookies and $13,000 for veterans and improvements in the pension and health care plans. Moreover, players were allowed to have agents.

However, harmony between the players and owners did not last long. In 1974, when the collective bargaining agreement ended, another strike occurred. The players wanted, among other things, total free agency, impartial arbitration of all disputes, elimination of the draft, and individual contracts. The owners, however, refused to negotiate with the union. This led to the players going out on strike on July 1. The strike was not a success, as the owners still refused to agree to any of the players' proposals because they believed they could win in the courts. Moreover, 25 percent of veteran players crossed the picket lines. These incidents led the players to abandon the strike on August 10. They did not, however, abandon their fight. Instead the players took the battle to the courts and the NLRB.

The court ruled in the players' favor in 1976, but an agreement was not finalized until 1977. The union won better benefits as well as impartial arbitration of noninjury grievances. However, while the free agency rules were modified, the costs of compensation to a free agent's team (giving up a first round draft pick) meant that there was very little player movement.

Following the end of the collective bargaining agreement in 1982, there was further labor unrest. A new television agreement resulted in a massive increase in revenue to the owners. Television revenue increased to $14.2 million from $5.8 million. Obviously, the players felt they deserved a share of the pie. Indeed, they wanted player salaries to be 55 percent of league revenue. Moreover, the NFLPA argued that revenues should be divided among players based on tenure in the league, playing time, and performance. The owners rejected the proposal.

This led the players to take a strike vote. However, before they could go on strike, the owners locked out the players. For the first time in NFL history, games were lost during the regular season. The lockout lasted fifty-seven days and, unlike the 1974 lockout, there was good player solidarity. Two issues led to a resolution. First, it was likely that the entire season would be canceled unless games resumed in early November. Second, the owners proposed a $1.28 billion package that would cover the 1983–87 seasons. This amounted to approximately 50 percent of league revenue. The players returned to work while the negotiations continued. An agreement was reached on December 5. As well as the revenue package, other benefits to the players included severance pay, an increase in the minimum salary, pension, preseason pay, and injury protection. However, the free agency question remained unresolved.

It could be argued that both the 1977 and 1982 agreements did not live up to player expectations. While in theory there was free agency, in practice there was very little player movement. Likewise, as Staudohar argued in 1988, while player salaries increased "from $90,000 in 1982 to $230,000 in 1987, most of this increase was due to opportunities for players to jump to USFL [United States Football League] clubs for a higher salary or to be paid more by their NFL clubs to stay." However, the NFLPA argued that while these agreements were not as good as the players wanted, they were never going to achieve great results in the short term due to the power and solidarity of the owners. Thus, it was necessary to modify some of their demands to achieve victory in the long term.

In the lead-up to the 1987 collective bargaining negotiations, there was labor disharmony. Unrestricted free agency was the NFLPA's number one priority. Under the existing contract only one out of a possible 500 free agents was offered a deal by another club. Once again, the owners rejected the players' demands. Following the players' strike authorization (which was a long way from unanimous) the owners, led by their spokesperson Jack Donlan, made preparations for scabs to replace the players. In a first, regular season games were played by scabs and 15 percent of veteran players who crossed the picket lines. Quite surprisingly, the NFLPA, as in 1982, was not really prepared for a strike. There was no strike fund or line of credit for the players. However, the American Federation of Labor-Congress of Industrial Organizations supported the NFLPA by urging its members to boycott games as well as forming picket lines at the grounds. Nevertheless, public opinion was on the side of the owners as fans, referees, and broadcasters generally all supported the owners. Moreover, the owners remained unified while the aforementioned 15 percent of players became scabs.

Faced with these obstacles, after a twenty-four-day strike the players returned to work without achieving any of their demands and completed the season without an agreement. It was a sad day for organized labor. However, the NFLPA had another tactic in mind.

On the day that the players returned to work, the NFLPA filled an antitrust lawsuit against the NFL. The NFLPA was initially successful, but the Eighth Circuit Court of Appeals reversed the decision. The court argued that because the NFLPA was a union, it could not sue the league for antitrust violations. In response, the NFLPA decertified itself and became a professional association. After a series of court victories by the players, the NFLPA and the owners agreed to a compromise deal to avoid further litigation. Owners agreed to free agency, but in return they wanted a salary cap. The NFLPA accepted this on the condition that it is only implemented if player costs exceed 67 percent of league revenue. Moreover, players' salaries must be at least 58 percent of league revenue. Following this victory the NFLPA once again became a certified union.

The history of player strikes/lockouts in the NFL is not one of great success. There was often a lack of the solidarity and planning necessary for any strike to succeed. The NFLPA achieved its greatest successes through the court system. Thus, in the end the players were victorious, just not through strike action.

MLB: Victory at a Price

There certainly has not been harmony between players and owners in baseball. There have been six strikes and three lockouts in Major League history. However, apart from a one-day strike in 1912 by the Detroit Tigers, there was labor peace, though not player satisfaction, until 1972.

It is fair to say that for a long time baseball players were exploited by owners. Even though the Major League Baseball Players' Association (MLBPA) had been in existence since the 1930s, it was weak and ineffectual. The MLBPA's only useful function was to collect and distribute a pension for the players. However, the MLBPA gained strength in the 1960s with the appointment of Marvin Miller, a longtime labor organizer.

The first strike in 1972 was over player pensions and binding arbitration. After a ten-day strike that delayed the start of the season, the players were successful in achieving their demands. The owners agreed to increase the pension fund by $500,000, and the players gained the right to salary arbitration. However, after no agreement could be reached on a collective bargaining agreement before the start of the 1973 season, the owners locked out the players. After a fourteen-day stoppage that resulted in eighty-six games being abandoned, once again the players were victorious. The pension plan was strengthened and the minimum salaries increased. Moreover, players not eligible for free agency were allowed to have their salaries decided by an arbitrator. Salary arbitration would be a frequent bone of contention in future collective bargaining negotiations.

There were similar victories for players in 1976 and 1980. In the 1976 negotiations, the MLBPA wanted free agency for players. After a seventeen-day lockout, a new agreement was signed that granted players free agency after six years. There was a similar strike in 1980, once again over free agency. After an eight-day strike at the end of spring training, a four-year agreement was signed, but it included a clause that allowed the contract to be reopened in 1981 in relation to free agency.

The 1981 stoppage was due to free agency compensation. The owners wanted compensation for losing a free agent player to another team. MLBPA argued that any form of compensation would diminish the point of free agency. The players authorized a strike to begin on May 29 if no agreement could be reached. Once again the players displayed a remarkable sense of solidarity; this was not true for the owners. Moreover, fans and the media supported the players. Most famously, *Sports Illustrated* had a cover article during the strike entitled: "Strike! The Walkout the Owners Provoked." The strike was the longest in Major League history at the time, lasting fifty days with 712 games being abandoned. Once again the players were victorious. Clubs would no longer be compensated directly for the loss of free agents, but they could retain players for six years and be compensated with other players from the draft. One legacy of the 1981 strike was the bitter relationship between Miller and the owners' representative Ray Grebey, which seems to have prolonged the strike. Their dislike was so fierce that they refused to be photographed together upon completion of negotiations.

There were two further minor work stoppages in 1985 and 1990. In 1985 there was a two-day strike in the middle of the season that led to the loss of twenty-five games (although they were eventually replayed). The players wanted a greater slice of league revenue and got it—the owners increased their contribution to the players' pension by $33 million for the period 1985–88 and $39 million in 1989. The minimum salary increased from $40,000 to $60,000. The owners had hoped that salary arbitration would reduce salaries, but it was an utter failure. Under the new agreement, a player had to have three years' experience before he could go for arbitration; previously a player needed only two years' experience.

Nearing the end of the previous five-year agreement, in 1990 the owners locked out the players during spring training for thirty-two days. Among other demands, the owners wanted a salary cap and to limit players' salaries to only 48 percent of revenue. The players were once again victorious. Owners agreed to contribute $55 million every year to the pension fund (a $16 million increase) and to increase the minimum salary to $100,000 from $60,000. Moreover, the agreement allowed the best 17 percent of players with between two and three years of experience to have salary arbitration. In other words, it was another success for the MLBPA. As is often the case, however, success came at a price. The price that the players paid was that the owners were sick of losing. They wanted to win at any cost. This set the stage for the 1994–95 strike, which eventually led to the cancellation of the World Series for only the second time in its history.

The 1994 season started without a collective bargaining agreement in place. Players' salaries were the main issue. From 1990 to 1993, the average player salary had increased 86 percent to $1.109 million from $597,000. However, while the owners voted to reopen negotiations in December 1992, they did not table a proposal to the union until June 14, 1994 (well after the season was under way). The owners wanted a seven-year contract, with the players receiving a maximum 50 percent of revenue and the elimination of salary arbitration. In return, players with four to six years of experience could become free agents. Moreover, they wanted a salary cap. On July 18 the MLBPA rejected the proposal. During the negotiations, the owners withheld $7.8 million that they were required to pay into the players' pension and benefit plans. This inflamed the situation. On July 28, the MLBPA authorized a strike beginning on August 12 if a settlement could not be reached; it could not. As Staudohar argued in 1997, the timing of the strike was significant as it was late in the season. Thus, the players had already received the majority of their salaries, while the owners receive 75 percent of their revenue during the postseason.

Hampering any potential settlement was that 75 percent of owners had to consent to an agreement, and the owners were split into three groups. Staudohar notes that "groups were largely based on market size, with the hawkish advocates of radical change from small market teams. . . . On the other end of the spectrum were owners with teams in large markets and some owners from smaller market teams that had recently built new stadiums and were doing well financially. . . . The remaining teams were somewhere in between, looking for moderate change, but susceptible to arm-twisting from either the hawks or doves."

After failing to come to an agreement, MLB acting commissioner Bud Selig canceled the season on September 14, to the general dismay of the public. The strike continued into the new year. While most of the league was willing to play the 1995 season with scabs, the Baltimore Orioles refused to use replacement players, and some coaches refused to work with the scabs. Moreover, the Ontario Labor Board stated that replacement umpires would not be allowed to work Toronto Blue Jays home games, as it would be a violation of Ontario law. The MLBPA argued that it would not call off the strike if scabs were used during the regular season. However, a resolution was near.

On March 27, 1995, the MLBPA filed an unfair labor practices complaint against the owners to the National Labor Relations Board (NLRB). Two days later, the NLRB agreed with the players in a three-to-two decision. The strike ended on March 31 when federal judge Sonia Sotomayor issued a preliminary injunction against the owners. She noted that at the end of a contract "the parties must not alter mandatory subjects until a new agreement is reached or a good-faith impasse is reached." The owners lost the court case because while they reopened negotiations in December 1992, they did not table a proposal until June 1994, and it contained radical changes. The judge's ruling ended the strike. The aftermath of the strike witnessed a 20 percent decline in attendance in 1995. Moreover, there was still no agreement in place. Eventually, an agreement was signed in November 1996, two years and three months after the strike began. Minimum salary increased to $150,000, but there were no changes to salary arbitration and free agency. Thus, a two-year battle resulted in very little change, a victory for the players and another defeat for the owners.

Strength in Numbers, Hardball, and Alternative Tactics

The strikes and lockouts in the NHL, NBA, NFL, and MLB usually came down to matters of principle. Like all employees, players wanted a larger share of the economic pie. They also wanted the same rights as other workers, especially the right to change employers without restriction. In virtually every other field, employers are not entitled to compensation if their employees move to a rival company. Why should professional sports be different?

One issue generally decided who was successful in professional sports disputes: solidarity. If players remained committed to the cause and did not cross the picket line, they were usually successful. The MLBPA offered the clearest demonstration of this point. It continually emerged victorious because the players repeatedly united behind strong and determined leadership, while the owners' unity often disintegrated in mutual recrimination. By contrast, where the owners remained more unified than the players, they usually succeeded, as demonstrated most starkly in the NHL and NFL, but also in the 1994–95 MLB lockout.

Interestingly, where players have not succeeded in collective bargaining, they have often won in court. They have done so because they have used the legal system to assert basic rights enjoyed by most workers, particularly the right to change employers. This right provides the foundation for many other rights and benefits because it increases player solidarity and decreases owner solidarity. Thus, while it may be difficult for most American workers to empathize with millionaire professional athletes, their struggles have been rooted in basic principles that most workers would probably embrace. They have fought for their freedom of movement, their right to the product of their labor, and to improve the conditions of their work. To the extent that they have some of the most powerful unions in the United States and engage in some of the most solidaristic activity, American workers, rather than condemning their greed (which pales in comparison to that of the owners), might look to professional athletes as examples to emulate.

See also: Strikes in the United States Since World War II, 226.

Bibliography

Brehm, Mike. "Lockout Chronology: 1995–2005." *USA Today*, February 16, 2005.

Coates, Dennis, and Brad R. Humphreys. "The Economic Consequences of Professional Sports Strikes and Lockouts." *Southern Economic Journal* 67, no. 3 (2001): 737–47.

Cosell, Howard. *What's Wrong with Sports.* New York: Simon & Schuster, 1991.

Kovach, Kenneth A., Patrizia Ricci, and Aladino Robles. "Is Nothing Sacred? Labor Strife in Professional Sports." *Business Horizons* 41, no. 1 (January–February 1998): 34–42.

Lahman, Sean. 1996. "A Brief History of Baseball: Part III: Labor Battles in the Modern Era." *The Baseball Archive.* Available at baseball1.com/bb-data/e-hist-3.html.

Matheson, Victor A. "The Effects of Labor Strikes on Consumer Demand in Professional Sports: Revisited." *Applied Economics* (June 10, 2006): 1173–79.

Staudohar, Paul D. "The Baseball Strike of 1994–95." *Monthly Labor Review* (March 1997): 21–27.

———. "The Football Strike of 1987: The Question of Free Agency." *Monthly Labor Review* (August 1988): 26–31.

———. "The Hockey Lockout of 2004–05." *Monthly Labor Review* (December 2005): 23–29.

———. "Labor Relations in Basketball: The Lockout of 1998–99." *Monthly Labor Review* (April 1999): 3–9.

Zirin, Dave. "How Owners Destroyed the NHL." *Anderson Valley Advertiser,* February 23, 2005.

———. 2005. "Shellacked! The Crushing of the NHL Players Association." *Edge of Sports.* Available at www.edgeofsports.com/2005-07-19-141/index.html.

NURSES ON STRIKE

Lisa Hayes

"Tomorrow we take a strike vote. If it's yes, which I know it will be, then two weeks from today four hundred nurses will walk out that door and we won't come back until we have a decent contract. If you work in a hospital, you want to have rules that protect the safety of the patients and the nurses."

—Sue, nurse and strike leader
in the play *Nurse!*

The banner proclaims "Striking Nurses Fighting for Quality Care in Petoskey—Longest R.N. Strike in the U.S.A." Headquartered in a storefront on the main road through this small Michigan town, Teamsters Local 406 went out on strike in November 2002 for over two years, fighting to secure a first contract for the nurses of Northern Michigan Hospital. Like workers in other industries, nurses have turned to unions to negotiate a variety of salary and benefit issues. However, in recent years, another major item has been added to the collective bargaining agenda for nurses: patient safety.

It is this concern for patient safety that over the last several years has had the greatest influence in moving nurses like those in Petoskey from the bedside to the picket line outside hospitals across the country. With a growing shortage of nurses and a health care system redesigned to "manage" patient care, nurses find themselves caring for more patients at a time than is safe. Where nurses may have once cared for four or five patients, they now may handle the needs of ten or twelve patients, all critically ill since only the sickest patients are hospitalized. At the same time that nurses are caring for more patients, they often are doing so on overtime, since hospital administrations have been employing the use of overtime, voluntary and forced work, to staff hospitals. A nurse who has just completed an eight-, ten-, or even twelve-hour shift can be mandated—that is, forced—to work another four, six, or eight hours. Nurses who refuse can be charged with "patient abandonment" and may face dismissal or loss of their license. Add to this the fact that nurses who are caring for too many patients and working too many hours are far more likely to make mistakes that endanger the lives of patients. Therefore, it is easy to see why patient safety has become the primary issue in collective bargaining for nurses.

This essay is the result of participant observation, research, and interviews over a period of years. Participant observation and interviews took place during a 104-day strike by nurses in the New York State Nurses Association at St. Catherine of Sienna Hospital in Smithtown, New York, in the winter of 2001–2, including attendance at a negotiating session during the strike. Participant observation and interviews also took place during a 1990–91 organizing campaign at Mercy Hospital in Buffalo, New York, and during many encounters with nurses over more than a decade. The essay and the epigraphs in it draw on the author's one-woman play *Nurse!*, which revolves around a nursing strike and debuted off-Broadway in May 2003 with sponsorship from the New York State Nurses Association (NYSNA).

Historical Context

I started out working per diem in a lot of different hospitals and saw right away how nurses were getting screwed. In this Catholic hospital where I worked, any time a nurse fulfilled her duty as a good Catholic girl—you know, had a baby—when she came back to work, whether in 3 months or 3 weeks, she went back to zero. No time accrued. Nothing. She could have been working at that hospital for 20 years and have zero time vested. . . . Or a nurse could have been asking, begging for a certain shift for 5 years, and a new hire could walk in, get that shift AND a higher salary. . . . One day I discovered that the gals in dietary at my hospital had dental coverage, we didn't, they had prescription coverage, we didn't, they had tuition reimbursement, we didn't. And you know why? Because they had a union. That's the day I picked up the phone and called the union. That's how I got involved in organizing.

—Sue, in *Nurse!*

As early as 1913, American nurses were forming unions to address workplace issues. Alice Henry wrote in her 1915 book *The Trade Union Woman:* "Nurses and attendants in several of the state institutions of Illinois have during the last two years formed unions. Already they have had hours shortened from the old irregular schedule of twelve, fourteen and even sixteen hours a day to an eight-hour workday for all, as far as practicable. The State Board is also entirely favorable to concede higher wages, one day off in seven, and an annual vacation of two weeks on pay . . ." Though some nurses may have formed unions as early as 1915, the practice was by no means common. The Nurse Associated Alumnae of the United States and Canada was created in 1896 and later renamed the American Nurses Association (ANA) in 1911. The organization was deemed necessary to address the issues of deplorable working conditions and the need to protect the public from incompetent women who claimed to be trained nurses.

The New York State Nurses Association, founded in 1903, was the first state nurses association. The NYSNA initiated legislation to regulate the practice of nursing in New York by permitting registration of qualified nurses and created the title of Registered Nurse (RN). In 1946, according to labor historian Philip Foner, the American Nurses Association endorsed collective bargaining by creating an Economic Security Program, but at the same time told its members not to confuse "collective bargaining" with labor unionism and that strikes were to be avoided at all costs. In 1957, the NYSNA approved their own comprehensive economic security program, which included collective bargaining, and three years later the organization was designated the exclusive representative of professional nurses in New York City's Department of Hospitals and by 1962 represented fifty-one bargaining units. According to its Web site, "In the 1970s, NYSNA became the largest collective bargaining agent for nurses in the country, representing nearly 30,000 nurses." Hospital workers, including nurses, were dealt a severe blow in 1947 with the passage of the Taft-Hartley Act, which exempted nonprofit institutions from the regulatory power of the National Labor Relations Act of 1935. This meant that workers in nonprofit hospitals were excluded from unemployment insurance, disability benefits, minimum wage protection, and the right to collective bargaining. Many workers were so poor that they needed to turn to welfare to survive. In 1966, nearly twenty years after the passage of the Taft-Hartley Act, salary issues led to a strike of 2,000 nurses in thirty-three San Francisco Bay Area hospitals, a "move that broke with tradition by using the strike as a tool for gaining economic objectives," according to Barbara Tone. That strike and the national attention it attracted helped spark the chain of events that resulted in the 1974 repeal of the Taft-Hartley prohibition on collective bargaining in charitable institutions.

From 1974 until the mid-1990s, the dozens of strikes or near strikes by American nurses centered around pay issues. Because the nursing workforce had been over 99 percent women, wages had been kept artificially low. A ninety-eight-day strike at Englewood Hospital in New Jersey in 1980 brought a 28 percent increase in wages over the three years of the contract, bringing the hourly wage up to $12.00 an hour. The leader of another 1980 nurse strike, this time in Waterbury, Connecticut, pointed out to the *New York Times* that the average weekly salary for a registered nurse at that hospital was $274 and that one of their nurses made more money in fifteen hours as a cocktail waitress than working forty hours as a nurse. However, the nursing shortage of the mid-1980s and the growing activism of women as a result of the women's movement enabled nurses to make major gains in salary and benefits. Then came the dramatic changes wrought by the rapid rise of managed care.

The Nursing Crisis and Managed Care

If you're in a car accident, you want a nurse putting painkillers in your IV who's so exhausted from working a double shift that she can't read the dosage? Or do you want a nurse who's running around looking after fifteen other patients and doesn't have time to help you to the bathroom so you ended up wetting the bed and you have to lay there and wait until somebody can change your sheets. And you talk about efficiency. These are people we're talking about. Sick people. They can't be organized and run like an office. You can't say when one person is going to have a heart attack and somebody else is going to throw up.

—Mary, a striking nurse in *Nurse!*

Mary's tirade touches on two major concerns of nurses today, those being mandatory overtime and nurse-to-patient ratios. With 75 percent of health maintenance organizations (HMOs) being for-profit corporations, the quest to maximize profits has led to the wholesale restructuring of patient care under the guidance of so-called efficiency experts. According to author Suzanne Gordon, "The use of unlicensed personnel, temporary and floating staff—which is a cornerstone of what hospitals call 'patient-centered' or 'patient-focused care'—is fast destroying the innovation of primary nursing. Patient-focused care is a concept designed by management consultants . . . to cut labor costs, streamline the process of patient care and increase competitiveness . . . cutting inpatient days and length of stays has become almost a religious principle in the United States." This all means that nurses have less time to care for even sicker patients. According to Patricia Ponte, "Nurses experienced a sense of loss as the pace of patient turnover hastened. They perceived the loss of ability to assess patients' knowledge about their illness and often discharged patients without the satisfaction of having taught them what they need to know. Nurses felt frustrated and ineffective when patients were discharged too early. . . . Nurses would come into their units wondering how bad the day would be, rather than wondering how yesterday's patients had progressed."

In August 2002, the Joint Commission on Accreditation of Healthcare Organizations published a white paper titled *Health Care at the Crossroads: Strategies for Addressing the Evolving Nursing Crisis.* A synthesis of material from roundtable discussions with leaders in hospital administrations, nursing unions and organizations, and nursing education, the report concludes that "too few nurses to care for critically ill patients for shorter lengths of stay characterizes the stressful work environments in most of America's hospitals. The factors that have undermined the desirability of nursing as a career must be eliminated." According to the report, currently 126,000 nursing positions remain unfilled in U.S. hospitals. As the baby boom generation ages, it is estimated that by 2020 the United States will have 400,000 fewer nurses than needed. The problem lies not only with the aging of the patient population but also with the aging of nurses. According to the Bureau of Nursing at the U.S. Department of Health and Human Services, the average age of RNs increased from thirty-six in 1980 to forty-five in 2000, with over two-thirds of RNs being forty or older. Only 12 percent of RNs in the workforce today are under the age of thirty, which represents a staggering 41 percent decline since 1983.

The number of nurses leaving patient care continues to rise as nurses seek less stressful and less physically demanding work. A survey conducted by the American Nurses Association found that 41 percent of nurses currently working report being dissatisfied with their jobs. Of these, 43 percent are burned out, and 22 percent are planning to leave their jobs in the next year (one-third of these are under age thirty). The ANA report also noted that 55 percent of nurses would not recommend nursing as a career to their children or friends. Nurses are subject to a variety of health and safety risks—needle sticks, physical assaults, fatigue, and back injuries. Respondents to the survey assert that unsafe working conditions are interfering with their ability to provide patient care. With too many patients and not enough support, nurses simply are not able to provide the level of care they once did. In a survey regarding their last shift, 31 percent of the nurses reported patients did not receive necessary skin care, 20 percent reported inadequate oral care, 28 percent were not able to provide patients and family with necessary education and instruction, 40 percent were unable to comfort or talk to patients, and 70 percent had to perform non-nursing tasks such as supply management, housekeeping, and food service.

Recent studies prove how dangerous this nursing crisis is. In a study that appeared in the *Journal of the American Medical Association* in October 2003, Linda Aiken and her colleagues reported that for each additional patient over four in an RN's workload, the risk of death increases by 7 percent for hospital patients. When nurses are caring for eight patients, those patients face a 31 percent higher risk of death than if the nurse was caring for just four patients. A recent study by Ann Rogers and her colleagues found that nurses working more than twelve-and-a-half consecutive hours are three times more likely to make errors than nurses working shorter hours and that working overtime increased the odds of making at least one error, regardless of how long the shift was originally scheduled. It is no wonder, then, that nurses are turning to unions for help or that collective bargaining for nurses often concerns issues of patient safety.

The availability of unions as an option for nurses was seriously compromised in 1994 when the Supreme Court upheld a ruling by the Sixth Circuit Court of Appeals in the case of *National Labor Relations Board v. Health Care and Retirement Corporation* stating that nurses fired from an Ohio nursing home were "supervisors" and not entitled to protection under the National Labor Relations Act. In a 1995 article that appeared in *Revolution: The Journal of Nurse Empowerment,* RN Harold Stearley described how this ruling prompted hospital administration to go on the offensive. Administrators at DePaul Hospital in St. Louis impounded ballots from a vote by nurses for a union. Management at DePaul spent over $200,000 to produce a movie—which nurses were required to see—showing the AFL-CIO to be a corrupt union. "Management was willing to lose a multi-million dollar contract, providing healthcare to members of the AFL-CIO in St. Louis, just to prevent their nurses from organizing." Stearley goes on to describe how administrators at Michigan Capital Medical Center in Lansing, Michigan, simply canceled the election regarding the formation of a nurses' union.

However, in early 1996 the National Labor Relations Board (NLRB), in the first cases since that 1994 Supreme Court decision, declared that nurses at an Alaskan hospital and licensed practical nurses at a New York nursing home were employees, not supervisors. The case hinged on deciding whether nurses in hospitals, nursing homes, and home health care were to be considered acting in a supervisory capacity, with "responsibility to direct," and direction "done with independent judgment." The decisions rendered by the NLRB stated that the majority of nurses in those situations are giving routine directions necessary in the functioning of the facility and are not supervisors, which paved the way for them to join unions.

The battle over who is a supervisor again took center stage in 2001 when the Supreme Court overturned the NLRB's ruling in what is referred to as the Kentucky River Case. The Court suggested that the NLRB needed to clarify its interpretation of the terms "independent judgment," "assign," and "responsibly to direct." The NLRB did just that with their ruling in favor of the employer in *Oakwood Healthcare Inc. and International Union, United Automobile, Aerospace and Agricultural Implement Workers of America (UAW), AFL–CIO*, announced on September 29, 2006. The Republican-dominated NLRB, in a three-to-two ruling, significantly expanded the definition of what constitutes a supervisor so that even if someone spends only 10 to 15 percent of their time on supervisory tasks, they are considered a supervisor, and as a supervisor no longer have the right to collective bargaining. It will be some time before the full impact of this decision can be assessed, but as the two dissenting NLRB members argued, the ruling "threatens to create a new class of workers under Federal labor law: workers who have neither the genuine prerogatives of management, nor the statutory rights of ordinary employees."

Nursing Strikes as a Tool for Change

Last night I was changing the dressings on this 75-year-old woman with third degree burns over most of her body. When I finished, she asked if I could just hold her hand for a couple of minutes. I had to say "no." They needed me on Nine South, because you know how many nurses they had on duty there? None. When I got a chance later on, I came back to check on her. She'd died. Scared and alone. That's some system, huh? When you can't take two minutes to hold a patient's hand. How screwed up is that?

—Sue, in *Nurse!*

In a 2004 *Newsweek* article, Paul Duke described how his work as an emergency room nurse has changed. Five years ago, he typically would be caring for four or five patients, but on an average day he now has ten or twelve. "Once I even had 22. On that night I was feeling swamped, so I went to the charge nurse for help. She was as busy as I was, so she told me to take the five sickest patients and keep them alive, and get to the rest when I could." He goes on to say, "Don't get me wrong—my colleagues are some of the hardest-working and most professional nurses you will find. But when you're given 20 patients when you should have six, well, you're only so good."

Situations such as those described by Duke are the reason more and more nurses feel they have no choice but to strike when hospitals refuse to provide the resources and support nurses need to provide quality patient care. When the largest of Honolulu's four hospitals announced in 1999 a plan to implement work role design, nurses feared that the other three hospitals would soon follow. With their contract expiring, the Hawaiian Nurses Association (HNA) wanted staffing and patient safety to be included in the contract negotiations. "We were at our wit's end," an HNA representative told journalists Bernice Buresh and Suzanne Gordon. "Everything we said to them about staffing and patient safety was falling on deaf ears. To change the employer's position, we knew we needed to get the support of the broader community." HNA brought in the communications director from the Massachusetts Nurses Association (MNA), which had been very successful gaining press attention and public support through a safe care campaign. Recognizing the HNA's need for political organizing as well as public relations, the MNA staffer said, "You need someone like Ralph Nader." So HNA hired Scott Foster, a former Nader employee, to help them mount a public relations campaign.

The first strategy was to present a national perspective by inviting respected journalist Suzanne Gordon to speak at a meeting with state government officials, health policy academics, nursing and health plan executives, and consumer activists during the state nurses' convention. Getting these people to attend that meeting prompted its own special campaign that included media kits, individually targeted letters, follow-up phone calls and more follow-up phone calls. The strategy of the "outside expert" worked, and the process created a strong relationship between HNA and the press. Nurses were coached on how to speak to the media. When management refused to put staffing and work design on the table, HNA kept the media apprised of the situation as nurses took strike votes. Nurses spoke eloquently in interviews. According to Buresh and Gordon, "When the hospitals released a report titled 'Hospitals' Bleeding Budget,' that insisted the state's hospitals didn't have money to maintain or enlarge their nursing staffs, the nurses assertively reframed the issue. They argued that the dispute was not primarily about wages, but about patient safety. Throughout the campaign, Foster had a lineup of nurses giving interviews to various media. When the nurses were at the HNA offices painting picket signs, TV reporters and camera crews were there too." The nurses won. Work role design was withdrawn and staffing was included in the negotiation.

The Massachusetts Nurses Association's public relations campaign played an important role in the forty-nine-day strike by nurses at St. Vincent's Hospital in Worcester, Massachusetts, in 2000. In 1997, the hospital was bought by the for-profit hospital chain that then became part of Tenet Healthcare, based in Santa Barbara, California. In 1998, a group of nurses began organizing, succeeded in getting a union, and began negotiating a first contract.

According to nurse Sandy Eaton, when Tenet kept insisting on the right to impose mandatory overtime, the nurses realized that Tenet, which was building the new Worcester Medical Center, was planning to staff the new units at minimal levels "with mandatory overtime, including a second 8-hour shift for those already on duty, if the patient census jumped up on a given day and with staff sent home without pay if the census fell." During the two years of negotiations, nurses focused on educating the community about issues of patient safety. By the time the nurses went out on strike the day before the grand opening of the new medical center, they had already gained enormous public support for their cause.

The strike was settled when the nurse negotiating team flew to Washington, DC, and met with Tenet executives from California at the office of Senator Ted Kennedy. According to Eaton, they succeeded in getting "no full-shift mandatory overtime and severe limits (no more than 4 hours) of required overtime, with nurses retaining the right to refuse if they felt they were too tired or ill." The following year (2001), another strike rocked the Massachusetts nursing community. Nurses in Brockton, Massachusetts, finally prevailed in a ninety-two-day strike seeking improved working conditions. They wanted to stop the hospital from using overtime and mandatory overtime as a means of staffing the hospital. In addition to strictly limiting the amount of mandatory overtime, the contract prohibited the inappropriate floating of nurses, provided a mechanism for nurses to monitor the hospital's recruiting efforts, and gave nurses a 13 percent salary increase over the three years of the contract.

In 2002, there were some eighteen nursing strikes in the United States involving 5,600 nurses, from as few as five at a clinic in Iowa to nearly 1,500 at the Oregon Health and Science University in Portland. The nurses of St. Catherine of Sienna in the Long Island community of Smithtown, New York, ended their 104-day strike in March 2002. Though the nurses won a salary increase, the strike was about improving working conditions and patient safety. The nurses secured staffing guidelines, with arbitration as an option if the nurses felt the hospital was not following the guidelines. To discourage the hospital's use of mandatory overtime, the new contract provided that in addition to the regular time-and-a-half pay, nurses would be paid $11.00 per hour for the first four hours of overtime, then $16.00 per hour after that. And though the nurses in Hawaii may have succeeded in gaining an excellent contract in 1999, they were again out on strike in December 2002 over issues regarding staffing and mandatory overtime, wages, and retiree benefits.

In 2002, there were eighteen nursing strikes in the United States, involving 5,600 nurses. The nurses of St. Catherine of Sienna in Smithtown, New York, ended their 104-day strike in March 2002. (*Courtesy:* The New York State Nurses Association.)

When the nurses of Northern Michigan Hospital in Petoskey, Michigan, walked out on strike on November 14, 2002, they had no idea they would find themselves embroiled in the longest nursing strike in U.S. history. In October 2001, the nurses voted to join the Teamsters. They wanted a voice in how patient care was delivered and in issues related to patient safety given the increasing workload. Bargaining began in April 2002, but by November negotiations were at an impasse and the nurses went out on strike. One of the main sticking points in negotiations was the nurses' proposal to set up a committee to address safe nursing practice so that their knowledge of patient care would be considered. Sandy Marquardt, a nurse who had been at the hospital for twenty-four years, told the *Petoskey News Review*, "I'm an old nurse, and I thought professional nurses didn't go on strike. But it came to the point that something had to change."

The hospital brought in a consulting firm that

helps employers keep unions out of the workplace. The consultants had the hospital recruit replacement nurses by offering interested nurses a free ski weekend with their families. Many nurses took the hospital up on its offer, though few had any intention of crossing the picket line. As a result the hospital lost $11 million in 2003, largely because it spent more than $14 million on replacement nurses. During the strike, management raised nurses' salaries three times as part of its strategy to lure striking nurses back to work.

In December 2004, hospital officials stopped recognizing the Teamsters as the bargaining agent for the nurses, saying they had received a petition signed by a majority of the nurses saying they no longer wanted to be union members. The union contested the way the signatures had been collected and 200 nurses remained on strike. However, after unfavorable rulings, in October 2006, the union chose to withdraw its complaint, figuring it would be quicker to have the nurses' petition for a new election. The withdrawal of the complaint prompted hospital officials to declare an "official" end to the four-year strike, though union representatives called this a "fantasy" and declared that the hospital does not decide "whether the strike is over or not." Nevertheless, the strike essentially ended.

The fact that the nurses remained on strike for so long, in spite of the offer of higher wages, is a strong indication that having a voice in patient care is more important than money. The nurses have become crusaders, fighting for patient safety and for the future of the nursing profession. As Patricia Beer, a nurse of forty-four years, told the Associated Press, "I'm doing this for nursing. I gain nothing from this strike. We have to stand up and make a difference, or there aren't going to be nurses to take care of people in the future."

Beyond Statistics—The Human Factor

After 30 years working in the same place, I was scared, terrified of working somewhere else. But I knew—well, we all knew—how important it was to work somewhere else during the strike, that if we were to have any hope of lasting longer than management we'd need to have a paycheck coming in. I've been working over at Central—they even asked us to go permanent. I know some of the gals are considering it, but I just don't want to leave here. You're my family. Walking the picket line with you, that has been just—I don't know how to—it's been incredible. What an amazing group of women we are. And men. I don't mean to leave out our wonderful men. This strike, I know this is weird to say, but this strike is the best thing that ever happened to me. I feel like I'm standing up for myself, for what I believe, for the first time in my life.

—Lily, in *Nurse!*

No matter what the profession, strikes are highly charged events that often have a life-changing impact on the participants, far beyond the actual issues involved. As Sue in *Nurse!* describes it, "I understand now why soldiers have a hard time coming back from war. You're happy to be home and back to a normal life, but at the same time you miss that other life, that sense of heightened reality, and camaraderie, and purpose. Look at us. Four hundred nurses took a stand. We walked out on strike together and stayed out for over a hundred days until we got a contract that would protect our patients and protect us. We walked the picket line together. We laughed together, we cried together."

As the St. Catherine of Sienna nurses geared up to go on strike in 2001, the leader of the strike began sending out daily e-mails to the nurses. These e-mails were an invaluable way of keeping the nurses up to date on the negotiations, dealing with the "rumor mill," and maintaining a support network and feeling of community among the 400 striking nurses who before the strike had known very few of their fellow nurses, other than those with whom they directly worked. On day three of the strike, an e-mail encouraged the nurses: "If you let fear get a hold on you, it will drive you back up the hill. We have had at least five agencies try to recruit us right off the line. There is a tremendous amount of work, at a rate higher than many are making now." Another e-mail described a meeting where one of the striking nurses asked how many were affected by mandatory overtime, since it had never been a problem for her. When 90 percent of the nurses in the room raised their hands, all she could say was, "Oh, my God." Since not all nurses had the same issues, the e-mails were a vital educational tool that helped make all of the nurses conversant on what the union was fighting for and feel a vested interest in the welfare of their colleagues. These e-mails also provided a forum to share funny stories, such as when a four-year-old grandchild came to the picket line. When the child's mother was fixing breakfast and asked "What do you want," the child replied, "A contract." And the e-mails were a forum to reach out for support when a child was born, a husband had a heart attack, or a family member died.

The crucial bonding for the nurses of Northern Michigan Hospital came not in the form of e-mails but in the unlikely shape of "the tent." For the entire first year of their strike, while management refused to negotiate, Teamsters Local 406 was based in a blue tarp tent, surrounded by bales of hay as insulation against the bitter northern Michigan winter. Manned twenty-four hours a day, seven days a week, the tent had a space heater, a coffeepot, a Crock-Pot, and eventually even florescent lights. Nurses learned to recognize each other by their eyes, since that was all that showed when they were bundled up against the cold. Like the nurses of St. Catherine, many of the nurses of NMH signed up with agencies and worked in other hospitals. The difficulty in Michigan, however, was the relative isolation of Petoskey, a resort community in northern Michigan, which meant that many nurses had to drive hundreds of miles to downstate hospitals to work. Those who could not travel had to find alternate sources of income, including cleaning houses and babysitting. One nurse became a beekeeper and three nurses started an organic gardening business called "The Soil Sisters."

Nurses from both St. Catherine and northern Michigan reached out to community leaders they felt they could trust, only to be disappointed. Because St. Catherine of Sienna is a part of the Catholic Healthcare System, one of the striking nurses approached the local priest after Mass one Sunday. She told him she was one of the striking nurses and that they really needed his help. He kissed her on the forehead, said "I'm praying for all of you," and turned his back to talk to someone else. One of the nurses in Petoskey, feeling that she had a relationship with one of the hospital's wealthy board members since she had been his private duty nurse, approached him after church one day. Before she got close and without speaking, the man ran away from her and then complained to the minister that she had harassed him.

The fact that nursing is still mostly a female workforce brings its own set of misconceptions and challenges. There is still a lingering perception that a woman's income is secondary and that she is usually covered by her husband's benefits, trivializing the nurses' demands for wage increases and health and retirement benefits. The truth is that many of these women are the main or sole support of their families. The head of St. Catherine of Sienna Hospital pleaded with one of the nurses not to go on strike because he had small children at home, and if the nurses went on strike, his wife might have to go to work. Also, because the workforce is predominantly female, the men (and it is usually men) who represent management in negotiations tend to be arrogant and condescending, a combination that can easily drag a strike out far longer than necessary. In the case of the St. Catherine of Sienna strike, management's lawyer yelled to a whole roomful of nurses, "You girls wanted a strike. You got it." When the nurse negotiating team from northern Michigan went to meet with management's lawyer, his small talk before the meeting included complaining that when he had taken his mother to the emergency room, all of "those" people (meaning those without insurance) were being seen before his mother. Of course, he was having this conversation with nurses who because of the length of the strike, were no longer eligible for COBRA, and thus faced being without insurance themselves.

Nurses have remained largely invisible, their skills and the vital role they play in patient care taken for granted and often trivialized by comments like "just a nurse" or things like a crossword puzzle answer being "TLC" for "what a nurse provides." Nurses will provide as much "tender loving care" as they have time for, but with so many very sick patients, their time is usually consumed with monitoring vital signs, administering medication, and performing hundreds of tasks that have a direct impact on a patient's condition. It is likely that with an anticipated nursing shortage of 400,000 by 2020, the number of nursing strikes will only increase over the coming years if extraordinary efforts are not made to address the problems of a health care system in critical condition.

How often are nurses included in the political discussions about health care? Almost never! It's always the doctors and administrators. But nurses are the ones who spend the most time with patients. We're the ones who see how all of these policies directly impact on the people the system is supposed to serve. So instead of just including a nurse or two when the topic is nursing, invite us into a discussion about the whole system. Maybe we can help!

—Sue, at the end of *Nurse!*

See also: Organizing Home Health Care Workers in New York City, 716.

Bibliography

Aiken, Linda H., et al. "Hospital Nurse Staffing and Patient Mortality, Nurse Burnout and Job Dissatisfaction." *Journal of the AMA* 288, no. 16 (October 23/30, 2002): 1987–93.

Associated Press. "Michigan Nurses Strike Hits One-Year Mark." *Associated Press,* November 14, 2003.

Buresh, Bernice, and Suzanne Gordon. *From Silence to Voice: What Nurses Know and Must Communicate to the Public.* Ithaca, NY: Cornell University Press, 2000.

Duke, Paul. "If ER Nurses Crash, Will Patients Follow?" *Newsweek,* February 2, 2004.

Eaton, Sandy. "A Look Back at the St. Vincent's Strike—A Victory for All Nurses." Available at www.massnurses.org/news/2000/000007/stvreview.htm.

Foner, Philip. *Women and the American Labor Movement.* Washington, DC: Free Press, 1982.

Gordon, Suzanne. *Life Support: Three Nurses on the Front Lines.* Boston: Little, Brown, 1997.

Henry, A. *The Trade Union Woman,* 1915. Available at www.boondocksnet.com/editions/tuw/tuw08.html.

Joint Commission of Health Care Organizations. "Health Care at the Crossroads: Strategies for Addressing the Evolving Nursing Crisis." White paper, August 7, 2002.

Piehl, Beth Anne. "Nurses' Ultimate Goal: Taking Care of Patient." *Petoskey News-Review,* November 7, 2003.

Ponte, Patricia Reid, et al. "Factors Leading to a Strike Vote and Strategies for Reestablishing Relationships." *Journal of Nursing Administration* 28, no. 2 (February 1998): 35–43.

Rogers, Ann E., et al. "The Working Hours of Hospital Staff Nurses and Patient Safety." *Health Affairs* 23, no. 4 (July/August 2004): 202–12.

Stearley, Harold. "Rise and Fall of the Nursing Union." *Revolution: The Journal of Nurse Empowerment* 5, no. 2 (Summer 1995): 56–59.

Tone, Barbara, "United American Nurses Announce New Roster." *Nurse Week,* November 1999.

U.S. Department of Health and Human Services, Bureau of Nursing. *National Sample Survey of Registered Nurses,* 1980–2000.

ORGANIZING HOME HEALTH CARE WORKERS IN NEW YORK CITY

Immanuel Ness

The current assault against government and public services poses new and important questions for the theoretical literature about the relationship of public employee unions to their members and the state, and the use of the strike as a tactic and strategy in gaining respect and dignity. Much of this literature, while recognizing the useful function that trade unions served initially in mobilizing disparate public sector workers, sanctions the belief that once public employee unions are recognized by government authorities, the unions should revert to the status of an interest group whose primary goal is to develop a professional cadre to serve member interests through collective bargaining with government. The literature stresses the functional need to establish professional union bureaucracies and routines whereby effective interaction with government labor negotiators is facilitated. This evolutionary perspective is informed by the pluralist assumption that unions will mature ineluctably into purposeful interest groups whose function is to influence and shape government policy through the political bargaining process. The ultimate goal of union representatives is to develop lines of access to government leaders in order to influence policy on behalf of their members.

As trade unions develop more sophisticated practices and procedures, they become more adept at negotiating with government officials; as a result, union leaders resort less often to more militant forms of political action, as collective bargaining at the top replaces membership mobilization and rank-and-file militancy. Although unions impose a financial cost on government, officials often prefer their presence, insofar as they temper worker discontent and channel any residual militancy away from the state. In New York City, public officials encouraged the formation of large municipal employee unions in the 1960s to reduce the power of radical trade union leaders by folding them into a larger association dominated by more moderate unions. Thus was born District Council 37 of the American Federation of State, Municipal, and County Employees (AFSCME DC 37). The expansion of DC 37 in the 1960s and 1970s facilitated comprehensive pattern bargaining for municipal workers employed in the delivery of public health, welfare, and municipal services. The public sector, dominated by service workers, was the primary source of trade union growth from the 1950s to the 1970s. Even as unionization in the private sector declined, public sector union growth continued into the early 1980s. The promise of greatly improved working conditions and higher wages and benefits through unionization encouraged vast numbers of workers to join public sector unions. In just over fifteen years, public sector trade union membership in the United States swelled from slightly over 1 million in 1960 to over 3 million in 1976, accounting for more than 80 percent of all trade union growth in the nation during the 1960s and 1970s.

Against the backdrop of the rapid ascendancy of public employee unions as a major social and political force in urban politics, a strong backlash emerged among pluralist reformers disturbed by what they saw as the undue influence of public employee unions on public policy; collective bargaining, it was argued, imposed unfair costs on city taxpayers. Political scientist Clyde Summers considered the influence exercised by public sector unions through collective bargaining to be disruptive of rational and democratic governance. Because public sector unions dominated and distorted the democratic process through collective bargaining, he argued, they could not be granted the same legitimacy as other interest groups. These unions, he held, were unlike private unions, whose influence was confined to the sphere of private capitalist enterprise. The influence of public employee unions was thereby presented as subverting the supposed impartiality of pluralist democratic politics, which subordinated the union interest in lighter work and higher wages to the greater public interest in more service and lower taxes. Voters, who far outnumbered public employees and who shared the employers' economic interest in maintaining low taxes, were unfairly excluded from the collective bargaining process. According to this perspective, the strike threat should be prohibited in public sector collective bargaining. To remedy the overwhelming political influence exercised by public employee unions through collective bargaining, Summers concluded, "disputes by public employees should be resolved through the customary channels of political decisionmaking" rather than through the bargaining process.

Emboldened by this critical perspective on public sector unionization, federal, state, and local officials have become all the more willing to resist union efforts to improve wages and working conditions for their members. A majority of public employee unions have become reluctant to employ the strike threat, and as a result have become relatively passive partners with management in attempting to convince members and the public of their weakness rather than their potential strength.

In turn, public employee unions from the mid-1970s to the mid-1990s considerably weakened their response to government-imposed austerity. Their activism in the 1960s and 1970s was followed by a period of conciliation, particularly in the aftermath of the municipal government fiscal crises in the mid-1970s and Ronald Reagan's summary dismissal of striking air traffic controllers in 1981. After their unions were officially recognized by government authorities, union leaders once willing to organize the rank and file in demonstrations, petition drives, and strikes tended to become moderate, accommodating, and in some cases sympathetic to fiscal restraints in response to budget cuts that encroached upon their members' wages and job security. Public sector union leaders have found it considerably more difficult to combat efforts by public authorities to restrain wages through budget cuts, privatization, mass layoffs, and programs of permanent job attrition. Even proponents of public sector unions based their defense of collective bargaining on its minimal effect on government spending and taxes. They appealed, for example, to research by political scientists Jeffrey Zax and Casey Ichniowski demonstrating that total budgets of cities with public sector unions were no higher than those without unions, indicating that collective bargaining occasions not an increase in public spending but simply its reallocation.

Political Action as Labor Market Action

Conventionally, public employee unions have influenced state budgeting policies by lobbying legislators and government officials to support programs beneficial to their members. While union lobbyists are skilled in conventional legislative bargaining tactics, public sector unions are under unprecedented pressure from government efforts to cut funding for programs in which their members are employed. In this environment of fiscal austerity, government retrenchment, and diminished government enthusiasm for human services programs, typical forms of lobbying and persuasion are rendered ever less effective. A return to the original organizing strategy of mobilizing members and communities is vital to defending and restoring public sector worker power.

In this environment, so hostile to public employee unions, a few activist unions have responded by attempting to persuade public opinion of the significant work their members perform and the justification for engaging in a more militant strategy against government cutbacks. These strategies are designed to counter divisive management tactics that tend to detach the interests of unions and their members from the public interest in communities. The labor-community organizing strategy is thus posed as an alternative to the management-labor cooperation strategy promoted by union leaders and public officials. Through organizing members and the public around joint causes, the labor-community strategy enables public employee unions to politicize the collective bargaining process and wield the strike threat more effectively in bargaining with management.

Home Care Worker Strikes in New York City

The labor-community mobilization around home care in the late 1980s represents an interesting deviation from conventional forms of union militant activity and strikes that emerged following the upsurge in public sector worker activism in the 1960s and 1970s. That home care workers mobilized and went on strike to improve their poverty-level wages in the late 1980s, at a time of government austerity and privatization of public services, makes their story noteworthy. Home care services, it should be remarked, were among the first government programs to be contracted out to private vendors. In 1987, unions representing home care workers in New York initiated a campaign to mobilize a relatively dormant membership. Although these workers had been organized into unions in the late 1970s and early 1980s, their wages and working conditions, unlike those of other public sector workers, were not improved in the initial wave of unionization. The 1987 home care workers mobilization was useful in gaining public attention that spurred political action to improve conditions in the industry.

Home care workers occupy a position at the margins of the labor force. Indeed, their wages and working conditions provide a stark contrast to the prevailing image of public sector workers as unfairly taking advantage of their position through collective bargaining, in the fashion portrayed by neo-pluralist critics. Before the upsurge of activism in the late 1980s, unionized home care workers in New York City still earned the minimum wage, with health benefits substantially inferior to those provided by Medicaid. To improve their conditions, the Local 1199 National Health and Human Service Employees Union politicized the disparate labor force of home care workers and encouraged their participation in political action and the fight for higher levels of state Medicaid funding for personal care services. The union's activism sprung from the emergence of a new, more activist leadership, which sought to legitimate its position through restoring the union's militant tradition of political action and membership mobilization.

Caring for the elderly and disabled was traditionally a job performed by females who looked after spouses, parents, or children who could not perform physical tasks related to personal care. However, changes in the family and the economy have transformed the character of home care in the last quarter of the twentieth century from a family responsibility into a multibillion-dollar industry employing hundreds of thousands of low-wage workers nationwide. This transformation was brought about in large measure by the meeting of two accelerating social and economic trends: the entry of large numbers of females into the paid labor force to supplement or replace the income of males, and attempts by government health care providers and insurance companies to shorten hospital stays in order to reduce the increasingly high cost of patient care. The widespread availability of modern medical technology for chronic and acute patient care in the home further facilitated the process of deinstitutionalization.

The rapid growth of home care services in New York City during the 1980s stemmed from local, state, and federal government decisions to reduce the cost of institutional services provided by hospitals and nursing homes by employing a low-wage labor force, overwhelmingly minority and female, in patient homes. Even after the union mobilization of home care workers in the late 1980s, worker compensation remains 35 percent below that of comparable semiskilled paraprofessionals who perform the same work in hospitals and nursing homes, according to health care analysts Rick Surpin, Kathryn Haslanger, and Steven Dawson. The low wages in the industry are painfully apparent to Local 1199's Home Care Division, which must employ full-time social workers to assist its members in obtaining food stamps, Medicaid, and other government benefits.

The wage structure in the industry is reinforced by traditional attitudes that home care aides perform female nurturing tasks usually provided without compensation as part of a woman's family obligation. By the 1980s the home health care aide was the most rapidly growing major occupational category in the United States economy. The number of workers employed as home health care aides rose from 123,000 in 1983 to 363,000 in 1993. In 1994, over 67,000 home care attendants serving 63,000 clients annually were employed in New York City's $1.2 billion personal care program, which provided help to home-bound people needing assistance with daily activities such as dressing, bathing, and taking medicine. New York State contributed 40 percent toward the cost of personal care services, which were covered under the national Medicaid program for low-income people, New York City contributed 10 percent, and the federal government 50 percent. By 1994, New York State received three-quarters of all federal Medicaid funding for personal care services and New York City received two-thirds of all New York State funding for Medicaid services.

Annual growth rates in all home health services averaged over 16 percent between 1989 and 1993, compared to a total health services growth rate of just over 4 percent. Personal and home health care aides represented a significant proportion of this growth in home health employment, rising 4.2 percentage points from 1990 through 1993. Much of the early growth in home health care was fueled by favorable changes in Medicare financing in 1988 that permitted elderly and disabled patients to receive part-time care. Previously, only patients requiring full-time care were qualified for home health care services. The number of home care agencies increased 38.5 percent, from 10,848 in 1987 to 15,024 in 1994, delivering health care to 7.1 million people nationwide. The expansion was underwritten primarily by expanding eligibility for Medicare and Medicaid, which reimbursed local home care agencies for the elderly and the indigent.

The demographic composition of the home care labor force reflects the industry's origin within the traditional family. In the United States, mostly middle-aged minority women perform their work at remarkably low wages with poor benefits. As demand for home health care services expanded in the 1990s, immigrant women have become the largest growing demographic category. In New York City, documented immigrants and naturalized citizens account for nearly 60 percent of all workers in the industry.

Local nonprofit vendors that receive New York State financing for their services employ home health care workers who care for elderly and disabled indigent clients in New York City. To qualify for home health care services, individuals must be eligible for Medicaid, provided through the New York City Human Resources Administration, the local arm of the New York State Department of Social Services. Individuals must have depleted all or most of their savings and have virtually no independent source of income. In New York City this population includes a large number of elderly residents who are eligible for full-time Medicaid services. Elderly persons who have not exhausted their personal savings are eligible only for part-time Medicare home care services, even if they are disabled and require around-the-clock care. Since federal, state, and local governments are the primary funding source for nonprofit agencies contracting to provide home care services, employees and their unions must appeal to legislators and government agencies to authorize improvements in wages and benefits. While trade unions representing home care workers must bargain collectively with voluntary home care agencies, wages and benefits are ultimately dependent on the level of government funding for home health care services.

The 1987-1988 Mobilization

In New York City, when home care workers were originally organized into unions in the late 1970s, they were employed by the New York City Department of Human Resources. Before their unionization, they received the federal minimum wage and no health benefits. Although with union representation they received modest wage gains and health insurance benefits, however inadequate, even these were eroded by state and local funding cuts and by inflationary pressures. In the immediate wake of unionization in 1980, New York City turned the program over to private vendors that served as contracting agencies for government-funded home care services. Over the next several years, wages and benefits eroded to a level barely above the minimum wage; this situation, coupled with working conditions that left workers isolated from each other, made employment in the industry undesirable. A United Hospital Fund study quoted by Surpin noted that "when a person works hard, and for long hours, and yet still depends on food stamps and other forms of public assistance to raise a family, that person is clearly not earning an adequate wage." The problem of low government reimbursements and wages began to hamper the ability of home care vendor agencies to recruit trained and reliable personal care aides. By the late 1980s, home care agencies were among the most vocal proponents of improving economic conditions for home care workers.

Although home care workers in New York City were organized into unions earlier than elsewhere, they were not mobilized for political action until 1987, when two of the three unions representing home care workers in the city—Local 1199, representing 20,000 workers, and Local 389 of AFSCME District Council 1707, representing about 6,000 workers—launched Justice for Home Care Workers. Together the unions worked to generate public support for increased state and local funding and reimbursement of home care agencies contracting to provide services. Service Employees International Union (SEIU) Local 32B-32J, which represented over 30,000 home care workers in New York City until the late 1990s, declined to participate in Justice for Home Care Workers, but its members benefited from the agreements reached by Local 1199 and DC 1707. In January 1987, the two unions had put together the New York Labor Coalition for Home Care Workers, a grouping that included, besides the unions themselves, representatives of the vendor agencies and various community groups. The primary objective was to encourage state legislators to improve the reimbursement system. General recognition of the poor economic and work conditions of home care workers helped to advance the union's efforts to improve wages and working conditions in the industry. Both unions demanded that the vendor agencies provide comprehensive health benefits for the first time, raise wages by $2.00 an hour, and pay overtime for those working over forty hours a week. Thus, the unions adopted a two-pronged strategy: to persuade home care agencies to raise wages and increase benefits, and to convince state and local authorities to raise Medicaid home care compensation so that the agencies could accede to these demands. A decisive factor in the campaign was gaining the support of the vendor agencies that had an interest in raising worker compensation so that they might more easily recruit skilled and responsible home care aides. Allen Rosen, president of the Home Care Council of New York City, an employers' association, told Manhattan borough president David Dinkins that "we cannot be expected to keep loyal and dedicated employees and thus provide the quality of care we would like if we do not treat employees fairly. . . . [Their] benefits . . . are far less than what city workers get and much worse than what Medicaid would provide if they chose not to work." The leadership of both 1199 and DC 1707 recognized early on the futility of traditional forms of collective bargaining that excluded the rank and file. Both unions understood that the success of their strategy required that they mobilize their members politically. "Most home care workers didn't know they belonged to a union," according to 1199 officials Gerald Hudson and Barbara Caress; "since they worked in isolation from each other, they were extremely difficult to organize and even harder to mobilize." The Campaign for Justice employed an array of tactics to overcome this atomization. The effort included public hearings, rank-and-file lobbying, polling, coalition building, rallies, organized press campaigns, and soliciting support from prominent leaders and public officials. Whereas at the start of the campaign, both unions were largely disconnected from the rank and file, they were able to mobilize their membership by identifying informal networks and reaching out directly to members. The same two officials noted that 15 percent of 1199's members became actively involved in the campaign, an astonishing demonstration of rank-and-file support.

The Campaign for Justice successfully appealed to Jesse Jackson (then a contender for the Democratic Party's presidential nomination), David Dinkins (then borough president of Manhattan), and John Cardinal O'Connor (of the Catholic Archdiocese of New York) to support the home care workers' struggle for a decent contract. The three leaders met at St. Patrick's Cathedral to appeal for government action to improve the wages for these poorly paid workers who cared for the elderly and disabled. Members of 1199 and DC 1707 rallied outside to demand higher wages. The home care workers' contract campaign became a rallying cry for the Jackson campaign, and the alliance of the two causes proved decisive in gaining a contract in April 1988. An appeal to the public conscience pressured the vendor agencies and government authorities to raise wages, then about $4.50 an hour. The contract settlement, which included wage and benefit increases of more than 50 percent, came on the heels of Jackson's surprising Democratic primary victory in Michigan and amid anticipation for a strong showing in the New York primary. On May 28, 1987, Jackson spoke at a coalition-sponsored rally of 10,000 workers intended to focus public attention on the poor conditions afflicting home care workers. Moreover, a position paper on the destitute condition of 1199 home care workers showed that the most common annual wage was less than $5,000 a year, further validating demands for a substantial wage increase.

The agreement reached in January 1988 between the two unions and the Home Care Council of New York City, which represented sixty nonprofit home care providers, was considered by 1199 officials, in a press release, to be "a major advance in addressing the woefully inadequate economic conditions of home care workers." Before it could be implemented, however, the agreement required the approval of city and state authorities, which contributed 50 percent of the cost of home health care services. The unions subsequently lobbied state authorities to increase Medicaid payments to the nonprofit agencies employing home care workers. The campaign included mobilizing members and directly appealing to Governor Mario Cuomo and the state legislature to authorize an increase in state reimbursement. On March 31, an 1199 press release reported that the state had agreed to increase Medicaid payments for home care by $315 million, which would allow home care agencies to raise the starting wage from $4.15 an hour to $5.90 over the length of the contract. SEIU Local 32B-32J, which bargained separately, accepted the same terms.

Perhaps the most significant consequence of the 1987–88 worker mobilization was the regard that home care workers developed for social movement unionism. Before the union campaign, home care workers were among the lowest-paid workers in New York City. The significantly improved wages and benefits in the new agreement demonstrated to members the importance of mass action and the role of state and local government in achieving wage gains.

Subsequent Mobilizations

Local 1199 continued to conduct campaigns in the public domain to increase public awareness of the wages and working conditions of home care workers and to seek to couple the interests of members with those of the public. Because collective bargaining agreements must be ratified by government agencies, the union routinely mobilized members and lobbied for higher reimbursement rates from state and local authorities. Although in 1991 the spotlight was not on the plight of home care workers as it had been in 1988, the unions were again successful in mobilizing members to pressure employers to negotiate an agreement that improved wages in the industry. According to *Crain's New York Business*, Norman Metzger, professor emeritus at Mount Sinai School of Medicine, was reported to have said, "The mayor won't come forward and say 'Give them what they want.' The governor won't come forward and say 'Give them what they want.' There is no pressure for anything but a normal settlement." Nonetheless, the unions successfully pressured the nonprofit health care agencies and state and city government to reach a favorable agreement.

In April 1991, the two health care unions called a one-day strike to publicize the fact that their members had been working without a contract for nine months. Home care workers joined student demonstrations protesting proposed budget cuts that would raise tuition at City University of New York campuses. According to police estimates, a crowd of 6,000 students and 1199 members marched together in Lower Manhattan to protest the budget cuts and the reluctance of the state to increase home care funding. In June 1991 a mass rally of home care workers and a second one-day strike influenced Dinkins, now mayor, to expedite contract talks through two city agencies, the Office of Municipal Labor Relations and the Human Resources Administration. According to a United Press International report, 1199 president Dennis Rivera met privately with David Dinkins as a crowd of 500 home care workers demonstrated outside in City Hall Park. The mayor later promised the demonstrators at the rally to work vigorously for a new contract. Although a two-year collective bargaining agreement was not reached until

January 1992, union members received a 5 percent wage increase retroactive to June 1990, when the preceding agreement had expired.

The success of Local 1199's ongoing efforts to improve conditions for home care workers depended on the extent to which the union could mobilize members as a bargaining strategy in an era of government austerity. Although unions were able to apply political pressure to Democratic governor Mario Cuomo, leading to increased state reimbursements for home care, the election of Republicans as mayor in 1993 and governor in 1994, along with the election of a Republican-controlled Congress, diminished the political advantage that home care workers had gained in the 1980s and early 1990s. Governor George Pataki and Mayor Rudolph Giuliani argued that New York City's home care program was too generous and recommended deep cuts in the program, which relied on $1.3 billion in federal, state, and city support each year. Pataki, with the mayor's support, proposed home care spending cuts of 30 percent as part of a plan to reduce state Medicaid spending by $1 billion. Both efforts contributed to sharp cuts in home care services, leading thousands of elderly and disabled people to lose their Medicaid eligibility for home care.

As a result, in the late 1990s thousands of home care workers lost their jobs or worked too few hours to support their households. The new state and local government restrictions on Medicaid eligibility for home care services heightened the importance of political action for Local 1199 and other unions that represented workers dependent on state disbursements for continuation of their programs. This was brought home once again when a collective bargaining agreement reached between unions and vendor agencies in March 1996—a pact that provided wage and benefit gains—was held up until New York State could approve the package and allocate additional funding. In such a climate it was necessary that unions mobilize their members, form coalitions with clients, and influence public opinion in order to pressure government officials to advance the interests of workers. Their success at political mobilization sparked a wave of organizing that led to the unionization of tens of thousands of home care workers in several states, including California, Illinois, and Washington. SEIU, the parent of Local 1199, translated its experience in New York and replicated its success elsewhere.

See also: Nurses on Strike, 707.

Note

A version of this essay was published as, "Organizing Home Health-Care Workers: A New York City Case Study." *Working USA* 3, no. 4 (November 1999): 59–95.

Bibliography

Agovino, Theresa. "Health Care Unions Seeking Big Pay Hike." *Crain's New York Business,* April 22, 1991.

Cimini, Michael H., and Susan L. Behrmann. "Pay Raise for Health Care Workers: Pact Between Local 1199 of the Drug, Hospital, and Health Care Employees Union and the Home Care Council of New York Inc." *Monthly Labor Review,* April 1992.

Dinkins, David N. *Plight of the Home Care Worker.* Report of the Manhattan Borough President's Hearing on April 29, 1987. New York: City of New York.

Fink, Leon, and Brian Greenberg. *Upheaval in the Quiet Zone: A History of Hospital Workers' Union Local 1199.* Chicago: University of Illinois Press, 1989.

Freeman, Laura. "Home-Sweet-Home Health Care: Home Health Services Growth." *Monthly Labor Review,* March 1995.

Hudson, Gerald, and Barbara Caress. "New York's 1199 in 1989: Rebuilding a Troubled Union." *Labor Research Review* 10, no. 1 (1991): 69–80.

Johnston, Paul. 1994. *Success While Others Fail: Social Movement Unionism and the Public Workplace.* Ithaca, NY: ILR Press.

Mandulo, Rhea. "Health Care Workers Join CUNY Rally." United Press International (April 17, 1991).

Summers, Clyde W. "Public Employee Bargaining: A Political Perspective." In *Public Sector Labor Relations: Analysis and Readings,* 2nd ed., ed. David Lewin, Peter Feuille, and Thomas A. Kochan. Sun Lakes, AZ: Thomas Horton, 1981.

Surpin, Rick, Kathryn Haslanger, and Steven Dawson. *Better Jobs, Better Care: Building the Home Care Work Force.* New York: United Hospital Fund of New York, 1994.

United Press International. "Short-lived Home Health Care Workers' Strike." (June 12, 1991).

Zax, Jeffrey, and Casey Ichniowski. "The Effects of Public Sector Unionism on Pay, Employment, Department Budgets, and Municipal Expenditures." In *When Public Sector Workers Unionize,* ed. Richard B. Freeman and Casey Ichniowski. Chicago: University of Chicago Press, 1988.

ADDITIONAL BIBLIOGRAPHY

Contributors to the *Encyclopedia of Strikes in American History* submitted additional sources related to strikes that will be of interest to readers. While these sources are organized into parts that correspond to the parts of the *Encyclopedia,* many of them address questions that cross these boundaries.

Part 1

Adamic, Louis. *Dynamite!* New York: Viking, 1934.

Anderson, John. *The Briggs Strike.* Cleveland, OH: Hera, 1983.

Aronowitz, Stanley. *False Promises: The Shaping of American Working Class Consciousness.* New York: McGraw-Hill, 1973.

Balser, Diane. *Sisterhood & Solidarity: Feminism and Labor in Modern Times.* Boston: South End, 1987.

Bebel, August, et al. "German Socialists and the General Strike." In *Modern Socialism,* ed. R. C. K. Ensor, 189–97. New York: Scribner's, 1908.

Biggs, Michael. "Positive Feedback in Collective Mobilization: The American Strike Wave of 1886." *Theory and Society* 32 (2003): 217–54.

Buhle, Paul. *Taking Care of Business: Samuel Gompers, George Meany, Lane Kirkland, and the Tragedy of American Labor.* New York: Monthly Review, 1999.

Cousineau, Jean-Michel and Robert Lacroix. "Imperfect Information and Strikes: An Analysis of the Canadian Experience, 1967–98." *Industrial and Labor Relations Review* 39 (1986): 377–87.

De Leon, Daniel. *What Means This Strike?* 1895. New York: Socialist Labor Party, 1914.

Dobbs, Farrell. *Teamster Rebellion.* New York: Monad, 1972.

Douglas, Sara, Norma Pecora, and Thomas Guback. "Work, Workers, and the Workplace: Is Local Newspaper Coverage Enough?" *Journalism Quarterly* 62, no. 4 (1985): 855–60.

Dunne, William F. *The Great San Francisco General Strike.* New York: Workers Library, 1934.

Filippelli, Ronald L., ed. *Labor Conflict in the United States: An Encyclopedia.* New York: Garland Publishing, 1990.

Foner, Philip, for United States Department of Labor. *Labor Firsts in America.* Washington, D.C.: U.S. Government Printing Office, 1977.

Fones-Wolf, Elizabeth A. *Selling Free Enterprise: The Business Assault on Labor and Liberalism, 1945–1960.* Urbana: University of Illinois Press, 1994.

Foster, William Z. *The Great Steel Strike and Its Lessons.* New York: B. W. Huebsch, 1920.

———. *Strike Strategy.* Chicago: Trade Union Educational League, 1926.

Fraser, Steve, and Gary Gerstle. *The Rise and Fall of the New Deal Order, 1930–1980.* Princeton, NJ: Princeton University Press, 1989.

Friedman, Gerald. *State-Making and Labor Movements: France and the United States, 1876–1914.* Ithaca, NY: Cornell University Press, 1998.

Gatlin, Rochelle. "A 'Society of Outsiders': Union W.A.G.E., Working-Class Feminism, and the Labor Movement." In *Culture, Gender, Race, and U.S. Labor History,* ed. Ronald C. Kent, Sara Markham, David R. Roediger, and Herbert Shapiro. Westport, CT: Greenwood, 1993.

Georgakas, Dan, and Marvin Surkin. *Detroit, I Do Mind Dying: A Study in Urban Revolution.* New York: St. Martin's, 1975.

Glaberman, Martin. *Wartime Strikes.* Detroit: Bewick, 1980.

Goldfield, Michael. *The Decline of Organized Labor in the United States.* Chicago: University of Chicago Press, 1987.

Gouldner, Alvin W. *Wildcat Strike.* Yellow Springs, OH: Antioch, 1954.

Green, James, ed. *Workers' Struggles, Past and Present: A 'Radical America' Reader.* Philadelphia: Temple University Press, 1983.

Hayek, Friedrich. *The Constitution of Liberty.* Chicago: University of Chicago Press, 1960.

Hyman, Richard. *Strikes.* London: Fontana, 1972.

Keller, Helen. "Strike Against War" (1916). In *Helen Keller: Her Socialist Years*, 75–81. New York: International, 1967.

Lee, Howard B. *Bloodletting in Appalachia: The Story of West Virginia's Four Major Mine Wars and Other Thrilling Incidents of Its Coal Fields.* Morgantown: West Virginia Press, 1969.

Lenin, V. I. "May Day Action by the Revolutionary Proletariat." In V. I. Lenin, *Collected Works.* Vol. 19. Moscow: Foreign Languages Publishing House, 1963.

Lichtenstein, Nelson. *Labor's War at Home: The CIO in World War II.* Cambridge, UK: Cambridge University Press, 1982.

Lipset, George. *Rainbow at Midnight: Labor and Culture in the 1940s.* Urbana: University of Illinois Press, 1994.

London, Jack. "Strike Methods: American and Australian" (1905). In *Jack London: American Rebel*, ed. Philip Foner, 405–10. Berlin: Seven Seas, 1958.

Luxemburg, Rosa. *The Mass Strike.* London: Bookmarks, 1986.

Moody, Kim. *An Injury to All: The Decline of American Unionism.* London: Verso, 1988.

———. *Workers in a Lean World: Unions in an International Economy.* London: Verso, 1997.

Muste, A. J. "The Battle of Toledo." *The Nation* 138 (June 6, 1934): 639–40.

Rachleff, Peter. *Hard-Pressed in the Heartland: The Hormel Strike and the Future of the Labor Movement.* Boston: South End, 1993.

Schwartz, Bob. *Strikes, Picketing, and Inside Campaigns: A Legal Guide For Unions.* Cambridge, MA: Work Rights Press, 2006.

Slater, Philip A. "The Railroad Strikes of 1877." *Marxist Quarterly* 1 (April–June 1937): 214–36.

Slaughter, Jane, ed. *A Troublemaker's Handbook* 2. Detroit: Labor Notes, 2005.

Tax, Merideth. *The Rising of the Women: Feminist Solidarity and Class Conflict, 1880–1917.* New York: Monthly Review, 1980.

Thompson, Edward P. *The Making of the English Working Class.* New York: Vintage, 1963.

Weir, Stan. *Singlejack Solidarity.* Minneapolis: University of Minnesota, 2004.

Part 2

Arnesen, Eric. *Brotherhoods of Color: Black Railroad Workers and the Struggle for Equality.* Cambridge, MA: Harvard University Press, 2001.

Biondi, Martha. *To Stand and Fight: The Struggle for Civil Rights in Postwar New York City.* Cambridge, MA: Harvard University Press, 2003.

Crane, Diana. *Fashion and Its Social Agendas.* Chicago: University of Chicago Press, 2000.

Dubofsky, Melvyn. *We Shall Be All: A History of the Industrial Workers of the World.* New York: Quadrangle, 1969.

Estes, Steve. "'I AM A MAN!': Race, Masculinity, and the 1968 Memphis Sanitation Strike." *Labor History* 41, no. 2 (May 2000): 53–70.

Ferris, Susan, and Ricardo Sandoval. *Fight in the Fields: Cesar Chavez and the Farmworkers Movement.* San Diego: Harcourt Brace, 1997.

Green, Archie. *Wobblies, Pile Butts, and Other Heroes: Laborlore Explorations.* Urbana: University of Illinois Press, 1993.

Green, Nancy. *Ready-to-Wear and Ready-to-Work: A Century of Industry and Immigrants in Paris and New York.* Durham, NC: Duke University, 1997.

Gutman, Herbert G. *Work, Culture, and Society in Industrializing America.* New York: Vintage Books, 1977.

Hoffus, Steve. "Charleston Hospital Workers' Strike, 1969." In *Working Lives: The Southern Exposure History of Labor in the South*, ed. Marc S. Miller. New York: Pantheon Books, 1980.

Jeineman, Kenneth J. *A Catholic New Deal: Religion and Reform in Depression Pittsburgh.* University Park: Pennsylvania State University Press, 1999.

Jensen, Joan M. "The Great Uprisings: 1900–1920." In *A Needle, a Bobbin, a Strike: Woman Needleworkers in America*, ed. Joan M. Jensen and Sue Davidson. Philadelphia: Temple University Press, 1984.

Levy, Jacques E. *Cesar Chavez: Autobiography of La Causa.* New York: Norton and Simon, 1975.

Lichtenstein, Nelson. *The Most Dangerous Man in Detroit: Walter Reuther and the Fate of American Labor.* New York: Basic Books, 1995.

Lichtenstein, Nelson, Susan Strasser, and Roy Rosenzweig. *Who Built America?: Working People and the Nation's Economy, Politics, Culture, and Society*, 2nd ed. Vol. 2. New York: Worth, 2000.

Lipsitz, George. *Rainbow at Midnight: Labor and Culture in the 1940s.* Urbana: University of Illinois Press, 1994.

Nelson, Bruce. *Divided We Stand: American Workers and the Struggle for Black Equality.* Princeton, NJ: Princeton University Press, 2001.

Pula, James S., and Eugene E. Dziedzic. *United We Stand: The Role of Polish Workers in the New York Mills Textile Strikes, 1912 and 1916.* New York: Columbia University Press, 1990.

Radzilowski, Thaddeus C. "The Second Generation: The Unknown Polonia." *Polish American Studies* 43, no. 1 (1986): 11.

Renkiewicz, Frank A. "An Economy of Self-Help: Fraternal Capitalism and the Evolution of Polish America."

In *Studies in Ethnicity: The East European Experience in America,* ed. Charles A. Ward, Philip Shashko, and Donald E. Pienkos. Boulder, CO: East European Monographs, 1980.

Romalis, Shelly. *Pistol Packin' Mama: Aunt Molly Jackson and the Politics of Folksong.* Urbana: University of Illinois Press, 1999.

Schwenning, G.T. "Prospects of Southern Textile Unionism." *The Journal of Political Economy* 39, no. 6 (December 1931).

Shockley, Megan Taylor. *"We, Too, Are Americans": African American Women in Detroit and Richmond, 1940–54.* Urbana: University of Illinois Press, 2003.

Taft, Philip. "The Association of Catholic Trade Unionists." *Industrial and Labor Relations Review* 2, no. 2 (January 1949): 210–18.

Part 3

Adamic, Louis. "Sitdown." *The Nation* 143, no. 23 (December 5, 1936): 652–54.

Adamic, Louis. "Sitdown: II." *The Nation* 143, no. 24 (December 12, 1936): 702–4.

Howard J. Woodford, Jr. "Frank Murphy and the Sit-Down Strikes of 1937." *Labor History* 1, no. 2 (Spring 1960): 103–40.

Kirstein, George. *Stores and Unions: A Study of the Growth of Unionism in Dry Goods and Department Stores.* New York: Fairchild Publications, 1950.

Kraus, Henry. *The Many and the Few: A Chronicle of the Dynamic Auto Workers,* 2nd ed. Urbana: University of Illinois Press, 1985 (1947).

Link, Monica. "Keep Unions Alive." *Solidarity* (December 2003): 15.

Mortimer, Wyndham. *Organize! My Life as A Union Man.* Boston: Beacon Press, 1971.

Nelson, Daniel. "The CIO at Bay: Labor Militancy and Politics in Akron, 1936–1938." *Journal of American History* 71, no. 3 (December 1984): 565–86.

Lichtenstein, Nelson. *State of the Union: A Century of American Labor.* Princeton, NJ: Princeton University Press, 2002.

Part 4

Anderson, Mary. *Woman at Work.* Westport, CT: Greenwood Press, 1973.

Eisenstein, Sarah. *Give Us Bread but Give Us Roses.* London: Routledge and Kegan Paul, 1983.

Glass, Fred, ed. *A History of the California Federation of Teachers, 1919–1989.* San Francisco: California Federation of Teachers, 1989.

Montgomery, David. *The Fall of the House of Labor: The Workplace, the State and American Labor Activism, 1865–1925.* Cambridge, MA: Cambridge University Press, 1987.

Murray, Robert. *Red Scare: A Study in National Hysteria, 1919–20.* Minneapolis: University of Minnesota Press, 1955.

Tax, Meredith. *The Rising of the Women.* New York: Monthly Review Press, 1980.

Part 5

Adams Graham, Jr. *Age of Industrial Violence, 1910–1915.* New York: Columbia University Press, 1966.

Arnesen, Eric. *Brotherhoods of Color: Black Railroad Workers and the Struggle for Equality.* Cambridge, MA: Harvard University Press, 2002.

Babcock, Robert H. "The Saint John Street Railwaymen's Strike and Riot, 1914." *Acadiensis* 11 (Spring 1982): 3–27.

———. "Will You Walk? Yes, We'll Walk! Popular Support for a Street Railway Strike in Portland, Maine." *Labor History* 35 (Summer 1994): 372–98.

Balderrama, Francisco E., and Rodríguez, Raymond. *Decade of Betrayal: Mexican Repatriation in the 1930s.* Albuquerque: University of New Mexico Press, 1995.

Bernstein, Aaron. *Grounded: Frank Lorenzo and the Destruction of Eastern Airlines.* New York: Simon & Schuster, 1990.

Bohstedt, John. *Riots and Community Politics in England and Wales, 1790–1810.* Cambridge, MA: Harvard University Press, 1983.

Brueggemann, John, and Cliff Brown. "The Decline of Industrial Unionism in the Meatpacking Industry: Event-Structure Analyses of Labor Unrest, 1946–1987." *Work and Occupations* 30, no. 3 (August 2003): 327–60.

Cardoso, Lawrence A. *Mexican Emigration to the United States, 1897–1931: Socio-Economic Patterns.* Tucson: University of Arizona Press, 1980.

Chandler Alfred D., Jr. *The Visible Hand: Managerial Revolution in American Business.* Cambridge, MA: Harvard University, 1977.

Ciabattari, Mark. "Urban Liberals and the Fight for Public Transit, San Francisco, 1897–1915." Ph.D. diss., New York University, 1988.

Craypo, Charles. "Meatpacking: Industry Restructuring and Union Decline." In *Contemporary Collective Bargaining in the Private Sector,* ed. Paula B. Voss. Madison, WI: Industrial Relations Research Association, 1994.

Cumbler, John. *Working-Class Community in Industrial America: Work Leisure, and Struggle in Two Industrial Cities, 1880–1930.* Westport, CT: Greenwood Press, 1979.

Daniel, Pete. *Breaking the Land: The Transformation of Cotton, Tobacco and Rice Cultures Since 1880.* Urbana: University of Illinois Press, 1985.

———. *The Shadow of Slavery: Peonage in the South, 1901–1969.* Urbana: University of Illinois Press, 1990.

Davies, Margery W. *Women's Place Is at the Typewriter.* Philadelphia: Temple University Press, 1982.

Davis, Mike. "Sunshine and the Open Shop: Ford and Darwin in 1920s Los Angeles." *Metropolis in the Making: Los Angeles in the 1920s,* ed. Tom Sitton and William Deverell. Berkeley: University of California Press, 2001.

DeFusco, Richard A., and Scott M. Fuess. "The Effects of Airline Strikes on Struck and Nonstruck Carriers." *Industrial & Labor Relations Review* 44, no. 2 (1991): 324–34.

DeVeaux, Scott. *Be Bop: A Social and Musical History.* Berkeley: University of California Press,1997.

Dubofsky, Melvyn. *We Shall Be All: A History of the Industrial Workers of the World.* New York: New York Times Publishing, 1969.

DuBois, W.E.B. *Black Reconstruction in America, 1860–1880.* New York: Atheneum, 1962.

Ducker, James H. *Men of the Steel Rails: Workers on the Atchison, Topeka & Santa Fe Railroad, 1869–1900.* Lincoln: University of Nebraska Press, 1983.

Dulles, Foster R., and Melvyn Dubofsky. *Labor in America: A History.* Wheeling, IL: Harlan Davidson, 1993.

Dutton, H.I., and J.E. King. *Ten Per Cent and No Surrender: The Preston Strike, 1853–54.* Cambridge, UK: Cambridge University Press, 1981.

Fahey, Michael, T. *Packing It In! The Hormel Strike 1985–1986, A Personal Perspective.* St. Paul, MN: Kirwin & Sons, 1989.

Feldberg, Roselyn L., and Evelyn N. Glenn. "Clerical Work: The Female Occupation." In *Women: A Feminist Perspective,* 3rd ed., ed. Jo Freeman. Palo Alto, CA: Mayfield, 1984.

Foley, Neil. *The White Scourge: Mexicans, Blacks and Poor Whites in the Texas Cotton Culture.* Berkeley: University of California Press, 1997.

Foner, Philip S. "The Battle to End Discrimination against Negroes on Philadelphia Streetcars." Two parts. *Pennsylvania History* 40 (July and October, 1973): 261–90, 355–79.

———. *The History of the Labor Movement in the United States: On the Eve of America's Entrance into World War I.* New York: International, 1982.

Genovese, Eugene D. *Roll, Jordan, Roll: The World the Slaves Made.* New York: Random House Vintage Books, 1974.

Gonzalez, Gilbert G., "The 1933 Los Angeles Country Farm Workers Strike." *New Political Science* 20, no. 4 (1998): 441–58.

Gutman, Herbert G. *Power and Culture: Essays on the American Working Class.* New York: Free Press, 1986.

Gutman, Herbert G. *Work, Culture and Society in Industrializing America.* New York: Knopf, 1977.

Hayes, Samuel P. *The Response to Industrialism, 1885–1914.* Chicago: University of Chicago, 1957.

Hendrick, Burton. "Great American Fortunes and Their Making: Street-Railway Financiers." *McClure's Magazine* 30 (November 1907): 33–48.

Joyce, Patrick. *Work, Politics and Society: The Culture of the Factory in Later Victorian England.* New Brunswick, NJ: Rutgers University Press, 1980.

Kahn, Mark L. "The National Airlines Strike: A Case Study." *Journal of Air Law and Commerce* 19, no. 1 (1952): 11–24.

Kassalow, Everett. "White Collar Unionism in the United States." In *White-Collar Trade Unions: Contemporary Developments in Industrialized Societies,* ed. Adolf Sturmthal, 305–64. Urbana: University of Illinois Press, 1966.

Kester, Howard. *Revolt Among the Sharecroppers.* New York: Covici Friede, 1936; reprint New York: Arno, 1969.

Krause, Paul. *The Battle for Homestead, 1880–1892: Politics, Culture and Steel.* Pittsburgh: University of Pittsburgh Press, 1992.

Kushner, Sam. *Long Road to Delano.* New York: International, 1975.

Lahne, Herbert J. *The Cotton Textile Worker.* New York: Farr & Rinehart, 1944.

Licht, Walter. *Working for the Railroads: The Organization of Work in the Nineteenth Century.* Princeton, NJ: Princeton University Press, 1983.

London, Joan, and Anderson, Henry. *So Shall Ye Reap.* New York: Crowell, 1970.

Mahon, William D. *Wage History of the Amalgamated Association of Street & Electric Railway Employes of America.* Detroit: Amalgamated Association, 1914.

Matthiessen, Peter. *Sal Si Puedes: César Chávez and the New American Revolution.* New York: Dell, 1969.

McCammon, Holly J. "Legal Limits on Labor Militancy: U.S. Labor Law and the Right to Strike since the New Deal." *Social Problems* 37, no. 2 (May 1990): 206–29.

McCartin, Joseph A. *Labor's Great War: The Struggle for Industrial Democracy and the Origins of Modern American Labor Relations, 1912–1921.* Chapel Hill: University of North Carolina Press, 1997.

Molloy, Scott. "Motormen, Moguls, and the Machine: Urban Mass Transit in Rhode Island, 1864–1902." Ph.D. diss., Providence College, 1991.

———. *Rhode Island Transit Album.* Cambridge, MA: Boston Street Railway Association, 1978.

Nelson, Eugene. *Huelga: The First Hundred Days of the Great Delano Grape Strike.* Delano, CA: Farm Worker Press, 1966.

Nordlund, Willis J. *Silent Skies: The Air Traffic Controllers' Strike.* Westport, CT: Praeger, 1998.

Norwood, Stephen. *Strikebreaking & Intimidation: Mercenaries and Masculinity in Nineteenth-Century America.* Chapel Hill: University of North Carolina Press, 2002.

Nicolaides, Becky M. *My Blue Heaven: Life and Politics in the Working-Class Suburbs of Los Angeles, 1920–1965.* Chicago: University of Chicago Press, 2002.

Oppenheimer, Martin. *White Collar Politics.* New York: Monthly Review Press, 1985.

Scopino, A.J. "Community, Class, and Conflict: The Waterbury Trolley Strike of 1903." *Connecticut History* 24 (1983): 29–46.

Scott, Carole E., and Richard D. Guynn. "The Atlanta Streetcar Strikes." *The Georgia Historical Quarterly* 80 (Fall 2000): 434–59.

Stover, John. *The Life and Decline of the American Railroad.* New York: Oxford University Press, 1970.

Stowell, David. *Streets, Railroads, and the Great Strike of 1877.* Chicago: University of Chicago Press, 1999.

Stromquist, Shelton. *A Generation of Boomers: The Pattern of Railroad Labor Conflict in Nineteenth Century America.* Chicago: University of Chicago Press, 1987.

Takaki, Ronald. *Strangers from a Different Shore: A History of Asian Americans.* Boston: Little, Brown, 1998.

Taplin, Eric. *Near to Revolution: The Liverpool General Transport Strike of 1911.* Liverpool: Bluecoat Press, 1994.

Taylor, Ronald B. *Chavez and the Farm Workers.* Boston: Beacon Press, 1975.

Tomasson, Robert E. "Growing Militancy Turns Strikes into Routine." *New York Times,* December 11, 1980.

Venkataramani, M.S. "Norman Thomas, Arkansas Sharecroppers, and the Roosevelt Agricultural Politicies, 1933–1937." *Mississippi Valley Historical Review* 47, no. 2 (September 1960): 225–46.

Ware, Norman J. *The Industrial Worker, 1840–1860.* Chicago: Quadrangle Books, 1924.

Ware, Norman J. *The Labor Movement in the United States, 1860–1895: A Study in Democracy.* New York: Vintage Books, 1964.

Wright, Chester M. "The Street Car Union and New York's Big Strike." *Pearson's Magazine* 36 (November 1916): 422–27.

Yearly, Clifton K. *Britons in American Labor: A History of the Influence of United Kingdom Immigrants on American Labor, 1820–1914.* Baltimore: Johns Hopkins University Press, 1957.

Young, Dina. "The St. Louis Streetcar Strike of 1900: Pivotal Politics at the Century's Dawn." *Gateway Heritage* 12 (Summer 1991): 4–17.

Zeigler, Robert E. "The Limits of Power: The Amalgamated Association of Street Railway Employees in Houston, Texas, 1897–1905." *Labor History* 18 (Winter 1971): 71–90.

Zieger, Robert H. *American Workers, American Unions.* Baltimore: Johns Hopkins University Press, 1994.

NAME INDEX

Page numbers in italics refer to illustrations

SUBJECT INDEX

Page numbers in italics refer to illustrations